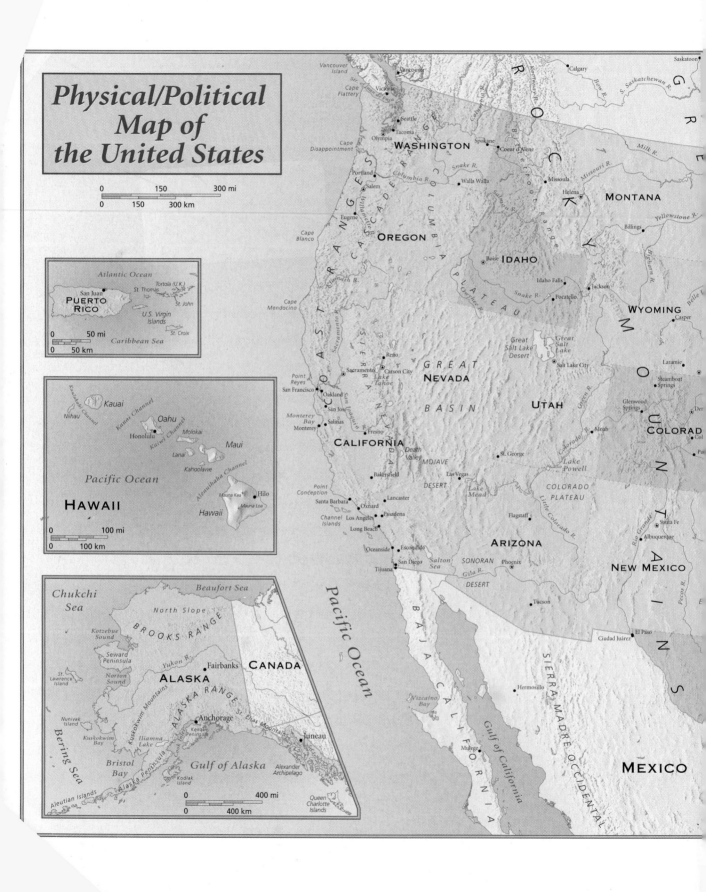

Physical/Political Map of the United States

0 150 300 mi
0 150 300 km

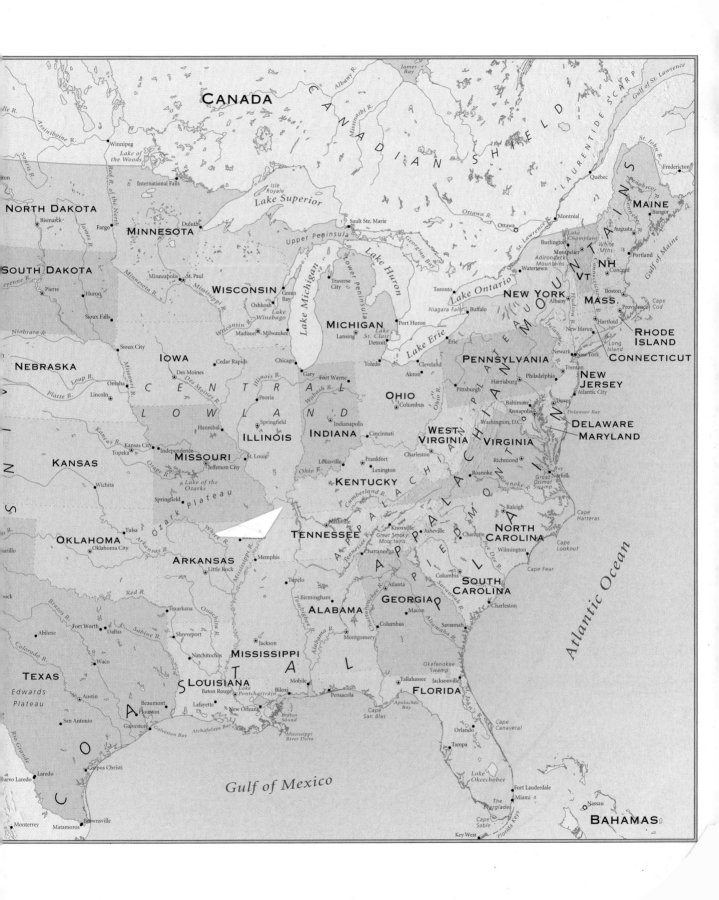

WE THE PEOPLE

An Introduction to American Politics

SHORTER FIFTH EDITION

WE THE PEOPLE

An Introduction to American Politics

BENJAMIN GINSBERG

THE JOHNS HOPKINS UNIVERSITY

THEODORE J. LOWI

CORNELL UNIVERSITY

MARGARET WEIR

UNIVERSITY OF CALIFORNIA AT BERKELEY

SHORTER FIFTH EDITION

W • W • NORTON & COMPANY • NEW YORK • LONDON

W. W. Norton & Company has been independent since its founding in 1923, when William Warder Norton and Mary D. Herter Norton first published lectures delivered at the People's Institute, the adult education division of New York City's Cooper Union. The Nortons soon expanded their program beyond the Institute, publishing books by celebrated academics from America and abroad. By mid-century, the two major pillars of Norton's publishing program—trade books and college texts—were firmly established. In the 1950s, the Norton family transferred control of the company to its employees, and today—with a staff of four hundred and a comparable number of trade, college, and professional titles published each year—W. W. Norton & Company stands as the largest and oldest publishing house owned wholly by its employees.

Editor: Stephen Dunn
Editorial assistant: Kelly Rolf
Project editor: Kim Yi
Production manager: Diane O'Connor
Book design: Chris Welch
Figures: John McAusland
Managing editor, College: Marian Johnson
Composition: TSI Graphics
Manufacturing: Quebecor/Versailles
Cover illustration: Mick Wiggins
Photo research: Neil Ryder Hoos
E-media editor: Denise Shanks

Library of Congress Cataloging-in-Publication Data

Ginsberg, Benjamin
    We the people: an introduction to American politics/Benjamin Ginsberg,
Theodore J. Lowi, Margaret Weir.—Shorter, 5th ed.
        p. cm.
Includes bibliographical references and index.

ISBN 0-393-92619-2

    1. United States—Politics and government. I. Lowi, Theodore J. II. Weir, Margaret, 1952-III.
Title.

JK271.G65 2005
320.473—dc22   2004058308

W. W. Norton & Company, Inc., 500 Fifth Avenue, New York, N.Y. 10110
                    www.wwnorton.com

W. W. Norton & Company Ltd., Castle House, 75/76 Wells Street, London W1T 3QT

 2 3 4 5 6 7 8 9 0

TO

SANDY, CINDY, AND ALEX GINSBERG

ANGELE, ANNA, AND JASON LOWI

NICHOLAS ZIEGLER

CONTENTS

Part I
FOUNDATIONS

2 THE FOUNDING AND THE CONSTITUTION 36

5 CIVIL RIGHTS   162

6   PUBLIC OPINION   210

Part II

POLITICS

9 POLITICAL PARTIES   326

10 CAMPAIGNS AND ELECTIONS   374

Part III
INSTITUTIONS

15 THE FEDERAL COURTS   614

PREFACE

This book has been and continues to be dedicated to developing a satisfactory response to the question more and more Americans are asking: Why should we be engaged with government and politics? Through the first four editions, we sought to answer this question by making the text directly relevant to the lives of the students who would be reading it. As a result, we tried to make politics interesting by demonstrating that students' interests are at stake and that they therefore need to take a personal, even selfish, interest in the outcomes of government. At the same time, we realized that students needed guidance in how to become politically engaged. Beyond providing students with a core of political knowledge, we needed to show them how they could apply that knowledge as participants in the political process. The "Get Involved: What You Can Do" conclusions to each chapter helped achieve that goal.

This fifth edition retains the same goals and methods as earlier editions, but goes beyond them. As events from the last four years have reminded us, "what government does" can be a matter of life and death. During that time, events have reinforced the centrality of government in citizens' lives. The U.S. government has fought a war abroad, while compromising the liberties of its citizens at home. The administration has adopted policies that have further polarized Democrats and Republicans and exacerbated the economic inequality in this country. These events have prompted more critical attention to the Bush administration specifically and to the practices of American government more broadly. America's role in the world is discussed daily both inside and outside the classroom. Moreover, students and younger Americans have become more aware of and involved in politics, as the 2004 campaign for president illustrated. Reflecting all of these trends, this new fifth edition shows more than any other book on the market (1) how American government is connected to the world; (2) how students are connected to government; and (3) why students should think critically about government and politics. These themes are incorporated in the following ways:

- **New "America in the World" boxes show students how American government is connected to the world.** These one-page boxes in every chapter illustrate the important political role the United States plays abroad. Topics include "Should America Export Democracy?" "The American Constitution: A Model for the World?" "Participation and Democracy in Iraq," and "Congress, the President, and Foreign Trade." These new boxes exemplify the critical-analytical approach that characterizes the new edition and include "For Critical Analysis" questions.

- **Chapter introductions focus on "What Government Does and Why It Matters."** During the past two decades, cynicism about "big government" has dominated the political zeitgeist. But critics of government often forget that governments do a great deal for citizens. Every year, Americans are the beneficiaries of billions of dollars of goods and services from government programs. Government "does" a lot, and what it does matters a great deal to everyone, including college students. At the start of each chapter, this theme is introduced and applied to the chapter's topic. The goal is to show students that government and politics mean something to their daily lives.

- **"Get Involved: What You Can Do" conclusions and new "Interactive Politics" boxes at the end of every chapter show students why political participation matters and how they can participate.** The "Get Involved" sections offer specific instructions and guidance on how college students can become involved in their own communities, as well as at the state and national level. The "Interactive Politics" boxes provide specific role-playing scenarios that encourage students to think about the many forms of political participation.

- **New "Previewing Liberty, Equality, and Democracy" and "Thinking Critically about …" content highlights the critical-analytical approach of this new edition.** American history reveals large gaps between the principles of liberty, equality, and democracy and the practice of American politics. Are these principles mere ideals? How are they applied? How effective is our government at upholding these ideals? Every chapter begins with a new "Previewing Liberty, Equality, and Democracy" section that sets the stage for how liberty, equality, and democracy apply to the chapter's topic, identifies the gap between those principles and actual government practice, and explores the potential conflict between those three principles. "Thinking Critically about …" sections later in the chapter show students how to apply a critical perspective to these issues. For example, in Chapter 10, "Campaigns and Elections," the preview emphasizes that while the essence of democracy is citizens participating equally in competitive elections, actual electoral practices seem inconsistent with our egalitarian values. The text explores whether the disproportionate role played by elites fails our democratic ideal of "government by the people." The "Thinking Critically about the Electoral Process" section further explores how the question of campaign finance illustrates a clash between equality and liberty in that Americans seem wary of the apparently sinister role that wealthy individuals and well-heeled interest groups play in elections, but efforts to make the electoral process more equal could come at the expense of liberty.

- **New "For Critical Analysis" questions are incorporated in the "America in the World" and "Policy Debate" boxes and appear throughout the chapter to prompt students' own critical thinking.** The "America in the World" boxes demonstrate the important role the United States plays in the world. The two "For Critical Analysis" questions that conclude each box get students to think critically about that role. For example, the Chapter 1 box "Should America Export Democracy?" describes U.S. attempts to export democracy to countries such as Iraq. The "For Critical Analysis" questions that conclude the box ask students to think about whether it is appropriate for America to try to shape the governmental institutions and political arrangements of other countries in the first place. "Policy Debate" boxes describe the various issues surrounding a policy conflict. For example, the box in Chapter 3 explores the debate on the 2002 No Child Left Behind Act. The "For Critical Analysis" questions that conclude the box ask students to consider "Why might the federal government be better able than state and local governments to ensure that low-income students receive a high-quality education?" and "Why do critics call this act an unfunded mandate that will harm low-income students?"

One remaining feature of our text that we hope will help students become informed and critical citizens is what we call our "Greek chorus." Each chapter includes a "Student Debate" that presents the opposing views of students on current issues. As with the chorus in Greek drama, our student chorus illustrates the range of enlightenment. We continue to hope that our book will itself be accepted as a form of enlightened political action. This fifth edition is another chance. It is an advancement toward our goal. We promise to keep trying.

ACKNOWLEDGMENTS

Our students at Cornell, Johns Hopkins, Harvard, and Berkeley have been an essential factor in the writings of this book. They have been our most immediate intellectual community, a hospitable one indeed. Another part of our community, perhaps a large suburb, is the discipline of political science itself. Our debt to the scholarship of our colleagues is scientifically measurable, probably to several decimal points, in the endnotes of each chapter. Despite many complaints that the field is too scientific or not scientific enough, political science is alive and well in the United States. It is an aspect of democracy itself, and it has grown and changed in response to the developments in government and politics that we have chronicled in our book. If we did a "time line" on the history of political science, it would show a close association with developments in "the American state." Sometimes the discipline has been out of phase and critical; at other times, it has been in phase and perhaps apologetic. But political science has never been at a loss for relevant literature, and without it, our job would have been impossible.

We are especially pleased to acknowledge our debt to the many colleagues who had a direct and active role in criticism and preparation of the manuscript. Our thanks go to

First Edition Reviewers
Sarah Binder, Brookings Institution
Kathleen Gille, Office of Representative David Bonior
Rodney Hero, University of Colorado at Boulder
Robert Katzmann, Brookings Institution
Kathleen Knight, University of Houston
Robin Kolodny, Temple University
Nancy Kral, Tomball College
Robert C. Lieberman, Columbia University
David A. Marcum, University of Wyoming
Laura R. Winsky Mattei, State University of New York at Buffalo
Marilyn S. Mertens, Midwestern State University
Barbara Suhay, Henry Ford Community College
Carolyn Wong, Stanford University
Julian Zelizer, State University of New York at Albany

Second Edition Reviewers
Lydia Andrade, University of North Texas
John Coleman, University of Wisconsin at Madison

Daphne Eastman, Odessa College
Otto Feinstein, Wayne State University
Elizabeth Flores, Delmar College
James Gimpel, University of Maryland at College Park
Jill Glaathar, Southwest Missouri State University
Shaun Herness, University of Florida
William Lyons, University of Tennessee at Knoxville
Andrew Polsky, Hunter College, City University of New York
Grant Reeher, Syracuse University
Richard Rich, Virginia Polytechnic
Bartholomew Sparrow, University of Texas at Austin

Third Edition Reviewers
Amy Jasperson, University of Texas at San Antonio
Loch Johnson, University of Georgia
Mark Kann, University of Southern California
Andrea Simpson, University of Washington
Brian Smentkowski, Southeast Missouri State University
Nelson Wikstrom, Virginia Commonwealth University

Fourth Edition Reviewers
M. E. Banks, Virginia Commonwealth University
Mark Cichock, University of Texas at Arlington
Del Fields, St. Petersburg College
Nancy Kinney, Washtenaw Community College
William Klein, St. Petersburg College
Christopher Muste, Louisiana State University
David Rankin, State University of New York at Fredonia
Paul Roesler, St. Charles Community College
J. Philip Rogers, San Antonio College
Greg Shaw, Illinois Wesleyan University
Tracy Skopek, Stephen F. Austin State University
Don Smith, University of North Texas
Terri Wright, Cal State, Fullerton

Fifth Edition Reviewers
Denise Dutton, Southwest Missouri State University
Rick Kurtz, Central Michigan University
Kelly McDaniel, Three Rivers Community College
Eric Plutzer, Pennsylvania State University
Daniel Smith, Northwest Missouri State University
Dara Strolovitch, University of Minnesota
Stacy Ulbig, Southwest Missouri State University

We also must pay thanks to the many collaborators we have had on this project: Robert J. Spitzer of the State University of New York at Cortland; Mark Kann and Marcella Marlowe of the University of Southern California.

We are also grateful for the talents and hard work of several research assistants, whose contributions can never be adequately compensated. In particular, Mingus

Mapps, Doug Harris, and Ben Bowyer put an enormous amount of thought and time into the figures, tables, and study aids that appear in the text. Israel Waismel-Manor also kept a close eye on keeping the book as up-to-date as possible.

We would like to give special thanks to Jacqueline Pastore at Cornell University, who not only prepared portions of the manuscript but also helped to hold the entire project together. We especially thank her for her hard work and dedication.

Perhaps above all, we wish to thank those at W. W. Norton. For its five editions, our editor, Steve Dunn, has helped us shape the book in countless ways. We thank Neil Ryder Hoos and Abigail Becker for devoting an enormous amount of time to finding new photos and selecting pieces for the "Student Debates." For our interactive Web site for the book, Denise Shanks has been an energetic and visionary editor. Patterson Lamb edited the manuscript with Marian Johnson's superb direction, and project editor Kim Yi devoted countless hours keeping on top of myriad details. Diane O'Connor has been dedicated in managing production. Finally, we wish to thank Roby Harrington, the head of Norton's college department.

We are more than happy, however, to absolve all these contributors from any flaws, errors, and misjudgments that will inevitably be discovered. We wish the book could be free of all production errors, grammatical errors, misspellings, misquotes, missed citations, etc. From that standpoint, a book ought to try to be perfect. But substantively we have not tried to write a flawless book; we have not tried to write a book to please everyone. We have again tried to write an effective book, a book that cannot be taken lightly. Our goal was not to make every reader a political scientist or a political activist. Our goal was to restore politics as a subject matter of vigorous and enjoyable discourse, recapturing it from the bondage of the thirty-second sound bite and the thirty-page technical briefing. Every person can be knowledgeable because everything about politics is accessible. One does not have to be a television anchorperson to profit from political events. One does not have to be a philosopher to argue about the requisites of democracy, a lawyer to dispute constitutional interpretations, an economist to debate a public policy. We would be very proud if our book contributes in a small way to the restoration of the ancient art of political controversy.

BENJAMIN GINSBERG
THEODORE J. LOWI
MARGARET WEIR

NOVEMBER 2004

WE THE PEOPLE

An Introduction to American Politics

SHORTER FIFTH EDITION

FOUNDATIONS

1 AMERICAN POLITICAL CULTURE

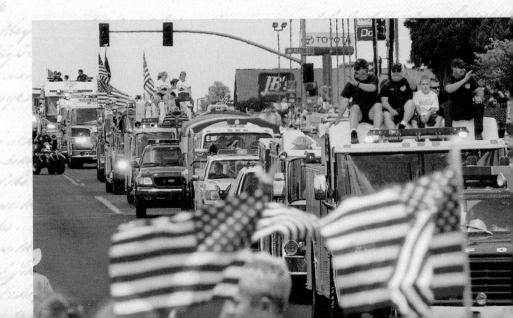

What Government Does and Why It Matters

AMERICANS SOMETIMES APPEAR to believe that the government is an institution that does things *to* them and from which they need protection. Business owners complain that federal health and safety regulations threaten their ability to make a profit. Farmers and ranchers complain that federal and state environmental rules intrude upon their property rights. Motorists allege that municipal "red light" cameras, designed to photograph traffic violators, represent the intrusion of "Big Brother" into their lives. Civil libertarians—including groups like the American Civil Liberties Union (ACLU), organized to defend First Amendment freedoms—express concern over what they view as sometimes overly aggressive police and prosecutorial practices. Everyone complains about federal, state, and local taxes.

Yet many of the same individuals who complain about what the government does *to* them also want the government to do a great deal *for* them. Business owners receive billions of dollars in federal assistance in the form of low-interest loans, marketing services, export assistance, and government contracts. Farmers are the beneficiaries of billions in federal subsidies and research programs. Motorists would have no roads upon which to be photographed by those hated cameras if not for the tens of billions of dollars spent each year on road construction and maintenance by federal, state, and municipal authorities. Individuals accused of crimes benefit from procedural safeguards and state-funded defense attorneys. And, as to those detested taxes, without them there would be no government benefits at all.

Americans' dependence on the government is brought into particularly sharp focus during times of danger. When Pearl Harbor was bombed on December 7, 1941, Americans listened to their radios, waiting for President Franklin D. Roosevelt to tell them how he intended to defend Americans' lives and property. In a similar vein, after the September 11, 2001, terrorist attacks on the World Trade Center and the Pentagon, followed by the delivery of anthrax-contaminated letters to government officials, media corporations, and other sites, Americans demanded government action. President George W. Bush responded by mobilizing powerful military forces and organizing an international coalition for what he defined as a lengthy and worldwide campaign against terrorism. This campaign began with an extensive military operation in Afghanistan, where it appeared that the terrorists responsible for the September 11 attacks were based. Bush also created an Office of Homeland Security (later reorganized as a cabinet department) and instituted massive new law-enforcement measures to combat terrorism. Subsequently, the president ordered that suspected foreign terrorists could be tried before special military tribunals, bypassing the civilian courts and their numerous procedural safeguards. Federal agencies, including the Justice Department and the Transportation Department (which houses the U.S. Coast Guard) developed antiterrorism programs. The Centers for Disease Control moved to develop methods for preventing bioterrorism. The Treasury Department began tracking funds used to support terrorist activities worldwide. The State Department sought to enhance international support for American antiterrorism efforts. At the president's behest, Congress authorized tens of billions of dollars in new federal expenditures to combat terrorism and to repair the damage already caused by terrorists. Congress also enacted legislation requested by the president aimed at safeguarding the nation's airports. The states mobilized their own police and national guard forces for duties such as airport security, and local police and public safety departments were placed on high alert.

In the face of this national emergency, few Americans seemed concerned with the civil liberties of individuals held without trial on suspicion of involvement in terrorist activities and fewer still were worried about the implications for democracy of the president's exercise of emergency powers virtually without congressional involvement. Indeed, Congress seemed almost irrelevant as the president ordered American forces into action in Afghanistan and again, in 2003, when the president launched a massive military campaign against Iraq, a nation he accused of supporting terrorism and developing weapons of mass destruction. At least in the short run, most Americans approved of the president's actions, though as time went on, his standing fell in response to a sluggish economy and concern over American casualties incurred during the occupation of Iraq. Nevertheless, in the face of danger, Americans had looked to the government for action and protection and were less likely to view government as a hostile force from which they needed protection. Former president Bill Clinton famously proclaimed that the era of "big government" was over. His proclamation, however, seems to have been premature. Apparently, like atheists, **libertarians** are scarce in foxholes. ■

libertarian one who favors minimal government and maximum individual freedom

- **In this chapter, we will explore the relationship between the government and the people it governs. First, we will assess what Americans think about their government.** Although Americans have always been distrustful of governmental power, they rely on government for many of their needs. In recent decades, however, trust in government and the belief that individuals can influence government have both been in decline. These trends have important consequences that we need to examine.

- **Second, we will explore the principle of democratic citizenship.** We believe that good citizenship begins with political knowledge—knowledge of government, of politics, and of democratic principles. With this knowledge, citizens can identify their interests and take advantage of their opportunities to influence politics.

- **Next, we will look at the principles of government and politics.** The relationship between a government and its citizens is especially dependent on the form that a government takes. In order to better understand the opportunities that citizens have to influence government, we will look at the alternative forms government can take and the key differences among them. We will also examine the factors that led to the emergence of representative democracy in the United States and elsewhere around the world. In doing so, we will consider one of the most fundamental and enduring problems of democratic politics: the relationship between government and the people it governs.

■ **Finally, we will look at American political culture.** Here, we will examine the political principles that serve as the basis for American government and assess how well government upholds these ideals. We will conclude by suggesting what ordinary citizens can do to make these American political ideals more of a reality.

■ Previewing Liberty, Equality, and Democracy

Liberty, equality, and democracy are key American political values. Liberty means personal freedom and a government whose powers are limited by law. Equality is the idea that all individuals should have a right to participate in political life and society on equivalent terms. Democracy implies placing considerable political power in the hands of ordinary people. Most Americans find it easy to affirm all three values in principle. In practice, however, matters are not always so clear. Policies and practices that seem to affirm one of these values may contradict another. Americans, moreover, are sometimes willing to subordinate liberty to security and have frequently tolerated significant departures from the principles of equality and democracy.

What Americans Think about Government

Since the United States was established as a nation, Americans have been reluctant to grant government too much power, and they have often been suspicious of politicians. But over the course of the nation's history, Americans have also turned to government for assistance in times of need and have strongly supported the government in periods of war, such as during the war against the Taliban in Afghanistan. For example, in 1933, the power of the government began to expand to meet the crises created by the stock market crash of 1929, the Great Depression, and the run on banks of 1933. Congress passed legislation that brought the government into the businesses of home mortgages, farm mortgages, credit, and relief of personal distress. Today, the national government is an enormous institution with programs and policies reaching into every corner of American life. It oversees the nation's economy; it is the nation's largest employer; it provides citizens with a host of services; it controls the world's most formidable military establishment; and it regulates a wide range of social and commercial activities in which Americans engage. Even in the realm of criminal law, a matter once left almost entirely to states and municipalities, the federal government has expanded its reach to deal with economic crimes, civil rights enforcement, narcotics trafficking, terrorism, and a host of other matters.

Citizens are so dependent upon government today that much of what they have come to take for granted—as, somehow, part of the natural environment—is in fact created by government. For example, a college student who drives her car to school may think that she is engaged in a purely private activity. Yet the simple act of driving an automobile is heavily dependent upon a multitude of government initiatives and is surrounded by a host of governmental rules. The roads upon which the student drives were constructed by a local government, probably with

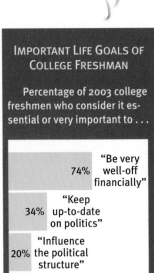

IMPORTANT LIFE GOALS OF COLLEGE FRESHMAN

Percentage of 2003 college freshmen who consider it essential or very important to . . .

74% "Be very well-off financially"

34% "Keep up-to-date on politics"

20% "Influence the political structure"

The Presence of Government in the Daily Life of a Student at "State University"

Box 1.1

Time of Day	Schedule
7:00 AM	Wake up. Standard time set by the national government.
7:10 AM	Shower. Water courtesy of local government, either a public entity or a regulated private company. Brush your teeth with toothpaste, with cavity-fighting claims verified by federal agency. Dry your hair with electric dryer, manufactured according to federal government agency guidelines.
7:30 AM	Have a bowl of cereal with milk for breakfast. "Nutrition Facts" on food labels are a federal requirement, pasteurization of milk required by state law, freshness dating on milk based on state and federal standards, recycling the empty cereal box and milk carton enabled by state or local laws.
8:30 AM	Drive or take public transportation to campus. Air bags and seat belts required by federal and state laws. Roads and bridges paid for by state and local governments, speed and traffic laws set by state and local governments, public transportation subsidized by all levels of government.
8:45 AM	Arrive on campus of large public university. Buildings are 70 percent financed by state taxpayers.
9:00 AM	First class: Chemistry 101. Tuition partially paid by a federal loan (more than half the cost of university instruction is paid for by taxpayers), chemistry lab paid for with grants from the National Science Foundation (a federal agency) and smaller grants from business corporations made possible by federal income tax deductions for charitable contributions.
Noon	Eat lunch. College cafeteria financed by state dormitory authority on land grant from federal Department of Agriculture.
2:00 PM	Second class: American Government 101 (your favorite class!). You may be taking this class because it's required by the state legislature or because it fulfills a university requirement.
4:00 PM	Third class: Computer lab. Free computers, software, and Internet access courtesy of state subsidies plus grants and discounts from IBM and Microsoft, the costs of which are deducted from their corporate income taxes; Internet built in part by federal government. Duplication of software protected by federal copyright laws.
6:00 PM	Eat dinner: hamburger and french fries. Meat inspected by federal agencies for bacteria.
7:00 PM	Work at part-time job at the campus library. Minimum wage set by federal government, books and journals in library paid for by state taxpayers.
10:00 PM	Go to local bar. Purchase and consumption of alcohol regulated by state law and enforced by city police.
11:00 PM	Go home. Street lighting paid for by county and city governments, police patrols by city government.
11:15 PM	Watch TV. Networks regulated by federal government, cable public-access channels required by city law. Weather forecast provided to broadcasters by a federal agency.
Midnight	Put out the garbage before going to bed. Garbage collected by city sanitation department, financed by "user charges."

the assistance of some fraction of the more than $20 billion in federal highway funds spent each year. The roads are maintained by municipal, county, and state governments. During the winter, snow is removed from the roads by local governments. Traffic is regulated by local governments. Road signs are placed and maintained by local and state governments. The student holds a driver's license issued by her state government, which has also registered her vehicle and inspected it for safety and compliance with emissions standards. The vehicle itself has been manufactured to meet safety and emissions standards set by the federal government. The contract under which the student purchased the automobile as well as the loan she signed if she borrowed money for the purchase were both governed by commercial sales and banking regulations established by the state and federal governments. The list goes on.

It might be possible for this student to drive to school without all this government assistance and regulation. In principle, roads could be privately owned, traffic unregulated, and neither drivers nor their autos required to meet any standards. Perhaps our student could still reach her destination in such an environment. Certainly, her driving experience would be markedly different from the current one.

The example of this driver could be applied in endless other situations. Government plays a role in everyone's activities and, by the same token, regulates almost everything we do. Figure 1.1 is a diagram of some of the governmental services received by and controls exerted upon any recent college graduate. Some of these governmental activities are federal; others are the province of state and local governments.

TRUST IN GOVERNMENT

Ironically, even as popular dependence upon it has grown, the American public's view of government has turned more sour. Public trust in government has declined, and Americans are now more likely to feel that they can do little to influence the government's actions. The decline in public trust among Americans is striking. In the early 1960s, three-quarters of Americans said they trusted government most of the time. By 1994, only one-quarter of Americans expressed trust in government; three-quarters stated that they did not trust government most of the time.[1] Different groups vary somewhat in their levels of trust: African Americans and Latinos actually express more confidence in the federal government than do whites. But even among the most supportive groups, more than half do not trust the government.[2] These developments are important because politically engaged citizens and public confidence in government are vital for the health of a democracy.

In the aftermath of the September 11 terrorist attacks, a number of studies reported a substantial increase in popular trust in government. For example, in October 2001, 60 percent of American college students surveyed said they trusted the government to "do the right thing" all or most of the time. Before September 11, only 36 percent expressed a similar view. In addition, 75 percent said they trusted the military, 69 percent expressed trust in the president, and 62 percent trusted Congress.[3] These views, expressed during a period of national crisis, may be indicative less of a renewed *trust* in government to do the right thing than of a fervent

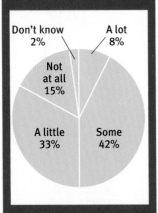

Perspectives on Politics

YOUNG AMERICANS' TRUST IN GOVERNMENT

"How much do you trust the government to do what is right for the country?"

Don't know 2%
A lot 8%
Not at all 15%
A little 33%
Some 42%

SOURCE: Center for Democracy and Citizenship and The Campaign for Young Voters Research Project. "2004 Youth Survey on Internet, Issues, Youth Engagement." Conducted November 2003. www.youngcitizensurvey.org.

Figure 1.1

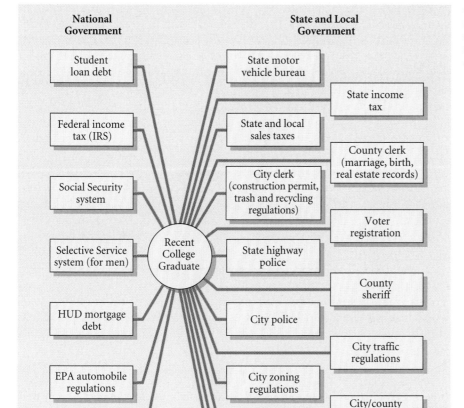

Government is a pervasive force in the lives of all Americans, especially at the state and local level. Think of the many ways in which government affects your life every day.

hope that it will. And, indeed, by July 2003, trust in government had returned to its pre-September 11 level, with only 36 percent of Americans indicating that they trusted the government most or all of the time (see Figure 1.2). During the same period, 48 percent said they would prefer a smaller government offering fewer services.[4] With the apparent waning of the emergency, libertarianism was free to reassert itself.

Levels of trust in government can also differ according to the political context. In early 2002, an ABC News poll found that 68 percent of Americans trusted the government to do what is right "when it comes to handling national security and the war on terrorism," but only 38 percent had the same trust "when it comes to handling social issues like the economy, health care, Social Security, and education."

Figure 1.2   Trust in Government, 1958–2003

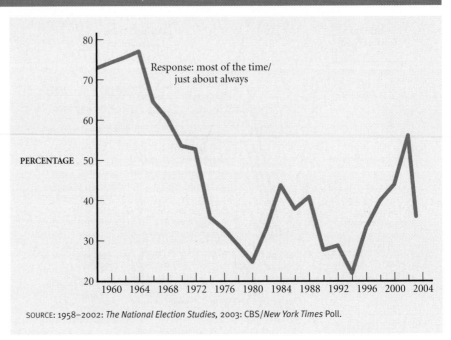

SOURCE: 1958–2002: *The National Election Studies,* 2003: CBS/*New York Times* Poll.

And congressional investigations into the security failures of September 11 may well erode the public's currently high levels of trust on national security issues.

In 2002, following revelations of misconduct by some of America's largest corporations—including the energy giant Enron, telecommunications conglomerate Worldcom, and the accounting firm Arthur Andersen—Americans wondered if they could trust the government to regulate business and the economy. Congress quickly enacted legislation designed to curb corporate abuses and restore public confidence in business. The full extent of the damage, however, will take some time to assess.

Does it matter if Americans trust their government? For the most part, the answer is yes. As we have seen, most Americans rely on government for a wide range of services and laws that they simply take for granted. But long-term distrust in government can result in public refusal to pay taxes adequate to support such widely approved public activities. Low levels of confidence may also make it difficult for government to attract talented and effective workers to public service.[5] The weakening of government as a result of prolonged levels of distrust may ultimately harm our capacity to defend our national interest in the world economy and may jeopardize our national security. Likewise, a weak government can do little to assist citizens who need help in weathering periods of sharp economic or technological change.

POLITICAL EFFICACY

Another important trend in American views about government has been a declining sense of **political efficacy,** the belief that citizens can affect what government does,

FOR CRITICAL ANALYSIS

Does the government deserve our trust? Has the behavior of the U.S. government over the past 50 years inspired or undermined popular trust? Why?

political efficacy the ability to influence government and politics

Americans' trust in their government has fluctuated widely over time and hit a high point in the 1960s. Hundreds of thousands of demonstrators joined the March on Washington in 1963 to demand civil rights for African Americans. These protesters sought justice from the federal government, which they saw as powerful enough to overcome racist laws in individual states. However, during the late 1960s, trust in the federal government began a precipitous decline that accelerated in the 1970s. The Watergate scandal originated with a break-in at the Democratic National Committee headquarters in Washington, D.C., and ended with the resignation of President Richard Nixon. The illegal tactics of the Nixon campaign and administration disgraced the office of the president and shook Americans' trust in government.

During the Reagan years, faith in government recovered somewhat. This trend coincided with Reagan's plan to scale back government. In this photo (left), he is signing a massive tax cut into law—apparently, his attempts to reduce the size of government improved people's perception of it. President Clinton waves his "veto pen" during his State of the Union address in 1994 (right). Universal health care was a central part of Clinton's platform, but his health care bill did not make it through Congress intact. This failure helped bring trust in government to a historic low.

In response to the terrorist attacks of September 11, 2001, Americans rallied around government officials and offered unprecedented support. Government employees like these firefighters became symbols of heroism and reliability. After the state of emergency abated somewhat, federal policy makers were subject to sharper scrutiny, and trust levels dropped.

Perspectives
on
Politics

THE POLITICAL EFFICACY OF YOUNG AMERICANS

"Do you agree or disagree that the government addresses the needs and concerns of young people like you?"

53%   Agree
44%   Disagree

SOURCE: The Center for Information and Reserach in Civic Learning & Engagement Research Project. "The Political and Civic Engagement of Young Adults in America." Conducted January 2002. www.civicyouth. org/research/products/national_ youth_survey.htm

that they can take action to make government listen to them. In recent decades, the public belief that government is responsive to ordinary citizens has declined. In 2000, 56 percent of Americans said that government officials don't care what people think; in 1960, only 25 percent felt so shut out of government. Accompanying this sense that ordinary people can't get heard is a growing belief—held by 61 percent of the public in 2000—that "government is run by a few big interests looking out only for themselves."[6] These views are widely shared across the age spectrum.

Many young Americans feel that government has ignored their views in particular. They feel that older officials cannot understand the challenges and problems facing the younger generation. For example, 72 percent of young people polled agreed that "our generation has an important voice but no one seems to hear it." But young Americans are not alone in feeling that government doesn't listen to them. In fact, most people of earlier generations feel even more strongly than young Americans that public officials have little interest in what they think.[7] The sense that government is out of touch and the feelings of powerlessness and lack of political efficacy that come with it seem to affect most Americans, regardless of age.

This widely felt loss of political efficacy is bad news for American democracy. The feeling that you can't affect government decisions can lead to a self-perpetuating cycle of apathy, declining political participation, and withdrawal from political life. Why bother to participate if you believe it makes no difference? Yet, the belief that you can be effective is the first step needed to influence government. Not every effort of ordinary citizens to influence government will succeed, but without any such efforts, government decisions will be made by a smaller and smaller circle of powerful people. Such loss of broad popular influence over government actions undermines the key feature of American democracy—government by the people.

Who Knows What?

Table 1.1

QUESTION	PERCENTAGE ANSWERING CORRECTLY
What is affirmative action?	31
When was the New Deal?	29
How long is a senator's term?	25
Name two First Amendment rights.	20
What is the Food and Drug Administration?	20
Name all three branches of government.	19
What was the New Deal?	15

SOURCE: Michael X. Delli Carpini and Scott Keeter, *What Americans Know about Politics and Why It Matters* (New Haven, CT: Yale University Press, 1996), pp. 58–94.

What Americans Know about Government

The first prerequisite to achieving an increased sense of political efficacy is knowledge. Political indifference is often simply a habit that stems from a lack of knowledge about how your interests are affected by politics and from a sense that you can do nothing to affect politics. But political efficacy is a self-fulfilling prophecy: if you think you cannot be effective, chances are you will never try. Most research suggests that people active in politics have a high sense of their efficacy. This means they believe they can make a difference—even if they do not win all the time. Most people do not want to be politically active every day of their lives, but it is essential to our political ideals that all citizens be informed and able to act.

Sadly, the state of political knowledge in the United States today is dismal. Most Americans know little about current issues or debates. A recent survey that tested the knowledge of the institutions and processes of government in the United States found that 70 percent of the respondents answered fewer than 60 percent of the questions correctly (see Table 1.1). In most colleges and universities, below 60 is a failing grade. But, rather than dwell on the widespread political ignorance of many Americans, we prefer to view this as an opportunity for the readers of this book. Those of you who make the effort to become among the knowledgeable few will be much better prepared to influence the political system regarding the issues and concerns that you care most about. Finally, bear in mind that no citizen has to be alone in the effort to influence government. An important aspect of political knowledge is knowing who shares your interests.

CITIZENSHIP: KNOWLEDGE AND PARTICIPATION

After September 11, many commentators noted a revival in Americans' sense of citizenship, as manifested by ubiquitous flag displays and other demonstrations of patriotic sentiment. There seems to be little doubt that millions of Americans experienced a renewed sense of identification with their nation. Citizenship, however, has a broader meaning than just patriotism.

Beginning with the ancient Greeks, citizenship has meant membership in one's community. In fact, the Greeks did not even conceive of the individual as a complete person. The complete person was the public person, the *citizen;* noncitizens and private persons were referred to as *idiotés.* Participation in public affairs was virtually the definition of citizenship. Citizenship was never defined as voting. Although voting was not excluded, the essence of citizen participation was talking. As one political philosopher put it, "What counts is argument among the citizens. . . . [T]he citizen who makes the most persuasive argument gets [his or her] way but can't use force, or pull rank, or distribute money; [the citizen] must talk about the issues at hand. . . . Citizens must come into the forum with nothing but their arguments."[8] Involvement in the public debate is the central, quintessential right of citizenship. Following the Greek ideal, the First Amendment to the U.S. Constitution makes freedom of speech the primary right of American citizenship.

Our meaning for **citizenship** derives from the Greek ideal: enlightened political engagement.[9] To be politically engaged in a meaningful way, citizens require resources, especially political knowledge and information. Democracy functions best when citizens are informed.

But to be a citizen in the full sense as understood first by the ancient Greeks requires more than an occasional visit to an election booth. A true citizen must have the knowledge needed to participate in political debate. If you want to be a citizen rather than an *idioté,* it is important that you acquire three forms of political knowledge from this course and this textbook:

> **citizenship** informed and active membership in a political community

1. *Knowledge of government.* Citizens must understand the "rules of the game." From the citizen's perspective, the most important rules concern one's own political rights, which can vary greatly according to the type of government under which one lives. In the United States, these rights are extensive and concrete, and they affect every citizen directly.
2. *Knowledge of politics.* We need to understand what is at stake in the political world. This understanding includes the capacity to discern our own interests in the political arena and identify the best means through which to realize them.
3. *Knowledge of democratic principles.* Although politics may divide Americans, democratic ideals hold them together. As citizens, we need to know what forms of political conduct are consistent with democratic principles. Democracy requires that both government and citizens be aware of and respect the constraints upon their political activities.

Political knowledge means more than having a few opinions to offer the pollster or to guide your decisions in a voting booth. It is important to know the rules and strategies that govern political institutions and the principles upon which they are based, but it is more important to know them in ways that relate to your own interests. Citizens need knowledge in order to assess their interests and know when to act upon them. Knowledgeable citizens are more attentive to and more engaged in politics because they understand how and why politics is relevant to their lives.

THE NECESSITY OF POLITICAL KNOWLEDGE

Political knowledge is the key to effective participation in political life. Without political knowledge, no citizen can be aware of her interests or stake in a political dispute.

In the year preceding the 2004 presidential election, for example, many of the prospective Democratic candidates presented rather detailed proposals on ways of changing the current American tax system. How many voters paid enough attention to the discussion to be able to meaningfully distinguish among the various proposals and their implications? Did you attempt to ascertain whether you and your family would be better off under the tax system envisioned by Kerry, Dean, Clark, or Sharpton rather than the system favored by President Bush? How could you participate intelligently without this knowledge? Interestingly, various public and private interest groups devote enormous time and energy to understanding alternative policy proposals and their implications so they will know whom to support. Interest groups understand something that every citizen should also understand: effective participation requires knowledge.

Citizens also need political knowledge to identify the best ways of acting upon their interests. If your road is rendered impassable by snow, what can you do? Is snow removal the responsibility of the federal government? Is it a state or municipal responsibility? Knowing that you have a stake in a clear road does not help much if you do not know that snow removal is a city or county responsibility and you cannot identify the municipal agency that deals with the problem. Americans are fond of complaining that government is not responsive to their needs, but is it not possible that many citizens simply lack the information they need to present their problems to the appropriate government officials?

Citizens need political knowledge, as well, to ascertain what they cannot or should not ask of politicians and the government. The famous Scottish economist Adam Smith once observed that in the economic realm the selfish pursuit of private interests improved the general good as if by "an invisible hand." Smith's idea is the basis for our belief in free markets today. It is not so clear, however, that Smith's logic applies as well to political life. One of the reasons that we take part in political life is that many of our most important collective goals, including defense, protection of the environment, and safety from crime, are unlikely to be achieved purely by individual action. We need to cooperate in order to defend our nation, protect our environment, and keep our homes safe. Thus, political knowledge includes knowing the limits upon, as well as the possibilities for pursuing, one's own individual interests through political action. This is, perhaps, the most difficult form of political knowledge to acquire.

The rest of this chapter will look at the forms of political knowledge that we believe are most critical for a citizen to possess. In the next section, we will examine the principles of government and politics. Following that, we will review the democratic principles upon which the United States is based and assess how well American government fulfills these principles. Finally, we will conclude with suggestions of what you and other ordinary citizens can do to become more knowledgeable and more engaged.

FOR CRITICAL ANALYSIS

Democracy implies some level of popular involvement and political knowledge. Many studies, though, seem to show that most Americans know very little about government and politics. Can we have democratic government without knowledgeable and aware citizens?

Government

Government is the term generally used to describe the formal institutions through which a land and its people are ruled. To govern is to rule. A government may be as simple as a tribal council that meets occasionally to advise the chief, or as complex as the vast establishments, with their forms, rules, and bureaucracies, found in the

government institutions and procedures through which a territory and its people are ruled

United States. A more complex government is sometimes referred to as "the state." In the history of civilization, governments have not been difficult to establish. There have been thousands of them. The hard part is establishing a government that lasts. Even more difficult is developing a stable government that is compatible with liberty, equality, and democracy.

IS GOVERNMENT NEEDED?

Americans have always harbored some suspicion of government and have wondered how extensive a role it should play in their lives. Thomas Jefferson famously observed that the best government was one that "governed least." Generally speaking, a government is needed to provide those services, sometimes called "public goods," that all citizens need but are not likely to be able to adequately provide for themselves. These might include defense against foreign aggression, maintenance of public order, enforcement of contractual obligations and property rights, and a guarantee of some measure of social justice. The precise extent to which government involvement in our society is needed has been debated throughout our history and will continue to be a central focus of political contention in America.

FORMS OF GOVERNMENT

Governments vary in their structure, in their size, and in the way they operate. Two questions are of special importance in determining how governments differ: Who governs? And how much government control is permitted?

In some nations, governing is done by a single individual—a king or dictator, for example. This state of affairs is called **autocracy.** Where a small group—perhaps landowners, military officers, or wealthy merchants—controls most of the governing decisions, that government is said to be an **oligarchy.** If more people participate and have some influence over decision making, that government is a **democracy.**

Governments also vary considerably in terms of how they govern. In the United States and a small number of other nations, governments are limited as to what they are permitted to control (substantive limits), as well as how they go about it (procedural limits). Governments that are limited in this way are called **constitutional governments,** or liberal governments. In other nations, including many in Europe as well as in South America, Asia, and Africa, though the law imposes few real limits, the government is nevertheless kept in check by other political and social institutions that the government is unable to control and must come to terms with—such as autonomous territories, an organized religion, organized business groups, or organized labor unions. Such governments are generally called **authoritarian.** In a third group of nations, including the Soviet Union under Joseph Stalin, Nazi Germany, and perhaps prewar Japan and Italy, governments not only are free of legal limits but also seek to eliminate those organized social groups that might challenge or limit their authority. These governments typically attempt to dominate or control every sphere of political, economic, and social life and, as a result, are called **totalitarian.**

Americans have the good fortune to live in a nation in which limits are placed on what governments can do and how they can do it. But such constitutional democracies are relatively rare in today's world; it is estimated that only twenty or

autocracy a form of government in which a single individual—a king, queen, or dictator—rules

oligarchy a form of government in which a small group—landowners, military officers, or wealthy merchants—controls most of the governing decisions

democracy a system of rule that permits citizens to play a significant part in the governmental process, usually through the election of key public officials

constitutional government a system of rule in which formal and effective limits are placed on the powers of the government

authoritarian government a system of rule in which the government recognizes no formal limits but may nevertheless be restrained by the power of other social institutions

totalitarian government a system of rule in which the government recognizes no formal limits on its power and seeks to absorb or eliminate other social institutions that might challenge it so of the world's nearly 200 governments could be included in this category. And constitutional democracies were unheard of before the modern era. Prior to the eighteenth and nineteenth centuries, governments seldom sought—and rarely received—the support of their ordinary subjects. The available evidence strongly suggests that the ordinary people had little love for the government or for the social order. After all, they had no stake in it. They equated government with the police officer, the bailiff, and the tax collector.[10]

Beginning in the seventeenth century, in a handful of Western nations, two important changes began to take place in the character and conduct of government. First, governments began to acknowledge formal limits upon their power. Second, a small number of governments began to provide the ordinary citizen with a formal voice in public affairs—through the vote. Obviously, the desirability of limits on government and the expansion of popular influence were at the heart of the American Revolution in 1776. "No taxation without representation," as we shall see in Chapter 2, was hotly debated from the beginning of the Revolution through the Founding in 1789. But even before the Revolution, a tradition of limiting government and expanding participation in the political process had developed throughout western Europe. Thus, to understand how the relationship between rulers and the ruled was transformed, we must broaden our focus to take into account events in Europe as well as in America. We will have to divide the transformation into its two separate parts. The first is the effort to put limits on government. The second is the effort to expand the influence of the people through access to government and politics.

LIMITING GOVERNMENT

The key force behind the imposition of limits on government power was a new social class, the bourgeoisie. *Bourgeois* is a French word for freeman of the city, or *bourg*. Being part of the bourgeoisie later became associated with being "middle class" and with being in commerce or industry. In order to gain a share of control of government, joining or even displacing the kings, aristocrats, and gentry who had dominated government for centuries, the bourgeoisie sought to change existing institutions—especially parliaments—into instruments of real political participation. Parliaments had existed for centuries, but were generally aristocratic institutions. The bourgeoisie embraced parliaments as means by which they could exert the weight of their superior numbers and growing economic advantage against their aristocratic rivals. At the same time, the bourgeoisie sought to place restraints on the capacity of governments to threaten these economic and political interests by placing formal or constitutional limits on governmental power.

Although motivated primarily by the need to protect and defend their own interests, the bourgeoisie advanced many of the principles that became the central underpinnings of individual liberty for all citizens—freedom of speech, freedom of assembly, freedom of conscience, and freedom from arbitrary search and seizure. It is important to note here that the bourgeoisie generally did not favor democracy as we know it. They were advocates of electoral and representative institutions, but they favored property requirements and other restrictions so as to limit participation to the middle classes. Yet once these institutions of politics and the protection of the right to engage in politics were established, it was difficult to limit them to the bourgeoisie.

ACCESS TO GOVERNMENT: THE EXPANSION OF PARTICIPATION

The expansion of participation from the bourgeoisie to ever-larger segments of society took two paths. In some nations, popular participation was expanded by the crown or the aristocracy, which ironically saw common people as potential political allies against the bourgeoisie. Thus in nineteenth-century Prussia, for example, it was the emperor and his great minister Otto von Bismarck who expanded popular participation in order to build political support among the lower orders.

In other nations, participation expanded because competing segments of the bourgeoisie sought to gain political advantage by reaching out and mobilizing the support of working- and lower-class groups who craved the opportunity to take part in politics—"lining up the unwashed," as one American historian put it.[11] To be sure, excluded groups often agitated for greater participation. But seldom was such agitation, by itself, enough to secure the right to participate. Usually, expansion of voting rights resulted from a combination of pressure from below and help from above.

This pattern of suffrage expansion by groups hoping to derive some political advantage has been typical in American history. After the Civil War, one of the chief reasons that Republicans moved to enfranchise newly freed slaves was to use the support of the former slaves to maintain Republican control over the defeated southern states. Similarly, in the early twentieth century, upper-middle-class "Progressives" advocated women's suffrage because they believed that women were likely to support the reforms espoused by the Progressive movement.

INFLUENCING THE GOVERNMENT THROUGH PARTICIPATION: POLITICS

Expansion of participation means that more and more people have a legal right to take part in politics. Politics is an important term. In its broadest sense, "politics" refers to conflicts over the character, membership, and policies of any organization to which people belong. As Harold Lasswell, a famous political scientist, once put it, politics is the struggle over "who gets what, when, how."[12] Although politics is a phenomenon that can be found in any organization, our concern in this book is more narrow. Here, **politics** will be used to refer only to conflicts and struggles over the leadership, structure, and policies of governments. The goal of politics, as we define it, is to have a share or a say in the composition of the government's leadership, how the government is organized, or what its policies are going to be. Having a share is called having **power** or influence.

Politics can take many forms, including everything from sending letters to government officials to voting, lobbying legislators on behalf of particular programs, and participating in protest marches and even violent demonstrations. A system of government that gives citizens a regular opportunity to elect the top government officials is usually called a **representative democracy** or **republic.** A system that permits citizens to vote directly on laws and policies is often called a **direct democracy.** At the national level, America is a representative democracy in which citizens select government officials but do not vote on legislation. Some states and cities,

politics conflict over the leadership, structure, and policies of governments

power influence over a government's leadership, organization, or policies

representative democracy/ republic a system of government in which the populace selects representatives, who play a significant role in governmental decision making

direct democracy a system of rule that permits citizens to vote directly on laws and policies however, have provisions for direct legislation through popular initiative and ballot referendum. These procedures allow citizens to collect petitions requiring an issue to be brought directly to the voters for a decision. In 2002, more than 200 initiatives appeared on state ballots. These dealt with matters ranging from taxes and education to animal cruelty and marijuana use. While most measures failed, a number were voted into law. In Oklahoma, for example, the electorate approved a ban on cock fighting; Florida voters approved a measure requiring more humane treatment of pregnant pigs. In California, Proposition 49, mandating more state spending on before- and after-school programs, was approved by the electorate. This initiative had been heavily promoted by actor Arnold Schwarzenegger, who, in 2003, became California's governor in a recall election. Mandated by a number of states, the recall is a form of election that permits voters to end the terms of state officials before they are due to expire. Schwarzenegger replaced Governor Gray Davis, who became the first state governor to be recalled in more than eighty years.

Groups and organized interests obviously do not vote (although their members do), but they certainly do participate in politics. Their political activities usually consist of such endeavors as providing funds for candidates, lobbying, and trying to influence public opinion. The pattern of struggles among interests is called group politics, or **pluralism.** Americans have always been ambivalent about pluralist politics. On one hand, the right of groups to press their views and compete for influence in the government is the essence of liberty. On the other hand, Americans often fear that organized groups may sometimes exert too much influence, advancing special interests at the expense of larger public interests. We will return to this problem in Chapter 11.

Sometimes, of course, politics does not take place through formal channels at all but instead involves direct action. **Direct action politics** can include either violent politics or civil disobedience, both of which attempt to shock rulers into behaving more responsibly. Direct action can also be a form of revolutionary politics, which rejects the system entirely and attempts to replace it with a new ruling group and a new set of rules. In recent years in the United States, groups ranging from animal-rights activists to right-to-life advocates to protesters against the war in Iraq have used direct action to underline their demands. Direct political action is protected by the U.S. Constitution. The country's Founders knew that the right to protest is essential to the maintenance of political freedom, even where the ballot box is available.

pluralism the theory that all interests are and should be free to compete for influence in the government. The outcome of this competition is compromise and moderation

direct action politics a form of politics, such as civil disobedience or revolutionary action, that takes place outside formal channels

FOR CRITICAL ANALYSIS

What type of government does the United States have? Is it the most democratic government possible? Do citizens make the decisions of government or do they merely influence them?

American Political Culture: Shared Values, but Disagreements over the Role of Government

Underlying and framing political life in the United States are agreements on basic political values but disagreements over the ends or goals of government. Values shape citizens' views of the world and define their sense of what is right and wrong, just and unjust, possible and impossible. If Americans shared no values, they would have difficulty communicating, much less agreeing upon a common system of government and politics. On the other hand, sharing broad values does not guarantee political consensus. We can agree on principles but disagree over their application.

For example, some critics claim that measures such as affirmative action have not promoted political inclusion and instead have condoned reverse discrimination and a segmented society. Far from fulfilling American ideals, they argue, these policies represent a movement away from our most fundamental values. An opposing perspective questions the progress that has been made in promoting equality. Pointing to the disproportionately high rates of poverty among women and minorities and continuing evidence of discrimination against these groups, this side questions whether Americans are serious about equality. Much of the debate over the role of government has been over what government should do and how far it should go to reduce the inequalities within our society and political system.

Even though Americans have disagreed over the meaning of such political ideals as equality, they still agree on the importance of these ideals. The shared values, beliefs, and attitudes that form our **political culture** and serve to hold the United States and its people together date back to the time of the founding of the union.

The essential documents of the American Founding—the Declaration of Independence and the Constitution—enunciated a set of political principles about the purposes of the new republic. In contrast with many other democracies, in the United States these political ideals did not just remain words on dusty documents. Americans actively embraced the principles of the Founders and made them central to the national identity. Let us look more closely at three of these ideals: liberty, equality, and democracy.

LIBERTY

No ideal is more central to American values than liberty. The Declaration of Independence defined three inalienable rights: "life, liberty and the pursuit of happiness." The preamble of the Constitution likewise identified the need to secure "the blessings of liberty" as one of the key reasons for drawing up the Constitution. For Americans, **liberty** means both personal freedom and economic freedom. Both are closely linked to the idea of **limited government.**

The Constitution's first ten amendments, known collectively as the Bill of Rights, above all preserve individual personal liberties and rights. In fact, liberty has come to mean many of the freedoms guaranteed in the Bill of Rights: freedom of speech and writing, the right to assemble freely, and the right to practice religious beliefs without interference from the government. Over the course of American history, the scope of personal liberties has expanded, as laws have become more tolerant and as individuals have successfully used the courts to challenge restrictions on their individual freedoms. Far fewer restrictions exist today on the press, political speech, and individual moral behavior than in the early years of the nation. Even so, conflicts persist over how personal liberties should be extended and when personal liberties violate community norms. For example, one of the most contentious issues in the last thirty years has been that of abortion. Whereas defenders of the right to choose abortion view it as an essential personal freedom for women, opponents view it as murder—something that no society should allow.

In addition to personal freedom, the American concept of liberty means economic freedom. Since the Founding, economic freedom has been linked to capital-

political culture broadly shared values, beliefs, and attitudes about how the government should function. American political culture emphasizes the values of liberty, equality, and democracy

liberty freedom from governmental control

limited government a principle of constitutional government; a government whose powers are defined and limited by a constitution ism, free markets, and the protection of private property. Free competition, unfettered movement of goods, and the right to enjoy the fruits of one's labor are all essential aspects of economic freedom and American capitalism.[13] In the first century of the Republic, support for capitalism often meant support for the doctrine of "laissez-faire" (translated literally as to "leave alone"). **Laissez-faire capitalism** allowed very little room for the national government to regulate trade or restrict the use of private property, even in the public interest. Americans still strongly support capitalism and economic liberty, but they now also endorse some restrictions on economic freedoms to protect the public. Federal and state governments now deploy a wide array of regulations in the name of public protection. These include health and safety laws, environmental rules, and workplace regulations. Not surprisingly, fierce disagreements often erupt over what the proper scope of government regulation should be. What some people regard as protecting the public, others see as an infringement on their own freedom to run their businesses and use their property as they see fit.

laissez-faire capitalism an economic system in which the means of production and distribution are privately owned and operated for profit with minimal or no government interference

EQUALITY

The Declaration of Independence declares as its first "self-evident" truth that "all men are created equal." As central as it is to the American political creed, however, equality has been a less well defined ideal than liberty because people interpret "equality" in different ways. Few Americans have wholeheartedly embraced full equality of results, but most Americans share the ideal of **equality of opportunity**—that is, the notion that each person should be given a fair chance to go as far as his or her talents will allow. Yet it is hard for Americans to reach agreement about what constitutes equality of opportunity. Must *past* inequalities be remedied in order to ensure equal opportunity in the *present*? Should inequalities in the legal, political, and economic spheres be given the same weight? In contrast to liberty, which requires limits on the role of government, equality implies an *obligation* of the government to the people.[14]

equality of opportunity a widely shared American ideal that all people should have the freedom to use whatever talents and wealth they have to reach their fullest potential

Americans do make clear distinctions between political equality and social or economic equality. **Political equality** means that members of the American political community have the right to participate in politics on equal terms. Beginning from a very restricted definition of political community, which originally included only propertied white men, the United States has moved much closer to an ideal of political equality that can be summed up as "one person, one vote." Broad support for the ideal of political equality has helped expand the American political community and extend the right to participate to all. Although considerable conflict remains over whether the political system makes it harder for some people to participate and easier for others and about whether the role of money in politics has drowned out the public voice, Americans agree that all citizens should have an equal right to participate and that government should enforce that right.

political equality the right to participate in politics equally, based on the principle of "one person, one vote"

In part because Americans believe that individuals are free to work as hard as they choose, they have always been less concerned about social or economic inequality. Many Americans regard economic differences as the consequence of individual choices, virtues, or failures. Because of this, Americans tend to be less supportive than most Europeans of government action to ensure equality. Yet

Since the Founding, liberty—
personal and economic
freedom—has been central to
the political values of
Americans. Patrick Henry's
famous "Give me liberty, or give
me death" speech demanded
freedom at any cost and has
resonated with Americans
throughout the nation's history.

The new country did not meet Henry's demand for freedom, at least not for all people.
Samuel Jennings painted this work, Liberty Displaying the Arts and Sciences, in 1792.
The books, instruments, and classical columns at the left of the painting contrast with the
kneeling slaves at the right—illustrating the divide between America's rhetoric of liberty
and the political and economic reality of slavery.

when major economic forces, such as the Great Depression of the 1930s, affect
many people or when systematic barriers appear to block equality of opportunity,
Americans support government action to promote equality. Even then, however,
Americans have endorsed only a limited government role designed to help people
get back on their feet or to open up opportunity.

DEMOCRACY

Americans' political devotion to
freedom manifests itself in
many everyday ways. For
example, all U.S. coins have
been inscribed with the word
"liberty" since 1792.

The essence of democracy is the participation of the people in choosing their rulers
and the people's ability to influence what those rulers do. In a democracy, political
power ultimately comes from the people. The idea of placing power in the hands of
the people is known as **popular sovereignty.** In the United States, popular sovereignty and political equality make politicians accountable to the people. Ideally,
democracy envisions an engaged citizenry prepared to exercise its power over
rulers. As we saw earlier, the United States is a representative democracy, meaning
that the people do not rule directly but instead exercise power through elected representatives. Forms of participation in a democracy vary greatly, but voting is a key
element of the representative democracy that the American Founders established.

American democracy rests on the principle of **majority rule** with **minority
rights.** Majority rule means that the wishes of the majority determine what gov-

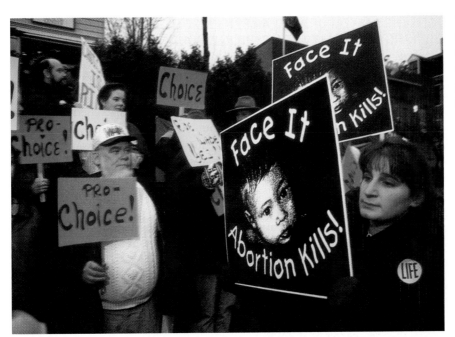

The issue of freedom plays out in a personal way in abortion rights. Politically, the debate hinges on the extent of government control over personal liberty.

ernment does. The House of Representatives—a large body elected directly by the people—was designed in particular to ensure majority rule. But the Founders feared that popular majorities could turn government into a "tyranny of the majority" in which individual liberties would be violated. Concern for individual rights has thus been a part of American democracy from the beginning. The rights enumerated in the Bill of Rights and enforced through the courts provide an important check on the power of the majority.

popular sovereignty a principle of democracy in which political authority rests ultimately in the hands of the people

majority rule/minority rights the democratic principle that a government follows the preferences of the majority of voters but protects the interests of the minority

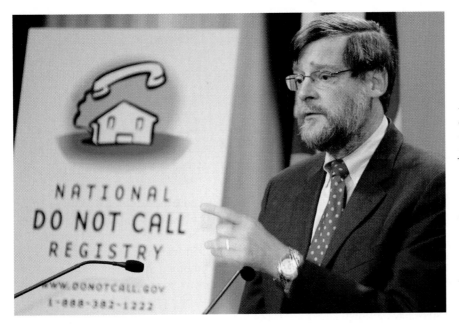

In 2003, the federal government created the National Do Not Call Registry to make it easier for Americans to stop getting unwanted telemarketing calls. Government regulations intended to protect the public are sometimes viewed by business as infringements on economic liberty. In this case, the Direct Marketing Association called the ban an infringement on the freedom of speech.

DOES THE SYSTEM UPHOLD AMERICAN POLITICAL VALUES?: THINKING CRITICALLY ABOUT LIBERTY, EQUALITY, AND DEMOCRACY

Clearly, the ideals of liberty, equality, and democracy are open to diverse interpretations. We should note, moreover, that debates about ideals are not only discussions of abstract principles but they also involve questions of who will benefit from the government's actions. In general, the assertion that individual liberty should be America's primary political value is an argument for limiting the government's power in America's economy and society. Frequently, though not always, this is an argument made on behalf of those who are satisfied with their place in the scheme of things and who fear that government intervention might threaten that place. In a similar vein, those who point to equality as the fundamental value also see themselves as potential beneficiaries of the powerful and activist government that would be needed to bring about a more egalitarian society. Debates over democracy, therefore, often pit forces satisfied with the current balance of power against those who would like to see new political procedures that might shake up the political establishment and bring new groups to power. Sometimes these debates are subtle. For example, some proponents of campaign finance reform—presented as a democratizing measure—see limits on campaign spending as a vehicle for protecting the status quo by preventing challengers from mounting well-financed campaigns against incumbents. Thus, debates over core values are also disputes over what the government should do and, more important, over who will benefit. Also, the ideals can easily conflict with one another in practice. When we examine American history, we can see that there have been large gaps between these ideals and the practice of American politics. We can also see that some ideals have been prized more than others at different historical moments. But it is also clear that as Americans have engaged in political conflict about who should participate in politics and how political institutions should be organized, they have called upon these ideals to justify their actions. Now let's reexamine these ideals, noting key historical conflicts and current controversies about what they should mean in practice.

Liberty   The central historical conflict regarding liberty in the United States was about the enslavement of blacks. The facts of slavery and the differential treatment of the races have cast a long shadow over all of American history. In fact, scholars today note that the American definition of freedom has been formed in relation to the concept of slavery. The right to control one's labor and the right to receive rewards for that labor have been central elements of our definition of freedom precisely because these freedoms were denied to slaves.[15]

Concerns about the meaning of liberty also arise in connection with government regulation of economic and social activity. Economic regulations imposed to ensure public health and safety are often decried by the affected businesses as infringements on their freedom. For example, in 1994, the Occupational Safety and Health Administration (OSHA) of the national government prepared to issue regulations intended to protect workers from repetitive stress injuries. Such injuries, which affect 700,000 workers a year, are caused by long hours on the assembly line or at the computer. OSHA's regulations would have required employers to provide specified work breaks and proper furniture and other equipment. Although such regulations might have been welcomed by workers, employers viewed them as intrusive and extremely costly. In the face of strong opposition from employers, OSHA backed down and decided not to issue the regulations.[16]

Social regulations prompt similar disputes. Some citizens believe that government should enforce certain standards of behavior or instill particular values in citizens. Examples of such activity abound: welfare rules that once denied benefits to women who were found with a "man in the house," the practice of saying prayers in school, laws that require parents to pay child support for their children even if those children no longer live with them, and laws that require citizens to wear seat belts are just a few examples. Deciding the proper scope of economic and social regulation is a topic of great concern and much conflict among Americans today.

More recently, concerns about liberty have arisen in relation to the government's efforts to combat terrorism. In November 2001, President Bush issued an executive order mandating that suspected foreign terrorists would be tried before special military tribunals rather than in the regular federal courts. Hypothetically, such tribunals could impose severe penalties—on the basis of evidence that might not be admitted in civilian courts. Earlier, the Justice Department had announced that federal investigators would be allowed to eavesdrop on conversations between terrorist suspects and their attorneys. In the months following September 11, hundreds of individuals—mainly of Middle Eastern origin—were arrested by federal authorities and held on immigration charges or by material witness warrants that allowed the government to incarcerate them without having to show any evidence they were linked to terrorist activities. The events of September 11 leave us with an extraordinary dilemma. On the one hand, we treasure liberty, but on the other hand, we recognize that the lives of thousands of Americans have already been lost and countless others are threatened by terrorism. Can we reconcile liberty and security? Liberty and order? In previous national emergencies, Americans accepted restrictions on liberty with the understanding that these would be temporary. For example, military tribunals were established during World War II to try German saboteurs who landed on the East Coast. President Bush, however, has said that the war against terrorism will last years and years. Clearly, the implications for American liberty will be profound.

Equality Because equality is such an elusive concept, many conflicts have arisen over what it should mean in practice. Americans have engaged in three kinds of controversies about the public role in addressing inequality. The first is determining what constitutes equality of access to public institutions. In 1896, the Supreme Court ruled in *Plessy v. Ferguson* that "separate but equal" accommodations for blacks and whites were constitutional. In 1954, in a major legal victory for the civil rights movement, the Supreme Court overturned the separate but equal doctrine in *Brown v. Board of Education* (see Chapter 5). Today, new questions have been raised about what constitutes equal access to public institutions. Some argue that the unequal financing of public schools in cities, suburbs, and rural districts is a violation of the right to equal education. To date, these claims have not been supported by the federal courts, which have rejected the notion that the unequal economic impacts of public policy outcomes are a constitutional matter.[17] Lawsuits arguing a right to "economic equal protection" stalled in 1973 when the Supreme Court ruled that a Texas school-financing law did not violate the Constitution even though the law affected rich and poor students differently.[18]

A second debate concerns the public role in ensuring equality of opportunity in private life. Although Americans generally agree that discrimination should not be

FOR CRITICAL ANALYSIS

Combating terrorism has entailed restrictions on civil liberties. Does America believe in liberty only when it is convenient? How can we reconcile civil liberty and national security? When we, as a nation, are compelled to make choices, are we better off opting for more liberty or for more security?

Table 1.2	American Attitudes about Equality

STATEMENT	PERCENTAGE WHO AGREE
Our society should do whatever is necessary to make sure that everyone has an equal opportunity to succeed.	82
We have gone too far in pushing equal rights in this country.	45
One of the big problems in this country is that we don't give everyone an equal chance.	48
It is not really that big a problem if some people have more of a chance in life than others.	37
The country would be better off if we worried less about how equal people are.	53
If people were treated more equally in this country, we would have many fewer problems.	83

SOURCE: Based on 1996 and 1998 data from the American National Election Studies, conducted by the University of Michigan, Center for Political Studies, and provided by the Inter-University Consortium for Political and Social Research, Ann Arbor, Michigan.

tolerated, people disagree over what should be done to ensure equality of opportunity (see Table 1.2). Controversies about affirmative action programs reflect these disputes. Supporters of affirmative action claim that such programs are necessary to compensate for past discrimination in order to obtain true equality of opportunity today. Opponents maintain that affirmative action amounts to reverse discrimination and that a society that espouses true equality should not acknowledge gender or racial differences. The question of the public responsibility for private inequalities is central to gender issues. The traditional view, still held by many today, sees the special responsibilities of women in the family as something that falls outside the range of public concern. Indeed, from this perspective, the role of women within families is essential to the functioning of a democratic society. In the past thirty years, especially, these traditional views have come under fire, as advocates for women have argued that women occupy a subordinate place within the family and that such private inequalities *are* a topic of public concern.[19]

A third debate about equality concerns differences in income and wealth. Unlike in other countries, income inequality has not been an enduring topic of political controversy in the United States, which currently has the largest gap in income and wealth between rich and poor citizens of any developed nation. But Americans have generally tolerated great differences among rich and poor citizens, in part because of a pervasive belief that mobility is possible and that economic success is the product of individual effort.[20] At times, however, concern about economic inequalities emerges, often around the issue of fair taxation. Some analysts today warn that the growing division between rich and poor may invigorate a politics of class and polarize political debate along income lines.[21]

Political participation was greatest during the nineteenth century. In George Caleb Bingham's Verdict of the People *(1853–54), a crowd seems half delighted with and half regretful about the outcome of the vote. But as this painting indicates, white men were virtually the only people who could vote at the time.*

Democracy Despite Americans' deep attachment to the *ideal* of democracy, many questions can be raised about our *practice* of democracy. The first is the restricted definition of the political community during much of American history. The United States was not a full democracy until the 1960s, when African Americans were at last guaranteed the right to vote. Property restrictions on the right to vote were eliminated by 1828; in 1870, the Fifteenth Amendment to the

Voting rights expanded dramatically during the civil rights movement, which forced the government to allow people to vote regardless of their race. Here, residents of Wilcox County, Alabama, line up to vote in 1966. Prior to the passage of the Voting Rights Act of 1965, Wilcox County had no registered black voters.

Should America Export Democracy?

Americans are justifiably proud of their democratic political institutions and often believe that the people of all nations would benefit from living under American-style democratic rule. Indeed, on a number of occasions Americans have sought to transform other nations into democracies—a policy called "democratization." In the aftermath of World War II, American military forces occupied Japan and the western portion of Germany. Before allowing these defeated powers to reclaim their political independence, the United States imposed new democratic governments to replace the dictatorial regimes blamed for launching the war. Today, both Germany and Japan are parliamentary democracies. More recently, after successful American military campaigns to overthrow the governments of Afghanistan and Iraq, the United States has undertaken an effort to build democratic governments in those nations. In November 2003, for example, the American-backed interim Afghan government unveiled a proposal for a new constitution similar to the U.S. Constitution, including an elected president and a bicameral legislature.

There are three reasons that exporting democracy might be seen as a desirable goal. The first of these is humanitarian. Generally speaking, individuals are better off when they possess civil liberties and political rights. President George W. Bush alluded to this purpose of democratization in his November 2003 speech to the National Endowment for Democracy, a government-sponsored institution designed to promote democratic political practices throughout the world. In his speech, Bush asserted that one of the main purposes of American policy in the Middle East was to bring democracy to the people of the region. "It is the calling of our country," Bush said.

A second reason sometimes given in support of American efforts to export democracy is the promotion of political stability. In a democracy, competing economic and social forces have a chance to work out their differences through lawful political struggle. Dictatorial regimes, by contrast, seldom provide opportunities for lawful political activity and usually seek to quash expressions of political dissent or opposition. Lacking lawful channels, when they are expressed, political grievances in nations ruled by dictatorships usually manifest themselves in such forms as public protest, political violence, and terrorism. Instability and violence in one country can easily spread beyond borders to pose threats elsewhere. In his November 2003 speech, President Bush alluded to the instability associated with dicta-

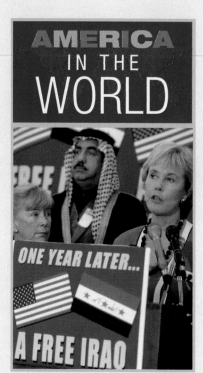

torial regimes as another reason the United States sought democratization, particularly in the Middle East. "As long as the Middle East remains a place where freedom does not flourish," said Bush, "it will remain a place of stagnation, resentment and violence ready for export. And with the spread of weapons that can bring catastrophic harm to our country and to our friends, it would be reckless to accept the status quo."

A third reason Americans might wish to support policies of democratization is that the spread of democracy may promote world peace. The connection between democracy and peace was first explored by the German philosopher Immanuel Kant in his famous 1795 essay "Toward Perpetual Peace." Kant observed that democratic regimes seldom made war on one another. Thus, he argued, the expansion of democracy would enhance the prospects for world peace. In recent years, a good deal of empirical research has supported Kant's hypothesis.

While a more democratic world might, indeed, be more humane, stable, and peaceful, a policy of democratization faces daunting prospects. First, a huge percentage of the world's population lives in nations that are not democracies. According to Freedom House, a nonprofit organization that has monitored international political developments since 1941, more than 100 of the world's 192 independent nations, accounting for two-thirds of the globe's population, were "not free" or only "partly free" in terms of their political practices and civil liberties. It seems unlikely that America could actually democratize so much of the globe. Second, many nations might not be capable of sustaining democratic regimes even if they were established. Democracy is most likely to flourish where there is a vigorous civil society and a stable economy—conditions that do not exist in many regions of the world. Finally, the process of democratization can, itself, be dangerous. As dictatorial regimes weaken and collapse, they can unleash long suppressed hatreds and rivalries—witness events in the former Yugoslavia. Thus, while it may ultimately produce peace and stability, democracy can be a dangerous export.

FOR CRITICAL ANALYSIS

1. What are some of the factors that might help to determine whether democratic politics can take root in a country that has not previously experienced democracy?

2. Is it appropriate for America to try to shape the governments and political arrangements of other countries?

Although Americans are no longer legally barred from voting on the basis of sex or race, political participation is minimal for most people. In the 2000 election, only 51 percent of eligible voters came to the polls (left). Special interests have been all too willing to influence government in the absence of popular political participation. Lobbyists not only attempt to convince politicians with their arguments; they also control large donations to political campaigns. Corporate donations support candidates, but this support has become something of a political liability after the Enron collapse (right).

Constitution granted African Americans the vote, although later exclusionary practices denied them that right; in 1920, the Nineteenth Amendment guaranteed women the right to vote; and in 1965, the Voting Rights Act finally secured the right of African Americans to vote.

Just securing the right to vote does not end concerns about democracy, however. The organization of electoral institutions can have a significant impact on access to elections and on who can get elected. During the first two decades of the twentieth century, states and cities enacted many reforms that made it harder to vote, including strict registration requirements and scheduling of elections. The aim was to rid politics of corruption but the consequence was to reduce participation. Other institutional decisions affect which candidates stand the best chance of getting elected (see Chapter 10).

A further consideration about democracy concerns the relationship between economic power and political power. Money has always played an important role in elections and governing in the United States. Many argue that the pervasive influence of money in American electoral campaigns today undermines democracy. With the decline of locally based political parties that depended on party loyalists to turn out the vote, and the rise of political action committees, political consultants, and expensive media campaigns, money has become the central fact of life in American politics. Money often determines who runs for office; it can exert a heavy influence on who wins; and, some argue, money affects what politicians do once they are in office.[22]

A final consideration that must be raised about democracy is the engagement of the citizenry. Low turnout for elections and a pervasive sense of apathy and cynicism characterize American politics today. Many people say that it does not matter if they participate because their votes will not make any difference. This disillusionment and sense of ineffectiveness undermines the vitality of democracy, which in turn reduces the accountability of the rulers to the ruled.

VALUES AND THE ENDS OF GOVERNMENT

Many of the most important dilemmas of American political life involve conflicts among fundamental political values when those values are put into operation. For example, Americans strongly value both liberty and equality, but often programs designed to promote one may impose restraints upon the other. Thus, affirmative action programs or statutes designed to prevent discrimination against the handicapped, such as the Americans with Disabilities Act, may promote equality but may also infringe upon the liberty of employers to hire whomever they wish. In a similar vein, democratic political processes may sometimes produce results that can challenge both liberty and equality. After all, Adolf Hitler and the Nazis came to power in Germany in the 1930s partly through democratic means. Even in America, political extremists who oppose both liberty and equality have been elected to office. As recently as 1991, a white supremacist, David Duke, was very nearly elected governor of Louisiana.

Conversely, in the name of equality or liberty, courts often hand down verdicts that undo decisions of democratically elected legislatures and even decisions reached in popular referenda. Principles that seem incontrovertible in the abstract become more problematic in operation. In the process of resolving conflicts among core beliefs, America's political principles change and evolve. Even core values should be understood as works in progress rather than immutable facts.

WHO BENEFITS FROM GOVERNMENT?

Government is not a neutral force in any society. Some groups always benefit more than others from the government's actions. Some regimes are run by small cliques or even by families for their own benefit. Our government is dominated by shifting coalitions of electoral forces along with interest groups; local, state, and national politicians; civic leaders; labor groups; ethnic and religious groups; professional associations; and a host of others. Almost every piece of legislation or governmental regulation bears the stamp of some set of interests that pushed for its enactment because it seemed to serve their purposes. In some instances, interests have turned getting what they want into a science. For example, the Enron Corporation, a now-bankrupt Texas energy giant, developed a computer program named "Matrix" that could evaluate the net impact upon the company of any proposed federal energy regulation. This information, in turn, guided the firm's lobbying efforts and campaign contributions, which were designed to influence the government's activities.[23]

Although we know that most pieces of legislation and many regulations have particular beneficiaries, we hope that the benefits and costs of our government's policies are not narrowly defined. That is, we hope that the net benefits of government do not always flow to the same groups. James Madison, the principal

FOR CRITICAL ANALYSIS

Think of some examples that demonstrate the gaps between the ideals of America's core political values and the practice of American politics. Describe how such gaps were reconciled in the past. Identify one current gap between Americans' values and their political practices. How might this discrepancy be reconciled?

author of the U.S. Constitution, argued that in a large and diverse republic there would be so many groups fighting for power that no one group or coalition of groups would always prevail. Today, we call this idea pluralism, and we fervently hope that in our society some benefits of government accrue to all citizens—or at least to all participants in the political process. We can certainly observe that even apparently powerful forces are sometimes defeated in the political arena and that for most political actors, power is short-lived. The once-mighty Enron Corporation was destroyed despite its grasp of sophisticated political techniques. Perhaps this is the best outcome for which we can hope—that political power will be dispersed and short-lived, so that government will benefit many and favor few for very long.

GET INVOLVED

What You Can Do:
Test the Political Waters

You may not be interested in politics. You probably distrust politicians. You certainly have other priorities. Why bother with politics? After all, there is not much you can do about children's access to guns or mounting tensions in the Middle East.

Before you decide that public life is strictly for other people, consider several factors. First, political involvement can be fascinating. It may put you at the center of challenging issues that have important effects on many people's lives. Should Americans promote environmental safeguards that protect some people's health but cost other people jobs? Should Americans spend scarce public resources on prenatal care for poor women or build libraries that provide Internet access to all community members?

Second, political engagement can be energizing. Imagine how it feels to be the person who organizes a group that gives voice to the concerns of elderly people who had previously been ignored or neglected. Consider how exciting it would be to participate in a coalition that places a referendum to save wildlife reserves on the state ballot, to feel the tension of campaign volunteers as the first election returns trickle in.

Third, political activism can produce political efficacy—the sense that you can make a difference. If you do nothing, you cannot be part of the solution. When you get involved, you can continue the efforts of those who precede you, try innovative approaches to old problems, and create a legacy for those who will follow. You may ease existing dilemmas and contribute to their resolution. Occasionally, one determined person does make a significant difference.

Accordingly, before you say no to political participation, consider the potential fascination, energy, and accomplishments that await you. Do more than consider. Test the political waters. Here are a few easy ways to see if political involvement can be meaningful and fulfilling to you.

- **Assess your political interests.**
  Read a newspaper or a weekly news magazine. Watch national or local news on television. Listen to a political talk show. What issues catch your eye? Which ones seem important to you? How do any of them affect your life? Identify one or two issues and follow them for a week or so. You may discover that political knowledge generates interest.

YOU ARE... producing a talk-radio show!

All Americans have political opinions, and many love to express them in very public ways, taking advantage of our freedom of speech to try and convince others to think as they do. American talk radio has long provided an opportunity for listeners to call in to discuss the pressing issues of the day, but famous hosts such as Rush Limbaugh, Mike Gallagher, and more recently Al Franken have elevated the talk show to a new level of popularity.

In this simulation, you are working with your boss, the on-air host, to air strong views. It is your job to screen the potential callers. You must determine their ideology and message, and decide whether they fit the themes of the day. The more that you have learned about the American values of liberty, equality, and democracy, as well as the disagreements about the role government should play in supporting these values, the better you will do your job.

Go to www.wwnorton.com/wtp5e

Questions to consider as you conduct the online simulation:

What values do Americans tend to share? Are there any values that are shared by all Americans?

Given that we have broad consensus in valuing liberty, equality, and democracy, why do we disagree so vehemently about the proper role of government in upholding those values?

When these values come into conflict with one another, how should we decide which values should take precedence?

- **Initiate a discussion with family members, friends, or classmates.**
  Ask a few people what they think about an issue that interests you. Do they care? Are they knowledgeable? Do they have a position on the issue? If so, how do they defend their position? Do you agree or disagree with them? The point here is to *listen* to and *learn* from other people's political viewpoints.
- **Articulate your own views on the issue.**
  Experiment with expressing your own views on the issue. Are they clear? Coherent? Cogent? Now see if you can articulate your views with enough force that other people take you seriously but also with sufficient civility to keep up the attention and interest of people who disagree with you.
- **Write a letter to the editor of a campus or community newspaper.**
  Write a letter to the editor expressing your view. Make the letter short, direct, and civil. That will increase the likelihood that it will be selected for publication. A few readers may answer your letter by submitting written responses to it.
- **Call in to a radio talk show.**
  State your point clearly and succinctly to the person who screens callers. If you get on air, state your main point, present your key arguments, and invite a response from the host or the call-in audience.

Democracy begins with discussion. Adopt an experimental attitude and join the discussion. It is not important to persuade other people that you are right. People change their minds very slowly. Instead, aim at expressing yourself clearly and knowledgeably so that your views will be communicated effectively. Often, it is as important to be taken seriously as it is to be heeded.

Summary

The citizen's role in political life begins with information and knowledge. A citizen's knowledge should include knowledge of government, of politics, and of democratic principles. Knowledgeable citizens are better able to identify and act upon their political interests. In short, knowledgeable citizens better understand how and why politics and government influence their lives.

The form that a government takes affects citizens because it determines who governs and how much governmental control is permitted. Americans live in a constitutional democracy, where limits are placed on what governments can do and how they can do it. Americans are also given access to government through legal rights to political participation. Through politics, Americans are able to struggle over the leadership, structure, and policies of governments.

Although politics may divide Americans from one another, the core values of American political culture—liberty, equality, and democracy—hold the United States and its people together. Although these values have been important since the time the United States was founded, during much of American history there have been large gaps between these ideals and the practice of American politics. Moreover, liberty, equality, and democracy often conflict with one another in American political life.

For Further Reading

Dahl, Robert. *Democracy and Its Critics.* New Haven, CT: Yale University Press, 1989.

Delli Carpini, Michael X., and Scott Keeter. *What Americans Know about Politics and Why It Matters.* New Haven, CT: Yale University Press, 1996.

Hibbing, John R., and Elizabeth Theiss-Morse. *Stealth Democracy: Americans' Belief about How Government Should Work.* New York: Cambridge University Press, 2002.

Huntington, Samuel P. *American Politics: The Promise of Disharmony.* Cambridge, MA: Harvard University Press, 1981.

Lasswell, Harold. *Politics: Who Gets What, When, How.* New York: Meridian Books, 1958.

Nie, Norman H., Jane Junn, and Kenneth Stehlik-Barry. *Education and Democratic Citizenship in America.* Chicago: University of Chicago Press, 1996.

Nye, Joseph S., Jr., Philip D. Zelikow, and David C. King, eds. *Why People Don't Trust Government.* Cambridge, MA: Harvard University Press, 1997.

Putnam, Robert. *Making Democracy Work: Civic Traditions in Modern Italy.* Princeton, NJ: Princeton University Press, 1993.

de Tocqueville, Alexis. *Democracy in America.* Trans. Phillips Bradley. New York: Knopf, Vintage Books, 1945; orig. published 1835.

Study Outline

www.wwnorton.com/wtp5e   Keyword: Review 1

What Americans Think about Government

1. In recent decades, the public's trust in government has declined considerably. Some Americans believe that government has grown too large and that government programs do not benefit them. As public distrust of government has increased, so has public dissatisfaction with the government's performance.
2. Americans today are less likely to think that they can influence what the government does. This view has led to increased apathy and cynicism among the citizenry.

What Americans Know about Government

1. Informed and active membership in a political community is the basis for citizenship. Citizens require political knowledge in order to be aware of their interests in a political dispute, to identify the best ways of acting upon their interests, and to know what political action can and cannot achieve. However, today many Americans have little political knowledge.

Government

1. Governments vary in their structure, in their size, and in the way they operate.
2. Beginning in the seventeenth century, two important changes began to take place in the governance of some Western nations: governments began to acknowledge formal limits on their power, and governments began to give citizens a formal voice in politics through the vote.
3. Political participation can take many forms: the vote, group activities, and even direct action, such as violent opposition or civil disobedience.

American Political Culture: Shared Values, but Disagreements over the Role of Government

1. Three important political values in American politics are liberty, equality, and democracy.
2. At times in American history there have been large gaps between the ideals embodied in Americans' core values and the practice of American government.
3. Many of the important dilemmas of American politics revolve around conflicts over fundamental political values. One such conflict involves the ideals of liberty and equality. Over time, efforts to promote equality may threaten liberty.

Practice Quiz

www.wwnorton.com/wtp5e   Keyword: Quiz 1

1. Political efficacy is the belief that
   a) government operates efficiently.
   b) government has grown too large.
   c) government cannot be trusted.
   d) one can influence what government does.

2. The famous political scientist Harold Lasswell defined politics as the struggle over
   a) who gets elected.
   b) who gets what, when, how.
   c) who protests.
   d) who gets to vote.

3. What is the basic difference between autocracy and oligarchy?
   a) the extent to which the average citizen has a say in government affairs
   b) the means of collecting taxes and conscripting soldiers
   c) the number of people who control governing decisions
   d) They are fundamentally the same thing.

4. According to the authors, good citizenship requires
   a) political knowledge.
   b) political engagement.
   c) a good education.
   d) both a and b

5. The principle of political equality can be best summed up as
   a) "equality of results."
   b) "equality of opportunity."
   c) "one person, one vote."
   d) "equality between the sexes."

6. Which of the following is an important principle of American democracy?
   a) popular sovereignty
   b) majority rule/minority rights
   c) limited government
   d) All of the above are important principles of American democracy.

7. Which of the following is not related to the American conception of "liberty"?
   a) freedom of speech
   b) free enterprise
   c) freedom of religion
   d) All of the above are related to liberty.

8. Which of the following is *not* part of the American political culture?
   a) belief in equality of results
   b) belief in equality of opportunity
   c) belief in individual liberty
   d) belief in free competition

9. Which of the following does *not* represent a current discrepancy between the ideal and practice of democracy in America?
   a) the use of property restrictions for voting in three remaining states
   b) the influence of money in electoral politics
   c) the low voter turnout in American elections
   d) All of the above represent discrepancies between the ideal and practice of democracy in modern America.

10. Americans' trust in their government
    a) declined steadily from the early 1960s to the mid-1990s but rose slightly since then.
    b) declined during Watergate, but rose again during the 1980s.
    c) has risen since 1990.
    d) rose during the 1970s and 1980s, but has declined since 1992.

Key Terms

www.wwnorton.com/wtp5e

Keyword: Vocabulary 1

authoritarian government (p. 16)
autocracy (p. 16)
citizenship (p. 14)
constitutional government (p. 16)
democracy (p. 16)
direct action politics (p. 19)

direct democracy (p. 18)
equality of opportunity (p. 21)
government (p. 15)
laissez-faire capitalism (p. 21)
libertarian (p. 5)
liberty (p. 20)
limited government (p. 20)
majority rule/minority rights (p. 23)
oligarchy (p. 16)
pluralism (p. 19)

political culture (p. 20)
political efficacy (p. 10)
political equality (p. 21)
politics (p. 18)
popular sovereignty (p. 23)
power (p. 18)
representative democracy (or republic) (p. 18)
totalitarian government (p. 16)

2 THE FOUNDING AND THE CONSTITUTION

What Government Does and Why It Matters

THE STORY OF AMERICA'S Founding and the Constitution is generally presented as something both inevitable and glorious: it was inevitable that the American colonies would break away from England to successfully establish their own country; and it was glorious in that it established the best of all possible forms of government under a new Constitution, which was easily adopted and quickly embraced, even by its critics. In reality, though, America's successful breakaway from England was by no means assured, and the Constitution that we revere today as one of the most brilliant creations of any nation was in fact highly controversial. Moreover, its ratification and durability were often in doubt. George Washington, the man revered as the father of the country and the person chosen to preside over the Constitutional Convention of 1787, thought the document produced that hot summer in Philadelphia would probably last no more than twenty years, at which time leaders would have to convene again to come up with something new.

That Washington's prediction proved wrong is, indeed, a testament to the enduring strength of the Constitution. But none of the Founders was Moses, and the Constitution was no Ten Commandments, carved by lightning in stone. The Constitution was a product of political bargaining and compromise, formed very much in the same way political decisions are made today. This fact is often overlooked because of what historian Michael Kammen has called the "cult of the Constitution"—a tendency of Americans, going back more than a century, to blindly venerate, sometimes to the point of near worship, the Founders and the document they created.[1] As this chapter will show, the Constitution reflects political self-interest, but high principle, too. It also defines the relationship between American citizens and their government.

Often, the story of the Founding and the Constitution is written to emphasize the framers' concerns regarding individual liberty and limits on government. And, of course, the framers had such concerns. It is important to note, however, that the primary goal of the framers was the creation of an *effective* government. They sought a government with the capacity to provide for the nation's safety in a sometimes hostile world: "Among the many objects to which a wise and free people find it necessary to direct their attention," wrote John Jay in *Federalist 3*, "that of providing for their safety seems to be the first." The framers endeavored to create a government with the power to maintain public order, promote prosperity, and secure the nation's independence, powers that the government under the Articles of Confederation lacked. The Constitution begins not with a statement of the limits on government, but with an affirmative statement of the ends a government is designed to achieve—to establish justice, insure domestic tranquility, and provide for the common defense and general welfare. ■

It has also become commonplace to accuse the framers of hostility to democracy and tolerance of the most extreme forms of inequality, including human slavery. There is, of course, some truth to both accusations. Some of the framers feared that "excessive" democracy would threaten property rights and several were, themselves, slave holders. Nevertheless, the framers believed that a powerful government required a broad popular base and, hence, opened the way for direct popular election of members of the House of Representatives. And, while the framers—products of a particular time and place—certainly did not share today's notions of racial and gender equality, they did provide equal political rights for the white males, regardless of wealth or social class background. By asserting this principle of equality, the framers made it more difficult to defend denying equal rights to African Americans, women, and others in subsequent centuries.

■ **In this chapter, we will first assess the political backdrop of the American Revolution, which led to the Declaration of Independence and the establishment of a governmental structure under the Articles of Confederation.**

■ **We will then consider the conditions that led to the Constitutional Convention of 1787 and the great issues that were debated by the framers.** To fully understand the character of the Founding and the meaning of the Constitution, it is essential to look beyond the myths and rhetoric and to explore the conflicting interests and forces at work during the period.

■ **Next, we will examine the Constitution that ultimately emerged as the basis for the national government.** Although the Constitution was the product of a particular set of political forces, the principles of government it established have had long-lasting significance. The framers sought to create a powerful national government, but guarded against possible misuse of that power through the separation of powers, federalism, and the Bill of Rights.

■ **We will then examine the first hurdle that the Constitution faced, the fight for ratification.** Two sides, the Federalists and the Antifederalists, vigorously debated the great political issues and principles at stake. The resolution of this debate created the framework for a national government that has lasted more than two hundred years.

■ **We will then look at how the Constitution has changed over the past two centuries.** The framers designed an amendment process so that the Constitution could change, but the process has succeeded only on rare occasions.

■ **Finally, we will ask what liberty, equality, and democracy meant to the framers of the Constitution.** Although the framers established a system of government that would eventually allow each of these political values to thrive, they championed liberty as the most important of the three.

■ Previewing Liberty, Equality, and Democracy

Liberty, equality, and democracy were all major themes of the founding period and are all elements of the U.S. Constitution. For the framers, individual liberty was the most important political value, and they distrusted both the "leveling spirit" of equality and "excessive" democracy. Nevertheless, the Constitution anticipates popular election of representatives and provides equal political rights for white males, not political equality by contemporary standards, but unusual for the time. Over the ensuing centuries, moreover, liberty opened the way for the expansion of political activity that, in turn, helped bring about the growth of democracy and greater political and social equality in America.

The First Founding: Interests and Conflicts

Competing ideals and principles often reflect competing interests, and so it was in Revolutionary America. The American Revolution and the American Constitution were outgrowths and expressions of a struggle among economic and political forces within the colonies. Five sectors of society had interests that were important in colonial politics: (1) the New England merchants; (2) the southern planters; (3) the "royalists"—holders of royal lands, offices, and patents (licenses to engage in a profession or business activity); (4) shopkeepers, artisans, and laborers; and (5) small farmers. Throughout the eighteenth century, these groups were in conflict over issues of taxation, trade, and commerce. For the most part, however, the southern planters, the New England merchants, and the royal office and patent holders—groups that together made up the colonial elite—were able to maintain a political alliance that held in check the more

The British helped radicalize colonists through bad policy decisions in the years before the Revolution. For example, Britain gave the ailing East India Company a monopoly on the tea trade in the American colonies. Colonists feared the monopoly would hurt colonial merchants' business and protested by throwing the East India Company tea into Boston Harbor. The Boston Tea Party of 1773 brought on oppressive retribution from Britain, which led to colonial resistance and, ultimately, revolution.

radical forces representing shopkeepers, laborers, and small farmers. After 1750, however, by seriously threatening the interests of New England merchants and southern planters, British tax and trade policies split the colonial elite, permitting radical forces to expand their political influence, and set into motion a chain of events that culminated in the American Revolution.[2]

BRITISH TAXES AND COLONIAL INTERESTS

Beginning in the 1750s, the debts and other financial problems faced by the British government forced it to search for new revenue sources. This search rather quickly led to the Crown's North American colonies, which, on the whole, paid remarkably little in taxes to their parent country. The British government reasoned that a sizable fraction of its debt was, in fact, attributable to the expenses it had incurred in defense of the colonies during the recent French and Indian wars, as well as to the continuing protection that British forces were giving the colonists from Indian attacks and that the British navy was providing for colonial shipping. Thus, during the 1760s, England sought to impose new, though relatively modest, taxes upon the colonists.

Like most governments of the period, the British regime had limited ways in which to collect revenues. The income tax, which in the twentieth century became the single most important source of governmental revenues, had not yet been developed. For the most part, in the mid-eighteenth century, governments relied on tariffs, duties, and other

Britain eventually sent troops to subdue the American colonists. Grant Wood's Midnight Ride of Paul Revere *(1931) depicts Revere alerting colonists to the British army's arrival. The subsequent battle between colonial and British forces at Concord and Lexington began the Revolutionary War.*

taxes on commerce, and it was to such taxes, including the Stamp Act, that the British turned during the 1760s.

The Stamp Act and other taxes on commerce, such as the Sugar Act of 1764, which taxed sugar, molasses, and other commodities, most heavily affected the two groups in colonial society whose commercial interests and activities were most extensive—the New England merchants and the southern planters. Under the famous slogan "no taxation without representation," the merchants and planters together sought to organize opposition to these new taxes. In the course of the struggle against British tax measures, the planters and merchants broke with their royalist allies and turned to their former adversaries—the shopkeepers, small farmers, laborers, and artisans—for help. With the assistance of these groups, the merchants and planters organized demonstrations and a boycott of British goods that ultimately forced the Crown to rescind most of its new taxes.

From the perspective of the merchants and planters, however, the British government's decision to eliminate most of the hated taxes represented a victorious end to their struggle with the mother country. They were anxious to end the unrest they had helped to arouse, and they supported the British government's efforts to restore order. Indeed, most respectable Bostonians supported the actions of the British soldiers involved in the Boston Massacre. In their subsequent trial, the soldiers were defended by John Adams, a pillar of Boston society and a future president of the United States. Adams asserted that the soldiers' actions were entirely justified, provoked by "a motley rabble of saucy boys, Negroes and mulattos, Irish teagues and outlandish Jack tars." All but two of the soldiers were acquitted.[3]

Despite the efforts of the British government and the better-to-do strata of colonial society, it proved difficult to bring an end to the political strife. The more radical forces representing shopkeepers, artisans, laborers, and small farmers, who had been mobilized and energized by the struggle over taxes, continued to agitate for political and social change within the colonies. These radicals, led by individuals like Samuel Adams, a cousin of John Adams, asserted that British power supported an unjust political and social structure within the colonies, and began to advocate an end to British rule.[4]

This picture of a segmented snake, printed in Benjamin Franklin's newspaper, urged the colonies to unite during the French and Indian War of the 1750s. Again during the Revolutionary War, cooperation among the states was crucial to the independence movement. Thirty years before the Constitution was written, Franklin recognized the importance of national concerns as well as state ones.

POLITICAL STRIFE AND THE RADICALIZING OF THE COLONISTS

The political strife within the colonies was the background for the events of 1773–74. In 1773, the British government granted the politically powerful East India Company a monopoly on the export of tea from Britain, eliminating a lucrative form of trade for colonial merchants. To add to the injury, the East India Company sought to sell the tea directly in the colonies instead of working through the colonial merchants. Tea was an extremely important commodity in the 1770s, and these British actions posed a mortal threat to the New England merchants. Together with their southern allies, the merchants once again called upon their radical adversaries for support. The most dramatic result was the Boston Tea Party of 1773, led by Samuel Adams.

This event was of decisive importance in American history. The merchants had hoped to force the British government to rescind the Tea Act, but they did not support any demands beyond this one. They certainly did not seek independence from Britain. Samuel Adams and the other radicals, however, hoped to provoke the British government to take actions that would alienate its colonial supporters and pave the

The year after fighting began between American colonists and the British army, the Continental Congress voted for independence, on July 2, 1776. The Declaration of Independence famously summarized the colonists' grievances against Britain and declared the "self-evident" rights of equality, "Life, Liberty, and the pursuit of Happiness."

way for a rebellion. This was precisely the purpose of the Boston Tea Party, and it succeeded. By dumping the East India Company's tea into Boston Harbor, Adams and his followers goaded the British into enacting a number of harsh reprisals. Within five months after the incident in Boston, the House of Commons passed a series of acts that closed the port of Boston to commerce, changed the provincial government of Massachusetts, provided for the removal of accused persons to England for trial, and most important, restricted movement to the West—further alienating the southern planters, who depended upon access to new western lands. These acts of retaliation confirmed the worst criticisms of England and helped radicalize Americans. Radicals like Samuel Adams and Christopher Gadsden of South Carolina had been agitating for more violent measures to deal with England. But ultimately they needed Britain's political repression to create widespread support for independence.

Thus, the Boston Tea Party set into motion a cycle of provocation and retaliation that in 1774 resulted in the convening of the First Continental Congress—an assembly of delegates from all parts of the country—that called for a total boycott of British goods and, under the prodding of the radicals, began to consider the possibility of independence from British rule. The eventual result was the Declaration of Independence.

THE DECLARATION OF INDEPENDENCE

In 1776, the Second Continental Congress appointed a committee consisting of Thomas Jefferson of Virginia, Benjamin Franklin of Pennsylvania, Roger Sherman of Connecticut, John Adams of Massachusetts, and Robert Livingston of New York to draft a statement of American independence from British rule. The Declaration of Independence, written by Jefferson and adopted by the Second Continental Congress, was an extraordinary document in both philosophical and political terms. Philosophically, the Declaration was remarkable for its assertion that certain rights, called "unalienable rights"—including life, liberty, and the pursuit of happiness— could not be abridged by governments. In the world of 1776, a world in which some kings still claimed to rule by divine right, this was a dramatic statement. Politically, the Declaration was remarkable because, despite the differences of interest that divided the colonists along economic, regional, and philosophical lines, the Declaration identified and focused on problems, grievances, aspirations, and principles that might unify the various colonial groups. The Declaration was an attempt to identify and articulate a history and set of principles that might help to forge national unity.[5]

THE ARTICLES OF CONFEDERATION

Having declared their independence, the colonies needed to establish a governmental structure. In November of 1777, the Continental Congress adopted the **Articles of Confederation and Perpetual Union**—the United States's first written constitution. Although it was not ratified by all the states until 1781, it was the country's operative constitution for almost twelve years, until March 1789.

The Articles of Confederation was a constitution concerned primarily with limiting the powers of the central government. The central government, first of all, was based entirely in a Congress. Since it was not intended to be a powerful government, it was given no executive branch. Execution of its laws was to be left to the individual states. Second, the Congress had little power. Its members were not much more than delegates or messengers from the state legislatures. They were chosen by the state legislatures, their salaries were paid out of the state treasuries, and they were subject to immediate recall by state authorities. In addition, each state, regardless of its size, had only a single vote.

The Congress was given the power to declare war and make peace, to make treaties and alliances, to coin or borrow money, and to regulate trade with the Native Americans. It could also appoint the senior officers of the United States army. But it could not levy taxes or regulate commerce among the states. Moreover, the army officers it appointed had no army to serve in because the nation's armed forces were composed of the state militias. Probably the most unfortunate part of the Articles of Confederation was that the central government could not prevent one state from discriminating against other states in the quest for foreign commerce.

In brief, the relationship between the Congress and the states under the Articles of Confederation was much like the contemporary relationship between the United Nations and its member states, a relationship in which virtually all governmental powers are retained by the states. It was properly called a **confederation** because, as provided under Article II, "each state retains its sovereignty, freedom, and independence, and every power, jurisdiction, and right, which is not by this Confederation expressly delegated to the United States, in Congress assembled." Not only was there no executive, there also was no judicial authority and no other means of enforcing the Congress's will. If there was to be any enforcement at all, it would be done for the Congress by the states.[6]

Articles of Confederation America's first written constitution; served as the basis for America's national government until 1789

confederation a system of government in which states retain sovereign authority except for the powers expressly delegated to the national governments

The Second Founding: From Compromise to Constitution

The Declaration of Independence and the Articles of Confederation were not sufficient to hold the new nation together as an independent and effective nation-state. From almost the moment of armistice with the British in 1783, moves were afoot to reform and strengthen the Articles of Confederation.

INTERNATIONAL STANDING AND BALANCE OF POWER

There was a special concern for the country's international position. Competition among the states for foreign commerce allowed the European powers to play the states off against one another, which created confusion on both sides of the Atlantic. At one point during the winter of 1786–87, John Adams of Massachusetts, a leader in the independence struggle, was sent to negotiate a new treaty with the British, one that would cover disputes left over from the war. The British government responded that since the United States under the Articles of Confederation was unable to enforce existing treaties, it would negotiate with each of the thirteen states separately.

At the same time, well-to-do Americans—in particular the New England merchants and southern planters—were troubled by the influence that "radical" forces exercised in the Continental Congress and in the governments of several of the states. The colonists' victory in the Revolutionary War had not only ended British rule but also significantly changed the balance of political power within the new states. As a result of the Revolution, one key segment of the colonial elite—the royal land, office, and patent holders—was stripped of its economic and political privileges. In fact, many of these individuals, along with tens of thousands of other colonists who considered themselves loyal British subjects, left for Canada after the British surrender. And while the pre-Revolutionary elite was weakened, the pre-Revolutionary radicals were now better organized than ever before and were the controlling forces in such states as Pennsylvania and Rhode Island, where they pursued economic and political policies that struck terror into the hearts of the pre-Revolutionary political establishment. In Rhode Island, for example, between 1783 and 1785, a legislature dominated by representatives of small farmers, artisans, and shopkeepers had instituted economic policies, including drastic currency inflation, that frightened business and property owners throughout the country. Of course, the central government under the Articles of Confederation was powerless to intervene.

THE ANNAPOLIS CONVENTION

The continuation of international weakness and domestic economic turmoil led many Americans to consider whether their newly adopted form of government might not already require revision. In the fall of 1786, many state leaders accepted an invitation from the Virginia legislature for a conference of representatives of all the states. Delegates from five states actually attended. This conference, held in Annapolis, Maryland, was the first step toward the second founding. The one positive thing that came out of the Annapolis Convention was a carefully worded resolution calling on the Congress to send commissioners to Philadelphia at a later time "to devise such further provisions as shall appear to them necessary to render the Constitution of the Federal Government adequate to the exigencies of the Union."[7] This resolution was drafted by Alexander Hamilton, a thirty-four-year-old New York lawyer who had played a significant role in the Revolution as George Washington's secretary and who would play a still more significant role in framing the Constitution and forming the new government in the 1790s. But the resolution did not necessarily imply any desire to do more than improve and reform the Articles of Confederation.

SHAYS'S REBELLION

It is quite possible that the Constitutional Convention of 1787 in Philadelphia would never have taken place at all except for a single event that occurred during the winter following the Annapolis Convention: Shays's Rebellion.

Daniel Shays, a former army captain, led a mob of farmers in a rebellion against the government of Massachusetts. The purpose of the rebellion was to prevent foreclosures on their debt-ridden land by keeping the county courts of western Massachusetts from sitting until after the next election. The state militia dispersed the mob, but for several days Shays and his followers terrified the state government by attempting to capture the federal arsenal at Springfield, provoking an appeal to the Congress to help restore order. Within a few days, the state government regained control and captured fourteen of the rebels (all were eventually pardoned). In 1787, a newly elected Massachusetts legislature granted some of the farmers' demands.

Although the incident ended peacefully, its effects lingered and spread. Washington summed it up: "I am mortified beyond expression that in the moment of our acknowledged independence we should by our conduct verify the predictions of our transatlantic foe, and render ourselves ridiculous and contemptible in the eyes of all Europe."[8]

The Congress under the Confederation had been unable to act decisively in a time of crisis. This provided critics of the Articles of Confederation with precisely the evidence they needed to push Hamilton's Annapolis resolution through the Congress. Thus, the states were asked to send representatives to Philadelphia to discuss constitutional revision. Delegates were eventually sent by every state except Rhode Island.

THE CONSTITUTIONAL CONVENTION

Delegates selected by the state governments convened in Philadelphia in May 1787, with political strife, international embarrassment, national weakness, and local

Opponents of the Articles called for a new Constitutional Convention to explore a stronger form of national government. George Washington, a hero of the Revolution, presided over the convention. In creating the Constitution, the convention faced a host of pitfalls caused by the dramatic differences between the states.

The Articles of Confederation created a weak national government at the end of the Revolutionary War. The states were largely left to make their own policy. In the winter of 1787, the Massachusetts legislature levied heavy taxes that hit the poor particularly hard. In protest, Daniel Shays led a makeshift army against the federal arsenal at Springfield. Shays's group was soon stopped, but the rebellion proved the Articles too weak to protect the fledgling nation.

rebellion fixed in their minds. Recognizing that these issues were symptoms of fundamental flaws in the Articles of Confederation, the delegates soon abandoned the plan to revise the Articles and committed themselves to a second founding—a second, and ultimately successful, attempt to create a legitimate and effective national system of government. This effort occupied the convention for the next five months.

A Marriage of Interest and Principle   Scholars have for years disagreed about the motives of the Founders in Philadelphia. Among the most controversial views of the framers' motives is the "economic interpretation" put forward by historian Charles Beard and his disciples.[9] According to Beard's account, America's Founders were a collection of securities speculators and property owners whose only aim was personal enrichment. From this perspective, the Constitution's lofty principles were little more than sophisticated masks behind which the most venal interests sought to enrich themselves.

Contrary to Beard's approach is the view that the framers of the Constitution *were* concerned with philosophical and ethical principles. Indeed, the framers sought to devise a system of government consistent with the dominant philosophical and moral principles of the day. But, in fact, these two views belong together; the Founders' interests were reinforced by their principles. The convention that drafted the American Constitution was chiefly organized by the New England merchants and southern planters. Although the delegates representing these groups did not all hope to profit personally from an increase in the value of their securities, as Beard would have it, they did hope to benefit in the broadest political and economic sense by breaking the power of their radical foes and establishing a system of government more compatible with their long-term economic and political interests. Thus, the framers sought to create a new government capable of promoting commerce and protecting property from radical state legislatures. At the same time, they hoped to fashion a government less susceptible than the existing state and national regimes to populist forces hostile to the interests of the commercial and propertied classes.

The Great Compromise   The proponents of a new government fired their opening shot on May 29, 1787, when Edmund Randolph of Virginia offered a resolution that proposed corrections and enlargements in the Articles of Confederation. The proposal, which showed the strong influence of James Madison, was not a simple motion. It provided for virtually every aspect of a new government. Randolph later admitted it was intended to be an alternative draft constitution, and it did in fact serve as the framework for what ultimately became the Constitution. (There is no verbatim record of the debates, but Madison was present during virtually all of the deliberations and kept full notes on them.)[10]

The portion of Randolph's motion that became most controversial was called the **Virginia Plan.** This plan provided for a system of representation in the national legislature based upon the population of each state or the proportion of each state's revenue contribution to the national government, or both. (Randolph also proposed a second branch of the legislature, but it was to be elected by the members of the first branch.) Since the states varied enormously in size and wealth, the Virginia Plan was thought to be heavily biased in favor of the large states.

While the convention was debating the Virginia Plan, additional delegates were arriving in Philadelphia and were beginning to mount opposition to it.

Virginia Plan a framework for the Constitution, introduced by Edmund Randolph, which called for representation in the national legislature based upon the population of each state

A stronger national government would have to overcome deep divisions between the states and their interests. "The Looking Glass for 1787" showcases Connecticut's debate about the newly drafted Constitution. In the cartoon, Federalists stand for trade and commerce. Antifederalists say "Tax Luxary" [sic] and "Success to Shays"—showing the cartoonist's Federalist leaning while implying that Antifederalists were troublemakers.

Their resolution, introduced by William Paterson of New Jersey and known as the **New Jersey Plan,** did not oppose the Virginia Plan point for point. Instead, it concentrated on specific weaknesses in the Articles of Confederation, in the spirit of revision rather than radical replacement of that document. Supporters of the New Jersey Plan did not seriously question the convention's commitment to replacing the Articles. But their opposition to the Virginia Plan's scheme of representation was sufficient to send its proposals back to committee for reworking into a common document. In particular, delegates from the less-populous states, which included Delaware, New Jersey, Connecticut, and New York, asserted that the more populous states, such as Virginia, Pennsylvania, North Carolina, Massachusetts, and Georgia, would dominate the new government if representation were determined by population. The smaller states argued that each state should be equally represented in the new regime regardless of that state's population.

The issue of representation was one that threatened to wreck the entire constitutional enterprise. Delegates conferred, factions maneuvered, and tempers flared. James Wilson of Pennsylvania told the small-state delegates that if they wanted to disrupt the union they should go ahead. The separation could, he said, "never happen on better grounds." Small-state delegates were equally blunt. Gunning Bedford of Delaware declared that the small states might look elsewhere for friends if they were forced. "The large states," he said, "dare not dissolve the confederation. If they do the small ones will find some foreign ally of more honor and good faith, who will take them by the hand and do them justice." These sentiments were widely shared. The union, as Oliver Ellsworth of Connecticut put it, was "on the verge of dissolution, scarcely held together by the strength of a hair."

New Jersey Plan a framework for the Constitution, introduced by William Paterson, which called for equal state representation in the national legislature regardless of population

Although there was much acrimonious debate and necessary compromise as the new Constitution was written, this print suggests that farmers, artisans, and gentlemen alike supported it after its ratification. Liberty is enshrined above the crowd, and the Constitution seems to have been accepted by all.

Great Compromise the agreement reached at the Constitutional Convention of 1787 that gave each state an equal number of senators regardless of its population, but linked representation in the House of Representatives to population

bicameral having a legislative assembly composed of two chambers or houses

The outcome of this debate was the Connecticut Compromise, also known as the **Great Compromise.** Under the terms of this compromise, in the first branch of Congress—the House of Representatives—the representatives would be apportioned according to the number of inhabitants in each state. This, of course, was what delegates from the large states had sought. But in the second branch—the Senate—each state would have an equal vote regardless of its size; this provision addressed the concerns of the small states. This compromise was not immediately satisfactory to all the delegates. Indeed, two of the most vocal members of the small-state faction, John Lansing and Robert Yates of New York, were so incensed by the concession that their colleagues had made to the large-state forces that they stormed out of the convention. In the end, however, both sets of forces preferred compromise to the breakup of the Union, and the plan was accepted.

The Question of Slavery: The Three-Fifths Compromise   The story so far is too neat, too easy, and too anticlimactic. If it were left here, it would only contribute to American mythology. After all, the notion of a **bicameral** (two-chambered) legislature was very much in the air in 1787. Some of the states had had bicameral legislatures for years. The Philadelphia delegates might well have gone straight to the adoption of two chambers based on two different principles of representation even without the dramatic interplay of conflict and compromise. But a far more fundamental issue had to be confronted before the Great Compromise could take place: the issue of slavery.

Many of the conflicts that emerged during the Constitutional Convention were reflections of the fundamental differences between the slave and the nonslave states—differences that pitted the southern planters and New England merchants against one another. This was the first premonition of a conflict that would almost destroy the Republic in later years. In the midst of debate over large versus small states, Madison observed,

> The great danger to our general government is the great southern and northern interests of the continent, being opposed to each other. Look to the votes in Congress, and most of them stand divided by the geography of the country, not according to the size of the states.[11]

More than 90 percent of the country's slaves resided in five states—Georgia, Maryland, North Carolina, South Carolina, and Virginia—where they accounted for 30 percent of the total population. In some places, slaves outnumbered nonslaves by as much as ten to one. If the Constitution were to embody any principle of national supremacy, some basic decisions would have to be made about the place of slavery in the general scheme. Madison hit on this point on several occasions as different aspects of the Constitution were being discussed. For example, he observed,

It seemed now to be pretty well understood that the real difference of interests lay, not between the large and small but between the northern and southern states. The institution of slavery and its consequences formed the line of discrimination. There were five states on the South, eight on the northern side of this line. Should a proportional representation take place it was true, the northern side would still outnumber the other: but not in the same degree, at this time; and every day would tend towards an equilibrium.[12]

Northerners and southerners eventually reached agreement through the **Three-fifths Compromise.** The seats in the House of Representatives would be apportioned according to a "population" in which five slaves would count as three free persons. The slaves would not be allowed to vote, of course, but the number of representatives would be apportioned accordingly.

The issue of slavery was the most difficult one faced by the framers, and it nearly destroyed the Union. Although some delegates believed slavery to be morally wrong, an evil and oppressive institution that made a mockery of the ideals and values espoused in the Constitution, morality was not the issue that caused the framers to support or oppose the Three-fifths Compromise. Whatever they thought of the institution of slavery, most delegates from the northern states opposed counting slaves in the distribution of congressional seats. Wilson of Pennsylvania, for example, argued that if slaves were citizens they should be treated and counted like other citizens. If, on the other hand, they were property, then why should not other forms of property be counted toward the apportionment of representatives? But southern delegates made it clear that if the northerners refused to give in, they would never agree to the new government. William R. Davie of North Carolina heatedly said that it was time "to speak out." He asserted that the people of North Carolina would never enter the Union if slaves were not counted as part of the basis for representation. Without such agreement, he asserted ominously, "the business was at an end." Even southerners like Edmund Randolph of Virginia, who conceded that slavery

Three-fifths Compromise the agreement reached at the Constitutional Convention of 1787 that stipulated that for purposes of the apportionment of congressional seats, every slave would be counted as three-fifths of a person

FOR CRITICAL ANALYSIS

Recount and explain the ideological, geographical, social, and political conflicts both at the time of the American Revolution and at the time of the writing of the United States Constitution. What experiences and interests informed the forces involved in each of these conflicts? How did the framers resolve these conflicts? Were there any conflicts left unresolved?

Despite its Enlightenment language, the new Constitution supported slavery. The Three-fifths Compromise made a concession to the slaveholding South by counting each slave as three-fifths of a person in apportioning seats in the House of Representatives. The Constitution explicitly prevented Congress from banning the slave trade until 1808. These cross-sectional views of a slave ship show the inhuman conditions that African slaves endured on the passage to America.

was immoral, insisted upon including slaves in the allocation of congressional seats. This conflict between the southern and northern delegates was so divisive that many came to question the possibility of creating and maintaining a union of the two. Pierce Butler of South Carolina declared that the North and South were as different as Russia and Turkey. Eventually, the North and South compromised on the issue of slavery and representation. Indeed, northerners even agreed to permit a continuation of the odious slave trade to keep the South in the union. But, in due course, Butler proved to be correct, and a bloody war was fought when the disparate interests of the North and the South could no longer be reconciled.

The Constitution

The political significance of the Great Compromise and the Three-fifths Compromise was to reinforce the unity of the mercantile and planter forces that sought to create a new government. The Great Compromise reassured those who feared that the importance of their own local or regional influence would be reduced by the new governmental framework. The Three-fifths Compromise temporarily defused the rivalry between the merchants and planters. Their unity secured, members of the alliance supporting the establishment of a new government moved to fashion a constitutional framework consistent with their economic and political interests.

In particular, the framers sought a new government that, first, would be strong enough to promote commerce and protect property from radical state legislatures such as Rhode Island's. This became the constitutional basis for national control over commerce and finance, as well as for the establishment of national judicial supremacy and the effort to construct a strong presidency. Second, the framers sought to prevent what they saw as the threat posed by the "excessive democracy" of the state and national governments under the Articles of Confederation. This led to such constitutional principles as bicameralism (division of the Congress into two chambers), **checks and balances,** staggered terms in office, and indirect election (selection of the president by an **electoral college** rather than by voters directly). Third, the framers, lacking the power to force the states or the public at large to accept the new form of government, sought to identify principles that would help to secure support. This became the basis of the constitutional provision for direct popular election of representatives and, subsequently, for the addition of the **Bill of Rights** to the Constitution. Finally, the framers wanted to be certain that the government they created did not pose even more of a threat to its citizens' liberties and property rights than did the radical state legislatures they feared and despised. To prevent the new government from abusing its power, the framers incorporated principles such as the **separation of powers** and **federalism** into the Constitution. Let us assess the major provisions of the Constitution's seven articles (listed in Box 2.1) to see how each relates to these objectives.

THE LEGISLATIVE BRANCH

The Constitution provided in Article I, Sections 1–7, for a Congress consisting of two chambers—a House of Representatives and a Senate. Members of the House of Representatives were given two-year terms in office and were to be elected directly

checks and balances mechanisms through which each branch of government is able to participate in and influence the activities of the other branches. Major examples include the presidential veto power over congressional legislation, the power of the Senate to approve presidential appointments, and judicial review of congressional enactments

electoral college the presidential electors from each state who meet after the popular election to cast ballots for president and vice president

Bill of Rights the first ten amendments to the U.S. Constitution, ratified in 1791; they ensure certain rights and liberties to the people

separation of powers the division of governmental power among several institutions that must cooperate in decision making

federalism a system of government in which power is divided, by a constitution, between a central government and regional governments

1. The Legislative Branch

House: two-year terms, elected directly by the people.

Senate: six-year terms (staggered so that only one-third of the Senate changes in any given election), appointed by state legislature (changed in 1913 to direct election).

Expressed powers of the national government: collecting taxes, borrowing money, regulating commerce, declaring war, and maintaining an army and a navy; all other power belongs to the states, unless deemed otherwise by the elastic ("necessary and proper") clause.

Exclusive powers of the national government: states are expressly forbidden to issue their own paper money, tax imports and exports, regulate trade outside their own borders, and impair the obligation of contracts; these powers are the exclusive domain of the national government.

2. The Executive Branch

Presidency: four-year terms (limited in 1951 to a maximum of two terms), elected indirectly by the electoral college.

Powers: can recognize other countries, negotiate treaties, grant reprieves and pardons, convene Congress in special sessions, and veto congressional enactment.

3. The Judicial Branch

Supreme Court: lifetime terms, appointed by the president with the approval of the Senate.

Powers: include resolving conflicts between federal and state laws, determining whether power belongs to the national government or the states, and settling controversies between citizens of different states.

4. National Unity and Power

Reciprocity among states: establishes that each state must give "full faith and credit" to official acts of other states, and guarantees citizens of any state the "privileges and immunities" of every other state.

5. Amending the Constitution

Procedure: requires approval by two-thirds of Congress and adoption by three-fourths of the states.

6. National Supremacy

The Constitution and national law are the supreme law of the land and cannot be overruled by state law.

7. Ratification

The Constitution became effective when approved by nine states.

by the people. Members of the Senate were to be appointed by the state legislatures (this was changed in 1913 by the Seventeenth Amendment, which instituted direct election of senators) for six-year terms. These terms were staggered so that the appointments of one-third of the senators would expire every two years. The Constitution assigned somewhat different tasks to the House and Senate. Though the approval of each body was required for the enactment of a law, the Senate alone was given the power to ratify treaties and approve presidential appointments. The House, on the other hand, was given the sole power to originate revenue bills.

The character of the legislative branch was directly related to the framers' major goals. The House of Representatives was designed to be directly responsible to the people in order to encourage popular consent for the new Constitution and to help enhance the power of the new government. At the same time, to guard against "excessive democracy," the power of the House of Representatives was checked by the Senate, whose members were to be appointed by the states for long terms rather than be elected directly by the people. The purpose of this provision, according to Alexander Hamilton, was to avoid "an unqualified complaisance to every sudden breeze of passion, or to every transient impulse which the people may receive."[13] Staggered terms of service in the Senate, moreover, were intended to make that body even more resistant to popular pressure. Since only one-third of the senators would be selected at any given time, the composition of the institution would be protected from changes in popular preferences transmitted by the state legislatures. This would prevent what James Madison called "mutability in the public councils arising from a rapid succession of new members."[14] Thus, the structure of the legislative branch was designed to contribute to governmental power, to promote popular consent for the new government, and at the same time to place limits on the popular political currents that many of the framers saw as a radical threat to the economic and social order.

The issues of power and consent were important throughout the Constitution. Section 8 of Article I specifically listed the powers of Congress, which include the authority to collect taxes, to borrow money, to regulate commerce, to declare war, and to maintain an army and navy. By granting Congress these powers, the framers indicated very clearly that they intended the new government to be far more influential than its predecessor. At the same time, by defining the new government's most important powers as belonging to Congress, the framers sought to promote popular acceptance of this critical change by reassuring citizens that their views would be fully represented whenever the government exercised its new powers.

As a further guarantee to the people that the new government would pose no threat to them, the Constitution implied that any powers not listed were not granted at all. This is the doctrine of **expressed power.** The Constitution grants only those powers specifically expressed in its text. But the framers intended to create an active and powerful government, and so they included the **elastic clause,** sometimes known as the necessary and proper clause, which signified that the enumerated powers were meant to be a source of strength to the national government, not a limitation on it. Each power could be used with the utmost vigor, but no new powers could be seized upon by the national government without a constitutional amendment. In the absence of such an amendment, any power not enumerated was conceived to be "reserved" to the states (or the people).

expressed powers specific powers granted to Congress under Article I, Section 8, of the Constitution

elastic clause Article I, Section 8, of the Constitution (also known as the "necessary and proper" clause), which enumerates the powers of Congress and provides Congress with the authority to make all laws "necessary and proper" to carry them out

THE EXECUTIVE BRANCH

The Constitution provided for the establishment of the presidency in Article II. As Alexander Hamilton commented, the presidential article aimed toward "energy in the Executive." It did so in an effort to overcome the natural tendency toward stalemate that was built into the bicameral legislature as well as into the separation of powers among the three branches. The Constitution afforded the president a measure of independence from the people and from the other branches of government—particularly the Congress.

In line with the framers' goal of increased power to the national government, the president was granted the unconditional power to accept ambassadors from other countries; this amounted to the power to "recognize" other countries. The president was also given the power to negotiate treaties, although their acceptance required the approval of the Senate. The president was given the unconditional right to grant reprieves and pardons, except in cases of impeachment. And the president was provided with the power to appoint major departmental personnel, to convene Congress in special session, and to veto congressional enactments. (The veto power is formidable, but it is not absolute, since Congress can override it by a two-thirds vote.)

The framers hoped to create a presidency that would make the federal government rather than the states the agency capable of timely and decisive action to deal with public issues and problems. This was the meaning of the "energy" that Hamilton hoped to impart to the executive branch.[15] At the same time, however, the framers sought to help the president withstand excessively democratic pressures by creating a system of indirect rather than direct election through a separate electoral college.

THE JUDICIAL BRANCH

In establishing the judicial branch in Article III, the Constitution reflected the framers' preoccupations with nationalizing governmental power and checking radical democratic impulses while guarding against potential interference with liberty and property from the new national government itself.

Under the provisions of Article III, the framers created a court that was to be literally a supreme court of the United States, and not merely the highest court of the national government. The most important expression of this intention was granting the Supreme Court the power to resolve any conflicts that might emerge between federal and state laws. In particular, the Supreme Court was given the right to determine whether a power was exclusive to the national government, concurrent with the states, or exclusive to the states. In addition, the Supreme Court was assigned jurisdiction over controversies between citizens of different states. The long-term significance of this provision was that as the country developed a national economy, it came to rely increasingly on the federal judiciary, rather than on the state courts, for the resolution of disputes.

Judges were given lifetime appointments in order to protect them from popular politics and from interference by the other branches. This, however, did not mean that the judiciary would remain totally impartial to political considerations or to the other branches, for the president was to appoint the judges, and the Senate to approve the appointments. Congress would also have the power to create inferior (lower) courts, to change the jurisdiction of the federal courts, to add or subtract federal judges, and even to change the size of the Supreme Court.

No direct mention is made in the Constitution of **judicial review**—the power of the courts to render the final decision when there is a conflict of interpretation of the Constitution or of laws between the courts and Congress, the courts and the executive branch, or the courts and the states. The Supreme Court eventually assumed the power of judicial review. Its assumption of this power, as we shall see in

judicial review the power of the courts to declare actions of the legislative and executive branches invalid or unconstitutional. The Supreme Court asserted this power in *Marbury v. Madison*

Chapter 15, was based not on the Constitution itself but on the politics of later decades and the membership of the Court.

NATIONAL UNITY AND POWER

Various provisions in the Constitution addressed the framers' concern with national unity and power, including Article IV's provisions for comity (reciprocity) among states and among citizens of all states. Each state was prohibited from discriminating against the citizens of other states in favor of its own citizens, with the Supreme Court charged with deciding in each case whether a state had discriminated against goods or people from another state. The Constitution restricted the power of the states in favor of ensuring enough power to the national government to give the country a free-flowing national economy.

The framers' concern with national supremacy was also expressed in Article VI, in the **supremacy clause,** which provided that national laws and treaties "shall be the supreme Law of the Land." This meant that all laws made under the "Authority of the United States" would be superior to all laws adopted by any state or any other subdivision, and the states would be expected to respect all treaties made under that authority. The supremacy clause also bound the officials of all governments—state and local as well as federal—to take an oath of office to support the national Constitution. This meant that every action taken by the United States Congress would have to be applied within each state as though the action were in fact state law.

supremacy clause Article VI of the Constitution, which states that laws passed by the national government and all treaties are the supreme law of the land and superior to all laws adopted by any state or any subdivision

AMENDING THE CONSTITUTION

The Constitution established procedures for its own revision in Article V. Its provisions are so difficult that Americans have availed themselves of the amending process only seventeen times since 1791, when the first ten amendments were adopted. Many other amendments have been proposed in Congress, but fewer than forty of them have even come close to fulfilling the Constitution's requirement of a two-thirds vote in Congress, and only a fraction have gotten anywhere near adoption by three-fourths of the states. Article V also provides that the Constitution can be amended by a constitutional convention. Occasionally, proponents of particular measures, such as a balanced-budget amendment, have called for a constitutional convention to consider their proposals. Whatever the purpose for which it were called, however, such a convention would presumably have the authority to revise America's entire system of government.

RATIFYING THE CONSTITUTION

The rules for the ratification of the Constitution were set forth in Article VII. Nine of the thirteen states would have to ratify, or agree upon, the terms in order for the Constitution to pass.

CONSTITUTIONAL LIMITS ON THE NATIONAL GOVERNMENT'S POWER

As we have indicated, although the framers sought to create a powerful national government, they also wanted to guard against possible misuse of that power. To that end, the framers incorporated two key principles into the Constitution—the separation of powers and federalism. A third set of limitations, in the form of the Bill of Rights, was added to the Constitution to help secure its ratification when opponents of the document charged that it paid insufficient attention to citizens' rights.

The Separation of Powers   No principle of politics was more widely shared at the time of the 1787 founding than the principle that power must be used to balance power. The French political theorist Baron de la Brède et de Montesquieu (1689–1755) believed that this balance was an indispensable defense against tyranny, and his writings, especially his major work, *The Spirit of the Laws*, "were taken as political gospel" at the Philadelphia Convention.[16] The principle of the separation of powers is not stated explicitly in the Constitution, but it is clearly built on Articles I, II, and III, which provide for the following:

1. Three separate and distinct branches of government (see Figure 2.1);
2. Different methods of selecting the top personnel, so that each branch is responsible to a different constituency. This is supposed to produce a "mixed regime," in which the personnel of each department will develop very different interests and outlooks on how to govern, and different groups in society will be assured some access to governmental decision making; and

The Separation of Powers   Figure 2.1

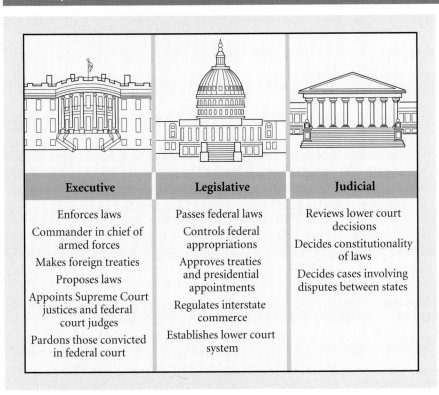

Executive	Legislative	Judicial
Enforces laws	Passes federal laws	Reviews lower court decisions
Commander in chief of armed forces	Controls federal appropriations	Decides constitutionality of laws
Makes foreign treaties	Approves treaties and presidential appointments	Decides cases involving disputes between states
Proposes laws		
Appoints Supreme Court justices and federal court judges	Regulates interstate commerce	
Pardons those convicted in federal court	Establishes lower court system	

Figure 2.2   **Checks and Balances**

Executive over Legislative
Can veto acts of Congress
Can call Congress into a special session
Carries out, and thereby interprets, laws passed by Congress
Vice president casts tie-breaking vote in the Senate

LEGISLATIVE

Legislative over Judicial
Can change size of federal court system and the number of Supreme Court justices
Can propose constitutional amendments
Can reject Supreme Court nominees
Can impeach and remove federal judges

Legislative over Executive
Can override presidential veto
Can impeach and remove president
Can reject president's appointments and refuse to ratify treaties
Can conduct investigations into president's actions
Can refuse to pass laws or to provide funding that president requests

Judicial over Legislative
Can declare laws unconstitutional
Chief justice presides over Senate during hearing to impeach the president

JUDICIAL

Executive over Judicial
Nominates Supreme Court justices
Nominates federal judges
Can pardon those convicted in federal court
Can refuse to enforce Court decisions

Judicial over Executive
Can declare executive actions unconstitutional
Power to issue warrants
Chief justice presides over impeachment of president

EXECUTIVE

FOR CRITICAL ANALYSIS

In many ways, the framers of the Constitution created a central government much stronger than the government created by the Articles of Confederation. Still, the framers seem to have taken great care to limit the power of the central government in various ways. Describe the ways in which the central government under the Constitution was stronger than the central government under the Articles. Describe the ways in which the framers limited the national government's power under the Constitution. Why might the framers have placed such limits on the government they had just created?

3. Checks and balances—a system under which each of the branches is given some power over the others. Familiar examples are the presidential veto power over legislation, the power of the Senate to approve presidential appointments, and judicial review of acts of Congress (see Figure 2.2).

One clever formulation of the separation of powers is that of a system not of separated powers but of "separated institutions sharing power,"[17] thus diminishing the chance that power will be misused.

Federalism   Compared with the confederation principle of the Articles of Confederation, federalism was a step toward greater centralization of power. The delegates agreed that they needed to place more power at the national level, without completely undermining the power of the state governments. Thus, they devised a system of two sovereigns—the states and the nation—with the hope that competition between the two would be an effective limitation on the power of both.

The Bill of Rights Late in the Philadelphia Convention, a motion was made to include a list of citizens' rights in the Constitution. After a brief debate in which hardly a word was said in its favor and only one speech was made against it, the motion was almost unanimously turned down. Most delegates sincerely believed that since the federal government was already limited to its expressed powers, further protection of citizens was not needed. The delegates argued that the states should adopt bills of rights because their greater powers needed greater limitations. But almost immediately after the Constitution was ratified, there was a movement to adopt a national bill of rights. This is why the Bill of Rights, adopted in 1791, comprises the first ten amendments to the Constitution rather than being part of the body of it. We will have a good deal more to say about the Bill of Rights in Chapter 4.

The Fight for Ratification

The first hurdle faced by the Constitution was ratification by state conventions of delegates elected by the people of each state. This struggle for ratification was carried out in thirteen separate campaigns. Each involved different people, moved at a different pace, and was influenced by local as well as national considerations. Two sides faced off throughout the states, however, calling themselves Federalists and Antifederalists (see Table 2.1). The **Federalists** (who more accurately should have called themselves "Nationalists," but who took their name to appear to follow in the revolutionary tradition) supported the Constitution and preferred a strong

Federalists those who favored a strong national government and supported the constitution proposed at the American Constitutional Convention of 1787

Federalists versus Antifederalists		Table 2.1
	FEDERALISTS	**ANTIFEDERALISTS**
Who were they?	Property owners, creditors, merchants	Small farmers, frontiersmen, debtors, shopkeepers
What did they believe?	Believed that elites were best fit to govern; feared "excessive democracy"	Believed that government should be closer to the people; feared concentration of power in hands of the elites
What system of government did they favor?	Favored strong national government; believed in "filtration" so that only elites would obtain governmental power	Favored retention of power by state governments and protection of individual rights
Who were their leaders?	Alexander Hamilton James Madison George Washington	Patrick Henry George Mason Elbridge Gerry George Clinton

Antifederalists those who favored strong state governments and a weak national government and who were opponents of the constitution proposed at the American Constitutional Convention of 1787

national government. The **Antifederalists** opposed the Constitution and preferred a federal system of government that was decentralized; they took their name by default, in reaction to their better-organized opponents. The Federalists were united in their support of the Constitution, while the Antifederalists were divided over what they believed the alternative to the Constitution should be.

During the struggle over ratification of the Constitution, Americans argued about great political issues and principles. How much power should the national government be given? What safeguards were most likely to prevent the abuse of power? What institutional arrangements could best ensure adequate representation for all Americans? Was tyranny to be feared more from the many or from the few?

FEDERALISTS VERSUS ANTIFEDERALISTS

During the ratification struggle, thousands of essays, speeches, pamphlets, and letters were presented in support of and in opposition to the proposed Constitution. The best-known pieces supporting ratification of the Constitution were the eighty-five essays written, under the name of "Publius," by Alexander Hamilton, James Madison, and John Jay between the fall of 1787 and the spring of 1788. These **Federalist Papers,** as they are collectively known today, defended the principles of the Constitution and sought to dispel fears of a national authority. The Antifederalists published essays of their own, arguing that the new Constitution betrayed the Revolution and was a step toward monarchy. Among the best of the Antifederalist works were the essays, usually attributed to New York Supreme Court justice Robert Yates, that were written under the name of "Brutus" and published in the *New York Journal* at the same time the Federalist Papers appeared. The Antifederalist view was also ably presented in the pamphlets and letters written by a former delegate to the Continental Congress and future U.S. senator, Richard Henry Lee of Virginia, using the pen name "The Federal Farmer." These essays highlight the major differences of opinion between Federalists and Antifederalists. Federalists appealed to basic principles of government in support of their nationalist vision. Antifederalists cited equally fundamental precepts to support their vision of a looser confederacy of small republics.

Federalist Papers a series of essays written by James Madison, Alexander Hamilton, and John Jay supporting the ratification of the Constitution

Representation One major area of contention between the two sides was the question of representation. The Antifederalists asserted that representatives must be "a true picture of the people, . . . [possessing] the knowledge of their circumstances and their wants."[18] This could be achieved, argued the Antifederalists, only in small, relatively homogeneous republics such as the existing states. In their view, the size and extent of the entire nation precluded the construction of a truly representative form of government. As Brutus put it, "Is it practicable for a country so large and so numerous . . . to elect a representation that will speak their sentiments? . . . It certainly is not."[19]

Federalists, for their part, saw no reason that representatives should be precisely like those they represented. In the Federalist view, one of the great advantages of representative government over direct democracy was precisely the possibility that the people would choose as their representatives individuals possessing ability, experience, and talent superior to their own. In Madison's words, rather than serve as a mirror or reflection of society, representatives must

Religious Freedom and School Prayer

The first two rights enshrined in the First Amendment bar the government from establishing a state religion and from inhibiting the free exercise of religion by individuals. Thus, the government is barred from breaching the "wall of separation" between church and state, so that religious liberty may find full expression. Yet is that wall breached if individuals wish to express their religious beliefs in schools? At first glance, the answer would appear to be yes. In the 1962 case of *Engel v. Vitale,* the Supreme Court barred government-organized and -led religious prayer. Since then, proponents of prayer in school have marshaled much support for a more flexible approach, arguing in part that courts have misunderstood the framers' intent. Proponents have also pushed for a constitutional amendment guaranteeing free religious expression in public schools.

Proponents of prayer in school argue that the Constitution's framers were pious men who were not out to drive religion from schools or other aspects of public life. Every congress since the Founding has opened its daily session with a prayer. Supreme Court sessions begin with the words "God save the United States and this Honorable Court." By now shunning any form of religious expression at a time when children seem increasingly in need of moral and spiritual guidance, schools are sending the wrong message to the nation's children. Moreover, the absence of school religion implicitly encourages another belief system—secularism.

School prayer need not be led by teachers or administrators, nor need it be required. Voluntary prayer led by students would pose no threat to the First Amendment. Instead, it would reflect the proper extension of religious liberty into schools. In short, an enlightened approach to school prayer requires neither a government stamp of approval nor any form of coercion.

Opponents of school prayer argue that both the First Amendment and American respect for individual freedom require that schools avoid any role in religious teaching, instruction, or prayer. They generally oppose even student-run religious activities associated with school functions. For example, groups opposed to school prayer applauded the Supreme Court's decision in *Doe v. Santa Fe Independent School District* (2000), in which the Court ruled that a public school's policy of allowing students to read prayers over the public address system during football games violated the First Amendment's Establishment Clause. Government meddling in religion drove many European settlers to America, and the Founders understood that keeping government out of religious matters was not an expression of hostility to religion, but a simple acknowledgment that both government and religion were better off if the former let the latter alone.

Although most Americans hold some form of religious belief, the range of those beliefs is wide and growing, meaning that any form of religious teaching or prayer is bound to offend the sensibilities of some religious groups. Moreover, the rights of nonbelievers are equal to those of believers. School actions that ostracize, penalize, or stigmatize nonbelievers violate their right to equal treatment and their right not to be subjected to religious teachings in what is a public and secular institution.

FOR CRITICAL ANALYSIS

1. What did the framers of the Constitution mean when they prohibited the "establishment" of a religion? Would the framers agree or disagree with recent Supreme Court decisions? Should we be bound by the framers' views or should Americans be free to reinterpret the Constitution in keeping with contemporary values?

2. The Constitution bans the establishment of religion and also prohibits Congress from interfering with the free exercise of religion. Could these provisions ever come into conflict?

Should School Prayer Be Allowed?

Yes In 1947, the U. S. Supreme Court bastardized the intentions of Thomas Jefferson and contrived public policy from one of his personal, private letters. This led to a systematic effort by organizations such as the American Civil Liberties Union to remove any recognition of God from the public arena.

The latest example of special interest groups utilizing the "separation of church and state" argument is found in Alabama, where a federal court ordered Chief Justice Roy Moore to remove the Ten Commandments monument in the Supreme Court Rotunda.

I don't intend to defend Moore's actions or methods, but this case has once again brought the arguments over religious liberty to a boil, and I would be remiss if I failed to defend true religious liberty.

Most would be surprised to hear that the U. S.Constitution contains no mention of a "separation of church and state." In fact, that phrase only was found in Jefferson's personal, private letter to the Danbury Baptist Association.

This is probably the sole time in history when national policy was created merely from a single and most private letter. The establishment clause found in the First Amendment simply reads, "Congress shall make no law respecting an establishment of religion, or prohibiting the free exercise thereof."

Secondly, when one looks at Jefferson's actions and words, it is easy to see he had no desire for the government to limit, restrict, regulate, or interfere with public religious practices. He simply believed the First Amendment had been enacted to protect religion from governmental oppression, prevent the federal establishment of a national denomination, and not allow the United States to become a theocracy.

In another private letter Jefferson wrote to Samuel Millar he stated: "I consider the government of the United States as interdicted [prohibited] by the Constitution from intermeddling with religious institutions . . . or exercises."

Jefferson, however, allowed church services to be held in the chambers of the Supreme Court.

Obviously, he did not fear or oppose religious exercises in the public square.

He further declared, "The power to prescribe any religious exercise . . . must rest with the states."

The federal courts directly violate the principles of the one they claim to derive their policy from. How can a federal court cite Jefferson then enforce its wishes on each state? It is clear to see Jefferson and the founders meant to leave this authority to the individual states.

Without a doubt, religion and the idea of God-given rights helped fuel the fires of the American Revolution and form the founding principles of the United States. Many of the founding fathers recognized the benefits of a religious and moral society in creating and guarding a free republic.

"It is religion and morality alone which can establish the principles upon which freedom can securely stand," John Adams said.

George Washington echoed Adams's sentiment when he asked, "Where is the security for property, for reputation, for life, if the sense of religious obligation desert the oaths, which are the instruments of investigation in Courts of Justice?"

The 1962 *Engel v. Vitale* case led the U. S. Supreme Court to banish public school prayer in the name of the supposed "wall" between church and state. Since then many student religious groups have been prevented from meeting on school property, Bibles have been removed from numerous public school libraries, and students who express their faith often do so at the risk of retribution from the administration. The removal of scores of Ten Commandments displays across the nation's public schools, city halls, public places, and courts such as the Alabama Supreme Court shows the resolve and the effectiveness of those who wish for people to only practice their faith in their prayer closet.

Can anyone testify to improved school life since prayer was removed? What improvements has it brought to our society? Gone are the days of petty school problems such as chewing gum and even merely smoking cigarettes in the bathroom. Now our public school students often enter war zones in their classrooms and deal with problems such as teen pregnancy and STDs. It is not hard to argue that our culture has been on a steady decline.

What are we to expect when we forbid the foundation of morality from being freely discussed, presented, or acknowledged in America's public places?

This also has created an environment where people of faith and religious leaders are afraid to speak out or admit to their faith in public. At the time of our founding, many ministers served in Congress and used the pulpit to further the revolution. Today it is difficult to find many religious leaders who will take a stand, and those who do are often criticized and dismissed as "religious-right zealots."

It is time for all to realize the true foundation of our nation. We can't expect to keep our greatness if we continue to forget what made us great in the first place. All people of faith need to claim the religious freedom our founders wanted for us and fight any oppression of their expression, public or private.

I only can pray that our leaders will place justices who truly understand the religious freedom Jefferson and the founders sought when they founded our great country.

Perhaps Jefferson made the argument best when he asked, "And can the liberties of a nation be though secure if we have lost the only firm basis, a conviction in the minds of the people that these liberties are the gift of God? That they are not to be violated but with His wrath?"

SOURCE: Jason Dore, "Separation Would Shake Foundation: Leave God Where Jefferson Put Him," *LSU Reveille* (Louisiana State University), August 27, 2003.

No

Religion, or its artistic representation, has no place on the grounds of a government building — end of story.

The removal of the ten Commandments statue from an Alabama judicial building should serve as a reminder to Americans. Our government does not and should not allow the promotion of any religion, be it through laws, funding, or within its buildings.

But the U. S. government does not prohibit religious expression in this country, nor should it. Americans are allowed to practice any religion they choose, or none at all. The purpose of "separation of church and state" has always been to respect the freedom of religion, not to infringe upon it.

The best way to preserve religion is to have a government that does not endorse any. According to the Americans United for Separation of Church and State Web site (www.au.org), as soon as government money or rhetoric is used to support a church, the citizens' incentive to promote and maintain their churches begins to dissipate. Truly, religious Americans should understand and support the separation of church from state.

Now, not many Americans are advocating an official Church of the United States.

However, lobbying for prayer in school and retaining "God" on our money is comparable to asking for a religious place within government. If religion is to be separate from state activities, allotted prayer time and the acknowledgment of a higher power on our currency run contradictory to that principle.

The point here is principle. If we, as Americans, start letting the church-state line blur, we are not allowing freedom of expression. We are allowing the religious voice to be heard where it does not belong. Freedom of expression means people are allowed to practice the religion of their choice; it does not mean the majority religion should be allowed to display and promote that religion through government means.

If you are a person who identifies with a religion, ask yourself these questions: Do I have the right to expect my country to favor my religion over all others? Should I defend the making of laws that support my religion or support religion over non-religion in general? Should I support legislation or actions that give obvious preference to religious-minded people like me? The answer should be "no" on all counts.

If you like living in a country that establishes your religion by law, then perhaps you should consider living in a theocracy, not a democracy. Otherwise, it is time that all Americans recognize the value of a country that keeps religion far from law-making, or as the case may be, our judicial buildings.

SOURCE: Stephanie Lovett, "Where Do Religious Representations Belong? Nowhere Near Government," *The University Daily Kansan* (University of Kansas), September 4, 2003.

be "[those] who possess [the] most wisdom to discern, and [the] most virtue to pursue, the common good of the society."[20]

Although the terms of discussion have changed, this debate over representation continues today. Some argue that representatives must be very close in life experience, race, and ethnic background to their constituents to truly understand the needs and interests of those constituents. This argument is made by contemporary proponents of giving the states more control over social programs. This argument is also made by proponents of "minority districts"—legislative districts whose boundaries are drawn so as to guarantee that minorities will be able to elect their own representative to Congress. Opponents of this practice, which we will explore further in Chapter 10, have argued in court that it is discriminatory and unnecessary; blacks, they say, can be represented by whites and vice versa. Who is correct? It would appear that this question can never be answered to everyone's complete satisfaction.

Tyranny of the Majority   A second important issue dividing Federalists and Antifederalists was the threat of **tyranny**—unjust rule by the group in power. Both opponents and defenders of the Constitution frequently affirmed their fear of tyrannical rule. Each side, however, had a different view of the most likely source of tyranny and, hence, of the way in which the threat was to be forestalled.

From the Antifederalist perspective, the great danger was the tendency of all governments—including republican governments—to become gradually more and more "aristocratic" in character, wherein the small number of individuals in positions of authority would use their stations to gain more and more power over the general citizenry. In essence, the few would use their power to tyrannize the many. For this reason, Antifederalists were sharply critical of those features of the Constitution that divorced governmental institutions from direct responsibility to the people—institutions such as the Senate, the executive, and the federal judiciary. The latter, appointed for life, presented a particular threat: "I wonder if the world ever saw . . . a court of justice invested with such immense powers, and yet placed in a situation so little responsible," protested Brutus.[21]

The Federalists, too, recognized the threat of tyranny, but they believed that the danger particularly associated with republican governments was not aristocracy, but instead, majority tyranny. The Federalists were concerned that a popular majority, "united and actuated by some common impulse of passion, or of interest, adverse to the rights of other citizens," would endeavor to "trample on the rules of justice."[22] From the Federalist perspective, it was precisely those features of the Constitution attacked as potential sources of tyranny by the Antifederalists that actually offered the best hope of averting the threat of oppression. The size and extent of the nation, for instance, was for the Federalists a bulwark against tyranny.

Governmental Power   A third major difference between Federalists and Antifederalists was the issue of governmental power. Both opponents and proponents of the Constitution agreed on the principle of **limited government.** They differed, however, on the fundamentally important question of how to place limits on governmental action. Antifederalists favored limiting and enumerating the powers granted to the national government in relation both to the states and to the people at large. To them, the powers given the national government ought to be "confined to certain defined national objects."[23] Otherwise, the national government would

tyranny oppressive and unjust government that employs cruel and unjust use of power and authority

limited government a government whose powers are defined and limited by a constitution "swallow up all the power of the state governments."[24] Antifederalists bitterly attacked the supremacy clause and the elastic clause of the Constitution as unlimited and dangerous grants of power to the national government.[25] Antifederalists also demanded that a bill of rights be added to the Constitution to place limits upon the government's exercise of power over the citizenry.

Federalists favored the construction of a government with broad powers. They wanted a government that had the capacity to defend the nation against foreign foes, guard against domestic strife and insurrection, promote commerce, and expand the nation's economy. Antifederalists shared some of these goals but still feared governmental power. Hamilton pointed out, however, that these goals could not be achieved without allowing the government to exercise the necessary power. Federalists acknowledged that every power could be abused but argued that the way to prevent misuse of power was not by depriving the government of the powers needed to achieve national goals. Instead, they argued that the threat of abuse of power would be mitigated by the Constitution's internal checks and controls. As Madison put it, "the power surrendered by the people is first divided between two distinct governments, and then the portion allotted to each subdivided among distinct and separate departments. Hence, a double security arises to the rights of the people. The different governments will control each other, at the same time that each will be controlled by itself."[26] The Federalists' concern with avoiding unwarranted limits on governmental power led them to oppose a bill of rights, which they saw as nothing more than a set of unnecessary restrictions on the government.

The Federalists acknowledged that abuse of power remained a possibility, but felt that the risk had to be taken because of the goals to be achieved. "The very idea of power included a possibility of doing harm," said the Federalist John Rutledge during the South Carolina ratification debates. "If the gentleman would show the power that could do no harm," Rutledge continued, "he would at once discover it to be a power that could do no good."[27] This aspect of the debate between the Federalists and the Antifederalists, perhaps more than any other, continues to reverberate through American politics. Should the nation limit the federal government's power to tax and spend? Should Congress limit the capacity of federal agencies to issue new regulations? Should the government endeavor to create new rights for minorities, the disabled, and others? What is the proper balance between promoting equality and protecting liberty? Though the details have changed, these are the same great questions that have been debated since the time of the Founding.

FOR CRITICAL ANALYSIS

What were the major points of contention between the Federalists and the Antifederalists? Were the Federalists correct?

REFLECTIONS ON THE FOUNDING

The final product of the Constitutional Convention would have to be considered an extraordinary victory for the groups that had most forcefully called for the creation of a new system of government to replace the Articles of Confederation. Antifederalist criticisms forced the Constitution's proponents to accept the addition of a bill of rights designed to limit the powers of the national government. In general, however, it was the Federalist vision of America that triumphed. The Constitution adopted in 1789 created the framework for a powerful national government that for more than 200 years has defended the nation's interests, promoted its commerce, and maintained national unity. In one notable instance, the national government fought and won a bloody war to prevent the nation from breaking apart. And despite this powerful government, the system of internal checks and balances has functioned reasonably well, as the Federalists predicted, to prevent the national government from tyrannizing its citizens.

Of course, the groups whose interests were served by the Constitution in 1789, mainly the merchants and planters, are not the same groups that benefit from the Constitution's provisions today. Once incorporated into the law, political principles often take on lives of their own and have consequences that were never anticipated by their original champions. Indeed, many of the groups that benefit from constitutional provisions today did not even exist in 1789. Who would have thought that the principle of free speech would influence the transmission of data on the Internet? Who would have predicted that commercial interests that once sought a powerful government might come, two centuries later, to denounce governmental activism as "socialist"? Perhaps one secret of the Constitution's longevity is that it did not confer permanent advantage upon any one set of economic or social forces.

Although they were defeated in 1789, the Antifederalists present us with an important picture of a road not taken and of an America that might have been. Would the country have been worse off if it had been governed by a confederacy of small republics linked by a national administration with severely limited powers? Were the Antifederalists correct in predicting that a government given great power in the hope that it might do good would, through "insensible progress," inevitably turn to evil purposes? Two hundred years of government under the federal Constitution are not necessarily enough to definitively answer these questions. Time must tell.

The Citizen's Role and the Changing Constitution

The Constitution has endured for more than two centuries as the framework of government. But it has not endured without change. Without change, the Constitution might have become merely a sacred text, stored under glass.

AMENDMENTS: MANY ARE CALLED, FEW ARE CHOSEN

amendment a change added to a bill, law, or constitution

The need for change was recognized by the framers of the Constitution, and the provisions for **amendment** incorporated into Article V were thought to be "an easy, regular and Constitutional way" to make changes, which would occasionally be necessary because members of Congress "may abuse their power and refuse their consent on that very account . . . to admit to amendments to correct the source of the abuse."[28] Madison made a more balanced defense of the amendment procedure in Article V: "It guards equally against that extreme facility, which would render the Constitution too mutable; and that extreme difficulty, which might perpetuate its discovered faults."[29]

Experience since 1789 raises questions even about Madison's more modest claims. The Constitution has proven to be extremely difficult to amend. In the history of efforts to amend the Constitution, the most appropriate characterization is "many are called, few are chosen." Between 1789 and 1996, more than 11,000 amendments were formally offered in Congress. Of these, Congress officially proposed only twenty-nine, and twenty-seven of these were eventually ratified by the states. But the record is even more severe than that. Since 1791, when the first ten amendments, the Bill of Rights, were added, only seventeen amendments have been adopted. And two of them—Prohibition and its repeal—cancel each other out, so that for all practical purposes, only fifteen amendments have been added to the Constitution since 1791. Despite vast changes in American society and its economy, only twelve amendments have been adopted since the Civil War amendments in 1868.

Four methods of amendment are provided for in Article V:

1. Passage in House and Senate by two-thirds vote; then ratification by majority vote of the legislatures of three-fourths (thirty-eight) of the states.
2. Passage in House and Senate by two-thirds vote; then ratification by conventions called for the purpose in three-fourths of the states.
3. Passage in a national convention called by Congress in response to petitions by two-thirds of the states; ratification by majority vote of the legislatures of three-fourths of the states.
4. Passage in a national convention, as in (3); then ratification by conventions called for the purpose in three-fourths of the states.

(Figure 2.3 illustrates each of these possible methods.) Since no amendment has ever been proposed by national convention, however, methods (3) and (4) have

Four Ways the Constitution Can Be Amended
Figure 2.3

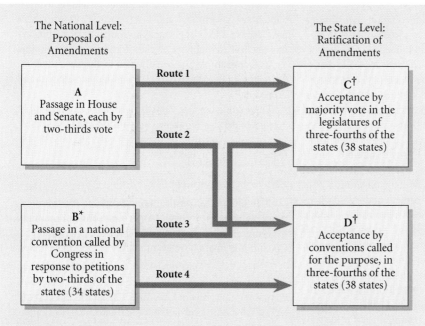

The National Level:
Proposal of Amendments

The State Level:
Ratification of Amendments

A
Passage in House and Senate, each by two-thirds vote

Route 1

Route 2

C†
Acceptance by majority vote in the legislatures of three-fourths of the states (38 states)

B*
Passage in a national convention called by Congress in response to petitions by two-thirds of the states (34 states)

Route 3

Route 4

D†
Acceptance by conventions called for the purpose, in three-fourths of the states (38 states)

*This method of proposal has never been employed. Thus amendment routes 3 and 4 have never been attempted.

†In each amendment proposal, Congress has the power to choose the method of ratification, the time limit for consideration by the states, and other conditions of ratification.

The American Constitution: A Model for the World?

The U.S. Constitution is often said to be both the world's oldest written constitution and a continuing model for the nations of the world. Both of these assertions are *partly* accurate. Nearly two millennia before the delegates to America's constitutional convention met in Philadelphia, a number of Greek city-states had produced written constitutions.[a] And closer to home, all the first American states possessed written constitutions. Indeed, to the embarrassment of the framers, most state constitutions included bills of rights that the framers hesitated to include in the national constitution. Nevertheless, it might be said that the U.S. Constitution is the world's oldest written document that formally organizes the governmental processes of an entire nation. What is sometimes callled America's first constitution—the Articles of Confederation—was more a compact among sovereign entities, the states, than an organic statute for a nation.

As to the second assertion, the U.S. Constitution has indeed frequently served as a model for others, but other nations' constitution writers often consciously sought to avoid rather than imitate American-style institutions and practices. One important American idea that has been widely copied is that of having a written constitution. After America wrote its constitution in 1789, both Poland and France adopted written constitutions in 1791. The French became so enamored of constitution writing that they put forth four different constitutions during the 1790s alone, as successive revolutionary governments seized power.[b] As revolutions swept Europe during the nineteenth and early twentieth centuries, every new government viewed a written constitution both as an important legitimating instrument and as a declaration that the new regime categorically rejected the despotic and arbitrary practices of its predecessor. Today, virtually all the world's democracies have written constitutions. Britain, Israel, and New Zealand remain important exceptions.[c] Ironically, possession of a written constitution has become such an important attribute of political legitimacy and symbol of freedom that even some despotic regimes have sham constitutions to provide the appearance, albeit not the substance, of popular government. For example, the former Soviet Union often boasted that it possessed the world's most democratic constitution.

Among the world's constitutional democracies, some have copied elements of the American Constitution but most have chosen patterns of government quite different

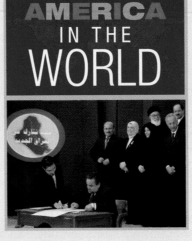

from the American model. Judicial review of statutes, an American political innovation, has been adopted by most democracies. In a number of instances, too, new constitutions have incorporated the principle of federalism to deal with the problem of ethnic or regional divisions. For example, with American encouragement, both Iraq and Afghanistan have made federalism an important principle in their new constitutional documents. Few democracies, however, have copied the American system of separation of powers and checks and balances, opting, instead, for parliamentary government. Even the Japanese and German constitutions, written under the supervision of American occupation authorities following World War II, created parliamentary systems. Presumably, the United States sought to discourage the emergence of a strong and independent executive in nations that had arguably suffered from an excess of executive power during the previous decade.

In addition to providing for parliamentary government, most of the world's constitutions have departed from the American model by providing extensive lists of political, social, cultural, and economic rights. For example, the constitution of the Czech Republic includes a lengthy "Charter of Fundamental Rights and Freedoms."

Thus, while the U.S. Constitution inspired many other nations to develop a written constitution, the precise form that national constitutions take can diverge considerably from the American model.

FOR CRITICAL ANALYSIS

1. Is America's Constitution appropriate for every nation? Which elements of the American Constitution might have universal validity? Which features of the American Constitution might be relevant mainly to the United States?

2. The U.S. Constitution is a very brief document whereas many new constitutions are lengthy documents containing long lists of governmental duties and citizens' rights. What are the advantages and disadvantages of America's constitutional model?

[a]Kim Lane Scheppele, "Constitutions around the World," National Constitution Center, www.constitutioncenter.org/explore/Originsofthecon-stitution/nccscholaressays, 2003, p. 1.
[b]Scheppele, p. 1.
[c]Scheppele, p. 2.

never been employed. And method (2) has only been employed once (the Twenty-first Amendment, which repealed the Eighteenth, or Prohibition, Amendment). Thus, method (1) has been used for all the others.

Now it should be clear why it has been so difficult to amend the Constitution. The requirement of a two-thirds vote in the House and the Senate means that any proposal for an amendment in Congress can be killed by only 34 senators or 136 members of the House. What is more, if the necessary two-thirds vote is obtained, the amendment can still be killed by the refusal or inability of only thirteen state legislatures to ratify it. Since each state has an equal vote regardless of its population, the thirteen holdout states may represent a very small fraction of the total American population.

THE CASE OF THE EQUAL RIGHTS AMENDMENT

The Equal Rights Amendment (ERA) is a case study of a proposed amendment that almost succeeded. In fact, the ERA is one of the very few proposals that got the necessary two-thirds vote in Congress yet failed to obtain the ratification of the requisite thirty-eight states.

On October 12, 1971, the U.S. House of Representatives approved the Equal Rights Amendment by the required two-thirds majority; the Senate followed suit on March 22, 1972. The amendment was simple:

Sec. 1. Equality of rights under the law shall not be denied or abridged by the United States or by any State on account of sex.
Sec. 2. The Congress shall have the power to enforce, by appropriate legislation, the provisions of this article.
Sec. 3. This amendment shall take effect two years after the date of ratification.

The congressional resolution provided for the accustomed method of ratification through the state legislatures rather than by state conventions—route (1) rather than route (2) in Figure 2.3—and that it had to be completed within seven years, by March 22, 1979.

Since the amendment was the culmination of nearly a half-century of efforts, and since the women's movement had spread its struggle for several years prior to 1971, the amendment was ratified by twenty-eight state legislatures during the very first year. But opposition forces quickly organized into the "Stop ERA" movement. By the end of 1974, five more states had ratified the amendment, but three states that had ratified it in 1973—Idaho, Nebraska, and Tennessee—had afterward voted to rescind their ratification. This posed an unprecedented problem: whether a state legislature had the right to rescind its approval. The Supreme Court refused to deal with this question, insisting that it was a political question to be settled by Congress. If the ERA had been ratified by the thirty-eight-state minimum, Congress would have had to decide whether to respect the rescissions or to count them as ratifications.

This point was rendered moot by events. By the end of 1978, thirty-five state legislatures had ratified the ERA—counting the three rescinding legislatures as ratifiers. But even counting them, the three additional state ratifications necessary to reach thirty-eight became increasingly difficult to get. In each of the remaining fifteen states, the amendment had already been rejected at least once. The only hope of the ERA forces was that the 1978 elections would change the composition of some of those state legislatures. Pinning their hopes on that, the ERA forces turned back to Congress and succeeded in getting an extension of the ratification deadline to June 30, 1982. This was an especially significant victory, because it was the first time Congress had extended the time limit since it began placing time restrictions on ratification in 1917. But this victory in Washington failed to impress any of the fifteen holdout legislatures. June 30, 1982, came and went, and the ERA was, for the time being at least, laid to rest. It was beaten by the efforts of Stop ERA and by the emergence of conservatism generally, which had culminated in Ronald Reagan's election as president.[30]

WHICH WERE CHOSEN? AN ANALYSIS OF THE TWENTY-SEVEN

There is more to the amending difficulties than the politics of campaigning and voting. It would appear that only a limited number of changes needed by society can actually be made through the Constitution. Although we shall see that the ERA fits the pattern of successful amendments, most efforts to amend the Constitution have failed because they were simply attempts to use the Constitution as an alternative to legislation for dealing directly with a public problem. A review of the successful amendments will provide two insights: First, it will give us some understanding of the conditions underlying successful amendments; and second, it will reveal a great deal about what constitutionalism means.

The purpose of the ten amendments in the Bill of Rights was basically structural, to give each of the three branches clearer and more restricted boundaries. The First Amendment clarified the jurisdiction of Congress. Although the powers of Congress under Article I, Section 8, would not have justified laws regulating religion, speech, and the like, the First Amendment made this limitation explicit: "Congress shall make no law. . . ." The Second, Third, and Fourth amendments similarly spelled out specific limits on the executive branch. This was seen as a necessity given the abuses of executive power Americans had endured under British rule.

The Fifth, Sixth, Seventh, and Eighth amendments contain some of the most important safeguards for individual citizens against the arbitrary exercise of government power. These amendments sought to accomplish their goal by defining the judicial branch more concretely and clearly than had been done in Article III of the Constitution. Table 2.2 analyzes the ten amendments included in the Bill of Rights.

Five of the seventeen amendments adopted since 1791 are directly concerned with the expansion of the electorate and, thus, political equality (see Table 2.3). The Founders were unable to establish a national electorate with uniform voting qualifications. They decided to evade it by providing in the final draft of Article I, Section 2, that eligibility to vote in a national election would be the same as "the Qualifications requisite for Electors of the most numerous Branch of the State Legislature." Article I, Section 4, added that Congress could alter state regulations as to the "Times, Places and Manner of holding Elections for Senators and Representatives." Nevertheless, this meant that any important *expansion* of the American electorate would almost certainly require a constitutional amendment.

Six more amendments are also electoral in nature, although they are not concerned directly with voting rights and the expansion of the electorate (see Table 2.4).

The Bill of Rights: Analysis of Its Provisions

Table 2.2

AMENDMENT	PURPOSE
I	*Limits on Congress:* Congress is not to make any law establishing a religion or abridging speech, press, assembly, or petition freedoms.
II, III, IV	*Limits on Executive:* The executive branch is not to infringe on the right of people to keep arms (II), is not to arbitrarily take houses for a militia (III), and is not to engage in the search or seizure of evidence without a court warrant swearing to belief in the probable existence of a crime (IV).
V, VI, VII, VIII	*Limits on Courts:* The courts are not to hold trials for serious offenses without provision for a grand jury (V), a petit (trial) jury (VII), a speedy trial (VI), presentation of charges (VI), confrontation of hostile witnesses (VI), immunity from testimony against oneself (V), and immunity from trial more than once for the same offense (V). Neither bail nor punishment can be excessive (VIII), and no property can be taken without just compensation (V).
IX, X	*Limits on National Government:* All rights not enumerated are reserved to the states or the people.

These six amendments are concerned with the elective offices themselves (the Twentieth, Twenty-second, and Twenty-fifth) or with the relationship between elective offices and the electorate (the Twelfth, Fourteenth, and Seventeenth). One could conclude that one effect was the enhancement of democracy.

Amending the Constitution to Expand the Electorate

Table 2.3

AMENDMENT	PURPOSE	YEAR PROPOSED	YEAR ADOPTED
XV	Extended voting rights to all races	1869	1870
XIX	Extended voting rights to women	1919	1920
XXIII	Extended voting rights to residents of the District of Columbia	1960	1961
XXIV	Extended voting rights to all classes by abolition of poll taxes	1962	1964
XXVI	Extended voting rights to citizens aged 18 and over	1971	1971*

*The Twenty-sixth Amendment holds the record for speed of adoption. It was proposed on March 23, 1971, and adopted on July 5, 1971.

| Table 2.4 | Amending the Constitution to Change the Relationship between Elected Offices and the Electorate |

AMENDMENT	PURPOSE	YEAR PROPOSED	YEAR ADOPTED
XII	Provided separate ballot for vice president in the electoral college	1803	1804
XIV	(Part 1) Provided a national definition of citizenship*	1866	1868
XVII	Provided direct election of senators	1912	1913
XX	Eliminated "lame duck" session of Congress	1932	1933
XXII	Limited presidential term	1947	1951
XXV	Provided presidential succession in case of disability	1965	1967

*In defining *citizenship*, the Fourteenth Amendment actually provided the constitutional basis for expanding the electorate to include all races, women, and residents of the District of Columbia. Only the "eighteen-year-olds' amendment" should have been necessary, since it changed the definition of citizenship. The fact that additional amendments were required following the Fourteenth suggests that voting is not considered an inherent right of U.S. citizenship. Instead, it is viewed as a privilege.

Another five amendments serve to expand or limit the power of government (see Table 2.5).[31] The Eleventh Amendment protected the states from suits by private individuals and took away from the federal courts any power to take suits by private individuals of one state (or a foreign country) against another state. The other three amendments in Table 2.5 are obviously designed to reduce state power (Thirteenth), to reduce state power and expand national power (Fourteenth), and to expand national power (Sixteenth). The Twenty-seventh put a limit on Congress's ability to raise its own salary.

The one missing amendment underscores the meaning of the rest: the Eighteenth, or Prohibition, Amendment. This is the only instance in which the country tried to *legislate* by constitutional amendment. In other words, it is the only amendment that was designed to deal directly with some substantive social problem. And it was the only amendment ever to have been repealed. Two other amendments—the Thirteenth, which abolished slavery, and the Sixteenth, which established the power to levy an income tax—can be said to have had the effect of legislation. But the purpose of the Thirteenth was to restrict the power of the states by forever forbidding them to treat any human being as property. As for the Sixteenth, it is certainly true that income tax legislation followed immediately; nevertheless, the amendment concerns itself strictly with establishing the power of Congress to enact such legislation. The legislation came later; and if down the line a majority in Congress had wanted to

Amending the Constitution to Expand or Limit the Power of Government

Table 2.5

Amendment	Purpose	Year Proposed	Year Adopted
XI	Limited jurisdiction of federal courts over suits involving the states	1794	1798
XIII	Eliminated slavery and eliminated the right of states to allow property in persons	1865*	1865
XIV	(Part 2) Applied due process of Bill of Rights to the states	1866	1868
XVI	Established national power to tax incomes	1909	1913
XXVII	Limited Congress's power to raise its own salary	1789	1992

*The Thirteenth Amendment was proposed January 31, 1865, and adopted less than a year later, on December 18, 1865.

abolish the income tax, they could also have done this by legislation rather than through the arduous path of a constitutional amendment repealing the income tax.

All of this points to the principle underlying the twenty-five existing amendments: all are concerned with the structure or composition of government. This is consistent with the dictionary, which defines *constitution* as the makeup or composition of something. And it is consistent with the concept of a constitution as "higher law," because the whole point and purpose of a higher law is to establish a framework within which government and the process of making ordinary law can take place. Even those who would have preferred more changes in the Constitution would have to agree that there is great wisdom in this principle. A constitution ought to enable legislation and public policies to take place, but it should not determine what that legislation or those public policies ought to be.

For those whose hopes for change center on the Constitution, it must be emphasized that the amendment route to social change is, and always will be, extremely limited. Through a constitution it is possible to establish a working structure of government, and through a constitution it is possible to establish basic rights of citizens by placing limitations on the powers of that government. Once these things have been accomplished, the real problem is how to extend rights to those people who do not already enjoy them. Of course, the Constitution cannot enforce itself. But it can and does have a real influence on everyday life because a

FOR CRITICAL ANALYSIS

It is very difficult to amend the Constitution. Should it be made easier? Would our system of government be more democratic if our Constitution could be revised more easily?

The Constitution has evolved through the amendment process—a process that continues today. In 2003, some conservatives, in an attempt to override several states' laws permitting gay marriage, began a push to add the Federal Marriage Amendment, a Constitutional amendment that defined marriage as a union legal only between a man and a woman, which would effectively ban gay marriages. In early 2004, conservatives stepped up their efforts in response to the Massachusetts Supreme Judicial Court's decision to grant marriage rights to same-sex couples and San Francisco Mayor Gavin Newsom's decision to give marriage licenses to gay and lesbian couples. In both Massachusetts and California, opinion was divided on the issue. The Massachusetts State House was the scene of protests both for (above left) and against (above right) gay marriage. Similar protests were held in California for (below left) and against (below right).

In July 2004, the amendment was defeated in the U.S. Senate. Opinion polls showed that although a large majority of Americans opposed gay marriage, many also opposed amending the Constitution to outlaw the practice. In line with the polls, senators expressed reluctance to alter the Constitution to include a divisive social issue, especially at the expense of tampering with traditional state prerogatives over marriage law. In general, attempts to legislate through the amendment process have proven unsuccessful throughout American political history.

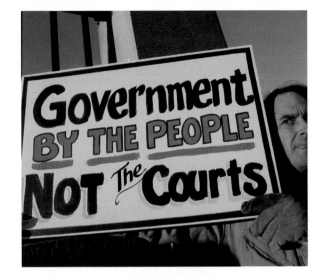

right or an obligation set forth in the Constitution can become a cause of action in the hands of an otherwise powerless person.

Private property is an excellent example. Property is one of the most fundamental and well-established rights in the United States; but it is well established not because it is recognized in so many words in the Constitution, but because legislatures and courts have made it a crime for anyone, including the government, to trespass or to take away property without compensation.

A constitution is good if it produces the cause of action that leads to good legislation, good case law, and appropriate police behavior. A constitution cannot eliminate power. But its principles can be a citizen's dependable defense against the abuse of power.

Thinking Critically about Liberty, Equality, and Democracy

The Constitution's framers placed individual liberty ahead of all other political values. Their concern for liberty led many of the framers to distrust both democracy and equality. They feared that democracy could degenerate into a majority tyranny in which the populace, perhaps led by a rabble-rousing demagogue, would trample on liberty. As to equality, the framers were products of their time and place; our contemporary ideas of racial and gender equality would have been foreign to them. The framers were concerned primarily with another manifestation of equality: they feared that those without property or position might be driven by what some called a "leveling spirit" to infringe upon liberty in the name of greater economic or social equality. Indeed, the framers believed that this leveling spirit was most likely to produce demagoguery and majority tyranny. As a result, the basic structure of the Constitution—separated powers, internal checks and balances, and federalism—was designed to safeguard liberty, and the Bill of Rights created further safeguards for liberty. At the same time, however, many of the Constitution's other key provisions, such as indirect election of senators and the president, as well as the appointment of judges for life, were designed to limit democracy and, hence, the threat of majority tyranny.

By championing liberty, however, the framers virtually guaranteed that democracy and even a measure of equality would sooner or later evolve in the United States. For liberty inevitably leads to the growth of political activity and the expansion of political participation. In James Madison's famous phrase, "Liberty is to faction as air is to fire."[32] Where they have liberty, more and more people, groups, and interests will almost inevitably engage in politics and gradually overcome whatever restrictions might have been placed upon participation. This is precisely what happened in the early years of the American Republic. During the Jeffersonian period, political parties formed. During the Jacksonian period, many state suffrage restrictions were removed and popular participation greatly expanded. Over time, liberty is conducive to democracy.

Liberty does not guarantee that everyone will be equal. It does, however, reduce the threat of inequality in one very important way. Historically, the greatest inequalities of wealth, power, and privilege have arisen where governments have used their power to allocate status and opportunity among individuals or groups. From the

FOR CRITICAL ANALYSIS
What are our Constitution's greatest strengths? What are its most pronounced weaknesses? If you were a framer, what changes would you make in the Constitution? Why?

aristocracies of the early modern period to the *nomenklatura* of twentieth-century despotisms, the most extreme cases of inequality are associated with the most tyrannical regimes.

The other side of the coin, however, is that the absence of government intervention in economic affairs—in the name of liberty—may mean that there is no antidote to the inevitable inequalities of wealth produced by the marketplace. Economic inequalities, in turn, may lead to inequalities in political power as wealthy groups and individuals use their superior resources to elect politicians friendly to them and their aims and to influence the legislative process. Thus, liberty is a complex matter. In the absence of liberty, inequality is virtually certain. The existence of liberty, however, poses its own threat to political equality. Can we fully reconcile liberty and equality? Doing so remains a constant challenge in a democratic society.

Another limitation of liberty as a political principle is that the idea of limits upon government action can also inhibit effective government. Take one of the basic tasks of government, the protection of citizens' lives and property. A government limited by concerns over the rights of those accused of crimes may be limited in its ability to maintain public order. Currently, the U.S. government is asserting that protecting the nation against terrorists requires law enforcement measures that seem at odds with legal and constitutional formalities. The conflict between liberty and governmental effectiveness is another tension at the heart of the American constitutional system.

FOR CRITICAL ANALYSIS

The framers of the Constitution were very concerned with creating an effective system of government. Yet whenever crises loom, critics charge that America's government is too cumbersome and too filled with checks on power to promote effective action. Does the war on terrorism reveal our constitutional government's effectiveness or lack of effectiveness? Are there ways in which we benefit from the government's occasional lack of efficiency?

GET INVOLVED

What You Can Do:
Become a Framer

Constitutions are "higher law." They spell out general principles and procedures for how people should interact, make decisions, and enforce them. Like the U.S. Constitution and the fifty state constitutions, they also structure politics. The U.S. Constitution outlines three major branches of government, limits their powers, and reserves authority for the states. State constitutions set up state institutions and processes, delegating some authority to regional and local governments. These constitutions declare or imply that the courts should interpret and enforce higher law to ensure that all government actions are consistent with it.

Very few people found new nations or frame constitutions; relatively few people propose and promote amendments to constitutions. However, students and citizens can and do get involved in setting forth general principles, establishing decision-making procedures, and structuring institutions on their campuses and in their communities.

For example, many college campuses have "principles of community" that are very much like constitutions. They articulate the aspirations and values that bind faculty, staff, alumni, and students into a cohesive community. Typically, principles of community highlight the educational mission of the institution and call on all members to show respect for people with diverse racial/ethnic backgrounds, religious beliefs, abilities and disabilities, and so forth. The principles may prohibit activities (such as the use of racial slurs) and outline processes for adjudicating and punishing infractions.

Organizations often frame "bylaws" that are similar to constitutions. Bylaws might include "mission statements," outline organization arrangements, detail procedures for choosing officers, specify decision-making processes, and set down the frequency and timing of meetings. Some colleges require student groups to establish bylaws in order to be eligible for funding. And many groups voluntarily frame bylaws to focus and structure their activities.

Common variations on constitutions are "charters." A state may share its power with city governments by approving city charters that authorize local officials to make some decisions without requiring explicit state approval. A local government may create an agency by issuing a charter that specifies the new agency's goals, structure, personnel, and timeline. Similarly, a college may approve the charter of a student organization to authorize it to exercise discretionary authority in distributing student-generated funds for a variety of campus activities.

Here are some possibilities for you to become a framer of "constitutions" on your campus and in your community.

- Identify a general problem on your campus. Perhaps administrators ignore student voices, tolerate long lines for financial aid, and serve poor-quality food in cafeterias. Working with a few classmates or an appropriate student organization, discuss, develop, circulate, and promote a "Student Bill of Rights" that expresses principles that protect students from abuse and promotes student voices on campus.
- If you are starting a group, such as a campus chapter of Human Rights Watch, consider drafting bylaws to focus and structure the group as well as to initiate a conversation about its goals and strategies. When you invite other students to be group founders and bylaw framers, they are likely to develop a sense of ownership that strengthens their commitment and loyalty to the group.
- If you are a member of a group, whether it is Campus Republicans or a youth service group, consider raising "constitutional" questions. Does the group have bylaws? If not, would they be useful? If so, perhaps current bylaws should be reexamined and amended. Take the constitutional pulse of your group.
- Perhaps you are working on a student government or community political campaign. Is the campaign inefficient, disorganized, and chaotic? Do workers and volunteers grumble because little is being accomplished? Many groups hit a low point marked by morale problems. To prevent or resolve morale problems, you might suggest that members draft a "mission statement." The drafting process encourages individuals to strengthen commitment, identifies sources of cohesion, and prods folks to set aside minor complaints to achieve major goals.

By articulating shared principles, framing and rethinking bylaws, or drafting mission statements, you do not directly accomplish group goals. However, you do clarify goals, establish processes, and set up structures that empower group members to collaborate and cooperate more effectively.

Summary

Political conflicts between the colonies and Britain, and among competing groups within the colonies, led to the first founding as expressed by the Declaration of Independence. The first constitution, the Articles of Confederation, was adopted one

INTERACTIVE
POLITICS

YOU ARE... a delegate to the Constitutional Convention!

It was a long, hot summer in Philadelphia in 1787. Following Shays's Rebellion, twelve states sent fifty-five delegates to try to repair the Articles of Confederation. Behind the closed doors of Independence Hall, the delegates were soon convinced that a whole new constitution was needed. But how could they create a government that on the one hand would be powerful enough to solve their problems without on the other hand degenerating into either tyranny or chaos?

Go to www.wwnorton.com/wtp5e

Questions to consider as you conduct the online simulation:

What did the various states share as common interests, and what were the competing values?

What would be the ideal federal relationship? How important is it to have a strong national government while protecting the autonomy of the states?

How can the interests of wealthy, populous states and smaller, agrarian states be balanced?

What compromises can create a document that both abolitionist northern interests and slave-dependent southern interests would sign?

year later (1777). Under this document, the states retained their sovereignty and the central government had few powers and no means of enforcing its will. The national government's weakness led to the Constitution of 1787, the second founding.

The Constitution's framers sought, first, to fashion a new government sufficiently powerful to promote commerce and protect property from radical state legislatures. Second, the framers sought to bring an end to the "excessive democracy" of the state and national governments under the Articles of Confederation. Third, the framers introduced mechanisms that helped secure popular consent for the new government. Finally, the framers made certain that their new government would not itself pose a threat to liberty and property.

The struggle for the ratification of the Constitution pitted the Antifederalists, who thought the proposed new government would be too powerful, against the Federalists, who supported the Constitution and were able to secure its ratification after a nationwide political debate.

This chapter also sought to convey an appreciation of constitutionalism itself. In addition to describing how the Constitution is formally amended, we analyzed the twenty-seven amendments in order to determine what they had in common, contrasting them with the hundreds of amendments that were offered but never adopted. We found that with the exception of the two Prohibition amendments, all amendments were oriented toward some change in the framework or structure of government. The Prohibition Amendment was the only adopted amendment that sought to legislate by constitutional means.

For Further Reading

Beard, Charles. *An Economic Interpretation of the Constitution of the United States.* New York: Macmillan, 1913.

Dahl, Robert A. *How Democratic Is the American Constitution?,* 2nd ed. New Haven: Yale University Press, 2002.

Hamilton, Alexander, James Madison, and John Jay. *The Federalist Papers.* Edited by Isaac Kramnick. New York: Viking, 1987.

Jensen, Merrill. *The Articles of Confederation.* Madison: University of Wisconsin Press, 1963.

Lipset, Seymour M. *The First New Nation: The United States in Historical and Comparative Perspective.* New York: Basic Books, 1963.

McDonald, Forrest. *The Formation of the American Republic.* New York: Penguin, 1967.

Main, Jackson Turner. *The Social Structure of Revolutionary America.* Princeton, NJ: Princeton University Press, 1965.

Rossiter, Clinton. *1787: Grand Convention.* New York: Macmillan, 1966.

Storing, Herbert, ed. *The Complete Anti-Federalist.* 7 vols. Chicago: University of Chicago Press, 1981.

Wills, Garry. *Explaining America.* New York: Penguin, 1982.

Wood, Gordon S. *The Creation of the American Republic.* New York: Norton, 1982.

Study Outline

www.wwnorton.com/wtp5e Keyword: Review 2

The First Founding: Interests and Conflicts

1. In an effort to alleviate financial problems, including considerable debt, the British government sought to raise revenue by taxing its North American colonies. This energized New England merchants and southern planters, who then organized colonial resistance.

2. Colonial resistance set into motion a cycle of provocation and reaction that resulted in the First Continental Congress and eventually the Declaration of Independence.

3. The Declaration of Independence was an attempt to identify and articulate a history and set of principles that might help to forge national unity.

4. The colonies established the Articles of Confederation and Perpetual Union. Under the Articles, the central government was based entirely in Congress, yet Congress had little power.

The Second Founding: From Compromise to Constitution

1. Concern over America's precarious position in the international community coupled with domestic concern that "radical forces" had too much influence in Congress and in state governments led to the Annapolis Convention in 1786.
2. Shays's Rebellion in Massachusetts provided critics of the Articles of Confederation with the evidence they needed to push for constitutional revision.
3. Recognizing fundamental flaws in the Articles, the delegates to the Philadelphia Convention abandoned the plan to revise the Articles and committed themselves to a second founding.
4. Conflict between large and small states over the issue of representation in Congress led to the Great Compromise, which created a bicameral legislature based on two different principles of representation.
5. The Three-fifths Compromise addressed the question of slavery by apportioning the seats in the House of Representatives according to a population in which five slaves would count as three persons.

The Constitution

1. The new government was to be strong enough to defend the nation's interests internationally, promote commerce and protect property, and prevent the threat posed by "excessive democracy."
2. The House of Representatives was designed to be directly responsible to the people in order to encourage popular consent for the Constitution. The Senate was designed to guard against the potential for excessive democracy in the House.
3. The Constitution grants Congress important and influential powers, but any power not specifically enumerated in its text is reserved specifically to the states.
4. The framers hoped to create a presidency with energy—one that would be capable of timely and decisive action to deal with public issues and problems.
5. The establishment of the Supreme Court reflected the framers' preoccupations with nationalizing governmental power and checking radical democratic impulses while guarding against potential interference with liberty and property from the new national government itself.
6. Various provisions in the Constitution addressed the framers' concern with national unity and power. Such provisions included clauses promoting reciprocity among states.

7. Procedures for amending the Constitution are provided in Article V. These procedures are so difficult that amendments are quite rare in American history.
8. To guard against possible misuse of national government power, the framers incorporated the principles of the separation of powers and federalism, as well as a Bill of Rights, in the Constitution.

9. The separation of powers was based on the principle that power must be used to balance power.
10. Although the framers' move to federalism was a step toward greater centralization of national government power, they retained state power by devising a system of two sovereigns.
11. The Bill of Rights was adopted as the first ten amendments to the Constitution in 1791.

The Fight for Ratification

1. The struggle for ratification was carried out in thirteen separate campaigns—one in each state.
2. The Federalists supported the Constitution and a stronger national government. The Antifederalists, on the other hand, preferred a more decentralized system of government and fought against ratification.
3. Federalists and Antifederalists had differing views regarding issues such as representation and the prevention of tyranny.
4. Antifederalist criticisms helped to shape the Constitution and the national government, but it was the Federalist vision of America that triumphed.

The Citizen's Role and the Changing Constitution

1. Provisions for amending the Constitution, incorporated into Article V, have proven to be difficult criteria to meet. Relatively few amendments have been made to the Constitution.
2. Most of the amendments to the Constitution deal with the structure or composition of the government.

Thinking Critically about Liberty, Equality, and Democracy

1. The Constitution's framers placed individual liberty ahead of all other political values. But by emphasizing liberty, the framers virtually guaranteed that democracy and equality would evolve in the United States.

Practice Quiz

www.wwnorton.com/wtp5e Keyword: Quiz 2

1. In the Revolutionary struggles, which of the following groups was allied with the New England merchants?
   a) artisans
   b) southern planters
   c) western speculators
   d) laborers

2. How did the British attempt to raise revenue in the North American colonies?
   a) income tax
   b) taxes on commerce
   c) expropriation and government sale of land
   d) government asset sales

3. The first governing document in the United States was
   a) the Declaration of Independence.
   b) the Articles of Confederation and Perpetual Union.
   c) the Constitution.
   d) none of the above.

4. Which state's proposal embodied a principle of representing states in the Congress according to their size and wealth?
   a) Connecticut
   b) Maryland
   c) New Jersey
   d) Virginia

5. Where was the execution of laws conducted under the Articles of Confederation?
   a) the presidency
   b) the Congress
   c) the states
   d) the expanding federal bureaucracy

6. Which of the following was *not* a reason that the Articles of Confederation seemed too weak?
   a) the lack of a single voice in international affairs
   b) the power of radical forces in the Congress
   c) the impending "tyranny of the states"
   d) the power of radical forces in several states

7. What mechanism was instituted in the Congress to guard against "excessive democracy"?
   a) bicameralism
   b) staggered Senate terms
   c) appointment of senators for long terms
   d) all of the above

8. Which of the following best describes the Supreme Court as understood by the Founders?
   a) the highest court of the national government
   b) arbiter of disputes within the Congress
   c) a figurehead commission of elders
   d) a supreme court of the nation and its states

9. Which of the following were the Antifederalists most concerned with?
   a) interstate commerce
   b) the protection of property
   c) the distinction between principles and interests
   d) the potential for tyranny in the central government

10. The draft constitution that was introduced at the start of the Constitutional Convention was authored by
    a) Edmund Randolph.
    b) Thomas Jefferson.
    c) James Madison.
    d) George Clinton.

Key Terms

www.wwnorton.com/wtp5e

Keyword: Vocabulary 2

amendment (p. 64)
Antifederalists (p. 58)
Articles of Confederation (p. 43)
bicameral (p. 48)
Bill of Rights (p. 50)

checks and balances (p. 50)
confederation (p. 43)
elastic clause (p. 52)
electoral college (p. 50)
expressed powers (p. 52)
federalism (p. 50)
Federalist Papers (p. 58)
Federalists (p. 57)
Great Compromise (p. 48)

judicial review (p. 53)
limited government (p. 62)
New Jersey Plan (p. 47)
separation of powers (p. 50)
supremacy clause (p. 54)
Three-fifths Compromise (p. 49)
tyranny (p. 62)
Virginia Plan (p. 46)

3 FEDERALISM

What Government Does
and Why It Matters

F YOU LIVE in Huntington, West Virginia, you might decide to spend a Saturday night cruising in a friend's new car; in Fargo, North Dakota, the same weekend plans would get you a ticket, as Fargo has an anti-cruising ordinance. And if you decide to take your car out to the highway, in Montana, during the day, you could go 75 miles per hour, but if you live in New York State, you would risk getting a speeding ticket if you drove over 65 miles per hour.

Driving is just one of the many areas for which where you live affects what you can do and what the government does. If you lose your job in New Hampshire, the highest level of unemployment insurance benefits you can get is $301 per week; in neighboring Massachusetts, you could receive as much as $646 per week. By giving the states power to set benefit levels on such social policies as unemployment insurance and welfare, the American system of federalism allows substantial inequalities to exist across the country. Likewise, what kinds of classes are offered in high schools, the taxes citizens pay for public schools, and the tuition you pay if you attend a state university or college are all affected by where you live. In fact, most of the rules and regulations that Americans face in their daily lives are set by state and local governments.[1]

State and local governments play such important roles in the lives of American citizens because the United States is a federal system. Throughout American history, lawmakers, politicians, and citizens have wrestled with questions about how responsibilities should be allocated across the different levels of government. Some responsibilities, such as international relations, clearly lie with the federal government. Others, such as the divorce laws, are controlled by state governments. However, the vast majority of government responsibilities are now shared in American federalism. These include such activities as building transportation systems (roads, bridges, airports, mass transit); providing education; protecting the health and safety of citizens; providing social benefits; protecting civil liberties; and administering criminal justice. Reflecting the Founders' mistrust of centralized power and the long-standing preference of Americans for local self-government as the best form of democracy, state and local governments have retained substantial power. Yet over the course of American history, the federal government has grown far more powerful. Especially since the New Deal in the 1930s, the national government has played a much more prominent role in protecting liberty and promoting equality. It has done so through a growing body of social programs and regulations, enacted by the federal government but often implemented by the states. In the 1980s, the tide turned against the federal government, as a new generation of lawmakers sought to enhance the responsibilities of the states. This shifting balance highlights an old debate in American politics; it traces back to the Founding, when the Federalists argued in favor of a stronger national government and the Antifederalists opposed them. ■

THE debate about "who should do what" remains one of the most important discussions in American politics. Much is at stake in how authority is divided up among the different levels of government. The debate about how responsibilities should be divided is often informed by conflicting principles and differing evaluations about what each level of government is best suited to do. For example, many people believe that the United States needs national goals and standards to ensure equal opportunities for citizens across the nation; others contend that state and local governments can do a better job at most things because they are closer to the people. For this reason the states have been called "laboratories of democracy": they can experiment with different policies to find measures that best meet the needs of their citizens.

But decisions about who should do what are also highly political. Groups that want government to do more to promote equality frequently prefer a stronger national role. After all, it was the national government that first implemented the civil rights policies in the 1960s and guaranteed civil liberties in all states. Groups that want less government, on the other hand, often favor shifting power to the states or localities. Many conservatives oppose a strong national role because they believe that nationwide regulations infringe on individual liberties. Furthermore, different interest groups argue for placing policy responsibilities at the level of government that they find easiest to influence. And politicians in national, state, and local governments often have quite different views about which level of government should be expected to do what.

Thus, both political principles and interests influence decisions about how power and responsibility should be sorted out across the levels of government. At various points in history, Americans have given different answers to questions about the appropriate role of national, state, and local governments. National power increased as the national government initiated new social and regulatory policies during the New Deal of the 1930s and the Great Society of the 1960s. But in the 1970s and 1980s, states began to claim more authority over these policies. The effort to increase state responsibility and reduce the national role received a boost when the Republicans took over Congress in 1995. With the support of a growing number of Republican governors, congressional Republicans advocated a strategy of devolution, in which the national government would grant the states more authority over a range of policies. For the most part, Republicans did not deliver on their promise to devolve more responsibility to state and local governments; in some areas, they actually increased federal control.

■ **In this chapter, we will first look at how federalism was defined in the Constitution.** The framers sought to limit national power with the creation of a separate layer of government in opposition to it. For the first 150 years of American government, the states were most important in governing the lives of American citizens. Over time, however, the Supreme Court interpreted the principle of federalism in a way that gave the national government more expansive powers.

■ **We will then examine how the federal framework has changed in recent years, especially in the growth of the national government's role.** After the 1930s, the national government began to expand, yet the states maintained most of their traditional powers.

■ **We will then assess how changes in federalism reflect the changes in how Americans perceive liberty, equality, and democracy.** American federalism has always been a work in progress. As federal, state, and local governments change, questions about the relationship between American political values and federalism continue to emerge.

■ **Finally, we will discuss how political participation by citizens at the local, state, and national levels affects the federal system.**

■ Previewing Liberty, Equality, and Democracy

American federalism promotes the value of democracy by allowing states to set their own standards for many of the issues that most affect people's lives. Variations in state laws reflect the distinctive priorities of each state. Yet, since

the 1930s, the federal government has played an expanded role in ensuring democracy, equality, and liberty. During the 1960s, it outlawed many obstacles to political participation in the American South. By funding social welfare programs and setting national standards, the federal government helps to limit inequality across the states. Federal laws also ensure that basic liberties are enforced in every state. In recent years, a trend to return more power to the states has allowed greater differences in the laws and social protections in the states. Though this trend has reduced the move toward greater equality, its proponents believe that it has in fact enhanced democracy.

The Federal Framework

The Constitution has had its most fundamental influence on American life through federalism. **Federalism** can be defined with misleading ease and simplicity as the division of powers and functions between the national government and the state governments. Governments can organize power in a variety of ways. One of the most important distinctions is between unitary and federal governments. In a **unitary system,** the central government makes the important decisions, and lower levels of government have little independent power. In such systems, lower levels of government primarily serve to implement decisions made by the central government. In France, for example, the central government was once so involved in the smallest details of local activity that the minister of education boasted that by looking at his watch he could tell what all French schoolchildren were learning at that time because the central government set the school curriculum. In a **federal system,** by contrast, the central government shares power or functions with lower levels of government, such as regions or states. Nations with diverse ethnic or language groupings, such as Switzerland and Canada, are most likely to have federal arrangements. In federal systems, lower levels of government often have significant independent power to set policy in some areas, such as education and social programs, and to impose taxes. Yet the specific ways in which power is shared vary greatly: no two federal systems are exactly the same.

federalism a system of government in which power is divided, by a constitution, between a central government and regional governments

unitary system a centralized government system in which lower levels of government have little power independent of the national government

federal system a system of government in which the national government shares power with lower levels of government, such as states

FEDERALISM IN THE CONSTITUTION

The United States was the first nation to adopt federalism as its governing framework. With federalism, the framers sought to limit the national government by creating a second layer of state governments. American federalism recognized two sovereigns in the original Constitution and reinforced the principle in the Bill of Rights by granting a few **expressed powers** to the national government and reserving all the rest to the states.

expressed powers specific powers granted to Congress under Article I, Section 8, of the Constitution

implied powers powers derived from the "necessary and proper" clause of Article I, Section 8, of the Constitution. Such powers are not specifically expressed, but are implied through the expansive interpretation of delegated powers

The Powers of the National Government   As we saw in Chapter 2, the "expressed powers" granted to the national government are found in Article I, Section 8, of the Constitution. These seventeen powers include the power to collect taxes, to coin money, to declare war, and to regulate commerce (which, as we will see, became a very important power for the national government). Article I, Section 8, also contains another important source of power for the national government: the **implied powers** that enable Congress "to make all Laws which shall be necessary and proper for carrying into Execution the foregoing Powers." Not until several decades after the Founding did the Supreme Court allow Congress to exercise the power granted in this **necessary and proper clause,** but, as we shall see later in this chapter, this doctrine allowed the national government to expand considerably the scope of its authority, although the process was a slow one. In addition to these expressed and implied powers, the Constitution affirmed the power of the national government in the supremacy clause (Article VI), which made all national laws and treaties "the supreme Law of the Land."

necessary and proper clause from Article I, Section 8, of the Constitution, it provides Congress with the authority to make all laws "necessary and proper" to carry out its expressed powers

The Powers of State Government   One way in which the framers sought to preserve a strong role for the states was through the Tenth Amendment to the Constitution. The Tenth Amendment states that the powers that the Constitution does not delegate to the national government or prohibit to the states are "reserved to the States respectively, or to the people." The Antifederalists, who feared that a strong central government would encroach on individual liberty, repeatedly pressed for such an amendment as a way of limiting national power. Federalists agreed to the amendment because they did not think it would do much harm, given the powers of the Constitution already granted to the national government. The Tenth Amendment is also called the **reserved powers** amendment because it aims to reserve powers to the states.

reserved powers powers, derived from the Tenth Amendment to the Constitution, that are not specifically delegated to the national government or denied to the states

The most fundamental power that is retained by the states is that of coercion—the power to develop and enforce criminal codes, to administer health and safety rules, to regulate the family via marriage and divorce laws. The states have the power to regulate individuals' livelihoods; if you're a doctor or a lawyer or a plumber or a barber, you must be licensed by the state. Even more fundamentally, the states had the power to define private property—private property exists because state laws against trespass define who is and is not entitled to use a piece of property. If you own a car, your ownership isn't worth much unless the state is willing to enforce your right to possession by making it a crime for anyone else to drive your car. These are fundamental matters, and the powers of the states regarding these domestic issues are much greater than the powers of the national government, even today.

A state's authority to regulate these fundamental matters is commonly referred to as the **police power** of the state and encompasses the state's power to regulate the health, safety, welfare, and morals of its citizens. Policing is what states do—they coerce you in the name of the community in order to maintain public order. And this was exactly the type of power that the Founders intended the states to exercise.

police power power reserved to the government to regulate the health, safety, and morals of its citizens

In some areas, the states share **concurrent powers** with the national government, wherein they retain and share some power to regulate commerce and to affect the currency—for example, by being able to charter banks, grant or deny corporate charters, grant or deny licenses to engage in a business or practice a trade, and regulate the quality of products or the conditions of labor. This issue of concurrent versus exclusive power has come up from time to time in our history, but wherever there is a direct conflict of laws between the federal and the state levels, the issue will most likely be resolved in favor of national supremacy.

concurrent powers authority possessed by *both* state and national governments, such as the power to levy taxes

State Obligations to One Another   The Constitution also creates obligations among the states. These obligations, spelled out in Article IV, were intended to promote national unity. By requiring the states to recognize actions and decisions taken in other states as legal and proper, the framers aimed to make the states less like independent countries and more like parts of a single nation.

Article IV, Section I, calls for "Full Faith and Credit" among states, meaning that each state is normally expected to honor the "public Acts, Records, and judicial Proceedings" that take place in any other state. So, for example, if a couple is married in Texas—marriage being regulated by state law—Missouri must also recognize that marriage, even though they were not married under Missouri state law.

full faith and credit clause provision from Article IV, Section 1, of the Constitution, requiring that the states normally honor the public acts and judicial decisions that take place in another state

This **full faith and credit clause** has recently become embroiled in the controversy over gay and lesbian marriage. In December 1999, the Vermont Supreme Court ruled that gay and lesbian couples should have the same rights as heterosexuals. The Vermont legislature responded with a new law that allowed gays and lesbians to form "civil unions." Although not legally considered marriages, such unions allow gay and lesbian couples most of the benefits of marriage, such as eligibility for the partner's health insurance, inheritance rights, and the right to transfer property. In 2003, the Massachusetts Supreme Court went further, ruling that gays and lesbians have the right to marry under state law. The Court directed the state legislature to amend state law to allow such marriages. The Vermont and Massachusetts decisions could have broad implications for other states. Thirty-eight states have passed "defense of marriage acts" that define marriage as a union between men and women only. Anxious to show its disapproval of gay marriage, Congress passed the Defense of Marriage Act in 1996, which declared that states will *not* have to recognize a same-sex marriage, even if it is legal in one state. The act also said that the federal government will not recognize gay marriage—even if it is legal under state law—and that gay marriage partners will not be eligible for the federal benefits, such as Medicare and Social Security, normally available to spouses.[2] The Massachusetts decision reenergized the movement to pass a constitutional amendment outlawing gay marriage. If successful, such an amendment would represent a significant encroachment on traditional state powers to regulate matters related to marriage. For a further discussion of gay and lesbian marriage, see Chapter 5.

Because of this controversy, the extent and meaning of the full faith and credit clause is sure to be considered by the Supreme Court. In fact, it is not clear that the clause requires states to recognize gay marriage because the Court's past interpretation of the clause has provided exceptions for "public policy" reasons: if states have strong objections to a law, they do not have to honor it. In 1997 the Court took up a case involving the full faith and credit clause. The case concerned a Michigan court order that prevented a former engineer for General Motors from testifying against the company. The engineer, who left the company on bad terms, later testified in a Missouri court about a car accident in which a woman died when her Chevrolet Blazer caught fire. General Motors challenged his right to testify, arguing that Missouri should give "full faith and credit" to the Michigan ruling. The Supreme Court ruled that the engineer could testify and that the court system in one state cannot hinder other state courts in their "search for the truth."[3]

privileges and immunities clause provision from Article IV, Section 2, of the Constitution, that a state cannot discriminate against someone from another state or give its own residents special privileges

Article IV, Section 2, known as the "comity clause," also seeks to promote national unity. It provides that citizens enjoying the **"privileges and immunities"** of one state should be entitled to similar treatment in other states. What this has come to mean is that a state cannot discriminate against someone from another state or give special privileges to its own residents. For example, in the 1970s, when Alaska passed a law that gave residents preference over nonresidents in obtaining work on the state's oil and gas pipelines, the Supreme Court ruled the law illegal because it discriminated against citizens of other states.[4] This clause also regulates criminal justice among the states by requiring states to return fugitives to the states from which they have fled. Thus, in 1952, when an inmate escaped from an Alabama prison and sought to avoid being returned to Alabama on the grounds that he was being subjected to "cruel and unusual punishment" there, the Supreme Court ruled that he must be returned according to Article IV, Section 2.[5] This example highlights the difference between the obligations among states and those among different countries. Recently, France refused to return an American fugitive because he might be subject to the death penalty, which does not exist in France.[6] The Constitution clearly forbids states from doing something similar.

States' relationships to one another are also governed by the interstate compact clause (Article I, Section 10), which states that "No State shall, without the Consent of Congress . . . enter into any Agreement or Compact with another State." The Court has interpreted the clause to mean that states may enter into agreements with one another, subject to congressional approval. Compacts are a way for two or more states to reach a legally binding agreement about how to solve a problem that crosses state lines. In the early years of the Republic, states turned to compacts primarily to settle border disputes. Today they are used for a wide range of issues but are especially important in regulating the distribution of river water, addressing environmental concerns, and operating transportation systems that cross state lines.[7]

Local Government and the Constitution   Local government occupies a peculiar but very important place in the American system. In fact, the status of American local government is probably unique in world experience. First, it must be pointed out that local government has no status in the American Constitution. *State* legislatures created local governments, and *state* constitutions and laws permit local governments to take on some of the responsibilities of the state governments. Most states amended their own constitutions to give their larger cities **home rule**—a guarantee of noninterference in various areas of local affairs. But local governments enjoy no such recognition in the Constitution. Local governments have always been mere conveniences of the states.[8]

Local governments became administratively important in the early years of the Republic because the states possessed little administrative capability. They relied on local governments—cities and countries—to implement the laws of the state. Local government was an alternative to a statewide bureaucracy (see Table 3.1).

home rule power delegated by the state to a local unit of government to manage its own affairs

87,576 Governments in the United States   Table 3.1

Type	Number
National	1
State	50
County	3,034
Municipal	19,429
Townships	16,504
School districts	13,506
Other special districts	35,052

SOURCE: *Statistical Abstract of the United States, 2003* (Washington, DC: U.S. Government Printing Office, 2003), Table 431.

Table 3.2	The Federal System: Specialization of Governmental Functions in the Traditional System (1800–1933)

NATIONAL GOVERNMENT POLICIES (DOMESTIC)	STATE GOVERNMENT POLICIES	LOCAL GOVERNMENT POLICIES
Internal improvements	Property laws (including slavery)	Adaptation of state laws to local conditions ("variances")
Subsidies	Estate and inheritance laws	Public works
Tariffs	Commerce laws	Contracts for public works
Public lands disposal	Banking and credit laws	Licensing of public accommodations
Patents	Corporate laws	Assessible improvements
Currency	Insurance laws	Basic public services
	Family laws	
	Morality laws	
	Public health laws	
	Education laws	
	General penal laws	
	Eminent domain laws	
	Construction codes	
	Land-use laws	
	Water and mineral laws	
	Criminal procedure laws	
	Electoral and political parties laws	
	Local government laws	
	Civil service laws	
	Occupations and professions laws	

RESTRAINING NATIONAL POWER WITH DUAL FEDERALISM, 1789–1937

dual federalism the system of government that prevailed in the United States from 1789 to 1937, in which most fundamental governmental powers were shared between the federal and state governments

As we have noted, the Constitution created two layers of government: the national government and the state governments. The consequences of this **dual federalism** are fundamental to the American system of government in theory and in practice; they have meant that states have done most of the fundamental governing. For evidence, look at Table 3.2. It lists the major types of public policies by which Americans were governed for the first century and a half under the Constitution. We call it the "traditional system" because it prevailed for three-quarters of American history and because it closely approximates the intentions of the framers of the Constitution.

Under the traditional system, the national government was quite small by comparison both to the state governments and to the governments of other Western nations. Not only was it smaller than most governments of that time, but it was also actually very narrowly specialized in the functions it performed. The national government built or sponsored the construction of roads, canals, and bridges (internal improvements). It provided cash subsidies to shippers and shipbuilders and distributed free or low-priced public land to encourage western settlement and business ventures. It placed relatively heavy taxes on imported goods (tariffs), not only to raise revenues but to protect "infant industries" from competition from the more advanced European enterprises. It protected patents and provided for a common currency, also to encourage and facilitate enterprises and to expand markets.

What do these functions of the national government reveal? First, virtually all its functions were aimed at assisting commerce. It is quite appropriate to refer to the traditional American system as a "commercial republic." Second, virtually none of the national government's policies directly coerced citizens. The emphasis of governmental programs was on assistance, promotion, and encouragement—the allocation of land or capital where they were insufficiently available for economic development.

Meanwhile, state legislatures were actively involved in economic regulation during the nineteenth century. In the United States, then and now, private property exists only in state laws and state court decisions regarding property, trespass, and real estate. American capitalism took its form from state property and trespass laws, as well as from state laws and court decisions regarding contracts, markets, credit, banking, incorporation, and insurance. Laws concerning slavery were a subdivision of property law in states where slavery existed. The practice of important professions, such as law and medicine, was and is illegal, except as provided for by state law. Marriage, divorce, and the birth or adoption of a child have always been regulated by state law. To educate or not to educate a child has been a decision governed more by state laws than by parents, and not at all by national law. It is important to note also that virtually all criminal laws—regarding everything from trespass to murder—have been state laws. Most of the criminal laws adopted by Congress are concerned with the District of Columbia and other federal territories.

All this (and more, as shown in the middle column of Table 3.2) demonstrates without any question that most of the fundamental governing in the United States was done by the states. The contrast between national and state policies, as shown by Table 3.2, demonstrates the difference in the power vested in each. The list of items in the middle column could actually have been made longer. Moreover, each item on the list is a category of law that fills many volumes of statutes and court decisions.

This contrast between national and state governments is all the more impressive because it is basically what the framers of the Constitution intended. Since the 1930s, the national government has expanded into local and intrastate matters, far beyond what anyone would have foreseen in 1790, 1890, or even in the 1920s. But this significant expansion of the national government did not alter the basic framework. The national government has become much larger, but the states have continued to be central to the American system of government.

Here lies probably the most important point of all: the fundamental impact of federalism on the way the United States is governed comes not from any particular provision of the Constitution but from the framework itself, which has determined the flow of government functions and, through that, the political development of the country. By allowing state governments to do most of the fundamental governing, the Constitution saved the national government from many policy decisions that might have proven too divisive for a large and very young country. There is no doubt that if the Constitution had provided for a unitary rather than a federal system, the war over slavery would have come in 1789 or 1809 rather than in 1860; and if it had come that early, the South might very well have seceded and established a separate and permanent slaveholding nation.

In helping the national government remain small and aloof from the most divisive issues of the day, federalism contributed significantly to the political stability of the nation, even as the social, economic, and political systems of many of the states and regions of the country were undergoing tremendous, profound, and sometimes violent, change.[9] As we shall see, some important aspects of federalism have changed, but the federal framework has survived two centuries and a devastating civil war.

FEDERALISM AND THE SLOW GROWTH OF THE NATIONAL GOVERNMENT'S POWER

Having created the national government, and recognizing the potential for abuse of power, the states sought through federalism to constrain the national government. The "traditional system" of a weak national government prevailed for over a century despite economic forces favoring its expansion and despite Supreme Court cases giving a pro-national interpretation to Article I, Section 8, of the Constitution.

That article delegates to Congress the power "to regulate commerce with foreign nations, and among the several States and with the Indian tribes." This **commerce clause** was consistently interpreted *in favor* of national power by the Supreme Court for most of the nineteenth century. The first and most important case favoring national power over the economy was *McCulloch v. Maryland*.[10] This case involved the question of whether Congress had the power to charter a national bank, since such an explicit grant of power was nowhere to be found in Article I, Section 8. Chief Justice John Marshall answered that the power could be "implied" from other powers that were expressly delegated to Congress, such as the "powers to lay and collect taxes; to borrow money; to regulate commerce; and to declare and conduct a war."

By allowing Congress to use the necessary and proper clause to interpret its delegated powers expansively, the Supreme Court created the potential for an unprecedented increase in national government power. Marshall also concluded that whenever a state law conflicted with a federal law (as in the case of *McCulloch v. Maryland*), the state law would be deemed invalid since the Constitution states that "the Laws of the United States . . . shall be the supreme Law of the Land." Both parts of this great case are pro-national, yet Congress did not immediately seek to expand the policies of the national government.

Another major case, *Gibbons v. Ogden* in 1824, reinforced this nationalistic interpretation of the Constitution. The important but relatively narrow issue was whether the state of New York could grant a monopoly to Robert Fulton's steamboat company to operate an exclusive service between New York and New Jersey. Chief Justice Marshall argued that New York State did not have the power to grant this particular monopoly. In order to reach this decision, it was necessary for Marshall to define what Article I, Section 8, meant by "commerce among the

commerce clause Article I, Section 8, of the Constitution, which delegates to Congress the power "to regulate commerce with foreign nations, and among the several States and with the Indian tribes." This clause was interpreted by the Supreme Court in favor of national power over the economy several states." He insisted that the definition was "comprehensive," extending to "every species of commercial intercourse." He did say that this comprehensiveness was limited "to that commerce which concerns more states than one," giving rise to what later came to be called "interstate commerce." *Gibbons* is important because it established the supremacy of the national government in all matters affecting interstate commerce.[11] But what would remain uncertain during several decades of constitutional discourse was the precise meaning of interstate commerce.

Article I, Section 8, backed by the implied powers decision in *McCulloch* and by the broad definition of "interstate commerce" in *Gibbons*, was a source of power for the national government as long as Congress sought to facilitate commerce through subsidies, services, and land grants. But later in the nineteenth century, when the national government sought to use those powers to *regulate* the economy rather than merely to promote economic development, federalism and the concept of interstate commerce began to operate as restraints on, rather than sources of, national power. Any effort of the national government to regulate commerce in such areas as fraud, the production of impure goods, the use of child labor, or the existence of dangerous working conditions or long hours was declared unconstitutional by the Supreme Court as a violation of the concept of interstate commerce. Such legislation meant that the federal government was entering the factory and the workplace—local areas—and was attempting to

The role of the national government in the economy has expanded gradually since the time of the Founding. In 1815, President James Madison called for a federally funded program of "internal improvements," which was one of the few policy roles for the national government during the first half of the nineteenth century. By improving transportation through the construction of roads and canals, the government fostered the growth of the market economy and boosted federal power (left). In 1916, the national government passed the Keating-Owen Child Labor Act, which excluded from interstate commerce all goods manufactured by children under fourteen. The act was ruled unconstitutional by the Supreme Court on the grounds that the regulation of interstate commerce could not extend to the conditions of labor. Despite this attempt at federal control, the regulation of child labor remained in the hands of state governments until the 1930s (right).

During the Great Depression, the national government became more active in regulating the economy and supporting the poor. New Deal programs sought to aid those affected by the Depression, such as residents of this Hooverville outside of Seattle, which was photographed in 1933 (left). The national government funded 90 percent of the cost of building more than 42,500 miles of interstate highways during the 1950s. State governments paid for the remaining 10 percent. Since the highways would improve interstate commerce, the federal government took the lead in funding them (right).

regulate goods that had not passed into commerce. To enter these local workplaces was to exercise police power—the power reserved to the states for the protection of the health, safety, and morals of their citizens. No one questioned the power of the national government to regulate businesses that intrinsically involved interstate commerce, such as railroads, gas pipelines, and waterway transportation. But well into the twentieth century, the Supreme Court used the concept of interstate commerce as a barrier against most efforts by Congress to regulate local conditions.

This aspect of federalism was alive and well during an epoch of tremendous economic development, the period between the Civil War and the 1930s. It gave the American economy a freedom from federal government control that closely approximated the ideal of free enterprise. The economy was never entirely free, of course; in fact, entrepreneurs themselves did not want complete freedom from government. They needed law and order. They needed a stable currency. They needed courts and police to enforce contracts and prevent trespass. They needed roads, canals, and railroads. But federalism, as interpreted by the Supreme Court for seventy years after the Civil War, made it possible for business to have its cake and eat it, too. Entrepreneurs enjoyed the benefits of national policies facilitating commerce and were protected by the courts from policies regulating commerce.[12]

All this changed after 1937, when the Supreme Court threw out the old distinction between interstate and intrastate commerce, converting the commerce clause from a source of limitations to a source of power for the national government. The Court began to refuse to review appeals challenging acts of Congress protecting the rights of employees to organize and engage in collective bargaining, regulating the amount of farmland in cultivation, extending low-interest credit to small businesses and farmers, and restricting the activities of corporations dealing in the stock market, and many other laws that contributed to the construction of the "welfare state."[13]

THE CHANGING ROLE OF THE STATES

As we have seen, the Constitution contained the seeds of a very expansive national government—in the commerce clause. For much of the nineteenth century, federal power remained limited. The Tenth Amendment was used to bolster arguments about **states' rights,** which in their extreme version claimed that the states did not have to submit to national laws when they believed the national government had exceeded its authority. These arguments in favor of states' rights were voiced less often after the Civil War. But the Supreme Court continued to use the Tenth Amendment to strike down laws that it thought exceeded national power, including the Civil Rights Act passed in 1875.

In the early twentieth century, however, the Tenth Amendment appeared to lose its force. Reformers began to press for national regulations to limit the power of large corporations and to preserve the health and welfare of citizens. The Supreme Court approved of some of these laws but it struck others down, including a law combating child labor. The Court stated that the law violated the Tenth Amendment because only states should have the power to regulate conditions of employment. By the late 1930s, however, the Supreme Court had approved such an expansion of federal power that the Tenth Amendment appeared irrelevant. The desire to promote equal conditions across the country had elevated the federal government over the states. In fact, in 1941, Justice Harlan Fiske Stone declared that the Tenth Amendment was simply a "truism," that it had no real meaning.[14]

Yet the idea that some powers should be reserved to the states did not go away. Indeed, in the 1950s, southern opponents of the civil rights movement revived the idea of states' rights. In 1956, ninety-six southern members of Congress issued a

states' rights the principle that the states should oppose the increasing authority of the national government. This principle was most popular in the period before the Civil War

States' rights have been embraced by many causes in the past fifty years. Governor George Wallace of Alabama defiantly turned back U.S. Attorney General Nicholas Katzenbach, who tried to enroll two black students at the University of Alabama at Tuscaloosa in 1963. Wallace, who proclaimed "segregation now, segregation tomorrow, segregation forever," was a vocal supporter of states' rights.

Especially in the mid-1990s, Republican Party leaders have contended that the national government has grown too powerful at the expense of the states and argue that the Tenth Amendment should restrict the growth of national power.

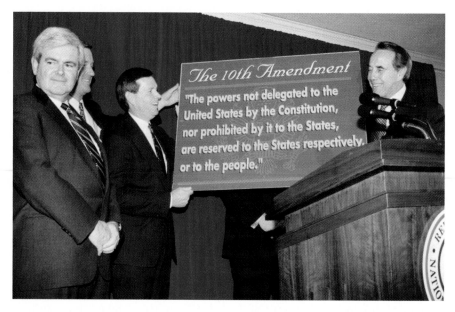

"Southern Manifesto" in which they declared that southern states were not constitutionally bound by Supreme Court decisions outlawing racial segregation. They believed that states' rights should override individual rights to liberty and formal equality. With the triumph of the civil rights movement, the slogan of "states' rights" became tarnished by its association with racial inequality.

Recent years have seen a revival of interest in the Tenth Amendment and important Supreme Court decisions limiting federal power. Much of the interest in the Tenth Amendment stems from conservatives who believe that a strong federal government encroaches on individual liberties. They believe such freedoms are

With the renewal of more state autonomy in recent decades, wide differences across the states in terms of economic and social policy benefits have emerged again. For example, some states set their minimum wages at levels higher than the federal level. States also differ in the amount of health-care coverage provided for poor children. California is currently the only state to have a paid family leave policy. Former governor Gray Davis is shown here celebrating its passage in September 2002.

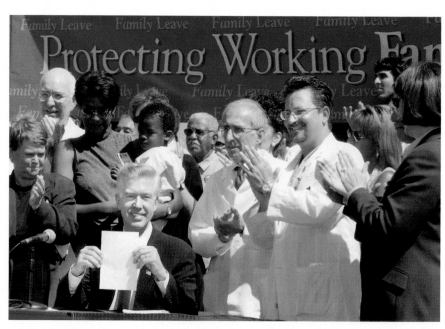

Global Governance and the States

The Constitution reserves for the federal government the power to make foreign policy and to enter into treaties. As the global economy has grown, the federal government has taken the lead in creating new international institutions to govern the global economy. Yet the expansion of international trade over the past three decades has also increased the importance of the international arena for state and local governments. As a result, many state governments have become international actors themselves and have built new capacities to monitor the international arena. As international economic activity has expanded, however, states have confronted new restrictions on their law-making powers.

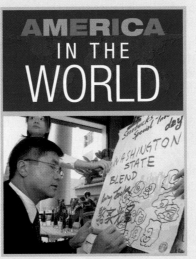

State officials have found it easiest to act in the international arena when they assume the role of economic ambassadors for their states. Many states have opened overseas offices to promote international trade, investment, and tourism. By the middle of the 1990s, states had set up more than 140 offices in countries all over the world. Governors now routinely lead trade missions to other countries to promote investment, and state economic development agencies offer a variety of assistance packages designed to make their states more attractive to foreign investors. By one estimate, states spend over $100 million a year on international trade development. The stakes are high: local economies now rise and fall due to international trade and investment.[a]

When states try to set their own standards in foreign policy, they face restrictions. In 1996, the Massachusetts legislature passed a law forbidding the state's procuring goods and services from companies that did business with Burma (Myanmar). Burma had been accused of major human rights violations, including the use of slave labor. Japan and the European Union challenged this law and a group of American companies later sued the state in federal court. The U.S. Supreme Court struck down the law in 2000, ruling that the federal government had preemptive authority over decisions regarding international business. In striking down the Massachusetts law, Supreme Court Justice Anthony Kennedy posed the problem: "Can we have 50 states passing resolutions denouncing different countries?"

States now also may face new restrictions when they act in more traditional arenas of domestic policy. This is because state lawmaking may run counter to the rules of international trade agreements. One of the most important such trade agreements is the North American Free Trade Act (NAFTA), a treaty signed by Canada, the United States, and Mexico in 1992 to open trade across the national borders of these three countries. It also created new trade rules that each national government is obligated to follow. Although American state governments were not involved in creating these trade rules, the new rules may significantly restrict their ability to enact their own policies, which may be challenged as a restraint on trade by other countries participating in the global governing arrangements. The potential for restricting state sovereignty is particularly high in the areas of economic development, environmental regulation, consumer protection, state procurement policies, and workplace regulation.

In the decade since NAFTA was signed, there has been a handful of challenges to national and state laws in Mexico, the United States, and Canada. In the United States, California's tough environmental laws have come under scrutiny. In 2003, a Canadian mining company threatened to sue the United States under NAFTA over a new California environmental regulation restricting open pit mining in the state. This case, and others like it, has not been settled and has aroused considerable concern because the decision about whether a state law violates NAFTA is made in a closed tribunal whose decision cannot be appealed.

States have responded to these new threats to their lawmaking powers by urging the federal government to ensure that the values of federalism are preserved in international trade agreements. The potential for trade agreements to restrict the traditional democratic decision-making powers of the states means that in the future, states will have to consider the international repercussions of their actions as a normal part of state lawmaking.

FOR CRITICAL ANALYSIS

1. What are some of the ways that American state governments have sought to advance their interests internationally? Why are states limited in how they can engage in international issues?

2. How do international treaties such as NAFTA and international organizations such as the World Trade Organization affect the sovereign powers of the states? Will states lose their independent policy-making power to international bodies? Are some kinds of state decisions subject to greater international scrutiny than others?

[a]Mark C. Gordon, *Democracy's New Challenge: Globalization, Governance, and the Future of American Federalism* (New York: Demos, 2001), www.demos-usa.org.

devolution a policy to remove a program from one level of government by delegating it or passing it down to a lower level of government, such as from the national government to the state and local governments

better protected by returning more power to the states through the process of **devolution.** In 1996, Republican presidential candidate Bob Dole carried a copy of the Tenth Amendment in his pocket as he campaigned, pulling it out to read at rallies.[15] The Supreme Court's ruling in *United States v. Lopez* in 1995 fueled further interest in the Tenth Amendment.[16] In that case, the Court, stating that Congress had exceeded its authority under the commerce clause, struck down a federal law that barred handguns near schools. This was the first time since the New Deal that the Court had limited congressional powers in this way. In 1997, the Court again relied on the Tenth Amendment to limit federal power in *Printz v. United States.*[17] The decision declared unconstitutional a provision of the Brady Handgun Violence Prevention Act that required state and local law enforcement officials to conduct background checks on handgun purchasers. The Court declared that this provision violated state sovereignty guaranteed in the Tenth Amendment because it required state and local officials to administer a federal regulatory program. The Court also limited the power of the federal government over the states in a 1996 ruling that prevented Native Americans from the Seminole tribe from suing the state of Florida in federal court. A 1988 law had given Indian tribes the right to sue a state in federal court if the state did not negotiate in good faith over issues related to gambling casinos on tribal land. The Supreme Court's ruling appeared to signal a much broader limitation on national power by raising new questions about whether individuals can sue a state if it fails to uphold federal law.[18] In 2003, the Court surprised many observers by ruling against the state of Nevada's challenge to the application of the federal Family and Medical Leave Act to Nevada state employees. The act guarantees workers time off (without pay) for family emergencies. The Court's decision, which required Nevada state government to abide by the family leave act, appeared to conflict with earlier decisions immunizing states against lawsuits on the basis of age and disability discrimination. Perhaps most surprising was the support of Chief Justice William Rehnquist, a strong proponent of federalism. In his opinion, Rehnquist argued that family care issues were so strongly gender related that the family leave act was necessary to prevent unconstitutional discrimination against women. Such protection against unconstitutional discrimination justified overriding state immunity in Rehnquist's view. Some analysts viewed the decision, in which the Court showed that on fundamental matters of civil rights federal law would supersede state sovereignty, as potentially a key turning point in judicial rulings on federalism.

The expansion of the power of the national government has not left the states powerless. The state governments continue to make the most of the fundamental laws; the national government did not expand at the expense of the states. The growth of the national government has been an addition, not a redistribution of power from the states. No better demonstration of the continuing influence of the federal framework can be offered than that the middle column of Table 3.2 is still a fairly accurate characterization of state government today.

FOR CRITICAL ANALYSIS

How have Supreme Court decisions affected the balance of power between the federal government and the states? Has the Supreme Court favored the federal government or the states?

Who Does What? The Changing Federal Framework

Questions about how to divide responsibilities between the states and the national government first arose more than 200 years ago, when the framers wrote the Constitution to create a stronger union. But they did not solve the issue of who should do what. There is no "right" answer to that question; each generation of Americans has provided its own answer. In recent years, Americans have grown distrustful of the federal government and have supported giving more responsibility to the states.[19] Even so, they still want the federal government to set standards and promote equality.

Political debates about the division of responsibility often take sides: some people argue for a strong federal role to set national standards, while others say the states should do more. These two goals are not necessarily at odds. The key is to find the right balance. During the first 150 years of American history, that balance favored state power. But the balance began to shift toward Washington in the 1930s. In this section, we will look at how the balance shifted, and then we will consider current efforts to reshape the relationship between the national government and the states.

EXPANSION OF THE NATIONAL GOVERNMENT

The New Deal of the 1930s signaled the rise of a more active national government. The door to increased federal action opened when states proved unable to cope with the demands brought on by the Great Depression. Before the Depression, states and localities took responsibility for addressing the needs of the poor, usually through private charity. But the extent of the need created by the Depression quickly exhausted local and state capacities. By 1932, 25 percent of the workforce was unemployed. The jobless lost their homes and settled into camps all over the country, called "Hoovervilles," after President Herbert Hoover. Elected in 1928, the year before the Depression hit, Hoover steadfastly maintained that there was little the federal government could do to alleviate the misery caused by the Depression. It was a matter for state and local governments, he said.

Yet demands mounted for the federal government to take action. In Congress, some Democrats proposed that the federal government finance public works to aid the economy and put people back to work. Other members of Congress introduced legislation to provide federal grants to the states to assist them in their relief efforts. None of these measures passed while Hoover remained in the White House.

When Franklin D. Roosevelt took office in 1933, he energetically threw the federal government into the business of fighting the Depression. He proposed a variety of temporary measures to provide federal relief and work programs. Most of the programs he proposed were to be financed by the federal government but administered by the states. In addition to these temporary measures, Roosevelt presided over the creation of several important federal programs designed to provide future economic security for Americans.

FEDERAL GRANTS

For the most part, the new national programs that the Roosevelt administration developed did not directly take power away from the states. Instead, Washington typically redirected states by offering them **grants-in-aid,** whereby Congress appropriates money to state and local governments on the condition that the money be spent for a particular purpose defined by Congress.

The principle of the grant-in-aid can be traced back to the nineteenth-century land grants that the national government made to the states for the improvement of agriculture and farm-related education. Since farms were not in "interstate

grants-in-aid programs through which Congress provides money to state and local governments on the condition that the funds be employed for purposes defined by the federal government commerce," it was unclear whether the Constitution permitted the national government to provide direct assistance to agriculture. Grants made to the states, but designated for farmers, presented a way of avoiding the question of constitutionality while pursuing what was recognized in Congress as a national goal.

Franklin Roosevelt's New Deal expanded the range of grants-in-aid into social programs, providing grants to the states for financial assistance to poor children. Congress added new grants after World War II, creating new programs to help states fund activities such as providing school lunches and building highways. Sometimes the national government required state or local governments to match the national contribution dollar for dollar, but in some programs, such as the development of the interstate highway system, the congressional grants provided 90 percent of the cost of the program.

categorical grants congressional grants given to states and localities on the condition that expenditures be limited to a problem or group specified by law

These types of federal grants-in-aid are also called **categorical grants,** because the national government determines the purposes, or categories, for which the money can be used. For the most part, the categorical grants created before the 1960s simply helped the states perform their traditional functions.[20] In the 1960s, however, the national role expanded and the number of categorical grants increased dramatically. For example, during the Eighty-ninth Congress (1965–66) alone, the number of categorical grant-in-aid programs grew from 221 to 379.[21] The value of categorical grants also rose dramatically, increasing in value from $2.3 billion in 1950 to $387 billion in 2003. The grants authorized during the 1960s announced national purposes much more strongly than did earlier grants. Central to that national purpose was the need to provide opportunities to the poor (see Figure 3.1).

| Figure 3.1 | Historical Trend of Federal Grants-in-Aid*, 1950–2003 |

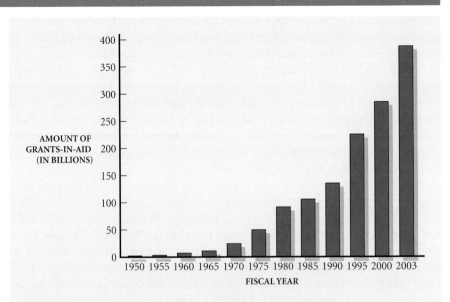

*Excludes outlays for national defense, international affairs, and net interest.
SOURCE: Office of Management and Budget, *Budget of the United States Government, Fiscal Year 2005, Analytical Perspectives* (Washington, DC: Government Printing Office, 2004), Table 8-3, p. 120.

Dual versus Cooperative Federalism

Figure 3.2

Dual Federalism

Cooperative Federalism

Cooperate on some policies {

National Government

State Governments

"Layer Cake"

National Government

State Governments

"Marble Cake"

In marble-cake federalism, national policies, state policies, and local policies overlap in many areas.

Many of the categorical grants enacted during the 1960s were **project grants,** which require state and local governments to submit proposals to federal agencies. In contrast to the older **formula grants,** which used a formula (composed of such elements as need and state and local capacities) to distribute funds, the new project grants made funding available on a competitive basis. Federal agencies would give grants to the proposals they judged to be the best. In this way, the national government acquired substantial control over which state and local governments got money, how much they got, and how they spent it.

project grants grant programs in which state and local governments submit proposals to federal agencies and for which funding is provided on a competitive basis

formula grants grants-in-aid in which a formula is used to determine the amount of federal funds a state or local government will receive

COOPERATIVE FEDERALISM

The growth of categorical grants created a new kind of federalism. If the traditional system of two sovereigns performing highly different functions could be called dual federalism, historians of federalism suggest that the system since the New Deal could be called **cooperative federalism.** The most important student of the history of American federalism, Morton Grozdins, characterized this as a move from "layer-cake federalism" to "marble-cake federalism,"[22] in which intergovernmental cooperation and sharing have blurred a once-clear distinguishing line, making it difficult to say where the national government ends and the state and local governments begin (see Figure 3.2). Figure 3.3 demonstrates the financial basis of the marble-cake idea.

For a while in the 1960s, however, it appeared as if the state governments would become increasingly irrelevant to American federalism. Many of the new federal grants bypassed the states and instead sent money directly to local governments and even to local nonprofit organizations. The theme heard repeatedly in Washington was that the states simply could not be trusted to carry out national purposes.[23]

One of the reasons that Washington distrusted the states was because of the way African American citizens were treated in the South. The southern states' forthright defense of segregation, justified on the grounds of states' rights, helped to tarnish the image of the states as the civil rights movement took hold. The national officials who planned the War on Poverty in the 1960s pointed to

cooperative federalism a type of federalism existing since the New Deal era in which grants-in-aid have been used strategically to encourage states and localities (without commanding them) to pursue nationally defined goals. Also known as "intergovernmental cooperation"

Figure 3.3   The Rise, Decline, and Recovery of Federal Aid

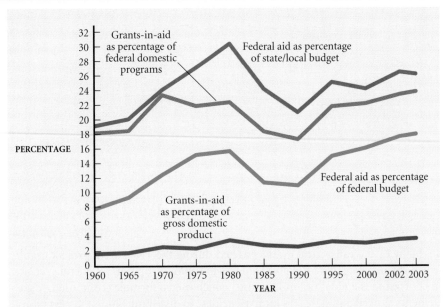

SOURCE: Office of Management and Budget, *Budget of the United States Government, Fiscal Year 2005, Analytical Perspectives* (Washington, DC: Government Printing Office, 2004), Table 8-3, p. 120.

the racial exclusion practiced in the southern states as a reason for bypassing state governments. Political scientist James Sundquist described how the "Alabama syndrome" affected the War on Poverty: "In the drafting of the Economic Opportunity Act, an 'Alabama syndrome' developed. Any suggestion within the poverty task force that the states be given a role in the administration of the act was met with the question, 'Do you want to give that kind of power to [Alabama governor] George Wallace?'"[24]

Yet, even though many national policies of the 1960s bypassed the states, other new programs, such as Medicaid—the health program for the poor—relied on state governments for their implementation. In addition, as the national government expanded existing programs run by the states, states had to take on more responsibility. These new responsibilities meant that the states were playing a very important role in the federal system.

REGULATED FEDERALISM AND NATIONAL STANDARDS

The question of who decides what each level of government should do goes to the very heart of what it means to be an American citizen. How different should things be when one crosses a state line? In what policy areas is it acceptable to have state differences and in what areas should states be similar? How much inequality across the states is acceptable? Supreme Court decisions about the fundamental rights of American citizens provide the most important answers to these questions. Over time, the Court has pushed for greater uniformity across the states. In addition to legal decisions, the national government uses two other tools to create similarities across the states: grants-in-aid and regulations.

Grants-in-aid, as we have seen, are a little like bribes: Congress gives money to state and local governments if they agree to spend it for the purposes Congress specifies. But as Congress began to enact legislation in new areas, such as environmental policy, it also imposed additional regulations on states and localities. Some political scientists call this a move toward **regulated federalism.**[25] The national government began to set standards of conduct or required the states to set standards that met national guidelines. The effect of these national standards is that state and local policies in the areas of environmental protection, social services, and education are more uniform from coast to coast than are other nationally funded policies.

Some national standards require the federal government to take over areas of regulation formerly overseen by state or local governments. Such **preemption** occurs when state and local actions are found to be inconsistent with federal requirements. If this occurs, all regulations in the preempted area must henceforth come from the national government. In many cases, the scope of the federal authority to preempt is decided by the courts. For example, in 1973 the Supreme Court struck down a local ordinance prohibiting jets from taking off from the airport in Burbank, California, between 11 P.M. and 7 A.M. It ruled that the Federal Aeronautics Act granted the Federal Aviation Administration all authority over flight patterns, takeoffs, and landings and that local governments could not impose regulations in this area. As federal regulations increased after the 1970s, Washington increasingly preempted state and local action in many different policy areas. This preemption has escalated since 1995, when Republicans gained control of Congress. Although the Republicans came to power promising to grant more responsibility to the states, they have reduced state control in many areas by preemption. For example, in 1998 Congress passed a law that prohibits states and localities from taxing Internet access services for the next three to six years. State and local governments often contest federal preemptions. For example, in 2001, Attorney General John Ashcroft declared that Oregon's law permitting doctor-assisted suicide was illegal under federal drug regulations. Oregon took the Justice Department to federal court, which ruled in favor of the local law, stating that the federal government had overstepped its boundaries. In other recent cases, federal preemption of local laws has been more successful, as in federal efforts to nullify the medical marijuana statutes passed by several states. Although voters in three states have approved medical use of marijuana, the federal government has conducted raids on dispensers of medical marijuana, charging that they violate federal law.

The growth of national standards has created some new problems and has raised questions about how far federal standardization should go. One problem that emerged in the 1980s was the increase in **unfunded mandates**—regulations or new conditions for receiving grants that impose costs on state and local governments for which they are not reimbursed by the national government. The growth of unfunded mandates was the product of a Democratic Congress, which wanted to achieve liberal social objectives, and a Republican president, who opposed increased social spending. Between 1983 and 1991, Congress mandated standards in many policy areas, including social services and environmental regulations, without providing additional funds to meet those standards. Altogether, Congress enacted twenty-seven laws that imposed new regulations or required states to expand

regulated federalism a form of federalism in which Congress imposes legislation on states and localities, requiring them to meet national standards

preemption the principle that allows the national government to override state or local actions in certain policy areas

FOR CRITICAL ANALYSIS

Is federal preemption of local laws desirable? Is preemption justified for some issues more than for others?

unfunded mandates regulations or conditions for receiving grants that impose costs on state and local governments for which they are not reimbursed by the federal government existing programs.[26] For example, in the late 1980s, Congress ordered the states to extend the coverage provided by Medicaid, the medical insurance program for the poor. The aim was to make the program serve more people, particularly poor children, and to expand services. But Congress did not supply additional funding to help states meet these new requirements; the states had to shoulder the increased financial burden themselves.

States and localities quickly began to protest the cost of unfunded mandates. Although it is very hard to determine the exact cost of federal regulations, the Congressional Budget Office estimated that between 1983 and 1990, new federal regulations cost states and localities between $8.9 and $12.7 billion.[27] States complained that mandates took up so much of their budgets that they were not able to set their own priorities.

These burdens became part of a rallying cry to reduce the power of the federal government—a cry that took center stage when a Republican Congress was elected in 1994. One of the first measures the new Congress passed was an act to limit the cost of unfunded mandates, the Unfunded Mandate Reform Act (UMRA). Under this law, Congress must estimate the cost of any proposal it believes will cost more than $50 million. It must then vote to approve the regulation, acknowledging the expenditure. At most, UMRA represented an effort to move the national-state relationship a bit further to the state side. But it has had no significant impact on mandates. The act does not prevent congressional members from passing unfunded mandates, but only makes them think twice before they do. Moreover, the act exempts several areas of regulation. States must still enforce antidiscrimination laws and meet other requirements to receive federal assistance.

Despite considerable talk about unfunded mandates, the federal government has not acted to help states pay for existing mandates, many of which have grown very costly over the years. For example, federal law requires states to offer education to disabled children. Despite its promises, the federal government has offered little new support for states confronting the rapidly rising costs of this responsibility. This issue became the focus of national attention in 2001 when Vermont Republican senator Jim Jeffords threatened to leave the Republican Party in part because congressional Republicans refused to provide full funding to the states for the costs of educating disabled children. In a dramatic move, Jeffords, a lifelong Republican, decided to switch his party affiliation to independent and to vote with the Democrats. His move robbed Republicans of their one-vote majority and turned control of the Senate over to Democrats.

New national problems inevitably raise the question of "who pays?" Since the terrorist attacks of 2001, state governments have grown deeply concerned about the costs of security. Although ensuring the common defense is traditionally a federal responsibility, where responsibility for homeland security lies is not clear. This is not surprising because no one had ever used the term *homeland security* before the terror attacks. Since 2001, the costs of homeland security have fallen heavily on the states. In 2003, states, faced with their worst fiscal crises in sixty years, complained that the federal assistance provided for homeland security was far too little. At its annual meetings that year, the National Governors' Association declared homeland security an unfunded mandate with which the federal government should help more. The relationship between national security needs and state and local capabilities remains an unsettled area.

FOR CRITICAL ANALYSIS

Should states be required to implement unfunded mandates? Are Americans better off or worse off as a result of devolution?

NEW FEDERALISM AND STATE CONTROL

In 1970, the mayor of Oakland, California, told Congress that there were twenty-two separate employment and training programs in his city but that few poor residents were being trained for jobs that were available in the local labor market.[28] National programs had proliferated as Congress enacted many small grants, but little effort was made to coordinate or adapt programs to local needs. Today many governors argue for more control over such national grant programs. They complain that national grants do not allow for enough local flexibility and instead take a "one size fits all" approach.[29] These criticisms point to a fundamental problem in American federalism: how to get the best results for the money spent. Do some divisions of responsibility between states and the federal government work better than others? Since the 1970s, as states have become more capable of administering large-scale programs, the idea of devolution—transferring responsibility for policy from the federal government to the states and localities—has become popular.

Proponents of more state authority have looked to **block grants** as a way of reducing federal control. Block grants are federal grants that allow the states considerable leeway in spending federal money. President Nixon led the first push for block grants in the early 1970s, as part of his **New Federalism.** Nixon's block grants consolidated programs in the areas of job training, community development, and social services into three large block grants. These grants imposed some conditions on states and localities for how the money should be spent, but not the narrow regulations contained in the categorical grants. In addition, Congress provided an important new form of federal assistance to state and local governments called **general revenue sharing.** Revenue sharing provided money to local governments and counties with no strings attached; localities could spend the money as they wished. In enacting revenue sharing, Washington acknowledged both the critical role that state and local governments play in implementing national priorities and their need for increased funding and enhanced flexibility in order to carry out that role (see Figure 3.4). Reagan's version of New Federalism also looked to block grants. Like Nixon, Reagan wanted to reduce the national government's control and return power to the states. In all, Congress created twelve new block grants between 1981 and 1990.[30]

Another way of letting the states do more is by having the national government do less. When Nixon implemented block grants he increased federal spending. But Reagan's block grants cut federal funding by 12 percent. His view was that the states could spend their own funds to make up the difference, if they chose to do so. Revenue sharing was also eliminated during the Reagan administration, leaving localities to fend for themselves. The Republican Congress elected in 1994 took this strategy even further, supporting block grants as well as substantial cuts in federal programs. Their biggest success was the 1996 welfare reform law, which delegated to states important new responsibilities. Most of the other major proposed block grants or spending reductions failed to pass Congress or were vetoed by President Clinton. The Republican congressional leadership had found that it was much easier to promise a "devolution revolution" than to deliver on that promise.[31]

Neither block grants nor reduced federal funding have proven to be magic solutions to the problems of federalism. For one thing, there is always a trade-off between accountability, that is, whether the states are using funds for the purposes intended, and flexibility. Accountability and proper use of funds continue to be troublesome issues. Even after block grants were created, Congress reimposed

block grants federal grants-in-aid that allow states considerable discretion in how the funds are spent

New Federalism attempts by Presidents Nixon and Reagan to return power to the states through block grants

general revenue sharing the process by which one unit of government yields a portion of its tax income to another unit of government, according to an established formula. Revenue sharing typically involves the national government providing money to state governments

Figure 3.4   Regulated versus New Federalism

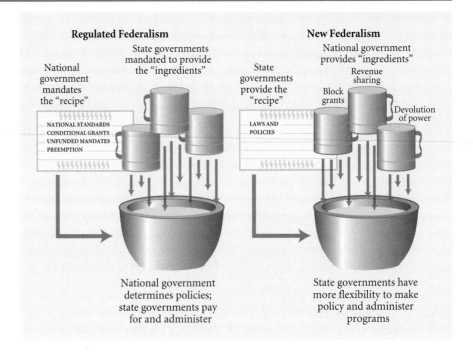

Regulated Federalism

National government mandates the "recipe"

State governments mandated to provide the "ingredients"

NATIONAL STANDARDS
CONDITIONAL GRANTS
UNFUNDED MANDATES
PREEMPTION

National government determines policies; state governments pay for and administer

New Federalism

National government provides "ingredients"

State governments provide the "recipe"

Revenue sharing

Block grants

Devolution of power

LAWS AND POLICIES

State governments have more flexibility to make policy and administer programs

regulations in order to increase the states' accountability. If the objective is to have accountable and efficient government, it is not clear that state bureaucracies are any more efficient or more capable than national agencies. In Mississippi, for example, the state Department of Human Services spent money from the child care block grant for office furniture and designer salt and pepper shakers that cost $37.50 a pair. As one Mississippi state legislator said, "I've seen too many years of good ol' boy politics to know they shouldn't [transfer money to the states] without stricter controls and requirements."[32]

Reduced federal funding may leave states with problems that they do not have the resources to solve. During the 1980s, many states had to raise taxes in order to make up for some of the cuts in federal funding. And in the early 1990s and again in 2002, when recession hit, states had to cut back services because they were short of funds even after raising taxes.

Most discussion of New Federalism has focused on increased state control over government spending programs. On balance, we have seen, states did gain more power over spending policies during the 1980s and 1990s. Yet, in other important respects, states lost power during the same time period. As discussed in the previous section, the federal government has used its power of preemption to limit state discretion. The Republican Congress has been especially active in asserting federal power in the areas of criminal law, securities law, and telecommunications. The imposition of federal standards has likewise continued to grow. The first major bipartisan legislation of the George W. Bush administration was No Child Left Behind, an education bill that gave schools more discretion over how they used federal dollars but, at the same time, imposed educational standards by requiring annual reading and math tests.

The States, the Federal Government, and Public Education

The United States stands out among developed nations for its early and strong support of free public education. The provision of primary and secondary education has historically been the responsibility of state and local governments. Not until the 1960s did the federal government provide substantial funding for public schools. Even so, primary and secondary education remains largely funded by state and local governments: today, the federal government provides only 10 percent of the total spending on K–12 education. Nonetheless, since the 1980s, presidents have sought to respond to widespread concerns about the quality of American public education. Despite all the talk about education in Washington, the federal effort to improve public education remained primarily symbolic until 2002, with the passage of President George W. Bush's No Child Left Behind law.

No Child Left Behind dramatically expanded the federal role in public education. The goal of the law is to improve the quality of education by holding schools accountable for results. It requires testing in reading and math from the third to the eighth grades. The test results, which are reported to parents and to the federal government, have to be broken down by school, grade, race, ethnicity, and income level. Schools that fail to show steady progress in all subgroups of students are required to take remedial actions, which include extra tutoring for students and additional professional training for teachers. Underperforming schools are required to allow students to transfer to schools that are not failing and they must provide transportation to those schools. Schools that continue to fail can ultimately be closed and their staffs replaced. The goal is to move all students up to proficiency in math and reading by 2014. The law provides extra funding to help schools meet this goal.

Defenders of the strong federal role in the No Child Left Behind act point out that many states and localities have failed to deliver quality education and have especially neglected low-income students. The uneven performance of states and localities means that federal action is required to ensure that all students receive a quality education. This is an appropriate federal role because an educated population is an important national resource. The country needs an educated population in order to compete internationally.

Moreover, the federal government is in the best position to enforce educational standards because many state

and local governments are unduly influenced by teachers' unions, which have long resisted standards and accountability in the schools. Federal action is particularly needed to ensure that low-income and minority students receive a quality education. Because their parents are not powerful and because their school districts are often resource poor, these students are frequently neglected by state and local districts. If all children are to have a fair chance to succeed, educational standards must be enforced in every school. Since states and localities have not ensured quality education for low-income students, it is up to the federal government to see that it happens.

Critics of No Child Left Behind denounce the law as an unfunded mandate. They argue that the federal government has not provided adequate resources to support the additional services that the law requires. Even though many of the services mandated in the law for failing schools are desirable, states simply do not have the money to pick up the tab. In fact, the law hurts poor schools and rural schools more than it helps them. It reduces their resources by forcing them to allow students to transfer and by requiring them to pay for transportation to other schools.

No Child Left Behind is an intrusive law. It imposes a "one size fits all" model on schools, which should respond to local needs. Many suburban parents and educators, for example, reject the law's emphasis on testing. They believe that education should promote critical thinking, not the rote learning required to succeed on standardized tests. Because needs are so diverse, education policy demands the kind of flexibility that only states and localities can ensure. In usurping the state role, No Child Left Behind not only undermines state sovereignty; it threatens the future of public education.

FOR CRITICAL ANALYSIS

1. Why do critics call the No Child Left Behind law an unfunded mandate that will harm low-income and minority students?

2. How does the No Child Left Behind law aim to provide better education to low-income and minority students? Why is the federal government better able than state and local governments to ensure that all children receive a high-quality education?

Does the No Child Left Behind Act Work?

Yes

If you asked a group of politically informed college students if they were pleased with President Bush's main domestic policy item of his term—the No Child Left Behind Act (NCLB)—chances are you wouldn't get a very warm response. Viscerally aware of the party dogma on decentralization, a lot of Republicans have reacted violently to NCLB's federal mandates: others, the more disconcerting band of Bush cheerleaders, usually give a nod of the head and a coy few words, perhaps a "well, he tried." On the Left, NCLB occupies a place on the official hit list of Senator John F. Kerry (D-Mass.), with the senator's blithe suggestion of a National Education Trust, a pool of money to fund schools "no questions asked"—in other workds, without federal mandates.

The good ol' boys at the National Education Association (NEA), the largest teacher's union, love this idea—so much so that they've been proposing it for nearly two decades. After what could be remembered by NEA apparatchiks as "the great betrayal," when Democrats including Kerry voted for the NCLB's planks on teacher and school accountability, the nominee-to-be has reversed himself, crudely plagiarizing the NEA's position papers and taking them as his own plan to "make sure every child gets the skills they need."

Kerry's peculiar support of decentralization on education issues can be explained by looking at the NEA's own political station. It's an organization that prefers to work in state capitals . . . it's a good bet that you can find an NEA satellite's office within three blocks of any state House. And on a community-by-community basis, the same school board system that allows the religious right to hijack school control in the South allows the NEA to do it elsewhere. It's pure fantasy to expect the NEA to pay more attention to the quality of students' education than teachers' salaries and benefits packages.

Nonetheless, that's the tune Dems keep playing. To hear it from the mouth of NEA President Reg Weaver's public comments, you'd think the NEA was all about education reform, standing up for children, and arguing against byzantine labor rules that protect bad teachers and keep good teachers where they are. . . . [But] the organiziation has done everything it can to obstruct even basic edutcation reforms on federal and state levels. The union was outraged with NCLB and Democrats, who flocked to support the law after Senator Edward M. Kennedy (D-Mass.), signed up as a co-sponsor. That as hardly a novel occurrence, though—every six years, when the Elementary and Secondary Education Act's mandatory reauthorization comes before Congress, it's the same song and dance. Accountability for failing teachers? No. Incentives for successful educators? Think again. Charter schools? Hardly. Vouchers of any kind? In your dreams. Actually, the only policy the NEA has ever favored on Capitol Hill is a rather straightforward one: giving more money to the nation's schools with few or no strings attached—the aforementioned policy that Kerry has recently usurped.

This is the root inspiration for the vague Democratic criticism of NCLB, not the fact that NCLB is unfunded. Indeed, the Bush administration has increased education spending 35.8 percent since it took office, a boost that accounts for the largest dollar increase of any domestic agency. Likewise, the reason why NCLB is being attacked is not because something went terrribly wrong with the implementation of the bill—on the contary, it's working exactly as planned, coercing states (with however much disregard for local hardships) to educate children better or forego federal dollars, and idea that the NEA has consistently opposed.

Now, though, it seems tha the NEA's campaign donations—95 percent of which go into the hands of Democrats—are paying off. Kerry's padded renunciation of the law he voted for—including the " National Education Trust" and the idea of making education reform a recommendation rather than a requirement—is hardly a courageous step for a Democrat and is a telling indicator of the NEA's hand in the matter.

SOURCE: Travis R. Kavulla, " The New Tune on NCLB, "*The Harvard Crimson* (Harvard University), March 9, 2004.

No

Earlier this month, The National Assessment of Educational Progress, considered the nation's report card, released its results on the reading proficiency of students across the nation. It found that when it comes to reading,

American students simply don't do well. Only about one-third of fourth, eighth, and twelfth-graders read at their appropriate grade level. And while the 31 percent proficiency of fourth-graders is a slight improvement of a 2 percent increase from four years ago, the proficiency of high school seniors had dropped by 4 percent.

Education Secretary Rod Paige is quoted by CNN as saying "There are no sciencific answers as to why our high school seniors have performed so poorly on this reading asssessment, but we're still searching for solutions to these daunting challenges."

Is America's pathetic record on financing primary and secondary education a scientific enough answer?

Education spending is always a popular way to garner votes during political campaigns, but little seems to come of these promises. In 2000, the George W. Bush campaign adopted the long-held Children's Defense Fund motto "Leave No Child Behind" as a slogan to illustrate how much Bush cares about education in America. The motto was even adopted as the name of education reform legislation Bush signed into law on Jan. 8, 2002.

However, like every other education-related promise, little will come of this law unless government officials prove that they are serious about change. If students are to succeed, schools must be provided with adequate resources to properly teach them.

Education funding must not be one of the first places grovernment officials cut spending, and "accountablility" must not be an excuse for the government to skimp on its obligations to American students.

The No Child Left Behind Act emphasizes the accountablility of schools. Students in schools that do not perform well are free to transfer at the expense of their original school. this policy, however, does little to help students. It only makes the situation of schools worse.

John Wilhelmi, principal of Marshall High School in Portland, Oregon, told *The Washington Post* how this policy affects his school: "For every thirty students we lose, we lose a teacher. You lose teachers, and you cut programs. You cut programs, and you attract fewer students. It's a vicious cycle downward."

The state of Texas is also guilty of forcing school districts into a " vicious cycle downward." Schools that perform poorly on the Texas assessment of Knowledge and Skills test get their funding cut as well, which is the exact opposite of what should happen. It's the poorer districts that are not performing well. Making them poorer by cutting the money supply makes absolutely no sense.

It's ridiculous to think that poorly performing schools will improve with less money— they didn't have enough money to begin with. Yes, schools should be accountable for their students' performances, but it is not solely the school's fault. The state and the national government are to blame for poorly performing students.

Schools need more money; it's as simple as that. Schools need money to hire more and better teachers. They need money to reduce class size. They need money to provide programs that will prepare students for the real world. Schools need money that does not seem to be forthcoming.

While the No Child Left Behind Act increased federal funding for schools by 40 percent, the funding still acccounts for less than 10 percent of K–12 spending nationally, according to *The Washington Post*. This leaves schools susceptible to large budget cuts when states need to free up some money. Due to the current economic crises faced by state governments, more than one-third of states are cutting school financing by millions, and in some cases— such as California—billions of dollars.

These budget cuts will only make the situation worse, and unless the national government does more to help American students, millions will be left behind.

Without better funding, there is no way the No Child Left Behind Act's goal that every student be proficient in reading by 2013 will be met. Right now, that goal is nothing more than a pipe dream.

SOURCE: Jenelle Wilson, "Funding Public Education," *The Battalion* (Texas A&M), June 30, 2003.

The debate over national versus state control is illustrated by the question of speed limits. The issue arose in 1973, when gas prices skyrocketed and supplies became scarce. Drivers nationwide were forced to wait in long lines at gas stations (right). The federal government responded to the gas crisis by instituting a national 55-mile-per-hour speed limit. The new limit was mandatory on all federal highways and was intended to reduce gas use (below).

redistributive programs economic policies designed to control the economy through taxing and spending, with the goal of benefiting the poor

DEVOLUTION: FOR WHOSE BENEFIT?

Since the expansion of the national government in the 1930s, questions about "who does what" have frequently provoked conflict in American politics. Why does such an apparently simple choice set off such highly charged political debate? One reason is that many decisions about federal versus state responsibility have implications for who benefits from government action.

Let's consider the benefits of federal control versus devolution in the realm of **redistributive programs.** These are programs designed primarily for the benefit of the poor. Many political scientists and economists maintain that states and localities should not be in charge of redistributive programs. They argue that since states and local governments have to compete with one another, they do not have the incentive to spend their money on the needy people in their areas. Instead, they want to keep taxes low and spend money on things that promote economic development.[33] In this situation, states might engage in a "race to the bottom": if one state cuts assistance to the poor, neighboring states will institute similar or deeper cuts both to reduce expenditures and to discourage poorer people from moving into their states. As one New York legislator put it, "The concern we have is that unless we make our welfare system and our tax and regulatory system competitive with the states around us, we will have too many disincentives for business to move here. Welfare is a big part of that."[34]

In 1996, when Congress enacted a major welfare reform law, it followed a different logic. By changing welfare from a combined federal-state program into a block grant to the states, Congress gave the states more responsibility for programs that serve the poor. One argument in favor of this decision was that states can act as "laboratories of democracy," by experimenting with many different approaches to find ones that best meet the needs of their citizens.[35] As states have altered their welfare programs in the wake of the new law, they have indeed designed diverse approaches. For example, Minnesota has adopted an incentive-based approach that offers extra assistance to families that take low-wage jobs. Other states, such as California, have more "sticks" than "carrots" in their new welfare programs. In the years since the passage of the law, welfare rolls have declined dramatically. On average they have declined by 47 percent from their peak in 1994; in six states the decline was 70 percent or higher. Politicians have cited these statistics to claim that the poor have benefited from greater state control of welfare, yet analysts caution that we do not yet know enough about the fate of those who have left welfare to judge the effect of welfare reform. Most studies have found that the majority of those leaving welfare remain in poverty. Many analysts are also concerned that the poor who rely on support from states become particularly vulnerable

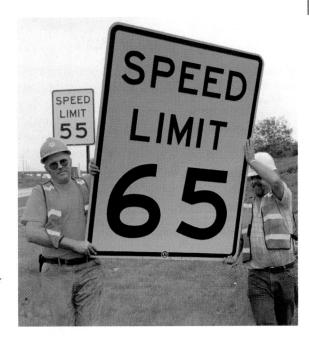

during economic recessions. Because states have to balance their budgets each year, they have little cushion to fall back on during an economic downturn. During the recession that began in 2001, the decline in welfare rolls halted but the numbers of recipients did not increase dramatically, as had been feared. In fact, the welfare caseload actually went down by a few percentage points between 2001 and 2003. By contrast, the numbers of people receiving food stamps—a federal

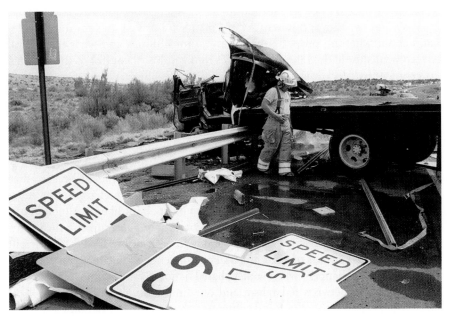

In 1995, Congress removed its speed limit restrictions and gave the states the right to determine their own road speeds. As a result, speed limits went up on many highways (above). Proponents of the states' right to set higher speed limits had insisted that it would not increase the number of accidents on the road. However, car accidents like this fatal crash—in which a truck carrying speed limit signs rolled over and caught fire—suggest that high speed limits may have dangerous consequences (left).

program—rose sharply between 2001 and 2003. For critics of welfare reform, this divergence in the welfare and food stamp caseloads demonstrated that the federal government is more responsive than the states to increased need during periods of recession. They believe that the poor would be better off with a national program that guaranteed a basic level of support for needy people. They contrast welfare to Social Security, a fully national program that has greatly reduced poverty among the elderly.

In other decisions about federalism, local concerns have been overridden in the name of the national interest. In the example of air traffic, which was cited in a previous section, local residents of Burbank, California, lost out to the national interest in having a smoothly operating air transportation system. The question of speed limits, discussed at the beginning of this chapter, raised a similar set of concerns. Speed limits had traditionally been a state and local responsibility. But in 1973, at the height of the oil shortage, Congress passed legislation to withhold federal highway funds from states that did not adopt a maximum speed limit of 55 miles per hour (mph). The lower speed limit, it was argued, would reduce energy consumption by cars. Although Congress had not formally taken over the authority to set speed limits, the power of its purse was so important that every state adopted the new speed limit. The national interest in energy conservation had outweighed local preferences for higher speed limits. As the crisis faded, concern about energy conservation diminished. The national speed limit lost much of its support, even though it was found to have reduced the number of traffic deaths. In 1995, Congress repealed the penalties for higher speed limits, and states once again became free to set their own speed limits. Many states with large rural areas raised their maximum to 75 mph; Montana initially set unlimited speeds in the rural areas during daylight hours. Research indicates that numbers of highway deaths have indeed risen in the states that increased the limits.[36]

Because the division of responsibility in the federal system has important implications for who benefits, few conflicts over state versus national control will ever be settled once and for all. As new evidence becomes available about the costs and benefits of different arrangements, it provides fuel for ongoing debates about what are properly the states' responsibilities and what the federal government should do. Likewise, changes in the political control of the national government usually provoke a rethinking of responsibilities as new leaders seek to alter federal arrangements for the benefit of the groups they represent.

Thinking Critically about Liberty versus Equality

It is often argued that liberals prefer a strong federal government because they value equality more than liberty. Conservatives are said to prefer granting more power to states and localities because they care most about liberty. Although this greatly oversimplifies liberal and conservative views about government, such arguments underscore the reality that ideas about federalism are linked to different views about the purposes of government. For what ends should government powers be used? What happens when widely shared national values conflict in practice? The connections between federalism and our fundamental national values have made federalism a focus of political contention throughout our nation's history.

The Constitution limited the power of the federal government in order to promote liberty. This decision reflected the framers' suspicions of centralized power, based on their experience with the British Crown. The American suspicion of centralized power lives on today in widespread dislike of "big government," which generally evokes a picture of a bloated federal government. But over the course of our history we have come to realize that the federal government is also an important guarantor of liberty. As we'll see in Chapter 4, it took enhanced federal power to ensure that local and state governments adhered to the fundamental constitutional freedoms in the Bill of Rights.

One of the most important continuing arguments for a strong federal government is its role in ensuring equality. A key puzzle of federalism is deciding when differences across states represent the proper democratic decisions of the states and when such differences represent inequalities that should not be tolerated. Sometimes a decision to eliminate differences is made on the grounds of equality and individual rights, as in the Civil Rights Act of 1964, which outlawed legal segregation. At other times, a stronger federal role is justified on the grounds of national interest, as in the case of the oil shortage and the institution of a 55 mph speed limit in the 1970s. Advocates of a more limited federal role often point to the value of democracy. Public actions can more easily be tailored to fit distinctive local or state desires if states and localities have more power to make policy. Viewed this way, variation across states can be an expression of democratic will.

In recent years, many Americans have grown disillusioned with the federal government and have supported efforts to give the states more responsibilities. A 1997 poll, for example, found that Americans tended to have the most confidence in governments that were closest to them. Thirty-eight percent expressed "a great deal" of confidence in local government, 32 percent in state government, and 22 percent in the federal government. Nearly two-thirds of those polled believed that shifting some responsibility to states and localities would help achieve excellence in government. After the terrorist attacks, however, support for the federal government soared. With issues of security topping the list of citizens' concerns, the federal government, which had seemed less important with the waning of the cold war, suddenly reemerged as the central actor in American politics. As one observer put it, "Federalism was a luxury of peaceful times."[37] Yet the newfound respect for the federal government is likely to be contingent on how well the government performs. If the federal government does not appear to be effective in the fight against terrorism, its stature may once again decline in the minds of many Americans.

American federalism remains a work in progress. As public problems shift and as local, state, and federal governments change, questions about the relationship between American values and federalism naturally emerge. The different views that people bring to this discussion suggest that concerns about federalism will remain a central issue in American democracy.

FOR CRITICAL ANALYSIS

Economic inequality has increased over the past three decades. Has devolution of government programs made it more difficult to reduce inequality? Are critics of devolution right in charging that the federal government needs to play a stronger role in combating inequality?

GET INVOLVED

What You Can Do: Participate at Different Levels of the Federal System

How can citizens contribute to the ongoing design of American federalism? To be effective participants in a federal system, citizens must first understand how responsibilities are divided among the different levels of government. They also need to be aware of how decisions made at one level of government may affect the possibilities for public action at other levels. In other words, if citizens are to be politically effective they must understand the connections among the levels of the federal system and target their activities where they will be most effective.

One of the striking features of political participation in the United States is the preference for engaging in politics at the state and local levels. One study of political participation found that 92 percent of Americans who participated beyond voting—by campaigning, contacting public officials, or sitting on a governing board, for example—engaged in an activity focused on state and local activity. Fifty-one percent of those questioned engaged only in state and local action, while 41 percent added some form of national participation to their state and local activities.[38] This pattern of participation makes sense because politics at these levels—especially the local level—is more personal and often easier to get involved in. Moreover, many of the things that people care most about are close to home. Here are two local arenas that may attract your interest.

1. *Public education.* State governments mandate the general requirements for curricula and minimal requirements for graduation, but these state mandates are administered by local school districts. In turn, local school districts are managed by superintendents who have considerable discretion in shaping elementary, middle, high school, and sometimes community college education. Most school districts and superintendents are accountable to local school boards. School board members are usually selected by voters in competitive elections in the same way that mayors or council members are chosen.

2. *Law enforcement.* Most states have several different police agencies, for example, state police or highway patrol, county sheriffs, and city or town peace officers. Other state and local officials may have police powers, too. We do not necessarily think of lifeguards or forest rangers as police personnel, but they often are.

Many police agencies practice community policing. Rather than simply reacting to crime, they try to prevent crime by promoting a local environment conducive to law-abiding behavior. They may sponsor after-school programs for at-risk youth; they may provide mediation services to settle domestic disputes; or they may host community forums aimed at easing racial tensions and promoting interracial cooperation.

To be broadly effective, citizens must also be able to engage in political activity at different levels of the federal system. For example, in the 1970s, community groups frustrated in their efforts to revitalize inner-city neighborhoods lobbied Congress to pass the Community Reinvestment Act, which requires banks to invest in the neighborhoods where they do business. With this federal law behind them, community organizations have been much more effective in promoting investment. But it is often not easy for groups of citizens to focus their activity at different levels of government as needed. Often they do not have the expertise or the contacts or the information to be effective in a different setting.

In recent years, as states have taken on a greater role in making public policy, it has become more important for citizens to become effective participants in state politics. Moreover, the media coverage of state politics is generally not as deep or informative as coverage of national politics. Citizens need a better knowledge of what states do today and more information about state politics simply as a first step to being effective participants in our federal system.

The federal system makes American democracy a flexible form of government for a large and diverse nation. But citizens must be knowledgeable about how public actions across the federal system are connected and they must be able to act at different levels if federalism is to be an effective and representative form of government.

Summary

In this chapter, we have examined one of the central principles of American government—federalism. The Constitution divides powers between the national government and the states, but over time national power has grown substantially. Many aspects of expanded federal power stem from struggles to realize the ideals of liberty and equality for all citizens.

The aim of federalism in the Constitution was to limit national power by creating two sovereigns—the national government and the state governments. The Founders hoped that this system of dual federalism would ensure the liberty of citizens by preventing the national government from becoming too powerful. But during the 1930s, American citizens used the democratic system to change the balance between federal and state governments. The failure of the states to provide basic economic security for citizens during the Great Depression led to an expansion of the federal government. Most Americans were supportive of this growing federal power because they believed that economic power had become too concentrated in the hands of big corporations and the common person was the loser. Thus, the ideal of equality—in this case, the belief that working people should have a fighting chance to support themselves—overrode fears that a strong federal government would abridge liberties. Expanded federal powers first took the form of grants-in-aid to states. Later, federal regulations became more common.

In recent years, many Americans have come to believe that the pendulum has swung too far in the direction of expanded federal power. A common charge is that the federal government is too big and, as a result, has encroached on fundamental liberties. State and local governments complain that they cannot govern because their powers have been preempted or because they have to use their own funds to fulfill unfunded mandates imposed by the federal government. The move to devolve more powers to the states has been called "New Federalism." Advocates of reduced federal power believe that states can protect liberty without creating unacceptable inequalities. Others continue to believe that a strong central government is essential to ensuring basic equalities. They argue that economic competition among the states means that states cannot ensure equality as well as the federal government can. Since September 11, Americans have looked to the federal government to ensure national security. Charges of "big government" have become less compelling as we face threats to domestic safety and national defense that only the federal government can address.

YOU ARE... a recent college graduate with a new job!

Federalism refers to the division of powers and functions among the national, state, and local governments. America seems to love governments, as there are more than 87,000 governments in the United States. All individual citizens interact with several different governments in the course of their daily lives. The relationship between national and state governments is complex, and the relationship between cities, towns, counties, and their state governments is often complicated.

The distribution of power among the national, state, and local levels of government has changed enormously since the Constitution was written. Overall, the balance of power has moved toward the national government because of its greater resources and the growing perception among many citizens that it is the level best able to handle problems requiring large collective action.

Go to www.wwnorton.com/wtp5

Questions to consider as you conduct the online simulation:

Why would it make sense to have differing levels of government responsible for different tasks?

What areas should be left to the states rather than to the national government?

Do you consider your links to your state government more or less important than your links to your national government?

What tasks do people need to complete every time they move to a new city in a new state?

For Further Reading

Bensel, Richard. *Sectionalism and American Political Development: 1880–1980.* Madison: University of Wisconsin Press, 1984.

Bowman, Ann O'M., and Richard Kearny. *The Resurgence of the States.* Englewood Cliffs, NJ: Prentice-Hall, 1986.

Donahue, John D. *Disunited States.* New York: Basic Books, 1997.

Dye, Thomas R. *American Federalism: Competition among Governments.* Lexington, MA: Lexington Books, 1990.

Elazar, Daniel. *American Federalism: A View from the States,* 3rd ed. New York: Harper & Row, 1984.

Grodzins, Morton. *The American System.* Chicago: Rand McNally, 1974.

Kelley, E. Wood. *Policy and Politics in the United States: The Limits of Localism.* Philadelphia: Temple University Press, 1987.

Kettl, Donald. *The Regulation of American Federalism.* Baltimore: Johns Hopkins University Press, 1987.

Peterson, Paul E. *The Price of Federalism.* Washington, DC: Brookings, 1995.

Study Outline

www.wwnorton.com/wtp5e   Keyword: Review 3

The Federal Framework

1. In an effort to limit national power, the framers of the Constitution established a system of dual federalism, wherein both the national and state governments would have sovereignty.

2. The Constitution granted a few "expressed powers" to the national government and, through the Tenth Amendment, reserved all the rest to the states.

3. The Constitution also created obligations among the states in the "full faith and credit" and "privileges and immunities" clauses.

4. Federalism and a restrictive definition of "interstate commerce" limited the national government's control over the economy.

5. Federalism allows a great deal of variation between states.

6. Under the traditional system of federalism, the national government was small and very narrowly specialized in its functions compared with other Western nations. Most of its functions were aimed at promoting commerce.

7. Under the traditional system, states rather than the national government did most of the fundamental governing in the country.

8. The system of federalism limited the expansion of the national government despite economic forces and expansive interpretations of the Constitution in cases such as *McCulloch v. Maryland* and *Gibbons v. Ogden.*

9. For most of U.S. history, the concept of interstate commerce kept the national government from regulating the economy. But in 1937, the Supreme Court converted the commerce clause from a source of limitations to a source of power for the national government.

10. Recent years have seen a revival of interest in returning more power to the states through devolution.

Who Does What? The Changing Federal Framework

1. The rise of national government activity after the New Deal did not necessarily mean that states lost power directly. Rather, the national government paid states through grants-in-aid to administer federal programs.

2. Some federal programs bypass the states by sending money directly to local governments or local organizations. The states are most important, however; they are integral to federal programs such as Medicaid.

3. The national government also imposed regulations on states and localities in areas such as environmental policy in order to guarantee national standards.

4. Under President Nixon, many categorical grants were combined into larger block grants that offered greater flexibility in the use of the money. The Nixon administration also developed revenue sharing that was not tied to any specific programs.

5. As states have become more capable of administering large-scale programs, the idea of devolution has become popular.

Thinking Critically about Liberty versus Equality

1. Some of the sharpest tensions among liberty, equality, and democracy are visible in debates over federalism.

2. The Constitution limited the power of the national government as a safeguard for liberty, but over the course of American history, a strong national government has been an important guarantor of liberty.

3. A key puzzle of federalism is deciding when differences across states represent the proper democratic decisions of the states and when such differences represent inequalities that should not be tolerated.

Practice Quiz

www.wwnorton.com/wtp5e   Keyword: Quiz 3

1. Which term describes the sharing of powers between the national government and the state governments?
   a) separation of powers
   b) federalism
   c) checks and balances
   d) shared powers

2. The system of federalism that allowed states to do most of the fundamental governing from 1789 to 1937 was
   a) home rule.
   b) regulated federalism.
   c) dual federalism.
   d) cooperative federalism.

3. Which of the following resulted from the federal system?
   a) It limited the power of the national government in relation to the states.
   b) It restrained the power of the national government over the economy.
   c) It allowed variation among the states.
   d) all of the above

4. The overall effect of the growth of national policies has been
   a) to weaken state government.
   b) to strengthen state government.
   c) to provide uniform laws in the nation.
   d) to make the states more diverse culturally.

5. Which amendment to the Constitution stated that the powers not delegated to the national government or prohibited to the states were "reserved to the states"?
   a) First Amendment
   b) Fifth Amendment
   c) Tenth Amendment
   d) Twenty-sixth Amendment

6. The process of returning more of the responsibilities of governing from the national level to the state level is known as
   a) dual federalism.
   b) devolution.
   c) preemption.
   d) home rule.

7. One of the most powerful tools by which the federal government has attempted to get the states to act in ways that are desired by the federal government is by
   a) providing grants-in-aid.
   b) requiring licensing.
   c) granting home rule.
   d) defending states' rights.

8. The form of regulated federalism that allows the federal government to take over areas of regulation formerly overseen by states or local governments is called
   a) categorical grants.
   b) formula grants.
   c) project grants.
   d) preemption.

9. To what does the term *New Federalism* refer?
   a) the national government's regulation of state action through grants-in-aid
   b) the type of federalism relying on categorical grants
   c) efforts to return more policy-making discretion to the states through the use of block grants
   d) the recent emergence of local governments as important political actors

10. A recent notable example of the process of giving the states more responsibility for administering government programs is
    a) campaign finance reform.
    b) prison reform.
    c) trade reform.
    d) welfare reform.

Key Terms

www.wwnorton.com/wtp5e

Keyword: Vocabulary 3

block grants (p. 103)
categorical grants (p. 98)
commerce clause (p. 90)
concurrent powers (p. 85)
cooperative federalism (p. 99)
devolution (p. 96)
dual federalism (p. 88)

expressed powers (p. 84)
federal system (p. 84)
federalism (p. 84)
formula grants (p. 99)
full faith and credit clause (p. 86)
general revenue sharing (p. 103)
grants-in-aid (p. 97)
home rule (p. 87)
implied powers (p. 84)
necessary and proper clause (p. 85)
New Federalism (p. 103)

police power (p. 85)
preemption (p. 101)
privileges and immunities clause (p. 86)
project grants (p. 99)
redistributive programs (p. 108)
regulated federalism (p. 101)
reserved powers (p. 85)
states' rights (p. 93)
unfunded mandates (p. 101)
unitary system (p. 84)

4 CIVIL LIBERTIES

What Government Does and Why It Matters

THE FIRST TEN AMENDMENTS of the United States Constitution, together called the **Bill of Rights,** are the basis for the freedoms we enjoy as American citizens. The Bill of Rights might well have been entitled the "Bill of Liberties," because the provisions that were incorporated in the Bill of Rights were seen as defining a private sphere of personal liberty, free of governmental restrictions. These freedoms include the right to free speech, the right to the free exercise of religion, prohibitions against unreasonable searches and seizures, guarantees of due process of law, and the right to privacy, including a woman's right to have an abortion.

As Jefferson put it, a bill of rights "is what people are entitled to against every government on earth. . . ." Note the emphasis—people *against* government. **Civil liberties** are *protections from* improper government action. Thus, the Bill of Rights is a series of "thou shalt nots"—restraints imposed upon government. Some of these restraints are **substantive liberties,** which put limits on *what* the government shall and shall not have power to do— such as establishing a religion, quartering troops in private homes without consent, or seizing private property without just compensation. Other restraints are **procedural liberties,** which deal with *how* the government is supposed to act. These procedural liberties are usually grouped under the general category of **due process of law,** which first appears in the Fifth Amendment provision that "no person shall be . . . deprived of life, liberty, or property, without due process of law." For example, even though the government has the substantive power to declare certain acts to be crimes and to arrest and imprison persons who violate criminal laws, it may not do so without meticulously observing procedures designed to protect the accused person. The best-known procedural rule is that an accused person is

Bill of Rights the first ten amendments to the Constitution, which guarantee certain rights and liberties to the people

civil liberties areas of personal freedom with which governments are constrained from interfering

substantive liberties restraints on what the government shall and shall not have the power to do

procedural liberties restraints on how the government is supposed to act; for example, citizens are guaranteed the due process of law

due process of law the right of every citizen against arbitrary action by national or state governments presumed innocent until proven guilty. This rule does not question the government's power to punish someone for committing a crime; it questions only the way the government determines who committed the crime. Substantive and procedural restraints together identify the realm of civil liberties.

Today, we may take the liberties contained within the Bill of Rights for granted. Few citizens of other countries can make such a claim. In fact, few people in recorded history have enjoyed such protections, including American citizens before the 1960s. For more than 170 years after its passage in 1789, the Bill of Rights meant little to most Americans. As we shall see in this chapter, guaranteeing the liberties articulated in the Bill of Rights to all Americans required a long struggle. As new challenges to the Bill of Rights arise, this struggle will likely continue.

As recently as the early 1960s, many of the freedoms we enjoy today were not guaranteed. At that time, abortion was illegal everywhere in the United States, criminal suspects in state cases did not have to be informed of their rights, some states required daily Bible readings and prayers in their public schools, and some communities regularly censored reading material that they deemed to be obscene. Since the early 1960s, the Supreme Court has expanded the scope of individual freedoms considerably. But since these liberties are constantly subject to judicial interpretation, their provisions are fragile and need to be vigilantly safeguarded, especially during times of war or a threat to national security, such as in the aftermath of September 11, 2001. ■

- **In this chapter, our first task is to define the Bill of Rights and establish its relationship to personal liberty.** As we shall see, it is through the Bill of Rights that Americans are protected from government.

- **We then turn to the process by which the Bill of Rights was applied, not only to the national government, but also to the state governments.** This nationalizing process has been long and selective in applying only certain provisions of the Bill of Rights.

■ **The bulk of this chapter is an analysis of the state of civil liberties today, beginning with the First Amendment and the freedom of religion.** Questions over the meaning of this First Amendment guarantee continue to be a focal point of judicial interpretation of the Bill of Rights.

■ **We then turn to the other First Amendment rights regarding the freedoms of speech and of the press.** Although freedom of speech and freedom of the press are critical for a democracy, some forms of speech are only conditionally protected.

■ **After briefly reviewing the Second Amendment right to bear arms, we move on to the rights of those accused of a crime.** These rights, contained in the Fourth, Fifth, Sixth, and Eighth Amendments, make up the due process of law, a concept that the Supreme Court continues to reinterpret.

■ **We then turn to a right that has become increasingly important in recent decades, the right to privacy.** This right takes many forms and, like the freedoms found directly in the Bill of Rights, has been subject to new judicial interpretations.

■ **We conclude by pondering the future of civil liberties in the United States.** As we emphasize throughout this chapter, the Bill of Rights is constantly subject to the interpretations of the Supreme Court. Will the Court try to limit the extent of civil liberties in the near future?

■ Previewing Liberty, Equality, and Democracy

Civil liberties require a delicate balance between governmental power and governmental restraint. The government must be kept in check, with severe limits on its powers; yet, at the same time, the government must be given enough power to defend liberty and its benefits from those who seek to deprive others of them. This chapter will explore how the status of civil liberties at any given time is a reflection of how that balance is being struck. We will also see how the Supreme Court, an undemocratic institution, is especially important in determining this balance. Civil liberties also reflect how well the democratic principle of majority rule with minority rights works. The rights enumerated in the Bill of Rights and enforced through the courts can provide an important check on the power of the majority.

A Brief History of the Bill of Rights

When the first Congress under the newly ratified Constitution met in late April of 1789, the most important item of business was the consideration of a proposal to add a bill of rights to the Constitution. Such a proposal had been turned down with little debate in the waning days of the Philadelphia Constitutional Convention in 1787, not because the delegates were against rights, but because, as the Federalists, led by Alexander Hamilton, later argued, it was "not only unnecessary in the proposed Constitution but would even be dangerous."[1]

Table 4.1 **Rights in the Original Constitution (Not in the Bill of Rights)**

CLAUSE	RIGHT ESTABLISHED
Article I, Sec. 9	guarantee of *habeas corpus*
Article I, Sec. 9	prohibition of **bills of attainder**
Article I, Sec. 9	prohibition of **ex post facto laws**
Article I, Sec. 9	prohibition against acceptance of titles of nobility, etc., from any foreign state
Article III	guarantee of trial by jury in state where crime was committed
Article III	treason defined and limited to the life of the person convicted, not to the person's heirs

bills of attainder laws that decree a person guilty of a crime without a trial

ex post facto laws laws that declare an action to be illegal after it has been committed

habeas corpus a court order demanding that an individual in custody be brought into court and shown the cause for detention

First, according to Hamilton, a bill of rights would be irrelevant to a national government that was given only delegated powers in the first place. To put restraints on "powers which are not granted" could provide a pretext for governments to claim more powers than were in fact granted: "For why declare that things shall not be done which there is no power to do?"[2] Second, the Constitution was to Hamilton and the Federalists a bill of rights in itself, or contained provisions that amounted to a bill of rights without requiring additional amendments (see Table 4.1). For example, Article I, Section 9, included the right of *habeas corpus,* which prohibits the government from depriving a person of liberty without an open trial before a judge.

Despite the power of Hamilton's arguments, when the Constitution was submitted to the states for ratification, Antifederalists, most of whom had not been delegates in Philadelphia, picked up on the argument of Thomas Jefferson (who also had not been a delegate) that the omission of a bill of rights was a major imperfection of the new Constitution. The Federalists conceded that in order to gain ratification they would have to make an "unwritten but unequivocal pledge" to add a bill of rights that would include a confirmation (in what became the Tenth Amendment) of the understanding that all powers not expressly delegated to the national government or explicitly prohibited to the states were reserved to the states.[3]

"After much discussion and manipulation . . . at the delicate prompting of Washington and under the masterful prodding of Madison," the House of Representatives adopted seventeen amendments; of these, the Senate adopted twelve. Ten of the amendments were ratified by the states on December 15, 1791; from the start these ten were called the Bill of Rights (see Box 4.1).[4]

NATIONALIZING THE BILL OF RIGHTS

The First Amendment provides that "Congress shall make no law . . ." But this is the only amendment in the Bill of Rights that addresses itself exclusively to the national government. For example, the Second Amendment provides that "the

Box 4.1

Amendment I: Limits on Congress

Congress cannot make any law establishing a religion or abridging freedoms of religious exercise, speech, assembly, or petition.

Amendments II, III, IV: Limits on the Executive

The executive branch cannot infringe on the right of the people to keep arms (II), cannot arbitrarily take houses for militia (III), and cannot search for or seize evidence without a court warrant swearing to the probable existence of a crime (IV).

Amendments V, VI, VII, VIII: Limits on the Judiciary

The courts cannot hold trials for serious offenses without provision for a grand jury (V), a trial jury (VII), a speedy trial (VI), presentation of charges and confrontation by the accused of hostile witnesses (VI), and immunity from testimony against oneself and immunity from trial more than once for the same offense (V). Furthermore, neither bail nor punishment can be excessive (VIII), and no property can be taken without "just compensation" (V).

Amendments IX, X: Limits on the National Government

Any rights not enumerated are reserved to the state or the people (X), but the enumeration of certain rights in the Constitution should not be interpreted to mean that those are the only rights the people have (IX).

right of the people to keep and bear Arms, shall not be infringed." And the Fifth Amendment says, among other things, that "no person shall . . . be twice put in jeopardy of life or limb" for the same crime. Since the First Amendment is the only part of the Bill of Rights that is explicit in its intention to put limits on Congress and therefore on the national government, a fundamental question inevitably arises: do the remaining provisions of the Bill of Rights put limits only on the national government, or do they limit the state governments as well?

The Supreme Court first answered this question in 1833 by ruling that the Bill of Rights limited only the national government and not the state governments.[5] But in 1868, when the Fourteenth Amendment was added to the Constitution, the question arose once again. The Fourteenth Amendment reads as if it were meant to impose the Bill of Rights upon the states:

> No *State* shall make or enforce any law which shall abridge the privileges or immunities of citizens of the United States; nor shall any *State* deprive any person of life, liberty, or property, without due process of law; nor deny to any person within its jurisdiction the equal protection of the laws [emphasis added].

This language sounds like an effort to extend the Bill of Rights in its entirety to all citizens, wherever they might reside.[6] Yet this was not the Supreme Court's interpretation of the amendment for nearly a hundred years. Within five years of ratification of the Fourteenth Amendment, the Court was making decisions as though the amendment had never been adopted.[7]

The only change in civil liberties during the first sixty years following the adoption of the Fourteenth Amendment came in 1897, when the Supreme Court held that the due process clause of the Fourteenth Amendment did in fact prohibit states from taking property for a public use without just compensation.[8] However, the Supreme Court had selectively "incorporated" into the Fourteenth Amendment only the property protection provision of the Fifth Amendment and no other clause of the Fifth or any other amendment of the Bill of Rights. In other words, although according to the Fifth Amendment "due process" applied to the taking of life and liberty as well as property, only property was incorporated into the Fourteenth Amendment as a limitation on state power.

No further expansion of civil liberties via the Fourteenth Amendment occurred until 1925, when the Supreme Court held that freedom of speech is "among the fundamental personal rights and 'liberties' protected by the due process clause of the Fourteenth Amendment from impairment by the states."[9] In 1931, the Court added freedom of the press to that short list protected by the Bill of Rights from state action; in 1939, it added freedom of assembly.[10]

But that was as far as the Court was willing to go. As late as 1937, the Supreme Court was still unwilling to nationalize civil liberties beyond the First Amendment. The Constitution, as interpreted as late as 1937 by the Supreme Court in *Palko v. Connecticut*, left standing the framework in which the states had the power to determine their own law on a number of fundamental issues. *Palko* established the principle of **selective incorporation,** by which the provisions of the Bill of Rights were to be considered one by one and selectively applied as limits on the states through the Fourteenth Amendment.[11] In order to make clear that "selective incorporation" should be narrowly interpreted, Justice Benjamin Cardozo, writing for an 8-to-1 majority, asserted that although many rights have value and importance, not all are of the same value and importance:

> [Not all rights are of] the very essence of a scheme of ordered liberty. To abolish them is not to violate a "principle of justice so rooted in the traditions and conscience of our people as to be ranked as fundamental." . . . What is true of jury trials and indictments is true also . . . of the immunity from compulsory self-incrimination [as in *Palko*]. . . . This too might be lost, and justice still be done. . . . If the Fourteenth Amendment has absorbed them [for example, freedom of thought and speech] the process of absorption has had its source in the belief that neither liberty nor justice would exist if they were sacrificed.

Palko left states with most of the powers they had possessed even before the adoption of the Fourteenth Amendment, including the power to pass laws segregating the races—a power in fact that the thirteen former Confederate states chose to continue to exercise on into the 1960s, despite *Brown v. Board of Education* in 1954. The constitutional framework also left states with the power to engage in searches and seizures without a warrant, to indict accused persons without a grand jury, to deprive accused persons of trial by jury, to deprive persons of their right not to have to testify against themselves, to deprive accused persons of their right to confront adverse witnesses, and to prosecute accused persons more than once for the same crime.[12] Few states chose to use these kinds of powers, but some states did, and the power to do so was available for any state whose legislative majority or courts so chose.

selective incorporation the process by which different protections in the Bill of Rights were incorporated into the Fourteenth Amendment, thus guaranteeing citizens protection from state as well as national governments

Incorporation of the Bill of Rights into the Fourteenth Amendment

Table 4.2

SELECTED PROVISIONS AND AMENDMENTS	NOT "INCORPORATED" UNTIL	KEY CASE
Eminent domain (V)	1897	*Chicago, Burlington, and Quincy R.R. v. Chicago*
Freedom of speech (I)	1925	*Gitlow v. New York*
Freedom of press (I)	1931	*Near v. Minnesota*
Free exercise of religion (I)	1934	*Hamilton v. Regents of the University of California*
Freedom of assembly (I)	1939	*Hague v. CIO*
Freedom from unnecessary search and seizure (IV)	1949	*Wolf v. Colorado*
Freedom from warrantless search and seizure (IV) ("exclusionary rule")	1961	*Mapp v. Ohio*
Freedom from cruel and unusual punishment (VIII)	1962	*Robinson v. California*
Right to counsel in any criminal trial (VI)	1963	*Gideon v. Wainwright*
Right against self-incrimination and forced confessions (V)	1964	*Mallory v. Hogan Escobedo v. Illinois*
Right to privacy (III, IV, & V)	1965	*Griswold v. Connecticut*
Right to remain silent (V)	1966	*Miranda v. Arizona*
Right against double jeopardy (V)	1969	*Benton v. Maryland*

So, until 1961, only the First Amendment and one clause of the Fifth Amendment had been clearly incorporated into the Fourteenth Amendment as binding on the states as well as on the national government.[13] After that, one by one, most of the important provisions of the Bill of Rights were incorporated into the Fourteenth Amendment and applied to the states. Table 4.2 shows the progress of this revolution in the interpretation of the Constitution.

But the controversy over incorporation lives on. Since liberty requires restraining the power of government, the general status of civil liberties can never be considered fixed and permanent. Every provision in the Bill of Rights is subject to interpretation, and in any dispute involving a clause of the Bill of Rights, interpretations will always be shaped by the interpreter's interest in the outcome. As we shall see, the Court continually reminds everyone that if it has the power to expand the Bill of Rights, it also has the power to contract it.[14]

The best way to examine the Bill of Rights today is the simplest way—to take the major provisions one at a time. Some of these provisions are settled areas of law, and others are not. Any one of them can be reinterpreted by the Court at any time.

The First Amendment and Freedom of Religion

> Congress shall make no law respecting an establishment of religion, or prohibiting the free exercise thereof; or abridging the freedom of speech, or of the press; or the right of the people peaceably to assemble, and to petition the Government for a redress of grievances.

The Bill of Rights begins by guaranteeing freedom, and the First Amendment provides for that freedom in two distinct clauses: "Congress shall make no law [1] respecting an establishment of religion, or [2] prohibiting the free exercise thereof." The first clause is called the "establishment clause," and the second is called the "free exercise clause."

SEPARATION BETWEEN CHURCH AND STATE

establishment clause the First Amendment clause that says that "Congress shall make no law respecting an establishment of religion." This law means that a "wall of separation" exists between church and state

The **establishment clause** has been interpreted quite strictly to mean that a virtual "wall of separation" exists between church and state. The separation of church and state was especially important to the great numbers of American colonists who had sought refuge from persecution for having rejected membership in state-sponsored churches. The concept of a "wall of separation" was Jefferson's own formulation, and this concept has figured in all of the modern Supreme Court cases arising under the establishment clause.

Despite the absolute sound of the phrase "wall of separation," there is ample room to disagree on how high the wall is or of what materials it is composed. For example, the Court has been consistently strict in cases of school prayer, striking down such practices as Bible reading,[15] nondenominational prayer,[16] a moment of silence for meditation, and pre-game prayer at public sporting events.[17] In each of these cases, the Court reasoned that school-sponsored observations, even of an apparently nondenominational character, are highly suggestive of school sponsorship and therefore violate the prohibition against establishment of religion. On the other hand, the Court has been quite permissive (and some would say inconsistent) about the public display of religious symbols, such as city-sponsored Nativity scenes in commercial or municipal areas.[18] And although the Court has consistently disapproved of government financial support for religious schools, even when the purpose has been purely educational and secular, the Court has permitted certain direct aid to students of such schools in the form of busing, for example. In 1971, after thirty years of cases involving religious schools, the Court attempted to specify some criteria to guide its decisions and those of lower courts, indicating, for example, in a decision invalidating state payments for the teaching of secular subjects in parochial schools, circumstances under which the Court might allow certain financial assistance. The case was *Lemon v. Kurtzman;* in its decision, the Supreme Court established three criteria to guide future cases, in what came to be called the **Lemon test.** The Court held that government aid to religious schools would be accepted as constitutional if (1) it had a secular purpose, (2) its effect was neither to advance nor to inhibit religion, and (3) it did not entangle government and religious institutions in each other's affairs.[19]

Lemon test a rule articulated in *Lemon v. Kurtzman* that government action toward religion is permissible if it is secular in purpose, does not lead to "excessive entanglement" with religion, and neither promotes nor inhibits the practice of religion

Although these restrictions make the *Lemon* test a hard test to pass, imaginative authorities are finding ways to do so, and the Supreme Court has demonstrated a

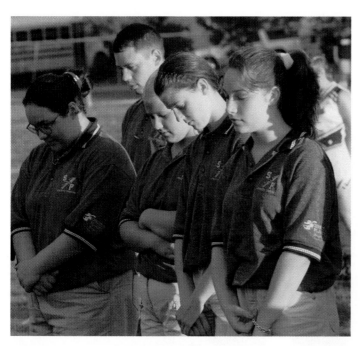

The First Amendment affects everyday life in a multitude of ways. Because of its ban on state-sanctioned religion, the Supreme Court ruled in 2000 that student-initiated public prayer at school is illegal. Pre-game prayer at public schools violates the establishment clause of the First Amendment.

willingness to let them. For example, in 1995, the Court narrowly ruled that a student religious group at the University of Virginia could not be denied student activities funds merely because it was a religious group espousing a particular viewpoint about a deity. The Court called the denial "viewpoint discrimination" that violated the free speech rights of the group.[20] This led two years later to a new, more conservative approach to the "separation of church and state." In 1997, the Court accepted the practice of sending public school teachers into parochial (religious) schools to provide remedial education to disadvantaged children.[21]

More recently, the establishment clause has been put under pressure by the school voucher and charter school movements. Vouchers financed by public revenues are supporting student tuitions at religious schools, where common prayer and religious instruction are known parts of the curriculum. In addition, many financially needy church schools are actively recruiting students with tax-supported vouchers, considering them an essential source of revenue to keep their schools operating. In both these respects, vouchers and charter schools are creating the impression that public support is aiding the establishment of religion.[22] Yet the Supreme Court has refused to rule on the constitutionality of these programs.

In 2004, the question of whether the phrase "under God" in the Pledge of Allegiance violates the "establishment clause" was brought before the Court. Written in 1892, the Pledge had been used in schools without any religious references. But in

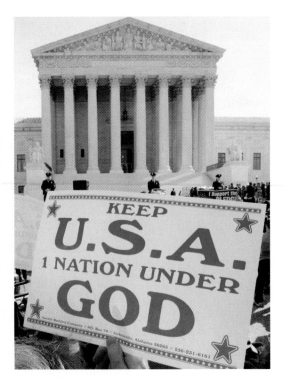

Despite the establishment clause, the United States still uses the motto "In God we trust" and calls itself "one nation, under God." This South Carolina license plate was introduced in 2002. But such displays of religious patriotism are not universally accepted. Michael Newdow (pictured) filed suit against his daughter's school district because the Pledge of Allegiance refers to God. Newdow was publicly reviled and received phone threats. As the Supreme Court prepared to decide whether the Pledge of Allegiance would remain intact, demonstrators stood outside the courthouse and repeatedly recited the pledge, emphasizing the words "under God." At the time of the case, one public-opinion poll found that 87 percent of Americans favored keeping the two words in the pledge. The Court ultimately found that Newdow did not have a sufficient personal stake in the case, and so "under God" was left in.

FOR CRITICAL ANALYSIS

Do you think that the daily recital of the Pledge of Allegiance in public schools represents an unconstitutional violation of the separation of church and state clause of the First Amendment? If another case is presented before the Supreme Court, how do you think the court will decide?

1954, in the midst of the Cold War, Congress voted to change the Pledge, in response to the "godless Communism" of the Soviet Union. The conversion was made by adding two key words, so that the revised version read: "I pledge allegiance to the flag of the United States of America and to the Republic for which it stands, one nation *under God,* indivisible, with liberty and justice for all."

Ever since the change was made, there has been a consistent murmuring of discontent from those who object to an officially sanctioned profession of belief in a deity as a violation of the religious freedom clause of the First Amendment. When saying the pledge, those who object to the phrase have often simply stayed silent during the two key words and then resumed for the rest of the Pledge. In 2003, Michael A. Newdow, the atheist father of a kindergarten student in a California elementary school, forced the issue to the surface when he brought suit against the local school district. Newdow argued that the reference to God turned the daily recitation of the pledge into a religious exercise. A federal court ruled that although students were not required to recite the Pledge at all, having to stand and listen to "under God" still violated the First Amendment's "establishment clause." The case was appealed to the Supreme Court and on June 14, 2004—exactly fifty years to the day after the adoption of "under God" in the pledge—the Court ruled that Newdow lacked a sufficient personal stake in the case to bring the complaint. This inconclusive decision by the Supreme Court left "under God" in the Pledge while keeping the issue alive for possible resolution in a future case.

FREE EXERCISE OF RELIGION

The **free exercise clause** protects the right to believe and to practice whatever religion one chooses; it also protects the right to be a nonbeliever. The precedent-setting case involving free exercise is *West Virginia State Board of Education v. Barnette* (1943), which involved the children of a family of Jehovah's Witnesses who refused to salute and pledge allegiance to the American flag on the grounds that their religious faith did not permit it. Three years earlier, the Court had upheld such a requirement and had permitted schools to expel students for refusing to salute the flag. But the entry of the United States into a war to defend democracy coupled with the ugly treatment to which the Jehovah's Witnesses' children had been subjected induced the Court to reverse itself and to endorse the free exercise of religion even when it may be offensive to the beliefs of the majority.[23]

free exercise clause the First Amendment clause that protects a citizen's right to believe and practice whatever religion he or she chooses

Although the Supreme Court has been fairly consistent and strict in protecting the free exercise of religious belief, it has taken pains to distinguish between religious beliefs and *actions* based on those beliefs. In one case, for example, two Native Americans had been fired from their jobs for smoking peyote, an illegal drug. They claimed that they had been fired from their jobs illegally because smoking peyote was a religious sacrament protected by the free exercise clause. The Court disagreed with their claim in an important 1990 decision,[24] but Congress supported the claim and it went on to engage in an unusual controversy with the Court, involving the separation of powers as well as the proper application of the separation of church and state. Congress literally reversed the Court's 1990 decision with the enactment of the Religious Freedom Restoration Act of 1993 (RFRA), forbidding any federal agency or state government from restricting a person's free exercise of religion unless the federal agency or state government demonstrates that its action "furthers a compelling government interest" and "is the least restrictive means of furthering that compelling governmental interest." One of the first applications of the RFRA was to a case brought by St. Peter's Catholic Church against the city of Boerne, Texas, which had denied permission to the church to enlarge its building because the building had been declared an historic landmark. The case went to federal court on the argument that the city had violated the church's religious freedom as guaranteed by Congress in RFRA. The Supreme Court declared RFRA unconstitutional, but on grounds rarely utilized, if not unique to this case: Congress had violated the separation of powers principle, infringing on the powers of the judiciary by going so far beyond its law making powers that it ended up actually expanding the scope of religious rights

Should Religious Freedom Be a Foreign Policy?

In 1917, President Woodrow Wilson proclaimed that America's purpose in entering World War I was "to make the world safe for democracy." This doctrine was translated into "self-determination"—a policy of partitioning former colonial territories and dependencies into new nation-states by drawing boundaries around recognized ethnic, religious, and "ethno-religious" groupings. Although admirable in theory, the Wilsonian policy of building new states on voluntary or imposed ethno-religious segregation was an initial solution to demands for statehood that proved a disaster for human rights. When a single religious orthodoxy rules the state, pluralism and religious freedom go out the window. This is a principal—possibly *the* principal—reason that there has been so little democracy or religious freedom in the countries stretching from the Balkans to Indonesia.

As Americans should have learned from their experience with the suppression and expulsion of religious dissenters, genuine religious liberty requires constitutions and laws, along with a nonsectarian government steadfastly committed to tolerance of all religious faiths and to policies that protect every sect in regard to its religious observances. One of the principal objectives of U.S. foreign policy with regard to the establishment of the United Nations was to have an international institution in which human rights could be advanced and egregious violations of established principles of human rights would be identified, exposed, and, to the extent possible, eliminated. This policy was ultimately implemented by inclusion of two early amendments to the UN Charter considered paramount to freedom of thought, conscience, and religion": the Genocide Convention and the Universal Declaration of Human Rights. And Congress has given some administrative clout to these principles by establishing a Bureau of Democracy, Human Rights and Labor in the State Department, dedicated to "elimination of all forms of intolerance and of discrimination based on religion or beliefs." This bureau has identified and exposed those regimes "hostile to minority or 'unapproved' religions" and has defined as "a particular problem" the countries of Central Asia, East Asia, and the Middle East. The current Bush administration added to the bureau an Office of International Religious

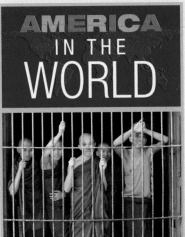

Freedom, giving it authority to oppose regimes that discriminate against minority religions in their country. The most extreme cases identified by the bureau in 2003 were (moving from the most to the least extreme) Burma [Myanmar], China, Cuba, Laos, North Korea, Vietnam, Iran, Iraq, Pakistan, Saudi Arabia, Sudan, Turkistan, and Uzbekistan. Various other states and their regimes are ranked at a somewhat lower level of misconduct toward religious minorities. The nature, extent, and character of the suppression and discrimination in all of these regimes are identified in fairly vivid detail.[a]

Exposure is a far cry from direct intervention, but expressions of disapproval of and moral revulsion against guilty regimes contribute to the strengthening of the moral conscience of the world and provide justification for international humanitarian intervention against the most extreme acts of state-sponsored mass expulsion or genocide—as has already been taken against "ethnic cleansing" in the Balkans, genocide by chemical and germ warfare in Iraq against the Kurds, and the Taliban regime in Afghanistan. Actually, there may now be a problem the other way around—the tendency to go too far, using human rights violations as a provocation or a pretext for "regime change" and "state building." Nevertheless, the dictators of the world have at last been put on notice that civilized nations will no longer tolerate policies of religious suppression and ethnic cleansing.

FOR CRITICAL ANALYSIS

1. In its foreign policies with Islamic states, what policies can the United States adopt to foster religious tolerance and freedom without destabilizing the region?

2. Should the U.S. ignore religious intolerance in other countries or actively combat it? If the latter, should humanitarian intervention be considered? If so, should the United States go it alone or involve other countries as allies?

[a]Source: U.S. Department of State, 2003 Executive Summary, International Religious Freedom Report, of the Bureau of Democracy, Human Rights and Labor, http://www.state.gov/g/drl/rls/irf.

rather than just enforcing them. The Court thereby implied that questions requiring a balancing of religious claims against public policy claims were reserved strictly to the judiciary.[25]

The *City of Boerne* case did settle some matters of constitutional controversy over the religious exercise and the establishment clauses of the First Amendment but left a lot more unsettled. What about polygamy, a practice allowed in the Mormon faith? What about snake worship? Or the refusal of Amish parents to send their children to school beyond eighth grade because exposing their children to "modern values" would undermine their religious commitment? In this last example, the Court decided in favor of the Amish and endorsed a very strong interpretation of the protection of free exercise.[26]

The First Amendment and Freedom of Speech and the Press

Congress shall make no law . . . abridging the freedom of speech, or of the press. . . .

Because democracy depends upon an open political process and because politics is basically talk, freedom of speech and freedom of the press are considered critical. For this reason, they were given a prominence in the Bill of Rights equal to that of freedom of religion. In 1938, freedom of speech (which in all important respects includes freedom of the press) was given extraordinary constitutional status when the Supreme Court established that any legislation that attempts to restrict these fundamental freedoms "is to be subjected to a more exacting judicial scrutiny . . . than are most other types of legislation."[27]

What the Court was saying is that the democratic political process must be protected at almost any cost. This higher standard of judicial review came to be called **strict scrutiny**. Strict scrutiny implies that speech—at least some kinds of speech—will be protected almost absolutely. But as it turns out, only some types of speech are fully protected against restrictions (see Figure 4.1). As we shall see, many forms of speech are less than absolutely protected—even though they are entitled to strict scrutiny. This section will look at these two categories of speech: (1) absolutely protected speech and (2) conditionally protected speech.

strict scrutiny test, used by the Supreme Court in racial discrimination cases and other cases involving civil liberties and civil rights, which places the burden of proof on the government rather than on the challengers to show that the law in question is constitutional

ABSOLUTELY PROTECTED SPEECH

There is one and only one absolute defense against efforts to place limitations on speech, oral or in print: the truth. The truth is protected even when its expression damages the person to whom it applies. And of all forms of speech, political speech is the most consistently protected.

Political Speech   Political speech was the activity of greatest concern to the framers of the Constitution, even though they found it the most difficult provision to observe. Within seven years of the ratification of the Bill of Rights in 1791, Congress adopted the infamous Alien and Sedition Acts, which, among other things, made it a crime to say or publish anything that might tend to defame or bring into disrepute the government of the United States. Quite clearly, the acts' intentions were to criminalize the very conduct given absolute protection by the First Amendment (see also

Figure 4.1   The Protection of Free Speech by the First Amendment

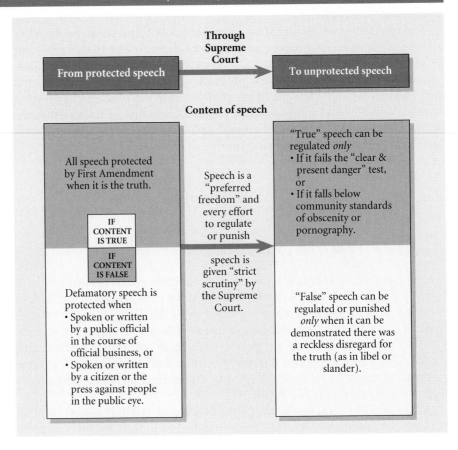

Chapter 9). Fifteen violators—including several newspaper editors—were indicted, and a few were actually convicted before the relevant portions of the acts were allowed to expire.

The first modern free speech case arose immediately after World War I. It involved persons who had been convicted under the federal Espionage Act of 1917 for opposing U.S. involvement in the war. The Supreme Court upheld the Espionage Act and refused to protect the speech rights of the defendants on the grounds that their activities—appeals to draftees to resist the draft—constituted a **"clear and present danger"** to security.[28] This is the first and most famous "test" for when government intervention or censorship could be permitted.

It was only after the 1920s that real progress toward a genuinely effective First Amendment was made. Since then, political speech has been consistently protected by the courts even when it has been deemed "insulting" or "outrageous." Here is the way the Supreme Court put it in one of its most important statements on the subject:

"clear and present danger" test
test to determine whether speech is protected or unprotected, based on its capacity to present a "clear and present danger" to society

The constitutional guarantees of free speech and free press do not permit a State to forbid or proscribe advocacy of the use of force or of law violation *except where such advocacy is directed to inciting or producing imminent lawless action and is likely to incite or produce such action* [emphasis added].[29]

This statement was made in the case of a Ku Klux Klan leader, Charles Brandenburg, who had been arrested and convicted of advocating "revengent" action against the president, Congress, and the Supreme Court, among others, if they continued "to suppress the white, Caucasian race. . . ." Although Brandenburg was not carrying a weapon, some of the members of his audience were. Nevertheless, the Supreme Court reversed the state courts and freed Brandenburg while also declaring Ohio's Criminal Syndicalism Act unconstitutional because it punished persons who "advocate, or teach the duty, necessity, or propriety [of violence] as a means of accomplishing industrial or political reform . . ."; or who publish materials or "voluntarily assemble . . . to teach or advocate the doctrines of criminal syndicalism." The Supreme Court argued that the statute did not distinguish "mere advocacy" from "incitement to imminent lawless action." It would be difficult to go much further in protecting freedom of speech.

Another area of recent expansion of political speech—the participation of wealthy persons and corporations in political campaigns—was opened up in 1976, with the Supreme Court's decision in *Buckley v. Valeo*. Campaign finance reform laws of the early 1970s, arising out of the Watergate scandal, sought to put severe limits on campaign spending, and a number of important provisions were declared unconstitutional on the basis of a new principle that spending money by or on behalf of candidates is a form of speech protected by the First Amendment. (For more details, see Chapter 10.) The issue came up again in 2003, with passage of a new and still more severe campaign finance law, the McCain-Feingold Campaign Reform Act. In *McConnell v. FEC* (Federal Election Commission), the five-four majority seriously reduced the area of speech protected by the *Buckley v. Valeo* decision by holding that Congress was well within its power to put limits on the amounts individuals could spend, plus severe limits on the amounts of "soft money" that could be spent by corporations and their PACs. The Court argued that "the selling of access . . . has given rise to the appearance of undue influence [that justifies] regulations impinging on First Amendment rights . . . in order to curb corruption or the appearance of corruption." [30]

Symbolic Speech, Speech Plus, and the Rights of Assembly and Petition   The First Amendment treats the freedoms of assembly and petition as equal to the freedoms of religion and political speech. Freedom of assembly and freedom of petition are closely associated with speech but go beyond it to speech associated with action. Since at least 1931, the Supreme Court has sought to protect actions that are designed to send a political message. (Usually the purpose of a symbolic act is not only to send a direct message but to draw a crowd—to do something spectacular in order to draw spectators to the action and thus strengthen the message.) Thus the Court held unconstitutional a California statute making it a felony to display a red flag "as a sign, symbol or emblem of opposition to organized government."[31] Although today there are limits on how far one can go with actions that symbolically convey a message, the protection of such action is very broad. Thus, although the Court upheld a federal statute making it a crime to burn draft cards to protest the Vietnam War on the grounds that the government had a compelling interest in preserving draft cards as part of the conduct of the war itself, it considered the wearing of black armbands to school a protected form of assembly for symbolic action.

Another example is the burning of the American flag as a symbol of protest. In 1984, at a political rally held during the Republican National Convention in Dallas, Texas, a political protester burned an American flag in violation of a Texas statute that prohibited desecration of a venerated object. In a 5-to-4 decision, the Supreme Court declared the Texas law unconstitutional on the grounds that flag burning was expressive conduct protected by the First Amendment.[32] Congress reacted immediately with a proposal for a constitutional amendment reversing the Court's Texas decision, and when the amendment failed to receive the necessary two-thirds majority in the Senate, Congress passed the Flag Protection Act of 1989. Protesters promptly violated this act and their prosecution moved quickly into the federal district court, which declared the new law unconstitutional. The Supreme Court, in another 5-to-4 decision, affirmed the lower court decision.[33] A renewed effort began in Congress to propose a constitutional amendment that would reverse the Supreme Court and place this form of expressive conduct outside the realm of protected speech or assembly. Since 1995, the House of Representatives has four times passed a resolution for a constitutional amendment to ban flag burning, but each time the Senate has failed to go along.[34] Further effort in Congress was probably killed by the Supreme Court's 2003 decision striking down a Virginia cross-burning statute. In that case, the Court ruled that states could make cross-burning a crime as long as the statute requires prosecutors to prove that the act of setting fire to the cross was intended to intimidate. Justice Sandra Day O'Connor wrote for the majority that the First Amendment permits the government to forbid cross-burning as a "particularly virulent form of intimidation" but not when the act was "a form of symbolic expression."[35] This decision will almost inevitably become a more generalized First Amendment protection of any conduct, including flag burning, that can be shown to be a form of symbolic expression.

Closer to the original intent of the assembly and petition clause is the category of **"speech plus"**—following speech with physical activity such as picketing, distributing leaflets, and other forms of peaceful demonstration or assembly. Such assemblies are consistently protected by courts under the First Amendment; state and local laws regulating such activities are closely scrutinized and frequently overturned. But the same assembly on private property is quite another matter and can in many circumstances be regulated. For example, the directors of a shopping center can lawfully prohibit an assembly protesting a war or supporting a ban on abortion. Assemblies in public areas can also be restricted under some circumstances, especially when the assembly or demonstration jeopardizes the health, safety, or rights of others. This condition was the basis of the Supreme Court's decision to uphold a lower court order that restricted the access abortion protesters had to the entrances of abortion clinics.[36]

speech plus speech accompanied by conduct such as sit-ins, picketing, and demonstrations; protection of this form of speech under the First Amendment is conditional, and restrictions imposed by state or local authorities are acceptable if properly balanced by considerations of public order

FREEDOM OF THE PRESS

For all practical purposes, freedom of speech implies and includes freedom of the press. With the exception of the broadcast media, which are subject to federal regulation, the press is protected under the doctrine against **prior restraint.** Beginning with the landmark 1931 case of *Near v. Minnesota,* the U.S. Supreme Court has held that, except under the most extraordinary circumstances, the First Amendment of the Constitution prohibits government agencies from seeking to prevent newspapers or magazines from publishing whatever they wish.[37] Indeed, in the case of *New York Times v. U.S.,* the so-called *Pentagon Papers* case, the Supreme Court ruled that the government could not even block publication of secret Defense Department documents furnished to the *New York Times* by an opponent of the Vietnam War who had obtained the documents illegally.[38] In a 1990 case, however, the Supreme Court upheld a lower-court order restraining Cable News Network (CNN) from broadcasting tapes of conversations between former Panamanian dictator Manuel Noriega and his lawyer, supposedly recorded by the U.S. government. By a vote of 7 to 2, the Court held that CNN could be restrained from broadcasting the tapes until the trial court in the Noriega case had listened to the tapes and had decided whether their broadcast would violate Noriega's right to a fair trial.

prior restraint an effort by a governmental agency to block the publication of material it deems libelous or harmful in some other way; censorship. In the United States, the courts forbid prior restraint except under the most extraordinary circumstances

CONDITIONALLY PROTECTED SPEECH

At least four forms of speech fall outside the absolute guarantees of the First Amendment and therefore outside the realm of absolute protection. Since they do enjoy some protection, they qualify as "conditionally protected" types of speech: (1) libel and slander, (2) obscenity and pornography, (3) fighting words, and (4) commercial speech. It should be emphasized once again that these four types of speech still enjoy considerable protection by the courts.

Libel and Slander Some speech is not protected at all. If a written statement is made in "reckless disregard of the truth" and is considered damaging to the victim because it is "malicious, scandalous, and defamatory," it can be punished as **libel.** If an oral statement of such nature is made, it can be punished as **slander.**

Today, most libel suits involve freedom of the press, and the realm of free press is enormous. Historically, newspapers were subject to the law of libel, which provided that newspapers that printed false and malicious stories could be compelled to pay damages to those they defamed. In recent years, however, American courts have greatly narrowed the meaning of libel and made it extremely difficult, particularly for politicians or other public figures, to win a libel case against a newspaper. In the important 1964 case of *New York Times v. Sullivan,* the Court held that to be deemed libelous a story about a public official not only had to be untrue, but also had to result from "actual malice" or "reckless disregard" for the truth.[39] In other words, the newspaper had to *deliberately* print false and malicious material. In practice, it is nearly impossible to prove that a paper deliberately printed maliciously false information, and it is especially difficult for a politician or other public figure to win a libel case. Essentially, the print media have been able to publish anything they want about a public figure.

However, in at least one recent case, the Court has opened up the possibility for public officials to file libel suits against the press. In 1985, the Court held that the press was immune from libel only when the printed material was "a matter of public concern." In other words, in future cases a newspaper would have to show

libel a written statement made in "reckless disregard of the truth" that is considered damaging to a victim because it is "malicious, scandalous, and defamatory"

slander an oral statement, made in "reckless disregard of the truth," which is considered damaging to the victim because it is "malicious, scandalous, and defamatory" that the public official was engaged in activities that were indeed *public*. This new principle has made the press more vulnerable to libel suits, but it still leaves an enormous realm of freedom for the press. For example, Reverend Jerry Falwell, the leader of the Moral Majority, lost his libel suit against *Hustler* magazine even though the magazine had published a cartoon of Falwell showing him having drunken intercourse with his mother in an outhouse. A unanimous Supreme Court rejected a jury verdict in favor of damages for "emotional distress" on the grounds that parodies, no matter how outrageous, are protected because "outrageousness" is too subjective a test and thus would interfere with the free flow of ideas protected by the First Amendment.[40]

Obscenity and Pornography   If libel and slander cases can be difficult because of the problem of determining the truth of statements and whether those statements are malicious and damaging, cases involving pornography and obscenity can be even more sticky. It is easy to say that pornography and obscenity fall outside the realm of protected speech, but it is impossible to draw a clear line defining exactly where protection ends and unprotected speech begins. Not until 1957 did the Supreme Court confront this problem, and it did so with a definition of obscenity that may have caused more confusion than it cleared up. Justice William Brennan, in writing the Court's opinion, defined obscenity as speech or writing that appeals to the "prurient interest"—that is, books, magazines, films, and other material whose purpose is to excite lust as this appears "to the average person, applying contemporary community standards. . . ." Even so, Brennan added, the work should be judged obscene only when it is "utterly without redeeming social importance."[41] Brennan's definition, instead of clarifying the Court's view, actually caused more confusion. In 1964, Justice Potter Stewart confessed that, although he found pornography impossible to define, "I know it when I see it."[42]

All attempts by the courts to define pornography and obscenity have proved impractical, because each instance required courts to screen thousands of pages of print material and feet of film alleged to be pornographic. The vague and impractical standards that had been developed meant ultimately that almost nothing could be banned on the grounds that it was pornographic and obscene. An effort was made to strengthen the restrictions in 1973, when the Supreme Court expressed its willingness to define pornography as a work that (1) as a whole, is deemed prurient by the "average person" according to "community standards"; (2) depicts sexual conduct "in a patently offensive way"; and (3) lacks "serious literary, artistic, political, or scientific value." This definition meant that pornography would be determined by local rather than national standards. Thus, a local bookseller might be prosecuted for selling a volume that was a best-seller nationally but that was deemed pornographic locally.[43] This new definition of standards did not help much either, and not long after 1973 the Court began again to review all such community antipornography laws, reversing most of them.

Consequently, today there is a widespread fear that Americans are free to publish any and all variety of intellectual expression, whether there is any "redeeming social value" or not. Yet this area of free speech is far from settled.

In recent years, the battle against obscene speech has been against "cyberporn"—pornography on the Internet. Opponents of this form of expression argue that it should be banned because of the easy access children have to the Internet.

The first major effort to regulate the content of the Internet occurred on February 1, 1996, when the 104th Congress passed major telecommunications legislation. Attached to the Telecommunications Act was an amendment, called the Communications Decency Act (CDA), that was designed to regulate the online transmission of obscene material. The constitutionality of the CDA was immediately challenged in court by a coalition of interests led by the ACLU. In the 1997 Supreme Court case of *Reno v. ACLU,* the Court struck down the CDA, ruling that it suppressed speech that "adults have a constitutional right to receive" and that governments may not limit the adult population to messages that are fit for children. Supreme Court Justice John Paul Stevens described the Internet as the "town crier" of the modern age and said that the Internet was entitled to the greatest degree of First Amendment protection possible.[44] Congress again tried limiting children's access to Internet pornography, with the 2001 Children's Internet Protection Act, which required public libraries to install antipornography filters on all library computers with Internet access. Though the act made cooperation a condition for receiving federal subsidies, it did permit librarians to unblock a site at the request of an adult patron. The law was challenged, and in 2003 the Court upheld it, asserting that its provisions did not violate library patrons' First Amendment rights.[45]

In 2000, the Supreme Court also extended the highest degree of First Amendment protection to cable (not broadcast) television. In *U.S. v. Playboy Entertainment Group,* the Court struck down a portion of the Telecommunications Act of 1996 that required cable TV companies to limit the broadcast of sexually explicit programming to late night hours. In its decision, the Court noted that the law already provided parents with the means to restrict access to sexually explicit cable channels through various blocking devices. Moreover, such programming could come into the home only if parents decided to purchase such channels in the first place.

Fighting Words   Speech can also lose its protected position when it moves toward the sphere of action. "Expressive speech," for example, is protected until it moves from the symbolic realm to the realm of actual conduct—to direct incitement of damaging conduct with the use of so-called **fighting words.** In 1942, the Supreme Court upheld the arrest and conviction of a man who had violated a state law forbidding the use of offensive language in public. He had called the arresting officer a "goddamned racketeer" and "a damn Fascist." When his case reached the Supreme Court, the arrest was upheld on the grounds that the First Amendment provides no protection for such offensive language because such words "are no essential part of any exposition of ideas."[46] This case was reaffirmed in a much more famous and important case decided at the height of the Cold War, when the Supreme Court held that "there is no substantial public interest in permitting certain kinds of utterances: the lewd and obscene, the profane, the libelous, and the insulting or 'fighting' words—those which by their very utterance inflict injury or tend to incite an immediate breach of the peace."[47]

fighting words speech that directly incites damaging conduct

Since that time, however, the Supreme Court has reversed almost every conviction based on arguments that the speaker had used "fighting words." But again, that does not mean that this is an absolutely settled area. In recent years, the increased activism of minority and women's groups has prompted a movement against words that might be construed as offensive to members of a particular group. This movement has come to be called, derisively, "political correctness" or "pc." In response to this movement, many organizations have attempted to impose codes of

Banned Books

One of the more visible issues of free speech in recent years has been the banning of books in public schools. Following is a list of the most-censored books of 2003, with the reasons they were banned:

1. *Alice* series, Phyllis Reynolds Naylor: sexually explicit, offensive language, and unsuited to age group
2. *Harry Potter* series, J. K. Rowling: wizardry and magic
3. *Of Mice and Men*, John Steinbeck: offensive language and unsuited to age group
4. *Arming America: The Origins of a National Gun*, Michael A. Bellesiles: inaccuracy
5. *Fallen Angels*, Walter Dean Myers: offensive language and unsuited to age group
6. *Go Ask Alice*, Anonymous: sexually explicit, offensive language, and drug use
7. *It's Perfectly Normal*, Robie Harris: homosexuality, nudity, sexual content, and sex education
8. *We All Fall Down*, Robert Cormier: offensive language and sexual content
9. *King and King*, Linda de Haan: homosexuality.
10. *Bridge to Terabithia*, Katherine Paterson: offensive language and occult/satanism

SOURCE: American Library Association

etiquette that acknowledge these enhanced sensitivities. These efforts to formalize the restraints on the use of certain words in public are causing great concern over their possible infringement of freedom of speech. But how should we determine what words are "fighting words" that fall outside the protections of the freedom of speech?

One category of conditionally protected speech is the free speech of high school students in public schools. In 1986, the Supreme Court backed away from a broad protection of student free-speech rights by upholding the punishment of a high school student for making sexually suggestive speech. The Court opinion held that such speech interfered with the school's goal of teaching students the limits of socially acceptable behavior.[48] Two years later, the Supreme Court took another conservative step and restricted student speech and press rights even further by defining them as part of the educational process not to be treated with the same standard as adult speech in a regular public forum.[49]

In addition, scores of universities have attempted to develop speech codes to suppress utterances deemed to be racial or ethnic slurs. What these universities find, however, is that the codes produce more problems than they solve. The University of Pennsylvania learned this when it first tried to apply its newly written "Harassment Code." Around midnight in January of 1993, Eden Jacobowitz and several other students trying to study yelled from their dorm windows at a noisy group of partying black sorority members: "Shut up, you water buffaloes." Other students also made rude comments, including racial and sexual slurs, but Jacobowitz was the only one who actually came forward and admitted to having yelled. Born in Israel and fluent in Hebrew, Jacobowitz explained that "water buffalo" loosely translated from Hebrew means "rude person." Nevertheless, the University of Pennsylvania brought Jacobowitz before a campus judicial inquiry board and charged him with racial harassment in violation of the new code. The black women at whom he had yelled also brought civil charges of racial harassment against Jacobowitz. Five months after the incident, all charges were dropped—both the civil charges and those brought by the university. After reviewing the matter, Penn officials confessed that the university's harassment code "contained flaws which could not withstand the stress of intense publicity and international attention."[50]

Such concerns are not limited to universities, although universities have probably moved furthest toward efforts to formalize "politically correct" speech guidelines. Similar developments have taken place in large corporations, both public and private, in which many successful complaints and lawsuits have been brought, alleging that the words of employers or their supervisors create a "hostile or abusive working environment." These cases arise out of the civil rights laws and will be addressed in more detail in Chapter 5. The Supreme Court has held that "sexual harassment" that creates a "hostile working environment" includes "unwelcome sexual advances, requests for sexual favors, and other *verbal* or physical conduct of a sexual nature" (emphasis added).[51] There is a fundamental free speech issue involved in these regulations of hostile speech. So far, the assumption favoring the regulation of hostile speech in universities and other workplaces is that "some speech must be shut down in the name of free speech because it tends to silence those disparaged by it,"[52] even though a threat of hostile action (usually embodied in "fighting words") is not present. The United States is on something of a collision course between the right to express hostile views and the protection of the sensitivities of minorities and women. The collisions will end up in the courts, but not before a lot more airing in public and balancing efforts by state legislatures and Congress.

Commercial Speech   Commercial speech, such as newspaper or television advertisements, does not have full First Amendment protection because it cannot be considered political speech. Initially considered to be entirely outside the protection of the First Amendment, commercial speech has made gains during the twentieth century. Some commercial speech is still unprotected and therefore regulated. For example, the regulation of false and misleading advertising by the Federal Trade Commission is an old and well-established power of the federal government. The Supreme Court long ago approved the constitutionality of laws prohibiting the electronic media from carrying cigarette advertising.[53] The Court has upheld a state university ban on Tupperware parties in college dormitories.[54] It has upheld city ordinances prohibiting the posting of all signs on public property (as long as the ban is total, so that there is no hint of censorship).[55] And the Supreme Court, in a heated 5-to-4 decision written by Chief Justice William Rehnquist, upheld Puerto Rico's statute restricting gambling advertising aimed at residents of Puerto Rico.[56]

However, the gains far outweigh the losses in the effort to expand the protection commercial speech enjoys under the First Amendment. "In part, this reflects the growing appreciation that commercial speech is part of the free flow of information necessary for informed choice and democratic participation."[57] For example, the Court in 1975 struck down a state statute making it a misdemeanor to sell or circulate newspapers encouraging abortions; the Court ruled that the statute infringed upon constitutionally protected speech and upon the right of the reader to make informed choices.[58] On a similar basis, the Court reversed its own earlier decisions upholding laws that prohibited dentists and other professionals from advertising their services. For the Court, medical service advertising was a matter of health that could be advanced by the free flow of information.[59] In a 1983 case, the Supreme Court struck down a congressional statute that prohibited the unsolicited mailing of advertisements for contraceptives. In 1996, the Supreme Court struck down Rhode Island laws and regulations banning the advertisement of liquor prices as a violation of the First Amendment.[60] And in a 2001 case, the Supreme Court ruled that a Massachusetts ban on all cigarette advertising violated the First Amendment right of the tobacco industry to advertise its products to adult consumers.[61] These instances of commercial speech are significant in themselves, but they are all the more significant because they indicate the breadth and depth of the freedom existing today to direct appeals broadly to a large public, not only to sell goods and services but also to mobilize people for political purposes.

FOR CRITICAL ANALYSIS

In a national poll conducted by the Center for Survey and Analysis at the University of Connecticut in October 2003, 74 percent of the respondents agreed that Americans should be allowed to express unpopular opinions. Yet when the questions were made more specific, support for such speech as "hate speech" dropped precipitously. Only 26 percent "strongly agree" on the right to express unpopular opinions offensive to religious groups. Only 18 percent "strongly agree" on the right to say something that might be offensive to racial groups. Is it contradictory that many who strongly support free thought and expression draw the line on protecting "thought we hate"? Should hate speech be protected?

The Second Amendment and the Right to Bear Arms

A well regulated Militia, being necessary to the security of a free State, the right of the people to keep and bear Arms, shall not be infringed.

The point and purpose of the Second Amendment is the provision for militias; they were to be the backing of the government for the maintenance of local public

The Second Amendment arouses at least as much controversy as the First. The right to bear arms is constitutionally guaranteed, although an estimated 80 percent of Americans support some form of gun control. States are allowed to regulate the sale of weapons by requiring a waiting period or a background check on the buyer.

order. "Militia" was understood at the time of the Founding to be a military or police resource for state governments, and militias were specifically distinguished from armies and troops, which came within the sole constitutional jurisdiction of Congress.

Thus, the right of the people "to keep and bear Arms" is based on and associated with participation in state militias. The reference to citizens keeping arms underscored the fact that in the 1700s, state governments could not be relied on to provide firearms to militia members, so citizens eligible to serve in militias (white males between the ages of eighteen and forty-five) were expected to keep their own firearms at the ready.

Recent controversy has arisen concerning some citizens who have sought to form their own *private* militias, unconnected with the government. Yet the Supreme Court made clear that the Second Amendment does not allow citizens to form their own militias free from government control. When a private militia tried to assert such a right, the Supreme Court denied it.[62]

Thus, while much public controversy over the gun control issue holds up the banner of the Second Amendment, it is mostly irrelevant to the modern gun control controversy. This point is underscored by the fact that no gun control law has ever been declared unconstitutional as a violation of the Second Amendment, including a local law that banned the possession of working handguns except for individuals who used handguns for their jobs, like police and security guards.[63] The gun control issue is one that will be settled through the political process, not by the courts.

President Reagan receives a lifetime membership in the National Rifle Association in this 1983 photo (left). The NRA is a well-disciplined group dedicated to preserving Americans' Second Amendment rights. The organization is so powerful a lobby that Reagan—who was himself shot in an assassination attempt in 1981—sought its support. Legal gun ownership is controversial because of its byproduct: gun violence. Former presidential press secretary James Brady, also shot during the attempted assassination of Reagan, never regained use of his legs. Here he speaks to the Democratic National Convention in support of a congressional bill to establish a waiting period and background checks for gun buyers (right). The Supreme Court declared part of the so-called Brady Bill to be in violation of the Second Amendment.

Since the Second Amendment entitles people to carry guns, police are used to facing gunfire. This can have tragic consequences: in 1998, New York police shot a sixteen-year-old boy seventeen times when he refused to drop his toy gun, which mimicked a semiautomatic weapon. Here, New York police sergeant Eric Adams calls for revised regulations dealing with toy guns.

Rights of the Criminally Accused

Except for the First Amendment, most of the battle to apply the Bill of Rights to the states was fought over the various protections granted to individuals who are accused of a crime, who are suspects in the commission of a crime, or who are brought before the court as a witness to a crime. The Fourth, Fifth, Sixth, and Eighth Amendments, taken together, are the essence of the due process of law, even though this fundamental concept does not appear until the very last words of the Fifth Amendment. In the next sections we will look at specific cases that illuminate the dynamics of this important constitutional issue. The procedural safeguards that we will discuss may seem remote to most law-abiding citizens, but they help define the limits of government action against the personal liberty of every citizen. Many Americans believe that "legal technicalities" are responsible for setting many actual criminals free. In many cases, that is absolutely true. In fact, setting defendants free is the very purpose of the requirements that constitute due process. One

exclusionary rule the ability of courts to exclude evidence obtained in violation of the Fourth Amendment

of America's traditional and most strongly held juridical values is that "it is far worse to convict an innocent man than to let a guilty man go free."[64] In civil suits, verdicts rest upon "the preponderance of the evidence"; in criminal cases, guilt has to be proven "beyond a reasonable doubt"—a far higher standard. The provisions for due process in the Bill of Rights were added in order to improve the probability that the standard of "reasonable doubt" will be respected.

THE FOURTH AMENDMENT AND SEARCHES AND SEIZURES

> The right of the people to be secure in their persons, houses, papers, and effects, against unreasonable searches and seizures, shall not be violated, and no Warrants shall issue, but upon probable cause, supported by Oath or affirmation, and particularly describing the place to be searched, and the persons or things to be seized.

The purpose of the Fourth Amendment is to guarantee the security of citizens against unreasonable (i.e., improper) searches and seizures. In 1990, the Supreme Court summarized its understanding of the Fourth Amendment brilliantly and succinctly: "A search compromises the individual interest in privacy; a seizure deprives the individual of dominion over his or her person or property."[65] But how are we to define what is reasonable and what is unreasonable?

The 1961 case of *Mapp v. Ohio* illustrates the beauty and the agony of one of the most important of the procedures that have grown out of the Fourth Amendment—the **exclusionary rule,** which prohibits evidence obtained during an illegal search from being introduced in a trial. Dollree (Dolly) Mapp was "a Cleveland woman of questionable reputation" (by some accounts), the ex-wife of one prominent boxer, and the fiancée of an even more famous one. Acting on a tip that Dolly Mapp was harboring a suspect in a bombing incident, several policemen forcibly entered Ms. Mapp's house claiming they had a warrant to look for the bombing suspect. The police did not find the bombing suspect but did find some materials connected to the local numbers racket (an illegal gambling operation) and a quantity of "obscene materials," in violation of an Ohio law banning possession of such materials. Although the warrant was never produced, the evidence that had been seized was admitted by a court, and Ms. Mapp was charged and convicted for illegal possession of obscene materials.

By the time Ms. Mapp's appeal reached the Supreme Court, the issue of obscene materials had faded into obscurity, and the question before the Court was whether any evidence produced under the circumstances of the search of her home was admissible. The Court's opinion affirmed the exclusionary rule: under the Fourth Amendment (applied to the states through the Fourteenth Amendment), "all evidence obtained by searches and seizures in violation of the Constitution . . . is inadmissible."[66] This means that even people who are clearly guilty of the crime of which they are accused must not be convicted if the only evidence for their conviction was obtained illegally. This idea was expressed by Supreme Court Justice Benjamin Cardozo nearly a century ago when he wrote that "the criminal is to go free because the constable has blundered."

The exclusionary rule is the most severe restraint ever imposed by the Constitution and the courts on the behavior of the police. The exclusionary rule is a dramatic restriction because it rules out precisely the evidence that produces a conviction; it frees those people who are *known* to have committed the crime of which they have been accused. Because it works so dramatically in favor of persons known to have committed a crime, the Court has since softened the application of the rule. In recent years, the federal courts have relied upon a discretionary use of the exclusionary rule, whereby they make a judgment as to the "nature and quality of the intrusion." It is thus difficult to know ahead of time whether a defendant will or will not be protected from an illegal search under the Fourth Amendment.[67]

Another recent issue involving the Fourth Amendment is the controversy over mandatory drug testing. Such tests are most widely used on public employees, and in an important case the Supreme Court has upheld the U.S. Customs Service's drug-testing program for its employees.[68] The same year the Court approved drug and alcohol tests for railroad workers if they were involved in serious accidents.[69] After Court approvals of those two cases in 1989, more than forty federal agencies initiated mandatory employee drug tests. The practice of drug testing was reinforced by a presidential executive order widely touted as the "campaign for a drug-free federal workplace." These growing practices gave rise to public appeals against the general practice of "suspicionless testing" of employees. Regardless of any need to limit the spread of drug abuse, working in this manner through public employees seemed patently unconstitutional, in violation of the Fourth Amendment. A 1995 case, in which the Court upheld a public school district's policy requiring all students participating in interscholastic sports to submit to random drug tests, surely contributed to the efforts of federal, state, and local agencies to initiate random and suspicionless drug and alcohol testing.[70] The most recent cases suggest, however, that the Court is beginning to consider limits on the war against drugs. In a decisive 8-to-1 decision, the Court applied the Fourth Amendment as a shield against "state action that diminishes personal privacy" when the officials in question are not performing high-risk or safety-sensitive tasks.[71] Using random and suspicionless drug testing as a symbol to fight drug use was, in the Court's opinion, carrying the exceptions to the Fourth Amendment too far.

The Constitution provides several major protections for those accused of a crime. In the case of Dollree Mapp v. Ohio, *the Supreme Court interpreted the Fourth Amendment to mean that if incriminating material is found through illegal search and seizure, it cannot be used as evidence in court. Mapp's case against the Cleveland Police Department resulted in the nationalization of the Fourth Amendment's exclusionary rule.*

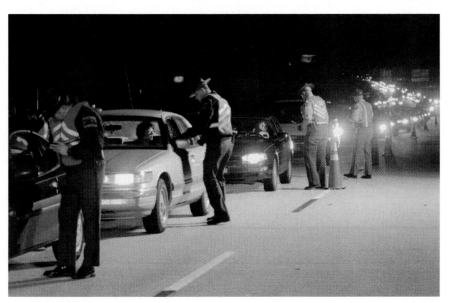

Drug testing has raised concerns about the Fourth Amendment—is a drug test an unreasonable search? Though the Supreme Court initially upheld drug and alcohol tests, the Court indicated in a 1997 case that such tests illegally invade privacy if they are conducted randomly and without suspicion of guilt. However, the Court allowed tests on those engaged in risky activities, such as driving. Here, North Carolina police conduct random alcohol tests at a roadblock.

More recently, the Court found it unconstitutional for police to use trained dogs in roadblocks set up to look for drugs in cars. Unlike drunk-driving roadblocks, where public safety is directly involved, narcotics roadblocks "cannot escape the Fourth Amendment's requirement that searches be based on suspicion of individual wrongdoing."[72] The Court also ruled that a public hospital cannot constitutionally test maternity patients for illegal drug use without their consent.[73] Finally, the Court found that the police may not use thermal imaging devices to detect suspicious patterns of heat emerging from private homes without obtaining the usual search warrant.[74]

THE FIFTH AMENDMENT

No person shall be held to answer for a capital, or otherwise infamous crime, unless on a presentment or indictment of a Grand Jury, except in cases arising in the land or naval forces, or in the Militia, when in actual service in time of War or public danger; nor shall any person be subject for the same offence to be twice put in jeopardy of life or limb; nor shall be compelled in any criminal case to be a witness against himself, nor be deprived of life, liberty, or property, without due process of law; nor shall private property be taken for public use, without just compensation.

grand jury jury that determines whether sufficient evidence is available to justify a trial; grand juries do not rule on the accused's guilt or innocence.

Grand Juries   The first clause of the Fifth Amendment, the right to a **grand jury** to determine whether a trial is warranted, is considered "the oldest institution known to the Constitution."[75] Grand juries play an important role in federal criminal cases. However, the provision for a grand jury is the one important civil liberties provision of the Bill of Rights that was not incorporated by the Fourteenth Amendment to apply to state criminal prosecutions. Thus, some states operate without grand juries. In such states, the prosecuting attorney simply files a "bill of information" affirming that there is sufficient evidence available to justify a trial. If the accused person is to be held in custody, the prosecutor must take the available information before a judge to determine that the evidence shows probable cause.

double jeopardy the Fifth Amendment right providing that a person cannot be tried twice for the same crime

Double Jeopardy   "Nor shall any person be subject for the same offence to be twice put in jeopardy of life or limb" is the constitutional protection from **double jeopardy,** or being tried more than once for the same crime. The protection from double jeopardy was at the heart of the *Palko* case in 1937, which, as we saw earlier in this chapter, also established the principle of selective incorporation of the Bill of Rights. In that case, the state of Connecticut had indicted Frank Palko for first-degree murder, but a lower court had found him guilty of only second-degree murder and sentenced him to life in prison. Unhappy with the verdict, the state of Connecticut appealed the conviction to its highest court, won the appeal, got a new trial, and then succeeded in getting Palko convicted of first-degree murder. Palko appealed to the Supreme Court on what seemed an open-and-shut case of double jeopardy. Yet, although the majority of the Court agreed that this could indeed be considered a case of double jeopardy, they decided that double jeopardy was *not* one of the provisions of the Bill of Rights incorporated in the Fourteenth Amendment as a restriction on the powers of the states. It took more than thirty years for the Court to nationalize the constitutional protection against double jeopardy. Palko was eventually executed for the crime, because he lived in the state of Connecticut rather than in some state whose constitution included a guarantee against double jeopardy.

Self-Incrimination Perhaps the most significant liberty found in the Fifth Amendment, and the one most familiar to many Americans who watch television crime shows, is the guarantee that no citizen "shall be compelled in any criminal case to be a witness against himself. . . ." The most famous case concerning self-incrimination is one of such importance that Chief Justice Earl Warren assessed its results as going "to the very root of our concepts of American criminal jurisprudence."[76] Twenty-three-year-old Ernesto Miranda was sentenced to between twenty and thirty years in prison for the kidnapping and rape of an eighteen-year-old woman. The woman had identified him in a police lineup, and, after two hours of questioning, Miranda confessed, subsequently signing a statement that his confession had been made voluntarily, without threats or promises of immunity. These confessions were admitted into evidence, served as the basis for Miranda's conviction, and also served as the basis of the appeal of his conviction all the way to the Supreme Court. In one of the most intensely and widely criticized decisions ever handed down by the Supreme Court, Ernesto Miranda's case produced the rules the police must follow before questioning an arrested criminal suspect. The reading of a person's "Miranda rights" became a standard scene in every police station and on virtually every dramatization of police action on television and in the movies. *Miranda* advanced the civil liberties of accused persons by expanding not only the scope of the Fifth Amendment clause covering coerced confessions and self-incrimination, but also by confirming the right to counsel (discussed later).

DEFENDANT		LOCATION	

SPECIFIC WARNING REGARDING INTERROGATIONS

1. You have the right to remain silent.

2. Anything you say can and will be used against you in a court of law.

3. You have the right to talk to a lawyer and have him present with you while you are being questioned.

4. If you cannot afford to hire a lawyer one will be appointed to represent you before any questioning, if you wish one.

SIGNATURE OF DEFENDANT		DATE
WITNESS		TIME
☐ REFUSED SIGNATURE	SAN FRANCISCO POLICE DEPARTMENT	PR.9.1.4

The Fifth Amendment provides additional protection from the government by barring double jeopardy and self-incrimination and by guaranteeing grand jury inquiries and eminent domain payments. The modern interpretation of the Fifth Amendment was shaped by the 1966 case Miranda v. Arizona. *In 1966, Ernesto Miranda confessed to kidnapping and rape. Since he was never told that he was not required to answer police questions, his case was appealed on the grounds that his right against self-incrimination had been violated. The trial resulted in the creation of* Miranda *rights, which must be read to those arrested to make them aware of their constitutional rights.*

Miranda rule the requirement, articulated by the Supreme Court in *Miranda v. Arizona,* that persons under arrest must be informed prior to police interrogation of their rights to remain silent and to have the benefit of legal counsel

eminent domain the right of government to take private property for public use

The Supreme Court under Burger and Rehnquist has considerably softened the *Miranda* restrictions, making the job of the police a little easier, but the **Miranda rule** still stands as a protection against egregious police abuses of arrested persons. The Supreme Court reaffirmed *Miranda* in *Dickerson v. United States* (2000).

Eminent Domain The other fundamental clause of the Fifth Amendment is the "takings clause," which extends to each citizen a protection against the "taking" of private property "without just compensation." Although this part of the Fifth Amendment is not specifically concerned with protecting persons accused of crimes, it is nevertheless a fundamentally important instance where the government and the citizen are adversaries. The power of any government to take private property for a public use is called **eminent domain.** This power is essential to the very concept of sovereignty. The Fifth Amendment neither invents eminent domain nor takes it away; its purpose is to put limits on that inherent power through procedures that require a showing of a public purpose and the provision of fair payment for the taking of someone's property. This provision is now universally observed in all U.S. principalities, but it has not always been meticulously observed.

Take the case of Mr. Berman, who in the 1950s owned and operated a "mom and pop" grocery store in a run-down neighborhood on the southwest side of the District of Columbia. In carrying out a vast urban redevelopment program, the city government of Washington, D.C., took Berman's property as one of a large number of privately owned lots to be cleared for new housing and business construction. Berman, and his successors after his death, took the government to court on the grounds that it was an unconstitutional use of eminent domain to take property from one private owner and eventually to turn that property back, in altered form, to another private owner. Berman and his successors lost their case. The Supreme Court's argument was a curious but very important one: the "public interest" can mean virtually anything a legislature says it means. In other words, since the overall slum clearance and redevelopment project was in the public interest, according to the legislature, the eventual transfers of property that were going to take place were justified.[77]

THE SIXTH AMENDMENT AND THE RIGHT TO COUNSEL

In all criminal prosecutions, the accused shall enjoy the right to a speedy and public trial, by an impartial jury of the State and district wherein the crime shall have been committed, which district shall have been previously ascertained by law, and to be informed of the nature and cause of the accusation; to be confronted with the witnesses against him; to have compulsory process for obtaining witnesses in his favor, and to have the Assistance of Counsel for his defence.

Like the exclusionary rule of the Fourth Amendment and the self-incrimination clause of the Fifth Amendment, the "right to counsel" provision of the Sixth Amendment is notable for freeing defendants who seem to the public to be patently guilty as charged. Other provisions of the Sixth Amendment, such as the right to a speedy trial and the right to confront witnesses before an impartial jury, are less controversial in nature.

Gideon v. Wainwright is the perfect case study because it involved a disreputable person who seemed patently guilty of the crime for which he was convicted. In and out of jails for most of his fifty-one years, Clarence Earl Gideon received a five-year sentence for breaking and entering a poolroom in Panama City, Florida. While serving time in jail, Gideon became a fairly well qualified "jailhouse lawyer," made his own appeal on a handwritten petition, and eventually won the landmark ruling on the right to counsel in all felony cases.[78]

The right to counsel has been expanded rather than contracted during the past few decades, when the courts have become more conservative. For example, although at first the right to counsel was met by judges assigning lawyers from the community as a formal public obligation, most states and cities now have created an office of public defender; these state-employed professional defense lawyers typically provide poor defendants with much better legal representation. And, although these defendants cannot choose their private defense attorney, they do have the right to appeal a conviction on the grounds that the counsel provided by the state was deficient. For example, in 2003 the Supreme Court overturned the death sentence for a Maryland death row inmate, holding that the defense lawyer had failed to fully inform the jury of the defendant's history of "horrendous childhood abuse."[79] Moreover, the right to counsel extends beyond serious crimes to any trial, with or without jury, that holds the possibility of imprisonment.[80]

THE EIGHTH AMENDMENT AND CRUEL AND UNUSUAL PUNISHMENT

The Eighth Amendment prohibits "excessive bail," "excessive fines," and "cruel and unusual punishment." Virtually all the debate over Eighth Amendment issues focuses on the last clause of the amendment: the protection from "cruel and unusual punishment." One of the greatest challenges in interpreting this provision consistently is that what is considered "cruel and unusual" varies from culture to culture and from generation to generation. And, unfortunately, it also varies by class and race.

By far the biggest issue of class and race inconsistency as constituting cruel and unusual punishment arises over the death penalty. In 1972, the Supreme Court overturned several state death penalty laws, not because they were cruel and unusual, but because they were being applied in a capricious manner—that is, blacks were much more likely than whites to be sentenced to death, and the poor more likely than the rich, and men more likely than women.[81] Very soon after that decision, a majority of states revised their capital punishment provisions to meet the Court's standards.[82] Since 1976, the Court has consistently upheld state laws providing for capital punishment, although the Court also continues to review numerous death penalty appeals each year.

Between 1976 and 2000, states executed 683 people. Most of those executions occurred in southern states, with Texas leading the way at 239. As of 2002, thirty-eight states had adopted some form of capital punishment, a move approved of by about three-quarters of all Americans.

Although virtually all criminal conduct is regulated by the states, Congress has also jumped on the bandwagon, imposing capital punishment for more than fifty federal crimes. Despite the seeming popularity of the death penalty, the debate has become, if anything, more intense. In 1997, for example, the American Bar Association passed a resolution calling for a halt to the death penalty until concerns about its fairness—that is, whether its application violates the principle of equality—and about ensuring due process are addressed. In 2000, the governor of Illinois imposed a moratorium on the death penalty and created a commission to review the capital punishment system. After a two-year study by the commission, Illinois adopted a number of reforms, including a ban on executions of the mentally retarded. In June 2002, the U.S. Supreme Court banned all executions of mentally retarded defendants, a decision that could move 200 or more people off death row.

Many death penalty supporters trumpet its deterrent effects on other would-be criminals. Although studies of capital crimes usually fail to demonstrate any direct deterrent effect, that may be due to the lengthy delays—typically years and even decades—between convictions and executions. A system that eliminates undue delays would surely enhance deterrence. And deterring even one murder or other heinous crime, proponents argue, is more than ample justification for such laws. Beyond this, the death penalty is seen as a proper expression of retribution, echoed in the biblical phrase "an eye for an eye." People who commit vicious crimes deserve to forfeit their lives in exchange for the suffering they have inflicted. If the world applauded the execution of Nazis after World War II, for example, how could it deny the right of society to execute a serial killer?

Constitutional objections to the death penalty often invoke the Eighth Amendment's protection against punishments that are "cruel and unusual." Yet the death penalty can hardly be considered a violation of this protection, say supporters, since the death penalty was commonly used in the eighteenth century and was supported by most early American leaders. And while the poor, males, and blacks and Latinos are more likely to find themselves sitting on death row, this fact reflects the painful reality that these categories of individuals are more likely to commit crimes.

Death penalty opponents are quick to point out that the death penalty has not been proven to deter crime, either in the United States or abroad. In fact, America is the only Western nation that still executes criminals. The fact that American states execute criminals debases, rather than elevates, society, by extolling vengeance. If the government is to serve as an example of proper behavior, say foes, it has no business sanctioning killing when incarceration will similarly protect society. As for the Constitution, most of the Founders surely supported the death penalty. But, foes note, they also countenanced slavery, and lived at a time when society was both less informed about, and more indifferent to, the human condition. Modern Americans' greater civility should be reflected in how it defines individual rights.

Furthermore, according to death penalty foes, execution is expensive—more expensive than life imprisonment—precisely because the government must make every effort to ensure that it is not executing an innocent person. Curtailing legal appeals would make the possibility of a mistake too great. And although most Americans do support the death penalty, people also support life without the possibility of parole as an alternative. Race also intrudes in death penalty cases: people of color (who are more likely to face economic deprivation) are disproportionately more likely to be sentenced to death, whereas whites charged with identical crimes are less likely to be given the ultimate punishment. Such disparity of treatment violates the principle of equal protection. And finally, according to opponents, a life sentence may be a worse punishment for criminals than the death penalty.

FOR CRITICAL ANALYSIS

Do you think the death penalty deters crime? Do you think that the death penalty is fairly and equally applied? In the United States, seventy-one inmates were executed in 2002: thirty-three in Texas, seven in Oklahoma, six in Missouri, four each in Georgia and Virginia, three each in Florida, South Carolina, and Ohio, two each in Alabama, Mississippi, and North Carolina, and one each in Louisiana and California; fifty-three were white, eighteen were black; sixty-nine were men, and two were women.

The Right to Privacy

Some of the people all of the time and all of the people some of the time would just like to be left alone, to have their own private domain into which no one—friends, family, government, church, or employer—has the right to enter without permission.

Many Jehovah's Witnesses felt that way in the 1930s. They risked serious punishment in 1940 by telling their children not to salute the flag or say the "Pledge of Allegiance" in school because of their understanding of the First Commandment's prohibition of the worship of "graven images." They lost their appeal, the children were expelled, and the parents were punished.[83] However, the Supreme Court concluded that the 1940 decision was "wrongly decided."[84] These two cases arose under the freedom of religion provisions of the First Amendment, but they were also the first cases to confront the possibility of another right that is not mentioned anywhere in the Constitution or the Bill of Rights: the right to be left alone. When the Court began to take a more activist role in the mid-1950s and 1960s, the idea of a **right to privacy** was revived. In 1958, the Supreme Court recognized "privacy in one's association" in its decision to prevent the state of Alabama from using the membership list of the National Association for the Advancement of Colored People in the state's investigations.[85]

right to privacy the right to be let alone, which has been interpreted by the Supreme Court to entail free access to birth control and abortions

Birth Control   The sphere of privacy was drawn in earnest in 1965, when the Court ruled that a Connecticut statute forbidding the use of contraceptives violated the right of marital privacy. Estelle Griswold, the executive director of the Planned Parenthood League of Connecticut, was arrested by the state of Connecticut for providing information, instruction, and medical advice about contraception to married couples. She and her associates were found guilty as accessories to the crime and fined $100 each. The Supreme Court reversed the lower court decisions and declared the Connecticut law unconstitutional because it violated "a right of privacy older than the Bill of Rights—older than our political parties, older than our school system."[86] Justice William O. Douglas, author of the majority decision in the *Griswold* case, argued that this right of privacy is also grounded in the Constitution, because it fits into a "zone of privacy" created by a combination of the Third, Fourth, and Fifth Amendments. A concurring opinion, written by Justice Arthur Goldberg, attempted to strengthen Douglas's argument by adding that "the concept of liberty . . . embraces the right of marital privacy though that right is not mentioned explicitly in the Constitution [and] is supported by numerous decisions of this Court . . . and *by the language and history of the Ninth Amendment*" (emphasis added).[87]

Abortion   The right to privacy was confirmed and extended in 1973 in the most important of all privacy decisions, and one of the most important Supreme Court decisions in American history: *Roe v. Wade*. This decision established a woman's right to seek an abortion and prohibited states from making abortion a criminal act.[88] The Burger Court's decision in *Roe* took a revolutionary step toward establishing the right to privacy. It is important to emphasize that the preference for privacy rights and for their extension to include the rights of women to control their own bodies was not something invented by the Supreme Court in a vacuum. Most states did not regulate abortions in any fashion until the 1840s, at which time only six of the twenty-six existing states had any regulations governing abortion at all. In addition, many states had begun to ease their abortion restrictions well before the 1973 *Roe* decision, although in recent years a number of states have reinstated some restrictions on abortion.

By extending the umbrella of privacy, this sweeping ruling dramatically changed abortion practices in America. In addition, it galvanized and nationalized the abortion debate. Groups opposed to abortion, such as the National Right to Life Committee, organized to fight the new liberal standard, while abortion rights groups sought to maintain that protection. In recent years, the legal standard shifted against abortion rights supporters in two key Supreme Court cases.

In *Webster v. Reproductive Health Services* (1989), the Court narrowly upheld (by a 5-to-4 majority) the constitutionality of restrictions on the use of public medical facilities for abortion.[89] And in the 1992 case of *Planned Parenthood v. Casey,* another 5-to-4 majority of the Court upheld *Roe* but narrowed its scope, refusing to invalidate a Pennsylvania law that significantly limits freedom of choice. The Court's decision defined the right to an abortion as a "limited or qualified" right subject to regulation by the states as long as the regulation does not constitute an "undue burden."[90] More recently, the Court had another opportunity to rule on what constitutes an undue burden. In the 2000 case of *Stenberg v. Carhart,* the Court, by a vote of 5 to 4, struck down Nebraska's ban on partial-birth abortions because the law had the "effect of placing a substantial obstacle in the path of a woman seeking an abortion."[91]

Homosexuality In the last two decades, the right to be left alone began to include the privacy rights of homosexuals. One morning in Atlanta, Georgia, in the mid-1980s, Michael Hardwick was arrested by a police officer who discovered him in bed with another man. The officer had come to serve a warrant for Hardwick's arrest for failure to appear in court to answer charges of drinking in public. One of Hardwick's unknowing housemates invited the officer to look in Hardwick's room, where he found Hardwick and another man engaging in "consensual sexual behavior." He was then arrested under Georgia's laws against heterosexual and homosexual sodomy. Hardwick filed a lawsuit against the state, challenging the constitutionality of the Georgia law. Hardwick won his case in the federal court of appeals. The state of Georgia, in an unusual move, appealed the court's decision to the Supreme Court. The majority of the Court reversed the lower court decision, holding against Mr. Hardwick, on the grounds that "the federal Constitution confers [no] fundamental right upon homosexuals to engage in sodomy," and that therefore there was no basis to invalidate "the laws of the many states that still make such conduct illegal and have done so for a very long time."[92] The Court majority concluded its opinion with a warning that it ought not and would not use its power to "discover new fundamental rights embedded in the Due Process Clause." In other words, the Court under Chief Justice Rehnquist was expressing its determination to restrict quite severely the expansion of the Ninth Amendment and the development of new substantive rights. The four dissenters argued that the case was not about a fundamental right to engage in homosexual sodomy, but was in fact about "the most comprehensive of rights and the right most valued by civilized men, [namely,] the right to be let alone."[93]

Seventeen years later and to most everyone's surprise, the Court overturned *Bowers v. Hardwick* with a dramatic pronouncement that gays are "entitled to respect for their private lives" as a matter of constitutional due process. With *Lawrence v. Texas* (2003), the state legislatures no longer had the authority to make private sexual behavior a crime.[94] Drawing from the tradition of negative liberty, the Court maintained: "In our tradition the State is not omnipresent in the home.

The USA PATRIOT Act

The objective of civil liberties is to create a "private sphere" in which individuals are autonomous and free from government interference. There is also a presumption that people have the right to be left alone, to have privacy.

Few would argue, however, that the right of privacy is absolute. No right is absolute, and we regularly compromise our privacy in return for something we value even more. Every new communications technology reduces our privacy. Note how casually we compromise our private lives every time we use our credit cards, subscribe to a periodical, run a red light, or send and receive e-mails, whether for business, personal, confidential, or illegal affairs. Even our Social Security and bank account numbers are up for grabs.

The most ardent civil libertarian would find it difficult to disagree with Attorney General Ashcroft when he said, "liberty is meaningless without security," in his defense of the USA PATRIOT Act. War is the most fundamental threat to liberty. President Lincoln abruptly and unilaterally suspended the power of our judiciary to issue writs of *habeas corpus* (requiring a show of cause why an individual is in custody). President Washington, as well as Lincoln and Franklin Roosevelt, set up military tribunals to try, without right of counsel, persons believed to be collaborators with, or merely sympathizers of, the enemy. Most dramatically, in 1942 Presidential Roosevelt ordered over 120,000 Japanese-Americans (most of them U.S. citizens) to internment camps for the duration of World War II, without consulting Congress and without accusing the internees of any sort of crime.

Six weeks after September 11, 2001, President Bush submitted to Congress the USA PATRIOT Act—"*Uniting and Strengthening America by Providing Appropriate Tools Required to Intercept and Obstruct Terrorism Act.*" The 342-page act gave the federal government power over many different types of beliefs and associations as well as over activities that could be interpreted as sympathetic to terrorism from whatever source.

Many of the provisions in the USA PATRIOT Act come under a "sunset clause" that provides that they will automatically terminate in 2005. However, not all provisions are covered. For example, the latitude to intercept all forms of Internet activity, including e-mail messages, is not included.

Nevertheless, there is a continuing willingness among Americans across the ideological spectrum to support the USA PATRIOT Act as a hedge against terrorism. But there is an unmistakable growth of opposition to many of its provisions, especially those that give the Attorney General immense discretionary power to detain and imprison "on suspicion" and to use information technology to engage in "fishing expeditions" within the United States, as though America were a foreign country. In 2001 many politicians voted for the Act as an emergency measure and accompanied their support with the assertion that the Act "can be fixed" by Justice Department interpretations, by judicial review, and even by Congress itself. However, in the three ensuing years, nothing in the Act has been amended to any extent by Congress or the courts, and many of the provisions have been expanded by Justice Department application beyond anything publicly anticipated in 2001. As a consequence, public discussion of the Act has taken on a rigid moral/ideological quality, "with neither side willing to concede an inch." Attorney General Ashcroft probably further deepened the polarization with his accusation that "To those who scare peace-loving people with phantoms of lost liberty, my message is this: Your tactics only aid terrorists, for they erode our national unity and diminish our resolve." The resolution of this polarized discourse will not consist of landing "somewhere in between" but of dispassionately analyzing each provision, eliminating those provisions proven to be extravagant or irrelevant, and surrounding justifiable security provisions with "fail-safe" procedures. Both American liberals and American conservatives fear a strong state. If we give up the "eternal vigilance" Jefferson counseled as the price of liberty, we will be giving the terrorists their victory without their having to fire another shot or explode another suicide bomb.

FOR CRITICAL ANALYSIS

1. What should be the proper balance between liberty and security? Where does the USA PATRIOT Act fall on this spectrum?

2. Do you agree with John Ashcroft that civil libertarians concerned about lost liberties "threatened by the USA PATRIOT Act are just aiding terrorists"? Should the provisions of the USA PATRIOT Act that are set to expire at the end of 2005 be renewed? Why or why not?

Is the USA PATRIOT Act a Threat to Liberty?

Yes

On Wednesday, November 13, 2002, a special federal appeals court gave the Justice Department broad new power to use wiretaps for intelligence investigations. The court's ruling came under the deceptively titled Uniting and Strengthening America by Providing Appropriate Tools Required to Intercept and Obstruct Terrorism Act (USA PATRIOT Act), passed just over a year ago. This piece of legislation dramatically changed the legal structure within which law enforcement and foreign intelligence agencies operate, allowing significant expansion of surveillance and information-gathering power in response to the September 11 terrorist attacks. However, considerable bipartisan concern regarding the act's ineffectiveness in combating terrorism, its reliance on executive command rather than congressional and judicial oversight, and, most important, its infringements on individual civil liberties, have proved this act unworthy for a nation that claims personal liberty as a founding principle.

National policy has hitherto separated domestic criminal investigations from the collection of foreign intelligence, as the requirements for obtaining a wiretap for intelligence-gathering are more lax than the strict standards required to wiretap in a criminal investigation. In their decision, the judge affirmed Attorney General John Ashcroft's assertion that the USA PATRIOT Act eliminates any distinction between the foreign and domestic sides of national security operations, going further to declare that this separation was never required or intended by Congress. "Effective counterintelligence," the panel wrote, "requires the wholehearted cooperation of all the government's personnel who can be brought to the task." The USA PATRIOT Act facilitates this cooperation by removing barriers that also serve as significant safeguards to American liberty. . . .

The legislative proposals that provided the basis for the USA PATRIOT Act were introduced in Congress within a week of the terrorist attacks, passing through both houses with minimal discussion, criticism, and debate. Acting under extreme pressure from Attorney General John Ashcroft and the Bush administration and in a national climate of fear, uncertainty, emotion, and mounting patriotism, Congressional members voted on the act even before the finalized text of the bill was available for assessment.

Nor has the media provided the necessary scrutiny. An informed citizenry is essential to democracy, and the media is the primary means by which American citizens obtain information about new laws. Through thorough political discourse, the public holds its government accountable. Yet in the months immediately following the September 11 attacks, news coverage, while heavy in terms of quantity, lacked journalistic quality in regard to breadth and completeness. Media inquiry was overwhelmingly deficient, promoting a jingoistic national atmosphere that discourages dissent. In order to remain consistent with the popular public sentiment of patriotism, little was said in opposition to the USA PATRIOT Act. Indeed, even a year after its passage, most Americans are not even aware of its existence, or know of the act simply as "anti-terrorism" legislation. The implication, for legislators and citizens, is that dissent is unpatriotic. Thus, the act persists in a country in which national security is the premium, and to these ends, some sacrifice of liberty is acceptable.

However, war does not legitimize disregarding the Bill of Rights and other Constitutional provisions that limit the powers of the government. Our history reveals a fallible nation prone to imprudent legislation in times of war: the Alien and Sedition Acts, the suspension of habeas corpus during the Civil War, the internment of Japanese-Americans during World War II, the McCarthy era witch hunt of supposed Communist sympathizers, and the Church Committee's surveillance and harassment of Dr. Martin Luther King, Jr. In his majority opinion for *Kennedy v. Mendoza Martinez*, a Supreme Court case involving draft evasion, Justice Arthur Goldberg wrote, "It is fundamental that the great powers of Congress to conduct war and to regulate the nation's foreign relations are subject to the constitutional requirements of due process. The imperative necessity for safeguarding these rights to procedural due process under the gravest of emergencies has existed throughout our constitutional history, for it is then, under the pressing exigencies of crisis, that there is the greatest temptation to dispense with fundamental constitutional guarantees, which, it is feared, will inhibit governmental action."

While not explicit in the Constitution, the Supreme Court has asserted the fundamental right to privacy. Despite such judicial precedent, the USA PATRIOT Act flaunts this right. Expansion of governmental surveillance and information-gathering powers affects all United States residents, not just the terrorists for whom it is intended. . . .

Congress and the judiciary must be called upon to exert governmental checks and balances, prevent abuses, and provide the necessary guardianship of privacy rights to ensure the protection of our liberties.

SOURCE: Theresa Nguyen, "Anti-Terrorist Law Violates Civil Rights," *Yale Herald* (Yale University), November 21, 2002.

No

The PATRIOT Act was started because of the terrorist attacks of September 11, 2001. Liberals would have you believe that those attacks were because of our foreign policy and because we meddled where we were not wanted. The favorite buzzword you hear from the left these days is the word "imperialism" in association with the U.S. military. But I'm getting ahead of myself.

The PATRIOT Act was actually just a federal combination of fifteen existing statutes that were then updated for the crises that we face now in fighting terrorism abroad. The "expansion" of the Act by Attorney General John Ashcroft was simply to close loopholes in those laws. The Act enables the government to give a judge the authority to allow the monitoring of a person making unauthorized encrypted communications from a computer. It allows the government the ability to make roving wiretaps. What this means is that the FBI can now follow a terrorist's calls, and not just one particular phone number. Sound horrible yet? Since many terrorists use student visas to gain entry into our country, the PATRIOT Act also allows the government to follow their progress and to (God forbid) pull their library records to see if a foreign national is reading *The Cat in the Hat* or *Did You Know You Can Make a Bomb Out of Fertilizer?* Since its inception, there have been terrorist cells arrested in Buffalo, Seattle, Portland, and Detroit, and now thousands of people hostile to Americans are under surveillance across the globe.

The arguments from the American Civil Liberties Union are knee-jerk and typical. Civil rights abuses you say? The PATRIOT Act requires the inspector general at the Department of Justice to investigate complaints. Of the 1,037 claims made of civil rights abuses, 34 were found to be credible, and even then, most of those stemmed from some ignorant prison guard verbally harassing a prisoner. Sound Orwellian yet?

Also, the government could go through your closet and find your *Playboy* magazine, then leak it later to destroy your reputation! Ladies and gentleman, I'm going to tell you that the government has been able to go through your stuff for years now. It's called a warrant, and you still need to go to a judge to get one. This is neither Nazi Germany in 1935 nor the horrors described in George Orwell's *1984*. The only thing I will concede about this legislation is that in some places it goes too far in protecting our country, but the Republican-controlled House and Senate have already scaled back those parts.

Finally, is there any doubt that we are constantly at war? There is war in Iraq, but there is also an intelligence war going on here. That Muhammed Atta and his cronies slipped by the CIA and FBI two years ago is unacceptable. The PATRIOT Act boosts the powers of those agencies so that something like September 11 will never happen again.

Those who think that the only reason that we are at risk from terrorism is because of Afghanistan and Iraq are deluded and are missing the point. September 11 made us realize more than ever how important it is for us to use our powers to modernize the world.

Feudal warlords in Afghanistan, 400,000 in mass graves in Iraq, women dying in a school fire in Iran because the religious military let the men out first—these are the real human-rights issues that are happening across the planet, and I am at a loss to explain why anyone would not want those problems stopped immediately. The people who perpetrate terrorism in our country are not affiliated with any country, and President Bush and the United States acknowledge that. Our battle is not one of vengeance, but rather one of responsibility. In the meantime, we need the PATRIOT Act to protect our citizens in these trying times, when America is trying to change the world, and in a positive way.

[Critics say] "privacy, in the White House, is a deeply held value until it's applied to somebody else." Nothing could be farther from the truth. President Bush and other neoconservatives believe that privacy is a value that should be held by everyone. The PATRIOT Act should do an excellent job protecting Americans while Bush's progressive foreign policy is put in motion.

SOURCE: Barney Keller, "Patriot Act: A Necessary Piece of National Security," *Chicago Maroon* (University of Chicago), December 2, 2003.

And there are other spheres of our lives and existence outside the home, where the State should not be a dominant presence." Explicitly encompassing lesbians and gay men within the umbrella of privacy, the Court concluded that the "petitioners are entitled to respect for their private lives. The State cannot demean their existence or control their destiny by making their private sexual conduct a crime." This decision added substance to the Ninth Amendment "right of privacy."[95]

The Right to Die   Another area ripe for litigation and public discourse is the so-called right to die. A number of highly publicized physician-assisted suicides in the 1990s focused attention on whether people have a right to choose their own death and to receive assistance in carrying it out. Can this become part of the privacy right or is it a new substantive right? A tentative answer came in 1997, when the Court ruled that a Washington state law establishing a ban on "causing" or "aiding" a suicide did not violate the Fourteenth Amendment or any clauses of the Bill of Rights incorporated in the Fourteenth Amendment.[96] Thus, if a state can constitutionally adopt such a prohibition, there is no constitutional right to suicide or assisted suicide. However, the Court left open the narrower question of "whether a mentally competent person who is experiencing great suffering has a constitutionally cognizable interest in controlling the circumstances of his or her imminent death."[97] "Americans are engaged in an earnest and profound debate about the morality, legality, and practicality of physician-assisted suicide. Our holding permits this debate to continue, as it should in a democratic society."[98] Never before has the Supreme Court more openly invited further litigation on a point.[99]

Thinking Critically about the Future of Civil Liberties: Does the War on Terrorism Affect It?

The next and final question for this chapter is whether the current Supreme Court, with its conservative majority, will try to reverse the nationalization of the Bill of Rights after a period of more than thirty-five years. Although such a move is possible, it is not certain. First of all, the Rehnquist Court has not actually reversed important decisions made by the Warren or Burger Courts, but instead has given narrower and more restrictive interpretations of earlier Court decisions. For example, in 1997, the Court made it easier for the police to search cars for drugs or other contraband when the cars have been pulled over only for traffic violations. Activists such as Justices Rehnquist, Antonin Scalia, and Clarence Thomas, who would prefer to overturn many of the Court's decisions from the 1960s and 1970s, do not yet command a majority on the Court. The most recent sign of the times is a case regarding the constitutionality of the 1994 Drivers' Privacy Protection Act. The purpose of the act was to protect privacy rights in general and the safety of women in particular by barring states from disclosing without consent the personal information contained in motor vehicle and driving license records. By selling these lists of registrants to anyone willing to buy them, information can be gained, by stalkers as well as by telemarketers, that many people go to great lengths to keep confidential. Justice Stephen Breyer observed that if the Court overturned this statute, it could on principle overturn "the entire body of law under which the

FOR CRITICAL ANALYSIS

Recount the history of the constitutional "right to privacy." How has this right affected American politics since the 1960s? How has this right interacted with the other rights in the Bill of Rights? Read the Third, Fourth, Fifth, and Ninth Amendments. In your opinion, do American citizens have a right to privacy?

FOR CRITICAL ANALYSIS

In many ways it seems that the Bill of Rights is an ambiguous document. Choose one protection offered in the Bill of Rights and explain how it has been interpreted in various ways. What does this say about the role of politics and the Constitution in defining the limits of governmental power? What does it say about the power of the Supreme Court in American politics?

authority of Congress to regulate interstate commerce has been understood to place corresponding limits on state authority." In a unanimous decision the Court rejected the states' rights challenge to the Drivers' Privacy Protection Act. Chief Justice William Rehnquist wrote the *Reno v. Condon* (2000) decision.

Meanwhile, the resurgence of federalism will play itself out in judicial territory. One certain trend in the Court that is likely to continue is its commitment to giving more discretion to the states, returning some of the power to state legislatures that was taken away during the "nationalization" of the Bill of Rights. But what if the state legislatures begin using their regained powers in ways they had used them before the nationalization of the Bill of Rights? What would be the reaction when states pass laws imposing further criminal restrictions on abortion? Permitting more religious practices in the public schools? Spreading the application of capital punishment to new crimes? Imposing stricter sentences on white-collar crimes? Terminating the use of buses to maintain desegregated schools? A great deal will depend upon the three or even four appointments that the president will likely be able to make as vacancies are produced by an aging Court membership. When that occurs, what would a majority on the Court do? Would the Court be equally respectful of state-level democracy then?

Finally, there will be even stronger and more lasting suspense as to whether the war on terrorism will have a permanent effect on civil liberties. Two months after the September 11 attacks, President Bush issued an executive order allowing the use of military tribunals.[100] Citing his authority as commander in chief, the order allowed the president to use military tribunals to try individuals who had engaged in terrorism or knowingly aided terrorists.

Several months of legal debate followed Bush's proposal. The administration emphasized the need for the military venue and procedures to allow quick, effective, and secure trials.[101] Supporters looked to a World War II case that permitted, as an extension of the commander in chief's powers endorsed by congressional legislation, the creation of a military commission to try German saboteurs.[102] Critics argued that Bush's order lacked congressional support and also compromised constitutional due-process guarantees by eliminating judicial review of tribunal verdicts, establishing a lesser standard of evidence, and not providing for jurors. In March 2002, the Pentagon issued rules for the tribunals that answered some of these concerns.[103] Attorney General John Ashcroft also moved to change how surveillance and detention of suspected terrorists are handled. Ashcroft approved a Justice Department rule to allow federal agents to monitor some meetings between federal inmates and their lawyers, if he determined that the inmates might use these conversations to communicate information about terrorism. Traditionally, attorney-client conversations are confidential. The USA PATRIOT Act gave the government more latitude to conduct searches and to detain uncharged suspects longer than normally allowed, a degree of authority many critics argued challenges the right to counsel and to be free from unreasonable searches and seizures.[104] Even some conservatives who generally approve of the direction this conservative Court has been taking are expressing concern over the initiatives taken by the Bush administration in dealing with thousands of American residents of Middle Eastern origin. For example, the eminent conservative *New York Times* columnist William Safire referred to the secretive processes in military tribunals as "kangaroo courts."[105] Even though these measures were justified as military emergencies, critics were focused on Justice Jackson's warning in the *Korematsu* case that an emergency measure once established as constitutional can be "a loaded

FOR CRITICAL ANALYSIS

The perennial trouble between war and civil liberties came to a head in early 1942 when hundreds of Japanese, many of them American citizens, were sent to "relocation camps" and kept there for the duration of the war. In 1944, the Supreme Court held this action to be constitutional, within "the war power of Congress and the Executive. . . ." In an eloquent dissent, Justice Jackson argued that holding it constitutional simply because it was necessary "is a far more subtle blow to liberty than the promulgation of the order itself. . . ." What does sixty years of experience since 1942 tell us about what we should do in this post–September 11 era to balance the needs of war and the protection of civil liberties?

weapon ready for the hand of any authority that can bring forward a plausible claim of an urgent need." In 2004, Justice O'Connor echoed Jackson's warning with a question she posed to the Deputy Solicitor General who was representing the government in its defense of its power to arrest American citizens and foreigners on American soil as "enemy combatants," and to detain them without grand jury indictments or legal counsel for an indefinite period. Her question was simply, "What if the emergency created by terrorism lasted twenty-five, even fifty years?" As if in answer to that important question, in separate cases from June 2004, the Court challenged the Bush administration's detention of those it deemed enemy combatants and ruled that both foreign detainees and American citizens held in open-ended detention at Guantanamo Bay, Cuba, and in the United States have the right to challenge their detention and designation as an "enemy combatant" before an impartial federal court.[106]

GET INVOLVED
What You Can Do: Defend Liberty

The civil liberties that Americans enjoy today have been won by the struggles of ordinary citizens. The Bill of Rights offers Americans who have been denied their civil liberties a remedy through the judicial system. Individuals such as Dolly Mapp, Ernesto Miranda, and Clarence Earl Gideon fought to defend their fundamental liberties, and through their efforts all Americans now possess a more clearly defined and protected right to the due process of law. The most central aspect of a woman's right to privacy started with the difficulties of a poor high school dropout in Texas. Norma McCorvey was a twenty-one-year-old pregnant, divorced carnival worker with a five-year-old daughter. McCorvey lived regularly on the edge of poverty, and as a high school dropout, her prospects were poor, all the poorer in Texas, where the carnival had moved, because Texas had prohibited abortion unless necessary to save the mother's life. "I found one doctor who offered to abort me for $500. Only he didn't have a license, and I was scared to turn my body over to him. So there I was—pregnant, . . . alone and stuck."

McCorvey bore her child and gave it up immediately for adoption, but in the process she was introduced to two recent graduates of the University of Texas Law School, Sarah Weddington and Linda Coffey. These three women decided to challenge the Texas abortion statute. In order to avoid any stigma attached to such an emotionally charged case, Norma McCorvey's name was changed to Jane Roe in the court documents. Her case alleged that "she was unmarried and pregnant; that she wished to terminate her pregnancy by an abortion . . . ; [and] that she was unable to get a 'legal' abortion because her life did not appear to be threatened by the continuation of her pregnancy. . . ." The Court's ruling in *Roe v. Wade* subsequently prohibited states from making abortion illegal.[107]

In 1995, a student group at the University of Virginia scored a dramatic legal victory before the U.S. Supreme Court. The university had refused to provide support from the student activities fund for *Wide Awake,* a magazine published by a Christian student group. Although other student publications received subsidies from the activities fund, university policy prohibited grants to religious groups. Ronald Rosenberger, a Virginia undergraduate and an editor of the magazine, and his fellow editors filed suit in federal court, charging, among other things, that the university's refusal to fund their magazine because of its religious focus violated their First Amendment right to freedom of speech. A federal district court ruled in favor of the university on the grounds that funding for a religious newspaper by a state university would violate the Constitution's prohibition against government support for religion. Rosenberger and his colleagues appealed, but lost again when the district court's decision was affirmed by the Fourth Circuit Court of Appeals, which said that the Constitution mandated a strict separation of church and state. Undeterred, the student editors appealed the circuit court's decision to the Supreme Court. As we saw earlier in this chapter, the Supreme Court ruled in favor of the student group, holding that the university's policies amounted to state support for some ideas but not others. This, said the Court, represented a fundamental violation of the First Amendment.[108] The *Rosenberger* decision represents a potential loosening of the Court's long-standing opposition to any government support for religious groups or ideas, and it demonstrates how much influence can be exerted by a determined group of students.

One way to become politically involved is to seize on a civil liberties issue that stimulates your emotions and start a campus group to defend your position on the issue. Precisely because civil liberties issues generate strong feelings, there is a good chance that you can identify a small core of committed students who are willing to lend their support, commitment, and time to the group. Talk to classmates and friends. Circulate your ideas around the dormitory. Ask for a few minutes to speak to campus Democrats or Republicans or whatever groups might be sympathetic to your position. With only three or four initial members, you can launch your group.

Most college campuses have a central student board that handles funding for student groups. If so, consider applying for funding. Money widens your options for action. However, even without funding, you can go far. You might announce an organization meeting in your political science class or in the upcoming events section of the student newspaper. Contact the campus radio station (if you have one) or post flyers on campus bulletin boards. Even if just a few people show up, here are some of the kinds of activities and events you can organize.

- Hold informal gatherings where members and interested people can brainstorm possible activities around your civil liberties issue.
- Host prominent speakers who will talk about your issue and address questions from the audience.
- Plan or participate in debates with students or campus groups that have different views on the issue.
- Invite professors and students to participate in a "roundtable discussion" about your civil liberties issue.
- Set up card tables in high-traffic locations at lunch time to disseminate information or to gather signatures for a petition relevant to your issue.
- Make contact with national political groups that share your position. They may be able to provide you materials for dissemination and other resources.

Starting a campus group is a great way to get involved, encourage others to become more politically active, and at the same time focus your energy on an issue that is important to you. You may be surprised to discover that a relatively small but entrepreneurial group can make a difference on campus and beyond.

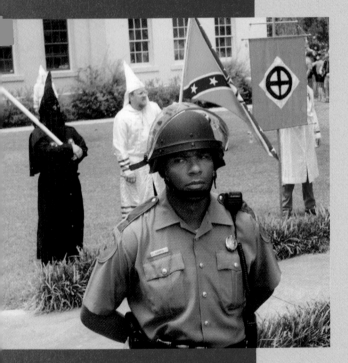

YOU ARE... a city council member!

John Stuart Mill argued that it is always wrong to silence minority opinion, no matter how objectionable, for it is only then that the majority might learn to change their mind or else strengthen their understanding of the truth. The Supreme Court has rejected his absolute approach, instead drawing lines between protected and unprotected speech.

What should a community do when some in the community want to speak out with extremely unpopular views—indeed views that are so offensive that others claim that the mere speech itself will do irreparable harm?

Serving on a city council in this country often means long hours and making tough decisions for little or no pay. Controversy often swirls around decisions that have lasting ramifications for the community.

Go to www.wwnorton.com/wtp5e

Questions to consider as you conduct the online simulation:

When rights to safety and security seem to conflict with fundamental civil liberties, how should we decide what to value more?

Should elected officials do what the majority desires or do what they think is best, even if very unpopular?

Should the time, place, and manner of speech matter when deciding whether the speech is constitutionally protected?

If hateful speech is political, does that make it more constitutionally protected?

If a small group cares more deeply about a conflict than the relatively "silent" majority, should the smaller group's opinion matter more?

Summary

The provisions of the Bill of Rights seek to protect citizens from improper government action. Civil liberties ought to be carefully distinguished from civil rights, which did not become part of the Constitution until the Fourteenth Amendment and its provision for "equal protection of the laws."

During its first century, the Bill of Rights was applicable only to the national government and not to the state governments. The Fourteenth Amendment (1868) seemed to apply the Bill of Rights to the states, but the Supreme Court continued to apply the Bill of Rights as though the Fourteenth Amendment had never been adopted. For sixty years following the adoption of the Fourteenth Amendment, only one provision was "incorporated" into the Fourteenth Amendment and applied as a restriction on the state governments: the Fifth Amendment "eminent domain" clause, which was incorporated in 1897. Even as recently as 1961, only the eminent domain clause and the clauses of the First Amendment had been incorporated into the Fourteenth Amendment and applied to the states. After 1961, one by one, most of the provisions of the Bill of Rights were finally incorporated and applied to the states, although a conservative Supreme Court tried to reverse this trend during the 1980s and 1990s. The status of the First Amendment seems to have been least affected by this conservative trend. Protection of purely political speech remains close to absolute. The categories of conditionally protected speech include "speech plus," libel and slander, obscenity and pornography, fighting words, and commercial speech. Nevertheless, the realm of free speech in all these areas is still quite broad.

Of the other amendments and clauses in the Bill of Rights, the ones most likely to receive conservative interpretations are the religious clauses of the First Amendment, illegal search and seizure cases arising under the Fourth Amendment, and cases involving the Eighth Amendment cruel and unusual punishment clause.

For Further Reading

Abraham, Henry J. *Freedom and the Court: Civil Rights and Liberties in the United States.* 6th ed. New York: Oxford University Press, 1994.

Bryner, Gary C., and A. Don Sorensen, eds. *The Bill of Rights: A Bicentennial Assessment.* Albany: State University of New York Press, 1993.

Eisenstein, Zillah. *The Female Body and the Law.* Berkeley: University of California Press, 1988.

Friendly, Fred W. *Minnesota Rag: The Dramatic Story of the Landmark Supreme Court Case that Gave New Meaning to Freedom of the Press.* New York: Vintage, 1982.

Glendon, Mary Ann. *Rights Talk: The Impoverishment of Political Discourse.* New York: Free Press, 1991.

Hentoff, Nat. *The First Freedom: The Tumultuous History of Free Speech in America.* New York: Basic Books, 1994.

Levy, Leonard. *Legacy of Suppression: Freedom of Speech and Press in Early American History.* New York: Harper, 1963.

Lewis, Anthony. *Gideon's Trumpet.* New York: Random House, 1964.

Meyer, Michael J., and William A. Parent. *The Constitution of Rights: Human Dignity and American Values.* Ithaca, NY: Cornell University Press, 1992.

Minow, Martha. *Making All the Difference: Inclusion, Exclusion, and American Law.* Ithaca, NY: Cornell University Press, 1990.

Silverstein, Mark. *Constitutional Faiths.* Ithaca, NY: Cornell University Press, 1984.

Stone, Geoffrey R., Richard A. Epstein, and Cass R. Sunstein, eds. *The Bill of Rights in the Modern State.* Chicago: University of Chicago Press, 1992.

Study Outline

www.wwnorton.com/wtp5e
Keyword: Review 4

A Brief History of the Bill of Rights

1. Despite the insistence of Alexander Hamilton that a bill of rights was both unnecessary and dangerous, adding a list of explicit rights was the most important item of business for the First Congress in 1789.
2. The Bill of Rights would have been more aptly named the "Bill of Liberties," because it is made up of provisions that protect citizens from improper government action.
3. Civil rights did not become part of the Constitution until 1868 with the adoption of the Fourteenth Amendment, which sought to provide for each citizen "the equal protection of the laws."
4. In 1833, the Supreme Court found that the Bill of Rights limited only the national government and not state governments.
5. Although the language of the Fourteenth Amendment seems to indicate that the protections of the Bill of Rights apply to state governments as well as the national government, for the remainder of the nineteenth century the Supreme Court (with only one exception) made decisions as if the Fourteenth Amendment had never been adopted.
6. As of 1961, only the First Amendment and one clause of the Fifth Amendment had been "selectively incorporated" into the Fourteenth Amendment. After 1961, however, most of the provisions of the Bill of Rights were incorporated into the Fourteenth Amendment and applied to the states.

The First Amendment and Freedom of Religion

1. The "establishment clause" of the First Amendment has been interpreted to mean the strict separation of church and state.
2. The "free exercise clause" protects the right to believe and to practice whatever religion one chooses; it also involves protection of the right to be a nonbeliever.

The First Amendment and Freedom of Speech and the Press

1. Although freedom of speech and freedom of the press hold an important place in the Bill of Rights, the extent and nature of certain types of expression are subject to constitutional debate.
2. Among the forms of speech that are absolutely protected are the truth, political speech, symbolic speech, and "speech plus," which is speech plus a physical activity such as picketing. The forms of speech that are currently only conditionally protected include libel and slander; obscenity and pornography; fighting words; and commercial speech.

The Second Amendment and the Right to Bear Arms

1. Constitutionally, the Second Amendment unquestionably protects citizens' rights to bear arms, but this right can be regulated by both state and federal law.

Rights of the Criminally Accused

1. The purpose of due process is to equalize the playing field between the accused individual and the all-powerful state.
2. The Fourth Amendment protects against unreasonable searches and seizures.
3. The Fifth Amendment requires a grand jury for most crimes, protects against double jeopardy, and provides that you cannot be forced to testify against yourself.
4. The Sixth Amendment requires a speedy trial and the right to witnesses and counsel.
5. The Eighth Amendment prohibits cruel and unusual punishment.

The Right to Privacy

1. In the case of *Griswold v. Connecticut,* the Supreme Court found a right of privacy in the Constitution. This right was confirmed and extended in 1973 in the case of *Roe v. Wade.*

Thinking Critically about the Future of Civil Liberties

1. Under Chief Justice William Rehnquist, the Court has somewhat restricted civil liberties without actually overturning any of the important decisions from the 1960s and 1970s that established many of the liberties enjoyed today.

Practice Quiz

www.wwnorton.com/wtp5e
Keyword: Quiz 4

1. From 1789 until the 1960s, the Bill of Rights put limits on
   a) the national government only.
   b) the state government only.
   c) both the national and state governments.
   d) neither the national nor the state governments.

2. The amendment that provided the basis for the modern understanding of the government's obligation to protect civil rights was the
   a) First Amendment.
   b) Ninth Amendment.
   c) Fourteenth Amendment.
   d) Twenty-second Amendment.

3. The so-called *Lemon* test, derived from the Supreme Court's ruling in *Lemon v. Kurtzman,* concerns the issue of
   a) school desegregation.
   b) aid to religious schools.
   c) prayer in school.
   d) obscenity.

4. The process by which some of the liberties in the Bill of Rights were applied to the states (or nationalized) is known as
   a) selective incorporation.
   b) judicial activism.
   c) civil liberties.
   d) establishment.

5. Which of the following provided that all of the protections contained in the Bill of Rights applied to the states as well as the national government?
   a) the Fourteenth Amendment
   b) *Palko v. Connecticut*
   c) *Gitlow v. New York*
   d) none of the above

6. Which of the following protections are not contained in the First Amendment?
   a) the establishment clause
   b) the free exercise clause
   c) freedom of the press
   d) All of the above are First Amendment protections.

7. Which of the following describes a written statement made in "reckless disregard of the truth" that is considered damaging to a victim because it is "malicious, scandalous, and defamatory"?
   a) slander
   b) libel
   c) fighting words
   d) expressive speech

8. The Fourth, Fifth, Sixth, and Eighth Amendments, taken together, define:
   a) due process of law.
   b) free speech.
   c) the right to bear arms.
   d) civil rights of minorities.

9. In what case was a right to privacy first found in the Constitution?
   a) *Griswold v. Connecticut*
   b) *Roe v. Wade*
   c) *Baker v. Carr*
   d) *Planned Parenthood v. Casey*

10. Which famous case deals with Sixth Amendment issues?
   a) *Miranda v. Arizona*
   b) *Mapp v. Ohio*
   c) *Gideon v. Wainwright*
   d) *Terry v. Ohio*

Key Terms

5 CIVIL RIGHTS

★ **The Struggle for Civil Rights**

What is the legal basis for civil rights?

How has the equal protection clause historically been enforced?

What is the critical Supreme Court ruling in the battle for equal protection?

How has Congress tried to make equal protection a reality?

In what areas did the civil rights acts seek to provide equal access and protection?

★ **The Universalization of Civil Rights**

What groups were spurred by the provision of the Civil Rights Act of 1964, outlawing discrimination in employment practices based on race, religion, and gender, to seek broader protection under the law?

What is the politics of the universalization of civil rights?

★ **Affirmative Action**

What is the basis for affirmative action? What forms does it take?

How does affirmative action contribute to the polarization of the politics of civil rights?

How does the debate about affirmative action reflect the debate over American political values?

What Government Does
and Why It Matters

N 1960, FOUR BLACK STUDENTS from North Carolina A&T made history: the four freshmen sat down at Woolworth's whites-only lunch counter in Greensboro, North Carolina, challenging the policies of segregation that kept blacks and whites in separate public and private accommodations across the South. Day after day the students sat at the counter, ignoring the taunts of onlookers, determined to break the system of segregation. Their actions and those of many other students, clergy members, and ordinary citizens finally did abolish such practices as separate white and black park benches, water fountains, and waiting rooms; the end of segregation meant opening access to public and private institutions on equal terms to all. But the victories of the civil rights movement did not come cheaply: many marchers, freedom riders, and sit-in participants were beaten; some were murdered.

Today, the Greensboro lunch counter is a part of history, on display at the Smithsonian Institution in Washington, D.C. Many goals of the civil rights movement that aroused such controversy in 1960 are now widely accepted as the proper expression of the American commitment to equal rights. But the question of what is meant by "equal rights" is hardly settled. While most Americans reject the idea that government should create equal outcomes for its citizens, they do widely endorse government action to prohibit public and private discrimination and they support the idea of equality of opportunity. However, even this concept is elusive. When past denial of rights creates unequal starting points for some groups, should government take additional steps to ensure equal opportunity? What kinds of groups should be specially protected against discrimination? Should the disabled receive special protection? Should gays and lesbians? Finally, what kinds of steps are acceptable to remedy discrimination, and who should bear the costs? These questions are at the heart of contemporary debates over **civil rights,** the obligation imposed on government to *take positive action* to protect citizens from any illegal action of government agencies as well as of other private citizens. ∎

civil rights obligation imposed on government to take positive action to protect citizens from any illegal action of government agencies as well as from other private citizens

discrimination use of any unreasonable and unjust criterion of exclusion

I N THE United States, the history of slavery and legalized racial **discrimination** against African Americans coexists uneasily with a strong tradition of individual liberty. Indeed, for much of our history Americans have struggled to reconcile such exclusionary racial practices with our notions of individual rights. With the adoption of the Fourteenth Amendment in 1868, civil rights became part of the Constitution, guaranteed to each citizen through "equal protection of the laws." This **equal protection clause** launched a century of political movements and legal efforts to press for racial equality. The African American quest for civil rights in turn inspired many other groups, including members of other racial and ethnic groups, women, the disabled, and gays and lesbians, to seek new laws and constitutional guarantees of their civil rights.

equal protection clause provision of the Fourteenth Amendment guaranteeing citizens "the equal protection of the laws." This clause has served as the basis for the civil rights of African Americans, women, and other groups

- **First, we review the legal developments and political movements that have expanded the scope of civil rights since the Fourteenth Amendment was adopted in 1868.** In this section, we look at the establishment of legal segregation in the South and the civil rights movement that overthrew it.

- **Second, we trace the broad impact that civil rights legislation has had on American life.** The Civil Rights Act of 1964 was especially critical in guaranteeing the "equal protection of the laws" set forth in the Fourteenth Amendment almost 100 years earlier.

- **We then explore how other groups, including women, Native Americans, Latinos, the disabled, and gays and lesbians, formed movements to win active protection of their rights as well.** This universalization of civil rights has become the new frontier of the civil rights struggle.

- **Next, we turn to the development of affirmative action and the controversies surrounding it.** The debate over affirmative action has intensified in recent years, revealing the ways in which Americans differ over the meaning of equality.

- **Finally, we review the role that citizens play in determining the meaning of civil rights.** As we see, students have often been in the forefront of the civil rights debate.

■ Previewing Liberty, Equality, and Democracy

In *Animal Farm* George Orwell wrote that "all animals are equal, but some animals are more equal than others." Apply this satirical, pessimistic comment to humans, and its truth is perhaps no more evident than in the history of civil rights in the United States. This chapter will show how inequalities between races and genders were tolerated, and even enforced by law. While the United States is based on the ideals of liberty, equality, and democracy, its history of civil rights reveals a gap between these principles and the actual practices. This history also reveals how the struggle to obtain those ideals has helped narrow this gap. Closer to the present day, the struggle for political and social equality also shows how liberty and equality are not mutually supportive. In fact, these principles are often in conflict with one another. This chapter's concluding discussion of affirmative action illustrates this conflict.

The Struggle for Civil Rights

For African Americans, the central fact of political life has been a denial of full citizenship rights for most of American history. By accepting the institution of slavery, the Founders embraced a system fundamentally at odds with the "Blessings of Liberty" promised in the Constitution. Their decision set the stage for two centuries of African American struggles to achieve full citizenship. For women as well, electoral politics was a decidedly masculine world. Until 1920, not only were women barred from voting in national politics, but electoral politics was closely tied to such male social institutions as lodges, bars, and clubs. Yet the exclusion of women from this political world did not prevent them from engaging in public life. Instead, women carved out a "separate sphere" for their public activities. Emphasizing female stewardship over the moral realm, women became important voices in social reform well before they won the right to vote.[1] For example, prior to the Civil War, women played leading roles in the abolitionist movement.

SLAVERY AND THE ABOLITIONIST MOVEMENT

No issue in the nation's history so deeply divided Americans as that of the abolition of slavery. The importation and subjugation of Africans kidnapped from their native lands was a practice virtually as old as the country itself: the first slaves brought to what became the United States arrived in 1619, a year before the Plymouth colony was established in Massachusetts. White southerners built their agricultural economy (especially cotton production) on a large slave labor force. By 1840, for example, nearly half of the populations of Alabama and Louisiana consisted of black slaves. Even so, only about a quarter of southern white families owned slaves.

The subjugation of blacks through slavery was so much a part of the southern culture that efforts to restrict or abolish slavery were met with fierce resistance. Despite the manifest cruelties of the slave system, southerners referred to the system by the quaint term "peculiar institution." The label meant little to slavery's opponents, however, and an abolitionist movement grew and spread among northerners in the 1830s (although abolitionist sentiment could be traced back to the pre-Revolutionary era). The movement was most closely identified with the writing of William Lloyd Garrison. Slavery had been all but eliminated in the North by this time, but few northerners favored outright abolition. In fact, most whites held attitudes toward blacks that would be considered racist today.

The abolitionist movement spread primarily through local organizations in the North. Antislavery groups coalesced in New York, Ohio, New Hampshire, Pennsylvania, New Jersey, and Michigan. In addition to forming antislavery societies, the movement spawned two political parties: the Liberty Party, a staunchly antislavery party, and the Free Soil Party, a larger but more moderate third party that sought primarily to restrict the spread of slavery into new western territories. Garrison noted his dismay at the Free Soil Party's more modest and pragmatic approach: "It is a party for keeping Free Soil and not for setting men free."

Some opponents of slavery took matters into their own hands, aiding in the escape of runaway slaves along the Underground Railroad. Even today, private homes and churches, scattered throughout the northeast, that were used to hide blacks on their trips to Canada, attest to the involvement of local citizenry. In the South, a similar, if contrary, fervor prompted mobs to break into post offices in order to seize and destroy antislavery literature.

The emotional power of the slavery issue was such that it precipitated the nation's most bloody conflict, the Civil War. From the ashes of the Civil War came the Thirteenth, Fourteenth, and Fifteenth Amendments, which would redefine civil rights from that day to this.

THE LINK TO THE WOMEN'S RIGHTS MOVEMENT

The quiet upstate New York town of Seneca Falls played host to what would later come to be known as the starting point of the modern women's movement. Convened in July 1848, and organized by activists Elizabeth Cady Stanton (who lived in Seneca Falls) and Lucretia Mott, the Seneca Falls Convention drew three hundred delegates to discuss and formulate plans to advance the political and social rights of women.

The centerpiece of the convention was its Declaration of Sentiments and Resolutions. Patterned after the Declaration of Independence, the Seneca Falls document declared, "We hold these truths to be self-evident: that all men and women are created equal," and "The history of mankind is a history of repeated injuries and usurpations on the part of man toward woman, having in direct object the establishment of an absolute tyranny over her." The most controversial provision of the declaration, nearly rejected as too radical, was the call for the right to vote for women. Although most of the delegates were women, about forty men participated, including the renowned abolitionist Frederick Douglass.

The link to the antislavery movement was not new. Stanton and Mott had attended the World Anti-slavery Convention in London in 1840, but had been denied delegate seats because of their sex. This rebuke helped precipitate the 1848 convention. The movements for women's rights and abolition of slavery were also closely linked with the temperance movement (because alcohol abuse was closely linked to male abuses of women). The convergence of the antislavery, temperance, and suffrage movements was reflected in the views and actions of other women's movement leaders, such as Susan B. Anthony.

The convention and its participants were subjected to widespread ridicule, but similar conventions were organized in other states, and in the same year, New York

State passed the Married Women's Property Act in order to restore the right of a married woman to own property.

THE CIVIL WAR AMENDMENTS TO THE CONSTITUTION

The hopes of African Americans for achieving full citizenship rights initially seemed fulfilled when three constitutional amendments were adopted after the Civil War: the **Thirteenth Amendment** abolished slavery; the **Fourteenth Amendment** guaranteed equal protection under the law; and the **Fifteenth Amendment** guaranteed voting rights for blacks. Protected by the presence of federal troops, African American men were able to exercise their political rights immediately after the war. During Reconstruction, blacks were elected to many political offices: two black senators were elected from Mississippi and a total of fourteen African Americans were elected to the House of Representatives between 1869 and 1877. African Americans also held many state-level political offices. As voters and public officials, black citizens found a home in the Republican Party, which had secured the ratification of the three constitutional amendments guaranteeing black rights. After the war, the Republican Party continued to reach out to black voters as a means to build party strength in the South.[2]

Thirteenth Amendment one of three Civil War amendments; abolished slavery

Fourteenth Amendment one of three Civil War amendments; guaranteed equal protection and due process

Fifteenth Amendment one of three Civil War amendments; guaranteed voting rights for African American men

This political equality was short-lived, however. The national government withdrew its troops from the South and turned its back on African Americans in 1877. In the Compromise of 1877, southern Democrats agreed to allow the Republican candidate, Rutherford B. Hayes, to become president after a disputed election. In exchange, northern Republicans dropped their support for the civil liberties and political participation of African Americans. After that, southern states erected a **"Jim Crow"** system of social, political, and economic inequality that made a mockery of the promises in the Constitution.

"Jim Crow" laws enacted by southern states following Reconstruction that discriminated against African Americans

Around the same time, some women pressed for the right to vote at the national level immediately after the Civil War, when male ex-slaves won the franchise. Politicians in both parties rejected women's suffrage as disruptive and unrealistic. Women also started to press for the vote at the state level in 1867 when a referendum to give women the vote in Kansas failed. Frustration with the general failure to win reforms in other states accelerated suffrage activism. In 1872, Susan B. Anthony and several other women were arrested in Rochester, New York, for illegally registering and voting in that year's national election. (The men who allowed the women to register and vote were also indicted; Anthony paid their expenses and eventually won presidential pardons for them.) At her trial, Judge Ward Hunt ordered the jury to find her guilty without deliberation. Yet Anthony was allowed to address the court, saying, "Your denial of my citizen's right to vote is the denial of my right of consent as one of the governed, the denial of my right of representation as one of the taxed, the denial of my right to a trial of my peers as an offender against the law."[3] Hunt assessed Anthony a fine of $100 but did not sentence her to jail. Anthony refused to pay the fine.

CIVIL RIGHTS AND THE SUPREME COURT: "SEPARATE BUT EQUAL"

Resistance to equality for African Americans in the South led Congress to adopt the Civil Rights Act of 1875, which attempted to protect blacks from discrimination by proprietors of hotels, theaters, and other public accommodations. But the

Court declared the Civil Rights Act of 1875 unconstitutional on the grounds that the act sought to protect blacks against discrimination by *private* businesses, while the Fourteenth Amendment, according to the Court's interpretation, was intended to protect individuals from discrimination only against actions by *public* officials of state and local governments.

In 1896, the Court went still further, in the infamous case of *Plessy v. Ferguson,* by upholding a Louisiana statute that *required* segregation of the races on trolleys and other public carriers (and by implication in all public facilities, including schools). Plessy, a man defined as "one-eighth black," had violated a Louisiana law that provided for "equal but separate accommodations" on trains and a $25 fine for any white passenger who sat in a car reserved for blacks or any black passenger who sat in a car reserved for whites. The Supreme Court held that the Fourteenth Amendment's "equal protection of the laws" was not violated by racial distinction as long as the facilities were equal, thus establishing the **"separate but equal" rule** that prevailed through the mid-twentieth century. People generally pretended that segregated accommodations were equal as long as some accommodation for blacks existed. The Court said that although "the object of the [Fourteenth] Amendment was undoubtedly to enforce the absolute equality of the two races before the law, . . . it could not have intended to abolish distinctions based on color, or to enforce so-cial, as distinguished from political, equality, or a commingling of the two races upon terms unsatisfactory to either."[4] What the Court was saying in effect was that the use of race as a criterion of exclusion in public matters was not unreasonable.

"separate but equal" rule doctrine that public accommodations could be segregated by race but still be equal

ORGANIZING FOR EQUALITY

The National Association for the Advancement of Colored People (NAACP) The creation of a "Jim Crow" system in the southern states and the lack of a legal basis for "equal protection under the laws" prompted the beginning of a long process in which African Americans built organizations and devised strategies for asserting their constitutional rights.

One such strategy sought to win political rights through political pressure and litigation. This approach was championed by the NAACP, established by a group of black and white reformers in 1909. Among the NAACP's founders was W. E. B. Du Bois, one of the most influential and creative thinkers on racial issues of the twentieth century. Because the northern black vote was so small in the early decades of the twentieth century, the organization primarily relied on the courts to press for black political rights. After the 1920s, the NAACP built a strong membership base, with some strength in the South, which would be critical when the civil rights movement gained momentum in the 1950s.

The great migration of blacks to the North beginning around World War I en-livened a protest strategy. Although protest organizations had existed in the nine-teenth century, the continuing migration of blacks to the North made protest an increasingly useful tool. Black labor leader A. Philip Randolph forced the federal government to address racial discrimination in hiring practices during World War II by threatening a massive march on Washington. The federal government also grew more attentive to blacks as their voting strength increased as a result of the northward migration. By the 1940s, the black vote had swung away from Re-publicans, but the Democratic hold on black votes was by no means absolute.

Women's Organizations and the Right to Suffrage   Suffragists used the occasion of the Constitution's centennial in 1887 to protest the continued denial of their rights. For these women, the centennial represented "a century of injustice." The unveiling of the Statue of Liberty, depicting liberty as a woman, in New York Harbor in 1886 prompted women's rights advocates to call it " the greatest hypocrisy of the nineteenth century," in that "not one single woman throughout the length and breadth of the Land is as yet in possession of political Liberty."[5]

The climactic movement toward suffrage was formally launched in 1878 with the introduction of a proposed constitutional amendment in Congress. Parallel efforts were made in the states. Many states granted women the right to vote before the national government did; western states with less-entrenched political systems opened politics to women earliest. When Wyoming became a state in 1890, it was the first state to grant full suffrage to women. Colorado, Utah, and Idaho all followed suit in the next several years. Suffrage organizations grew—the National American Woman Suffrage Association (NAWSA), formed in 1890, claimed two million members by 1917—and staged mass meetings, parades, petitions, and protests. NAWSA organized state-by-state efforts to win the right for women to vote. A more militant group, the National Women's Party, staged pickets and got arrested in front of the White House to protest President Wilson's opposition to a constitutional amendment granting women this right. Finally in 1920, the Nineteenth Amendment was ratified, guaranteeing women the right to vote.

LITIGATING FOR EQUALITY AFTER WORLD WAR II

The shame of discrimination against black military personnel during World War II, plus revelations of Nazi racial atrocities, moved President Harry S. Truman finally to bring the problem to the White House and national attention, with the appointment in 1946 of the President's Commission on Civil Rights. In 1948, the commission submitted its report, *To Secure These Rights*, which laid bare the extent of the problem of racial discrimination and its consequences. The report also revealed the success of experiments with racial integration in the armed forces during World War II to demonstrate to southern society that it had nothing to fear. But the committee recognized that the national government had no clear constitutional authority to pass and implement civil rights legislation. The committee proposed tying civil rights legislation to the commerce power, although it was clear that discrimination was not itself part of the flow of interstate commerce.[6] The committee even suggested using the treaty power as a source of constitutional authority for civil rights legislation.[7]

As for the Supreme Court, it had begun to change its position on racial discrimination before World War II by being stricter about the criterion of equal facilities in the "separate but equal" rule. In 1938, for example, the Court rejected Missouri's policy of paying the tuition of qualified blacks to out-of-state law schools rather than admitting them to the University of Missouri Law School.[8]

After the war, modest progress resumed. In 1950, the Court rejected Texas's claim that its new "law school for Negroes" afforded education equal to that of the all-white University of Texas Law School. Without confronting the "separate but equal" principle itself, the Court's decision anticipated its future civil rights rulings by opening the question of whether *any* segregated facilities could be truly equal.[9]

But the Supreme Court, in ordering the admission of blacks to all-white state law schools, did not directly confront the "separate but equal" rule because the Court needed only to recognize the absence of any *equal* law school for blacks. The same was true in 1944, when the Supreme Court struck down the southern practice of "white primaries," which legally excluded blacks from participation in the nominating process. Here the Court simply recognized that primaries could no longer be regarded as the private affairs of the parties but were an integral aspect of the electoral process. This made parties "an agency of the State," and therefore any practice of discrimination against blacks was "state action within the meaning of the Fifteenth Amendment."[10] The most important pre-1954 decision was probably *Shelley v. Kraemer,* in which the Court ruled against the widespread practice of "restrictive covenants," whereby the seller of a home added a clause to the sales contract requiring the buyer to agree not to sell the home later to any non-Caucasian, non-Christian, and so on. The Court ruled that although private persons could sign such restrictive covenants, they could not be judicially enforced since the Fourteenth Amendment prohibits any organ of the state, including the courts, from denying equal protection of its laws.[11]

Although none of those pre-1954 cases confronted "separate but equal" and the principle of racial discrimination as such, they were extremely significant to black leaders in the 1940s and gave them encouragement enough to believe that there was at last an opportunity and enough legal precedent to change the constitutional framework itself. Much of this legal work was done by the Legal Defense and Educational Fund of the NAACP. Until the late 1940s, lawyers working for the Legal Defense Fund had concentrated on winning small victories within that framework. Then, in 1948, the Legal Defense Fund upgraded its approach by simultaneously filing suits in different federal districts and through each level of schooling from unequal provision of kindergarten for blacks to unequal sports and science facilities in all-black high schools. After nearly two years of these mostly successful equalization suits, the lawyers decided the time was ripe to confront the "separate but equal" rule head-on, but they felt they needed some heavier artillery to lead the attack. Their choice was African American lawyer Thurgood Marshall, who had been fighting, and often winning, equalization suits since the early 1930s. Marshall was pessimistic about the readiness of the Supreme Court for a full confrontation with segregation itself and the constitutional principle sustaining it. But the unwillingness of Congress after the 1948 election to consider fair employment legislation seems to have convinced Marshall that the courts were the only hope.

The Supreme Court must have come to the same conclusion because during the four years following 1948 there emerged a clear impression that the Court was willing to take more civil rights cases on appeal. Yet this was no guarantee that the Court would reverse *on principle* the separate but equal precedent of *Plessy v. Ferguson.* All through 1951 and 1952, as cases were winding slowly through the lower-court litigation maze, intense discussions and disagreements arose among NAACP lawyers as to whether a full-scale assault on *Plessy* was good strategy or whether it might not be better to continue with specific cases alleging unequal treatment and demanding relief with a Court-imposed policy of equalization.[12] But for some lawyers like Marshall, these kinds of victories could amount to a defeat. South Carolina, for example, under the leadership of Governor James F. Byrnes, a former Supreme Court justice, had undertaken a strategy of equalization of school services on a large scale in order to satisfy the *Plessy* rule and to head off or render moot litigation against the principle of separate but equal.

In the fall of 1952, the Court had on its docket cases from Kansas, South Carolina, Virginia, Delaware, and the District of Columbia challenging the constitutionality of school segregation. Of these, the case filed in Kansas became the chosen one. It seemed to be ahead of the pack in its district court, and it had the special advantage of being located in a state outside the Deep South.[13]

Oliver Brown, the father of three girls, lived "across the tracks" in a low-income, racially mixed Topeka neighborhood. Every school-day morning, Linda Brown took the school bus to the Monroe School for black children about a mile away. In September 1950, Oliver Brown took Linda to the all-white Sumner School, which was closer to home, to enter her into the third grade in defiance of state law and local segregation rules. When they were refused, Brown took his case to the NAACP, and soon thereafter **Brown v. Board of Education** was born. In mid-1953, the Court announced that the several cases on their way up would be reargued within a set of questions having to do with the intent of the Fourteenth Amendment. Almost exactly a year later, the Court responded to those questions in one of the most important decisions in its history.

In deciding the *Brown* case, the Court, to the surprise of many, basically rejected as inconclusive all the learned arguments about the intent and the history of the Fourteenth Amendment and committed itself to considering only the consequences of segregation:

> Does segregation of children in public schools solely on the basis of race, even though the physical facilities and other "tangible" factors may be equal, deprive the children of the minority group of equal educational opportunities? We believe that it does. . . . We conclude that in the field of public education the doctrine of "separate but equal" has no place. Separate educational facilities are inherently unequal.[14]

The *Brown* decision altered the constitutional framework in two fundamental respects. First, after *Brown,* the states no longer had the power to use race as a criterion of discrimination in law. Second, the national government from then on had the power (and eventually the obligation) to intervene with strict regulatory policies against the discriminatory actions of state or local governments, school boards, employers, and many others in the private sector.

CIVIL RIGHTS AFTER *BROWN V. BOARD OF EDUCATION*

Brown v. Board of Education withdrew all constitutional authority to use race as a criterion of exclusion, and it signaled more clearly the Court's determination to use the **strict scrutiny** test in cases related to racial discrimination. This meant that the burden of proof would fall on the government—not on the challengers—to show that the law in question *was* constitutional.[15] Although the use of strict scrutiny in cases relating to racial discrimination would give an advantage to those attacking racial discrimination, the historic decision in *Brown v. Board of Education* was merely a small opening move. First, most states refused to cooperate until sued, and many ingenious schemes were employed to delay obedience (such as paying the tuition for white students to attend newly created "private" academies). Second, even as southern school boards began to cooperate by eliminating their legally enforced

Brown v. Board of Education the 1954 Supreme Court decision that struck down the "separate but equal" doctrine as fundamentally unequal. This case eliminated state power to use race as a criterion of discrimination in law and provided the national government with the power to intervene by exercising strict regulatory policies against discriminatory actions

FOR CRITICAL ANALYSIS

Describe the changes in American society between the *Plessy v. Ferguson* and the *Brown v. Board of Education* decisions. Using this as an example, explain how changes in society can lead to changes in civil rights policy or other types of government policy. How might changes in society have predicted the changes in civil rights policy in America since the *Brown* case? How might the changes in civil rights policy have changed American society?

strict scrutiny test, used by the Supreme Court in racial discrimination cases and other cases involving civil liberties and civil rights, which places the burden of proof on the government rather than on the challengers to show that the law in question is constitutional

The push for equality for African Americans began in the nineteenth century. African Americans won the right to vote after the Civil War with the passage of the Thirteenth, Fourteenth, and Fifteenth Amendments, and many former slaves began registering and voting in state elections as early as 1867. This political influence soon evaporated in the face of Jim Crow laws and the end of Reconstruction.

de jure literally, "by law"; legally enforced practices, such as school segregation in the South before the 1960s

de facto literally, "by fact"; practices that occur even when there is no legal enforcement, such as school segregation in much of the United States today

The 1896 Supreme Court case of Plessy v. Ferguson upheld legal segregation and created the "separate but equal" rule, which fostered national segregation. This 1941 photograph of a rural Georgia school for black students shows the inferior conditions that African Americans faced under the Plessy *ruling (left). Overt discrimination in public accommodations was common (right).*

(**de jure**) school segregation, there remained extensive actual (**de facto**) school segregation in the North as well as in the South, as a consequence of racially segregated housing that could not be reached by the 1954–55 *Brown* principles. Third, discrimination in employment, public accommodations, juries, voting, and other areas of social and economic activity were not directly touched by *Brown*.

School Desegregation, Phase One   Although the District of Columbia and some of the school districts in the border states began to respond almost immediately to court-ordered desegregation, the states of the Deep South responded with a carefully planned delaying tactic commonly called "massive resistance" by the more demagogic southern leaders and "nullification" and "interposition" by the centrists. Either way, southern politicians stood shoulder-to-shoulder to declare that the Supreme Court's decisions and orders were without effect. The legislatures in these states enacted statutes ordering school districts to maintain segregated schools and state superintendents to terminate state funding wherever there was racial mixing in the

In the 1950s, school segregation came under attack at the federal level. "Massive resistance" among white southerners attempted to block the desegregation attempts of the national government. For example, at Little Rock Central High School in 1957, an angry mob of white students prevented black students from entering the school. As a result, the federal government sent troops to protect the black students and to uphold the desegregation plan.

classroom. Some southern states violated their own long traditions of local school autonomy by centralizing public school authority under the governor or the state board of education and by giving states the power to close the schools and to provide alternative private schooling wherever local school boards might be tending to obey the Supreme Court.

The 1964 Civil Rights Act made desegregation a legal requirement. One government remedy was court-ordered busing from black schools to white schools. Busing bitterly divided the black and white communities in Boston. In 1976, a mob of white protesters outside the Boston federal courthouse sought to impale this innocent black bystander—a lawyer on his way to his office—on a flag. In the face of institutional and white resistance, school desegregation remains incomplete fifty years after it began.

Most of these plans of "massive resistance" were tested in the federal courts and were struck down as unconstitutional.[16] But southern resistance was not confined to legislation. For example, in Arkansas in 1957, Governor Orval Faubus mobilized the Arkansas National Guard to intercede against enforcement of a federal court order to integrate Central High School of Little Rock, and President Eisenhower was forced to deploy U.S. troops and literally place the city under martial law. The Supreme Court considered the Little Rock confrontation so historically important that the opinion it rendered in that case was not only agreed to unanimously but was, unprecedentedly, signed personally by every one of the justices.[17] The end of massive resistance, however, became simply the beginning of still another southern strategy, "pupil placement" laws, which authorized school districts to place each pupil in a school according to a whole variety of academic, personal, and psychological considerations, never mentioning race at all. This put the burden of transferring to an all-white school on the nonwhite children and their parents, making it almost impossible for a single court order to cover a whole district, let alone a whole state. This delayed desegregation a while longer.[18]

Social Protest and Congressional Action   Ten years after *Brown,* fewer than 1 percent of black school-age children in the Deep South were attending schools with whites.[19] A decade of frustration made it fairly obvious to all observers that adjudication alone would not succeed. The goal of "equal protection" required positive, or affirmative, action by Congress and by administrative agencies. And given massive southern resistance and a generally negative national public opinion toward racial integration, progress would not be made through courts, Congress, or federal agencies without intense, well-organized support. Table 5.1 shows the increase in civil rights demonstrations for voting rights and public accommodations during the fourteen years following *Brown.* It shows that organized civil rights demonstrations began to mount slowly but surely after *Brown v. Board of Education.* By the 1960s, the many organizations that made up the civil rights movement had accumulated experience and built networks capable of launching massive direct-action campaigns against southern segregationists. The Southern Christian Leadership Conference, the Student Nonviolent Coordinating Committee, and many other organizations had built a movement that stretched across the South. The movement used the media to attract nationwide attention and support. In the massive March on Washington in 1963, the Reverend Martin Luther King, Jr., staked out the movement's moral claims in his famous "I Have a Dream" speech. The image of protesters being beaten, attacked by police dogs, and set upon with fire hoses did much to win broad sympathy for the cause of black civil rights and to discredit state and local governments in the South. In this way, the movement created intense pressure for a reluctant federal government to take more assertive steps to defend black civil rights.

The first modern effort to legislate in the field of civil rights was made in 1957, but the law contained only a federal guarantee of voting rights, without any powers of enforcement, although it did create the Civil Rights Commission to study abuses. Much more important legislation for civil rights followed, especially the Civil Rights Act of 1964. It is important to observe here the mutual dependence of the courts and legislatures: not only do the legislatures need constitutional authority to act, but the courts need legislative and political assis-

Peaceful Civil Rights Demonstrations, 1954–68

Table 5.1

YEAR	TOTAL	FOR PUBLIC ACCOMMODATIONS	FOR VOTING
1954	0	0	0
1955	0	0	0
1956	18	6	0
1957	44	9	0
1958	19	8	0
1959	7	11	0
1960	173	127	0
1961	198	122	0
1962	77	44	0
1963	272	140	1
1964	271	93	12
1965	387	21	128
1966	171	15	32
1967	93	3	3
1968	97	2	0

NOTE: This table is drawn from a search of the *New York Times Index* for all references to civil rights demonstrations during the years the table covers. The table should be taken simply as indicative, for the data—news stories in a single paper—are very crude. The classification of the incident as peaceful or violent and the subject area of the demonstration are inferred from the entry in the *Index*, usually the headline from the story. The two subcategories reported here—public accommodations and voting—do not sum to the total because demonstrations dealing with a variety of other issues (e.g., education, employment, police brutality) are included in the total.

SOURCE: Jonathan D. Casper, *The Politics of Civil Liberties* (New York: Harper & Row, 1972), p. 90.

tance, through the power of the purse and the power to organize administrative agencies to implement court orders, and through the focusing of political support. Consequently, even as the U.S. Congress finally moved into the field of school desegregation (and other areas of "equal protection"), the courts continued to exercise their powers, not only by placing court orders against recalcitrant school districts, but also by extending and reinterpreting aspects of the "equal protection" clause to support legislative and administrative actions (see Figure 5.1).

THE CIVIL RIGHTS ACTS

The right to equal protection of the laws could be established and, to a certain extent, implemented by the courts. But after a decade of very frustrating efforts, the courts and Congress ultimately came to the conclusion that the federal courts alone were not adequate to the task of changing the social rules, and that legislation and administrative action would be needed.

Three civil rights acts were passed during the first decade after the 1954 Supreme Court decision in *Brown v. Board of Education*. But these acts were of only marginal importance. The first two, in 1957 and 1960, established that the Fourteenth Amendment of the Constitution, adopted almost a century earlier,

Figure 5.1 — Cause and Effect in the Civil Rights Movement

Political action and government action spurred each other to produce dramatic changes in American civil rights policies.

Judicial and Legal Action	Political Action
1954 *Brown v. Board of Education*	
1955 *Brown* II—Implementation of *Brown* I	**1955** Montgomery, Alabama, bus boycott
1956 Federal courts order school integration, especially one ordering Autherine Lucy admitted to University of Alabama, with Governor Wallace officially protesting	
1957 Civil Rights Act creating Civil Rights Commission; President Eisenhower sends paratroops to Little Rock, Arkansas, to enforce integration of Central High School	**1957** Southern Christian Leadership Conference (SCLC) formed, with Martin Luther King, Jr. as president
1960 First substantive Civil Rights Act, primarily voting rights	**1960** Student Nonviolent Coordinating Committee formed to organize protests, sit-ins, freedom rides
1961 Interstate Commerce Commission orders desegregation on all buses and trains, and in terminals	
1961 JFK favors executive action over civil rights legislation	
1963 JFK shifts, supports strong civil rights law; assassination; LBJ asserts strong support for civil rights	**1963** Nonviolent demonstrations in Birmingham, Alabama, lead to King's arrest and his "Letter from the Birmingham Jail"
	1963 March on Washington
1964 Congress passes historic Civil Rights Act covering voting, employment, public accommodations, education	
1965 Voting Rights Act	**1965** King announces drive to register 3 million blacks in the South
1966 War on Poverty in full swing	**Late 1960s** Movement dissipates: part toward litigation, part toward community action programs, part toward war protest, part toward more militant "Black Power" actions

could no longer be disregarded, particularly with regard to voting. The third, the Equal Pay Act of 1963, was more important, but it was concerned with women, did not touch the question of racial discrimination, and had no enforcement mechanisms.

By far the most important piece of legislation passed by Congress concerning equal opportunity was the Civil Rights Act of 1964. It not only put some teeth in the voting rights provisions of the 1957 and 1960 acts but also went far beyond voting to attack discrimination in public accommodations, segregation in the schools, and at long last, the discriminatory conduct of employers in hiring, promoting, and laying off their employees. Discrimination against women was also included, extending the important 1963 provisions. The 1964 act seemed bold at the time, but it was enacted ten years after the Supreme Court had declared racial discrimination "inherently unequal" under the Fifth and Fourteenth Amendments. And it was enacted long after blacks had demonstrated that discrimination was no longer acceptable. The choice in 1964 was not between congressional action or inaction but between legal action and expanded violence.

Public Accommodations   After the passage of the 1964 Civil Rights Act, public accommodations quickly removed some of the most visible forms of racial discrimination. Signs defining "colored" and "white" restrooms, water fountains, waiting rooms, and seating arrangements were removed and a host of other practices that relegated black people to separate and inferior arrangements were ended. In addition, the federal government filed more than 400 antidiscrimination suits in federal courts against hotels, restaurants, taverns, gas stations, and other "public accommodations."

Many aspects of legalized racial segregation—such as separate Bibles in the courtroom—seem like ancient history today. But the issue of racial discrimination in public settings is by no means over. In 1993, six African American Secret Service agents filed charges against the Denny's restaurant chain for failing to serve them; white Secret Service agents at a nearby table had received prompt service. Similar charges citing discriminatory service at Denny's restaurants surfaced across the country. Faced with evidence of a pattern of systematic discrimination and numerous lawsuits, Denny's paid $45 million in damages to plaintiffs in Maryland and California in what is said to be the largest settlement ever in a public accommodation case.[20] The Denny's case shows how effective the Civil Rights Act of 1964 can be in challenging racial discrimination. In addition to the settlement, the chain vowed to expand employment and management opportunities for minorities in Denny's restaurants. Other forms of racial discrimination in public accommodations are harder to challenge, however. For example, there is considerable evidence that taxicabs often refuse to pick up black passengers.[21] Such practices may be common, but they are difficult to prove and remedy through the law.

School Desegregation, Phase Two   The 1964 Civil Rights Act also declared discrimination by private employers and state governments (school boards, etc.) illegal, then went further to provide for administrative agencies to help the courts implement these laws. Title IV of the act, for example, authorized the executive branch, through the Justice Department, to implement federal court orders to desegregate schools, and to do so without having to wait for individual parents to bring complaints. Title VI of the act vastly strengthened the role of the executive branch and the credibility of court orders by providing that federal grants-in-aid to state and local governments for education must be withheld from any school system practicing racial segregation. Title VI became the most effective weapon for desegregating schools outside the South, because the situation in northern communities was more subtle and difficult to reach. In the South, the problem was segregation by law coupled with overt resistance to the national government's efforts to change the situation. In contrast, outside the South, segregated facilities were the outcome of hundreds of thousands of housing choices made by individuals and families. Once racial residential patterns emerged, racial homogeneity, property values, and neighborhood schools and churches were defended by realtors, neighborhood organizations, and the like. Thus, in order to eliminate discrimination nationwide, the 1964 Civil Rights Act (1) gave the president through the Office for Civil Rights of the Justice Department the power to withhold federal education grants,[22] and (2) gave the attorney general of the United States the power to initiate suits (rather than having to await complaints) wherever there was a "pattern or practice" of discrimination.[23]

In the decade following the 1964 Civil Rights Act, the Justice Department brought legal action against more than 500 school districts. During the same period, administrative agencies filed actions against 600 school districts, threatening to suspend federal aid to education unless real desegregation steps were taken.

Busing   One step taken toward desegregation was busing children from poor urban school districts to wealthier suburban ones. In 1971, the Supreme Court held that state-imposed desegregation could be brought about by busing children across school districts, even where relatively long distances were involved:

> If school authorities fail in their affirmative obligations judicial authority may be invoked. Once a right and a violation have been shown, the scope of a district court's equitable powers to remedy past wrongs is broad. . . . Bus transportation [is] a normal and accepted tool of educational policy.[24]

But the decision went beyond that, adding that under certain limited circumstances even racial quotas could be used as the "starting point in shaping a remedy to correct past constitutional violations," and that pairing or grouping of schools and reorganizing school attendance zones would also be acceptable.

Three years later, however, this principle was severely restricted when the Supreme Court determined that only cities found guilty of deliberate and de jure racial segregation would have to desegregate their schools.[25] This ruling had the effect of exempting most northern states and cities from busing because school segregation in northern cities is generally de facto segregation that follows from segregated housing and from thousands of acts of private discrimination against blacks and other minorities.

Boston provides the best illustration of the agonizing problem of making further progress in civil rights in the schools under the constitutional framework established by these decisions. Boston school authorities were found guilty of deliberately building school facilities and drawing school districts "to increase racial segregation." After vain efforts by Boston school authorities to draw up an acceptable plan to remedy the segregation, federal judge W. Arthur Garrity ordered an elaborate desegregation plan of his own, involving busing between the all-black neighborhood of Roxbury and the nearby white, working-class community of South Boston. Opponents of this plan were organized and eventually took the case to the Supreme Court, where *certiorari* (the Court's device for accepting appeals; see Chapter 15) was denied; this had the effect of approving Judge Garrity's order. The city's schools were so segregated and uncooperative that even the conservative administration of President Richard Nixon had already initiated a punitive cutoff of funds. But many liberals also criticized Judge Garrity's plan as being badly conceived, because it involved two neighboring communities with a history of tension and mutual resentment. The plan worked well at the elementary school level but proved so explosive at the high school level that it generated a continuing crisis for the city of Boston and for the whole nation over court-ordered, federally directed desegregation in the North.[26]

Additional progress in the desegregation of schools is likely to be extremely slow unless the Supreme Court decides to permit federal action against de facto segregation and against the varieties of private schools and academies that have sprung up for the purpose of avoiding integration. The prospects for further school integration diminished with a Supreme Court decision handed down on January 15, 1991. The opinion, written for the Court by Chief Justice William Rehnquist, held that lower federal courts could end supervision of local school boards if those boards could show compliance "in good faith" with court orders to desegregate and could show that "vestiges of past discrimination" had been eliminated "to the extent practicable."[27] It is not necessarily easy for a school board to prove that the new standard has been met, but this was the first time since *Brown* and the 1964 Civil Rights Act that the Court had opened the door at all to retreat.

That door of retreat was opened further by a 1995 decision in which the Court ruled that the remedies being applied in Kansas City, Missouri, were improper.[28] In accordance with a lower court ruling, the state was pouring additional funding into salaries and remedial programs for Kansas City schools, which had a history of segregation. The aim of the spending was to improve student performance and to attract white students from the suburbs into the city schools. The Supreme Court declared the interdistrict goal improper and reiterated its earlier ruling that states can free themselves of court orders by showing a good faith effort. This decision indicated the Court's new willingness to end desegregation plans even when predominantly minority schools continue to lag significantly behind white suburban schools.

Outlawing Discrimination in Employment Despite the agonizingly slow progress of school desegregation, some progress was made in other areas of civil rights during the 1960s and 1970s. Voting rights were established and fairly quickly began to revolutionize southern politics. Service on juries was no longer denied to minorities. But progress in the right to participate in politics and government dramatized the relative lack of progress in the economic domain, and it was in this area that battles over civil rights were increasingly fought.

The federal courts and the Justice Department entered this area through Title VII of the Civil Rights Act of 1964, which outlawed job discrimination by all private and public employers, including governmental agencies (such as fire and police departments) that employed more than fifteen workers. We have already seen (in Chapter 3) that the Supreme Court gave "interstate commerce" such a broad definition that Congress had the constitutional authority to cover discrimination by virtually any local employers.[29] Title VII makes it unlawful to discriminate in employment on the basis of color, religion, sex, or national origin, as well as race.

Title VII delegated some of the powers to enforce fair employment practices to the Justice Department's Civil Rights Division and others to a new agency created in the 1964 act, the Equal Employment Opportunity Commission (EEOC). By executive order, these agencies had the power of the national government to revoke public contracts for goods and services and to refuse to engage in contracts for goods and services with any private company that could not guarantee that its rules for hiring, promotion, and firing were nondiscriminatory. Executive orders in 1965, 1967, and 1969 by Presidents Johnson and Nixon extended and reaffirmed nondiscrimination practices in employment and promotion in the federal government service. And in 1972, President Nixon and a Democratic Congress cooperated to strengthen the EEOC by giving it authority to initiate suits rather than wait for grievances.

But one problem with Title VII was that the complaining party had to show that deliberate discrimination was the cause of the failure to get a job or a training opportunity. Rarely does an employer explicitly admit discrimination on the basis of race, sex, or any other illegal reason. Recognizing the rarity of such an admission, the courts have allowed aggrieved parties (the plaintiffs) to make their case if they can show that an employer's hiring practices had the *effect* of exclusion. A leading case in 1971 involved a "class action" by several black employees in North Carolina attempting to show with statistical evidence that blacks had been relegated to only one department in the Duke Power Company, which involved the least desirable, manual-labor jobs, and that they had been kept out of contention for the better jobs because the employer had added attainment of a high school education and the passing of specially prepared aptitude tests as qualifications for higher jobs. The Supreme Court held that although the statistical evidence did not prove intentional discrimination, and although the requirements were race-neutral in appearance, their effects were sufficient to shift the burden of justification to the employer to show that the requirements were a "business necessity" that bore "a demonstrable relationship to successful performance."[30] The ruling in this case was subsequently applied to other hiring, promotion, and training programs.[31]

Voting Rights Although 1964 was the *most* important year for civil rights legislation, it was not the only important year. In 1965, Congress significantly strengthened legislation protecting voting rights by barring literacy and other tests as a condition for voting in six southern states,[32] by setting criminal penalties for interference with efforts to vote, and by providing for the replacement of local registrars with federally appointed registrars in counties designated by the attorney general as significantly resistant to registering eligible blacks to vote. The right to vote was further strengthened with ratification in 1964 of the Twenty-fourth Amendment, which abolished the poll tax, and in 1975 with legislation permanently outlawing literacy tests in all fifty states and mandating bilingual ballots or oral assistance for Spanish, Chinese, Japanese, Koreans, Native Americans, and Eskimos.

In the long run, the laws extending and protecting voting rights could prove to be the most effective of all the great civil rights legislation, because the progress in black political participation produced by these acts has altered the shape of American politics. In 1965, in the seven states of the Old Confederacy covered by the Voting Rights Act, 29.3 percent of the eligible black residents were registered to vote, compared to 73.4 percent of the white residents (see Table 5.2). Mississippi was the extreme case, with 6.7 percent black and 69.9 percent white registration. In 1967, a mere two years after implementation of the voting rights laws, 52.1 percent of the eligible blacks in the seven states were registered, comparing favorably to 79.5 percent of the eligible whites, a gap of 27.4 points. By 1972, the gap between black and white registration in the seven states was only 11.2 points, and in Mississippi the gap had been reduced to 9.4 points. At one time, white leaders in Mississippi attempted to dilute the influence of this growing black vote by **gerrymandering** districts to ensure that no blacks would be elected to Congress. But the black voters changed Mississippi before Mississippi could change them. In 1988, 11 percent of all elected officials in Mississippi were black. This was up one full percentage point from 1987 and closely approximates the size of the national black electorate, which at the time was just over 11 percent of the American voting-age population. Mississippi's blacks had made significant gains (as was true in other Deep South states) as elected state and local representatives, and Mississippi was one of only eight states in the country in which a black judge presided over the highest state court. (Four of the eight were Deep South states.)[33]

The 2000 elections reminded black leaders that even basic rights, such as voting, must be monitored. The U.S. Commission on Civil Rights conducted hearings on the election in Florida, at which black voters testified about being turned away

gerrymandering apportionment of voters in districts in such a way as to give unfair advantage to one racial or ethnic group or political party

---

Registration by Race and State in Southern States Covered by the Voting Rights Act

Table 5.2

	BEFORE THE ACT*			AFTER THE ACT* 1971–72		
	WHITE	**BLACK**	**GAP†**	**WHITE**	**BLACK**	**GAP†**
Alabama	69.2%	19.3%	49.9%	80.7%	57.1%	23.6%
Georgia	62.6	27.4	35.2	70.6	67.8	2.8
Louisiana	80.5	31.6	48.9	80.0	59.1	20.9
Mississippi	69.9	6.7	63.2	71.6	62.2	9.4
North Carolina	96.8	46.8	50.0	62.2	46.3	15.9
South Carolina	75.7	37.3	38.4	51.2	48.0	3.2
Virginia	61.1	38.3	22.8	61.2	54.0	7.2
TOTAL	73.4	29.3	44.1	67.8	56.6	11.2

*Available registration data as of March 1965 and 1971–72.
†The gap is the percentage point difference between white and black registration rates.
SOURCE: U.S. Commission on Civil Rights, *Political Participation* (1968), Appendix VII: Voter Education Project, Attachment to Press Release, October 3, 1972.

from the polls, about being wrongly purged from the voting rolls, and about the unreliable voting technology in their neighborhoods. On the basis of this testimony and after an analysis of the vote, the Commission charged that there had been extensive racial discrimination. A subsequent thorough analysis of the Florida vote by a consortium of newspapers showed that black precincts had three times the number of rejected ballots as white precincts even after the effects of income, education, and ballot design were taken into account.[34]

Housing   The Civil Rights Act of 1964 did not address housing, but in 1968, Congress passed another civil rights act specifically to outlaw housing discrimination. Called the Fair Housing Act, the law prohibited discrimination in the sale or rental of most housing—eventually covering nearly all the nation's housing. Housing was among the most controversial of discrimination issues because of deeply entrenched patterns of residential segregation across the United States. Such segregation was not simply a product of individual choice. Local housing authorities deliberately segregated public housing, and federal guidelines had sanctioned discrimination in Federal Housing Administration mortgage lending, effectively preventing blacks from joining the exodus to the suburbs in the 1950s and 1960s. Nonetheless, Congress had been reluctant to tackle housing discrimination, fearing the tremendous controversy it could arouse. But just as the housing legislation was being considered in April 1968, civil rights leader Martin Luther King, Jr., was assassinated; this tragedy brought the measure unexpected support in Congress.

Although it pronounced sweeping goals, the Fair Housing Act had little effect on housing segregation because its enforcement mechanisms were so weak. Individuals believing they had been discriminated against had to file suit themselves. The burden was on the individual to prove that housing discrimination had occurred, even though such discrimination is often subtle and difficult to document. Although local fair-housing groups emerged to assist individuals in their court claims, the procedures for proving discrimination proved a formidable barrier to effective change. These procedures were not altered until 1988, when Congress passed the Fair Housing Amendments Act. This new law put more teeth in the enforcement procedures and allowed the Department of Housing and Urban Development (HUD) to initiate legal action in cases of discrimination. With vigorous use, these provisions may prove more successful than past efforts at combating housing discrimination.[35]

Other avenues for challenging residential segregation also had mixed success. HUD tried briefly in the early 1970s to create racially "open communities" by withholding federal funds to suburbs that refused to accept subsidized housing. Confronted with charges of "forced integration" and bitter local protests, however, the administration quickly backed down. Efforts to prohibit discrimination in lending have been somewhat more promising. Several laws passed in the 1970s required banks to report information about their mortgage lending patterns, making it more difficult for them to engage in **redlining,** the practice of refusing to lend to entire neighborhoods. The 1977 Community Reinvestment Act required banks to lend in neighborhoods in which they do business. Through vigorous use of this act, many neighborhood organizations have reached agreements with banks that, as a result, have significantly increased investment in some poor neighborhoods.

FOR CRITICAL ANALYSIS

There are many who believe that despite the significance of the *Brown v. Board of Education* decision, it has failed to fulfill its promise. What did *Brown v. Board* really accomplish? Can courts bring about social change?

redlining a practice in which banks refuse to make loans to people living in certain geographic locations

The Universalization of Civil Rights

Even before equal employment laws began to have a positive effect on the economic situation of blacks, something far more dramatic began happening—the universalization of civil rights. The right not to be discriminated against was being successfully claimed by the other groups listed in Title VII of the 1964 Civil Rights Act—those defined by sex, religion, or national origin—and eventually by still other groups defined by age or sexual preference. This universalization of civil rights has become the new frontier of the civil rights struggle.

As gender discrimination began to be seen as an important civil rights issue, other groups arose demanding recognition and active protection of their civil rights. Under Title VII, any group or individual can try, and in fact is encouraged to try, to convert goals and grievances into questions of rights and of the deprivation of those rights. A plaintiff must establish only that his or her membership in a group is an unreasonable basis for discrimination—that is, that it cannot be proven to be a "job-related" or otherwise clearly reasonable and relevant decision. In America today, the list of individuals and groups claiming illegal discrimination is lengthy.

WOMEN AND GENDER DISCRIMINATION

Title VII provided a valuable tool for the growing women's movement in the 1960s and 1970s. In fact, in many ways the law fostered the growth of the women's movement. The first major campaign of the National Organization for Women (NOW) involved picketing the Equal Employment Opportunity Commission (EEOC) for its refusal to ban sex-segregated employment advertisements. NOW also sued the *New York Times* for continuing to publish such ads after the passage of Title VII. Another organization, the Women's Equity Action League (WEAL), pursued legal action on a wide range of sex discrimination issues, filing lawsuits against law schools and medical schools for discriminatory admission policies, for example.

Building on these victories and the growth of the women's movement, feminist activists sought an "Equal Rights Amendment" (ERA) to the Constitution. The proposed amendment was short: its substantive passage stated that "equality of rights under the law shall not be denied or abridged by the United States or by any State on account of sex." The amendment's supporters believed that such a sweeping guarantee of equal rights was a necessary tool for ending all discrimination against women and for making gender roles more equal. Opponents charged that it would be socially disruptive and would introduce changes—such as coed restrooms—that most Americans did not want. The amendment easily passed Congress in 1972 and won quick approval in many state legislatures, but it fell three states short of the thirty-eight needed to ratify the amendment by the 1982 deadline for its ratification.[36]

Despite the failure of the ERA, gender discrimination expanded dramatically as an area of civil rights law. In the 1970s, the conservative Burger Court (under Chief Justice Warren Burger) helped to establish gender discrimination as a major and highly visible civil rights issue. Although the Burger Court refused to treat gender discrimination as the equivalent of racial discrimination,[37] it did make it easier for

intermediate scrutiny test used by the Supreme Court in gender discrimination cases, which places the burden of proof partially on the government and partially on the challengers to show that the law in question is constitutional

plaintiffs to file and win suits on the basis of gender discrimination by applying an "intermediate" level of review to these cases.[38] This **intermediate scrutiny** is midway between traditional rules of evidence, which put the burden of proof on the plaintiff, and the doctrine of strict scrutiny, which requires the defendant to show not only that a particular classification is reasonable but also that there is a need or compelling interest for it. Intermediate scrutiny shifts the burden of proof partially onto the defendant, rather than leaving it entirely on the plaintiff.

One major step was taken in 1992, when the Court decided in *Franklin v. Gwinnett County Public Schools* that violations of Title IX of the 1972 Education Act could be remedied with monetary damages.[39] Title IX forbade gender discrimination in education, but it initially sparked little litigation because of its weak enforcement provisions. The Court's 1992 ruling that monetary damages could be awarded for gender discrimination opened the door for more legal action in the area of education. The greatest impact has been in the areas of sexual harassment—the subject of the *Franklin* case—and in equal treatment of women's athletic programs. The potential for monetary damages has made universities and public schools take the problem of sexual harassment more seriously. Colleges and universities have also started to pay more attention to women's athletic programs. In the two years after the *Franklin* case, complaints to the Education Department's Office for Civil Rights about unequal treatment of women's athletic programs nearly tripled. In several high-profile legal cases, some prominent universities have been ordered to create more women's sports programs; many other colleges and universities have begun to add more women's programs in order to avoid potential litigation.[40] In 1997, the Supreme Court refused to hear a petition by Brown University challenging a lower court ruling that the university establish strict sex equity in its athletic programs. The Court's decision meant that in colleges and universities across the country, varsity athletic positions for men and women must now reflect their overall enrollment numbers.[41]

In 1996, the Supreme Court made another important decision about gender and education by putting an end to all-male schools supported by public funds. It ruled that the policy of the Virginia Military Institute not to admit women was unconstitutional.[42] Along with the Citadel, another all-male military college in South Carolina, VMI had never admitted women in its 157-year history. VMI argued that the unique educational experience it offered—including intense physical training and the harsh treatment of freshmen—would be destroyed if women students were admitted. The Court, however, ruled that the male-only policy denied "substantial equality" to women. Two days after the Court's ruling, the Citadel announced that it would accept women. VMI considered becoming a private institution in order to remain all-male, but in September 1996, the school board finally voted to admit women. The legal decisions may have removed formal barriers to entry, but the experience of the new female cadets at these schools has not been easy. The first female cadet at the Citadel, Shannon Faulkner, won admission in 1995 under a federal court order but quit after four days. Although four women were admitted to the Citadel after the Supreme Court decision, two of the four quit several months later. They charged harassment from male students, including attempts to set the female cadets on fire.[43]

Courts began to find sexual harassment a form of sex discrimination during the late 1970s. Although sexual harassment law applies to education, most of the

Women were not originally outlawed from voting by the Constitution. Although a few women could vote in the early American republic, such as these New Jersey women who satisfied state property qualifications, laws were soon enacted to block women from the ballot box. At the beginning of the nineteenth century, no American woman could legally vote.

law of sexual harassment has been developed by courts through interpretation of Title VII of the Civil Rights Act of 1964. In 1986, the Supreme Court recognized two forms of sexual harassment—the quid pro quo type, which involves sexual extortion, and the hostile environment type, which involves sexual intimidation.[44] Employers and many employees have worried that hostile-environment sexual harassment is too ambiguous. When can an employee bring charges? When is the employer liable? In 1986, the Court said that sexual harassment may be legally actionable even if the employee did not suffer tangible economic or job-related losses in relation to it. In 1993, the Court said that sexual harassment may be legally actionable even if the employee did not suffer tangible psychological costs

People had been agitating for women's right to vote since the 1830s, especially during the Civil War era. However, the Fourteenth Amendment explicitly referred to voters as men, squelching women's hope for the vote. Another suffragist push in the 1910s reinvigorated the fight for women's political equality with men. Here, a police officer arrests two suffragists in front of the White House. Women finally gained the constitutional right to vote in 1920.

Political equality did not end discrimination against women in the workplace or in society at large. African Americans' struggle for civil rights in the 1950s and 1960s spurred a parallel equal rights movement for women in the 1960s and 1970s. Activists sought to add the Equal Rights Amendment (ERA) to the Constitution as a way to end sex discrimination permanently. Despite Congressional and state support, it mustered approval from only thirty-five of the necessary thirty-eight state legislatures and failed to become law in 1982.

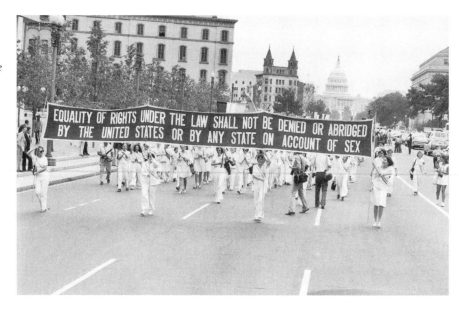

The ERA never passed, but women's struggle against gender discrimination continued. Under the Civil Rights Act of 1964 and the Education Act of 1972, women could legally demand treatment equal to men. One result of this has been that college athletics programs must be gender-balanced. Colleges and universities have added more women's sports programs to comply with government regulations.

as a result of it.[45] In two 1998 cases, the Court further strengthened the law when it said that whether or not sexual harassment results in economic harm to the employee, an employer is liable for the harassment if it was committed by someone with authority over the employee—by a supervisor, for example. But the Court also said that an employer may defend itself by showing that it had a sexual harassment prevention and grievance policy in effect.[46]

The development of gender discrimination as an important part of the civil rights struggle has coincided with the rise of women's politics as a discrete movement in American politics. As with the struggle for racial equality, the relationship between changes in government policies and political action suggests that changes in government policies to a great degree produce political action. Today, the existence of a powerful women's movement derives in large measure from the enactment of Title VII of the Civil Rights Act of 1964 and from the Burger Court's vital steps in applying that law to protect women. The recognition of women's civil rights has become an issue that in many ways transcends the usual distinctions of American political debate. In the heavily partisan debate over the federal crime bill enacted in 1994, for instance, the section of the bill that enjoyed the widest support was the Violence Against Women Act, whose most important feature was that it defined gender-biased violent crimes as a matter of civil rights, and created a civil rights remedy for women who have been the victims of such crimes. But since the act was ruled unconstitutional by the Supreme Court in 2000, the struggle for women's rights will likely remain part of the political debate.

LATINOS AND ASIAN AMERICANS

The labels "Latino"/"Hispanic" and "Asian American" encompass a wide range of groups with diverse national origins, distinctive cultural identities, and particular experiences. For example, the early political experiences of Mexican Americans were shaped by race and by region. In 1898, Mexican Americans were given formal political rights, including the right to vote. In many places,

America's International Role in Promoting Human Rights

Although the United States was a bit late in committing to using its military, diplomatic, and moral resources to advance the cause of human rights throughout the world, two recent human rights interventions by the United States are worthy of note. The first is the UN Protocol to Prevent, Suppress and Punish Trafficking in Persons, especially women and children, adopted in November 2000. The United States took the initiative on this issue by passing an Act of Congress—a full month before the UN passed its protocol. Recognizing such trafficking as one of the "greatest human rights challenges of our time," the United States set up an "Office to Monitor and Combat Trafficking Persons" in order to meet a congressional requirement that an annual report on Trafficking in Persons (TIP) be issued to Congress to guide the effort against human trafficking. Data and documents on each country are assimilated into a rating of the conduct of each of those countries in terms of their compliance with the minimum standards set by Congress. Sanctions are to be imposed, notably the withholding of certain kinds of assistance, including blockage of access to international financial institutions, such as the International Monetary Fund and the World Bank. Although it is far too early to make a definitive judgment, there is already some evidence that many countries are making efforts to move into compliance with the standards.

The second intervention is that of U.S. initiative in the matter of women's rights. The stress on women's rights results from several factors. The first is our increasing involvement in the Middle East, not only because of oil but because of trade in general; globalization and the inevitable modernization that follows tend to threaten traditional societies. Another related factor is that in traditional Islamic countries in particular, women are discriminated against as a matter of culture and law. Add to this the high population growth rate in these countries, which contributes to the swelling of illegal international trade in hungry, exploitable people, particularly women and children.

Although this commitment to women's rights is worldwide, the U.S. approach is country by country. The United States sponsored a UN commitment to the involvement of women on an equal basis in public life, including the holding of decision-making positions in governmental bodies at

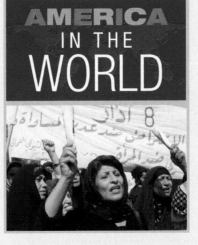

all levels. All members of the UN monitor the "efforts"; implementation of this policy by the United States occurs one country at a time, with concentration on the countries in the Middle East. The constitution drawn up by the post-Saddam Iraqi Governing Council provides for a bill of rights ensuring equal rights for all Iraqis regardless of gender; the United States succeeded in getting at least three women on the Governing Council. One woman holds the key post of Minister of Public Works, and another was appointed Principal Representative of Iraq to the United States. Six out of thirty-seven members of the Baghdad City Council are women, and over eighty women serve on neighborhood and district councils around the capital. Even more striking in a country that has so severely subordinated women, already in 2004, just months before the turning of sovereignty back to the Iraqis, over one hundred women were recruited as security officers, police, prison guards, and so on. Still more promising is the role Iraqi women played in successfully opposing a resolution adopted by the Governing Council in December 2003 that transferred family law matters from civil administration to religious law. Almost immediately, Iraqi women's rights groups bore down on Council members until they repealed the resolution.

These commitments to human rights are not merely political actions to placate women's and other reformist interest groups in the United States or to make friends at the UN. This is realistic, hard-headed foreign policy, based on a well-tested principle that democratic—or even democratizing—countries don't go to war against each other. Advancing the interests of women meets a fundamental requirement of democracy, and the advancement of democracy, although a good in itself, is also a stroke for peace.

FOR CRITICAL ANALYSIS

1. As Secretary of State, how would you deal with discrimination against women in Islamic countries where religious beliefs justify, even require, women's inequality?

2. In the international advancement of human rights, should the United States ever act unilaterally? Should we form multilateral coalitions for the purpose? Should we work entirely through the UN and its agencies?

however, and especially in Texas, Mexican Americans were segregated and prevented from voting through such means as the white primary and the poll tax.[47] Region made a difference too. In contrast to the northeastern and midwestern cities to which most European ethnics immigrated, the Southwest did not have a tradition of ethnic mobilization associated with machine politics. Particularly after the political reforms enacted in the first decade of the twentieth century, city politics in the Southwest was dominated by a small group of Anglo elites. In the countryside, when Mexican Americans participated in politics, it was often as part of a political organization dominated by a large white landowner, or *patron.*

The earliest Mexican American independent political organizations, the League of United Latin American Citizens (LULAC) and the GI Forum, worked to stem discrimination against Mexican Americans in the years after World War II. By the late 1950s, the first Mexican American was elected to Congress, and four others followed in the 1960s. In the late 1960s a new kind of Mexican American political movement was born. Inspired by the black civil rights movement, Mexican American students launched boycotts of high school classes in East Los Angeles, Denver, and San Antonio. Students in colleges and universities across California joined in as well. Among their demands were bilingual education, an end to discrimination, and more cultural recognition. In Crystal City, Texas, which had been dominated by Anglo politicians despite a population that was overwhelmingly Mexican American, the newly formed La Raza Unida Party took over the city government.[48]

Since that time, Mexican American political strategy has developed along two tracks. One is a traditional ethnic-group path of voter registration and voting along ethnic lines. The second is a legal strategy using the various civil rights laws designed to ensure fair access to the political system. The Mexican American Legal Defense Fund (MALDEF) has played a key role in designing and pursuing the latter strategy.

The early Asian experience in the United States was shaped by a series of naturalization laws dating back to 1790, the first of which declared that only white aliens were eligible for citizenship. Chinese immigrants had begun arriving in California in the 1850s, drawn by the boom of the Gold Rush, but they were immediately met with hostility. The virulent antagonism toward Chinese immigrants in California led Congress to declare Chinese immigrants ineligible for citizenship in 1870. In 1882, the first Chinese Exclusion Act suspended the entry of Chinese laborers.

At the time of the Exclusion Act, the Chinese community was composed predominantly of single male laborers, with few women and children. The few Chinese children in San Francisco were initially denied entry to the public schools; only after parents of American-born Chinese children pressed legal action were the children allowed to attend public school. Even then, however, they were segregated into a separate Chinese school. American-born Chinese children could not be denied citizenship, however; this right was confirmed by the Supreme Court in 1898, when it ruled in *United States v. Wong Kim Ark* that anyone born in the United States was entitled to full citizenship.[49] Still, new Chinese immigrants were barred from the United States until 1943, after China had become a key wartime ally and Congress repealed the Chinese Exclusion Act and permitted Chinese residents to become citizens.

Immigration climbed rapidly after the 1965 Immigration Act, which lifted discriminatory quotas. In spite of this and other developments, limited English proficiency barred many Asian Americans and Latinos from full participation in American life. Two developments in the 1970s, however, established rights for language minorities. In 1974, the Supreme Court ruled in *Lau v. Nichols,* a suit filed on behalf of Chinese students in San Francisco, that school districts have to provide education for students whose English is limited.[50] It did not mandate bilingual education but it established a duty to provide instruction that the students could understand. The 1970 amendments to the Voting Rights Act permanently outlawed literacy tests in all fifty states and mandated bilingual ballots or oral assistance for those who speak Spanish, Chinese, Japanese, Korean, Native American languages, or Eskimo languages.

Asian Americans and Latinos have also been concerned about the impact of immigration laws on their civil rights. Many Asian American and Latino organizations opposed the Immigration Reform and Control Act of 1986 because it imposed sanctions on employers who hire undocumented workers. Such sanctions, they feared, would lead employers to discriminate against Latinos and Asian Americans. These suspicions were confirmed in a 1990 report by the General Accounting Office that found employer sanctions had created a "widespread pattern of discrimination" against Latinos and others who appear foreign.[51] Organizations such as MALDEF and the Asian Law Caucus monitor and challenge such discrimination. These groups have turned their attention to the rights of legal and illegal immigrants, as anti-immigrant sentiment has grown in recent years.

The Supreme Court has ruled that illegal immigrants are eligible for education and medical care but can be denied other social benefits; legal immigrants are to be treated much the same as citizens. But growing immigration—including an estimated 300,000 illegal immigrants per year—and mounting economic insecurity have undermined these practices. Groups of voters across the country now strongly support drawing a sharper line between immigrants and citizens. Not surprisingly, the movement to deny benefits to noncitizens began in California, which experienced sharp economic distress in the early 1990s and has the highest levels of immigration of any state. In 1994, Californians voted in favor of Proposition 187, denying illegal immigrants all services except emergency medical care. Supporters of the measure hoped to discourage illegal immigration and to pressure illegal immigrants already in the country to leave. Opponents contended that denying basic services to illegal immigrants risked creating a subclass of residents in the United States whose lack of education and poor health threaten all Americans. In 1994 and 1997, a federal court declared most of Proposition 187 unconstitutional, affirming previous rulings that illegal immigrants should be granted public education. A booming economy helped to reduce public concern about illegal immigration, but supporters of Proposition 187 promised to reintroduce similar measures in the future.

In January 2004, President Bush released a plan to revamp American immigration laws to enable all undocumented immigrants "to obtain legal status as temporary workers." Amnesty was proposed but rejected in Congress on the grounds that it "encourages the violation of our laws and perpetuates illegal immigration." The Bush proposal would first substantially increase the number of "green cards" available for legal immigration. For illegal immigrants, he proposed a new "temporary worker program" procedure, whereby every illegal immigrant could apply for a work permit that would last for three years, and would be renewable for another

FOR CRITICAL ANALYSIS
Should illegal immigrants have access to U.S. courts for civil rights grievances in cases of employer discrimination? Given that illegal immigrants now depend on employers for their legal status, does this amount to a sub-caste of low-wage labor without providing a mechanism for these workers to achieve permanent residence or citizenship? Will the number of newly legalized "guest workers" lower wages and deprive citizens of these jobs? What policy might maintain some equity between the newly documented low-wage workers and the existing workforce?

three—provided, however, that the temporary or "guest worker" *already had a job*—*those who failed to stay employed or who broke the law would be deported.* Under the plan, employers controlled the work permits, so that the continued status of the guest worker depended entirely upon the discretion of the employer.

The question of the rights of legal immigrants poses an even tougher problem. Congress has the power to deny public benefits to this group but doing so would go against long-standing traditions in American political culture. Legal immigrants have traditionally enjoyed most of the rights and obligations (such as paying taxes) of citizens. As constitutional scholar Theodore Bikel points out, the Constitution begins with "We the People of the United States"; likewise the Bill of Rights refers to the rights of *people,* not citizens.[52]

NATIVE AMERICANS

The political status of Native Americans was left unclear in the Constitution. But by the early 1800s, the courts had defined each of the Indian tribes as a nation. As members of an Indian nation, Native Americans were declared noncitizens of the United States. The political status of Native Americans changed in 1924, when congressional legislation granted citizenship to those who had been born in the United States. A variety of changes in federal policy toward Native Americans during the 1930s paved the way for a later resurgence of their political power. Most important was the federal decision to encourage Native Americans on reservations to establish local self-government.[53]

The Native American political movement gathered force in the 1960s, as Native Americans began to use protest, litigation, and assertion of tribal rights to improve their situation. In 1968, Dennis Banks cofounded the American Indian Movement (AIM), the most prominent Native American protest organization. AIM won national attention in 1969 when 200 of its members, representing twenty different tribes, took over the famous prison island of Alcatraz in San Francisco Bay, claiming it for Native Americans. In 1971, AIM members took over the town of Wounded Knee, South Dakota, the site of the massacre of over two hundred Sioux men, women, and children by the U.S. Army in December 1890. The federal government responded to the rise in Indian activism with the Indian Self-Determination and Education Assistance Act, which began to give Indians more control over their own land.[54]

As a language minority, Native Americans were also affected by the 1975 amendments to the Voting Rights Act and the *Lau* decision. The *Lau* decision established the right of Native Americans to be taught in their own languages. This marked quite a change from the boarding schools once run by the Bureau of Indian Affairs, at which members of Indian tribes had been forbidden to speak their own languages. In addition to these language-related issues, Native Americans have sought to expand their rights on the basis of their sovereign status. Since the 1920s and 1930s, Native American tribes have sued the federal government for illegally seizing land, seeking monetary reparations and land as damages. Both types of damages have been awarded in such suits, but only in small amounts. Native American tribes have been more successful in winning federal recognition of their sovereignty. Sovereign status has, in turn, allowed them to exercise greater self-determination. Most significant economically was a 1987 Supreme Court decision that freed Native American tribes from most state regulations prohibiting gambling. The establishment of casino gambling on Native American lands has brought a substantial flow of new income into desperately poor reservations.

DISABLED AMERICANS

The concept of rights for the disabled began to emerge in the 1970s as the civil rights model spread to other groups. The seed was planted in a little-noticed provision of the 1973 Rehabilitation Act, which outlawed discrimination against individuals on the basis of disabilities. As in many other cases, the law itself helped give rise to the movement demanding rights for the handicapped.[55] Modeling itself on the NAACP's Legal Defense Fund, the disability movement founded a Disability Rights Education and Defense Fund to press their legal claims. The movement achieved its greatest success with the passage of the Americans with Disabilities Act (ADA) of 1990, which guarantees equal employment rights and access to public businesses for the disabled. Claims of discrimination in violation of this act are considered by the Equal Employment Opportunity Commission. The impact of the law has been far-reaching, as businesses and public facilities have installed ramps, elevators, and other devices to meet the act's requirements.[56] In 1998, the Supreme Court interpreted the ADA to apply to people with HIV. Until then, ADA was interpreted as covering people with AIDS but not people with HIV. The case arose when a dentist was asked to fill a cavity for a woman with HIV; he refused unless the procedure was done in a hospital setting. The woman sued, and her complaint was that HIV had already disabled her because it was discouraging her from having children. (The act prohibits discrimination in employment, housing, and in health care.) Although there have been widespread concerns that the ADA was being expanded too broadly and the costs were becoming too burdensome, corporate America did not seem to be disturbed by the Court's ruling. Stephen Bokat, General Counsel of the U.S. Chamber of Commerce, said businesses in general had already been accommodating people with HIV as well as with AIDS and that the case presented no serious problem.[57]

THE AGED

Age discrimination in employment is illegal. The 1967 federal Age Discrimination in Employment Act (ADEA) makes age discrimination illegal when practiced by employers with at least twenty employees. Many states have added to the federal provisions with their own age discrimination laws, and some such state laws are stronger than the federal provisions. The major lobbyist for seniors, the American Association of Retired Persons (AARP, see Chapter 11), with its claim to over thirty million members, has been active in keeping these laws on the books and making sure that they are vigorously implemented.

GAYS AND LESBIANS

In less than thirty years, the gay and lesbian movement has become one of the largest civil rights movements in contemporary America. Beginning with street protests in the 1960s, the movement has grown into a well-financed and sophisticated lobby. The Human Rights Campaign Fund is the primary national political action committee

(PAC) focused on gay rights; it provides campaign financing and volunteers to work for candidates endorsed by the group. The movement has also formed legal rights organizations, including the Lambda Legal Defense and Education Fund.

Gay and lesbian rights drew national attention in 1993, when President Bill Clinton confronted the question of whether gays should be allowed to serve in the military. As a candidate, Clinton had said he favored lifting the ban on homosexuals in the military. The issue set off a huge controversy in the first months of Clinton's presidency. After nearly a year of deliberation, the administration enunciated a compromise: their "Don't ask, don't tell" policy. This policy allows gays and lesbians to serve in the military as long as they do not openly proclaim their sexual orientation or engage in homosexual activity. The administration maintained that the ruling would protect gays and lesbians against witch-hunting investigations, but many gay and lesbian advocates expressed disappointment, charging the president with reneging on his campaign promise.

But until 1996, there was no Supreme Court ruling or national legislation explicitly protecting gays and lesbians from discrimination. The first gay rights case that the Court decided, *Bowers v. Hardwick,* ruled against a right to privacy that would protect consensual homosexual activity.[58] After the *Bowers* decision, the gay and lesbian rights movement sought suitable legal cases to test the constitutionality of discrimination against gays and lesbians, much as the black civil rights movement did in the late 1940s and 1950s. As one advocate put it, "lesbians and gay men are looking for their *Brown v. Board of Education.*"[59] Among the cases tested were those stemming from local ordinances restricting gay rights (including the right to marry), job discrimination, and family law issues such as adoption and parental rights. In 1996, the Supreme Court, in *Romer v. Evans,* explicitly extended fundamental civil rights protections to gays and lesbians, by declaring unconstitutional a 1992 amendment to the Colorado state constitution that prohibited local governments from passing ordinances to protect gay rights.[60] The decision's forceful language highlighted the connection between gay rights and civil rights as it declared discrimination against gay people unconstitutional.

In *Lawrence v. Texas* (2003), the Court overturned *Bowers* and struck down a Texas statute criminalizing certain intimate sexual conduct between consenting partners of the same sex.[61] A victory for lesbians and gays every bit as significant as *Roe v. Wade* was for women, *Lawrence v. Texas* extends at least one aspect of civil liberties to sexual minorities: the right to privacy. However, this decision by itself does not undo the various exclusions that deprive lesbians and gays full civil rights, including the right to marry, which became a hot-button issue in 2004.

In early 2004, the Supreme Judicial Court of Massachusetts ruled that under that state's constitution, gay men and lesbians were entitled to marry. The state senate then requested the court to rule on whether a civil-union statute (avoiding the word "marriage") would, as it did in Vermont, satisfy the court's ruling—to which the court ruled negatively, asserting that civil unions were too much like the "separate but equal" doctrine that maintained legalized racial segregation from 1896 to 1954. Meanwhile, in San Francisco hundreds of gays and lesbians responded to the opportunity provided by the mayor, who had directed the city clerk to issue marriage licenses to same-sex couples in defiance of California law. At the same time, signs were that Massachusetts might move toward a state constitutional amendment that would ban gay unions by whatever name. Voters in Missouri and

Louisiana approved a ban on same-sex marriages, joining Alaska, Hawaii, Nebraska, and Nevada in implementing such a ban. Voters in eleven other states approved similar bans in the November 2004 elections.

Affirmative Action

Not only has the politics of rights spread to increasing numbers of groups in American society since the 1960s but it has also expanded its goal. The relatively narrow goal of equalizing opportunity by eliminating discriminatory barriers evolved into the far broader goal of **affirmative action**—compensatory action to overcome the consequences of past discrimination. An affirmative action policy tends to involve two novel approaches: (1) positive or benign discrimination in which race or some other status is actually taken into account, but for compensatory action rather than mistreatment; and (2) compensatory action to favor members of the disadvantaged group who themselves may never have been the victims of discrimination. Quotas may be but are not necessarily involved in affirmative action policies.

affirmative action government policies or programs that seek to redress past injustices against specified groups by making special efforts to provide members of these groups with access to educational and employment opportunities

President Lyndon Johnson put the case emotionally in 1965: "You do not take a person who, for years, has been hobbled by chains . . . and then say you are free to compete with all the others, and still just believe that you have been completely fair."[62] Johnson attempted to inaugurate affirmative action by executive orders directing agency heads and personnel officers to pursue vigorously a policy of minority employment in the federal civil service and in companies doing business with the national government. But affirmative action did not become a prominent goal of the national government until the 1970s.

Affirmative action also took the form of efforts by the agencies in the Department of Health, Education, and Welfare to shift their focus from "desegregation" to "integration."[63] Federal agencies—sometimes with court orders and sometimes without them—required school districts to present plans for busing children across district lines, for pairing schools, for closing certain schools, and for redistributing faculties as well as students, under pain of loss of grants-in-aid from the federal government. The guidelines issued for such plans literally constituted preferential treatment to compensate for past discrimination, and without this legislatively assisted approach to integration orders, there would certainly not have been the dramatic increase in black children attending integrated classes. The yellow school bus became a symbol of hope for many and a signal of defeat for others.

Affirmative action was also initiated in the area of employment opportunity. The Equal Employment Opportunity Commission often has required plans whereby employers must attempt to increase the number of their minority employees, and the office of Federal Contract Compliance in the Department of Labor has used the threat of contract revocation for the same purpose.

THE SUPREME COURT AND THE BURDEN OF PROOF

Efforts by the executive, legislative, and judicial branches to shape the meaning of affirmative action today tend to center on a key issue: what is the appropriate level of review in affirmative action cases—that is, on whom should the burden of proof be placed, the plaintiff or the defendant? The issue of qualification versus minority preference was addressed formally by the Supreme Court in the case of Allan Bakke. Bakke, a white male, brought suit against the University of California at Davis Medical School on the grounds that in denying him admission the school had discriminated against him on the basis of his race (that year the school had reserved 16 of 100 available slots for minority applicants). He argued that his grades and test scores had ranked him well above many students who had been accepted at the school and that the only possible explanation for his rejection was that those others accepted were black or Latino while he was white. In 1978, Bakke won his case before the Supreme Court and was admitted to the medical school, but he did not succeed in getting affirmative action declared unconstitutional. The Court rejected the procedures at the University of California because its medical school had used both a quota *and* a separate admissions system for minorities. The Court agreed with Bakke's argument that racial categorizations are suspect categories that place a severe burden of proof on those using them to show a "compelling public purpose." The Court went on to say that achieving "a diverse student body" was such a public purpose, but the method of a rigid quota of student slots assigned on the basis of race was incompatible with the equal protection clause. Thus, the Court permitted universities (and presumably other schools, training programs, and hiring authorities) to continue to take minority status into consideration, but limited severely the use of quotas to situations in which (1) previous discrimination had been shown, and (2) it was used more as a guideline for social diversity than as a mathematically defined ratio.[64]

For nearly a decade after *Bakke,* the Supreme Court was tentative and permissive about efforts by corporations and governments to experiment with affirmative action programs in employment.[65] But in 1989, the Court returned to the *Bakke* position that any "rigid numerical quota" is suspect. In *Wards Cove v. Atonio,* the Court backed away further from affirmative action by easing the way for employers to prefer white males, holding that the burden of proof of unlawful discrimination should be shifted from the defendant (the employer) to the plaintiff (the person claiming to be the victim of discrimination).[66] This decision virtually overruled the Court's prior holding.[67] That same year, the Court ruled that any affirmative action program already approved by federal courts could be subsequently challenged by white males who allege that the program discriminates against them.[68]

In 1991, Congress enacted a piece of legislation designed to undo the effects of the decisions limiting affirmative action. Under the terms of the Civil Rights Act of 1991, the burden of proof in employment discrimination cases was shifted back to employers. In addition, the act made it more difficult to mount later challenges to consent decrees in affirmative action cases. Despite Congress's actions, however, the federal judiciary will have the last word as cases under the new law reach the courts. In a 5-to-4 decision in 1993, the Supreme Court ruled that employees had to prove their employers intended discrimination, again placing the burden of proof on employees.[69]

In 1995, the Supreme Court's ruling in *Adarand Constructors v. Pena* further weakened affirmative action. This decision stated that race-based policies, such as preferences given by the government to minority contractors, must survive strict scrutiny, placing the burden on the government to show that such affirmative action programs serve a compelling government interest and are narrowly tailored to address identifiable past discrimination.[70] President Clinton responded to the *Adarand* decision by ordering a review of all government affirmative action policies and practices. Although many observers suspected that the president would use the review as an opportunity to back away from affirmative action, the conclusions of the task force largely defended existing policies. Reflecting the influence of the Supreme Court's decision in *Adarand,* President Clinton acknowledged that some government policies would need to change. But on the whole, the review found that most affirmative action policies were fair and did not "unduly burden nonbeneficiaries."[71]

Although Clinton sought to "mend, not end" affirmative action, developments in the courts and the states continued to restrict affirmative action in important ways. One of the most significant was the *Hopwood* case, in which white students challenged admissions practices in the University of Texas Law School, charging that the school's affirmative action program discriminated against whites. In 1996, a federal court (the U.S. Court of Appeals for the Fifth Circuit) ruling on the case stated that race could never be considered in granting admissions and scholarships at state colleges and universities.[72] This decision effectively rolled back the use of affirmative action permitted by the 1978 *Bakke* case. In *Bakke,* as discussed earlier, the Supreme Court had outlawed quotas but said that race could be used as one factor among many in admissions decisions. Many universities and colleges have since justified affirmative action as a way of promoting racial diversity among their student bodies. What was new in the *Hopwood* decision was the ruling that race could *never* be used as a factor in admissions decisions, even to promote diversity.

In 1996, the Supreme Court refused to hear a challenge to the *Hopwood* case. This meant that its ruling remains in effect in the states covered by the Fifth Circuit—Texas, Louisiana, and Mississippi—but does not apply to the rest of the country. The impact of the *Hopwood* ruling is greatest in Texas because Louisiana and Mississippi are under conflicting court orders to desegregate their universities. In Texas, in the year after the *Hopwood* case, minority applications to Texas universities declined. Concerned about the ability of Texas public universities to serve the state's minority students, the Texas legislature quickly passed a new law granting students who graduate in the top 10 percent of their classes automatic admission to the state's public universities. It is hoped that this measure will ensure a racially diverse student body.[73]

The weakening of affirmative action in the courts was underscored in a case the Supreme Court agreed to hear in 1998. A white schoolteacher in New Jersey who had lost her job had sued her school district, charging that her layoff was racially motivated: a black colleague hired on the same day was not laid off. Under President George Bush, the Justice Department had filed a brief on her behalf in 1989, but in 1994 the Clinton administration formally reversed course in a new brief supporting the school district's right to make distinctions based on race as long as it did not involve the use of quotas. Three years later, the administration, worried that the case was weak and could result in a broad decision against affirmative action, reversed course again. It filed a brief with the Court urging a narrow ruling in favor of the dismissed worker. Because the school board had justified its actions on the grounds of preserving diversity, the administration feared that a broad ruling by the

Affirmative action programs seek to overcome past discrimination against a group by practicing benign discrimination—providing additional opportunities for those who face discrimination. Here, women's rights advocates call for more opportunities for women and equal pay for equal work.

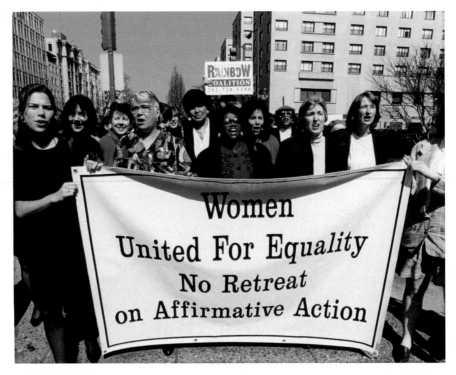

Supreme Court could totally prohibit the use of race in employment decisions, even as one factor among many designed to achieve diversity. But before the Court could issue a ruling, a coalition of civil rights groups brokered and arranged to pay for a settlement. This unusual move reflected the widespread fear of a sweeping negative decision. Cases involving dismissals, as the New Jersey case did, are generally viewed as much more difficult to defend than cases that concern hiring. In addition, the particular facts of the New Jersey case—two equally qualified teachers hired on the same day—were seen as unusual and unfavorable to affirmative action.[74]

This betwixt and between status affirmative action was how things stood in 2003, when the Supreme Court took two cases against the University of Michigan that were virtually certain to clarify, if not put closure on, affirmative action. The first suit, *Gratz v. Bollinger* (the university president), was against the University of Michigan's undergraduate admissions policy and practices, alleging that by using a point-based ranking system that automatically awarded 20 points (out of 150) to African American, Latino, and Native American applicants, the university discriminated unconstitutionally against white students of otherwise equal or superior academic qualifications. The Supreme Court agreed, 6 to 3, arguing that something tantamount to a quota was involved because undergraduate admissions lacked the necessary "individualized consideration," employing instead a "mechanical one," based too much on the favorable minority points.[75] The Court's ruling in *Gratz v. Bollinger* was not surprising, given *Bakke's* (1978) holding against quotas and given recent decisions calling for strict scrutiny of all racial classifications, even those that are intended to remedy past discrimination or promote future equality.

The second case, *Grutter v. Bollinger*, broke new ground. Grutter sued the Law School on the grounds that it had discriminated in a race-conscious way against

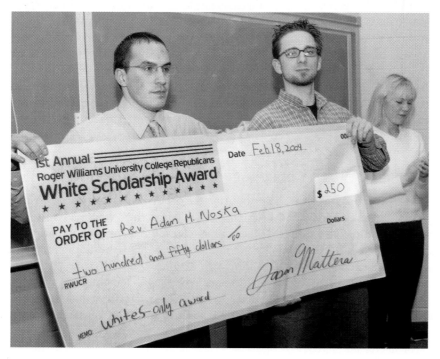

Especially in colleges and universities, affirmative action remains controversial. At many schools across the United States, student groups have debated the merits of the program. The College Republicans at Roger Williams University in Bristol, Rhode Island (bottom left), went so far as to create a "whites-only" scholarship as a statement against affirmative action. At the University of Michigan (top left), the defendant in two major affirmative action cases in 2003, student groups supporting affirmative action were prevalent. The two plaintiffs in these cases, Jennifer Gratz (shown signing a petition) and Barbara Grutter (far right), also led a campaign to let Michigan voters decide in November 2004 whether affirmative action should continue in universities and other public agencies. The petition campaign failed, but leaders of this effort said they plan to push for a similar initiative in 2006.

white applicants with equal or superior grades and law boards. A precarious majority of 5 to 4 aligned the majority of the Supreme Court with Justice Powell's lone plurality opinion in *Bakke* for the first time. In *Bakke*, Powell argued that (1) diversity in education is a compelling state interest and (2) race could be constitutionally considered as a plus factor in admissions decisions. In *Grutter*, the

Court reiterated Powell's holding and, applying strict scrutiny to the Law School's policy, found that the Law School's admissions process is narrowly tailored to the school's compelling state interest in diversity because it gives a "highly individualized, holistic review of each applicant's file" in which race counts but is not used in a "mechanical" way.[76] The Court's ruling that racial categories can be deployed to serve a compelling state interest puts affirmative action on stronger ground.

REFERENDUMS ON AFFIRMATIVE ACTION

The courts have not been the only center of action: during the 1990s, challenges to affirmative action also emerged in state and local politics. One of the most significant state actions was the passage of the California Civil Rights Initiative, also known as Proposition 209, in 1996. Proposition 209 outlawed affirmative action programs in the state and local governments of California, thus prohibiting state and local governments from using race or gender preferences in their decisions about hiring, contracting, or university admissions. The political battle over Proposition 209 was heated, and supporters and defenders took to the streets as well as the airwaves to make their cases. When the referendum was held, the measure passed with 54 percent of the vote, including 27 percent of the black vote, 30 percent of the Latino vote, and 45 percent of the Asian American vote.[77] In 1997, the Supreme Court refused to hear a challenge to the new law. California's Proposition 209 was framed as a civil rights initiative: "the state shall not discriminate against, or grant preferential treatment to, any individual or group on the basis of race, sex, color, ethnicity, or national origin." Different wording can produce quite different outcomes, as a 1997 vote on affirmative action in Houston revealed. There, the ballot initiative asked voters whether they wanted to ban affirmative action in city contracting and hiring, not whether they wanted to end preferential treatment. Fifty-five percent of Houston voters decided in favor of affirmative action.[78]

THINKING CRITICALLY ABOUT THE AFFIRMATIVE ACTION DEBATE

Affirmative action efforts have contributed to the polarization of the politics of civil rights. At the risk of grievous oversimplification, we can divide the sides by two labels: liberals and conservatives.[79] The conservatives' argument against affirmative action can be reduced to two major points. The first is that rights in the American tradition are *individual* rights, and affirmative action violates this concept by concerning itself with "group rights," an idea said to be alien to the American tradition. The second point has to do with quotas. Conservatives would argue that the Constitution is "color-blind," and that any discrimination, even if it is called positive or benign discrimination, ultimately violates the equal protection clause.

The liberal side agrees that rights ultimately come down to individuals, but argues that since the essence of discrimination is the use of unreasonable and unjust criteria of exclusion to deprive *an entire group* of access to something valuable the society has to offer, then the phenomenon of discrimination itself has to be attacked on a group basis. Liberals can also use Supreme Court history to support their side because the first definitive interpretation of the Fourteenth Amendment by the Court in 1873 stated explicitly that

Affirmative Action

The sweeping civil rights laws enacted in the 1960s officially ended state-sanctioned segregation. They did not, however, end racism, or erase stark inequities between the races in such areas as employment and education. As a consequence, affirmative action policies were enacted to ensure some equality between the races.

Proponents of affirmative action cite the continued need for such programs, especially for African Americans, because of the nation's long history of discrimination and persecution. Racism was institutionalized throughout most of the country's history; indeed, the Constitution specifically recognized, and therefore countenanced, slavery. For example, it rewarded slaveowners with the Three-fifths Compromise, giving slaveowners extra representation in the House of Representatives, a provision excised from the Constitution only after the Civil War. Moreover, few would deny that racism still exists in America. Given these facts, it follows that equal treatment of unequals perpetuates inequality. Programs that give an extra boost to traditionally disadvantaged groups offer the only sure way to overcome structural inequality.

To take the example of university and college admissions, affirmative action opponents argue that admissions decisions should be based on merit, not race. Yet affirmative action does not disregard merit, and in any case, admissions does not operate purely based on merit, however defined, for any college or university. Institutions of higher education rely on such measures as grade point average, board scores, and letters of recommendation. But they also consider such nonmerit factors as region, urban vs. rural background, family relationship to alumni and wealthy donors, athletic ability, and other specialized factors unrelated to the usual definition of merit. The inclusion of race as one of these many admissions criteria is as defensible as the inclusion of any other; moreover, it helps ensure a more diverse student body, which in itself is a laudable educational goal. In addition, such programs do not guarantee educational success, but simply assure that individuals from disadvantaged groups have a chance to succeed, an idea most Americans

support. Affirmative action programs have in fact succeeded in providing opportunity to millions who would not otherwise have had it.

Opponents of affirmative action argue that such programs, while based on good intentions, do more harm than good. The belief that persons who gain employment or college admission from such programs did not earn their positions stigmatizes those who are supposed to benefit, creating self-doubt among the recipients and mistrust in others. In the realm of education, students admitted to colleges and universities under these special programs have lower graduation rates. Affirmative action also violates the fundamental American value of equality of opportunity. Although all may not possess the same opportunity, the effort expended to provide special advantages to some would be better directed toward making sure that the principles of equal opportunity and merit are followed.

America's history of discrimination, though reprehensible, should not be used as a basis for employment or educational decisions, because it is unreasonable to ask Americans today to pay for the mistakes of their ancestors. Moreover, the track record of affirmative action programs reveals another problem: the groups that have benefited most are middle-class African Americans and women. If anything, preferential programs should focus on *economic* disadvantage, regardless of race, and better education early in life. Good intentions notwithstanding, there are limits to what government social engineering can accomplish, and most Americans favor the abandonment of race-based preference programs.

FOR CRITICAL ANALYSIS

1. Supporters of affirmative action argue that it is intended not only to compensate for past discrimination but also to level an uneven playing field in which discrimination still exists. What do you think? To what extent is our society free from discrimination?

2. What is the impact of affirmative action on society today? What alternatives to affirmative action policies exist?

Is Affirmative Action Fair?

Yes

While many minorities and women support affirmative action, a growing number say its benefits are no longer worth its side effect: the perception that their achievement is undeserved.

For those who are unaware, affirmative action is a policy that gives minorities and women special consideration in employment, college admission, and other assessments when compared to similarly qualified applicants. Institutions with affirmative action policies generally set aside seats or give preference to minorities and women while recruiting employees as a means of achieving diversity. Thus, an employer or counselor faced with two equally qualified applicants might choose the minority over a white person or a similarly capable woman instead of a man. However, some angry white men blame affirmative action for robbing them of promotions and other opportunities.

Affirmative action is meant to level the playing field so minorities and women have the chance to compete in education and business. However, even with affirmative action in place, white men hold 95 percent to 97 percent of high-level corporate jobs, tilting the playing field in favor of white men. . . . By and large, minorities and women are in much lower paying jobs and still face discrimination. For every dollar earned by men, women earn 74 cents, black women earn 63 cents and Hispanic women earn 57 cents.

I have a right-wing friend who said affirmative action results in admitting students with weaker academic records. He said that statistically, minorities and women have larger failure rates, and because they aren't really good candidates, institutions would be setting them up for letdown. To dispel this myth, I would like to say that most well-known institutions accept the best candidates because there is a standard to maintain. Some studies have shown that women work harder than men.

I do not support arguments that claim affirmative action is justified morally and constitutionally as a means to ensure equality by compensating past discrimination and slavery. There really is no compensation for slavery, and to attempt such compensation would only make a mockery of race.

I do not think affirmative action is the "be all and end all" of awarding equal civil rights, but as long as something good comes out of it, it's worth it. Besides, does it really hurt to reserve a few seats for minorities and women? Veterans often get preferences in workplaces and on campuses. The children of alumni get preferential treatment in admission to some colleges. Friends help others get jobs. Affirmative action helps open doors for women and minorities who don't have these connections.

Another pressing question on this issue: Why should special rights be secured for particular races? Isn't that enforcing racism in some erroneous manner?

Race should not be a factor in employment and education because it perpetuates the belief that we are all fundamentally different, and that destroys integrity. Some feel affirmative action violates the principle of equal protection under the law. The opposition says if minorities and women are intelligent and capable, then they would get hired anyway.

But today's world doesn't believe in "colorblindness." I remember reading about a survey conducted at the top fifty companies in the country, and about 80 percent of the applicants they invited back for an interview had names that sounded white, not black or Latino.

Racism prevents talented minority candidates from landing the job they want. Despite improvements made by the civil rights and women's rights movements, women and minorities still face impediments in business and education. What do we do with affirmative action now?

I would have to agree with Bill on this one. In support of the issue, President Clinton said, "Mend it, but don't end it."

SOURCE: Shouger Merchant, "Affirmative and Negative Action," *Daily Illini* (University of Illinois), April 26, 2004.

No

Lately, I've noted my professors and TAs citing the recent University of Michigan affirmative action case as an example of the discretionary powers that universities have in their admissions processes or to point out that different schools deal with this issue in a variety of ways. However, it seems these educators are hesitant to discuss this topic more in-depth, somewhat restricting a healthy dialogue.

The University of Wisconsin viewed the University of Michigan decision as support for its current practice of considering a student's race when making admissions decisions. While the UW does not have specific admissions guidelines in place for admitting students of color, it does actively recruit these groups of students to help accomplish its goal of greater racial diversity on campus.

To do this, the UW takes into account all other admissions criteria such as GPA, ACT scores, rigor of course load, etc. and then looks at the student's ethnicity and socioeconomic background.

Therefore, some students, faculty, and administration proclaimed the University of Michigan verdict to be a "huge victory" for minority students here. I cannot help but see it as a glaring setback for minorities as well as for race relations, but I do not believe this based solely on the typical reasons that you may hear many conservatives draw on, and we've all heard them: that affirmative action isn't fair for white students, it is actually reverse discrimination, or that administrations should not be responsible for any injustice that their ancestors may have created in the past.

The court attempted to apply a quick legal Band-Aid instead of looking at the actual source of the wound: inequality. OK, so it did overturn one aspect of the University of Michigan's admission process. The Supreme Court threw out the point system that the University of Michigan uses, saying that race shouldn't carry as much weight as the 20 automatic points that this university had been awarding minority students. However, as long as universities continue to use race as even a small part of admission decisions, we will not be able to move past the inequality that these very institutions are trying to prevent.

Minority students are struggling to prove that they are as intelligent, creative and successful as other students if they are given the same opportunities. However, as long as imbalanced admissions practices continue to exist, minority students will continue to struggle. That is because right now, no matter how hard a student of color works to be admitted to a particular school, he or she can be criticized: "He only got in because he's black" or "She's Hispanic, so her grades don't have to be as good as mine to be accepted." It's easy to see that our current situation is a far cry from equality.

Students of color should not have to constantly defend themselves and their accomplishments. It's time for them to be seen as equals, and the only way to achieve this is to start treating them as equals. By using an identical admissions process for each and every student, members of society will have no basis for claims that certain students did not earn their way into the university.

The Supreme Court made the easy decision. Rather than think about how to really deal with the problem of racial discrimination for the long term, it decided to temporarily please minorities by using a quick fix for right now. In fact, this decision actually damages race relations even more. Though it is helping students of color get into college today, it is ensuring more discrimination for tomorrow.

By reaffirming that race is a credible aspect to consider when admitting students to college, the Court sent a message saying that despite years of hard work or a lot of talent, students need to be aware of how their race will affect their future. And didn't civil rights leaders in the past envision a society whose members would be measured solely by their personal merit rather than by the color of their skin? We need to stop telling students that they are disadvantaged simply because their ancestors came from a particular region of the world.

How will this decision affect those who have really embraced racial diversity? The number of biracial children and families is constantly growing. Which race should be considered when making an admissions decision? The "white" side? The "black"? It is getting harder and harder to classify students according to one race or another. Many students can't choose which ethnicity they want to identify them, and they shouldn't have to.

Yes, the Supreme Court may have pleased the university and some minority students for now. However, don't be surprised if, in the future, this case is viewed as a missed opportunity to improve race relations for our country.

SOURCE: Nicole Marklein, "Affirmative Action Decision a Missed Opportunity," *Badger Herald* (University of Wisconsin—Madison), October 1, 2003.

the existence of laws in the state where the newly emancipated Negroes resided, which discriminated with gross injustice and hardship against them *as a class,* was the evil to be remedied by this clause [emphasis added].[80]

Liberals also have a response to the other conservative argument concerning quotas. The liberal response is that the Supreme Court has already accepted ratios—a form of quota—that are admitted as evidence to prove a "pattern or practice of discrimination" sufficient to reverse the burden of proof—to obligate the employer to show that there was *not* an intent to discriminate. Liberals can also argue that benign quotas often have been used by Americans both to compensate for some bad action in the past or to provide some desired distribution of social characteristics—sometimes called diversity. For example, a long and respected policy in the United States is that of "veteran's preference," on the basis of which the government automatically gives extra consideration in hiring to persons who have served the country in the armed forces. The justification is that ex-soldiers deserve compensation for having made sacrifices for the good of the country. And the goal of social diversity has justified "positive discrimination," especially in higher education, the very institution where conservatives have most adamantly argued against positive quotas for blacks and women. For example, all of the Ivy League schools and many other private colleges and universities regularly and consistently reserve admissions places for some students whose qualifications in a strict academic sense are below those of others who are not admitted. These schools not only recruit students from minority groups, but they set aside places for the children of loyal alumni and of their own faculty, even when, in a pure competition solely and exclusively based on test scores and high school records, many of those same children would not have been admitted. These practices are not conclusive justification in themselves, but they certainly underscore the liberal argument that affirmative or compensatory action for minorities who have been unjustly treated in the past is not alien to American experience.

If we think of the debate about affirmative action in terms of American political values, it is clear that conservatives emphasize liberty, whereas liberals stress equality. Conservatives believe that using government actively to promote equality for minorities and women infringes on the rights of white men. Lawsuits challenging affirmative action often cite this "reverse discrimination" as a justification. Liberals, on the other hand, traditionally have defended affirmative action as the best way to achieve equality. In recent years, however, the debate over affirmative action has become more complex and has created divisions among liberals. These divisions stem from growing doubts among some liberals about whether affirmative action can be defended as the best way to achieve equality and about the tensions between affirmative action and democratic values. One recent study of public opinion found that many self-identified liberals were angry about affirmative action.[81] These liberals felt that in the name of equality, affirmative action actually violates norms of fairness and equality of opportunity by giving special advantages to some. Moreover, it is argued, affirmative action is broadly unpopular and is therefore questionable in terms of democratic values. Because our nation has a history of slavery and legalized racial discrimination, and because discrimination continues to exist (although it has declined over time), the question of racial justice, more than any other issue, highlights the difficulty of reconciling our values in practice.

Americans' Opinions on Affirmative Action

Table 5.3

	BLACKS	WHITES
Do you favor affirmative action programs for racial minorites?	70%	44% (responding yes)
Do affirmative active programs give preferential treatment to minorities in school admissions and job hirings even when those minorities are less qualified than other applicants?	20	56

SOURCE: The Gallup Poll, June 2003, reprinted in *USA Today*, June 23, 2003.

Although the problems of rights in America are agonizing, they can be looked at optimistically. The United States has a long way to go before it constructs a truly just, "equally protected" society. But it also has come very far in a relatively short time. Groups pressing for equality have been able to use government to change a variety of discriminatory practices. The federal government has become an active partner in ensuring civil rights and political equality. All explicit de jure barriers to minorities have been dismantled. Many de facto barriers have also been dismantled, and thousands upon thousands of new opportunities have been opened. Deep and fundamental differences have polarized many Americans (see Table 5.3), but political and governmental institutions have proven themselves capable of maintaining balances between them. This kind of balancing can be done without violence so long as everyone recognizes that policy choices, even about rights, cannot be absolute.

GET INVOLVED

What You Can Do:
Mobilize for Civil Rights

Citizens have played the leading role in determining the meaning of civil rights, and students have often been in the forefront of conflicts about civil rights. As we saw in the introduction to this chapter, students played a pivotal role in the civil rights movement in the 1960s. When the movement seemed to be at an impasse in 1960, students helped to reenergize it with their sit-in at the Woolworth's lunch counter. Sit-ins had been used by labor unions seeking recognition in the 1930s, but it was students who first applied this tactic in civil rights struggles. Likewise, "Freedom Summer," a movement launched in 1964 to register southern blacks to vote, was run by students, four of whom lost their lives registering people to vote that summer.

How have students been involved in civil rights issues in more recent years? Reflecting the conflicting views about what civil rights should mean today,

INTERACTIVE POLITICS

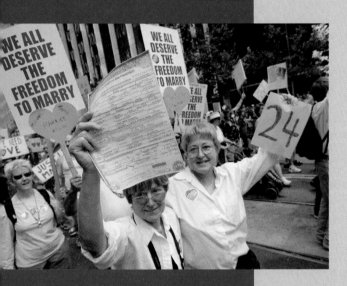

YOU ARE... an activist!

A central tenet of republican democracy is that the people themselves have power to influence outcomes. The people are only effective sovereigns if they are adequately informed and if, when things are going wrong, they take the steps required to force change.

Strategies and tactics vary tremendously for groups seeking redress of grievances, from working within the legislative process, to peaceful marches and public protest, to public relations campaigns, to violent insurrection. The appropriateness and effectiveness of specific tactics will vary by situation and timing.

Recent events in the controversy regarding gay marriage have prompted activists supporting and opposing the practice to increase their efforts and alter tactics. In this simulation, you will push for the outcomes you prefer.

Go to www.wwnorton.com/wtp5e

Questions to consider as you conduct the online simulation:

When the system is not producing the desired changes, how long must a group wait before going outside the normal system and engaging in extraordinary politics?

What makes one social movement's aims legitimate when its opponents also have strong preferences?

What strategies and tactics, if any, are "over the line" and illegitimate, regardless of how strongly a group feels?

How should we balance the preferences of majority rule against the justice of minority rights?

students have been actively involved on both sides of the issue. Students across California were active in the debate about Proposition 209, staging protests and other efforts to persuade voters to reject or support the measure. Since the *Hopwood* decision, students in Texas have held rallies and teach-ins to inform other students about the issues involved. They hope to create a national movement to reinstate affirmative action. Students opposing affirmative action have been less visibly active, but their voices, too, have been heard. For example, the student newspaper at the University of California at Berkeley, *The Californian*, endorsed Proposition 209. Many students on both sides of the issue attended events with speakers presenting arguments for and against affirmative action. Participating in such public events and developing informed opinions is an important kind of political activity.

It is probable that struggles for civil rights are currently taking place on your college campus. Many higher education institutions have student groups organized around specific identities, for example, African American students, Jewish students, women students, gay and lesbian students, and so forth. These identity groups often seek to promote rights and opportunities for their members by appealing for student support and lobbying campus officials to prohibit some activities (such as racist speech) and promote other activities (such as Black History Month). Also, many colleges have campus affiliates of national or international civil rights organizations such as Amnesty International and Human Rights Watch. Numerous campuses have opened up administrative offices aimed at protecting and advancing the civil rights of particular student populations. For example, your school might have a Student Disabilities Office that monitors campus compliance with the Americans with Disabilities Act of 1990.

One way to get involved in the struggle for civil rights is to join a student identity group or volunteer to work in a relevant campus office. Once you have established your presence and membership, consider the range of activities that your group might organize to further the struggle for civil rights. Suppose that your group's immediate goal is to raise campus awareness of civil rights issues. Here are some activities that student groups use to achieve that goal:

- Sponsor a gay and lesbian rights parade.
- Conduct a "Take Back the Night" march opposing violence against women.
- Organize a noon rally to protest the lack of a Latino Studies department.
- Set up a photographic display of human rights violations around the world.
- Hold campus forums designed to facilitate multiracial dialogue and cooperation.

When you plan events, be clear about your goals and match them to appropriate means. Accordingly, you may want to orchestrate highly publicized events to build public support, but you may consider quiet negotiations to work out new policies with campus administration. Finally, learn from the past. Think back to the civil rights struggles of the 1950s and 1960s, study the creative strategies that were used to build a national movement, and then update those strategies and innovate on them to build a foundation for civil rights in this new millennium.

Summary

The constitutional basis of civil rights is the "equal protection" clause. This clause imposes a positive obligation on government to advance civil rights, and its original motivation seems to have been to eliminate the gross injustices suffered by "the newly emancipated Negroes . . . as a class." Civil rights call for the expansion of governmental power rather than restraints upon it. This expanded power allows the government to take an active role in promoting equality. But there was little advancement in the interpretation or application of the "equal protection" clause until after World War II. The major breakthrough came in 1954 with *Brown v. Board of Education,* and advancements came in fits and starts during the succeeding ten years.

After 1964, Congress finally supported the federal courts with effective civil rights legislation that outlawed a number of discriminatory practices in the private sector and provided for the withholding of federal grants-in-aid to any local government, school, or private employer as a sanction to help enforce the civil rights laws. From that point, civil rights developed in two ways. First, the definition of civil rights was expanded to include other, nonblack victims of discrimination. Second, the definition of civil rights became increasingly positive; affirmative action has become an official term. Judicial decisions, congressional statutes, and administrative agency actions all have moved beyond the original goal of eliminating discrimination, toward creating new opportunities for minorities and, in some areas, compensating today's minorities for the consequences of discriminatory actions not directly against them but against members of their group in the past. Because compensatory civil rights action has sometimes relied upon quotas, Americans have engaged in intense debate over the constitutionality as well as the desirability of affirmative action, part of a broader debate over American political values. Citizens' involvement in the civil rights movement played a leading role in determining the meaning of civil rights, although recent conflicts over affirmative action have raised questions about what is effective political action.

The story has not ended and is not likely to end. The politics of rights will remain an important part of American political discourse.

For Further Reading

Garrow, David J. *Bearing the Cross: Martin Luther King and the Southern Christian Leadership Conference: A Personal Portrait.* New York: Morrow, 1986.

Glendon, Mary Ann. *Rights Talk: The Impoverishment of Political Discourse.* New York: Free Press, 1991.

Greenberg, Jack. *Crusaders in the Courts: How a Dedicated Band of Lawyers Fought for the Civil Rights Revolution.* New York: Basic Books, 1994.

Kelly, Christine. *Tangled Up in Red, White, and Blue: Social Movements in America.* New York: Rowman & Littlefield, 2001.

Kinder, Donald, and Lynn Sanders. *Divided by Color: Racial Politics and Democratic Ideals.* Chicago: University of Chicago Press, 1996.

Klinkner, Philip A., and Rogers M. Smith. *The Unsteady March: The Rise and Decline of Racial Equality in America.* Chicago: University of Chicago Press, 1999.

Massey, Douglas S., and Nancy A. Denton. *American Apartheid: Segregation and the Making of the Underclass.* Cambridge, MA: Harvard University Press, 1993.

Mink, Gwendolyn. *Hostile Environment: The Political Betrayal of Sexually Harassed Women.* Ithaca, NY: Cornell University Press, 1999.

Nava, Michael. *Created Equal: Why Gay Rights Matter to America.* New York: St. Martin's, 1994.

Rosenberg, Gerald N. *The Hollow Hope: Can Courts Bring About Social Change?* Chicago: University of Chicago Press, 1991.

Study Outline

www.wwnorton.com/wtp5e
Keyword: Review 5

The Struggle for Civil Rights

1. From 1896 until the end of World War II, the Supreme Court held that the Fourteenth Amendment's equal protection clause was not violated by racial distinction as long as the facilities were equal.
2. After World War II, the Supreme Court began to undermine the separate but equal doctrine, eventually declaring it unconstitutional in *Brown v. Board of Education.*

3. The *Brown* decision marked the beginning of a difficult battle for equal protection in education, employment, housing, voting, and other areas of social and economic activity.
4. The first phase of school desegregation was met with such massive resistance in the South that, ten years after *Brown,* fewer than 1 percent of black children in the South were attending schools with whites.
5. In 1971, the Supreme Court held that state-imposed desegregation could be brought about by busing children across school districts.
6. Title VII of the Civil Rights Act of 1964 outlawed job discrimination by all private and public employers, including governmental agencies, that employed more than fifteen workers.
7. In 1965, Congress significantly strengthened legislation protecting voting rights by barring literacy and other tests as a condition for voting in southern states. In the long run, the laws extending and protecting voting rights could prove to be the most effective of all civil rights legislation, because increased political participation by minorities has altered the shape of American politics.

The Universalization of Civil Rights

1. The protections won by the African American civil rights movement spilled over to protect other groups as well, including women, Latinos, Asian Americans, Native Americans, disabled Americans, and gays and lesbians.

Affirmative Action

1. By seeking to provide compensatory action to overcome the consequences of past discrimination, affirmative action represents the expansion of the goals of groups championing minority rights.

2. Affirmative action has been a controversial policy. Opponents charge that affirmative action creates group rights and establishes quotas, both of which are inimical to the American tradition. Proponents of affirmative action

argue that the long history of group discrimination makes affirmative action necessary and that efforts to compensate for some bad action in the past are well within the federal government's purview. Recent conflicts over affirmative action have raised questions about what is effective political action.

Practice Quiz

www.wwnorton.com/wtp5e
Keyword: Quiz 5

1. When did civil rights become part of the Constitution?
   a) in 1789 at the Founding
   b) with the adoption of the Fourteenth Amendment in 1868
   c) with the adoption of the Nineteenth Amendment in 1920
   d) in the 1954 *Brown v. Board of Education* case

2. Which civil rights case established the "separate but equal" rule?
   a) *Plessy v. Ferguson*
   b) *Brown v. Board of Education*
   c) *Bakke v. Regents of the University of California*
   d) *Adarand Constructors v. Pena*

3. "Massive resistance" refers to efforts by southern states during the late 1950s and early 1960s to
   a) build public housing for poor blacks.
   b) defy federal mandates to desegregate public schools.
   c) give women the right to have an abortion.
   d) bus black students to white schools.

4. Which of the following organizations established a Legal Defense Fund to challenge segregation?
   a) the Association of American Trial Lawyers
   b) the National Association for the Advancement of Colored People
   c) the Student Nonviolent Coordinating Committee
   d) the Southern Christian Leadership Council

5. Which of the following made discrimination by private employers and state governments illegal?
   a) the Fourteenth Amendment
   b) *Brown v. Board of Education*
   c) the 1964 Civil Rights Act
   d) *Bakke v. Board of Regents*

6. In what way does the struggle for gender equality most resemble the struggle for racial equality?
   a) There has been very little political action in realizing the goal.
   b) Changes in government policies to a great degree produced political action.
   c) The Supreme Court has not ruled on the issue.
   d) No legislation has passed adopting the aims of the movement.

7. Which of the following is *not* an example of an area in which women have made progress since the 1970s in guaranteeing certain civil rights?
   a) sexual harassment
   b) integration into all-male publicly supported universities
   c) more equal funding for college women's varsity athletic programs
   d) the passage of the Equal Rights Amendment

8. Which of the following civil rights measures dealt with access to public businesses and accommodations?
   a) the 1990 Americans with Disabilities Act
   b) the 1964 Civil Rights Act
   c) neither a nor b
   d) both a and b

9. Which of the following cases represents the *Brown v. Board of Education* case for lesbians and gay men?
   a) *Bowers v. Hardwick*
   b) *Lau v. Nichols*
   c) *Romer v. Evans*
   d) There has not been a Supreme Court ruling explicitly protecting gays and lesbians from discrimination.

10. In what case did the Supreme Court find that "rigid quotas" are incompatible with the equal protection clause of the Fourteenth Amendment?
   a) *Bakke v. Board of Regents*
   b) *Brown v. Board of Education*
   c) *United States v. Nixon*
   d) *Immigration and Naturalization Service v. Chadha*

Key Terms

www.wwnorton.com/wtp5e
Keyword: Vocabulary 5

affirmative action (p. 193)
Brown v. Board of Education (p. 171)
civil rights (p. 164)
de facto (p. 172)

de jure (p. 172)
discrimination (p. 164)
equal protection clause (p. 164)
Fifteenth Amendment (p. 167)
Fourteenth Amendment (p. 167)
gerrymandering (p. 181)
intermediate scrutiny (p. 184)

Jim Crow (p. 167)
redlining (p. 182)
"separate but equal" rule (p. 168)
strict scrutiny (p. 171)
Thirteenth Amendment (p. 167)

POLITICS

6 PUBLIC OPINION

⭐ **Political Values**

In what ways do Americans agree on fundamental values but disagree on fundamental issues?

How are political values and beliefs formed? What influences individuals' political beliefs?

What do the differences between liberals and conservatives reveal about American political debate?

⭐ **How We Form Political Opinions**

What influences the way we form political opinions?

How are political issues marketed and managed by the government, private groups, and the media?

⭐ **Measuring Public Opinion**

How can public opinion be measured?

What problems arise from public opinion polling?

⭐ **Thinking Critically about Public Opinion and Democracy**

How responsive is the government to public opinion?

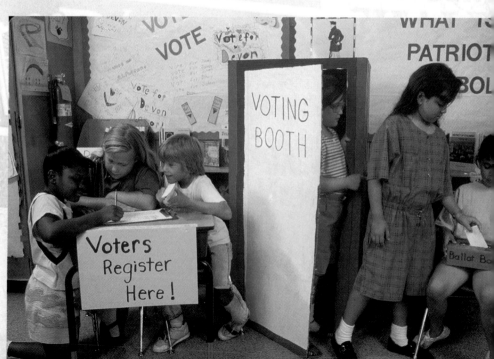

What Government Does and Why It Matters

N RECENT YEARS, American politics seems to have lost some of its vitality, as growing numbers of citizens have turned away from politics. Participation in most kinds of political activities—with the exception of contributing money—is declining. Instead of a distinctively American optimism, a sense of pessimism pervades our politics. Individuals express a sense of powerlessness, frustration, and disengagement from the political system. Among youth such feelings are especially strong. Many students feel that the political system is not relevant to their lives and that politics will not solve the problems in the world. Only about one in five eighteen- to twenty-year-olds vote, and political organizations that aim to represent the views of young people have a hard time staying afloat.[1] Why is this? What can be done to counteract this disturbing trend?

One solution that has been implemented in many areas of the country is "service learning." Though we generally conceive of participation as connoting volunteerism, in some areas of the country young people are actually being required to participate in community or civic affairs. For example, the state of Maryland now mandates fulfillment of a "student service learning" requirement as a condition for high school graduation. Students must sign up for public service jobs with charitable, civic, and public interest groups. These jobs, usually undertaken in conjunction with class work, include work with public interest groups such as the Sierra Club, positions in hospitals and nursing homes, shopping for the elderly, caring for abandoned animals, teaching ecology lessons to small children, and demonstrating eighteenth-century farm crafts including yo-yo making.[2] Students who fail to complete the requisite number of service hours are not allowed to graduate. In 1998, thirty Maryland high school students were denied diplomas because they did not meet their obligation to provide seventy-five hours of community service over four years.[3] Other states are beginning to follow the Maryland example.

At the college level, the presidents of fifty-one American colleges and universities signed a declaration of their commitment to civic responsibility and community participation in July 1999. The declaration called upon colleges to encourage their students to learn about and engage in politics and community service. The declaration came at a conference sponsored by Campus Compact, a fifteen-year-old organization based at Brown University and composed of more than 540 college and university presidents who support the integration of public and community service into academic studies.[4] At the same time, California governor Gray Davis proposed that community service be made a mandatory requirement for graduation from California's public colleges and universities. It remains to be seen whether these efforts will change citizens' attitudes about government and politics. ■

public opinion citizens' attitudes about political issues, leaders, institutions, and events

values (or beliefs) basic principles that shape a person's opinions about political issues and events

political ideology a cohesive set of beliefs that forms a general philosophy about the role of government

attitude (or opinion) a specific preference on a particular issue

The term **public opinion** is used to denote the values and attitudes that people have about issues, events, and personalities. Although the terms are sometimes used interchangeably, it is useful to distinguish between values and beliefs on the one hand, and attitudes or opinions on the other. **Values (or beliefs)** are a person's basic orientations to politics. Values represent deep-rooted goals, aspirations, and ideals that shape an individual's perceptions of political issues and events. Liberty, equality, and democracy are basic political values that most Americans hold. Another useful term for understanding public opinion is *ideology*. **Political ideology** refers to a complex set of beliefs and values that, as a whole, form a general philosophy about government. As we shall see, liberalism and conservatism are important ideologies in America today.

For example, the idea that governmental solutions to problems are inherently inferior to solutions offered by the private sector is a belief held by many Americans. This general belief, in turn, may lead individuals to have negative views of specific government programs even before they know much about them. An **attitude (or opinion)** is a specific view about a particular issue, personality, or event. An individual may have an opinion about Bill Clinton or an attitude toward American policy in Iraq. The attitude or opinion may have emerged from a broad belief about Democrats or military intervention, but an attitude itself is very specific. Some attitudes may be short-lived.

This chapter will examine the role of public opinion in American politics.

■ **First, we examine the political values and beliefs that inform how Americans perceive the political process.** After reviewing the most basic American political values, we analyze how values and beliefs are formed and how certain processes and institutions influence their formation. We conclude this introductory section by looking at how a person's values and beliefs relate to political ideology.

■ **Second, we turn to the process of how political opinions are formed.** We begin by assessing the relative importance of ideology in this process. We then look at the roles that one's knowledge of politics and influence of political leaders, private groups, and the media have on the formation of political views.

■ **Third, we view the science of gathering and measuring public opinion.** The reliability of public opinion is directly related to the way in which it is gathered. Despite the limitations of public opinion polls, they remain an important part of the American political process.

■ Previewing Liberty, Equality, and Democracy

The United States was the first nation in which public opinion polling became a major industry, and no wonder. Questions about public opinion are inextricably linked to America's core political values. Liberty implies the freedom to express one's opinions even if they are critical of the government. Democracy implies that the opinions of the people will have some impact on the government. Equality implies that one person's opinion is as important as another's. Even in America, however, public opinion does not always drive the government's actions. Nor, perhaps, should it.

Political Values

When we think of opinion, we often think in terms of differences of opinion. The media are fond of reporting and analyzing political differences between blacks and whites, men and women (the so-called gender gap), the young and old, and so on. Certainly, Americans differ on many issues, and often these differences do seem to be associated with race, religion, gender, age, or other social characteristics. Today, Americans seem sharply divided on truly fundamental questions about the role of government in American society, the proper place of religious and moral values in public life, and how best to deal with racial conflicts.

FUNDAMENTAL VALUES

As we review these differences, however, it is important to remember that Americans also agree on a number of matters. Indeed, most Americans share a common set of values, including a belief in the principles—if not always the actual practice—of liberty, equality, and democracy. **Equality of opportunity** has always been an important theme in American society. Americans believe that all individuals should be allowed to seek personal and material success. Moreover, Americans

equality of opportunity a widely shared American ideal that all people should have the freedom to use whatever talents and wealth they have to reach their fullest potential

| Figure 6.1 | Americans' Support for Fundamental Values |

SOURCE: 1992 American National Election Studies; Herbert McCloskey and John Zaller, *The American Ethos: Public Attitudes toward Capitalism and Democracy* (Cambridge, MA: Harvard University Press, 1984), p. 25; and Robert S. Erikson, Norman R. Luttbeg, and Kent L. Tedin, *American Public Opinion: Its Origins, Content, and Impact*, 4th ed. (New York: Macmillan, 1991), p. 108.

liberty freedom from government control

democracy a system of rule that permits citizens to play a significant part in the governmental process, usually through the election of key public officials

generally believe that such success should be linked to personal effort and ability, rather than to family "connections" or other forms of special privilege. Similarly, Americans have always voiced strong support for the principle of individual **liberty.** They typically support the notion that governmental interference with individuals' lives and property should be kept to the minimum consistent with the general welfare (although in recent years Americans have grown accustomed to greater levels of governmental intervention than would have been deemed appropriate by the founders of liberal theory). And most Americans also believe in **democracy.** They presume that every person should have the opportunity to take part in the nation's governmental and policy-making processes and to have some "say" in determining how they are governed.[5] Figure 6.1 above offers some indication of this American consensus on fundamental values: 95 percent of those polled believed in equal opportunity, 89 percent supported free speech regardless of the views being expressed, and 95 percent supported majority rule.

One indication that Americans of all political stripes share these fundamental political values is the content of the acceptance speeches delivered by John Kerry and George W. Bush upon receiving their parties' presidential nominations in 2004. Kerry and Bush differed on many issues and policies. Yet the political visions they presented reveal an underlying similarity. A major emphasis of both candidates was equality of opportunity. Kerry referred frequently to opportunity in his speech and, indeed, referred to his running mate, Senator John Edwards as a "man whose life is the story of the American dream . . . the son of a mill worker [now] ready to lead." Bush struck a similar note in his acceptance speech when he said,

"And we will extend the promise of prosperity to every forgotten corner of this country; to every man and every woman a chance to succeed . . ." Thus, however much the two candidates differed on means and specifics, their understandings of the fundamental goals of government were quite similar.

Obviously, the principles that Americans espouse have not always been put into practice. For two hundred years, Americans were able to believe in the principles of equality of opportunity and individual liberty while denying them in practice to generations of African Americans. Yet it is important to note that the strength of the principles ultimately helped to overcome practices that deviated from those principles. Proponents of slavery and, later, of segregation, were defeated in the arena of public opinion because their practices differed so sharply from the fundamental principles accepted by most Americans. Ironically, in contemporary politics, Americans' fundamental commitment to equality of opportunity has led to divisions over racial policy. In particular, both proponents and opponents of affirmative action programs cite their belief in equality of opportunity as the justification for their position. Proponents see these programs as necessary to ensure equality of opportunity, while opponents believe that affirmative action is a form of preferential treatment that violates basic American values.[6]

FORMS OF DISAGREEMENT

Agreement on fundamentals by no means implies that Americans do not differ with one another on a wide variety of issues. American political life is characterized by vigorous debate on economic policy, foreign policy, and social policy issues; race relations; environmental affairs; and a host of other matters.

As we shall see later in this chapter, differences of political opinion are often associated with such variables as income, education, and occupation. Similarly, factors such as race, gender, ethnicity, age, religion, and region, which not only influence individuals' interests but also shape their experiences and upbringing, have enormous influence on their beliefs and opinions. For example, individuals whose incomes differ substantially have different views on the desirability of a number of important economic and social programs. In general, the poor—who are the chief beneficiaries of these programs—support them more strongly than do those who are more wealthy, and pay more of the taxes that fund the programs. Similarly, blacks and whites have different views on questions of civil rights and civil liberties—presumably reflecting differences of interest and historical experience. In recent years, many observers have begun to take note of a number of differences between the views expressed by men and those supported by women, especially on foreign policy questions, where women appear to be much more concerned with the dangers of war. Let us see how such differences develop.

HOW POLITICAL VALUES ARE FORMED

The attitudes that individuals hold about political issues and personalities tend to be shaped by their underlying political beliefs and values. For example, an individual who has basically negative feelings about government intervention into America's economy and society would probably be predisposed to oppose the development of new health care and social programs. Similarly, someone who distrusts the military would likely be suspicious of any call for the use of American

Perspectives on Politics

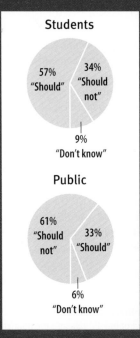

HOW THE OPINION OF COLLEGE STUDENTS ON GAY MARRIAGE DIFFERS FROM THE GENERAL PUBLIC

"Do you think marriages between homosexuals should or should not be recognized by the law as valid, with the same rights as traditional marriages?"

Students

57% "Should"
34% "Should not"
9% "Don't know"

Public

61% "Should not"
33% "Should"
6% "Don't know"

SOURCE: Institute of Politics, Harvard University. "Attitudes toward Politics and Public Service: A National Survey of College Undergraduates." Conducted March 13–23, 2004. www.iop.harvard.edu/programs/other/natlsurvey/april_2004_topline.pdf

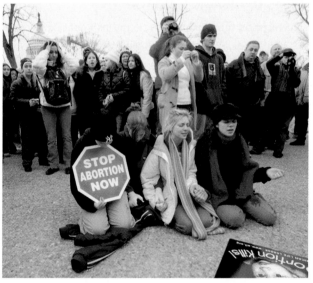

One of the hallmarks of American democracy has been vigorous debate on important policy issues. During the 1960s and early 1970s, anti–Vietnam War protestors staged numerous demonstrations across the nation in opposition to America's foreign policies in Southeast Asia (above). Public opposition to the war and the draft played a major role in forcing President Richard Nixon to withdraw American military forces from Vietnam.

In recent years, differences of opinion on policy have sparked protests and demonstrations. For example, the 2003 war in Iraq led to numerous protests all over the United States, such as this one on the Washington Mall. Opponents and proponents of a woman's right to choose often clash with one another.

political socialization the induction of individuals into the political culture; learning the underlying beliefs and values upon which the political system is based

agencies of socialization social institutions, including families and schools, that help to shape individuals' basic political beliefs and values

troops. The processes through which these underlying political beliefs and values are formed are collectively called **political socialization.**

The process of political socialization is important. Probably no nation, and certainly no democracy, could survive if its citizens did not share some fundamental beliefs. If Americans had few common values or perspectives, it would be very difficult for them to reach agreement on particular issues. In contemporary America, some elements of the socialization process tend to produce differences in outlook, whereas others promote similarities. Four of the most important **agencies of socialization** that foster differences in political perspectives are the family, membership in social groups, education, and prevailing political conditions.

The debate over gay marriage in early 2004 also sparked mass protests in Massachusetts, California, and Washington, D.C. Despite these deep divisons, in recent years public protest as an expression of public opinion has rarely led to violence. One exception was the 1999 Seattle demonstrations protesting the policies of the World Trade Organization. Indeed, throughout the course of American political history, protest politics have generally been channeled into the electoral arena. The voting booth gives voters a more peaceful and institutionalized forum for expressing their opinions.

No inventory of agencies of socialization can fully explain the development of a given individual's basic political beliefs. In addition to the factors that are important for everyone, forces that are unique to each individual play a role in shaping political orientations. For one person, the character of an early encounter with a member of another racial group can have a lasting impact on that individual's view of the world. For another, a highly salient political event, such as the Vietnam War, can leave an indelible mark on that person's political consciousness. For a third person, some deepseated personality characteristic, such as paranoia, for example, may strongly influence the formation of political beliefs. Nevertheless, knowing that we cannot fully explain the development of any given individual's political outlook, let us look at some of the most important agencies of socialization that do affect one's beliefs.

INFLUENCES ON OUR POLITICAL VALUES

The Family   Most people acquire their initial orientation to politics from their families. As might be expected, differences in family background tend to produce divergent political outlooks. Although relatively few parents spend much time teaching their children about politics, political conversations occur in many households and children tend to absorb the political views of parents and other caregivers, perhaps without realizing it. Studies have suggested, for example, that party preferences are initially acquired at home. Children raised in households in which the primary caregivers are Democrats tend to become Democrats themselves, whereas children raised in homes where their caregivers are Republicans tend to favor the GOP (Grand Old Party, a traditional nickname for the Republican Party).[7] Similarly, children reared in politically liberal households are more likely

Gay Marriage

The idea that all Americans are entitled to equal treatment is today a widely accepted principle. More controversial, however, is the matter of how that principle ought to apply to homosexuals. Most Americans embrace a live-and-let-live philosophy regarding homosexuality; at the same time, however, many Americans are uneasy with some highly publicized efforts to define or extend civil rights for gays. This unease is reflected in voters' rejection of some local and state resolutions barring discrimination based on sexual preference.

Central to this debate has been the question of whether states should officially sanction gay marriage. Marriage itself is a private decision, but such a union between two people must also be approved by the state through the issuance of a marriage license if the couple is to receive many of the benefits of marriage, from tax breaks to insurance protection. Complicating this debate is the "full faith and credit" clause of the Constitution (Article IV, Section 1), which says that all states must honor the public acts of any other state, including marriage licenses. Thus, if gay marriage is recognized in even one state, other states are obliged to recognize its legality, too. In 1996, Congress enacted the Defense of Marriage Act, which provided that no state was required to recognize a same-sex marriage performed in another state. Vermont has legalized same-sex marriage, and in November 2003, the Massachusetts supreme court ruled that same-sex couples had the right to marry under the state's constitution. As a result, a constitutional test of the Defense of Marriage Act is likely to come before the Supreme Court.

Supporters of gay marriage point out that homosexuality is neither a fad nor a choice, but an involuntary condition. Given this, loving relationships are inevitable, and it is a denial of equality to discriminate against gays because they seek the same bond of marriage as heterosexuals. "It's a good idea," said one proponent of same-sex marriage responding to the Massachusetts court decision. "How can someone else tell you who you can love and who you can marry? Whoever you love is your own business."[a] Civil marriage for gays would amount to formal public recognition of a homosexual union, making it in principle the same as a heterosexual marriage. Such recognition would actually encourage traditional values of fidelity and stability among homosexuals. It would also ease financial, insurance, and other problems, because gay partners could receive health, life insurance, and

pension benefits, and it would clarify such matters as inheritance, property, and adoption rights. Some localities have extended such rights through domestic-partnership laws, but these enactments are relatively uncommon and vary in their applicability.

Opponents of gay marriage argue that marriage, as it is traditionally defined by law and religion, does and ought to apply only to heterosexual unions. If state governments officially sanctioned gay marriage, they would, in effect, be endorsing a lifestyle that society simply does not equate with heterosexual marriage. Law reflects society's moral values, and those values do not countenance gay unions. Furthermore, a traditional purpose of marriage is the creation of children, and that cannot occur within the confines of a gay marriage (without the intervention of a third person). Many gay couples would seek to adopt children, but not enough research exists to demonstrate whether children would be harmed by such a situation. "God . . . told us to multiply and replenish the earth. That's why we're here," said a same-sex marriage opponent.[b]

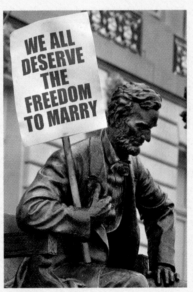

The issue of same-sex marriage has posed difficulties for all politicians. Democrats want to please their liberal core constituencies, which favor gay marriage, but are reluctant to alienate moderate voters. At the same time, Republicans need to please their conservative core constituents, who oppose gay marriage, without alienating moderate voters. President Bush declared his opposition to gay marriage and his support for a proposed constitutional amendment that would define marriage as a union between a man and a woman.

FOR CRITICAL ANALYSIS

1. Rules governing marriage have traditionally been the province of the states, but in recent years some people have advocated a constitutional amendment prohibiting same-sex marriage. Should marriage become a federal matter? Why or why not?

2. Why has gay marriage become an important political issue? What are the positions of your senators and congressional representatives on the topic? Perhaps their Web sites or calls to their offices can provide the answer.

[a]Michael Janovsky, "Amid Acceptance of Gays, a Split on Marriage Issue," *New York Times*, November 24, 2003, p. A12.
[b]Quoted in Janovsky.

than not to develop a liberal outlook, whereas children raised in politically conservative settings are prone to see the world through conservative lenses. Obviously, not all children absorb their parents' political views. Two of former conservative Republican president Ronald Reagan's three children, for instance, rejected their parents' conservative values. Moreover, even those children whose views are initially shaped by parental values may change their minds as they mature and experience political life for themselves. Nevertheless, the family is an important initial source of political orientation for everyone.

Social Groups   Another important source of divergent political orientations and values are the social groups to which individuals belong. Social groups include those to which individuals belong involuntarily—gender and racial groups, for example—as well as those to which people belong voluntarily—such as political parties, labor unions, and educational and occupational groups. Some social groups have both voluntary and involuntary attributes. For example, individuals are born with a particular social-class background, but as a result of their own efforts people may move up—or down—the class structure.

Membership in social groups can affect political values in a variety of ways. Membership in a particular group can give individuals important experiences and perspectives that shape their view of political and social life. In American society, for example, the experiences of blacks and whites can differ significantly. Blacks are a minority and have been victims of persecution and discrimination throughout American history. Blacks and whites also have different educational and occupational opportunities, often live in separate communities, and may attend separate schools. Such differences tend to produce distinctive political outlooks. For example, in 1995 blacks and whites had very different reactions to the murder trial of former football star O. J. Simpson, who was accused of killing his ex-wife and one of her friends. Seventy percent of the white Americans surveyed believed that Simpson was guilty, based on the evidence presented by the police and prosecutors. But an identical 70 percent of the black Americans surveyed immediately after the trial believed that the police had fabricated evidence and had sought to convict Simpson of a crime he had not committed; these beliefs were presumably based on blacks' experiences with and perceptions of the criminal justice system.[8] In a similar vein, Reverend Al Sharpton's 2003–04 campaign for the Democratic presidential nomination was not taken seriously by most white voters and received little attention from the mainstream news media. Black voters, on the other hand, were quite attuned to Sharpton's candidacy, which received considerable coverage in the African American news media. Indeed, Sharpton received considerable financial backing from black media executives.[9]

According to other recent surveys, blacks and whites in the United States differ on many issues. For example, among middle-income Americans (defined as those earning between $30,000 and $75,000 per year), 65 percent of black respondents and only 35 percent of white respondents thought racism was a major problem in the United States today. Within this same group of respondents, 63 percent of blacks and only 39 percent of whites thought the federal government should provide more services even at the cost of higher taxes.[10] Nearly three-quarters of white Americans but only one-third of black Americans favored going to war against Iraq in 2003. Other issues show a similar pattern of disagreement, reflecting the differences in experience, background, and interests between blacks and whites in America (see Figure 6.2 on page 222).

Perspectives on Politics

PARENTAL IMPACT ON POLITICAL EFFICACY

"Of those who grew up with political discussion in the home, 75% are registered to vote (vs. 57% among those who did not have political discussion in the home); 71% trust government (vs. 53%); 68% believe voting is important (vs. 33%); 57% believe politicians pay attention to their concerns (vs. 39%)."

▪ Those who grew up with political discussion
◪ Those who did not have political discussion in the home.

"...Are registered to vote"

"...Trust Government"

"...Believe voting is important"

"...Believe politicians pay attention to our concerns"

SOURCE: The Center for Information and Research in Civic Learning & Engagement Research Project. "The Political and Civic Engagement of Young Adults in America." Conducted January 2002. www.civicyouth.org/ research/products/national_youth_ survey.htm

Should Gay Marriage Be Legal?

Yes

The Massachusetts Supreme Judicial Court made a groundbreaking ruling in the struggle for gay rights Tuesday.

In the 4-3 decision, the court declared laws banning gay marriages were in violation of the state's constitution. They stated attorneys "failed to identify any constitutionally adequate reason" to prohibit same-sex couples from marrying.

While Massachusetts is the first state to legalize gay marriages, Vermont and California already extend marriage benefits and rights to same-sex couples through domestic and civil unions.

Nevertheless, this ruling has been extremely controversial in Massachusetts, as well as across the nation.

In fact, President Bush has criticized the ruling, saying it violates the sanctity of marriage and Massachusetts Governor Mitt Romney said he would immediately work toward overturning the decision.

Some Republican legislators also are discussing an amendment to the U.S. Constitution which would prohibit gay marriages.

However, the politicians' arguments are based upon maintaining the "traditional family." But such perspectives on the appropriate family are based in religion, not law. Therefore they have no place in our legal system.

Despite such strong opposition to the ruling, we are pleased to see government officials making a long-overdue step toward eliminating the gross injustices experienced by gays and lesbians.

Homosexual Americans deserve the same civil rights enjoyed by all citizens, yet the law has frequently permitted discrimination against them.

Why should a devoted same-sex couple not experience the same rights and benefits as heterosexual couples?

Nevertheless, some politicians in opposition to the Massachusetts Supreme Court ruling insist the majority of the consituents they represent also oppose legalized same-sex marriages.

Although this may be true, it is important to remember that one of the primary functions of the U.S. Constitution is to protect the rights of citizens who are in the minority.

After all, African Americans only make up a minority of the population, and it is safe to say more than one hundred years ago the majority of Americans would have opposed voting rights for blacks.

Today there is no question that all people, despite race, gender, religion, or sexual orientation, should have the right to represent themselves through voting.

Hopefully one hundred years from now, there will be no question whether all people have the right to choose whom they want to marry.

SOURCE: [Staff Editorial], "Same-Sex Couples Deserve Equal Rights", *The Murray State News* (Murray State University), November 21, 2003.

No The gay marriage debate currently being waged in America is a difficult path to follow. It has thousands of twists and turns, and even more thoughts to be pondered and considered.

This entire debate, and many other hotly contested debates, comes from something that began more than 200 years ago. This something is the process of "judicial review," a power not granted in the Constitution, but rather a power the United States Supreme Court developed for itself in 1803.

Judicial review is the process by which a court determines that a law violates either the function or the will of our Constitution, and casts the law aside. It has had more detrimental effects than positive.

For all of its good effects *(Brown v. Board of Education)* it has its negatives *(Roe v. Wade)*. But in the end, the entire gay marriages debate springs from this.

What has stimulated the most recent wave of action against gay marriage is the ruling by the Massachusetts Supreme Court that the law developed in that state defining a marriage as a union between a man and a woman violates the state constitution. Judicial review at work: thwarting the will of the people and subjugating it to the will of a few judges.

Unfortunately, it doesn't stop there. In California, we have a state that made gay marriage illegal by a voter intiative. This wasn't some right-wing legislature that made this decision; it was the citizens of the state, but in the end it doesn't really matter what the people want. Mayor Gavin Newsom has violated California law by issuing marriage licenses to homosexuals wishing to be wed. According to the law, he is in violation and should be ordered to stop, and possibly be arrested, but activist judges in California are dragging their feet, refusing to stop acts that violate state law.

In Indiana, our law banning gay marriage is being challenged. Last week, state Republicans attempted to bring a "blast" motion to the floor, which would have resulted in a constitutional amendment, thus prohibiting the state supreme court from overruling the will of the people. The Democrats in this state have stopped this motion from even being brought to a vote.

Last week, the president of the United States gave his support to a proposed constitutional amendment defining marriage as a union between one man and one woman. This amendment is the only way to supersede radical liberal judges who do not care about the will of the people, only about implementing their personal agenda. This amendment is not hateful or divisive. It does not ban civil unions, an arrangement that offers ALL of the same benefits homosexuals allegedly seek, without cheapening the institution of marriage. The amendment does defend the institution of marriage and keeps it from being expanded to include one man and three women, a man and his dog, or a man and his daughter.

Marriage is between a man and a woman. Its roots are in religious law, not that of the secular government. If homosexuals want to make [their] marriage legal, they should do so through the state legislatures or through the United States legislative branch. Unfortunately, they have chosen to use the will of a select few liberal judges to overrule the clear majority of American people. That should be unconstitutional.

SOURCE: Russell Greim, "Judicial Review Unreliable Base for Policy Decisions," *Ball State Daily News* (Ball State University), March 1, 2004.

Figure 6.2 Disagreement Among Blacks and Whites

African Americans and white Americans have strong differences of opinion on certain issues.

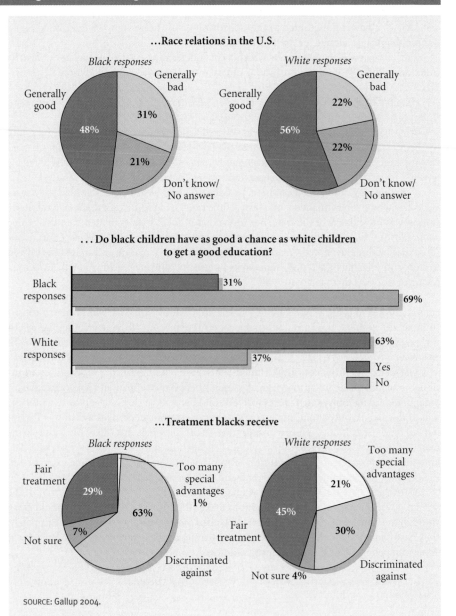

...Race relations in the U.S.

Black responses
- Generally good: 48%
- Generally bad: 31%
- Don't know/No answer: 21%

White responses
- Generally good: 56%
- Generally bad: 22%
- Don't know/No answer: 22%

... Do black children have as good a chance as white children to get a good education?

Black responses: Yes 31%, No 69%

White responses: Yes 63%, No 37%

Yes
No

...Treatment blacks receive

Black responses
- Fair treatment: 29%
- Too many special advantages: 1%
- Discriminated against: 63%
- Not sure: 7%

White responses
- Too many special advantages: 21%
- Fair treatment: 45%
- Discriminated against: 30%
- Not sure: 4%

SOURCE: Gallup 2004.

Disagreements among Men and Women on Issues of War and Peace

Table 6.1

GOVERNMENT ACTION	PERCENTAGE APPROVING OF ACTION	
	MEN	WOMEN
Prefer cease-fire over NATO airstrikes on Yugoslavia (1999)	44	51
Favor unilateral military action against Iraq (1998)	55	35
Support military operation against Somali warlord (1993)	72	60
Support going to war against Iraq (1991)	72	53
Agree with sending U.S. troops to Saudi Arabia in response to Iraqi invasion of Kuwait (1991)	78	54
Believe U.S. should mount long-term war in Afghanistan (2002)	64	42
Support going to war against Iraq (2003)	78	66

SOURCE: Gallup Poll, 1991, 1993, 1998, 1999, 2002, 2003.

Men and women have important differences of opinion as well. Reflecting differences in social roles, political experience, and occupational patterns, women tend to be less militaristic than men on issues of war and peace, more likely than men to favor measures to protect the environment, and more supportive than men of government social and health care programs (see Table 6.1). Perhaps because of these differences on issues, women are more likely than men to vote for Democratic candidates.[11] This tendency for men's and women's opinions to differ is called the **gender gap.**

Political party membership can be another factor affecting political orientations.[12] Partisans tend to rely on party leaders and spokespersons for cues on the appropriate positions to take on major political issues. In recent years, congressional redistricting and partisan realignment in the South have reduced the number of conservative Democrats and all but eliminated liberal Republicans from the Congress and from positions of prominence in the party. As a result, the leadership of the Republican Party has become increasingly conservative while that of the Democratic Party has become more and more liberal. These changes in the positions of party leaders have been reflected in the views of party adherents and sympathizers in the general public. According to recent studies, differences between Democratic and Republican partisans on a variety of political and policy questions are greater today than during any other period for which data are available. On issues of national security, for example, Republicans have become very "hawkish" while Democrats have become quite "dovish." In October 2003, for instance, 85 percent of Republicans compared to 39 percent of the Democrats surveyed thought America's war against Iraq had been a good idea. Gaps on domestic social and economic issues were nearly as broad.[13]

Membership in a social group can affect individuals' political orientations in another way: through the efforts of groups themselves to influence their members. Labor unions, for example, often seek to "educate" their members through meetings, rallies, and literature. These activities are designed to shape union members'

gender gap a distinctive pattern of voting behavior reflecting the differences in views between women and men understanding of politics and to make them more amenable to supporting the political positions favored by union leaders. Similarly, organization can sharpen the impact of membership in an involuntary group. Women's groups, black groups, religious groups, and the like usually endeavor to structure their members' political views through intensive educational programs. The importance of such group efforts can be seen from the impact of group membership on political opinion. Women who belong to women's organizations, for example, are likely to differ more from men in their political views than women without such group affiliation.[14] Other analysts have found that African Americans who belong to black organizations are likely to differ more from whites in their political orientations than blacks who lack such affiliations.[15]

In many cases, no particular efforts are required by groups to affect their members' beliefs and opinions. Often, individuals will consciously or unconsciously adapt their views to those of the groups with which they identify. For example, an African American who is dubious about affirmative action is likely to come under considerable peer pressure and internal pressure to modify his or her views. In this and other cases, dissenters are likely gradually to shift their own views to conform to those of the group. Political psychologist Elisabeth Noelle-Neumann has called this process the "spiral of silence."[16]

A third way that membership in social groups can affect political beliefs is through what might be called objective political interests. On many economic issues, for example, the interests of the rich and poor differ significantly. Inevitably, these differences of interest will produce differences of political outlook. James Madison and other framers of the Constitution thought that the inherent gulf between the rich and the poor would always be the most important source of conflict in political life. Certainly today, struggles over tax policy, welfare policy, health care policy, and so forth are fueled by differences of interest between wealthier and poorer Americans. In a similar vein, objective differences of interest between "senior citizens" and younger Americans can lead to very different views on such diverse issues as health care policy, Social Security, and criminal justice. To take another example, in recent decades major differences of opinion and political orientation have developed between American civilians and members of the armed services. Military officers, in particular, are far more conservative in their domestic and foreign policy views than the public-at-large and are heavily Republican in their political leanings.[17] Interestingly, support for the Republicans among military officers climbed sharply during the 1980s and 1990s, decades in which the GOP championed large military budgets. Could this be another case of objective interests swaying ideology?

It is worth pointing out again that, like the other agencies of socialization, group membership can never fully explain a given individual's political views. One's unique personality and life experiences may produce political views very different from those of the group to which one might nominally belong. This is why some African Americans are conservative Republicans, or why an occasional wealthy industrialist is also a socialist. Group membership is conducive to particular outlooks, but it is not determinative.

Differences in Education   A third important source of differences in political perspectives comes from a person's education. In some respects, of course, schooling is a great equalizer. Governments use public education to try to teach all children a common set of civic values. It is mainly in school that Americans acquire their basic belief in liberty, equality, and democracy. In history classes, students are taught that the Founders fought for the principle of liberty. Through participation in class elections and student government, students are taught the virtues of democracy. In the course of studying such topics as the Constitution, the Civil War, and the civil rights movement, students are taught the importance of equality. These lessons are repeated in every grade in a variety of contexts. No wonder they are such an important element in Americans' beliefs.

At the same time, however, differences in educational attainment are strongly associated with differences in political outlook. In particular, those who attend college are often exposed to philosophies and modes of thought that will forever distinguish them from their friends and neighbors who do not pursue college diplomas. Table 6.2 outlines some general differences of opinion that are found between college graduates and other Americans.

In recent years, conservatives have charged that liberal college professors indoctrinate their students with liberal ideas. College does seem to have some "liberalizing" effect upon students, but, more significantly, college seems to convince students of the importance of political participation and of their own capacity to have an impact on politics and policy. Thus, one of the major differences between college graduates and other Americans can be seen in levels of political participation. College graduates vote, write "letters to the editor," join campaigns, take part in protests, and, generally, make their voices heard. Does this mean that college graduates are turned into dangerous radicals by liberal professors? Quite the contrary: college seems to convince individuals that it is important to involve themselves in the nation's politics. What perspective could be more conservative?

Education and Public Opinion in 2000

Table 6.2

The figures show the percentage of respondents in each category agreeing with the statement.

	EDUCATION			
ISSUES	DROP-OUT	HIGH SCHOOL	SOME COLLEGE	COLLEGE GRAD.
1. Women and men should have equal roles.	45%	72%	84%	85%
2. Abortion should never be allowed.	31	16	11	5
3. The government should adopt national health insurance.	50	43	38	37
4. The U.S. should not concern itself with other nations' problems.	27	34	27	12
5. Government should see to fair treatment in jobs for African Americans.	24	33	32	43
6. Government should provide fewer services to reduce government spending.	18	13	19	31

SOURCE: The American National Election Studies, 2000 data, provided by the Inter-University Consortium for Political and Social Research, University of Michigan.

IMPACT OF SEPTEMBER 11 ON COLLEGE STUDENTS' ATTITUDES ABOUT POLITICS AND GOVERNMENT

"Have the attacks of September 11 made you more or less likely to participate in politics and voting?"

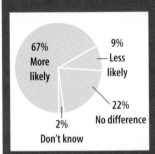

67% More likely

9% Less likely

22% No difference

2% Don't know

SOURCE: The Center for Information and Research in Civic Learning & Engagement Research Project. "The Political and Civic Engagement of Young Adults in America." Conducted January 2002. www.civicyouth.org/research/products/national_youth_survey.htm

Political Conditions A fourth set of factors that shape political orientations and values are the conditions under which individuals and groups are recruited into and involved in political life. Although political beliefs are influenced by family background and group membership, the precise content and character of these views is, to a large extent, determined by political circumstances. For example, in the nineteenth century, millions of southern Italian peasants left their homes. Some migrated to cities in northern Italy; others came to cities in the United States. Many of those who moved to northern Italy were recruited by socialist and communist parties and became mainstays of the forces of the Italian Left. At the same time, their cousins and neighbors who migrated to American cities were recruited by urban patronage machines and became mainstays of political conservatism. In both instances, group membership influenced political beliefs. Yet the character of those beliefs varied enormously with the political circumstances in which a given group found itself.

In a similar vein, the views held by members of a particular group can shift drastically over time, as political circumstances change. For example, American white southerners were staunch members of the Democratic Party from the Civil War through the 1960s. As members of this political group, they became key supporters of liberal New Deal and post–New Deal social programs that greatly expanded the size and power of the American national government. Since the 1960s, however, southern whites have shifted in large numbers to the Republican Party. Now they provide a major base of support for efforts to scale back social programs and to sharply reduce the size and power of the national government. The South's move from the Democratic to the Republican camp took place because of white southern opposition to the Democratic Party's racial policies and because of determined Republican efforts to win white southern support. It was not a change in the character of white southerners but a change in the political circumstances in which they found themselves that induced this major shift in political allegiances and outlooks in the South.

The moral of this story is that a group's views cannot be inferred simply from the character of the group. College students are not inherently radical or inherently conservative. Jews are not inherently liberal. Southerners are not inherently conservative. Men are not inherently supportive of the military. Any group's political outlooks and orientations are shaped by the political circumstances in which that group finds itself, and those outlooks can change as circumstances change. Quite probably, the generation of American students now coming of political age will have a very different view of the use of American military power than their parents—members of a generation that reached political consciousness during the 1960s, when opposition to the Vietnam War and military conscription was an important political phenomenon.

FROM POLITICAL VALUES TO IDEOLOGY

As we have seen, people's beliefs about government can vary widely. But for some individuals, this set of beliefs can fit together into a coherent philosophy about government. This set of underlying orientations, ideas, and beliefs through which we come to understand and interpret politics is called a political ideology. Ideologies take many different forms. Some people may view politics primarily in religious terms. During the course of European political history, for example, Protestantism and Catholicism were often political ideologies as much as they were religious

S upports abortion rights.

Opposes prayer in the public schools.

Supports affirmative action.

Advocates universal health insurance.

Favors a multilateral approach to foreign policy and security issues.

Proposes higher taxes on wealthy taxpayers.

Advocates a $100 billion job creation fund.

creeds. Each set of beliefs not only included elements of religious practice but also involved ideas about secular authority and political action. Other people may see politics through racial lenses. Nazism was a political ideology that placed race at the center of political life and sought to interpret politics in terms of racial categories.

In America today, people often describe themselves as liberals or conservatives. Liberalism and conservatism are political ideologies that include beliefs about the role of the government, ideas about public policies, and notions about which groups in society should properly exercise power (see Boxes 6.1 and 6.2). These ideologies can be seen as the end results of the process of political socialization that was discussed in the preceding section.

W ants to trim the size of the federal government and transfer power to state and local governments. Wants to diminish government regulation of business.

Favors prayer in the public schools.

Opposes gay rights legislation.

Supports programs that would allow children and parents more flexibility in deciding what school to attend.

Supports strict regulation of pornography.

Favors making most abortions illegal.

Would eliminate some environmental regulations.

Supports harsher treatment of criminals.

Opposes many affirmative action programs.

Opposes allowing women to serve in military combat units.

Questions U.S. participation in international organizations.

Favors tax cuts.

Supports high levels of military spending.

liberal today this term refers to those who generally support social and political reform; extensive governmental intervention in the economy; the expansion of federal social services; more vigorous efforts on behalf of the poor, minorities, and women; and greater concern for consumers and the environment

conservative today this term refers to those who generally support the social and economic status quo and are suspicious of efforts to introduce new political formulae and economic arrangements. Conservatives believe that a large and powerful government poses a threat to citizens' freedom

Today, the term **liberal** has come to imply support for political and social reform, extensive government intervention in the economy, the expansion of federal social services, and more vigorous efforts on behalf of the poor, minorities, and women, as well as greater concern for consumers and the environment. In social and cultural areas, liberals generally support abortion rights, are concerned with the rights of persons accused of crime, and oppose state involvement with religious institutions and religious expression. In international affairs, liberal positions are usually seen as including support for arms control, opposition to the development and testing of nuclear weapons, support for aid to poor nations, opposition to the use of American troops to influence the domestic affairs of developing nations, and support for international organizations such as the United Nations. Of course, liberalism is not monolithic. For example, among individuals who view themselves as liberal, many support American military intervention when it is tied to a humanitarian purpose, as in the case of America's military action in Kosovo in 1998–99. Most liberals supported President Bush's war on terrorism, even when some of the president's actions seemed to curtail civil liberties.

By contrast, the term **conservative** today is used to describe those who generally support the social and economic status quo and are suspicious of efforts to introduce new political formulae and economic arrangements. Conservatives believe strongly that a large and powerful government poses a threat to citizens' freedom. Thus, in the domestic arena, conservatives generally oppose the expansion of governmental activity, asserting that solutions to social and economic problems can be developed in the private sector. Conservatives particularly oppose efforts to impose government regulation on business, pointing out that such regulation is frequently economically inefficient and costly and can ultimately lower the entire nation's standard of living. As to social and cultural positions, many conservatives oppose abortion, support school prayer, are more concerned for the victims than for the perpetrators of crimes, oppose school busing, and support traditional family arrangements. In international affairs, conservatism has come to mean support for the maintenance of American military power. Like liberalism, conservatism is far from a monolithic ideology. Some conservatives support many government social programs. Republican George W. Bush calls himself a "compassionate conservative" to indicate that he favors programs that assist the poor and needy. Other conservatives oppose efforts to outlaw abortion, arguing that government intrusion in this area is as misguided as government intervention in the economy. Such a position is sometimes called "libertarian." In a similar vein, Pat Buchanan has angered many fellow conservatives by opposing most American military intervention in other regions. Many conservatives charge Buchanan with advocating a form of American "isolationism" that runs counter to contemporary conservative doctrine. The real political world is far too complex to be seen in terms of a simple struggle between liberals and conservatives.

To some extent, contemporary liberalism and conservatism can be seen as differences of emphasis with regard to the fundamental American political values of liberty and equality. For liberals, equality is the most important of the core values. Liberals are willing to tolerate government intervention in such areas as college admissions and business decisions when these seem to result in high levels of race, class, or gender inequality. For conservatives, on the other hand, liberty is the core value. Conservatives oppose most efforts by the government, however well intentioned, to intrude into private life or the marketplace. For example, in October and

November 2001, conservatives delayed the enactment of airport safety legislation because they opposed plans for a government takeover of airline baggage inspection. Conservatives charged that private security firms could handle the job more effectively. This simple formula for distinguishing liberalism and conservatism, however, is not always accurate, because political ideologies seldom lend themselves to neat or logical characterizations. Often political observers search for logical connections among the various positions identified with liberalism or with conservatism, and they are disappointed or puzzled when they are unable to find a set of coherent philosophical principles that define and unite the several elements of either of these sets of beliefs. On the liberal side, for example, what is the logical connection between opposition to U.S. government intervention in the affairs of foreign nations and calls for greater intervention in America's economy and society? On the conservative side, what is the logical relationship between opposition to governmental regulation of business and support for a government ban on abortion? Indeed, the latter would seem to be just the sort of regulation of private conduct that conservatives claim to abhor.

Frequently, the relationships among the various elements of liberalism or of conservatism are political rather than logical. One underlying basis of liberal views is that all or most represent criticisms of or attacks on the foreign and domestic policies and cultural values of the business and commercial strata that have been prominent in the United States for the past century. In some measure, the tenets of contemporary conservatism represent this elite's defense of its positions against its enemies, who include organized labor, minority groups, and some intellectuals and professionals. Thus, liberals attack business and commercial elites by advocating more governmental regulation, including consumer protection and environmental regulation, opposing new military weapons programs, and supporting expensive social programs. Conservatives counterattack by asserting that governmental regulation of the economy is ruinous and that new military weapons are needed in a changing world, and they seek to stigmatize their opponents for showing no concern for the rights of "unborn" Americans.

Of course, it is important to note that many people who call themselves liberals or conservatives accept only part of the liberal or conservative ideology. During the 1980s, many political commentators asserted that Americans were becoming increasingly conservative. Indeed, it was partly in response to this view that the Democrats in 1992 selected a presidential candidate, Bill Clinton, drawn from the party's moderate wing. Although it appears that Americans have adopted more conservative outlooks on some issues, their views in most areas have remained largely unchanged or even have become more liberal in recent years. Thus, many individuals who are liberal on social issues are conservative on economic issues. There is nothing illogical about these mixed positions. They simply indicate the relatively open and fluid character of American political debate. As Figure 6.3 indicates, Americans are often apt to shift their ideological preferences.

How We Form Political Opinions

An individual's opinions on particular issues, events, and personalities emerge as he or she evaluates these phenomena through the lenses of the beliefs and orientations that, taken together, comprise his or her political ideology. Thus, if

FOR CRITICAL ANALYSIS

Describe the differences between liberal and conservative ideologies in American politics. Using one social or demographic group as an example, describe some of the factors that may have shaped the ideological orientation of that particular group. What factors may explain inconsistencies in that group's political ideology or issue positions?

Perspectives on Politics

COLLEGE STUDENTS' POLITICAL IDEOLOGY

"Do you consider yourself a liberal, conservative, or a moderate?*"

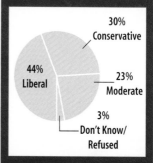

30% Conservative

44% Liberal

23% Moderate

3% Don't Know/ Refused

*The categories for liberal and conservative include those respondents who identified themselves as moderates who lean to one end of the spectrum.

SOURCE: Institute of Politics, Harvard University. "Attitudes Toward Politics and Public Service: A National Survey of College Undergraduates." Conducted March 13–23, 2004. www.iop.harvard.edu/programs/ other/natlsurvey/april_2004_ topline.pdf

Figure 6.3
Americans' Shifting Ideology, 1972—2002

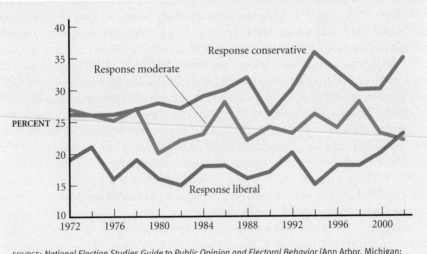

SOURCE: *National Election Studies Guide to Public Opinion and Electoral Behavior* (Ann Arbor, Michigan: Inter-University Consortium for Political and Social Research, 2004).

a conservative is confronted with a plan to expand federal social programs, he or she is likely to express opposition to the endeavor without spending too much time pondering the specific plan. Similarly, if a liberal is asked to comment on conservative former president Ronald Reagan, he or she is not likely to hesitate long before offering a negative view. Underlying beliefs and ideologies tend to automatically color people's perceptions and opinions about politics.

Opinions on particular issues, however, are seldom fully shaped by underlying ideologies. Few individuals possess ideologies so cohesive and intensely held that they will automatically shape all their opinions. Indeed, when we occasionally encounter individuals with rigid worldviews, who see everything through a particular political lens, we tend to dismiss them as "ideologues," or lacking common sense.

Although ideologies color our political perspectives, they seldom fully determine our views. This is true for a variety of reasons. First, as noted earlier, most individuals' ideologies contain internal contradictions. Take, for example, a conservative view of the issue of abortion. Should conservatives favor outlawing abortion as an appropriate means of preserving public morality, or should they oppose restrictions on abortion because these represent government intrusions into private life? Or take the issue of America's response to terrorism. Should conservatives support President Bush's plans to try terrorists before military tribunals as a properly harsh reaction to international criminals or should they oppose the president's plans as an unwarranted expansion of the government's power? In this instance, as in many others, ideology can point in different directions.

Second, individuals may have difficulty linking particular issues or personalities to their own underlying beliefs. Some issues defy ideological characterization. Should conservatives have supported or opposed the 1999 "Patient's Bill of Rights" that made it easier for individuals to file suit against the widely unpopular health maintenance organizations (HMOs), which came to dominate American health care in the 1990s? What should liberals think about America's 1998–99 bombing campaign against Serbia, our 2001–02 war in Afghanistan, and continued conflict with Iraq? Each of these policies combines a mix of issues and is too complex to be viewed through simple ideological lenses.

Finally, most people have at least some conflicting underlying attitudes. Most conservatives support *some* federal programs—defense, or tax deductions for businesses, for example—and wish to see them, and hence the government, expanded. Many liberals favor American military intervention in other nations for what they deem to be humanitarian purposes, but generally oppose American military intervention in the affairs of other nations.

Thus, most individuals' attitudes on particular issues do not spring automatically from their ideological predispositions. It is true that most people have underlying beliefs that help to shape their opinions on particular issues, but two other factors are also important: a person's knowledge of political issues, and outside influences on that person's views.

POLITICAL KNOWLEDGE

As we have seen, general political beliefs can guide the formation of opinions on specific issues, but an individual's beliefs and opinions are not always consistent with one another. Studies of political opinion have shown that most people don't hold specific and clearly defined opinions on every political issue. As a result, they are easily influenced by others. What best explains whether citizens are generally consistent in their political views or inconsistent and open to the influence of others? The key is knowledge and information about political issues. In general, knowledgeable citizens are better able to evaluate new information and determine whether it is relevant to and consistent with their beliefs and opinions. As a result, better-informed individuals can recognize their political interests and act consistently on behalf of them.

One of the most obvious and important examples of this proposition is voting. Despite the predisposition of voters to support their own party's candidates (see Chapter 9 for a discussion of party identification), millions of voters are affected by the information they receive about candidates during a campaign. During the 2000 presidential campaign, for instance, voters weighed the arguments of Al Gore against those of George W. Bush about who was better fit to run the U.S. economy based on what they (the voters) knew about the country's economic health. Some Republican voters actually supported Gore because they approved of the economic policies followed during the Clinton years. Thus citizens can use information and judgment to overcome their predispositions. Without some political knowledge, citizens would have a difficult time making sense of the complex political world in which they live.

This point brings up two questions, however. First, how much political knowledge is necessary for one to act as an effective citizen? And second, how is political knowledge distributed throughout the population? In a recent study of political knowledge in the United States, political scientists Michael X. Delli Carpini and Scott Keeter found that the average American exhibits little knowledge of political institutions, processes, leaders, and policy debates. Many Americans cannot even name their own congressional representative.[18] Does this ignorance of key political facts matter?

political efficacy the ability to influence government and politics

Another important concern is the character of those who possess and act upon the political information that they acquire. Political knowledge is not evenly distributed throughout the population. Those with higher education, income, and occupational status and who are members of social or political organizations are more likely to know about and be active in politics. An interest in politics reinforces an individual's sense of **political efficacy** and provides more incentive to acquire additional knowledge and information about politics. Those who don't think they can have an effect on government tend not to be interested in learning about or participating in politics. As a result, individuals with a disproportionate share of income and education also have a disproportionate share of knowledge and influence and are better able to get what they want from government.

Political Knowledge and Political Inequality If knowledge is power, lack of knowledge can be an enormous source of political weakness and contribute greatly to political inequality. When individuals are unaware of their interests or how to pursue them, it is virtually certain that political outcomes will not favor them. One example is in the realm of taxation. Over the past several decades, the United States has substantially reduced the rate of taxation paid by its wealthiest citizens. Most recently, tax cuts signed into law by President Bush in 2001 provided a tax break mainly for the top 1 percent of the nation's wage earners while further tax cuts proposed by the president offer additional benefits to this privileged stratum. Surprisingly, however, polling data show that millions of middle-class and lower-middle-class Americans who do not stand to benefit from the president's tax cuts seem to favor them, nonetheless. The explanation for this odd state of affairs appears to be lack of political knowledge. Millions of individuals who are unlikely to derive much advantage from President Bush's tax policy think they will. Political scientist Larry Bartels has called this phenomenon "misplaced self-interest."[19] Upper-bracket taxpayers, who are usually served by an army of financial advisers, are unlikely to suffer from this problem.

FOR CRITICAL ANALYSIS

Americans vary enormously in their knowledge about government and politics, yet we treat all opinions as having equal weight. The polls certainly do not distinguish between informed and uninformed opinions. Should all political opinions be treated equally?

THE INFLUENCE OF POLITICAL LEADERS, PRIVATE GROUPS, AND THE MEDIA

When individuals attempt to form opinions about particular political issues, events, and personalities, they seldom do so in isolation. Typically, they are confronted—sometimes bombarded—by the efforts of a host of individuals and groups seeking to persuade them to adopt a particular point of view. Someone trying to decide what to think about George W. Bush, Colin Powell, or Dick Cheney could hardly avoid an avalanche of opinions expressed through the media, in meetings, or in conversations with friends. The **marketplace of ideas** is the interplay of opinions and views that takes place as competing forces attempt to persuade as many people as possible to accept a particular position on a particular event. Given constant exposure to the ideas of others, it is virtually impossible for most individuals to resist some modification of their own beliefs. For example, as we saw earlier, African Americans and white Americans disagree on a number of matters. Yet, as political scientists Paul Sniderman and Edward Carmines have shown, considerable cross-racial agreement has evolved on fundamental issues of race and civil rights.[20]

marketplace of ideas the public forum in which beliefs and ideas are exchanged and compete

The marketplace of ideas has created a common ground on which the discussion of issues is encouraged, based on common understandings. Despite the many and often sharp divisions that exist in the twentieth century—between liberals and conservatives or different income groups—most Americans see the world through similar lenses. This idea market makes it possible for ideas of all sorts to compete for attention and acceptance.

Few ideas spread spontaneously. Usually, whether they are matters of fashion, science, or politics, ideas must be vigorously promoted to become widely known and accepted. For example, the clothing, sports, and entertainment fads that occasionally seem to appear from nowhere and sweep the country before being replaced by some other new trend are almost always the product of careful marketing campaigns by some commercial interest, rather than spontaneous phenomena. Like their counterparts in fashion, successful—or at least widely held—political ideas are usually the products of carefully orchestrated campaigns by government or by organized groups and interests, rather than the results of spontaneous popular enthusiasm. In general, new ideas are presented in ways that make them seem consistent with, or even logical outgrowths of, Americans' more fundamental beliefs. For example, proponents of affirmative action generally present the policy as a necessary step toward racial equality. Or opponents of a proposed government regulation will vehemently assert that the rule is inconsistent with liberty. Both supporters and opponents of campaign finance reform seek to wrap their arguments in the cloak of democracy.[21]

Three forces that play important roles in shaping opinions are the government, private groups, and the news media.

Government and the Shaping of Public Opinion All governments attempt, to a greater or lesser extent, to influence, manipulate, or manage their citizens' beliefs. But the extent to which public opinion is actually affected by governmental public relations efforts is probably limited. The government—despite its size and power—is only one source of information and evaluation in the United States. Very often, governmental claims are disputed by the media, by interest groups, and at times by opposing forces within the government itself. Often, too, governmental efforts to manipulate public opinion backfire when the public is made aware of the government's tactics. Thus, in 1971, the United States government's efforts to build popular support for the Vietnam War were hurt when CBS News aired its documentary "The Selling of the Pentagon," which purported to reveal the extent and character of governmental efforts to sway popular sentiment. In this documentary, CBS demonstrated the techniques, including planted news stories and faked film footage, that the government had used to misrepresent its activities in Vietnam. These revelations, of course, undermined popular trust in all governmental claims.

A hallmark of the Clinton administration was the steady use of techniques like those used in election campaigns to bolster popular enthusiasm for White House initiatives. The president established a political "war room," similar to the one that operated in his campaign headquarters, where representatives from all departments met daily to discuss and coordinate the president's public relations efforts. Many of the same consultants and pollsters who directed the successful Clinton campaign were also employed in the selling of the president's programs.[22]

Indeed, the Clinton White House made more sustained and systematic use of public-opinion polling than any previous administration. For example, during his

BOB GORRELL
Courtesy Richmond Times-Dispatch/
Copley News Service

Because of the importance of public opinion, most presidents have made major efforts both to ascertain the public's views and to promote opinions favorable to themselves and their policies. FDR was the first president to use professional pollsters and make systematic use of newspapers, movie newsreels, and the radio to reach out to the public and attempt to shape opinion on domestic and foreign policies. FDR's famous "fireside chats" brought him into every American home via the radio.

America's two most recent presidents, Bill Clinton and George W. Bush, established elaborate White House communications efforts to convince the American people of the wisdom of the president's policies. Clinton was often criticized for retaining a number of pollsters to chart shifts in public opinion on a daily basis.

Bush established a communications office to deliver the president's message to the nation in an effort to stay ahead of the headlines by providing the media with stories and sound bites that would dominate coverage for days. His efforts to shape public opinion haven't always worked. For instance, while onboard the aircraft carrier USS Abraham Lincoln, President Bush declared "mission accomplished" at the end of major combat in Iraq. Yet the continuing guerrilla warfare and suicide bombings in Iraq contributed to a sharp decline in his public approval rating. And in 2003, Bush signed a ban on "partial birth" abortions while surrounded by a group of all men. The controversial nature of the ban and the context within which it was presented to the public alienated moderate voters, particularly moderate women voters.

presidency Bill Clinton relied heavily on the polling firm of Penn & Schoen to help him decide which issues to emphasize and what strategies to adopt. During the 1995–96 budget battle with Congress, the White House commissioned polls almost every night to chart changes in public perceptions about the struggle. Poll data suggested to Clinton that he should present himself as struggling to save Medicare from Republican cuts. Clinton responded by launching a media attack against what he claimed were GOP efforts to hurt the elderly. This proved to be a successful strategy and helped Clinton defeat the Republican budget.[23]

After he assumed office in 2001, President George W. Bush asserted that political leaders should base their programs upon their own conception of the public interest rather than the polls. This, however, did not mean that Bush ignored public opinion. Bush has relied on pollster Jan van Lohuizen to conduct a low-key operation, sufficiently removed from the limelight to allow the president to renounce polling while continuing to make use of survey data.[24] At the same time, the Bush White House developed an extensive public relations program, led by former presidential aide Karen P. Hughes, to bolster popular support for the president's policies. Hughes, working with conservative TV personality Mary Matalin, coordinated White House efforts to maintain popular support for the administration's war against terrorism. These efforts included presidential speeches, media appearances by administration officials, numerous press conferences, and thousands of press releases presenting the administration's views.[25] The White House also made a substantial effort to sway opinion in foreign countries, even sending officials to present the administration's views on television networks serving the Arab world.

Another example of a Bush administration effort to shape public opinion is a series of commercials it produced at taxpayer expense in 2004 to promote the new Medicare prescription drug program. The commercials, prominently featuring the president, were designed to look like actual news stories and were aired in English and Spanish by hundreds of local television stations. Called a "video news release," this type of commercial is designed to give viewers the impression that they are watching a real news story. The presumption is that viewers are more likely to believe what they think is news coverage than material they know to be advertising. Democrats, of course, accused the administration of conducting a partisan propaganda campaign with public funds, but Republicans pointed out that the Clinton administration had engaged in similar practices.

Private Groups and the Shaping of Public Opinion   We have already seen how the government tries to shape public opinion. But the ideas that become prominent in political life are also developed and spread by important economic and political groups searching for issues that will advance their causes. One example is the "right-to-life" issue that has inflamed American politics over the past twenty years.

The notion of right-to-life, whose proponents seek to outlaw abortion and overturn the Supreme Court's *Roe v. Wade* decision, was developed and heavily promoted by conservative politicians who saw the issue of abortion as a means of uniting Catholic and Protestant conservatives and linking both groups to the Republican Party. These politicians convinced Catholic and evangelical Protestant leaders that they shared similar views on the question of abortion, and they worked with religious leaders to focus public attention on the negative issues in the abortion debate. To advance their cause, leaders of the movement sponsored well-publicized Senate

FOR CRITICAL ANALYSIS

Former president Bill Clinton polled public opinion on an almost daily basis to try to stay in touch with shifts in popular sentiment. President George W. Bush places less emphasis on polling, apparently believing that leaders should use their own judgment rather than follow popular sentiment on every issue. Which of these views would be supported by the framers of the Constitution? Which of these views is more appropriate for a politician in a democracy?

hearings, where testimony, photographs, and other exhibits were presented to illustrate the violent effects of abortion procedures. At the same time, publicists for the movement produced leaflets, articles, books, and films such as *The Silent Scream* to highlight the agony and pain ostensibly felt by the "unborn" when they were being aborted. All this underscored the movement's claim that abortion was nothing more or less than the murder of millions of innocent human beings. Finally, Catholic and evangelical Protestant religious leaders were organized to denounce abortion from their church pulpits and, increasingly, from their electronic pulpits on the Christian Broadcasting Network (CBN) and the various other television forums available for religious programming. Religious leaders also organized demonstrations, pickets, and disruptions at abortion clinics throughout the nation.[26] The abortion rights issue remains a potent one; it even influenced the debate over health care reform.

Typically, ideas are marketed most effectively by groups with access to financial resources, public or private institutional support, and sufficient skill or education to select, develop, and draft ideas that will attract interest and support. Thus, the development and promotion of conservative themes and ideas in recent years have been greatly facilitated by the millions of dollars that conservative corporations and business organizations such as the Chamber of Commerce and the Public Affairs Council spend each year on public information and what is now called in corporate circles "issues management." In addition, conservative business leaders have contributed millions of dollars to such conservative institutions as the Heritage Foundation, the Hoover Institution, and the American Enterprise Institute.[27] Many of the ideas that helped those on the right influence political debate were first developed and articulated by scholars associated with institutions such as these.

Although they do not usually have access to financial assets that match those available to their conservative opponents, liberal intellectuals and professionals have ample organizational skills, access to the media, and practice in creating, communicating, and using ideas. During the past three decades, the chief vehicle through which liberal intellectuals and professionals have advanced their ideas has been the "public interest group," an institution that relies heavily on voluntary contributions of time, effort, and interest on the part of its members. Through groups like Common Cause, the National Organization for Women, the Sierra Club, Friends of the Earth, and Physicians for Social Responsibility, intellectuals and professionals have been able to use their organizational skills and educational resources to develop and promote ideas.[28] Often, research conducted in universities and in liberal "think tanks" such as the Brookings Institution provides the ideas on which liberal politicians rely. For example, the welfare reform plan introduced by the Clinton administration in 1994 originated with the work of former Harvard professor David Ellwood. Ellwood's academic research led him to the conclusion that the nation's welfare system would be improved if services to the poor were expanded in scope but limited in duration. His idea was adopted by the 1992 Clinton campaign, which was searching for a position on welfare that would appeal to both liberal and conservative Democrats. The Ellwood plan seemed perfect: it promised liberals an immediate expansion of welfare benefits, yet it held out to conservatives the idea that welfare recipients would receive benefits only for a limited period of time. The Clinton welfare reform plan even borrowed phrases from Ellwood's book *Poor Support.*[29]

Journalist and author Joe Queenan has correctly observed that although political ideas can erupt spontaneously, they almost never do. Instead, he says, issues are usually manufactured by tenured professors and obscure employees of think tanks.... It is inconceivable that the American people, all by themselves, could independently arrive at the conclusion that the depletion of the ozone layer poses a dire threat to our national well-being, or that an immediate, across-the-board cut in the capital-gains tax is the only thing that stands between us and the economic abyss. The American people do not have that kind of sophistication. *They have to have help.*[30]

The Media and Public Opinion   The communications media are among the most powerful forces operating in the marketplace of ideas. As we shall see in Chapter 7, the mass media are not simply neutral messengers for ideas developed by others. Instead, the media have an enormous impact on popular attitudes and opinions. Over time, the ways in which the mass media report political events help to shape the underlying attitudes and beliefs from which opinions emerge.[31] For example, for the past thirty years, the national news media have relentlessly investigated personal and official wrongdoing on the part of politicians and public officials. This continual media presentation of corruption in government and venality in politics has undoubtedly fostered the general attitude of cynicism and distrust that exists in the general public.

At the same time, the ways in which media coverage interprets or frames specific events can have a major impact on popular responses and opinions about these events.[32] Because media framing can be important, the Bush administration sought to persuade broadcasters to follow its lead in its coverage of terrorism and America's response to terrorism in the months following the September 11 attacks. Broadcasters, who found themselves targets of anthrax-contaminated letters apparently mailed by terrorists, needed little persuasion. For the most part, the media praised the president for his leadership and presented the administration's military campaign in Afghanistan and domestic antiterrorist efforts in a positive light. Even newspapers like the *New York Times,* which had strongly opposed Bush in the 2000 election and questioned his fitness for the presidency, asserted that he had grown into the job. In the aftermath of the 2003 Iraq war, however, media coverage of the Bush administration became more critical. Formerly supportive media accused the president of failing both to anticipate the chaos and violence of postwar Iraq and to develop a strategy that would allow America to extricate itself from its involvement in Iraq. The president, for his part, accused the media of failing to present an accurate picture of his administration's successes in Iraq.

FOR CRITICAL ANALYSIS

Politicians, governments, and a host of groups endeavor to shape public perceptions of issues, events, and personalities. What are some of the major ways these actors try to mold opinion? How can we distinguish between information and propaganda?

Measuring Public Opinion

As recently as fifty years ago, American political leaders gauged public opinion by people's applause and by the presence of crowds at meetings. This direct exposure to the people's views did not necessarily produce accurate knowledge of public opinion. It did, however, give political leaders confidence in their public support—and therefore confidence in their ability to govern by consent.

Abraham Lincoln and Stephen Douglas debated each other seven times in the summer and autumn of 1858, two years before they became presidential nominees. Their debates took place before audiences in parched cornfields and courthouse squares. A century later, the presidential debates, although seen by millions, take place before a few reporters and technicians in television studios that might as well be on the moon. The public's response cannot be experienced directly. This distance between leaders and followers is one of the agonizing problems of modern democracy. The media send information to millions of people, but they are not yet as efficient at getting information back to leaders. Is government by consent possible where the scale of communication is so large and impersonal? In order to compensate for the decline in their ability to experience public opinion for themselves, leaders have turned to science, in particular to the science of opinion polling.

It is no secret that politicians and public officials make extensive use of **public opinion polls** to help them decide whether to run for office, what policies to support, how to vote on important legislation, and what types of appeals to make in their campaigns. President Lyndon Johnson was famous for carrying the latest Gallup and Roper poll results in his pocket, and it is widely believed that he began to withdraw from politics because the polls reported losses in public support. All recent presidents and other major political figures have worked closely with polls and pollsters.

CONSTRUCTING PUBLIC OPINION FROM SURVEYS

The population in which pollsters are interested is usually quite large. To conduct their polls they first choose a **sample** of the total population. The selection of this sample is important. Above all, it must be representative: the views of those in the sample must accurately and proportionately reflect the views of the whole. To a large extent, the validity of the poll's results depends on the sampling procedure used.

Sampling Techniques and Selection Bias   The most common techniques for choosing such a sample are probability sampling and random digit dialing. In the case of **probability sampling,** the pollster begins with a listing of the population to be surveyed. This listing is called the "sampling frame." After each member of the population is assigned a number, a table of random numbers or a computerized random selection process is used to select those to be surveyed. This technique is appropriate when the entire population can be identified. For example, all students registered at Texas colleges and universities can be identified from college records, and a sample of them can easily be drawn. When the pollster is interested in a national sample of Americans, however, this technique is not feasible, as no complete list of Americans exists.[33] National samples are usually drawn using a technique called **random digit dialing.** A computer random number generator is used to produce a list of as many ten-digit numbers as the pollster deems necessary. Given that more than 95 percent of American households have telephones, this technique usually results in a random national sample.

The importance of sampling was brought home early in the history of political polling. A 1936 *Literary Digest* poll predicted that Republican presidential candidate Alf Landon would defeat Democrat Franklin D. Roosevelt in that year's presidential election. The actual election, of course, ended in a Roosevelt landslide. The main problem with the survey was what is called **selection bias** in drawing the sample. The pollsters had relied on telephone directories and automobile registration rosters to produce a sampling frame. During the Great Depression, only wealthier Americans owned telephones and automobiles. Thus, the millions of working class Americans who constituted Roosevelt's principal base of support were excluded from the sample. A more recent instance of polling error caused by selection bias was the 1998 Minnesota gubernatorial election. A poll conducted by

public opinion polls scientific instruments for measuring public opinion

sample a small group selected by researchers to represent the most important characteristics of an entire population

probability sampling a method used by pollsters to select a representative sample in which every individual in the population has an equal probability of being selected as a respondent

random digit dialing polls in which respondents are selected at random from a list of ten-digit telephone numbers, with every effort made to avoid bias in the construction of the sample

selection bias polling error that arises when the sample is not representative of the population being studied which create errors in overrepresenting or underrepresenting some opinions

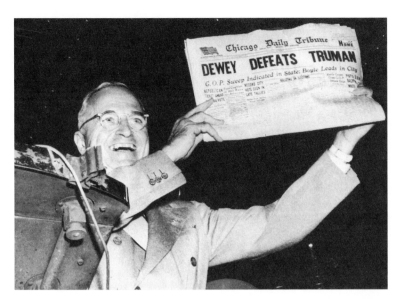

Though public opinion is important, it is not always easy to interpret, because very often, the pollsters ask individuals to answer questions about which they actually have no opinion. At best, the polls offer some indication of the relative name recognition of the candidates, and often, fail to accurately predict how Americans will vote. In 1948, election-night polls showed Dewey defeating Truman for the presidency.

the *Minneapolis Star Tribune* just six weeks before the election showed Jesse Ventura running a distant third to Democratic candidate Hubert Humphrey III, who seemed to have the support of 49 percent of the electorate, and the Republican Norm Coleman, whose support stood at 29 percent. Only 10 percent of those polled said they were planning to vote for Ventura. On election day, of course, Ventura outpolled both Humphrey and Coleman. Analysis of exit-poll data showed why the preelection polls had been so wrong. In an effort to be more accurate, preelection pollsters' predictions often take account of the likelihood that respondents will actually vote. This is accomplished by polling only people who have voted in the past or correcting for past frequency of voting. The *Star Tribune* poll was conducted only among individuals who had voted in the previous election. Ventura, however, brought to the polls not only individuals who had not voted in the last election but many people who had never voted before in their lives. Twelve percent of Minnesota's voters in 1998 said they came to the polls only because Ventura was on the ballot. This surge in turnout was facilitated by the fact that Minnesota permits

In Minnesota's 1998 gubernatorial election, pre-election polling failed to account for Jesse Ventura's appeal among first-time voters, who, thanks to the state's same-day voter registration rule, swept Ventura into office.

Table 6.3   Two Pollsters and Their Records (1948–2004)

	HARRIS	GALLUP	ACTUAL OUTCOME
2004			
Bush	49	49	51
Kerry	48	49	48
Nader	1	1	0
2000			
Bush	47%	48%	48%
Gore	47	46	49
Nader	5	4	3
1996			
Clinton	51%	52%	49%
Dole	39	41	41
Perot	9	7	8
1992			
Clinton	44%	44%	43%
Bush	38	37	38
Perot	17	14	19
1988			
Bush	51%	53%	54%
Dukakis	47	42	46
1984			
Reagan	56%	59%	59%
Mondale	44	41	41
1980			
Reagan	48%	47%	51%
Carter	43	44	41
Anderson		8	
1976			
Carter	48%	48%	51%
Ford	45	49	48
1972			
Nixon	59%	62%	61%
McGovern	35	38	38
1968			
Nixon	40%	43%	43%
Humphrey	43	42	43
Wallace	13	15	14
1964			
Johnson	62%	64%	61%
Goldwater	33	36	39
1960			
Kennedy	49%	51%	50%
Nixon	41	49	49
1956			
Eisenhower	NA	60%	58%
Stevenson		41	42
1952			
Eisenhower	47%	51%	55%
Stevenson	42	49	44
1948			
Truman	NA	44.5%	49.6%
Dewey		49.5	45.1

All figures except those for 1948 are rounded. NA = Not asked.

SOURCE: Data from the Gallup Poll and the Harris Survey (New York: Chicago Tribune–New York News Syndicate, various press releases 1964–2004). Courtesy of the Gallup Organization and Louis Harris Associates.

same-day voter registration (see Chapter 10 for a discussion of the consequences of registration rules). Thus, the pollsters were wrong because Ventura changed the composition of the electorate.[34]

In recent years, the issue of selection bias has been further complicated by the fact that growing numbers of individuals refuse to answer pollsters' questions or use such devices as answering machines and "Caller ID" to screen unwanted callers. If pollsters could be certain that those who responded to their surveys simply reflected the views of those who refused to respond, there would be no problem. Some studies, however, suggest that the views of respondents and nonrespondents can differ, especially along social class lines. Middle and upper middle class individuals are more likely to be willing to respond to surveys than their working class counterparts.[35] Thus far, "nonresponse bias" has not undermined a major national survey, but the possibility of a future *Literary Digest* fiasco should not be ignored.

Sample Size The degree of reliability in polling is also a function of sample size. The same sample is needed to represent a small population as to represent a large population. The typical size of a sample ranges from 450 to 1,500 respondents. This number, however, reflects a trade-off between cost and degree of precision desired. The degree of accuracy that can be achieved with even a small sample can be seen from the polls' success in predicting election outcomes. The chance that the sample used does not accurately represent the population from which it is drawn is called the **sampling error** or *margin of error*. A typical survey of 1,500 respondents will have a sampling error of approximately 3 percent. When a preelection poll indicates 51 percent of voters surveyed favor the Republican candidate and 49 percent support the Democratic candidate, the outcome is too close to call because it is within the margin of error of the survey. A figure of 51 percent means that between 54 and 48 percent of voters in the population favor the Republicans, while a figure of 49 percent indicates that between 52 and 46 percent of all voters support the Democrats. Thus, in this example, a 52-to-48 percent Democratic victory would still be consistent with polls predicting a 51-to-49 percent Republican triumph.

sampling error polling error that arises based on the small size of the sample

Table 6.3 shows how accurate two of the major national polling organizations actually have been in predicting the outcomes of presidential elections. Pollsters have been mostly correct in their predictions.

Survey Design Even with reliable sample procedures, surveys may fail to reflect the true distribution of opinion within a target population. One frequent source of **measurement error** is the wording of survey questions. The precise words used in a question can have an enormous impact on the answers it elicits. The validity of survey results can also be adversely affected by poor question format, faulty ordering of questions, inappropriate vocabulary, ambiguity of questions, or questions with built-in biases. Often, seemingly minor differences in the wording of a question can convey vastly different meanings to respondents and thus produce quite different response patterns (see Box 6.3). For example, for many years the University of Chicago's National Opinion Research Center has asked respondents whether they think the federal government is spending too much, too little, or about the right amount of money on "assistance for the poor." Answering the question posed this way, about two-thirds of all respondents seem to believe that the government is spending too

measurement error failure to identify the true distribution of opinion within a population because of errors such as ambiguous or poorly worded questions

It Depends on How You Ask

The public's desire for tax cuts can be hard to measure. Pollsters asking what should be done with the nation's budget surplus got different results depending on the specifics of the question.

The Question

President Clinton has proposed setting aside approximately two-thirds of an expected budget surplus to fix the Social Security system. What do you think the leaders in Washington should do with the remainder of the surplus?

Variation 1

Should the money be used for a tax cut, or should it be used to fund new government programs?

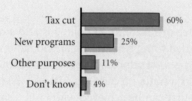

Tax cut	60%
New programs	25%
Other purposes	11%
Don't know	4%

Variation 2

Should the money be used for a tax cut, or should it be spent on programs for education, the environment, health care, crime-fighting, and military defense?

Tax cut	22%
Programs	69%
Other purposes	6%
Don't know	3%

SOURCE: Pew Research Center, reported in *The New York Times*, January 30, 2000, p. WK 3.

---

little. However, the same survey also asks whether the government spends too much, too little, or about the right amount for "welfare." When the word "welfare" is substituted for "assistance for the poor," about half of all respondents indicate that too much is being spent.[36]

Push Polling In recent years, a new form of bias has been introduced into surveys by the use of a technique called **push polling.** This technique involves asking a respondent a loaded question about a political candidate designed to elicit the response sought by the pollster and, simultaneously, to shape the respondent's perception of the candidate in question. For example, during the 1996 New Hampshire presidential primary, push pollsters employed by the campaign of one of Lamar Alexander's rivals called thousands of voters to ask, "If you knew that Lamar Alexander had raised taxes six times in Tennessee, would you be less inclined or more inclined to support him?"[37] More than one hundred consulting firms across the nation now specialize in push polling.[38] Calling push polling the "political equivalent of a

push polling a polling technique in which the questions are designed to shape the respondent's opinion drive-by shooting," Representative Joe Barton (R-Tex.) launched a congressional investigation into the practice.[39] Push polls may be one reason that Americans are becoming increasingly skeptical about the practice of polling and increasingly unwilling to answer pollsters' questions.[40]

Illusion of Saliency   In the early days of a political campaign when voters are asked which candidates they do, or do not, support, the answer they give often has little significance, because the choice is not yet important to them. Their preferences may change many times before the actual election. This is part of the explanation for the phenomenon of the postconvention "bounce" in the popularity of presidential candidates, which was observed after the Democratic and Republican national conventions in 1992 and 1996.[41] Respondents' preferences reflected the amount of attention a candidate had received during the conventions rather than strongly held views.

Salient interests are interests that stand out beyond others, that are of more than ordinary concern to respondents in a survey or to voters in the electorate. Politicans, social scientists, journalists, or pollsters who assume something is important to the public, when in fact it is not, are creating an **illusion of saliency.** This illusion can be created and fostered by polls despite careful controls over sampling, interviewing, and data analysis. In fact, the illusion is strengthened by the credibility that science gives survey results.

The problem of saliency has become especially acute as a result of the proliferation of media polls. The television networks and major national newspapers all make heavy use of opinion polls. Increasingly, polls are being commissioned by local television stations and local and regional newspapers as well.[42] On the positive side, polls allow journalists to make independent assessments of political realities—assessments not influenced by the partisan claims of politicians.

At the same time, however, media polls can allow journalists to make news when none really exists. Polling diminishes journalists' dependence upon news makers. A poll commissioned by a news agency can provide the basis for a good story even when candidates, politicians, and other news makers refuse to cooperate by engaging in newsworthy activities. Thus, on days when little or nothing is actually taking place in a political campaign, poll results, especially apparent changes in candidate popularity margins, can provide exciting news. Several times during the 2004 presidential campaign, for example, small changes in the relative standing of the Democratic and Republican candidates produced banner headlines around the country. Stories about what the candidates actually did or said often took second place to reporting the "horse race."

Interestingly, because rapid and dramatic shifts in candidate margins tend to take place when voters' preferences are least fully formed, horse-race news is most likely to make the headlines when it is actually least significant.[43] In other words, media interest in poll results is inversely related to the actual salience of voters' opinions and the significance of the polls' findings. However, by influencing perceptions, especially those of major contributors, media polls can influence political realities.

Bandwagon Effect   The most noted, but least serious, of polling problems is the **bandwagon effect,** which occurs when polling results influence people to support the candidate marked as the probable victor. Some scholars argue that this bandwagon effect can be offset by an "underdog effect" in favor of the candidate who is trailing in

salient interests attitudes and views that are especially important to the individual holding them

illusion of saliency the impression conveyed by polls that something is important to the public when actually it is not

bandwagon effect a shift in electoral support to the candidate that public opinion polls report as the front-runner

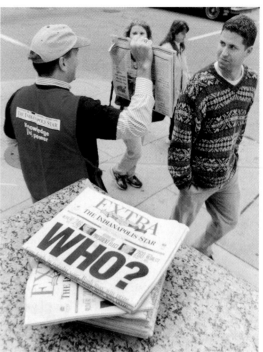

In 2000, the major networks announced, on the basis of their exit polls, that Al Gore had defeated George W. Bush. Later, they were forced to retract their prediction. The pollsters' inability to accurately project the winner in Florida left the nation in suspense. Ultimately, of course, "Who won?" was not known until after a lengthy recount and a series of court cases.

the polls.[44] However, a candidate who demonstrates a lead in the polls usually finds it considerably easier to raise campaign funds than a candidate whose poll standing is poor. With these additional funds, poll leaders can often afford to pay for television time and other campaign activities that will cement their advantage.

Thinking Critically about Public Opinion and Democracy

A major purpose of democratic government, with its participatory procedures and representative institutions, is to ensure that political leaders will heed public opinion. And, indeed, a good deal of evidence suggests that they do. There are many instances in which public policy and public opinion do not coincide, but in general the government's actions are consistent with citizens' preferences. One study, for example, found that between 1935 and 1979, in about two-thirds of all cases, significant changes in public opinion were followed within one year by changes in government policy consistent with the shift in the popular mood.[45] Other studies have come to similar conclusions about public opinion and government policy at the state level.[46] Some recent studies, however, have suggested that the responsiveness of government to public opinion has been declining, reaching an all-time low during President Clinton's first term. These findings imply that, contrary to popular beliefs, elected leaders don't always pander to the results of public opinion polls, but instead use polling to sell their policy proposals and shape the public's views.[47]

In addition, areas of disagreement always arise between opinion and policy. For example, the majority of Americans favored stricter governmental control of handguns for years before Congress finally adopted the modest restrictions on firearms purchases embodied in the Brady bill and the Violent Crime Control Act, passed in 1993 and 1994, respectively. Similarly, most Americans—blacks as well as whites—oppose school busing to achieve racial balance, yet such busing continues to be used in many parts of the nation. Most Americans are far less concerned with the rights of the accused than the federal courts seem to be. Most Americans usually oppose U.S. military intervention in other nations' affairs, yet such interventions continue to take place in such regions as Bosnia, Haiti, and Iraq, where American troops are currently stationed, and often win public approval after the fact. Of course, the overwhelming majority of Americans supported the Bush administration's decision to attack Afghanistan after September 11.

Several factors can contribute to a lack of consistency between opinion and governmental policy. First, the nominal majority on a particular issue may not be as intensely committed to its preference as the adherents of the minority viewpoint. An intensely committed minority may often be more willing to commit its time, energy, efforts, and resources to the affirmation of its opinions than an apathetic, even if large, majority. In the case of firearms, for example, although the proponents of gun control are by a wide margin the majority, most do not regard the issue as one of critical importance to themselves and are not willing to commit much effort to advancing their cause. The opponents of gun control, by contrast, are intensely committed, well organized, and well financed, and as a result are usually able to carry the day.

A second important reason that public policy and public opinion may not coincide has to do with the character and structure of the American system of government. The framers of the American Constitution, as we saw in Chapter 2, sought to create a system of government that was based upon popular consent but that did not invariably and automatically translate shifting popular sentiments into public policies. As a result, the American governmental process includes arrangements such as an appointed judiciary that can produce policy decisions that may run contrary to prevailing popular sentiment—at least for a time.

Perhaps the inconsistencies between opinion and policy could be resolved if we made broader use of a mechanism currently employed by a number of states—the initiative and referendum. This procedure allows propositions to be placed on the ballot and voted into law by the electorate, bypassing most of the normal machinery of representative government. In recent years, several important propositions sponsored by business and conservative groups have been enacted by voters in certain states.[48] For example, California's Proposition 209, approved by the state's voters in 1996, prohibited the state and local government agencies in California from using race or gender preferences in hiring, contracting, or university admissions decisions. Responding to conservatives' success, liberal groups launched a number of ballot initiatives in 2000. For example, in Washington state, voters were asked to consider propositions sponsored by teachers' unions that would have required annual cost-of-living raises for teachers and more than $1.8 billion in additional state spending over the next six years.[49] And, as we saw in Chapter 1, more than 400 ballot initiatives were presented to voters in 2002.

Initiatives such as these seem to provide the public with an opportunity to express its will. The major problem, however, is that government by initiative offers little opportunity for reflection and compromise. Voters are presented with a proposition, usually sponsored by a special interest group, and are asked to take it or leave it. Perhaps the true will of the people, not to mention their best interest,

How Americans View the World and Vice Versa

When they are not being accused of seeking to conquer the world, Americans are often charged with failing to pay enough attention to international affairs. It is true that many Americans lack a basic knowledge of world history and geography and have considerable difficulty naming the leaders of other nations. Several surveys have indicated that some Americans think Canada is one of the 50 states. Nevertheless, Americans do have strong opinions about which foreign nations are America's friends in the world and which are her foes. Topping the list of friends is Great Britain, seen by 74 percent of recent poll respondents as a "close ally." Curiously, 2 percent of those surveyed viewed Britain as an enemy. Perhaps they have not forgotten King George's mistreatment of the colonists in 1775. When it comes to China, now one of America's most important trading partners, only 9 percent of Americans believe China is a close ally while 54 percent think China is not friendly or even America's enemy. It is interesting to note also that France, traditionally an American ally, came to be viewed less favorably than Russia, America's Cold War adversary, in the wake of vocal French opposition to America's Middle East policy.

Just as Americans have opinions about the world, citizens of other nations have their own opinions about America. Americans sometimes complain that their efforts on behalf of other nations are not properly appreciated and feel envied and disliked by the rest of the world. Interestingly, however, much of the world seems to view America more favorably than Americans see others. Canadian, Italian, and British respondents to a recent survey had an overwhelmingly positive view of America. Surprisingly, the Vietnamese had positive views of the United States, despite the lingering scars of a bitter war. Even most French respondents reported favorable attitudes toward America. Only respondents in the Middle East had a uniformly negative view of America, although, according to the survey, people in these countries tend to view all outsiders with almost the same degree of distrust and ill will.

During the first year of the American occupation of Iraq, antagonism toward American foreign policy hardened even more in most Muslim countries. For example, a clear majority of those polled in Jordan, Pakistan, and Morocco said that suicide bombings against Americans in Iraq were justified. The enduring popularity of Osama bin Laden in these countries also reinforces Muslim attitudes generally toward the United States. Worldwide, a majority of people, except those in Britain, believed that the United States' war on terror was actually an attempt to control the Middle East's oil or to dominate the world. Whether the world's opposition to the Bush administration's conduct of foreign policy translates more broadly into ill will toward America remains to be seen.

FOR CRITICAL ANALYSIS

1. What are the factors shaping the ways Americans view other nations and others view America?

2. Should Americans care about how they are seen around the world? Why or why not?

The World's View of America

	PERCENTAGE FAVORABLE	PERCENTAGE UNFAVORABLE
Canada	72	27
United Kingdom	75	16
Italy	70	23
France	63	34
Russia	61	33
Pakistan	10	69
Mexico	64	25
South Korea	53	44
Japan	72	26
Kenya	80	15
Vietnam	71	27
Egypt	6	69
Jordan	25	75

Source: The Harris Poll and the Pew Research Center for the People and the Press.

might lie somewhere between the positions taken by various interest groups. Perhaps, for example, California voters might have wanted affirmative action programs to be modified but not scrapped altogether as Proposition 209 mandated. In a representative assembly, as opposed to a referendum campaign, a compromise position might have been achieved that was more satisfactory to all the residents of the state. This is one reason the framers of the U.S. Constitution strongly favored representative government rather than direct democracy.

When all is said and done, even without the initiative and referendum, there can be little doubt that in general the actions of the American government do not remain out of line with popular sentiment for very long. One could take these as signs of a vital and thriving democracy.

GET INVOLVED
What You Can Do:
Become Politically Knowledgeable

In a democracy, one central role of the citizen is to be informed and knowledgeable. Many eighteenth- and nineteenth-century political theorists believed that popular government required an informed, aware, and involved citizenry, and wondered whether this condition could be met. The Frenchman Alexis de Tocqueville, writing in the early nineteenth century, asserted that to participate in democratic politics ordinary citizens needed to be aware of their own interests and to understand how those interests might be affected by contemporary issues. Tocqueville and others have feared that participation by the unenlightened might be worse than no participation at all, since the ignorant could easily be swayed by demagogues to support foolish or even evil causes. Contemporary public opinion research indicates that better-informed citizens are considerably better able than their uninformed counterparts to exert influence in the political arena and to benefit from the government's actions. Knowledge, indeed, seems to be power.[50]

Fortunately, the most basic element of citizenship is also one of the simplest to achieve. Viewed correctly, reading a daily newspaper is an important political act! Watching a television news or discussion program is an important form of political participation. For some, visiting and comparing the Web sites of several candidates are ways of becoming politically involved, albeit in cyberspace.

Those who use newspapers, magazines, television, and computers to become politically knowledgeable and aware have taken a huge first step toward becoming politically influential. Those who limit their newspaper reading to the sports page and their television viewing to situation comedies are also abdicating the responsibilities and opportunities inherent in democratic citizenship. If a person opts to be indifferent or cynical about politics, his or her decision must be based on an informed indifference or cynicism to be truly meaningful.

Summary

Americans disagree on many issues, but they nevertheless share a number of important values, including liberty, equality of opportunity, and democracy. Although factors such as race, education, gender, and social class produce important

FOR CRITICAL ANALYSIS

In the American system of government, public opinion seems to be an important factor in political and governmental decision making. In what ways does the public, through opinion, control its political leaders? In what ways do political leaders control public opinion? What are the positive and negative consequences of governing by popular opinion?

INTERACTIVE
POLITICS

YOU ARE... a pollster!

Americans seem to have a love/hate relationship with polls. We decry them as fulfilling the old adage about "lies . . . damned lies . . . and statistics," but increasingly we expect to see the results from polls on more and more subjects. Evidence suggests that the presentation of polling data actually shapes people's opinions.

Active citizens must learn to become careful consumers of poll results. Advocates who understand the impact they can have will often present data in a way that is most favorable to their position. The margin of error within poll results is often misunderstood, leading to misinterpretation of data. Poorly constructed poll questions or sampling techniques will produce very unreliable or invalid results.

In this simulation, you will play the role of a professional pollster hired by those who want to measure public opinion on the controversial subject of gay marriage.

Go to www.wwnorton.com/wtp5e

Questions to consider as you conduct the online simulation:

How responsive should government be to what is popular?

What are the problems with opinion polls, and how can the science of polling overcome these problems?

Which methods of sampling opinion are the most effective, and why?

How can the public tell the difference between valid and invalid poll results?

differences in outlook, Americans probably agree more on fundamental values than do the citizens of most other nations.

Most people acquire their initial orientation to political life from their families. Subsequently, political views are influenced by interests, personal experiences, group memberships, and the conditions under which citizens are first mobilized into politics. Opinions on particular issues may also be influenced by political leaders and the mass media. The media help determine what Americans know about politics.

Most governments, including the U.S. government, endeavor to shape their citizens' political beliefs. In democracies, private groups compete with government to shape opinion.

Public opinion is generally measured by polling. However, polls can also distort opinion, imputing salience to issues that citizens care little about or creating the illusion that most people are moderate or centrist in their views.

Over time, the government's policies are strongly affected by public opinion, although there can be lags and divergences, especially when an intense minority confronts a more apathetic majority.

For Further Reading

Gallup, George. *The Pulse of Democracy.* New York: Simon and Schuster, 1940.

Ginsberg, Benjamin. *The Captive Public: How Mass Opinion Promotes State Power.* New York: Basic Books, 1986.

Herbst, Susan. *Numbered Voices: How Opinion Polling Has Shaped American Politics.* Chicago: University of Chicago Press, 1993.

Herbst, Susan. *Reading Public Opinion: How Political Actors View the Democratic Process.* Chicago: University of Chicago Press, 1998.

Jacobs, Lawrence R., and Robert Y. Shapiro. *Politicians Don't Pander: Political Manipulation and the Loss of Democratic Responsiveness.* Chicago: University of Chicago Press, 2000.

Key, V. O. *Public Opinion and American Democracy.* New York: Knopf, 1961.

Lippman, Walter. *Public Opinion.* New York: Harcourt, Brace, 1922.

Mayer, William G. *The Changing American Mind: How and Why American Public Opinion Changed between 1960 and 1988.* Ann Arbor: University of Michigan Press, 1992.

Mutz, Diana C. *Impersonal Influence: How Perceptions of Mass Collectives Affect Political Attitudes.* New York: Cambridge University Press, 1998.

Neuman, W. Russell. *The Paradox of Mass Politics: Knowledge and Opinion in the American Electorate.* Cambridge, MA: Harvard University Press, 1986.

Page, Benjamin I., and Robert Y. Shapiro. *The Rational Public: Fifty Years of Trends in Americans' Policy Preferences.* Chicago: University of Chicago Press, 1992.

Rinehart, Sue Tolleson. *Gender Consciousness and Politics.* New York: Routledge, 1992.

Schuman, Howard, Charlotte Steeh, and Lawrence Bobo. *Racial Attitudes in America.* Cambridge, MA: Harvard University Press, 1990.

Traugott, Michael, and Paul Lavrakas. *The Voter's Guide to Election Polls.* 2nd ed. New York: Chatham House, 2000.

Study Outline

www.wwnorton.com/wtp5e   Keyword: Review 6

Political Values

1. Although Americans have many political differences, they share a common set of values, including liberty, equality of opportunity, and democracy.

2. Agreement on fundamental political values is probably more widespread in the United States than anywhere else in the Western world.

3. Often for reasons associated with demographics, Americans' opinions do differ widely on a variety of issues.

4. Most people acquire their initial orientation to politics from their families.

5. Membership in both voluntary and involuntary social groups can affect an individual's political values through personal experience, the influence of group leaders, and recognition of political interests.

6. One's level of education is an important factor in shaping political beliefs.

7. Conditions under which individuals and groups are recruited into political life also shape political orientations.

8. Many Americans describe themselves as either liberal or conservative in political orientation.

How We Form Political Opinions

1. Although ideologies shape political opinions, they seldom fully determine one's views.
2. Political opinions are influenced by an individual's underlying values, knowledge of political issues, and external forces such as the government, private groups, and the media.

Measuring Public Opinion

1. In order to construct public opinion from surveys, a polling sample must be large and the views of those in the sample must accurately and proportionately reflect the views of the whole.

Thinking Critically about Public Opinion and Democracy

1. Government policies in the United States are generally consistent with popular preferences. There are, however, always some inconsistencies.
2. Disagreements between opinion and policy come about because on some issues, such as gun control, an intensely committed minority can defeat a more apathetic majority. Moreover, the American system of government is not designed to quickly transform changes in opinion into changes in government programs.

Practice Quiz

www.wwnorton.com/wtp5e   Keyword: Quiz 6

1. The term "public opinion" is used to describe
   a) the collected speeches and writings made by a president during his term in office.
   b) the analysis of events broadcast by news reporters during the evening news.
   c) the beliefs and attitudes that people have about issues.
   d) decisions of the Supreme Court.

2. Variables such as income, education, race, gender, and ethnicity
   a) often create differences of political opinion in America.
   b) have consistently been a challenge to America's core political values.
   c) have little impact on political opinions.
   d) help explain why public opinion polls are so unreliable.

3. Which of the following is an agency of socialization?
   a) the family
   b) social groups
   c) education
   d) all of the above

4. When men and women respond differently to issues of public policy, they are demonstrating an example of
   a) liberalism.
   b) educational differences.
   c) the gender gap.
   d) party politics.

5. The process by which Americans learn political beliefs and values is called
   a) brainwashing.
   b) propaganda.
   c) indoctrination.
   d) political socialization.

6. In addition to one's basic political values, what other two factors influence one's political opinions?
   a) ideology and party identification
   b) political knowledge and the influence of political leaders, private groups, and the media
   c) the gender gap and the education gap
   d) sample size and the bandwagon effect

7. Which of the following is (are) not an important external influence on how political opinions are formed?
   a) the government and political leaders
   b) private interest groups
   c) the media
   d) the Constitution

8. Which of the following is the term used in public opinion polling to denote the small group representing the opinions of the whole population?
   a) control group
   b) sample
   c) micropopulation
   d) respondents

9. When politicians, pollsters, journalists, or social scientists assume something is important to the public when in fact it is not, they are creating
   a) an illusion of saliency.
   b) an illusion of responsibility.
   c) a gender gap.
   d) an elitist issue.

10. A familiar polling problem is the "bandwagon effect," which occurs when
    a) the same results are used over and over again.
    b) polling results influence people to support the candidate marked as the probable victor in a campaign.
    c) polling results influence people to support the candidate who is trailing in a campaign.
    d) background noise makes it difficult for a pollster and a respondent to communicate with each other.

Key Terms

www.wwnorton.com/wtp5e

Keyword: Vocabulary 6

agencies of socialization (p. 216)
attitude (or opinion) (p. 212)
bandwagon effect (p. 243)
conservative (p. 228)
democracy (p. 214)

equality of opportunity (p. 213)
gender gap (p. 223)
illusion of saliency (p. 243)
liberal (p. 228)
liberty (p. 214)
marketplace of ideas (p. 232)
measurement error (p. 241)
political efficacy (p. 232)
political ideology (p. 212)
political socialization (p. 216)

probability sampling (p. 238)
public opinion (p. 212)
public opinion polls (p. 238)
push polling (p. 242)
random digit dialing (p. 238)
salient interests (p. 243)
sample (p. 238)
sampling error (p. 241)
selection bias (p. 238)
values (or beliefs) (p. 212)

7 THE MEDIA

What Government Does and Why It Matters

ONE AREA IN WHICH our government's role is intended to be minimal is the realm of the news media. The Constitution's First Amendment guarantees freedom of the press and most Americans believe that a free press is an essential condition for both liberty and democratic politics. Certainly, the press is usually ready to denounce any government actions that smack of censorship or news manipulation. Nevertheless, attempts to silence or discredit the opposition press have a long history in America. The infamous Alien and Sedition Acts were enacted by the Federalists in an attempt to silence the Republican press. In more recent times, during the McCarthy era of the 1950s, right-wing politicians used charges of communist infiltration to intimidate the liberal news media. During President Richard Nixon's administration, the White House attacked its critics in the media by threatening to take action to bar the television networks from owning local affiliates, as well as by illegally wiretapping the phones of government officials suspected of leaking information to the press. In the early 1980s, conservative groups financed a series of libel suits against CBS News, *Time* magazine, and other media organizations, in an attempt to discourage them from publicizing material critical of Reagan administration policies.[1] In 1998, President Clinton's political allies accused the national news media of engaging in tabloid journalism and invading the president's privacy in order to discredit him by publicizing the intimate details of Clinton's sexual relationship with former White House intern Monica Lewinsky. In a similar vein, in October 2003, President Bush accused the media of failing to report American successes in the occupation of Iraq while dwelling only on apparent failures of U.S. policy. In 2004, an article by investigative reporter Seymour Hersh in the *New Yorker* along with a story on *60 Minutes II* revealed that American soldiers had abused Iraqi prisoners in their custody. The story prompted a televised apology from President Bush, congressional hearings, and calls for the resignation of Defense Secretary Donald Rumsfeld. As the abuse scandal widened, it became a major issue in the 2004 presidential race. The Bush administration was furious but, as was the case during previous presidencies, could do little to silence its media critics. In all these instances, attempts to browbeat and intimidate the press failed. ■

- **In this chapter, we will examine the place of the media in American politics. First, we will look at the organization and regulation of the American news media.** The media industry continues to grow larger and more centralized, resulting in little variety in what is reported about national issues. Despite the central importance of freedom of the press in the United States, the media are still subject to some regulation by the government.

- **Second, we will discuss the factors that help to determine "what's news."** The agenda of issues and type of coverage that the media provide are affected most by those who create the news and those who consume the news.

- **Third, we will examine the scope of media power in politics.** What the media report can have far-reaching effects on public perceptions of political events, issues, leaders, and institutions.

■ Previewing Liberty, Equality, and Democracy

Freedom of the press and other news media is essential for the preservation of both liberty and democracy. When an unfettered and vigorous press publicizes abuse of power, it helps to bolster liberty, and when the media carry news of political events they promote democracy. The media also play a role in sustaining political equality. Information, as we saw in Chapter 1, is an important source of political influence. Without the media, information would be monopolized by a small number of political insiders, contributing to the concentration of political power. However, important as the media are for preserving American political values, the power of the national media itself has become a matter of political concern. We conclude this chapter by addressing the question of responsibility: to whom, if anyone, are the media accountable for the use of their formidable power? The answer to this question has great implications for American democracy.

The Media Industry and Government

The American news media are among the world's most vast and most free. Americans literally have thousands of available options to find political reporting. This wide variety of newspapers, newsmagazines, and broadcast media regularly present information that is at odds with the government's claims, as well as editorial opinions sharply critical of high-ranking officials. The freedom to speak one's mind is one of the most cherished of American political values—one that is jealously safeguarded by the media. Yet although thousands of media companies exist across the United States, surprisingly little variety appears in what is reported about national events and issues.

TYPES OF MEDIA

Americans get their news from three main sources: broadcast media (radio, television), print media (newspapers and magazines), and, increasingly, the Internet (see Figure 7.1 on the next page). Each of these sources has distinctive characteristics. Television news reaches more Americans than any other single news source. Tens of millions of individuals watch national and local news programs every day. Television news, however, covers relatively few topics and provides little depth of coverage. Television news is more like a series of newspaper headlines connected to pictures. It serves the extremely important function of alerting viewers to issues and events, but provides little more than a series of "sound bites," brief quotes and short characterizations of the day's events. Because they are aware of the character of television news coverage, politicians and other newsmakers often seek to manipulate the news by providing the media with sound bites that will dominate news coverage for at least a few days. George Bush's famous 1988 sound bite, "Read my lips, no new taxes," received a great deal of media coverage. Two years later he was, in effect, bitten by his own sound bite when he signed legislation that included new taxes. The twenty-four-hour news stations like Cable News Network (CNN) offer more detail and commentary than the networks' half-hour evening news shows. Even CNN and the others, however, offer more headlines than analysis, especially during their prime-time broadcasts.

Politicians generally view the local broadcast news as a friendlier venue than the national news. National reporters are often inclined to criticize and question while local reporters often accept the pronouncements of national leaders at face value. For this reason, presidents often introduce new proposals in a series of short visits to a number of cities—indeed, sometimes flying from airport stop to airport stop—in addition to or instead of making a national presentation. For example, in February 2002, President Bush introduced his idea for a new national volunteer corps during his State of the Union message and then made a number of local speeches around the country promoting the same theme. While national reporters questioned the president's plans, local news coverage was overwhelmingly positive.

Radio news is also essentially a headline service, but without pictures. In the short time—usually five minutes per hour—they devote to news, radio stations announce the day's major events without providing much detail. In major cities, all-news stations provide a bit more coverage of major stories, but for the most part these stations fill the day with repetition rather than detail. All-news stations like Washington, D.C.'s WTOP or New York's WCBS assume that most listeners are in their cars and that, as a

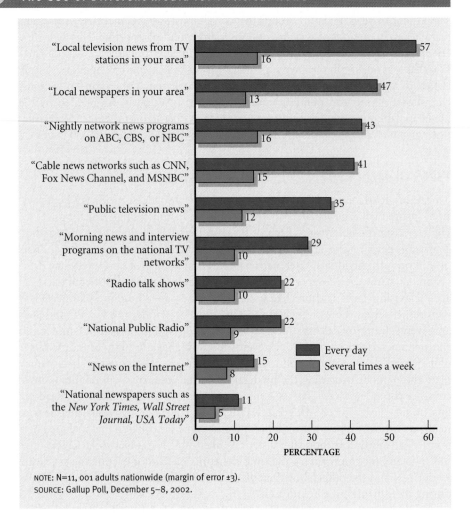

Figure 7.1   **The Use of Different Media for Political News**

NOTE: N=11, 001 adults nationwide (margin of error ±3).
SOURCE: Gallup Poll, December 5–8, 2002.

result, the people in the audience change markedly throughout the day as listeners reach their destinations. Thus, rather than use their time to flesh out a given set of stories, they repeat the same stories each hour to present them to new listeners. In recent years, radio talk shows have become important sources of commentary and opinion. A number of conservative radio hosts such as Rush Limbaugh and Dr. Laura Schlesinger have huge audiences and have helped to mobilize support for conservative political causes and candidates. Liberals have had less success in the world of talk radio. In 2003, however, a group of wealthy liberal political activists led by Anita

Drobny, a major Democratic Party donor, announced plans for the creation of a liberal talk-radio network designed to combat conservative dominance of this important medium. One executive of the developing network said, "There are so many right-wing talk shows, we think it's created a hole in the market you could drive a truck through." Liberals hoped their network would be entertaining as well as informative, specializing in parody and political satire.[2]

The most important source of news is the old-fashioned newspaper. Newspapers remain critically important even though they are not the primary news source for most Americans. The print media are important for three reasons. First, as we shall see later in this chapter, the broadcast media rely upon leading newspapers such as the *New York Times* and the *Washington Post* to set their news agenda. The broadcast media engage in very little actual reporting; they primarily cover stories that have been "broken," or initially reported, by the print media. For example, sensational charges that President Bill Clinton had an affair with a White House intern were reported first by the *Washington Post* and *Newsweek* before being trumpeted around the world by the broadcast media. It is only a slight exaggeration to observe that if an event is not covered in the *New York Times,* it is not likely to appear on the *CBS Evening News.* Second, the print media provide more detailed and complete information, offering a better context for analysis. Third, the print media are important because they are the prime source of news for educated and influential individuals. The nation's economic, social, and political elites rely upon the detailed coverage provided by the print media to inform and influence their views about important public matters. The print media may have a smaller audience than their cousins in broadcasting, but they have an audience that matters.

A relatively new source of news is the Internet. Every day, several million Americans scan one of many news sites on the Internet for coverage of current events. For the most part, however, the Internet provides electronic versions of coverage offered by print sources. One great advantage of the Internet is that it allows frequent updating. It potentially can combine the depth of coverage of a newspaper with the timeliness of television and radio, and probably will become a major news source in the next decade. In 2000, many Americans relied on Web sites such as CNN.com for up-to-the-minute election news during the campaign and, especially, during the dramatic post-election battle in Florida. Acknowledging the growing importance of the Internet as a political communications medium, the U.S. Supreme Court posted its decisions in the Florida election cases as soon as they were issued. After the September 11 terrorist attacks, millions of Americans relied on the Internet for news about terrorism, bioterrorism, and the military campaign in Afghanistan. Web sites providing information on anthrax and other biological threats also reported hundreds of thousands of visits. Online magazines such as *Slate* have a growing audience and often feature the work of major political writers such as Christopher Hitchens and Ed Finn. Also, a number of political entrepreneurs have sought to organize online advocacy groups that would be able to raise money, make their positions known through e-mail and letter campaigns, and provide support for politicians who accepted their views. One of the most successful of these enterprises is MoveOn.org, founded by two liberal Silicon Valley entrepreneurs. MoveOn seeks to build electronic advocacy groups, allowing members to propose issues and strategies and acting on behalf of those that appear to have the highest level of member support. In 1998, MoveOn worked vigorously to defeat the

GOP's effort to impeach Bill Clinton, and in 2001, MoveOn launched a "peace campaign" to build support for nonmilitary responses to the September 11 terrorist attacks. More than 100,000 individuals signed MoveOn's electronic petition calling on President Bush to find a peaceful response to terrorism.

In addition, hundreds of thousands of readers turn to more informal sources of Internet news and commentary called *web logs* or "blogs." Blogs are intermittently published online by thousands of individuals and generally feature personal opinion and commentary on national and world events. Some "bloggers," as the authors of blogs are called, achieve fame, or at least notoriety, among online readers for their political and social views. Many blogs invite readers to post comments and can become online discussion forums. In 2002 and 2003, the Howard Dean presidential campaign relied on hundreds of friendly bloggers to publicize the candidate's views and tout his virtues. Bloggers also helped Dean raise tens of millions of dollars in small contributions to finance his unsuccessful presidential bid. The various blogs served as a communications network linking thousands of Dean supporters and some 900 pro-Dean groups around the country in a structure that Dean campaign manager Joe Trippi called a grid modeled on the Internet itself.[3] For many Dean supporters, this national, online network provided a sense of fellowship and belonging that appealed to them as much as, or more than, the candidate's policy positions. As online access becomes simpler and faster, the Internet could open Americans to unprecedented quantities of up-to-the-minute information. If only computers could also give Americans the ability to make good use of that information!

FOR CRITICAL ANALYSIS

Does news coverage on the Internet differ from news presented via the traditional media? What impact might the Internet have on American politics?

REGULATION OF THE BROADCAST MEDIA

In some countries, the government controls media content. In other countries, the government owns the broadcast media (e.g., the BBC in Britain) but it does not tell the media what to say. In the United States, the government neither owns nor controls the communications networks, but it does regulate the content and ownership of the broadcast media.

As we saw in Chapter 4, in the United States, the print media are essentially free from government interference. The broadcast media, on the other hand, are subject to federal regulation. American radio and television are regulated by the Federal Communications Commission (FCC), an independent regulatory agency established in 1934. Radio and TV stations must have FCC licenses that must be renewed every five years. Licensing provides a mechanism for allocating radio and TV frequencies to prevent broadcasts from interfering with and garbling one another. License renewals are almost always granted automatically by the FCC. Indeed, renewal requests are now filed by postcard.

Through regulations prohibiting obscenity, indecency, and profanity, the FCC has also sought to prohibit radio and television stations from airing explicit sexual and excretory references between 6 A.M. and 10 P.M. These are the hours when children are most likely to be in the audience. The FCC has enforced these rules haphazardly. Since 1990, nearly half the $5 million in fines levied by the agency have involved Howard Stern, a "shock jock" whose programs are built around sexually explicit material. In 2004, after another set of FCC fines, Stern's program was dropped by a major outlet, Clear Channel Communication. Stern charged that the Bush administration had singled him out for censure because of his known opposition to the president.

For more than sixty years, the FCC also sought to regulate and promote competition in the broadcast industry, but in 1996 Congress passed the Telecommunications Act, a broad effort to do away with most regulations in effect since 1934. The act loosened restrictions on media ownership and allowed for telephone companies, cable television providers, and broadcasters to compete with one another for telecommunication services. Following the passage of the act, several mergers between telephone and cable companies and between different segments of the entertainment media produced an even greater concentration of media ownership.

The Telecommunications Act of 1996 also included an attempt to regulate the content of material transmitted over the Internet. This law, known as the Communications Decency Act, made it illegal to make "indecent" sexual material on the Internet accessible to those under eighteen years old. The act was immediately denounced by civil libertarians and brought to court as an infringement of free speech. The case reached the Supreme Court in 1997 and the act was ruled an unconstitutional infringement of the First Amendment's right to freedom of speech (see Chapter 4).

Although the government's ability to regulate the content of the electronic media on the Internet has been questioned, the federal government has used its licensing power to impose several regulations that can affect the political content of radio and TV broadcasts. The first of these is the **equal time rule,** under which broadcasters must provide candidates for the same political office equal opportunities to communicate their messages to the public. If, for example, a television station sells commercial time to a state's Republican gubernatorial candidate, it may not refuse to sell time to the Democratic candidate for the same position.

The second regulation affecting the content of broadcasts is the **right of rebuttal,** which requires that individuals be given the opportunity to respond to personal attacks. In the 1969 case of *Red Lion Broadcasting Company v. FCC,* for example, the U.S. Supreme Court upheld the FCC's determination that a radio station was required to provide a liberal author with an opportunity to respond to an attack from a conservative commentator that the station had aired.[4]

For many years, a third important federal regulation was the **fairness doctrine.** Under this doctrine, broadcasters who aired programs on controversial issues were required to provide time for opposing views. In 1985, however, the FCC stopped enforcing the fairness doctrine on the grounds that there were so many radio and television stations—to say nothing of newspapers and newsmagazines—that in all likelihood many different viewpoints were already being presented without having to require each station to try to present all sides of an argument. Critics of this FCC decision charge that in many media markets the number of competing viewpoints is small. Nevertheless, a congressional effort to require the FCC to enforce the fairness doctrine was blocked by the Reagan administration in 1987.

equal time rule the requirement that broadcasters provide candidates for the same political office an equal opportunity to communicate their messages to the public

right of rebuttal a Federal Communications Commission regulation giving individuals the right to have the opportunity to respond to personal attacks made on a radio or television broadcast

fairness doctrine a Federal Communications Commission (FCC) requirement for broadcasters who air programs on controversial issues to provide time for opposing views. The FCC ceased enforcing this doctrine in 1985

ORGANIZATION AND OWNERSHIP OF THE MEDIA

The United States boasts more than 1,000 television stations, approximately 1,800 daily newspapers, and more than 9,000 radio stations (20 percent of which are devoted to news, talk, or public affairs).[5]

Even though the number of TV and radio stations and daily newspapers reporting news in the United States is enormous, the number of sources of national news is actually quite small—several wire services, four broadcast networks, public radio and television, two elite newspapers, three newsmagazines, and a scattering of other sources such as the national correspondents of a few large local papers and the small independent radio networks. More than three-fourths of the daily newspapers in the United States are owned by large media conglomerates such as the Hearst, Knight Ridder, or Gannett corporations; thus the diversity of coverage and editorial opinion in American newspapers is not as broad as it might seem. Much of the national news that is published by local newspapers is provided by one wire service, the Associated Press, while additional coverage is provided by services run by several major newspapers like the *New York Times* and the *Chicago Tribune.* More than five hundred of the nation's television stations are affiliated with one of the four networks and carry that network's evening news reports. Dozens of others carry PBS (Public Broadcasting System) news. Several hundred local radio stations also carry network news or National Public Radio news broadcasts. At the same time, although there are only three truly national newspapers, the *Wall Street Journal,* the *Christian Science Monitor,* and *USA Today,* two other papers, the *New York Times* and the *Washington Post,* are read by political leaders and other influential Americans throughout the nation. Such is the influence of these two "elite" newspapers that their news coverage sets the standard for virtually all other news outlets. Stories carried in the *New York Times* or the *Washington Post* influence the content of many other papers as well as of the network news. Note how often this text, like most others, relies upon *New York Times* and *Washington Post* stories as sources for contemporary events. National news is also carried to millions of Americans by the three major newsmagazines—*Time, Newsweek,* and *U.S. News & World Report.* Beginning in the late 1980s, CNN became another major news source for Americans, especially after its spectacular coverage of the Persian Gulf War. At one point, CNN was able to provide live reports of American bombing raids on Baghdad, Iraq, after the major networks' correspondents had been forced to flee to bomb shelters. However, the number of news sources has remained essentially the same. Even the availability of new electronic media on the Internet has failed to expand the number of news sources. Most national news available on the World Wide Web, for example, consists of electronic versions of the conventional print or broadcast media.

The trend toward the homogenization of national news has been hastened by dramatic changes in media ownership, which became possible in large part due to the relaxation of government regulations in the 1980s and 1990s. The enactment of the 1996 Telecommunications Act opened the way for further consolidation in the media industry, and a wave of mergers and consolidations has further reduced the field of independent media across the country. Since that time, among the major news networks, ABC was bought by the Walt Disney corporation, CBS was bought by Westinghouse Electric and later merged with Viacom, the owner of MTV and Paramount Studios, and CNN was bought by Time Warner. NBC has been owned by General Electric since 1986. Australian press baron Rupert Murdoch owns the Fox network plus a host of radio, television, and newspaper properties around the world. A small number of giant corporations now controls a wide swath of media holdings, including television networks, movie studios, record companies, cable channels and local cable providers, book publishers, magazines, and newspapers. These developments have prompted questions about whether enough competition exists among the media to produce a diverse set of views on political and corporate matters[6] or whether the U. S. has become the prisoner of media monopolies.

Regulation of Media Ownership

In June 2003 the Federal Communications Commission (FCC) announced a set of rules that would permit major media corporations to expand their control of print and broadcast properties. Under the new rules, a company would be allowed to own newspapers and television stations that, together, could reach 45 percent of the nation's viewers (an increase from 35 percent under the old rule). A single company would also be permitted to own the most important newspaper and as many as three television and eight radio stations in a single market, effectively dominating news coverage within that market. Various public interest groups and members of Congress were outraged by the FCC's action, charging that the Commission was promoting the development of media monopolies. Both the House and the Senate considered legislation to reverse the FCC's decision, and several lawsuits were filed to block its enforcement.

Those who favor rules to limit the market power of media corporations make three major arguments. These have to do with quality, diversity of opinion, and political competitiveness. As to the first of these arguments, proponents of rules regulating competition assert that the quality of the print and broadcast media is improved by vigorous competition among a large number of newspaper, radio, and television outlets, each striving to attract readers, listeners, or viewers. As the number of competitors diminishes, regulatory proponents argue, the quality of news and feature programming is reduced as media outlets feel less competitive incentive to aim for quality and innovation.

The second argument made by proponents of regulation concerns diversity of opinion. Regulation is needed, the argument goes, to ensure that as many different opinions and perspectives as possible will be presented by the print and broadcast media. Concentration of ownership inevitably means that fewer perspectives will find their way into print or be presented on radio and television. This could mean that less-popular views would seldom receive media coverage. For example, during the 2003 Iraq war, the five television networks all presented a favorable account of American military efforts. Only viewers with access to foreign television coverage were presented with alternative perspectives.

The third argument, political competitiveness, is related to the second. Just as concentration of media ownership may diminish the availability of diverse outlooks, so it may also stifle political competition. If, for example, there was only a handful of media companies and they united behind a single party or candidate, their influence would be difficult to overcome. This state of affairs has, to some extent, come about in Italy. Italian prime minister Silvio Berlusconi is a media magnate who controls many of the nation's most important print and broadcast properties. Control of major portions of the media has given Berlusconi a commanding voice in Italian politics.

Opponents of regulation, for their part, are not against quality, diversity, and political competitiveness. They argue, however, that regulation of media ownership is unnecessary and may be counterproductive. Quality, say opponents of regulation, is enhanced by open competition in the marketplace and not by rules tha give small print and broadcast companies sheltered market niches where they are safe from powerful rivals. This, they say, is a recipe for mediocrity. And as to diversity of viewpoints, opponents of regulation note that so many media outlets exist in the United States, including online magazines and thousands of "blogs," that there is no danger that a single media corporation or small number of corporations can dominate coverage. It is regulation, rather than market competition, say opponents, that poses a threat to political and ideological diversity.

FOR CRITICAL ANALYSIS

1. Why might we be concerned about media concentration? Should we seek government action to curb concentration or should we rely on market forces to maintain diversity?

2. Some nations restrict foreign ownership of major media outlets. Should the United States adopt such a policy?

Should Government Regulate Media Ownership?

Yes

Competition. This cornerstone of our nation's economy means lower prices, more motivation for improvement and innovation and a built-in safeguard against monopolies. In the modern-day American media, however, a foundational principle of capitalism is quickly vanishing.

It's been seven years since the Federal Communications Commission loosened the reigns on merger regulations for radio stations, creating as it did a nationalized playlist, determined each week by Clear Channel Communications and Infinity Broadcasting, which together now control most of the nation's broadcast stations. In the years that followed this move, the two corporations (and several others like them) began gobbling up locally owned stations across the country, slowly destroying a distinction between radio stations from New Orleans to Raleigh to San Francisco to Detroit.

Not surprisingly, the decreased competition in radio markets has led to—surprise—less improvement and innovation, fewer choices for consumers, and virtual monopolies in many markets. This bold experiment in deregulation has been a disaster for members of the listening public with any discerning taste in the music and information they hear on the radio. This group of consumers, though, has little to do with the FCC's governing process.

Deregulation, however, has been an unprecedented success for conglomerates like Clear Channel, whose vast wealth and resources make them a major player in the political processes that determine the fate of the American communications industry. In the seven short years of anything-goes, merge-happy radio, this undisputed king of American radio has grown from 43 stations to almost 1,200.

It is no surprise, then, that television conglomerates would be the next to line up at the bottomless trough of deregulation.

Until this summer, the TV giants were held in check, albeit loosely, by a provision that prohibited the same company from owning both a major newspaper and major network affiliate in the same major market. They were also limited to one station per market and their combined holdings could never reach more than 35 percent of the U.S. television audience at anytime.

A 3-2 FCC vote on June 2 changed all that by eliminating the restriction on dual TV-newspaper ownership in a major market, raising the percentage of the market one conglomerate can reach to 45 percent, and allowing one company to own up to three TV stations in the same market.

Despite the bleak landscape that many predicted after the landmark vote, an unexpected counterpunch was dealt to the FCC—and the evil, three-headed Viacoms of the world—from an unlikely source last week: bipartisan legislation approved by the U.S. Senate.

One week ago the Senate overturned all the June 2 changes with a rarely employed tool called a "resolution of disapproval," which allows them to invalidate the policies and regulations of federal agencies. Although sponsored by Byron Dorgan (D-N.D.), much of the credit for this rare moment of Senatorial coherency should be given to Trent Lott (R-Ms.), who co-sponsored the legislation and led twelve Republicans who pushed the resolution over the top by a 55-40 vote.

Not only did these courageous Republicans refute the FCC, which is controlled by members of their own party, but they also stood firm against the White House, which supports media deregulation and has stated that President Bush would veto such a measure if it managed to pass both houses.

Sadly, the Senate vote will likely be a Pyrrhic vector for forces dedicated to local control and media competition. Although more and more Senate Republicans have begun to realize that the "ClearChannelization" of American radio might not be the best model to transfer to television, their counterparts in the House, led by Billy "Big Business" Tauzin (R-La.), remain unconvinced.

Commenting on the chances of the approved Senate legislation being addressed in the House, Tauzin's spokesman said, "It can be held at the speaker's desk collecting dust and cobwebs for the rest of recorded time."

Kudos to Lott and Co. for standing up to big business, Big Billy, and Big Bush, even if it's all for naught in the long run. My advice for the day is to enjoy the Fox News-CNN or New York Times-Wall Street Journal debates while you can—pretty soon, the same stock abbreviation will own them all.

SOURCE: Bradley Aldrich, "Radio/TV Conglomerates Make More of the Same," *LSU Reveille* (Louisiana State University), September 23, 2003.

No On Monday, the FCC acted as expected and relaxed media ownership rules, allowing, among other things, networks to own broadcast stations, which reach up to forty-five percent of a viewing audience (the rule was previously thirty-five percent) as well as easing rules on cross-ownership of television and radio stations along with newspapers. Note that as of press time, the sky has yet to fall.

As the myriad of protests went, supposedly such relatively cosmetic changes to FCC regulatory structure would lead to the eventual consolidation of all media, an end to all diversity of viewpoints, and complete homogenization of media content. Critics point to the deregulation of radio ownership rules, which has since allowed Clear Channel Communications (the bane of anti-corporate types) to dominate the radio station market across the country, providing nationalized playlists and content that critics decry as "the death of local radio."

Overlooked in this calculation, of course, is the argument that Clear Channel's local stations could not be a success if they failed to appeal to their listeners' desires—with the proliferation of cheap car CD-players and the advent of the CD-R drive and satellite radio, local radio hardly constitutes a captive audience. Indeed, listeners who prove dissatisfied with the choices in content provided not only have more choices today in the types of music they can select in terms of the number of stations and formats, they also have more alternatives to traditional radio than ever before, rendering the objection to Clear Channel's chokehold on the market more an objection by music elitists to the plebeian taste of the masses than a salient critique of deregulation. The very fact of Clear Channel's success is simply a manifestation of regular market forces at work. If the tastes of the listening public are largely undiscriminating, the result will be swill filling the airwaves—deregulation has nothing to do with this.

Likewise, the same can be said for both the expansion of network ownership along with cross-ownership rules. When the rules were originally conceived, not only were there only three major networks (Fox proving to be a very contradiction to the claim that the oligopoly would prevent the emergence of new players), but there was no Internet and satellite television was unheard of. Today's consumer can not only obtain television and news from around the world (a prime example would be Qatar-based Al Jazeera's coverage of the Iraq war), but the very elements of information distribution have become less centralized, not more so. No one news corporation can put a bottleneck on the flow of information by both independent journalists and competing foreign media over the Internet, nor can they stop individuals from seeking out these alternate avenues for news and information.

All of this leads up the very authority these regulations are put forth upon to begin with—by its Congressional authorization, the FCC must put forth rules that explicitly demonstrate their own necessity for preserving and enhancing competition. Indeed, the Supreme Court has also upheld this standard, striking down previous regulations in *Fox v. FCC* on the grounds that they did not justify why such rules were necessary to safeguard or enhance competition. Ultimately, the onus is on regulators to demonstrate why regulations must be kept in order to safeguard competition—not the other way around.

. . .[T]he ultimate mistake that proponents of tight regulation make is in assuming media consumers are a captive audience, which as the explosion of nontraditional media shows, they are clearly not. Indeed, market forces prove far more adaptive to consumer demand than any regulator can.

SOURCE: Steve Skutnik, "New FCC Rules Aren't As Bad As They Seem," *Iowa State Daily* (Iowa State University), June 3, 2003.

In June 2003, the Federal Communication Commission (FCC) announced a set of rules that seemed to pave the way for even more concentration in the media industry. The FCC mandated that the major networks could now own TV stations that would collectively reach 45 percent of all viewers, up from the 35 percent permitted under existing rules. The new rules also allowed a single company to own the leading newspaper and multiple television and radio outlets in a single market. In the largest cities, this could include a newspaper, three television stations, and as many as eight radio stations. Major media companies, which had long lobbied for the right to expand their activities, welcomed the new FCC rules. Critics, however, expressed concern that the decision would result in a narrowing of the range of views and issues presented to the general public. Congressional opponents of the FCC's action sought to overturn the new rules but were stymied by opposition from the House Republican leadership as well as a threatened presidential veto. In 2004, however, a federal appeals court placed the new regulations on hold and ordered the FCC to justify or modify its approach to setting numerical limits on media ownership.

Media Ownership and Political Equality   Increasing concentration of media ownership raises a number of major issues (see Policy Debate on p. 261). One of the most important relates to political equality. Access to the print and broadcast media is such an important political resource that for all intents and purposes, political forces that lack media access have only a very limited opportunity to influence the political process. As major newspapers, television stations, and radio networks fall into fewer and fewer hands, the risk increases that less popular or minority viewpoints and the politicians who express them will have difficulty finding a public forum in which to disseminate their ideas. Increasingly, such individuals turn to the Internet and its numerous blogs and Web sites to express their views. The problem, however, is that ideas presented on the Internet tend to be read mainly by those who already agree with them. The Internet can be an important mechanism for linking communities of adherents, but it is less effective than radio, television, and the print media for reaching new audiences. Hence, growing concentration and consolidation in the print and broadcast industries are important policy problems.

FOR CRITICAL ANALYSIS

In recent years, a number of major media corporations have acquired numerous newspapers, television stations, and radio properties. Is media concentration a serious problem? Why?

NATIONALIZATION OF THE NEWS

In general, the national news media cover more or less the same sets of events, present similar information, and emphasize similar issues and problems. Indeed, the national news services watch one another quite carefully. It is very likely that a major story carried by one service will quickly find its way into the pages or programming of the others. As a result, in the United States a rather centralized national news has developed, through which a relatively similar picture of events, issues, and problems is presented to the entire nation.[7] The nationalization of the news began at the turn of the century, was accelerated by the development of radio networks in the 1920s and 1930s and by the creation of the television networks after the 1950s, and has been further strengthened by the recent trends toward concentrated media ownership. This nationalization of news content has very important consequences for the American political system.

Nationalization of the news has contributed greatly to the nationalization of politics and of political perspectives in the United States. Prior to the development of the national media and the nationalization of news coverage, news traveled very slowly. Every region and city saw national issues and problems primarily through a local lens. Concerns and perspectives varied greatly from region to region, city to city, and village to village. Today, in large measure as a result of the nationalization of the media, residents of all parts of the country share a similar picture of the day's events.[8] They may not agree on everything, but most see the world in similar ways.

The exception to this pattern can be found with those Americans whose chief source of news is something other than the "mainstream" national media. Despite the nationalization and homogenization of the news, in some American cities, alternative news coverage is available. Such media markets are known as **news enclaves.** For example, some African Americans rely on newspapers and radio stations that aim their coverage primarily at black audiences. This general strategy is known as "narrowcasting" (to distinguish it from broadcasting). As a result, these individuals may interpret events differently from white Americans and even other blacks.[9] The existence of a black-focused media helps to explain why many African Americans and white Americans reacted differently to the 1995 trial of O. J. Simpson in Los Angeles. While national media outlets generally portrayed Simpson as guilty of the murder of his former wife, African American media outlets depicted Simpson as a victim of a racist criminal justice system. This latter view came to be held by a large number of African Americans.

In a similar vein, some radio stations and print media are aimed exclusively at religious and social conservatives. These individuals are also likely to develop and retain a perception of the news that is quite different from that of "mainstream" America. For example, the rural midwesterners who rely on the ultraconservative People's Radio Network for their news coverage may become concerned about the alleged efforts of the United Nations to subordinate the United States in a world government, a viewpoint unfamiliar to most Americans.

Internet newsgroups are another form of news enclave. Newsgroups are informal and tend to develop around the discussion of a particular set of issues. Individuals post their views for others to read; comments are also posted. In some instances, posted comments are attacked by other members of the community. In general, users seem to seek out and exchange postings with those who share their opinions. Perhaps the long-term significance of the Internet is that it will increasingly allow contacts among individuals with unconventional viewpoints who are geographically dispersed and might otherwise be unaware of the existence of others who share their views. In the mid-1990s, Internet newsgroups played a role in the mobilization of "antigovernment" fringe groups.

The same principle seems to hold for another form of discussion on the Internet, known as a chat room. Chat rooms are online forums in which anonymous individuals form groups spontaneously and converse with one another. The topics change often as participants leave and are replaced by newcomers. Like newsgroups, chat rooms seem to function as opinion enclaves where like-minded individuals from across the nation can congregate and reinforce one another's views.

news enclave a group seeking specialized information not provided by the mainstream media

News Coverage

Because of the important role the media can play in national politics, understanding the factors that affect media coverage is vitally important.[10] What accounts for the media's agenda of issues and topics? What explains the character of coverage—why does a politician receive good or bad press? What factors determine the interpretation or "spin" that a particular story will receive? Although a host of minor factors plays a role, three major factors are important: (1) the journalists, or producers of the news; (2) the sources or topics of the news; and (3) the audience for the news.

JOURNALISTS

Media content and news coverage are inevitably affected by the views, ideals, and interests of those who seek out, write, and produce news and other stories. At one time, newspaper publishers exercised a great deal of influence over their papers' news content. Publishers such as William Randolph Hearst and Joseph Pulitzer became political powers through their manipulation of news coverage. Hearst, for example, almost single-handedly pushed the United States into war with Spain in 1898 through his newspapers' relentless coverage of the alleged brutality employed by Spain in its efforts to suppress a rebellion in Cuba, at that time a Spanish colony. The sinking of the American battleship *Maine* in Havana harbor under mysterious circumstances gave Hearst the ammunition he needed to force a reluctant President McKinley to lead the nation into war. Today, few publishers have that kind of power. Most publishers are concerned more with the business operations of their newspapers than with editorial content, although a few continue to impose their interests and tastes on the news.

More important than publishers, for the most part, are the reporters. Those who cover the news for the national media generally have a good deal of discretion or freedom to interpret stories and, as a result, have an opportunity to interject their views and ideals into news stories. For example, the personal friendship and respect that some reporters felt for Franklin Roosevelt or John Kennedy helped to generate more favorable news coverage for these presidents. Likewise, the dislike and distrust felt by many reporters for Richard Nixon was also communicated to the public. In the case of Ronald Reagan, the disdain that many journalists felt for the president was communicated in stories suggesting that he was often asleep or inattentive when important decisions were made.

Conservatives have long charged that the liberal biases of reporters and journalists result in distorted news coverage. A 1996 survey of Washington newspaper bureau chiefs and correspondents seems to support this charge.[11] The study, conducted by the Roper Center and the Freedom Forum, a conservative foundation, found that 61 percent of the bureau chiefs and correspondents polled called themselves "liberal" or "liberal to moderate." Only 9 percent called themselves "conservative" or "conservative to moderate." In a similar vein, 89 percent said they had voted for Democrat Bill Clinton in 1992, while only 7 percent indicated that they had voted for Republican George Bush. Fifty percent said they were Democrats, and only 4 percent claimed to be Republicans.[12] Generally speaking, reporters for major national news outlets tend to be more liberal than their local counterparts who often profess moderate or even conservative views.

The linkage between journalists and liberal ideas is by no means absolute. Most reporters, to be sure, attempt to maintain some measure of balance or objectivity whatever their personal political views. Moreover, over the past several years a conservative media complex has emerged in opposition to the liberal media. This complex includes two major newspapers, the *Wall Street Journal* and the *Washington*

Times, several magazines such as the *American Spectator,* and a host of conservative radio and television talk programs. Also important is media baron Rupert Murdoch, creator of Fox Network News and the financial force behind the *Weekly Standard.* Murdoch sees Fox as a conservative alternative to the more liberal networks and has staffed Fox with rather conservative broadcast personalities. The emergence of this conservative media complex has meant that liberal policies and politicians are virtually certain to come under attack even when the "liberal media" are sympathetic to them.

Probably more important than ideological bias is a selection bias in favor of news that the media view as having a great deal of audience appeal because of its dramatic or entertainment value. In practice, this bias often results in news coverage that focuses on crimes and scandals, especially those involving prominent individuals, despite the fact that the public obviously looks to the media for information about important political debates. For example, even though most journalists may be Democrats, this partisan predisposition did not prevent an enormous media frenzy in January 1998 when reports surfaced that President Clinton might have had an affair with White House intern Monica Lewinsky. Once a hint of blood appeared in the water, partisanship and ideology were swept away by the piranhalike instincts often manifested by journalists.

SUBJECTS OF THE NEWS

News coverage is also influenced by the individuals or groups who are subjects of the news or whose interests and activities are actual or potential news topics. The president, in particular, has the power to set the news agenda through his speeches and actions. All politicians, for that matter, seek to shape or manipulate their media images by cultivating good relations with reporters as well as through news leaks and staged news events. For example, during the lengthy investigation of President Clinton conducted by Special Counsel Kenneth Starr, both the Office of the Special Counsel and the White House frequently leaked information to the press designed to bolster their respective positions in the struggle. Starr admitted speaking to reporters on a not-for-attribution basis about aspects of his investigation of the president. One journalist, Steven Brill, accused a number of prominent reporters of serving as "lap dogs" for the Special Counsel by reporting as fact the information fed to them by Starr.[13] Some politicians become extremely adept image makers—or at least skilled at hiring publicists who are skillful image makers. Indeed, press releases drafted by skillful publicists often become the basis for reporters' stories. A substantial percentage of the news stories published every day are initially drafted by publicists and later rewritten only slightly, if at all, by busy reporters and editors.

Furthermore, political candidates often endeavor to tailor their images for specific audiences. For example, to cultivate a favorable image among younger voters during his 1992 campaign, Bill Clinton made several appearances on MTV, and he continued to grant interviews to MTV after his election. His MTV forays came to an end, however, when he was severely criticized for discussing his preferred type of underwear with members of an MTV audience.

President George W. Bush's administration has developed a highly sophisticated communications office under the leadership of former presidential aide Karen Hughes. Hughes, who resigned in April 2002, and her staff endeavored to craft a new media message every few days in order to continually shape the nation's

FOR CRITICAL ANALYSIS

There is a great deal of talk about the liberal bias of the media in American politics. To what extent is the media liberal? To what extent, do you think, is it biased? Considering the growing importance of conservative talk radio and news enclaves that support conservative causes, describe the ways in which discussions of a liberal bias in the media should be qualified.

During the 2003 Iraq war, the Bush administration went to great lengths to influence media coverage so that the U.S. military's efforts were presented in a positive light. For example, the U.S. Central Command headquarters in Doha, Qatar, included an elaborate $1.5 million media center with multiple flat plasma television screens, high speed telephone lines, and an espresso bar. Each day of the heavy combat phase of the war, a military spokesperson updated the media on the progress made. The briefing had a predictable routine: the spokesperson iterated the successes on the battlefield, including video clips of "shock and awe" strikes on Iraqi targets; gave a few solemn words memorializing fallen comrades and made expressions of condolences for their families who had sacrificed a loved one for the cause; offered one or two anecdotes about the extreme cruelty of Saddam Hussein's regime; and concluded by answering questions from the press corps for about 45 minutes—typically with answers of "we don't discuss military operations" or "no comment."

Prior to the war, the administration also invited more than one hundred news correspondents and photographers to accompany American forces into battle. These "embedded" journalists rode in tanks with the troops, sharing their hardships and dangers. As the administration hoped, the embedded journalists developed considerable rapport with the soldiers and provided generally sympathetic war coverage, often beginning their accounts of military actions with the pronoun "we."

Public support for the president's military policies faltered in late 2003 and 2004, when the occupation of Iraq produced a steady stream of U.S. casualties. And in April 2004, 60 Minutes II's broadcast of the story of American soldiers' abuse of Iraqi inmates at Abu Ghraib prison was seen around the world and led to accusations of brutality, abuse, and torture. Initial efforts by the Bush administration to contain the Iraq prison torture scandal and limit the blame to a handful of soldiers and immediate senior officers failed. Even President Bush took part in the media campaign when, soon after the scandal became public, he gave interviews to Al Arabiya and Al-Hurra (which is financed by the U.S. government) to mitigate Arab anger.

press coverage. For example, Bush's reference to nations supporting terrorist groups as an "axis of evil" in February 2002 was designed to give the media a catch phrase that would dominate the headlines and provide **sound bites**—short, attention-grabbing summaries of a story—for the broadcast media for days. By the time the media tired of the "axis of evil," the White House hoped to have developed a new sound bite for the reporters. The Bush team also pays enormous attention to the visual elements of a story. For example, in summer 2002, the president delivered a speech at Mount Rushmore. His media advisers positioned the platform for television crews off to one side so that the cameras would show the president in profile, perfectly aligned with the heads of the four presidents carved into the mountain. In a similar vein, in May 2003, the president spoke in Indiana on his economic plan. Staffers asked people in the audience who might be seen on camera to remove their ties so that they would look more like the ordinary individuals the president said would benefit from his tax cuts.[14]

sound bites short snippets of information aimed at dramatizing a story rather than explaining its substantive meaning

The capacity of news subjects to influence the news is hardly unlimited. Media consultants and issues managers may shape the news for a time, but it is generally not difficult for the media to penetrate the smoke screens thrown up by news sources if they have a reason to do so. Thus, for example, despite the administration's media management, by fall 2003 reporters in Iraq were filing numerous accounts of the resistance American occupation forces were encountering. Unfavorable media coverage placed President Bush under enormous pressure to modify his policies in Iraq, and in November 2003, the president intimated that he would speed up efforts to return control of Iraq affairs to an interim local government.

Occasionally, however, a politician proves incredibly adept at surviving repeated media attacks. Bill Clinton, for example, was able to survive repeated revelations of sexual improprieties, financial irregularities, lying to the public, and illegal campaign fund-raising activities. Clinton and his advisers crafted what the *Washington Post* called a "toolkit" for dealing with potentially damaging media revelations. This toolkit included techniques such as chiding the press, browbeating reporters, referring inquiries quickly to lawyers who would not comment, and acting quickly to change the agenda. These techniques helped Clinton maintain a favorable public image despite the Monica Lewinsky scandal and even the humiliation of a formal impeachment and trial.

THE POWER OF CONSUMERS

The print and broadcast media are businesses that, in general, seek to show a profit. This means that like any other business, they must cater to the preferences of consumers. This has very important consequences for the content and character of the news media.

Catering to the Audience   In general, and especially in the political realm, the print and broadcast media and the publishing industry are not only responsive to the interests of consumers generally, but are particularly responsive to the interests and views of the better educated and more affluent segments of their audience. The preferences of these audience segments have a profound effect on the content and orientation of the press, of radio and television programming, and of books, especially in the areas of news and public affairs.[15]

Although affluent consumers do watch television programs and read periodicals whose contents are designed simply to amuse or entertain, the one area that most directly appeals to the upscale audience is that of news and public affairs. The affluent—who are also typically well educated—are the core audience of newsmagazines, journals of opinion, books dealing with public affairs, such newspapers as the *New York Times* and the *Washington Post,* and broadcast news and weekend and evening public-affairs programs. Although other segments of the public also read newspapers and watch television news, their level of interest in world events, national political issues, and the like is closely related to their level of education. As a result, upscale Americans are overrepresented in the news and public-affairs audience. The concentration of these strata in the audience makes news, politics, and public affairs potentially very attractive topics to advertisers, publishers, radio broadcasters, and television executives. As a result, topics in which the upper-middle-class is interested, such as the stock market, scientific and literary affairs, and international politics, receive extensive coverage.

At the same time, however, entire categories of events, issues, and phenomena of interest to lower-middle- and working-class Americans receive scant attention from the national print and broadcast media. For example, trade-union news and events are discussed only in the context of major strikes or revelations of corruption. No network or national periodical routinely covers labor organizations. Religious and church affairs receive little coverage. The activities of veterans', fraternal, ethnic, and patriotic organizations are also generally ignored.

The Media and Conflict   While the media respond most to the upscale audience, groups who cannot afford the services of media consultants and issues managers can publicize their views and interests through protest. Frequently, the media are accused of encouraging conflict and even violence as a result of the fact that the audience mostly watches news for the entertainment value that conflict can provide. Clearly, conflict can be an important vehicle for attracting the attention and interest of the media, and thus may provide an opportunity for media attention to groups otherwise lacking the financial or organizational resources to broadcast their views. But while conflict and protest can succeed in drawing media attention, these methods ultimately do not allow groups from the bottom of the social ladder to compete effectively in the media.

The chief problem with protest as a media technique is that, in general, the media upon which the protesters depend have considerable discretion in reporting and interpreting the events they cover. For example, should the media focus on the conflict itself, rather than the issues or concerns that created the conflict? The answer to this question is typically determined by the media, not by the protesters. This means that media interpretation of protest activities is more a reflection of the views of the groups and forces to which the media are responsive—as we have seen, usually segments of the upper-middle class—than it is a function of the wishes of the protesters themselves. It is worth noting that civil rights protesters received their most favorable media coverage when a segment of the white upper-middle class saw blacks as potential political allies in the Democratic party.

Typically, upper-middle-class protesters—student demonstrators and the like—have little difficulty securing favorable publicity for themselves and their causes. Upper-middle-class protesters are often more skilled than their lower-class counterparts in the techniques of media manipulation. That is, they typically have a better sense—often as a result of formal courses on the subject—of how to package messages for media consumption. For example, it is important to know what time of day a protest should occur if it is to be carried on the evening news. Similarly, the setting, definition of the issues, character of the rhetoric used, and so on, all help to determine whether a protest will receive favorable media coverage, unfavorable coverage, or no coverage at all. Moreover, upper-middle-class protesters can often produce their own media coverage through "underground" newspapers, college papers, student radio and television stations, and, now, over the Internet. The same resources and skills that generally allow upper-middle-class people to publicize their ideas are usually not left behind when segments of this class choose to engage in disruptive forms of political action. This helps to explain why small groups of demonstrators in Seattle, Washington, were able to garner enormous media coverage in the winter of 1999 for their protests against the World Trade Organization.

Media Power in American Politics

The content and character of news and public affairs programming—what the media choose to present and how they present it—can have far-reaching political consequences. Media disclosures can greatly enhance—or fatally damage—the careers of public officials. Media coverage can rally support for—or intensify opposition to—national policies. The media can shape and modify, if not fully form, public perceptions of events, issues, and institutions.

SHAPING EVENTS

In recent American political history, the media have played a central role in at least three major events. First, the media were a critically important factor in the civil rights movement of the 1950s and 1960s. Television photos showing peaceful civil rights marchers attacked by club-swinging police helped to generate sympathy among northern whites for the civil rights struggle and greatly increased the pressure on Congress to bring an end to segregation.[16] Second, the media were instrumental in compelling the Nixon administration to negotiate an end to American involvement in the Vietnam War. Beginning in 1967, the national media, reacting in part to a shift in elite opinion, portrayed the war as misguided and unwinnable and, as a result, helped to turn popular sentiment against continued American involvement.[17]

Finally, the media were central actors in the Watergate affair, which ultimately forced President Richard Nixon, landslide victor in the 1972 presidential election, to resign from office in disgrace. It was the relentless series of investigations launched by the *Washington Post,* the *New York Times,* and the television networks that led to

Millions of Americans depend upon newspapers, television, the radio, and, increasingly, the Internet for reporting and analysis of the major events of the day. The way in which the media portray or "frame" an event often has a major impact on popular perceptions. Media accounts critical of the Vietnam War helped to turn public opinion against the war and hastened the withdrawal of American troops. This famous photograph of the aftermath of a napalm attack was one of many media images that shaped the American public's views on the war.

Civil rights protesters in the 1960s learned a variety of techniques designed to elicit favorable media coverage. Media accounts of the brutal treatment of protesters in some communities turned public opinion against the Jim Crow system of racial segregation and helped bring about the enactment of laws aimed at prohibiting racial discrimination. Television images of police brutality in Alabama led directly to the enactment of the 1965 Civil Rights Act.

the disclosures of the various abuses of which Nixon was guilty and ultimately forced Nixon to choose between resignation and almost certain impeachment.

THE SOURCES OF MEDIA POWER

Agenda Setting   The power of the media stems from several sources. The first is **agenda setting,** which means that the media help to set the agenda for political

agenda setting the power of the media to bring public attention to particular issues and problems

During President Richard Nixon's second term in office, media accounts of the president's misdeeds, including complicity in a break-in at 1972 Democratic campaign headquarters in Washington's Watergate Hotel, led to congressional investigations that forced Nixon to resign from office. Washington Post *reporters Robert Woodward and Carl Bernstein played an important role in uncovering the Watergate conspiracy (left).*

In the late 1990s, President Bill Clinton was nearly driven from office by media revelations of his sexual misconduct with White House intern Monica Lewinsky (right). The media relentlessly pursued Clinton's evasions, lies, and indiscretions and provided fuel for a congressional effort to impeach the president.

discussion. Groups and forces that wish to bring their ideas before the public in order to generate support for policy proposals or political candidacies must somehow secure media coverage. If the media are persuaded that an idea is newsworthy, then they may declare it an "issue" that must be confronted or a "problem" to be solved, thus clearing the first hurdle in the policy-making process. On the other hand, if an idea lacks or loses media appeal, its chance of resulting in new programs or policies is diminished.

For example, in 2003, Democratic presidential candidate Al Sharpton sought to make poverty the central issue of his bid for office. Sharpton appeared at numerous events to speak out against poverty and offered a plan that he said would improve our national security by promoting education, health care, and housing. Sharpton also promised to raise the minimum wage and increase tax credits for the working poor. While this topic was popular among some liberal and labor groups, the national media seemed to regard it as old hat and did not make Sharpton's plan a central theme in its coverage of the presidential race. Other candidates ignored the Sharpton effort since the media failed to label it as a major issue in the race.

On the other hand, Democrats were able to persuade the media that regulation of health maintenance organizations (HMOs) was an issue worthy of discussion. During well-publicized congressional hearings in the fall of 1999, Democrats presented many witnesses who testified that their HMOs had prevented them from receiving adequate treatment. Democrats called for a "Patient's Bill of Rights" to allow HMO physicians more autonomy and to permit unhappy patients redress in the courts. Republicans initially charged that the Democrats were simply doing the bidding of the trial lawyers, major contributors to the Democratic Party, who saw HMOs as rich targets for litigation. Media coverage of the disgruntled HMO patients, however, made it impossible for Republicans to dismiss the issue from the agenda and led eventually to the enactment of legislation close to the Democratic proposal.

In the fall of 2001, President Bush had little difficulty convincing the media that terrorism and his administration's campaign to combat terrorist attacks merited a dominant place on the agenda. In 2002 and 2003, American military campaigns in Afghanistan and Iraq easily dominated the news. Some stories have such overwhelming significance that political leaders' main concern is not whether the story will receive attention but whether they will figure prominently and positively in media accounts. In many instances, the media serve as conduits for agenda-setting efforts by competing groups and forces. Occasionally, however, journalists themselves play an important role in setting the agenda of political discussion. For example, whereas many of the scandals and investigations surrounding President Clinton were initiated by his political opponents, the Watergate scandal that destroyed Nixon's presidency was in some measure initiated and driven by the *Washington Post* and the national television networks.

framing the power of the media to influence how events and issues are interpreted

Framing   A second source of the media's power, known as **framing**, is their power to decide how political events and results are interpreted by the American people. For example, during the 1995–96 struggle between President Clinton and congressional Republicans over the nation's budget—a struggle that led to several partial shutdowns of the federal government—the media's interpretation of events forced the Republicans to back down and agree to a budget on Clinton's terms. At the beginning of the crisis, congressional Republicans, led by then House Speaker Newt Gingrich, were confident that they could compel Clinton to accept their budget, which called for substantial cuts in domestic social programs. Republicans calculated that Clinton would fear being blamed for lengthy government shutdowns and would quickly accede to their demands, and that once Americans saw that life went on with government agencies closed, they would support the Republicans in asserting that the United States could get along with less government.

For the most part, however, the media did not cooperate with the GOP's plans. Media coverage of the several government shutdowns during this period emphasized the hardships imposed upon federal workers who were being furloughed in the weeks before Christmas. Indeed, Newt Gingrich, who was generally portrayed as the villain who caused the crisis, came to be called the "Gin*grinch*" who stole Christmas from the children of hundreds of thousands of federal workers. Rather than suggest that the shutdown demonstrated that America could carry on with less government, media accounts focused on the difficulties encountered by Washington tourists unable to visit the capital's monuments, museums, and galleries. The woes of American travelers whose passports were delayed were given considerable attention. Thus, the "dominant frame" became the hardship and disruption caused by the Republicans. The GOP's "competing frame" was dismissed.[18] This sort of coverage eventually convinced most Americans that the government shutdown was bad for the country. In the end, Gingrich and the congressional Republicans were forced to surrender and to accept a new budget reflecting many of Clinton's priorities. The Republicans' defeat in the budget showdown contributed to the unraveling of the GOP's legislative program and, ultimately, to the Republicans' poor showing in the 1996 presidential elections and 1998 congressional races. The character of media coverage of an event thus had enormous repercussions for how Americans interpreted it.

Media frames were quite important during the 2000 election. Early in the campaign, the national media presented Bush as lacking in intelligence and Gore as somewhat dishonest. These characterizations were reinforced by many stories. For example, when Bush responded to a question about his favorite book from childhood by naming a well-known children's book, *The Very Hungry Caterpillar,* news accounts suggested that the book was one of his current favorites.[19] As for Gore, the media frequently played up what it considered his tendency to exaggerate, with stories poking fun at his claims of having worked on a farm in his youth and his contention that he played a role in the development of the Internet. These media frames helped to shape voters' perceptions of the two candidates. Strikingly, in one instance, a media frame shaped a candidate's perception of himself. After the first presidential debate, the news media presented Gore as overly aggressive. Not only did the public accept this characterization, but Gore himself responded to the image presented by the media by completely changing his behavior in the second debate. While he had been extremely critical of Bush in their first encounter, Gore went out of his way to praise Bush during their second meeting.[20] In this case, a media frame affected the participants as much as it did the viewers.

After he assumed office in 2001, George W. Bush sought to frame media coverage by introducing a new issue—education, taxes, the budget—every week. Bush hoped to attract media attention, control the headlines, and demonstrate that his administration was vigorously undertaking the people's work. After the debut of the president's tax-cut initiative in February 2001, Bush embarked on a multi-state

Sources of Media Power

Setting the Agenda for Political Discussion

Groups wishing to generate support for policy proposals or political candidacies must secure media coverage. The media must be persuaded that an item is newsworthy.

Framing

The media's interpretation or evaluation of an event or political action can sometimes determine how people perceive the event or result.

Priming

Most citizens will never meet their political leaders, but will base opinions of these leaders on their media images. The media has a great deal of control over how a person is evaluated or whether an individual even receives public attention. The media are also able to shape how a policy issue is perceived by the public.

speaking tour in support of his program. The president hoped to dominate local news coverage in a number of key states as a way of putting pressure on members of Congress to support his proposals. For its part, the news media combined several stories involving financial improprieties on the part of corporate executives such as those of the Enron Corporation and framed a major account of "corporate greed" in 2002. What might have been seen as white collar crime—a page 10 story—became a page 1 story and a central political issue in the 2002 elections.

The importance of framing was underlined by the Bush administration in the fall of 2001, when presidential aides held extensive discussions with network executives and even Hollywood filmmakers about their treatment of America's war against terrorism. The White House asked the media to sound a patriotic note and frame the war as a national necessity. By all accounts, media executives responded positively, indicating that they would present the war news in a favorable light.[21] In 2004, the Bush campaign sought to "reframe" the issue of John Kerry's service in the Vietnam War by raising questions about Kerry's conduct after the war and whether he actually deserved his medals. For its part, the Kerry campaign sought to reframe the issue by portraying Bush as a draft dodger and military shirker.

priming process of preparing the public to take a particular view of an event or political actor

Priming A third important media power is **priming.** This occurs when media coverage affects the way the public evaluates political leaders or candidates for office. For example, nearly unanimous media praise for President Bush's speeches to the nation in the wake of the September 11 terrorist attacks prepared, or "primed," the public to view Bush's subsequent response to terrorism in an extremely positive light, even though some aspects of the administration's efforts, most notably those in the realm of bioterrorism, were quite problematic.

In the case of political candidates, the media have considerable influence over whether a particular individual will receive public attention, whether a particular individual will be taken seriously as a viable contender, and whether the public will evaluate a candidate's performance favorably. Thus, if the media find a candidate interesting, they may treat him or her as a serious contender even though the facts of the matter seem to suggest otherwise. In a similar vein, the media may declare that a candidate has "momentum," a mythical property that the media confer upon candidates if they happen to exceed the media's expectations. Momentum has no substantive meaning—it is simply a media prediction that a particular candidate will do even better in the future than in the past. Such media prophecies can become self-fulfilling as contributors and supporters jump on the bandwagon of the candidate possessing this "momentum." In 1992, when Bill Clinton's poll standings surged in the wake of the Democratic National Convention, the media determined that Clinton had enormous momentum. In fact, nothing that happened during the remainder of the race led the media to change its collective judgment.

Typically, media coverage of election campaigns focuses on the "horse race" to the detriment of attention to issues and candidate records. During the 2000 presidential primaries, Senator John McCain of Arizona was able to use his Senate committee chairmanship to raise enough money to mount a challenge to Bush for the Republican nomination. In reality, McCain had little chance of defeating the front-runner. Seeing the possibility of a "horse race," however, the media gave McCain a great deal of generally positive coverage and helped him mount a noisy, if brief, challenge to Bush. McCain's hopes were dashed, though, when he was trounced by Bush in a series of primaries, including those held in South Carolina and other GOP strongholds. In the

What the Media Tell Americans about the World and the World about America

It is often said that we live in an age of "globalization," when events anywhere in the world affect everyone in the world. Nevertheless, the American news media are surprisingly parochial in their orientation. Few news organizations have foreign bureaus or foreign correspondents. Indeed, in the face of globalization, the number of foreign bureaus operated by major news organizations has actually decreased. One veteran CBS reporter, Tom Fenton, said that when he joined the network in 1970, "I was one of three correspondents in the Rome bureau. We had bureaus in Paris, Bonn, Warsaw, Cairo, and Nairobi. Now you can count the number of foreign correspondents on two hands and have three fingers left over. Before, we had stringers all over the world. Now no one can afford that."[a] Despite vital American interests in the Middle East—a region in which the United States has fought three wars in the past decade and a half—most reporters know very little about the history, culture, and languages of the region. U.S. correspondents sent to cover the Iraq war could not speak directly with Iraqis or understand Arabic news media.[b]

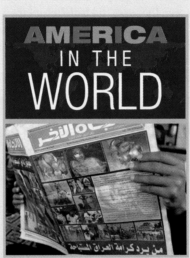

A brief survey of recent American newspapers offers a sense of the character of news coverage of international affairs. On November 16, 2003, a typical fall Sunday, most American newspapers devoted roughly 20 percent of their news coverage to international events.

Interestingly, the bulk of the international news featured in these papers involved war, terrorism, and political violence. To the extent that Americans derive their understanding of the world from the newspapers, they might reasonably see much of it as a very dangerous place. Indeed, the focus on violence and danger far exceeds even the blood-spattered domestic coverage for which some newspapers are famous.

However, before we agree with Tom Fenton and dismiss the American news media as parochial, it is interesting to compare U.S. coverage of international events with that presented on the same day in November by one of the world's oldest and most famous newspapers, the *Times* of London. The *Times* did, indeed, devote a considerably greater portion of its news coverage to international events than did the American newspapers. Slightly more than 44 percent of the stories in the *Times* focused on world affairs—twice the percentage found in the typical American paper and considerably greater even than in the internationally minded *New York Times*. And, while the London *Times* hardly ignored war, revolution, and political turmoil, its international stories also dealt with more peaceful and prosaic matters—political maneuvering in Sweden, marital customs in India, and other matters that might remind readers that the world outside their borders was filled with ordinary people like themselves engaged in mundane activities and was not simply a hotbed of violence and danger.

The *Times* and other international newspapers devote enormous attention to the United States because America's economic and military power mean that American actions are likely to have important consequences throughout the world. In their news pages and editorial commentary, newspapers in Europe, Asia, Africa, Latin America, and the Middle East seek to dissect every nuance of American policy to understand its intentions and significance for their own nation. Often, this coverage is less than flattering, even when American policy appears to be successful. For example, one of France's most influential newspapers, *Le Monde*, saw the capture of Saddam Hussein as an act of revenge designed to allow America to present itself as "a righter of wrongs." Many newspapers depict the United States as an international bully intent on pursuing its own economic and political interests without much regard for the views and needs of others. The influential Jordanian daily *Al-Dustour* described American troops in Iraq as "a gang of murderers." Most European newspapers were sharply critical of the Bush administration's decision to go to war against Iraq without UN approval. Newspapers throughout the Middle East view America's "war on terrorism" as a war on Muslims. Is the United States a malevolent force or is the world simply envious of America's wealth and power?

FOR CRITICAL ANALYSIS

1. American news coverage of the abuse of Iraqi prisoners by U.S. soldiers shocked the world. Should the American media seek to present a more positive image of the United States to foreigners?

2. American newspapers offer more coverage of local events than of world affairs. What factors might help to explain the local focus of the American press?

[a]Michael Massing, "The Unseen War," *New York Review of Books*, May 29, 2003, p. 17.

[b]Ibid.

year preceding the 2004 national elections, the various contenders for the Democratic presidential nomination—Howard Dean, John Kerry, Joe Lieberman, Al Sharpton, Wesley Clark, John Edwards, Dennis Kucinich, Carol Moseley-Braun, and Dick Gephardt—sought to take advantage of the media's horse-race orientation. These Democrats traveled around the nation debating the major issues of the day. They hoped that the debates would enhance media coverage of the candidates precisely because they would trigger endless speculation about who was ahead and who was behind and who was gaining and who was losing political momentum. And indeed, for nearly a year, the news media followed the Democratic debaters around the country generally focusing less on the substance of the debates than on the tactics of the debators and how they might affect the outcome of the race.

Bill Clinton and George W. Bush made good use of appearances on entertainment programs. Clinton played his saxophone on the Arsenio Hall program and discussed his choice of underwear with a teenage interviewer on MTV (left). Bush (right) appeared on The Tonight Show, as did Arnold Schwarzenegger, who officially announced that he would run for governor of California on Jay Leno's show (top). Some politicians believe that entertainment and "soft interview" programs like Larry King Live give them excellent exposure without subjecting them to the sometimes difficult questions and commentary they face in press conferences and news and interview shows.

The media's power to influence people's evaluation of public figures is not absolute. Throughout the last decade, politicians implemented new techniques for communicating with the public and shaping their own images. For instance, Bill Clinton pioneered the use of town meetings and television entertainment programs as a means of communicating directly with voters in the 1992 election. During the 2000 presidential race between Bush and Gore, both candidates made use of town meetings, as well as talk shows and entertainment programs like *The Oprah Winfrey Show*, *The Tonight Show with Jay Leno*, and *Saturday Night Live*, to reach mass audiences. During a town meeting, talk show, or entertainment program, politicians are free to craft their own images without interference from journalists. Thus, it is not surprising that actor-turned-politician Arnold Schwarzenegger announced his candidacy in California's 2003 gubernatorial recall election on *The Tonight Show with Jay Leno* rather than in a more formal setting.

In 2000, George W. Bush was also able to shape his image by effectively courting the press through informal conversation and interaction. Bush's "charm offensive" was successful. Journalists concluded that Bush was a nice fellow, albeit inexperienced, and refrained from subjecting him to harsh criticism and close scrutiny. Al Gore, on the other hand, seemed to offend journalists by remaining aloof and giving an impression of disdain for the press. Journalists responded by portraying Gore as "stiff." The result was unusually positive coverage for the Republican candidate and unusually negative coverage for the Democratic candidate. In 2004, John Kerry struggled to portray himself as a "regular guy" despite his wealth and what is perceived as his "patrician" manner.

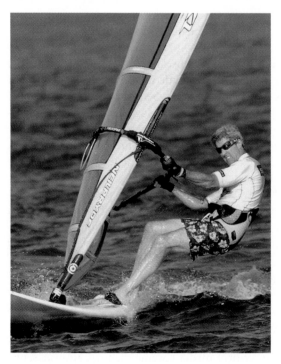

In spite of political candidates' efforts to define their public image, it's the media that typically determines how candidates are viewed by the public. During the 2004 campaign, John Kerry consistently tried to portray himself as a "regular guy," but the media frequently circumvented these efforts. For example, during the Republican National Convention, the media mercilessly mocked Kerry for windsurfing instead of responding to President Bush's attacks on him or campaigning. Images of Kerry windsurfing played into the negative stereotype his opponents tried to play up—that of the out-of-touch, elitist Massachusetts liberal.

THE RISE OF ADVERSARIAL JOURNALISM

The political power of the news media vis-à-vis the government has greatly increased in recent years through the growing prominence of "adversarial journalism"—a form of reporting in which the media adopt a hostile posture toward the government and public officials.

During the nineteenth century, American newspapers were completely subordinate to the political parties. Newspapers depended upon official patronage—legal notice and party subsidies—for their financial survival and were controlled by party leaders. (A vestige of that era survived into the twentieth century in such newspaper names as the *Springfield Republican* and the *St. Louis Globe-Democrat*.) At the turn of the century, with the development of commercial advertising, newspapers became financially independent. This made possible the emergence of a formally nonpartisan press.

Presidents were the first national officials to see the opportunities in this development. By communicating directly to the electorate through newspapers and magazines, Theodore Roosevelt and Woodrow Wilson established political constituencies for themselves, independent of party organizations, and strengthened their own power relative to Congress. President Franklin Roosevelt used the radio, most notably in his famous fireside chats, to reach out to voters throughout the nation and to make himself the center of American politics. FDR was also adept at developing close personal relationships with reporters that enabled him to obtain favorable news coverage despite the fact that in his day a majority of newspaper owners and publishers were staunch conservatives. Following Roosevelt's example, subsequent presidents have all sought to use the media to enhance their popularity and power. For example, through televised news conferences, President John F. Kennedy mobilized public support for his domestic and foreign policy initiatives.

During the 1950s and early 1960s, a few members of Congress also made successful use of the media—especially television—to mobilize national support for their causes. Senator Estes Kefauver of Tennessee became a major contender for the presidency and won a place on the 1956 Democratic national ticket as a result of his dramatic televised hearings on organized crime. Senator Joseph McCarthy of Wisconsin made himself a powerful national figure through his well-publicized investigations of alleged communist infiltration of key American institutions. These senators, however, were more exceptional than typical. Through the mid-1960s, the executive branch continued to generate the bulk of news coverage, and the media served as a cornerstone of presidential power.

The Vietnam War shattered this relationship between the press and the presidency. During the early stages of U.S. involvement, American officials in Vietnam who disapproved of the way the war was being conducted leaked information critical of administrative policy to reporters. Publication of this material infuriated the White House, which pressured publishers to block its release—on one occasion, President Kennedy went so far as to ask the *New York Times* to reassign its Saigon correspondent. However, the national print and broadcast media—the network news divisions, the national newsweeklies, the *Washington Post*, and the *New York Times*—discovered that there was an audience for critical coverage and investigative reporting among segments of the public skeptical of administration policy. As the Vietnam conflict dragged on, critical media coverage fanned antiwar sentiment. Moreover, growing opposition to the war among liberals encouraged some members of Congress, most notably Senator J. William Fulbright, chair of the Senate Foreign Relations Committee, to break with the president. In turn, these shifts in popular and congressional sentiment emboldened journalists and publishers to continue to present critical news reports. Through this process, journalists developed a commitment to adversarial journalism, while a constituency emerged that would rally to the defense of the media when it came under White House attack.

This pattern, established during the Vietnam War, endured through the 1970s and into the 1980s. Political forces opposed to presidential policies, many members of Congress, and the national news media began to find that their interests often overlapped. Opponents of the Nixon, Carter, Reagan, and Bush administrations welcomed news accounts critical of the conduct of executive agencies and officials in foreign affairs and in such domestic areas as race relations, the environment, and regulatory policy. In addition, many senators and representatives found it politically advantageous to champion causes favored by the antiwar, consumer, or environmental movements because, by conducting televised hearings on such issues, they were able to mobilize national constituencies, to become national figures, and in a number of instances to become serious contenders for their party's presidential nomination.

For their part, aggressive use of the techniques of investigation, publicity, and exposure allowed the national media to enhance their autonomy and carve out a prominent place for themselves in American government and politics. The power derived by the press from adversarial journalism is one of the reasons that the media seem to relish opportunities to attack political institutions and to publish damaging information about important public officials. Increasingly, media coverage has come to influence politicians' careers, the mobilization of political constituencies, and the fate of issues and causes.

Adversarial, or "attack," journalism has become commonplace in America, and some critics have suggested that the media have contributed to popular cynicism and the low levels of citizen participation that characterize contemporary American political processes. But before we begin to think about means of compelling the media to adopt a more positive view of politicians and political issues, we should consider the possibility that media criticism is one of the major mechanisms of political accountability in the American political process. Without aggressive media coverage would we have known of Bill Clinton's misdeeds or, for that matter, those of Richard Nixon? Without aggressive media coverage would important questions be raised about the conduct of American foreign and domestic policy? It is easy to criticize the media for their aggressive tactics, but would our democracy function effectively without the critical role of the press? A vigorous and critical media are needed as the "watchdogs" of American politics. Of course, in October 2001, the adversarial relationship between the government and the media was at least temporarily transformed into a much more supportive association as the media helped rally the American people for the fight against terrorism.

The adversarial relationship between the government and segments of the press, however, resumed in the wake of the 2003 Iraq war. Such newspapers as the *Washington Post* and the *New York Times* castigated President Bush for going to war without the support of some of America's major allies. When American forces failed to uncover evidence that Iraq possessed weapons of mass destruction—a

FOR CRITICAL ANALYSIS

In wartime, can media criticism of government action actually aid the nation's enemies? Should there be limits on media criticism of the government during time of war? Or does criticism actually enhance the nation's strength?

major reason cited by the administration for launching the war—these newspapers intimated that the war had been based on intelligence failures, if not outright presidential deceptions. The president, as noted earlier, denounced the media for distorting his record. Thus, after a brief interlude of post–September 11 harmony, the customary hostilities between the government and the press manifested themselves once again.

Thinking Critically about Media Power and Democracy

The free media are an institution absolutely essential to democratic government. Ordinary citizens depend upon the media to investigate wrongdoing, to publicize and explain governmental actions, to evaluate programs and politicians, and to bring to light matters that might otherwise be known to only a handful of governmental insiders. In short, without free and active media, popular government would be virtually impossible. Citizens would have few means through which to know or assess the government's actions—other than the claims or pronouncements of the government itself. Moreover, without active—indeed, aggressive—media, citizens would be hard-pressed to make informed choices among competing candidates at the polls. Often enough, the media reveal discrepancies between candidates' claims and their actual records, and between the images that candidates seek to project and the underlying realities. Of course, by continually emphasizing deceptions and wrongdoing on the part of political figures, the media encourage the public to become cynical and distrustful, not only of the people in office, but of the government and the political process themselves. A widespread sense that all politics is corrupt or deceptive can easily lead to a sense that nothing can be done. In this way, the media's adversarial posture may contribute to the low levels of political participation seen in America today.

At the same time, the declining power of party organizations (as we will see in Chapter 9) has made politicians ever more dependent upon favorable media coverage. National political leaders and journalists have had symbiotic relationships, at least since FDR's presidency, but initially politicians were the senior partners. They benefited from media publicity, but they were not totally dependent upon it as long as they could still rely upon party organizations to mobilize votes. Journalists, on the other hand, depended upon their relationships with politicians for access to information and would hesitate to report stories that might antagonize valuable sources for fear of being excluded from the flow of information in retaliation. Thus, for example, reporters did not publicize potentially embarrassing information, widely known in Washington, about the personal lives of such figures as Franklin Roosevelt and John F. Kennedy.

With the decline of party organizations, the balance of power between politicians and journalists has been reversed. Now that politicians have become heavily dependent upon the media to reach their constituents, journalists have less fear that their access to information can be restricted in retaliation for negative coverage.

Such freedom gives the media enormous power. The media can make or break reputations, help to launch or to destroy political careers, and build support for or rally opposition to programs and institutions.[22] Wherever there is so much power, there exists at least the potential for its abuse or overly zealous use. All things considered, free media are so critically important to the maintenance of a democratic

FOR CRITICAL ANALYSIS

If the public receives most of its information about politics from the media, how accurate is its knowledge of government and politics? How does the media itself distort political reality? How do politicians use the media for their own purposes? What are the consequences for American democracy when the electorate is informed through such a filter? How might the quality of political information in America be improved?

society that Americans must be prepared to take the risk that the media will occasionally abuse their power. The forms of governmental control that would prevent the media from misusing their power would also certainly destroy freedom. The ultimate beneficiaries of a free and active media are the American people.

What You Can Do: Analyze News Sources

In their relationship to the media, most Americans adopt a passive stance. They read, they watch, or they listen to media accounts of events. However, it is relatively easy to become an active rather than a passive media user. One way to become an active media user is through letter-writing. Every newspaper and newsmagazine, and some television programs as well, provides a forum for citizen commentary. Letter writers have an opportunity to object to editorials with which they disagree, correct errors in news coverage, and even respond to other letter writers.

On one particular day, for example, the *New York Times* published eleven letters from readers. Several objected to the paper's editorial views, two asserted that news stories published in the paper had misrepresented important facts, and others commented on issues discussed in the paper. On the same day, the *Washington Post* published three long letters objecting to facts alleged in prior *Post* stories on German politics and on global warming. Obviously, a few letters cannot completely counterbalance all the errors or biases that may affect a newspaper's coverage. But if a newspaper or magazine were truly biased, it probably would not publish letters pointing out its biases.

Most newspapers and magazines feel some obligation to publish letters critical of their published materials. Even more important, letters can make editors aware of significant errors and omissions in the paper's coverage, perhaps leading them to admonish or reassign the journalists responsible. Letters to the editor can even compel college newspapers to correct errors in news coverage. In November 1997, for example, the University of Buffalo's student newspaper published an apology and retraction after letter writers pointed out significant errors in a news story.[23] As commercial enterprises, the media are very eager to maintain a high level of customer satisfaction.

Citizens must also learn to be critical consumers of the media. It is very important to be alert to the possible biases or hidden messages in any news story. First, when watching the news or reading a story, be alert to the author or reporter's implicit assumptions. For example, the media tend to be naive about the motives of any group claiming to work on behalf of the "public interest" or "citizens" and to take the claims of such groups at face value, especially if the group is criticizing business or the government. You should think carefully about the claims and facts being presented. Second, watch for stereotypes. Many newspapers and radio and television stations make an effort to avoid the racial and gender stereotypes that were once common. However, many other stereotypes are prevalent in the news. For example, some government programs such as the space program enjoy "good press" and generally receive positive coverage despite the often dubious claims made by their backers. Other programs, such as public-assistance programs and the highway program, are treated as "wasteful" or "pork-barrel projects," despite the good they may do. Critical consumers need to make up their own minds rather than allow media stereotypes to color their judgment.

INTERACTIVE
POLITICS

YOU ARE...
a newspaper reporter!

The media provide the lens through which citizens view political events. Newspapers, television, and the Internet vie to be the most favored source of news and analysis for the people. Americans often base their opinions on the media they trust. Unfortunately, while still providing the vital watchdog role, the media are also businesses that must compete with one another for our attention. This competition can lead to sensationalistic reporting.

In this simulation, you are cast in the role of editor in chief of a significant daily newspaper. Your task is to make decisions about the stories on your front page while answering to your readers and your publisher.

Go to www.wwnorton.com/wtp5e

Questions to consider as you conduct the online simulation:

Do you tend to seek the news source that is the most balanced or the most entertaining? How does your favorite news source compare to C-SPAN, with its gavel-to-gavel coverage of political events?

How do editors decide what is the most important news for the day?

Which forces manipulate the media more often: policy elites or persuasive personalities?

Where should the line be drawn between hard news and "infotainment"?

Third, take note of news sources. Very often, reporters rely upon the views of a small number of top officials or influential figures who make it their business to cultivate journalists. When Henry Kissinger was secretary of state, he was such a successful manipulator of the media that most news about American foreign policy reflected his views. Often, politicians and interest groups retain public relations firms to contact journalists and disseminate their views. Always ask yourself whose interests might be served by a particular story. Often, those interests turn out to be the source of the story.

Finally, it is important to rely upon more than one source of news. The best approach is to make use of news sources with disparate ideological perspectives. For example, residents of Washington, D.C., sometimes read both the liberal *Washington Post* and the conservative *Washington Times.* Anyone can subscribe to both a liberal magazine, such as *The Public Interest,* and a conservative one, such as the *Weekly Standard,* that often cover the same topics. The importance of using such disparate news sources is to obtain different perspectives on the same events. This, in turn, will help you see more than one possibility and, ultimately, to make up your own mind.[24]

Summary

The American news media are among the world's most free. The print and broadcast media regularly present information and opinions critical of the government, political leaders, and policies.

The media help to determine the agenda or focus of political debate in the United States, to shape popular understanding of political events and results, and to influence popular judgments of politicians and leaders.

Over the past century, the media have helped to nationalize American political perspectives. Media coverage is influenced by the perspectives of journalists, the activities of news subjects, and, most important, by the media's need to appeal to upscale audiences. The attention that the media give to conflict is also a function of audience factors.

Free media are an essential ingredient of popular government.

For Further Reading

Ansolabehere, Stephen, and Shanto Iyengar. *Going Negative: How Attack Ads Shrink and Polarize the Electorate.* New York: Free Press, 1995.

Bagdikian, Ben. *The Media Monopoly.* 5th ed. Boston: Beacon, 1997.

Cook, Timothy. *Governing with the News: The News Media as a Political Institution.* Chicago: University of Chicago Press, 1997.

Davis, Richard, and Diana Owen. *New Media and American Politics.* New York: Oxford University Press, 1998.

Graber, Doris, et al. *The Politics of News, The News of Politics.* Washington, DC: Congressional Quarterly Press, 1998.

Hallin, Daniel C. *The Uncensored War.* Berkeley and Los Angeles: University of California Press, 1986.

Hart, Roderick. *Seducing America: How Television Charms the Modern Voter.* New York: Oxford University Press, 1994.

Hess, Stephen. *Live from Capitol Hill: Studies of Congress and the Media.* Washington, DC: Brookings, 1991.

Kurtz, Howard. *Spin Cycle: Inside the Clinton Propaganda Machine.* New York: Free Press, 1998.

Sparrow, Bartholomew H. *Uncertain Guardians: The News Media as a Political Institution.* Baltimore, MD: Johns Hopkins University Press, 1998.

West, Darrell. *Air Wars: Television Advertising in Election Campaigns, 1952–1992.* Washington, DC: Congressional Quarterly Press, 1993.

Study Outline

www.wwnorton.com/wtp5e   Keyword: Review 7

The Media Industry and Government

1. Americans obtain their news from radio, television, newspapers, magazines, and the Internet. Even though television news reaches more Americans than any other single news source, the print media are still important because they often set the agenda for the broadcast media and because they reach a more influential audience.

2. Since the passage of the Telecommunications Act of 1996, a wave of mergers and consolidations in the media industry has reduced the number of independent media in the United States.

3. The nationalization of the American news media, through which a relatively uniform picture of events, issues, and problems is presented to the entire nation, has contributed greatly to the nationalization of politics and of political perspectives in the United States.

4. Despite the widespread nationalization of news in America, news enclaves exist in which some demographic and ideological groups receive alternative news coverage.

5. Part of the Telecommunications Act of 1996, known as the Communications Decency Act, attempted to regulate the content of material transmitted over the Internet, but the law was overruled by the Supreme Court in the 1997 case *Reno v. American Civil Liberties Union.*

6. Under federal regulations, broadcasters must provide candidates seeking the same political office equal time to communicate their messages to the public.

7. Regulations also require that individuals be granted the right to rebut personal attacks.

8. Although recently diminished in importance, the fairness doctrine for many years required that broadcasters who aired programs on controversial issues provide time for opposing views.

News Coverage

1. Media content and news coverage are inevitably affected by the views, ideals, and interests of the journalists who seek out, write, and produce news stories.

2. News coverage is also influenced by the individuals or groups who are subjects of the news or whose interests and activities are actual or potential news topics.

3. Because the print and broadcast media are businesses that generally seek to show a profit, they must cater to the preferences of consumers.

4. The print and broadcast media, as well as the publishing industry, are particularly responsive to the interests and views of the upscale segments of their audiences.

5. Protest is one way that groups who cannot afford the services of media consultants and "issues managers" can publicize their views and interests.

Media Power in American Politics

1. In recent political history, the media have played a central role in the civil rights movement, the ending of American involvement in the Vietnam War, and in the Watergate investigation.

2. The power of the media stems from several sources, all of which contribute to the media's great influence in setting the political agenda, shaping electoral outcomes, and interpreting events and political results.

3. The political power of the news media has greatly increased in recent years through the growing prominence of investigative reporting.

Thinking Critically about Media Power and Democracy

1. Because the media provide the information citizens need for meaningful participation in the political process, they are essential to democratic government.

2. The decline of political parties has given the media enormous power, which creates a great potential for abuse.

Practice Quiz

www.wwnorton.com/wtp5e   Keyword: Quiz 7

1. The nationalization of the news has been influenced by which of the following trends in ownership of the media?
   a) the purchase of influential newspapers by foreign corporations
   b) the fragmentation of ownership of all media in the United States
   c) the wave of mergers and consolidations following the passage of the 1996 Telecommunications Act
   d) the purchase of the major news networks by the national government

2. Which of the following best describes national news in the United States?
   a) fragmented and localized
   b) nationalized and centralized
   c) centralized but still localized
   d) none of the above

3. Which of the following Supreme Court cases overruled the government's attempt to regulate the content of the Internet?
   a) *Near v. Minnesota*
   b) *New York Times v. United States*
   c) *Red Lion Broadcasting Company v. FCC*
   d) *Reno v. American Civil Liberties Union*

4. How do journalists compare to the general public in their political attitudes?
   a) Journalists are more conservative than the general public.
   b) The two groups' views are about the same.
   c) Journalists are more liberal than the general public.
   d) Journalists tend to be more Republican than the general public.

5. Which of the following have an impact on the nature of media coverage of politics?
   a) reporters
   b) political actors
   c) news consumers
   d) all of the above

6. Which of the following is a strategy available to poor people to increase their coverage by the news media?
   a) protest
   b) media consultants
   c) television advertising
   d) newspaper advertising "time sharing"

7. The media's powers to determine what becomes a part of the political discussion and to shape how political events are interpreted by the American people are known as
   a) issue definition and protest power.
   b) agenda setting and framing.
   c) the illusion of saliency and the bandwagon effect.
   d) the equal time rule and the right of rebuttal.

8. Which of the following can be considered an example of a news enclave?
   a) Internet chat rooms
   b) letters to the editor
   c) readers of *The New York Times*
   d) people who watch CNN

9. Which of the following exemplifies the liberal bias in the news media?
   a) talk radio programs
   b) the *Wall Street Journal*
   c) the *American Spectator*
   d) none of the above

10. The newspaper publisher William Randolph Hearst was responsible for encouraging U.S. involvement in which war?
    a) the Spanish-American War
    b) the Vietnam War
    c) the U.S. war with Mexico
    d) the Gulf War

Key Terms

www.wwnorton.com/wtp5e
Keyword: Vocabulary 7

agenda setting (p. 273)
equal time rule (p. 259)
fairness doctrine (p. 259)

framing (p. 274)
news enclave (p. 265)
priming (p. 276)

right of rebuttal (p. 259)
sound bites (p. 269)

8 POLITICAL PARTICIPATION AND VOTING

★ **Political Participation**
  In what different ways do Americans participate in politics? Why is voting
  the most important form of political participation?

★ **Who Participates, and How?**
  What is the history of suffrage in the United States?

★ **Explaining Political Participation**
  What explains levels of participation? Why has participation declined
  over time?

★ **Thinking Critically about Political Participation and
  Liberty, Equality, and Democracy**
  What roles do political institutions play in promoting participation and
  fulfilling American political values? Have attempts to increase
  participation succeeded? Why or why not? What are the implications
  for democracy?

What Government Does and Why It Matters

T O A CONSIDERABLE EXTENT, citizen participation in political life is a function of the government's policies, through which a government can make it easier or harder for citizens to participate. The most obvious example is the institution of the democratic election. When they introduce elections and grant citizens the right to vote, or *suffrage,* governments facilitate participation in politics. As we shall see, however, institutional factors such as voter registration rules strongly affect participation. Holding elections on weekends, as is the custom in much of Europe, promotes participation. Political institutions can also promote participation by mobilizing citizens to vote. The most effective forms of mobilization involve face-to-face interactions. In recent decades, American political institutions moved away from such direct mobilization toward political advertising aimed at those already likely to participate. However, in 2004, with the country so evenly divided politically, parties and other political organizations launched major direct mobilization campaigns in nearly twenty battleground states. Thus, the policies of the government and the practices of political institutions such as parties play a very important role in determining the extent and effectiveness of what is, at first glance, a voluntary activity. If we want more Americans to participate effectively in politics, we should endeavor to develop policies that foster, rather than discourage, participation. ∎

■ In this chapter, we will examine the role of citizen participation in American politics. We will first examine patterns of contemporary political participation, discussing the different forms that participation can take.

■ We then review the kinds of access to the political system that groups of different social backgrounds and cultural beliefs fought for and subsequently enjoyed. We will see that such identities do not always provide the basis for shared political activity.

■ We will then consider the reasons for declining participation in recent decades. We will see that individual beliefs, such as a sense of efficacy, are important, but that most significant is the failure of our institutions to mobilize people into politics.

■ Previewing Liberty, Equality, and Democracy

For much of American history, formal barriers restricted the right to vote and created a pattern of unequal participation in politics. By the 1960s, the political struggles of women and members of racial minorities had succeeded in extending voting rights to all citizens. The extension of the franchise to those eighteen and older in 1971 underscored the importance of political participation to our democratic values. Although most formal barriers to participation have been eliminated, voter participation has declined since the 1960s. Reduced participation has created a pattern of inequality in which citizens with higher socioeconomic status participate more than citizens with lower socioeconomic status. One explanation for the decline in participation is American political institutions, which are geared toward raising money, not toward mobilizing the population to participate. Yet the right to contribute financially to political causes is defended as a basic liberty. The decline in participation is one of the major challenges facing American democracy. We conclude by analyzing the implications of this development.

Political Participation

political participation political activities, such as voting, contacting political officials, volunteering for a campaign, or participating in a protest, whose purpose is to influence government

Political participation makes the ideals of liberty and equality come alive. But by many measures, Americans are participating less and less. For example, in the 1996 presidential election only 49 percent of eligible voters cast ballots, the lowest percentage in a presidential election in more than seventy years. In 2000, voter turnout rose only slightly to 50.7 percent. Citizens can, however, participate in ways other than voting. In this section we will examine the different ways that Americans participate in politics. We will look for changes in rates and methods of participation over time and describe the differences in participation among groups. In the second half of the chapter, we will explore the causes for the patterns we observe. Two questions in particular will concern us: Why has participation declined? Why do people with higher levels of education and wealth participate most? Finally, we will consider the role that political institutions play in promoting participation.

FORMS OF PARTICIPATION

Today, voting has come to be seen as the normal or typical form of citizen political activity. Yet ordinary people took part in politics long before the advent of the election or any other formal mechanism of popular involvement in political life. If there is any natural or spontaneous form of popular political participation, it is the riot rather than the election. The urban riot and the rural uprising were common in both Europe and America prior to the nineteenth century and not entirely uncommon even in the twentieth century. Urban riots played an important role in American politics in the 1960s and 1970s. Even as recently as 1999, riots during the Seattle, Washington, meeting of the World Trade Organization helped labor unions and other opponents of trade liberalization to slow the pace of change in the rules governing world trade.

Most Americans would not consider taking part in a riot. Yet in recent years, fewer numbers of Americans are exercising their right to vote. Participation in presidential elections has dropped significantly over the past forty years. In 1960, 64 percent of eligible voters cast ballots; in 2000, only about half of the electorate turned out. In 2004, major efforts to get out the vote brought turnout to over 59 percent. This was the first significant increase in voting in recent years. Turnout for midterm elections is typically lower, for local elections, even lower.[1]

Fortunately, voting and rioting are not the only forms of participation available to Americans. Citizens can contact political officials, sign petitions, attend public meetings, join organizations, give money to a politician or a political organization, volunteer in a campaign, write a letter to the editor or write an article about an issue, or participate in a protest or rally. Such activities differ from voting because they can communicate much more detailed information to public officials than voting can. Voters may support a candidate for many reasons but their actual votes do not indicate specifically what they like and don't like, nor do they tell officials how intensely voters feel about issues. A vote can convey only a general sense of approval or disapproval. By writing a letter or engaging in other kinds of political participation, people can convey much more specific information, telling public officials exactly what issues they care most about and what their views on those issues are. For that reason these other political activities are often more satisfying than voting. And citizens who engage in these other activities are more likely to try to influence state and local politics rather than national politics; in voting, people find the national scene more interesting than state and local politics.[2]

Nonelectoral political activity takes many forms: some of the most prominent in recent years include *lobbying, public relations, litigation,* and *protest.*

Lobbying is an effort by groups or individuals to take their case directly to elected or appointed officials. By voting, citizens seek to determine who will govern. By lobbying, citizens attempt to determine what those in power will do. As we shall see in Chapter 11, many interest groups employ professional lobbyists to bring their views to lawmakers. At the same time, however, thousands of volunteers lobby Congress and the bureaucracy each year on behalf of citizen groups like the National Organization for Women (NOW), the Sierra Club, and the Home School Legal Defense Fund.[3] The hundreds of thousands of citizens who call or write members of Congress each year, seeking to influence their votes, are also engaged in lobbying.

lobbying a strategy by which organized interests seek to influence the passage of legislation by exerting direct pressure on members of the legislature

public relations an attempt, usually through the use of paid consultants, to establish a favorable relationship with the public and influence its political opinions

Public relations is an effort to sway public opinion on behalf of an issue or cause. Corporations and interest groups typically employ professional public relations firms to produce print, radio, and television advertising in support of their goals. At times, corporations use public relations strategies to influence specific pieces of legislation. For example, in 2002, the auto industry sponsored an advertising campaign against a bill that would have raised fuel economy standards for the first time since the 1980s. The ads claimed that stricter standards for fuel economy would lead to the extinction of S.U.V.s and pickup trucks. In other instances, corporations launch public relations efforts to create goodwill in the public and fend off possible future regulations. Oil companies routinely air television commercials and print advertisements that affirm their support for a clean environment. At the same time, public relations tactics are also used by numerous citizen groups to promote issues and causes dear to them.

In 2003, the American Association of Retired Persons (AARP), the main lobbying group for the elderly, launched a series of influential radio, television, and newspaper advertisements endorsing a controversial major reform of Medicare, the federal program that provides health care for the elderly. As is increasingly common, the group's executive director had a career in public relations before taking charge at the AARP.

A favorite tactic of citizen groups is the press release designed to shape news coverage. In 1999, for example, citizen groups favoring affirmative action released data purporting to show that affirmative action programs were successful. Groups opposing affirmative action released data purporting to show the opposite. The same pattern was manifest in debates about gun control, capital punishment, policy toward the homeless, and the use of school vouchers. In each of these issue areas citizen groups conducted political warfare through public relations.

litigation a lawsuit or legal proceeding; as a form of political participation, an attempt to seek relief in a court of law

Litigation is an attempt to use the courts to achieve a goal. In recent years, the federal courts have been used more and more frequently by citizen groups and even individuals to affect public policy. Using the so-called citizen-suit provisions of a number of federal statutes, citizen groups play an active role in shaping policy in such areas as air and water quality, preservation of endangered species, civil rights, and the rights of persons with disabilities. Use of the courts by citizen groups is encouraged by federal and state fee-shifting provisions that allow plaintiffs (those bringing a case in court) to recover legal fees from the government or defendant, as well as by class-action rules that allow an individual to bring suit on behalf of large groups. We will learn more about this form of participation in Chapter 15.

protest participation that involves assembling crowds to confront a government or other official organization

Though most Americans reject violent **protest** or terrorism for political ends, peaceful protest is generally recognized as a legitimate and important form of political activity and is protected by the First Amendment. During the 1960s and 1970s, hundreds of thousands of Americans took part in peaceful protests that helped bring an end to legalized racial segregation. In recent years, peaceful marches and demonstrations have been employed by a host of groups ranging from opponents of the war in Iraq to antiabortion activists. Protest is widely valued as a strategy that is available to all groups. In 2003, when the federal government used an obscure law to charge the environmental group Greenpeace with conspiracy in connection with a protest, groups across the political spectrum expressed fear that the federal government was seeking to limit the right to protest. While protests can occur anywhere, favorite spots for demonstrations include the

Political Participation: How Much? About What?

Figure 8.1

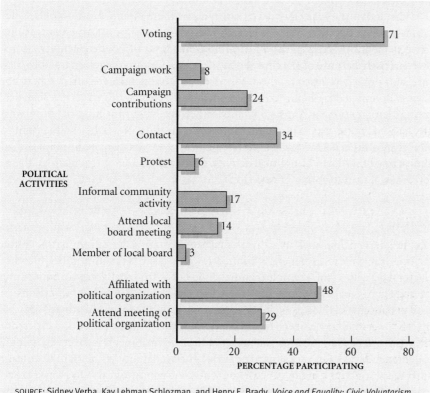

SOURCE: Sidney Verba, Kay Lehman Schlozman, and Henry E. Brady, *Voice and Equality: Civic Voluntarism in American Politics* (Cambridge, MA: Harvard University Press, 1995), p. 51.

park in front of the White House and the members' parking lot in front of the Capitol. These two areas have been the sites of demonstrations by large groups of Native Americans, by proponents and opponents of abortion rights, by veterans' groups, and by the handicapped. Occasionally, protests by unpopular groups lead to counterprotests by others. For example, in 1999, planned rallies in New York and Washington by a handful of Ku Klux Klan members led to counterdemonstrations by tens of thousands of people protesting the Klan's presence in their city. Thousands of police officers were mobilized to protect the Klan members and to safeguard their First Amendment rights.

Alternative forms of political action generally require more time, effort, or money than voting does. It is not surprising, then, that far fewer people engage in these forms of political participation than vote. A recent study of participation, for example, found that about a third of those questioned said they had contacted a public official; almost a quarter reported that they had made a campaign contribution; and fewer than 10 percent said they had been active in a political campaign (see Figure 8.1). Nearly half, however, said they were involved in an organization that took positions on political issues.[4] In contrast to the sharp decline in voting, involvement in these other activities has not fallen off nearly so much and, by some measures, has actually increased. For example, Americans are more likely to contribute money to political organizations and campaigns than in the past, but they are less likely to belong to political organizations.[5]

Whether voting is as effective or satisfying as these other forms of political action is an open question. What is clear, however, is that for most Americans voting remains the most accessible and most important form of political activity. Moreover, precisely because of the time, energy, and money often required to lobby, litigate, and even demonstrate, these forms of political action are often, albeit not always, dominated by better educated and wealthier Americans. As we shall see, voting participation in America is also somewhat biased in favor of those with greater wealth and, especially, higher levels of education. Nevertheless, the right to vote gives ordinary Americans a more equal chance to participate in politics than almost any other form of political activity. In the remainder of this chapter, therefore, we will turn to voting in America.

VOTING

Despite the availability of an array of alternatives, in practice citizen participation in American politics is generally limited to voting and a small number of other electoral activities (for example, campaigning). It is true that voter turnout in the United States is relatively low. But when, for one reason or another, Americans do seek to participate, their participation generally takes the form of voting.

The preeminent position of voting in the American political process is not surprising. The American legal and political environment is overwhelmingly weighted in favor of electoral participation. The availability of the right to vote, or **suffrage,** is, of course, a question of law. And civic education, also to a large extent mandated by law, encourages citizens to believe that electoral participation is the appropriate way to express opinions and grievances. Although all American citizens over the age of eighteen now have the right to vote and most learn about the importance of the vote in school, electoral participation has declined in recent decades. What is most alarming about declining electoral participation is that the least well-off Americans are the least likely to vote and the most advantaged are the most likely to vote. Because this pattern of class bias in participation conflicts so strongly with the American ideal of equal political rights, it has raised considerable concern.

suffrage the right to vote; also called franchise

Voting Rights   In principle, states determine who is eligible to vote. During the nineteenth and early twentieth centuries, the right to vote was not distributed equally across the American population. Voter eligibility requirements often varied greatly from state to state. Some states openly abridged the right to vote on the basis of race; others did not. Some states imposed property restrictions on voting; others had no such restrictions. Most states mandated lengthy residency requirements, which meant that persons moving from one state to another sometimes lost their right to vote for as much as a year. In more recent years, however, constitutional amendments, federal statutes, and federal court decisions have limited states' discretion in the area of voting rights. Individual states may establish brief residency requirements, generally fifteen days, for record-keeping purposes. Beyond this, states have little or no power to regulate suffrage.

Today in the United States, all native-born or naturalized citizens over the age of eighteen, with the exception of convicted felons in most states, have the right to vote. During the colonial and early national periods of American history, the right to vote was generally restricted to white males over the age of twenty-one. Many states also limited voting to those who owned property or paid more than a specified amount of annual tax. Property and tax requirements began to be rescinded during the 1820s, however, and had generally disappeared by the end of the Civil War.

By the time of the Civil War, blacks had won the right to vote in most northern states. In the South, black voting rights were established by the Fifteenth Amendment, ratified in 1870, which prohibited denial of the right to vote on the basis of race. Despite the Fifteenth Amendment, the voting rights of African Americans were effectively rescinded during the 1880s by the states of the former Confederacy. During this period, the southern states created what was called the "Jim Crow" system of racial segregation. As part of this system, a variety of devices, such as **poll taxes** and literacy tests, were used to prevent virtually all blacks from voting. During the 1950s and 1960s, through the civil rights movement led by Dr. Martin Luther King, Jr., and others, African Americans demanded the restoration of their voting rights. Their goal was accomplished through the enactment of the 1965 Voting Rights Act, which provided for the federal government to register voters in states that discriminated against minority citizens. The result was the reenfranchisement of southern blacks for the first time since the 1860s.

poll tax a state-imposed tax upon voters as a prerequisite for registration. Poll taxes were rendered unconstitutional in national elections by the Twenty-fourth Amendment, and in state elections by the Supreme Court in 1966

Women won the right to vote in 1920, with the adoption of the Nineteenth Amendment. This amendment resulted primarily from the activities of the women's suffrage movement, led by Elizabeth Cady Stanton, Susan B. Anthony, and Carrie Chapman Catt during the late nineteenth and early twentieth centuries. The "suffragettes," as they were called, held rallies, demonstrations, and protest marches for more than half a century before achieving their goal. The cause of women's suffrage was ultimately advanced by World War I. President Woodrow Wilson and members of Congress were convinced that women would be more likely to support the war effort if they were granted the right to vote. For this same reason, women were given the right to vote in Great Britain and Canada during World War I.

The most recent expansion of the right to vote in the United States took place in 1971, during the Vietnam War, when the Twenty-sixth Amendment was ratified, lowering the voting age from twenty-one to eighteen. Unlike black suffrage and women's suffrage, which came about in part because of the demands of groups that had been deprived of the right to vote, the Twenty-sixth Amendment was not a response to the demands of young people to be given the right to vote. Instead, many policy makers hoped that the right to vote would channel the disruptive protest activities of students involved in the anti–Vietnam War movement into peaceful participation at the ballot box.

FOR CRITICAL ANALYSIS

Describe the expansion of suffrage in the United States since the Founding. Why might the government have denied participation to so many for so long? What forces influenced the expansion of voting rights?

Voting and Civic Education   Laws, of course, cannot completely explain why most people vote rather than riot or lobby. If public attitudes were completely unfavorable to elections, it is doubtful that legal remedies alone would have much impact.

Positive public attitudes about voting do not come into being in a completely spontaneous manner. Americans are taught to equate citizenship with electoral participation. Civic training, designed to give students an appreciation for the American system of government, is a legally required part of the curriculum in

More Americans tend to vote in presidential election years than in years when only congressional and local elections are held.

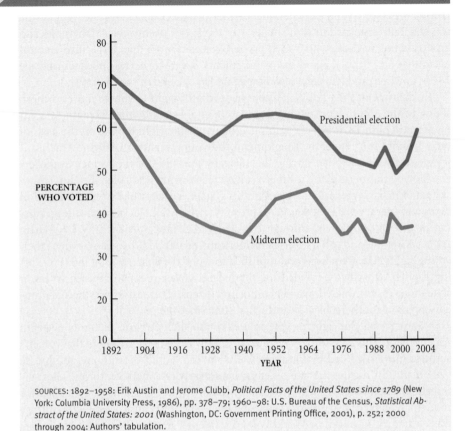

SOURCES: 1892–1958: Erik Austin and Jerome Clubb, *Political Facts of the United States since 1789* (New York: Columbia University Press, 1986), pp. 378–79; 1960–98: U.S. Bureau of the Census, *Statistical Abstract of the United States: 2001* (Washington, DC: Government Printing Office, 2001), p. 252; 2000 through 2004: Authors' tabulation.

every elementary and secondary school. Although it is not as often required by law, civic education usually manages to find its way into college curricula as well.

Voter Participation   Although the United States has developed a system of civic education and a legal basis for nearly universal suffrage, America's rate of voter participation, or **turnout,** is very low. About 50 percent of those eligible participate in national presidential elections, while barely one-third of eligible voters take part in midterm congressional elections (see Figure 8.2). Turnout in state and local races that do not coincide with national contests is typically even lower. In most European countries and other Western democracies, by contrast, national voter turnout is usually between 70 and 90 percent[6] (see Figure 8.3).

Figure 8.4 shows the marked differences in voter turnout linked to ethnic group, education level, employment status, and age. This trend has created a political process whose class bias is so obvious and egregious that, if it continues, Americans may have to begin adding a qualifier when they describe their politics as democratic. Perhaps the terms "semidemocratic," "quasidemocratic," or "neodemocratic" are in order to describe a political process in which ordinary voters have as little influence as they do in contemporary America.

turnout the percentage of eligible individuals who actually vote

Voter Turnout in Comparative Perspective 1991–2000*

Figure 8.3

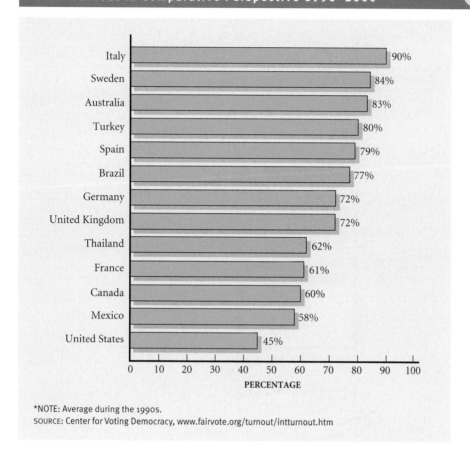

*NOTE: Average during the 1990s.

SOURCE: Center for Voting Democracy, www.fairvote.org/turnout/intturnout.htm

Who Participates, and How?

The original **American political community** consisted of a rather limited group of white male property holders. Over the ensuing two centuries, "we the people" became a larger and more inclusive body as a result of such forces as the abolitionist movement, the women's suffrage movement, and the civil rights movement (see Chapter 5). This expansion of the political community was marked by enormous conflicts involving questions of race, gender, religious identity, and age. Today, these conflicts continue in the form of struggles over such issues as affirmative action, welfare reform, abortion, the gender gap, the political mobilization of religious groups, and the rise and fall of minority voting districts; the ongoing participation of groups with distinctive social and cultural identities has transformed politics, altering political coalitions and changing political debates. This section examines the experiences of different kinds of cultural and social groups in American politics: racial and ethnic, gender, religious, and age-based groups. It asks to what extent members of these particular groups have recognized common interests and have sought to act politically on those interests.

American political community
citizens who are eligible to vote and participate in American political life

Figure 8.4 The Percentage of Americans Who Voted, 1976–2000

Whether or not Americans are likely to vote depends in part on their ethnic group, education level, employment status, and age.

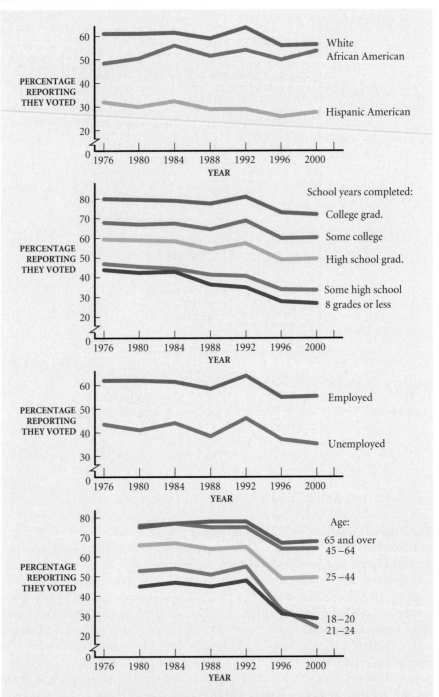

SOURCES: U.S. Bureau of the Census, *Statistical Abstract of the United States: 2001* (Washington, DC: Government Printing Office, 2001), p. 251; and www.census.gov/population/socdemo/voting/history/vot23.txt (accessed 7/11/02).

Participation and Democracy in Iraq

In contemporary American democracy, a high value is placed on active participation of the citizens in selecting their representatives. This was not always the case. Prior to the adoption of the Seventeenth Amendment to the Constitution in 1913, senators were appointed by state legislatures. This indirect form of democracy reflected the elite status of the Senate and the idea that the Senate should be more attuned to the interests of property than those of the population. Although the practice of broad popular participation in American elections is now taken for granted, when the United States promotes democracy in other countries, it does not always advocate direct participation in elections.

The question of how to organize democratic participation was one of the toughest problems faced by the American government after the 2003 war in Iraq. After the war, the United States announced that one of its major goals was to establish a popular democracy in Iraq to replace the dictatorship of Saddam Hussein. Yet establishing democracy was a difficult task in a country ruled since its creation by military leaders, monarchs, and dictators. Recognizing this difficulty, American officials advocated an indirect form of democracy at the outset.

At the local level, Americans supported the creation of governing councils, appointed by the U.S. military and the Research Triangle Institute, a U.S.-based research group advising the American government on how to establish democracy in Iraq. Local councils were the site of democracy training classes across the country, in which American trainers sought to convey the principles of divided government and self-rule to Iraqis. The councils were responsible for electing their own leadership, which was rotated in order to develop leadership skills in the population. The U.S. decision to rely on appointed councils reflected its belief that direct elections could lead to outcomes that the United States did not support, such as the exclusion of women or discrimination by religion. In addition, American occupation officials hoped that the council governments would help establish a pattern of local self-rule that would contribute to building a democratic culture.

The United States also proposed an indirect approach to participation in its initial proposals for selecting a new Iraqi national government. The plan called for the American-appointed National Governing Council and Iraqi local councils to choose a National assembly, which would establish an interim Iraqi government. This government would then write a new Iraqi constitution. Americans preferred this caucus style of participation to direct participation and majority rule for several reasons. Because Iraq is an ethnically divided country, direct majority rule could mean domination of government by one group, the Shiite Muslims, who had suffered under Saddam Hussein. Moreover, it was feared that the Shiite majority would support the establishment of an Islamic theocracy opposed to the United States.

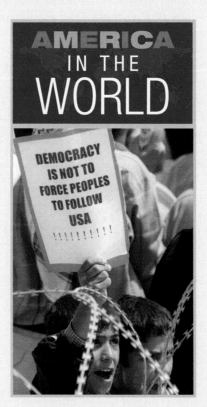

This American plan was challenged by leaders of the Shiites, who instead supported direct election of the new Iraqi government. As one of the most important Shiite clerics put it, "No one has the right to appoint the members of the constitutional assembly. We see no alternative but to go back to the people for choosing their representatives."[a]

The demands for direct elections posed a dilemma for American officials. Critics of the United States claimed that American reluctance to support popular elections demonstrated that the United States was not interested in promoting democracy in Iraq but only a government sympathetic to the United States. In answer, American officials claimed that indirect forms of participation were most likely to build a stable democracy that would endure long after the occupation forces departed.

FOR CRITICAL ANALYSIS

1. What are the barriers to establishing a democracy governed by direct elections in Iraq? Why is it so difficult to transplant American-style democracy to Iraq?

2. Why did Americans initially propose an indirect style of democracy in Iraq? Would indirect democracy ultimately promote the creation of a stable Iraqi democracy? Was the United States hypocritical in not supporting majority-rule elections, as some Iraqis charged?

[a]Alex Berenson, "The World: Iraq's Shiites Insist on Democracy," *New York Times*. November 30, 2003, Section 4, p. 5.

AFRICAN AMERICANS

As we saw in Chapter 5, political and legal pressure and protest all played a part in the modern civil rights movement, which took off in the 1950s. The movement drew on an organizational base and network of communication rooted in black churches, the NAACP, and black colleges.

The nonviolent protest tactics adopted by local clergy members, including Rev. Martin Luther King, Jr., eventually spread across the South and brought national attention to the movement. The clergy organized into a group called the Southern Christian Leadership Conference (SCLC). Students also played a key role. The most important student organization was the Student Nonviolent Coordinating Committee (SNCC). In 1960, four black students sat down at the lunch counter of the Greensboro, North Carolina, Woolworth's department store, which like most southern establishments did not serve African Americans. Their sit-in was the first of many. Through a combination of protest, legal action, and political pressure, the civil rights movement compelled a reluctant federal government to enforce black civil and political rights.

The victories of the civil rights movement made blacks full citizens and stimulated a tremendous growth in the number of black public officials at all levels of government, as blacks exercised their newfound political rights. Yet despite these successes, racial segregation remains a fact of life in the United States, and new problems have emerged. Most troubling is the persistence of black urban poverty, now coupled with deep social and economic isolation.[7] These conditions raise new questions about African American political participation. One question concerns black political cohesion: Will blacks continue to vote as a bloc, given the sharp economic differences that now divide a large black middle class from an equally large group of deeply impoverished African Americans? A second question concerns the benefits of participation: How can political participation improve the lives of African Americans, especially of the poor?

Public opinion and voting evidence indicate that African Americans continue to vote as a bloc despite their economic differences.[8] Surveys of black voters show that blacks across the income spectrum believe that their fates are linked because of their race. This sense of shared experience and a common fate has united blacks at the polls and in politics.[9] Since the 1960s, blacks have overwhelmingly chosen Democratic candidates and black candidates have sought election under the Democratic banner. Republican hostility to affirmative action and other programs of racial preference is likely to sharply check any large-scale black migration to the Republican Party.

At the same time, however, the black community and its political leadership has been considerably frustrated about the benefits of loyalty to the Democratic Party. Some analysts argue that the structure of party competition makes it difficult for African Americans to win policy benefits through political participation. Because Republicans have not sought to win the black vote and Democrats take it for granted, neither party is willing to support bold measures to address the mounting problems of poor African Americans.

LATINOS

For many years, analysts called the Latino vote "the sleeping giant" because as a group Latinos had relatively low levels of political mobilization. Two important

THE SHACKLE BROKEN — BY THE GENIUS OF FREEDOM.

During the nineteenth century, universal white manhood suffrage became the rule in America, but women and most African Americans were denied voting rights. After the Civil War, the Fifteenth Amendment to the Constitution appeared to guarantee black voting rights. Blacks were elected to many political offices during Reconstruction, including a majority of seats in the South Carolina House of Representatives (right). But with the end of Reconstruction in the 1870s, African Americans were effectively deprived of the right to vote in most southern states, first by violence and intimidation and then by institutional barriers such as literacy tests. It was not until the 1965 Voting Rights Act that millions of African Americans were enfranchised.

reasons for the low mobilization levels among Latinos were the low rates of voter registration and low rates of naturalization. Among those who were eligible to vote, registration and turnout rates were relatively low.

Today, Latinos are viewed as a political group of critical importance. Rapid population growth, increased political participation, and uncertain party attachment all magnify the importance of the Latino vote in the coming decade. The Latino population grew some 60 percent between 1990 and 2002, to an estimated 38.8 million. This makes Hispanics larger in numbers than African Americans. Moreover, since 1996, Latino voters have begun to register and vote in unprecedented numbers. In 2000, Hispanics accounted for 7 percent of the total national vote, and it is estimated they were 9 or 10 percent of the vote in 2004.[10] Latinos have traditionally voted heavily Democratic: Vice President Al Gore received two-thirds of the Hispanic vote in 2000. But Republicans also believe they can attract Hispanic voters because Democratic Hispanic voters tend to be more socially conservative than those of non-Hispanic Democrats. Many pollsters now see Latinos as a key "swing" vote that can tip elections toward either party. President Bush actively courted Hispanic voters and received 44 percent of their vote in 2004. At rallies and meetings involving Hispanic groups, the president routinely displayed his Spanish-speaking abilities. He also appointed Latinos to high-level cabinet positions and nominated conservative Hispanics for important judicial positions. Bush's proposal in early 2004 to provide legal status for undocumented workers was widely seen as an initiative that would draw more Latino support for the Republican Party. The power of the Latino vote means that politicians at all levels of government are now paying close attention to what Latinos want from government.

ASIAN AMERICANS

The diversity of national backgrounds among Asian Americans has impeded the development of group-based political power. No one national group dominates among the Asian American population. This diversity means that Asian Americans—or, to use the broader census-based category, Asian Pacific Islanders (commonly referred to as Asian Pacific Americans or APAs)—often have different political concerns stemming from their different national backgrounds and experiences in the United States. Historically, these groups have united most effectively around common issues of ethnic discrimination or anti-Asian violence in the United States. For example, discriminatory immigration policies or discrimination in access to federal mortgage policies provided a common focus in the past.

With the population of 10.6 million in 2000, APAs are too small a group to exercise significant influence in national politics. However, in particular states, such as California, where 40 percent of APAs live, this group has the potential to become an important political presence. Politically, APAs are a diverse group: a 2000–01 survey showed that 36 percent of APAs identified as Democrats and 14 percent as Republicans. However, 49 percent claimed no party attachment, either identifying as independents, stating that they were not sure which party they preferred, or indicating that they did not think in terms of party affiliation.[11] In recent years there have been efforts to mobilize a more united Asian American political presence. In 1997, controversy erupted over illegal donations to President Clinton's re-election campaign by a Chinese American named John Huang. Many Asian Americans felt that the attention to this matter unfairly cast suspicion on all Asian Americans who participated in political fund-raising. This experience prompted the formation of several organizations aiming to enhance the power of the Asian vote. In Los Angeles, a group called CAUSE—Vision 21 formed in order to register Asian American voters and to highlight the importance of their vote. In addition, an effort called the 80/20 initiative was formed to persuade Asian Americans to support the candidate who promises the most to Asian voters.

WOMEN VERSUS MEN

gender gap a distinctive pattern of voting behavior reflecting the differences in views between men and women

The ongoing significance of gender issues in American politics is best exemplified by the emergence of a **gender gap**—a distinctive pattern of male and female voting decisions—in electoral politics. Although proponents of women's suffrage had expected women to make a distinctive impact on politics as soon as they won the vote, not until the 1980s did voting patterns reveal a clear difference between male and female votes. In 1980, men voted heavily for Republican candidate Ronald Reagan; women divided their votes between Reagan and the incumbent Democratic president, Jimmy Carter. Since that election, gender differences have emerged in congressional and state elections, as well. Women tend to vote in higher numbers for Democratic candidates, while Republicans win more male votes. In the 2004 election, Bush narrowed the gender gap substantially, winning 48 percent of the female vote.[12] Behind these voting patterns are differing assessments of key policy issues. For one thing, more women than men take liberal positions on political issues; women are more likely than men to oppose military activities and support social spending. For example, 54 percent of women approved of the U.S. decision to send troops to Saudi Arabia in 1991, compared to 78 percent of men.

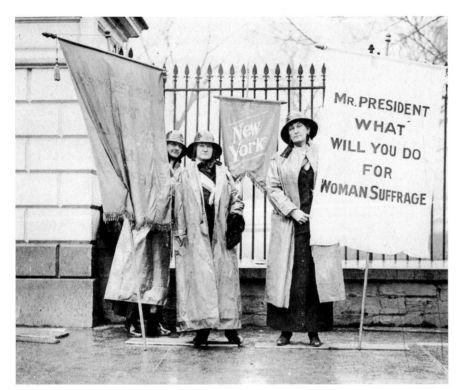

Women won the right to vote with the adoption of the Nineteenth Amendment in 1920. While suffragettes had been demanding enfranchisement for decades, it took World War I to bring women the right to vote, one reason being that many officials were convinced that women's suffrage would increase female support for the war effort.

The military campaign in Afghanistan was a rare exception to this pattern of gender differences: 85 percent of women and 89 percent of men expressed support for the war in Afghanistan.[13] The gender gap returned with the war in Iraq. During the war, 79 percent of men supported the war compared to 65 percent of women. This split continued during the occupation of Iraq, with 52 percent of men saying the war was worth it and only 44 percent of women saying it was worth it by November 2003.[14] On social spending, these trends reverse: 69 percent of women favor increased spending on Social Security, compared to 57 percent of men; 83 percent of women favor improving the nation's health care, compared to 76 percent of men; 72 percent of women advocate more spending on programs for the homeless, compared to 63 percent of men.[15] It is important to note that these differences do not mean that all women vote more liberally than all men. In fact, the voting differences between women who are homemakers and women who are in the workforce are almost as large as the differences between men and women. The sharpest differences are found between married men and single women, with single women tending to take the most liberal positions.[16]

Another key development in gender politics in recent years is the growing number of women in political office (see Figure 8.5). Journalists dubbed 1992 the "Year of the Woman" because so many women were elected to Congress: women doubled their numbers in the House and tripled them in the Senate. By 2002, women held 13.5 percent of the seats in the House of Representatives and 13 percent in the Senate; 22.6 percent of state legislators in 2002 were women.[17] Organizations supporting female candidates have worked to encourage more

Figure 8.5   Increase in Number of Women in Elective Office, 1975–2003

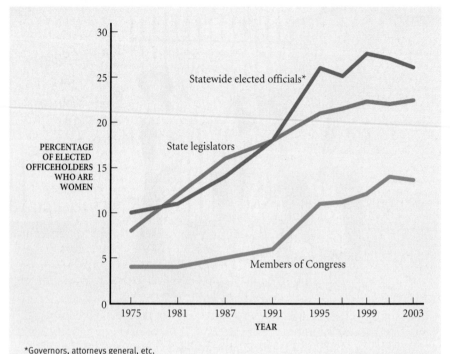

*Governors, attorneys general, etc.
SOURCE: Cynthia Costello, Shari Miles, and Anne J. Stone, eds., *The American Woman, 2001–2002* (New York: W. W. Norton, 2002), p. 328, and Center for American Women and Politics, "Women in Elective Office 2004," www.cawp.rutgers.edu/Facts/Officeholders/elective.pdf.

women to run for office and have supported them financially. In addition to the bipartisan NWPC, the Women's Campaign Fund and EMILY's List provide pro-choice Democratic women with early campaign financing, which is critical to establishing electoral momentum (the acronym of the latter group stands for Early Money Is Like Yeast). Recent research has shown that the key to increasing the numbers of women in political office is to encourage more women to run for election. Women are disadvantaged as candidates not because they are women but because male candidates are more likely to have the advantage of incumbency.[18] Although women in public office by no means take uniform positions on policy issues, surveys show that, on the whole, women legislators are more supportive of women's rights, health care spending, and children's and family issues.[19]

RELIGIOUS IDENTITY AND POLITICS

Religious identity plays an important role in American life. For some people, religious groups provide an organizational infrastructure for participating in politics around issues of special group concern. Black churches, for example, were instrumental in the civil rights movement, and black religious leaders continue to play important roles in national and local politics. Jews have also been active as a group in politics, but less through religious bodies than through a variety of social action agencies. Such agencies include the American Jewish Congress, the Anti-Defamation League, and the American Jewish Committee.

For most of American history, religious values have been woven deeply into the fabric of public life. Public school students began the day with prayers or Bible reading; city halls displayed crèches during the Christmas season. Practices that were religiously proscribed—most notably abortion—were also forbidden under law. But over the past thirty-five years, a variety of court decisions greatly reduced this kind of religious influence on public life. In 1962, the Supreme Court ruled in *Engel v. Vitale* that prayer in public schools was unconstitutional—that government should not be in the business of sponsoring official prayers. Bible reading was prohibited the following year. By 1973, with *Roe v. Wade*, the Court had made abortion legal.[20]

These decisions drew the condemnation of many Catholic and Protestant leaders. They also helped to spawn a countermovement of religious activists seeking to roll back these decisions and to find a renewed role for religion in public life. The mobilization of religious organizations and other groups that aim to reintroduce their view of morality into public life has been one of the most significant political developments of the past two decades. Some of the most divisive conflicts in politics today, such as that over abortion, hinge on differences over religious and moral issues. These divisions have become so significant and so broad that they now constitute a major clash of cultures with repercussions throughout the political system and across many different areas of policy.

Politically, one of the most significant elements of this new politics has been the mobilization of white evangelical Protestants into a cohesive and politically shrewd organization aligned with the Republican Party. The Moral Majority, the first broad political organization of evangelical Christians, showed its political muscle in the 1980 election, when it aligned with the Republican Party, eventually backing Ronald Reagan for president. Over the next few years, evangelicals strengthened their movement by registering voters and mobilizing them with sophisticated, state-of-the-art political techniques. Their success was evident in the 1984 election, when 80 percent of evangelical Christian voters cast their ballots for Reagan. The 1988 election was a turning point in the political development of the Christian Right. Televangelist Pat Robertson ran for president and, although his candidacy was unsuccessful, his effort laid the groundwork for future political strength. Robertson's supporters gained control of some state Republican parties and won positions of power in others. With this new organizational base and sharply honed political skills, Robertson formed a new organization, the Christian Coalition. This organization became one of the most important groups in American politics during the 1990s because of its ability to reach and mobilize a large grassroots base. The Christian Coalition was credited with helping to elect the Republican Congress in 1994.

President Bush has been closely aligned with religious conservatives. Many analysts viewed the president's faith-based initiative, which sought to funnel government assistance to religious groups engaged in charitable work, as a way to reward conservative Christian groups for supporting his election. In fact, conservative religious groups initially turned against the initiative because they feared that government control would accompany federal dollars.[21]

By the early 2000s, the political power of the religious Right had become uncertain. On the one hand, some of its strongest organizations, such as the Christian Coalition, had fallen into disarray and others had retreated from direct political engagement. On the other hand, the sympathy of President Bush for many of the goals of religious conservatives meant that their ideas were well represented in government. As Ralph Reed, former head of the Christian Coalition and current chairman of the Georgia Republican Party, put it, "You're no longer throwing rocks at the building; you're in the building."[22]

AGE AND PARTICIPATION

One of the most significant patterns in political participation is the generational divide. Older people have much higher rates of participation than young people. This division is especially apparent in the different voting rates of the two groups. In the 2000 election, the overall turnout was 50.7 percent. The elderly were significantly above the average, with 67.6 percent of people over sixty-five voting. Young people were far below the average, with only 28.4 percent of people between the ages of eighteen and twenty and 24.2 percent of those between twenty-one and twenty-four reporting that they voted.[23] Although these two groups make up a similar portion of the population—in 2000, there were 26.8 million potential voters between the ages of eighteen and twenty-four and 32.8 million potential voters over sixty-five—the political voice of the elderly is much stronger because of their higher voting rates. When the Twenty-sixth Amendment to the Constitution granted eighteen- to twenty-year-olds the right to vote in 1971, many believed this group would be a significant new voice in politics. Instead, voting participation of the young has declined quite dramatically. Between 1980 and 2000, the percent of twenty-one- to twenty-four-year-olds who voted dropped by over 20 percent, compared with a 5 percent overall decline.

One reason that younger people vote less is that political campaigns rarely target young voters. A study of political advertising in the 2000 elections found that 64 percent of campaign television advertising was directed at people over fifty. Only 14.2 percent of advertising was aimed at eighteen- to thirty-four-year-olds.[24] This creates a vicious cycle: the less political campaigns appeal to younger voters, the less likely they are to participate, and the less they participate, the less likely they will be targeted by political campaigns.

Another reason that political campaigns target older voters is that the elderly are better organized to participate than young people. The most important organization representing the elderly is the American Association of Retired Persons (AARP), which has a membership of more than 33 million. Although only a small fraction of the members are active in the organization, the AARP's ability to mobilize many thousands of individuals to weigh in on policy proposals has made the organization one of the most powerful in Washington, D.C. Young people have no comparable organization. The United States Student Association has represented college students since the 1950s, but its numbers are much smaller and it does not have the same organizational capacity to mobilize its members as the AARP. Other organizations, such as Third Millennium, have emerged to represent the voice of young people in politics. But, like most advocacy organizations, these groups do not have a membership base and have little capacity to mobilize.

Since the early 1990s, several campaigns have been designed to increase the participation of young voters. Rock the Vote, which began in 1990, uses musicians

In 1971, the Twenty-sixth Amendment lowered the voting age from 21 to 18. The impetus for the reform was antiwar protest. Public officials thought that the right to vote would encourage disgruntled students to take their concerns from the streets into the polling place. That prediction has not been borne out as many young Americans have opted not to participate. As a result, voter registration drives, such as the MTV-sponsored "Choose or Lose," are frequently held on college campuses (left).

College students are not the only group to not participate in politics in great numbers. Voter turnout in general is far lower in the United States than in other Western democracies. One factor is America's large population of immigrants who have not learned the ins and outs of democratic politics. The Latino community, for example, has not been fully integrated into American political processes and, consequently, shows low rates of voting participation. The size of the Latino community, however, makes it something of a "sleeping giant" in the American political system. Increasing rates of naturalization and voter registration could make the Latino vote a powerful force in American politics (right).

and actors to urge young people to vote. It has spawned other initiatives aimed at young voters including Rap the Vote and Rock the Vote a lo Latino. In the 2004 election, many political analysts believed that young voters could be an important swing vote. Polls showed that most young voters (41 percent) did not identify with either political party but also indicated that more young people than usual intended to vote in the 2004 election. Several initiatives sought to increase youth participation by registering young people to vote. Smackdown Your Vote (sponsored by the unlikely combination of the World Wrestling Entertainment Group, the Hip-Hop Summit Action Network, and the League of Women Voters) sought to register 2 million young voters. The New Voter's Project targeted six states where the 2000 elections were won by less than 4 percent of the vote. The project aimed to register 260,000 young people (in fact, they registered 348,197 young voters) and increase their turnout by 5 percent in the 2004 election.

The disengagement of youth from politics contrasts with their strong record in community service. More than 70 percent of young people volunteer in their own communities.[25] One recent national survey found that a majority of students believed that community service was the best way to deal with national problems. By

FOR CRITICAL ANALYSIS

When the Twenty-sixth Amendment changed the voting age from 21 to 18 in 1971, observers expected that the youth vote would add a significant new voice to American politics. Why has the youth vote turned out to be less important than was hoped? What changes would engage more young people in the political system?

contrast, they tended to view politics and politicians with cynicism. The declining levels of youth participation do not bode well for the future of American politics. Although participation rates increase with age, political participation is a habit that is acquired young. Low levels of youth participation today signify a more disengaged population in the future.

Explaining Political Participation

Participation is skewed toward those with more education and more money. To understand these current patterns we must go back to a basic question: Why do people participate in politics? Simple as it seems, there are different ways to answer this question.

SOCIOECONOMIC STATUS

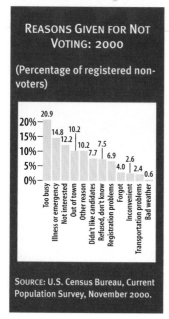

REASONS GIVEN FOR NOT VOTING: 2000

(Percentage of registered non-voters)

SOURCE: U.S. Census Bureau, Current Population Survey, November 2000.

The first explanation for participation points to the characteristics of individuals. One of the most important and consistent results of surveys about participation is that Americans with higher levels of education, more income, and higher-level occupations—what social scientists call **socioeconomic status**—participate much more in politics than do those with less education and less income. Education level alone is the strongest predictor of most kinds of participation, but income becomes important—not surprisingly—when it comes to making contributions. In addition to education and income, other individual characteristics also affect participation. For example, African Americans and Latinos are less likely to participate than are whites, although when differences in education and income are taken into account, both groups participate at the same levels or higher levels than do whites. Finally, young people are far less likely to participate in politics than are older people. The proportion of young people that vote has declined in almost every single election since 1972.[26]

Although they give us a picture of who participates and who does not, explanations based on individual characteristics leave many questions open. One of the biggest questions is why the relationship between education and participation—so strong in surveys—does not seem to hold true over time. As Americans have become more educated, with more people finishing high school and attending college, we would expect to see more people participating in politics. Yet participation has declined, not increased.[27] In the nineteenth century, participation in presidential elections was 20 percent higher than current levels. Moreover, politics was a much more vibrant and encompassing activity: large numbers of people joined in parades, public meetings, and electioneering.[28] This puzzle about declining participation suggests that we need to look beyond the characteristics of individuals to the larger social and political setting to understand changes in patterns of participation over time.

socioeconomic status status in society based on level of education, income, and occupational prestige

CIVIC ENGAGEMENT

civic engagement a sense of concern among members of the political community about public, social, and political life, expressed through participation in social and political organizations

The social setting can affect political participation in a variety of ways. One recent study argued that participation depends on three elements: resources (including time, money, and know-how), **civic engagement** (are you concerned about public issues and do you feel that you can make a difference?), and recruitment (are you

Does Higher Voter Participation Really Matter?

One of the great contradictions of American politics is the fact that our elections—the hallmark of democracy—are plagued by low, and declining, voter turnout. From a high point of about 65 percent turnout in 1960 to a seven-decade low of 49 percent in the 1996 presidential election, Americans are staying away from the polls in record numbers. By comparison, voter turnout in virtually every other democratic nation of the world is significantly higher, typically in the range of 70 to 90 percent in their comparable national elections. But is this anything to worry about?

Yes, say many. Part of the problem lies in the tangle of rules that regulate voting, which are more complicated than those found in almost any other nation. Most of these rules were enacted decades ago to discourage "undesirables"— African Americans, immigrants, the poor—from voting. In many nations, voting is easier because citizens are automatically registered to vote, do not have to worry about local residency requirements, and elections are held on the weekends. A government that cares about its elections should certainly do more to make the act of voting easier. Turnout matters to campaigns, because those who run for office tailor their campaign issues and strategies to those who are likely to vote. Thus, the needs and concerns of the nonvoters—generally those with lower incomes and less education and members of disadvantaged groups—are likely to be ignored, with the result that policy fails to address the nation's most pressing needs. Three states have experimented with making voting easier. In Texas, citizens have been allowed since 1991 to vote any time during the two weeks prior to election day. In Oregon, turnout has risen since the state made balloting by mail easy, more than a decade ago. In 2000, Arizona began experimenting with voting via the Internet. These pioneering efforts demonstrate that the government could do more to make voting easier, and should do so, many argue, because the ever-declining percentage of voting casts a shadow over the very legitimacy of the government that is elected. How can a president, or other elected leaders, claim a mandate to govern when less than a quarter of eligible voters cast ballots for the winner?

Skeptics counter these arguments by asserting that the negative consequences of nonvoting have been greatly overstated. In 1993, Congress passed the "Motor Voter" law, which allowed citizens to register to vote when they applied for a driver's license. Even though millions of new voters registered by this means, it had little or no effect on voting rates, suggesting that existing election laws may have little to do with voting rates. Further, research has demonstrated that there is often less difference between voters and nonvoters than many assume. A study of the 1988 election, for example, showed that, contrary to expectations, nonvoters would have supported the winning presidential candidate, George Bush, over challenger Michael Dukakis. This and similar research supports the idea that the interests of nonvoters are not so different from those of voters. Beyond this, nonvoting is not necessarily a sign of alienation from the political system. To some extent at least, it can be interpreted as citizen satisfaction with the overall course of the country's affairs. While indifference is a less than noble sentiment, it can at least be taken as a green light for the nation's political leaders. When crises have arisen in the past, from the Great Depression to the Gulf War, Americans have turned close attention to their political leaders. Finally, voting is only one method of political expression, and citizens with concerns ranging from race to abortion to guns increasingly express their views through means other than the ballot box, from interest group activity to the Internet. Voting is still the most frequent political activity, but citizens are free to express themselves in an ever-wider array of methods.

FOR CRITICAL ANALYSIS

1. Why is it important to vote even if the voter feels that he or she is only choosing between the "lesser of two evils"?

2. Why do many Americans believe that it makes no difference if they vote? Does it make sense to avoid voting but concentrate on other forms of political activity?

Is It Important That Everyone Vote?

Yes

Campaign ads are dominating the airwaves in Kansas City and St. Louis. Democratic hopefuls John Kerry, John Edwards, Al Sharpton, and Howard Dean have all traveled to one or both of those cities to make their pitch to Missouri voters. Save for a weekend appearance by Edwards's wife, Columbia has hardly fit the image of a campaign-saturated Missouri we keep reading and hearing about. There's a reason the candidates have largely ignored Columbia—it's a college town. It is full of 18- to 24-year-olds, grounds enough for candidates to keep on truckin' down Interstate 70 toward Missourians who might actually vote.

It seems every four years, pundits try to answer the question, "Why don't young people vote?" And each time we regurgitate the same tired, empty responses: We don't care. We're not engaged. Politics are too political. We don't like negative ads. My vote doesn't count.

It's a perennial exercise in shirking responsibility for our own inaction, a wave of excuses that boils down to a complaint that politicians don't listen to young people.

It's hard to listen to someone who isn't saying anything.

If a candidate were to talk to us, what would he or she talk about? College campuses tried, with varying degrees of success, to get upset about a war in Iraq, so should "our" candidate talk about peace and diplomacy? If so, what are we to make of myriad studies indicating a substantial shift to the right among young Americans? Choosing issues that will resonate with youths must surely be tough when barely a third of the youths in question define their concerns at the polls.

Old people have earned the political clout they enjoy. They vote, so the power to shape platforms of candidates whose future depends on their support is, understandably, theirs. We can't expect candidates to focus solely on us at the expense of winning, thereby precluding accomplishing anything for anyone.

November's general election will determine the winner not only of a political clash, but also of an ideological one. All the viable Democratic candidates appear ready to operate under a philosophy much different than President Bush's, and with the economy (read: your ability to get a job), the war on terrorism (read: your safety from further attacks), and with a plethora of social issues in the balance, it matters which direction the country takes. It matters now, it matters in a few years when we all graduate, and it matters for years after that. Which of these competing ideologies you choose is of secondary importance to making a choice in the first place.

And it's so easy! The Boone County clerk's Web site, www.showmeboone.com/clerk, can help you find your polling place quickly and easily, and requesting an absentee ballot, either from a different county in Missouri or from another state, ain't exactly rocket science. It's too late now to vote absentee in Missouri's primary, but the general election is only a few months away. Those who never got around to registering—another ridiculously easy procedure—also ought to look toward November and the prospect of voting in the general election.

Learning about the candidates, choosing one, and voting isn't a difficult process. It's not hard, it's not time-consuming, and it's incredibly important. And if you're about to feed us the preposterous "My vote doesn't count" line, save it. Tell someone in Dade County, Florida, that one vote didn't count in 2000. This election is shaping up to be as close, if not even closer, than the one in 2000, which means each vote counts. If the 74 percent of American youths who sat out the 2000 election woke up and voted this time, we're willing to bet it would impact the outcome of the race.

It's time to get off the apathetic high horse from which our generation avoids the dangers of our own complacency. Politicians will listen if we speak up, and they'll do what it takes to make us happy. All we have to do is start giving a damn about the decisions that will affect our lives.

SOURCE: Editorial Board, "Vicious Cycle Is Ours to Break, *The Maneater* (University of Missouri), February 3, 2004.

This republic established by the blueprint of the Constitution is a beautiful thing. The citizens' right to vote in elections allows us to provide peaceful feedback to what the government is doing. This is the reason our government works so well . . . or better than most other governments.

The ruling government, while given the freedom to direct the country where it thinks we ought to go, can never stray too far from the people's interest, lest the people elect another government. It's like a hand being able to tell the brain to let go of a red-hot firebrand.

The critical factor in this equation is the interest of the people. In a country this large, it is not hard to find good people. Yes, that's right—it is not hard. It is only hard to elect them when the people's interest in the government wanes. Then, leaders are elected by style, not substance. Things tend to go to crap under these circumstances. The hand has fallen asleep and no longer minds when it gets placed into a container full of used needles.

It's kind of like current day Washington, D.C.

There are a lot of "grass roots" organizations trying to combat declining interest in politics by getting more people to vote. Even MTV is doing its part with the "Choose or Lose" campaign. Of course, MTV has the ulterior motive of getting more clueless twenty-somethings to vote in order to help its guys get elected.

All the while, these groups knowingly work under the false assumption that decreasing voter turnout is the cause for our politicians' ineptitude and give those who vote (who vote randomly for all intents and purposes) a sense of accomplishment. In this case, they are treating the symptoms to further hide the disease. Continuing the metaphor, they're numbing the hand to the pricks of the needles.

The problem with those who are apathetic toward politics is not when they stay home during an election but when they vote. The apathetic, uninformed voter can easily fall on either side of the fence, depending on the emotions of the voter.

When he or she votes in excess of the informed voters, candidates are selected by the equivalent of a coin toss.

From personal experience, there are plenty of liberals who are convinced President Bush is recklessly cutting the federal budgets. Of course, he isn't. Any conservative is pained to admit quite the opposite. This is a perfect example of people who emotionally label a person or party and then believe and vote accordingly. When a lot of people vote for or against Bush based solely on their feelings toward him (e.g., Democrats say he's evil; Republicans say he's a saint), then that effectively dilutes those who vote based on important things.

Given this, is it any wonder that presidential politics have been so evenly divided for the last four years? Not really.

This random selection is what causes the disconnect between what we want (good people) and what we get (Hillary Clinton).

So how do we fix things in politics? Simple really—go out and don't vote. That's right, don't vote. An uninformed vote is most easily eliminated when people simply don't vote. It is too difficult and impractical to eliminate it the other way through diligent research.

So the next time you're in the voting booth, only vote for those candidates that you know a significant amount about. If that's no one, then you have some research to do if you want to vote for anyone the next time.

A good place to start is www.votesmart.org.

SOURCE: James Peterson, "Uniformed People Shouldn't Vote in November," *Iowa State Daily*, September 14, 2004.

asked to participate, especially by someone you know?).[29] Whether people have resources, feel engaged, and are recruited depends very much on their social setting—what their parents are like, whom they know, what associations they belong to. In the United States, churches are a particularly important social institution in helping to foster political participation. Through their church activities people learn the civic skills that prepare them to participate in the political world more broadly. It is often through church activities that people learn to run meetings, write newsletters, or give speeches and presentations. Churches are also an important setting for meeting people and creating networks for recruitment, since people are more likely to participate if asked by a friend or an acquaintance.

As this model suggests, if fewer people belong to social organizations, they may be less likely to participate in politics. The United States has often been called a nation of joiners because of our readiness to form local associations to address common problems. As early as the 1830s, the Frenchman Alexis de Tocqueville singled out this tendency to form associations as a most distinctive American trait.[30] There is evidence, however, that Americans no longer join organizations as much as they did in the past. This declining membership raises concerns that the civic engagement that ordinary Americans once had is deteriorating. These concerns are magnified by declining levels of social trust, which further contribute to the tendency to pull back from public engagement.[31] There are many possible reasons for the decline in organizational membership and social trust, and consequently in civic engagement. Television, for example, keeps people in their houses and away from meetings or other, more civic, engagements.[32] Crime can also reduce civic engagement by reducing social trust, making people suspicious and unwilling to take part in neighborhood activities.

Another way to explain the decline in civic engagement is to look at how the experiences of different generations might make them more or less oriented toward civic engagement. The generation that came of age during the Great Depression and World War II has been called the "long civic generation" because this group tends to participate in politics and associational life much more than previous or later generations. During the 1930s, people looked to government to help them with economic hardships, and in the 1940s, the same generation fought World War II, a popular war in which the entire country pulled together.[33] Later generations have not experienced such popular common causes to bring them together in the public sphere: their wars have been less popular and their great social causes more divisive. In addition, political life has seemed much less inspiring, filled with accusations of wrongdoing and constant investigations into possible scandal. Such a generational perspective makes sense because people form habits and beliefs in their early years that are very important in how they participate later in life. A generational perspective also helps explain why participation did not decline during the twentieth century, but instead started out low in the early 1900s, rose from the 1930s through the 1960s, and then began to fall once again.

Arguments about declining public trust and generational effects don't pay enough attention to the political setting in which participation takes place. The organization of politics itself plays a key role in channeling participation in particular directions and in encouraging or discouraging people from participating. Participation depends on whether there are formal obstacles in the political system, what people think political engagement has to offer them, and most important, whether political parties and politicians try to mobilize people into politics.

FORMAL OBSTACLES

Formal obstacles can greatly decrease participation. As we saw earlier in the chapter, in the South prior to the 1960s, the widespread use of the poll tax and other measures such as the **white primary** essentially deprived black Americans (and many poor whites) of the right to vote during the first part of this century. This system of legal segregation meant that there were few avenues for black Americans in the South to participate in politics. With the removal of these legal barriers in the 1960s, black political participation shot up, with rates of turnout approaching those of southern whites, as early as 1968.[34]

Another important political factor reducing voter turnout in the United States is our nation's peculiar registration rules. In every American state but North Dakota, individuals who are eligible to vote must register with the state election board before they are actually allowed to vote. Registration requirements were introduced at the end of the nineteenth century in response to the demands of the Progressive movement. Progressives hoped to make voting more difficult both to reduce multiple voting and other forms of corruption and to discourage immigrant and working-class voters from going to the polls. When first introduced, registration was extremely difficult and, in some states, reduced voter turnout by as much as 50 percent. In the last several decades, 80 to 90 percent of registered voters have participated in presidential elections. Clearly, registration requirements are the major hurdle in getting Americans to the polling booth.

Registration requirements particularly depress the participation of those with little education and low incomes because registration requires a greater degree of political involvement and interest than does the act of voting itself. To vote, a person need be concerned only with the particular election campaign at hand. Requiring individuals to register before the next election forces them to make a decision to participate on the basis of an abstract interest in the electoral process rather than a simple concern with a specific campaign. Such an abstract interest in electoral politics is largely a product of education. Those with relatively little education may become interested in political events once the issues of a particular campaign become salient, but by that time it may be too late to register. Young people tend to assign a low priority to registration even if they are well educated. Moreover, because young people tend to move more often than older people, registration requirements place a greater burden on them. As a result, personal registration requirements not only diminish the size of the electorate but also tend to create an electorate that is, on average, better educated, higher in income and social status, and composed of fewer young people, African Americans, and other minorities than the citizenry as a whole (see Figure 8.6). In Europe, there is typically no registration burden on the individual voter; voter registration is handled automatically by the government. This is one reason that voter turnout rates in Europe are higher than those in the United States.

As might be expected, in states that do not require registration (North Dakota) or that allow registration on the day of the election (Minnesota) voter turnout is not only higher than average, but younger and less affluent voters turn out in larger percentages.[35] Minnesota's same-day rule played an important role in the surprise 1998 gubernatorial victory of colorful former professional wrestler Jesse Ventura. Ventura won the votes of many young men who had not been registered until they came to the polls on election day. Without same-day registration, Ventura's electoral chances would have been considerably lessened.

white primary primary election in which only white voters are eligible to participate

The percentage of Americans who are registered to vote varies according to education level, employment status, ethnic group, and age.

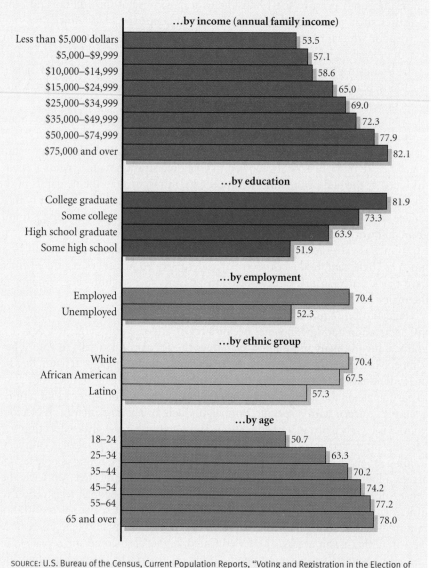

SOURCE: U.S. Bureau of the Census, Current Population Reports, "Voting and Registration in the Election of November 2000" (February 2002), www.census.gov/population/www/socdemo/voting.html

Over the years, voter registration restrictions have been modified somewhat to make registration easier. But the removal of formal obstacles is not enough to ensure that people participate, as the example of the National Voter Registration Act passed in 1993 shows. Popularly known as the Motor Voter Act, the law aimed to increase participation by making it easier to register to vote. The cumbersome process of registering (and staying registered after moving) has often been singled out as a barrier to participation. The new law aimed to remove this obstacle by allowing people to register when they apply for a driver's license and at other public facilities. Although voter registration increased, turnout did not. An estimated 3.4 million people registered to vote as a result of the Motor Voter Act, but turnout in the 1996 election—the first presidential election held after the law went into effect—actually declined by 6 percent from that in 1992.[36] The very limited success of the Motor Voter Act suggests that people need motivation to participate, not simply the removal of barriers.

One formal obstacle to participation that has grown more important in recent years is the restriction on the voting rights of people who have committed a felony. Forty-eight states and the District of Columbia prohibit prison inmates who are serving a felony sentence from voting.[37] In thirty-three states, felons on probation or parole are not permitted to vote. There are also numerous restrictions on the voting rights of felons who have served their sentences. In twelve states, a felony record can result in a lifetime ban on voting. With the sharp rise in incarceration rates in the 1980s and 1990s, these restrictions have had a significant impact on voting rights. By one estimate, 4.6 million people—2 percent of the voting-age population—have lost their voting rights as a result of these restrictions. These restrictions disproportionately affect minorities because 60 percent of the prison population is black or Latino. One in eight black men cannot vote because of a criminal record. In the states that deny the vote to all ex-felons, one in nearly three black men has lost the right to vote. Concern over the impact of these voting restrictions has led to campaigns to restore voting rights to people who have committed a felony. Since 1996, eight states have reduced voting restrictions for people with a felony record. In the five states that implemented the most substantial reforms, an estimated 471,000 people regained the right to vote. Such reforms may have an important impact on politics: one study showed that if all people with felony records had been allowed to vote, Al Gore would have won the 2000 election.[38] The impact of felon disenfranchisement has been especially strong in the South, where Republican candidates have benefited from the reduction in the numbers of minority voters.

Another type of formal obstacle has received less attention. In the United States, elections are held on Tuesdays, regular working days. By contrast, in most European counties, elections are held on Sundays or holidays. In some countries, such as India, polls remain open for several days. The United States has addressed this problem somewhat by expanding the use of absentee ballots and instituting early voting or voting by mail. In states with easy access to the absentee ballot, such as California, 25 percent of the vote was cast via absentee ballot in the 2000 election. In Texas, 39 percent of voters cast early ballots in the 2000 election. Oregon has gone the furthest in instituting new ways of voting: in 1998, Oregon voters approved a measure allowing voters to cast their ballots by mail. Although the public is enthusiastic about these new methods of voting, research shows that they have increased turnout only modestly.

POLITICAL MOBILIZATION

The political setting can play an important role in motivating people to vote. When elections are closely contested, more people tend to vote. And in political settings where they think their input will make a difference, people are more likely to participate. One study of black political participation, for example, found that blacks were more likely to vote, participate in campaigns, and contact public officials in cities run by a black mayor. Their greater attention to city politics and their belief that city government is more responsive to their concerns helps to spark participation.[39]

But the most significant factor affecting participation is whether people are mobilized by parties, candidates, interest groups, and social movements. A recent comprehensive study of the decline in participation in the United States found that fully half of the drop-off could be accounted for by reduced **mobilization** efforts.[40]

mobilization the process by which large numbers of people are organized for a political activity

During the nineteenth century, America's political parties worked hard to mobilize voters, using everything from barbecues to bribes to get out the vote. On the day of a presidential election, hundreds of thousands of party workers handed out leaflets, knocked on doors, and even provided free transportation to those unable to get to the polls on their own.

People are much more likely to participate when someone—preferably someone they know—asks them to get involved.

The importance of personal contact for mobilizing voters has been demonstrated in a series of experiments recently conducted by political scientists Donald Green and Alan Gerber. Evaluating the results of several get-out-the-vote drives, Green and Gerber showed that face-to-face interaction with a canvasser greatly increased the chances that the person contacted would go to the polls. They estimated that personal contact boosted turnout from 44.5 percent to 56 percent. The impact of direct mail was much smaller, causing only a 2.2 percent increase in voting.[41] Impersonal calls from a phone bank had no effect on voter turnout. Green and Gerber have also evaluated the impact of mobilization on young voters, studying a series of get-out-the-vote campaigns conducted near college campuses during the 2000 election. In these campaigns, phone contacts that were more chatty and informal than standard phone bank messages increased turnout by an estimated 5 percent. Face-to-face contact again proved even more powerful, increasing turnout by 8.5 percent.[42]

In previous decades, political parties, organizations, and social movements relied on personal contact to mobilize voters. As we will see in Chapter 9, during the nineteenth century, American political party machines employed hundreds of thousands of workers to organize and mobilize voters as well as to bring them to the polls. The result was an extremely high rate of turnout, typically more than 90 percent of eligible voters.[43] But political party machines began to decline in strength in the beginning of the twentieth century and by now have, for the most part, disappeared. Without party workers to encourage them to go to the polls and even to bring them there if necessary, many eligible voters will not participate.

Rather than mobilizers of people, political parties became essentially fund-raising and advertising organizations. The experience of a Connecticut woman dur-

Today, political parties are not as strong as they were in the nineteenth century, but other groups and organizations endeavor to mobilize voters. In 2004, a number of new efforts to register and mobilize new voters were undertaken by a variety of independent groups and organizations. For example, Hip-Hop Summit Action Network, led by Russell Simmons, joined forces with World Wrestling Entertainment's Smackdown Your Vote, led by Vince McMahon, to launch a nonpartisan campaign to register two million 18-to-30-year-olds. Numerous recording artists joined the campaign to recruit youth voters in 2004. HeadCount, Music for America, PunkVoter, and Vote for Change were just some of the groups taking part in pop music tours aimed at inspiring voters and, in some cases, changing their minds. Vote for Change—a partisan group led by Bruce Springsteen with the obvious goal of electing John Kerry—included members of the Dave Matthews Band, the Dixie Chicks, Pearl Jam, and others. The Vote for Change tour focused exclusively on the battleground states such as Michigan, Pennsylvania, and Florida. While celebrity efforts such as these are successful in drumming up publicity, most political scientists are skeptical of their actual success in mobilizing voters or influencing their vote choices.

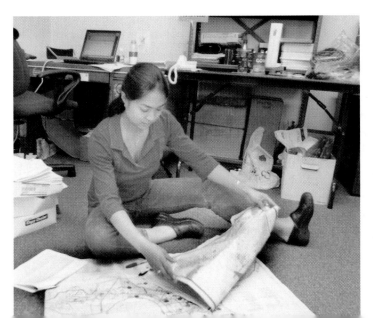

Despite the challenges of mobilizing young voters, millions of college students were expected to vote in the 2004 presidential election and thousands were active in various campaigns. For example, Joan Javier of the New Voters Project, shown here looking over voting-district maps, took part in a student-led voter participation campaign that registered 18,000 new voters among New Jersey college students and planned to use fliers, phone banks, and shuttle buses to encourage them to go to the polls on Election Day.

FOR CRITICAL ANALYSIS

Why is voter turnout so low in the United States? What are the consequences of low levels of voter turnout? Some critics charge that the United States cannot claim to be a democracy when so few of its citizens actually vote. Is there any basis to this charge?

ing the 1996 election is typical. Hoping to participate in the campaign, she sent a check to the Democratic Party and asked how she could volunteer. She subsequently received many more requests to donate money but she was never informed of any other way to become involved.[44] Interest groups also reduced their efforts at direct mobilization. Although the number of interest groups has grown dramatically in recent decades, the connection that most interest-group members had to these groups often extended no further than their checkbook. Rather than being a means for contact by a friend or an acquaintance to take part in a political activity, belonging to an organization was likely to bring requests through the mail for donations. And rather than providing a venue for meeting new people and widening your circle of engagement, organizational membership was more likely to land your name on yet another mailing list, generating still more requests for funds. In the past, social movements, such as the labor movement in the 1930s and the civil rights movement of the 1960s, played an important role in mobilizing people into politics.

In recent elections, parties and candidates have begun to reemphasize direct voter mobilization using a blend of old and new technologies. In the 2002 midterm elections, for example, Georgia Republicans built strong support through traditional door-to-door political mobilization. In the last three days before the election, they organized a "72-hour task force" of volunteers who made sure their voters went to the polls. The spectacular success of the strategy—an unexpected Republican sweep in Georgia—meant that both parties sought to deploy such strategies in the 2004 election.

These grassroots strategies were especially important in twenty battleground states, where the margin of victory for the presidential election was expected to be very close. Republicans built grassroots organizations in eighteen states with more than 1.4 million volunteers. These volunteers were trained to make calls to 18 million potential voters, go door to door to register voters, write letters to the editor in support of President Bush, post blogs on the Web, and phone in to local radio talk shows. Discussing the goals of the grassroots operation, one Republican strategist declared, "We're going to find every Bush voter, we're going to call them, we're going to write them, we're going to knock on their doors, and when the day comes, we're going to physically take them to the polls."[45] Republicans aimed to register three million new Republican voters with this strategy.

Democrats, busy fighting the primary elections, were far behind in building grassroots voter mobilizations in the states. But several groups aligned with the Democratic Party had already begun to create voter mobilization capabilities similar to those of the Republicans. Called 527 committees after their status in the tax code, these organizations constituted a virtual "shadow Democratic Party." The most important of these groups engaged in voter mobilization was Americans Coming Together (ACT), which united representatives from organized labor, environmental groups, and women's organizations. ACT drew on union members as well as other volunteers for its door-to-door operations and focused in particular on registering and turning out voters in low-income and minority communities most likely to vote Democratic. At its best, this style of politics does more than get people to the polls: it also educates them, making them understand what is at stake in elections and showing them how their vote matters. As such, it addresses the lack of motivation and understanding that keeps a great number of nonvoters away from the polls.

In addition to these party and interest group mobilization efforts, new forms of political engagement have emerged on the Internet. The most significant is

MoveOn.org, originally started as a Web site to organize against the impeachment of President Bill Clinton. In 2003, MoveOn.org emerged as a significant liberal political force with over a million members whom it can mobilize rapidly to raise funds for an issue advertisement or for other kinds of participation. In the primaries, Howard Dean had also pioneered new ways of using the Internet to mobilize supporters. Dean-Link aimed to create a broad network of campaign supporters connected through common acquaintances and through information such as photos and comments posted on the Web. Through Meetup.com, Dean supporters turned Internet contacts into face-to-face meetings of supporters. This new style of campaigning created a base of dedicated and intense supporters, particularly appealing to young voters.

It is too soon to tell if these efforts to energize voters are the first steps toward institutionalizing a more mobilized style of politics and whether they will become sufficiently broad to overcome the class bias entrenched in political participation. Although these initiatives are significant, they coexist with other features of politics that are fundamentally demobilizing. Negative advertising, which has been shown to reduce turnout, continues to be an important component of political campaigns. The longer-term impact of attack style politics is to reinforce the mistrust with which many Americans view politicians and the distance they feel from politics as having an impact on their lives.

FOR CRITICAL ANALYSIS

Why do efforts at direct mobilization seem to be more successful than television advertising in promoting voter turnout? How might the Internet become an important tool for increasing political participation?

Thinking Critically about Political Participation and Liberty, Equality, and Democracy

Over the course of our history, as we have seen, the American political community has expanded to make our politics more closely match our fundamental values of liberty, equality, and democracy. But more recently, our **political institutions** have ceased to mobilize an active citizenry. Furthermore, our uneven pattern of political participation is at odds with our notions of equality and democracy. These problems highlight the tension among our basic values and raise questions about whether our institutions could help provide a better balance among them. Two questions about institutions are particularly pressing: Is "checkbook democracy" enough? Do our public institutions do enough to bring us together to engage in common problem-solving? Both questions raise a third: Does the contemporary pattern of political participation in the United States reinforce inequality by providing a stronger voice for more-advantaged groups?

"Checkbook democracy" refers to the new importance of money in politics, both in electoral campaigns and in interest-group activity. Checkbook democracy is a major aspect of inequality in politics because citizens with fatter wallets are much better positioned to participate in this form of politics. Because it has been associated with declining participation and a greater inequality in participation patterns, checkbook politics has been the target of reformers who want to limit the role of money in politics. But the Supreme Court greatly limited the scope for reform in an important decision in 1976, when it ruled that individual contributions to candidates were a form of free speech and that it would be a curtailment of liberty to forbid such spending so long as it was not formally connected with a political campaign.[46] Many reformers remain dissatisfied with the Court's decision because they believe that allowing money to play such an important role in politics undermines political equality. Critics also do not think that restricting direct

political institution an organization that connects people to politics, such as a political party, or a governmental organization, such as the Congress or the courts

As voter turnout has declined, inequality in political participation has become more severe. Why are upper-income Americans more likely to be voters than lower-income Americans? What are the most promising ways to alter the class bias in political participation?

spending on candidates is a significant infringement of liberty. The McCain-Feingold campaign finance reform act (upheld by the Supreme Court in 2003) limited donations to parties. But because interest groups quickly created new organizations to attract funds, the law did little to reduce the importance of money in campaigns. (See Chapter 10 for a discussion of this reform.)

The other charge against checkbook politics is that it saps the energy from democracy because most members have only very loose connections with the groups who receive their checks. This not only allows interest groups to lobby in Washington with little direct accountability to their membership, it also fails to mobilize people directly and thus does not build the personal connections that promote broad political engagement. Defenders of this style of politics say it does not drain democracy, it only makes it more efficient. In other words, people no longer have to go to meetings; they can simply send a check to the organizations they like and avoid the organizations they dislike.[47] These different views provoke questions about whether we need more direct participation to promote political equality and a vibrant democracy. They also cause us to ask what kinds of changes in social and political institutions would promote more direct participation.

Public institutions can play an important role in helping people understand our values in practice and find acceptable balances among them. Yet there are indications that our institutions are increasingly less able to perform this role. Some people argue that the behavior of American elites—the upper-middle class and the corporate community—has been the driving factor in the weakening of American democracy. Many American elites no longer participate in broad public institutions; instead, they send their children to private schools, obtain their medical care from generous private insurance plans, and hire private police to ensure their security. This "secession of the rich" has had damaging consequences for American democracy because these groups no longer have a stake in what happens in the public sector. Their main interest is in keeping taxes low and protecting themselves from public problems.[48] Yet clearly individuals have the right to participate as they wish and to purchase the services they think they need. But what happens when these individual choices undermine our ability to bring people together to hammer out their differences about what our values should mean in practice?

American political culture has supplied a core set of values that has helped knit together a culturally diverse nation. But the scope and meaning of these values has shifted over the course of history. In the past, these values were applied selectively, and some people were excluded from the definition of the American political community. Today, a more inclusive definition has evolved. Nonetheless, new questions about the role of our institutions in promoting political engagement and broad-based participation have emerged. We now face serious questions about what our values mean in a political system that seems irrelevant to many people and in which higher-income citizens have a disproportionately strong voice. The answers given to these questions today will shape the meaning of the American dream for future generations.

GET INVOLVED

What You Can Do: Become a Voter

In a sense, the role of the citizen in a democracy is obvious. Citizens have a right to participate. If citizens do not participate, then liberty, equality, and democracy become meaningless terms. The most common way for U.S. citizens to get involved in politics is to cast a vote in elections. Many political scientists believe that voting in competitive elections is the most important form of political participation in a democracy. It is the main means by which citizens give their consent to government, choose their governors, and hold them accountable for their actions. Furthermore, voting links people to every level of government. Citizens may be called on to cast ballots for local propositions; school board and city council members; county district attorneys and judges; state governors and treasurers; and federal officials such as the president and U.S. senators. Often, voters' choices for several levels of government are consolidated into one ballot and take place on the same day; other times, elections for different issues and levels of government are put on separate ballots and held at different times of the year.

If you are a U.S. citizen who is eighteen years old or older, you are *eligible* to vote, but you must *register* to vote with your own state government. Registration is not automatic, but it is a fairly painless process. Voter registration forms are usually available at state government offices and many other government offices, too. Post offices, motor vehicle departments, schools, and public libraries often distribute voter registration forms. You can call your local city hall to find out where you can get one. Prior to elections, you are likely to find groups on campus conducting voter registration drives. They make the forms readily accessible to you and, if you need assistance, they may help you fill out the form.

Once you have the form, completing it is fairly straightforward. You must provide general identification information such as name, address, date of birth, and so forth. The form will also ask you to declare your political party affiliation. You can list a specific political party or you can check "no party" if you do not wish to have a party affiliation. In some states, it is important to designate your party preference because that makes you eligible to vote in the primary election of your designated party. In other states, however, all registered voters are eligible to vote for all candidates running in primary elections.

When you have filled out the voter registration form, mail it to the address shown on the form or return it to the people conducting the voter registration drive. Note that different states have different deadlines regarding when you must be registered in order to be eligible to vote in an upcoming election.

After you are registered to vote, there is a strong probability that you will receive multiple campaign mailings from interest groups, political action committees, direct mail professionals, political parties, and candidates as an election approaches. These mailings may consist of a lot of junk; however, they sometimes contain useful information to help you think through your position on important issues or choose among the competing candidates. For even more information, log on to the Internet, put an issue, a political party, or a candidate's name into a search engine, and see what you can find.

In some states, prior to an election, you should receive a sample ballot, which will lay out all of the offices and choices in the election. The sample ballot will tell you where your polling place is (where you vote on Election Day). It will also have a form on it that you can use to request an absentee ballot (if you are unable to appear at your polling place on Election Day). You may also receive information from both government sources and private sources about propositions that may appear on the ballot, the pros and cons of the propositions, and perhaps the costs (if any) to taxpayers should the propositions pass.

INTERACTIVE POLITICS

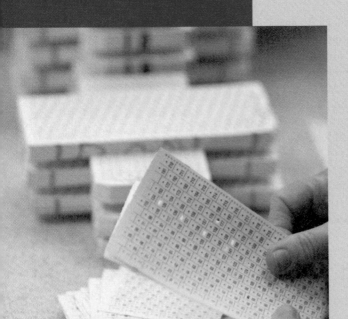

YOU ARE... an election commissioner!

The 2000 presidential election was one of the closest on record, and the results from a single state could have made the difference in the outcome. Even so, the odds that any single vote in an election will tip the balance and create a winner are remote. Given the tiny probability that an individual's vote will determine the winner in an election, mobilizing voters becomes a difficult challenge for those seeking to increase turnout.

In a democracy, low turnout is highly problematic because if people are not vested in the system, it loses legitimacy. Election officials and political scientists are often working very hard to increase voter turnout.

In this simulation, you are cast in the role of your state's election commissioner, charged with increasing turnout in the next elections. Will you be able to reverse the reductions of the recent decades?

Go to www.wwnorton.com/wtp5e

Questions to consider as you conduct the online simulation:

What factors help determine whether people will be likely to vote?

What rules and procedures can a state change that would actually increase the number of voters?

Do incumbents and challengers really have the same goals regarding increasing turnout?

Would some reforms help one political party's candidates more than another's?

Assuming that you do not cast an absentee ballot, you need to go to your polling place on Election Day. Depending on where you vote, you will encounter one of the five voting systems currently used in the United States. One involves putting check marks next to your preferences on a paper ballot. A second lists all options and requires you to pull a mechanical lever next to your choices. A third system requires that you punch holes in a card to indicate your choices. A fourth system has you darken circles or rectangles beside your choices. A fifth voting method, called Direct Recording Electronic (DRE), asks you to use a touch-screen or push buttons to indicate your preferences. Regardless of the system, your polling place will be staffed by community volunteers who will answer questions about how to cast your votes.

To make democracy more vital and effective, however, citizens need to do more than vote. There are many opportunities for citizens, including college students, to become actively involved in the political process. Political parties and political campaigns are eager to sign on volunteer workers. Usually, the addresses and phone numbers of campaign offices are well publicized before elections. In addition, information about how to become involved with campaigns is available on the Internet from candidates' Web sites. Political work can be fun and rewarding. Campaign workers can make a real difference in bolstering voter turnout and even in persuading undecided voters one way or the other.

In some instances the effectiveness of citizens' political participation is easy to discern. Lobbying and demonstrations by members of the American Association for Retired Persons (AARP) has had direct and immediate effects upon legislation affecting Social Security and health care for the elderly. By writing letters and making phone calls, individuals frequently secure the assistance of members of Congress with immigration problems. Student "sit-ins" often force college administrators to revise their policies. Lobbying and demonstrating, however, are activities in which most citizens seldom, if ever, engage. Voting is the form of political participation that engages the energy of the largest number of Americans on a routine basis.

There can be little doubt that the electorate's choices can have significant implications for government and policy in the United States. When, for example, Americans elected Ronald Reagan to the presidency in 1980, they were choosing a president who promised to cut taxes, expand military spending, and limit social spending. Reagan worked successfully to implement all those promises. By the same token, when voters chose Bill Clinton in 1992, they knew they were opting for a president who would work to undo some of the consequences of Reaganism and seek to expand the role of government in the provision of social services. Clinton worked to accomplish this goal, though achieving only mixed success. In both these cases, though, citizens' participation had important implications for America's political leadership and public policies.

FOR CRITICAL ANALYSIS

In December 1941, following the Japanese attack on American naval forces stationed at Pearl Harbor, President Franklin D. Roosevelt called upon Americans to prepare themselves for service and sacrifice. In September 2001, following terrorist attacks in New York and Washington, D.C., President George W. Bush called upon Americans to go on with their normal routines. Has popular participation become less important over the past six decades? Does the government still need the involvement of ordinary Americans to be effective?

Summary

Political participation can take many forms, including lobbying, public relations, litigation, protest, and voting. Voting is the most common and important form of participation. At the time of America's Founding, the right to vote was generally limited to white males over the age of twenty-one. Many states also limited voting rights to those who owned property. Over the years, voting rights were expanded to give all adult Americans the right to participate in elections. Despite this, only about half of all American citizens over the age of eighteen actually vote in presidential elections.

An individual's socioeconomic status is the most important characteristic determining whether he or she participates in politics. But the efforts of political institutions to mobilize people are especially significant if we wish to understand patterns of participation over time. In recent decades political institutions, such as parties, have done less to mobilize people to participate in politics. The fact that many Americans do not participate gives the American political process a quasi-democratic character.

For Further Reading

Drew, Elizabeth. *The Corruption of American Politics: What Went Wrong and Why*. New York: Birch Lane, 1999.

Eliasoph, Nina. *Avoiding Politics: How Americans Produce Apathy in Everyday Life*. Cambridge, England: Cambridge University Press, 1998.

Frantzich, Stephen E. *Citizen Democracy: Political Activists in a Cynical Age*. New York: Rowman and Littlefield, 1999.

Green, Donald P., and Alan S. Gerber. *Get Out the Vote! How to Increase Voter Turnout*. Washington, DC: Brookings Institution Press, 2004.

Miller, Warren, and J. Merrill Shanks. *The New American Voter*. Cambridge, MA: Harvard University Press, 1996.

Putnam, Robert D. *Bowling Alone: The Collapse and Revival of American Community*. New York: Simon & Schuster, 2000.

Rosenstone, Steven J, and John Mark Hansen. *Mobilization, Participation and Democracy in America*. New York: Macmillan, 1993.

Schudson, Michael. *The Good Citizen: A History of American Civic Life*. New York: Free Press, 1998.

Verba, Sidney, Kay Lehman Schlotzman, and Henry Brady. *Voice and Equality: Civic Voluntarism in American Politics*. Cambridge, MA: Harvard University Press, 1995.

Study Outline

www.wwnorton.com/wtp5e   Keyword: Review 8

Political Participation

1. Political participation can take many forms. The most common today are lobbying, public relations, litigation, protest, and, most important, voting.
2. Throughout American history, there has been a progressive, if uneven, expansion of suffrage to groups such as African Americans, women, and youths.
3. Americans are taught to equate citizenship with electoral participation.
4. Though the United States now has a system of universal suffrage, voter turnout continues to be low.

Who Participates, and How?

1. Several strategies of mobilization emerged to guide African Americans' quest for equality in the twentieth century, including political pressure, legal strategies, and protest. But the question remains whether political participation can improve the lives of African Americans, especially the poor.
2. In recent years, Latino political organizations have attempted to mobilize members of their community. This effort, if successful, would tap a "sleeping giant" of political influence.
3. The diversity of national backgrounds among Asian Americans has impeded the development of group-based political power.
4. The ongoing significance of gender issues in American politics is indicated by three trends: the gender gap, the increase in the number of women holding public office, and the continued importance of political issues of special concern to women.
5. A significant element of modern religious politics has been the mobilization of evangelical Protestants into a cohesive and politically active organization aligned with the Republican party.
6. One of the most significant patterns in political participation is that older people have much higher rates of participation than young people.

Explaining Political Participation

1. Several factors explain political participation. They include socioeconomic status, levels of civic engagement, formal obstacles, and efforts by political institutions to mobilize people. The most significant political factor affecting participation is whether people are mobilized by parties, candidates, interest groups, and social movements.

2. In recent decades, political in-stitutions have ceased to mobi-lize an active citizenry. As a result, the ties between elected leaders and members of the upper and middle classes, who tend to vote more regularly, have been strengthened.

3. The quasidemocratic features of the American electoral system reveal its inherent inequality.

Practice Quiz

www.wwnorton.com/wtp5e   Keyword: Quiz 8

1. Which of the following is *not* a form of political participation?
   a) volunteering in a campaign
   b) attending an abortion-rights rally
   c) contributing to the Democratic Party
   d) watching the news on television

2. What is the most common form of political participation?
   a) lobbying
   b) contributing money to a campaign
   c) protesting
   d) voting

3. Which of the following best describes the electorate in the United States prior to the 1820s?
   a) landowning white males over the age of twenty-one
   b) all white males
   c) all literate males
   d) "universal suffrage"

4. Women won the right to vote in _____ with the adop-tion of the _____ Amendment.
   a) 1791; Fifth
   b) 1868; Fourteenth
   c) 1920; Nineteenth
   d) 1971; Twenty-sixth

5. Civic education takes place during
   a) elementary school.
   b) high school.
   c) election campaigns.
   d) all of the above

6. Which of the following negatively impacts voter turnout in the United States?
   a) registration requirements
   b) weak parties
   c) neither a nor b
   d) both a and b

7. Of all the factors explaining political participation, which is the most important?
   a) the mobilization of people by political institutions
   b) socioeconomic status
   c) civic engagement
   d) level of education

8. Which of the following are examples of obstacles to political participation for African Americans?
   a) mobilization and levels of civic engagement
   b) the Civil Rights Acts of 1957 and 1964
   c) poll taxes and white primaries
   d) churches and community centers

9. After passage of the Motor Voter Act in 1993, participation in the 1996 elections
   a) increased dramatically.
   b) increased somewhat.
   c) declined somewhat.
   d) was not affected, since few people registered to vote as a result of the act.

10. Americans who do vote tend to be _____ than the population as a whole.
    a) wealthier
    b) whiter
    c) more educated
    d) all of the above

Key Terms

www.wwnorton.com/wtp5e
Keyword: Vocabulary 8

American political community (p. 297)
civic engagement (p. 308)

gender gap (p. 302)
litigation (p. 292)
lobbying (p. 291)
mobilization (p. 315)
political institution (p. 319)
political participation (p. 290)
poll tax (p. 295)

protest (p. 292)
public relations (p. 292)
socioeconomic status (p. 308)
suffrage (p. 294)
turnout (p. 296)
white primary (p. 313)

9 POLITICAL PARTIES

What Government Does and Why It Matters

OLITICAL PARTIES ARE organizations that seek to control the government. This seems to be a simple idea, but the relationship between parties and government is more complex than we sometimes think. In modern history, political parties have been the chief points of contact between governments, on the one side, and groups and forces in society, on the other. Through organized political parties, social forces can gain some control over governmental policies and personnel. Simultaneously, governments often seek to organize and influence important groups in society through political parties. All political parties have this dual character: they are instruments through which citizens and governments attempt to influence one another. In some nations, such as the People's Republic of China, the leading political party serves primarily the interests of the government. In others, such as the United States, political parties force the government to concern itself with the needs of its citizens.

The idea of political parties was not always accepted in the United States. In the early years of the Republic, parties were seen as threats to the social order. In his 1796 "Farewell Address," President George Washington warned his countrymen to shun partisan politics:

> Let me warn you in the most solemn manner against the baneful effects of the spirit of party generally. This spirit exists under different shapes in all government, more or less stifled, controlled, or repressed, but in those of the popular form it is seen in its greater rankness and is truly their worst enemy.

Often, those in power viewed the formation of political parties by their opponents as acts of treason that merited severe punishment. Thus, in 1798, the Federalist Party, which controlled the national government, in effect sought to outlaw its Jeffersonian Republican opponents through the infamous Alien and Sedition Acts, which, among other things, made it a crime to publish or say anything that might tend to defame or bring into disrepute either the president or the Congress. Under this law, fifteen individuals—including several Republican newspaper editors—were arrested and convicted.[1] Jeffersonian opposition to the Alien and Sedition Acts helped to strengthen the foundations for civil liberties in the United States. And, subsequently, the party-building activities of the Jeffersonians, Jacksonians, and their successors made American politics more egalitarian and democratic.

Obviously, over the past 200 years, Americans' conception of political parties has changed considerably—from subversive organizations to bulwarks of democracy. In this chapter, we will examine the realities underlying these changing conceptions. ■

- **We begin by explaining why political parties exist.** In doing so, we will see that parties play a significant role in key aspects of the political process.

- **We then examine the history of the American two-party system.** As we will see, the history of parties has followed an interesting pattern that has had important consequences for governance.

- **In the next three sections, we look at parties as organizations, parties in the electorate, and the role of parties in the campaign process.** We will see that although party organizations remain strong, the electorate's identification with parties and the role of parties in the electoral process have been declining in recent decades.

- **We then assess the impact of parties on government and the policy-making process.** We will see that the differences between the two major parties can and do have an effect on policy.

■ Previewing Liberty, Equality, and Democracy

This chapter will show how liberty, equality, and democracy depend on the existence of strong political parties and energetic party competition. Liberty requires coherent and well-organized opposition to those in power. Political equality is enhanced when parties organize the collective political energies of those who, as individuals, might lack the resources and knowledge to compete with elites and interest groups. Democracy is promoted when parties mobilize large numbers of individuals to participate in the political arena. Unfortunately, political parties in America today may not be sufficiently vigorous or well organized to bolster participation or to provide a democratic counterweight to the power of special interests. The chapter concludes by analyzing the health of America's parties today and its consequences for democracy.

What Are Political Parties?

Political parties, like interest groups, are organizations that seek influence over government. Ordinarily, they can be distinguished from interest groups on the basis of their orientation. A party seeks to control the entire government by electing its members to office and thereby controlling the government's personnel. Interest groups usually accept government and its personnel as a given and try to influence government policies through them.

As long as political parties have existed, they have been criticized for introducing selfish, "partisan" concerns into public debate and national policy. Yet political parties are extremely important to the proper functioning of a democracy. As we shall see, parties expand popular political participation, promote more effective choice, and smooth the flow of public business in the Congress. Our problem in America today is not that political life is too partisan but that our parties are not strong enough to function effectively. This is one reason, as we shall see, that America has such low levels of popular political involvement. Unfortunately, some reforms currently being implemented, such as restrictions on so-called soft money, might further erode party strength in America.

political parties organized groups that attempt to influence the government by electing their members to important government offices

OUTGROWTHS OF THE ELECTORAL PROCESS

Political parties as they are known today developed along with the expansion of suffrage and can be understood only in the context of elections. The two are so intertwined that American parties actually take their structure from the electoral process. The shape of party organization in the United States has followed a simple rule: for every district where an election is held, there should be some kind of party unit. Republicans failed to maintain units in most counties of the southern states between 1900 and 1952; Democrats were similarly unsuccessful in many areas of New England. But for most of the history of the United States, two major parties have had enough of an organized presence to oppose each other in elections in most of the nation's towns, cities, and counties. This makes the American party system one of the oldest political institutions in the history of democracy.

Compared with political parties in Europe, parties in the United States have always seemed weak. They have no criteria for party membership—no cards for their members to carry, no obligatory participation in any activity. Today, they seem weaker than ever; they inspire less loyalty and are less able to control nominations. Some people are even talking about a "crisis of political parties," as though party politics were being abandoned. But there continues to be at least some substance to party organizations in the United States.

OUTGROWTHS OF THE POLICY-MAKING PROCESS

Political parties are also essential elements in the process of making policy. Within the government, parties are coalitions of individuals with shared or overlapping interests who, as a rule, will support one another's programs and initiatives. Even though there may be areas of disagreement within each party, a common party label in and of itself gives party members a reason to cooperate. Because they are permanent coalitions, parties greatly facilitate the policy-making process. If alliances had to be formed from scratch for each legislative proposal, the business of government would slow to a crawl or halt altogether. Parties create a basis for coalition and thus sharply reduce the time, energy, and effort needed to advance a legislative proposal. For example, in 2001, when newly elected president George Bush considered a series of new policy initiatives, he met first with the House and Senate leaders of the Republican Party. Although some congressional Republicans disagreed with the president's approach to a number of issues, all felt they had a stake in cooperating with him to burnish the party's image in preparation for the next round of national elections. Without the support of a party, the president would be compelled to undertake the daunting and probably impossible task of forming a completely new coalition for every individual policy proposal. As political scientist John Aldrich has noted, no group of politicians in our democracy has ever come up with a way to achieve their goals without political parties.[2]

The Two-Party System in America

two-party system a political system in which only two parties have a realistic opportunity to compete effectively for control

Although George Washington, and in fact many other leaders of his time, deplored partisan politics, the **two-party system** emerged early in the history of the new Republic. Beginning with the Federalists and the Jeffersonian Republicans in the late 1780s, two major parties would dominate national politics, although which particular two parties they were would change with the times and issues. This two-party system has culminated in today's Democrats and Republicans (see Figure 9.1).

HISTORICAL ORIGINS

Historically, parties form in one of two ways. The first, which could be called "internal mobilization," occurs when political conflicts break out and government officials and competing factions seek to mobilize popular support. This is precisely what happened during the early years of the American Republic. Competition in the Congress between northeastern mercantile and southern agrarian factions led first the southerners and then the northeasterners to attempt to organize popular followings. The result was the foundation of America's first national parties—the Jeffersonians, whose primary base was in the South, and the Federalists, whose strength was greatest in the New England states.

The second common mode of party formation, which could be called "external mobilization," takes place when a group of politicians outside the established governmental framework develops and organizes popular support to win governmental power. For example, during the 1850s, a group of state politicians who opposed slavery, especially the expansion of slavery in America's territorial possessions, built what became the Republican Party by constructing party organizations and mobilizing popular support in the Northeast and West.

America's two major parties now, of course, are the Democrats and the Republicans. Each has had an important place in U.S. history.

How the Party System Evolved

Figure 9.1

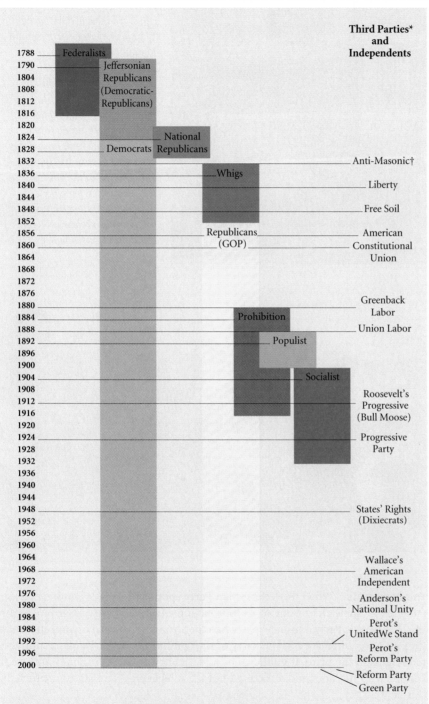

*Or in some cases, fourth party; most of these parties lasted through only one term.
†The Anti-Masonics had the distinction of being not only the first third party, but also the first party to hold a national nominating convention and the first to announce a party platform.

The Democratic Party of the United States is the world's oldest political party. The Democrats can trace their history back to Thomas Jefferson's Jeffersonian Republicans and, later, to Andrew Jackson's Jacksonian Democrats. The Jacksonians brought patronage politics—the spoils system—and modern campaign techniques to the political arena and, in so doing, expanded voter participation and ushered in the political era of the common person, as shown in this image of Jackson's inauguration celebration on the White House lawn.

In the late nineteenth century, the Democrats organized an incongruous coalition of southerners and northern immigrant voters into powerful urban "machines," such as New York's Tammany Hall machine and Chicago's Cook County machine (run for many years by Mayor Richard J. Daley, behind podium). These machines were capable of mobilizing hundreds of thousands of voters for the party's candidates.

The Democrats   When the Jeffersonian Party splintered in 1824, Andrew Jackson emerged as the leader of one of its four factions. In 1830, Jackson's group became the Democratic Party. This new party had the strongest national organization of its time and presented itself as the party of the common man. Jacksonians supported reductions in the price of public lands and a policy of cheaper money and credit. Laborers, immigrants, and settlers west of the Alleghenies were quickly attracted to this new party.

From 1828, when Jackson was elected president, to 1860, the Democratic Party was the dominant force in American politics. For all but eight of those years, the Democrats held the White House. In addition, a Democratic majority controlled the Senate for twenty-six years and the House for twenty-four years

Even at the height of their strength during and following the New Deal, the Democrats were never fully united. Many conservative southern Democrats opposed the party's embrace of African Americans and civil rights. After the 1948 national convention, southern segregationists broke from the party and formed the States' Rights Democratic Party, popularly known as the "Dixiecrats," and nominated Strom Thurmond (behind podium) of South Carolina for president.

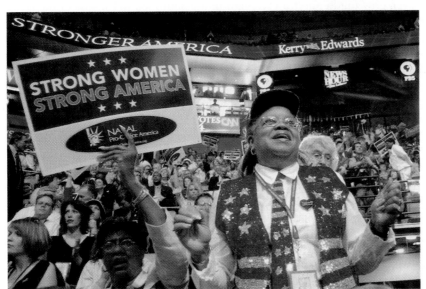

By the 1960s, the Democratic Party had evolved into a liberal-labor coalition that supported minority rights and a variety of domestic social programs. In matters of foreign policy, the Democrats were divided, leading many voters to believe that the Democratic Party was weak on national defense. In 2004, Democratic presidential nominee John Kerry ran a campaign that sought to appeal to the party's core constituencies while reassuring other voters that Democrats were for a "stronger America" too.

during the same time period. These nineteenth-century Democrats emphasized the importance of interpreting the Constitution literally, upholding states' rights, and limiting federal spending.

In 1860, the issue of slavery split the Democrats along geographic lines. In the South, many Democrats served in the Confederate government. In the North, one faction of the party (the Copperheads) opposed the war and advocated negotiating a peace with the South. Thus, for years after the war, Republicans denounced the Democrats as the "party of treason."

The Democratic Party was not fully able to regain its political strength until the Great Depression. In 1933, Democrat Franklin D. Roosevelt entered the White House and the Democrats won control of Congress as well. Roosevelt's New Deal coalition, composed of Catholics, Jews, blacks, farmers, intellectuals, and members of organized labor, dominated American politics until the 1970s and served as the basis for the party's expansion of federal power and efforts to remedy social problems.

The Democrats were never fully united. In Congress, southern Democrats often aligned with Republicans in the "conservative coalition" rather than with members of their own party. But the Democratic Party remained America's majority party, usually controlling both Congress and the White House, for nearly four decades after 1932. By the 1980s, the Democratic coalition faced serious problems. The once-solid South often voted for the Republicans, along with many white, blue-collar northern voters. On the other hand, the Democrats increased their strength among African American voters and women. The Democrats maintained a strong base in the bureaucracies of the federal government and the states, in labor unions, and in the not-for-profit sector of the economy. During the 1980s and 1990s, moderate Democrats were able to take control of the party nominating process and sought to broaden middle-class support for the Democrats. This helped the Democrats elect a president in 1992. In 1994, however, growing Republican strength in the South led to the loss of the Democrats' control of both houses of Congress for the first time since 1946. Although President Clinton, a Democrat, was able to win re-election to the White House in 1996 over the weak opposition of Republican Bob Dole, Democrats were unable to recapture control of either house of Congress.

Employing a strategy his aides called "triangulation," President Clinton sought to pursue a moderate course that placed him midway between the positions of conservative Republicans and liberal Democrats. This strategy helped Clinton and the Democratic Party as a whole, which gained strength and nearly regained control of the House of Representatives in the 1998 national elections. In 2000, Vice President Al Gore won the party's nomination for president, and Gore, like Clinton, sought to keep his campaign and the Democratic Party firmly anchored in the political center. Late in the presidential race, in which he was trailing in the polls, Gore shifted course and sought to appeal to the party's liberal, African American, and union-based wing. This strategy may have cost Gore some support among moderate Democrats. Despite the lessons of Clinton's "triangulation," the Democratic Party has not yet found a way to firmly unite its liberal and more moderate wings. Disagreements between the two wings of the party were evident during the campaign for the Democratic presidential nomination in 2003 and 2004. Moderate Democrat Joseph Lieberman, for example, supported President Bush's decision to launch a war against Iraq, while liberal Democrats such as Howard Dean and Al Sharpton strongly criticized the president's military policies. The party's eventual nominee, Senator John Kerry of Massachusetts, had originally supported the war but sought to stake out a position in opposition to Bush's policies that would satisfy liberal Democrats but not appear to be indecisive.

The Republicans The 1854 Kansas-Nebraska Act overturned the Missouri Compromise of 1820 and the Compromise of 1850, which had barred the expansion of slavery in the American territories. The Kansas-Nebraska Act gave each territory the right to decide whether to permit slavery. Opposition to this policy galvanized antislavery groups and led them to create a new party, the Republicans. It drew its membership from existing political groups—former Whigs, Know-Nothings, Free Soilers, and antislavery Democrats. In 1856, the party's

The Republican Party was formed during the 1850s as a coalition of antislavery and other forces. The party's nomination of Abraham Lincoln for the presidency at the 1860 convention (left) sparked the secession of the South and of the Civil War.

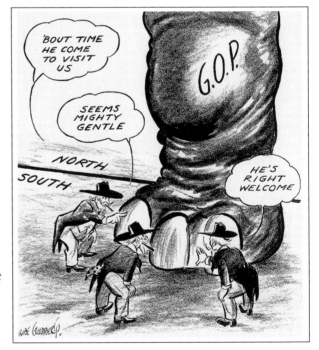

Beginning in the 1940s, but especially during the 1960s and 1970s, Democratic Party support for the civil rights movement divided the party and led white southerners to the Republican camp. Starting in 1952, this bolstered the GOP's strength and gave it a decided edge in presidential elections. Between 1968 and 1988, Republicans won five of six presidential elections.

first presidential candidate, John C. Fremont, won one-third of the popular vote and carried eleven states.

The early Republican platforms appealed to commercial as well as antislavery interests. The Republicans favored homesteading, internal improvements, the construction of a transcontinental railroad, and protective tariffs as well as the containment of slavery. In 1858, the Republican Party won control of the House of

Representatives; in 1860, the Republican presidential candidate, Abraham Lincoln, was victorious in a four-way race.

For almost seventy-five years after the North's victory in the Civil War, the Republicans were America's dominant political party, especially after 1896. Between 1860 and 1932, Republicans occupied the White House for fifty-six years and controlled the Senate for sixty years and the House for fifty. During these years, the Republicans came to be closely associated with big business. The party of Lincoln became the party of Wall Street.

The Great Depression ended Republican hegemony, however. The voters held President Herbert Hoover responsible for the economic catastrophe, and by 1936, the party's popularity was so low that Republicans won only eighty-nine seats in the House and seventeen in the Senate. The Republican presidential candidate in 1936, Governor Alfred M. Landon of Kansas, carried only two states. The Republicans won only four presidential elections between 1932 and 1980, and they controlled Congress for only four of those years (1947–49 and 1953–55).

In 1994, Republicans took control of both houses of Congress for the first time in four decades and promised to implement a conservative agenda under the rubric of a "Contract with America." However, the GOP's ultimately unsuccessful effort to impeach Democratic president Bill Clinton diverted Republican energies from other tasks.

The Republican Party, also known as the GOP (which stands for "Grand Old Party"), has widened its appeal over the last five decades. Groups previously associated with the Democratic Party—particularly white, blue-collar workers and white southern Democrats—have been increasingly attracted to Republican presidential candidates (for example, Dwight D. Eisenhower, Richard Nixon, Ronald Reagan, George H. W. Bush, and George W. Bush). Yet Republicans generally did not do as well at the state and local levels and, until recently, had little chance of capturing a majority in either the House or the Senate. In 1994, however, the Republican Party finally won a majority in both houses of Congress, in large part because of the party's growing strength in the South.

During his presidency, President George W. Bush united his party around core Republican issues such as tax cuts and military strength. The Republican's 2004 convention featured speaker after speaker touting Bush's leadership of a "nation at war."

During the 1990s, conservative religious groups, who had been attracted to the Republican camp by its opposition to abortion and support for school prayer, made a concerted effort to expand their influence within the party. This effort led to conflict between these members of the "religious Right" and more traditional "country-club" Republicans, whose major concerns were matters such as taxes and federal regulation of business. The coalition between these two wings won control of both houses of Congress in 1994 and was able to retain control of both houses in 1996, despite President Clinton's re-election. In 1998, however, severe strains began to show in the GOP coalition. In 2000, George W. Bush sought to unite the party's centrist and right wings behind a program of tax cuts, education reform, military strength, and family values. Bush avoided issues that divided the GOP camp, like abortion. Bush's candidacy boded well for the future of the GOP insofar as Bush was able to find a political formula that could unite the party. Republicans hoped that future candidates might apply this formula to restore the GOP to its glory years.

PARTY SYSTEMS

Our understanding of American party history would be incomplete if we considered each party only in isolation. America's political parties compete with one another over offices, policies, and power, and the history of each party is inextricably linked to that of its major rival. Historians often refer to the constellation of parties that are important at any given time as a nation's "party system." The most obvious feature of a party system is the number of major parties competing for power. The United States has usually had a two-party system, meaning that only two parties have a serious chance to win national elections. Of course, we have not always had the same two parties, and, as we shall see below, minor parties often put forward candidates.

The term *party system*, however, refers to more than just the number of parties competing for power. It also connotes the organization of the parties, the balance of power between and within party coalitions, the parties' social and institutional bases, and the issues and policies around which party competition is organized. Seen from this broader perspective, the character of a nation's party system can change even though the number of parties remains the same and even when the same two parties seem to be competing for power. Today's American party system is very different from the country's party system of fifty years ago, but the Democrats and Republicans continue to be the major competing forces. The character of a nation's party system can have profound consequences for the relative influences of social forces, the importance of political institutions, and even the types of issues and policies that reach the nation's political agenda. For example, the contemporary American political parties mainly compete for the support of different groups of middle-class Americans. As a result, issues that concern the middle and upper-middle classes, such as the environment, health care, retirement benefits, and taxation, are very much on the political agenda while issues that concern working-class and poorer Americans, such as welfare and housing, receive short shrift from both parties.[3] Over the course of American history, changes in political forces and alignments have produced six distinctive party systems.

The First Party System: Federalists and Jeffersonian Republicans   The first party system emerged in the 1790s and pitted the Federalists against the Jeffersonian

Republicans. The Federalists spoke mainly for New England mercantile groups and supported a program of protective tariffs to encourage manufactures, assumption of the states' Revolutionary War debts, the creation of a national bank, and resumption of commercial ties with England. The Jeffersonians, led by southern agrarian interests, opposed these policies and instead favored free trade, the promotion of agrarian over commercial interests, and friendship with France. The Federalists sought, unsuccessfully, to use the force of law against the Jeffersonians by enacting the Alien and Sedition Acts to outlaw criticism of the government. These acts, however, proved virtually impossible to enforce, and the Jeffersonians gradually expanded their base from the South into the Middle Atlantic states. In the election of 1800, Jefferson defeated incumbent Federalist president John Adams and led his party to power. Over the ensuing years, the Federalists gradually weakened. The party disappeared altogether after the pro-British sympathies of some Federalist leaders during the War of 1812 led to charges that the party was guilty of treason.

From the collapse of the Federalists until the 1830s, America had only one political party, the Jeffersonian Republicans, who gradually came to be known as the Democrats. This period of one-party politics is sometimes known as the "era of good feelings" to indicate the absence of party competition. Throughout this period, however, there was intense factional conflict within the Democratic Party, particularly between the supporters and opponents of General Andrew Jackson, America's great military hero of the War of 1812. Jackson's opponents united to deny him the presidency in 1824, but Jackson won election in 1828 and again in 1832. Jackson's base of support was in the South and in the West, and he generally espoused a program of free trade and monetary expansionism that appealed to those regions. During the 1830s, groups opposing Jackson for reasons of personality and politics united to form a new political force—the Whig Party—thus giving rise to the second American party system.

The Second Party System: Democrats and Whigs During the 1830s and 1840s, the Democrats and Whigs built party organizations throughout the nation; they both sought to enlarge their bases of support by expanding the suffrage through the elimination of property restrictions and other barriers to voting—at least voting by white males. This would not be the last time that party competition paved the way for expansion of the electorate. Support for the new Whig Party was stronger in the Northeast than in the South and West and stronger among mercantile groups than among small farmers. Hence, in some measure, the Whigs were the successors of the Federalists. Yet, conflict between the two parties revolved more around personalities than policies. The Whigs were a diverse group united more by opposition to the Democrats than by agreement on programs. In 1840, the Whigs won their first presidential election under the leadership of General William Henry Harrison, a military hero known as "Old Tippecanoe." The Whig campaign carefully avoided issues—since the party could agree on almost none—and emphasized the personal qualities and heroism of the candidate. The Whigs also invested heavily in campaign rallies and entertainment to win the hearts, if not exactly the minds, of the voters. The 1840 campaign came to be called the "hard cider" campaign to denote the then-common practice of using food and especially drink to win votes.

In the late 1840s and early 1850s, conflicts over slavery produced sharp divisions within both the Whig and the Democratic parties despite the efforts of party leaders like Henry Clay and Stephen Douglas to develop sectional compromises that would bridge the increasing gulf between the North and the South. By 1856, the Whig Party had all but disintegrated under the strain, and many Whig politicians and voters, along with antislavery Democrats, joined the new Republican Party, which pledged to ban slavery from the western territories. In 1860, the Republicans nominated Abraham Lincoln for the presidency. Lincoln's victory strengthened southern calls for secession from the Union and, soon thereafter, for all-out civil war.

The Civil War and Post–Civil War Party System: Republicans and Democrats

During the course of the war, President Lincoln depended heavily on Republican governors and state legislatures to raise troops, provide funding, and maintain popular support for a long and bloody military conflict. The secession of the South had stripped the Democratic Party of many of its leaders and supporters, but the Democrats remained politically competitive throughout the war and nearly won the 1864 presidential election because of war weariness on the part of the northern public. With the defeat of the Confederacy in 1865, some congressional Republicans sought to convert the South into a Republican bastion through a program of Reconstruction that enfranchised newly freed slaves while disfranchising many white voters and disqualifying many white politicians from seeking office. This Reconstruction program collapsed in the 1870s as a result of dissension within the Republican Party in Congress and violent resistance to Reconstruction by southern whites. With the end of Reconstruction, the former Confederate states regained full membership in the Union and full control of their internal affairs. Throughout the South, African Americans were deprived of political rights, including the right to vote, despite post–Civil War constitutional guarantees to the contrary. The post–Civil War South was solidly Democratic in its political affiliation, and with a firm Southern base, the national Democratic Party was able to confront the Republicans on a more or less equal basis. From the end of the Civil War to the 1890s, the Republican Party remained the party of the North, with strong business and middle-class support, while the Democrats were the party of the South, with support from working-class and immigrant groups in the North. Republican candidates campaigned by waving the "bloody shirt" of the Civil War and urging their supporters to "Vote the way you shot." Democrats emphasized the issue of the tariff, which they claimed was ruinous to agricultural interests.

The System of 1896: Republicans and Democrats

During the 1890s, profound and rapid social and economic changes led to the emergence of a variety of protest parties, including the Populist Party, which won the support of hundreds of thousands of voters in the South and West. The Populists appealed mainly to small farmers but also attracted western mining interests and urban workers as well. In the 1892 presidential election, the Populist Party carried four states and elected governors in eight. In 1896, the Populist Party effectively merged with the Democrats, who nominated William Jennings Bryan, a Democratic senator with pronounced Populist sympathies, for the presidency. The Republicans nominated conservative senator William McKinley. In the ensuing campaign, northern and midwestern business made an all-out effort to defeat what it saw as a radical threat from the Populist-Democratic alliance. When the dust settled, the Republicans had won a resounding victory. The GOP had carried the northern and midwestern states and confined the Democrats to their bastions in the South and far West. For the next thirty-six years, the Republicans were the nation's majority party, carrying seven of nine presidential elections and controlling both houses of Congress in fifteen of eighteen contests. The Republican Party of this era was very much the party of American business, advocating low taxes, high tariffs, and a minimum of government regulation. The Democrats were far too weak to offer much opposition. Southern Democrats, moreover, were too concerned with maintaining the region's autonomy on issues of race to challenge the Republicans on other fronts.

The New Deal Party System: Reversal of Fortune   Soon after Republican presidential candidate Herbert Hoover won the 1928 presidential election, the nation's economy collapsed. The "Great Depression," which produced unprecedented economic hardship, stemmed from a variety of causes, but from the perspective of millions of Americans the Republican Party did not do enough to promote economic recovery. In 1932, Americans elected Franklin D. Roosevelt (FDR) and a solidly Democratic Congress. FDR developed a program for economic recovery that he dubbed the "New Deal." Under the auspices of the New Deal, the size and reach of America's national government increased substantially. The federal government took responsibility for economic management and social welfare to an extent that was unprecedented in American history. Roosevelt designed many of his programs specifically to expand the political base of the Democratic Party. He rebuilt the party around a nucleus of unionized workers, upper-middle-class intellectuals and professionals, southern farmers, Jews, Catholics, and African Americans that revitalized the Democrats. This so-called New Deal coalition made the Democrats the nation's majority party for the next thirty-six years. Republicans groped for a response to the New Deal and often wound up supporting popular New Deal programs like Social Security in what was sometimes derided as "me too" Republicanism.

The New Deal coalition was severely strained during the 1960s by conflicts over civil rights and the Vietnam War. The struggle over civil rights initially divided northern Democrats who supported the civil rights cause from white southern Democrats who defended the system of racial segregation. Subsequently, as the civil rights movement launched a northern campaign aimed at securing access to jobs and education and an end to racial discrimination in such realms as housing, northern Democrats also split, often along income lines. The struggle over the Vietnam War further divided the Democrats, with upper-income liberal Democrats strongly opposing the Johnson administration's decision to send U.S. forces to fight in Southeast Asia. These schisms within the Democratic Party provided an opportunity for the GOP, which returned to power in 1968 under the leadership of Richard Nixon.

The Contemporary American Party System   In the 1960s, conservative Republicans argued that "me-tooism" was a recipe for continual failure and sought to reposition the GOP as a genuine alternative to the Democrats. In 1964, for example, Republican presidential candidate Barry Goldwater, author of a book entitled *Conscience of a Conservative,* argued in favor of substantially reduced levels of taxation and spending, less government regulation of the economy, and the elimination of many federal social programs. Though Goldwater was defeated by Lyndon Johnson, the ideas he espoused continued to be major themes for the Republican

Party. It took Richard Nixon's "southern strategy" to give the GOP the votes it needed to end Democratic dominance of the political process. Nixon appealed strongly to disaffected white southerners, and with the help of independent candidate and former Alabama governor George Wallace, he sparked the shift of voters that eventually gave the once-hated "party of Lincoln" a strong position in all the states of the former Confederacy. In the 1980s, under the leadership of Ronald Reagan, Republicans added another important group to their coalition: religious conservatives who were offended by Democratic support for abortion and gay rights as well as alleged Democratic disdain for traditional cultural and religious values.

While Republicans built a political base around economic and social conservatives and white southerners, the Democratic Party maintained its support among unionized workers and upper-middle-class intellectuals and professionals. Democrats also appealed strongly to racial minorities. The 1965 Voting Rights Act had greatly increased black voter participation in the South and helped the Democratic Party retain some House and Senate seats in southern states. And while the GOP appealed to social conservatives, the Democrats appealed strongly to Americans concerned with abortion rights, gay rights, feminism, environmentalism, and other progressive social causes. The result, thus far, has been a very even balance between the two parties. The 2000 presidential election ended in a virtual tie between George W. Bush and Al Gore, and the two houses of Congress are almost evenly divided between the two parties.

ELECTORAL ALIGNMENTS AND REALIGNMENTS

The points of transition between party systems in American history are sometimes called periods of **electoral realignment.** During these periods, the electoral coalitions that support the parties and the balance of power between the parties are redefined. Figure 9.2 charts the sequence of party systems and realignments in American history. Party loyalties in contemporary America continue to be in a state of flux, perhaps reflecting the organizational weakness of contemporary American parties. Some scholars have referred to modern-day partisan shifts as **dealignment** rather than realignment.

Although there are disputes among scholars about the timing of realignments, there is some agreement that five have occurred since the Founding. The first took place around 1800 when the Jeffersonian Republicans defeated the Federalists and became the dominant force in American politics. The second realignment took place in about 1828 when the Jacksonian Democrats seized control of the White House and the Congress. The third period of realignment centered on 1860. During this period, the newly founded Republican party led by Abraham Lincoln won power, in the process destroying the Whig Party, which had been one of the nation's two major parties since the 1830s. During the fourth realignment, centered on the election of 1896, the Republicans reasserted their dominance of the national government, which had been weakening since the 1880s. The fifth realignment took place during the period 1932–36, when the Democrats, led by Franklin Delano Roosevelt, took control of the White House and Congress and, despite sporadic interruptions, maintained control of both through the 1960s. Since that time, American party politics has been characterized primarily by **divided government,** wherein the presidency is controlled by one party while the other party controls one or both houses of Congress.

electoral realignment the point in history when a new party supplants the ruling party, becoming in turn the dominant political force. In the United States, this has tended to occur roughly every thirty years

dealignment large-scale weakening of partisan ties in the electorate

divided government the condition in American government wherein the presidency is controlled by one party while the opposing party controls one or both houses of Congress

| Figure 9.2 | Electoral Realignments |

Political scientists disagree over whether an electoral realignment occurred in 1968, because no one party clearly dominated the national government after that election.

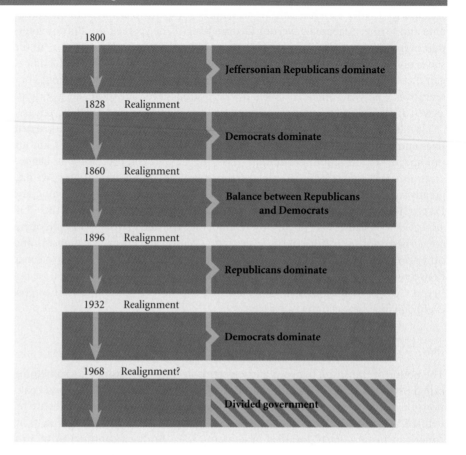

Historically, realignments occur when new issues combined with economic or political crises mobilize new voters and persuade large numbers of voters to reexamine their traditional partisan loyalties and permanently shift their support from one party to another. For example, during the 1850s, diverse regional, income, and business groups supported one of the two major parties, the Democrats or the Whigs, on the basis of their positions on various economic issues, such as internal improvements, the tariff, monetary policy, and banking. This economic alignment was shattered during the 1850s. The newly formed Republican Party campaigned on the basis of opposition to slavery and, in particular, opposition to the expansion of slavery into the territories. The issues of slavery and sectionalism produced divisions within both the Democratic and the Whig parties, ultimately leading to the dissolution of the latter, and these issues compelled voters to reexamine their partisan allegiances. Many northern voters who had supported the Whigs or the Democrats on the basis of their economic stands shifted their support to the Republicans as slavery replaced tariffs and economic concerns as the central item on the nation's political agenda. Many southern Whigs shifted their support to the Democrats. The new sectional alignment of forces that emerged was solidified by the trauma of the Civil War and persisted almost to the turn of the century.

In 1896, this sectional alignment was at least partially supplanted by an alignment of political forces based on economic and cultural factors. During the economic crises of the 1880s and 1890s, the Democrats forged a coalition consisting of economically hard-pressed midwestern and southern farmers, as well as small-town and rural economic interests. These groups tended to be native-stock, fundamentalist Protestants. The Republicans, on the other hand, put together a coalition comprising most of the business community, industrial workers, and city dwellers. In the election of 1896, Republican candidate William McKinley, emphasizing business, industry, and urban interests, defeated Democrat William Jennings Bryan, who spoke for sectional interests, farmers, and fundamentalism. Republican dominance lasted until 1932.

Such periods of electoral realignment in American politics have had extremely important institutional and policy results. Realignments occur when new issue concerns coupled with economic or political crises weaken the established political elite and permit new groups of politicians to create coalitions of forces capable of capturing and holding the reins of governmental power. The construction of new governing coalitions during these realigning periods has effected major changes in American governmental institutions and policies. Each period of realignment represents a turning point in American politics. The choices made by the national electorate during these periods have helped shape the course of American political history for a generation.[4]

AMERICAN THIRD PARTIES

Although the United States is said to have a two-party system, the country has always had more than two parties. Typically, **third parties** in the United States have represented social and economic interests that for one or another reason were not given voice by the two major parties.[5] Such parties have had a good deal of influence on ideas and elections in the United States. The Populists, a party centered in the rural areas of the West and Midwest, and the Progressives, spokesmen for the urban middle classes in the late nineteenth and early twentieth centuries, are the most important examples in the past 100 years. More recently, Ross Perot, who ran in 1992 as an independent and in 1996 as the Reform Party's nominee, impressed voters with his folksy style; he garnered almost 19 percent of the votes cast in the 1992 presidential election. Table 9.1 shows a listing of all the parties that offered candidates in one or more states in the presidential election of 2004, as well as independent candidates who ran. Including Ralph Nader, the third-party and independent candidates together polled only 1.05 million votes. They gained no electoral votes for president, and most of them disappeared immediately after the presidential election. The significance of Table 9.1 is that it demonstrates the large number of third parties running candidates and appealing to voters. Third-party candidacies also arise at the state and local levels. In New York, the Liberal and Conservative parties have been on the ballot for decades. In 1998, Minnesota elected a third-party governor, former professional wrestler Jesse Ventura.

Although the Republican Party was only the third American political party to make itself permanent (by replacing the Whigs), other third parties have enjoyed an influence far beyond their electoral size. This was because large parts of their programs were adopted by one or both of the major parties, who sought to appeal to the voters mobilized by the new party, and so to expand their own electoral

third parties parties that organize to compete against the two major American political parties

Table 9.1 · Parties and Candidates in 2004

In the 2004 presidential election, in addition to the Democratic and Republican nominees, at least fifteen candidates appeared on the ballot in one or more states.

Candidate	Party	Vote Total*	Percentage of Vote*
George W. Bush	Republican	58,978,616	51%
John F. Kerry	Democratic	55,384,497	48%
Ralph Nader	Independent	394,578	0%
Michael Badnarik	Libertarian	377,940	0%
Michael A. Peroutka	Constitution	129,842	0%
David Cobb	Green	105,525	0%
Leonard Peltier	Peace and Freedom	21,616	0%
Walter F. Brown	Independent	10,258	0%
James Harris	Socialist Workers	6,699	0%
Roger Calero	Socialist Workers	5,274	0%
Thomas J. Harens	Other	2,395	0%
Bill Van Auken	Independent	2,078	0%
Gene Amondson	Libertarian	1,896	0%
John Parker	Liberty Union	1,159	0%
Charles Jay	Personal Choice	867	0%
Stanford "Andy" E. Andress	Unaffiliated	720	0%
Earl F. Dodge	Prohibition	122	0%
None of the above	—	3,646	0%

*With 99 percent of votes tallied.
SOURCE: www.washingtonpost.com/wp-srv/elections/2004/page/295001 (Accessed 11/8/04).

FOR CRITICAL ANALYSIS

Historically, third parties have developed in America when certain issues or constituencies have been ignored by the existing parties. Considering the similarities and differences between the Democratic and Republican parties, where might a budding third party find a constituency? What issues might it adopt? Finally, what structural and ideological obstacles might that third party face?

strength. The Democratic Party, for example, became a great deal more liberal when it adopted most of the Progressive program early in the twentieth century. Many Socialists felt that President Roosevelt's New Deal had adopted most of their party's program, including old-age pensions, unemployment compensation, an agricultural marketing program, and laws guaranteeing workers the right to organize into unions.

This kind of influence explains the short lives of third parties. Their causes are usually eliminated when the major parties absorb their programs and draw their supporters into the mainstream. There are, of course, additional reasons for the short duration of most third parties. One is the usual limitation of their electoral support to one or two regions. Populist support, for example, was primarily midwestern. The 1948 Progressive Party, with Henry Wallace as its candidate, drew nearly half its votes from the state of New York. The American Independent Party polled nearly 10 million popular votes and 45 electoral votes for George Wallace in 1968—the most electoral votes ever polled by a third-party candidate. But all of Wallace's electoral votes and the majority of his popular vote came from the states of the Deep South.

Americans usually assume that only the candidates nominated by one of the two major parties have any chance of winning an election. Thus, a vote cast for a third-party or independent candidate is often seen as a vote wasted. Voters who would prefer a third-party candidate may feel compelled to vote for the major-party candidate whom they regard as the "lesser of two evils" to avoid wasting their vote in a futile gesture. Third-party candidates must struggle—usually without success—to overcome the perception that they cannot win. Thus, in 1996, many voters who favored Ross Perot gave their votes to Bob Dole or Bill Clinton on the presumption that Perot was not really electable.

Under federal election law, any minor party receiving more than 5 percent of the national presidential vote is entitled to federal funds, though considerably less than the major parties receive. The Reform Party qualified by winning 8.2 percent in 1996. Ralph Nader, the Green Party candidate in 2000, hoped to win the 5 percent of the vote that would entitle the Green Party to federal funds. Though Nader may have drawn enough liberal votes in New Hampshire and Florida to give those states—and the national election—to the GOP, hopes of achieving the 5 percent threshold were dashed. Nader, nevertheless, resumed his presidential campaign in 2004, to the dismay of the Democrats.

Third parties are not active in presidential races only. During the 2002 off-year elections, third-party candidates ran for state office and for congressional seats in many states. Libertarian Party gubernatorial candidates received at least 2 percent of the vote in fifteen states, including a whopping 11 percent of the vote in Wisconsin. Green Party candidates also were active throughout the nation. While the Green Party generally draws votes that might have been cast for Democrats, the Libertarians tend to be supported by individuals who might otherwise have voted for the GOP's candidate. Thus, the Libertarians' strong showing in Wisconsin helped to bring about a Democratic victory in that state in 2002.

As many scholars have pointed out, third-party prospects are also hampered by America's **single-member-district** plurality election system. In many other nations, several individuals can be elected to represent each legislative district. This is called a system of **multiple-member districts.** With this type of system, the candidates of weaker parties have a better chance of winning at least some seats, and voters, less concerned about wasting ballots, are usually more willing to support minor-party candidates.

Reinforcing the effects of the single-member district, the **plurality system** of voting (see Chapter 10) generally has the effect of setting what could be called a high threshold for victory. To win a plurality race, candidates usually must secure many more votes than they would need under most European systems of **proportional**

While the Republicans and Democrats are America's dominant parties, many minor parties have presented candidates for political office throughout American history. In the nineteenth century, parties ranging from the Anti-Masons to the Vegetarians to the People's (or Populist) Party competed for votes. Typically, third parties in the United States have been considered short-lived coalitions of disgruntled outsiders, as shown in this satiric view of the People's Party as a "party of patches."

single-member district an electorate that is allowed to select only one representative from each district; the normal method of representation in the United States

multiple-member district an electorate that selects all candidates at large from the whole district; each voter is given the number of votes equivalent to the number of seats to be filled

plurality system a type of electoral system in which, to win a seat in the parliament or other representative body, a candidate need only receive the most votes in the election, not necessarily a majority of votes cast

proportional representation a multiple-member district system that allows each political party representation in proportion to its percentage of the total vote

representation. For example, to win an American plurality election in a single-member district where there are only two candidates, a politician must win more than 50 percent of the votes cast. To win a seat from a European multiple-member district under proportional rules, a candidate may need to win only 15 or 20 percent of the votes cast. This high American threshold discourages minor parties and encourages the various political factions that might otherwise form minor parties to minimize their differences and remain within the major-party coalitions.[6]

Though few minor parties survive more than one or two campaigns, they sometimes introduce new issues into politics and affect the outcome of the race by taking votes from the major party candidates. In 1992, Ross Perot (right) created the Reform Party, emphasizing such issues as the federal budget deficit and term limits, and won nearly 19 percent of the vote. Perot made it impossible for the major parties to ignore budget issues. By 2000, the major parties had appropriated Perot's issues, and Reform Party candidate Pat Buchanan won barely one-half of a percent of the popular vote.

Campaigning as the candidate of the Green Party in 2000, Ralph Nader (left) focused on global economic issues and carried 3 percent of the vote, mainly at the expense of Democratic candidate Al Gore. In 2004, Nader ran again but as an independent candidate after the Green Party rebuffed him as their nominee. Unlike in 2000, in 2004, Nader received only 0.3 percent of the vote. Third-party presidential candidates received a mere 0.9 percent in 2004. Third parties seldom survive because American electoral rules are stacked against them. America's winner-take-all system encourages voters to choose between the parties that have the best chance of winning in order to avoid throwing away their votes. In Europe, most elections are based upon systems of proportional representation that can give legislative seats to second, third, and fourth place finishers.

However, it would be incorrect to assert (as some scholars have) that America's single-member plurality election system is the major cause of its historical two-party pattern. All that can be said is that American election law depresses the number of parties likely to survive over long periods of time in the United States. There is nothing magical about two. Indeed, the single-member plurality system of election can also discourage second parties. After all, if one party consistently receives a large plurality of the vote, people may eventually come to see their vote *even for the second party* as a wasted effort. This happened to the Republican Party in the Deep South before World War II.

Party Organization

In the United States, **party organizations** exist at virtually every level of government (see Figure 9.3). These organizations are usually committees made up of a

party organization the formal structure of a political party, including its leadership, election committees, active members, and paid staff

How American Parties Are Organized

Figure 9.3

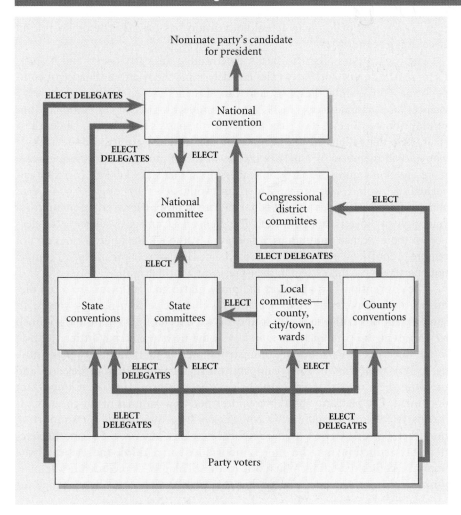

caucus (political) a normally closed meeting of a political or legislative group to select candidates, plan strategy, or make decisions regarding legislative matters

national convention a national party political institution that serves to nominate the party's presidential and vice presidential candidates, establish party rules, and write and ratify the party's platform

platform a party document, written at a national convention, that contains party philosophy, principles, and positions on issues

number of active party members. State law and party rules prescribe how such committees are constituted. Usually, committee members are elected at local party meetings—called **caucuses**—or as part of the regular primary election. The best-known examples of these committees are at the national level—the Democratic National Committee and the Republican National Committee.

NATIONAL CONVENTION

At the national level, the party's most important institution is the quadrennial **national convention.** The convention is attended by delegates from each of the states; as a group, they nominate the party's presidential and vice presidential candidates, draft the party's campaign platform for the presidential race, and approve changes in the rules and regulations governing party procedures. Before World War II, presidential nominations occupied most of the time, energy, and effort expended at the national convention. The nomination process required days of negotiation and compromise among state party leaders and often required many ballots before a nominee was selected. In recent years, however, presidential candidates have essentially nominated themselves by capturing enough delegate support in primary elections to win the official nomination on the first ballot. The actual convention has played little or no role in selecting the candidates.

The convention's other two tasks, determining the party's rules and its platform, remain important. Party rules can determine the relative influence of competing factions within the party and can also increase or decrease the party's chances for electoral success. In 1972, for example, the Democratic National Convention adopted a new set of rules favored by the party's liberal wing. Under these rules, state delegations to the Democratic convention were required to include women and members of minority groups in rough proportion to those groups' representation among the party's membership in that state. Liberals correctly calculated that women and African Americans would generally support liberal ideas and candidates. The rules also called for the use of proportional representation—a voting system liberals thought would give them an advantage by allowing the election of more women and minority delegates. (Although Republican rules do not require proportional representation, some state legislatures have moved to compel both parties to use this system in their presidential primaries.)

The convention also approves the party **platform.** Platforms are often dismissed as documents filled with platitudes that are seldom read by voters. To some extent this criticism is well founded. Not one voter in a thousand so much as glances at the party platform, and even the news media pay little attention to the documents. Furthermore, the parties' presidential candidates make little use of the platforms in their campaigns; usually they prefer to develop and promote their own themes. Nonetheless, the platform can be an important document. The platform should be understood as a contract in which the various party factions attending the convention state their terms for supporting the ticket. For one faction, welfare reform may be a key issue. For another faction, tax reduction may be more important. For a third, the critical issue might be deficit reduction. When one of these "planks" is included in the platform, its promoters are asserting that this is what they want in exchange for

Are More Parties Better Than Two Parties?

Despite occasionally strong performances by third parties, America is one of the few nations that has maintained an enduring two-party political system, beginning with the Federalist and Antifederalist parties in the postcolonial period. Today's Democratic Party is the world's oldest viable party; the younger Republican Party dates from the 1850s. America's stubborn loyalty to its two parties has been complicated by persistent criticisms of both of them, including charges that they are little different from each other and that they monopolize political power, choke off new ideas, and restrict the influx of new leaders with different ideas.

These and other criticisms have produced support for the idea of a multiparty system (any political system with three or more active parties is considered a multiparty system). American history supports the idea that third parties can help the political process. First, new parties can raise new and important issues ignored by the two major parties. In the pre–Civil War era, the Liberty and Free Soil parties advanced the cause of slavery abolition when the dominant Democratic and Whig parties were unable to come to grips with the issue. Early in the twentieth century, the Progressive Party advanced a vast array of social and political reforms that were eventually embraced by Democrats and Republicans. Ross Perot's Reform Party moved issues like deficit spending and budgetary responsibility to center stage in 1992. Second, as these examples suggest, a third-party option gives voters more choices among candidates and issues, addressing a persistent voter complaint. Third, most democratic nations have a multiparty system, showing that the idea not only is viable, but is a routine part of the workings of democracy. Fourth, new parties might spark renewed voter interest in an electoral system that now attracts fewer than half of the eligible adult electorate to the voting booth. And fifth, states like Minnesota and New York have maintained an active multiparty tradition (although in these states, the two major parties still dominate), suggesting that some version of the idea could indeed work on a national level.

Supporters of two-partyism argue that the virtues of the existing system are taken for granted. First and foremost, a two-party system produces automatic majorities, for the obvious reason that one will always receive over 50 percent of the vote. In a nation as large and diverse as America, governance could easily become impossible, or at least far more difficult, if multiple parties produced a bevy of candidates with no clear winner, or if American legislatures were populated with representatives from many different parties, barring any one party from organizing power. A second and related point is that the compromises that produce two candidates from two large parties also generally encourage moderation, compromise, and stability. Multiple parties might well heighten polarization and paralysis in America in a way that would make contemporary political gridlock seem tame by comparison. And while many democracies have multiparty systems, politics in those nations is often polarized and unstable. The Italian multiparty system, for example, produced over forty different governing coalitions in its first fifty years after the end of World War II. Third, the charge of exclusion of new factions and ideas by the two parties misses the fact that the two American parties are very large and diverse. In other nations, political conflict is played out between multiple parties. In America, much of that conflict occurs within the parties, especially during the nomination process. Fourth, America's enduring two-party system is a product of its political culture and historical development. The idea that a multiparty system could simply be transplanted onto the American political landscape is a leap of faith little supported by actual experience.

FOR CRITICAL ANALYSIS

1. Third parties are formed in the United States every year, but few last more than one or two electoral cycles. Why do third parties tend to be short-lived?

2. Should voters support a third party that has no chance of winning or should they vote for the major party candidate they dislike least?

Are More Parties Better Than Two Parties?

Yes

To many Democrats the two words are enough to make them turn red with anger.

But despite the invective spewed his way over the past three and a half years, the seventy-year-old consumer advocate has decided to return for another run at the presidency, this time as an independent.

With all the rage exploding on the campaign trail over this decision, one thing can be said: This is a great thing for America.

No, not because Nader stands to steal votes from Democratic nominee Senator John Kerry (D-Mass.) but because a debate will be reopened as to the necessity of multiple parties in today's system.

As Nader claimed on NBC's *Meet the Press*, today's two major parties are failing.

"[Corporate interests are] taking our country apart," Nader said. "Basically, it's a question between both parties flunking . . . one with a D–, the Republicans; one with a D+, the Democrats."

For this Nader and all other third-party candidates deserve a place in the presidential debates.

America has not been at its best when ruled from the center. The bold, near-Socialist initiatives of President Franklin D. Roosevelt pushed our nation out of the Depression. Ronald Reagan's government-cutting, strong-military agenda made the 1980s a golden era.

Third parties also allow for debates to open on previously ignored issues.

"Nader might force the candidates to talk about environmental issues," said political science professor Catherine Wilson.

Now the two parties toe the middle and just represent "Version 1" and "Version 1a."

Republicans and Democrats both call for tax cuts. Republicans and Democrats both do not go out on the limb with regards to universal health care. And, as Nader claims, both are too receptive to the causes of big business.

Even within their own party, nonmoderate candidates are shunned. Look at Ohio Republican Dennis Kucinich, who pushed for a progressive agenda with an exact, broad plan for all of America, all while being shunned in his own party in favor of the "electable" Kerry.

So, since Kerry is so "electable" Democrats need not fear Nader, you'd think?

If only America knew the whole picture.

Today, it is safe to say many Americans fit within the general ideals of Libertarians, championing smaller government. Today's structure, however, does not allow for people to hold beliefs outside of the mainstream; otherwise, they are branded as "extreme."

Nader still faces a stiff challenge to even get on the ballot in most states, requiring, for example, 25,000 signatures of registered voters in Illinois who did not vote in the March 16 primary.

His fight, however, must be recommended.

Sure, questions exist. How can we have a debate with a double-digit number of candidates? We will find a big enough stage. Wouldn't these debates take forever? We are picking our president. It is worth the time and effort.

An election looms 213 days from today, and many Americans view their choice as between the lesser of two evils.

Too bad, especially when it does not have to be that way.

SOURCE: Troy Appel, "Nader: Welcome Guest for Dull Parties," *Daily Northwestern* (Northwestern University), April 2, 2004.

No It is fashionable in liberal quarters these days to grumble about the Democratic Party "establishment," and to call for a revival of what Howard Dean called the "Democratic wing of the Democratic Party"—a not-so-subtle dig at the centrist Democratic Leadership Council. Moderate Democrats like Senator Joe Lieberman are viewed with a contempt usually reserved only for those whom a friend recently called "flamboyant Republicans." Disillusioned young progressives look farther to the left, beyond the mainstream, and toward the likes of Ralph Nader, revered champion of America's third parties. Idealists by nature, they urge their peers to reject the cynical, calculating tactics espoused by Democrats (myself included) who rallied behind John Kerry and his "electability," and instead to join them in "voting their consciences." How, they demand, can American democracy ever escape the evil clutches of the two-party system if its voters continue to submit complacently to the status quo?

To them I say, what is so great about multi-party systems, anyway? No matter how you look at it, it is still essentially the majority who govern. And if you want to be part of the majority, you need to find a way to agree with at least half of America's voters—you've got your labor unions, your impoverished urbanites, your "soccer moms," your educators, your trial lawyers, your pretentious movie stars who didn't even graduate from high school and don't know crap about politics but nevertheless have the audacity to peer down at us lowly Americans from their lofty pulpit at the Oscars and bestow upon us their profound insight regarding American foreign policy—take your pick!

Perhaps the idealists would accuse me at this point of advocating the compromise of one's beliefs. And they would be precisely correct! To be sure, there are times when there is something to be said for taking a stand, but let us not forget that compromise is the very essence of democracy. It is the art of compromise that allows us to proceed from a seeming impasse of squabbling voices and divergent interests to a peaceful and fluid process of governance.

Nor is compromise any less a part of multi-party systems than of our two-party system. The alternative to a majority party composed of diverse factions, after all, is but a majority coalition composed of diverse parties. In a multi-party system, you can "vote your conscience," but the party you choose must compromise with other parties if it is to participate in the governing coalition. So the question is not whether or not to compromise, but rather, should compromise occur at the voter level or at the party level?

This, of course, is not to say that there is no difference between multi- and two-party systems, nor that one is superior to the other. One might admire, for example, the dynamism of party coalitions, compared to the stagnation and entrenchment of party factions. Or perhaps one system, it might be argued, is more effective than the other in certain mystical euphoria that surrounds the multi-party system, which surely is centered in part around its exotic appeal, but which also is based perhaps on the fallacy that a multiplicity of parties somehow renders compromise obsolete. And nothing would please me more than to spoil this euphoria as cruelly as Ralph Nader spoiled the 2000 election . . .

SOURCE: Rob Tobin, "Third Parties Can Stick It," *The New Hampshire* (University of New Hampshire), March 26, 2004.

their support for the ticket, while other party factions are agreeing that the position seems reasonable and appropriate. Thus, party platforms should be seen more as internal party documents than as public pledges. The 2004 Democratic platform, for example, promised to protect the environment against the potentially damaging consequences of globalization. Again, this issue has little meaning to most voters but is of great concern to liberal environmentalists, an important Democratic constituency, who believe that American trade agreements should contain provisions essentially imposing U.S. environmental standards on other nations.

NATIONAL COMMITTEE

Between conventions, each national political party is technically headed by its national committee. For the Democrats and Republicans, these are called the Democratic National Committee (DNC) and the Republican National Committee (RNC), respectively. These national committees raise campaign funds, head off factional disputes within the party, and endeavor to enhance the party's media image. The actual work of each national committee is overseen by its chairperson. Governor Jim Gilmore of Virginia, chair of the Republican National Committee, is a political ally of President George W. Bush. The Democratic National Committee is chaired by real estate developer Terry McAuliffe, a close ally of former president Bill Clinton and one of the party's leading fund-raisers. Other committee members are generally major party contributors or fund-raisers and serve in a largely ceremonial capacity. Prior to the enactment of campaign finance reforms in 2002, during every election cycle the DNC and RNC each raised tens of millions of dollars of so-called soft money that could be used to support party candidates throughout the nation. The 2002 Bipartisan Campaign Reform Act (BCRA), sometimes known as the McCain-Feingold Act, outlawed this practice. To circumvent BCRA, however, each party has established a set of "shadow parties." These are groups nominally organized to promote and publicize political issues and, as such, can claim tax-exempt status under Section 527 of the Internal Revenue Code, which defines and provides tax-exempt status for nonprofit political advocacy groups. Such groups are sometimes called **527 Committees** because of this provision of the tax code.

527 Committees nonprofit independent groups that receive and disburse funds to influence the nomination, election, or defeat of candidates. Named after Section 527 of the Internal Revenue Code, which defines and provides tax-exempt status for nonprofit advocacy groups

Under the law, 527 Committees can raise and spend unlimited amounts of money as long as their activities are not coordinated with those of the formal party organizations. While some 527 Committees are actually independent, many are directed by former Republican and Democratic party officials and run shadow campaigns on behalf of the parties. On the Republican side, a major shadow is the Republican Club for Growth, which raises and spends millions of dollars for GOP television ads. Democratic shadows include such groups as Americans Coming Together (ACT) and the Media Fund, which together raised tens of millions of dollars in support of Senator John Kerry's presidential bid. In a recent decision, the Federal Election Commission (FEC) affirmed the legality of unlimited spending by 527 groups.[7]

For whichever party controls the White House, the party's national committee chair is appointed by the president. Typically, this means that that party's national committee becomes little more than an adjunct to the White House staff. For a first-term president, the committee devotes the bulk of its energy to the re-election campaign. The national committee chair of the party not in control of the White House is selected by the committee itself and usually takes a broader view of the party's needs, raising money and performing other activities on behalf of the party's members in Congress and in the state legislatures.

CONGRESSIONAL CAMPAIGN COMMITTEES

Each party also forms House and Senate campaign committees to raise funds for House and Senate election campaigns. Their efforts may or may not be coordinated with the activities of the national committees. For the party that controls the White House, the national committee and the congressional campaign committees are often rivals, since both groups are seeking donations from the same people but for different candidates: the national committee seeks funds for the presidential race while the congressional campaign committees approach the same contributors for support for the congressional contests. In recent years, the Republican Party has attempted to coordinate the fund-raising activities of all its committees. Republicans have sought to give the GOP's national institutions the capacity to invest funds in those close congressional, state, and local races where they can do the most good. The Democrats have been slower to coordinate their various committee activities, and this may have placed them at a disadvantage in recent congressional and local races.

STATE AND LOCAL PARTY ORGANIZATIONS

Each of the two major parties has a central committee in each state. The parties traditionally also have county committees and, in some instances, state senate district committees, judicial district committees, and in the case of larger cities, city-wide party committees and local assembly district "ward" committees as well. Congressional districts also may have party committees.

Some cities also have precinct committees. Precincts are not districts from which any representative is elected but instead are legally defined subdivisions of wards that are used to register voters and set up ballot boxes or voting machines. A precinct is typically composed of 300 to 600 voters. Well-organized political parties—especially the famous old machines of New York, Chicago, and Boston—provided for "precinct captains" and a fairly tight group of party members around them. Precinct captains were usually members of long standing in neighborhood party clubhouses, which were important social centers as well as places for distributing favors to constituents.[8]

In the nineteenth and early twentieth centuries, many cities and counties and even a few states upon occasion have had such well-organized parties that they were called **machines** and their leaders were called "bosses." Some of the great reform movements in American history were motivated by the excessive powers and abuses of these machines and their bosses. But few, if any, machines are left today. Traditional party machines depended heavily upon **patronage,** their power to control government jobs. With thousands of jobs to dispense, party bosses were able to recruit armies of political workers who, in turn, mobilized millions of voters. Today, because of civil service reform, party leaders no longer control many positions. Nevertheless, state and local party organizations are very active in recruiting candidates and conducting voter registration drives. In addition, under

machines strong party organizations in late-nineteenth- and early-twentieth-century American cities. These machines were led by "bosses" who controlled party nominations and patronage

patronage the resources available to higher officials, usually opportunities to make partisan appointments to offices and to confer grants, licenses, or special favors to supporters current federal law, state and local party organizations can spend unlimited amounts of money on "party-building" activities such as voter registration and get-out-the-vote drives (though in some states such practices are limited by state law). As a result, for many years the national party organizations, which have enormous fund-raising abilities but were restricted by law in how much they could spend on candidates, transferred millions of dollars to the state and local organizations. The state and local parties, in turn, spent these funds, sometimes called **"soft money,"** to promote the candidacies of national, as well as state and local, candidates. In this process, local organizations became linked financially to the national parties and American political parties became somewhat more integrated and nationalized than ever before. At the same time, the state and local party organizations came to control large financial resources and play important roles in elections despite the collapse of the old patronage machines.[9]

The McCain-Feingold campaign reform act of 2002 (BCRA) prohibited such soft money contributions. This legislation may weaken political parties and strengthen interest groups, which remain free to spend as much as they wish so long as their expenditures are not formally coordinated with a candidate's own campaign. As we saw, the parties also moved to circumvent BCRA restrictions by forming fund-raising units nominally unaffiliated with the national party organizations and thus not subject to the new law's restrictions.

Parties and the Electorate

Party organizations are more than just organizations; they are made up of millions of rank-and-file members. Individual voters tend to develop **party identification** with one of the political parties. Although it is a psychological tie, party identification also has a rational component. Voters generally form attachments to parties that reflect their views and interests. Once those attachments are formed, however, they are likely to persist and even to be handed down to children, unless some very strong factors convince individuals that their party is no longer an appropriate object for their affections. In some sense, party identification is similar to brand loyalty in the marketplace: consumers choose a brand of automobile for its appearance or mechanical characteristics and stick with it out of loyalty, habit, and unwillingness to constantly reexamine their choices, but they may eventually change if the old brand no longer serves their interests.

Although the strength of partisan ties in the United States has declined in recent years, most Americans continue to identify with either the Republican Party or the Democratic Party (see Figure 9.4). Party identification gives citizens a stake in election outcomes that goes beyond the particular race at hand. This is why strong party identifiers are more likely than other Americans to go to the polls and, of course, are more likely than others to support the party with which they identify. **Party activists** are drawn from the ranks of the strong identifiers. Activists are those who not only vote but also contribute their time, energy, and effort to party affairs. Activists ring doorbells, stuff envelopes, attend meetings, and contribute money to the party cause. No party could succeed without the thousands of volunteers who undertake the mundane tasks needed to keep the organization going.

Figure 9.4

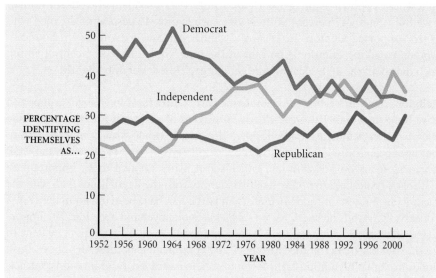

SOURCE: Harold W. Stanley and Richard G. Niemi, *Vital Statistics on American Politics, 2001–2002* (Washington, DC: Congressional Quarterly Press, 2001), p. 115, and *National Election Studies Guide to Public Opinion and Political Behavior.*

GROUP AFFILIATIONS

The Democratic and Republican parties are America's only national parties. They are the only political organizations that draw support from most regions of the country and from Americans of every racial, economic, religious, and ethnic group. The two parties do not draw equal support from members of every social stratum, however. When we refer to the Democratic or Republican "coalition," we mean the groups that generally support one or the other party. In the United States today, a variety of group characteristics are associated with party identification. These include race and ethnicity, gender, religion, class, ideology, and region.

Race and Ethnicity   Since the 1930s and Franklin Roosevelt's New Deal, African Americans have been overwhelmingly Democratic in their party identification. More than 90 percent of African Americans describe themselves as Democrats and support Democratic candidates in national, state, and local elections. Approximately 25 percent of the Democratic Party's support in presidential races comes from African American voters.

Latino voters do not form a monolithic bloc, by contrast. Cuban Americans are generally Republican in their party affiliations, whereas Mexican Americans favor the Democrats by a small margin. Other Latino voters, including those from Puerto Rico, are overwhelmingly Democratic. Asian Americans tend to be divided as well, but along class lines. The Asian American community's influential business and professional stratum identifies with the Republicans, but less-affluent Asian Americans tend to support the Democrats.

Gender   Women are somewhat more likely to support Democrats, and men somewhat more likely to support Republicans, in surveys of party affiliation. This difference is known as the **gender gap.** In the 1992 presidential election, women gave Bill Clinton 47 percent of their votes, while only 41 percent of the men who voted supported Clinton. In 1996, the gender gap was even more pronounced: women voted for Clinton 54 percent of the time, while only 43 percent of voting men did so. In the 2000 election, the gender gap closed, but only slightly.

Religion   Jews are among the Democratic Party's most loyal constituent groups and have been since the New Deal. Nearly 90 percent of all Jewish Americans describe themselves as Democrats. Catholics were also once a strongly pro-Democratic group but have been shifting toward the Republican Party since the 1970s, when the GOP began to focus on abortion and other social issues deemed to be important to Catholics. Protestants are more likely to identify with the Republicans than with the Democrats. Protestant fundamentalists, in particular, have been drawn to the GOP's conservative stands on social issues, such as school prayer and abortion. The importance of religious conservatives to the Republican Party became quite evident in 2001. After his victory in the November 2000 presidential election, George W. Bush announced that his administration would seek to award federal grants and contracts to religious groups. By using so-called faith-based groups as federal contractors, Bush was seeking to reward religious conservatives for their past loyalty to the GOP and to ensure that these groups would have a continuing stake in Republican success.

Class   Upper-income Americans are considerably more likely to affiliate with the Republicans, whereas lower-income Americans are far more likely to identify with the Democrats. This divide is reflected by the differences between the two parties on economic issues. In general, the Republicans support cutting taxes and social spending—positions that reflect the interests of the wealthy. The Democrats, however, favor increasing social spending, even if this requires increasing taxes—a position consistent with the interests of less-affluent Americans. One important exception to this principle is that relatively affluent individuals who work in the public sector or such related institutions as foundations and universities also tend to affiliate with the Democrats. Such individuals are likely to appreciate the Democratic Party's support for an expanded governmental role and high levels of public spending.

Ideology   Ideology and party identification are very closely linked. Most individuals who describe themselves as conservatives identify with the Republican Party, whereas most who call themselves liberals support the Democrats. This division has increased in recent years as the two parties have taken very different positions on social and economic issues. Before the 1970s, when party differences were more blurred, it was not uncommon to find Democratic conservatives and Republican liberals. Both of these species are rare today.

Region   Between the Civil War and the 1960s, the "Solid South" was a Democratic bastion. Today, the South is becoming solidly Republican, as is much of the West and Southwest. The area of greatest Democratic Party strength is the Northeast. The Midwest is a battleground, more or less evenly divided between the two parties.

Perspectives on Politics

COLLEGE STUDENTS' PARTY IDS

"Do you consider yourself to be a Democrat, a Republican, or an Independent?"

Democrat	Republican	Independent
32%	24%	41%

SOURCE: Institute of Politics, Harvard University, "Attitudes Toward Politics and Public Service: A National Survey of College Undergraduates," Conducted March 13–23, 2004. www.iop.harvard.edu/programs/other/natlsurvey/april_2004_topline.pdf. NOTE: Roughly 2–3% refused to answer or were affiliated with another party.

The explanations for these regional variations are complex. Southern Republicanism has come about because conservative white southerners identify the Democratic Party with the civil rights movement and with liberal positions on abortion, school prayer, and other social issues. Republican strength in the South and in the West is also related to the weakness of organized labor in these regions, as well as to the dependence of the two regions upon military programs supported by the Republicans. Democratic strength in the Northeast is a function of the continuing influence of organized labor in the large cities of this region, as well as of the region's large population of minority and elderly voters, who benefit from Democratic social programs.

Age   Age is another factor associated with partisanship. At the present time, individuals younger than fifty or older than sixty-five are fairly evenly divided between Democrats and Republicans, while those between the ages of fifty and sixty-four are much more likely to be Democrats. There is nothing about a particular numerical age that leads to a particular party loyalty. Instead, individuals from the same age cohort are likely to have experienced a similar set of events during the period when their party loyalties were formed. Thus, Americans between the ages of fifty and sixty-four came of political age during the cold-war, Vietnam, and civil-rights eras. Apparently among voters whose initial perceptions of politics were shaped during this period, more responded favorably to the role played by the Democrats than to the actions of the Republicans. Interestingly, among the youngest group of Americans, a group that came of age during an era of political scandals that tainted both parties, the majority describe themselves as Independents.

Figure 9.5 indicates the relationship between party identification and a number of social criteria. Race, religion, and income seem to have the greatest influence on Americans' party affiliations. None of these social characteristics are inevitably linked to partisan identification, however. There are black Republicans, southern white Democrats, Jewish Republicans, and even an occasional conservative Democrat. The general party identifications just discussed are broad tendencies that both reflect and reinforce the issue and policy positions the two parties take in the national and local political arenas.

FOR CRITICAL ANALYSIS

What are the major components of each party's political coalition? What factors tie these groups to their respective parties?

Parties and Elections

Parties play an important role in the electoral process. They provide the candidates for office, get out the vote, and facilitate mass electoral choice.

RECRUITING CANDIDATES

One of the most important but least noticed party activities is the recruitment of candidates for local, state, and national office. Each election year, candidates must be found for thousands of state and local offices as well as congressional seats. Where they do not have an incumbent running for re-election, party leaders attempt to identify strong candidates and to interest them in entering the campaign.

An ideal candidate will have an unblemished record and the capacity to raise enough money to mount a serious campaign. Party leaders are usually not willing to

Figure 9.5   Party Identification by Social Groups, 2002

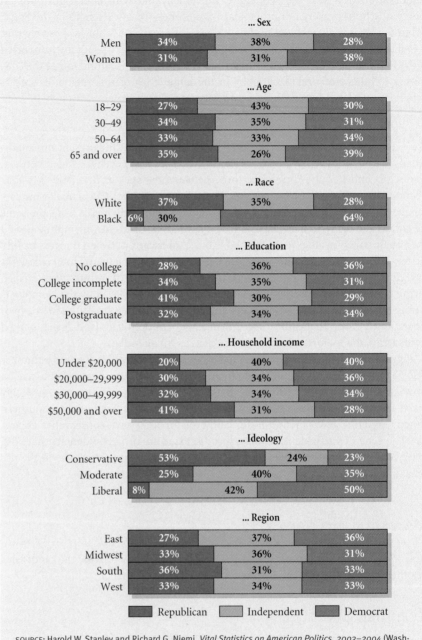

... Sex

	Republican	Independent	Democrat
Men	34%	38%	28%
Women	31%	31%	38%

... Age

	Republican	Independent	Democrat
18–29	27%	43%	30%
30–49	34%	35%	31%
50–64	33%	33%	34%
65 and over	35%	26%	39%

... Race

	Republican	Independent	Democrat
White	37%	35%	28%
Black	6%	30%	64%

... Education

	Republican	Independent	Democrat
No college	28%	36%	36%
College incomplete	34%	35%	31%
College graduate	41%	30%	29%
Postgraduate	32%	34%	34%

... Household income

	Republican	Independent	Democrat
Under $20,000	20%	40%	40%
$20,000–29,999	30%	34%	36%
$30,000–49,999	32%	34%	34%
$50,000 and over	41%	31%	28%

... Ideology

	Republican	Independent	Democrat
Conservative	53%	24%	23%
Moderate	25%	40%	35%
Liberal	8%	42%	50%

... Region

	Republican	Independent	Democrat
East	27%	37%	36%
Midwest	33%	36%	31%
South	36%	31%	33%
West	33%	34%	33%

■ Republican   ■ Independent   ■ Democrat

SOURCE: Harold W. Stanley and Richard G. Niemi, *Vital Statistics on American Politics, 2003–2004* (Washington, DC: Congressional Quarterly Press, 2003), Table 3-2, p. 119.

provide financial backing to candidates who are unable to raise substantial funds on their own. For a House seat this can mean several hundred thousand dollars; for a Senate seat a serious candidate must be able to raise several million dollars. Often, party leaders have difficulty finding attractive candidates and persuading them to run. Candidate recruitment is problematic in an era when political campaigns often involve mudslinging and candidates must assume that their personal lives will be intensely scrutinized in the press.[10]

NOMINATIONS

Article I, Section 4, of the Constitution makes only a few provisions for elections. It delegates to the states the power to set the "times, places, and manner" of holding elections, even for U.S. senators and representatives. It does, however, reserve to Congress the power to make such laws if it chooses to do so. The Constitution has been amended from time to time to expand the right to participate in elections. Congress has also occasionally passed laws about elections, congressional districting, and campaign practices. But the Constitution and the laws are almost completely silent on nominations, setting only citizenship and age requirements for candidates. The president must be at least thirty-five years of age, a natural-born citizen, and a resident of the United States for fourteen years. A senator must be at least thirty, a U.S. citizen for at least nine years, and a resident of the state he or she represents. A member of the House must be at least twenty-five, a U.S. citizen for seven years, and a resident of the state he or she represents.

Nomination is the process by which a party selects a single candidate to run for each elective office. The nominating process can precede the election by many months, as it does when the many candidates for the presidency are eliminated from consideration through a grueling series of debates and state primaries until there is only one survivor in each party—the party's nominee.

Nomination is the parties' most serious and difficult business. When more than one person aspires to an office, the choice can divide friends and associates. In comparison to such an internal dispute, the electoral campaign against the opposition is almost fun, because there the fight is against the declared adversaries.

nomination the process through which political parties select their candidates for election to public office

GETTING OUT THE VOTE

The actual election period begins immediately after the nominations. Historically, this has been a time of glory for the political parties, whose popular base of support is fully displayed. All the paraphernalia of party committees and all the committee members are activated into local party work forces.

The first step in the electoral process involves voter registration. This aspect of the process takes place all year round. There was a time when party workers were responsible for virtually all of this kind of electoral activity, but they have been supplemented (and in many states virtually displaced) by civic groups such as the League of Women Voters, unions, and chambers of commerce.

Those who have registered have to decide on Election Day whether to go to the polling place, stand in line, and actually vote for the various candidates and referenda on the ballot. Political parties, candidates, and campaigning can make a big difference in convincing the voters to vote. In recent years, each of the two parties has developed extensive data files on hundreds of millions of potential voters. The GOP has called its archive "Voter Vault," while the Democratic file has been designated "Demzilla." Democrats claim their files contain the names, addresses, voting preferences, contribution history, ethnic backgrounds, and other information on some 165 million Americans. Republican files contain similar data on nearly 200 million individuals. These elaborate data files allow the two parties to bring their search for votes, contributions, and campaign help down to named individuals. Voter mobilization, once an art, has now become a science.

FACILITATING VOTER CHOICE

On any general election ballot, there are likely to be only two or three candidacies where the nature of the office and the characteristics and positions of the candidates are well known to voters. But what about the choices for judges, the state comptroller, the state attorney general, and many other elective positions? And what about referenda? This method of making policy choices is being used more and more as a means of direct democracy. A referendum may ask: Should there be a new bond issue for financing the local schools? Should there be a constitutional amendment to increase the number of county judges? In 1996, Californians approved Proposition 201, a referendum that called for an end to most statewide affirmative action programs, including those employed for college admission. Another famous proposition on the 1978 California ballot was a referendum to reduce local property taxes. It started a taxpayer revolt that spread to many other states. By the time it had spread, most voters knew where they stood on the issue. But the typical referendum question is one on which few voters have clear and knowledgeable positions. Parties and campaigns help most by giving information when voters must choose among obscure candidates and vote on unclear referenda.

Parties and Government

When the dust of the campaign has settled, does it matter which party has won? It can.

PARTIES AND POLICY

One of the most familiar observations about American politics is that the two major parties try to be all things to all people and are therefore indistinguishable from each other. Data and experience give some support to this observation. Parties in the United States are not programmatic or ideological, as they have sometimes been in Britain or other parts of Europe. But this does not mean there are no differences between them. Since the 1980s, important differences have emerged between the positions of Democratic and Republican party leaders on a number of key issues, and these differences are still apparent today. For example, the national leadership of the Republican Party supports maintaining high levels of military spending, cuts in social programs, tax relief for middle- and upper-income voters, tax incentives to businesses, and the "social agenda" backed by members of conservative religious denominations. The national Democratic leadership, on the other hand, supports expanded social welfare spending, cuts in military spending, increased regulation of business, and a variety of consumer and environmental programs.

These differences reflect differences in philosophy and differences in the core constituencies to which the parties seek to appeal. The Democratic Party at the national level seeks to unite organized labor, the poor, members of racial minorities, and liberal upper-middle-class professionals. The Republicans, by contrast, appeal to business, upper-middle- and upper-class groups in the private sector, and social conservatives. Often, party leaders will seek to develop issues they hope will add new groups to their party's constituent base. During the 1980s, for example, under the leadership of Ronald Reagan, the Republicans devised a series of "social issues," including support for school prayer, opposition to abortion, and opposition to affirmative action, designed to cultivate the support of white southerners. This effort was extremely successful in increasing Republican strength in the once solidly Democratic South. In the 1990s, under the leadership of Bill Clinton, who called himself a "new Democrat," the Democratic Party sought to develop new social programs designed to solidify the party's base among working-class and poor voters, and new, somewhat more conservative economic programs aimed at attracting the votes of middle- and upper-middle-class voters. In 2000, George W. Bush labeled himself a "compassionate conservative" to signal the Republican base that he was a conservative while seeking to reassure moderate and independent voters that he was not an opponent of federal social programs.

As these examples suggest, parties do not always support policies just because they are already favored by their constituents. Instead, party leaders can play the role of **policy entrepreneurs,** seeking ideas and programs that will expand their party's base of support while eroding that of the opposition. It is one of the essential characteristics of party politics in America that a party's programs and policies often lead, rather than follow, public opinion. Like their counterparts in the business world, party leaders seek to identify and develop "products" (programs and policies) that will appeal to the public. The public, of course, has the ultimate voice. With its votes it decides whether or not to "buy" new policy offerings.

Thus, for example, in 1999, Democratic presidential hopefuls Al Gore and Bill Bradley both proposed new programs in the realms of health care, education, and social services, which they hoped would expand their own political bases as well as increase support for the Democratic Party. On the Republican side, Senator John McCain championed the issue of campaign finance reform, and George W. Bush pledged that he would be the "education president." In a similar vein, in 2003, Howard Dean promised to repeal President Bush's tax cuts in order to balance the budget and pave the way for more social spending. Carol Moseley-Braun advocated universal health care and Dennis Kucinich proposed rewriting trade agreements to protect jobs and the environment.

PARTIES IN CONGRESS

The ultimate test of the party system is its relationship to and influence on the institutions of government. Congress, in particular, depends more on the party system than is generally recognized. For one thing, the speakership of the House is essentially a party office. All the members of the House take part in the election of the Speaker. But the actual selection is made by the **majority party,** that is, the party that holds a majority of seats in the House. (The other party is known as the **minority party.**) When the majority party caucus presents a nominee to the entire House, its choice is then invariably ratified in a straight vote along party lines.

The committee system of both houses of Congress is also a product of the two-party system. Although the rules organizing committees and the rules defining the jurisdiction of each are adopted like ordinary legislation by the whole membership,

policy entrepreneur an individual who identifies a problem as a political issue and brings a policy proposal into the political agenda

FOR CRITICAL ANALYSIS

It was once said that "politics stops at the water's edge." This adage meant that parties should refrain from criticizing one another's foreign policies for fear of presenting a picture of division to foreign foes. For the most part, Democrats have supported President Bush's campaign against terrorism, but some Democrats have criticized the president's policies involving the war in Iraq. Should partisan politics stop at the "water's edge"? Is partisan politics compatible with effective governance?

majority party the party that holds the majority of legislative seats in either the House or the Senate

minority party the party that holds a minority of legislative seats in either the House or the Senate

Political Parties and the World

Few Americans are aware of the international involvements of our two major political parties. Both parties maintain close, informal links to like-minded political parties in other countries. For example, the Republican Party has very good relations with Britain's Conservatives while the Democrats have long-standing ties to the British Labour Party. Making use of these cross-national partisan ties can allow U.S. politicians to claim that their programs and policies have international backing—sometimes an important political asset. Indeed, both sides can benefit from the relationship. For example, in 2002–03, President Bush was very eager to have British political and military backing for his plan to attack Iraq and depose Iraqi dictator Saddam Hussein. Bush was supported by British prime minister Tony Blair, but many members of Blair's own Labour Party opposed the war. In February 2003, Labour dissidents called for a vote of no confidence, which could have forced Blair to call new elections and would almost certainly have prevented him from supporting Bush's Iraq policy. Usually, a British prime minister can count on the full support of his own party and the opposition of all members of the competing party. With the Labour Party divided, Conservative opposition might have doomed Blair's government and undermined President Bush's foreign policy. To prevent this development, Bush called on the leaders of the Republican Party to use their ties to British Conservatives. Republicans made numerous calls to British Conservative Party leaders to urge them to support Blair. In the end, more than 100 Labor members of Parliament deserted the government, but the virtually unanimous support of the Conservatives assured Blair's political survival.

In addition to informal ties to like-minded politicians, since the mid-1980s each political party has been associated with a formal foreign policy institute. The International Republican Institute (IRI) was founded in 1983, and the National Democratic Institute for International Affairs (NDI) was established in 1985. Both were funded by the National Endowment for Democracy (NED), a Reagan-era congressional initiative to promote democratic political practices around the world. Today, both party institutes continue to receive public funding from the NED as well as contributions from private donors. Each party's institute is led by a cadre of the party's former officials and elected office holders.

Both the IRI and the NDI work to encourage citizen participation and democracy throughout the world, particularly in regions that lack a historical and institutional base for democratic politics. Both party institutes work with local politicians, civic leaders, and community activists to encourage understanding of democratic political techniques and respect for democratic values.

While the programs of the party institutes have many similarities, they also diverge in ways that reflect the differences between the two American political parties. NDI programs pay special attention to women and young people—groups cultivated by the Democratic Party in the United States—and to trade unions, another bulwark of the U.S. Democratic Party. Thus, for example, an NDI program in Senegal was designed to increase the involvement of women in local government and in the leadership of the nation's political parties. The IRI, for its part, has emphasized cultivating relationships with government officials and business leaders, and while the NDI's approach is decidedly grass roots in character, the IRI, like the Republican Party, emphasizes political technology. For example, in Macedonia, the IRI has taught public officials the elements of media relations, public-opinion polling, and "message development." These techniques are typically emphasized by conservative parties, whose hands-on contact with ordinary voters is limited.

Through their international programs, the two U.S. political parties hope not only to promote democratization abroad but also to cultivate friends and allies throughout the world who will strengthen their own political positions in the United States. As President Bush and Prime Minister Blair discovered, in today's world friends abroad can be important at home.

FOR CRITICAL ANALYSIS

1. What are the similarities and differences between the NDI and the IRI? Do these parallel the similarities and differences between the Democratic and Republican parties?

2. In what ways do the parties' foreign policy institutes advance American interests abroad? How do the parties benefit from their institutes?

all other features of the committees are shaped by parties. For example, each party is assigned a quota of members for each committee, depending upon the percentage of total seats held by the party. On the rare occasions when an independent or third-party candidate is elected, the leaders of the two parties must agree against whose quota this member's committee assignments will count. Presumably the member will not be able to serve on any committee until the question of quota is settled.

As we shall see in Chapter 12, the assignment of individual members to committees is a party decision. Each party has a "committee on committees" to make such decisions. Permission to transfer to another committee is also a party decision. Moreover, advancement up the committee ladder toward the chair is a party decision. Since the late nineteenth century, most advancements have been automatic—based upon the length of continual service on the committee. This seniority system has existed only because of the support of the two parties, however, and either party can depart from it by a simple vote. During the 1970s, both parties reinstituted the practice of reviewing each chair—voting anew every two years on whether each committee's chair would continue to be held by the same person. In their 1994 campaign document, the "Contract with America," House Republican candidates pledged to limit committee and subcommittee chairs to three two-year terms if the GOP won control of Congress. For years, Republicans had argued that entrenched Democratic committee chairs had become powerful, arrogant, and indifferent to the popular will. When Republicans took control of Congress in 1994, they reaffirmed their pledge to limit the terms of committee and subcommittee chairs. As they approached the 2000 congressional elections, however, some GOP leaders now regretted the commitment they had made six years earlier. Powerful Republican committee chairs were not very enthusiastic about the idea of surrendering their positions if the GOP maintained control of the House. Some Republican committee chairs hoped to trade positions with one another and begin new stints in charge of new panels. Younger members who had hoped to benefit from the three-term rule by claiming the vacated chairs were prepared to fight for what they now regarded as their due. Thus, a pledge made in 1994 when the GOP was out of power seemed to portend sharp conflicts among Republican members if the GOP retained power in 2000. However, in 2001, Republicans lived up to their 1995 pledge to limit House committee chairs to three terms. Existing chairmen were forced to step down but were generally replaced by the most senior Republican member of each committee.

The continuing importance of parties in Congress became especially evident after the Republicans won control of Congress in 1994. During the first few months of the 104th Congress, the Republican leadership was able to maintain nearly unanimous support among party members on vote after vote as it sought to implement the GOP's legislative agenda. Between 1995 and 1999, however, splits within the party began to surface over issues such as welfare reform and balancing the budget. This legislative struggle and its continuation after the 2000 elections will be discussed further in Chapter 12.

PRESIDENT AND PARTY

As we saw earlier, the party that wins the White House is always led, in title anyway, by the president. The president normally depends upon fellow party members in Congress to support legislative initiatives. At the same time, members of the party in Congress hope that the president's programs and personal prestige will help them raise campaign funds and secure re-election. During his two terms in office, President Bill Clinton had a mixed record as party leader. In the realm of trade policy, Clinton sometimes found more support among Republicans than among Democrats. In addition, although Clinton proved to be an extremely successful fund-raiser, congressional Democrats often complained that he failed to share his largesse with them. At the same time, however, a number of Clinton's policy initiatives seemed calculated to strengthen the Democratic Party as a whole. Clinton's early health care initiative would have linked millions of voters to the Democrats for years to come, much as FDR's Social Security program had done in a previous era. But by the middle of Clinton's second term, the president's acknowledgment of his sexual affair with a White House intern threatened his position as party leader. Initially, Democratic candidates nationwide feared that the scandal would undermine their own chances for election, and many moved to distance themselves from the president. The Democrats' surprisingly good showing in the 1998 elections, however, strengthened Clinton's position and gave him another chance to shape the Democratic agenda.

Between the 1998 and 2000 elections, however, the president's initiatives on Social Security and nuclear disarmament failed to make much headway in a Republican-controlled Congress. The GOP was not prepared to give Clinton anything for which Democrats could claim credit in the 2000 elections. Lacking strong congressional leadership, however, the GOP did agree to many of Clinton's budgetary proposals in 1999 and dropped its own plan for large-scale cuts in federal taxes.

When he assumed office in 2001, George W. Bush called for a new era of bipartisan cooperation. The new president did receive the support of some conservative Democrats, such as Georgia senator Zell Miller, who spoke in favor of Bush at the 2004 GOP convention. Generally, however, Bush depended upon near-unanimous backing from his own party in Congress to implement his plans, which included a substantial cut in federal income taxes. After the September 11 terrorist attacks, both parties united behind the president's military response. Even then, however, the parties were divided on a number of matters. Democrats, for example, favored the creation of a federal force of airline baggage screeners, while Republicans supported a private-sector approach to airport security. Ultimately, the Democrats prevailed, and the president signed into law a bill that federalized baggage inspection. Having given in to political necessity, the president claimed full credit for the legislation.

Thinking Critically about the Role of Parties in a Democracy

Democracy and political parties arose together in the modern world. Without democracy, a system of competing political parties never could have emerged. At the same time, without a system of competing political parties, democracy never could have flourished. Without a strong opposition, rulers never would have surrendered power, and without well-organized parties, ordinary people never could have acquired or used the right to vote. It is because of this strong historical association between democracy and political parties that the current weakness of American political parties is a matter of concern.

FOR CRITICAL ANALYSIS

Describe the factors that have contributed to the overall weakening of political parties in America. How are parties weaker? How do they remain important? What are the advantages of a political system with weak political parties? What are the disadvantages? How do weaker parties affect democracy?

Healthy political parties are extremely important for maintaining political equality, democracy, and liberty in America. First, strong parties are generally an essential ingredient for effective electoral competition by groups lacking substantial economic or institutional resources. Party building has typically been the strategy pursued by groups that must organize the collective energies of large numbers of individuals to counter their opponents' superior material means or institutional standing. Historically, disciplined and coherent party organizations were generally developed first by groups representing the political aspirations of the working classes. Parties, French political scientist Maurice Duverger notes, "are always more developed on the Left than on the Right because they are always more necessary on the Left than on the Right."[11] In the United States, the first mass party was built by the Jeffersonians as a counterweight to the superior social, institutional, and economic resources that could be deployed by the incumbent Federalists. In a subsequent period of American history, the efforts of the Jacksonians to construct a coherent mass party organization were impelled by a similar set of circumstances. Only by organizing the power of numbers could the Jacksonian coalition hope to compete successfully against the superior resources that could be mobilized by its adversaries.

In the United States, the political success of party organizations forced their opponents to copy them in order to meet the challenge. It was, as Duverger points out, "contagion from the Left" that led politicians of the Center and Right to attempt to build strong party organizations.[12] These efforts were sometimes successful. In the United States during the 1830s, the Whig Party, which was led by northeastern business interests, carefully copied the effective organizational techniques devised by the Jacksonians. The Whigs won control of the national government in 1840. But even when groups nearer the top of the social scale responded in kind to organizational efforts by their inferiors, the net effect nonetheless was to give lower-class groups an opportunity to compete on a more equal footing. In the absence of coherent mass organization, middle- and upper-class factions almost inevitably have a substantial competitive edge over their lower-class rivals. When both sides organize, the net effect is to erode the relative advantage of the well-off.

Second, political parties are bulwarks of liberty. The Constitution certainly provides for freedom of speech, freedom of assembly, and freedom of the press. Maintaining these liberties, though, requires more than parchment guarantees. Of course, as long as freedom is not seriously threatened, abstract guarantees suffice to protect it. If, however, those in power actually threaten citizens' liberties, the preservation of freedom may come to depend upon the presence of a coherent and well-organized opposition. As we saw earlier in this chapter, in the first years of the Republic, it was not the Constitution or the courts that preserved free speech in the face of Federalist efforts to silence the government's critics; it was the vigorous action of the Jeffersonian-Republican opposition that saved liberty. To this day, the presence of an opposition party serves as a fundamentally important check on attempts by those in power to skirt the law and infringe upon citizens' liberties. For example, twenty-five years ago, although it was the news media that revealed President Richard Nixon's abuses of power, the concerted efforts of Nixon's Democratic opponents in Congress were required finally to drive the president from office.

Third, parties promote voter turnout. Party competition has long been known to be a key factor in stimulating voting. As political scientists Stanley Kelley, Richard Ayres, and William Bowen note, competition gives citizens an incentive to vote and politicians an incentive to get them to vote.[13] The origins of the American national electorate can be traced to the competitive organizing activities of the Jeffersonian Republicans and the Federalists. According to historian David Fischer,

> During the 1790s the Jeffersonians revolutionized electioneering. . . . Their opponents complained bitterly of endless "dinings," "drinkings," and celebrations; of handbills "industriously posted along every road"; of convoys of vehicles which brought voters to the polls by the carload; of candidates "in perpetual motion."[14]

The Federalists, although initially reluctant, soon learned the techniques of mobilizing voters: "mass meetings, barbecues, stump-speaking, festivals of many kinds, processions and parades, runners and riders, door-to-door canvassing, the distribution of tickets and ballots, . . . free transportation to the polls, outright bribery and corruption of other kinds."[15]

The result of this competition for votes was described by historian Henry Jones Ford in his classic *Rise and Growth of American Politics*.[16] Ford examined the popular clamor against John Adams and Federalist policies in the 1790s that made government a "weak, shakey affair" and appeared to contemporary observers to mark the beginnings of a popular insurrection against the government.[17] Attempts by the Federalists initially to suppress mass discontent, Ford observed, might have "caused an explosion of force which would have blown up the government."[18] What intervened to prevent rebellion was Jefferson's "great unconscious achievement," the creation of an opposition party that served to "open constitutional channels of political agitation."[19] The creation of the Jeffersonian Republican Party diverted opposition to the administration into electoral channels. Party competition gave citizens a sense that their votes were valuable and that it was thus not necessary to take to the streets to have an impact upon political affairs. Whether or not Ford was correct in crediting party competition with an ability to curb civil unrest, it is clear that competition between the parties promoted voting.

Finally, political parties make democratic government possible. We often do not appreciate that democratic government is a contradiction in terms. Government implies policies, programs, and decisive action. Democracy, on the other hand, implies an opportunity for all citizens to participate fully in the governmental process. The contradiction is that full participation by everyone is often inconsistent with getting anything done. At what point should participation stop and governance begin? How can we make certain that popular participation will result in a government capable of making decisions and developing needed policies? The problem of democratic government is especially acute in the United States because of the system of separated powers bequeathed to us by the Constitution's framers. Our system of separated powers means that it is very difficult to link popular participation and effective decision making. Often, after the citizens have spoken and the dust has settled, no single set of political forces has been able to win control of enough of the scattered levers of power to actually do anything. Instead of government, we have a continual political struggle.

Strong political parties are a partial antidote to the inherent contradiction between participation and government. Strong parties can both encourage popular involvement and convert participation into effective government. More than fifty years ago, a committee of the academic American Political Science Association (APSA) called for the development of a more "responsible" party government. By

responsible party government, the committee meant political parties that mobilized voters and were sufficiently well organized to develop and implement coherent programs and policies after the election. Strong parties can link democratic participation and government.

Although they are significant factors in politics and government, American political parties today are not as strong as the "responsible parties" advocated by the APSA. Many politicians are able to raise funds, attract volunteers, and win office without much help from local party organizations. Once in office, these politicians have no particular reason to submit to party discipline; instead, they steer independent courses. They are often supported by voters who see independence as a virtue and party discipline as "boss rule." Sometimes analysts refer to this pattern as a "candidate-centered" politics to distinguish it from a political process in which parties are the dominant forces. The problem with a candidate-centered politics is that it tends to be associated with low turnout, high levels of special-interest influence, and a lack of effective decision making. In short, many of the problems that have plagued American politics in recent years can be traced directly to the independence of American voters and politicians and the candidate-centered nature of American national politics.

The health of America's parties should be a source of concern to all citizens who value liberty, equality, and democracy. Can political parties be strengthened? The answer is, in principle, yes. For example, political parties could be strengthened if the rules governing campaign finance were revised to make candidates more dependent financially upon state and local party organizations rather than on personal resources or private contributors. Such a reform, to be sure, would require more strict regulation of party fund-raising practices. The potential benefit, however, of a greater party role in political finance could be substantial. If parties controlled the bulk of the campaign funds, they would become more coherent and disciplined, and might come to resemble the responsible parties envisioned by the APSA. In 2002, Congress enacted campaign finance reforms that diminished the role of the national party organizations in financing campaigns. Time will tell what consequences will be brought about by this change. Political parties have been such important features of American democratic politics that we need to think long and hard about how to preserve and strengthen them.

responsible party government
a set of principles that idealizes a strong role for parties in defining their stance on issues, mobilizing voters, and fulfilling their campaign promises once in office

FOR CRITICAL ANALYSIS

What are the principal issues dividing the two major parties today? What are the chief areas of agreement between the two parties? Do the parties agree or disagree on questions of liberty and democracy?

GET INVOLVED

What You Can Do:
Become a Party Activist

American political parties are very open to citizen involvement. Students who attend local party meetings and volunteer to assist with communication and fund-raising efforts are usually welcome. In the nineteenth century, the national parties could rely upon the efforts of tens of thousands of patronage employees who were obligated to engage in political work. Today, the parties rely upon volunteers and enthusiasts.

How do you become a party activist? First, decide which political party best represents your own values and visions. Most Americans who identify with a particular political party choose the Democratic Party or the Republican Party. If you think these parties are too close together on important issues, or if you are not

YOU ARE... running for your party's nomination for the office of county clerk!

The selection of candidates must occur for thousands of races across the nation every cycle. Parties select their standard-bearer for each race, and this process is often lengthy and very competitive for attractive offices. Nominees for county-level office are often determined by primaries, although occasionally by caucuses or convention.

In this simulation, you must find the best strategies to ensure your nomination. Where will you spend your very scarce resources, and how will you position yourself on the issues to maximize your chances in the primary?

Go to www.wwnorton.com/wtp5e

Questions to consider as you conduct the online simulation:

What motivates regular citizens to run for local offices, given that the positions usually offer low pay and many challenges?

What are the advantages and disadvantages of winning a partisan nomination for an office?

What resources do local parties contribute to local campaigns?

What criteria will party members use to select a nominee for an office like county clerk, when many voters know little about what the job entails and even less about the candidates?

What choices will increase your chances of winning the primary?

MARRIAGE LICENSES
ISSUED
MONDAY thru FRIDAY
8:00 A.M. to 4:00 P.M.

BIRTH
CERTIFICATES
ARE ACROSS THE
HALL IN
ROOM 110

ABSENTEE BALLOTS MUST
BE OBTAINED FROM YOUR
CITY, TOWN OR

particularly enamored of party politics "as usual," you may want to consider the Reform Party, the Green Party, the Natural Law Party, the Peace and Freedom Party, or other parties soliciting members and support. Determine which political party best captures your sympathies and passions.

Next, see if your campus has a student organization that is affiliated with the party that interests you. Many campuses have student chapters of the Democratic and Republican parties as well as some of the smaller parties. These campus chapters are likely to be linked to other campus chapters as well as to the local and state offices of the parties. These affiliates are always looking for new members with interest, enthusiasm, and commitment.

Alternatively, your school or political science department may have an internship program or an intern coordinating office. Local branches of political parties regularly work with internship offices to attract young people to their parties as well as to get energetic volunteers to perform innumerable labor-intensive tasks such as stuffing envelopes, manning phone banks, and knocking on doors. The advantages of taking this route to party activism are (1) program contacts should make it relatively easy for you to connect with the party of your choice and (2) you may be able to receive academic credit for your party involvement.

For some students, such volunteer work is the first step in a political career. For example, Cruz Bustamante, who in 1997 became the first Latino elected to be Speaker of the California state assembly, began his political career as a volunteer worker for local Democratic politicians in the Fresno, California, area. Interested in such issues as immigration, health care, and the status of farm workers, Bustamante saw politics as the best vehicle for doing something about these issues. In 1973, at the age of nineteen, he went to Washington as a congressional intern. He was not paid for his internship and needed support from his parents and five brothers and sisters, who worked in the fields as agricultural laborers. After returning to California, Bustamante worked as a staff assistant to several Democratic legislators, and was elected to the legislature in 1993. In 1997, Bustamante replaced Assembly Speaker Willie Brown, who was unable to seek re-election because of the state's new term-limits law.[20]

Much of the work undertaken by party organizations at the local level is quite mundane. Thousands of envelopes are filled and sealed. Many meetings are held. Politics at the "grass roots" is not very glamorous. However, if politics were only glamorous it could not be democratic. Grassroots party activity helps to ensure that the more glamorous world of Washington remains tied and responsive to Bozeman, Long Beach, Raleigh, and Utica. State and even national party leaders pay close attention to the views of local party organizations and activists. They depend upon these local organizations for ideas, for campaign workers, and often, for candidates. Many prominent politicians, including former president Clinton, were themselves once young volunteers in a local party organization.

Summary

Political parties seek to control government by controlling its personnel. Elections are one means to this end. Thus, parties take shape from the electoral process.

The two-party system dominates U.S. politics. During the course of American history, the government has generally been dominated by one or the other party for long periods of time. This is generally followed by a period of realignment during which new groups attempt to seize power and the previously dominant party may be displaced by its rival. There have been five electoral realignments in American political history.

Third parties are short-lived for several reasons. They have limited electoral support, the tradition of the two-party system is strong, and a major party often adopts the platform of a third party. Single-member districts with two competing parties also discourage third parties.

Party organizations exist at every level of American government. The national party organizations are generally less important than the state and local party units. Each party's national committee and congressional campaign committees help to recruit candidates and raise money. The national conventions have, for the most part, lost their nominating functions, but still play an important role in determining party rules and party platforms.

Parties influence voting through the ties of party identification, particularly the strong ties formed with party activists. A variety of group characteristics can influence party identification, including race and ethnicity, gender, religion, class, ideology, region, and age.

Nominating and electing are the basic functions of parties. Parties are critical for getting out the vote, recruiting candidates, facilitating popular choice, and organizing the government. Strong parties are essential to the continuing vitality of American democracy.

For Further Reading

Aldrich, John H. *Why Parties? The Origin and Transformation of Political Parties in America.* Chicago: University of Chicago Press, 1995.

Andersen, Kristi. *After Suffrage: Women in Partisan and Electoral Politics before the New Deal.* Chicago: University of Chicago Press, 1996.

Carmines, Edward G., and James A. Stimson. *Issue Evolution: Race and the Transformation of American Politics.* Princeton, NJ: Princeton University Press, 1989.

Edsall, Thomas Byrne, and Mary D. Edsall. *Chain Reaction: The Impact of Race, Rights, and Taxes on American Politics.* New York: Norton, 1993.

Gerring, John. *Party Ideologies in America.* New York: Cambridge University Press, 1998.

Gilmour, John B. *Strategic Disagreement: Stalemate in American Politics.* Pittsburgh, PA: University of Pittsburgh Press, 1995.

Green, John C., and Daniel M. Shea, eds. *The State of the Parties: The Changing Role of Contemporary Parties.* 2nd ed. Lanham, MD: Rowman and Littlefield, 1996.

Lawson, Kay, and Peter Merkl. *When Parties Fail: Emerging Alternative Organizations.* Princeton, NJ: Princeton University Press, 1988.

Milkis, Sidney. *The President and the Parties: The Transformation of the American Party System since the New Deal.* New York: Oxford University Press, 1993.

Shefter, Martin. *Political Parties and the State: The American Historical Experience.* Princeton, NJ: Princeton University Press, 1994.

Study Outline

Keyword: Review 9
www.wwnorton.com/wtp5e

1. In modern history, political parties have been the chief points of contact between governments and groups and forces in society. By organizing political parties, social forces attempt to gain some control over government policies and personnel.

What Are Political Parties?

1. Political parties as they are known today developed along with the expansion of suffrage, and actually took their shape from the electoral process.
2. Political parties, as coalitions of those with similar interests, are also important in making policy.

The Two-Party System in America

1. Historically, parties originate through either internal or external mobilization by those seeking to win governmental power.
2. The Democratic Party originated through a process of internal mobilization, as the Jeffersonian Party splintered into four factions in 1824, and Andrew Jackson emerged as the leader of one of these four groups.
3. The Republican Party grew through a process of external mobilization as antislavery groups formed a new party to oppose the 1854 Kansas-Nebraska Act.
4. The United States has experienced five realigning eras, which occur when the established political elite weakens sufficiently to permit the creation of new coalitions of forces capable of capturing and holding the reins of government.

5. American third parties have always represented social and economic protests ignored by the other parties.

Party Organization

1. Party organizations exist at virtually every level of American government—usually taking the form of committees made up of active party members.
2. Although national party conventions no longer have the power to nominate presidential candidates, they are still important in determining the party's rules and platform.
3. The national committee and the congressional campaign committees play important roles in recruiting candidates and raising money.

Parties and the Electorate

1. Individuals tend to form psychological ties with parties, called "party identification." This identification often follows demographic, ideological, and regional lines.

Parties and Elections

1. Parties are important in the electoral process for recruiting and nominating candidates for office.
2. Though not as important today as in the past, parties also can make a big difference in convincing voters to vote.
3. Parties also help voters choose among candidates.

Parties and Government

1. The differences between the two parties reflects a general difference in philosophy but also an attempt to appeal to core constituencies. These differences are often reflected in the policy agenda that party leaders adopt.
2. Political parties help to organize Congress. Congressional leadership and the committee system are both products of the two-party system.
3. The president serves as an informal party head by seeking support from congressional members of the party and by supporting their bids for re-election.

Thinking Critically about the Role of Parties in a Democracy

1. Democracy depends on strong parties, which promote electoral competition and voter turnout and enable governance through their organizations in Congress.
2. The ties that parties have to the electorate are currently weak; the resulting "candidate-centered" politics has some negative consequences, including lower voter turnout, increased influence of interest groups, and a lack of effective decision making by elected leaders.
3. Parties could be strengthened by changes in campaign finance laws.

Practice Quiz

Keyword: Quiz 9
www.wwnorton.com/wtp5e

1. A political party is different from an interest group in that a political party
   a) seeks to control the entire government by electing its members to office and thereby controlling the government's personnel.
   b) seeks to control only limited, very specific, functions of government.
   c) is entirely nonprofit.
   d) has a much smaller membership.

2. The periodic episodes in American history in which an "old" dominant political party is replaced by a "new" dominant political party are called
   a) constitutional revolutions.
   b) party turnovers.
   c) presidential elections.
   d) electoral realignments.

3. Through which mechanism did Boss Tweed and other party leaders in the late nineteenth and early twentieth centuries maintain their control?
   a) civil service reform
   b) soft money contributions
   c) machine politics
   d) electoral reform

4. On what level are U.S. political parties organized?
   a) national
   b) state
   c) county
   d) all of the above

5. Contemporary national party conventions are important because they
   a) determine the party's presidential candidate.
   b) determine the party's rules and platform.
   c) Both a and b are correct.
   d) Neither a nor b is correct.

6. Which party was founded as a political expression of the antislavery movement?
   a) American Independent
   b) Prohibition
   c) Republican
   d) Democratic

7. Historically, when do realignments occur?
   a) typically, every twenty years
   b) whenever a minority party takes over Congress
   c) when large numbers of voters permanently shift their support from one party to another
   d) in odd-numbered years

8. Parties today are most important in the electoral process in
   a) recruiting and nominating candidates for office.
   b) financing all of the campaign's spending.
   c) providing millions of volunteers to mobilize voters.
   d) creating a responsible party government.

9. What role do parties play in Congress?
   a) They select leaders, e.g., Speaker of the House.
   b) They assign members to committees.
   c) Both a and b are correct.
   d) Parties play no role in Congress.

10. Parties are important to democracy because they
    a) encourage electoral competition.
    b) promote voter turnout.
    c) make governance possible by organizing elected leaders into governing coalitions.
    d) all of the above.

Key Terms

Keyword: Vocabulary 9
www.wwnorton.com/wtp5e

caucus (political) (p. 348)
dealignment (p. 341)
divided government (p. 341)
electoral realignment (p. 341)
527 Committees (p. 352)
gender gap (p. 356)

machines (p. 353)
majority party (p. 361)
minority party (p. 361)
multiple-member district (p. 345)
national convention (p. 348)
nomination (p. 359)
party activists (p. 354)
party identification (p. 354)
party organization (p. 347)
patronage (p. 353)

platform (p. 348)
plurality system (p. 346)
policy entrepreneur (p. 361)
political parties (p. 329)
proportional representation (p. 346)
responsible party government (p. 367)
single-member district (p. 345)
soft money (p. 354)
third parties (p. 343)
two-party system (p. 330)

10 CAMPAIGNS AND ELECTIONS

STRONGER AT HOME
RESPECTED IN THE WORLD

John Kerry
PRESIDENT

APPROVED BY JOHN KERRY AND PAID FOR BY JOHN KERRY FOR PRESIDENT, INC

What Government Does and Why It Matters

VER THE PAST two centuries, elections have come to play a significant role in the political processes of most nations. The forms that elections take and the purposes they serve, however, vary greatly from nation to nation. The most important difference among national electoral systems is that some provide the opportunity for opposition while others do not. Democratic electoral systems, such as those that have evolved in the United States and western Europe, allow opposing forces to compete against and even to replace current officeholders. Authoritarian electoral systems, by contrast, do not allow the defeat of those in power. In the authoritarian context, elections are used primarily to mobilize popular enthusiasm for the government, to provide an outlet for popular discontent, and to persuade foreigners that the regime is legitimate—i.e., that it has the support of the people. In the former Soviet Union, for example, citizens were required to vote even though no opposition to Communist Party candidates was allowed.

In democracies, elections can also serve as institutions of legitimation and as safety valves for social discontent. But beyond these functions, democratic elections facilitate popular influence, promote leadership accountability, and offer groups in society a measure of protection from the abuse of governmental power. Citizens exercise influence through elections by determining who should control the government. The chance to decide who will govern serves as an opportunity for ordinary citizens to make choices about the policies, programs, and directions of government action. In the United States, for example, recent Democratic and Republican candidates have differed significantly on issues of taxing, social spending, and governmental regulation. As American voters have chosen between the two parties' candidates, they have also made choices about these issues.

Elections promote leadership accountability because the threat of defeat at the polls exerts pressure on those in power to conduct themselves in a responsible manner and to take account of popular interests and wishes when they make their decisions. As James Madison observed in the Federalist Papers, elected leaders are "compelled to anticipate the moment when their power is to cease, when their exercise of it is to be reviewed, and when they must descend to the level from which they were raised, there forever to remain unless a faithful discharge of their trust shall have established their title to a renewal of it."[1] It is because of this need to anticipate the dissatisfaction of their constituents that elected officials constantly monitor public opinion polls as they decide what positions to take on policy issues.

suffrage the right to vote; also called franchise

Furthermore, the right to vote, or **suffrage,** can serve as an important source of protection for groups in American society. The passage of the 1965 Voting Rights Act, for example, enfranchised millions of African Americans in the South, paving the way for the election of thousands of new black public officials at the local, state, and national levels and ensuring that white politicians could no longer ignore the views and needs of African Americans. The Voting Rights Act was one of the chief spurs for the elimination of many overt forms of racial discrimination as well as for the diminution of racist rhetoric in American public life.

Finally, while elections allow citizens a chance to participate in politics, they also allow the government a chance to exert a good deal of control over when, where, how, and which of its citizens will participate. Electoral processes are governed by a variety of rules and procedures that allow those in power a significant opportunity to regulate the character—and perhaps also the consequences—of mass political participation. ■

■ **In this chapter, we will examine the place of elections in American political life. We will first examine some of the formal aspects of electoral participation in the United States.** These include types of elections, the ways that election winners are determined, electoral districts, the ballot, and the electoral college. As we shall see, all of these factors affect the type and level of influence that citizens have through the electoral process.

■ **In the next two sections, we will see how election campaigns are conducted in the United States.** The campaign for any political office consists of a number of steps. Election campaigns are also becoming increasingly expensive to wage.

■ **Next, we assess the various factors that influence voters' decisions.** Despite the growing importance of money to elections, it is still voters who decide the outcomes.

■ **We then turn to the broader issue of money and elections.** Raising campaign funds is now a crucial factor for winning. Although attempts to reform campaign finance have been made, the money keeps pouring in. As we will see, this development produces a clash between liberty and equality.

■ Previewing Liberty, Equality, and Democracy

Popular selection of public officials in competitive elections is the essence of democracy. Moreover, through democratic elections citizens have an opportunity to safeguard their liberties. And to the extent that political power is actually exercised through the ballot, every citizen is equal to every other citizen. Thus, electoral politics and American political values are fundamentally intertwined. In recent decades, however, many Americans have not bothered to vote and some of our electoral practices have seemed inconsistent with egalitarian conceptions of politics. This chapter concludes by analyzing critically the implications of these developments.

Elections in America

In the United States, elections are held at regular intervals. National presidential elections take place every four years, on the first Tuesday in November; congressional elections are held every two years on the same Tuesday. (Congressional elections that do not coincide with a presidential election are sometimes called **midterm elections.**) Elections for state and local office also often coincide with national elections. Some states and municipalities, however, prefer to schedule their local elections for times that do not coincide with national contests to ensure that local results will not be affected by national trends.

midterm elections congressional elections that do not coincide with a presidential election; also called off-year elections

In the American federal system, the responsibility for organizing elections rests largely with state and local governments. State laws specify how elections are to be administered, determine the boundaries of electoral districts, and specify candidate and voter qualifications. Elections are administered by state, county, and municipal election boards that are responsible for establishing and staffing polling places and verifying the eligibility of individuals who come to vote.

TYPES OF ELECTIONS

Three types of elections are held in the United States: primary elections, general elections, and runoff elections. Americans occasionally also participate in a fourth voting process, the referendum, but the referendum is not actually an election.

primary elections elections used to select a party's candidate for the general election

Primary elections are used to select each party's candidates for the general election. In the case of local and statewide offices, the winners of primary elections face one another as their parties' nominees in the general election. At the presidential level, however, primary elections are indirect; they are used to select state delegates to the national nominating conventions, at which the major party presidential candidates are chosen. America is one of the only nations in the world to use primary elections. In most countries, nominations are controlled by party officials, as they once were in the United States. The primary system was introduced at the turn of the century by Progressive reformers who hoped to weaken the power of party leaders by taking candidate nominations out of their hands.

closed primary a primary election in which voters can participate in the nomination of candidates, but only of the party in which they are enrolled for a period of time prior to primary day

open primary a primary election in which the voter can wait until the day of the primary to choose which party to enroll in to select candidates for the general election

Under the laws of some states, only registered members of a political party may vote in a primary election to select that party's candidates. This is called a **closed primary.** Other states allow all registered voters to decide on the day of the primary in which party's primary they will participate. This is called an **open primary.**

The primary is followed by the general election—the decisive electoral contest. The winner of the general election is elected to office for a specified term. In some states, however, mainly in the southeast, if no candidate wins an absolute majority in the primary, a runoff election is held before the general election. This situation is most likely to arise if there are more than two candidates, none of whom receives a majority of the votes cast. A runoff election is held between the two candidates who received the largest number of votes.

referendum the practice of referring a measure proposed or passed by a legislature to the vote of the electorate for approval or rejection

Twenty four states also provide for referendum voting, as we saw in Chapter 1. The **referendum** process allows citizens to vote directly on proposed laws or other governmental actions. In recent years, voters in several states have voted to set limits on tax rates, to block state and local spending proposals, and to prohibit social services for illegal immigrants. Although it involves voting, a referendum is not an election. The election is an institution of representative government. Through an election, voters choose officials to act for them. The referendum, by contrast, is an institution of direct democracy; it allows voters to govern directly without intervention by government officials. The validity of referenda results, however, is subject to judicial action. If a court finds that a referendum outcome violates the state or national constitution, it can overturn the result. This happened in the case of a 1995 California referendum curtailing social services to illegal aliens.[2] Generally, elected officials do not like ballot referenda, which they see as interfering with their prerogatives. In 2004, several state legislatures have sought to place limits on referenda. In Florida, for example, Governor Jeb Bush is leading an effort to make the use of citizen referenda more difficult.

recall procedure to allow voters an opportunity to remove state officials from office before their terms expire

Eighteen states also have legal provisions for **recall** elections. The recall is an electoral device introduced by turn-of-the-century Populists to allow voters to remove governors and other state officials from office prior to the expiration of their terms. Federal officials, such as the president and members of Congress, are not subject to recall. Generally speaking, a recall effort begins with a petition campaign. For example, in California, the site of a tumultuous recall battle in 2003, if 12 percent of those who voted in the last general election sign petitions demanding a special recall election, one must be scheduled by the state board of elections. Such petition campaigns are relatively common, but most fail to garner enough signatures to bring the matter to a statewide vote. In the California case, however, a conservative Republican member of Congress, Darrell Issa, led a successful effort to recall Democratic governor Gray Davis. Generally dissatisfied with Davis's performance, voters were particularly unhappy about the state's economy and blamed Davis for the state's $38 billion budget deficit. Issa and his followers were able to secure enough signatures to force a vote, and in October 2003, Davis became only the second governor in American history to be recalled by his state's electorate. The first was North Dakota governor Lynn Frazier, who was recalled in 1921. Under California law, voters in a special recall election are also asked to choose a replacement for the official whom they dismiss. Californians in 2003 elected movie star Arnold Schwarzengger to be their governor. Ironically, the new Republican governor had starred in such films as *The Terminator, Running Man,* and *Total Recall.* While critics charged that the Davis recall had been a "political circus," the campaign had the effect of greatly increasing voter interest and involvement in the political process. More than 400,000 new voters registered in California in 2003, many drawn into the political arena by the opportunity to participate in the recall campaign.

THE CRITERIA FOR WINNING

In some countries, to win a seat in the parliament or other governing body, a candidate must receive an absolute majority (50 percent + 1) of all the votes cast in the relevant district. This type of electoral system is called a **majority system** and, in the United States, is used in primary elections by some southern states. Majority systems usually include a provision for a runoff election between the two top candidates, because if the initial race draws several candidates, there is little chance that any one will receive a majority.

In other nations, candidates for office need not win an absolute majority of the votes cast to win an election. Instead, victory is awarded to the candidate who receives the most votes, regardless of the actual percentage this represents. A candidate receiving 50 percent, 30 percent, or 20 percent of the vote can win if no other candidate received more votes. This type of electoral system is called a **plurality system** and is used in virtually all general elections in the United States.

Most European nations employ a third type of electoral system, called **proportional representation.** Under proportional rules, competing political parties are awarded legislative seats in rough proportion to the percentage of the popular votes cast that each party won. A party that wins 30 percent of the vote will receive roughly 30 percent of the seats in the parliament or other representative body. In the United States, proportional representation is used by many states in presidential primary elections.

In general, proportional representation works to the advantage of smaller or weaker groups in society, whereas plurality and majority rules tend to help larger and more powerful forces. Proportional representation benefits smaller or weaker groups because it usually allows a party to win legislative seats with fewer votes than would be required under a majority or plurality system. In Europe, for example, a party that wins 10 percent of the national vote might win 10 percent of the parliamentary seats. In the United States, by contrast, a party that wins 10 percent of the vote would probably win no seats in Congress. Because they give small parties little chance of success,

majority system a type of electoral system in which, to win a seat in the parliament or other representative body, a candidate must receive a majority of all the votes cast in the relevant district

plurality system a type of electoral system in which, to win a seat in the parliament or other representative body, a candidate need only receive the most votes in the election, not necessarily a majority of votes cast

proportional representation a multiple-member district system that allows each political party representation in proportion to its percentage of the total vote plurality and majority systems tend to reduce the number of competitive political parties. Proportional representation, on the other hand, tends to increase the number of parties. It is in part because of its use of plurality elections that the United States has usually had only two significant political parties, while with proportional representation, many European countries have developed multiparty systems.

ELECTORAL DISTRICTS

redistricting the process of redrawing election districts and redistributing legislative representatives. This happens every ten years to reflect shifts in population or in response to legal challenges in existing districts

The boundaries for congressional and state legislative districts in the United States are redrawn by the states usually every ten years in response to population changes determined by the decennial census. This redrawing of district boundaries is called **redistricting.** The character of district boundaries is influenced by several factors. Some of the most important influences have been federal court decisions. In the 1963 case of *Gray v. Sanders,* and in the 1964 cases of *Wesberry v. Sanders* and *Reynolds v. Sims,* the Supreme Court held that legislative districts within a state must include roughly equal populations, so as to accord with the principle of "one person, one vote."[3] During the 1980s, the Supreme Court also declared that legislative districts should, insofar as possible, be contiguous, compact, and consistent with existing political subdivisions.[4]

Despite judicial intervention, state legislators routinely seek to influence electoral outcomes by manipulating the organization of electoral districts. This strat-

The translation of votes into legislative seats and other political offices in the United States is shaped by the drawing of electoral districts. Districting for congressional races and state legislative contests is always a matter of controversy, with opponents accusing one another of "gerrymandering"—drawing district boundaries in such a way as to serve a particular group's interests. The original gerrymander was a districting plan attributed to Massachusetts governor Elbridge Gerry (1744–1814), who was said to have designed a district shaped like a salamander.

Redistricting usually takes place at the expense of the party out of power. For example, in 2002, the Democratically controlled Georgia legislature redrew boundaries to create a "safe" district for the Democrats. In 2003, the Republican-controlled Texas legislature attempted to redraw districts to the Republican's advantage. In recent years, many districting plans have been challenged and the federal courts have taken the position that districts should be compact, contiguous, and respectful of established political jurisdictions such as towns and counties. However, in 2004, the Supreme Court declined to overturn a partisan gerrymander in Pennsylvania.

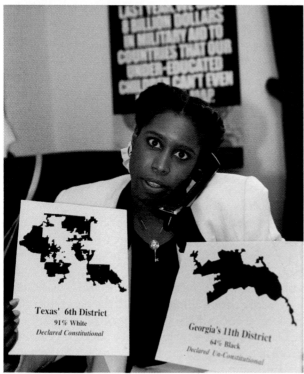

Texas' 6th District
91% White
Declared Constitutional

Georgia's 11th District
64% Black
Declared Un-Constitutional

The courts also have scrutinized districting plans for evidence of racial discrimination. In a number of recent cases, both black and white voters in the South have claimed to be the victims of racial gerrymanders. For instance, in 1995 the Supreme Court held that Cynthia McKinney's district, which was 64 percent African American, was unfairly based on race. Meanwhile, no challenge was made to Texas's 6th District, which was predominantly white. Blacks have charged old-fashioned racial discrimination, while whites have charged that they are the victims of so-called benign gerrymandering plans designed to help increase black representation.

gerrymandering apportionment of voters in districts in such a way as to give unfair advantage to one racial or ethnic group or political party

benign gerrymandering attempts to draw district boundaries so as to create districts made up primarily of disadvantaged or underrepresented minorities

minority district a gerrymandered voting district that improves the chances of minority candidates by making selected minority groups the majority within the district

egy is called **gerrymandering,** named for a nineteenth-century Massachusetts governor, Elbridge Gerry, who was alleged to have designed a district in the shape of a salamander to promote his party's interests. The principle of gerrymandering is simple: different distributions of voters among districts can produce different electoral results. For example, by dispersing the members of a particular group across two or more districts, state legislators can dilute their voting power and prevent them from electing a representative in any district. Alternatively, by concentrating the members of a group or the adherents of the opposing party in as few districts as possible, state legislators can try to ensure that their opponents will elect as few representatives as possible. In recent years, the federal government has supported what is sometimes called **benign gerrymandering** through the creation of congressional districts made up primarily of minority group members. This practice was intended to increase the number of African Americans elected to public office. The Supreme Court has viewed this effort as constitutionally dubious, however. Beginning with the 1993 case of *Shaw v. Reno,* the Court has undermined efforts to create such **minority districts.**[5]

Traditionally, district boundaries have been redrawn only once a decade, following the decennial national census. In recent years, however, the Republican Party has adopted an extremely aggressive redistricting strategy, in some instances not waiting for a new census before launching a redistricting effort that could serve its political interests. In Texas, for example, after the GOP took control of both houses of the state legislature in the 2002 elections, Republican lawmakers sought to enact a redistricting plan that promised to shift as many as five congressional seats to the Republican column. This Republican effort was masterminded by U.S. House Majority Leader Tom DeLay, who is himself a Texan. DeLay saw an opportunity to increase the Republican majority in the House and reduce Democratic prospects for regaining control of Congress. In an effort to block DeLay's plan, fifty-one Democratic legislators refused to attend state legislative sessions, leaving the Texas legislature without a quorum and unable to conduct its business. The legislature's Republican leadership ordered the state police to apprehend the missing Democrats and return them to the Capitol. The Democrats responded by escaping to Oklahoma, beyond the jurisdiction of the Texas police. Eventually, the Democrats capitulated and the GOP was able to enact its redistricting plan. The entire matter, however, is now before the courts. A similar GOP redistricting effort in Pennsylvania was upheld by the United States Supreme Court in 2004.

THE BALLOT

Prior to the 1890s, voters cast ballots according to political parties. Each party printed its own ballots, listed only its own candidates for each office, and employed party workers to distribute its ballots at the polls. Because only one party's candidates appeared on any ballot, it was very difficult for a voter to cast anything other than a straight party vote.

The advent of a new, neutral ballot represented a significant change in electoral procedure. The new ballot was prepared and administered by the state rather than the parties. Each ballot was identical and included the names of all candidates for office. This ballot reform made it possible for voters to make their choices on the basis of the individual rather than the collective merits of a party's candidates. Because all candidates for the same office now appeared on the same ballot, voters

Electoral Redistricting and Race

The process of redrawing election districts to take account of population shifts is both necessary and controversial. America's two major political parties have always vied to obtain political advantage through redistricting in the hope that redrawn district lines will help their candidates, or hurt the opposing candidates. Yet redistricting has also been used as a weapon to minimize the electoral influence of selected groups, especially African Americans, a process many consider an undemocratic denial of equality. To remedy this problem, Congress amended the 1965 Voting Rights Act in 1982 to compel states with significant African American and Latino populations to redraw district lines in such a way as to make more likely the election of representatives from these groups. This redistricting was carried out in thirteen states after the 1990 census, and it produced the desired effect. Before the 1990 reapportionment, the House of Representatives had a record-high twenty-five African American members (5.7 percent of members). After the reapportionment, which included the creation of districts having black majorities, thirty-nine African Americans were elected (9 percent of the House); Latino representatives increased from ten to seventeen. Yet many of these race-based reapportionment schemes were challenged in court.

Supporters of race-based redistricting argue that such drastic measures are necessary to overcome traditional white dominance. Southern blacks, in particular, traditionally have been frozen out of public office, since most American elections follow the winner-take-all system, meaning that election districts with substantial nonwhite populations could always be outvoted by a white majority. Indeed, studies have shown that race matters to voters. In a study from the 1980s, more than 80 percent of white North Carolina voters reported that they would not vote for an African American candidate, even if there was no other choice on the ballot. North Carolina did not elect an African American to Congress in the twentieth century until after the 1990 reapportionment, despite the fact that between one-fifth and one-third of the state's population was black.

Although race-based redistricting has produced some odd-shaped congressional districts, it increased not only the number of nonwhite representatives in Congress but

also increased their political voice and clout. This larger number of representatives has exerted more influence over national policy making in such areas as crime and gun control. It also has increased the pool of potential office-seekers. The persistence of racism, and the resistance of institutions to change, has made such "minority" districts necessary.

Critics have argued that race-based redistricting is nothing more than racial gerrymandering and that it perpetuates the very problem it claims to solve. While the number of minority representatives in Congress has increased, race-based reapportionment has also purged surrounding districts of nonwhite voters, transforming many of these districts from racially and politically competitive to uniformly white and Republican, a fact reflected in the shift of twelve seats to Republican candidates in the thirteen states where these changes took place (because of the shifting of Democratic-voting blacks from these formerly competitive districts). Thus, black voters have been walled off from more conservative white voters.

The shoestring shape of many of these districts—some portions of some districts are no wider than an interstate highway—reveals their blatant gerrymandering. Even though the purpose of providing more representation for African Americans and Latinos may be praiseworthy, the method violates the principle of equal protection, as the Supreme Court has noted in recent decisions. Winner-take-all elections do often disguise the preferences of minority groups, but the remedy is stronger electoral competition and greater pressure from constituent groups. Reapportionment based on race is unacceptable, regardless of which race benefits.

FOR CRITICAL ANALYSIS

1. Is it ever appropriate to use race and ethnicity as criteria for drawing legislative district boundaries?

2. What are some of the most important U.S. Supreme Court decisions concerning race and districting? How has the Court's position changed over time?

SOURCE: Lani Guinier, "Don't Scapegoat the Gerrymander," *New York Times Magazine*, January 8, 1995.

Is Redistricting Fair?

Yes

When Senator John Whitmire returned to Texas this past Labor Day weekend, he ended a two-month old stalemate in the Texas Senate. To block Republican efforts at redistricting, the Senate Democrats have left Texas twice to break quorum, once fleeing to Oklahoma and more recently to New Mexico for more than a month. Both times the Democrats have ground this state's government operations to a halt and cost the taxpayers an incredible amount of money in the process.

Now that the Senate Republicans can force quorum, and therefore a vote on the issue that they have the numbers to pass, the question on everyone's mind is what Governor Rick Perry and the rest of the Republicans will do next. Will Governor Perry call a third special session to deal with the redistricting issue? Perhaps the question that Republicans should ask themselves is whether or not he should call that session.

Certainly Democrats have reason to keep this issue from passing, but their motivations for skipping out are entirely selfish and partisan. For their part, the Republicans aren't exactly saints either. While they certainly have reason to redistrict (the state votes overwhelmingly Republican, yet Texas sends more Democrats to Congress than Republicans), to push the redistricting plan in so blatantly a partisan effort is, in a word, cheap.

The fact of the matter is that the state lines should be redrawn, and that the congressional representation of this state should reflect its voting patterns. If that means less Democrats, so be it—better to face the issue head on than to turn tail and run away. Instead of running, the Democrats should have worked hard to draw up a less partisan map that would still reflect the voting patterns of the state, but they took the coward's way out: run and whine.

When the Democrats showed their cowardly colors, they doomed themselves. Not only is running from problems the irresponsible thing to do, it is un-American, un-Texan, and just plain childish. These Democrats do not represent their constituents, they do not represent Texas, and they have shown that they would rather play partisan hardball than deal with important issues for the good of the people and the state. They will not be in office after the next elections, and that is why the Republicans and Governor Perry should not call a third special session.

Americans (and Texans) are plain tired of partisan bickering and a government that is put on hold because of it. The Republicans should recognize this and drop the issue of redistricting for now. Doing so will have myriad good effects on their party, which will in the end win them the majority with or without redistricting. First, it shows that Republicans can rise above the partisan politics that have torn this country apart. Second, it will show that the Republicans are more interested in tackling other issues (such as budget, education, etc.) than boosting their congressional numbers. Third, and most importantly, it would prove to Texas and America that they are responsible with their power. It is a wise man that knows just because you can doesn't mean you should.

Sure, the Republicans could call their session, cast their votes, and get their boost. They could force the power play and claim victory—but would they really have won? Forcing the issue in a third special session only perpetuates the partisan politics that plague our country, and it's high time someone rose above the childish bickering.

Republicans have the opportunity to do exactly that right here, and they would be fools not to take it. Uncle Ben was right: with great power comes great responsibility—maybe the Republican should start using their power with a grain of responsibility instead of a pound of partisanship. Doing so would earn a ton of respect, and more than a few votes.

SOURCE: Richard Whitrock, "Use Power Wisely, Republicans," *The Daily Cougar* (University of Houston), September 8, 2003.

No I love the Fourth of July. I love the barbeques, I love the flags, but most of all, I love the fireworks—and with congressional redistricting on for the special legislative session, I'm sure there will be plenty of fireworks in the state capitol.

For most of us on campus, it's hard to see why congressional redistricting matters: What does it mean for us? How will it affect our lives? Who cares?

On the surface, the whole redistricting issue just seems like boring political maneuvering and partisan bickering. The Republicans accuse the Democrats of being chicken and running away from their duties (ouch), and the Democrats blame the Republicans for abusing their majority by trying to smite the Texas Democratic Party in Congress (double ouch).

But redistricting does matter beyond the partisan name calling, and it is especially relevant as we are about to celebrate America's 227th Independence Day.

Congressional redistricting is about representation, one of the basic rights Americans fought for in the Revolution. (Remember the whole "No taxation without representation" stuff?) Well, that's what redistricting is all about—the right to be able to elect politicians who can represent our interest. Not just Congress.

Ideally, districts are areas defined by a community, or a region, within the state that elects one politician to the U.S. House of Representatives. Usually, districts are changed and reshaped once very ten years (after a national census) to reflect demographic shifts. (Texas just did this in 2001, using the court because the legislature could not come to an agreement.)

But when redistricting is used as a political tool, like the Republicans are doing here in Texas, it can create weirdly shaped districts that can tip the scales, giving one party an electoral advantage. (This is known as "gerrymandering," named after Massachusetts Governor Elbridge Gerry, who, in 1812, reshaped districts for political purposes, making some of them look like salamanders.)

One gerrymandering Texas Republican plan creates a district that runs from one block in downtown Austin all the way down to the Mexican border. Newly created districts like this one may not reflect any regional or group interests. Instead they are shaped without a coherent constituent character. The character and needs of a constituent in downtown Austin are completely different from those of someone living near the border—how can they be in the same district, represented by the same person?

This kind of congressional redistricting, as controlled by partisanship and wrought with gerrymandering, abuses our fundamental right to proper representation.

And when I hear the argument that congressional redistricting actually helps to create a more "realistic" picture of the Texas electorate, as it seeks to reflect the number of people voting Republican, I say the ends do not justify the means. Instead, we risk creating districts that may fail to reflect any region or constituent group, undermining the goal of a representative government itself.

What's more, congressional redistricting as it is about to happen here in Texas is part and parcel of a larger national Republican agenda (just ask Representative Tom DeLay), that seeks to permanently quiet dissenting voices, carried out at the expense of our right to proper representation.

The fireworks of this Fourth of July should remind us that we live in interesting political times, marked by intense partisan debate. But when our politicians try to push something like redistricting for strategic gain, they trade our democratic ideals for instant political advantage, and they weaken the ground upon which all government rests: the ideal of true representation.

SOURCE: Gabriel Levine, "Redistricting Matters To All," *Daily Texan* (University of Texas-Austin), July 3, 2003.

split-ticket voting the practice of casting ballots for the candidates of at least two different political parties in the same election

straight-ticket voting the practice of casting ballots for candidates of only one party

were no longer forced to choose a straight party ticket. This gave rise to the phenomenon of split-ticket voting in American elections.

If a voter supports candidates from more than one party in the same election, he or she is said to be casting a **split-ticket vote.** Voters who support only one party's candidates are casting a **straight-ticket vote.** Straight-ticket voting occurs

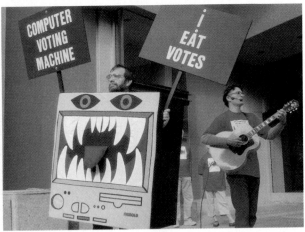

A variety of the devices used to record votes in the United States are notably prone to errors that can affect election results. For example, in the state of Florida, the cumbersome methods used to tally votes may have affected the result of the 2000 presidential election. Some voters were confused by the "butterfly ballot" in Palm Beach County, which made it difficult to match candidates and votes and possibly led more than 3,000 people to vote for Pat Buchanan instead of the candidate they intended to vote for, Al Gore. Reports of election irregularities and the closeness of the vote in Florida led to a statewide recount, including close scrutiny of "hanging" or "dimpled" chads on thousands of punch card ballots. Six months after the 2000 election, the Florida state legislature overwhelmingly passed a voting reform act designed to eliminate the controversial punch-card ballots.

In the aftermath of the 2000 debacle, Congress passed the Help America Vote Act to overhaul the nation's election system. The law encouraged states to move away from punch cards and explore other voting technologies. In the 2004 elections, approximately 30 percent of the nation's 150 million voters cast their ballots on electronic touch-screen machines. Critics of touch-screen voting systems, however, questioned the machines for their accuracy and security against fraud.

most often when a voter casts a ballot for a party's presidential candidate and then "automatically" votes for the rest of that party's candidates. The result of this voting pattern is known as the **coattail effect.**

Prior to the reform of the ballot, it was not uncommon for an entire incumbent administration to be swept from office and replaced by an entirely new set of officials. In the absence of a real possibility of split-ticket voting, any desire on the part of the electorate for change could be expressed only as a vote against all candidates of the party in power. Because of this, there always existed the possibility, particularly at the state and local levels, that an insurgent slate committed to policy change could be swept into power. The party ballot thus increased the potential impact of elections upon the government's composition. Although this potential may not always have been realized, the party ballot at least increased the chance that electoral decisions could lead to policy changes. By contrast, because it permitted choice on the basis of candidates' individual appeals, ticket splitting led to increasingly divided partisan control of government.

The actual ballots used by voters vary from county to county across the United States. Some counties employ paper ballots; others use mechanical voting machines. Some use punch-card systems; still others have introduced electronic and computerized systems. Not surprisingly, the controversy surrounding Florida's presidential vote in 2000 led to a closer look at the different balloting systems, and it became apparent that some of them produced unreliable results. Indeed, faulty ballots in Florida and other states may have changed the outcome of the 2000 election. Many counties moved to introduce computerized voting system, which they hoped would lessen the chance of spoiled or incorrectly counted ballots. Some critics of computerized systems, however, warn that they may be vulnerable to unauthorized use or "hacking," which could call the result of an entire election into question.

coattail effect the result of voters casting their ballot for president or governor and "automatically" voting for the remainder of the party's ticket

THE ELECTORAL COLLEGE

In the early history of popular voting, nations often made use of indirect elections. In these elections, voters would choose the members of an intermediate body. These members would, in turn, select public officials. The assumption underlying such processes was that ordinary citizens were not really qualified to choose their leaders and could not be trusted to do so directly. The last vestige of this procedure in America is the **electoral college,** the group of electors who formally select the president and vice president of the United States.

When Americans go to the polls on election day, they are technically not voting directly for presidential candidates. Instead, voters within each state are choosing among slates of electors selected by each state's party and pledged, if elected, to support that party's presidential candidate. In each state (except Maine and Nebraska), the slate that wins casts all the state's electoral votes for its party's candidate.[6] Each state is entitled to a number of electoral votes equal to the number of the state's senators and representatives combined, for a total of 538 electoral votes for the fifty states and the District of Columbia. Occasionally, an elector will break his or her pledge and vote for the other party's candidate. For example, in 1976, when the Republicans carried the state of Washington, one Republican elector from that state refused to vote for Gerald Ford, the Republican presidential nominee. Many states have now enacted statutes formally binding electors to their pledges, but some constitutional authorities doubt whether such statutes are enforceable.

electoral college the presidential electors from each state who meet after the popular election to cast ballots for president and vice president

In each state, the electors whose slate has won proceed to the state's capital on the Monday following the second Wednesday in December and formally cast their ballots. These are sent to Washington, and tallied by the Congress in January; then the name of the winner is formally announced. If no candidate were to receive a majority of all electoral votes, the names of the top three candidates would be submitted to the House, where each state would be able to cast one vote. Whether a state's vote would be decided by a majority, plurality, or some other fraction of the state's delegates would be determined under rules established by the House.

In 1800 and 1824, the electoral college failed to produce a majority for any candidate. In the election of 1800, Thomas Jefferson, the Jeffersonian Republican Party's presidential candidate, and Aaron Burr, that party's vice presidential candidate, received an equal number of votes in the electoral college, throwing the election into the House of Representatives. (The Constitution at that time made no distinction between presidential and vice presidential candidates, specifying only that the individual receiving a majority of electoral votes would be named president.) Some members of the Federalist Party in Congress suggested that they should seize the opportunity to damage the Republican cause by supporting Burr and denying Jefferson the presidency. Federalist leader Alexander Hamilton put a stop to this mischievous notion, however, and made certain that his party supported Jefferson. Hamilton's actions enraged Burr and helped lead to the infamous duel between the two men, in which Hamilton was killed. The Twelfth Amendment, ratified in 1804, was designed to prevent a repetition of such an inconclusive election by providing for separate electoral college votes for president and vice president.

In the 1824 election, four candidates—John Quincy Adams, Andrew Jackson, Henry Clay, and William H. Crawford—divided the electoral vote; no one of them received a majority. The House of Representatives eventually chose Adams over the others, even though Jackson had won more electoral and popular votes. After 1824, the two major political parties had begun to dominate presidential politics to such an extent that by December of each election year, only two candidates remained for the electors to choose between, thus ensuring that one would receive a majority. This freed the parties and the candidates from having to plan their campaigns to culminate in Congress, and Congress very quickly ceased to dominate the presidential selection process.

On all but three occasions since 1824, the electoral vote has simply ratified the nationwide popular vote. Since electoral votes are won on a state-by-state basis, it is mathematically possible for a candidate who receives a nationwide popular plurality to fail to carry states whose electoral votes would add up to a majority. Thus, in 1876, Rutherford B. Hayes was the winner in the electoral college despite receiving fewer popular votes than his rival, Samuel Tilden. In 1888, Grover Cleveland received more popular votes than Benjamin Harrison, but received fewer electoral votes. And in 2000, Al Gore outpolled his opponent, George W. Bush, by more than 500,000 votes, but narrowly lost the electoral college by a mere four electoral votes.

Election Campaigns

campaign an effort by political candidates and their staffs to win the backing of donors, political activists, and voters in the quest for political office

A **campaign** is an effort by political candidates and their supporters to win the backing of donors, political activists, and voters in their quest for political office.

Campaigns precede every primary and general election. Because of the complexity of the campaign process, and because of the amount of money that candidates must raise, presidential campaigns usually begin almost two years before the November presidential elections. The campaign for any office consists of a number of steps. Candidates must first organize groups of supporters who will help them raise funds and bring their name to the attention of the media and potential donors. This step is relatively easy for a candidate currently in the office. The current officeholder is called an **incumbent.** Incumbents usually are already well known and have little difficulty attracting supporters and contributors, unless of course they have been subject to damaging publicity while in office.

incumbent a candidate running for a position that he or she already holds

ADVISERS

The next step in a typical campaign involves recruiting advisers and creating a formal campaign organization (see Figure 10.1). Most candidates, especially for national or statewide office, will need a campaign manager, a media consultant, a

The Typical Organization of a National Political Campaign

Figure 10.1

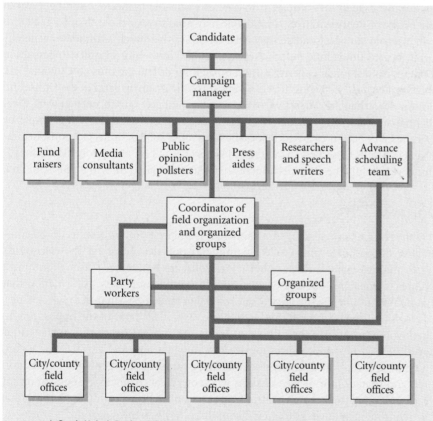

SOURCE: L. Sandy Maisel, *Parties and Elections in America,* 2nd ed. (New York: McGraw-Hill, 1993), p. 190. Copyright © 1993, McGraw-Hill. Used with permission.

pollster, a financial adviser, and a press spokesperson, as well as a staff director to coordinate the activities of volunteer and paid workers. For a local campaign, candidates generally need hundreds of workers. State-level campaigns call for thousands of workers, and presidential campaigns require tens of thousands of workers nationwide.

Professional campaign workers, including the managers, consultants, and pollsters required in a modern campaign, prefer to work for candidates who seem to have a reasonable chance of winning. Candidates seen as having little chance of winning often have difficulty hiring the most experienced professional consultants. Professional political consultants have taken the place of the old-time party bosses who once controlled political campaigns. Most consultants who direct campaigns specialize in politics, although some are drawn from the ranks of corporate advertising and may work with commercial clients in addition to politicians. Campaign consultants conduct public opinion polls, produce television commercials, organize direct-mail campaigns, and develop the issues and advertising messages the candidate will use to mobilize support. George W. Bush's chief political strategist, Karl Rove, not only played a key role in two presidential campaigns, but is also widely credited for crafting the strategy that brought about a Republican victory in the 2002 national congressional races.

Together with their advisers, candidates must begin serious fund-raising efforts at an early stage in the campaign. To have a reasonable chance of winning a seat in the House of Representatives, a candidate may need to raise more than $500,000. To win a Senate seat, a candidate may need ten times that much. Candidates generally begin raising funds long before they face an election. Once in office, members of Congress find it much easier to raise campaign funds and are thus able to outspend their challengers (see Figure 10.2).[7] Members of the majority party in the House and Senate are particularly attractive to donors who want access to those in power.[8] Presidential candidates in particular must raise huge amounts of money. For example, by December 1999, almost a year before the November 2000 national elections, Republican George W. Bush had already raised some $63 million to support his bid for office. A year before the 2004 election, Bush had already raised more than $100 million.

POLLING

Another important element of a campaign is public-opinion polling. To be competitive, a candidate must collect voting and poll data to assess the electorate's needs, hopes, fears, and past behavior. Polls are conducted throughout most political campaigns. Surveys of voter opinion provide the basic information that candidates and their staffs use to craft campaign strategies—that is, to select issues, to assess their own strengths and weaknesses as well as those of the opposition, to check voter response to the campaign, and to measure the degree to which various constituent groups may be responsive to campaign appeals. The themes, issues, and messages that candidates present during a campaign are generally based upon polls and smaller face-to-face sessions with voters, called "focus groups." In recent years, pollsters have become central figures in most national campaigns, and some have continued as advisers to their clients after they win the election.

In the months leading up to the 2004 presidential election, Democrats conducted extensive polls to assess President Bush's political strengths and weak-

House and Senate Campaign Expenditures, 1980–2000 (Net Dollars)   **Figure 10.2**

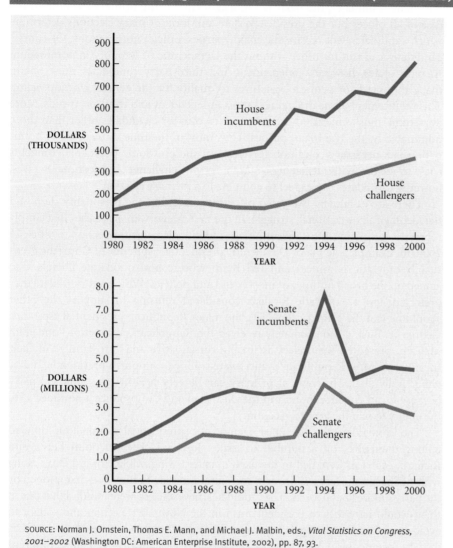

SOURCE: Norman J. Ornstein, Thomas E. Mann, and Michael J. Malbin, eds., *Vital Statistics on Congress, 2001–2002* (Washington DC: American Enterprise Institute, 2002), pp. 87, 93.

nesses. Their data suggested that Bush's main area of strength, national security policy, had been undermined by public concerns over his policies in Iraq. They also indicated widespread concern about Bush's economic stewardship, even though the economy seemed to be improving. These data led Democrats to fashion attacks on the president aimed at raising further questions about Iraq and suggesting that the economic recovery would be limited in scope—a so-called jobless recovery.[9]

THE PRIMARIES

For many candidates, the next step in a campaign is the primary election. In the case of all offices but the presidency, state and local primary elections determine which candidates will receive the major parties' official nominations. Of course, candidates can run for office without the Democratic or Republican nomination. In most states, however, independent and third-party candidates must obtain many thousands of petition signatures to qualify for the general election ballot. This requirement alone discourages most independent and third-party bids. More important, most Americans are reluctant to vote for candidates other than those nominated by the two major parties. Thus most of the time, a major party nomination is a necessary condition for electoral success. Some popular incumbents coast to victory without having to face a serious challenge. In most major races, however, candidates can expect to compete in a primary election.

There are essentially two types of primary contests: the personality clash and the ideological, or factional, struggle. In the first category are primaries that simply represent competing efforts by ambitious individuals to secure election to office. In 2000, for example, the major Democratic presidential aspirants, Al Gore (the eventual Democratic nominee) and Bill Bradley, were both moderate liberals who agreed on the broad outlines of most issues and policies. Whichever candidate they preferred, few Democratic loyalists considered refusing to support the other should he win the primary. Similarly, the major Republican presidential aspirants, George W. Bush (who ultimately received the Republican nomination) and John McCain, presented themselves as fiscally conservative and "pro-family" in their social views. Most Republican loyalists were willing to support a presidential bid by either individual. This type of primary can be very healthy for a political party because it can enhance interest in the campaign and can produce a nominee with the ability to win the general election.

The contenders for the 2004 Democratic presidential nomination differed among themselves on a number of issues. Joseph Lieberman, John Kerry, and Richard Gephardt were tied to the party's centrist wing, while Howard Dean along with Al Sharpton, Dennis Kucinich, and Carol Moseley Braun were championed by the party's more liberal forces. The candidates, nevertheless, were mindful that one of them would have to face President Bush in the November election and sought to avoid an acrimonious struggle on divisive issues that might ultimately help the GOP.

The second type of primary—the ideological struggle—can have different consequences. Ideological struggles usually occur when one wing of a party decides that an incumbent is too willing to compromise or too moderate in his or her political views. For example, in 1992, former president George H. W. Bush was challenged for the Republican presidential nomination by conservative columnist Pat Buchanan. Buchanan charged Bush with being too willing to compromise conservative principles. Such ideological challenges not only reveal rifts within a party coalition, but the friction and resentment they cause can undermine a party's general election chances. Through his ideological crusade, Buchanan damaged President Bush's re-election chances in 1992.

Ideological struggles can also produce candidates who are too liberal or too conservative to win the general election. Primary electorates are much smaller and tend to be ideologically more extreme than the general electorate: Democratic primary voters are somewhat more liberal than the general electorate, and Republican primary voters are typically more conservative than the general electorate. Thus, the winner of an intraparty ideological struggle may prove too extreme for the general election. In 1994, for example, archconservative Oliver North won the Virginia Republican senatorial primary over a moderate opponent, but was drubbed in the general election. Many moderate Republicans, including Virginia's other senator, John Warner, refused to support North.

Presidential Elections

Although they also involve primary elections, the major party presidential nominations follow a pattern that is quite different from the nominating process employed for other political offices. In some years, particularly when an incumbent president is running for re-election, one party's nomination may not be contested. If, however, the Democratic or Republican presidential nomination is contested, candidates typically compete in primaries or presidential nominating caucuses in all fifty states, attempting to capture national convention delegates. Most states use primary elections to choose the delegates for national conventions. A few states use the **caucus,** a nominating process that begins with precinct-level meetings throughout the state. Some caucuses, called **open caucuses,** are open to anyone wishing to attend. Other states use **closed caucuses,** open only to registered party members. Citizens attending the caucuses typically elect delegates to statewide conventions at which delegates to the national party conventions are chosen.

The primaries and caucuses usually begin in February of a presidential election year and end in June (see Figure 10.3). The early ones are most important because they can help front-running candidates secure media attention and financial support. Gradually, the primary and caucus process has become "front loaded," with states vying with one another to increase their political influence by holding their nominating processes first. Traditionally, the New Hampshire primary and the Iowa caucuses are considered the most important of the early events, and candidates spend months courting voter support in these two states. A candidate who performs well in Iowa and New Hampshire will usually be able to secure support and better media coverage for subsequent races. A candidate who fares badly in these two states may be written off as a loser.

As noted in Chapter 9, the Democratic Party requires that state presidential primaries allocate delegates on the basis of proportional representation; Democratic candidates win delegates in rough proportion to their percentage of the primary vote. The Republican Party does not require proportional representation, but most states have now written proportional representation requirements into their election laws. A few states use the **winner-take-all system,** by which the candidate with the most votes wins all the party's delegates in that state.

When the primaries and caucuses are concluded, it is usually clear which candidates have won their parties' nominations. For example, in 2004, John Kerry was the Democratic winner long before the party faithful assembled in Boston.

THE CONVENTION

The one major step that remains before a nomination is actually awarded is the national party convention. The Democratic and Republican national party conventions occur every four years to formally certify each party's presidential and

caucus (political) a normally closed meeting of a political or legislative group to select candidates, plan strategy, or make decisions regarding legislative matters

open caucus a presidential nominating caucus open to anyone who wishes to attend

closed caucus a presidential nominating caucus open only to registered party members

winner-take-all system a system in which all of a state's presidential nominating delegates are awarded to the candidate who wins the most votes, while runners-up receive no delegates

Figure 10.3 — The 2004 Presidential Election Season

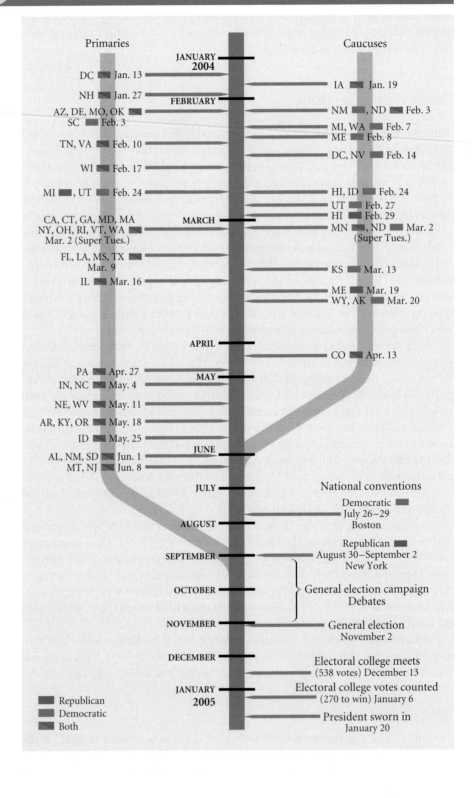

Primaries

Caucuses

JANUARY 2004

DC — Jan. 13

IA — Jan. 19

NH — Jan. 27

FEBRUARY

AZ, DE, MO, OK

NM, ND — Feb. 3

SC — Feb. 3

MI, WA — Feb. 7

ME — Feb. 8

TN, VA — Feb. 10

DC, NV — Feb. 14

WI — Feb. 17

MI, UT — Feb. 24

HI, ID — Feb. 24

UT — Feb. 27

HI — Feb. 29

CA, CT, GA, MD, MA
NY, OH, RI, VT, WA
Mar. 2 (Super Tues.)

MARCH

MN, ND — Mar. 2
(Super Tues.)

FL, LA, MS, TX
Mar. 9

KS — Mar. 13

IL — Mar. 16

ME — Mar. 19

WY, AK — Mar. 20

APRIL

CO — Apr. 13

PA — Apr. 27

MAY

IN, NC — May. 4

NE, WV — May. 11

AR, KY, OR — May. 18

ID — May. 25

AL, NM, SD — Jun. 1

JUNE

MT, NJ — Jun. 8

JULY

National conventions

Democratic
July 26–29
Boston

AUGUST

Republican
August 30–September 2
New York

SEPTEMBER

General election campaign
Debates

OCTOBER

NOVEMBER

General election
November 2

DECEMBER

Electoral college meets
(538 votes) December 13

JANUARY 2005

Electoral college votes counted
(270 to win) January 6

President sworn in
January 20

Republican
Democratic
Both

vice presidential nominees. In addition, the conventions draft a statement of party principles, called a **platform,** and determine the rules that will govern party activities for the next four years.

The History of Political Conventions   For more than fifty years after America's founding, presidential nominations were controlled by each party's congressional caucus—all the party's members in the House and the Senate. Critics referred to this process as the "King Caucus" and charged that it did not take proper account of the views of party members throughout the nation. In 1824, the King Caucus method came under severe attack when the Democratic Party caucus failed to nominate Andrew Jackson, the candidate with the greatest support among both party members and activists outside the capital. In the 1830s, the party convention was devised as a way of allowing party leaders and activists throughout the nation to participate in selecting presidential candidates. The first party convention was held by the Anti-Masonic Party in 1831. The Democratic Party held its first convention in 1832, when Andrew Jackson was nominated for a second term.

As it developed during the course of the next century, the convention became the decisive institution in the presidential nominating processes of the two major parties. The convention was a genuine deliberative body in which party factions argued, negotiated, and eventually reached a decision. The convention was composed of delegations from each state. The size of a state's delegation depended on the state's population, and each delegate was allowed one vote for the purpose of nominating the party's presidential and vice presidential candidates. Before 1936, victory required the support of two-thirds of the delegates. Until 1968, state delegations voted according to the **unit rule,** which meant that all the members of the state delegation would vote for the candidate favored by the majority of the state's delegates. This practice was designed to maximize a state's influence in the nominating process. The unit rule was abolished in 1968.

Between the 1830s and World War II, national convention delegates were generally selected by a state's party leaders. Usually the delegates were public officials, political activists, and party notables from all regions of the state, representing most major party factions. Some delegates would arrive at the convention having pledged in advance to give their support to a particular presidential candidate. Most delegates were uncommitted, however. This fact, coupled with the unit rule, allowed state party leaders (i.e., the delegates) to negotiate with one another and with presidential candidates for their support. State party leaders might agree to support a candidate in exchange for a promise to name them or their followers to important national positions, or in exchange for promises of federal programs and projects for their state. During the course of a convention, alliances of states would form, dissolve, and re-form in the course of tense negotiations. Typically, many votes were needed before the nomination could be decided. Often, deadlocks developed between the most powerful party factions, and state leaders would be forced to find a compromise, or "dark-horse," candidate. Among the more famous dark-horse nominees were James Polk in 1844 and Warren Harding in 1920. Although he was virtually unknown, Polk won the Democratic nomination when it became clear that none of the more established candidates could win. Similarly, Harding, another political unknown, won his nomination after the major candidates had fought one another to a standstill.

In its day, the convention was seen as a democratic reform. In later years, however, new generations of reformers came to view the convention as a symbol of rule by party leaders. The convention also strengthened the independence and power of the presidency, by taking the nominating process out of the hands of Congress.

Contemporary Party Conventions Whereas the traditional party convention was a deliberative assembly, the contemporary convention acts more to ratify than to determine the party's presidential and vice presidential nominations. Today, as we saw earlier in this chapter, the nomination is actually determined in a series of primary elections and local party caucuses held in virtually all fifty states during several months prior to the convention. These primaries and caucuses determine how each state's convention delegates will vote. Candidates now arrive at the convention knowing who has enough delegate support in hand to assure a victory in the first round of balloting. State party leaders no longer serve as power brokers, and the party's presidential and vice presidential choices are made relatively quickly.

Even though the party convention no longer controls presidential nominations, it still has a number of important tasks. The first of these is the adoption of party rules concerning such matters as convention delegate selection and future presidential primary elections. In 1972, for example, the Democratic convention accepted rules requiring convention delegates to be broadly representative of the party's membership in terms of race and gender. After those rules were passed, the convention refused to seat several state delegations that were deemed not to meet this standard.

Another important task for the convention is the drafting of a party platform—a statement of principles and pledges around which the delegates can unite. Although the two major parties' platforms tend to contain many similar principles and platitudes, differences between the two platforms can be significant. In recent years, for example, the Republican platform has advocated tax cuts and taken strong positions on such social issues as affirmative action and abortion. The Democratic platforms, on the other hand, have focused on the importance of maintaining welfare and regulatory programs. A close reading of the party platforms can reveal some of the ideological differences between the parties.

delegates political activists selected to vote at a party's national convention

Convention Delegates Today, convention **delegates** are generally political activists with strong positions on social and political issues. Generally, Republican delegates tend to be more conservative than Republican voters as a whole, whereas Democratic delegates tend to be more liberal than the majority of Democratic voters. In states such as Michigan and Iowa, local party caucuses choose many of the delegates who will actually attend the national convention. In most of the remaining states, primary elections determine how a state's delegation will vote, but the actual delegates are selected by state party officials. Delegate votes won in primary elections are apportioned to candidates on the basis of proportional representation. Thus a candidate who received 30 percent of the vote in the California Democratic primary would receive roughly 30 percent of the state's delegate votes at the party's national convention.

As was mentioned earlier, the Democratic Party requires that a state's convention delegation be representative of that state's Democratic electorate in terms of race, gender, and age. Republican delegates, by contrast, are more likely to be male and white. The Democrats also reserve slots for elected Democratic Party officials, called **superdelegates.** All the Democratic governors and about 80 percent of the party's members of Congress now attend the national convention as delegates.

superdelegate a convention delegate position, in Democratic conventions, reserved for party officials

Convention Procedure   Each party convention lasts several days. The convention usually begins with the selection of party committees, including the credentials, rules, and platform committees, and the election of a temporary convention chairperson. This individual normally delivers a keynote address highlighting the party's appeals and concerns. After all the delegates have been seated by the credentials committee, a permanent chair is elected. This person presides over the presidential and vice presidential nominations, the adoption of a party platform, and any votes on rules that are proposed by the rules committee.

Although the actual presidential nomination is effectively decided before the convention, the names of a number of candidates are generally put in nomination and speeches made on their behalf at the convention. To be nominated is considered an honor, and ambitious politicians are eager for the media attention, however brief, that such a nomination brings.

All the nominating speeches, as well as speeches by party notables, are carefully scrutinized by the mass media, which report and analyze the major events of the convention. In the 1950s and 1960s, the television networks provided "gavel-to-gavel" coverage of the Democratic and Republican national conventions. Today, however, the major television networks carry convention highlights only. Because the parties are eager to receive as much media coverage as possible, they schedule convention events in order to reach large television audiences. The parties typically try to present the actual presidential nomination and the nominee's acceptance speech during prime viewing time, normally between 8:00 and 11:00 P.M. on a weeknight. In 1996, the major networks proclaimed that both national conventions were essentially too boring to merit detailed coverage. One important news program, ABC's *Nightline,* halted its coverage of the Republican convention earlier than had been scheduled after the program's anchor, Ted Koppel, decided that the GOP convention was little more than a staged media event.

After the nominating speeches are concluded, the voting begins. The names of the states are called alphabetically and the state delegation's vote reported by its chairperson. During this process, noisy and colorful demonstrations are staged in support of the nominees. When the nomination is formally decided, a lengthy demonstration ensues, with bands and colorful balloons celebrating the conclusion of the process. The party's vice presidential candidate is usually nominated the next day. This individual is almost always selected by the presidential nominee, and the choice is merely ratified by the convention. In 2000 and 2004, George W. Bush selected Dick Cheney, who had previously served as his father's secretary of defense, while John Kerry designated North Carolina senator John Edwards as his running mate in 2004. Kerry hoped Edwards would appeal to southern voters.

Once the nominations have been settled and most other party business has been resolved, the presidential and vice presidential nominees deliver acceptance speeches. These speeches are opportunities for the nominees to begin their formal campaigns on a positive note, and they are usually meticulously crafted to make as positive an impression on the electorate as possible.

THE GENERAL ELECTION CAMPAIGN AND HIGH-TECH POLITICS

For those candidates lucky enough to survive the nominating process, the last hurdle is the general election. There are essentially two types of general election in the United States today. The first type is the organizationally driven, labor-intensive election. In general, local elections and many congressional races fall into this category. Candidates campaign in such elections by recruiting large numbers of volunteer workers to hand out leaflets and organize rallies. The candidates make appearances at receptions, community group meetings, and local events, and even in shopping malls and on busy street corners. Generally, local and congressional campaigns depend less upon issues and policy proposals and more upon hard work designed to make the candidate more visible than his or her opponent. Statewide campaigns, some congressional races, and, of course, the national presidential election fall into the second category: the media-driven, capital-intensive electoral campaign.

In the nineteenth and early twentieth centuries, political campaigns were waged by the parties' enormous armies of patronage workers. Throughout the year, party workers cultivated the support of voters by helping them with legal problems, helping them find jobs, and serving as liaisons with local, state, and federal agencies. On Election Day throughout the nation hundreds of thousands of party workers marched from house to house reminding their supporters to vote, helping the aged and infirm to reach the polls, and calling in the favors they had accrued during the year. Campaigns resembled the maneuvers of huge infantries vying for victory. Historians have, in fact, referred to this traditional style of party campaigning as "militarist."

Contemporary political campaigns rely less on infantries and more on "air power." That is, rather than deploy huge armies of workers, contemporary campaigns make use of a number of communications techniques to reach voters and bid for their support. Six techniques are especially important.

Polling   Surveys of voter opinion provide the information that candidates and their staffs use to craft campaign strategies. Candidates employ polls to select issues, to assess their own strengths and weaknesses (as well as those of the opposition), to check voter response to the campaign, and to determine the degree to which various constituent groups are susceptible to campaign appeals. Virtually all contemporary campaigns for national and statewide office as well as many local campaigns make extensive use of opinion polling. As we saw in Chapter 6, President Clinton relied heavily on polling data both during and after the 1996 presidential election to shape his rhetoric and guide his policy initiatives.

The Broadcast Media   Extensive use of the broadcast media, television in particular, has become the hallmark of the modern political campaign. Generally, media campaigns attempt to follow the guidelines indicated by a candidate's polls, emphasizing issues and personal characteristics that appear important in the poll data. The broadcast media are now so central to modern campaigns that most candidates' activities are tied to their media strategies.[10] Candidate activities are designed expressly to stimulate television news coverage. For instance, members of Congress running for re-election or for president almost always sponsor committee or subcommittee hearings to generate publicity.

Extensive use of radio and television has become the hallmark of the modern statewide or national political campaign. One commonly used broadcast technique is the fifteen-, thirty-, or sixty-second television **spot advertisement,** which permits a candidate's message to be delivered to a target audience before uninterested or hostile viewers can tune it out. Examples of effective spot ads include George Bush's 1988 "Willie Horton" ad, which implied that Bush's opponent, Michael Dukakis, coddled criminals, and Lyndon Johnson's 1964 "daisy girl" ad, which suggested that his opponent, Barry Goldwater, would lead the United States into nuclear war. Television spot ads are used to establish candidate name recognition, to create a favorable image of the candidate and a negative image of the opponent, to link the candidate with desirable groups in the community, and to communicate the candidate's stands on selected issues. Media campaigns generally follow the trail outlined by a candidate's polls, emphasizing issues and personal characteristics that appear important in the poll data.

> **spot advertisement** a fifteen-, thirty-, or sixty-second television campaign commercial that permits a candidate's message to be delivered to a target audience

The 1992 presidential campaign introduced three new media techniques, all of which are still important today: the talk show interview, the "electronic town hall meeting," and the "infomercial." Candidates used television and radio interview programs to reach the large audiences drawn to this newly popular entertainment program format. Some of these programs allow audience members to telephone the show with questions, which gives candidates a chance to demonstrate that they are interested in the views of ordinary people. The **town meeting** format allows candidates the opportunity to appear in an auditoriumlike setting and interact with ordinary citizens, thus underlining the candidates' concern with the views and needs of the voters. Moreover, both the talk show appearance and the town meeting allow candidates to deliver their messages to millions of Americans without the input of journalists or commentators who might criticize or question the candidates' assertions.

> **town meeting** a media format in which candidates meet with ordinary citizens. Allows candidates to deliver messages without the presence of journalists or commentators

The **infomercial** is a lengthy presentation, often lasting thirty minutes. Although infomercials are designed to have the appearance of news programs, they are actually presentations of a candidate's views. Independent candidate Ross Perot made frequent use of infomercials during the 1992 campaign.

> **infomercial** a lengthy campaign advertisement on television

Another use of the broadcast media in contemporary campaigns is the televised candidate debate. Televised presidential debates began with the famous 1960 Kennedy-Nixon clash. Today, both presidential and vice presidential candidates hold debates, as do candidates for statewide and even local offices. Debates allow candidates to reach voters who have not fully made up their minds about the election. Moreover, debates can increase the visibility of lesser-known candidates. In 1960, John F. Kennedy's strong performance in the presidential debate was a major factor in bringing about his victory over the much-better-known Richard Nixon.

Phone Banks   Through the broadcast media, candidates communicate with voters en masse and impersonally. Phone banks, on the other hand, allow campaign workers to make personal contact with hundreds of thousands of voters. Personal contacts of this sort are thought to be extremely effective. Again, polling data serve to identify the groups that will be targeted for phone calls. Computers select phone numbers from areas in which members of these groups are concentrated. Staffs of paid or volunteer callers, using computer-assisted dialing systems and prepared scripts, then place calls to deliver the candidate's message. The targeted groups are generally those identified by polls as either uncommitted or weakly committed, as well as strong supporters of the candidate who are contacted simply to encourage them to vote.

Direct Mail   Direct mail serves both as a vehicle for communicating with voters and as a mechanism for raising funds. The first step in a direct-mail campaign is the purchase or rental of a computerized mailing list of voters deemed to have some particular perspective or social characteristic. Often sets of magazine subscription lists or lists of donors to various causes are employed. For example, a candidate interested in reaching conservative voters might rent subscription lists from the *National Review, Human Events,* or *Conservative Digest*; a candidate interested in appealing to liberals might rent subscription lists from the *New York Review of Books* or *The Nation*. Considerable fine-tuning is possible. After obtaining the appropriate mailing lists, candidates usually send pamphlets, letters, and brochures describing themselves and their views to voters believed to be sympathetic. Different types of mail appeals are made to different electoral subgroups. Often the letters sent to voters are personalized. The recipient is addressed by name in the text and the letter appears actually to have been signed by the candidate. Of course, these "personal" letters are written and even signed by a computer.

In addition to its use as a political advertising medium, direct mail has also become an important source of campaign funds. Computerized mailing lists permit campaign strategists to pinpoint individuals whose interests, background, and activities suggest that they may be potential donors to the campaign. Letters of solicitation are sent to these potential donors. Some of the money raised is then used to purchase additional mailing lists. Direct-mail solicitation can be enormously effective.[11]

Professional Public Relations   Modern campaigns and the complex technology upon which they rely are typically directed by professional public relations consultants. Virtually all serious contenders for national and statewide office retain the services of professional campaign consultants. Increasingly, candidates for local office, too, have come to rely upon professional campaign managers. Consultants offer candidates the expertise necessary to conduct accurate opinion polls, produce television commercials, organize direct-mail campaigns, and make use of sophisticated computer analyses.

The number of technologically oriented campaigns increased greatly after 1971. The Federal Election Campaign Act of 1971 prompted the creation of large numbers of political action committees (PACs) by a host of corporate and ideological groups. This development increased the availability of funds to political candidates—conservative candidates in particular—which meant in turn that the new technology could be used more extensively. Initially, the new techniques were employed mainly by individual candidates who often made little or no effort to coordinate their campaigns with those of other political aspirants sharing the same party label. For this reason, campaigns employing new technology sometimes came to be called "candidate-centered" efforts, as distinguished from the traditional party-coordinated campaign. Nothing about the new technology, however, precluded its use by political party leaders seeking to coordinate a number of campaigns. In recent years, party leaders have learned to make good use of modern campaign technology. The difference between the old and new political methods is not that the latter are inherently candidate-centered while the former are strictly a party tool; it is a matter of the types of political resources upon which each method depends.

The Internet   Still another new media technique was introduced in the 1996 presidential campaign. This was the use of the Internet as a political medium. The major candidates and many minor candidates created Web pages that provided biographical data, information about the candidates' positions on various issues, and even photographs of the candidates and their family members. The Web pages also provided voters with information about how to become involved in the candidates' campaign efforts. As discussed in Chapter 7, candidate Web sites are most likely to be visited by individuals who already agree with the candidate's views and hence are not likely to change many votes. Nevertheless, these sites may help reinforce the commitments of loyalists and can encourage the faithful to work on behalf of their candidate.

In addition to Web sites, candidates are beginning to use the Internet for targeted advertising campaigns. In the 2000 contest, the politician who made the most extensive use of the Internet was John McCain. McCain used his Web site to mobilize volunteers and to raise hundreds of thousands of dollars for his unsuccessful bid for the Republican presidential nomination.

During the 2004 presidential contest, Democratic hopeful Howard Dean made extensive use of the Internet as a communication and fund-raising tool. Thousands of bloggers maintained discussion forums that promoted Dean's candidacy and solicited funds. By the end of 2003, Dean had amassed a war chest of more than $15 million, much of it raised on the Internet. Dean Internet guru Joe Trippi hoped to persuade 2 million Americans to each give "one hundred dollars online," to match the money that President Bush was expected to accumulate through traditional fund-raising methods.[12] In the end, though, Dean's Internet campaign was overcome by John Kerry's more traditional campaign tactics.

One consultant now refers to politics on the Internet as "netwar" and asserts that "small, smart attackers" can defeat more powerful opponents in the new, information-age "battlespace."[13] Although the Internet has not yet become a dominant force in political campaigns, most politicians and consultants believe that its full potential for customizing political appeals is only now beginning to be realized.

CAMPAIGN AND POLITICAL EQUALITY: FROM LABOR-INTENSIVE TO CAPITAL-INTENSIVE POLITICS

The displacement of organizational methods by the new political technology is, in essence, a shift from labor-intensive to capital-intensive competitive electoral practices. Campaign tasks that were once performed by masses of party workers with some cash now require fewer personnel but a great deal more money, for the new political style depends on polls, computers, and other electronic paraphernalia. Of course, even when workers and organization were the key electoral tools, money had considerable political significance. Nevertheless, during the nineteenth century, national political campaigns in the United States employed millions of people. Indeed, as many as 2.5 million individuals did political work during the

FOR CRITICAL ANALYSIS

In recent years, the Internet has become a prominent campaign tool. Does the Internet make electoral campaigns more democratic, does it make them less democratic, or are its effects neutral?

American Campaign Techniques Conquer the World

Since the 1950s, American election campaigns have been characterized by a reliance on technology in place of organization and personnel and by the rise of a new type of campaigner, the professional political consultant, in place of the old-time party boss. More and more, these campaign methods and even the consultants who wield them have spread to other parts of the world. American campaign consultants with their polls and phone banks and spot ads have directed campaigns in Europe, Latin America, and Asia. One American consultant, Joseph Napolitan, was instrumental in forming the International Association of Political Consultants (IAPC), which, working closely with the American Association of Political Consultants and the International Republican Institute (IRI), has helped to disseminate American-style campaign techniques throughout the world. One American consultant recently said, "[We have] worked a lot in South America, Israel, [and the] Philippines and one of the things that I've discovered through that work is that the tools and techniques and strategies that we have developed here are applicable everywhere."[a]

This phenomenon, which Europeans sometimes call the Americanization of politics, has important political implications. For the most part, the substitution of technology for organization in political campaigns works to the advantage of politicians and political forces representing the upper ends of the social spectrum versus those representing the lower classes. Strong party organization was generally introduced by working-class parties as a way of maximizing their major political resource—the power of numbers. Their middle-class opponents might copy them but when politics is based mainly on organization and numbers, working-class parties can compete quite successfully. The growing use of technology in place of organization shifts the advantage to middle- and upper-class parties, which generally have better access to the financial resources needed to fuel the polls and television ads on which new-style campaigns depend. In the United States, the shift to high-tech politics was led by the Republicans and such conservative consultants as Richard Viguerie, the pioneer of direct-mail fund-raising and advertising. Democrats followed the GOP's lead but found themselves fighting on the opponents' terrain. Moreover, since technology is most effectively used by those Democrats with the best access to corporate and other financial resources, high-tech politics has generally served the interests of more moderate and conservative forces within the Democratic Party—Bill Clinton's "New Democrats," for example.

The development of the new technology in Europe and other parts of the world followed the American pattern. New techniques were introduced first by conservative parties and then copied, usually with less success, by their opponents. In Germany, for example, American-style politics was introduced by the Christian Democrats in the 1960s and then copied by the Social Democrats. In Britain, the Conservatives began to employ mass media campaign techniques in the 1970s, initially importing American campaign consultants, leading to Margaret Thatcher's victory in 1979. Subsequently, Labor followed suit. In France, professional public relations, polling, and mass media campaigns were first introduced by Charles de Gaulle's party, the Union pour la Nouvelle République (UNR) in the 1980s.[b] As in the British case, French conservatives initially relied on the services of American consultants—in particular, Joseph Napolitan—before developing homegrown talent. Where working-class and labor parties have sought to use the new campaign techniques, the more conservative and business-oriented factions within those parties have usually been the chief beneficiaries—Tony Blair's "New Labor" in England, for example. Thus, as American-style politics has conquered the world, it has also helped to bring about changes in political patterns and party formations, making the world more like America.

FOR CRITICAL ANALYSIS

1. Which foreign political parties were first to adopt American-style campaign techniques? Why?

2. What are the political implications and consequences of the shift from old-fashioned campaign styles to American-style, technology-intensive politics?

[a]Quoted in Paul Baines, Fritz Plasser, and Christian Scheucher, "Operationalising Political Marketing: A Comparison of US and Western European Consultants and Managers," Middlesex University Discussion Paper Series, No. 7, July 1999.
[b]Benjamin Ginsberg, *The Captive Public* (New York: Basic Books, 1986), pp. 172–73.

1880s.[14] The direct cost of campaigns, therefore, was relatively low. For example, in 1860, Abraham Lincoln spent only $100,000—which was approximately twice the amount spent by his chief opponent, Stephen Douglas.

Modern campaigns depend heavily on money. Each element of the new political technology is enormously expensive. A sixty-second spot announcement on prime-time network television costs hundreds of thousands of dollars each time it is aired. Opinion surveys can be quite expensive; polling costs in a statewide race can easily reach or exceed the six-figure mark. Campaign consultants can charge substantial fees. A direct-mail campaign can eventually become an important source of funds but is very expensive to initiate. The inauguration of a serious national direct-mail effort requires at least $1 million in "front-end cash" to pay for mailing lists, brochures, letters, envelopes, and postage.[15] Although the cost of televised debates is covered by the sponsoring organizations and the television stations and is therefore free to the candidates, even debate preparation requires substantial staff work, research, and, of course, money. It is the expense of the new technology that accounts for the enormous cost of recent American national elections.

Certainly "people power" is not irrelevant to modern political campaigns. Candidates continue to utilize the political services of tens of thousands of volunteer workers. Nevertheless, in the contemporary era, even the recruitment of campaign workers has become a matter of electronic technology. Employing a technique called "instant organization," paid telephone callers use phone banks to contact individuals in areas targeted by a computer (which they do when contacting potential voters, as we discussed before). Volunteer workers are recruited from among these individuals. A number of campaigns—Richard Nixon's 1968 presidential campaign was the first—have successfully used this technique.

The displacement of organizational methods by the new political technology has the most far-reaching implications for the balance of power among contending political groups. Labor-intensive organizational tactics allowed parties whose chief support came from groups nearer the bottom of the social scale to use the numerical superiority of their forces as a partial counterweight to the institutional and economic resources more readily available to the opposition. The capital-intensive technological format, by contrast, has given a major boost to the political fortunes of those forces whose sympathizers are better able to furnish the large sums now needed to compete effectively.[16] Indeed, the new technology permits financial resources to be more effectively harnessed and exploited than was ever before possible.

Dominated by the new technology, electoral politics has become a contest in which the wealthy and powerful have a decided advantage. Perhaps the use of the Internet is the only exception. Furthermore, both political parties are compelled to rely heavily on the support of well-funded special interests—a situation that has become clear in the fund-raising scandals that have plagued both parties in recent years. We shall return to this topic later in this chapter.

How Voters Decide

Whatever the capacity of those with the money and power to influence the electoral process, it is the millions of individual decisions on Election Day that ultimately determine electoral outcomes. Sooner or later the choices of voters weigh more heavily than the schemes of campaign advisers or the leverage of interest groups.

Three factors influence voters' decisions at the polls: partisan loyalty, issue and policy concerns, and candidate characteristics.

PARTISAN LOYALTY

Many studies have shown that most Americans identify more or less strongly with one or the other of the two major political parties. Partisan loyalty was considerably stronger during the 1940s and 1950s than it is today. But even now most voters feel a certain sense of identification or kinship with the Democratic or Republican party. This sense of identification is often handed down from parents to children and is reinforced by social and cultural ties. Partisan identification predisposes voters in favor of their party's candidates and against those of the opposing party (see Figure 10.4). At the level of the presidential contest, issues and candidate personalities may become very important, although even here many Americans supported George W. Bush or John Kerry in the 2004 race only because of partisan loyalty. But partisanship is more likely to assert itself in the less-visible races, where issues and the candidates are not as well known. State legislative races, for example, are often decided by voters' party ties. Once formed, voters' partisan loyalties seldom change. Voters tend to keep their party affiliations unless some crisis causes them to reexamine the bases of their loyalties and to conclude that they have not given their support to the appropriate party. During these relatively infrequent periods of electoral change, millions of voters can change their party ties. For example, at the beginning of the New Deal era, between 1932 and 1936, millions of former Republicans transferred their allegiance to Franklin Roosevelt and the Democrats.

Figure 10.4   The Effect of Party Identification on the Vote, 2004

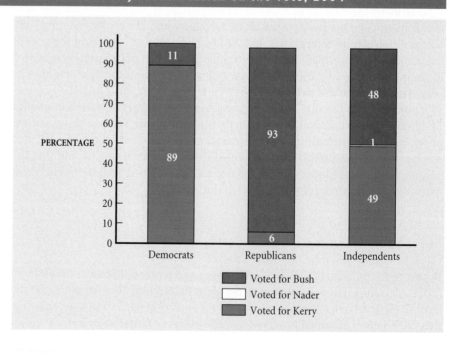

ISSUES

Issues and policy preferences are a second factor influencing voters' choices at the polls. Voters may cast their ballots for the candidate whose position on economic issues they believe to be closest to their own. Similarly, they may select the candidate who has what they believe to be the best record on foreign policy. Issues are more important in some races than others. If candidates actually "take issue" with one another, that is, articulate and publicize very different positions on important public questions, then voters are more likely to be able to identify and act on whatever policy preferences they may have.

The ability of voters to make choices on the basis of issue or policy preferences is diminished, however, if competing candidates do not differ substantially or do not focus their campaigns on policy matters. Very often, candidates deliberately take the safe course and emphasize topics that will not be offensive to any voters. Thus, candidates often trumpet their opposition to corruption, crime, and inflation. Presumably, few voters favor these things. Although it may be perfectly reasonable for candidates to take the safe course and remain as inoffensive as possible, this candidate strategy makes it extremely difficult for voters to make their issue or policy preferences the basis for their choices at the polls.

Voters' issue choices usually involve a mix of their judgments about the past behavior of competing parties and candidates and their hopes and fears about candidates' future behavior. Political scientists call choices that focus on future behavior **prospective voting,** while those based on past performance are called **retrospective voting.** To some extent, whether prospective or retrospective evaluation is more important in a particular election depends on the strategies of competing candidates. Candidates always endeavor to define the issues of an election in terms that will serve their interests. Incumbents running during a period of prosperity will seek to take credit for the economy's happy state and define the election as revolving around their record of success. This strategy encourages voters to make retrospective judgments. By contrast, an insurgent running during a period of economic uncertainty will tell voters it is time for a change and ask them to make prospective judgments. Thus, Bill Clinton focused on change in 1992 and prosperity in 1996, and through well-crafted media campaigns was able to define voters' agenda of choices.

In 2004, President Bush emphasized his efforts to protect the nation from terrorists, and his strong commitment to religious and moral values. Democratic candidate John Kerry on the other hand, attacked Bush's decision to invade Iraq, questioned the president's leadership in the war on terror, and charged that the president's economic policies had failed to produce prosperity. When asked by exit pollsters which issue mattered most in deciding how they voted for president, 22 percent of all voters cited "moral values" as their chief concern. More than 80 percent of these voters supported President Bush. The economy was cited as the most important issue by 20 percent of those who voted, and 80 percent of these Americans voted for Senator Kerry. Terrorism ranked third in terms of the number of voters who indicated it was the most important issue for them. President Bush received more than 80 percent of the votes of those Americans concerned mainly with terrorism.

The Economy As we identify the strategies and tactics employed by opposing political candidates and parties, we should keep in mind that the best-laid plans of politicians often go awry. Election outcomes are affected by a variety of forces that candidates for office cannot fully control. Among the most important of these

prospective voting voting based on the imagined future performance of a candidate

retrospective voting voting based on the past performance of a candidate

Perspectives on Politics

THE ISSUES THAT COLLEGE STUDENTS CARE MOST ABOUT

"What is the one issue that concerns you most?"

33% — War/terrorism/security
20% — Economy/jobs
21% — Education/gay marriage/other social issues
9% — Foreign policy
6% — Health care
11% — Don't know/none

SOURCE: Institute of Politics, Harvard University. "Attitudes Toward Politics and Public Service: A National Survey of College Undergraduates." Conducted March 13–23, 2004. www.iop.harvard.edu/programs/other/natlsurvey/april_2004_topline.pdf

Figure 10.5   Consumer Confidence and Presidential Elections

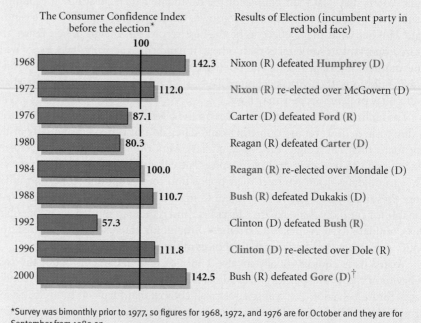

The Consumer Confidence Index before the election*

100

Year	Index	Results of Election (incumbent party in red bold face)
1968	142.3	Nixon (R) defeated **Humphrey (D)**
1972	112.0	**Nixon (R)** re-elected over McGovern (D)
1976	87.1	Carter (D) defeated **Ford (R)**
1980	80.3	Reagan (R) defeated **Carter (D)**
1984	100.0	**Reagan (R)** re-elected over Mondale (D)
1988	110.7	**Bush (R)** defeated Dukakis (D)
1992	57.3	Clinton (D) defeated **Bush (R)**
1996	111.8	**Clinton (D)** re-elected over Dole (R)
2000	142.5	Bush (R) defeated **Gore (D)**[†]

*Survey was bimonthly prior to 1977, so figures for 1968, 1972, and 1976 are for October and they are for September from 1980 on.
†Gore won the popular vote but Bush was elected by the Electoral College.

SOURCE: Bloomberg Financial Markets

forces is the condition of the economy. If voters are satisfied with their economic prospects, they tend to support the party in power, while voter unease about the economy tends to favor the opposition. Thus, George H. W. Bush lost in 1992 during an economic downturn even though his victory in the Middle East had briefly given him a 90 percent favorable rating in the polls. And Bill Clinton won in 1996 during an economic boom even though voters had serious concerns about his moral fiber. Over the past quarter-century, the "Consumer Confidence Index," calculated by the Conference Board, a business research group, has been a fairly accurate predictor of presidential outcomes. The index is based on surveys asking voters how optimistic they are about the future of the economy. It would appear that a generally rosy view, indicated by a score over 100, augers well for the party in power. An index score under 100, suggesting that voters are pessimistic about the economy's trend, suggests that incumbents should worry about their own job prospects (see Figure 10.5).

CANDIDATE CHARACTERISTICS

Candidates' personal attributes always influence voters' decisions. Some analysts claim that voters prefer tall candidates to short ones, candidates with shorter names to candidates with longer names, and candidates with lighter hair to candidates with darker hair. Perhaps these rather frivolous criteria do play some role. But the more important candidate characteristics that affect voters' choices are race, ethnicity, religion, gender, geography, and social background. In general, voters prefer candidates who are closer to themselves in terms of these categories; voters presume that such candidates are likely to have views and perspectives close to their own. Moreover, they may be proud to see someone of their ethnic, religious, or geographic background in a position of leadership. This is why, for many years, politicians sought to "balance the ticket," making certain that their party's ticket included members of as many important groups as possible.

Just as candidates' personal characteristics may attract some voters, they may repel others. Many voters are prejudiced against candidates of certain ethnic, racial, or religious groups. And for many years voters were reluctant to support the candidacies of women, although this appears to be changing.

Voters also pay attention to candidates' personality characteristics, such as "decisiveness," "honesty," and "vigor." In recent years, integrity has become a key election issue. During the 1992 campaign, George Bush accused Bill Clinton of seeking to mislead voters about his anti–Vietnam War activities and his efforts to avoid the draft during the 1960s. This, Bush said, revealed that Clinton lacked the integrity required of a president. Clinton, in turn, accused Bush of resorting to mudslinging because of his poor standing in the polls—an indication of Bush's own character deficiencies. In the 2004 presidential race, President Bush and the Republicans accused Senator Kerry of being inconsistent, a "flip-flopper" who continually changed his positions when it was expedient to do so. Bush, on the other hand, emphasized his own constancy. "I say what I mean and I do what I say" was the president's frequent refrain. The president also pointed to his strong religious commitment as evidence of his exemplary character. For their part, Democrats emphasized Senator Kerry's intelligence, empathy for ordinary Americans, and record of wartime heroism which, they said, stood in sharp contrast to Bush's own somewhat blemished military record. In the end, the GOP's characterization of Kerry as a "flip-flopper" and Bush as an individual with deep moral and religious commitments seemed to resonate with voters. Among those who said that it was important for the president to take a clear stand on issues, 80 percent voted for President Bush; among those for whom strong religious faith was important, 90 percent voted for Bush; and among those who cited honesty as the quality that mattered most, more than 70 percent gave their votes to Bush. On the other hand, among Americans who thought a president should be empathetic and care about people like them, Kerry received 75 percent support. And among those who thought intelligence was the most important personal characteristic of a president, 91 percent voted for Kerry and only 9 percent for Bush.

FOR CRITICAL ANALYSIS
Do American political campaigns help voters make decisions or do they produce more confusion than enlightenment?

The 2004 Elections

In 2004, President George W. Bush led the Republican party to a solid electoral victory, winning 51 percent of the popular vote versus Senator John Kerry's 48 percent, a 286–252 majority in the Electoral College (see Figure 10.6), and helping

Figure 10.6   **Distribution of Electoral Votes in the 2004 Election**

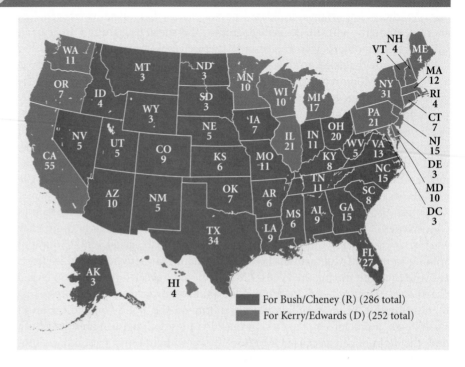

For Bush/Cheney (R) (286 total)
For Kerry/Edwards (D) (252 total)

to solidify what had been shaky Republican control of both houses of Congress. Republicans added four seats in the Senate, giving them a 55–44 majority (with one independent) and five seats in the House of Representatives to gain a 234–200 majority in the lower chamber (with one independent). To further embarrass the Democrats, Senate Democratic leader Tom Daschle was defeated by his Republican opponent in a hard-fought South Dakota campaign.

The roots of this GOP triumph go back nearly three years. In the wake of George W. Bush's disputed Electoral College victory in 2000, many pundits predicted that Bush would be a weak president. Bush had lost the popular vote to Democrat Al Gore and held office only because of a controversial Supreme Court decision that, in effect, awarded him Florida's electoral votes. The conventional wisdom held that, lacking a popular mandate, Bush would be unable to govern effectively and would have difficulty in a quest for a second term. The conventional wisdom, however, did not anticipate the events of September 11, 2001. On that day, Al Qaeda terrorists, under the direction of Osama bin Laden, inflicted serious damage upon the Pentagon and destroyed New York's World Trade Center, which incurred an enormous loss of American lives.

President Bush responded forcefully to the attack. In a series of speeches and dramatic visits to the sites of the strikes, Bush rallied the nation for what he warned would become a lengthy "war on terror." As the first campaign of that war, Bush ordered a massive American, air and ground assault on Afghanistan. That nation's Taliban regime was closely associated with bin Laden and provided sanctuary and support for Al Qaeda. After weeks of fierce fighting, American troops and their Afghan allies routed the Taliban, killed many of the most important Al Qaeda leaders, and installed a pro-American regime in Kabul, Afghanistan. The first American campaign of the war on terror appeared to result in a great triumph for the president.

By responding to Al Qaeda's attack on the United States with the successful Afghan campaign, Bush temporarily silenced all but the most intransigent of his critics. The president's popular approval approached a stratospheric 90 percent, and pundits who had previously called him an ineffectual and illegitimate leader now praised Bush and proclaimed that his presidency had been transformed. The circumstances of George W. Bush's election were all but forgotten.

Despite this triumph, Bush and his advisers knew that his political future was far from assured. During the course of American history, military victory has been no guarantee of lasting political success. Indeed, popular gratitude to wartime leaders tends to be short-lived. When the danger has passed, the public usually returns to its mundane economic and social concerns and is as likely as not to send its wartime champions into political retirement. This was precisely the fate of Bush's father, President George H. W. Bush. The first Bush had been enormously popular after he led the nation in a victorious campaign against Iraq in 1991. He was, nevertheless, defeated by Bill Clinton in the 1992 presidential election when the public was more concerned with an ongoing economic recession than with the previous year's martial glory.

BUILDING BLOCKS OF REPUBLICAN SUCCESS

George W. Bush was determined not to fall victim to his father's fate. The administration's political strategists, led by senior adviser Karl Rove, believed that three ingredients would combine to solidify the president's political strength and ensure his reelection in 2004. The first of these was an expansive economic policy. The Bush administration pursued a program of tax cuts and low interest rates that it hoped would produce a booming economy by election time. Generally, presidents who preside during times of economic expansion are returned to office. The second ingredient was money. Early in his term, President Bush embarked upon an unprecedented fund-raising effort, building a $100 million campaign chest before the Democrats were even close to nominating a candidate.

The final ingredient was the war on terror. The war on terror entailed new risks but, politically speaking, also produced new opportunities. A war of indefinite duration would mean that on a permanent and ongoing basis the American public would look to its government, especially to its president, for protection and reassurance. So long as the public remained convinced that President Bush was making an effective effort to safeguard the nation, it would be unlikely to deprive him of office. And, precisely in order to convince the public that his administration stood between it and mortal danger, the president organized a massive "homeland security" program that included far-reaching government reorganization and sweeping new powers for law enforcement agencies. Many elements of this program, such as enhanced inspection of passengers and freight in the nation's transport system, were designed to thwart terrorists. Other elements of the homeland security program, including a color-coded national alert system, seemed designed to remind Americans of the ongoing threat and the efforts of the Bush administration to protect the nation. Coupled with fund-raising activities and economic expansion, the war on terror appeared to promise political success for President Bush.

DEMOCRATIC OPPORTUNITIES

In the aftermath of September 11, President Bush seemed virtually guaranteed of political success. A new set of political circumstances, however, emerged to diminish the president's political standing and to threaten his grip on power. The first of these was the economy. Despite the administrations' efforts, economic growth was slow and job growth anemic during Bush's first term in office. The sluggish economy allowed Democrats to declare that Bush was the only president in recent history to preside over a net loss of jobs during his administration. Ultimately more important then the economy was the Iraq war. In March, 2003, American military forces launched a full-scale invasion of Iraq aimed at occupying the country and toppling the government of President Saddam Hussein. The invasion followed months of demands by the United States that Iraq acknowledge possessing outlawed weapons of mass destruction (WMDs) and agree to destroy them. The administration also charged that Iraq had been conspiring with Al Qaeda against the United States. Iraq denied American claims and even though UN weapons inspectors failed to find WMDs in Iraq, the Bush administration was convinced that the Iraqis were lying and that the United Nations was inept. After a brief war in which American forces performed at their customarily high level, the Iraqis were overwhelmed and forced to surrender. A short time later Saddam Hussein was captured. Most Americans initially supported the war, and early battlefield success seemed to bolster President Bush's standing. It soon became apparent, however, that whatever Iraqi WMD program might once have existed had been largely abandoned by Saddam Hussein's regime. The Bush administration, moreover, failed to prove a connection between Saddam and terrorism. Thus the president's stated war aims seemed to have been mistaken. To make matters worse, armed resistance to the American occupation of Iraq gradually stiffened, producing a steady drumbeat of American casualties. The Iraq war, though militarily successful, appeared to have been pointless, and suddenly made Bush politically vulnerable.

Adding to the president's problems and to the Democrats' opportunities was the effort by rich liberal activists—George Soros, for example—to form new independent groups, known as 527 Committees, specifically to defeat President Bush (527 Committees are discussed in more detail later in the chapter). Beyond raising millions of dollars to defeat Bush, these groups also registered millions of new Democratic voters. This influx of registrants posed a substantial threat to the GOP, not only at the presidential level but in congressional and local races as well.

But Democrats still faced formidable obstacles in their effort to unseat Bush. The first problem, of course, was identifying a viable candidate. After months of candidate debates and primaries, Senator John Kerry of Massachusetts, a Senate veteran and Vietnam War hero, captured the party's nomination. Kerry named North Carolina senator John Edwards as his running mate. Edwards, a former trial lawyer, lacked a particularly distinguished record in the Senate but was seen as an excellent fund-raiser who might help the Democrats among Southern and rural voters.

Democrats understood that to have any serious chance of defeating President Bush, they must somehow undermine the president's strongest political claim—that he responded forcefully to the September 11 attacks and continued to protect the country from the threat of terrorism. As long as voters accepted the president's contentions, he could not be defeated. As far back as the winter of 2002, Congressional Democrats hoped that a probe of the Bush administration's failure to anticipate the September 11 attacks might embarrass the president in an election year and undermine public confidence in his ability to protect the nation's security. However, their party did not control either house of Congress and, therefore, lacked access to the House or Senate's formal investigative machinery. Nevertheless, Democrats demanded an investigation and, ultimately, through public pressure, forced Congressional Republicans to agree to the creation of an ad hoc, bipartisan investigative panel to be appointed by the leaders of the two parties in Congress. Recognizing the president's peril and seeking to limit any political damage from the 9/11 Commission's findings, the GOP insisted that an investigation be completed and its report released by July 2004, some four months before the 2004 election. The Commission hearings in March and April suggested that the Bush administration had not been sufficiently attentive to the terrorist threat prior to September 2001. Bush was now clearly vulnerable, and throughout the campaign, Democrats charged that the president had failed to heed warnings of a terrorist attack and had subsequently focused on an imaginary threat from Iraq rather than the real danger from Al Qaeda. This was a theme emphasized by Senator Kerry during all three presidential debates.

REPUBLICAN STRATEGY

Republicans were hardly idle while their Democratic foes enrolled new voters and castigated the president. To deal with the threat posed by newly registered Democratic voters, the GOP began its own voter registration effort. Armed with data on millions of voters and potential voters, GOP operatives in every state—especially in so-called battleground states such as Ohio, Florida, Iowa, and Pennsylvania—embarked upon an ambitious effort to register millions of conservative voters. Religious conservatives were a particular target of GOP efforts. The president had appealed to these voters for four years with his stand against abortion and stem-cell research, his support for religious education, and his "faith-based initiative" to allow church-affiliated organizations to win federal contracts to deliver social services. Bush also made much of his own religious faith in televised and personal appearances.

To ensure that the growing legion of religious conservatives actually went to the polls on November 2, Republican campaign materials emphasized moral themes and the president's religious and moral commitments and the GOP launched a series of ballot initiatives on such "hot button" issues as same-sex marriage and abortion. Republicans calculated that these initiatives in such battleground states as Ohio and Florida would bring religious conservatives to the polls. Once at their polling places, they would also vote for President Bush. This strategy seems to have been especially successful in Ohio, where religious conservatives mobilized furiously behind an initiative to ban same-sex marriage. Ohio turned out to be essential to Bush's reelection.

Ultimately, competitive Democratic and Republican registration efforts produced the highest level of voter turnout in nearly four decades. Slightly more than 59 percent of eligible Americans went to the polls in 2004, an increase of almost 5 percentage points over 2000. Ultimately, more new voters supported Kerry than Bush, but the margin was not overwhelming. The Democratic effort to overwhelm the GOP with new registrants had been blunted.

In addition to enrolling their own new voters and emphasizing the religious themes deemed to be important to these voters, Republicans worked to discredit Kerry as a plausible president. Bush and other Republican campaigners accused Kerry of continually "flip-flopping" on important issues. Republicans also sought to undermine one of Kerry's strongest moral claims, his record of heroism during the Vietnam war. Just as Democrats had raised questions about Bush's leadership during September 11, Republicans raised questions about Kerry's war record. The GOP organized a group of conservative veterans called "Swift Boat Veterans for Truth" who traveled around the country making appearances and seeking media attention. The "Swifties" succeeded in raising questions about Kerry's claims of wartime heroism and converting what had been a given into a "he said, she said" situation. The GOP's efforts seemed to bear fruit. Throughout the fall of 2004, President Bush maintained a solid lead in the polls despite months of Democratic attacks.

THE END GAME

In October, however, Bush's lead appeared to evaporate in the wake of the presidential debates. The two parties had agreed to engage in three nationally televised presidential debates and one vice-presidential debate, with the first set for September 30, 2004. In most national elections, the first debate is crucial. Usually, much of the nation watches or listens to the first debate, and the audience diminishes in size during the subsequent debates. In 2004, most observers agreed that President Bush's performance in the first debate was a political disaster. The president appeared ill-at-ease, some commentators described him as irritable, while Senator Kerry was articulate and quite presidential in demeanor. The national news media declared the debate to have been a major Kerry victory. Republicans were stunned and Democrats elated. Bush rallied in the subsequent debates, but most of the media continued to declare Kerry the victor and to award Edwards the victory in the vice-presidential clash. In the aftermath of the debates, the polls indicated that the two tickets were now running neck and neck.

As the election approached, each side realized that success would depend upon its ability to produce high levels of turnout among its most loyal partisans in the ten or so states that could swing to either party. Democrats relied upon their traditional allies such as labor unions and African-American churches, as well as seeking to ensure high levels of turnout among their new registrants. For example, to encourage newly registered college students to go to the polls, the Kerry campaign charged that President Bush was planning to reinstitute military conscription—a factually baseless but politically useful claim. For their part, Republicans relied heavily upon such conservative groups as the Home School Legal Defense Fund and a host of religious organizations to bring out their voters. In this so-called ground game, each party made use of enormous computer data banks to identify likely voters and volunteers.

In the end, the GOP's superior on-the-ground organization prevailed. Republicans registered and brought to the polls tens of millions of religious conservatives who gave President Bush the margin of victory in such key states as Florida, Ohio, and Missouri. The importance of religious conservatives is manifest in the exit poll data, which indicates that on a national basis 22 percent of all voters cited moral values as the issue that mattered most to them—more than cited the economy, terrorism, the Iraq war, or any other issue. Of these morally committed Americans, an astonishing 82 percent gave their votes to President Bush.

For the most part, each candidate ran well among voters who normally support his party. Kerry won the support of union members, Jews, African Americans, and women. Bush was successful among white males, upper-income wage earners, and southerners. Neither candidate reached much beyond his political base, though Bush was somewhat more successful in 2004 than in 2000 among women, Hispanics, and Catholics. After hundreds of millions of dollars in expenditures and years of planning and maneuvering, the key to victory was old-fashioned voter turnout. After the issues had been debated, charges made and answered, claims made and debunked, Bush and the GOP prevailed because a record number of Republicans went to the polls on November 2—a democratic conclusion to an untidy but thoroughly democratic process.

Money and Politics

Modern national political campaigns are fueled by enormous amounts of money. In a national race, millions of dollars are spent on media time, as well as on public opinion polls and media consultants. In 2000, political candidates and independent groups spent a total of more than $3 billion on election campaigns. The average winning candidate that year in a campaign for a seat in the House of Representatives spent more than $630,000; the average winner in a senatorial campaign spent $5.6 million.[17] In 2004, Kerry and Bush raised nearly $500 million in private contributions during the presidential primary season. The 2004 Democratic and Republican presidential candidates received a total of $150 million in public funds to run their general campaigns.[18] Both presidential candidates were also helped by hundreds of millions of dollars in so-called independent expenditures by individuals and groups. As long as such political expenditures are not formally coordinated with a candidate's campaign, they are considered to be constitutionally protected free speech and are not subject to legal limitation or even reporting requirements.

SOURCES OF CAMPAIGN FUNDS

Federal Election Commission data suggest that approximately one-fourth of the private funds spent on political campaigns in the United States is raised through small, direct-mail contributions; about one-fourth is provided by large, individual gifts; and another fourth comes from contributions from PACs. The remaining fourth is drawn from the political parties and from candidates' personal or family resources.[19] Another source of campaign funds, which are not required to be reported to the Federal Election Commission, is independent expenditure is by interest groups and parties.

Individual Donors   Direct mail serves both as a vehicle for communicating with voters and as a mechanism for raising funds. Direct-mail fund-raising efforts begin with the purchase or rental of computerized mailing lists of voters deemed likely to support the candidate because of their partisan ties, interests, or ideology. Candidates send out pamphlets, letters, and brochures describing their views and appealing for funds. Tens of millions of dollars are raised by national, state, and local candidates through direct mail and the Internet each year, usually in contributions of $200 or less, although in 2000, Bush and Gore collected about three-quarters of their donor contributions from individuals giving the then-$1,000 maximum amount.[20]

Individual supporters of the parties and candidates are important not only as donors but also as fund-raisers. Each party depends on networks of wealthy and prominent individuals who solicit funds for candidates from their friends and business associates. For example, the Bush campaign relied heavily on a network of "Bush Pioneers," individuals who each raised $100,000 or more for George W. Bush. Many of the Bush Pioneers were wealthy business people who hoped their support for the president would help them influence the policy-making process.[21]

political action committee (PAC)
a private group that raises and distributes funds for use in election campaigns

Political Action Committees   Political action committees (PACs) are organizations established by corporations, labor unions, or interest groups to channel the contributions of their members into political campaigns. Under the terms of the 1971 Federal Elections Campaign Act, which governs campaign finance in the United States, PACs are permitted to make larger contributions to any given candidate than individuals are allowed to make (see Box 10.1). Individuals may donate a maximum of $2,000 to any single candidate, but a PAC may donate as much as $5,000 to each candidate. Moreover, allied or related PACs often coordinate their campaign contributions, greatly increasing the amount of money a candidate actually receives from the same interest group. More than 4,500 PACs are registered with the Federal Election Commission, which oversees campaign finance practices in the United States. Nearly two-thirds of all PACs represent corporations, trade associations, and other business and professional groups. Alliances of bankers, lawyers, doctors, and merchants all sponsor PACs. One example of a PAC is the National Beer Wholesalers' Association PAC, which, for many years, was known as "SixPAC." Labor unions also sponsor PACs, as do ideological, public interest, and nonprofit groups. The National Rifle Association sponsors a PAC as does the Sierra Club. Many congressional and party leaders have established PACs, known as leadership PACs, to provide funding for their political allies.

In recent years, PACs have raised hundreds of millions of dollars for political campaigns, but while these organizations have been important fund-raising tools,

Federal Campaign Finance Regulation

Box 10.1

Campaign Contributions

No individual may contribute more than $2,000 to any one candidate in any single election. Individuals may contribute as much as $25,000 to a national party committee and up to $5,000 to a political action committee. Full disclosure is required by candidates of all contributions over $100. Candidates may not accept cash contributions over $100. Contribution limits are raised for individuals facing "millionaire" opponents.

Political Action Committees

Any corporation, labor union, trade association, or other organization may establish a political action committee (PAC). PACs must contribute to the campaigns of at least five different candidates and may contribute as much as $5,000 per candidate in any given election.

Soft Money

The national parties are prohibited from raising campaign funds to be transferred to state party organizations.

Broadcast Advertising

Unions, corporations, and nonprofit agencies may not broadcast "issue ads" mentioning federal candidates within sixty days of a general election and thirty days of a primary election.

Presidential Elections

Candidates in presidential primaries may receive federal matching funds if they raise at least $5,000 in each of twenty states. The money raised must come in contributions of $250 or less. The amount raised by candidates in this way is matched by the federal government, dollar for dollar, up to a limit of $5 million. In the general election, major-party candidates' campaigns are fully funded by the federal government. Candidates may spend no money beyond their federal funding. Independent groups may spend money on behalf of a candidate so long as their efforts are not directly tied to the official campaign. Minor-party candidates may get partial federal funding.

Federal Election Commission (FEC)

The six-member FEC supervises federal elections, collects and publicizes campaign finance records, and investigates violations of federal campaign finance law.

the money from PACs has been overshadowed by so-called **soft money** contributed to the political parties and then recycled into campaigns. Soft money was not subject to the limitations of the FEC act; as a result, well-heeled individuals and interests often prefer to make large, anonymous soft-money contributions rather than—or in addition to—relatively small and publicly recorded contributions to PACs. By 2000, as many as three soft-money dollars were spent for every dollar of "hard money" given directly to candidates and PACs and thus subject to FEC regulation. The 2002 campaign finance reform act (BCRA) outlawed many, albeit not

soft money money contributed directly to political parties for voter registration and organization

Rules governing campaign finance have been the object of intense debate in recent years. Many Americans believe that government is for sale to the highest bidder and shudder when they watch political candidates raise millions of dollars from corporations, labor unions, lobby groups, and wealthy individuals. President Bush, shown here greeting supporters in Buena Vista, Florida, has been a prodigious fundraiser, raising close to $260 million for the primary phase of his re-election campaign, more than double the $106 million he raised for the 2000 primaries. John Kerry raised $233 million, a high mark for Democrats.

527 Committee nonprofit independent groups that receive and disburse funds to influence the nomination, election, or defeat of candidates. Named after Section 527 of the Internal Revenue Code, which defines and provides tax-exempt status for nonprofit advocacy groups

issue advocacy independent spending by individuals or interest groups on a campaign issue but not directly tied to a particular candidate

all, forms of soft money and potentially will increase the importance of political action committees in the funding process. As we have seen, however, parties and candidates have been able to evade some of the act's restrictions. Thus, the importance of PACs may continue to be overshadowed by soft-money contributions.

The Candidates On the basis of the Supreme Court's 1976 decision in *Buckley v. Valeo*, the right of individuals to spend their *own* money to campaign for office is a constitutionally protected matter of free speech and is not subject to limitation. Thus, extremely wealthy candidates often contribute millions of dollars to their own campaigns. Democrat Jon Corzine, for example, spent approximately $60 million of his own funds in a successful New Jersey Senate bid in 2000.

Independent Spending As noted above, "independent" spending by individuals and so-called **527 Committees** is also free from regulation; private groups, and wealthy individuals, engaging in what is called **issue advocacy,** may spend as much as they wish to help elect one candidate or defeat another, as long as these expenditures are not coordinated with any political campaign. Many business and ideological groups engage in such activities. Some estimates suggest that groups and individuals spent as much as $400 million on issue advocacy—generally through television advertising—during the 2000 elections. The National Rifle Association, for example, spent $3 million reminding voters of the importance of the right to bear arms, while the National Abortion and Reproductive Rights League spent nearly $5 million to express its support for Al Gore.

Some groups are careful not to mention particular candidates in their issue ads to avoid any suggestion that they might merely be fronts for a candidate's campaign committee. Most issue ads, however, are attacks on the opposing candidate's record or character. Organized labor spent more than $35 million in 1996 to attack

In 2002, Congress passed the Bipartisan Campaign Reform Act (BCRA), also known as McCain-Feingold after its two sponsors, pictured here with campaign finance reform activist Doris "Granny D" Haddock, who walked 3,200 miles from Los Angeles to Washington, D.C. in order to bring more public attention to the issue of campaign finance. Critics of the BCRA charged that the act would weaken political parties while merely diverting campaign funds to alternate channels. Indeed, during the 2004 presidential campaign, dozens of independent 527 committees spent hundreds of millions of dollars on television advertising. One of the most motorious of these ads was the "Swift Boat Veterans for Truth", which challenged John Kerry's military record and activism against the Vietnam War.

a number of Republican candidates for the House of Representatives. Business groups launched their own multimillion-dollar issue campaign to defend the GOP House members targeted by labor.[22] In 2000, liberal groups ran ads bashing Bush's record on capital punishment, tax reform, and Social Security. Conservative groups attacked Gore's views on gun ownership, abortion, and environmental regulation. In 2004, pro-Republican groups sponsored a series of ads portraying President Bush as protecting the nation by fighting terrorism while his political opponents tried to undermine him, and by extension, the nation. Democratic groups, for their part, attacked Bush's economic policies and handling of the Iraq war.

Parties and Soft Money   Before 2002, most campaign dollars took the form of "soft money," or unregulated contributions to the national parties nominally to assist in party-building or voter registration efforts rather than for particular campaigns. The amount the national parties could accept from any individual or PAC for the support of candidates for national office was limited by law. To circumvent the limits, the national parties forwarded much of the money they raised to state and local party organizations—again, nominally, for party-building purposes. At the state and local levels, political party units used most of these funds in thinly disguised campaign activities such as advertising campaigns that stopped just short of urging citizens to vote for or against a particular candidate. For example, in

1996, commercials sponsored by state Democratic Party organizations looked just like commercials for Bill Clinton. They praised the president's record while criticizing the GOP. However, because these ads did not specifically ask viewers to vote for Clinton or against his opponent, they were considered issue ads rather than campaign appeals and thus did not fall under the authority of the FEC. In 2000, the Democratic and Republican parties together raised nearly $1 billion in soft money mainly from corporate and professional interests.

Federal campaign finance legislation crafted by Senators John McCain and Russell Feingold and enacted in 2002 sought to ban soft money by prohibiting the national parties from soliciting and receiving contributions from corporations, unions, or individuals and prevented them from directing such funds to their affiliated state parties. The act, know as BCRA or the Bipartisan Campaign Reform Act of 2002, also prohibited issue ads within sixty days of a national election. BCRA may have the effect of weakening political parties, but as we saw in Chapter 9, both parties have moved aggressively to circumvent the new law. Democratic and Republican activists have formed organizations that are nominally unaffiliated with the two parties—and are thus not subject to most BCRA provisions—but that plan to participate vigorously in electoral contests. These groups, which are sometimes called "527 Committees" because of the section of the tax code that defines them, are raising millions of dollars. For example, financier George Soros has donated more than $12 million to groups working for the defeat of George W. Bush. For their part, Republican sympathizers have established groups such as Americans for a Better Country to solicit funds from Republican donors and work on behalf of GOP candidates. So long as these efforts are not coordinated with those of a campaign, they represent constitutionally protected free speech and are not subject to BCRA limitations. Late in 2002, portions of BCRA were invalidated by a federal appeals court. In December 2003, however, the U.S. Supreme Court overturned the lower court decision and upheld BCRA's key provisions.

Public Funding The Federal Elections Campaign Act also provides for public funding of presidential campaigns. As they seek a major party presidential nomination, candidates become eligible for public funds by raising at least $5,000 in individual contributions of $250 or less in each of twenty states. Candidates who reach this threshold may apply for federal funds to match, on a dollar-for-dollar basis, all individual contributions of $250 or less they receive. The funds are drawn from the Presidential Election Campaign Fund. Taxpayers can contribute $3 to this fund, at no additional cost to themselves, by checking a box on the first page of their federal income tax returns. Major party presidential candidates receive a lump sum (currently nearly $75 million) during the summer prior to the general election. They must meet all their general expenses from this money. Third-party candidates are eligible for public funding only if they received at least 5 percent of the vote in the previous presidential race. This stipulation effectively blocks preelection funding for third-party or independent candidates, although a third party that wins more than 5 percent of the vote can receive public funding after the election. In 1980, John Anderson convinced banks to lend him money for an independent candidacy on the strength of poll data showing that he would receive more than 5 percent of the vote and thus would obtain public funds with which to repay the loans. Under current law, no candidate is required to accept public funding for either the nominating races or general presidential election. Candidates who do not accept public funding are not

FOR CRITICAL ANALYSIS

Campaign finance reforms enacted in 2002 banned the use of soft money in national elections. What is soft money? Who benefits and who loses from restrictions on the role of soft money?

affected by any expenditure limits. Thus, in 1992 Ross Perot financed his own presidential bid and was not bound by the $55 million limit to which the Democratic and Republican candidates were held that year. Perot accepted public funding in 1996. In 2000, George W. Bush refused public funding and raised enough money to finance his own primary campaign. Eventually, Bush raised and spent nearly $200 million—more than twice the limit to which matching funds would have subjected him. Al Gore accepted federal funding and was nominally bound by the associated spending limitations. Soft money and independent spending, however, not limited by election law at the time, allowed Gore to close the gap with his opponent.

In 2004, neither President Bush nor Senator John Kerry accepted public funding prior to receiving the Republican and Democratic presidential nominations. Thus, Kerry raised private funds to compete in the lengthy Democratic primary process. Both candidates accepted public funding for their general election campaigns, each receiving approximately $75 million. In addition, private groups spent hundreds of millions more on behalf of the two candidates.

IMPLICATIONS FOR DEMOCRACY

The important role played by private funds in American politics affects the balance of power among contending social groups. Politicians need large amounts of money to campaign successfully for major offices. This fact inevitably ties their interests to the interests of the groups and forces that can provide this money. In a nation as large and diverse as the United States, to be sure, campaign contributors represent many different groups and often represent clashing interests. Business groups, labor groups, environmental groups, and pro-choice and right-to-life forces all contribute millions of dollars to political campaigns. Through such PACs as EMILY's List, women's groups contribute millions of dollars to women running for political office. One set of trade associations may contribute millions to win politicians' support for telecommunications reform, while another set may contribute just as much to block the same reform efforts. Insurance companies may contribute millions of dollars to Democrats to win their support for changes in the health care system, while physicians may contribute equal amounts to prevent the same changes from becoming law.

Interests that donate large amounts of money to campaigns expect and often receive favorable treatment from the beneficiaries of their largesse. For example, in 2000 a number of major interest groups with specific policy goals made substantial donations to the Bush presidential campaign. These interests included airlines, energy producers, banks, tobacco companies, and a number of others. After Bush's election, these interests pressed the new president to promote their legislative and regulatory agendas. For example, MBNA America Bank was a major donor to the 2000 Bush campaign. The bank and its executives gave Bush $1.3 million. The bank's president helped raise millions more for Bush and personally gave an additional $100,000 to the president's inaugural committee after the election. All told, MBNA and other banking companies donated $26 million to the GOP in 2000. Within weeks of his election, President Bush signed legislation providing MBNA and the others with something they had sought for years—bankruptcy laws making it more difficult for consumers to escape credit card debts. Such laws could potentially enhance the earnings of large credit card issuers like MBNA by tens of millions of dollars every year.

In a similar vein, a coalition of manufacturers led by the U.S. Chamber of Commerce and the National Association of Manufacturers also provided considerable

FOR CRITICAL ANALYSIS

What are the sources of campaign money in American politics? Why do candidates for public office need to raise so much money? How has the government sought to balance the competing ideals of free expression and equal representation in regard to campaign financing? Is this yet another example of a conflict between liberty and democracy?

support for Bush's 2000 campaign. This coalition sought, among other things, the repeal of federal rules promulgated in 2000 by the federal Occupational Safety and Health Administration (OSHA), which were designed to protect workers from repetitive motion injuries. Again, within weeks of his election, the president approved a resolution rejecting the rules. In March 2001, the House and Senate both voted to kill the ergonomic regulations.

Despite the diversity of contributors, not all interests play a role in financing political campaigns. Only those interests that have a good deal of money to spend can make their interests known in this way. These interests are not monolithic, but they do not completely reflect the diversity of American society. The poor, the destitute, and the downtrodden also live in America and have an interest in the outcome of political campaigns. Who is to speak for them? Who benefits from the American system of private funding of campaigns?

Thinking Critically about The Electoral Process

FOR CRITICAL ANALYSIS

Democratic elections are virtually an American invention, yet voter participation in the United States today is lower than voting rates in many other nations. Why is this so? What might be done to enhance the democratic character of American electoral politics?

As we have seen throughout this book, Americans' most fundamental values often clash, leaving us perplexed as to the best way to proceed. In the realm of electoral politics, the question of campaign finance produces such a clash of values. On the one hand, most Americans are wary of the high cost of campaigns and the apparently sinister role of campaign contributions in the political process. Through their contributions, wealthy individuals and well-heeled interest groups seek to influence election outcomes, the behavior of elected officials, and, through so-called issue advertising, even the tenor of the political debate.

The problem, however, is that we find ourselves with a case of competing political ends. While reform of spending practices might appear to advance the goal of political equality, it might do so at the expense of liberty. Don't we want to encourage vigorous and lively political debate—even though it may be expensive? Should not any group of citizens be free to promote its political ideas at its own expense? These are questions worth pondering, and as we often see in political life, they are dilemmas with no quick and easy solution.

What You Can Do: Campaign on Campus

GET INVOLVED

The most visible aspect of American politics may be election campaigns. Candidates do their best to get the names, images, ideas, and sound bites disseminated among potential donors and voters. They seek television and radio talk show appearances and they buy television time and radio advertisements. They hold fund-raising dinners. They often participate in mass mailings and telephone calling to targeted publics. They engineer media events to get print coverage. Generally, they seek to inundate the public with positive messages about themselves and negative messages about their opponents. Campaigning in a democracy is a high-visibility affair.

At any given moment, someone in America is considering, setting up, or actually running a campaign for elected office at the local, state, or national level. You can certainly get involved in a political campaign but your participation is likely to be highly restricted and guided. That is because today's political campaigns are increasingly orchestrated and conducted by professional political consultants who, along with the candidate, make the key decisions and then tell the amateurs what to do.

Your amateur status notwithstanding, you can participate in orchestrating and conducting a political campaign for elected office if you focus your sights on your own student government. In this area, all contenders are amateurs. Is a classmate, colleague, or friend running for the student senate or the student programming board? She will need strategists to figure out how best to get the attention and support of likely voters. She will need managers to recruit volunteers and coordinate their activities. Campaigning is hard work; it can be tiring; but it also can be exhilarating. Here are some practical suggestions for thinking through your campaign strategy.

- Gauge the preferences of the student body. Ask students what changes they think are needed or desirable. See if the concerns of residential students differ from those of commuter students or those involved in sororities and fraternities or students of particular racial, national, or religious identities. Know your electorate.
- Determine which students are most likely to vote. Student apathy on most campuses means that relatively few students will turn out for elections. Nevertheless, think strategically. What issues are likely to rouse students from apathy to action? Do students who are affiliated with particular groups have higher turnout rates than the general student population? How do you direct your appeal to likely voters?
- Develop a plan for getting your candidate known. Posters, signs, and flyers are common ways to get her name out in public. Can you get coverage in the student newspaper or on the student radio station? Can you create a catchy slogan that is likely to stick in people's minds? In an electoral campaign, gaining name recognition is half the battle.
- Figure out how to communicate your candidate's stand on key issues. Consider sponsoring or participating in candidate debates or forums, scheduling visits to student organizations and dormitories, forging alliances with student interest organizations likely to support your candidate's views, or having her spend time talking to students in a central area of campus.
- As the election approaches, devote your energy to getting out the vote among those students most likely to support your candidate. Call the leaders of allied groups and urge them to get their members to vote. Hang "get out the vote" brochures on dormitory door handles. Place posters in strategic places. On the day of the election, remind students to vote (and suggest that they vote for your wonderful candidate).
- Finally, the best strategy is useless unless you have the organization and volunteers to survey student preferences and voting patterns, gain name recognition, set up debates, visits, and alliances, and get out the vote. Accordingly, work out a strategy for recruiting, coordinating, and deploying a cadre of volunteers.

Once you get past some of the frustrations of campaigning and share in its joys, you may decide to run for student office yourself. Perhaps you can make a positive difference on your campus. Which position should you seek? Should you go after a low-profile position with limited autonomy and responsibility? Or should you run for

INTERACTIVE
POLITICS

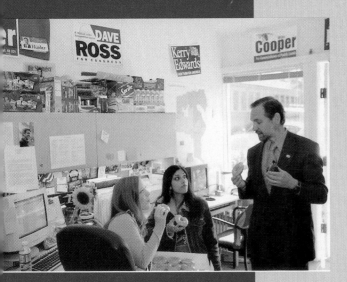

YOU ARE... a candidate for Congress!

Americans seem to love the sport of political campaigns. Although local races are sometimes one-sided, it is clear that the national races have become very competitive as is evidenced by the nearly evenly split Congress of the extremely close 2000 presidential election.

In this simulation, you will try your hand as a candidate for Congress, attempting to wrest the seat away from an incumbent. Can you manage a campaign effectively?

Go to www.wwnorton.com/wtp5e

Questions to consider as you conduct the online simulation:

Why are incumbents for state legislatures or Congress so often unopposed for reelection?

Why do incumbents have such significant advantages over challengers?

What helps make a candidate a competitive, "quality" challenger?

Does negative advertising tend to help or backfire against a candidate?

Is the advice of professional campaign consultants worth the cost?

student body president? Talk to people already involved in student government. Find out the options and the responsibilities each position entails. Then consider the time and energy involved in running for office and the likely workload if you are elected to office. If you still have an interest and think you can handle the workload, go for it.

Summary

At the time of America's Founding, the right to vote was generally limited to white males over the age of twenty-one. Many states also limited voting rights to those who owned property. Over the years, voting rights were expanded to give all adult Americans the right to participate in elections. Despite this, only about half of all American citizens over the age of eighteen actually vote in presidential elections. Turnout is limited by America's voter registration requirements and the absence of a strong party system to "get out the vote."

Three types of elections are held in the United States: general elections, primary elections, and runoff elections. In most contests, the candidate winning a plurality of the vote is the victor. In some contests, however, victory requires a majority of the votes cast, while others rely on proportional representation. State legislatures draw the boundaries of electoral districts. Often, political forces use a redistricting technique called gerrymandering to attempt to gain political advantage. Presidential elections are different from other American electoral contests. The president is elected indirectly through the electoral college.

Election campaigns are directed by candidates and their advisers. Candidates must secure endorsements, construct an organization, and raise money for both the primary and the general elections. Funds are raised from individuals and from political action committees. Presidential candidates must campaign in a series of statewide primaries and caucuses that lead up to the national party conventions, where the formal Democratic and Republican nominations take place. In addition to candidates' efforts, election outcomes are decided by partisan loyalty, voter response to issues, and voter response to candidates' personalities and qualifications.

The fact that many Americans do not vote gives the American political process a quasidemocratic character. Nonvoters tend to be drawn from low-income, low-education, and minority groups. Neither political party has shown much interest in vigorously promoting voter participation.

For Further Reading

Black, Earl, and Merle Black. *The Vital South: How Presidents Are Elected.* Cambridge, MA: Harvard University Press, 1992.

Carmines, Edward G., and James Stimson. *Issue Evolution: The Racial Transformation of American Politics.* Princeton, NJ: Princeton University Press, 1988.

Fowler, Linda, and Robert D. McClure. *Political Ambition: Who Decides to Run for Congress.* New Haven, CT: Yale University Press, 1989.

Ginsberg, Benjamin, and Martin Shefter. *Politics by Other Means: Institutional Conflict and the Declining Significance of Elections in America.* New York: Norton, 1999.

Sorauf, Frank. *Inside Campaign Finance: Myths and Realities.* New Haven, CT: Yale University Press, 1992.

Tate, Katherine. *From Protest to Politics: The New Black Voters in American Elections.* Cambridge, MA: Harvard University Press, 1994.

Wilcox, Clyde. *God's Warriors: The Christian Right in Twentieth-Century America.* Baltimore: Johns Hopkins University Press, 1991.

Witt, Linda, Karen Paget, and Glenna Matthews. *Running as a Woman: Gender and Power in American Politics.* New York: Free Press, 1994.

Study Outline

www.wwnorton.com/wtp5e
Keyword: Review 10

1. In democratic systems, elections can be used to replace current officeholders as well as to serve as institutions of legitimation.
2. Elections also help to promote government accountability and serve as a source of protection for groups in society.

Elections in America

1. In the American federal system, the responsibility for organizing elections rests largely with state and local governments.
2. State legislators routinely seek to influence electoral outcomes by manipulating the organization of electoral districts.
3. Prior to the 1890s, voters cast ballots according to political parties. The advent of the neutral ballot allowed voters to choose individual candidates rather than a political party as a whole.
4. Americans do not vote directly for presidential candidates. Rather, they choose electors who are pledged to support a party's presidential candidate.

Election Campaigns

1. The first step in campaigning involves the organization of supporters to help the candidate raise funds and create public name recognition.
2. The next steps of campaigning involve hiring experts—campaign managers, media consultants, pollsters, and others—to aid in developing issues and a message and communicating them to the public.
3. Because most of the time a major-party nomination is necessary for electoral success, candidates must seek a party's nomination in primary elections.

Presidential Elections

1. Presidential candidates secure a party's nomination by running in state party primaries and caucuses.
2. Nominations of presidential candidates were first made in caucuses of a party's members of Congress. This system was replaced, in the 1830s, by nominating conventions, which were designed to be a more democratic, deliberative method of nominating candidates.
3. Contemporary conventions merely ratify a party's presidential and vice presidential nominations, although conventions still draft the party platform and adopt rules governing the party and its future conventions.
4. In recent years, the role of the parties during the general campaign has been transformed by the introduction of high-tech campaign techniques, including polls, using the broadcast media, phone banks, direct mail, and professional public relations.
5. In capital-intensive campaigns, the main technique is to use the broadcast media to present the electorate with themes and issues that will induce them to support one candidate over another.

How Voters Decide

1. Three factors influence voters' decisions at the polls: partisan loyalty, issues, and candidate characteristics.
2. Partisan loyalty predisposes voters in favor of their party's candidates and against those of the opposing party.
3. The impact of issues and policy preferences on electoral choice is diminished if competing candidates do not differ substantially or do not focus their campaigns on policy matters.
4. Candidates' attributes and personality characteristics always influence voters' decisions.
5. The salience of these three bases of electoral choice varies from contest to contest and from voter to voter.

Money and Politics

1. Campaign funds in the United States are provided by small, direct-mail contributions, large gifts, PACs, political parties, candidates' personal resources, and public funding. In 2000, some candidates also benefited from issue advocacy.
2. Campaign finance is regulated by the Federal Elections Campaign Act of 1971. Following the 1996 and 2000 elections, the role of soft money was scrutinized. The McCain-Feingold bill, a bipartisan attempt to restrict soft money contributions and issue advocacy, was passed by Congress in 2002.
3. The role played by private money in American politics affects the relative power of social groups. As a result, less affluent groups have considerably less power in the political system.

Practice Quiz

www.wwnorton.com/wtp5e
Keyword: Quiz 10

1. What is the most important difference between democratic and authoritarian electoral systems?
   a) The latter do not allow the defeat of those in power.
   b) There are no elections in authoritarian systems.
   c) Democratic systems use elections as a safety valve for social discontent.
   d) Authoritarian elections are not organized by party.

2. The neutral ballot made it possible for voters to
   a) vote the party line.
   b) split-ticket vote.
   c) send clear mandates for policy change.
   d) both a and b

3. What is the difference between an open and a closed primary?
   a) You must pay a poll tax to vote in a closed primary.
   b) Open primaries allow voters to split the ticket.
   c) In closed primaries, only registered members of a political party may vote to select that party's candidates.
   d) They are fundamentally the same thing.

4. What are the potential consequences of ideological struggles in primary contests?
   a) General election chances may be undermined.
   b) Party extremists may win the nomination.
   c) Typical party supporters may refuse to support the party's nominee.
   d) all of the above

5. What is the most fundamental change in national conventions in the twentieth century?
   a) They no longer nominate presidential candidates.
   b) Now party platforms are written at the convention.
   c) The participation of electoral officials in conventions has continued to decline.
   d) none of the above

6. Which of the following is not an example of a media technique introduced in the 1992 presidential campaign?
   a) the spot advertisement
   b) the town meeting
   c) the infomercial
   d) a, b, and c were all introduced in 1992.

7. In *Buckley v. Valeo,* the Supreme Court ruled that
   a) PAC donations to campaigns are constitutionally protected.
   b) The right of individuals to spend their own money to campaign is constitutionally protected.
   c) The political system is corrupt.
   d) The Federal Elections Campaign Act is unconstitutional.

8. Partisan loyalty
   a) is often handed down from parents to children.
   b) changes frequently.
   c) has little impact on electoral choice.
   d) is mandated in states with closed primaries.

9. Which of the following is *not* a factor that influences voters' decisions?
   a) partisanship
   b) issues
   c) candidate characteristics
   d) the electoral system used to determine the winner

10. If a state has ten members in the U.S. House of Representatives, how many electoral votes does that state have?
    a) two
    b) ten
    c) twelve
    d) can't tell from this information

Key Terms

www.wwnorton.com/wtp5e
Keyword: Vocabulary 10

benign gerrymandering (p. 382)
campaign (p. 388)
caucus (political) (p. 393)
closed caucus (p. 393)
closed primary (p. 378)
coattail effect (p. 387)
delegates (p. 396)
electoral college (p. 387)
527 Committee (p. 416)
gerrymandering (p. 382)

incumbent (p. 389)
infomercial (p. 399)
issue advocacy (p. 416)
majority system (p. 379)
midterm elections (p. 377)
minority district (p. 382)
open caucus (p. 393)
open primary (p. 378)
platform (p. 395)
plurality system (p. 379)
political action committee (PAC) (p. 414)
primary elections (p. 378)
proportional representation (p. 379)

prospective voting (p. 405)
recall (p. 378)
redistricting (p. 380)
referendum (p. 378)
retrospective voting (p. 405)
soft money (p. 415)
split-ticket voting (p. 386)
spot advertisement (p. 399)
straight-ticket voting (p. 386)
suffrage (p. 376)
superdelegate (p. 397)
town meeting (p. 399)
unit rule (p. 395)
winner-take-all system (p. 393)

11 GROUPS AND INTERESTS

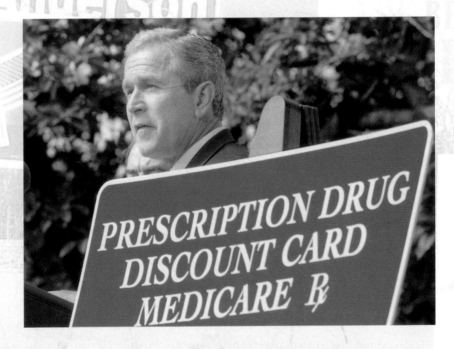

What Government Does
and Why It Matters

FOR MORE THAN TWO DECADES, lobbyists for senior citizens, led by the AARP (formerly called the American Association of Retired Persons), have sought to add a prescription drug benefit to the Medicare program on which most seniors depend for their health care. Many members of Congress have opposed such a benefit because it would cost hundreds of billions of dollars. The pharmaceutical industry also feared that such a Medicare prescription plan would open the way for government regulation of drug prices as well as other aspects of the industry. Through its political arm, the Pharmaceutical Research and Manufacturers of America (PhRMA), the pharmaceutical industry is one of the most powerful lobby groups in Washington. Drug company executives and corporate PACs have contributed more than $60 million to political campaigns since 2000, and a number of drug industry lobbyists and executives are currently major donors to and fund-raisers for the Bush presidential campaign. The drug industry's political clout was, for years, an enormous impediment to the enactment of a Medicare prescription drug plan.

By the early 2000s, however, the industry had begun to face a number of economic and political problems. To begin with, the high prices charged for prescription drugs were producing enormous pressure in Congress to reduce the patent protection enjoyed by drug company products; this would allow cheaper generic drugs to enter the marketplace more rapidly. Second, many consumers had discovered that they could purchase drugs in Canada and Europe for as much as 75 percent less than what they cost in the United States. These foreign purchases, while illegal, are difficult to monitor and are costing the drug companies millions of dollars in profits. Finally, growing numbers of senior citizens were not able to afford their prescription drugs at all and so were simply not buying medicine—another source of lost profit for the industry.

In the face of these problems, PhRMA changed its lobbying strategy. Rather than continue to resist a Medicare drug plan, the industry moved to craft a plan of its own. In 2002, the pharmaceutical industry formed an alliance with several other health industry groups, including nursing home and hospital interests, to develop a new Medicare bill. The AARP had a number of misgivings about the bill but lent its support, calculating that once a law was enacted, the "senior lobby" could secure favorable amendments over the ensuing years. The resulting legislation, enacted by Congress in November 2003, after the drug industry spent nearly $40 million lobbying on its behalf, appeared to be perfectly tailored to suit the industry's needs. Under the new plan, Medicare will subsidize drug purchases for all seniors who agree to pay a modest monthly fee. The plan prohibits the government from attempting to force the companies to lower drug prices, leaves in place the ban on imported drugs, and does not address the issue of generic drugs. Once in place in 2006, the Medicare prescription plan is expected to lead to substantially higher drug purchases and to increase industry profits by as much as $13 billion a year at a cost of tens of billions of dollars a year to the federal treasury.[1] PhRMA's nursing home and hospital allies also won favorable treatment under the plan.[2] Seniors at long last will get their drug plan but in a form that will cost the nation an enormous amount of money, funds that will be transferred from the pockets of hard-pressed middle-class taxpayers into the coffers of an already fabulously wealthy industry. ■

THE case of the pharmaceutical industry exemplifies the power of interest groups in action. The framers of the American Constitution feared the power that could be wielded by organized interests. Yet they believed that interest groups thrived because of liberty—the freedom that all Americans enjoy to organize and express their views. If the government were given the power to regulate or in any way to forbid efforts by organized interests to interfere in the political process, the government would in effect have the power to suppress liberty. The solution to this dilemma was presented by James Madison:

Take in a greater variety of parties and interest [and] you make it less probable that a majority of the whole will have a common motive to invade the rights of other citizens. . . . [Hence the advantage] enjoyed by a large over a small republic.[3]

According to the Madisonian theory, a good constitution encourages multitudes of interests so that no single interest, which he called a "faction," can ever tyrannize the others. The basic assumption is that competition among interests will produce balance, with all the interests regulating each other.[4] Today, this Madisonian principle of regulation is called **pluralism.** According to pluralist theory, all interests are and should be free to compete for influence in the United States. Moreover, according to a pluralist doctrine, the outcome of this competition is compromise and moderation, since no group is likely to be able to achieve any of its goals without accommodating itself to some of the views of its many competitors.[5]

Tens of thousands of organized groups have formed in the United States, ranging from civic associations to huge nationwide groups like the National Rifle Association (NRA), whose chief cause is opposition to restrictions on gun ownership, or Common Cause, a public-interest group that advocates a variety of liberal political reforms. Despite the array of interest groups in American politics, however, we can be sure neither that all interests are represented equally nor that the results of this group competition are consistent with the common good. One criticism of interest-group pluralism is its class bias in favor of those with greater financial resources. As one critic put it, "The flaw in the pluralist heaven is that the heavenly chorus sings with a strong upper-class accent."[6] Another assumption of pluralism is that all groups have equal access to the political process and that achieving an outcome favorable to a particular group depends only on that group's strength and resources, not on biases inherent in the political system. But, as we shall see, group politics is a political format that has worked and continues to work more to the advantage of some types of interests than others.

- **In this chapter, we will examine some of the antecedents and consequences of interest-group politics in the United States.** We will first seek to understand the character of interest groups. We will look at types of interests, the organizational components of groups, and the characteristics of members. We will also examine the important question of why people join interest groups.

- **Second, we will assess the growth of interest-group activity in recent American political history.** The number of interest groups has proliferated in recent years and we will examine the reasons.

- **Third, we will review and evaluate the strategies that competing groups use in their struggles for influence.** The quest for political influence takes many forms.

pluralism the theory that all interests are and should be free to compete for influence in the government. The outcome of this competition is compromise and moderation

■ Previewing Liberty, Equality, and Democracy

Political liberty almost inevitably paves the way for competition among organized groups and interests. Such competition, however, may seem inconsistent with democracy and may undermine political equality since not all political forces have an equal ability to take part in group politics. Efforts to regulate interest groups, however, are often incompatible with political liberty. We conclude by evaluating some of the potential problems in trying to reduce the influence of interest groups in the political process.

The Character of Interest Groups

interest group individuals who
organize to influence the government's programs and policies

An **interest group** is an organized group of people that makes policy-related appeals to government. This definition of interest groups includes membership organizations but also businesses, corporations, universities, and other institutions that
do not accept members. Individuals form groups in order to increase the chance
that their views will be heard and their interests treated favorably by the government. Interest groups are organized to influence governmental decisions.

Interest groups are sometimes referred to as "lobbies." Interest groups are also
sometimes confused with political action committees, which are actually groups
that focus on influencing elections rather than trying to influence the elected. One
final distinction that we should make is that interest groups are also different from
political parties: interest groups tend to concern themselves with the *policies* of
government; parties tend to concern themselves with the *personnel* of government.

There is an enormous number of interest groups in the United States, and millions of Americans are members of one or more groups, at least to the extent of
paying dues or attending an occasional meeting. By representing the interests of
such large numbers of people and encouraging political participation, organized
groups can and do enhance American democracy. Organized groups educate their
members about issues that affect them. Groups lobby members of Congress and
the executive, engage in litigation, and generally represent their members' interests
in the political arena. Groups mobilize their members for elections and grassroots
lobbying efforts, thus encouraging participation. Interest groups also monitor government programs to make certain that their members are not adversely affected
by these programs. In all these ways, organized interests can be said to promote
democratic politics. But because not all interests are represented equally, interest-
group politics works to the advantage of some and the disadvantage of others.

WHAT INTERESTS ARE REPRESENTED?

Business and Agricultural Groups   Interest groups come in as many shapes and
sizes as the interests they represent. When most people think about interest groups,
they immediately think of groups with a direct economic interest in governmental
actions. These groups are generally supported by groups of producers or manufacturers in a particular economic sector. Examples of this type of group include the
National Petroleum Refiners Association and the American Farm Bureau Federation. At the same time that broadly representative groups such as these are active in
Washington, specific companies, such as Shell Oil, IBM, and General Motors, may
be active on certain issues that are of particular concern to them.

Labor Groups   Labor organizations are equally active lobbyists. The AFL-CIO, the
United Mine Workers, and the Teamsters are all groups that lobby on behalf of organized labor. In recent years, groups have arisen to further the interests of public
employees, the most significant among these being the American Federation of
State, County, and Municipal Employees.

Professional Associations   Professional lobbies like the American Bar Association
and the American Medical Association have been particularly successful in furthering their members' interests in state and federal legislatures. Financial institutions,

Interest Groups Go Global

One consequence of economic globalization is that interest groups can no longer limit themselves to activities within a single country. Decisions made in one nation can have enormous consequences around the world. Major corporations, in particular, are likely to be concerned about the policies of governments throughout the world, to say nothing of the policies of international organizations. European and Asian firms that export products to the United States have a vital stake in every aspect of American trade and economic policy. In a similar vein, American firms seeking to export goods to Europe worry about the policies of the individual European governments and the rules put forth by the European Union on behalf of most of the major European states. In recent years, for example, the American biotechnology and agricultural industries have fought against European restrictions on American bioengineered food crops while the Europeans have demanded better access to the American weapons market.

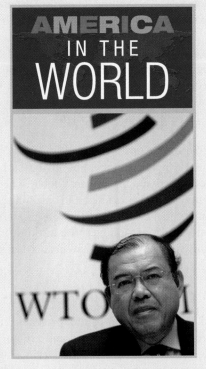

Dealing with these cross-national problems has become the speciality of a new breed of interest-group representative: the international trade lobbyist. International trade lobbyists operate in most major countries; their main task is to guide foreign firms through the intricacies of local laws and customs and to introduce foreign business executives to local government officials, power brokers, and movers and shakers.

One such firm in Washington, D.C., is the Carmen Group, headed by former ambassador Gerald Carmen. Since the 1970s, the Carmen Group has helped foreign firms to understand and gain access to the U.S. market and, especially, to overcome trade barriers, legal impediments, opposition from labor unions, and efforts by American rivals to mobilize political support against them. In recent years, according to the Carmen Group's literature, it has helped an Asian auto manufacturer successfully enter the U.S. market, assisted a Korean manufacturer in resolving a lawsuit brought by an American rival, and helped persuade Congress not to enact punitive trade legislation against a former Soviet republic believed to have violated trade agreements with the United States.

Engaged in similar activities on the other side of the Atlantic is Hill & Knowlton (H&K), a venerable British public relations firm; its international trade practice is headquartered in Brussels, where it assists clients in their dealings with the European Union (EU). H&K helps clients lobby EU bureaucrats and legislators; it also coordinates public information campaigns designed to create favorable image for the clients products. H&K boasts that in recent years it has helped a number of Asian and American interests overcome local opposition and succeed in the European market. For example, H&K has worked with the Japanese Automobile Manufacturers Association, a group that represents all Japanese auto manufacturers, to overcome tariff and customs barriers and to expand Japanese auto sales in Europe. Similarly, H&K helped a major American company, the Ethyl Corporation, overcome European objections to one of its products, the fuel additive MMT, which enhances auto performance but allegedly poses serious environmental risks.

Though they are sometimes seen as corporate traitors, international trade representatives play an important role in the global economy. They work to overcome impediments to world trade and, in that way, contribute to general economic well-being. Often, of course, international trade representatives come under attack in their own countries for promoting foreign business interests. How do they respond? Well, of course, they hire lobbyists to promote their cause.

FOR CRITICAL ANALYSIS

1. Should international trade lobbyists be seen as traitors to their own countries or promoters of world trade and prosperity?

2. Under what circumstances would a corporation seek the services of an international trade lobbyist?

represented by organizations such as the American Bankers Association and the National Savings & Loan League, although often less visible than other lobbies, also play an important role in shaping legislative policy.

Public Interest Groups   Recent years have witnessed the growth of a powerful "public interest" lobby, purporting to represent interests whose concerns are not addressed by traditional lobbies. These groups have been most visible in the consumer protection and environmental policy areas, although public interest groups cover a broad range of issues. The Natural Resources Defense Council, the Sierra Club, the Union of Concerned Scientists, and Common Cause are all examples of public interest groups.

Ideological Groups   Closely related to and overlapping public interest groups are ideological groups, organized in support of a particular political or philosophical perspective. People for the American Way, for example, promotes liberal values, whereas the Christian Coalition focuses on conservative social goals and the National Taxpayers Union campaigns to reduce the size of the federal government.

Public-Sector Groups   The perceived need for representation on Capitol Hill has generated a public-sector lobby in the past several years, including the National League of Cities and the "research" lobby. The latter group comprises think tanks and universities that have an interest in obtaining government funds for research and support, and it includes such institutions as Harvard University, the Brookings Institution, and the American Enterprise Institute. Indeed, universities have expanded their lobbying efforts even as they have reduced faculty positions and course offerings.[7]

WHAT INTERESTS ARE NOT REPRESENTED?

A similar categorization of unrepresented interests cannot be provided precisely because they are not organized and are not able to present us (or governments) their identity and their demands. David Truman tried to put a gentle turn on this phenomenon in what, after fifty years, is still the most systematic treatment of interest groups, *The Governmental Process*. He referred to these interests as "potential interest groups."[8] And he is undoubtedly correct that at any time, as long as there is freedom, any interest shared by a lot of people can develop through "voluntary association" into a genuine interest group that can demand, usually successfully, to get some representation. But the fact remains that many interests—very widely shared interests—do not get organized and recognized.

Under these special circumstances the best we can do is to provide an informed, and distinctly incomplete, inventory of unorganized and unrepresented "potential interest groups":

single mothers	adjunct college instructors
minimum-wage service workers	graduate TAs
nurses' aides	undergrads
medical interns	residents of Middle Eastern origin
the homeless	low-rent and public housing tenants
personal service labor	college athletes
midwives	

ORGANIZATIONAL COMPONENTS

Although there are many interest groups, most share certain key organizational components. These include leadership, money, an agency or office, and members.

First, every group must have a leadership and decision-making structure. For some groups, this structure is very simple. For others, it can be quite elaborate and involve hundreds of local chapters that are melded into a national apparatus. Interest-group leadership is, in some respects, analogous to business leadership. Many interest groups are initially organized by political entrepreneurs with a strong commitment to a particular set of goals. Such entrepreneurs see the formation of a group as a means both for achieving those goals and for enhancing their own influence in the political process. Just as is true in the business world, however, successful groups often become bureaucratized; the initial entrepreneurial leadership is replaced by a paid professional staff. In the 1960s, for example, Ralph Nader led a loosely organized band of consumer advocates ("Nader's Raiders") in a crusade for product safety that resulted in the enactment of a number of pieces of legislation and numerous regulations, such as the requirement that all new cars be equipped with air bags. Today, Nader remains active in the consumer movement, and his ragtag band of raiders has been transformed into a well-organized and well-financed phalanx of interlocked groups, including Public Citizen, the Center for the Study of Responsive Law, and the Center for Science in the Public Interest. All of these groups are now led by professional staffs.

Second, every interest group must build a financial structure capable of sustaining an organization and funding the group's activities. Most interest groups rely on membership dues and voluntary contributions from sympathizers. Many also sell some ancillary services to members, such as insurance and vacation tours. Third, most groups establish an agency that actually carries out the group's tasks. This may be a research organization, a public relations office, or a lobbying office in Washington or a state capital.

Finally, almost all interest groups must attract and keep members. Somehow, groups must persuade individuals to invest the money, time, energy, or effort required to take part in the group's activities. Members play a larger role in some groups than in others. In **membership associations,** group members actually serve on committees and engage in projects. In the case of labor unions, members may march on picket lines, and in the case of political or ideological groups, members may participate in demonstrations and protests. In another set of groups, **staff organizations,** a professional staff conducts most of the group's activities; members are called on only to pay dues and make other contributions. Among the well-known public interest groups, some, such as the National Organization for Women (NOW), are membership groups; others, such as Defenders of Wildlife and the Children's Defense Fund, are staff organizations.

The "Free Rider" Problem   Whether they need individuals to volunteer or merely to write checks, both types of groups need to recruit and retain members. Yet many groups find this task difficult, even when it comes to recruiting members who agree strongly with the group's goals. Why? As economist Mancur Olson explains, the benefits of a group's success are often broadly available and cannot be denied to nonmembers.[9] Such benefits can be called **collective goods.** This term is usually associated with certain government benefits, but it can also be applied to beneficial

membership association an organized group in which members actually play a substantial role, sitting on committees and engaging in group projects

staff organization a type of membership group in which a professional staff conducts most of the group's activities

collective goods benefits, sought by groups, that are broadly available and cannot be denied to nonmembers outcomes of interest-group activity. Following Olson's own example, suppose a number of private property owners live near a mosquito-infested swamp. Each owner wants this swamp cleared. But if one or a few of the owners were to clear the swamp alone, their actions would benefit all the other owners as well, without any effort on the part of those other owners. Each of the inactive owners would be a **free rider** on the efforts of the ones who cleared the swamp. Thus, there is a disincentive for any of the owners to undertake the job alone.

Since the number of concerned owners is small in this particular case, they might eventually be able to organize themselves to share the costs as well as enjoy the benefits of clearing the swamp. But suppose the numbers of interested people are increased. Suppose the common concern is not the neighborhood swamp but polluted air or groundwater involving thousands of residents in a region, or in fact millions of residents in a whole nation. National defense is the most obvious collective good whose benefits are shared by every resident, regardless of the taxes they pay or the support they provide. As the number of involved persons increases, or as the size of the group increases, the free rider phenomenon becomes more of a problem. Individuals do not have much incentive to become active members and supporters of a group that is already working more or less on their behalf. The group would no doubt be more influential if all concerned individuals were active members—if there were no free riders. But groups will not reduce their efforts just because free riders get the same benefits as dues-paying activists. In fact, groups may try even harder precisely because there are free riders, with the hope that the free riders will be encouraged to join in.

Why Join? Despite the free rider problem, interest groups offer numerous incentives to join. Most important, they make various "selective benefits" available only to group members. These benefits can be information-related, material, solidary, or purposive. Table 11.1 gives some examples of the range of benefits in each of these categories.

Informational benefits are the most widespread and important category of selective benefits offered to group members. Information is provided through conferences, training programs, and newsletters and other periodicals sent automatically to those who have paid membership dues.

Material benefits include anything that can be measured monetarily, such as special services, goods, and even money. A broad range of material benefits can be offered by groups to attract members. These benefits often include discount purchasing, shared advertising, and, perhaps most valuable of all, health and retirement insurance.

Another option identified on Table 11.1 is that of **solidary benefits.** The most notable of this class of benefits are the friendship and "networking" opportunities that membership provides. Another benefit that has become extremely important to many of the newer nonprofit and citizen groups is what has come to be called "consciousness-raising." One example of this can be seen in the claims of many women's organizations that active participation conveys to each member of the organization an enhanced sense of her own value and a stronger ability to advance individual as well as collective civil rights. A similar solidary or psychological benefit has been the mainstay of the appeal of group membership to discouraged and disillusioned African Americans since their emergence as a constitutionally free and equal people.

---

free riders those who enjoy the benefits of collective goods but did not participate in acquiring them

informational benefits special newsletters, periodicals, training programs, conferences, and other information provided to members of groups to entice others to join

material benefits special goods, services, or money provided to members of groups to entice others to join

solidary benefits selective benefits of group membership that emphasize friendship, networking, and consciousness-raising

Selective Benefits of Interest Group Membership

Table 11.1

Category	Benefits
Informational benefits	Conferences
	Professional contacts
	Training programs
	Publications
	Coordination among organizations
	Research
	Legal help
	Professional codes
	Collective bargaining
Material benefits	Travel packages
	Insurance
	Discounts on consumer goods
Solidary benefits	Friendship
	Networking opportunities
Purposive benefits	Advocacy
	Representation before government
	Participation in public affairs

SOURCE: Adapted from Jack Walker, Jr., *Mobilizing Interest Groups in America: Patrons, Professions, and Social Movements* (Ann Arbor: University of Michigan Press, 1991), p. 86.

A fourth type of benefit involves the appeal of the purpose of an interest group. The benefits of religious interest groups provide us with the best examples of such **purposive benefits.** The Christian Right is a movement made up of a number of interest groups that offer virtually no material benefits to their members. The growth and success of these groups depend on the religious identifications and affirmations of their members. Many such religiously based interest groups have arisen, especially at state and local levels, throughout American history. For example, both the abolition and the prohibition movements were driven by religious interest groups whose main attractions were nonmaterial benefits.

Ideology itself, or the sharing of a commonly developed ideology, is another important nonmaterial benefit. Many of the most successful interest groups of the past twenty years have been citizen groups or public interest groups, whose members are brought together largely around shared ideological goals, including government reform, election and campaign reform, civil rights, economic equality, "family values," or even opposition to government itself.

purposive benefits selective benefits of group membership that emphasize the purpose and accomplishments of the group

The AARP and the Benefits of Membership One group that has been extremely successful in recruiting members and mobilizing them for political action is the AARP (formerly called the American Association of Retired Persons). The AARP was founded in 1958 as a result of the efforts of a retired California high school principal, Ethel Percy Andrus, to find affordable health insurance for herself and for the thousands of members of the National Retired Teachers Association

(NRTA). In 1955 she found an insurer who was willing to give NRTA members a low, group rate. In 1958, partly at the urging of the insurer (who found that insuring the elderly was quite profitable), Andrus founded the AARP. For the insurer it provided an expanded market; for Andrus it was a way to serve the ever-growing elderly population, whose problems and needs were expanding along with their numbers and their life expectancy.

Today, the AARP is a large and powerful organization with an annual income of $540 million. In addition, the organization receives $90 million in federal grants. Its national headquarters in Washington, D.C., staffed by 1,750 full-time employees, is so large that it has its own zip code. Its monthly periodical, *Modern Maturity,* has a circulation larger than the combined circulations of *Time, Newsweek,* and *US News & World Report.*[10]

How did this large organization overcome the free rider problem and recruit thirty-five million older people as members? First, no other organization on earth has ever provided more successfully the selective benefits necessary to overcome the free rider problem. It helps that the AARP began as an organization to provide affordable health insurance for aging members rather than as an organization to influence public policy. But that fact only strengthens the argument that members need short-term individual benefits if they are to invest effort in a longer-term and less concrete set of benefits. As the AARP evolved into a political interest group, its leadership also added more selective benefits for individual members. They provided guidance against consumer fraud, offered low-interest credit cards, evaluated and endorsed products that were deemed of best value to members, and provided auto insurance and a discounted mail-order pharmacy.

In a group as large as the AARP, members are bound to disagree on particular subjects, often creating serious factional disputes. But the resources of the AARP are so extensive that its leadership has been able to mobilize itself for each issue of importance to the group. One of its most successful methods of mobilization for political action is the "telephone tree," with which AARP leaders can quickly mobilize thousands of members for and against proposals that affect Social Security, Medicare, and other questions of security for the aging. A "telephone tree" in each state enables the state AARP chair to phone all of the AARP district directors, who then can phone the presidents of the dozens of local chapters, who can call their local officers and individual members. Within twenty-four hours, thousands of individual AARP members can be contacting local, state, and national officials to express their opposition to proposed legislation. It is no wonder that the AARP is respected and feared throughout Washington, D.C. AARP support for the Bush administration's Medicare prescription drug plan made it virtually impossible for congressional Democrats to oppose the bill, even though many had misgivings about the bill's provisions and about handing the administration an important victory in the year before a presidential election.

THE CHARACTERISTICS OF MEMBERS

Membership in interest groups is not randomly distributed in the population. People with higher incomes, higher levels of education, and management or professional occupations are much more likely to become members of groups than those who occupy the lower rungs on the socioeconomic ladder (see Figure 11.1).[11] Well-educated, upper-income business and professional people are more likely to

FOR CRITICAL ANALYSIS

Are all interests organized? Why does it seem that some interests are more amenable to organization than others?

Interest Group Membership by Income Level

Figure 11.1

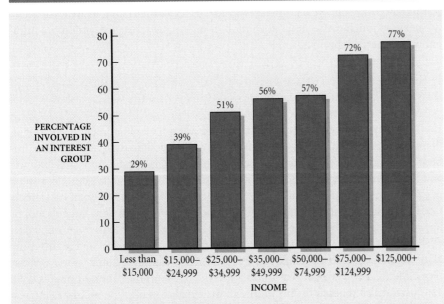

PERCENTAGE INVOLVED IN AN INTEREST GROUP

INCOME

The percentage of Americans who report that they are involved in an organization that takes a stand on political issues increases with income level.

SOURCE: Kay Lehman Scholzman, "Voluntary Organizations in Politics: Who Gets Involved?" in *Representing Interests and Interest Group Representation,* ed. William Crotty, Mildred A. Schwartz, and John C. Green (Lanham, MD: University Press of America, 1994), p. 76.

have the time and the money and to have acquired through the educational process the concerns and skills needed to play a role in a group or association. Moreover, for business and professional people, group membership may provide personal contacts and access to information that can help advance their careers. At the same time, of course, corporate entities—businesses and the like—usually have ample resources to form or participate in groups that seek to advance their causes.

The result is that interest-group politics in the United States tends to have a very pronounced upper-class bias. Certainly, there are many interest groups and political associations that have a working-class or lower-class membership—labor organizations or welfare-rights organizations, for example—but the great majority of interest groups and their members are drawn from the middle and upper-middle classes. In general, the "interests" served by interest groups are the interests of society's "haves." Even when interest groups take opposing positions on issues and policies, the conflicting positions they espouse usually reflect divisions among upper-income strata rather than conflicts between the upper and lower classes.

In general, to obtain adequate political representation, forces from the bottom rungs of the socioeconomic ladder must be organized on the massive scale associated with political parties. Parties can organize and mobilize the collective energies of large numbers of people who, as individuals, may have very limited resources. Interest groups, on the other hand, generally organize smaller numbers of the better-to-do. Thus, the relative importance of political parties and interest groups

FOR CRITICAL ANALYSIS

Could college students be organized as an interest group? What would such a group advocate? What might be some impediments to the creation of a National Organization of College Students?

in American politics has far-ranging implications for the distribution of political power in the United States. As we saw in Chapter 9, political parties have declined in influence in recent years. Interest groups, on the other hand, as we shall see in the next section, have become much more numerous, more active, and more influential in American politics.

The Proliferation of Groups

Interest groups and concerns about them are not a new phenomenon. As long as there is government, as long as government makes policies that add value or impose costs, and as long as there is liberty to organize, interest groups will abound; and if government expands so will interest groups. There was, for example, a spurt of growth in the national government during the 1880s and 1890s, arising largely from the first government efforts at economic intervention to fight large monopolies and to regulate some aspects of interstate commerce. In the latter decade, a parallel spurt of growth occurred in national interest groups, including the imposing National Association of Manufacturers (NAM) and numerous other trade associations. Many groups organized around specific agricultural commodities, as well. This period also marked the beginning of the expansion of trade unions as interest groups. Later, in the 1930s, interest groups with headquarters and representation in Washington began to grow significantly, concurrent with that decade's historic and sustained expansion within the national government (see Chapter 3).

Over the past thirty-five years, there has been an even greater increase both in the number of interest groups seeking to play a role in the American political process and in the extent of their opportunity to influence that process. This explosion of interest-group activity has two basic origins: first, the expansion of the role of government during this period; and second, the coming of age of a new and dynamic set of political forces in the United States—forces that have relied heavily on "public interest" groups to advance their causes.

As long as there is government, there will be interests trying to influence it. During the 1890s, for instance, business interests fought for protective tariffs from Congress and President McKinley. This 1897 cartoon satirizes their success in capturing Congress.

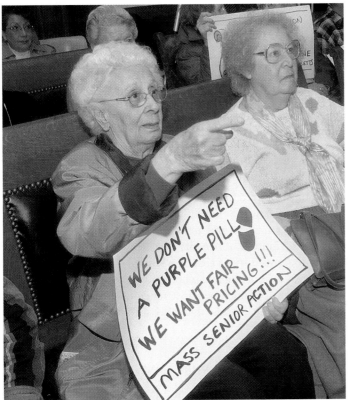

Ever since the 1930s and the expansion of federal social programs that benefit the elderly, such as Social Security and Medicare, senior citizen groups have become a powerful political force. During the 2003 national debate over Medicare reform and prescription drug pricing, it was the support of senior groups for a new Medicare bill that ultimately allowed the bill to prevail in Congress.

While there have always been groups trying to influence the government, since the 1960s the number of organized interests in Washington, D.C., has increased substantially. This growth includes a large number of new public interest groups representing a wide variety of issues, such as consumer protection, women's rights, and environmental protection. For instance, consumer activist Ralph Nader, shown here at a demonstration in support of mandatory airbags in cars, founded a network of consumer advocacy groups in the 1960s. Among the groups Nader founded was the Public Interest Research Group (PIRG), which evolved into an alliance of state-based, citizen-funded organizations that advocate for the public interest. State PIRGs use investigative research, media exposés, grassroots organizing, advocacy, and litigation in their battles to protect the environment, encourage a fair marketplace for consumers, and foster responsive, democratic government. For example, the New York PIRG created a campaign finance database that allows quick access to information about corporations or special interest groups trying to support or gain influence with politicians.

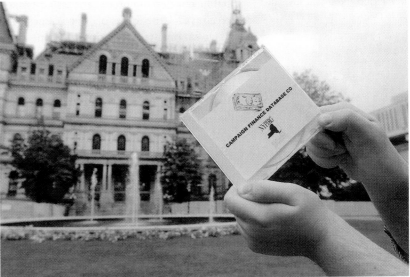

THE EXPANSION OF GOVERNMENT

Modern governments' extensive economic and social programs have powerful politicizing effects, often sparking the organization of new groups and interests. The activities of organized groups are usually viewed in terms of their effects upon governmental action. But interest-group activity is often as much a consequence as an antecedent of governmental programs. Even when national policies are initially responses to the appeals of pressure groups, government involvement in any area can be a powerful stimulus for political organization and action by those whose interests are affected. For example, during the 1970s, expanded federal regulation of the automobile, oil, gas, education, and health care industries impelled each of these interests to increase substantially its efforts to influence the government's behavior. These efforts, in turn, spurred the organization of other groups to augment or counter the activities of the first.[12] Similarly, federal social programs have occasionally sparked political organization and action on the part of clientele groups seeking to influence the distribution of benefits and, in turn, the organization of groups opposed to the programs or their cost. For example, federal programs and court decisions in such areas as abortion and school prayer were the stimuli for political organization and action by fundamentalist religious groups. Thus, the expansion of government in recent decades has also stimulated increased group activity and organization.

THE NEW POLITICS MOVEMENT AND PUBLIC INTEREST GROUPS

The second factor accounting for the explosion of interest-group activity in recent years has been the emergence of a new set of forces in American politics that can collectively be called the "New Politics" movement.

New Politics movement a political movement that began in the 1960s and 1970s, made up of professionals and intellectuals for whom the civil rights and antiwar movements were formative experiences. The New Politics movement strengthened public interest groups

The **New Politics movement** is made up of upper-middle-class professionals and intellectuals for whom the civil rights and antiwar movements were formative experiences, just as the Great Depression and World War II had been for their parents. The crusade against racial discrimination and the Vietnam War led these young men and women to see themselves as a political force in opposition to the public policies and politicians associated with the nation's postwar regime. In more recent years, the forces of New Politics have focused their attention on such issues as environmental protection, women's rights, and nuclear disarmament.

Members of the New Politics movement constructed or strengthened public interest groups such as Common Cause, the Sierra Club, the Environmental Defense Fund, Physicians for Social Responsibility, and the National Organization for Women. New Politics forces were able to influence the media, Congress, and even the judiciary and enjoyed a remarkable degree of success during the late 1960s and early 1970s in securing the enactment of policies they favored. New Politics activists played a major role in securing the enactment of environmental, consumer, and occupational health and safety legislation.

Among the factors contributing to the rise and success of New Politics forces was technology. In the 1970s and 1980s, computerized direct mail campaigns allowed public interest groups to reach hundreds of thousands of potential sympathizers and contributors. Today, the Internet and e-mail serve the same function. Electronic communication allows relatively small groups to efficiently identify and mobilize their adherents throughout the nation. Individuals with perspectives that might be in the minority can become conscious of one another and mobilize for national political action through the magic of electronic politics.

New Politics groups seek to distinguish themselves from other interest groups—business groups, in particular—by styling themselves as **public interest groups,** terminology that suggests they serve the general good rather than their own selfish interest. These groups' claims to represent *only* the public interest should be viewed with caution, however. It is not uncommon to find decidedly private interests seeking to hide behind the term "public interest."

public interest groups groups that claim they serve the general good rather than only their own particular interest

Strategies: The Quest for Political Power

Interest groups work to improve the probability that they and their policy interests will be heard and treated favorably by all branches and levels of the government. The quest for political influence or power takes many forms. Insider strategies include access to key decision makers and using the courts. Outsider strategies include going public and using electoral politics. These strategies do not exhaust all the possibilities, but they paint a broad picture of ways that groups utilize their resources in the fierce competition for power (see Figure 11.2).

Many groups employ a mix of insider and outsider strategies. For example, environmental groups like the Sierra Club lobby members of Congress and key congressional staff members, participate in bureaucratic rule-making by offering comments and suggestions to agencies on new environmental rules, and bring lawsuits under various environmental acts like the Endangered Species Act, which authorizes groups and citizens to come to court if they believe the act is being violated. At the same time, the Sierra Club attempts to influence public opinion through media campaigns and to influence electoral politics by supporting candidates whom they believe share their environmental views and opposing candidates whom they view as foes of environmentalism.

DIRECT LOBBYING

Lobbying is an attempt by a group to influence the policy process through persuasion of government officials. Most Americans tend to believe that interest groups exert their influence through direct contact with members of Congress, but lobbying encompasses a broad range of activities that groups engage in with all sorts of government officials and the public as a whole.

lobbying an attempt by a group to influence the policy process through persuasion of government officials

The 1946 Federal Regulation of Lobbying Act defines a lobbyist as "any person who shall engage himself for pay or any consideration for the purpose of attempting to influence the passage or defeat of any legislation of the Congress of the United States." The 1995 Lobbying Disclosure Act requires all organizations employing lobbyists to register with Congress and to disclose whom they represent, whom they lobby, what they are looking for, and how much they are paid. More than 7,000 organizations, collectively employing many thousands of lobbyists, are currently registered.

Lobbying involves a great deal of activity on the part of someone speaking for an interest. Lobbyists badger and buttonhole legislators, administrators, and committee staff members with facts about pertinent issues and facts or claims about

| Figure 11.2 | How Interest Groups Influence Congress |

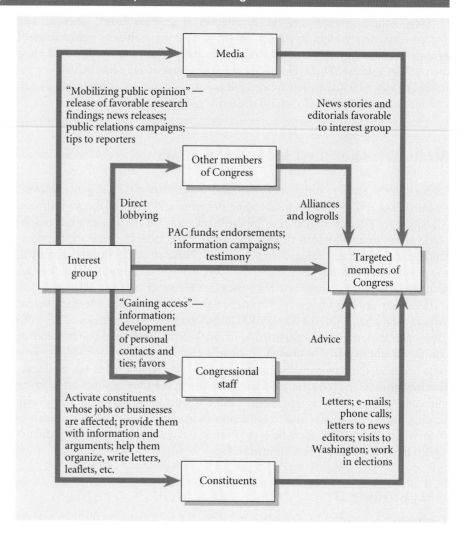

public support of certain issues or facts.[13] Lobbyists can serve a useful purpose in the legislative and administrative processes by providing this kind of information. In 1978, during debate on a bill to expand the requirement for lobbying disclosures, Democratic senators Edward Kennedy of Massachusetts and Dick Clark of Iowa joined with Republican senator Robert Stafford of Vermont to issue the following statement: "Government without lobbying could not function. The flow of information to Congress and to every federal agency is a vital part of our democratic system."[14]

Lobbying Congress   Today, lobbyists attempt to influence the policy process in a variety of ways.[15] Traditionally, however, the term *lobbyist* referred mainly to individuals who sought to influence the passage of legislation in the Congress. The First Amendment to the Constitution provides for the right to "petition the Government for a redress of grievances." But as early as the 1870s, "lobbying" became the common term for petitioning—and it is not an inaccurate one. Petitioning cannot take place on the floor of the House or Senate. Therefore, petitioners must confront members of Congress in the lobbies of the legislative chamber; this activity gave rise to the term "lobbying."

In many instances, the influence of lobbyists is based on networks of personal relationships and behind-the-scenes services that they are able to perform for lawmakers. For example, one of Washington's most successful lobbyists is J. Steven Hart, a senior partner at Williams & Jensen, a well-known Washington, D.C., lobbying and law firm. Hart's roster of clients includes such firms as Dell. Inc. and Bass Enterprises. What does Hart offer such clients? The most important service Hart provides is direct access to the leadership of Congress. Hart, as it happens, serves as the personal attorney for House majority leader Tom Delay as well as a number of other members of the House leadership. Often, this legal work is performed at a nominal fee, as a "loss leader."[16] As a result of this personal relationship with the majority leader, Hart is able to promise clients that their case will be heard by the nation's most important officials. Hart, for example, organized a meeting at DeLay's office in September 2001 in which airline executives were able to convince congressional leaders of the need for an airline bailout package in the wake of September 11. On the whole, about 50 percent of Washington lobbyists have prior government experience. Other lobbyists present at the September meeting included Rebecca Cox, wife of influential congressman Chris Cox of California. Ms. Cox is counsel for Continental Airlines, one of the firms seeking the bailout. Chris and Rebecca Cox are one example of a standard Washington phenomenon—a legislator married to a lobbyist. For instance, Hadassah Lieberman, wife of Connecticut senator and former Democratic presidential candidate Joseph Lieberman, was for many years a lobbyist for the pharmaceutical industry. Lobbyists married to powerful legislators can certainly promise their clients access to the highest level of government.

Interest groups also have substantial influence in setting the legislative agenda and in helping to craft specific language in legislation. Today, sophisticated lobbyists win influence by providing information about policies to busy members of Congress. As one lobbyist noted, "You can't get access without knowledge. . . . I can go in to see [former Energy and Commerce Committee chair] John Dingell, but if I have nothing to offer or nothing to say, he's not going to want to see me.[17] In recent years, interest groups have also begun to build broader coalitions and comprehensive campaigns around particular policy issues.[18] These coalitions do not rise from the grass roots but instead are put together by Washington lobbyists who launch comprehensive lobbying campaigns that combine stimulated grassroots activity with information and campaign funding for members of Congress. In recent years, the Republican leadership worked so closely with lobbyists that critics charged that the boundaries between lobbyists and legislators had been erased, and that lobbyists had become "adjunct staff to the Republican leadership."[19]

Lobbyists also often testify on behalf of their clients at congressional committee and agency hearings. Lobbyists talk to reporters, place ads in newspapers, and organize letter-writing, e-mail, and telegram campaigns. Lobbyists also play an important role in fund-raising, helping to direct clients' contributions to members of Congress and presidential candidates.

What happens to interests that do not engage in extensive lobbying? They often find themselves "Microsofted." In 1998, the software giant was facing antitrust action from the Justice Department and had few friends in Congress. One member of the House, Representative Billy Tauzin (R-La.), told Microsoft chairman Bill Gates that without an extensive investment in lobbying, the corporation would continue to be "demonized." Gates responded by quadrupling Microsoft's lobbying expenditures and hiring a group of lobbyists with strong ties to Congress. The result was congressional pressure on the Justice Department resulting in a settlement of the Microsoft suit on terms favorable to the company. Similarly, in 1999, member of Congress advised Wal-Mart that its efforts to win approval to operate savings and loans in its stores were doomed to failure if the retailer did not greatly increase its lobbying efforts. "They don't give money. They don't have congressional representation—so nobody here cares about them," said one influential member. Like Microsoft, Wal-Mart learned its lesson, hired more lobbyists, and got what it wanted.[20]

Lobbying the President　　So many individuals and groups clamor for the president's time and attention that only the most skilled and well-connected members of the lobbying community can hope to influence presidential decisions. One Washington lobbyist who fills this bill is Tom Kuhn, president of the Edison Electric Institute, a lobbying organization representing the electric power industry. Kuhn is a friend and former college classmate of President George W. Bush. In 2000, Kuhn was among the leading "Pioneers"—individuals who raised at least $100,000 for the Bush election campaign. Later, the electric power companies represented by Kuhn gave nearly $20 million to congressional candidates in the 2001–2002 election cycle. Kuhn's close relationship with the president and his efforts on behalf of the president's election have given Kuhn enormous leverage with the White House. During the 2000 transition, candidates for a presidential nomination to head the EPA felt compelled to pay "courtesy calls" to Kuhn. Subsequently, Kuhn led a successful effort to delay and weaken proposed new EPA controls on electric-power-plant emissions of mercury, a toxic substance linked to neurological damage, especially in children.[21] This was a victory for the electric power industry that promised to save the industry hundreds of millions of dollars a year and illustrates the influence that can be brought to bear by a powerful lobbyist.

Lobbying the Executive Branch　　Even when an interest group is very successful at getting its bill passed by Congress and signed by the president, the prospect of full and faithful implementation of that law is not guaranteed. Often, a group and its allies do not pack up and go home as soon as the president turns their lobbied-for new law over to the appropriate agency. On average, 40 percent of interest-group representatives regularly contact both legislative and executive branch organizations, while 13 percent contact only the legislature and 16 percent only the executive branch.[22]

In some respects, interest-group access to the executive branch is promoted by federal law. The Administrative Procedure Act, first enacted in 1946 and frequently amended in subsequent years, requires most federal agencies to provide notice and an opportunity for comment before implementing proposed new rules and regulations. So-called "notice and comment rule-making" is designed to allow interests an opportunity to make their views known and to participate in the implementation of federal legislation that affects them. In 1990, Congress enacted the Negotiated Rulemaking Act to encourage administrative agencies to engage in direct and open negotiations with affected interests when developing new regulations. These two pieces of legislation—which have been strongly enforced by the federal courts—have played an important role in opening the bureaucratic process to interest-group influence. Today, few federal agencies would consider attempting to implement a new rule without consulting affected interests, who are sometimes known as "stakeholders" in Washington.[23]

CULTIVATING ACCESS

Exerting influence on Congress or government agencies by providing them with information about issues, support, and even threats of retaliation requires easy and constant access to decision makers. Figure 11.3 illustrates one of the most important access patterns in recent American political history: that of the defense industry. Each such pattern, or **iron triangle,** is almost literally a triangular shape, with one point in an executive branch program, another point in a Senate or House legislative committee or subcommittee, and a third point in some highly stable and well-organized interest group. The points in the triangular relationship are mutually

iron triangle the stable, cooperative relationship that often develops among a congressional committee, an administrative agency, and one or more supportive interest groups

| The Iron Triangle in the Defense Sector | Figure 11.3 |

Defense contractors are powerful actors in shaping defense policy; they act in concert with defense committees and subcommittees in Congress and executive agencies concerned with defense.

Congress
(House National Security and Senate Armed Services committees, and Defense Appropriations subcommittees; Joint Committee on Defense Production; Joint Economic Committee; House and Senate members from districts with interests in defense industry)

Executive Agencies
(Department of Defense, National Aeronautics and Space Administration, Department of Energy)

Defense Contractors
(Boeing, Lockheed Martin, Northrop Grumman, Hercules)

Lobbyists are a frequent sight in the halls of power. Frank Gladics (left) is a lobbyist for the U.S. timber industry. While the most common image is that of a lobbyist meeting with a member of Congress, lobbyists also lobby the president. Former President George H. W. Bush is seen here with lobbyists from the group Citizens for a Sound Economy (right).

Lobbyists represent not only thousands of private and public interests but also the different branches of government. For instance, President Bill Clinton employed John Hilley, pictured here, as his chief congressional lobbyist for matters concerning the federal budget.

supporting; they count as access only if they last over a long period of time. For example, access to a legislative committee or subcommittee requires that at least one member of it support the interest group in question. This member also must have built up considerable seniority in Congress. An interest cannot feel comfortable about its access to Congress until it has one or more of its "own" people with ten or more years of continuous service on the relevant committee or subcommittee.

A number of important policy domains, such as the environmental and welfare arenas, are controlled not by highly structured and unified iron triangles but by rival **issue networks.** These networks consist of like-minded politicians, consultants, public officials, political activists, and interest groups who have some concern with the issue in question. Activists and interest groups recognized as being involved in the area are sometimes called "stakeholders" and are customarily invited to testify before congressional committees or give their views to government agencies considering action in their domain.

With the growing influence of the lobbying industry, stricter guidelines regulating the actions of lobbyists have been adopted in the last decade. For example, as of 1993, businesses may no longer deduct lobbying costs as a business expense. Trade associations must report to members the proportion of their dues that goes to lobbying, and that proportion of the dues may not be reported as a business expense either. The most important attempt to limit the influence of lobbyists was the 1995 Lobbying Disclosure Act, which significantly broadened the definition of people and organizations that must register as lobbyists. According to the filings under the Lobbying Disclosure Act of 1995, there were almost 11,500 lobbyists working the halls of Congress.

In 1996, Congress passed legislation limiting the size of gifts to its own members: no gift could be more than $50, and no member could receive more than

In recent years, foreign interests and governments have also employed lobbyists in Washington. For example, Otilie English, a lobbyist for the Afghan Northern Alliance, is shown here shaking hands with Representative Juanita Millender-McDonald during a Congressional Women's Caucus briefing in December 2001.

Lobbyists are now likely to have prior professional experience in government. For example, 144 former members of Congress have stayed in Washington as registered lobbyists. Howard Metzenbaum, pictured here, is a former senator from Ohio now working as a lobbyist for the Consumer Federation of America.

$100 from a single source. It also banned the practice of honoraria for giving speeches, which had been used by special interests to supplement congressional salaries. But Congress did not limit payment by lobby groups for travel of representatives, senators, their spouses, or congressional staff members. Interest groups can pay for congressional travel as long as a trip is related to legislative business and is disclosed on congressional reports within 30 days. On these trips, meals and entertainment expenses are not limited to $50 per event and $100 annually. The rules of Congress allow its members to travel on corporate jets as long as they pay an amount equal to first-class airfare.

issue network a loose network of elected leaders, public officials, activists, and interest groups drawn together by a specific policy issue

USING THE COURTS (LITIGATION)

Interest groups sometimes turn to litigation when they lack access or when they are dissatisfied with government in general or with a specific government program and feel they have insufficient influence to change the situation. Interest groups can use the courts to affect public policy in at least three ways: (1) by bringing suit directly on behalf of the group itself, (2) by financing suits brought by individuals, or (3) by filing a companion brief as "*amicus curiae*" (literally "friend of the court") to an existing court case (see Chapter 15 for a discussion of *amicus curiae* briefs).

Among the most significant modern illustrations of the use of the courts as a strategy for political influence are those that accompanied the "sexual revolution" of the 1960s and the emergence of the movement for women's rights.

The 1973 Supreme Court case of *Roe v. Wade*, which took away a state's power to ban abortions, sparked a controversy that brought conservatives to the fore on a national level.[24] These conservative groups made extensive use of the courts to whittle away the scope of the privacy doctrine. They obtained rulings, for example, that prohibit the use of federal funds to pay for voluntary abortions. And in 1989, right-to-life groups were able to use a strategy of litigation that significantly undermined the *Roe v. Wade* decision, namely in the case of *Webster v. Reproductive Health Services* (see Chapter 4), which restored the right of states to place restrictions on abortion.[25] The *Webster* case brought more than 300 interest groups on both sides of the abortion issue to the Supreme Court's door.

Another extremely significant set of contemporary illustrations of the use of the courts as a strategy for political influence are those found in the history of the NAACP. The most important of these court cases was, of course, *Brown v. Board of Education of Topeka, Kansas,* in which the U.S. Supreme Court held that legal segregation of the schools was unconstitutional.[26]

Business groups are also frequent users of the courts because of the number of government programs applied to them. Litigation involving large businesses is most mountainous in such areas as taxation, antitrust, interstate transportation, patents, and product quality and standardization. Often a business is brought to litigation against its will by virtue of initiatives taken against it by other businesses or by government agencies. But many individual businesses bring suit themselves in order to influence government policy. Major corporations and their trade associations pay tremendous amounts of money each year in fees to the most prestigious Washington law firms. Some of this money is expended in gaining access. A great proportion of it, however, is used to keep the best and most experienced lawyers prepared to represent the corporations in court or before administrative agencies when necessary.

New Politics forces made significant use of the courts during the 1970s and 1980s, and judicial decisions were instrumental in advancing their goals. Facilitated by changes in the rules governing access to the courts ("standing" is discussed in Chapter 15), the New Politics agenda was clearly visible in court decisions handed down in several key policy areas. In the environmental policy area, New Politics groups were able to force federal agencies to pay attention to environmental issues, even when the agency was not directly involved in activities related to environmental quality. For example, the Federal Trade Commission (FTC) became very responsive to the demands of New Politics activists during the 1970s and 1980s. The FTC stepped up its activities considerably, litigating a series of claims arising under regulations prohibiting deceptive advertising in cases ranging from false claims for over-the-counter drugs to inflated claims about the nutritional value of children's cereal.

Feminists and equal rights activists enjoyed enormous success in litigating discrimination claims under Title VII of the Civil Rights Act of 1964, and anti–nuclear power activists succeeded in virtually shutting down the nuclear power industry. Challenges to power plant siting and licensing regulations were instrumental in discouraging energy companies from pursuing nuclear projects over the long term.[27]

MOBILIZING PUBLIC OPINION

Going public is a strategy that attempts to mobilize the widest and most favorable climate of opinion. Many groups consider it imperative to maintain this climate at all times, even when they have no issue to fight about. An increased use of this kind of strategy is usually associated with modern advertising. As early as the 1930s, political analysts were distinguishing between the "old lobby" of direct group representation before Congress and the "new lobby" of public relations professionals addressing the public at large to reach Congress.[28]

Institutional Advertising   One of the best-known ways of going public is the use of **institutional advertising.** A casual scanning of important mass circulation magazines and newspapers will provide numerous examples of expensive and well-designed ads by the major oil companies, automobile and steel companies, other large corporations, and trade associations. The ads show how much these organizations are doing for the country, for the protection of the environment, or for the defense of the American way of life. Their purpose is to create and maintain a strongly positive association between the organization and the community at large in the hope that these favorable feelings can be drawn on as needed for specific political campaigns later on.

institutional advertising advertising designed to create a positive image of an organization

Social Movements   Many groups resort to going public because they lack the resources, the contacts, or the experience to use other political strategies. The sponsorship of boycotts, sit-ins, mass rallies, and marches by Martin Luther King, Jr.'s Southern Christian Leadership Conference (SCLC) and related organizations in the 1950s and 1960s is one of the most significant and successful cases of going public to create a more favorable climate of opinion by calling attention to abuses. The success of these events inspired similar efforts on the part of women. Organizations such as the National Organization for Women (NOW) used public strategies in their drive for legislation and in their efforts to gain ratification of the Equal Rights Amendment. In 1993, gay rights groups organized a mass rally as part of their effort to eliminate restrictions on military service and other forms of discrimination based on individuals' sexual preferences. Gay rights leaders met with President Clinton in mid-April 1993 and were assured of his support for a demonstration in Washington to be held at the end of the month.[29] Although President Clinton had campaigned actively for gay and lesbian support during the election, he did not attend the march for fear of offending religious conservatives.

Grassroots Mobilization   Another form of going public is **grassroots mobilization.** In such a campaign, a lobby group mobilizes its members and their families throughout the country to write to their elected representatives in support of the group's position.

grassroots mobilization campaign in which a group mobilizes its membership to contact government officials in support of the group's position

Among the most effective users of the grassroots effort in contemporary American politics is the religious Right. Networks of evangelical churches have the capacity to generate hundreds of thousands of letters and phone calls to Congress and the White House. For example, the religious Right was outraged when President Clinton announced soon after taking office that he planned to end the military's ban on gay and lesbian soldiers. The Reverend Jerry Falwell, an evangelical leader, called upon viewers of his television program to dial a telephone number that would add their names to a petition urging Clinton to retain the ban on gays in the military. Within a few hours, 24,000 people had called to support the petition.[30]

Grassroots campaigns have been so effective throughout the last few years that a number of Washington consulting firms have begun to specialize in this area. One example is Bonner and Associates, which was reportedly paid $3 million by a single trade association to generate a grassroots effort to defeat one bill on the Senate floor.[31] The annual tab for grassroots lobbying has been estimated at $1 billion.

Grassroots lobbying has become more prevalent in Washington over the last couple of decades because the adoption of congressional rules limiting gifts to members has made traditional lobbying more difficult. This circumstance makes all the more compelling the question of whether grassroots campaigning has reached an intolerable extreme. One case in particular may have tipped it over: in 1992, ten giant companies in the financial services, manufacturing, and technology industries began a grassroots campaign and spent untold millions of dollars over the next three years to influence a congressional decision that would limit their investors' ability to sue them for fraud. Retaining an expensive consulting firm, these corporations paid for the use of specialized computer software to persuade Congress that there was "an outpouring of popular support for the proposal." Thousands of letters from individuals flooded Capitol Hill. Many of those letters were written and sent by people who sincerely believed that investor lawsuits are often frivolous and should be curtailed. But much of the mail was phony, generated by the Washington-based campaign consultants; the letters came from people who had no strong feelings or even no opinion at all about the issue. More and more people, including leading members of Congress, are becoming quite skeptical of such methods, charging that these are not genuine grassroots campaigns but instead represent "Astroturf lobbying" (a play on the name of an artificial grass used on many sports fields). Such Astroturf campaigns have increased in frequency in recent years as members of Congress have grown more and more skeptical of Washington lobbyists and far more concerned about demonstrations of support for a particular issue by their constituents. But after the firms mentioned above spent millions of dollars and generated thousands of letters to members of Congress, they came to the somber conclusion that "it's more effective to have one hundred letters from your district where constituents took the time to write and understand the issue," because "Congress is sophisticated enough to know the difference."[32]

USING ELECTORAL POLITICS

In addition to attempting to influence members of Congress and other government officials, interest groups also seek to use the electoral process to elect the right legislators in the first place and to ensure that those who are elected will owe them a debt of gratitude for their support. To put matters into perspective, groups invest far more resources in lobbying than in electoral politics. Nevertheless, financial support and campaign activism can be important tools for organized interests.

Political Action Committees By far the most common electoral strategy employed by interest groups is that of giving financial support to the parties or to particular candidates. But such support can easily cross the threshold into outright bribery. Therefore, Congress has occasionally made an effort to regulate this strategy. For example, the Federal Election Campaign Act of 1971 (amended in 1974) limits campaign contributions and requires that each candidate or campaign committee itemize the full name and address, occupation, and principal business of each person who contributes more than $100. These provisions have been effective up to a point, considering the rather large number of embarrassments, indictments, resignations, and criminal convictions in the aftermath of the Watergate scandal.

The Watergate scandal was triggered by the illegal entry of Republican workers into the office of the Democratic National Committee in the Watergate apartment building. But an investigation quickly revealed numerous violations of campaign finance laws, involving millions of dollars in unregistered cash from corporate executives to President Nixon's re-election committee. Many of these revelations were made by the famous Ervin Committee, whose official name and jurisdiction was the Senate Select Committee to Investigate the 1972 Presidential Campaign Activities.

Reaction to Watergate produced further legislation on campaign finance in 1974 and 1976, but the effect was to restrict individual rather than interest-group campaign activity. Today, individuals may contribute no more than $2,000 to any candidate for federal office in any primary or general election. A **political action committee (PAC),** however, can contribute $5,000, provided it contributes to at least five different federal candidates each year. Beyond this, the laws permit corporations, unions, and other interest groups to form PACs and to pay the costs of soliciting funds from private citizens for the PACs. In other words, PACs are interest groups that choose to operate in the electoral arena, in addition to whatever they do within the interest-group system. The option to form a PAC was made available by law only in the early 1970s. Until then, it was difficult—if not downright illegal—for corporations, including unions, to get directly involved in elections by supporting parties and candidates.

political action committee (PAC)
a private group that raises and distributes funds for use in election campaigns

Electoral spending by interest groups has been increasing steadily despite the flurry of reform following Watergate. Table 11.2 presents a dramatic picture of the growth of PACs as the source of campaign contributions. The dollar amounts for

Political Action Committee Spending, 1977–2002   Table 11.2

Years	Contributions
1977–78 (est.)	$ 77,800,000
1979–80	131,153,384
1981–82	190,173,539
1983–84	266,822,476
1985–86	339,954,416
1987–88	364,201,275
1989–90	357,648,557
1991–92	394,785,896
1993–94	388,102,643
1995–96	429,887,819
1997–98	470,830,847
1999–2000	579,358,330
2001–2002	685,305,553

SOURCE: Federal Election Commission.

Growth of Political Action Committees, 1977–2002

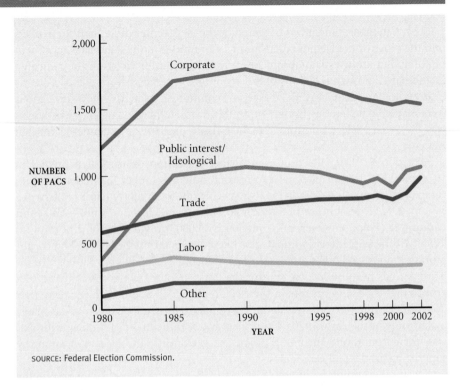

NUMBER OF PACS

Corporate

Public interest/
Ideological

Trade

Labor

Other

YEAR

SOURCE: Federal Election Commission.

Concern about business having too much influence in Washington dates back to the early days of the country. Here, a mid-nineteenth-century cartoon lampoons the ease with which corporate executives could bribe members of Congress (left), and an 1889 cartoon bitingly portrays the close relationship between big business and the political establishment of the time (right).

each year reveal the growth in electoral spending. The number of PACs has also increased significantly—from 480 in 1972 to more than 4,000 in 2002 (see Figure 11.4). Although the reform legislation of the early and mid-1970s attempted to reduce the influence that special interests have over elections, the effect has been almost the exact opposite. Opportunities for legally influencing campaigns are now widespread. The total extent of spending on national elections for 2000 was

Today, the concern about the influence of big business is greater than ever. President Clinton, shown above with Indonesian businessman John Huang, came under great scrutiny for accepting millions of dollars of donations from foreign interests. Huang himself was accused of soliciting illegal foreign donations to the Democratic National Committee. The current Bush administration has frequently been criticized for its close ties to the energy industry and its unwillingness to reveal the exact nature of those ties. For example, protesters outside of the annual stockholders meeting of Halliburton—the world's largest oil-and-gas services company that Vice President Cheney led from 1995 to 2000—questioned the integrity of Halliburton receiving up to $7 billion in government contracts for work in Iraq (right).

approximately $3 billion. PACs spent $579 million and contributed $260 million of this amount.

Given the enormous costs of television commercials, polls, computers, and other elements of the new political technology (see Chapter 10), most politicians are eager to receive PAC contributions and are at least willing to give a friendly hearing to the needs and interests of contributors. Most politicians probably will not simply sell their services to the interests that fund their campaigns, but there is some evidence that interest groups' campaign contributions do influence the overall pattern of political behavior in Congress and in the state legislatures.

Indeed, PACs and campaign contributions provide organized interests with such a useful tool for gaining access to the political process that calls to abolish PACs have been quite frequent among political reformers. Concern about PACs grew through the 1980s and 1990s, creating a constant drumbeat for reform of federal election laws. Proposals were introduced in Congress on many occasions, perhaps the most celebrated being the McCain-Feingold bill, which became the Bipartisan Campaign Reform Act (BCRA) of 2002. When originally proposed in 1996, McCain-Feingold was aimed at reducing or eliminating PACs. But in a stunning about-face, when campaign finance reform was adopted in 2002, it did not restrict PACs in any significant way. Rather, it eliminated unrestricted "soft money" donations to the national political parties (see Chapter 10). One consequence of this reform, as we saw in Chapters 9 and 10, was the creation of a host of new organizations known as 527 Committees. These are often directed by former party officials but nominally unaffiliated with the two parties. This change probably will have the effect of strengthening interest groups and weakening parties.

The campaign spending of activist groups is carefully kept separate from party and candidate organizations to avoid the restrictions of federal campaign finance laws. As long as a group's campaign expenditures are not coordinated with those of a candidate's own campaign, the group is free to spend as much money as it wishes. Such expenditures are viewed as "issue advocacy" and are protected by the First Amendment. This view was recently reaffirmed by the Federal Election Commission, which ruled in May 2004 that spending by 527 Committees was not limited by BCRA.

Campaign Activism   Financial support is not the only way that organized groups seek influence through electoral politics. Sometimes, activism can be even more important than campaign contributions. Campaign activism on the part of conservative groups played a very important role in bringing about the Republican capture of both houses of Congress in the 1994 congressional elections. For example, Christian Coalition activists played a role in many races, including ones in which Republican candidates were not overly identified with the religious Right. One postelection study suggested that more than 60 percent of the more than 600 candidates supported by the Christian Right were successful in state, local, and congressional races in 1994.[33] The efforts of conservative Republican activists to bring voters to the polls is one major reason that turnout among Republicans exceeded Democratic turnout in a midterm election for the first time since 1970. This increased turnout was especially marked in the South, where the Christian Coalition was most active. In many congressional districts, Christian Coalition efforts on behalf of the Republicans were augmented by grassroots campaigns launched by the NRA and the National Federation of Independent Business (NFIB). The NRA had been outraged by Democratic support for gun control legislation, while the NFIB had been energized by its campaign against employer mandates in the failed Clinton health care reform initiative. Both groups are well organized at the local level and were able to mobilize their members across the country to participate in congressional races.

One remarkable fact about the political activity of interest groups is how infrequently major interest groups have tried to form their own party. The fact that they have rarely done so is to a large extent attributable to the strength of the two-party tradition in the United States. But there is also a significant negative influence: the barriers erected by state laws regarding the formation of new political parties. As a consequence, significant interests such as "the working class," women, and African Americans have not been able to find clear expression in the electoral process. Their interests are always being adulterated by other interests within their chosen party. Yet this situation has a positive side: the two-party system has—unintentionally—softened social demarcations by cutting across classes, races, and other fundamental interests that deeply divide people. These interests are adulterated and softened, subduing what might otherwise become the kind of class conflict that we see so often in European history, where class, race, and ethnic interests have become radicalized when they are not forced to reconcile themselves with other interests in a broad political party.[34]

The Initiative   Another political tactic sometimes used by interest groups is sponsorship of ballot initiatives at the state level. The initiative, a device adopted by a

Regulating Political Spending

In December 2003, the U.S. Supreme Court, in a 5–4 decision, upheld the major provisions of the Bipartisan Campaign Reform Act (BCRA). The Court upheld the act's restrictions on so-called soft money contributions to the national party organizations as well as the act's ban on the use of unregulated funds for issue advertising that mentions a candidate's name within sixty days of a general election or thirty days of a primary election. The Court justified its decision on evidence that the electoral process was surrounded with the appearance of corruption and "the danger that officeholders will decide issues not on the merits or the desires of their constituencies but according to the wishes of those who have made large financial contributions valued by the officeholder."

Supporters of BCRA (including five justices of the U.S. Supreme Court) argue that well-heeled individuals and special interests have for too long been dominant forces in the American political process. In the 1970s, Congress enacted the Federal Elections Campaign Act (FECA) to deal with the corrupt practices revealed during the Watergate inquiry. FECA limited the amounts of money that individuals and political action committees were allowed to contribute to candidates. In the wake of FECA, however, tens of millions of dollars in unregulated or "soft" money began to flow into the coffers of the national political parties. Though this money was ostensibly to be used for voter registration and party-building activities, much of it was spent to elect candidates, circumventing FECA restrictions. In addition, wealthy individuals and groups discovered that they could launch campaign efforts on behalf of candidates without being limited by FECA restrictions as long as their efforts were not coordinated with the candidates' official campaigns. These activities usually took the form of "issue advertising" on a candidate's behalf. The intent of FECA had been to level the playing field and to prevent wealthy individuals and interests from essentially buying influence not available to ordinary voters. FECA clearly had failed. Democratic and Republican politicians alike seemed to be in the thrall of the donors on whose dollars they depended. Thus, according to BCRA supporters, further reform was needed to restrict the use of soft money and to block deceptive issue advertising.

Critics of BCRA concede that money is a powerful force in the political process. They argue, however, that BCRA will be both ineffective and harmful. Critics note that BCRA is filled with loopholes that are already being exploited by contending political forces. One loophole, discussed in this chapter, allows groups to raise and spend unlimited political funds as long as the groups are not formally affiliated with parties or candidates. A number of new organizations, "527 Committees," have been formed by Democratic and Republican activists. BCRA proponents, of course, argue that loopholes can be dealt with as they come to light. They hope the law will be expanded and tightened over the years, perhaps leading to full public funding of election campaigns.

BCRA critics, however, assert that the law has fundamental defects that cannot be cured by further tinkering. First, say critics, BCRA interferes with free speech and political expression, most notably by limiting issue ads. Second, they see BCRA as undermining political parties by outlawing soft money while allowing "hard money" contributions directly to candidates. Political parties have played an important role in American history, and BCRA threatens to rob them of their remaining vitality. Third, critics claim that BCRA makes it more difficult for challengers to defeat incumbents. Challengers must raise and spend far more money than incumbents to have a chance to win a House or Senate seat. To the extent that it slows the flow of money into political contests, BCRA is characterized by its critics as "incumbent protection legislation." Finally, critics charge that BCRA is one more step in the direction of full public funding of elections. While most BCRA supporters view this as a positive feature, critics say that full public funding would give those in power too much control over the electoral process and would lead to a system in which competing parties would have less incentive to pay attention to public preferences since their funding would come from the government.

FOR CRITICAL ANALYSIS

1. Under BCRA, the government has placed limits on political advertising. Are these limits necessary or do they constitute an infringement on First Amendment rights?

2. Many reformers advocate public funding of political campaigns, but critics charge that full public funding in Europe has made political parties less concerned with their constituents. How might public funding in the United States have this consequence? Do the potential benefits of public funding justify the potential problems?

Is BCRA Good for the Political System?

Yes On December 10, 2003, soft money took its rightful place beside libel, obscenity, and false advertising as a form of speech prohibited in the name of the public good. In a surprise decision, the Supreme Court upheld nearly all the major provisions of the Bipartisan Campaign Reform Act (BCRA)—including a ban on unlimited donations to political parties, known as soft money, and new laws regulating television advertising bought on behalf of candidates by their corporate and union supporters.

BCRA's opponents had claimed that banning soft money and restricting advertising was tantamount to limiting the right to free speech of corporations, unions, and special interest groups. In rejecting this argument, the Supreme Court declared, in effect, that the importance of protecting these means of speech was outweighed by the need to prevent the appearance of corruption in politics. The Court was right to make the reduction of apparent corruption a primary concern. In a country where the more monied candidates win 90 percent of the elections, the influence of wealthy donors cannot be denied. The Framers certainly would not have wanted political parties catering to the blank checks of special interests.

At the heart of campaign finance reform is the notion that the rich shouldn't be allowed to unduly influence politics. The appearance of this undue influence—real or imagined—was widespread before the signing of the BCRA. Companies gave most to the very politicians who sat on the committees charged with regulating them. And they spent heavily on the campaigns of their strongest political advocates. Senator Richard C. Shelby (R-Ala.) a recipient of over $74,000 of auto industry donations from 1995 to 2000, led the fight against new rollover-potential ratings for SUVs: a cause he dropped only after the Firestone-Ford debacle brought rollover tragedies to the forefront. When the House was still considering whether to fund the Justice Department's lawsuit against the tobacco companies in 2000, the 207 House members who voted to block this funding received an average of five times more money from the tobacco companies in the last two election cycles than those who voted for the funding. These kinds of examples, where only a few dots need be connected to infer political corruption, are what the BCRA and campaign finance reform in general will stop for good.

By accepting the main provisions of the BCRA, the Court established a strong, lasting precedent in favor of the practical consideration of reducing the appearance of corruption. With politicians now forced to rely on small, maximum $2,000 donations called hard money, the $200 check written by an autoworker or a dry cleaner carries more meaning than ever. With BCRA regulations in effect, the most successful fundraisers will win the distinction with the sheer number of donations they solicit, not with the buying power of a few wealthy executives. With so many voices behind a candidate's campaign, the politician is more likely to cater to the public interest, instead of a few special ones.

Building on this victory, congressional supporters of campaign finance reform have introduced two other significant measures to fix additional problems with the system. The first seeks to shore up public funding for presidential campaigns, which provides candidates with matching public funds if they adopt voluntary spending limits. The current upper bound to these funds is too low—a fact illustrated by George W. Bush's, Howard Dean's, and Senator John F. Kerry's decisions to forego federal funds in their primaries. This proposal is a necessary outgrowth of the BCRA, since it will encourage the adoption of spending limits and reduce further candidates' exposure to special interest money. The second proposal, a bill introduced by Senator John S. McCain (R-Ariz.) to reorganize the Federal Elections Commission (FEC), which is tasked with enforcing campaign finance laws, also deserves congressional support. The FEC must be given greater authority and legitimacy to implement these new laws. With campaign finance–related investigations already launching, including one against House Majority Leader Tom DeLay (R-Texas), the FEC needs clout and power to make campaign finance reform the unchallenged law of the new political landscape. Additional measures like these will guarantee that the Supreme Court's decision truly transfers power from the special interests back to the American voters, where it belongs.

SOURCE: The Crimson Staff, "Disappearing Corruption," *Harvard Crimson* (Harvard University), January 26, 2004.

No

Two months after the Supreme Court upheld 2001's Bipartisan Campaign Reform Act (BCRA) in the face of a challenge by Senator Mitch McConnell, objection again was raised in the form of a House bill that would repeal those sections of the "reform" that opponents say infringe upon basic freedoms. This measure, introduced February 12 by Roscoe Bartlett (R-Md.), is the latest expression of discontent with John McCain's pet legislation; the BCRA has previously drawn fire from such diverse critics as the AFL-CIO and the Libertarian Party. McConnell had been supported in his court challenge by, to name a few, the Christian Coalition, the ACLU, and Thomas E. McInerney, private citizen.

These groups and Representative Bartlett have ample cause for concern—legislation such as this has great potential for doing more harm than good. The act was McCain's flagship issue in his bid for the 2000 Republican presidential nomination, and though he received plenty of media attention in his self-styled role of reformer, the actual details of the legislation, which he later succeeded in passing, did not receive similar attention. The nebulous label "campaign finance reform" was often substituted by the media for any real scrutiny of the BCRA's provisions. However, those who were watching more closely saw reason for alarm in the following:

- The bill prohibits groups and organizations from running television or radio ads that mention the name of a local member of Congress for thirty days before a state's congressional primary, and for another sixty days before the general election. If federal courts were to strike down this rule, a new restriction would come into effect making it illegal to air any broadcast ad that supports or criticizes a congressman or a candidate if the ad is deemed to suggest that a person vote for or against the candidate.
- McCain added a last-minute amendment that places restrictions on the rights of lobbying groups to communicate with the public through any medium, including print and telephone calls, if the communication is deemed to be in connection with an election—even if the groups are acting independently, sans any collaboration with a candidate.
- It bans political parties from accepting soft money contributions, and places limits on individual contributions.
- It requires television stations to give discounted advertising to political candidates, and also stipulates that if an organization pays for an issue ad that praises or criticizes a candidate, that group must reveal which of its members or contributors donated $1,000 or more to the group.

Proponents claimed that these measures would level the playing field and cut out corruption in the form of "special interest" influence. In spite of such glowing self-written reviews, this false panacea appears (to borrow an apt comparison from the ACLU's Marvin Johnson) to be a case of "burning down a house to roast a pig."

The act flies in the face of Supreme Court rulings that have equated freedom of speech with freedom to spend money to express opinions. One such case is *Buckley v. Valeo* (1976), the verdict of which stated that campaign contributions and expenditures have First Amendment protection. In addition, the law lends a severe advantage to the incumbent by way of its free speech restrictions and soft money bans—strictures that can limit the funds and the means that political parties have to support challenger candidates.

However, the fatal flaw in this legislation lies in a core, mistaken assumption: that restricting freedom of expression is worth any potential, indirect reduction in abuse of power.

Corruption is indeed a problem, but the solution doesn't lie in limiting the rights of private organizations and individuals to express themselves and to petition and interact with their government. The root of corruption is not in the retention of these rights by the public, but rather in the decisions of elected officials to engage in misconduct.

Short of cauterizing the Constitution of all of the freedoms which allow for individual and collective participation in the political process (thereby reducing opportunity for shady negotiations), no law can guarantee prevention of such decisions and consequent elimination of political corruption, and no law should try.

When is comes to the BCRA, the cure is worse than the disease.

SOURCE: Sarah Taylor, "Reform Bill: Wolf in Sheep's Clothing," *Indiana Statesman* (Indiana State University), March 3, 2004.

FOR CRITICAL ANALYSIS

Describe the different techniques of influence used by organized interests. When is one technique preferable to another? With the rise of the New Politics movement, different techniques are now used more frequently. Which ones? Why are these techniques so well suited to New Politics?

number of states around 1900, allows proposed laws to be placed on the general election ballot and submitted directly to the state's voters. This procedure bypasses the state legislature and governor. The initiative was originally promoted by late-nineteenth-century Populists as a mechanism that would allow the people to govern directly. Populists saw the initiative as an antidote to interest group influence in the legislative process.

Ironically, many studies have suggested that most initiative campaigns today are actually sponsored by interest groups seeking to circumvent legislative opposition to their goals. In recent years, for example, initiative campaigns have been sponsored by the insurance industry, trial lawyers' associations and tobacco companies. [35] The role of interest groups in initiative campaigns should come as no surprise since such campaigns can cost millions of dollars.

Thinking Critically about Groups and Interests: The Dilemmas of Reform

We would like to think that policies are products of legislators' concepts of the public interest. Yet the truth of the matter is that few programs and policies ever reach the public agenda without the vigorous support of important national interest groups. In the realm of economic policy, social policy, international trade policy, and even such seemingly interest-free areas as criminal justice policy—where, in fact, private prison corporations lobby for longer sentences for law breakers—interest-group activity is a central feature. Of course, before we throw up our hands in dismay, we should remember that the untidy process and sometimes undesirable outcomes of interest-group politics are virtually inherent aspects of democratic politics.

FOR CRITICAL ANALYSIS

How do interest groups differ from political parties? In terms of America's core values of liberty and democracy, should we prefer a political process dominated by parties or one in which interest groups are more important?

James Madison wrote that "liberty is to faction as air is to fire."[36] By this he meant that the organization and proliferation of interests were inevitable in a free society. To seek to place limits on the organization of interests, in Madison's view, would be to limit liberty itself. Madison believed that interests should be permitted to regulate themselves by competing with one another. So long as competition among different interests was free, open, and vigorous—that is, so long as pluralism thrives—there would be some balance of power among them and no one interest would be able to dominate the political or governmental process.

There is considerable competition among organized groups in the United States. For example, prochoice and antiabortion forces continue to be locked in a bitter struggle. Nevertheless, interest-group politics is not as free of bias as Madisonian theory might suggest. Although the weak and poor do occasionally become organized to assert their rights, interest-group politics is generally a form of political competition in which the wealthy and powerful are best able to engage. In the realm of group politics, liberty seems inconsistent with equality.

Moreover, although groups sometimes organize to promote broad public concerns, interest groups more often represent relatively narrow, selfish interests. Small, self-interested groups can be organized much more easily than large and more diffuse collectives. For one thing, the members of a relatively small group—say, bankers or hunting enthusiasts—are usually able to recognize their shared interests and the need to pursue them in the political arena. Members of large and more diffuse groups—say, consumers or potential victims of firearms—often find it difficult to recognize their shared interests or the need to engage in collective action to achieve them.[37] This is why causes presented as public interests by their proponents often turn out, upon examination, to be private interests wrapped in a public mantle. Thus, group politics often appears to be inconsistent with democracy.

To make matters still more complicated, group politics seems to go hand-in-hand with government. As we saw earlier, government programs often lead to a proliferation of interest groups as competing forces mobilize to support, oppose, or take advantage of the government's actions. Often, the government explicitly encourages the formation of interest groups. From the perspective of a government agency, nothing is more useful than a well-organized constituency for its programs. Agencies such as the Department of Veterans Affairs, the Social Security Administration, and the Department of Agriculture devote a great deal of energy to the organization and mobilization of groups of "stakeholders" to support the agencies and their efforts. This strategy, a variant of what is sometimes called "interest-group liberalism," can be very effective. One reason that the Social Security program is considered politically invulnerable despite its fiscal shortcomings is that it is so strongly supported by a powerful group—the AARP. Significantly, the Social Security Administration played an important early role in the formation of the AARP, precisely because agency executives realized that this group could become a useful ally.

The responsiveness of government agencies to interest groups is a challenge to democracy. Groups seem to have a greater impact than voters upon the government's policies and programs. Yet, before we decide that we should do away with interest groups, we should think carefully: if there were no organized interests, would the government pay more attention to ordinary voters, or would the government simply pay no attention to anyone? In his great work *Democracy in America*, Alexis de Tocqueville argued that the proliferation of groups promoted democracy by encouraging governmental responsiveness. Does group politics foster democracy or impede democracy? It does both.

Thus, we have dilemmas for which there is no ideal answer. To regulate interest-group politics is, as Madison warned, to limit freedom and to expand governmental power. Not to regulate interest-group politics, on the other hand, may be to ignore equality and democracy. Those who believe that there are simple solutions to the issues of political life would do well to ponder this problem.

What You Can Do:
Join an Interest Group

The dilemmas posed by group politics raise questions for citizens, as well. If you can't beat them, should you join them?

Like political parties, interest groups are always looking for volunteers and members. Given the enormous number of groups in America today, every student should be able to find several whose causes seem worthwhile.

Inventory your interests. Which issue or issues rouse your passions? What injustices do you consider intolerable? Who is not being properly represented in public life? Which class discussions have you found most provocative? What issues do you discuss with friends late into the night? What have you studied or written about that moves you? Ask yourself which issue or issue area is compelling to the point that you want to get involved in it.

For any interest that you find compelling, there are likely to be many other people who share that interest. Furthermore, there are likely to be some people who have organized a group or association aimed at promoting that interest. Consider seeking out interest groups that are already organized and active in the area that concerns you. How can you begin your search?

It is often easiest to begin on your own campus. Ask students, faculty, and staff if they know of any campus groups working on gun control, human rights, legalization of marijuana, or whatever your particular interest is. See if your college publishes a directory of student organizations. Make a point of reading posted flyers and notifications of coming events in the campus newspaper. Observe who sets up card tables or sponsors marches to pursue their causes on campus.

Do not be discouraged if your campus search is unsuccessful. Interest groups abound in communities, at the regional and state level, and nationwide. Talk to your family and neighbors, particularly those who are politically savvy and involved. Try the local telephone book. It may have a section on community groups. Experiment with a search engine on the Internet. Persevere. Know that while you are looking for an interest group that fits your priorities, there are likely to be several appropriate interest groups hoping to make contact with people just like you.

Once you identify the appropriate interest group, make contact, ask questions, and discuss how you can contribute to the group's efforts. Interest groups generally carry out multiple functions. They try to enhance public awareness, raise money, build coalitions, find sympathetic candidates, and influence how public officials think and act. Working for an interest group can be one of the most effective ways of participating in politics.

While Steve Ma was growing up in suburban New Jersey, he didn't realize that his home state ranked last in the nation in industry compliance with clean water legislation. The extent of the problem and his ability to act became clear, however, when in high school he happened upon a protest over the Exxon *Valdez* oil spill. Concerned that government was taking inadequate action both in environmental legislation and in promoting citizen awareness, Ma began to search for a venue to make his voice heard. He found the place in the Student Public Interest Research Group (PIRG) of New Jersey at Rutgers University.

PIRGs exist in numerous states to promote various consumer rights, including minimizing student tuition increases, protecting the environment, and fighting homelessness. One of Ma's first activities with PIRG was to publish a guide to the goods and services available in New Brunswick, New Jersey, including critiques of landlords and apartment buildings, restaurant recommendations, and ratings of bookstores that paid for returned textbooks. As the year progressed, he worked on larger projects: he and his chapter worked with local businesses to find cost-effective ways to reduce pollution emissions, saving both the environment and the money necessary to clean contaminated areas. He also worked as an intern at New Jersey PIRG, researching and helping to write a report on the failed implementation of the New Jersey Motor Voter Bill, which required the state's Department of Motor Vehicles to distribute voter registration information to customers.

Over the next year, New Jersey PIRG lobbied heavily for the Clean Water Enforcement Act, a bill that would make New Jersey's clean water laws the most stringent in the nation. "We did so much against millions of dollars of industry lobbying," says Ma. "I actually lobbied the governor himself."[38] The bill passed by a close vote. Since then, New Jersey's compliance with water regulations has increased from last in the nation to fifteenth. "There is really an opportunity at the state level to create the issue," says Ma. "It sounds clichéd, but states are the laboratories of democracy. We were really effective; we had our heads on straight, an eye on the future, and an incredible ability to organize. Classrooms are good, but good internships in which you can do things like lobby the governor and organize meetings are invaluable."[40]

But what about the Madisonian dilemma? Should you become involved in group politics? Would you be contributing to the solution or exacerbating the problem?

Summary

Interest groups are pervasive in America. James Madison predicted that special interest groups would proliferate in a free society, but that competition among them would lead to moderation and compromise. Today, this theory is called pluralism. Individuals join or form groups to enhance their influence. To succeed, groups need leadership, a financial base, and active members. Recruiting new members can be difficult because of the "free rider" problem. Interest groups overcome this problem by offering selective benefits to members only. These include information, material benefits, solidary benefits, or purposive benefits.

The number of interest groups in America has increased because of the expansion of the government into new areas. This increase has included not only economic interests, but also "public interest" groups whose members do not seek economic gain. Both economic and public interest groups seek influence through a variety of techniques.

Lobbying is the act of petitioning legislators. Lobbyists—individuals who receive some form of compensation for lobbying—are required to register with the House and Senate. In spite of an undeserved reputation for corruption, lobbyists serve a useful function, providing members of Congress with a vital flow of information.

Access is participation in government. Groups with access have less need for lobbying. Most groups build up access over time through great effort. They work years to get their members into positions of influence on congressional committees.

Litigation sometimes serves interest groups when other strategies fail. Groups may bring suit on their own behalf, finance suits brought by individuals, or file *amicus curiae* briefs.

Going public is an effort to mobilize the widest and most favorable climate of opinion. Advertising is a common technique in this strategy. Other techniques are boycotts, strikes, rallies, and marches.

Groups engage in electoral politics either by embracing one of the major parties, usually through financial support, or through a nonpartisan strategy. Interest groups' campaign contributions now seem to be flowing into the coffers of candidates at a faster rate than ever before.

INTERACTIVE
POLITICS

YOU ARE... a legislative affairs director for an interest group!

Candidates for office regularly decry the power of the wealthy special interests. The implication is that they have undue access and influence and take advantage of their power at the expense of "regular folks." Yet, in fact, while there are risks to allowing special interest groups to form they can also enhance pluralistic democracy.

In this simulation, you are called to lead the charge for your group's interests on Capitol Hill. It is your job as Legislative affairs director to prioritize where you will spend your money and energy. Should you try inside or outside strategies? Should you give to your friends or opponents? Party leaders or committee chairs? What strategies and tactics will be successful for you?

Go to www.wwnorton.com/wtp5e

Questions to consider as you conduct the online simulation:

How are interest groups different from political parties?

What strategies and tactics can groups use to influence political outcomes?

What are the possible positive effects of allowing "special interests" to meet with members of Congress and the executive branch?

How do interest groups manage to recruit and retain members?

For Further Reading

Cigler, Allan J., and Burdett A. Loomis, eds. *Interest Group Politics.* Washington, DC: Congressional Quarterly Press, 1983.

Clawson, Dan, Alan Neustadt, and Denise Scott. *Money Talks: Corporate PACs and Political Influence.* New York: Basic Books, 1992.

Day, Christine. *What Older Americans Think: Interest Groups and Aging Policy.* Princeton, NJ: Princeton University Press, 1990.

Hansen, John Mark. *Gaining Access: Congress and the Farm Lobby, 1919–1981.* Chicago: University of Chicago Press, 1991.

Heinz, John P., Edward O. Laumann, Robert L. Nelson, and Robert H. Salisbury. *The Hollow Core: Private Interests in National Policy Making.* Cambridge, MA: Harvard University Press, 1993.

Lowi, Theodore J. *The End of Liberalism.* New York: Norton, 1979.

Moe, Terry M. *The Organization of Interests.* Chicago: University of Chicago Press, 1980.

Olson, Mancur, Jr. *The Logic of Collective Action: Public Goods and the Theory of Groups.* Cambridge, MA: Harvard University Press, 1971.

Petracca, Mark, ed. *The Politics of Interests: Interest Groups Transformed.* Boulder, CO: Westview, 1992.

Schlozman, Kay Lehman, and John T. Tierney. *Organized Interests and American Democracy.* New York: Harper & Row, 1986.

Truman, David. *The Governmental Process: Political Interests and Public Opinion.* New York: Knopf, 1951.

Vogel, David. *Fluctuating Fortunes.* New York: Basic Books, 1989.

Study Outline

www.wwnorton.com/wtp5e

Keyword: Review 11

The Character of Interest Groups

1. An enormous number of diverse interest groups exist in the United States.
2. Most interest groups share key organizational components, such as mechanisms for member recruitment, financial and decision-making processes, and agencies that actually carry out group goals.
3. Interest-group politics in the United States tends to have a pronounced upper-class bias because of the characteristics of interest-group members.

4. Because of natural disincentives to join interest groups, groups offer material, solidary, and purposive benefits to entice people to join.

The Proliferation of Groups

1. The modern expansion of governmental economic and social programs has contributed to the enormous increase in the number of groups seeking to influence the American political system.
2. The second factor accounting for the explosion of interest-group activity in recent years was the emergence of a new set of forces in American politics: the New Politics movement.

Strategies: The Quest for Political Power

1. Lobbying is an effort by outsiders to influence Congress or government agencies by providing them with information about issues, giving them support, and even threatening them with retaliation.
2. Access is actual involvement and influence in the decision-making process.
3. Interest groups often turn to litigation when they lack access or feel they have insufficient influence over the formulation and implementation of public policy.
4. Going public is a strategy that attempts to mobilize the widest and most favorable climate of opinion.
5. Many groups use a nonpartisan strategy in electoral politics to avoid giving up access to one party by embracing the other.

Thinking Critically about Groups and Interests: The Dilemmas of Reform

1. The organization of private interests into groups to advance their own views is a necessary and intrinsic element of the liberty of citizens to pursue their private lives, and to express their views, individually and collectively.
2. The organization of private interests into groups is biased in favor of the wealthy and the powerful, who have superior knowledge, opportunity, and resources with which to organize.

Practice Quiz

www.wwnorton.com/wtp5e
Keyword: Quiz 11

1. The theory that competition among organized interests will produce balance with all the interests regulating one another is
   a) pluralism.
   b) elite power politics.
   c) democracy.
   d) socialism.

2. To overcome the free rider problem, groups
   a) provide general benefits.
   b) litigate.
   c) go public.
   d) provide selective benefits.

3. Politically organized religious groups often make use of
   a) material benefits.
   b) solidary benefits.
   c) purposive benefits.
   d) none of the above.

4. Which of the following best describes the reputation of the AARP in the Washington community?
   a) It is respected and feared.
   b) It is supported and well liked by all political forces.
   c) It is believed to be ineffective.
   d) It wins the political battles it fights.

5. Which types of interest groups are most often associated with the New Politics movement?
   a) public interest groups
   b) professional associations
   c) government groups
   d) labor groups

6. Access politics, exemplified by defense contractors acting in concert with congressional committees and executive agencies, is an example of
   a) campaign activism.
   b) public interest politics.
   c) an iron triangle.
   d) the role of conservative interest groups.

7. In which of the following ways do interest groups use the courts to affect public policy?
   a) filing *amicus* briefs
   b) bringing lawsuits
   c) financing those bringing suit
   d) all of the above

8. According to this text, what is the limit a PAC can contribute to a primary or general election campaign?
   a) $1,000
   b) $5,000
   c) $10,000
   d) $50,000

9. Which of the following is not an activity in which interest groups frequently engage?
   a) starting their own political party
   b) litigation
   c) lobbying
   d) contributing to campaigns

Key Terms

www.wwnorton.com/wtp5e
Keyword: Vocabulary 11

collective goods (p. 433)
free riders (p. 434)
grassroots mobilization (p. 449)
informational benefits (p. 434)
institutional advertising (p. 449)

interest group (p. 430)
iron triangle (p. 445)
issue network (p. 447)
lobbying (p. 441)
material benefits (p. 434)
membership association (p. 433)
New Politics movement (p. 440)
pluralism (p. 429)

political action committee (PAC) (p. 451)
public interest groups (p. 441)
purposive benefits (p. 435)
solidary benefits (p. 434)
staff organization (p. 433)

INSTITUTIONS

12 CONGRESS

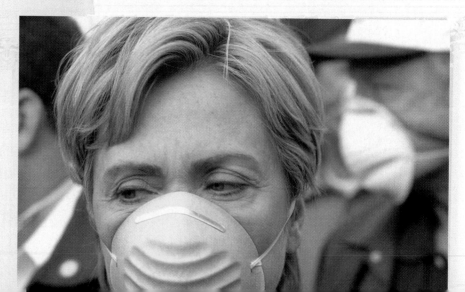

What Government Does and Why It Matters

FTER BEGINNING THE DAY with a speech to labor activists, the new junior senator from New York, Hillary Clinton, moved on to meet with a group from New York's theater district to consider how to bring Broadway back from its post–September 11 slump. During the rest of the day in her home state, Hillary Clinton participated in a panel discussion on terrorism; met with the families of victims of a downed airliner that had taken off from Kennedy airport; held a conference with the visiting president of the Philippines; and had a reunion party with her campaign staff. During the same week, Senator Clinton could be seen in Washington poring over documents as she attended a joint meeting of the House and Senate education committees. Easily the most famous member of the Senate due to her status as former first lady, Hillary Clinton began her term determined to be a Senate workhorse.[1] Her typical workweek offers a glimpse of the many different roles that members of Congress must fulfill: legislator, constituency servant, policy expert, campaigner, and "mentor-communicator" representing her New York constituency in Washington.[2]

If you want to find out what your congressional representative or senator has been doing lately, there are many ways to do so. You can watch your mailbox—most congressional offices send newsletters to constituents to report the office's activities. You can find your representative's home page on the World Wide Web at thomas.loc.gov. To get a sense of what is happening in Congress you can tune your television to C-SPAN; chances are that some congressional debate or committee hearing will be in progress. If you want to make your views known to your congressional representative, that is also pretty easy. You can send a postcard or a letter—the address of your representative can usually be found in the blue pages of your local telephone book. You can also call or fax his or her Washington office. The number isn't hard to get; consult your local phone book or call Washington, D.C., directory information. ■

DESPITE these many different ways people can learn about Congress and contact their representatives and senators, citizens regularly complain that Congress is "out of touch." In one poll, only 12 percent of Americans said they believed that congressional representatives "pay a good deal of attention to the people who elect them when deciding what to do in Congress." Eighty percent felt that members of Congress lost touch with their constituents soon after being elected.[3] Many Americans believe there is something about politics in Washington that is corrupting. One voter described what happens to members of Congress in this way: "You find so many good people going in and the next thing you know they're corrupted."[4] Congress seems to be the least trusted of America's national institutions.

What is puzzling is that these feelings of distrust and alienation from Congress have grown stronger precisely as access to Congress and its members has increased. Most of the proceedings of Congress have been open to the public since the passage of numerous "sunshine reforms" in the 1970s; today Congress conducts very few secret hearings. Public opinion polls taken before Congress became more accessible and open showed higher levels of trust and a greater belief that citizens could influence their representatives' decisions. Why has trust in Congress dropped rather than increased as new forms of access and increased openness have been put into place?

One answer to this puzzle is the growing professionalization of Congress as an institution. Professionalization means that Congress has grown more complex as an institution, with more powerful committees, longer terms for members, larger staffs, and higher salaries.[5] In many ways, professionalization makes Congress more capable of reaching informed decisions and makes it easier for members of Congress to serve their constituents. But professionalization also has a downside. It enhances the independence of individual congressional members, often making it harder for the institution as a whole to reach decisions. Moreover, as Congress has professionalized, narrowly focused, well-funded professional interest groups have formed to influence Congress. The growth and sophistication of these groups has made many ordinary citizens feel shut out, canceling out the positive side of the new openness and professionalization of Congress in the public mind. The public feeling of distance from Congress is compounded by the decline of political parties among the electorate. A crucial link that once connected Congress with voters has been severed.

In this chapter, we will try to understand the relationship between Congress and the American people. Congress is central to American democracy because it serves as the voice of the people and because it controls a formidable battery of powers that it uses to shape policies.

Congress has vast authority over the two most important powers given to any government: the power of force (control over the nation's military forces); and the power over money. Specifically, in Article I, Section 8, Congress can "lay and collect Taxes," deal with indebtedness and bankruptcy, impose duties, borrow and coin money, and generally control the nation's purse strings. It also may "provide for the common Defense and general welfare," regulate interstate commerce, undertake public works, acquire and control federal lands, promote science and "useful Arts" (pertaining mostly to patents and copyrights), and regulate the militia.

In the realm of foreign policy, Congress has the power to declare war, deal with piracy, regulate foreign commerce, and raise and regulate the armed forces and military installations. These powers over war and the military are supreme—even the president, as commander in chief of the military, must obey the laws and orders of Congress *if* Congress chooses to assert its constitutional authority. (In the past century, Congress has usually surrendered this authority to the president.) Further, the Senate has the power to approve treaties (by a two-thirds vote) and to approve the appointment of ambassadors. Capping these powers, Congress is charged to make laws "which shall be necessary and proper for carrying into Execution the foregoing Powers, and all other Powers vested by this Constitution in the Government of the United States, or in any Department or Officer thereof."

If it seems to the reader that many of these powers belong to the president, from war power to spending power, that is because modern presidents do exercise great authority in these areas. The modern presidency is a more powerful institution than it was 200 years ago, and much of that power has come from Congress, either because Congress has delegated the power to the president by law, or because Congress has simply allowed, or even urged, presidents to be more active in these areas. This also helps explain why the executive branch seems like a more important branch of government today than Congress. Still, the constitutional powers of Congress remain intact in the document. This takes us to Congress's pivotal role as a representative institution.

- **To understand the pivotal role that Congress plays in American democracy, we will first examine the concept of representation.** We will look closely at what it means to say that Congress represents the people. We will also look at how members of Congress act on behalf of their constituents and how the electoral process affects the relationship between Congress and the people.

- **Next, we will discuss the legislative process.** We will study the building blocks of congressional organization, including political parties, the committee system, congressional staff, and caucuses. We then turn to the rules of congressional procedure, through which laws are formulated.

- **We then look at congressional decision making, examining the influences on the legislation that Congress produces.** The complex legislative process is subject to a variety of influences from inside and outside government, including constituencies, interest groups, and party leaders.

- **We next turn to other powers that allow Congress to influence the process of government.** In addition to the power to make law, Congress has an array of instruments to use in its relationship with the president and the executive branch.

■ Previewing Liberty, Equality, and Democracy

Congress plays a pivotal role in American democracy. Of all our national institutions, Congress is most important in bringing our democratic values to life. This is because Congress represents in Washington the voice of the people across America. Yet, there are worries today that Congress does not represent all voices equally. Declining political participation among lower income voters and the growing importance of money in politics may make Congress more responsive to higher income voters and resource-rich interest groups. Congress can balance the tensions between liberty, equality, and democracy only when all groups are fairly represented. We conclude by assessing whether Congress fulfills these principles.

Congress: Representing the American People

constituency the district comprising the area from which an official is elected

Congress is the most important representative institution in American government. Each member's primary responsibility is to the district, to his or her **constituency,** not to the congressional leadership, a party, or even Congress itself. Yet the task of representation is not a simple one. Views about what constitutes fair and effective representation differ and constituents can make very different kinds of demands on their representatives. Members of Congress must consider these diverse views and demands as they represent their districts.

HOUSE AND SENATE: DIFFERENCES IN REPRESENTATION

bicameral having a legislative assembly composed of two chambers or houses; opposite of unicameral

The framers of the Constitution provided for a **bicameral** legislature—that is, a legislative body consisting of two chambers. As we saw in Chapter 2, the framers intended each of these chambers, the House of Representatives and the Senate, to serve a different constituency. Members of the Senate, appointed by state legislatures for six-year terms, were to represent the elite members of society and to be more attuned to the interests of property than of population. Today, members of the House and Senate are elected directly by the people. The 435 members of the House are elected from districts apportioned according to population; the 100 members of the Senate are elected by state, with two senators from each. Senators continue to have much longer terms in office and usually represent much larger and more diverse constituencies than do their counterparts in the House (see Table 12.1).

The House and Senate play different roles in the legislative process. In essence, the Senate is the more deliberative of the two bodies—the forum in which any and all ideas can receive a thorough public airing. The House is the more centralized and organized of the two bodies—better equipped to play a routine role in the governmental process. In part, this difference stems from the different rules governing the two bodies. These rules give House leaders more control over the legislative process and allow House members to specialize in certain legislative areas. The rules of the much-smaller Senate give its leadership relatively little power and discourage specialization.

Both formal and informal factors contribute to differences between the two chambers of Congress. Differences in the length of terms and requirements for

Differences Between the House and the Senate

Table 12.1

	HOUSE	SENATE
Minimum age of member	25 years	30 years
U.S. citizenship	At least 7 years	At least 9 years
Length of term	2 years	6 years
Number per state	Depends on population: 1 per 30,000 in 1789; now 1 per 660,000	2 per state
Constituency	Tends to be local	Both local and national

holding office specified by the Constitution generate differences in how members of each body develop their constituencies and exercise their powers of office. The result is that members of the House most effectively and frequently serve as the agents of well-organized local interests with specific legislative agendas—for instance, used-car dealers seeking relief from regulation, labor unions seeking more favorable legislation, or farmers looking for higher subsidies. The small size and relative homogeneity of their constituencies and the frequency with which they must seek re-election make House members more attuned to the legislative needs of local interest groups.

Senators, on the other hand, serve larger and more heterogeneous constituencies. As a result, they are somewhat better able than members of the House to serve as the agents for groups and interests organized on a statewide or national basis. Moreover, with longer terms in office, senators have the luxury of considering "new ideas" or seeking to bring together new coalitions of interests, rather than simply serving existing ones.

SOCIOLOGICAL VERSUS AGENCY REPRESENTATION

We have become so accustomed to the idea of representative government that we tend to forget what a peculiar concept representation really is. A representative claims to act or speak for some other person or group. But how can one person be trusted to speak for another? How do we know that those who call themselves our representatives are actually speaking on our behalf, rather than simply pursuing their own interests?

There are two circumstances under which one person reasonably might be trusted to speak for another. The first of these occurs if the two individuals are so similar in background, character, interests, and perspectives that anything said by one would very likely reflect the views of the other as well. This principle is at the heart of what is sometimes called **sociological representation**—the sort of representation that takes place when representatives have the same racial, ethnic, religious, or educational backgrounds as their constituents. The assumption is

sociological representation a type of representation in which representatives have the same racial, ethnic, religious, or educational backgrounds as their constituents. It is based on the principle that if two individuals are similar in background, character, interests, and perspectives, then one could correctly represent the other's views that sociological similarity helps to promote good representation; thus, the composition of a properly constituted representative assembly should mirror the composition of society.

The second circumstance under which one person might be trusted to speak for another occurs if the two are formally bound together so that the representative is in some way accountable to those he or she purports to represent. If representatives can somehow be punished or held to account for failing to speak properly for their constituents, then we know they have an incentive to provide good representation even if their own personal backgrounds, views, and interests differ from those they represent. This principle is called **agency representation**—the sort of representation that takes place when constituents have the power to hire and fire their representatives.

agency representation the type of representation by which representatives are held accountable to their constituency if they fail to represent that constituency properly. This is the incentive for good representation when the personal backgrounds, views, and interests of the representative differ from those of his or her constituency

Both sociological and agency representation play a role in the relationship between members of Congress and their constituencies.

The Social Composition of the U.S. Congress   The extent to which the U.S. Congress is representative of the American people in a sociological sense can be seen by examining the distribution of important social characteristics in the House and Senate today. It comes as no surprise that the religious affiliations of members of both the House and Senate are overwhelmingly Protestant—the distribution is very close to the proportion in the population at large—although the Protestant category is composed of more than fifteen denominations. Catholics are the second

For its first 128 years, Congress was a decidedly masculine world. In 1917, three years before the ratification of the Nineteenth Amendment, Jeanette Rankin (pictured back row, far right) became the first woman to serve in Congress. One of her first actions was to introduce a bill that would have allowed women citizenship independent of their husbands.

The first opportunity for African Americans to serve in Congress came during Reconstruction, when two black senators and fourteen black House representatives were elected. These numbers dropped precipitously, however, with the implementation of the Jim Crow system throughout the South. Not until the early 1970s did the number of African Americans in Congress start to increase again. In 1973, Barbara Jordan, here about to deliver the keynote speech at the 1976 Democratic National Convention, was elected as the first African American congresswoman from the South.

A key development in recent years is the growing number of women in elective office. Journalists dubbed 1992 the "Year of the Woman" because so many women were elected to Congress. And in 2002, Nancy Pelosi became the first woman in American history to lead a major party in the U.S. Congress when the Democrats elected her as the house minority leader. With more women in Congress, policy issues of special concern to women have more frequently become a part of the congressional agenda. For example, in 2003 Nancy Pelosi (left), actress Holly Hunter (center), and U.S. women's soccer team star Julie Foudy (right) announced a lobbying campaign to preserve Title IX gender equity funding. Title IX of the Educational Amendments of 1972 is the landmark legislation that bans sex discrimination in schools, whether it be in academics or athletics.

The increase in the number of African Americans in Congress in the last thirty-five years is shown by the membership of the Congressional Black Caucus. In 2004, the caucus had thirty-nine members. Since 1970, the caucus has fought for policies of special importance to African Americans, such as equal access to health care, voting rights, equal justice, and minority business development. Caucus members are shown here with filmmaker Michael Moore at a press conference talking about the war in Iraq and how African Americans are disproportionately dying in the war.

Figure 12.1 Women, African Americans, and Latinos in the U.S. Congress, 1971–2003

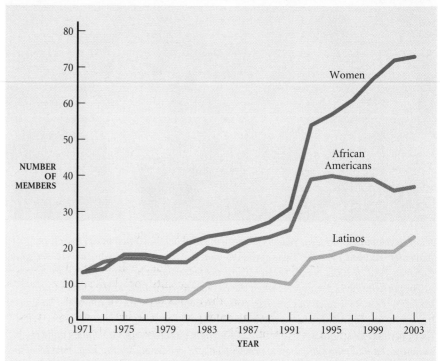

SOURCE: Harold W. Stanley and Richard G. Niemi, eds., *Vital Statistics on American Politics 2003–2004* (Washington, DC: Congressional Quarterly Press, 2003), Table 5–2, p. 207.

largest category of religious affiliation, and Jews a much smaller third category.[6] Religious affiliations directly affect congressional debate on a limited range of issues where different moral views are at stake, such as abortion.

African Americans, women, Hispanic Americans, and Asian Americans have increased their congressional representation in the past two decades (see Figure 12.1). In 2003, fifty-nine women served in the House (up from only twenty-nine in 1990). Also in 2003, Nancy Pelosi (D-Calif.) became Democratic whip, the highest congressional leadership position ever held by a woman. Thirteen women now serve in the Senate. However, the representation of women and minorities in Congress is still not comparable to their proportions in the general population. Since many important contemporary national issues do cut along racial and gender lines, a considerable amount of clamor for reform in the representative process is likely to continue until these groups are fully represented.

The occupational backgrounds of members of Congress have always been a matter of interest because so many issues cut along economic lines that are relevant to occupations and industries. The legal profession is the dominant career of most members of Congress prior to their election. Public service or politics is also a significant background. In addition, many members of Congress also have important ties to business and industry.[7] One composite portrait of a typical member of Congress has been that of "a middle-aged male lawyer whose father was of the professional or managerial class; a native-born 'white,' or—if he cannot avoid being an immigrant—a product of northwestern or central Europe or Canada, rather than of eastern or southern Europe, Latin America, Africa, or Asia."[8] This is not a portrait of the U.S. population. Congress is not a sociological microcosm of American society, and it probably can never become one.

Is Congress still able to legislate fairly or to take account of a diversity of views and interests if it is not a sociologically representative assembly? The task is certainly much more difficult. Yet there is reason to believe it can. Representatives, as we shall see shortly, can serve as the agents of their constituents, even if they do not precisely mirror their sociological attributes. Yet, sociological representation is a matter of some importance, even if it is not an absolute prerequisite for fair legislation on the part of members of the House and Senate. At the least, the social composition of a representative assembly is important for symbolic purposes— to demonstrate to groups in the population that they are taken seriously by the government. If Congress is not representative symbolically, then its own authority and indeed that of the entire government would be reduced.[9]

Representatives as Agents A good deal of evidence indicates that whether or not members of Congress share their constituents' sociological characteristics, they *do* work very hard to speak for their constituents' views and serve their constituents' interests in the governmental process. The idea of representative as agent is similar to the relationship of lawyer and client. True, the relationship between the member of Congress and as many as 660,000 "clients" in the district, or the senator and millions of "clients" in the state, is very different from that of the lawyer and client. But the criteria of performance are comparable. One expects at the very least that each representative will constantly be seeking to discover the interests of the constituency and will be speaking for those interests in Congress and in other centers of government.[10]

There is constant communication between constituents and congressional offices. For example, each year the House and Senate post offices handle nearly 100 million pieces of incoming mail, and in recent years, members of Congress have spent as much as $112 million annually to send out 458 million pieces of mail.[11]

The seriousness with which members of the House attempt to behave as representatives can be seen in the amount of time spent on behalf of their constituents. Well over a quarter of their time and nearly two-thirds of the time of their staff members is devoted to constituency service (called "case work"). This service is not merely a matter of writing and mailing letters. It includes talking to constituents, providing them with minor services, presenting special bills for them, and attempting to influence decisions by regulatory commissions on their behalf.[12]

Although no members of Congress are above constituency pressures (and they would not want to be), on many issues constituents do not have very strong views and representatives are free to act as they think best. Foreign policy issues often fall into this category. But in many districts there are two or three issues on which constituents have such pronounced opinions that representatives feel they have little freedom of choice. For example, representatives from districts that grow wheat,

FOR CRITICAL ANALYSIS

Why is sociological representation important? If congressional representatives have racial, religious, or educational backgrounds similar to those of their constituents, are they better representatives? Why?

cotton, or tobacco probably will not want to exercise a great deal of independence on relevant agricultural legislation. In the oil-rich states (such as Oklahoma, Texas, and California), senators and members of the House are likely to be leading advocates of oil interests. For one thing, representatives are probably fearful of voting against their district interests; for another, the districts are unlikely to have elected representatives who would *want* to vote against them.

The influence of constituencies is so pervasive that both parties have strongly embraced the informal rule that nothing should be done to endanger the re-election chances of any member. Party leaders obey this rule fairly consistently by not asking any member to vote in a way that might conflict with a district interest.

THE ELECTORAL CONNECTION

The sociological composition of Congress and the activities of representatives once they are in office are very much influenced by electoral considerations. Three factors related to the U.S. electoral system affect who gets elected and what they do once in office. The first set of issues concerns who decides to run for office and which candidates have an edge over others. The second issue is that of incumbency advantage. Finally, the way congressional district lines are drawn can greatly affect the outcome of an election. Let us examine more closely the impact that these considerations have on representation.

Who Runs for Congress?   Voters' choices are restricted from the start by who decides to run for office. In the past, decisions about who would run for a particular elected office were made by local party officials. A person who had a record of service to the party, or who was owed a favor, or whose "turn" had come up might be nominated by party leaders for an office. Today, few party organizations have the power to slate candidates in that way. Instead, parties try to ensure that well-qualified candidates run for Congress. In the 1990s, the Republican party developed "farm teams" of local officials who were groomed to run for Congress. Their success led Democrats to attempt a similar strategy. Even so, the decision to run for Congress is a personal choice. One of the most important factors determining who runs for office is a candidate's individual ambition.[13] A potential candidate may also assess whether he or she can attract enough money to mount a credible campaign. The ability to raise money depends on connections with other politicians, interest groups, and national party organizations. In the past, the difficulty of raising campaign funds posed a disadvantage to female candidates. Since the 1980s, however, a number of powerful **political action committees (PACs)** have emerged to recruit women and fund their campaigns. The largest of them, EMILY's List, has become one of the most powerful fund-raisers of all PACs. Recent research shows that money is no longer the barrier it once was to women running for office.[14]

Features distinctive to each congressional district also affect the field of candidates. Among them are the range of other political opportunities that may lure potential candidates away. In addition, the way the congressional district overlaps with state legislative boundaries may affect a candidate's decision to run. A state-level representative or senator who is considering running for the U.S. Congress is more likely to assess her prospects favorably if her state district coincides with the congressional district (because the voters will already know her). And for any

political action committee (PAC)
a private group that raises and distributes funds for use in election campaigns

candidate, decisions about running must be made early, because once money has been committed to already-declared candidates, it is harder for new candidates to break into a race. Thus, the outcome of a November election is partially determined many months earlier, when decisions to run are finalized.

Incumbency Incumbency plays a very important role in the American electoral system and in the kind of representation citizens get in Washington. Once in office, members of Congress possess an array of tools that they can use to stack the deck in favor of their re-election. The most important of these is constituency service: taking care of the problems and requests of individual voters. Through such services and through regular newsletter mailings, the incumbent seeks to establish a "personal" relationship with his or her constituents. The success of this strategy is evident in the high rates of re-election for congressional incumbents: as high as 98 percent for House members and 90 percent for members of the Senate in recent years (see Figure 12.2). It is also evident in what is called "sophomore surge"—the tendency for candidates to win a higher percentage of the vote when seeking future terms in office.

As in past elections, voters returned large numbers of congressional incumbents to office in 2004—specifically, 98.5 percent to the House and 96 percent to the Senate.

Incumbency can help a candidate by scaring off potential challengers. In many races, potential candidates may decide not to run because they fear that the incumbent simply has too much money or is too well liked or too well known. Potentially strong challengers may also decide that a district's partisan leanings are too

incumbency holding a political office for which one is running

---

The Power of Incumbency

Figure 12.2

Members of Congress who run for re-election have a very good chance of winning.

SOURCE: Norman J. Ornstein et al., eds., *Vital Statistics on Congress, 1999–2000* (Washington, DC: AEI Press, 2000), pp. 57–58; authors' update.

unfavorable. The efforts of incumbents to raise funds to ward off potential challengers start early. Colorado Republican Bob Beauprez, who was elected to Congress in 2002 by 121 votes, began immediately raising money for his next race. He received early assistance from the Republican "Retain Our Majority Program," which provides funds for vulnerable first-term members of Congress. Representative Thomas M. Davis III of Virginia decided to run for the House in 1994 when he saw that the incumbent had only $25,000 in her campaign war chest. As he noted, "If she had had $250,000 in the bank, I guarantee I wouldn't have run." Most incumbents are aware of the importance of fund-raising and they are able to use their connections to constituents and to other politicians to discourage opponents. The advantages of incumbents tend to grow over time. Democratic Wisconsin senator Herb Kohl first won office in 1988 by 4 percentage points; in his next race, the margin was 17 percent. As the 2000 election approached, his strength as an incumbent had discouraged potentially strong challengers from running against him.[15]

The advantage of incumbency thus tends to preserve the status quo in Congress. This fact has implications for the social composition of Congress. For example, incumbency advantage makes it harder for women to increase their numbers in Congress because most incumbents are men. Women who run for open seats (for which there are no incumbents) are just as likely to win as male candidates.[16] Supporters of **term limits** argue that such limits are the only way to get new faces into Congress. They believe that incumbency advantage and the tendency of many legislators to view politics as a career mean that very little turnover will occur in Congress unless limits are imposed on the number of terms a legislator can serve.

Yet the percentage of incumbents who are returned to Congress after each election also depends on how many members decide to run again. Because each year some members decide to retire, turnover in Congress is greater than the re-election rates of incumbents suggest. On average, 10 percent of the House and Senate decide to retire each election. In some years, the number of retirements is higher, as in 1992, when 20 percent of House members decided to retire; thus, the 90 percent of incumbents who were re-elected that year were a subset of all the eligible incumbents (80 percent). Opponents of term limits argue that, over time, such retirements ensure that there is sufficient turnover in Congress despite the high rates at which incumbents are re-elected.

Redistricting   The final factor that affects who wins a seat in Congress is the way congressional districts are drawn. Every ten years, state legislatures must redraw congressional districts to reflect population changes. Because the number of congressional seats has been fixed at 435 since 1929, redistricting is a zero-sum process. States with population growth gain additional seats and states with population declines lose seats. Over the past several decades, the shift of the American population to the South and the West has greatly increased the size of the congressional delegations from these regions (see Figure 12.3). In the redistricting that followed the 2000 census, this trend continued: eight largely northern and midwestern states (the exceptions were Mississippi and Oklahoma) lost one representative, and two states (New York and Pennsylvania) lost two seats. By contrast, the congressional delegations from southern and western states grew. The big winners were Arizona, Texas, Florida, and Georgia, which each gained two seats (see Figure 12.4).

term limits legally prescribed limits on the number of terms an elected official can serve

Apportionment of House Seats by Region, 1910 and 2000

Figure 12.3

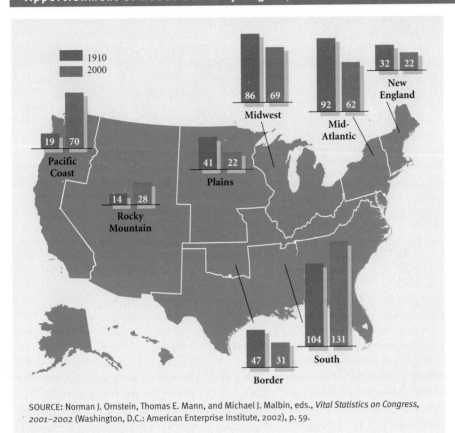

1910
2000

Pacific Coast: 19 | 70
Rocky Mountain: 14 | 28
Plains: 41 | 22
Midwest: 86 | 69
Mid-Atlantic: 92 | 62
New England: 32 | 22
South: 104 | 131
Border: 47 | 31

SOURCE: Norman J. Ornstein, Thomas E. Mann, and Michael J. Malbin, eds., *Vital Statistics on Congress, 2001–2002* (Washington, D.C.: American Enterprise Institute, 2002), p. 59.

Not surprisingly, **redistricting** is a highly political process: districts are shaped to create an advantage for the majority party in the state legislature, which controls the redistricting process. In this complex process, those charged with drawing districts use sophisticated computer technologies to come up with the most favorable district boundaries. Redistricting can create open seats and pit incumbents of the same party against one another, ensuring that one of them will lose. Redistricting can also give an advantage to one party by clustering voters with some ideological or sociological characteristics in a single district, or by separating those voters into two or more districts.

In the 2000 redistricting, the close balance of power in the House—with party control hinging on only six seats—made the process especially charged. Both Republicans and Democrats went to court to challenge remaps that they viewed as unfair. In 2002, Texas Republicans took the unprecedented step of redrawing the lines set in 2001. Those lines were drawn by a judicial panel when the politically divided legislature could not agree on a plan. In 2002, Texas elected seventeen Democrats and fifteen Republicans to the House. Republican leaders felt that the

redistricting the process of redrawing election districts and redistributing legislative representatives. This happens every ten years to reflect shifts in population or in response to legal challenges to existing districts

Figure 12.4

Results of Congressional Redistricting, 2000

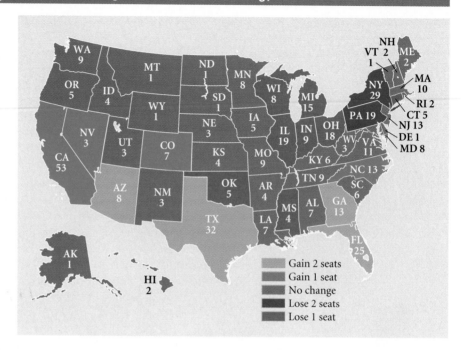

strong Democratic showing was the result of a flawed redistricting plan since Republicans won the overall vote in Texas with 53 percent of the vote for House seats. When the 2001 elections gave Republicans control of both houses of the Texas legislature as well as the governor's office, they sought to redraw the map. Republican congressional majority leader Tom DeLay played a central role in pushing the Texas legislature to take this step. The effort produced high drama when Texas Democratic legislators fled to first Oklahoma and later New Mexico to prevent passage of the plan. After forty-five days in New Mexico in July and August 2003, eleven state senators returned to Texas. The state legislature quickly approved the new map, which promised to be far more favorable to Republicans. It is unclear whether the strategy of additional redistricting in mid-decade will become a common practice across the states. Colorado's Supreme Court ruled against a similar redistricting effort in that state, writing that redistricting should occur only once a decade. In 2004, the U.S. Supreme Court refused to hear a challenge to the Colorado decision, effectively letting the state court's rejection of additional redistricting stand.

As we saw in Chapter 10, since the passage of the 1982 amendments to the 1964 Civil Rights Act, race has become a major—and controversial—consideration in drawing voting districts. These amendments, which encouraged the creation of districts in which members of racial minorities have decisive majorities, have greatly increased the number of minority representatives in Congress. After the 1991–92 redistricting, the number of predominantly minority districts doubled, rising from twenty-six to fifty-two. Among the most fervent supporters of the new minority districts were white Republicans, who used the opportunity to create more districts dominated by white Republican voters. These developments raise thorny questions about representation. Some analysts argue that the system may grant minorities greater sociological representation but has made it more difficult for minorities to win substantive policy goals. Others dispute this argument, noting that the strong surge of Republican voters was more significant than any losses due to racial redistricting.[17]

In 1995, the Supreme Court limited racial redistricting in *Miller v. Johnson,* in which the Court stated that race could not be the predominant factor in creating electoral districts.[18] Yet concerns about redistricting and representation have not disappeared. The distinction between race being a "predominant" factor and its being one factor among many is very hazy. Moreover, the practice of political redistricting has come under fire, as Democrats, angered by the aggressive Republican use of gerrymandering after the 2000 census, sought to challenge political gerrymandering. In 2002, Pennsylvania Democrats brought suit against the Republican remap of Pennsylvania, charging that the redistricting would cost Democrats an unconstitutional number of seats in the House. The justices upheld the Pennsylvania plan on the grounds that there were no clear standards for ruling against it. Because the drawing of district boundaries affects incumbents as well as the field of candidates who decide to run for office, it continues to be a key battleground on which political parties fight about the meaning of representation.

DIRECT PATRONAGE

As we saw in the preceding discussion, members of Congress often have an opportunity to provide direct benefits, or **patronage,** for their constituents. The most important of these opportunities for direct patronage is in legislation that has been described half-jokingly as the **pork barrel.** This type of legislation specifies a project to be funded or other authorizations, as well as the location of the project within a particular district. Many observers of Congress argue that pork-barrel bills are the only ones that some members are serious about moving toward actual passage, because they are seen as so important to members' re-election bids.

A common form of pork barreling is the "earmark," the practice through which members of Congress insert into otherwise pork-free bills language that provides special benefits for their own constituents. For example, by one count, the major spending legislation passed in 2004 (which rolled eleven of the annual appropriations bills into a single giant omnibus spending bill) contained 7,000 earmarks and projects worth more than $7.5 billion for House members' districts or senators' states.[19]

Highway bills are a favorite vehicle for congressional pork-barrel spending. The 2004 highway bill was full of such items, containing more than 3,000 projects earmarked for specific congressional districts. Among them were such projects as $3.5 million for horse trails in Virginia and $5 million for a parking garage in downtown Bozeman, Montana. These measures often have little to do with transportation needs, instead serving as evidence that congressional members can bring federal dollars back home. Perhaps the most extravagant—and least needed for transportation—item in the 2004 bill was a bridge in Alaska designed to connect a barely populated island to the town of Ketchikan, population just under 8,000. At a cost that could soar to $2 billion, the bridge would replace an existing five-minute ferry ride. Alaska representative Don Young (R) proudly claimed credit for such pork-barrel

FOR CRITICAL ANALYSIS

How does redistricting alter the balance of power in Congress? Why do political parties care so much about the redistricting process?

patronage the resources available to higher officials, usually opportunities to make partisan appointments to offices and to confer grants, licenses, or special favors to supporters

pork barrel appropriations made by legislative bodies for local projects that are often not needed but that are created so that local representatives can win re-election in their home districts projects. At the suggestion that Alaska's senior senator Ted Stevens (R), chairman of the Senate Appropriations committee, might be the reason Alaska got these projects, Young pretended to be offended, saying, "If he's the chief porker, I'm upset."[20]

A limited amount of other direct patronage also exists (see Figure 12.5). One important form of constituency service is intervention with federal administrative agencies on behalf of constituents. Members of the House and Senate and their staff members spend a great deal of time on the telephone and in administrative offices seeking to secure favorable treatment for constituents and supporters. Among the kinds of services that members of Congress offer to constituents is assistance for senior citizens who are having Social Security or Medicare benefit eligibility problems. They may also assist constituents in finding federal grants for which they may be eligible to apply. As Representative Pete Stark (D-Calif.) said on his Web site, "We cannot make the decision for a federal agency on such matters, but we can make sure that you get a fair shake."[21] A small but related form of patronage is getting an appointment to one of the military academies for the child of a constituent. Traditionally, these appointments are allocated one to a district.

A different form of patronage is the **private bill**—a proposal to grant some kind of relief, special privilege, or exemption to the person named in the bill. The private bill is a type of legislation, but it is distinguished from a public bill, which is supposed to deal with general rules and categories of behavior, people, and institutions. As many as 75 percent of all private bills introduced (and one-third of the ones that pass) are concerned with providing relief for foreign nationals who cannot get

private bill a proposal in Congress to provide a specific person with some kind of relief, such as a special exemption from immigration quotas

---

Figure 12.5   **How Members of Congress Represent Their Districts**

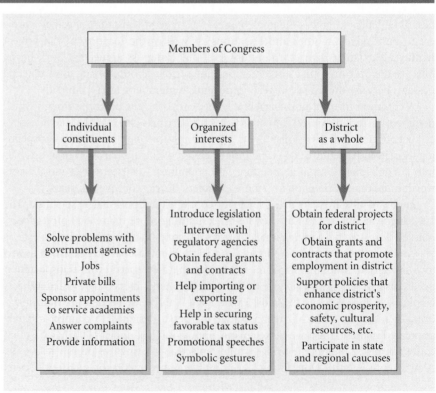

permanent visas to the United States because the immigration quota for their country is filled or because of something unusual about their particular situation.[22]

Private legislation is a congressional privilege that is often abused, but it is impossible to imagine members of Congress giving it up completely. It is one of the easiest, cheapest, and most effective forms of patronage available to each member. It can be defended as an indispensable part of the process by which members of Congress seek to fulfill their role as representatives. And obviously they like the privilege because it helps them win re-election.

The Organization of Congress

The United States Congress is not only a representative assembly. It is also a legislative body. For Americans, representation and legislation go hand in hand. As we saw earlier, however, many parliamentary bodies are representative without the power to legislate. It is no small achievement that the U.S. Congress both represents *and* governs.

It is extraordinarily difficult for a large, representative assembly to formulate, enact, and implement laws. The internal complexities of conducting business within Congress—the legislative process—alone are daunting. In addition, there are many individuals and institutions that have the capacity to influence the legislative process. For example, legislation to raise the salaries of members of the House of Representatives received input from congressional leaders of both parties, special legislative task forces, the president, the national chairs of the two major parties, public interest lobbyists, the news media, and the mass public before it became law in 1989. Since successful legislation requires the confluence of so many distinct factors, it is little wonder that most of the thousands of bills considered by Congress each year are defeated long before they reach the president.

Before an idea or proposal can become a law, it must pass through a complex set of organizations and procedures in Congress. Collectively, these are called the policy-making process, or the legislative process. Understanding this process is central to understanding why some ideas and proposals eventually become law while most do not.

Over its more than 200-year history, Congress has established procedures for creating a division of labor, setting an agenda, maintaining order through rules and procedures, and placing limits on debate and discussion. Still, congressional policy making often is an unwieldy process and the often tortuous deliberation affects the kind of legislation that Congress ultimately produces. To win support for their ideas within this complex framework, sponsors of legislation must build compromises that accommodate a broad range of interests. As a consequence, it is far easier to pass bills that represent incremental change than those designed to lead to comprehensive reform. In addition, legislation often resembles a Christmas tree—festooned with a variety of measures added on by individual congressional representatives. Although such measures may have little to do with the policy under consideration, they are needed to build majority support in Congress.

To exercise its power to make the law, Congress must first bring about something close to an organizational miracle. The building blocks of congressional organization include the political parties, the committee system, congressional staff, the caucuses, and the parliamentary rules of the House and Senate. Each of these factors plays a key role in the organization of Congress and in the process through which Congress formulates and enacts laws.

PARTY LEADERSHIP IN THE HOUSE AND SENATE

conference a gathering of House Republicans every two years to elect their House leaders. Democrats call their gathering the caucus

caucus (political) a normally closed meeting of a political or legislative group to select candidates, plan strategy, or make decisions regarding legislative matters

Speaker of the House the chief presiding officer of the House of Representatives. The Speaker is elected at the beginning of every Congress on a straight party vote. The Speaker is the most important party and House leader, and can influence the legislative agenda, the fate of individual pieces of legislation, and members' positions within the House

majority leader the elected leader of the majority party in the House of Representatives or in the Senate. In the House, the majority leader is subordinate in the party hierarchy to the Speaker of the House

minority leader the elected leader of the minority party in the House or Senate

Every two years, at the beginning of a new Congress, the members of each party gather to elect their House leaders. This gathering is traditionally called the **conference** (House Democrats call theirs the **caucus**). The elected leader of the majority party is later proposed to the whole House and is automatically elected to the position of **Speaker of the House,** with voting along straight party lines. The House majority conference or caucus then also elects a **majority leader.** The minority party goes through the same process and selects the **minority leader.** Both parties also elect whips to line up party members on important votes and to relay voting information to the leaders.

Next in line of importance for each party after the Speaker and majority or minority leader is its Committee on Committees (called the Steering and Policy Committee by the Democrats), whose tasks are to assign new legislators to committees and to deal with the requests of incumbent members for transfers from one committee to another. Currently, the Speaker serves as chair of the Republican Committee on Committees, while the minority leader chairs the Democratic Steering and Policy Committee. (The Republicans have a separate Policy Committee.) At one time, party leaders strictly controlled committee assignments, using them to enforce party discipline. Today, in principle, representatives receive the assignments they want. But assignments on the most important committees are often sought by several individuals, which gives the leadership an opportunity to cement alliances (and, perhaps, make enemies) as it resolves conflicting requests.

Generally, representatives seek assignments that will allow them to influence decisions of special importance to their districts. Representatives from farm districts, for example, may request seats on the Agriculture Committee.[23] Seats on powerful committees such as Ways and Means, which is responsible for tax legislation, and Appropriations are especially popular.

Within the Senate, the president pro tempore exercises primarily ceremonial leadership. Usually, the majority party designates a member with the greatest seniority to serve in this capacity. Real power is in the hands of the majority leader and minority leader, each elected by party conference. Together they control the Senate's calendar, or agenda for legislation.

At the end of 2002, Trent Lott (R-Miss.) became the first Senate majority leader forced to step down from that office. Lott had made racially insensitive remarks at the hundredth birthday party for one-time segregationist (now deceased) Senator Strom Thurmond (R-S.C.). As criticism mounted, the White House played an important role in supporting the challenge of Senator Bill Frist (R-Tenn.), who wanted Lott's position. Lacking strong support and hurting from the behind-the-scenes pressure of the White House, Lott relinquished his post, paving the way for Frist, a close ally of President Bush, to become Senate majority leader.

In addition to the majority leader and the minority leader, the senators from each party elect a whip. Each party also elects a Policy Committee, which advises the leadership on legislative priorities. The structure of majority party leadership in the House and the Senate is shown in Figures 12.6 and 12.7.

Majority Party Structure in the House of Representatives

Figure 12.6

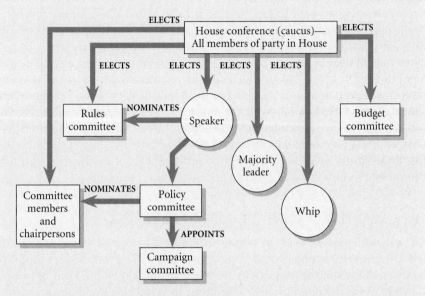

*Includes Speaker (chair), majority leader, chief and deputy whips, caucus chair, four members appointed by the Speaker, and twelve members elected by regional caucuses.

Majority Party Structure in the Senate

Figure 12.7

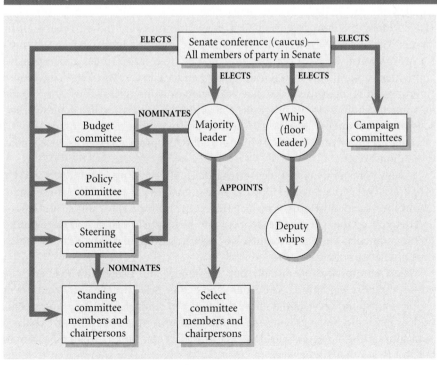

Along with these tasks of organization, congressional party leaders may also seek to establish a legislative agenda. Since the New Deal, presidents have taken the lead in creating legislative agendas (this trend will be discussed in the next chapter). When congressional leaders have been faced with a White House controlled by the opposing party, they have attempted to devise their own agendas. Democratic leaders of Congress sought to create a common Democratic perspective in 1981 when Ronald Reagan became president. The Republican Congress elected in 1994 expanded on this idea, calling its agenda the "Contract with America." More recently, with both houses of Congress in the hands of Republicans, congressional leaders have worked closely with the White House. President Bush's aggressive campaigning in the 2002 congressional elections helped to cement strong relationships with Republican members. Although minor tensions between Congress and the White House have emerged, congressional Republicans for the most part have been very responsive to the legislative priorities of the president.

THE COMMITTEE SYSTEM: THE CORE OF CONGRESS

The committee system is central to the operation of Congress. At each stage of the legislative process, Congress relies on committees and subcommittees to do the hard work of sorting through alternatives and writing legislation. There are several different kinds of congressional committees; these include standing committees, select committees, joint committees, and conference committees.

standing committee a permanent committee with the power to propose and write legislation that covers a particular subject, such as finance or appropriations

Standing committees are the most important arenas of congressional policy making. These committees continue in existence from one session of Congress to the next; they have the power to propose and write legislation. The jurisdiction of each standing committee covers a particular subject matter, which in most cases parallels the major departments or agencies in the executive branch (see Table 12.2). Among the most important standing committees are those in charge of finances. The House Ways and Means Committee and the Senate Finance Committee are powerful because of their jurisdiction over taxes, trade, and expensive entitlement programs such as Social Security and Medicare. The Senate and House Appropriations committees also play important ongoing roles because they decide how much funding various programs will actually receive; they also determine exactly how the money will be spent. A seat on an appropriations committee allows a member the opportunity to direct funds to a favored program—perhaps one in his or her home district.

Except for the House Rules Committee, all standing committees receive proposals for legislation and process them into official bills. The House Rules Committee decides the order in which bills come up for a vote on the House floor and determines the specific rules that govern the length of debate and opportunity for amendments. The Senate, which has less formal organization and fewer rules, does not have a rules committee.

select committee a (usually) temporary legislative committee set up to highlight or investigate a particular issue or address an issue not within the jurisdiction of existing committees

Select committees are usually not permanent and usually do not have the power to report legislation. (The House and Senate Select Intelligence committees are permanent, however, and do have the power to report legislation.) These committees may hold hearings and serve as focal points for the issues they are charged with considering. Congressional leaders form select committees when they want to take up issues that fall between the jurisdictions of existing committees, to highlight an issue, or to investigate a particular problem. Examples of select committees

Permanent Committees of Congress

Table 12.2

HOUSE COMMITTEES

Agriculture	Judiciary
Appropriations	Resources
Armed Services	Rules
Budget	Science
Education and the Workforce	Select Intelligence
Energy and Commerce	Small Business
Financial Services	Standards of Official Conduct
Government Reform	Transportation and Infrastructure
House Administration	Veterans Affairs
International Relations	Ways and Means

SENATE COMMITTEES

Agriculture, Nutrition, and Forestry	Foreign Relations
Appropriations	Governmental Affairs
Armed Services	Judiciary
Banking, Housing, and Urban Affairs	Health, Education, Labor, and Pensions
Budget	Rules and Administration
Commerce, Science, and Transportation	Select Intelligence
Energy and Natural Resources	Small Business
Environment and Public Works	Veterans Affairs
Finance	

investigating political scandals include the Senate Watergate Committee of 1973, the committees set up in 1987 to investigate the Iran-Contra affair, and the White-water Committee of 1995–96. Select committees set up to highlight ongoing issues have included the House Select Committee on Hunger, established in 1984, and the House Select Narcotics Committee. A few select committees have remained in existence for many years, such as the select committees on aging; hunger; children, youth, and families; and narcotics abuse and control. In 1995, however, congressional Republicans abolished most of these select committees, both to streamline operations and to remove a forum used primarily by Democratic representatives and their allies. In 2003, an important select committee, the House Select Homeland Security Committee, was created to oversee the new Department of Homeland Security. Unlike most select committees, this one has the ability to report legislation. Initially the committee had only temporary status; Congress was scheduled to decide whether to make it a permanent committee in 2005.

Joint committees involve members from both the Senate and the House. There are four such committees: economic, taxation, library, and printing. These joint committees are permanent, but they do not have the power to report legislation. The Joint Economic Committee and the Joint Taxation Committee have often played important roles in collecting information and holding hearings on economic and financial issues.

joint committee a legislative committee formed of members of both the House and the Senate

conference committee a joint committee created to work out a compromise on House and Senate versions of a piece of legislation

Finally, **conference committees** are temporary committees whose members are appointed by the Speaker of the House and the presiding officer of the Senate. These committees are charged with reaching a compromise on legislation once it has been passed by the House and the Senate. Conference committees play an extremely important role in determining what laws are actually passed, because they must reconcile any differences in the legislation passed by the House and Senate.

In 2003, conference committees became controversial when Democrats prevented several of them from convening. The Democrats took this action to protest their near-exclusion from conference committees on major energy, health care, and transportation laws. When control of Congress is divided between two parties, each is guaranteed significant representation in conference committees. When a single party controls both houses, the majority party is not obligated to offer such representation to the minority party.

Assignments to standing committees are made by a "committee on committees" appointed by the leadership of each party in each chamber of Congress. For the most part, these committees try to accommodate the requests of individual members for assignments. The decision about which committee seats to pursue is the most important choice an incoming member of Congress faces. Members are guided by different considerations in requesting committee assignments, but most prominent are serving constituent interests, making good public policy, and winning more influence in Congress.[24]

seniority priority or status ranking given to an individual on the basis of length of continuous service on a committee in Congress

Within each committee, hierarchy has usually been based on seniority. **Seniority** is determined by years of continuous service on a particular committee, not years of service in the House or Senate. In general, each committee is chaired by the most senior member of the majority party. But the principle of seniority is not absolute. Both Democrats and Republicans have violated it on occasion. When the Republicans took over the House in 1995, they violated the principle of seniority in the selection of key committee chairs. Newt Gingrich, House Speaker at the time, defended the new practice with an allusion to football, saying that "You've got to carry the moral responsibility of fielding the team that can win or you cheat the whole conference."[25] Since then, Republicans have continued to depart from the principle of seniority in selecting committee chairs, often choosing on the basis of loyalty or fund-raising abilities rather than seniority.

Over the years, Congress has reformed its organizational structure and operating procedures. Most changes have been made to improve efficiency, but some reforms have also represented a response to political considerations. In the 1970s, for example, a series of reforms substantially altered the organization of power in Congress. Among the most important changes put into place at that time were an increase in the number of subcommittees; greater autonomy for subcommittee chairs; the opening of most committee deliberations to the public; and a system of multiple referral of bills, which allowed several committees to consider one bill at the same time. One of the driving impulses behind these reforms was an effort to reduce the power of committee chairs. In the past, committee chairs exercised considerable power; they determined hearing schedules, selected subcommittee members, and appointed committee staff. Some chairs used their power to block consideration of bills they opposed. Because of the seniority system, many of the key committees were chaired by southern Democrats who stymied liberal legislation throughout the 1960s and early 1970s. By enhancing subcommittee power and allowing more members to chair subcommittees and appoint subcommittee staff, the reforms undercut the power of committee chairs.

Yet the reforms of the 1970s created new problems for Congress. As a consequence of the reforms, power has become more fragmented, making it harder to reach agreement on legislation. With power dissipated over a large number of committees and subcommittees, members spend more time in unproductive "turf battles." In addition, as committees expanded in size, members found they had so many committee responsibilities that they had to run from meeting to meeting. Thus their ability to specialize in a particular policy area has diminished as their responsibilities have increased.[26] The Republican leadership of the 104th Congress (1995–96) sought to reverse the fragmentation of congressional power and concentrate more authority in the party leadership. Toward this end they reduced the number of subcommittees and limited the time committee chairs could serve to three terms. They made good on this promise in 2001, when they replaced thirteen committee chairs. As a consequence of these changes, committees have not regained the central role they once held in policy making. Sharp partisan divisions among members of Congress and divisions among Republicans have made it difficult for committees to deliberate and bring bipartisan expertise to bear on policy making as in the past. With committees less able to engage in effective decision making and often unable to act, it has become more common in recent years for party-driven legislation to go directly to the floor, bypassing committees.[27]

THE STAFF SYSTEM: STAFFERS AND AGENCIES

A congressional institution second in importance only to the committee system is the staff system. Every member of Congress employs many staff members, whose tasks include handling constituency requests and, to a large and growing extent, dealing with legislative details and the activities of administrative agencies. Increasingly, staffers bear the primary responsibility for formulating and drafting proposals, organizing hearings, dealing with administrative agencies, and negotiating with lobbyists. Indeed, legislators typically deal with one another through staff, rather than through direct, personal contact. Representatives and senators together employ nearly 11,000 staffers in their Washington and home offices. Today, staffers even develop policy ideas, draft legislation, and in some instances, have a good deal of influence over the legislative process.

In addition to the personal staffs of individual senators and representatives, Congress also employs roughly 2,000 committee staffers. These individuals make up the permanent staff who stay attached to every House and Senate committee regardless of turnover in Congress and who are responsible for organizing and administering the committee's work, including doing research, scheduling, organizing hearings, and drafting legislation. Committee staffers can come to play key roles in the legislative process. One example of the importance of committee staffers is the success of the House Transportation and Infrastructure Committee. In a period when many committees have become less able to deliberate or have been unable to get their expenditures approved in the budget process, the Transportation Committee has been notably successful in passing very expensive legislation. One key to the committee's success is its staff. As is common for committee staff, most of the transportation committee senior staff are trained as lawyers. The committee's chief of staff has been a committee aide for over twenty-four years and has vast knowledge of the legislative process and transportation policy in particular. The combination of legal, political, and budgetary expertise that staffers accumulate is critical to the success of the large and complex bills considered in the Transportation Committee.[28]

The number of congressional staff members grew rapidly during the 1960s and 1970s, leveled off in the 1980s, and decreased dramatically in 1995. This sudden drop fulfilled the Republican congressional candidates' campaign promise to reduce the size of committee staffs.

staff agency a legislative support agency responsible for policy analysis

Not only does Congress employ personal and committee staff but it has also established **staff agencies** designed to provide the legislative branch with resources and expertise independent of the executive branch. These agencies enhance Congress's capacity to oversee administrative agencies and to evaluate presidential programs and proposals. They include the Congressional Research Service, which performs research for legislators who wish to know the facts and competing arguments relevant to policy proposals or other legislative business; the General Accounting Office, through which Congress can investigate the financial and administrative affairs of any government agency or program; and the Congressional Budget Office, which assesses the economic implications and likely costs of proposed federal programs, such as health care reform proposals. A fourth agency, the Office of Technology Assessment, which provided Congress with analyses of scientific or technical issues, was abolished in 1995.

INFORMAL ORGANIZATION: THE CAUCUSES

caucus (congressional) an association of members of Congress based on party, interest, or social group, such as gender or race

In addition to the official organization of Congress, there also exists an unofficial organizational structure—the caucuses. **Caucuses** are groups of senators or representatives who share certain opinions, interests, or social characteristics. They include ideological caucuses such as the liberal Democratic Study Group, the conservative Democratic Forum (popularly known as the "boll weevils"), and the moderate Republican Wednesday Group. At the same time, there is a large number of caucuses composed of legislators representing particular economic or policy interests, such as the Travel and Tourism Caucus, the Steel Caucus, the Mushroom Caucus, and Concerned Senators for the Arts. Legislators who share common backgrounds or social characteristics have organized caucuses such as the Congressional Black Caucus, the Congressional Caucus for Women's Issues, and the Hispanic Caucus. All these caucuses seek to advance the interests of the groups they represent by promoting legislation, encouraging Congress to hold hearings, and pressing administrative agencies for favorable treatment. In recent years, some caucuses have evolved into powerful lobbying organizations, well funded by interest groups. For example, the Sportsmen's Caucus receives funds from a nonprofit foundation that itself benefits from donations from the National Rifle Association, sports equipment manufacturers, and firearms manufacturers.

Rules of Lawmaking: How a Bill Becomes a Law

bill a proposed law that has been sponsored by a member of Congress and submitted to the clerk of the House or Senate

The institutional structure of Congress is a key factor in shaping the legislative process. A second and equally important set of factors is the rules of congressional procedure. These rules govern everything from the introduction of a **bill** through its submission to the president for signing (see Figure 12.8). Not only do these

How a Bill Becomes a Law

Figure 12.8

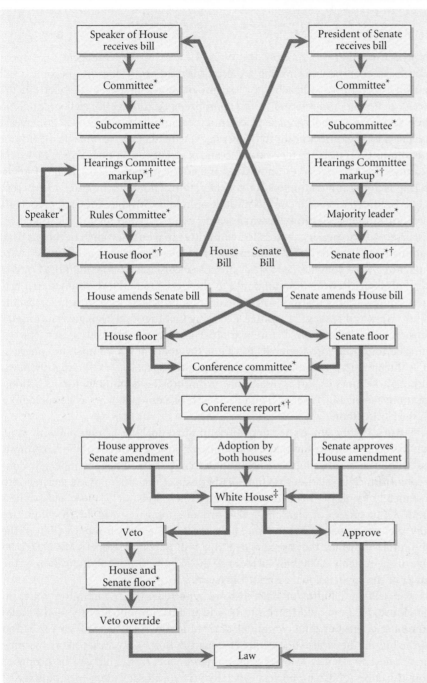

*Points at which a bill can be amended.
†Points at which a bill can die.
‡If the president neither signs nor vetoes a bill within ten days, it automatically becomes law.

regulations influence the fate of every bill but they also help to determine the distribution of power in the Congress.

COMMITTEE DELIBERATION

Even if a member of Congress, the White House, or a federal agency has spent months developing and drafting a piece of legislation, it does not become a bill until it is submitted officially by a senator or representative to the clerk of the House or Senate and referred to the appropriate committee for deliberation. No floor action on any bill can take place until the committee with jurisdiction over it has taken all the time it needs to deliberate. During the course of its deliberations, the committee typically refers the bill to one of its subcommittees, which may hold hearings, listen to expert testimony, and amend the proposed legislation before referring it to the full committee for consideration. The full committee may accept the recommendation of the subcommittee or hold its own hearings and prepare its own amendments. Sessions in which committees rewrite bills to reflect changes discussed during hearings are called **committee markup** sessions. In the partisan fighting that characterized the 108th Congress, Democrats charged that they were often not given enough time to study proposed legislation before markup. Conflict over this issue drew the Capitol police to the House and almost resulted in a fist-fight among representatives when Democrats protested their treatment by the House Ways and Means Committee. Charging that they had been given a complex pension bill only ten hours before markup, House Democrats walked out. The ensuing commotion, with Republicans calling the police and a Democratic congressman threatening a Republican, presented a sorry spectacle for the nightly news. Although Democrats lost a resolution to censure the committee for its actions, committee chair Bill Thomas (R-Calif.) later broke down in tears as he apologized on the House floor.

Frequently, the committee and subcommittee do little or nothing with a bill that has been submitted to them. Many bills are simply allowed to "die in committee" with little or no serious consideration given to them. Often, members of Congress introduce legislation that they neither expect nor desire to see enacted into law, merely to please a constituency group. These bills die a quick and painless death. Other pieces of legislation have ardent supporters and die in committee only after a long battle. But in either case, most bills are never reported out of the committees to which they are assigned. In a typical congressional session, 95 percent of the roughly 8,000 bills introduced die in committee—an indication of the power of the congressional committee system.

The relative handful of bills that are reported out of committee must, in the House, pass one additional hurdle within the committee system—the Rules Committee. This powerful committee determines the rules that will govern action on the bill on the House floor. In particular, the Rules Committee allots the time for debate and decides to what extent amendments to the bill can be proposed from the floor. A bill's supporters generally prefer a **closed rule,** which puts severe limits on floor debate and amendments. Opponents of a bill usually prefer an **open rule,** which permits potentially damaging floor debate and makes it easier to add amendments that may cripple the bill or weaken its chances for passage. Thus, the outcome of the Rules Committee's deliberations can be extremely important and the committee's hearings can be an occasion for sharp conflict.

committee markup session in which a congressional committee rewrites legislation to incorporate changes discussed during hearings on the bill

closed rule a provision by the House Rules Committee limiting or prohibiting the introduction of amendments during debate

open rule a provision by the House Rules Committee that permits floor debate and the addition of new amendments to a bill

DEBATE

Party control of the agenda is reinforced by the rule giving the Speaker of the House and the president of the Senate the power of recognition during debate on a bill. Usually the chair knows the purpose for which a member intends to speak well in advance of the occasion. Spontaneous efforts to gain recognition are often foiled. For example, the Speaker may ask, "For what purpose does the member rise?" before deciding whether to grant recognition.

In the House, virtually all the time allotted by the Rules Committee for debate on a given bill is controlled by the bill's sponsor and by its leading opponent. In almost every case, these two people are the committee chair and the ranking minority member of the committee that processed the bill—or those they designate. These two participants are, by rule and tradition, granted the power to allocate most of the debate time in small amounts to members who are seeking to speak for or against the measure. Preference in the allocation of time goes to the members of the committee whose jurisdiction covers the bill.

In the Senate, the leadership has much less control over floor debate. Indeed, the Senate is unique among the world's legislative bodies for its commitment to unlimited debate. Once given the floor, a senator may speak as long as he or she wishes. On a number of memorable occasions, senators have used this right to prevent action on legislation that they opposed. Through this tactic, called the **filibuster,** small minorities or even one individual in the Senate can force the majority to give in. During the 1950s and 1960s, for example, opponents of civil rights legislation often sought to block its passage by staging a filibuster. Democrats have used the threat of filibuster to block some of President Bush's judicial nominees, much as Republicans used the same tactic to derail Clinton nominees. In 2003, Senate Republicans staged a thirty-hour marathon, bringing cots and sleeping bags into the Senate, to protest Democratic use of the tactic. The votes of three-fifths of the Senate, or sixty votes, are needed to end a filibuster. This procedure is called **cloture.**

Although it is the best known, the filibuster is not the only technique used to block Senate debate. Under Senate rules, members have a virtually unlimited ability to propose amendments to a pending bill. Each amendment must be voted on before the bill can come to a final vote. The introduction of new amendments can be stopped only by unanimous consent. This, in effect, can permit a determined minority to filibuster-by-amendment, indefinitely delaying the passage of a bill. This tactic was briefly used by Republicans in 1994 to delay the Clinton administration's health care initiative. Senators can also place "holds," or stalling devices, on bills to delay debate. Senators place holds on bills when they fear that openly opposing them will be unpopular. Because holds are kept secret, the senators placing the holds do not have to take public responsibility for their actions. Such holds blocked bipartisan efforts to enact popular health insurance reforms for much of 1996. In 1997, opponents of this practice introduced an amendment that would have required publicizing the identity of the senator putting a bill on hold. But when the Senate voted on the measure, the proposal to end the practice of anonymous holds had "mysteriously disappeared."[29] Although no one took credit for killing the measure, it was evident that the majority of senators wanted to maintain the practice.

Once a bill is debated on the floor of the House and the Senate, the leaders schedule it for a vote on the floor of each chamber. By this time, congressional

filibuster a tactic used by members of the Senate to prevent action on legislation they oppose by continuously holding the floor and speaking until the majority backs down. Once given the floor, senators have unlimited time to speak, and it requires a vote of three-fifths of the Senate to end a filibuster

cloture a rule allowing a majority of two-thirds or three-fifths of the members in a legislative body to set a time limit on debate over a given bill leaders know what the vote will be; leaders do not bring legislation to the floor unless they are fairly certain it is going to pass. As a consequence, it is unusual for the leadership to lose a bill on the floor. On rare occasions, the last moments of the floor vote can be very dramatic, as each party's leadership puts its whip organization into action to make sure that wavering members vote with the party. The passage of Medicare reform in 2003 was one such occasion. Republican party leaders took the unprecedented step of keeping the vote open for two hours and fifty-one minutes while they looked high and low for the remaining votes needed to pass the law. It was nearly 6 A.M. by the time the bill passed.

CONFERENCE COMMITTEE: RECONCILING HOUSE AND SENATE VERSIONS OF LEGISLATION

Getting a bill out of committee and through one of the houses of Congress is no guarantee that a bill will be enacted into law. Frequently, bills that began with similar provisions in both chambers emerge with little resemblance to each other. Alternatively, a bill may be passed by one chamber but undergo substantial revision in the other chamber. In such cases, a conference committee composed of the senior members of the committees or subcommittees that initiated the bills may be required to iron out differences between the two pieces of legislation. Sometimes members or leaders will let objectionable provisions pass on the floor with the idea that they will get the chance to change what they want in conference. Usually, conference committees meet behind closed doors. Agreement requires a majority of each of the two delegations. Legislation that emerges successfully from a conference committee is more often a compromise than a clear victory of one set of forces over another.

When a bill comes out of conference, it faces one more hurdle. Before a bill can be sent to the president for signing, the House-Senate conference committee's version of the bill must be approved on the floor of each chamber. Usually such approval is given quickly. Occasionally, however, a bill's opponents use this round of approval as one last opportunity to defeat a piece of legislation.

PRESIDENTIAL ACTION

veto the president's constitutional power to turn down acts of Congress. A presidential veto may be overridden by a two-thirds vote of each house of Congress

pocket veto a presidential veto that is automatically triggered if the president does not act on a given piece of legislation passed during the final ten days of a legislative session

Once adopted by the House and Senate, a bill goes to the president, who may choose to sign the bill into law or **veto** it. The veto is the president's constitutional power to reject a piece of legislation. To veto a bill, the president returns it unsigned within ten days to the house of Congress in which it originated. If Congress adjourns during the ten-day period, and the president has taken no action, the bill is also considered to be vetoed. This latter method is known as the **pocket veto.** The possibility of a presidential veto affects how willing members of Congress are to push for different pieces of legislation at different times. If they think a proposal is likely to be vetoed they might shelve it for a later time.

A presidential veto may be overridden by a two-thirds vote in both the House and Senate. A veto override says much about the support that a president can expect from Congress, and it can deliver a stinging blow to the executive branch. Presidents will often back down from a veto threat if they believe that Congress will override the veto.

How Congress Decides

What determines the kinds of legislation that Congress ultimately produces? According to the simplest theories of representation, members of Congress would respond to the views of their constituents. In fact, the process of creating a legislative agenda, drawing up a list of possible measures, and deciding among them is a very complex process, in which a variety of influences from inside and outside government play important roles. External influences include a legislator's constituency and various interest groups. Influences from inside government include party leadership, congressional colleagues, and the president. Let us examine each of these influences individually and then consider how they interact to produce congressional policy decisions.

CONSTITUENCY

Because members of Congress, for the most part, want to be re-elected, we would expect the views of their constituents to be a primary influence on the decisions that legislators make. Yet constituency influence is not so straightforward. In fact, most constituents do not even know what policies their representatives support. The number of citizens who *do* pay attention to such matters—the attentive public—is usually very small. Nonetheless, members of Congress spend a lot of time worrying about what their constituents think, because these representatives realize that the choices they make may be scrutinized in a future election and used as ammunition by an opposing candidate. Because of this possibility, members of Congress try to anticipate their constituents' policy views.[30] Legislators are more likely to act in accordance with those views if they think that voters will take them into account during elections. In October 1998, for example, thirty-one House Democrats broke party ranks and voted in favor of an impeachment inquiry

The typical day in the life of a member of Congress is hectic. Political scientists use the term "hill style" to refer to a member's schedule in Washington and "home style" to refer to a member's activities in her district. Committee meetings, such as this conference committee's attempt to reconcile the differences between House and Senate versions of a bill, are a major component of a member's day.

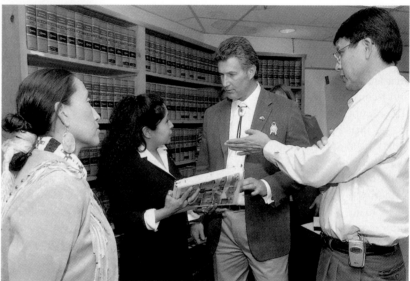

Members often meet constituents in their Capitol Hill offices. Pennsylvania representative Paul McHale (left) sets aside an "Open Till Midnight" evening every few weeks during which constituents can call him directly. Members of Congress also spend a great deal of time in their electoral districts meeting with constituents. Congressman Rick Renzi of Arizona is shown here meeting with some constituents in the Congressman's new office on the Navajo Nation.

against President Clinton because they believed a "no" vote could cost them re-election that November. The White House successfully pressed to schedule the vote authorizing the use of force in Iraq right before the 2002 elections in order to pressure members to vote for it. In this way, constituents may affect congressional policy choices even when there is little direct evidence of their influence.

INTEREST GROUPS

Interest groups are another important external influence on the policies that Congress produces. When members of Congress are making voting decisions, those interest groups that have some connection to constituents in particular members' districts are most likely to be influential. For this reason, interest groups with the ability to mobilize followers in many congressional districts may be especially influential in Congress. In recent years, Washington-based interest groups with little grassroots strength have recognized the importance of locally generated activity. They have, accordingly, sought to simulate grassroots pressure, using a strategy

Before a vote, members of Congress are pressed by outside influences. Here, Congressman Tom Barrett of Michigan meets with lobbyists from the auto industry (above). Sometimes the president influences congressional decision making. President Bush meets here with members of Congress to discuss Medicare reform (right).

that has been nicknamed "Astroturf lobbying." Such campaigns encourage constituents to sign form letters or postcards, which are then sent to congressional representatives. Sophisticated "grassroots" campaigns set up toll-free telephone numbers for a system in which simply reporting your name and address to the listening computer will generate a letter to your congressional representative. One Senate office estimated that such organized campaigns to demonstrate "grassroots" support account for two-thirds of the mail the office received. As such campaigns increase, however, they become less influential, because members of Congress are aware of how rare constituent interest actually is.[31]

Many interest groups now also use legislative "scorecards" that rate how members of Congress vote on issues of importance to that group. A high or low rating by an important interest group may provide a potent weapon in the next election. Interest groups can increase their influence over a particular piece of legislation by signaling their intention to include it in their scoring. Among the most influential groups that use scorecards, often posting them on their Web sites for members to see, are the National Federation of Independent Business, the AFL-CIO, National Right to Life, the League of Conservation Voters, and the National Rifle Association.

Interest groups also have substantial influence in setting the legislative agenda and in helping to craft specific language in legislation. Today, sophisticated lobbyists win influence by providing information about policies to busy members of Congress. As one lobbyist noted, "You can't get access without knowledge. . . . I can go in to see [former Energy and Commerce Committee chair] John Dingell, but if I have nothing to offer or nothing to say, he's not going to want to see me."[32] In recent years, interest groups have also begun to build broader coalitions and comprehensive campaigns around particular policy issues. These coalitions do not rise from the grass roots, but instead are put together by Washington lobbyists who launch comprehensive lobbying campaigns that combine simulated grassroots activity with information and campaign funding for members of Congress.

PARTY DISCIPLINE

In both the House and Senate, party leaders have a good deal of influence over the behavior of their party members. This influence, sometimes called "party discipline," was once so powerful that it dominated the lawmaking process. At the turn of the century, party leaders could often command the allegiance of more than 90 percent of their members. A vote on which 50 percent or more of the members of one party take one position while at least 50 percent of the members of the other party take the opposing position is called a **party vote.** At the beginning of the twentieth century, nearly half of all **roll-call votes** in the House of Representatives were party votes. Today, straight party-line voting is less common in Congress. But the increased partisan polarization in Congress during the 1990s and the strong Republican leadership of the House has greatly strengthened party discipline in recent years.

Typically, party unity is greater in the House than in the Senate. House rules grant greater procedural control of business to the majority party leaders, which gives them more influence over House members. In the Senate, however, the leadership has few sanctions over its members. Senate minority leader Tom Daschle once observed that a Senate leader seeking to influence other senators has as incentives "a bushel full of carrots and a few twigs."[33]

Though it has not reached nineteenth-century levels, party unity has been on the rise in the last decade because the divisions between the parties have deepened on many high profile issues such as abortion, affirmative action, the minimum wage, and school vouchers (see Figure 12.9). Party unity scores rise when congressional leaders try to put a partisan stamp on legislation. For example, in 1995, then-Speaker Newt Gingrich sought to enact a Republican Contract with America that few Democrats supported. The result was more party unity in the House than in any year since 1954. In 1998, party unity scores rose as bitter divisions between Democrats and Republicans over impeachment reduced either party's willingness to compromise on legislation.

To some extent, party unity is based on ideology and background. Republican members of Congress are more likely than Democrats to be drawn from rural or suburban areas. Democrats are likely to be more liberal on economic and social questions than their Republican colleagues. These differences certainly help to

party vote a roll-call vote in the House or Senate in which at least 50 percent of the members of one party take a particular position and are opposed by at least 50 percent of the members of the other party. Party votes are rare today, although they were fairly common in the nineteenth century

roll-call vote a vote in which each legislator's yes or no vote is recorded as the clerk calls the names of the members alphabetically

Party Unity Scores by Chamber

Figure 12.9

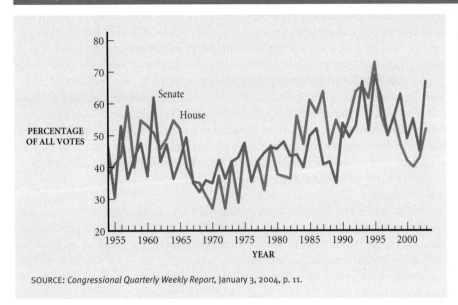

The party unity score is the percentage of times that members voted with the majority of their party on votes on which a majority of one party voted against the majority of the other party.

SOURCE: *Congressional Quarterly Weekly Report,* January 3, 2004, p. 11.

explain roll-call divisions between the two parties. Ideology and background, however, are only part of the explanation of party unity. The other part has to do with party organization and leadership. Although party organization has weakened since the beginning of the twentieth century, today's party leaders still have some resources at their disposal: (1) leadership PACs, (2) committee assignments, (3) access to the floor, (4) the whip system, (5) logrolling, and (6) the presidency. These resources are regularly used and are often effective in securing the support of party members.

Leadership PACs Leaders have increased their influence over members in recent years with aggressive use of leadership political action committees. Leadership PACs are organizations that members of Congress use to raise funds that they then distribute to other members of their party running for election. Republican congressional leaders pioneered the aggressive use of leadership PACs to win their congressional majority in 1995, and the practice has spread widely since that time. For example, House Speaker J. Dennis Hastert established a leadership PAC called Keep Our Majority PAC in preparation for the 2000 election. The influential House Majority Leader Tom DeLay (R-Tex.) has been especially aggressive in raising funds, creating several important PACs, including Americans for a Republican Majority (ARMPAC), Retain Our Majority Program (ROMP), and the Republican Majority Issues Committee. In the 2002 election cycle, there were nearly 200 leadership PACs, which raised nearly $34 million. Republicans have been in the forefront of the movement to create leadership PACs. Money from these PACs can be directed to the most vulnerable candidates or to candidates who are having trouble raising money. As such, the PACs enhance the power of the party and create a bond between the leaders and the members who receive their help.[34]

Party Discipline

Party discipline is maintained through a number of sources:

Committee assignments: by giving favorable committee assignments to members, party leaders create a sense of debt.

Access to the floor: ranking committee members in the Senate, and the Speaker of the House, control the allocation of floor time, so House and Senate members want to stay on good terms with these party leaders in order that their bills get time on the floor.

Whip system: party leaders use whips to track how many votes they have for a given piece of legislation; if the vote is close, they can try to influence members to switch sides.

Logrolling: members who may have nothing in common can agree to support one another's legislation because each needs the other's vote.

Presidency: the president's legislative proposals are often the most important part of Congress's agenda. Party leaders use the president's support to rally members.

whip system a communications network in each house of Congress; whips take polls of the membership in order to learn their intentions on specific legislative issues and to assist the majority and minority leaders in various tasks

Committee Assignments   Leaders can create debts among members by helping them get favorable committee assignments. These assignments are made early in the congressional careers of most members and cannot be taken from them if they later balk at party discipline. Nevertheless, if the leadership goes out of its way to get the right assignment for a member, this effort is likely to create a bond of obligation that can be called upon without any other payments or favors. This is one reason the Republican leadership gave freshmen favorable assignments when the Republicans took over Congress in 1995. When she assumed the position of House minority leader in late 2002, Nancy Pelosi dusted off an old rule of the Democratic caucus and limited the number of committee positions that each member could have in order to make room for more Democrats to sit on committees. By offering attractive committee assignments to members in competitive races, she sought to boost her party's chances in the 2004 election.

Access to the Floor   The most important everyday resource available to the parties is control over access to the floor. With thousands of bills awaiting passage and most members clamoring for access in order to influence a bill or to publicize themselves, floor time is precious. In the Senate, the leadership allows ranking committee members to influence the allocation of floor time—who will speak for how long; in the House, the Speaker, as head of the majority party (in consultation with the minority leader), allocates large blocks of floor time. Thus, floor time is allocated in both houses of Congress by the majority and minority leaders. More important, the Speaker of the House and the majority leader in the Senate possess the power of recognition. Although this power may not appear to be substantial, it is a formidable authority and can be used to stymie a piece of legislation completely or to frustrate a member's attempts to speak on a particular issue. Because the power is significant, members of Congress usually attempt to stay on good terms with the Speaker and the majority leader to ensure that they will continue to be recognized.

Some House members, Republicans in particular, have also taken advantage of "special orders," under which members can address the floor after the close of business. These addresses are typically made to an empty chamber, but are usually carried live by C-SPAN, a cable television channel. As the 106th Congress ended, Speaker Dennis Hastert addressed an empty House chamber to proclaim that the Congress had "made great progress in preparing America for the next century."[35] Knowing that the press would highlight the meager accomplishments of the conflict-ridden post-impeachment Congress, Hastert was ensured that his own more positive assessment would directly reach television audiences.

The Whip System   Some influence accrues to party leaders through the **whip system,** which is primarily a communications network. Between twelve and twenty assistant and regional whips are selected to operate at the direction of the majority or minority leader and the whip. They take polls of all the members in order to learn their intentions on specific bills. This enables the leaders to know if they have enough support to allow a vote as well as whether the vote is so close that they need to put pressure on a few undecided members. Leaders also use the whip system to convey their wishes and plans to the members, but only in very close votes do they actually exert pressure on a member. In those instances, the Speaker or a lieutenant will go to a few party members who have indicated they will switch if their vote is essential. The whip system helps the leaders limit pressuring members to a few times per session.

The whip system helps maintain party unity in both houses of Congress, but it is particularly critical in the House of Representatives because of the large number of legislators whose positions and votes must be accounted for. The majority and minority whips and their assistants must be adept at inducing compromise among legislators who hold widely differing viewpoints. The whips' personal styles and their perception of their function significantly affect the development of legislative coalitions and influence the compromises that emerge. As Republican House Whip from 1995 to 2002, Tom DeLay (R-Tex.) established a reputation as an effective vote counter and a tough leader, earning the nickname "the hammer." DeLay also expanded the reach of the whip, building alliances with Republicans outside of Congress, particularly those in ideological and business-oriented groups. Under DeLay's leadership these lobbyists effectively worked as part of the whip operation. As whip, DeLay also began a campaign to pressure trade associations to hire Republicans as their lobbyists, which has since been continued by his successor Roy Blunt (R-Mo.).

Logrolling   An agreement between two or more members of Congress who have nothing in common except the need for support is called **logrolling.** The agreement states, in effect, "You support me on bill X and I'll support you on another bill of your choice." Since party leaders are the center of the communications networks in the two chambers, they can help members create large logrolling coalitions. Hundreds of logrolling deals are made each year, and although there are no official record-keeping books, it would be a poor party leader whose whips did not know who owed what to whom. In some instances, logrolling produces strange alliances. A most unlikely alliance emerged in Congress in October 1991, which one commentator dubbed "the corn for porn plot."[36] The alliance joined Senate supporters of the National Endowment for the Arts (NEA) with senators seeking limits on the cost of grazing rights on federal lands. The NEA, which provides federal funding to the arts, had been under fire from conservative senator Jesse Helms (R-N.C.) for funding some controversial artists whose work Helms believed to be indecent. In an effort to prevent federal support for such works, Helms attached a provision to the NEA's funding that would have prohibited the agency from awarding grants to any work that in a "patently offensive way" depicted "sexual or excretory activities or organs." Supporters of the NEA condemned such restrictions as a violation of free speech and pointed out that many famous works of art could not have been funded under such restrictions. When it appeared that the amendment would pass, NEA supporters offered western senators a deal. In exchange for voting down the Helms amendment, they would eliminate a planned hike in grazing fees. Republican senators from sixteen western states switched their votes and defeated the Helms amendment. Although Helms called his defeat the product of "backroom deals and parliamentary flimflam," his amendment was simply the victim of the time-honored congressional practice of logrolling.[37]

logrolling a legislative practice wherein agreements are made between legislators in voting for or against a bill. Unlike in bargaining, logrolling parties have nothing in common but their desire to exchange support

The Presidency   Of all the influences that maintain the clarity of party lines in Congress, the influence of the presidency is probably the most important. Indeed, the office is a touchstone of party discipline in Congress. Since the late 1940s, under President Harry Truman, presidents each year have identified a number of bills to be considered part of their administration's program. By the mid-1950s, both parties in Congress began to look to the president for these proposals, which became the most significant part of Congress's agenda. The president's support is a criterion for party loyalty, and party leaders are able to use it to rally some members.

WEIGHING DIVERSE INFLUENCES

Clearly, many different factors affect congressional decisions. But at various points in the decision-making process, some factors are likely to be more influential than others. For example, interest groups may be more effective at the committee stage, when their expertise is especially valued and their visibility is less obvious. Because committees play a key role in deciding what legislation actually reaches the floor of the House or Senate, interest groups can often put a halt to bills they dislike, or they can ensure that the options that do reach the floor are those that the group's members support.

Once legislation reaches the floor and members of Congress are deciding among alternatives, constituent opinion will become more important. Legislators are also influenced very much by other legislators: many of their assessments about the substance and politics of legislation come from fellow members of Congress.

The influence of the external and internal forces described in the preceding section also varies according to the kind of issue being considered. On policies of great importance to powerful interest groups—farm subsidies, for example—those groups are likely to have considerable influence. On other issues, members of Congress may be less attentive to narrow interest groups and more willing to consider what they see as the general interest.

Finally, the mix of influences varies according to the historical moment. The close balance in Congress between Republicans and Democrats and the determination of Republicans to benefit from controlling Congress for the first time in forty years have made party leaders especially important in decision making during the last decade.

Beyond Legislation: Other Congressional Powers

In addition to the power to make the law, Congress has at its disposal an array of other instruments through which to influence the process of government. The Constitution gives the Senate the power to approve treaties and appointments. And Congress has a number of other powers through which it can share with the other branches the capacity to administer the laws.

OVERSIGHT

Oversight, as applied to Congress, refers not to something neglected, but to the effort to oversee or to supervise how legislation is carried out by the executive branch. Oversight is carried out by committees or subcommittees of the Senate or the House, which conduct hearings and investigations in order to analyze and evaluate bureaucratic agencies and the effectiveness of their programs. Their purpose may be to locate inefficiencies or abuses of power, to explore the relationship between what an agency does and what a law intended, or to change or abolish a

FOR CRITICAL ANALYSIS

Describe the process by which a bill becomes a law. At the various stages of this process, assess who—both within government and outside of government—makes and influences decisions. Are there stages at which the process is more democratic than it is at others? Are there stages at which the people have less influence? In your judgment, is the overall process democratic?

oversight the effort by Congress, through hearings, investigations, and other techniques, to exercise control over the activities of executive agencies

In 2004, Congress's oversight function in matters of foreign policy included investigations into the Abu Ghraib prison abuse scandal, the status of Iraqi weapons of mass destruction, and the organization of the U.S. intelligence community. U.S. weapons inspector David Kay is pictured here testifying before the Senate Armed Services Committee.

The Senate's approval power is significant. Occasionally, presidential appointments are given high levels of scrutiny by the Senate. For instance, when Clarence Thomas was nominated to the Supreme Court by George H.W. Bush, the Senate Judiciary Committee brought in numerous witnesses, including Anita Hill, who claimed that she had been sexually harassed by Thomas. Thomas's nomination received approval from a bare majority of both the committee and the Senate as a whole.

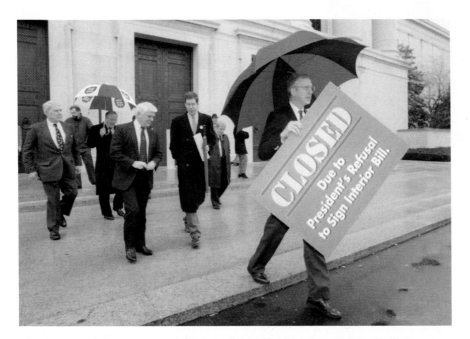

The appropriations process is one of Congress's essential functions. Without funding, government cannot operate. In December 1995, when Congress and the president could not agree on a budget bill, a partial shutdown of the federal government occurred.

Congress, which constitutionally has the right to declare war, plays an important part in foreign policy making. In fall 2002, President George W. Bush held several meetings with members of Congress, such as the one shown here in the White House, briefing them on U.S. intelligence on Iraq and courting their approval to go to war.

appropriations the amounts of money approved by Congress in statutes (bills) that each unit or agency of government can spend

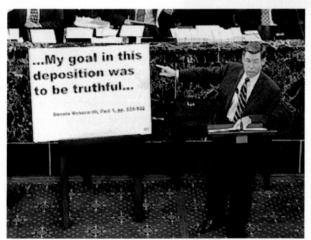

...My goal in this deposition was to be truthful...

The Senate also possesses the power to impeach federal officials. In American history, sixteen federal officials have been impeached, including two presidents, Andrew Johnson and Bill Clinton, who was impeached for lying under oath. During Clinton's trial in the House, House Manager Bill McCollum argued that lying under oath was sufficient grounds for Clinton's removal from office.

program. Most programs and agencies are subject to some oversight every year during the course of hearings on **appropriations,** that is, the funding of agencies and government programs.

Committees or subcommittees have the power to subpoena witnesses, take oaths, cross-examine, compel testimony, and bring criminal charges for contempt (refusing to cooperate) and perjury (lying). Hearings and investigations are similar in many ways, but they differ on one fundamental point. A hearing is usually held on a specific bill, and the questions asked are usually intended to build a record with regard to that bill. In an investigation, the committee or subcommittee does not begin with a particular bill, but examines a broad area or problem and then concludes its investigation with one or more proposed bills. One example of an investigation is the Senate hearings on the abuse of prisoners in Iraq's Abu Ghraib prison. Many Democrats and some Republicans complained that congressional oversight of the entire Iraq war had been too lax. Reflecting on the prison abuse scandal, Representative Christopher Shays (R-Conn.) stated, "I believe our failure to do proper oversight has hurt our country and the administration. Maybe they wouldn't have gotten into some of this trouble if our oversight had been better.[38]

ADVICE AND CONSENT: SPECIAL SENATE POWERS

The Constitution has given the Senate a special power, one that is not based on lawmaking. The president has the power to make treaties and to appoint top executive officers, ambassadors, and federal judges—but only "with the Advice and

What Is Congress's Role in Foreign Policy?

During World War II, national security dominated the congressional agenda. With the massive mobilization of American troops and economic production geared to support the war effort, domestic policy commanded only modest attention in Congress. Congress focused on supporting the president as the nation faced total mobilization for war. In other periods, Congress has been much less supportive of the president's foreign policy. For example, in the late 1960s, as widespread doubts about the wisdom of the Vietnam War began to grow, Congress convened hearings that questioned administration assumptions and priorities.

Americans disagree about Congress's proper role in foreign policy. Such disagreements become especially salient in times of war. Should Congress primarily support the president, as commander in chief of the armed forces? Or should Congress play the role of watchdog, delving into the details of foreign policy to ensure that the president's policies best serve the public interest? These questions become particularly hard to answer in prolonged "shadow wars" such as the Cold War and the current war on terrorism, when the nature and degree of the danger we confront is uncertain.

Intensive congressional scrutiny of the president's foreign policy is counterproductive, say those who believe Congress should unite behind the president. In order to manage the nation's defense effectively, it is important that the national government speak with one voice. Congressional objections to the president's priorities only strengthen the nation's enemies by weakening our resolve to take the measures needed to ensure our defense. There is always the danger that sensitive foreign policy matters are easily turned into political footballs in the hands of Congress. Congress is more likely to adopt a short term, politicized perspective than the president. Congress is also more likely to put domestic concerns ahead of foreign policy priorities. For example, in 2003, Congress, responding to popular pressure, initially sought to replace the grants in the president's aid package to Iraq with loans. Such a move would have undermined the administration's efforts to enlist other nations in the reconstruction of Iraq. In the end, presidents are better equipped than Congress to know what needs to be done to conduct a successful foreign policy. They have a large national security apparatus with extensive expertise and they are able to keep the big picture in mind.

Critics disagree, arguing that Congress has a vital role to play in foreign policy. Unless there is strong and ongoing congressional scrutiny of foreign policy, there can be abuses of presidential power. Democratic checks and balances must extend to foreign policy. For example, it is essential that the Congress investigate why President Bush claimed that the United States had evidence that Iraq was developing and already possessed weapons of mass destruction. The president's 2003 State of the Union address contained claims about Iraq's nuclear program that were later shown to be false. Such false claims undermine America's credibility with its allies. Congress must closely monitor the executive to ensure that the arguments and evidence for U.S. foreign policy is sound. Such monitoring will only strengthen American foreign policy.

President Bush's handling of the war in Iraq and the general war on terrorism shows that the president is even more likely than Congress to politicize foreign policy issues. This is because the president's reputation rests much more heavily on his success in foreign policy than do the reputations of members of Congress. Claims that Congress is too responsive to popular pressure are misguided. It is highly appropriate for domestic opinion to influence foreign policy; a democracy must be responsive to the wishes of the people. Foreign policy is no exception.

FOR CRITICAL ANALYSIS

1. Why is the president better equipped than Congress to conduct foreign policy, especially in matters such as the war against terrorism?

2. Why is congressional oversight essential to good foreign policy? How does the experience of the war in Iraq point to the importance of strong congressional involvement in foreign policy?

Should Congress Follow the President in Matters of Foreign Policy?

Yes

"If we fail to respond today, Saddam and all those who follow in his footsteps will be emboldened tomorrow. The stakes couldn't be higher. Someday, some way, I guarantee you he will use his arsenal."

With the drumbeat of war against Iraq coming out of Washington these days, one might think that these were the words of Bush, Cheney, Rumsfeld, or General Tommy Franks. However, these words were not spoken by any member of the Bush administration; rather, this quote is attributed to former President Bill Clinton. Clinton was giving a speech on February 17, 1998, and made the case for military action against Iraq. Clinton's words came just weeks after the passage of Senate Concurrent Resolution 71, which was co-sponsored by Senator Tom Daschle and about a dozen other Democrats. The Senate resolution urged Clinton to "take all necessary and appropriate actions to respond to the threat posed by Iraq's refusal to end its weapons of mass destruction programs."

The full Senate never took action on this resolution, because Saddam agreed suddenly to allow UN weapons inspectors into Iraq; a promise that he broke just days later when he threw the inspectors out of Iraq. Daschle's response: "If nothing changes, the use of force at some point would be inevitable."

Clearly Saddam is more capable of attacking America in some way than he was four years ago. He has been hard at work developing chemical and biological weapons to use against his enemies, specifically the United States. President Bush is trying to drum up support to take out Saddam's regime, and Daschle and many of the same Democrats who supported action against Iraq in 1998 are playing politics with this issue, and it is just plain sickening.

Clinton was right in 1998 and President Bush is right today: Saddam Hussein needs to be taken out. But why are the Democrats, who supported Clinton going into Iraq in 1998, now playing politics with an issue as important as this one? Those who supported Clinton in 1998 but now give Bush a hard time on Iraq are spineless and transparent. Certainly they understand the gravity of the situation at hand, but with the midterm elections coming up, they smell blood in the water. It is really sad.

Daschle and company seem to want to handle Saddam Hussein in much the same way our government handled Osama bin Laden for years prior to September 11. We allowed him to operate his terrorist network under the radar with little disruption, and the result was a steady buildup of terrorist activity that culminated with the September 11 attacks on New York, Washington, and Pennsylvania. Previous to September 11, bin Laden's terrorist network killed Americans in bombings on the *U.S.S. Cole* and at U.S. embassies in Africa. Clinton did not want to offend American pacifists or those in the Arab world by going after bin Laden, lest he would be considered "anti-Muslim," which would undoubtedly ruin his precious legacy. Politics prevented the Clinton administration from going after bin Laden, and we paid a hefty price for it. . . .

By turning a deaf ear and a blind eye to what is going on in Iraq, we are playing Russian roulette with our own futures. I keep hearing many on the left screaming and hollering for the United Nations to approve any military action against Iraq, and so far the response from nations that should be favorable toward us has not been so favorable. Canada, Germany, and France have been less than supportive of an invasion, but there is no surprise there. France and Germany both have large hate-America left populations, and Germany specifically is no surprise. Chancellor Gerhard Schroeder is up for re-election and is running far behind in the polls, and so he has made a last-ditch effort to mobilize the hate-America left voters into his corner. Clearly politics on this issue isn't exclusive to Washington. France and Germany don't want to rock the cradle because Saddam poses no similar immediate threat to their countries as he does to ours. In times like these we learn who our allies are.

I don't envy President Bush's position right about now. He has to fight two different wars: one in Washington against those who are playing politics for personal gain, and one abroad against terrorism. However, Bush himself is not playing politics. His plan to topple Saddam is the right thing to do, even if his political opponents try to smear him.

No one likes war and no one wants to see bloodshed, but sometimes it achieves a greater good. This is one of those times. A true leader will tell people not what they want to hear, but what they need to hear. President Bush is doing just that.

SOURCE: Sean Williams, "America Must Not Hesitate: Iraq is a Threat," *The Daily Campus*, (University of Connecticut), September 13, 2002.

No

In a shameless act of legislative brashness, Congress has voted to create a nationwide Do Not Call list, which was signed into law by President Bush on September 29. The wildly popular measure, which will forbid telemarketers to call households on the list, passed by a margin of 95-0 in the Senate and 412-8 in the House. Representative Billy Tauzin, the Louisiana Republican who sponsored the bill, suggested afterward that the measure be called "The This Time We Really Mean It Act," referring to an earlier court ruling that blocked the implementation of the program.

As a pointless bit of Congressional self-indulgence, the Do Not Call list is matched only by last spring's renaming of french fries and french toast. Given the enormous popularity of the measure, Congress' support of the Do Not Call list was not so heroic as Tauzin's remarks would suggest. And given the benign nature of most telemarketing calls, it hardly seems necessary that Congress should, with lightening speed and rock-solid conviction, create a federally administered system for eliminating them.

But the Do Not Call list, like "freedom fries" and "freedom toast," provided Congress with an irresistible opportunity to pander to public sentiment, striking out boldly against feeble enemies in a righteous display of legislative indignation. Indeed, such childish bravado has increasingly come to replace actual leadership as Congress has abdicated its constitutional responsibilities in the face of a hostile world and a domineering administration.

In order to comprehend the pathetic state of the American Congress, one need only compare its swift, decisive action against telemarketers with its utter passivity in matters such as the Iraq war and the Bush administration's antiterrorism initiatives.

Last fall, the administration began calling for the ouster of Saddam Hussein and the establishment of a new, democratic Iraqi regime. The project was one of staggering implications—having devised a new policy of preemptive warfare, the administration proposed to sacrifice billions of dollars and an unknown number of lives in a bold effort to oust a foreign regime and remake an entire region.

But despite the obvious importance of the war debate and its outcome, Congress uttered scarcely a word. Indeed, there was no national dialogue to speak of, except for the administration's daily calls for regime change. Throughout the yearlong buildup to war, Congress remained mute and ultimately passed a bill authorizing Bush to resolve the conflict as he saw fit, neither declaring war nor expressing opposition to it.

Congress has also offered its meek acquiescence in the administration's domestic antiterrorism initiatives. The most notorious case of this legislative passivity was that of the USA PATRIOT Act, which was signed into law on October 26, 2001. The PATRIOT Act vastly expanded the administration's law enforcement powers at the expense of America's time-honored civil liberties, yet its passage was the subject of minimal debate in Congress. Indeed, the 342-page bill, which made revisions to fifteen different statutes, passed by a large majority in both houses just weeks after the September 11 attacks.

Worthwhile arguments can be made for and against the administration's antiterrorism initiatives, but it is alarming that so few of these arguments have been made in Congress. To declare war is the sole prerogative of Congress, but the recent conflict in Iraq was fought at the insistance of the administration, without any legislative input. To write legislation is similarly the preserve of Congress, but the PATRIOT Act was proposed by the Justice Department and passed without any significant debate or revision.

Rather than exercising leadership in a time of national crisis, America's legislators have become a craven mob, tripping over themselves to claim credit for popular, but ultimately meaningless, measures, while failing utterly to address the vital issues of freedom and security in a world plagued by terrorism. In a matter of hours, Congress assembled a large, bipartisan majority in support of the Do Not Call list and Tauzin issued his bold warning against judicial interference with the program. But where is this passion on issues of substance?

If Congress is to reclaim its power to write laws, declare war, and generally oversee the war on terrorism, it must approach these matters of state with the same vigor it has applied to telemarketers and french fries. Senators and congressmen can be forgiven an occasional moment of popularity-seeking, but they cannot lose sight of their larger responsibilities. America's problems are far greater than a phone call at dinner.

SOURCE: Alec Solotorovsky, "Our Dysfunctional Congress," *The Cavalier Daily*, (University of Virginia), September 30, 2003.

Consent of the Senate" (Article II, Section 2). For treaties, two-thirds of those present must concur; for appointments, a simple majority is required.

The power to approve or reject presidential requests also involves the power to set conditions. The Senate only occasionally exercises its power to reject treaties and appointments. For example, only a handful of judicial nominees have been rejected by the Senate during the past century, whereas hundreds have been approved.

executive agreement an agreement, made between the president and another country, that has the force of a treaty but does not require the Senate's "advice and consent"

Most presidents make every effort to take potential Senate opposition into account in treaty negotiations and will frequently resort to **executive agreements** with foreign powers instead of treaties. The Supreme Court has held that such agreements are equivalent to treaties, but they do not need Senate approval.[39] In the past, presidents sometimes concluded secret agreements without informing Congress of the agreements' contents, or even their existence. For example, American involvement in the Vietnam War grew in part out of a series of secret arrangements made between American presidents and the South Vietnamese during the 1950s and 1960s. Congress did not even learn of the existence of these agreements until 1969. In 1972, Congress passed the Case Act, which requires that the president inform Congress of any executive agreement within sixty days of its having been reached. This provides Congress with the opportunity to cancel agreements that it opposes. In addition, Congress can limit the president's ability to conduct foreign policy through executive agreement by refusing to appropriate the funds needed to implement an agreement. In this way, for example, executive agreements to provide American economic or military assistance to foreign governments can be modified or even canceled by Congress.

IMPEACHMENT

impeachment the formal charge by the House of Representatives that a government official has committed "Treason, Bribery, or other high Crimes and Misdemeanors"

The Constitution also grants Congress the power of **impeachment** over the president, vice president, and other executive officials. Impeachment means to charge a government official (president or otherwise) with "Treason, Bribery, or other high Crimes and Misdemeanors" and bring them before Congress to determine their guilt. Impeachment is thus like a criminal indictment in which the House of Representatives acts like a grand jury, voting (by simple majority) on whether the accused ought to be impeached. If a majority of the House votes to impeach, the impeachment trial moves to the Senate, which acts like a trial jury by voting whether to convict and forcibly remove the person from office (this vote requires a two-thirds majority of the Senate).

Controversy over Congress's impeachment power has arisen over the grounds for impeachment, especially the meaning of "high Crimes and Misdemeanors." A strict reading of the Constitution suggests that the only impeachable offense is an actual crime. But a more commonly agreed upon definition is that "an impeachable offense is whatever the majority of the House of Representatives considers it to be at a given moment in history."[40] In other words, impeachment, especially impeachment of a president, is a political decision.

The political nature of impeachment was very clear in the two instances of impeachment that have occurred in American history. In the first, in 1867, President Andrew Johnson, a southern Democrat who had battled a congressional Republican majority over Reconstruction, was impeached by the House but saved from conviction by one vote in the Senate. In 1998, the House impeached President Bill Clinton on two counts, for lying under oath and obstructing justice, in the investigation into his sexual affair with White House intern Monica Lewinsky. The vote was highly partisan, with only five Democrats voting for impeachment on each charge. In the Senate, where a two-thirds majority was needed to convict the president, only forty-five senators voted to convict on the first count of lying and fifty voted to convict on the second charge of obstructing justice. As in the House, the vote for impeachment was highly partisan with all Democrats and only five Republicans supporting the president's ultimate acquittal.

The impeachment power is a considerable one; its very existence in the hands of Congress is a highly effective safeguard against the executive tyranny so greatly feared by the framers of the Constitution.

Thinking Critically about Congress and Democracy

Much of this chapter has described the major institutional components of Congress and has shown how they work as Congress makes policy. But what do these institutional features mean for how Congress represents the American public? Does the organization of Congress promote the equal representation of all Americans? Or are there institutional features of Congress that allow some interests more access and influence than others?

As we noted at the beginning of this chapter, Congress instituted a number of reforms in the 1970s to make itself looser and more accessible. These reforms sought to respond to public views that Congress had become a stodgy institution ruled by a powerful elite that made decisions in private. We have seen that these reforms increased the number of subcommittees, prohibited most secret hearings, and increased the staff support for Congress. These reforms spread power more evenly throughout the institution and opened new avenues for the public to contact and influence Congress.

But the opening of Congress ultimately did not benefit the broad American public, as reformers had envisioned. In fact the congressional reforms enacted in the 1970s actually made Congress less effective and, ironically, more permeable to special interests. Open committee meetings made it possible for sophisticated interest groups to monitor and influence every aspect of developing legislation. The unanticipated, negative consequences of these reforms highlighted the trade-off between representation and effectiveness in Congress.[41] Efforts to improve representation by opening Congress up made it difficult for Congress to be effective.

More recently, the concern about congressional effectiveness has waned because of the ability of the Republican-controlled Congress to enact much of the president's agenda in the 108th Congress. Yet, concerns about congressional representativeness have persisted. For the Founders, Congress was the national institution that best embodied the ideals of representative democracy. Throughout our history, Congress has served as the symbol of the American commitment to democratic values. Members of Congress, working to represent their constituents, bring these democratic values to life. A member of Congress can interpret his job as representative in two different ways: as a delegate or as a trustee. As a **delegate,** a member of Congress acts on the express preferences of his constituents; as a

FOR CRITICAL ANALYSIS

Two of Congress's chief responsibilities are representation and lawmaking. Describe the ways in which these two responsibilities might conflict with each other. How do these responsibilities support and reinforce one another? What would Congress be like if its sole function were representative? What would it be like if it were solely legislative?

delegate the role of a representative who votes according to the preferences of his or her constituency

Congress, the President, and Foreign Trade

International trade has been one of the most controversial issues confronting Congress since the 1990s. Although Congress has constitutional authority to regulate trade with other countries, for most of the twentieth century, it voluntarily delegated some of that authority to the president. In the past decade, as trade has become more politically controversial, many members of Congress have opposed the delegation of trade authority to the executive branch. On several occasions, in fact, Congress denied the president the discretion to negotiate trade agreements.

In 1934, Congress gave its authority over tariffs to the executive branch, which was more likely to be able to resist the demands of individual industries for trade protection. Congress gave the president the authority to reduce American tariffs by 50 percent once an agreement was reached with a trading partner that it would reduce its tariffs by the same amount. This new system meant that Congress would not have to pass individual trade bills every few years. Instead, the terms of trade with other countries would be negotiated by the executive branch.

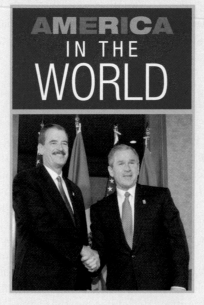

This system worked smoothly for nearly thirty years. By then, however, tariffs had been reduced so much that trade negotiations shifted to other kinds of barriers to trade, such as domestic subsidies of industries, import quotas, and licensing requirements. Because Congress had to approve each decision, presidents feared that they would not be able to negotiate effectively with other countries. American trading partners would have no reason to trust that agreements negotiated with the executive would be honored because Congress could alter or disregard the terms of an agreement. To remedy this problem, President Richard Nixon asked for "fast-track" authority in which the president would negotiate an agreement and Congress would have ninety days to vote the legislation up or down. Congress could not amend the agreement.

By the 1990s, however, Congress started questioning the wisdom of giving the president fast-track authority. Members of Congress who believed that foreign trade resulted in lost jobs and failed businesses did not want to grant the president the discretion to negotiate agreements that would hurt their constituents. A bitter fight erupted when the first President Bush sought to extend his fast-track authority. Members of Congress from areas hurt by trade voted to deny the president the authority. One senator declared that fast-track authority was "like a gun to your head" once a treaty was brought to Congress.[a] Congress ultimately approved fast track for Bush but for a limited time only.

When President Clinton sought to renew fast track in 1994, Congress denied his request. Opponents did not support Clinton's efforts to make labor and environmental protections part of his negotiating powers. Whereas organized labor had fought against fast track during the first Bush administration, businesses lobbied Congress to reject fast track under Clinton, fearing that trade agreements would include restrictive labor or environmental conditions.

President George W. Bush made it a priority to regain fast-track authority, which Congress had failed to approve since 1994. Congress initially voted against Bush's request. Opposition came from different quarters. Democrats concerned about the negative impact of trade sought to include enforceable labor and environmental protections in fast-track authority. Other members of Congress objected to the grant of congressional authority to the president. Congress ultimately approved fast-track authority, or trade promotion authority as Bush called it, in 2002.

Since the White House won fast-track authority, it has negotiated trade agreements with Chile and Singapore. Congress was able to influence the agreements through advisory markup sessions, in which it suggested several changes. The process of consultation led the administration to alter some features of the agreements. Despite these successes, trade continues to be extremely controversial in the light of job losses in the United States. Although President Bush won fast-track authority, Congress may well exercise its power to say no to agreements that are seen to threaten American jobs and living standards.

FOR CRITICAL ANALYSIS

1. Why did Congress delegate some of its power over trade to the executive branch in the 1930s? How does "fast-track" authority give the president increased power over trade?

2. Why do some members of Congress now want to reassert full congressional authority over trade? How will greater congressional authority alter the politics of trade agreements?

[a]David S. Cloud, "Hill Gives Bush Green Light to Negotiate Trade Pacts," *CQ Weekly*, May 25, 1991, p. 1358.

trustee, the member is more loosely tied to constituents and makes the decisions he thinks best. The delegate role appears to be the most democratic because it forces the representative to heed the desires of his constituents. But this requires the representative to be in constant touch with constituents; it also requires constituents to follow each policy issue very closely. The problem with this form of representation is that most people do not follow every issue so carefully; instead they focus only on extremely important issues or issues of particular interest to them. Many people are too busy to get the information necessary to make informed judgments even on issues they care about. Thus, adhering to the delegate form of representation risks that the voices of only a few active and informed constituents get heard. Although it seems more democratic at first glance, the delegate form of representation may actually open Congress up even more to the influence of the voices of special interests.

If a congressional member acts as a trustee, on the other hand, there is a danger that she will not pay sufficient attention to the wishes of constituents. In this scenario, the only way the public can exercise influence is by voting every two years for representatives or every six years for senators. Yet, most members of Congress take this electoral check very seriously. They try to anticipate the wishes of their constituents even when they don't know exactly what those interests are, because they know that unpopular decisions can be used against them in the coming election.

The public understands the trade-offs entailed in these different forms of representation and is, in fact, divided on how members of Congress should represent it. In a recent poll, 69 percent of respondents agreed that when a congressional representative votes, the views of the district should be the most important; only 25 percent believed that the representative's own principles and judgment should prevail. Yet the public also recognizes that representatives are often better informed about issues than the public. On a different survey, 65 percent of respondents agreed that, in making a decision members, of Congress should ask themselves how the majority of the public would think if they were well informed on all sides of the issue; only 29 percent said the representative should be guided instead by what the majority actually thinks.[42]

What the public dislikes most about Congress stems from suspicions that Congress acts as neither a trustee nor a delegate of the broad public interest, but instead is swayed by narrow special interests with lots of money.[43] There is some evidence to support such suspicions. One study of congressional policy making that sought to measure responsiveness found that senators were far more responsive to their affluent constituents.[44] Drawing on survey data that gauged the views of constituents in different income categories, the study showed that on key pieces of legislation, such as those dealing with the minimum wage and civil rights, the views of constituents in the top quarter of income distribution were far more likely to be represented than were the views of those in the bottom quarter of the income distribution.

Although political scientists have not been able to pinpoint the causes of such unequal representation, it is clear that interest group lobbying and the role of money in politics are important factors skewing congressional responsiveness toward the affluent. As we saw in Chapter 11, high-income people are far more likely to become active in an interest group. Interest groups that represent business have grown stronger over the past three decades while groups that represent labor have

trustee the role of a representative who votes based on what he or she thinks is best for his or her constituency

FOR CRITICAL ANALYSIS

For over a century, Congress has faced charges that it is dominated by special interests that drown out the public voice. Why is it so hard to make the voice of the public heard over the special interests in Congress? What reforms can enhance the public's influence in congressional deliberations?

weakened. And as we saw in Chapter 8, higher-income people are more likely to vote and to contact their congressional representatives. These patterns of group representation and political participation mean that members of Congress are more likely to hear the voices of higher-income Americans than of those who are less well-off. For most of the past half century, class politics was a prominent feature of European politics but not of the more fluid American politics. The United States has long prided itself on having a political system that responds to all Americans regardless of income. The sharp bias in our contemporary patterns of interest representation and participation raise questions about whether the American political system is contributing to new forms of inequality.

Ideally, representative democracy grants all citizens equal opportunity to select their leaders and to communicate their preferences to these elected representatives. Yet, in reality, some citizens have more wealth, are more politically savvy, or belong to more effective organizations. Despite past efforts to reform Congress, these advantages provide special access to some interests even as they mute the voice of much of the American public. The dilemma that congressional reformers confront is how to devise safeguards that reduce the voice of special interests while allowing Congress to remain open to public influence.

FOR CRITICAL ANALYSIS

What are the reasons that members of Congress may be more responsive to upper-income Americans? What would it take to alter this bias in responsiveness?

GET INVOLVED

What You Can Do: Make Contact with Congress

Are ordinary citizens powerless in the face of such activity by special-interest groups? The changing tactics of interest-group politics suggest that citizens, when they are organized and active, can greatly influence representatives. After all, what the most sophisticated interest groups are doing today is trying to convince members of Congress that there is genuine widespread grassroots support for their cause. This reflects the belief—rooted in long experience—that what really sways representatives most is evidence that their constituents care about particular issues. To influence all of Congress, it is particularly important to build a grassroots organization that is geographically broad. If members of Congress from many parts of the country are getting the same message from their constituents, there is a greater chance of successfully influencing policy.

The experience of some groups that have organized such broad-based grassroots activity indicates that ordinary citizens can affect what Congress does. In recent years, significant grassroots activism has emerged to influence government spending for research on diseases. The striking success of AIDS activists in dramatically increasing funding for AIDS research has inspired other groups to try similar strategies. One example is the National Breast Cancer Coalition, which represents 350 separate organizations around the country. Its aim has been to increase expenditures for federally sponsored research on breast cancer. When the coalition formed in 1991, the federal government spent $90 million a year on breast cancer research; by 1997 that amount had increased to $509 million.[45] Building on its grassroots strength and borrowing tactics from highly successful AIDS activists, the coalition sent 600,000 letters to Congress and to the White House in its first year alone. Initially told that the National Cancer Institute's priorities could not be changed so easily, they turned to the Defense Department, which had already spent some funds for breast cancer research. Today, the Defense Department is the second largest funder of breast cancer research, and citizens can monitor and affect its agenda through an independent panel overseeing the program. Both the increased expenditures and the ongoing public influence over the research agenda were a direct result of the grassroots activity of these local groups organized into a national coalition.

Organizing such grassroots groups takes time, expertise, and some resources. But the example of such groups as the Breast Cancer Coalition and AIDS activists indicates that, when organized, ordinary citizens can be effective. It is important for individuals who feel that Congress is out of touch to recognize that the path of influence may require considerable effort, but that it is available. One way for you to make Congress more approachable and accessible is to make contact with its nearest embodiment, your congressional representative's local field office.

All U.S. senators and representatives have offices in Washington, D.C. But they also have one or more local field offices in their home districts. These field offices are generally run by deputies who have the job of keeping their bosses visible among voters and donors as well as keeping them informed about local events, issues, and electoral concerns. While members of Congress do not spend much time in their field offices when Congress is in session, they regularly return to them for special occasions and during congressional recesses.

Making contact with a member's local field office is fairly simple. Most telephone directories have a section near the beginning that lists government offices. Your local directory is likely to name your U.S. senators and representative, as well as provide addresses and phone numbers for their nearest field offices. Alternatively, call your local city hall and request contact information for your representatives' field offices.

Summary

The U.S. Congress plays a vital role in American democracy. It is both the key national representative body and the focal point for decision making in Washington, D.C. Throughout American history, Congress has sought to combine representation and power as it made policy. In recent years, however, many Americans have become disillusioned with the ability of Congress to represent fairly and to exercise power responsibly.

Both sociological and agency representation play a role in the relationship between members of Congress and their constituencies. However, Congress is not fully representative because it is not a sociological microcosm of the United States. Members of Congress do seek to act as agents for their constituents by representing the views and interests of those constituents in the governmental process.

The activities of members of Congress are strongly influenced by electoral considerations. Who gets elected to Congress is influenced by who runs for office, the power of incumbency, and the way congressional districts are drawn. In order to assist their chances of re-election, members of Congress provide services and patronage to their constituents.

In order to make policy, Congress depends on a complex internal organization. Six basic dimensions of Congress affect the legislative process: (1) the parties, (2) the committees, (3) the staff, (4) the caucuses, (5) the rules, and (6) the presidency.

YOU ARE... a member of Congress!

It is Congress's job to make important, often controversial decisions. There are always different interests (all who seem to care deeply about the issues) who try to influence that decision process. Given that they are pushed and pulled by so many competing interests, how should members of Congress decide on vital questions of policy?

In this simulation, you will make a last-minute decision about a key amendment to an appropriations bill, possibly risking a veto as you seek to make the right choice for yourself, your district, and your party. What will you decide?

Go to www.wwnorton.com/wtp5e

Questions to consider as you conduct the online simulation:

Should Congressional members do what a majority of their constituents want, even if they personally disagree, or should the people trust the member's best judgment?

On highly salient issues, where members are hearing conflicting opinions, how should they cast their vote?

How much attention do voters really give to the voting record of their representative to Congress? What does that mean for democracy?

Is the primary goal of most congressional members good public policy, or to be reelected? Is that good or bad for democratic government?

Since the Constitution provides only for a presiding officer in each house, some method had to be devised for conducting business. Parties quickly assumed the responsibility for this. In the House, the majority party elects a leader every two years. This individual becomes Speaker. In addition, a majority leader, a minority leader, and party whips are elected. Each party has a committee whose job it is to make committee assignments. Party structure in the Senate is similar, except that the vice president of the United States is the Senate president.

The committee system surpasses the party system in its importance in Congress. In the early nineteenth century, standing committees became a fundamental aspect of Congress. They have, for the most part, evolved to correspond to executive branch departments or programs and thus reflect and maintain the separation of powers.

Congress also establishes rules of procedure to guide policy making. The Senate has a tradition of unlimited debate, on which the various cloture rules it has passed have had little effect. Filibusters still occur. The rules of the House, on the other hand, restrict talk and support committees; deliberation is recognized as committee business. The House Rules Committee has the power to control debate and floor amendments. The rules prescribe the formal procedure through which bills become law. Generally, the parties control scheduling and agenda, but the committees determine action on the floor. Committees, seniority, and rules all limit the ability of members to represent their constituents. Yet, these factors enable Congress to maintain its role as a major participant in government.

Many different factors affect how Congress ultimately decides on legislation. Among the most important influences are constituency preferences, interest group pressures, and party discipline. Typically party discipline is stronger in the House than in the Senate. Parties have several means of maintaining discipline: (1) favorable committee assignments create obligations; (2) floor time in the debate on one bill can be allocated in exchange for a specific vote on another; (3) the whip system allows party leaders to assess support for a bill and convey their wishes to members; (4) party leaders can help members create large logrolling coalitions; and (5) the president can champion certain pieces of legislation and thereby muster support along party lines. In most cases, party leaders accept constituency obligations as a valid reason for voting against the party position.

In addition to the power to make law, Congress possesses other formidable powers in its relationship with the executive branch. Among these are oversight, advice and consent on treaties and appointments, and the power to impeach executive officials. In spite of its array of powers, Congress is often accused of being ineffective and out of touch with the American people. At the heart of these criticisms lies the debate over whether members of Congress should act more as delegates or as trustees. An even more important concern facing Congress is whether it has become beholden to special interests and has, in effect, shut ordinary citizens out of the political process.

For Further Reading

Burrell, Barbara C., *A Woman's Place Is in the House: Campaigning for Congress in the Feminist Era.* Ann Arbor: University of Michigan Press, 1994.

Dodd, Lawrence, and Bruce I. Oppenheimer, eds. *Congress Reconsidered.* 5th ed. Washington, DC: Congressional Quarterly Press, 1993.

Fenno, Richard F. *Congressmen in Committees.* Boston: Little, Brown, 1973.

Fenno, Richard F. *Homestyle: House Members in Their Districts.* Boston: Little, Brown, 1978.

Fiorina, Morris. *Congress: Keystone of the Washington Establishment.* 2nd ed. New Haven, CT: Yale University Press, 1989.

Fowler, Linda, and Robert McClure. *Political Ambition: Who Decides to Run for Congress?* New Haven, CT: Yale University Press, 1989.

Mayhew, David R. *Congress: The Electoral Connection.* New Haven, CT: Yale University Press, 1974.

Thomas, Sue. *How Women Legislate.* New York: Oxford University Press, 1994.

Study Outline

www.wwnorton.com/wtp5e

Keyword: Review 12

Congress: Representing the American People

1. The House and Senate play different roles in the legislative process. The Senate is more deliberative, whereas the House is characterized by greater centralization and organization.
2. House members are more attuned to localized narrow interests in society, whereas senators are more able than House members to represent statewide or national interests.
3. In recent years, the House has exhibited more partisanship and ideological division than the Senate.
4. Congress is not fully representative because it is not a sociological microcosm of American society.
5. Members of Congress frequently communicate with constituents and devote a great deal of staff time to constituency service.
6. Electoral motivations have a strong impact on both sociological and agency representation in Congress.
7. Incumbency affords members of Congress resources such as constituency service and mailing to help secure re-election.
8. In recent years, turnover rates in Congress have increased, although this is due more to incumbent retirement than to the defeat of incumbents in elections.
9. Members of Congress can supply benefits to constituents by passing pork-barrel legislation. Pork-barrel votes are exchanged by members of Congress for votes on other issues.

The Organization of Congress

1. At the beginning of each Congress, Democrats and Republicans gather to select their leaders. The leader of the majority party in the House of Representatives is elected Speaker of the House by a strict party vote.
2. In the Senate, the president pro tempore serves as the presiding officer, although the majority and minority leaders control the calendar and agenda of the Senate.
3. The committee system provides Congress with a second organizational structure that is more a division of labor than the party-based hierarchies of power.
4. With specific jurisdiction over certain policy areas and the task of processing proposals of legislation into bills for floor consideration, standing committees are the most important arenas of congressional policy making.
5. Power within committees is based on seniority, although the seniority principle is not absolute.
6. In the 1970s, reforms fragmented power in Congress—the committee system, specifically—by increasing both the number of subcommittees and the autonomy of subcommittee chairpersons.
7. Each member of Congress has a personal staff that deals with constituency requests and, increasingly, with the details of legislative and administrative oversight.
8. Groups of senators or representatives who share certain opinions, interests, or social characteristics form informal organizations called caucuses.

Rules of Lawmaking: How a Bill Becomes a Law

1. Committee deliberation is necessary before floor action on any bill.
2. Many bills receive little or no committee or subcommittee action; they are allowed to "die in committee."
3. Bills reported out of committee in the House must go through the House Rules Committee before they can be debated on the floor. The Rules Committee allots the time for floor debate on a bill and the conditions under which a bill may (or may not) be amended.
4. In the Senate, rules of debate are much less rigid. In fact, senators may delay Senate action on legislation by refusing to yield the floor; this is known as a filibuster.
5. Conference committees are often required to reconcile House and Senate versions of bills that began with similar provisions but emerged with significant differences.
6. After being adopted by the House and the Senate, a bill is sent to the president, who may choose to sign the bill or veto it. Congress can override a president's veto by a two-thirds vote in both the House and the Senate.

How Congress Decides

1. Creating a legislative agenda, drawing up a list of possible measures, and deciding among them is a complex process in which a variety of influences from inside and outside government play important roles.
2. Interest groups can influence congressional decision making by mobilizing followers in congressional districts, setting the agenda, or writing legislative language.
3. Party discipline is still an important factor in congressional voting, despite its decline throughout the twentieth century.
4. Party unity is typically greater in the House than in the Senate. Party unity on roll-call votes has increased in recent sessions of Congress.
5. Party unity is a result of a combination of the ideology and background of individual members and the resources party leaders have at their disposal.
6. The influence of the presidency is probably the most important of all the resources that maintain party discipline in Congress.

Beyond Legislation: Other Congressional Powers

1. Congress has increasingly relied on legislative oversight of administrators.
2. The Senate also has the power of approving or rejecting presidential treaties and appointments.
3. Congress has the power to impeach executive officials.

Thinking Critically about Congress and Democracy

1. Congressional reforms of the 1970s fragmented power in Congress and made it more open to special interests.
2. What the public dislikes most about Congress stems from suspicions that Congress does not act as a trustee or as a delegate of any broad interest but that it is swayed by narrow special interests with money.

Practice Quiz

ON THE WEB

www.wwnorton.com/wtp5e
Keyword: Quiz 12

1. Members of Congress can work as agents of their constituents by
   a) providing direct patronage.
   b) taking part in a party vote.
   c) joining a caucus.
   d) supporting term limits.

2. Why has public approval of Congress as an institution declined since the 1970s?
   a) Constituents don't like their own representatives in Congress.
   b) Congress has become increasingly inaccessible to the public since the 1970s.
   c) Citizens can now see members of Congress on television every night.
   d) Congress has increasingly opened itself up to the control of special interests.

3. Because they have larger and more heterogeneous constituencies, senators
   a) are more attuned to the needs of localized interest groups.
   b) care more about re-election than House members.
   c) can better represent the national interest.
   d) face less competition in elections than House members.

4. Sociological representation is important in understanding the U.S. Congress because
   a) members often vote based on their religion.
   b) Congress is a microcosm of American society.
   c) the symbolic composition of Congress is important for the political stability of the United States.
   d) there is a distinct "congressional sociology."

5. What type of representation is described when constituents have the power to hire and fire their representative?
   a) agency representation
   b) sociological representation
   c) democratic representation
   d) trustee representation

6. Incumbency is an important factor in deciding who is elected to Congress because
   a) incumbents have tools they can use to help ensure re-election.
   b) potentially strong challengers may be dissuaded from running because of the strength of the incumbent.
   c) Both a and b are true.
   d) Neither a nor b is true.

7. Some have argued that the creation of minority congressional districts has
   a) lessened the sociological representation of minorities in Congress.
   b) made it more difficult for minorities to win substantive policy goals.
   c) been a result of the media's impact on state legislative politics.
   d) lessened the problem of "pork barrel" politics.

8. Which of the following is *not* an important influence on how members of Congress vote on legislation?
   a) the media
   b) constituency
   c) interest groups
   d) party leaders

9. Which of the following types of committees does *not* include members of both the House and the Senate?
   a) standing committee
   b) joint committee
   c) conference committee
   d) No committees include both House members and senators.

10. An agreement between members of Congress to trade support for each other's bill is known as
   a) oversight.
   b) filibuster.
   c) logrolling.
   d) patronage.

Key Terms

www.wwnorton.com/wtp5e

Keyword: Vocabulary 12

agency representation (p. 472)
appropriations (p. 504)
bicameral (p. 470)
bill (p. 490)
caucus (congressional) (p. 490)
caucus (political) (p. 484)
closed rule (p. 492)
cloture (p. 493)
committee markup (p. 492)
conference (p. 484)
conference committee (p. 488)
constituency (p. 470)

delegate (p. 509)
executive agreement (p. 508)
filibuster (p. 493)
impeachment (p. 508)
incumbency (p. 477)
joint committee (p. 487)
logrolling (p. 501)
majority leader (p. 484)
minority leader (p. 484)
open rule (p. 492)
oversight (p. 502)
party vote (p. 498)
patronage (p. 481)
pocket veto (p. 494)

political action committee (PAC) (p. 476)
pork barrel (p. 481)
private bill (p. 482)
redistricting (p. 479)
roll-call vote (p. 498)
select committee (p. 486)
seniority (p. 488)
sociological representation (p. 471)
Speaker of the House (p. 484)
staff agency (p. 490)
standing committee (p. 486)
term limits (p. 478)
trustee (p. 511)
veto (p. 494)
whip system (p. 500)

13 THE PRESIDENCY

LTHOUGH THE FIRST domestic impact of war is inevitably on civil liberties, war has ramifications throughout all governmental and political institutions as well as public policies. For example, President Abraham Lincoln's 1862 declaration of martial law and Congress's 1863 legislation giving the president the power to make arrests and imprisonments through military tribunals amounted to a "constitutional dictatorship," which lasted through the war and Lincoln's re-election in 1864. But these measures were viewed as emergency powers that could be taken back once the crisis of union was resolved. In less than a year after Lincoln's death, Congress had reasserted its power, leaving the presidency in many respects the same as, if not weaker than, it had been before.

War also transformed the presidency of Woodrow Wilson. In 1917, one of Congress's rare declarations of war provided America with another "constitutional dictatorship." In addition to restrictions on civil liberties, Congress gave the president a number of significant powers: to censor not only all international communications but also to take over and operate the railroads and all other common carriers; to seize and operate all telephone and telegraph lines; to regulate at his discretion the manufacture and distribution of all foods and related commodities; to fix prices on all such commodities and on stock exchanges; and to take over all aspects of mines and factories. As one leading constitutional history treatise puts it, "Legislative delegation [to the president] on this scale was unprecedented and little short of revolutionary. . . . [However,] if Wilson was in any sense a dictator, it was because Congress in certain spheres came close to a virtual delegation of its entire legislative power to the president *for the duration of the war*" [emphasis added]. The setting of a precise time limit on the duration of emergency powers later came to be called a "sunset" provision. In hindsight, some of the strengthening of the presidency did last beyond Wilson and the sunset provision. Fortunately for America, civil liberties not only survived the war restrictions but First Amendment rights actually flourished afterward.

During World War II, Franklin D. Roosevelt, like Lincoln, did not bother to wait for Congress but took executive action first and expected Congress to follow. Roosevelt brought the United States into an undeclared naval war against Germany a year before Pearl Harbor, and he ordered the unauthorized use of wiretaps and other surveillance as well as the investigation of suspicious persons for reasons not clearly specified. The most egregious (and revealing) of these was his segregation and eventual confinement of 120,000 individuals of Japanese descent, many of whom were American citizens. Even worse, the Supreme Court validated Roosevelt's treatment of the Japanese, on the flimsy grounds of military necessity. One dissenter on the Court called the president's assumption of emergency powers "a loaded weapon ready for the hand of any authority that can bring forward a plausible claim of an urgent need."

The "loaded weapon" was seized again on September 14, 2001, when Congress defined the World Trade Center and Pentagon attacks as an act of war and proceeded to adopt a joint resolution authorizing the president to use "all necessary and appropriate force against those nations, organizations or persons he determines planned, authorized, committed or aided the terrorist attacks that occurred on September 11, 2001, or harbored such organizations or persons. . . ." Congress did attach a "sunset provision" to the authorization resolution and planned for congressional oversight during the war, but it remains to be seen whether President George W. Bush's handling of the war against terrorism will lead to more power for the presidency beyond this particular war.

National emergencies are one source of presidential power, but presidents are also empowered by democratic political processes and, increasingly, by their ability to control and expand the institutional resources of the office. In this chapter, we will examine the foundations of the American presidency and assess the origins and character of presidential power in the twenty-first century. ∎

The task of this chapter is to explain why the American system of government could be described as presidential government and how it got to be that way. Another task is to explore how and why the president, however powerful, is also particularly vulnerable to the popular will. In other words, as the presidency became a powerful center of government, its foundation rested upon a virtually untamable mass popular democracy.

■ **Our focus in the first two parts of this chapter is to explore the constitutional basis and resources of presidential power.** The Constitution provides an array of expressed powers to the president. The Constitution also allows for Congress to delegate to the president the power to implement or execute its will. Finally, some presidents have asserted, especially during times of war or national emergency, that the office includes inherent powers. We will explain and review these categories of presidential power.

■ **We turn next to the institutional resources that presidents use as tools of management.** Without these resources, such as the Cabinet, presidents would be unable to use the powers provided by the Constitution.

■ **We will then examine the contemporary bases of presidential power.** Presidents rely on their party, the media, and public opinion to build support for their programs and persuade Congress to cooperate. These resources offer great strength to the president but, as we will see, can also be a great liability. As a result, contemporary presidents have increasingly turned to their administrative capabilities in order to increase the power of their office.

■ Previewing Liberty, Equality, and Democracy

Democracy helped to make the presidency a powerful institution by linking presidents to huge popular constituencies and allowing them to claim that they possessed a popular mandate for their actions. And, in a dangerous world, a powerful presidency may be necessary to protect the nation's security. Ironically, today it is the decline of democratic politics that has helped presidents gain power at the expense of the Congress. Excessive presidential power can pose a threat to civil liberties and leave Americans without a voice in their nation's affairs.

The Constitutional Basis of the Presidency

The presidency was established by Article II of the Constitution. Article II begins by asserting, "The executive power shall be vested in a President of the United States of America." It goes on to describe the manner in which the president is to be chosen and defines the basic powers of the presidency. By vesting the executive power in a single president, the framers were emphatically rejecting proposals for various forms of collective leadership. Some delegates to the Constitutional Convention had argued in favor of a multiheaded executive or an "executive council" in order to avoid undue concentration of power in the hands of one individual. Most of the framers, however, were anxious to provide for "energy" in the executive. They hoped to have a president capable of taking quick and aggressive action. These framers thought a unitary executive would be more energetic than some form of collective leadership. They believed that a powerful executive would help to protect the nation's interests vis-à-vis other nations and promote the federal government's interests relative to the states.

Immediately following the first sentence of Section 1, Article II of the Constitution defines the manner in which the president is to be chosen. This is a very odd sequence, but it does say something about the struggle the delegates were having over how to provide great power of action or energy to the executive and at the same time to balance that power with limitations. The struggle was between those delegates who wanted the president to be selected by, and thus responsible to, Congress and those delegates who preferred that the president be elected directly by the people. Direct popular election would create a more independent and more powerful presidency. With the adoption of a scheme of indirect election through an electoral college in which the electors would be selected by the state legislatures (and close elections would be resolved in the House of Representatives), the framers hoped to achieve a "republican" solution: a strong president responsible to state and national legislators rather than directly to the electorate. This indirect method of electing the president probably did dampen the power of most presidents in the nineteenth century.

The presidency was strengthened somewhat in the 1830s with the introduction of the national convention system of nominating presidential candidates. Until then, presidential candidates had been nominated by their party's congressional delegates. This was the **caucus** system of nominating candidates, and it was derisively called "King Caucus" because any candidate for president had to be beholden to the party's leaders in Congress to get the party's nomination and the support of the party's congressional delegation in the presidential election. The national nominating convention arose outside Congress to provide some representation for a party's voters who lived in districts where they weren't numerous enough to elect a member of Congress. The political party in each state made its own provisions for selecting delegates to attend the presidential nominating convention, and in virtually all states the selection was dominated by the party leaders (called "bosses" by the opposition party). Only in recent decades have state laws intervened to regularize the selection process and to provide (in all but a few instances) for open election of delegates. The convention system quickly became the most popular method of nominating candidates for all elective offices and remained so until well into the twentieth century, when it succumbed to the criticism that it was a nondemocratic method dominated by a few leaders in a "smoke-filled room." But in the nineteenth century, it was seen as a victory for democracy against the congressional elite. And the national convention gave the presidency a base of power independent of Congress.

This additional independence did not immediately transform the presidency into the office we recognize today, but the national convention did begin to open the presidency to larger social forces and newly organized interests in society. In other words, it gave the presidency a mass popular base that would eventually support and demand increased presidential power. Improvements in telephone, telegraph, and other forms of mass communication allowed individuals to share their

FOR CRITICAL ANALYSIS

In 2000, the Electoral College gave the presidency to George W. Bush even though he won fewer votes than his opponent. Is it time to abolish the Electoral College? What are the advantages and disadvantages of this indirect method of electing the president?

caucus (political) a normally closed meeting of a political or legislative group to select candidates, plan strategy, or make decisions regarding legislative matters complaints and allowed national leaders—especially presidents and presidential candidates—to reach out directly to people to ally themselves with, and even sometimes to create, popular groups and forces. Eventually, though more slowly, the presidential selection process began to be further democratized, with the adoption of primary elections through which millions of ordinary citizens were given an opportunity to take part in the presidential nominating process by popular selection of convention delegates.

But despite political and social conditions favoring the enhancement of the presidency, the development of presidential government as we know it today did not mature until the middle of the twentieth century. For a long period, even as the national government began to grow, Congress was careful to keep tight reins on the president's power. The real turning point in the history of American national government came during the administration of Franklin Delano Roosevelt. Since FDR, the tug of war seems to have been won for the chief executive presidency, because after FDR every president has been strong whether he was committed to the strong presidency or not.

The Constitutional Powers of the Presidency

While Section I of Article II explains how the president is to be chosen, Sections 2 and 3 outline the powers and duties of the president. These two sections identify two sources of presidential power. Some presidential powers are specifically established by the language of the Constitution. For example, the president is authorized to make treaties, grant pardons, and nominate judges and other public officials. These specifically defined powers are called the **expressed powers** of the office and cannot be revoked by the Congress or any other agency without an amendment to the Constitution. Other expressed powers include the power to receive ambassadors and command of the military forces of the United States.

In addition to the president's expressed powers, Article II declares that the president, "shall take Care that the Laws be faithfully executed." Since the laws are enacted by Congress, this language implies that Congress is to delegate to the president the power to implement or execute its will. Powers given to the president by Congress are called **delegated powers.** In principle, Congress delegates to the president only the power to identify or develop the means through which to carry out its decisions. So, for example, if Congress determines that air quality should be improved, it might delegate to a bureaucratic agency in the executive branch the power to identify the best means of bringing about such an improvement as well as the power to actually implement the cleanup process. In practice, of course, decisions about how to clean the air are likely to have an enormous impact on businesses, organizations, and individuals throughout the nation. As it delegates power to the executive, Congress substantially enhances the importance of the presidency and the executive branch. In most cases, Congress delegates power to bureaucratic agencies in the executive branch rather than to the president. As we shall see, however, contemporary presidents have found ways to capture a good deal of this delegated power for themselves.

Presidents have claimed a third source of power beyond expressed and delegated powers. These are powers not specified in the Constitution or the law but

expressed powers specific powers granted to Congress under Article I, Section 8, of the Constitution

delegated powers constitutional powers that are assigned to one governmental agency but that are exercised by another agency with the express permission of the first

inherent powers powers claimed by a president that are not expressed in the Constitution, but are inferred from it

said to stem from "the rights, duties and obligations of the presidency."[1] They are referred to as the **inherent powers** of the presidency and are most often asserted by presidents in times of war or national emergency. For example, after the fall of Fort Sumter and the outbreak of the Civil War, President Abraham Lincoln issued a series of executive orders for which he had no clear legal basis. Without even calling Congress into session, Lincoln combined the state militias into a ninety-day national volunteer force, called for 40,000 new volunteers, enlarged the regular army and navy, diverted $2 million in unspent appropriations to military needs, instituted censorship of the U.S. mails, ordered a blockade of southern ports, suspended the writ of habeas corpus in the border states, and ordered the arrest by military police of individuals whom he deemed to be guilty of engaging in or even contemplating treasonous actions.[2] Lincoln asserted that these extraordinary measures were justified by the president's inherent power to protect the nation.[3] Subsequent presidents, including Franklin D. Roosevelt and George W. Bush, have had similar views.

EXPRESSED POWERS

The president's expressed powers, as defined by Sections 2 and 3 of Article II, fall into several categories:

1. *Military.* Article II, Section 2, provides for the power as "Commander in Chief of the Army and Navy of the United States, and of the Militia of the several States, when called in to the actual Service of the United States."
2. *Judicial.* Article II, Section 2, also provides the power to "grant Reprieves and Pardons for Offences against the United States, except in Cases of Impeachment."
3. *Diplomatic.* Article II, Section 2, also provides the power "by and with the Advice and Consent of the Senate to make Treaties." Article II, Section 3, provides the power to "receive Ambassadors and other public Ministers."
4. *Executive.* Article II, Section 3, authorizes the president to see to it that all the laws are faithfully executed; Section 2 gives the chief executive power to appoint, remove, and supervise all executive officers and to appoint all federal judges.
5. *Legislative.* Article I, Section 7 and Article II, Section 3 give the president the power to participate authoritatively in the legislative process.

commander in chief the power of the president as commander of the national military and the state national guard units (when called into service)

Military   The president's military powers are among the most important exercised by the chief executive. The position of **commander in chief** makes the president the highest military authority in the United States, with control of the entire defense establishment. The president is also head of the nation's intelligence network, which includes not only the Central Intelligence Agency (CIA) but also the National Security Council (NSC), the National Security Agency (NSA), the Federal Bureau of Investigation (FBI), and a host of less well known but very powerful international and domestic security agencies.

War and Inherent Presidential Power   The Constitution, of course, gives Congress the power to declare war. Presidents, however, have gone a long way toward captur-

THE WORLD'S CONSTABLE.

President Theodore Roosevelt, who staked out a new role for himself and the United States as the policeman of the Western Hemisphere, claimed that the president had the power to do anything that the needs of the nation demanded.

ing this power for themselves. Congress has not declared war since December 1941, and yet, since then American military forces have engaged in numerous campaigns throughout the world under the orders of the president. When North Korean forces invaded South Korea in June 1950, Congress was actually prepared to declare war but President Harry S. Truman decided not to ask for congressional action. Instead, Truman asserted the principle that the president and not Congress could decide when and where to deploy America's military might. Truman dispatched American forces to Korea without a congressional declaration, and in the face of the emergency, Congress felt it had to acquiesce. Congress passed a resolution approving the president's actions and this became the pattern for future congressional-executive relations in the military realm. The wars in Vietnam, Bosnia, Afghanistan, and Iraq, as well as a host of lesser conflicts, were all fought without declarations of war.

In 1973, Congress responded to presidential unilateralism by passing the **War Powers Resolution** over President Nixon's veto. This resolution reasserted the principle of congressional war power, required the president to inform Congress of any planned military campaign, and stipulated that forces must be withdrawn within sixty days in the absence of a specific congressional authorization for their continued deployment. Presidents, however, have generally ignored the War Powers Resolution, claiming inherent executive power to defend the nation. Thus, for example, in 1989, President George H. W. Bush ordered an invasion of Panama without consulting Congress. In 1990, the same President Bush received congressional authorization to attack Iraq but had already made it clear that he was prepared to go to war with or without congressional assent. In 1995, President Clinton

War Powers Resolution a resolution of Congress that the president can send troops into action abroad only by authorization of Congress, or if American troops are already under attack or serious threat

The term the imperial presidency *was popularized in 1973 by a book of that name written during the Vietnam era. President Lyndon B. Johnson, pictured here greeting American troops in Vietnam, believed that his presidential powers allowed the Gulf of Tonkin resolution to mean that any of the nation's resources could be used to fight the war in Vietnam. His critics thought otherwise.*

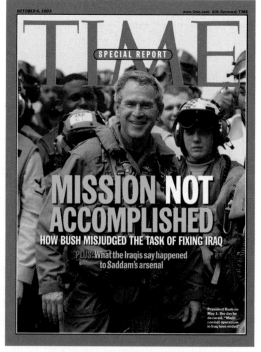

Given the national and Congressional reaction to Johnson's and Nixon's handling of Vietnam, presidents since 1973 have proceeded a little more cautiously in committing American troops to world trouble spots. Soon after the terrorist attacks of September 11, President Bush spoke before a joint session of Congress, where he presented his plan for the war on terrorism. Likewise, before taking action in Iraq, Bush sought Congress's approval. Bush's subsequent actions, however, provoked criticism that the imperial presidency had returned to the White House. Critics argued that adopting the USA PATRIOT Act as a means of fighting the war on terror deprived Americans of their liberties. Critics also charged that Bush led the United States into war under false pretenses and with little regard to is execution and aftermath.

The President versus the World:
How Presidents Seized Control of the War Power

The 1973 War Powers Resolution provided that presidents could not use military forces for more than sixty days without securing congressional authorization. Many in Congress saw this time limit as a restraint on presidential action though it gave the president more discretion than had been provided by the framers of the Constitution. President Gerald Ford had carefully followed the letter of the law when organizing a military effort to rescue American sailors held by North Korea. But this was the first and last time that the War Powers Act was fully observed. Between 1982 and 1986, President Reagan presented Congress with a set of military *faits accomplis* that undermined the War Powers Act and, in effect, asserted a doctrine of sole presidential authority in the security realm. In August 1982, Reagan sent U.S. forces to Lebanon, claiming a constitutional authority to do so.[a] After terrorist attacks killed a number of Marines, Congress pressed Reagan to withdraw American forces. To underscore its displeasure, Congress activated the sixty-day War Powers clock, but after the administration accused lawmakers of undermining America's military efforts, Congress extended the president's authority to deploy troops to Lebanon for another eighteen months.

In October 1983, while American forces were still in Lebanon, President Reagan ordered an invasion of the Caribbean island of Grenada after a coup had led to the installation of a pro-Cuban government on the island. Congress threatened to invoke the War Powers Act, but Reagan withdrew American troops before the Senate acted. In 1986, Reagan orderd the bombing of Libya in response to a terrorist attack in Berlin that the administration blamed on Libyan agents. In all three cases, Reagan acted without consulting Congress and claimed that his authority had come directly from the Constitution.

Reagan's successor, George H. W. Bush, ordered an invasion of Panama designed to oust Panamanian strongman General Manuel Noriega. Congress made no official response to the invasion. In 1990–91, the Bush administration sent a huge American military force into the Persian Gulf in response to Iraq's invasion and occupation of Kuwait. Both houses of Congress voted to authorize military action against Iraq—the Senate by the narrowest of margins—but the president made it clear that he did not feel bound by any congressional declaration and was prepared to go to war with or without Congress's assent. Indeed, the president later pointed out that he had specifically avoided asking Capitol Hill for "authorization" since such a request might improperly imply that Congress "had the final say in . . . an executive decision."[b]

President Clinton in 1994 planned an invasion of Haiti under the cover of a UN Security Council resolution. The president hoped to oust the military dictatorship that had seized power in a coup and to reinstall President Jean-Bertrand Aristide. Congress expressed strong opposition to Clinton's plans, but he pressed forward, nonetheless, claiming that he did not need congressional approval. In a similar vein, between 1994 and 1998, the administration undertook a variety of military actions in the former Yugoslavia, including an intensive bombing campaign directed against Serbian forces and installations, without formal congressional authorization.

By the end of the Clinton administration, it was no longer clear what war powers, if any, remained in the hands of the Congress. Ronald Reagan, George H. W. Bush, and Bill Clinton had all ordered American forces into combat on their own authority; outmaneuvered, bullied, or ignored the Congress; and repeatedly asserted the principle that the president controlled security policy and especially the use of military force. This set the stage for President George W. Bush's policies in Afghanistan and Iraq.

FOR CRITICAL ANALYSIS

1. Article I of the Constitution gives Congress the power to declare war. Why have presidents consistently refrained from asking Congress for such a declaration?

2. The late Edward Corwin said that the Constitution invited the president and Congress to struggle over war powers. What advantages have allowed presidents to gradually prevail in this struggle over the past century?

[a]Louis Fisher, *Congressional Abdication on War and Spending* (College Station: Texas A&M University Press, 2000), p. 68.
[b]George Bush and Brent Scowcroft, *A World Transformed* (New York: Knopf, 1998), p. 441.

ordered a massive bombing campaign against Serbian forces in the former nation of Yugoslavia without congressional authorization. And, of course, President George W. Bush responded to the 2001 attacks by Islamic terrorists by organizing a major military campaign to overthrow the Taliban regime in Afghanistan, which had sheltered the terrorists. In 2002, Bush ordered a major American campaign against Iraq, which he accused of posing a threat to the United States. U.S. forces overthrew the government of Iraqi dictator Saddam Hussein and occupied the country. In both instances, Congress passed resolutions approving the president's actions, but the president was careful to assert that he did not need congressional authorization. The War Powers Resolution was barely mentioned on Capitol Hill and was ignored by the White House.

Military Sources of Domestic Power   The president's military powers extend into the domestic sphere. Article IV, Section 4, provides that the "United States shall [protect] every State . . . against Invasion . . . and . . . domestic Violence," Congress has made this an explicit presidential power through statutes directing the president as commander in chief to discharge these obligations.[4] The Constitution restrains the president's use of domestic force by providing that a state legislature (or governor when the legislature is not in session) must request federal troops before the president can send them into the state to provide public order. Yet this proviso is not absolute. First, presidents are not obligated to deploy national troops merely because the state legislature or governor makes such a request. And more important, the president may deploy troops in a state or city without a specific request from the state legislature or governor if the president considers it necessary to maintain an essential national service during an emergency, to enforce a federal judicial order, or to protect federally guaranteed civil rights.

One historic example of the unilateral use of presidential emergency power to protect the states against domestic disorder, even when the states don't request it, was the decision by President Dwight Eisenhower in 1957 to send troops into Little Rock, Arkansas, literally against the wishes of the state of Arkansas, to enforce court orders to integrate Little Rock's Central High School. The governor of Arkansas, Orval Faubus, had actually posted the Arkansas National Guard at the entrance of Central High School to prevent the court-ordered admission of nine black students. After an effort to negotiate with Governor Faubus failed, President Eisenhower reluctantly sent a thousand paratroopers to Little Rock; they stood watch while the black students took their places in the all-white classrooms. This case makes quite clear that the president does not have to wait for a request by a state legislature or governor before acting as a domestic commander in chief.[5]

However, in most instances of domestic disorder—whether from human or from natural causes—presidents tend to exercise unilateral power by declaring a "state of emergency," thereby making available federal grants, insurance, and direct assistance. In 1992, in the aftermath of the devastating riots in Los Angeles and the hurricanes in Florida, American troops were very much in evidence, sent in by the president, but more in the role of good Samaritans than of military police.

Military emergencies have typically also led to expansion of the domestic powers of the executive branch. This was true during the First and Second World Wars and has been true in the wake of the "war on terrorism" as well. Within a month of the September 11 attacks, the White House had drafted and Congress had enacted

Iraq and Presidential Power

During the months following September 11 and the campaign against Al Qaeda and the Taliban in Afghanistan, advisers in the White House and the Pentagon convinced President Bush that Iraq was not only one of the key countries in the new "axis of evil" but was the principal one, because it was the country most likely to use or provide weapons of mass destruction for world terrorism. By summer 2002, President Bush had apparently come to the conclusion that another war with Iraq was close to inevitable. These were his words during the debate in the House and Senate on the resolution authorizing the president to go to war if and when he chose:

> While there are many dangers in the world, the threat from Iraq stands alone, because it gathers the most serious dangers of our age in one place.... Iraq's weapons of mass destruction are controlled by a murderous tyrant who has already used chemical weapons to kill thousands of people.

This request for a congressional resolution was a curious turn of events because the president had been arguing all along that he already had constitutional power to make a unilateral, preemptive, or preventive strike without any word whatsoever from Congress or the United Nations. His argument was based on congressional approval of the Persian Gulf War against Iraq in 1991 and UN Security Council resolutions imposing severe disarmament obligations on Saddam Hussein, which Hussein wantonly and frequently violated or just plain disregarded. Nevertheless, the president sought both: the authorizing resolution from Congress and one or more resolutions from the United Nations Security Council that would reimpose new and more stringent and enforceable disarmament, supervised by a UN team without any restrictions or conditions whatsoever. If Saddam Hussein persisted, he would, in effect, be bringing more upon himself and his own people. The Bush proposal to Congress was for authorization "to use all means . . . including force . . . to enforce UN Security Council resolutions [and] to restore peace and security *in the region*." [Emphasis added.]

During the debate in Congress, Senator Robert Byrd (D-W.V.) argued that the president could not make war without a declaration of war and that the Constitution provided that Congress and only Congress has the power to declare war. Never mind that only five times in all of American history has Congress seen fit to declare war: the War of 1812, the Mexican War of 1846, the Spanish-American War of 1898, and the two World Wars. Senator Byrd managed to garner only twenty-two votes along with his own against the resolution. And, as there was no equivalent opposition leader in the House, the ultimate opposition vote was only 133, with 296 voting yea.

Meanwhile, the real debate was not over whether there was to be a resolution but over the wording of the congressional resolution. Bush asked for "all means appropriate"; the opposition demanded "all means necessary and appropriate." President Bush asked for authorization covering the entire region, which could have meant all countries in the Middle East, or all Islamic countries. Bush set no time limit on the resolution, and Congress demanded he inform them within forty-eight hours of any military action and at least every sixty days thereafter.

Bush accepted the changes demanded by the opposition, and the decisive vote followed within four days. No one claimed that the changes were in any real way a defeat for President Bush. The "means" were his to determine; the obligation to keep Congress informed was already in the law as a result of the almost forgotten War Powers Resolution of 1973. And there was absolute silence on the role of the president, the armed forces, or the money that would be required after the inevitable victory was achieved and military occupation, "regime change," and "state-building" were undertaken.

FOR CRITICAL ANALYSIS

1. How does the 2002 congressional resolution authorizing President Bush to go to war differ from a constitutional declaration of war?

2. How did the congressional resolution, and the president's subsequent actions, differ from the requirements of the 1973 War Powers Act?

SOURCES: Hendrik Hertzberg, "Comment: Declarations," *The New Yorker*, September 30, 2002, pp. 45–48; Lawrence McQuillan and Kathy Kiely, "Bush, Key Lawmakers Settle on Iraq Resolution," *USA Today*, October 3, 2002, p. 9A; Kenneth T. Walsh, "Another Step Closer to War," *U.S. News & World Report*, October 21, 2002, pp. 30–32; and Mile Pomper, "Senate Democrats in Disarray after Gephardt's Deal on Iraq," and "Daschle's Grip on Majority Could Slip in Tussle over Iraq, Homeland Votes," *Congressional Quarterly*, October 5, 2002, pp. 2606–10.

Does the President's Foreign Policy Threaten Liberty?

Yes

World War II is often remembered as a time of great heroism and courage. Yet for the 120,000 Japanese Americans who were forced into relocation camps by an executive order from former President Roosevelt, World War II was a time when some lost what American soldiers fought the enemy to preserve: Freedom.

This relocation policy has been a sore spot in American history, which is the reason America offered reparations to survivors in 1988 during Reagan's administration.

It is surprising then that the Bush administration backed a similar policy in the War on Terror by detaining nearly 600 suspects in Guantanamo Bay, Cuba shortly after September 11. The administration has refused these detainee's due process for the last three years.

Since some of the detainees are U.S. citizens, many have contended that the administration violated the Sixth Amendment, which states: "in all criminal prosecutions, the accused shall enjoy the right to a speedy and public trial, by an impartial jury of the state and district wherein the crime shall have been committed."

The administration has claimed that the detainees are not being held on sovereign U.S. soil, and therefore they are not within the jurisdiction of U.S. courts. Yet, it was the policy of the Bush administration to forcibly place these prisoners where the courts could not reach.

To solve this constitutional disagreement, the Supreme Court stepped in to set the record straight. On June 28, the Court ruled that the terror suspects were able to challenge their detention in U.S. courts. Experts suspect that hundreds of new appeals will be presented to U.S. courts on behalf of the terror suspects.

This ruling opened a proud new chapter in the history of the Supreme Court. The Court reversed the wrongs done during World War II in the *Korematsu v. United States* case where the Court gave the Roosevelt administration permission to detain any person deemed harmful to the United States in the time of war.

This ruling is the largest setback for the Bush administration's war on terror. CNN reports that to comply with the ruling, the administration has set up a three-person panel of U.S. military officers that will begin to review the cases of the detainees. Appeals to U.S. courts will determine if this solution is permissible in light of the new ruling.

By forcing the Bush administration to give the detainees a trial, the Supreme Court affirmed that the judicial system could not be avoided at the whim of a president. "The president now has to act with the understanding that the court won't simply bow down in deference to any procedure he sets up," said David Cole, a Georgetown law professor and lawyer for the Center for Constitutional Rights.

The *Fort Worth Star-Telegram* reports that the Pentagon might release some Guantanamo Bay detainees instead of giving them access to civilian courts. The fact that the Bush administration now hints at releasing some of the detainees without having them go through the aforementioned review process is an indication that some of the terror suspects were probably held without enough evidence to punish them in a court of law.

Knowing the administration's policies toward preemptive action, it is not surprising that Bush wished to detain suspects that were not officially criminals.

The court system does not consider pre-crime to be a punishable offense, so the administration's efforts to dodge the court system shows a deep disrespect for the method of justice that we have in this country.

If we destroy the Constitution to save America, we have not saved anything.

Justice Sandra Day O'Connor said that a state of war was "not a blank check for the president when it comes to the rights of the nation's citizens." If presidents are allowed to hold Americans based on them being a loosely defined threat to America, nothing prevents future administrations from detaining those who hold views contrary to their official policy.

As Americans spread democracy to places across the world, they must make sure that the foundation of America's republic is secure. The bipartisan ruling shows America that the judicial system is one branch of government that works across party lines to secure American's freedoms.

If the U.S. court system is found to be lacking in its ability to remove harmful people from society as a whole, there is no possible way for America to exist in the form it was intended to. What the Bush administration must learn is that the U.S. court system will continue to work towards making America a safer place.

A government that can easily rid itself of hypocrisy can better reflect the will of the people. This balance of power has been the backbone of the American government, and is the primary reason our freedoms have been secured for so long.

Benjamin Franklin once wrote, "They who would give up an essential liberty for temporary security, deserve neither liberty or security." In this case, any administration that ignores freedoms guaranteed in the Bill of Rights to fight the war on terrorists helps the terrorists destroy the most important ideal on which America was founded: Liberty.

SOURCE: Jonathan Smith, "Terror Suspects Must Undergo Trials Despite Administration Opposition," *The Battalion* (Texas A & M University), July 5, 2004.

No

In response to Jonathan Smith's July 5 column:

The contention surrounding the issue of detainees being held in Guantanamo Bay is a sticky issue that deservedly merits our attention.

At some point we have to accept that the international and American law concerning the detention of such individuals is outdated at best.

Since information obtained from these individuals could mean the difference between life and death for American citizens I can understand the rationale that led to the Bush administration to characterize the detainees as enemy combatants rather than POWs, which under the Geneva conventions, only have to give their name and rank, whereas enemy combatants can be interrogated.

This distinction can rightly be made since the al Qaida terrorists are not characterized by the Geneva convention's definition of someone who could be a POW, that is, "having a fixed distinctive sign recognizable at a distance . . . of carrying arms openly . . . of conducting their operations in accordance with the laws and customs of war."

The detainees have been treated in line with the spirit of the Geneva convention, have been accommodated humanly, and in such instances that they were not, court marshals were given to the perpetrators. As to whether the detainees are entitled to a trial, most are not U.S. citizens and it should be noted that there is a provision within the Constitution (Section 9 Clause 2) that "The Privilege of the Writ of Habeas Corpus shall not be suspended, unless when in Cases of Rebellion or Invasion the public Safety may require it."

Bush is not the first wartime president to evoke this clause; Abraham Lincoln did so during the Civil War. As for those detainees who are American citizens such as John Walker Lindh, the American Taliban member, who was caught aiding and abetting the enemy, he is a traitor and should be treated as such.

It is true that the suspension of habeas corpus is a power delegated to Congress, and Americans like Jose Padilla are being held in breach of the Fifth Amendment.

I'm willing to give Bush the benefit of the doubt; at least he's doing something about terrorism, unlike the previous administration that did next to nothing in the face of the Cole bombing, 1993 WTC attack, African embassy bombings, and the Khobar tower bombings, though he was able to incinerate David Koresh, pass up a deal to get bin Laden, and allow the Gorelick memo to hamper the flow of intelligence through the FBI pre-September 11.

SOURCE: Kevin Sewell, "Bush Was Right to Detain Terror Suspects," *The Battalion* (Texas A & M University), July 6, 2004.

the USA PATRIOT Act, expanding the power of government agencies to engage in domestic surveillance activities, including electronic surveillance, and restricting judicial review of such efforts. The act also gave the attorney general greater authority to detain and deport aliens suspected of having terrorist affiliations. The following year, Congress created the Department of Homeland Security, combining offices from twenty-two federal agencies into one huge new cabinet department that would be responsible for protecting the nation from attack. The new agency, with a tentative budget of $40 billion, was to include the Coast Guard, Transportation Safety Administration, Federal Emergency Management Administration, Immigration and Naturalization Service, and offices from the departments of Agriculture, Energy, Transportation, Justice, Health and Human Services, Commerce, and the General Services Administration. The actual reorganization plan was drafted by the White House, but Congress weighed in to make certain that the new agency's workers had civil service and union protections.

Judicial   The presidential power to grant reprieves, pardons, and amnesties involves the power of life and death over all individuals who may be a threat to the security of the United States. Presidents may use this power on behalf of a particular individual, as did Gerald Ford when he pardoned Richard Nixon in 1974 "for all offenses against the United States which he . . . has committed or may have committed." Or they may use it on a large scale, as did President Andrew Johnson in 1868, when he gave full amnesty to all southerners who had participated in the "Late Rebellion," and President Carter in 1977, when he declared an amnesty for all the draft evaders of the Vietnam War. President Clinton issued a number of controversial pardons during his last weeks in office. This power of life and death over others helped elevate the president to the level of earlier conquerors and kings by establishing him as the person before whom supplicants might come to make their pleas for mercy.

Diplomatic   The president is America's "head of state"—its chief representative in dealings with other nations. As head of state the president has the power to make treaties for the United States (with the advice and consent of the Senate). When President Washington received Edmond Genêt ("Citizen Genêt") as the formal emissary of the revolutionary government of France in 1793 and had his cabinet officers and Congress back his decision, he established a greatly expanded interpretation of the power to "receive Ambassadors and other public Ministers," extending it to the power to "recognize" other countries. That power gives the president the almost unconditional authority to review the claims of any new ruling groups to determine whether they indeed control the territory and population of their country, so that they can commit it to treaties and other agreements.

In recent years, presidents have expanded the practice of using executive agreements instead of treaties to establish relations with other countries.[6] An **executive agreement** is exactly like a treaty because it is a contract between two countries, but an executive agreement does not require a two-thirds vote of approval by the Senate. Ordinarily, executive agreements are used to carry out commitments already made in treaties, or to arrange for matters well below the level of policy. But when presidents have found it expedient to use an executive agreement in place of a treaty, Congress typically acquiesced.

executive agreement an agreement, made between the president and another country, that has the force of a treaty but does not require the Senate's "advice and consent"

Executive Power   The most important basis of the president's power as chief executive is to be found in Article II, Section 3, which stipulates that the president must see that all the laws are faithfully executed, and Section 2, which provides that the president will appoint, remove, and supervise all executive officers, and appoint all federal judges (with Senate approval). The power to appoint the principal executive officers and to require each of them to report to the president on subjects relating to the duties of their departments makes the president the true chief executive officer (CEO) of the nation. In this manner, the Constitution focuses executive power and legal responsibility on the president. The famous sign on President Truman's desk, "The buck stops here," was not merely an assertion of Truman's personal sense of responsibility but was in fact recognition by him of the legal and constitutional responsibility of the president. The president is subject to some limitations, because the appointment of all such officers, including ambassadors, ministers, and federal judges, is subject to a majority approval by the Senate. But these appointments are at the discretion of the president, and the loyalty and the responsibility of each appointee are presumed to be directed toward the president.

Another component of the president's power as chief executive is **executive privilege.** Executive privilege is the claim that confidential communications between a president and close advisers should not be revealed without the consent of the president. Presidents have made this claim ever since George Washington refused a request from the House of Representatives to deliver documents concerning negotiations of an important treaty. Washington refused (successfully) on the grounds that, first, the House was not constitutionally part of the treaty-making process and, second, that diplomatic negotiations required secrecy.

Executive privilege became a popular part of the "checks and balances" counterpoint between president and Congress, and presidents have usually had the upper hand when invoking it. The expansion of executive privilege into a claim of "uncontrolled discretion" to refuse Congress's request for information came when President Nixon was beginning to get into political trouble over the Vietnam War in 1971.[7] It was President Nixon's claim to an almost absolute immunity to congressional inquiry that led to a Supreme Court rejection of the doctrine as a constitutional feature of the presidency in *United States v. Nixon* (418 U.S. 683, 1974). Although the doctrine continued to be invoked by succeeding presidents, the occasions were usually when presidents had something to hide that was of questionable legality (Iran-Contra) or potentially scandalous (Clinton's various scrapes). The exercise of presidential power through the executive-privilege doctrine has been all the more frequent in the past twenty years, when we have been living nearly 90 percent of the time under conditions of "divided government," where the party not in control of the White House is in control of one or both of the chambers of Congress.

executive privilege the claim that confidential communications between a president and close advisers should not be revealed without the consent of the president

The President's Legislative Power   The president plays a role not only in the administration of government but also in the legislative process. Two constitutional provisions are the primary sources of the president's power in the legislative arena. The first of these is the provision in Article II, Section 3, providing that the president "shall from time to time give to the Congress Information of the State of the Union, and recommend to their Consideration such Measures as he shall judge necessary and expedient." The second of the president's legislative powers is of course the veto power assigned by Article I, Section 7.[8]

Delivering a "State of the Union" address does not at first appear to be of any great import. It is a mere obligation on the part of the president to make recommendations for Congress's consideration. But as political and social conditions began to favor an increasingly prominent role for presidents, each president, especially since Franklin Delano Roosevelt, began to rely on this provision to become the primary initiator of proposals for legislative action in Congress and the principal source for public awareness of national issues, as well as the most important single individual participant in legislative decisions. Few today doubt that the president and the executive branch together are the primary source for many important congressional actions.[9]

veto the president's constitutional power to turn down acts of Congress. A presidential veto may be overridden by a two-thirds vote of each house of Congress

The **veto** is the president's constitutional power to turn down acts of Congress (see Figure 13.1). It alone makes the president the most important single legislative

---

Figure 13.1   **The Veto Process**

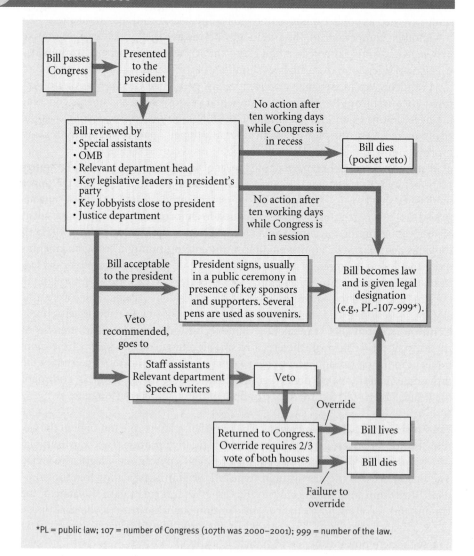

*PL = public law; 107 = number of Congress (107th was 2000–2001); 999 = number of the law.

leader.[10] No bill vetoed by the president can become law unless both the House and Senate override the veto by a two-thirds vote. In the case of a **pocket veto,** Congress does not even have the option of overriding the veto, but must reintroduce the bill in the next session. A pocket veto can occur when the president is presented with a bill during the last ten days of a legislative session. Usually, if a president does not sign a bill within ten days, it automatically becomes law. But this is true only while Congress is in session. If a president chooses not to sign a bill presented within the last ten days that Congress is in session, then the ten-day limit does not expire until Congress is out of session, and instead of becoming law, the bill is vetoed. In 1996, a new power was added to the president's lineup—the **line-item veto**—giving the president power to strike specific spending items from appropriations bills passed by Congress, unless reenacted by a two-thirds vote of both House and Senate. In 1997, President Clinton used this power eleven times to strike eighty-two items from the federal budget. But in 1998 the Supreme Court ruled that the Constitution does not authorize the line-item veto. Only a constitutional amendment would restore this power to the president.

Use of the veto varies according to the political situation that each president confronts. During Bill Clinton's first two years in office, when Democrats controlled both houses of Congress, he vetoed no bills. Following the congressional elections of 1994, however, Clinton confronted a Republican-controlled Congress with a definite agenda, and he began to use his veto power more vigorously.

Clinton also recaptured some of his leadership by finding the path of legislative initiative that he had lost with the Republican takeover of the House and Senate after the 1994 congressional elections. Although not explicitly stated, the Constitution provides the president with the power of **legislative initiative.** To "initiate" means to originate, and in government that can mean power. The framers of the Constitution clearly saw legislative initiative as one of the keys to executive power. Initiative obviously implies the ability to formulate proposals for important policies, and the president, as an individual with a great deal of staff assistance, is able to initiate decisive action more frequently than Congress, with its large assemblies that have to deliberate and debate before taking action. With some important exceptions, Congress banks on the president to set the agenda of public policy. And quite clearly, there is power in initiative; there is power in being able to set the terms of discourse in the making of public policy.

For example, during the weeks immediately following September 11, Bush took many presidential initiatives to Congress, and each was given almost unanimous support—from commitments to pursue al Qaeda to the removal of the Taliban, the reconstitution of the Afghanistan regime, all the way to almost unlimited approval for mobilization of both military power and power over the regulation of American civil liberties. After winning reelection in 2004, Bush sought to push forward his legislative domestic agenda, including changes in the nation's Social Security system and comprehensive tax reform. Bush also called on Congress to act quickly to limit lawsuit awards against doctors, and to push for tougher educational standards for high schools. Bush said "I earned capital in this campaign, political capital, and now I intend to spend it. . . . There is a feeling that the people have spoken and embraced your point of view, and that's what I intend to tell the Congress."[11]

The president's initiative does not end with policy making involving Congress and the making of laws in the ordinary sense of the term. The president has still

pocket veto a presidential veto that is automatically triggered if the president does not act on a given piece of legislation passed during the final ten days of a legislative session

line-item veto the power of the executive to veto specific provisions (lines) of a bill passed by the legislature

legislative initiative the president's inherent power to bring a legislative agenda before Congress

executive order a rule or regulation issued by the president that has the effect and formal status of legislation

another legislative role (in all but name) within the executive branch. This is designated as the power to issue **executive orders.** The executive order is first and foremost simply a normal tool of management, a power possessed by virtually any CEO to make "company policy"—rules setting procedures, etiquette, chains of command, functional responsibilities, and so on. But evolving out of this normal management practice is a recognized presidential power to promulgate rules that have the effect and the formal status of legislation. Most of the executive orders of the president provide for the reorganization of structures and procedures or otherwise direct the affairs of the executive branch—either to be applied across the board to all agencies or applied in some important respect to a single agency or department. One of the most important examples is Executive Order No. 8248, September 8, 1939, establishing the divisions of the Executive Office of the President. Another one of equal importance is President Nixon's executive order establishing the Environmental Protection Agency in 1970–71, which included establishment of the Environmental Impact Statement. President Reagan's Executive Order No. 12291 of 1981 provided a regulatory reform process that was responsible for more genuine deregulation in the past twenty years than was accomplished by any acts of congressional legislation. President Clinton's most important policy toward gays and gay rights in the military took the form of an executive order referred to as "Don't ask, don't tell."

This legislative or policy leadership role of the presidency is an institutionalized feature of the office that exists independent of the occupant of the office. That is to say, anyone duly elected president would possess these powers regardless of his or her individual energy or leadership characteristics.[12]

DELEGATED POWERS

Many of the powers exercised by the president and the executive branch are not found in the Constitution but are the products of congressional statutes and resolutions. Over the past three-quarters of a century, Congress has voluntarily delegated a great deal of its own legislative authority to the executive branch. To some extent, this delegation of power has been an almost inescapable consequence of the expansion of government activity in the United States since the New Deal. Given the vast range of the federal government's responsibilities, Congress cannot execute and administer all the programs it creates and the laws it enacts. Inevitably, Congress must turn to the hundreds of departments and agencies in the executive branch or, when necessary, create new agencies to implement its goals. Thus, for example, in 2002, when Congress sought to protect America from terrorist attacks, it established a Department of Homeland Security and gave it broad powers in the realms of law enforcement, public health, and immigration. Similarly, in 1970, when Congress enacted legislation designed to improve the nation's air and water quality, it assigned the task of implementing its goals to a new Environmental Protection Agency (EPA) created by an executive order issued by President Nixon. Congress gave the EPA substantial power to set and enforce air and water quality standards.

As they implement congressional legislation, federal agencies collectively develop thousands of rules and regulations and issue thousands of orders and findings every year. Agencies interpret Congress's intent, promulgate rules aimed at implementing that intent, and issue orders to individuals, firms, and organizations throughout the nation designed to impel them to conform to the law. When it establishes an agency, Congress sometimes grants it only limited discretionary authority, providing very specific guidelines and standards that must be followed by the administrators charged with the program's implementation. Take the Internal Revenue Service (IRS), for example. Most Americans view the IRS as a powerful agency whose dictates can have an immediate and sometimes unpleasant impact on their lives. Yet congressional tax legislation is very specific and detailed and leaves little to the discretion of IRS administrators.[13] The agency certainly develops numerous rules and procedures to enhance tax collection. It is Congress, however, that establishes the structure of tax liabilities, tax exemptions, and tax deductions that determine each taxpayer's burdens and responsibilities.

In most instances, however, congressional legislation is not very detailed. Often, Congress defines a broad goal or objective and delegates enormous discretionary power to administrators to determine how that goal is to be achieved. For example, the 1970 act creating the Occupational Safety and Health Administration (OSHA) states, as Congress's purpose, "to assure so far as is possible every working man and woman in the nation safe and healthful working conditions." The act, however, neither defines such conditions nor suggests how they might be achieved.[14] The result is that agency administrators have enormous discretionary power to draft rules and regulations that have the effect of law. Indeed, the courts treat these administrative rules like congressional statutes. For all intents and purposes, when Congress creates an agency like OSHA or the EPA, giving it broad mandate to achieve some desirable outcome, it transfers its own legislative power to the executive branch.

In the nineteenth and early twentieth centuries, Congress typically wrote laws that provided fairly clear principles and standards to guide executive implementation. For example, the 1923 tariff act empowered the president to increase or decrease duties on certain manufactured goods in order to reduce the difference in costs between domestically produced products and those manufactured abroad. The act authorized the president to make the final determination, but his discretionary authority was quite constrained. The statute listed the criteria the president was to consider, fixed the permissible range of tariff changes, and outlined the procedures to be used to calculate the cost differences between foreign and domestic goods. When an importer challenged a particular executive decision as an abuse of delegated power, the Supreme Court had no difficulty finding that the president was merely acting in accordance with Congress's directives.[15]

At least since the New Deal, however, Congress has tended to give executive agencies broad mandates and to draft legislation that offers few clear standards or guidelines for implementation by the executive. For example, the 1933 National Industrial Recovery Act gave the president the authority to set rules to bring about *fair competition* in key sectors of the economy without ever defining what the term meant or how it was to be achieved.[16] Similarly, the 1938 Agricultural Adjustment Act, which led to a system of commodity price supports and agricultural production restrictions, authorized the secretary of agriculture to make agricultural marketing "orderly" without offering any guidance regarding the commodities to be affected, how markets were to be organized, or how prices should be determined. All these decisions were left to the discretion of the secretary and his agents.[17] This

The Roles of the President

Chief of State (acting on behalf of all Americans)

Commander in Chief (in charge of military)

Chief Jurist (judicial responsibilities)

Chief Diplomat (managing our relations with other nations)

Chief Executive (as "boss" of executive branch)

Chief Legislator (legislative powers)

Chief Politician (party leadership)

FOR CRITICAL ANALYSIS

Presidents have expressed, delegated, and inherent sources of power. Which of the three do you think most accounts for the powers of the presidency? Is it, in fact, possible to discern among these the true source of presidential power? Select a president and discuss the ways in which that particular president used each source of power to succeed in the presidency.

The Cabinet Departments

Department Created	Year
State	1789
Treasury	1789
Defense*	1947
Justice	1789
Interior†	1849
Agriculture	1889
Commerce	1913
Labor	1913
Health and Human Services††	1953
Housing and Urban Development	1965
Transportation	1966
Energy	1977
Education	1979
Veterans Affairs	1989
Homeland Security	2002

*Formerly the War and Navy Departments, created in 1789 and 1798, respectively.
†Created in 1862; made part of Cabinet in 1889.
††Formerly Health, Education, and Welfare; reorganized in 1979 (when separate Department of Education was created).

Cabinet the secretaries, or chief administrators, of the major departments of the federal government. Cabinet secretaries are appointed by the president with the consent of the Senate

pattern of broad delegation became typical in the ensuing decades. The 1972 Consumer Product Safety Act, for example, authorizes the Consumer Product Safety Commission to reduce unreasonable risk of injury from household products but offers no suggestions to guide the commission's determination of what constitutes reasonable and unreasonable risks or how these are to be reduced.[18]

This shift from the nineteenth-century pattern of relatively well-defined congressional guidelines to administrators to the more contemporary pattern of broad delegations of congressional power to the executive branch is, to be sure, partially a consequence of the great scope and complexity of the tasks that America's contemporary government has undertaken. During much of the nineteenth century, the federal government had relatively few domestic responsibilities and Congress could pay close attention to details. Today, the operation of an enormous executive establishment and literally thousands of programs under varied and changing circumstances requires that administrators be allowed some considerable measure of discretion to carry out their jobs. Nevertheless, the end result is to shift power from Congress to the executive branch.

The Presidency as an Institution

The framers of the Constitution, as we saw, created a unitary executive because they thought this would make the presidency a more energetic institution. Nevertheless, since the ratification of the Constitution, the president has been joined by thousands of officials and staffers who work for, assist, or advise the chief executive (see Figure 13.2). Collectively, these individuals could be said to make up the institutional presidency and to give the president a capacity for action that no single individual, however energetic, could duplicate. The first component of the institutional presidency is the president's *Cabinet*.

THE CABINET

In the American system of government, the **Cabinet** is the traditional but informal designation for the heads of all the major federal government departments. The Cabinet has no constitutional status. Unlike in England and many other parliamentary countries, where the cabinet *is* the government, the American Cabinet is not a collective body. It meets but makes no decisions as a group. Each appointment must be approved by the Senate, but Cabinet members are not responsible to the Senate or to Congress at large. Cabinet appointments help build party and popular support, but the Cabinet is not a party organ. The Cabinet is made up of directors, but is not a true board of directors.

Aware of this fact, the president tends to develop a burning impatience with and a mild distrust of Cabinet members; to make the Cabinet a rubber stamp for actions already decided on; and to demand results, or the appearance of results, more immediately and more frequently than most department heads can provide. Since Cabinet appointees generally have not shared political careers with the president or with each other, and since they may meet literally for the first time after their selection, the formation of an effective governing group out of this motley collection of appointments is unlikely. Although President Clinton's insistence on a

The Institutional Presidency

Figure 13.2

The President

The White House Staff

Executive Office of the President

White House Office
Office of Management and Budget
Council of Economic Advisers
National Security Council
Office of National Drug Control Policy

Office of the U.S. Trade Representative
Council on Environmental Quality
Office of Science and Technology Policy
Office of Policy Development
Office of Administration
Vice President

The Cabinet

Department of Justice	Department of Defense	Department of State	
Department of Homeland Security	Department of Health and Human Services	Department of the Treasury	Department of Agriculture
Department of Housing and Urban Development	Department of the Interior	Department of Commerce	Department of Labor
Department of Education	Department of Transportation	Department of Energy	Department of Veterans Affairs

Independent Establishments and Government Corporations

Cabinet diverse enough to resemble American society could be considered an act of political wisdom, it virtually guaranteed that few of his appointees had ever spent much time working together or even knew the policy positions or beliefs of the other appointees.[19]

Some presidents have relied more heavily on an "inner Cabinet," the **National Security Council (NSC)**. The NSC, established by law in 1947, is composed of the president, the vice president, the secretaries of state, defense, and the treasury, the attorney general, and other officials invited by the president. It has its own staff of foreign-policy specialists run by the special assistant to the president for national security affairs. For these highest appointments, presidents turn to people from outside Washington, usually longtime associates. George W. Bush's "inner Cabinet" is composed largely of former and proven senior staffers and Cabinet members of former Republican administrations, most particularly Vice President Cheney, Defense Secretary Rumsfeld, Secretary of State Powell, and National Security Adviser Condoleezza Rice.

Presidents have obviously been uneven and unpredictable in their reliance on the NSC and other subcabinet bodies because executive management is inherently a personal matter. Despite all the personal variations, however, one generalization can be made: presidents have increasingly preferred the White House staff instead of the Cabinet as their means of managing the gigantic executive branch.

THE WHITE HOUSE STAFF

The **White House staff** is composed mainly of analysts and advisers.[20] Although many of the top White House staff members are given the title "special assistant" for a particular task or sector, the types of judgments they are expected to make and the kinds of advice they are supposed to give are a good deal broader and more generally political than those coming from the Executive Office of the President or from the Cabinet departments. The members of the White House staff also tend to be more closely associated with the president than other presidentially appointed officials.

From an informal group of fewer than a dozen people (popularly called the **Kitchen Cabinet**), and no more than four dozen at the height of the domestic Roosevelt presidency in 1937, the White House staff has grown substantially with each successive president.[21] Richard Nixon employed 550 people in 1972. President Carter, who found so many of the requirements of presidential power distasteful, and who publicly vowed to keep his staff small and decentralized, built an even larger and more centralized staff. President Clinton reduced the White House staff by 20 percent, but a large White House staff is still essential.

THE EXECUTIVE OFFICE OF THE PRESIDENT

The development of the White House staff can be appreciated only in its relation to the still-larger **Executive Office of the President (EOP).** Created in 1939, the EOP is a major part of what is often called the "institutional presidency"—the permanent agencies that perform defined management tasks for the president. The most important and the largest EOP agency is the Office of Management and Budget (OMB). Its roles in preparing the national budget, designing the president's program, reporting on agency activities, and overseeing regulatory proposals make OMB personnel part of virtually every conceivable presidential responsibility. The status and power of the

National Security Council (NSC) a presidential foreign policy advisory council composed of the president; the vice president; the secretaries of state, defense, and the treasury; the attorney general; and other officials invited by the president

White House staff analysts and advisers to the president, often given the title "special assistant"

Kitchen Cabinet an informal group of advisers to whom the president turns for counsel and guidance. Members of the official Cabinet may or may not also be members of the Kitchen Cabinet

Executive Office of the President (EOP) the permanent agencies that perform defined management tasks for the president. Created in 1939, the EOP includes the Office of Management and Budget, the Council of Economic Advisers, the National Security Council, and other agencies

OMB have grown in importance with each successive president. The process of budgeting at one time was a "bottom-up" procedure, with expenditure and program requests passing from the lowest bureaus through the departments to "clearance" in OMB and hence to Congress, where each agency could be called in to reveal what its "original request" had been before OMB revised it. Now the budgeting process is "top-down"; OMB sets the terms of discourse for agencies as well as for Congress. The director of OMB is now one of the most powerful officials in Washington.

The staff of the Council of Economic Advisers (CEA) constantly analyzes the economy and economic trends and attempts to give the president the ability to anticipate events rather than to wait and react to events. The Council on Environmental Quality was designed to do the same for environmental issues as the CEA does for economic issues. The National Security Council (NSC) is composed of designated Cabinet officials who meet regularly with the president to give advice on the large national security picture. The staff of the NSC assimilates and analyzes data from all intelligence-gathering agencies (CIA, etc.). Other EOP agencies perform more specialized tasks.

Somewhere between 1,500 and 2,000 highly specialized people work for EOP agencies.[22] The importance of each agency in the EOP varies according to the personal orientation of each president. For example, the NSC staff was of immense importance under President Nixon, especially because it served essentially as the personal staff of presidential assistant Henry Kissinger. But it was of less importance to President George H. W. Bush, who looked outside the EOP altogether for military policy matters, turning much more to the Joint Chiefs of Staff and its chair at the time, General Colin Powell.

THE VICE PRESIDENCY

The vice presidency is a constitutional anomaly even though the office was created along with the presidency by the Constitution. The vice president exists for two purposes only: to succeed the president in case of death, resignation, or incapacitation and to preside over the Senate, casting a tie-breaking vote when necessary.[23]

The main value of the vice presidency as a political resource for the president is electoral. Traditionally, a presidential candidate's most important rule for the choice of a running mate is that he or she bring the support of at least one state (preferably a large one) not otherwise likely to support the ticket. Another rule holds that the vice presidential nominee should provide some regional balance and, wherever possible, some balance among various ideological or ethnic subsections of the party. It is very doubtful that John Kennedy would have won in 1960 without his vice presidential candidate, Lyndon Johnson, and the contribution Johnson made to winning in Texas. George W. Bush's choice of Dick Cheney in 2000 was completely devoid of direct electoral value, since Cheney came from one of our least populous states (Wyoming, which casts only three electoral votes). But given Cheney's stalwart right-wing record both in Congress and as President Bush's secretary of defense, coupled with his even more prominently right-wing wife, Lynne Cheney, his inclusion on the Republican ticket was clearly an effort to consolidate the support of the restive right wing of his party. In 2004, John Kerry chose Senator John Edwards of North Carolina as his vice-presidential running mate. Edwards was viewed as an effective campaigner and fund-raiser who might bolster the Democratic ticket's prospects in the South and in rural parts of the

Throughout history, presidential wives have played an important, even decisive role in the administrations of their spouses. The nation's first first lady, Martha Washington, called herself "the hostess of the nation." Prior to becoming first lady, Martha Washington helped feed and nurse wounded American troops during the long winter at Valley Forge.

Midwest. In the end, the Democrats failed to carry a single Southern state, losing even North Carolina. Edwards also created a controversy with his comments about the sexual orientation of Vice President Cheney's daughter during their nationally televised debate.

As the institutional presidency has grown in size and complexity, most presidents of the past twenty-five years have sought to use their vice presidents as a management resource after the election. George H. W. Bush, as vice president, was "kept within the loop" of decision making because President Reagan delegated so much power. A copy of virtually everything made for Reagan was made for Bush, especially during the first term, when Bush's close friend James Baker was chief of staff. Former President Bush did not take such pains to keep Dan Quayle "in the loop," but President Clinton relied greatly on his vice president, Al Gore, and Gore emerged as one of the most trusted and effective figures in the Clinton White House. Gore's most important task was to oversee the National Performance Review (NPR), an ambitious program to "reinvent" the way the federal government conducts its affairs. The presidency of George W. Bush has resulted in unprecedented power and responsibility for his vice president, Dick Cheney. Before becoming vice president, Cheney served as chief executive of Halliburton—the world's largest oil-and-gas services company—for five years (from 1995 to 2000), and developed the reputation, among supporters and critics, for being a "man who gets things done." Known as a hands-on vice president, he plays an active role in cabinet meetings and policy formation, and directed the National Energy Policy Development Group, for which the Bush administration received some criticism when the Enron scandal unfolded in 2002. Cheney is widely viewed as one of the most influential, if not the most influential, vice presidents in American history.

THE FIRST LADY

The president serves as both chief executive and chief of state—the equivalent of Great Britain's prime minister and king rolled into one, simultaneously leading the government and serving as a symbol of the nation at official ceremonies and func-

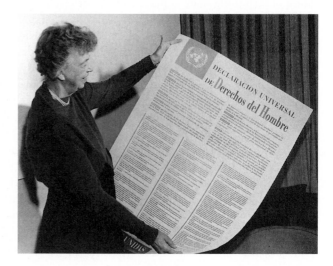

Eleanor Roosevelt was the first first lady to hold regular press conferences; she served as the administration's spokesperson on matters pertaining to race relations and human rights.

tions. For their part, most first ladies (all presidents so far have been men) limit their activities to the ceremonial portion of the presidency. First ladies greet foreign dignitaries, visit other countries, attend important national ceremonies, and otherwise act as America's "queen" when the president is called upon to serve in a kingly capacity.

Because the first lady is generally associated exclusively with the head of state aspect of America's presidency, she is usually not subject to the same sort of media scrutiny or partisan attack as that aimed at the president. Yet this has changed in recent times as first ladies have begun to exert more influence over policy. Franklin Roosevelt's wife, Eleanor, was widely popular, but also widely criticized, for her active role in many elements of her husband's presidency. She was a tireless advocate for the poor, the working class, and African Americans. She was also the first first lady to hold a former government post—assistant director of the Office of Civil Defense. Lyndon Johnson's wife, Lady Bird, headed the national campaign to beautify America. More recently, Jimmy Carter's wife, Rosalynn, sat in on Cabinet meetings, and was considered a close adviser to her husband on policy matters. President Reagan's wife, Nancy, exercised great control over her husband's schedule and over who could and could not see him. Hillary Clinton played a major political and policy role in Bill Clinton's presidency. During the 1992 campaign, Bill Clinton often implied that she would be active in the administration by joking that voters would get "two for the price of one." After the election, Hillary took a leading role in many policy areas, most notably heading the administration's health care reform effort. Like Eleanor Roosevelt, Hillary Clinton was fiercely criticized for exercising too much influence over her husband's administration. She also became the first first lady to seek public office on her own when she ran for and won a seat in the U.S. Senate in New York in 2000.

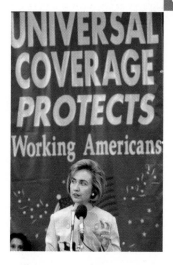

Hillary Rodham Clinton was active in White House policy making, most notably as head of the Task Force on National Health Care Reform, one of the policy priorities of the Clinton adminstration. Some complained about the prominent role of the first lady, and many blamed her for the failure to pass health care reform.

THE PRESIDENT AND POLICY

The president's powers and institutional resources, taken together, give the chief executive a substantial voice in the nation's policy-making processes. Strictly speaking, presidents cannot introduce legislation. Only members of Congress can formally propose new programs and policies. Nevertheless, a great many of the major bills acted on by the Congress are crafted by the president and his aides and then introduced by friendly legislators. Congress has come to expect the president to propose the government's budget, and the nation has come to expect presidential initiatives to deal with major problems. Some of these initiatives have come in the form of huge packages of programs—Franklin Roosevelt's "New Deal" and Lyndon Johnson's "Great Society." Sometimes presidents

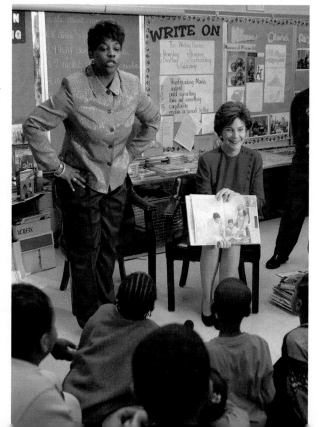

Former schoolteacher Laura Bush's policy focus has been on education and literacy. She frequently visits elementary schools and also sponsors White House events focused on American literature.

mandate a claim by a victorious candidate that the electorate has given him or her special authority to carry out promises made during the campaign

craft a single program they hope will have a significant impact on the nation and on their political fortunes. For example, Bill Clinton developed a major health care reform initiative whose political defeat marked a significant setback for his presidency. George Bush made the "War on Terrorism" the centerpiece of his administration. To fight this war, Bush brought about the creation of a new cabinet department—the Department of Homeland Security—and the enactment of such pieces of legislation as the USA PATRIOT Act to give the executive branch more power to deal with the terrorist threat. Going beyond terrorism, Bush also presided over the enactment of a huge expansion of the Medicare program to provide prescription drug benefits for senior citizens. All this from a president who was said to lack a popular **mandate** in the wake of the controversial 2000 election. Bush may have lacked a mandate, but the expressed and delegated powers of the office gave him the resources through which to prevail.

At one time, historians and journalists liked to debate the question of strong versus weak presidents. Some presidents, such as Lincoln and FDR, were called "strong" for their leadership and ability to guide the nation's political agenda. Others, like Buchanan and Coolidge, were seen as "weak" for failing to develop significant legislative programs and seeming to observe rather than shape political events. Today, the strong versus weak categorization has become moot. *Every president is strong.* This strength is not so much a function of personal charisma or political savvy as it is a reflection of the increasing power of the institution of the presidency. Let us see how this came about.

The Contemporary Bases of Presidential Power

In the nineteenth century, Congress was America's dominant institution of government whose members sometimes treated the president with disdain. Today, however, no one would assert that the presidency is an unimportant institution. Presidents seek to dominate the policy-making process and claim the inherent power to lead the nation in time of war. The expansion of presidential power over the course of the past century has not come about by accident but as the result of an ongoing effort by successive presidents to enlarge the powers of the office. Some of these efforts have succeeded and others have failed. As the framers of the Constitution predicted, presidential *ambition* has been a powerful and unrelenting force in American politics.

Generally, presidents can expand their power in three ways: party, popular mobilization, and administration. In the first instance, presidents may construct or strengthen national partisan institutions with which to exert influence in the legislative process and through which to implement their programs. Alternatively, or in addition to the first tactic, presidents may use popular appeals to create a mass base of support that will allow them to subordinate their political foes. This tactic has sometimes been called the strategy of "going public" or the "rhetorical" presidency.[24] Third, presidents may seek to bolster their control of established executive agencies or to create new administrative institutions and procedures that will reduce their dependence on Congress and give them a more independent governing and policy-making capability. Presidents' use of executive orders to achieve their policy goals in lieu of seeking to persuade Congress to enact legislation is, perhaps, the most obvious example.

PARTY AS A SOURCE OF POWER

All presidents have relied on the members and leaders of their own party to implement their legislative agendas. President Bush, for example, has worked closely with congressional GOP leaders on such matters as energy policy and Medicare reform. But the president does not control his own party; party members have considerable autonomy. Moreover, in America's system of separated powers, the president's party may be in the minority in Congress and unable to do much for the chief executive's programs (see Figure 13.3). Consequently, although their party is valuable to chief executives, it has not been a fully reliable presidential tool. As a result, contemporary presidents are more likely to use two other methods—popular mobilization and executive administration—to achieve their political goals.

GOING PUBLIC

Popular mobilization as a technique of presidential power has its historical roots in the presidencies of Theodore Roosevelt and Woodrow Wilson and has, subsequently,

The Presidential Batting Average: Presidential Success on Congressional Votes* (1953–2003)

Figure 13.3

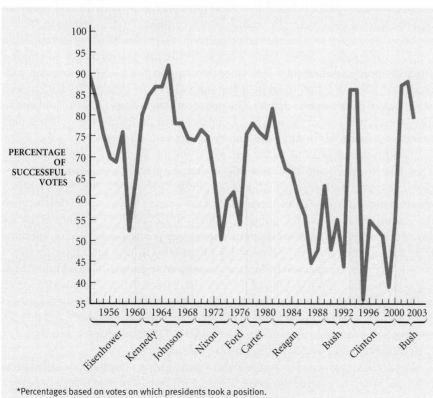

*Percentages based on votes on which presidents took a position.
SOURCE: *Congressional Quarterly Weekly Report*, January 3, 2004, p. 18.

President Theodore Roosevelt was the model for the twentieth-century president through his cultivation of a direct relationship with the American public. Roosevelt saw the presidency as a "bully pulpit," a terrific platform from which to persuasively advocate his agenda. Three decades later, President Franklin D. Roosevelt's direct appeals to the American people allowed FDR to "reach over the heads" of congressional opponents and force them to follow his lead because their constituents demanded it.

become a weapon in the political arsenals of most presidents since the mid-twentieth century. During the nineteenth century, it was considered rather inappropriate for presidents to engage in personal campaigning on their own behalf or in support of programs and policies. When Andrew Jackson broke this unwritten rule and made a series of speeches vehemently seeking public support for his Reconstruction program, even some of Johnson's most ardent supporters were shocked at what was seen as his lack of decorum and dignity. The president's opponents cited his "inflammatory" speeches in one of the articles of impeachment drafted by the Congress pursuant to the first effort in American history to oust a sitting president.[25]

The first presidents to make systematic use of appeals to the public were Theodore Roosevelt and Woodrow Wilson, but the president who used public appeals most effectively was Franklin D. Roosevelt. Political scientist Sydney Milkis observes that FDR was "firmly persuaded of the need to form a direct link between the executive office and the public."[26] Roosevelt developed a number of tactics aimed at forging such a link. Like his predecessors, he often embarked on speaking trips around the nation to promote his programs. On one such tour, he told a crowd, "I regain strength just by meeting the American people."[27] In addition, FDR made limited but important use of the new electronic medium, the radio, to reach millions of Americans. In his famous "fireside chats," the president, or at least his voice, came into every living room in the country to discuss programs and policies and generally to assure Americans that Franklin Delano Roosevelt was aware of their difficulties and working diligently toward solutions.

Roosevelt was also an innovator in the realm of what now might be called press relations. When he entered the White House, FDR faced a mainly hostile press typically controlled by conservative members of the business establishment. As the

President Bill Clinton was a master of the televised town meeting, in which the president gives the appearance of consulting average citizens on important policy issues. Clinton's technique illustrated how campaign-style events could become tools to shape and sell national policy. President George W. Bush also made direct appeals to the public in cozy voter forums. One Bush innovation was to distribute tickets to these forums in advance so that the audience was comprised of his supporters.

president wrote, "All the fat-cat newspapers—85 percent of the whole—have been utterly opposed to everything the Administration is seeking."[28] Roosevelt hoped to be able to use the press to mold public opinion, but to do so he needed to circumvent the editors and publishers who were generally unsympathetic to his goals. To this end, the president worked to cultivate the reporters who covered the White House. Roosevelt made himself available for biweekly press conferences where he offered candid answers to reporters' questions and made certain to make important policy announcements that would provide the reporters with significant stories to file with their papers.[29] Roosevelt was the first president to designate a press secretary (Stephen Early) who was charged with organizing the press conferences and making certain that reporters observed the informal rules distinguishing presidential comments that were off the record from those that could be attributed directly to the president.

Every president since FDR has sought to craft a public relations strategy that would emphasize the incumbent's strengths and maximize his popular appeal. For Kennedy, handsome and quick-witted, the televised press conference was an excellent public relations vehicle. Johnson and Nixon lacked Kennedy's charisma but both were effective television speakers, usually reading from a prepared text. Jimmy Carter and Bill Clinton occasionally addressed the nation and sometimes held press conferences, but both preferred other media formats. Both men made extensive use of televised town meetings—carefully staged events in which the president would not be asked the sorts of pointed questions preferred by reporters and gave the president an opportunity to appear to consult with rank-and-file citizens about his goals and policies. Like other presidents, Clinton also relied on friendly journalists to write favorable stories about the administration.

One Clinton innovation was to make the White House Communications Office an important institution within the Executive Office of the President (EOP). In a practice continued by George W. Bush, the Communications Office became responsible not only for responding to reporters' queries but for developing and implementing a coordinated communications strategy—promoting the president's policy goals, developing responses to unflattering news stories, and making certain that a favorable image of the president would, insofar as possible, dominate the news. The Communications Office, in effect, institutionalized the functions undertaken on an ad hoc basis by media-savvy presidents like the Roosevelts and their staffers. George W. Bush's first communications director, Karen Hughes, sought to put the office "ahead of the news," constantly developing stories that would dominate the headlines, present the president in a favorable light, and deflect criticism. For example, after the administration responded to the September 11 terrorist attacks against the World Trade Center and Pentagon with a massive military campaign in Afghanistan, the Communications Office developed several stories that made it difficult for administration critics to gain much traction. One such story concerned the brutal treatment of women by Afghanistan's fundamentalist Taliban regime, and this treatment was underlined in several speeches by First Lady Laura Bush and communicated to the press in hundreds of news releases. The wave of publicity the Communications Office was able to generate concerning the Taliban's harsh and demeaning posture toward women was one factor that made it extremely difficult for the Bush administration's liberal critics to utter even a word of protest regarding America's determined effort to oust the Taliban from power.

In addition to utilizing the media, recent presidents, particularly Bill Clinton, have reached out directly to the American public to gain its approval. President Clinton's enormously high public profile, as is indicated by the number of public appearances he made (see Figure 13.4), is only the most recent dramatic expression of the presidency as a **"permanent campaign"** for re-election. A study by political scientist Charles O. Jones shows that President Clinton engaged in campaignlike activity throughout his presidency and was the most-traveled American president in history. In his first twenty months in office, he made 203 appearances outside of Washington, compared with 178 for George H. W. Bush and 58 for Ronald Reagan. President George W. Bush might outdo them all. During his first hundred days, Bush gave speeches and other public appearances in twenty-six states; Clinton's and former president Bush's record during their first hundred days was fifteen states. Reagan went to a mere two states. In light of the need to mobilize the American people after September 11, 2001, Bush's number of appearances outside of Washington far exceeded that of Bill Clinton.

The permanent campaign serves two major purposes related to re-election: building mass popularity and raising campaign funds. Despite the growing controversy over campaign-finance abuses in 1997 and after, President Clinton attended numerous events to raise money to pay off the $30 million of debt from his 1996 presidential campaign. In fact, even during the most intense moments of the Monica Lewinsky scandal of early 1998, Clinton continued his fund-raising for the party, and the Democratic National Committee had to add staff to answer all the telephone calls and letters that were responding positively to President Clinton's appeals.

permanent campaign description of presidential politics in which all presidential actions are taken with re-election in mind

Public Appearances by Presidents, 1929–95

Figure 13.4

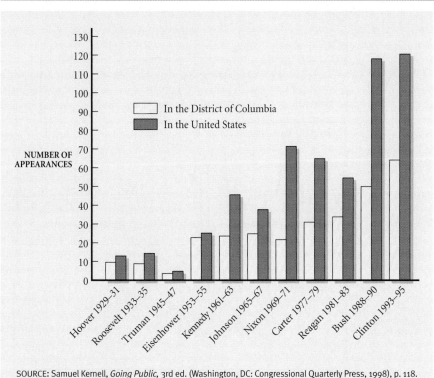

SOURCE: Samuel Kernell, *Going Public,* 3rd ed. (Washington, DC: Congressional Quarterly Press, 1998), p. 118.

President Bill Clinton made more public appearances in his first three years in office than any of his predecessors did in their first three years.

The Limits of Going Public Some presidents have been able to make effective use of popular appeals to overcome congressional opposition. Popular support, though, has not been a firm foundation for presidential power. To begin with, popular support is notoriously fickle. President George W. Bush maintained an approval rating of over 70 percent for more than a year following the September 11 terrorist attacks. By 2003, however, his approval rating had fallen nearly twenty points as American casualties in Iraq mounted. After America's triumph in the 1990 Persian Gulf War, President George H. W. Bush scored a remarkable 90 percent approval rating in the polls. Two years later, however, after the 1991 budget crisis, Bush's support plummeted and the president was defeated in his bid for reelection. During his first two years in office, Ronald Reagan's approval score ranged from a high of 59 percent in 1981 to a low of 37 percent in early 1983.[30] As Reagan's poll standing fell, his ability to overawe Democratic opponents and retain the support of wavering Republicans diminished sharply. Such declines in popular approval during a president's term in office are nearly inevitable and follow a predictable pattern (see Figure 13.5).[31] Presidents generate popular support by promising to undertake important programs that will contribute directly to the well-being of large numbers of Americans. Almost inevitably, presidential performance falls short of promises and popular expectations, leading to a sharp decline in public support and ensuing collapse of presidential influence.[32]

Presidents have certainly not abandoned "going public," but they no longer do so as frequently as they once did—there has been, for example, a decline in presidential

Presidential Performance Ratings from Kennedy to Bush

In presidential performance rating polls, respondents are asked, "Do you approve of the way the president is handling his job?" This graph shows the percentage of positive responses.

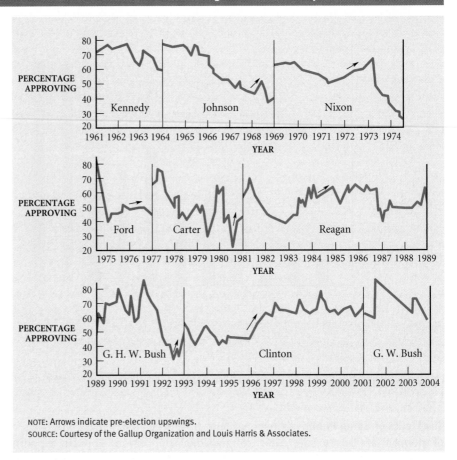

NOTE: Arrows indicate pre-election upswings.
SOURCE: Courtesy of the Gallup Organization and Louis Harris & Associates.

appearances on prime-time television over the past four administrations.[33] Instead, presidents have employed institutionalized public and media relations efforts more to create a generally favorable public image than to promote specific policies. Thus, in 2002, President George W. Bush made several speeches to boost the proposed creation of a Homeland Security department. At the same time, however, the White House Communications office was engaged in a nonstop, seven-day-a-week effort to promote news and feature stories aimed at bolstering the president's more general public image. Stories emphasized the president's empathy for retirees hurt by the downturn of stock prices; the president's anger over corporate abuses; the president's concern for the environment; the president's determination to prevent terrorism; the president's support for Israel; and so forth. These are all examples of image-polishing rather than going public on behalf of specific programs. Confronted with the limitations of a strategy of popular mobilization, presidents have shifted from an offensive strategy to a more defensive mode in this domain. The limitations of going public as a route to presidential power have also led contemporary presidents to make use of a third technique: expansion of their administrative capabilities.

THE ADMINISTRATIVE STATE

Contemporary presidents have increased the administrative capabilities of their office in three ways. First, they have enhanced the reach and power of the Executive Office of the President (EOP). Second, they have sought to increase White House control over the federal bureaucracy. Third, they have expanded the role of executive orders and other instruments of direct presidential governance. Taken together, these three components of what might be called the White House "administrative strategy" have given presidents a capacity to achieve their programmatic and policy goals even when they are unable to secure congressional approval. Indeed, some recent presidents have been able to accomplish quite a bit without much congressional, partisan, or even public support.

The Executive Office of the President   The Executive Office of the President has grown from six administrative assistants in 1939 to today's 400 employees working directly for the president in the White House office along with some 1,400 individuals staffing the several (currently eight) divisions of the Executive Office.[34] The creation and growth of the White House staff gives the president an enormously enhanced capacity to gather information, plan programs and strategies, communicate with constituencies, and exercise supervision over the executive branch. The staff multiplied the president's eyes, ears, and arms, becoming a critical instrument of presidential power.[35]

In particular, the Office of Management and Budget (OMB) serves as a potential instrument of presidential control over federal spending and hence a mechanism through which the White House has greatly expanded its power. The OMB has the capacity to analyze and approve all legislative proposals, not only budgetary requests, emanating from all federal agencies before being submitted to Congress. This procedure, now a matter of routine, greatly enhanced the president's control over the entire executive branch. All legislation emanating from the White House as well as all executive orders also go through the OMB.[36] Thus, in one White House agency, the president has the means to exert major influence over the flow of money as well as the shape and content of national legislation.

Regulatory Review   A second tactic that presidents have used to increase their power and reach is the process of regulatory review, through which presidents have sought to seize control of rule making by the agencies of the executive branch (also see Chapter 14). Whenever Congress enacts a statute, its actual implementation requires the promulgation of hundreds of rules by the agency charged with administering the law and giving effect to the will of Congress. Some congressional statutes are quite detailed and leave agencies with relatively little discretion. Typically, however, Congress enacts a relatively broad statement of legislative intent and delegates to the appropriate administrative agency the power to fill in many important details.[37] In other words, Congress typically says to an administrative agency, "Here is the problem: deal with it."[38]

The discretion Congress delegates to administrative agencies has provided recent presidents with an important avenue for expanding their own power. For example, President Clinton believed the president had full authority to order agencies of the executive branch to adopt such rules as the president thought appropriate.

During the course of his presidency, Clinton issued 107 directives to administrators ordering them to propose specific rules and regulations. In some instances, the language of the rule to be proposed was drafted by the White House staff; in other cases, the president asserted a priority but left it to the agency to draft the precise language of the proposal. Presidential rule-making directives covered a wide variety of topics. For example, Clinton ordered the Food and Drug Administration (FDA) to develop rules designed to restrict the marketing of tobacco products to children. White House and FDA staffers then spent several months preparing nearly 1,000 pages of new regulations affecting tobacco manufacturers and vendors.[39] Republicans, of course, denounced Clinton's actions as a usurpation of power.[40] However, after he took office, President George W. Bush made no move to surrender the powers Clinton had claimed. Quite the contrary. Bush continued the Clinton era practice of issuing presidential directives to agencies to spur them to issue new rules and regulations.

Governing by Decree: Executive Orders   A third mechanism through which contemporary presidents have sought to enhance their power to govern unilaterally is through the use of executive orders and other forms of presidential decrees, including executive agreements, national security findings and directives, proclamations, reorganization plans, the signing of statements, and a host of others.[41] Executive orders have a long history in the United States and have been the vehicles for a number of important government policies, including the purchase of Louisiana, the annexation of Texas, the emancipation of the slaves, the internment of the Japanese, the desegregation of the military, the initiation of affirmative action, and the creation of important federal agencies, among them the EPA, FDA, and Peace Corps.[42]

While wars and national emergencies produce the highest volume of executive orders, such presidential actions also occur frequently in peacetime (see Figure 13.6). In the realm of foreign policy, unilateral presidential actions in the form of executive agreements have virtually replaced treaties as the nation's chief foreign policy instruments.[43] Presidential decrees, however, are often used for purely domestic purposes.

Presidents may not use executive orders to issue whatever commands they please. The use of such decrees is bound by law. If a president issues an executive order, proclamation, directive, or the like, in principle he does so pursuant to the powers granted to him by the Constitution or delegated to him by Congress, usually through a statute. When presidents issue such orders, they generally state the constitutional or statutory basis for their actions. For example, when President Truman ordered the desegregation of the armed services, he did so pursuant to his constitutional powers as commander in chief. In a similar vein, when President Johnson issued Executive Order 11246, he asserted that the order was designed to implement the 1964 Civil Rights Act, which prohibited employment discrimination. Where an executive order has no statutory or constitutional basis, the courts have held it to be void. The most important case on this point is *Youngstown Co. v. Sawyer,* the so-called steel seizure case of 1952.[44] Here, the Supreme Court ruled that President Truman's seizure of the nation's steel mills during the Korean War had no statutory or constitutional basis and was thus invalid.

A number of court decisions, though, have established broad boundaries that leave considerable room for presidential action. By illustration, the courts have

Significant Executive Orders, 1900–1996

Figure 13.6

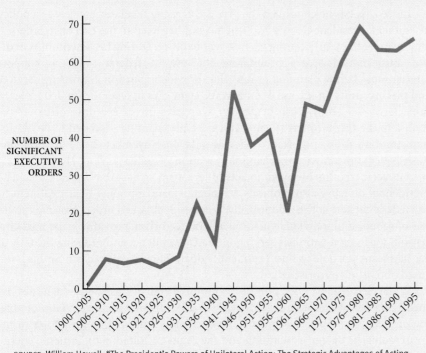

NUMBER OF SIGNIFICANT EXECUTIVE ORDERS

SOURCE: William Howell, "The President's Powers of Unilateral Action: The Strategic Advantages of Acting Alone" (Ph.D. diss., Stanford University, 1999).

held that Congress might approve presidential action after the fact or, in effect, ratify presidential action through "acquiescence," for example, by not objecting for long periods of time or by continuing to provide funding for programs established by executive orders. In addition, the courts have indicated that some areas, most notably the realm of military policy, are presidential in character and have allowed presidents wide latitude to make policy by executive decree. Thus, within the very broad limits established by the courts, presidential orders can be and have been important policy tools.

President Clinton issued numerous orders designed to promote a coherent set of policy goals: protecting the environment, strengthening federal regulatory power, shifting America's foreign policy from a unilateral to a multilateral focus, expanding affirmative action programs, and helping organized labor in its struggles with employers.[45] As in his use of regulatory review, President Clinton was able to craft a policy agenda through executive orders that he could not accomplish through legislation. Faced with a hostile Congress, Clinton turned to unilateral instruments of executive power including regulatory review, executive orders, and the like. Clinton certainly did not issue more executive orders than previous presidents. His innovation was to take an instrument that had been used sporadically and show that an activist president could develop and implement a significant policy agenda without legislation—a lesson that surely will not be lost on Clinton's successors.

Indeed, just as he continued the practice of using regulatory review as a policy instrument, President George W. Bush has not hesitated to use executive orders—issuing more than forty during his first year in office. During his first months in office, Bush issued orders prohibiting the use of federal funds to support international family planning groups that provided abortion-counseling services and placing limits on the use of embryonic stem cells in federally funded research projects. Subsequently, Bush made very aggressive use of executive orders in response to the threat of terrorism—which the president has declared to be his administration's most important policy agenda. In November 2001, for example, Bush issued a directive authorizing the creation of military tribunals to try noncitizens accused of involvement in acts of terrorism against the United States. The presidential directive also prohibits defendants from appealing their treatment to any federal or state court. Additionally, the president issued orders freezing the assets of groups and individuals associated with terrorism, providing expedited citizenship for foreign nationals serving in the U.S. military, and ordering the CIA to use all means possible to oust President Saddam Hussein of Iraq, whom Bush accused of plotting terrorist actions.

While terrorism was certainly at the top of President Bush's agenda, he also issued a number of executive orders having to do with domestic policy. For example, the president was able to overcome congressional resistance to his efforts to increase domestic energy exploration and the rapid exploitation of domestic energy resources. Like Clinton, however, President Bush discovered that an executive order can often substitute for legislation. In May 2001, Bush signed an executive order that closely followed a recommendation from the American Petroleum Institute, an oil industry trade association, to free energy companies from a number of federal regulations.

The Advantages of the Administrative Strategy   Through the course of American history, party leadership and popular appeals have played important roles in presidential efforts to overcome political opposition. Both party and appeals to the people continue to be instruments of presidential power. Reagan's tax cuts and Clinton's budget victories were achieved with strong partisan support. George W. Bush, lacking the oratorical skills of a Reagan or a Roosevelt, nevertheless has made good use of sophisticated communications strategies to promote his agenda. Yet, as we saw, in the modern era parties have waned in institutional strength while the effects of popular appeals have often proven evanescent. The limitations of the alternatives have increasingly impelled presidents to try to expand the administrative capabilities of the office and their own capacity for unilateral action as means of achieving their policy goals. And in recent decades, the expansion of the Executive Office, the development of regulatory review, and the use of executive orders, the signing of statements, and the like have given presidents a substantial capacity to achieve significant policy results despite congressional opposition to their legislative agendas.

To be sure, the administrative strategy does not always succeed. In some instances over the years the federal courts have struck down unilateral actions by the president. And, occasionally, Congress acts to reverse presidential orders. For example, in 1999, Congress enacted legislation prohibiting the Department of Education from carrying out a presidential directive to administer national education tests.[46] In 2000, Congress went even a step further. In response to President Clinton's aggressive regulatory review program, the Republican-controlled Congress moved to strengthen its capacity to block the president's use of administrative directives by enacting the Congressional Review Act (CRA). This piece of legislation requires federal agencies to send all proposed regulations to Congress for review sixty days before they take effect. The act also creates a fast-track procedure to allow the House and Senate to enact a joint resolution of disapproval that not only would void the regulation but also would prohibit the agency from subsequently issuing any substantially similar rule. The first test of the act came after Clinton left office. In the early weeks of the Bush administration, Congress passed a joint resolution repealing an ergonomics standard that had been supported by the Clinton administration and adopted by the Occupational Safety and Health Administration (OSHA). President Bush, who opposed the standard, signed the resolution and the ergonomics standard was voided. While this outcome may be seen as an effective effort by Congress to thwart a presidential directive, it seems clear that Congress was successful only because Clinton was out of office. Had his term not expired, Clinton would almost certainly have vetoed the resolution. Indeed, one reason Clinton was willing to sign CRA into law in the first place was that the president retained the power to veto any action undertaken by Congress under the statute's authority.

In principle, perhaps, Congress could respond more vigorously than it has to unilateral policy making by the president. Certainly a Congress willing to impeach a president should have the mettle to overturn his administrative directives. But the president has significant advantages in such struggles with Congress. In battles over presidential directives and orders, Congress is on the defensive, reacting to presidential initiatives. The framers of the Constitution saw "energy," or the ability to take the initiative, as a key feature of executive power.[47] When the president takes action by issuing an order or an administrative directive, Congress must initiate the cumbersome and time-consuming law-making process, overcome internal divisions, and enact legislation that the president may ultimately veto. Moreover, as Terry Moe has argued, in such battles Congress faces a significant collective action problem insofar as members are likely to be more sensitive to the substance of a president's actions and its effects on their constituents than to the more general implications of presidential power for the long-term vitality of their institution.[48]

FOR CRITICAL ANALYSIS

In recent years, the power of the presidency has expanded significantly as presidents have increasingly relied on executive orders, executive agreements, and other unilateral instruments to govern. Is the United States becoming a "presidential republic"? Is this a development to be feared or welcomed?

Thinking Critically about Presidential Power and Democracy

As is often noted by the media and in the academic literature, popular participation in American political life has declined precipitously since its nineteenth-century apogee. Voter turnout in national presidential elections barely exceeds the 50 percent mark while hardly a third of those eligible participate in off-year congressional races. Turnout in state and local contests is typically even lower. These facts are well known and their implications for the representative character of American government frequently deplored.

The decay of popular political participation, however, also has profoundly important institutional implications that are not often fully appreciated. To put the matter succinctly, the decline of voting and other forms of popular involvement in American political life reduces congressional influence while enhancing the power of the presidency. This is a development with which we should be deeply concerned. For all its faults and foibles, the Congress is the nation's most representative political institution and remains the only entity capable of placing limits on unwise or illegitimate presidential conduct. Certainly, the courts have seldom been capable of thwarting a determined president, especially in the foreign policy realm. Unfortunately, however, in recent decades our nation's undemocratic politics has undermined the Congress while paving the way for aggrandizement of power by the executive and the presidential unilateralism that inevitably follows.

The framers of the Constitution created a system of government in which the Congress and the executive branch were to share power. In recent years, however, the powers of Congress have waned while those of the presidency have expanded dramatically. To begin with the most recent instance of congressional retreat in the face of presidential assertiveness, in October 2002, pressed by President George W. Bush, both houses of Congress voted overwhelmingly to authorize the White House to use military force against Iraq. The resolution adopted by Congress allowed the president complete discretion to determine whether, when, and how to attack Iraq. The president had rejected language that might have implied even the slightest limitations on his prerogatives. Indeed, Bush's legal advisers had pointedly declared that the president did not actually need specific congressional authorization to attack Iraq if he deemed such action to be in America's interest. "We don't want to be in the legal position of asking Congress to authorize the use of force when the president already has that full authority," said one senior administration official. Few members of Congress even bothered to object to this apparent rewriting of the U.S. Constitution. Several months later, however, demonstrating that it was not completely irrelevant, the House of Representatives boldly responded to French efforts to thwart the president's Iraq policy by substituting "freedom" for "French" in the menu listings for the fried potatoes and crusty bread served in its dining room.

There is no doubt that Congress continues to be able to harass presidents and even, on occasion, to hand the White House a sharp rebuff. In the larger view, however, presidents' occasional defeats—however dramatic—have to be seen as temporary setbacks in a gradual and decisive shift toward increased presidential power in the twenty-first century. Louis Fisher, America's leading authority on the separation of powers, recently observed that in what are arguably the two most important policy arenas, national defense and the federal budget, the powers of Congress have shown a "precipitous decline" for at least the past fifty years. The last occasion on which Congress exercised its constitutional power to declare war was December 8, 1941, and yet, since that time, American forces have been committed to numerous battles on every continent by order of the president. The much-hailed 1973 War Powers Resolution, far from serving as a limit on presidential power, actually allowed the president considerably more discretionary authority than he was granted by the Constitution. The War Powers Act gave the president the authority to deploy forces abroad without congressional authority for sixty days. The Constitution, though, seems to require congressional authorization before troops can be deployed for even one day.

As to spending powers, the framers of the Constitution conceived the "power of the purse" to be Congress's most fundamental prerogative and for more than a century this power was jealously guarded by powerful congressional leaders like Taft-era House Speaker "Uncle" Joe Cannon, who saw congressional control of the budget as a fundamental safeguard against "Prussian-style" militarism and autocracy. Since the New Deal, however, successive Congresses have yielded to steadily increasing presidential influence over the budget process. In 1939, Congress allowed Franklin D. Roosevelt to take a giant step toward presidential control of the nation's purse strings when it permitted FDR to bring the Bureau of the Budget (BoB) into the newly created Executive Office of the President. Roosevelt and his successors used the BoB (now called the White House Office of Management and Budget or OMB) to effectively seize the nation's legislative and budgetary agenda. In 1974, Congress attempted to respond to Richard Nixon's efforts to further enhance presidential control of spending when it enacted the Budget and Impoundment Control Act. This piece of legislation centralized Congress's own budgetary process and seemed to reinforce congressional power. Yet, less than ten years later, Congress watched as President Ronald Reagan essentially seized control over the congressional budget process. Subsequently, as Fisher observes, lacking confidence in its own ability to maintain budgetary discipline, Congress has surrendered more and more power to the president, even attempting to hand the chief executive a line-item veto in 1995.

Representative assemblies like the United States Congress derive their influence from the support of groups and forces in civil society that believe these institutions serve their interests. Britain's Parliament ultimately overcame the Crown because it gradually won the confidence and support of the most important forces in civil society. A chief executive, like the president of the United States, on the other hand, fundamentally derives its power from its command of bureaucracies, armies, and the general machinery of the state. Presidents can certainly benefit from popular support. If we imagine, however, a fully demobilized polity in which neither institution could count on much support from forces in civil society, the president would still command the institutions of the state while Congress would be without significant resources. In a fully mobilized polity, on the other hand, Congress might have a chance to counterbalance the president's institutional powers with the support of significant social forces.

A powerful presidency, a weak Congress, and a partially demobilized electorate are a dangerous mix. Presidents have increasingly asserted the right to govern unilaterally and now appear able to overcome most institutional and political constraints. Presidential power, to be sure, can be a force for good. To cite one example from the not-so-distant past, it was President Lyndon Johnson, more than Congress or the judiciary, who faced up to the task of smashing America's apartheid system. Yet, as the framers knew, unchecked power is always dangerous. Americans of the founding generation feared that unchecked presidential power would lead to *monocracy*—a republican form of monarchy without a king. Have we not taken more than one step in that direction? Inevitably, there is a price to be paid for our undemocratic politics.

FOR CRITICAL ANALYSIS

At times, the Congress has been the dominant branch of government. At other times, the presidency has predominated. Describe the changes in the relationship between the presidency and the Congress throughout American history. What factors contributed to the dominance of Congress? What factors contributed to the resurgence of the presidency? Which branch of government dominates now? Why do you think so?

FOR CRITICAL ANALYSIS

The presidency and the Congress are both democratic institutions. Which is the more democratic of the two? Why?

What You Can Do: Work in the White House

Johanna Atienza was a twenty-year-old junior majoring in political science at a West Coast university when she learned from other students that her school had a

INTERACTIVE
POLITICS

⬤ **YOU ARE...** a presidential aide in the West Wing!

The president is the single most important person in the free world, and invitations to events he attends are the most coveted tickets in town. The president's time is very valuable, and he hopes to maximize his accomplishments at these events, and counts on his aides to insure that he is meeting with people who can advance his goals.

In this simulation, you are the "body" aide to the president, steering him to the meetings that can help him the most in winning his objectives. How much political acumen do you possess? Can you get the president to meet the most helpful people at a simple event?

Go to www.wwnorton.com/wtp5e

Questions to consider as you conduct the online simulation:

⬤ How is the president, the single most powerful man in the world, limited in his power to act as he pleases?

⬤ Why must the president resort to the power of his "bully pulpit" in order to accomplish many of his goals?

⬤ What are the formal and informal resources available to the president as he attempts to persuade others to help meet his goals?

⬤ Even though most modern democracies favor parliamentary or semi-presidential systems over a strong presidential system, why has the United States Congress been willing to delegate so much authority to our chief executive?

Washington, D.C., internship program. She was immediately interested: "What better way is there to learn about politics than from the inside?" She also felt that a semester in the nation's capital would help her to understand if the people who worked in the federal government really cared about the average citizen.

A speaker at the information session she attended spelled out the options for internships in Washington, D.C. Some were in government. Others were with the media, interest groups, and other private organizations involved in politics. Johanna's ears perked up when she learned that the White House had an intern program. The speaker suggested that she call the White House directly.

That first phone call was the beginning of her trip into what sometimes seemed like a fantasyland. After speaking directly to the White House director of the internship program, who answered her questions, Johanna received an application that asked for basic information, such as her name, address, telephone numbers, and so forth; two essays, one on why she wanted to be a White House intern and the other describing a formative experience in her life; a writing sample of approximately 500 words; and two letters of recommendation. Johanna filled out the form, devoted considerable thought and effort to the essays, and submitted the first page of a paper she had written for one of her classes as her writing sample.

Between Thanksgiving and Christmas, she received a large envelope with a return address that read, "The White House—Washington." Johanna's immediate reaction: "I was screaming!" She had been accepted into the program. Still, she needed to pass one more test. She had to fill out a form (for the FBI) that asked such questions as "Do you advocate the overthrow of the U.S. Government?" and "Have you taken illegal drugs?" The form also asked her to detail her addresses for the past seven or eight years. Johanna submitted the form. She assumed that she passed the FBI security test because she never heard anything more about it.

Several weeks later, she moved to the nation's capital. Her assignment was to work with the people who scheduled travel for the president and the first lady. Over the next three months, Johanna met and worked with some of the top officials in the White House. She also had the opportunity to meet President Bill Clinton and Hillary Clinton. While it was exciting to wander around the maze of offices in the White House, Johanna reports, she was often so busy that she had little time to realize that she was indeed wandering through White House corridors.

What did Johanna learn from her three-month participation in the day-to-day life of White House politics that she was unlikely to learn in a classroom? First, she was struck by the incredible complexity of the presidency and Washington politics. Procedures are detailed and time-consuming. Things moved remarkably slowly, if at all. Second, however, she gained tremendous respect for the people who work in the White House. In general, the staff believed that "you can do some good, you really can." They were dedicated people who worked long hours, often for little money. Even the older aides worked long hours and devoted themselves to public service.

Johanna went to the White House asking herself whether the staff and politicians in Washington, D.C., really care about the people back home. She returned to the West Coast with a strong sense that the people who work in the White House for the president of the United States do indeed strive to make life a little better for the rest of us.

Should other students apply for the White House intern program—even though the application process takes time and effort? Johanna answers without hesitation, "Definitely." See if your school has a Washington, D.C., program. If not, call the

White House directly and ask for the intern office. At this time next year, you could be one of the bright young people wandering their way through the West Wing.

Summary

The foundations for presidential government were laid in the Constitution, which provides for a unitary executive who is head of state as well as head of government. The first section of this chapter reviewed the powers of each: the head of state with its military, judicial, and diplomatic powers; the head of government with its executive, military, and legislative powers.

The second and third sections of this chapter focused on the president's institutional and political resources. The Cabinet, the other top appointments, the White House staff, and the Executive Office of the President are some of the impressive institutional resources of presidential power. The president's political party, the supportive group coalitions, and access to the media, and through that, access to the millions of Americans who make up the general public are formidable political resources that can be used to bolster a president's power. But these resources are not cost- or risk-free. A direct relationship with the public is the president's most potent modern resource, but it is also the most problematic.

The final section of this chapter traced the rise of modern presidential government after the much longer period of congressional dominance. There is no mystery in the shift to government centered on the presidency. Congress built the modern presidency by delegating to it not only the power to implement the vast new programs of the 1930s but also by delegating its own legislative power to make the policies themselves. Presidential government is now an established fact of American politics.

For Further Reading

Barber, James David. *The Presidential Character*. Englewood Cliffs, NJ: Prentice-Hall, 1992.

Issacharoff, Samuel, et al. *When Elections Go Bad: The Law of Democracy and the Presidential Election of 2000*. Rev. ed. New York: Foundation Press, 2001.

Jones, Charles O. *Clinton and Congress, 1993–1996: Risk, Restoration, and Re-Election*. Norman: University of Oklahoma Press, 1999.

Kernell, Samuel. *Going Public: New Strategies of Presidential Leadership*. Washington, DC: Congressional Quarterly Press, 1997.

Lowi, Theodore J. *The Personal President: Power Invested, Promise Unfulfilled*. Ithaca, NY: Cornell University Press, 1985.

Milkis, Sidney M. *The President and the Parties: The Transformation of the American Party System since the New Deal*. New York: Oxford University Press, 1993.

Neustadt, Richard E. *Presidential Power: The Politics of Leadership from Roosevelt to Reagan*. Rev. ed. New York: Free Press, 1990.

Pfiffner, James P. *The Modern Presidency*. New York: St. Martin's, 2000.

Schumaker, Paul, and Burdett A. Loomis, eds. *Choosing a President: The Electoral College and Beyond*. New York: Chatham House, 2001.

Skowronek, Stephen. *The Politics Presidents Make: Leadership from John Adams to Bill Clinton*. Cambridge, MA: The Belknap Press of Harvard University Press, 1997.

Tulis, Jeffrey. *The Rhetorical Presidency*. Princeton, NJ: Princeton University Press, 1987.

Study Outline

www.wwnorton.com/wtp5e

Keyword: Review 13

The Constitutional Basis of the Presidency

1. The framers thought a unitary executive would be energetic and thus better able to protect the nation's interests.

2. Presidents are selected in indirect elections through the electoral college.

The Constitutional Powers of the Presidency

1. The president's expressed powers fall into five categories—military, judicial, diplomatic, executive, and legislative—that are the source of some of the most important powers on which the president can draw.
2. The position of commander in chief makes the president the highest military authority in the United States, with control of the entire military establishment.
3. The Constitution delegates to the president, as commander in chief, the obligation to protect every state against invasion and domestic violence.

4. The presidential power to grant reprieves, pardons, and amnesties allows the president to choose freedom or confinement, and even life or death for all individuals who have violated, or are suspected of having violated, federal laws, including people who directly threaten the security of the United States.
5. The power to receive representatives of foreign countries allows the president almost unconditional authority to determine whether a new ruling group can indeed commit its country to treaties and other agreements.
6. The president's executive power, consists of the ability to appoint and supervise all executive officers.
7. The president's legislative power consists of the obligation to make recommendations for consideration by Congress and the ability to veto legislation.

The Presidency as an Institution

1. Presidents have at their disposal a variety of institutional resources—such as the power to fill high-level political positions—that directly affect a president's ability to govern.
2. Presidents increasingly have preferred the White House staff to the Cabinet as a tool for managing the gigantic executive branch.
3. The White House staff, which is composed primarily of analysts and advisers, has grown from an informal group of fewer than a dozen people to a new presidential bureaucracy.
4. The Executive Office of the President, often called the institutional presidency, is larger than the White House staff, and comprises the president's permanent management agencies.
5. As the institutional presidency has grown in size and complexity, most presidents of the past twenty-five years have sought to use their vice presidents as a management resource after the election.

The Contemporary Bases of Presidential Power

1. Generally, presidents have expanded their power in three ways: party, popular mobilization, and administration.
2. Although all presidents rely on the members and leaders of their own party to implement their legislative agendas, during periods of divided government, the president's party is in the minority in Congress.
3. "Going public" as a source of presidential power has been especially significant in the past fifty years. But popular support for the president can be fickle and it tends to decline over the course of a president's administration.
4. Contemporary presidents have increased the administrative capabilities and power of their office by enhancing the reach and power of the Executive Office of the President, increasing White House control over the federal bureaucracy, and expanding the role of executive orders and other instruments of direct presidential governance.

Thinking Critically about Presidential Power and Democracy

1. The decline of voting and other forms of popular involvement in American political life reduces congressional influence while enhancing the power of the presidency.

Practice Quiz

www.wwnorton.com/wtp5e
Keyword: Quiz 13

1. Which article of the Constitution establishes the presidency?
   a) Article I
   b) Article II
   c) Article III
   d) none of the above

2. Which of the following does not represent a classification of a constitutional provision designating the president as head of state?
   a) legislative
   b) military
   c) judicial
   d) diplomatic

3. Which of the following does not require the advice and consent of the Senate?
   a) an executive agreement
   b) a treaty
   c) Supreme Court nominations
   d) All of the above require the advice and consent of the Senate.

4. Which of the following terms has been used to describe the presidency as it has used constitutional and other powers to make itself more powerful?
   a) "the delegated presidency"
   b) "the imperial presidency"
   c) "the personal presidency"
   d) "the preemptive presidency"

5. By what process can Congress reject a presidential veto?
   a) veto override
   b) pocket veto
   c) executive delegation
   d) impeachment

6. Which of the following describes the presidential foreign policy advisory council composed of the president; the vice president; the secretaries of state, defense, and the treasury; the attorney general; and others?
   a) the "inner Cabinet"
   b) the National Security Council
   c) both a and b
   d) neither a nor b

7. The Office of Management and Budget is part of
   a) the Executive Office of the President.
   b) the White House staff.
   c) the Kitchen Cabinet.
   d) both a and b.

8. Which twentieth-century presidency transformed the American system of government from a Congress-centered to a president-centered system?
   a) Woodrow Wilson's
   b) Franklin Roosevelt's
   c) Richard Nixon's
   d) Jimmy Carter's

9. How many people work for agencies within the Executive Office of the President?
   a) 25 to 50
   b) 700 to 1,000
   c) 1,500 to 2,000
   d) 4,500 to 5,000

Key Terms

www.wwnorton.com/wtp5e
Keyword: Vocabulary 13

Cabinet (p. 540)
caucus (political) (p. 524)
commander in chief (p. 526)
delegated powers (p. 525)

executive agreement (p. 534)
Executive Office of the President (EOP) (p. 542)
executive privilege (p. 535)
executive order (p. 538)
expressed powers (p. 525)
inherent powers (p. 526)
Kitchen Cabinet (p. 542)
legislative initiative (p. 537)

line-item veto (p. 537)
mandate (p. 546)
National Security Council (NSC) (p. 542)
permanent campaign (p. 550)
pocket veto (p. 537)
veto (p. 536)
War Powers Resolution (p. 527)
White House staff (p. 542)

14 BUREAUCRACY IN A DEMOCRACY

What Government Does and Why It Matters

AMERICANS DEPEND ON government bureaucracies to accomplish the most spectacular achievements as well as the most mundane. Yet they often do not realize that public bureaucracies are essential for providing the services that they use every day and that they rely on in emergencies. On a typical day, a college student might check the weather forecast, drive on an interstate highway, mail the rent check, drink from a public water fountain, check the calories on the side of a yogurt container, attend a class, log on to the Internet, and meet a relative at the airport. Each of these activities is possible because of the work of a government bureaucracy: the U.S. Weather Service, the U.S. Department of Transportation, the U.S. Postal Service, the Environmental Protection Agency, the Food and Drug Administration, the student loan programs of the U.S. Department of Education, the Advanced Research Projects Agency (which developed the Internet in the 1960s), and the Federal Aviation Administration. Without the ongoing work of these agencies, many of these common activities would be impossible, unreliable, or more expensive. Even though bureaucracies provide essential services that all Americans rely on, they are often disparaged by politicians and the general public alike. Criticized as "big government," many federal bureaucracies come into public view only when they are charged with fraud, waste, and abuse.

In emergencies, the national perspective on bureaucracy and, indeed, on "big government" shifts. After the September 11 terrorist attacks, all eyes turned to Washington. The federal government responded by strengthening and reorganizing the bureaucracy to undertake a whole new set of responsibilities designed to keep America safe.

In the biggest government reorganization in over half a century, Congress created the Department of Homeland Security in 2002. The massive new department merged twenty-two existing agencies into a single department employing nearly 170,000 workers. The operation of the new department is a gargantuan management challenge. The Department of Homeland Security combined under one umbrella established agencies with vastly different cultures and no history of working together. For example, the Coast Guard, the old Immigration and Naturalization Service, and the Federal Emergency Management Agency are all part of the new department. In addition to combining these existing agencies, the department had to create its own intelligence unit and oversee the fledgling Transportation Security Agency, which was set up in the aftermath of the September 11 attacks to make transportation safe.

At the same time, the Bush administration launched a major push to contract out government jobs to private employers. In an effort to lower costs, the administration made changes in the rules for government contracting that could turn 850,000 government jobs over to private employers.

The two initiatives, apparently headed in different directions, illustrate the conflicts that arise in an era when most Americans believe that government is more necessary than ever but have significant doubts about whether the existing government is up to the job. Privatization raises questions about whether the private sector is, in fact, more cost effective than government and whether privatization is compatible with our national security needs and with democratic accountability. It also raises questions about equality: federal jobs have long been viewed as "good jobs," with decent pay and excellent benefits. Critics charge that, by replacing these jobs with private jobs, the government is undermining unions and reinforcing economic trends that have created the large gap between rich and poor. ■

Both routine and exceptional tasks require the organization, specialization, and expertise found in bureaucracies. Table 14.1 identifies the basic characteristics of bureaucracy. To provide services, government bureaucracies employ specialists such as meteorologists, doctors, and scientists. To do their jobs effectively, these specialists require resources and tools (ranging from paper to blood samples); they have to coordinate their work with others (for example, the traffic engineers must communicate with construction engineers); and there must be effective outreach to the public (for example, private doctors must be made aware of health warnings). Bureaucracy offers a way to coordinate the many different parts that must work together for the government to provide good services.

- **We begin this chapter by clarifying what we mean by "bureaucracy."** Before we can understand the nature and character of the executive branch of the U.S. government, we must first examine why bureaucracy is necessary. From there, we turn to the size, role, functions, and characteristics of the federal bureaucracy and bureaucrats.

- **We next examine the organization of the executive branch as a whole, looking at the Cabinet departments, agencies, and bureaus that make up its operating parts.** Since the executive branch is vast and there are far too many agencies for us to identify here, we will instead evaluate the different broad purposes that federal agencies serve.

- **We next turn to ways in which the size and role of the federal bureaucracy can be reduced.** Although efforts to downsize government have been popular in recent years, we question whether these attempts are effective or even address the most pressing problem regarding the control of the federal bureaucracy.

■ Previewing Liberty, Equality, and Democracy

Bureaucracy is essential for carrying out the tasks of government. At its best, bureaucracy is a key tool of democracy. It ensures that the public will is implemented. The rules that govern bureaucracy aim to ensure that public programs are implemented in accordance with congressional intent. In this way, bureaucracy promotes the values of equality and liberty embodied in federal legislation. Yet, because government bureaucracies operate outside the public eye, they raise important concerns about democratic accountability. As the federal bureaucracy grew in the twentieth century, new management techniques sought to promote greater efficiency and public responsiveness in it. Since the terrorist attacks of September 11, 2001, there has been a move toward more secrecy in the federal bureaucracy. Domestic security needs have created new conflict about the proper balance between democratic accountability and effective bureaucracy. We conclude by assessing this delicate balance.

Bureaucracy and Bureaucrats

Bureaucracy is nothing more nor less than a form of organization, as defined by the attributes in Table 14.1. To gain some objectivity, and to appreciate the universality of bureaucracy, let us take the word and break it into its two main parts—*bureau* and *cracy*. *Bureau*, a French word, can mean either "office" or "desk." *Cracy* is the Greek word for "rule" or "form of rule." Taken together, *bureau* and *cracy* produce a very interesting definition: **Bureaucracy** is a form of rule by offices and

bureaucracy the complex structure of offices, tasks, rules, and principles of organization that are employed by all large-scale institutions to coordinate effectively the work of their personnel

Table 14.1	The Six Primary Characteristics of Bureaucracy

Characteristic	**Explanation**
Division of labor	Workers are specialized. Each worker develops a skill in a particular job and performs the job routinely and repetitively, thereby increasing productivity.
Allocation of functions	Each task is assigned. No one makes a whole product; each worker depends on the output of other workers.
Allocation of responsibility	Each task becomes a personal responsibility— a contractual obligation. No task can be changed without permission.
Supervision	Some workers are assigned the special task of watching over other workers rather than contributing directly to the creation of the product. Each supervisor watches over a few workers (a situation known as "span of control"), and communications between workers or between levels move in a prescribed fashion (known as "chain of command").
Purchase of full-time employment	The organization controls all the time the worker is on the job, so each worker can be assigned and held to a task. Some part-time and contracted work is tolerated, but it is held to a minimum.
Identification of career within the organization	Workers come to identify with the organization as a way of life. Seniority, pension rights, and promotions are geared to this relationship.

desks. Each member of an organization has an office, meaning a place as well as a set of responsibilities. That is, each "office" comprises a set of tasks that are specialized to the needs of the organization, and the person holding that office (or position) performs those specialized tasks. Specialization and repetition are essential to the efficiency of any organization. Therefore, when an organization is inefficient, it is almost certainly because it is not bureaucratized enough!

THE SIZE OF THE FEDERAL SERVICE

For over two decades, politicians from both parties have asserted that the federal government is too big. Ronald Reagan led the way with his 1981 statement that government was the problem, not the solution. Fifteen years later President Bill Clinton abandoned the traditional Democratic defense of government, declaring that "the era of big government is over." President George W. Bush voiced similar sentiments when he accepted his party's nomination for president in 2000, proclaiming "Big government is not the answer!" Despite fears of bureaucratic growth getting out of hand, however, the federal service has hardly grown at all during the past twenty-five years; it reached its peak postwar level in 1968 with 3.0 million civilian employees plus an additional 3.6 million military personnel (a figure swollen by Vietnam). The number of civilian federal employees has since fallen to approximately 2.8 million in 2003; the number of military personnel totals only 1.5 million.[1]

The growth of the federal service over the past fifty years is even less imposing when placed in the context of the total workforce and when compared to the size of state and local public employment. Figure 14.1 indicates that since 1950, the ratio of federal employment to the total workforce has been steady, and in fact has *declined* slightly in the past thirty years. In 1950, there were 4.3 million state and local civil service employees (about 6.5 percent of the country's workforce). In 2000, there were almost 18.0 million (nearly 13 percent of the workforce). Federal employment, in contrast, exceeded 5 percent of the workforce only during World War II (not shown), and almost all of that momentary growth was military. After the demobilization, which continued until 1950 (as shown in Figure 14.1), the federal service has tended to grow at a rate that keeps pace with the economy and society. That is demonstrated by the lower line on Figure 14.1, which shows a constant relation between federal civilian employment and the size of the U.S. workforce.

Employees in the Federal Service and in the National Workforce, 1946–2003

Figure 14.1

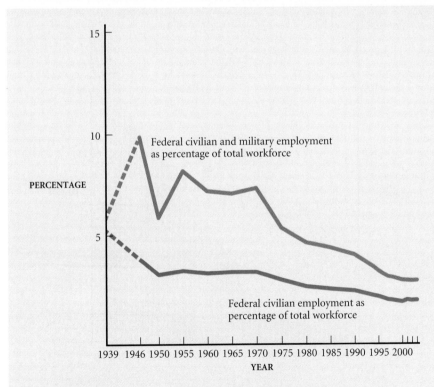

SOURCES: Office of Management and Budget, *Budget of the United States Government, FY, 2005, Historical Tables* (Washington, DC: Government Printing Office, 2004), p. 304, and U.S. Department of Labor, Bureau of Labor Statistics, *Employment and Earnings* (monthly).

Variations in federal employment since 1946 have been in the military and are directly related to war and the Cold War (as shown by the top line on Figure 14.1).

Another useful comparison is to be found in Figure 14.2. Although the dollar increase in federal spending shown by the bars looks impressive, the trend line indicating the relation of federal spending to the Gross Domestic Product (GDP) shows that in 2002, this percentage was barely higher than in 1960.

In sum, the national government is indeed "very large," but it has not been growing any faster than the economy or the society. The same is roughly true of the growth pattern of state and local public personnel. Bureaucracy keeps pace with society, despite people's seeming dislike for it, because the control towers, the prisons, the Social Security system, and other essential elements cannot be operated without bureaucracy. The United States certainly could not hope to protect the nation against terrorism without a large military and civilian bureaucracy.

Although the federal executive branch is large and complex, everything about it is commonplace. Bureaucracies are commonplace because they touch so many

Figure 14.2   Annual Federal Outlays, 1960–2005

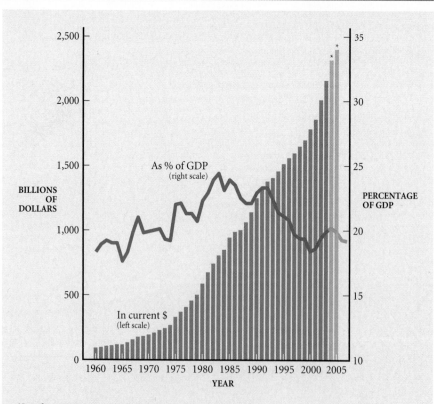

*Data from 2004–2005 are estimated.
SOURCE: Office of Management and Budget, *Historical Tables, Budget of the United States Government, Fiscal Year 2005* (Washington, DC: Government Printing Office, 2004).

aspects of daily life. Government bureaucracies implement the decisions made by the political process. Bureaucracies are full of routine because that assures the regular delivery of services and ensures that each agency fulfills its mandate. Public bureaucracies are powerful because legislatures and chief executives, and indeed the people, delegate to them vast power to make sure a particular job is done—enabling citizens to be more free to pursue their private ends.

BUREAUCRATS

"Government by offices and desks" conveys to most people a picture of hundreds of office workers shuffling millions of pieces of paper. There is a lot of truth in that image, but we have to look more closely at what papers are being shuffled and why. More than seventy years ago, an astute observer defined bureaucracy as "continuous routine business."[2] As we saw at the beginning of this chapter, almost any organization succeeds by reducing its work to routines, with each routine being given to a different specialist. But specialization separates people from each other; one worker's output becomes another worker's input. The timing of such relationships is essential, and this requires that these workers stay in communication with each other. Communication is the key. In fact, bureaucracy was the first information network. Routine came first; voluminous routine came as bureaucracies grew and specialized.

What Do Bureaucrats Do? Bureaucrats, whether in public or in private organizations, communicate with each other in order to coordinate all the specializations within their organization. This coordination is necessary to carry out the primary task of bureaucracy, which is **implementation,** that is, implementing the objectives of the organization as laid down by its board of directors (if a private company) or by law (if a public agency). In government, the "bosses" are ultimately the legislature and the elected chief executive.

When the bosses—Congress, in particular, when it is making the law—are clear in their instructions to bureaucrats, implementation is a fairly straightforward process. Bureaucrats translate the law into specific routines for each of the employees of an agency. But what happens to routine administrative implementation when there are several bosses who disagree as to what the instructions ought to be? This requires yet another job for bureaucrats: interpretation. Interpretation is a form of implementation, in that the bureaucrats still have to carry out what they believe to be the intentions of their superiors. But when bureaucrats have to interpret a law before implementing it, they are in effect engaging in *lawmaking.* Congress often deliberately delegates to an administrative agency the responsibility of lawmaking. Members of Congress often conclude that some area of industry needs regulating or some area of the environment needs protection, but they are unwilling or unable to specify just how that should be done. In such situations, Congress delegates to the appropriate agency a broad authority within which the bureaucrats have to make law, through the procedures of **rule making** and **administrative adjudication.**

Rulemaking is exactly the same as legislation; in fact, it is often referred to as "quasi-legislation." The rules issued by government agencies provide more detailed and specific indications of what the policy actually will mean. For example, the

implementation the efforts of departments and agencies to translate laws into specific bureaucratic routines

rule making a quasi-legislative administrative process that produces regulations by government agencies

administrative adjudication applying rules and precedents to specific cases to settle disputes with regulated parties

Occupational Safety and Health Administration (OSHA) is charged with ensuring that our workplaces are safe. OSHA regulates the use of chemicals and other well-known health hazards. In recent years, the widespread use of computers in the workplace has been associated with a growing number of cases of repetitive stress injury, which hurts the hands, arms, and neck. To repond to this new threat to workplace health, OSHA issued a new set of ergonomic rules in November 1999 that tell employers what they must do to prevent and address such injuries among their workers. Such rules only take force after a period of public comment. Reaction from the people or businesses that will be subject to the rules may cause an agency to modify the rules they first issue. The rules about ergonomic safety in the workplace, for example, were strongly contested by many businesses, which viewed them as too costly. Two months into his presidency, Bush signed a bill repealing the ergonomic regulations that had been scheduled to go into effect later in 2001. The rule-making process is thus a highly political one. Once rules are approved, they are published in the *Federal Register* and have the force of law.

Administrative adjudication is very similar to what the judiciary ordinarily does: applying rules and precedents to specific cases to settle disputes. In administrative adjudication, the agency charges the person or business suspected of violating the law. The ruling in an adjudication dispute applies only to the specific case being considered. Many regulatory agencies use administrative adjudication to make decisions about specific products or practices. For example, in December 1999, the Consumer Product Safety Commission held hearings on the safety of bleachers, sparked by concern over the death of children after falls from bleachers. It then issued guidelines about bleacher construction designed to prevent falls. These guidelines have the force of law. Likewise, product recalls are often the result of adjudication.

A good case study of the role agencies can play is the story of how ordinary federal bureaucrats created the Internet. Yes, it's true: what became the Internet was developed largely by the U.S. Department of Defense, and defense considerations still shape the basic structure of the Internet. In 1957, immediately following the profound American embarrassment over the Soviet Union's launching of *Sputnik,* Congress authorized the establishment of the Advanced Research Projects Agency (ARPA) to develop, among other things, a means of maintaining communications in the event the existing telecommunications network (the telephone system) was disabled by a strategic attack. Since the telephone network was highly centralized and therefore could have been completely disabled by a single attack, ARPA developed a decentralized, highly redundant network. Redundancy in this case improved the probability of functioning after an attack. The full design, called by the pet name of ARPANET, took almost a decade to create. By 1971, around twenty universities were connected to the ARPANET. The forerunner to the Internet was born.[3]

Government bureaucrats do essentially the same things that bureaucrats in large private organizations do, and neither type deserves the disrespect embodied in the term "bureaucrat." But because of the authoritative, coercive nature of government, far more constraints are imposed on public bureaucrats than on private bureaucrats, even when their jobs are the same. During the 1970s and 1980s, the length of time required to develop an administrative rule from a proposal to actual publication in the *Federal Register* (when it takes on full legal status) grew from an average

FOR CRITICAL ANALYSIS

Often the efficiency of public bureaucracies is judged in terms of the efficiency of private business and other organizations. In many instances, government has been expected to do things that businesses in the marketplace have chosen not to do or have found unprofitable. Might the tasks that government is asked to perform be more prone to inefficiency? Think about the ways in which business might be able to perform some tasks that government currently performs. Would business necessarily perform these tasks more efficiently? Should efficiency be the only priority in the public enterprise?

of 15 months to an average of 35 to 40 months. Inefficiency? No. Most of the increased time is attributable to new procedures requiring more public notice, more public hearings, more hearings held out in the field rather than in Washington, more cost-benefit analysis, and stronger legal obligations to prepare "environmental impact statements" demonstrating that the proposed rule or agency action will not have an unacceptably large negative impact on the human or physical environment.[4] Thus, a great deal of what is popularly paraded as the lower efficiency of public agencies can be attributed to the political, judicial, legal, and public-opinion restraints and extraordinarily high expectations imposed on public bureaucrats.

We will have more to say at the end of this chapter about bureaucratic accountability and the potential role of citizens in it. Suffice it to say here that if a private company such as Microsoft were required to open up all its decision processes and management practices to full view by the media, their competitors, and all interested citizens, Microsoft—despite its profit motive and the pressure of competition—would appear far less efficient, perhaps no more efficient than public bureaucracies.

The Merit System: How to Become a Bureaucrat   In return for all these inconveniences, public bureaucrats are rewarded in part with greater job security than employees of most private organizations enjoy. More than a century ago, the federal government attempted to imitate business by passing the Civil Service Act of 1883, which was followed by almost universal adoption of equivalent laws in state and local governments. These laws required that appointees to public office be qualified for the job to which they are appointed. This policy came to be called the **merit system;** its ideal was not merely to put an end to political appointments under the "spoils system" but also to require adequate preparation for every job by holding competitive examinations through which the very best candidates were to be hired. At the higher levels of government agencies, including such posts as cabinet secretaries and assistant secretaries, many jobs are filled with political appointees not part of the merit system.

As a further safeguard against political interference (and to compensate for the lower-than-average pay given to public employees), merit system employees—genuine civil servants—were given a form of tenure: legal protection against being fired without a show of cause. Reasonable people may disagree about the value of job tenure and how far it should extend in the civil service, but the justifiable objective of tenure—cleansing bureaucracy of political interference while upgrading performance—cannot be disputed.

merit system a product of civil service reform, in which appointees to positions in public bureaucracies must objectively be deemed qualified for the position

The Organization of the Executive Branch

Cabinet departments, agencies, and bureaus are the operating parts of the bureaucratic whole. Figure 14.3 is an organizational chart of one of the largest and most important of the fifteen **departments,** the Department of Agriculture. At the top is the head of the department, who in the United States is called the "secretary" of the department.[5] Below the secretary and the deputy secretary is a second tier of "undersecretaries" who have management responsibilities for one or more operating agencies, shown in the smaller print directly below each undersecretary. Those operating agencies are the third tier of the department, yet they are the highest level of

department the largest subunit of the executive branch. The secretaries of the fourteen departments form the Cabinet

Figure 14.3   Organizational Chart of the Department of Agriculture, 1998

SOURCE: U.S. Department of Agriculture World Wide Web home page, www.usda.gov/agencies/agchart.htm (accessed 5/11/98).

responsibility for the actual programs around which the entire department is organized. This third tier is generally called the "bureau level." Each bureau-level agency is usually operating under a statute, adopted by Congress, that set up the agency and gave it its authority and jurisdiction. The names of these bureau-level agencies are often quite well known to the public—the Forest Service and the Agricultural Research Service, for example. These are the so-called line agencies, or agencies that deal directly with the public. Sometimes these agencies are officially called "bureaus," as in the Federal Bureau of Investigation (FBI), which is a part of the third tier of the Department of Justice. But "bureau" is also the conventional term for this level of administrative agency, even though many agencies or their supporters have preferred over the years to adopt a more palatable designation, such as "service" or "administration." Each bureau is, of course, subdivided into still other units, known as divisions, offices, or units—all are parts of the bureaucratic hierarchy.

Not all government agencies are part of Cabinet departments. Some **independent agencies** are set up by Congress outside the departmental structure altogether, even though the president appoints and directs the heads of these agencies. Independent agencies usually have broad powers to provide public services that are either too expensive or too important to be left to private initiatives. Some examples of independent agencies are the National Aeronautics and Space Administration (NASA), the Central Intelligence Agency (CIA), and the Environmental Protection Agency (EPA). **Government corporations** are a third type of government agency, but are more like private businesses performing and charging for a market service, such as delivering the mail (the United States Postal Service) or transporting railroad passengers (Amtrak).

Yet a fourth type of agency is the independent regulatory commission, given broad discretion to make rules. The first regulatory agencies established by Congress, beginning with the Interstate Commerce Commission in 1888, were set up as independent regulatory commissions because Congress recognized that regulatory agencies are "minilegislatures," whose rules are exactly the same as legislation but require the kind of expertise and full-time attention that is beyond the capacity of Congress. Until the 1960s, most of the regulatory agencies that were set up by Congress, such as the Federal Trade Commission (1914) and the Federal Communications Commission (1934), were independent regulatory commissions. But beginning in the late 1960s and the early 1970s, all new regulatory programs, with two or three exceptions (such as the Federal Election Commission), were placed within existing departments and made directly responsible to the president. Since the 1970s, no major new regulatory programs have been established, independent or otherwise.

The different agencies of the executive branch can be classified into three main groups by the services that they provide to the American public. The first category of agencies provide services and products that seek to promote the public welfare. The second group of agencies work to promote national security. The third group provides services that help to maintain a strong economy. Let us look more closely at what each set of agencies offers to the American public.

independent agency an agency that is not part of a Cabinet department

government corporation a government agency that performs a service normally provided by the private sector

PROMOTING THE PUBLIC WELFARE

One of the most important activities of the federal bureaucracy is to promote the public welfare. Americans often think of government welfare as a single program that goes only to the very poor; but a number of federal agencies provide services, build infrastructure, and enact regulations designed to enhance the well-being of the vast majority of citizens. Departments that have important responsibilities for promoting the public welfare in this sense include the Department of Housing and Urban Development, the Department of Health and Human Services, the Department of Veterans Affairs, the Department of the Interior, the Department of Education, and the Department of Labor. Ensuring the public welfare is also the main activity of agencies in other departments, such as the Department of Agriculture's Food and Nutrition Service, which administers the federal school lunch program and food stamps. In addition, a variety of independent regulatory agencies enforce regulations that aim to safeguard the public health and welfare.

How Do Federal Bureaucracies Promote the Public Welfare?   To get a sense of the diverse services, products, and regulations provided by public bureaucracies let us take a closer look at several of these agencies. The Department of Health and Human Services (HHS) administers the program that comes closest to the popular understanding of welfare—Temporary Assistance to Needy Families (TANF). Yet this program is one of the smallest activities of the department. HHS also oversees the National Institutes of Health (NIH), which is responsible for cutting-edge biomedical research. The NIH occupies a large campus-like setting with seventy-five buildings outside of Washington, D.C. In their own labs and in the grants they provide to outside researchers, the NIH's central aim is to advance knowledge about health and diseases. Five of the scientists working in NIH labs have been awarded Nobel prizes for their research. The NIH is one of the leaders in experimenting with gene therapy, which is expected to open new possibilities for curing diseases in the future. HHS is also responsible for the two major health programs provided by the federal government: Medicaid, which provides health care for low-income families

The government promotes the public welfare in myriad ways. For instance, regulatory agencies have a strong presence in the lives of all Americans. One example of that presence is the subjection of the foods we eat to numerous restrictions from federal, state, and local agencies.

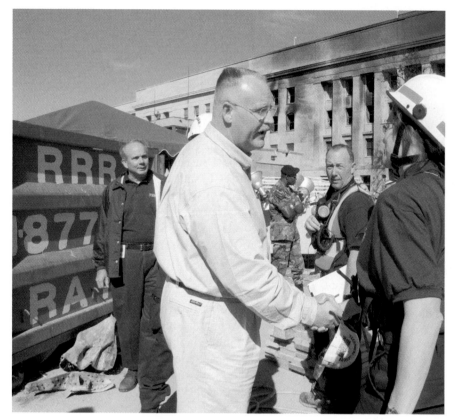

In emergencies, government bureaucracies are often the main source of organizational expertise to address urgent needs. For example, after September 11, the Federal Emergency Management Agency (FEMA) coordinated the cleanup of the sites of the terrorist attacks. FEMA also managed the cleanup when four separate hurricanes struck Florida in September 2004. Here, FEMA director Joe M. Allbaugh meets with Urban Search and Rescue teams at the Pentagon.

and for many elderly and disabled people in nursing homes, and Medicare, which is the health insurance available to all elderly people in the United States. The Administration on Aging is another agency under HHS; it provides services to the elderly such as "meals on wheels," which is designed to help keep the elderly independent. Also under HHS auspices is the Centers for Disease Control and Prevention (CDC), which is responsible for fighting bioterrorism. The CDC is charged with identifying the causes of outbreaks of sickness and assembling a national pharmaceutical stockpile to be used in responding to major health emergencies.

A different notion of the public welfare but one highly valued by most Americans is provided by the National Park Service, which is under the Department of the Interior. First created in 1916, the National Park Service is responsible for the care and upkeep of national parks. The Park Service also preserves historic sites, including Civil War battlegrounds such as Gettysburg, where President Lincoln made his famous address. Over 280 million people visit national parks each year. The Department of the Interior also houses the U.S. Fish and Wildlife Service, which is one of the oldest public conservation agencies in the world. The Fish and Wildlife Service seeks to protect wildlife habitats and since 1973 has also been charged with administering the Endangered Species Act. Since the nineteenth century, Americans have seen protection of the natural environment as an important public goal and have looked to federal agencies to implement laws and administer programs that preserve natural areas and keep them open to the public.

The Environmental Protection Agency is another federal agency working toward the public welfare—for instance, preventing the pollution of groundwater. Here, EPA project manager Bonnie Arthur examines a plastic liner that catches acid runoff from an abandoned copper mine in Nevada.

regulatory agencies departments, bureaus, or independent agencies whose primary mission is to impose limits, restrictions, or other obligations on the conduct of individuals or companies in the private sector

The United States has no "Department of Regulation" but has many **regulatory agencies.** Some of these are bureaus within departments, such as the Food and Drug Administration (FDA) within the Department of Health and Human Services, the Occupational Safety and Health Administration (OSHA) in the Department of Labor, and the Animal and Plant Health Inspection Service in the Department of Agriculture. As we saw earlier, other regulatory agencies are independent regulatory commissions, such as the Federal Communications Commission (FCC) and the Environmental Protection Agency (EPA). But whether departmental or independent, an agency or commission is regulatory if Congress delegates to it relatively broad powers over a sector of the economy or a type of commercial activity and authorizes it to make rules restricting the conduct of people and businesses within that jurisdiction. Rules made by regulatory agencies have the force and effect of law.

The activities of these agencies seek to promote the welfare of all Americans, often working behind the scenes. The FDA, for example, works to protect public health by setting standards for food processing and inspecting plants to ensure that those standards are met. The EPA sets standards to limit polluting emissions from automobiles. The regulations required automobile manufacturers to change the way they designed cars and the result has been cleaner air in many metropolitan areas.

Bureaucracies, Clienteles, and the Public   Some of the public agencies that provide services that enhance well-being are tied to a specific group or segment of American society that is often thought of as the main clientele of that agency. For

The Centers for Disease Control and Prevention protects the health and safety of people through its work to reduce and eliminate infectious diseases, including those caused by bioterrorism and chemical terrorism.

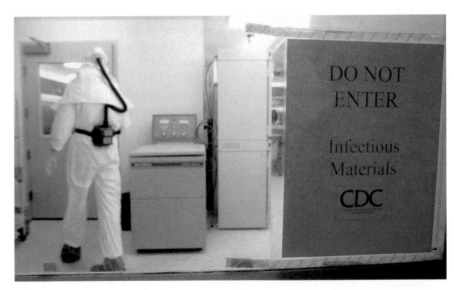

example, the Department of Agriculture was established in 1862 to promote the interests of farmers. The current Departments of Commerce and of Labor were founded in 1903 as a single department "to foster, promote, and develop the foreign and domestic commerce, the mining, the manufacturing, the shipping, and fishing industries, and the transportation facilities of the United States."[6] They remained one department until 1913, when Congress separated them into two. Likewise, the Department of Veterans Affairs has strong links to veterans' organizations, such as the American Legion and the Veterans of Foreign Wars. The Department of Education relies on teachers' organizations for support. Figure 14.4 is a representation of this type of politics. This configuration is known as an **iron triangle,** a pattern of stable relationships between an agency in the executive branch,

iron triangle the stable, cooperative relationships that often develop between a congressional committee, an administrative agency, and one or more supportive interest groups. Not all of these relationships are triangular, but the iron triangle is the most typical

Iron Triangles　　　　　　　　　　　　Figure 14.4

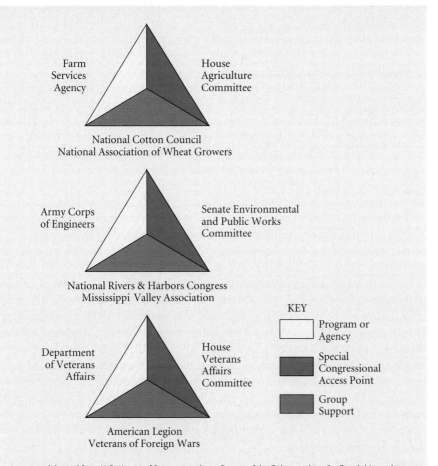

Farm Services Agency

House Agriculture Committee

National Cotton Council
National Association of Wheat Growers

Army Corps of Engineers

Senate Environmental and Public Works Committee

National Rivers & Harbors Congress
Mississippi Valley Association

Department of Veterans Affairs

House Veterans Affairs Committee

American Legion
Veterans of Foreign Wars

KEY

☐ Program or Agency

▨ Special Congressional Access Point

▨ Group Support

SOURCES: Adapted from U.S. House of Representatives, *Report of the Subcommittee for Special Investigations of the Committee on Armed Services,* 86th Cong., 1st sess. (Washington, DC: Government Printing Office, 1960), p. 7. Reprinted from Theodore J. Lowi, *Incomplete Conquest: Governing America,* 2nd ed. (New York: Holt, Rinehart and Winston, 1981), p. 139.

a congressional committee or subcommittee, and one or more organized groups of agency clientele. (Iron triangles were discussed in detail in Chapter 11.)

These relationships with particular clienteles are often important in preserving agencies from political attack. During his 1980 campaign, Ronald Reagan promised to dismantle the Department of Education as part of his commitment to get government "off people's backs." After his election, President Reagan even appointed a secretary of the department who was publicly committed to eliminating it. Yet, by the end of his administration, the Department of Education was still standing and barely touched. In 1995, the Republican Congress vowed to eliminate the Department of Education, along with two other departments, but it, too, failed. The educational constituency of the department mobilized to save it each time.

Such clientele groups generally have more influence over federal agencies than do people who are not part of the clientele group. But the ability of clientele groups to get their way is not automatic, as agencies have to balance limited resources, competing interests, and political pressures. For example, the Department of Veterans Affairs long resisted the efforts of Vietnam veterans to be compensated for exposure to Agent Orange, a chemical defoliant used extensively during the Vietnam War. Veterans charged that exposure to Agent Orange had left them with a variety of diseases ranging from cancer to severe birth defects in their children. Only after decades of lobbying, lawsuits, and federally sponsored studies did the Department of Veterans Affairs provide assistance to affected veterans.

Moreover, federal agencies increasingly seek public support outside their direct clients for their activities. In some cases, key clientele groups will work to build more widespread support for agency activities. For example, the AFL-CIO, which represents organized labor, built a broad coalition of student organizations, church groups, consumer groups, and civil rights activists opposed to sweatshops in the United States. These groups helped to support the Department of Labor's campaign to uncover and eliminate such manufacturing practices in the United States. Agency failure to consider public opinion can result in embarrassing incidents, which bureaucrats prefer to avoid. In 1981, the Department of Agriculture's Food and Nutrition Service, which administers the federal school lunch program, had to retract its cost-cutting decision to classify ketchup as a vegetable after a public outcry that the agency was harming children.

Attentiveness to the public often means making the public aware of services and improving the way services are delivered. The Social Security Administration is an independent agency that administers old-age and disability insurance, the federal government's most important and expensive welfare program. Old-age insurance, or Social Security, is supported by the AARP, an interest group representing people over 50, generally considered to be the most powerful interest group operating in the United States today. But worried that younger workers are losing confidence in Social Security, the agency has recently begun to issue annual statements to each worker, outlining the benefits that they can count on from Social Security when they retire and indicating what benefits are available if they become disabled before retirement.

PROVIDING NATIONAL SECURITY

One of the remarkable features of American federalism is that the most vital agencies for providing security for the American people are located in state and local

FOR CRITICAL ANALYSIS

What is the impact of iron triangles on inequality in the United States? Do the ties among agencies, congressional committees, and organized groups promote inequality? How?

governments—namely the police. But some agencies vital to maintaining national security do exist in the national government, and they can be grouped into two categories: (1) agencies for control of conduct defined as a threat to internal national security and (2) agencies for defending American security from external threats. The departments of greatest concern in these two areas are Homeland Security, Justice, Defense, and State.

Agencies for Internal Security The task of maintaining domestic security changed dramatically after the terrorist attacks of September 11, 2001. The creation of the Department of Homeland Security in late 2002 signaled the high priority that domestic security would now have. The orientation of domestic agencies shifted as well, as agencies geared up to prevent terrorism, a task that differed greatly from their former charge of investigating crime. Along with this shift in responsibility, these agencies have acquired broad new powers—many of them controversial—including the power to detain terrorist suspects and to engage in extensive domestic intelligence-gathering about possible terrorists.

Prior to September 11, most of the effort put into maintaining national security took the form of legal work related to prosecuting federal crimes. The largest and most important unit of the Justice Department is the Criminal Division. Lawyers in the Criminal Division represent the United States government when it is the plaintiff enforcing the federal criminal laws, except for those cases (about 25 percent) specifically assigned to other divisions or agencies. Criminal litigation is handled by U.S. attorneys, who are appointed by the president. There is one U.S. attorney in each of the ninety-four federal judicial districts; he or she supervises the work of a number of assistant U.S. attorneys.

The Civil Division of the Justice Department deals with litigation in which the United States is the defendant being sued for injury and damages allegedly inflicted by a government official. The missions of the other divisions of the Justice Department—Antitrust, Civil Rights, Environment and Natural Resources, and Tax—are described by their names.

When terrorism prevention took center stage, the Justice Department reoriented its activities accordingly. It was aided in its new mission by the USA PATRIOT Act, passed soon after September 11. The act gave the Justice Department broad new powers, allowing the attorney general to detain any foreigner suspected of posing a threat to internal security. The department launched a nationwide dragnet to detain potential suspects, using minor criminal charges or immigration violations as the legal rationale. It also initiated a voluntary program to question more than 5,000 young men from the Middle East about their views on terrorist activities and radical Islamic groups. Other new measures included the suspension of confidentiality of conversations between detainees and their attorneys. The PATRIOT Act also expanded the government's ability to use wiretaps and to issue search warrants without notifying suspects immediately. It required public libraries to keep lists of the public's book and Internet usage for federal inspection. Although initially popular with most Americans, these measures created concern about civil liberties. By 2004, dissatisfaction with these sweeping new powers had become widespread. More than 240 state and local governments had passed resolutions condemning the act, and Congress began to consider new legislation rolling back parts of the PATRIOT Act to protect people's civil liberties.

Along with state and local police, the federal government provides for domestic security, a role that changed dramatically after the September 11 attacks. The first step was the creation of the Office of Homeland Security with Tom Ridge as its head. Ridge is shown here at the Homeland Coordination Center in Washington, D.C., where security officials work together to prevent another attack.

The federal government has also assumed a new role in airport security. Armed forces were a common sight at airports following September 11. With the passage of the Secure Aviation and Transportation Act, the federal government also became involved with screening passengers and baggage.

The best-known bureau of the Justice Department is the Federal Bureau of Investigation (FBI). The FBI handles no litigation but instead serves as the principal information-gathering agency for the department and for the president. Established in 1908, the FBI expanded and advanced in stature during the 1920s and 1930s under the direction of J. Edgar Hoover.

Despite its professionalism and its fierce pride in its autonomy, the FBI has not been unresponsive to the partisan commitments of Democratic and Republican administrations. Although the FBI has always achieved its best publicity from the spectacular apprehension of famous criminals, such as John Dillinger, George "Machine Gun" Kelly, and Bonnie and Clyde,[7] it has followed the president's direction in focusing on particular crime problems. Thus it has infiltrated Nazi and Mafia organizations; it operates the vast loyalty and security investigation programs covering all federal employees since the Truman presidency; it monitored and infiltrated the Ku Klux Klan and the civil rights movement in the 1950s and 1960s; and it infiltrated radical political groups, extreme religious cults, and survivalist militias in the 1980s and 1990s.

To fight the war on terrorism, the FBI undertook a variety of new roles. It greatly beefed up its counterintelligence and counterterrorism activities. FBI agents now work closely with military intelligence to build information systems about terrorism. The agency is also increasingly involved in international activities. The FBI's international role expanded when it investigated the embassy bombings in Kenya and Tanzania during the 1990s. FBI agents played a key role in interrogat-

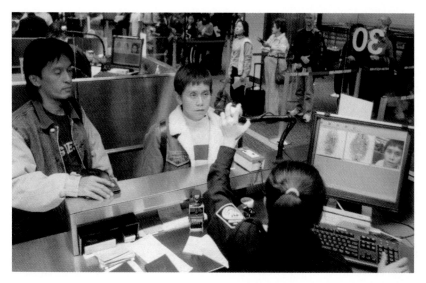

The federal government's response to the terrorist attacks includes the US-VISIT, or U.S. Visitor and Immigrant Status Indicator Technology, which is designed to fingerprint and photograph all visitors entering the United States. It will check up to an estimated 24 million foreigners each year.

FOR CRITICAL ANALYSIS

Why was the Department of Homeland Security created? What problems has the new agency faced?

ing suspects in Afghanistan. This new international role has made the agency more attentive to questions of diplomacy. Once simply a law enforcement agency, in recent years the FBI "has at times resembled a spy agency, diplomatic mission, and military adviser all in one."[8]

Since its creation in 2002, the Department of Home-land Security has joined the Justice Department as the major bureaucracy charged with domestic security. The new department took over some of the security-oriented agencies previously controlled by other departments (see Table 14.2). For example, the Immigration and Natural-ization Service (INS) was moved from Justice to Home-land Security. Once inside the new department, the INS was abolished. Immigration services were consolidated into U.S. Citizenship and Immigration Services. The en-forcement functions of the old INS were combined with the U.S. Customs Services (formerly part of the Treasury Department) to create a new Bureau of Immigration and Customs Enforcement, known as ICE, in the Department of Homeland Security. ICE has extensive investigative capacities, with field offices around the United States and bureaus in over thirty countries. Other agencies that were transferred to the Department of Homeland Security include the Coast Guard, the Secret Service, and the Federal Emergency Management Agency.

Growing pains were evident in the department's first years as different bureau-cratic cultures, now part of a single operation, sought to work together. The new department also quickly became embroiled in turf battles with the FBI (which re-mained in the Justice Department) as the two departments attempted to sort out their respective responsibilities for homeland security. Because the reorganization that created the Department of Homeland Security was so massive, it will take many years before we know whether the decision to bring these different agencies under one management has improved our domestic security.

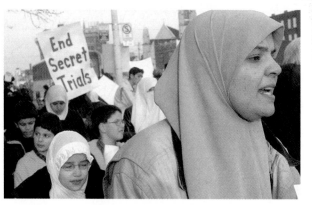

At least one aspect of the government's efforts to provide increased domestic security was controversial. The USA PATRIOT Act gave the attorney general the power to detain foreigners suspected of being potential security threats. The subsequent detention of more than 1,000 suspects led to protests, such as the one pictured here, claiming that the detainees were being denied their due process rights.

Table 14.2   The Shape of a Domestic Security Department

DEPARTMENT OF HOMELAND SECURITY	The agencies and departments that were moved to the main divisions of the Department of Homeland Security under the legislation creating the new department:	Department or agency they were previously under:	From President Bush's budget for the 2003 fiscal year:	
			Budget request, in millions:	Estimated number of employees:
Border and Transportation Security	Immigration and Naturalization Service enforcement functions*	Justice Dept.	$ 6,416	39, 459
	Transportation Security Administration	Transportation Dept.	4,800	41,300
	Customs Service	Treasury Dept.	3,796	21,743
	Federal Protective Services	General Services Administration	418	1,408
	Animal and Plant Health Inspection Service (parts)	Agriculture Dept.	402	3,974
Emergency Preparedness and Response	Federal Emergency Management Agency	*(Independent agency)*	$ 6,174	5,135
	Chemical, biological, radiological and nuclear response units	Health and Human Services Dept.	2,104	150
	Nuclear incident response teams	Energy Dept.	91	†
	National Domestic Preparedness Office	FBI	2	15
	Office of Domestic Preparedness	Justice Dept.	§	§
	Domestic Emergency Support Teams	*From various depts. and agencies*	*Not applicable*	*Not applicable*
Science and Technology	Civilian biodefense research programs	Health and Human Services Dept.	$ 1,993	150
	National Biological Warfare Defense Analysis Center	*(Proposed in fiscal 2003 budget)*	420	Not available
	Plum Island Animal Disease Center	Agriculture Dept.	25	124
	Lawrence Livermore National Laboratory (parts)	Energy Dept.	*Not available*	*Not available*
Information Analysis and Infrastructure Protection	National Communications System	Defense Dept.	$ 155	91
	National Infrastructure Protection Center	FBI	151	795
	Critical Infrastructure Assurance Office	Commerce Dept.	27	65
	National Infrastructure Simulation and Analysis Center	Energy Dept.	20	2
	Federal Computer Incident Response Center	General Services Administration	11	23
Secret Service	Secret Service, including presidential protection units	Treasury Dept.	$ 1,248	6,111
Coast Guard	Coast Guard	Transportation Dept.	$ 7,274	43, 639
		TOTAL	**$35,527**	**164,184**

Source: The White House   *Immigration services became a separate bureau within the department. †Classified §Included in FEMA budget request.

Agencies for External National Security   Two departments occupy center stage in maintaining external national security: the departments of State and Defense.

The State Department's primary mission is diplomacy. As the United States geared up to invade Afghanistan in 2001 and Iraq in 2003, Secretary of State Colin Powell took the lead in building the case for American action. Although diplomacy is the primary task of the State Department, diplomatic missions are only one of its organizational dimensions. As of 2004, the State Department comprised twenty-seven bureau-level units, each under the direction of an assistant secretary. Six of these are geographic or regional bureaus concerned with all problems within a defined region of the world; thirteen are "functional" bureaus, handling such things as economic and business affairs, intelligence and research, and international organizations. Four are bureaus of internal affairs, which handle such areas as security, finance and management, and legal issues.

These bureaus support the responsibilities of the elite of foreign affairs, the foreign service officers (FSOs), who staff U.S. embassies around the world and who hold almost all of the most powerful positions in the department below the rank of ambassador.[9] The ambassadorial positions, especially the plum positions in the major capitals of the world, are filled by presidential appointees, many of whom get their positions by having been important donors to the victorious political campaign.

Despite the importance of the State Department in foreign affairs, fewer than 20 percent of all U.S. government employees working abroad are directly under its authority. By far the largest number of career government professionals working abroad are under the authority of the Defense Department.

The creation of the Department of Defense by legislation between 1947 and 1949 was an effort to unify the two historic military departments, the War Department and the Navy Department, and to integrate them with a new department, the Air Force. Real unification, however, did not occur. The Defense Department simply added more pluralism to an already pluralistic national security establishment.

The American military, following worldwide military tradition, is organized according to a "chain of command"—a tight hierarchy of clear responsibility and rank, made clearer by uniforms, special insignia, and detailed organizational charts and rules of order and etiquette. The "line agencies" in the Department of Defense are the military commands, distributed geographically by divisions and fleets to deal with current or potential enemies. The "staff agencies," such as logistics, intelligence, personnel, research and development, quartermaster, and engineering, exist to serve the "line agencies." At the top of the military chain of command are chiefs of staff (called chief of naval operations in the navy, and commandant in the marines). These chiefs of staff also constitute the membership of the Joint Chiefs of Staff—the center of military policy and management.

In 2002, for the first time in our nation's history, the Defense Department created a regional commander in chief charged with homeland defense and command of military operations inside the nation's borders. The U.S. Northern Command is charged with providing emergency backup to state and local governments, who are the first responders to any security disaster. It also provides security when military personnel or equipment is needed. For example, during the 2004 Super Bowl the Northern Command deployed aircraft to patrol airspace above Houston's Reliant Stadium, which had been declared a no-fly zone. The creation of a regional command within the United States is an unprecedented move, breaching a long-standing line between domestic law enforcement and foreign military operations.

USAID and American Foreign Aid

As the modern world's first democracy, the United States has always regarded its international role as one that should not only project the nation's military power but also embody American values. In the second half of the twentieth century, as the Cold War pitted the United States against the Soviet Union in struggles around the world, the need to project American values onto the world stage became more urgent.

To fulfill this role, Congress created the U.S. Agency for International Development (USAID) in 1961. USAID's mission was to promote long-term economic and social development around the world. Officially an independent agency, USAID works under the guidance of the State Department. Thus, USAID has always been closely tied to American foreign policy objectives. As such, it has often been the target of critics who argue that the agency mainly serves American economic and political interests abroad. They charge that USAID not only fails to promote American values, but actually undermines democracy, equality, and liberty in many of the countries where it provides assistance.

Some of USAID's earliest projects included promoting economic development in Latin America and stemming communism in Southeast Asia. The agency's activities in Southeast Asia were particularly controversial. In helping to support anticommunism, USAID became embroiled in the Vietnam War. Critics claimed that the agency operated as a tool of the American military, focusing on short-term military goals, not long-term economic and social issues.

Today, USAID's major goals are to support economic growth, agricultural development, and trade with the developing world; promote global health; advance democracy and peace; and provide humanitarian assistance. The agency has field offices all over the world and works closely with a wide range of nongovernmental organizations, which receive USAID contracts to support their work.

To promote democracy, USAID works in new or unstable democracies, supporting projects that encourage respect for law and human rights, competitive elections, public participation, and the development of accountability in governing institutions. For example, USAID aims to strengthen democracy in Eastern Europe with programs that train judges and lawyers and efforts to promote an in-

dependent media. In Africa, the agency's global health objectives are at the forefront.

USAID has also played a leading role in the reconstruction of Afghanistan and Iraq. In addition to providing basic humanitarian assistance, it has sought to promote democracy in these countries. Toward this goal it has launched programs that supply training in democratic government, promote literacy for women, and rebuild education systems.

Although criticism of USAID is not as vocal today as it was during the Vietnam War, some charge that the agency continues to promote America's narrow economic and political interests at the expense of its deepest values. For example, critics contend that many of the agricultural programs supported by USAID replace local farming with cheaper American food sources. In so doing, they help open markets for American agricultural products but undermine local development and thus exacerbate rather than alleviate poverty. In Iraq, several major nongovernmental organizations refused to work with USAID because the agency was working under guidance from the Pentagon. Nongovernmental organizations that were working under USAID contracts in Iraq were especially troubled in 2003 when USAID head Andrew Natsios told them they had to do a better job of highlighting their ties with the Bush administration in order to receive further funding.[a]

As the world's richest nation and only superpower, the United States is uniquely situated to project its values internationally. As an agency that supports both American foreign policy and foreign aid programs designed to promote American values, USAID often finds itself in the crosshairs when the two conflict.

FOR CRITICAL ANALYSIS

1. Why did the United States create an agency devoted to promoting American values in the developing world? Is this a good use of taxpayer dollars?

2. Why has USAID often been the target of critics? How do its missions of promoting American values abroad and serving American foreign policy conflict with one another?

[a]Alan Beattie, "NGOs under Pressure on Relief Funds," *Financial Times*, June 13, 2003, p. 11.

The 9/11 Commission's Proposal to Reorganize Security In 2004, the National Commission on Terrorist Attacks upon the United States (the 9/11 Commission) issued a widely read report that called for a major reorganization of bureaucratic responsibilities for internal and external security.[10] The report revealed that different departments of the American government had information that, if handled properly, might have prevented the attacks of September 11, 2001. The commission found that the federal government's attempts to improve security after September 11 still did not address the critical problems with duplication, prioritization, and coordination in the current system. To correct this, the commission made major recommendations designed to promote unity of effort across the bureaucracy.

Topping the list were proposals designed to bridge the divide between domestic and foreign security efforts. Prior to September 11, the FBI, which collects domestic information, did not talk to the CIA, and the Defense Department collected mountains of information that was not shared with either the FBI or the CIA. The commission recommended the creation of a National Counterterrorism Center. The NCTC would function like a superbrain that would analyze all sources of intelligence and plan appropriate operational responses that could be carried out by existing agencies, such as the State Department, the CIA, the FBI, the Department of Homeland Security, and others. The commission also recommended that the President create a new position: National Intelligence Director. The director would oversee all intelligence activities in the federal government and advise the president about intelligence issues. Reporting to the national intelligence director would be the head of the CIA, the undersecretary of defense for intelligence, and the FBI's executive assistant director for intelligence. The national intelligence director's prime responsibilities would be to survey the range of future issues that threaten American security and see to it that necessary information was collected, and appropriate action taken. Under this new reorganization, the new director would have the budgetary authority to shift money between different intelligence agencies, as necessary. This was sure to displease the Department of Defense, which controls 80 percent of the intelligence budget. It was also sure to be opposed by the CIA, whose director would no longer have overall responsibility for intelligence.

The 9/11 Commission's high-profile televised hearings and its serious, nonpartisan approach to questions of national security gave it enormous public credibility. Because of this, politicians had to pay attention to its recommendations. A bipartisan group of congressional members introduced bills in the House and the Senate to enact most of the report's provisions. Although President Bush did not initially favor creating the commission and appeared lukewarm towards its recommendations, he eventually embraced one of its key recommendations when he announced his support for appointing a new national intelligence director with full budgetary authority. Even with the president's backing, the road to such a major bureaucratic reorganization was politically difficult. Many interests, including the Department of Defense and the CIA, lobbied fiercely to retain their autonomy and control over funds. However, the strong political momentum behind the report and its visibility in an election year where national security issues were front and center meant that the recommendations stood a good chance of becoming law.

National Security and Democracy Of all the agencies in the federal bureaucracy, those charged with providing national security most often come into tension with the norms and expectations of American democracy. Two issues in particular arise as these agencies work to ensure the national security: (1) the trade-offs between respecting the personal rights of individuals versus protecting the general public and (2) the need for secrecy in matters of national security versus the public's right to know what the government is doing. Standards about what is an acceptable trade-off in each area vary depending on whether the country is at war or peace. The nature of the threat facing national security also affects judgments about the appropriate trade-offs. Needless to say, Americans often disagree about such threats and therefore take different views about what activities the government should be able to pursue to defend our national security. At the outset of the war on terrorism, the nation was unusually united in its support for a wide range of government security measures that would have been highly controversial in any other circumstance.

When national security is at stake, federal agencies have taken actions that are normally considered incompatible with individual rights. For example, in World War II, thousands of American citizens of Japanese descent were interned for national security reasons. Although the Supreme Court declared this action justified, the federal government has since acknowledged that it constituted unjustified discrimination and has offered reparations to those who were interned. In the 1960s, FBI director J. Edgar Hoover authorized extensive wiretaps to eavesdrop on telephone calls of civil rights leader Martin Luther King, Jr.; most people today would regard this an illegal invasion of his personal privacy. With the advent of the war on terrorism, the government gained unprecedented powers to detain foreign suspects, carry out wiretaps and searches, conduct secret military tribunals, and build an integrated law enforcement and intelligence system. Congress hastily enacted many of these sweeping provisions of the PATRIOT Act several weeks after the terrorist attacks, with little debate. Since then, extensive doubts about the broad powers of the PATRIOT Act have emerged. As denunciations of the act spread from civil libertarians on the left to libertarians on the right and to groups such as librarians and city governments, who object to its surveillance provisions, Congress began to consider measures that would restrict federal power in order to protect individual liberties. The Bush administration, seeking to preserve the new powers, threatened to wield what would be its first veto against any efforts to roll back the PATRIOT Act.

Protecting the national security often requires the government to conduct its activities in secret. Yet, as Americans have come to expect a more open government in the past three decades, many critics believe that federal agencies charged with national security keep too many secrets from the American public. In the words of one critic, "the United States government must rest, in the words of the Declaration of Independence, on 'the consent of the governed.' And there can be no meaningful consent where those who are governed do not know to what they are consenting."[11] The effort to make information related to national security more available to the public began in 1966 with the passage of the Freedom of Information Act. Strengthened in 1974 after Watergate, the act allows any person to request classified information from any federal agency. It is estimated that the federal government spends $80 million a year responding to 600,000 requests for information.[12]

The information obtained through the Freedom of Information Act often reveals unflattering or unsuccessful aspects of national security activities. One private organization, the National Security Archive, makes extensive use of the Freedom of Information Act to obtain information about the activities of national security agencies. These include documents about a wide range of activities such as American involvement in the Cuban Bay of Pigs invasion in 1961 and human rights abuses in Latin America and the Caribbean in the past three decades. Such documents are often kept secret not because they threaten national security but because they are embarrassing or show that federal agencies violated accepted norms of human rights. The National Security Archive has published many of these documents on its Web site and maintains an archive in Washington, D.C., that is open to the public.

The tension between secrecy and democracy has sharpened dramatically with the war on terrorism. The Freedom of Information Act (FOIA) has been curtailed, and the range of information deemed sensitive has greatly expanded. President Bush defended the new secrecy, declaring, "We're an open society, but we're at war. Foreign terrorists and agents must never again be allowed to use our freedoms against us." While most Americans agreed that enhanced secrecy was needed to ensure domestic security, concerns about excessive secrecy mounted. Some analysts worried that secrecy would prevent Congress from carrying out its basic oversight responsibilities. They also claimed that much of the secrecy had nothing to do with national security. As head of the commission appointed to investigate the events of September 11, including related intelligence failures, former New Jersey Governor Tom Kean became a critic of the level of secrecy in the Bush administration. "I've been reading these highly, highly classified documents. In most cases, I finish with them, I look up and say, 'Why is this classified?' And so one of the things that I hope is that maybe out of our work and maybe others, a lot of these documents that are classified will be unclassified."[13] Others charged that the Bush administration was reversing the trend toward a more open government on issues that had nothing to do with domestic security (see Figure 14.5). Indeed, even as the war on terrorism was the central issue on the public's mind, the administration faced lawsuits from historians for blocking the release of routine documents from the Reagan administration. And in an unprecedented move, the Government Accountability Office, the investigative arm of Congress, sued the administration for failing to disclose information about Vice President Dick Cheney's task force on energy. The Supreme Court sent the case back to a lower court in 2003.

There are no easy answers to the questions about how the needs for national security should be reconciled with the values of a democratic society. It is clear, however, that in an era when national security is foremost in the public's mind, conflicts between democracy and secrecy are sure to increase.

MAINTAINING A STRONG ECONOMY

In our capitalist economic system, the government does not directly run the economy. Yet many federal government activities are critical to maintaining a strong economy. Foremost among these are the agencies responsible for fiscal and monetary policy. Other agencies, such as the Internal Revenue Service (IRS), transform private resources into use for public purposes. Tax policy may also strengthen the economy through decisions about whom to tax, how much, and when. Finally, the federal government, through such agencies as the Department of Transportation,

Figure 14.5 **Keeping Secrets**

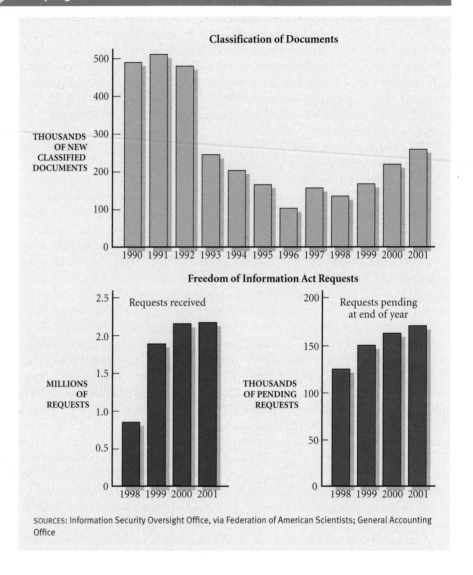

Classification of Documents

THOUSANDS OF NEW CLASSIFIED DOCUMENTS

Freedom of Information Act Requests

Requests received

MILLIONS OF REQUESTS

Requests pending at end of year

THOUSANDS OF PENDING REQUESTS

SOURCES: Information Security Oversight Office, via Federation of American Scientists; General Accounting Office

the Commerce Department, and the Energy Department may directly provide services or goods that bolster the economy.

fiscal policy the use of taxing, monetary, and spending powers to manipulate the economy

Fiscal and Monetary Agencies   The best term for government activity affecting or relating to money is **fiscal policy.** The *fiscus* was the Roman imperial treasury; "fiscal" can refer to anything and everything having to do with public finance. However, we in the United States choose to make a further distinction, reserving *fiscal* for taxing and spending policies and using *monetary* for policies having to do with banks, credit, and currency. Yet a third term, *welfare,* deserves to be treated as an equal member of this redistributive category.[14]

The administration of fiscal policy occurs primarily in the Treasury Department. In addition to collecting income, corporate, and other taxes, the Treasury is also re-

Secrecy and Openness
in the War on Terrorism

During the 1950s and 1960s, in the early decades of the cold war, the federal government argued that secrecy was essential to ensure national security. Information about a diverse range of government activities was routinely classified so that the public had no access to it. The 1973–74 Watergate scandal marked a sea change in this culture of secrecy. The Watergate hearings revealed that under the mantle of national security, the government had initiated unlawful activities and engaged in unjustifiable invasions of individual privacy. As a consequence, new legislation opened the bureaucracy up to greater public scrutiny, and the 1974 Freedom of Information Act allowed individuals to request access to classified information. In the aftermath of the September 11 terrorist attacks, President Bush defended the need to reimpose greater secrecy in the interests of national security. His administration immediately took significant measures to limit public access to information about government activities. After September 11, the administration removed hundreds of thousands of public documents from the Internet. Some of these documents are available for consultation by special request in a government facility. Others are entirely off limits to the public. The administration also refused to reveal the identities of more than 1,100 people held in custody—but not charged—for suspected terrorism. And in a move designed to weaken one of the most important tools promoting public disclosure, Attorney General John Ashcroft issued a directive to government agencies to use greater caution in responding to freedom of information requests.

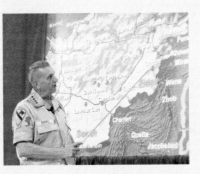

Supporters of enhanced secrecy contend that standards of openness prevalent in peacetime must give way during a war. Although most of the war on terrorism is not visible to the public, the need for secrecy may be even greater than in other wars in which the United States has been involved. Terrorists rely on publicly available sources of information to plan their attacks. Apparently innocuous information about the location of facilities, such as nuclear power plants or water treatment facilities, provides terrorists with vulnerable targets. When such information is available on the Internet, the job of the terrorist is even easier. Potential targets can be researched half a world away from the United States. Furthermore, counterterrorism is a delicate task. If the sources of information on which counterintelligence agencies rely become public, these sources may become unavailable in the future. For example, until 1998, the government tracked the activities of Osama bin Laden through calls he made on his satellite phone. When this knowledge became publicly available, bin Laden apparently stopped using the phone, making him much harder to track.

Critics contend that the administration has gone too far in its quest for secrecy. They agree that standards for government disclosure of information must be tightened to fight against terrorism but charge that the administration is taking advantage of the situation. The administration has claimed a right to secrecy on issues that have nothing to do with national security, as in its refusal to divulge the proceedings of its energy task force. Even in matters of national security, the administration has gone overboard, according to critics. Without access to information, Congress cannot exercise its oversight responsibilities, which are vital to democratic accountability. And, as in the past, secrecy that is officially justified by national security concerns may result in gross violations of the civil liberties of individuals who have nothing to do with terrorism. The secrecy surrounding those jailed as part of the terrorism probe distorts the American system of justice, since very few of these individuals were actually charged with a crime.

Finally, critics charge that secrecy will eventually erode public confidence in the government, thus undermining the war on terrorism. When information leaked that President Bush had been briefed in August 2001 about Al Qaeda's interest in hijacking American airplanes, the public began for the first time to question the administration's secrecy. In a public opinion poll, 68 percent of those questioned said that the administration should have revealed this information earlier. In the post-Watergate climate of Washington, it is much harder to keep secrets than it was in the Cold War era. Nothing will hurt the war on terrorism more, critics charge, than a cynical public that does not believe its government.

FOR CRITICAL ANALYSIS

1. Why is greater government secrecy necessary since the terrorist attacks in 2001?

2. How does secrecy undermine basic American values? How can the United States guard against terrorism without destroying the fundamental liberties that define our nation?

Can the Government Withhold Information?

Yes Americans already uneasy about the terrorist attacks on the United States should not have to worry about their government spreading misleading information. Since September 11, rumors circulated about what was actually going on. If releasing information conflicts with maintaining national security, then don't release the information to the press. Don't spread misleading information at press conferences or through government leaks. That is irresponsible. Explain to the press and the American public why information can't be released. No one wants to endanger American troops or the security of the nation. Media organizations will understand, even if they still ask the questions.

If the government does not act responsibly with its information, it will chip away at the public's trust at a time when it's needed most. It is unfair to lie to the public and the press. During *Meet the Press* on September 16, Vice President Dick Cheney said he needed to be careful in answering questions about the military's actions. He said it would be inappropriate to talk about specific military operations. We agree. But we are still left weary after conflicting reports that came forward regarding the plane that crashed in Pennsylvania. Initial reports came in that the plane crashed for unknown reasons. Then it was said to have been shot down by U.S. military forces. Now it appears that brave passengers on the plane struggled with the terrorists.

During televised press conferences before the attack on Afghanistan, U.S. Secretary of Defense Donald H. Rumsfeld didn't answer reporters' questions about where troops would be going or if they had already left. He was trying to protect the troops and the government's military strategy, and we agree with his actions. But maintaining the public's trust in the government's word is difficult to do after previous misleading information. According to a *Washington Post* story published September 25, Pentagon officials lied about the deployment of a U.S. aircraft carrier to the Persian Gulf in 1988. This is unacceptable. The government should not use the media to spin its tales to the American people. We want the truth, to the best of the government's ability, and we don't want to be used as pawns.

The First Amendment protects against a tyrannical government that uses the media for propaganda. We don't consider our government tyrannical, and we want to continue that tradition. We want to keep our First Amendment rights. And we agree with President George W. Bush, who was quoted about the present situation in the same *Washington Post* story, that his administration would not talk about how it gathers information and what it finds.

We understand the sensitivity of the issue. We understand that the safety of the country is in question. Yet the American citizens' questions need to be asked. They deserve to know if their sons and daughters will be called to fight—but not necessarily where they will fight. It's a matter of balance, respect, and trust. Let the people of the United States know as much as they can without hurting the nation's security. And above all, the government should not lie about information. Because it's the freedom of speech, the freedom of the press, and the freedom of the American people for which we're fighting this war.

SOURCE: Editorial Board, "Spinning Games," *Daily Nebraskan* (University of Nebraska), October 16, 2001.

No If you are among the 42 percent of Americans who, according to a recent study, feel the First Amendment goes too far in the rights it guarantees the press, consider the case of the Pentagon Papers. By 1971, the United States was entrenched in an increasingly bloody and hopeless war in Vietnam. Body bags were piling up, military and political officials were without an exit strategy, and protests at home were gaining momentum. Despite this, then-President Richard Nixon and his administration continued to assure Americans that victory would be won.

Meanwhile, circulating the Pentagon was a top-secret study of U.S. involvement in Southeast Asia since World War II that painted a much different picture. The Pentagon Papers, as the report was known, detailed how four successive presidential administrations deceived the American public about U.S. intentions in Vietnam as well as the risks, dangers, and prospects of achieving publicly stated goals. When a disillusioned former military official disclosed the 7,000-page history to the *New York Times,* the government filed an injunction to stop publication. The ensuing legal battle culminated in the landmark Supreme

Court ruling that lifted the prior restraints, permitting continued publication of the Pentagon Papers and allowing American citizens to read firsthand how the government had acted in their name. U.S. democracy, the court understood, would be better for it. In his historic opinion, Justice Hugo Black wrote, "paramount among the responsibilities of a free press is the duty to prevent any part of the government from deceiving the people and sending them off to distant lands to die of foreign fevers and foreign shot and shell."

More than thirty years later, we find ourselves navigating one of the most crucial periods in human history. The threats of terrorism, nuclear proliferation, and growing disparities in wealth and opportunity are among the enormous problems of our unstable world. To understand the shape of these dilemmas, America needs a vibrant and aggressive free press. But many government restrictions imposed after September 11, 2001 have obstructed journalists from doing their jobs. More broadly, the curtailing of civil liberties of all Americans, and many noncitizens who live here, has called into question our long-standing commitment to openness and equal justice. From restrictions on information to detentions without charge and military tribunals, the George W. Bush administration seems to presume that secrecy equals security. And the public, for the most part, doesn't mind.

Black's brilliant words, thirty years on, seem to have been lost on many Americans.

Public regard for the First Amendment is at a new low. The Freedom Forum, a Washington, D.C.,-based think tank, surveyed American attitudes toward the freedoms of speech and press in 2002 and found that more than 49 percent of Americans feel the First Amendment gives us "too much freedom." That's up from 22 percent in the 2000 study. The report also revealed that more than 40 percent of Americans feel newspapers should not be allowed to freely criticize the U.S. military about its strategy and performance.

The lack of appreciation for the First Amendment allows the government considerable room to curb freedoms. With but a whimper of opposition, Congress passed the USA PATRIOT Act, the Homeland Security Act, and other legislation after the September 11 attacks, which eroded civil liberties in the name of security. Pending bills would further expand government secrecy. The result is that today, the government can more easily intercept our e-mail messages and tap our telephone conversations. Noncitizens can be detained indefinitely, veiled from public scrutiny. Military tribunals, closed to the public, can be invoked to try suspected terrorists. Information once available on government Web sites or through the Freedom of Information Act is now restricted or obstructed for fear it could aid terrorists.

Americans, it seems, agree with Bush's claim that terrorists "attacked us because of our freedoms." And they've offered their civil liberties as national sacrifice. But has restricting our freedoms actually made us more secure? It's unlikely.

Democracy demands an informed citizenry make decisions to collectively solve problems. While it's true the executive branch and law enforcement now have broader authority, they also are less accountable. When information is limited and not independently verifiable, our ability to make those democratic decisions is hindered. How can we protect ourselves if we don't know what the problem is? The answer, according to the administration, is to put blind faith in government. A quick survey of U.S. history, however, suggests this is not a good idea. Recall McCarthy-era witch hunts, or the J. Edgar Hoover-era FBI, or the Watergate scandal. Democracy, we've learned, whithers without sunshine.

Just ask H.R. Haldeman. A key player in the Nixon White House and Watergate, Haldeman had this to say about unquestioningly trusting government: "out of the gobbledygook comes a very clear thing: . . . you can't believe what they say; and you can't rely on their judgment; and the implicit infallibility of presidents, which has been an accepted thing in America, is badly hurt by this, because it shows that people do things the president wants to do even though it's wrong, and the president can be wrong."

The First Amendment didn't come cheap. Americans have for more than 200 years fought and died for the ideals it embodies. A proud tradition of leaders—from James Madison and Thomas Jefferson to Ida Tarbell and Martin Luther King, Jr.—have cherished, nurtured, and aggressively defended these freedoms. A new generation must continue this fight. To do otherwise would be, frankly, un-American.

SOURCE: Todd Milbourn, "Why The First Amendment Matters," *The Minnesota Daily* (University of Minnesota), February 24, 2003.

sponsible for managing the enormous national debt—$3.91 trillion in 2003. (The national debt was a mere $710 billion in 1980.)[15] Debt is not simply something the country owes; it is something a country has to manage and administer. The debt is also a fiscal instrument in the hands of the federal government that can be used—through manipulation of interest rates and through the buying and selling of government bonds—to slow down or to speed up the activity of the entire national economy, as well as to defend the value of the dollar in international trade.

The Treasury Department is also responsible for printing the U.S. currency, but currency represents only a tiny proportion of the entire money economy. Most of the trillions of dollars used in the transactions of the private and public sectors of the U.S. economy exist in computerized accounts, not in currency.

Federal Reserve System a system of twelve Federal Reserve Banks that facilitates exchanges of cash, checks, and credit; regulates member banks; and uses monetary policies to fight inflation and deflation

Another important fiscal agency (although for technical reasons it is called an agency of monetary policy) is the **Federal Reserve System,** which is headed by the Federal Reserve Board. The Federal Reserve System (called simply the Fed) has authority over the interest rates and lending activities of the nation's most important banks. Congress established the Fed in 1913 as a clearinghouse responsible for adjusting the supply of money and credit to the needs of commerce and industry in different regions of the country. The Fed is also responsible for ensuring that banks do not overextend themselves, a policy that guards against a chain of bank failures during a sudden economic scare, such as occurred in 1929. The Federal Reserve Board directs the operations of the twelve district Federal Reserve Banks, which are essentially "bankers' banks," serving the monetary needs of the hundreds of member banks in the national banking system.[16] The Fed has become one of the most important actors in economic policy through its power to raise and lower interest rates. Leading financial actors in the banking industry and in the stock market anxiously anticipate quarterly meetings of the Federal Reserve Board, in which decisions about interest rates are made.

revenue agencies agencies responsible for collecting taxes. Examples include the Internal Revenue Service for income taxes, the U.S. Customs Service for tariffs and other taxes on imported goods, and the Bureau of Alcohol, Tobacco, and Firearms for collection of taxes on the sales of those particular products

Revenue Agencies One of the first actions of Congress under President George Washington was to create the Department of the Treasury, and probably its oldest function is the collection of taxes on imports, called tariffs. Now housed in the United States Customs Service, federal customs agents are located at every U.S. seaport and international airport to oversee the collection of tariffs. But far and away the most important of the **revenue agencies** is the Internal Revenue Service (IRS). The Customs Service and the IRS are two of at least twelve bureaus within the Treasury Department.

The IRS is not unresponsive to political influences, especially given the fact that it must maintain cooperative relationships with the two oldest and most important congressional committees, the House Ways and Means Committee and the Senate Finance Committee. Nonetheless, as one expert put it, "probably no organization in the country, public or private, creates as much clientele *dis*favor as the Internal Revenue Service. The very nature of its work brings it into an adversary relationship with vast numbers of Americans every year."[17] Complaints against the IRS have cascaded during the past decade, particularly since 1996 presidential candidate Steve Forbes staged his entire campaign on the need to abolish the IRS and the income tax itself. But aside from the principle of the income tax, all the other complaints against the IRS are against its needless complexity, its lack of sensitivity and responsiveness to individual taxpayers, and its overall lack of efficiency. As one of its critics put it, "Imagine a company that's owed $216 billion plus interest, a company with a 22-percent error rate. A company that spent $4 billion to update a computer system—with little success. It all describes the Internal Revenue Service."[18]

Such complaints led Congress to pass the IRS Restructuring and Reform Act of 1998, which instituted a number of new protections for taxpayers. The new laws aim to make IRS agents more "customer-friendly" and limit the agency's ability to collect money owed through liens on individual income or wages. Moreover, the new law mandates the firing of IRS employees who harass taxpayers or violate their rights. While many applaud the new law, there is also mounting concern that it has made tax agents too timid and that revenue collection is declining as a consequence of the law.[19] There are also charges that the IRS is biased toward wealthy taxpayers and big corporations in the way it carries out its work. In recent years, the IRS has stepped up its scrutiny of low-income filers who claim the Earned Income Tax Credit at the same time that it has relaxed its focus on wealthy taxpayers who can hide their money in complex ways that are expensive and time-consuming to unravel. Moreover, the IRS has been unable to resolve its computer problems. As part of the 1998 reform, the IRS launched an $8 billion effort to update its computer system, contracting with a private firm to design a new system. The IRS relies on a forty-year-old computer system because two previous update efforts failed. The current attempt at upgrading is years behind schedule and substantially over budget. Its success is vital to the future of the IRS, not least because the IRS employees who know how to operate the current system are facing retirement.[20]

The politics of the IRS is most interesting because although thousands upon thousands of individual corporations and wealthy individuals have a strong and active interest in American tax policy, key taxation decisions are set by agreements between the president, the Treasury Department, and the leading members of the two tax committees in Congress. External influence is not spread throughout the fifty states but is much more centralized in the majority political party, a few key figures in Congress, and a handful of professional lobbyists. Suspicions of unfair exemptions and favoritism are widespread, and they do exist, but these exemptions come largely from Congress, *not* from the IRS itself.

Economic Development Agencies   Federal agencies also conduct programs designed to strengthen particular segments of the economy or to provide specific services aimed to strengthen the entire economy. Created in 1889, the Department of Agriculture is the fourth oldest cabinet department. Its initial mission, to strengthen American agriculture through research and assist farmers by providing information about effective farming practices, reflected the enormous importance of agriculture in the American economy. Through its Agricultural Extension Service, the Department of Agriculture established an important presence in rural areas throughout the country. It also built strong support for its activities among the nation's farmers and at the many land grant colleges, where agricultural research has been conducted for over one hundred years.

At first glance, the Department of Transportation, which oversees the nation's highway and air traffic systems, may seem to have little to do with economic development. But effective transportation is the backbone of a strong economy. The interstate highway system, for example, is widely acknowledged as a key factor in promoting economic growth in the decades after World War II. The Departments of Commerce and Energy also oversee programs designed to ensure a strong economy. The Small Business Administration in the Department of Commerce provides loans and technical assistance to small businesses across the country.

In recent decades dissatisfaction with government has led to calls to keep government out of the economy. Yet if the federal government were to disappear, chances are high that the economy would fall into chaos. There is widespread agreement that the federal government should set the basic rules for economic activity and intervene—through such measures as setting interest rates—to keep the economy strong. Some analysts argue that the government role should go beyond rule setting to include more active measures such as investment in infrastructure. These advocates of government action point to the economic benefits of government investments in the interstate highway system and the government research in the 1960s that led to the creation of the Internet.

Can Bureaucracy Be Reinvented?

When citizens complain that government is too bureaucratic, what they often mean is that government bureaucracies seem inefficient and waste money. The poster child for such bureaucratic inefficiency in the late 1980s was the Department of Defense, which was revealed to have spent $640 apiece for toilet seats and $435 apiece for hammers.[21] Many citizens also had personal experience with the federal government: a mountain of forms to fill out, lengthy waits, and unsympathetic service. Why can't government do better? many citizens asked. The application of new technologies and innovative management strategies in the private sector during the 1980s made government agencies look even more lumbering and inefficient by comparison. People were coming to expect faster service and more customer-friendly interactions in the private sector. But how can public sector bureaucracies change their ways when they are not subject to tests of efficiency and cost-effectiveness that often prompt innovation in the private sector?

In 1993, President Clinton launched the National Performance Review (NPR)—a part of his promise to "reinvent government"—to make the federal bureaucracy more efficient, accountable, and effective. Vice President Al Gore took charge of the new effort. The National Performance Review sought to prod federal agencies into adopting flexible, goal-driven practices. Clinton promised that the result would be a government that would "work better and cost less." Virtually all observers agreed that the NPR made substantial progress. Its original goal was to save more than $100 billion over five years, in large part by cutting the federal workforce by 12 percent (more than 270,000 jobs) by the end of 1999. Actually, by the end of 1999, $136 billion in savings were already assured through legislative or administrative action, and the federal workforce had been cut by 377,000.[22]

The NPR also focused on cutting red tape, streamlining procurement (how the government purchases goods and services), improving the coordination of federal management, and simplifying federal rules. For instance, the OMB abolished the notorious 10,000-page Federal Personnel Manual and the Standard Form 171, the government's lengthy job application form. Another example, even more revealing of the nature of the NPR's work, was the employee-designed reform of the Defense Department's method for reimbursing its employees' travel expenses: a process that used to take seventeen steps and two months was streamlined to a four-step, computer-based procedure taking less than fifteen minutes, with anticipated savings of $1 billion over five years.

Another fact about administrative reform is that no reform movement will survive a change of president. Thus, although Republicans have an equal or better record than Democrats in the history of administrative reform, one of the first things that happened as President Bush took the oath of office in January 2001 was the termination of NPR. Reform of public bureaucracies is always complex because strong constituencies may attempt to block changes that they believe will harm them. Instead Bush sought to fulfill his promise of smaller government by launching a far-reaching effort to contract out government jobs. The president introduced new procedures that would subject more than 800,000 federal jobs—nearly half the federal civilian workforce—to competitive outsourcing. If it were determined that a private company could do the job more efficiently, the work would be contracted out. Not surprisingly, Bush's effort aroused considerable opposition from government workers. It also caused controversy in Congress, where it sparked a countermovement to restrict the conditions under which federal jobs could be contracted out.

Bush's efforts to streamline the federal bureaucracy were further complicated by the new demands put on the federal government by the war on terrorism. As we have already seen, the Department of Homeland Security presents a massive management challenge and may not achieve its goal of greater coordination of domestic security agencies for many years. At the same time, the new demands of domestic and international security have made it difficult to reduce the size of government. Although the number of federal civil servants has declined by about 2 percent since Bush took office, the numbers of people employed under federal contracts and grants has grown substantially. The Brookings Institution's Center for Public Service, a Washington-based research organization, estimates that the "true size" of government, including both federal civil service and contract and grant-generated jobs, grew by 10 percent from 1999 to 2002.[23] President Bush thus faces the difficult task of pushing for a controversial reform at the same time that he is managing new government responsibilities and a major governmental reorganization designed to enhance domestic security.

Can the Bureaucracy Be Reduced?

Does bureaucracy serve the interests of all the American people? Or does it provide special benefits for influential interest groups, ignoring public needs? Or does bureaucracy mainly benefit government workers themselves, wasting public money by providing inefficient services? During the 1980s and 1990s, the reputation of the federal bureaucracy was at a low point. The belief that bureaucracy benefited entrenched interests and wasted taxpayer dollars was widespread. The negative image of the federal bureaucracy led to numerous efforts to reduce (or to use the popular contemporary word, "downsize") the bureaucracy. This downsizing could be achieved in at least three ways: termination, devolution, or privatization.

In the last twelve years, there have been several attempts to "reinvent" government. In 1993, President Bill Clinton and Vice President Al Gore established the National Performance Review to reinvent government. Gore promoted this on David Letterman's show, where he railed against the government's procurement requirements, which even specified the number of pieces into which a government ashtray may shatter.

Gore and Clinton also succeeded in cutting back the number of rules promulgated by federal regulatory agencies and touted their success with a press conference on the south lawn of the White House, along with a forklift loaded up with the discarded regulations.

TERMINATION

The only *certain* way to reduce the size of the bureaucracy is to eliminate programs. Variations in the levels of federal personnel and expenditures (as was shown in Figures 14.1 and 14.2) demonstrate the futility of trying to make permanent cuts in existing agencies. Furthermore, most agencies have a supportive constituency that will fight to reinstate any cuts that are made. Termination is the only way to ensure an agency's reduction; this is a rare occurrence, even in the Reagan administration and the first Bush administration, both of which proclaimed a strong commitment to the reduction of the national government. In fact, not a single national government agency or program was terminated during the twelve years of Reagan and Bush.

The Republican-led 104th Congress (1995–96) was even more committed to the termination of programs. Newt Gingrich, Speaker of the House, took Congress by storm with his promises of a virtual revolution in government. But when the dust had settled at the end of the first session of the first Gingrich-led Congress, no significant progress had been made toward downsizing through termination of agencies and programs.[24] The only two agencies eliminated were the Office of Technology Assessment, which provided research for Congress, and the Advisory Council on Intergovernmental Relations, which studied the relationship between the federal government and the states. Significantly, neither of these agencies had a strong constituency to defend it.

The overall lack of success in terminating bureaucracy is a reflection of Americans' love/hate relationship with the national government. As antagonistic as Americans may be toward bureaucracy in general, they benefit from the services being rendered and protections being offered by particular bureaucratic agencies; that is, they fiercely defend their favorite agencies while perceiving no incon-

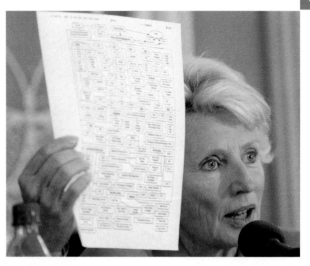

Other aspects of reinventing government have been harder to achieve, often because of the political pressures applied by those who will be affected by the change. For example, closing military bases has been difficult. Members of Congress used to try to overturn decisions to close bases in their districts. Because that is no longer possible, members of Congress such as Dianne Feinstein of California have sought to convert military bases for other government purposes. Critics say this isn't reducing bureaucracy, just shifting it around. The latest case of reinventing government is the largest and most complex yet, the creation of the Department of Homeland Security. Reorganizing the bureaucracy on this level has been a complicated procedure, as the organizational chart being held by Congresswoman Jane Harman attests.

sistency between that defense and their antagonistic attitude toward the bureaucracy in general. A good case in point is the agonizing problem of closing military bases in the wake of the Cold War with the former Soviet Union, when the United States no longer needed so many bases. Since every base was in some congressional member's district, it proved impossible for Congress to decide to close any of them. Consequently, between 1988 and 1990, Congress established a Defense Base Closure and Realignment Commission to decide on base closings, taking the matter out of Congress's hands altogether.[25] And even so, the process was slow and agonizing.

Elected leaders have come to rely on a more incremental approach to downsizing the bureaucracy. Much has been done by budgetary means, reducing the budgets of all agencies across the board by small percentages, and cutting some less-supported agencies by larger amounts. Yet these changes are still incremental, leaving the existence of agencies unaddressed.

An additional approach has been taken to thwart the highly unpopular regulatory agencies, which are so small (relatively) that cutting their budgets contributes virtually nothing to reducing the deficit. This approach is called **deregulation,** simply defined as a reduction in the number of rules promulgated by regulatory agencies. President Reagan used this strategy successfully and was very proud of it. Presidents Bush, Clinton, and George W. Bush have proudly followed Reagan's lead.

DEVOLUTION

The next best approach to genuine reduction of the size of the bureaucracy is **devolution**—downsizing the federal bureaucracy by delegating the implementation of programs to state and local governments. Devolution often alters the pattern of

deregulation a policy of reducing or eliminating regulatory restraints on the conduct of individuals or private institutions

devolution a policy to remove a program from one level of government by delegating it or passing it down to a lower level of government, such as from the national government to the state and local governments

A new strategy to reduce the cost of government is privatization. The United States's military operations have increasingly been privatized. This 2003 photo of Camp Bondsteel, the main U.S. military base in Kosovo, shows private military personnel from one contractor being served by private personnel of another contractor. Private military personnel were also prevalent in Iraq in 2003 and 2004. This photo shows Paul Bremer, the top U.S. administrator in Iraq, being escorted by his private security force.

who benefits most from government programs. Opponents of devolution in social policy, for example, charge that it reduces the ability of the government to remedy inequality. They argue that state governments, which cannot run deficits like the federal government and which have more limited taxing capabilities, will inevitably cut spending on programs that serve low-income residents. They point to the State Child Health Insurance Program, which was created in 1997 to extend health insurance to all low-income children. When the economy was booming, states added children to the rolls and some even extended benefits to their parents. By 2002, however, as states faced their worst budget crisis in decades, many cut back on the Child Health Insurance Program. By one estimate, thirty-four states had cut back on health programs for the poor. In some states, the cuts were very deep: in Texas, an estimated 500,000 low-income people—the majority of whom were children—were in danger of losing their health insurance.[26]

Often the central aim of devolution is to provide more efficient and flexible government services. Yet, by its very nature, devolution entails variation across the states. In some states, government services may improve as a consequence of devolution. In other states, services may deteriorate as the states use devolution as an opportunity to cut spending and reduce services. This has been the pattern in the implementation of the welfare reform passed in 1996, the most significant devolution of federal government social programs in many decades. Some states, such as Wisconsin, have used the flexibility of the reform to design innovative programs that respond to clients' needs; other states, such as Idaho, have virtually dismantled their welfare programs. Because the legislation placed a five-year lifetime limit on receiving welfare, the states will take on an even greater role in the future as existing clients lose their eligibility for federal benefits. Welfare reform has been praised by many for reducing welfare rolls and responding to the public desire that welfare be a temporary program. At the same time, it has placed more low-income women and their children at risk for being left with no form of assistance at all, depending on the state in which they live.

This is the dilemma that devolution poses. To a point, variation can be considered one of the virtues of federalism. But there are dangers inherent in large variations in the provisions of services and benefits in a democracy.

PRIVATIZATION

Privatization seems like a synonym for termination, but that is true only at the extreme. Most of what is called "privatization" is not termination at all but the provision of government goods and services by private contractors under direct government supervision. Except for top-secret strategic materials, virtually all of the production of military hardware, from boats to bullets, is done on a privatized basis by private contractors. Billions of dollars of research services are bought under contract by governments; these private contractors are universities as well as ordinary industrial corporations and private "think tanks." **Privatization** simply means that a formerly public activity is picked up under contract by a private company or companies. But such programs are still very much government programs; they are paid for by government and supervised by government. Privatization downsizes the government only in that the workers providing the service are no longer counted as part of the government bureaucracy.

privatization removing all or part of a program from the public sector to the private sector

The central aim of privatization is to reduce the cost of government. When private contractors can perform a task as well as government but for less money, taxpayers win. Often the losers in such situations are the workers. Government workers are generally unionized and therefore receive good pay and benefits. Private sector workers are less likely to be unionized and private firms often provide lower pay and fewer benefits. For this reason, public sector unions have been one of the strongest voices arguing against privatization. Other critics of privatization observe that private firms may not be more efficient or less costly than government. This is especially likely when there is little competition among private firms and when public bureaucracies are not granted a fair chance to bid in the contracting competition. When private firms have a monopoly on service provision, they may be less efficient than government and more expensive. In fact there is no good evidence that privatization saves the government money. And problems of accountability arise with private contractors just as they do with government workers. The Education Department found that one of its contractors had kept $6.6 million in student loan interest payments that it should have returned. In 2003 the giant company Halliburton, where Vice President Dick Cheney was CEO from 1995 to 2000, became a focus of public attention when it was awarded $9 billion in government contracts related to the Iraq war, with no competitive bidding. Halliburton performed tasks ranging from supplying fuel for the military to providing cafeteria meals. Yet questions emerged about how efficiently it was performing these jobs. Critics charged that Halliburton's gasoline costs were excessive and Pentagon auditors found that Halliburton may have overcharged the government $61 million. Halliburton's meal contracts allowed the company to get paid for 42,000 meals when it only served 14,000 meals. (Fewer soldiers than anticipated ate the Halliburton meals, which they regarded as unpalatable. Soldiers instead paid to eat at local food outlets.)[27] Clearly contracting out is no guarantee of efficiency. Even when there is substantial contracting out, the government continues to play an essential role in monitoring private activity to ensure that money is spent effectively and in accordance with the public will. Accountability and government

FOR CRITICAL ANALYSIS

Many Americans do not believe that the federal bureaucracy serves the public interest. These dissatisfied citizens have supported a range of reforms, including termination of agencies, devolution of responsibility to lower levels of government, and privatization. Are such reforms likely to make the bureaucracy more responsive to public wishes? Who benefits and loses from these reforms?

monitoring became vitally important in the Iraq war where extensive use of private security firms raised troubling questions. One estimate put the number of private security personnel in Iraq at 20,000, compared with 130,000 military personnel. Initially operating without clear rules of engagement or oversight, these private employees confronted dangerous situations with potentially important repercussions for the course of the conflict in Iraq.

FOR CRITICAL ANALYSIS

Private security firms played a significant role in the Iraq War. What are the advantages and disadvantages of relying of private firms in wartime? Can government provide adequate oversight of these private companies?

When government seeks to privatize jobs that are being performed by government workers, privatization can become a political hot potato. Although the term *federal bureaucracy* conjures up images of faceless office workers in Washington, D.C., cubicles, federal jobs are in fact located all over the country. This is one of the reasons that members of Congress from both parties challenged the reach of President Bush's privatization initiative. They sought to limit the scope of competitive outsourcing by declaring some areas off-limits, such as the Department of Interior, which administers the national park system, and much of federal aviation. Congress also sought to improve the terms on which federal agencies can compete to keep the work in house. Depending on how it is conducted, competitive outsourcing may not lead to extensive privatization; instead, competition may improve government performance by forcing federal agencies to reexamine how they can do their work more efficiently.

Can Bureaucracy Be Controlled?

The title of this chapter, "Bureaucracy in a Democracy," is intended to convey the sense that the two are contradictory.[28] Americans cannot live with bureaucracy, but they also cannot live without it. The task is neither to retreat from bureaucracy nor to attack it, but to take advantage of its strengths while making it more accountable to the demands of democratic politics and representative government. This task will be the focus of the remainder of this chapter.

Two hundred years, millions of employees, and trillions of dollars after the Founding, we must return to James Madison's observation, "You must first enable the government to control the governed; and in the next place oblige it to control itself."[29] Today the problem is the same, only now the process has a name: administrative accountability. Accountability implies that there is some higher authority by which the actions of the bureaucracy will be guided and judged. The highest authority in a democracy is *demos*—the people—and the guidance for bureaucratic action is the popular will. But that ideal of accountability must be translated into practical terms by the president and Congress.

THE PRESIDENT AS CHIEF EXECUTIVE

In 1937, President Franklin Roosevelt's Committee on Administrative Management gave official sanction to an idea that had been growing increasingly urgent: "The president needs help." The national government had grown rapidly during the preceding twenty-five years, but the structures and procedures necessary to manage the burgeoning executive branch had not yet been established. The response to the call for "help" for the president initially took the form of three management policies: (1) All communications and decisions that related to executive policy decisions must pass through the White House. (2) In order to cope with such a flow, the

White House must have adequate staffs of specialists in research, analysis, legislative and legal writing, and public affairs. (3) The White House must have additional staff to follow through on presidential decisions—to ensure that those decisions are made, communicated to Congress, and carried out by the appropriate agency.

Making the Managerial Presidency   Establishing a management capacity for the presidency began in earnest with FDR, but it did not stop there.[30] The story of the modern presidency can be told largely as a series of responses to the plea for managerial help. Indeed, each expansion of the national government into new policies and programs in the twentieth century was accompanied by a parallel expansion of the president's management authority. This pattern began even before FDR's presidency, with the policy innovations of President Woodrow Wilson between 1913 and 1920. Congress responded to Wilson's policies with the 1921 Budget and Accounting Act, which turned over the prime legislative power of budgeting to the White House. Each successive president has continued this pattern, creating what we now know as the "managerial presidency."

Presidents John Kennedy and Lyndon Johnson were committed both to government expansion and to management expansion, in the spirit of their party's hero, FDR. President Nixon also strengthened and enlarged the managerial presidency, but for somewhat different reasons. He sought the strongest possible managerial hand because he had to assume that the overwhelming majority of federal employees had sympathies with the Democratic Party, which had controlled the White House and had sponsored governmental growth for twenty-eight of the previous thirty-six years.[31]

President Jimmy Carter was probably more preoccupied with administrative reform and reorganization than any other president in the twentieth century. His reorganization of the civil service will long be recognized as one of the most significant contributions of his presidency. The Civil Service Reform Act of 1978 was the first major revamping of the federal civil service since its creation in 1883. The 1978 act abolished the century-old Civil Service Commission (CSC) and replaced it with three agencies, each designed to handle one of the CSC's functions on the theory that the competing demands of these functions had given the CSC an "identity crisis." The Merit Systems Protection Board (MSPB) was created to defend competitive merit recruitment and promotion from political encroachment. A separate Federal Labor Relations Authority (FLRA) was set up to administer collective bargaining and individual personnel grievances. The third new agency, the Office of Personnel Management (OPM), was created to manage recruiting, testing, training, and the retirement system. The Senior Executive Service was also created at this time to recognize and foster "public management" as a profession and to facilitate the movement of top, "supergrade" career officials across agencies and departments.[32]

Carter also tried to impose a stringent budgetary process on all executive agencies. Called "zero-base budgeting," it was a method of budgeting from the bottom up, wherein each agency was required to rejustify its entire mission rather than merely its next year's increase. Zero-base budgeting did not succeed, but the effort was not lost on President Reagan. Although Reagan gave the impression of being a laid-back president, he actually centralized management to an unprecedented degree. From Carter's "bottom-up" approach, Reagan went to a "top-down" approach, whereby the initial budgetary decisions would be made in the White House and the agencies would be required to fit within those decisions. This process converted the Office of Management and Budget (OMB) into an agency of policy determination and presidential management.[33] President Bush took Reagan's centralization strategy even further in using the White House staff instead of cabinet secretaries for managing the executive branch.[34]

President Clinton was often criticized for the way he managed his administration. His easygoing approach to administration led critics to liken his management style to college "bull sessions" complete with pizza and "all-nighters." Yet, as we have seen, Clinton also inaugurated one of the most systematic efforts "to change the way government does business" in his National Performance Review. Heavily influenced by the theories of management consultants who prized decentralization, customer responsiveness, and employee initiative, Clinton sought to infuse these new practices into government.[35]

George W. Bush was the first president with a degree in business. His management strategy followed a standard business school dictum: select skilled subordinates and delegate responsibility to them. Bush followed this model closely in his appointment of highly experienced officials to cabinet positions and in his selection of Dick Cheney for vice president. Indeed, at the outset of his term, Bush often appeared overshadowed by these appointees (and the vice president in particular). Many observers had the impression that Bush did not lead his own administration. The president's performance during the wars in Afghanistan and Iraq and the war on terrorism dispelled many doubts about his executive capabilities.

Decades of reform have increased the managerial capacity of the presidency, but such reforms themselves do not ensure democratic accountability—presidents must put their managerial powers to use. Although Ronald Reagan was an enormously popular president, he was faulted for his disengaged management style. During his administration, the National Security Council staff was not prevented from running its own policies toward Iran and Nicaragua for at least two years (1985–86) after Congress had explicitly restricted activities toward Nicaragua and the president had forbidden negotiations with Iran. The Tower Commission, appointed to investigate the Iran-Contra affair, concluded that although there was nothing fundamentally wrong with the institutions involved in foreign-policy making—the Department of State, the Department of Defense, the White House, and Congress—there had been a "flawed process," "a failure of responsibility," and a thinness of the president's personal engagement in the issues. The Tower Commission found that "at no time did [President Reagan] insist upon accountability and performance review."[36]

Presidents may also use their managerial capacities to limit democratic accountability if they believe it is a hindrance to effective government. Even in the unusual circumstances of the war on terrorism, critics question whether the Bush administration has been too quick to assert **executive privilege** and shield its actions from public scrutiny. In such circumstances, the separation of powers between the branches of government may be the best way to ensure democratic accountability.

executive privilege power that presidents assert in order to protect the executive branch from Congress and the judiciary. Executive privilege allows presidents to refuse some requests for information from Congress or the judiciary. Justified on the basis of the separation of powers, not the Constitution, executive privilege is subject to limitation by the courts

Thinking Critically about Responsible Bureaucracy in a Democracy

Congress is constitutionally essential to responsible bureaucracy because ultimately the key to bureaucratic responsibility is legislation. When a law is passed and its intent is clear, the accountability for implementation of that law is also clear. Then the president knows what to "faithfully execute," and the responsible agency understands what is expected of it. But when Congress enacts vague legislation, agencies must resort to their own interpretations. The president and the federal courts often step in to tell agencies what the legislation intended. And so do the most intensely interested groups. Yet when everybody, from president to courts to interest groups, gets involved in the actual interpretation of legislative intent, to whom and to what is the agency accountable? Even when the agency wants to behave responsibly, how shall accountability be accomplished?

Congress's answer is **oversight.** The more power Congress has delegated to the executive, the more it has sought to reinvolve itself in directing the interpretation of laws through committee and subcommittee oversight of each agency. The standing committee system in Congress is well suited for oversight, inasmuch as most of the congressional committees and subcommittees have jurisdictions roughly parallel to one or more departments and agencies, and members of Congress who sit on these committees can develop expertise equal to that of the bureaucrats. Appropriations committees as well as authorization committees have oversight powers—as do their respective subcommittees. In addition to these, the Government Reform and Oversight Committee in the House and the Governmental Affairs Committee in the Senate have oversight powers not limited by departmental jurisdiction.

> **oversight** the effort by Congress, through hearings, investigations, and other techniques, to exercise control over the activities of executive agencies

The best indication of Congress's oversight efforts is the use of public hearings, before which bureaucrats and other witnesses are summoned to discuss and defend agency budgets and past decisions. The data drawn from systematic studies of congressional committee and subcommittee hearings and meetings show quite dramatically that Congress has tried through oversight to keep pace with the expansion of the executive branch. Between 1950 and 1980, for example, the annual number of committee and subcommittee meetings in the House of Representatives rose steadily from 3,210 to 7,022; in the Senate, the number of such meetings rose from 2,607 to 4,265 (in 1975–76). Beginning in 1980 in the House and 1978 in the Senate, the number of committee and subcommittee hearings and meetings slowly began to decline, reaching 4,222 in the House and 2,597 in the Senate by the mid-1980s. New questions about the ability of Congress to exercise oversight arose when the Republicans took over Congress in 1995. Reductions in committee staffing and an emphasis on using investigative oversight to uncover scandal meant much less time spent on programmatic oversight. Moreover, congressional Republicans complained that they could not get sufficient information about programs from the White House to conduct effective oversight. Congressional records show that in 1991–92, when Democrats controlled the House, they issued reports on fifty-five federal programs, while in 1997–98, the Republican Congress issued only fourteen.[37] On issues of major national importance multiple committees may initiate oversight hearings simultaneously. In the months after the terror attacks in 2001, Congress exercised little of its oversight powers around issues of national security. At the time it seemed more important to support the president. Since then, however, many congressional committees have convened hearings related to the war on terrorism. These investigations cover a broad range of issues, including intelligence failures prior to the attacks, the financial war on terrorism, the implementation of the PATRIOT Act, and the reconstruction of Iraq after the war. Even so, critics maintain that strong party ties between President Bush and the Republican Congress have resulted in weaker congressional oversight.

The report of the 9/11 Commission drew attention to the problems with congressional oversight of the intelligence community. Noting that "congressional oversight may be among the most difficult and important" of all its recommendations, the Commission declared that current arrangements were "dysfunctional."[38] It found that the existing intelligence committees in Congress had insufficient power and expertise to provide adequate oversight. The Commission recommended the creation of a joint congressional committee or a single committee in either house with the ability to authorize and appropriate expenditures. The committees would be small and have a balanced partisan membership that would serve for an indefinite period of time, in order to develop the expertise and political credibility to oversee intelligence activities.

The Commission also recommended reorganizing congressional oversight of homeland security. Given that "the leaders of the Department of Homeland Security now appear before 88 committees and subcommittees of Congress,"[39] responsibility was spread so thinly that it was impossible to achieve accountability. The Commission advised that Congress create a single permanent standing committee in the House and in the Senate to provide a "principal point of oversight and review for homeland security."[40]

Although congressional oversight is potent because of Congress's power to make, and therefore to change, the law, often the most effective and influential lever over bureaucratic accountability is "the power of the purse"—the ability of the House and Senate committees and subcommittees on appropriations to look at agency performance through the microscope of the annual appropriations process (see Chapter 12). This annual process makes bureaucrats attentive to Congress because they know that Congress has a chance each year to reduce their funding.[41]

Oversight can also be carried out by individual members of Congress. Such inquiries addressed to bureaucrats are considered standard congressional "case work" and can turn up significant questions of public responsibility even when the motivation is only to meet the demand of an individual constituent. Oversight also takes place through communications between congressional staff and agency staff. The number of congressional staff has been enlarged tremendously since the Legislative Reorganization Act of 1946, and the legislative staff, especially the staff of the committees, is just as professionalized and specialized as the staff of executive agencies. In addition, Congress has created for itself three large agencies whose obligations are to engage in constant research on problems taking place in or confronted by the executive branch. These are the General Accounting Office (GAO), the Congressional Research Service (CRS), and the Congressional Budget Office (CBO). Each of these agencies is designed to give Congress information independent of the information it can get directly from the executive branch through hearings and other communications.[42] Normally a low-visibility agency, the GAO stepped into the national spotlight in 2002 when it sued the Bush administration for the release of information about its energy-policy task force. It was the first time the GAO had ever sued an administration in its eighty-year history. Another source of information for oversight is direct from citizens through the Freedom of Information Act (FOIA), which we have seen gives ordinary citizens the right to access agency files and agency data to determine whether derogatory information exists in the file about the citizens themselves and to learn about what the agency is doing in general. Nevertheless, the information gained by citizens through FOIA can be effective only through the institutionalized channels of congressional committees and, on a few occasions, through public-interest litigation in the federal courts.

The Bush administration's effort to expand the scope of contracting out raises new questions about democratic accountability. When government work is contracted out, federal monitoring is essential to ensure that funds are spent in accordance with the public will and to confirm that the costs are fair. Yet, even with monitoring, accountability may be hard to achieve. Many of the mechanisms of democratic accountability do not apply to private firms that contract to perform public work. For example, private corporations can resist FOIA requests, and they are not constrained by the same ethics rules as public employees. Moreover, because private firms do not have to disclose information about their operations in the same way that public bureaucracies do, Congress has much more limited oversight. The move to contracting out clearly presents major challenges to democratic accountability in the future.

As the president and Congress seek to translate the ideal of democratic accountability into practice, they struggle to find the proper balance between administrative discretion and the public's right to know. An administration whose every move is subject to intense public scrutiny may be hamstrung in its efforts to carry out the public interest. On the other hand, a bureaucracy that is shielded from the public eye may wind up pursuing its own interests rather than those of the public. The last century has seen a double movement toward strengthening the managerial capacity of the presidency and ensuring that bureaucratic decision making is more transparent. The purpose of these reforms has been to create an effective, responsive bureaucracy. But reforms alone cannot guarantee democratic accountability. Presidential and congressional vigilance in defense of the public interest is essential.

GET INVOLVED
What You Can Do:
Get Inside the Bureaucracy

Whether it has to do with taxes and the IRS, or passports and the State Department, or the motor vehicles agency or absentee voting or traffic cops at the state and local levels, citizens have more tools available to them than they may think. Public access to the workings of bureaucracies has been vastly facilitated in the past thirty years, in large part due to FOIA, which was enacted in 1966. Under FOIA, ordinary citizens can request documents from any government agency; even CIA and FBI files are available under certain conditions. It takes a lot of time and effort to get such files, but it can be done. The news media can (and do) also use FOIA, which is why newspapers and their reporters have so much more access to public bureaucracies than they ever had before. The public in general and interested citizens in particular gain from this access. Moreover, although general newspapers have limited space and resources for reporting on all agencies, specialized newspapers are actively involved in investigating and reporting on agency activities. This textbook regularly cites the *Congressional Quarterly,* which reports on the activities of the legislative branch but which often has information on agencies in the executive branch, as well. The *National Journal* also reports extensively on government agencies. There are innumerable trade magazines, whose subscribers are

---

FOR CRITICAL ANALYSIS

Describe the ways in which the public controls its bureaucracy. How much and what kind of control should the public exercise? Through elected officials—i.e., the president and the Congress—the public can achieve some control over the bureaucracy. What are the relative advantages and disadvantages of presidential and congressional control of the bureaucracy?

INTERACTIVE POLITICS

YOU ARE... the director of a federal agency

The federal bureaucratic agencies, largely composed of career civil service professionals, see presidents and their priorities come and go through the years. The agencies tend to prefer presidents that support their work with additional resources and attention.

In this simulation, you are cast in the role of agency director of a significant executive agency that answers to the president of the United States. You need to carry out your agency's mission, while competing with other agencies for resources and space on the national agenda.

Go to www.wwnorton.com/wtp5e

Questions to consider as you conduct the online simulation:

What are the primary goals of government agencies, and how do they prioritize those goals?

How does the president determine the national agenda when there are so many agencies and issues that require attention?

Which government jobs are considered to be the best in Washington, and what criteria can we use to compare them?

What strategies are available to bureaucrats when they disagree with politicians?

largely the companies and individuals who earn their livings in a particular trade or sector of the economy; these publications perform superbly as critics and exposers of the agencies and decisions within their area of concern.

The activities of important "think tanks" (independently financed policy-research organizations in Washington, D.C., and elsewhere around the country) revolve around the formation and implementation of public policy. The Brookings Institution, for example, has been studying government policies and agencies for more than six decades, and although considered to be more favorably disposed toward Democratic administrations, it is widely respected in all quarters. The same might be said of the best-known conservative-leaning think tank, the American Enterprise Institute, which has been a particularly important source of analysis and criticism of policies and agencies for the past twenty years.

Many of these information sources are already on the Internet. The same is true for a wide variety of government-provided publications of information on agencies and policies. Such access to information can help make bureaucracies more responsive to citizens' demands. In the first place, bureaucrats who know that their actions will be open to public scrutiny are more likely to take public wishes into account in their daily work. Second, when questionable bureaucratic practices are uncovered, citizens, through their congressional representatives, can work to change the laws and procedures that bureaucracies follow. The 1998 reform of the IRS, which, among other things, shifted the burden of proof from citizens to the government when there is a dispute, provides an example of this process. Finally, citizen dissatisfaction with bureaucracy can push politicians to institute reforms. When Clinton came to office, he wanted to take a more active governing approach than his Republican predecessors but realized that public distrust of government stood in the way. His effort to reinvent government, making bureaucracies more "customer-friendly," was a direct response to widespread public dissatisfaction.

The bad news is that, although citizen influence on bureaucracy is definitely possible, it can be expensive—in time and money. This gives it an upper-middle-class bias. The poor and uneducated lack virtually all the resources necessary to use the channels and opportunities available. But this class bias exists in all endeavors and walks of life; it is not particularly worse in the realm of bureaucracy. In fact, in many respects, now that political parties play less of a role in running the government, interaction with federal, state, and local agencies may be less daunting and discouraging than trying to influence legislatures.

Summary

Bureaucracy is a universal form of organization, found in businesses, churches, foundations, and universities as well as in the public sphere. All essential government services and regulations are carried out by bureaucracies—specifically, by administrative agencies. Bureaucrats are appointed to their offices based on the "merit system."

The agencies of the executive branch can be grouped according to the services they provide: (1) promoting the public welfare, (2) promoting national security, and (3) maintaining a strong economy. All of these agencies are alike in that they are all bureaucratic. These agencies differ in the way they are organized, in the way they participate in the political process, and in their levels of responsiveness to political authority. In recent years, attempts have been made to "downsize" the bureaucracy by termination, devolution, and privatization. Although these efforts are popular with the American people, they cannot reduce the size of the bureaucracy by much.

The executive and the legislative branches do the toughest job any government is called on to do: making the bureaucracy accountable to the people. Democratizing bureaucracy is the unending task of politics in a democracy.

For Further Reading

Arnold, Peri E. *Making the Managerial Presidency: Comprehensive Organization Planning.* Princeton, NJ: Princeton University Press, 1986.

Fesler, James W., and Donald F. Kettl. *The Politics of the Administrative Process.* Chatham, NJ: Chatham House, 1991.

Skowronek, Stephen. *Building a New American State: The Expansion of National Administrative Capacities, 1877–1920.* New York: Cambridge University Press, 1982.

Wildavsky, Aaron. *The New Politics of the Budget Process.* 2nd ed. New York: HarperCollins, 1992.

Wilson, James Q. *Bureaucracy: What Government Agencies Do and Why They Do It.* New York: Basic Books, 1989.

Wood, Dan B. *Bureaucratic Dynamics: The Role of Bureaucracy in a Democracy.* Boulder, CO: Westview, 1994.

Study Outline ON THE WEB

www.wwnorton.com/wtp5e

Keyword: Review 14

Bureaucracy and Bureaucrats

1. Bureaucracy is simply a form of organization. Specialization and repetition are essential to the efficiency of any organization.
2. Despite fears of bureaucratic growth, the federal service has grown little during the past twenty-five years. The national government is large, but the federal service has not been growing any faster than the economy or the society.
3. The primary task of bureaucracy is to implement the laws passed by Congress.
4. Because statutes and executive orders often provide only vague instructions, one important job of the bureaucrat is to interpret the intentions of Congress and the president prior to implementation of orders.
5. The lower efficiency of public agencies can be attributed to the added constraints put on them, as compared to those put on private agencies.
6. Through civil service reform, national and state governments have attempted to reduce political interference in public bureaucracies by granting certain public bureaucrats legal protection from being fired without a show of cause.

The Organization of the Executive Branch

1. Cabinet departments, agencies, and bureaus are the operating parts of the bureaucracy. Not all government agencies are part of Cabinet departments. Independent agencies, government corporations, and independent regulatory commissions also are part of the executive branch.

2. The different agencies of the executive branch can be classified into three main groups by the services that they provide to the American public. The first category of agencies provides services and products that seek to promote the public welfare. Some of these agencies are particularly tied to a specific group or segment of American society that is often thought of as the main clientele of that agency.

3. The second category of agencies work to promote national security from internal and external threat.

4. The third group of agencies provides services that help to maintain a strong economy. Foremost among these are the agencies that are responsible for fiscal and monetary policy. In addition, the federal government may directly provide services or goods that bolster the economy.

Can Bureaucracy Be Reinvented?

1. The National Performance Review was an effort to make the bureaucracy more efficient, accountable, and effective.
2. While government bureaucracies can be made more responsive and efficient, reform is not simply a matter of management techniques but also a political matter.

Can the Bureaucracy Be Reduced?

1. The bureaucracy can be reduced in three ways: termination, devolution, and privatization.

Can Bureaucracy Be Controlled?

1. Each expansion of the national government in the twentieth century was accompanied by a parallel expansion of presidential management authority, but the expansion of presidential power cannot guarantee responsible bureaucracy.

2. Although Congress attempts to control the bureaucracy through oversight, a more effective way to ensure accountability may be to clarify legislative intent.

Practice Quiz

www.wwnorton.com/wtp5e
Keyword: Quiz 14

1. Which of the following best describes the growth of the federal service in the past twenty-five years?
   a) rampant, exponential growth
   b) little growth at all
   c) decrease in the total number of federal employees
   d) vast, compared to the growth of the economy and the society

2. What task must bureaucrats perform if Congress charges them with enforcing a law through explicit directions?
   a) implementation
   b) interpretation
   c) lawmaking
   d) quasi-judicial decision making

3. Which of the following was *not* a component of the Civil Service Act of 1883?
   a) the merit system
   b) a type of tenure system
   c) a spoils system
   d) All of the above were associated with the Civil Service Act of 1883.

4. Which of the following is a way in which the bureaucracy might be reduced?
   a) devolution
   b) termination
   c) privatization
   d) all of the above

5. Which of the following is *not* an example of a clientele agency?
   a) Department of Justice
   b) Department of Commerce
   c) Department of Agriculture
   d) Department of Housing and Urban Development

6. The concept of oversight refers to the effort made by
   a) Congress to make executive agencies accountable for their actions.
   b) the president to make Congress accountable for its actions.
   c) the courts to make executive agencies responsible for their actions.
   d) the states to make the executive branch accountable for its actions.

7. Which president instituted the bureaucratic reform of the National Performance Review?
   a) Richard Nixon
   b) Lyndon Johnson
   c) Jimmy Carter
   d) Bill Clinton

8. Which of the following are *not* part of the executive branch?
   a) cabinet departments
   b) government corporations
   c) independent regulatory commissions
   d) All of the above are parts of the executive branch.

Key Terms

www.wwnorton.com/wtp5e
Keyword: Vocabulary 14

administrative adjudication (p. 573)
bureaucracy (p. 569)
department (p. 575)
deregulation (p. 601)
devolution (p. 601)
executive privilege (p. 606)
Federal Reserve System (p. 596)
fiscal policy (p. 592)
government corporation (p. 577)
implementation (p. 573)
independent agency (p. 577)
iron triangle (p. 581)
merit system (p. 575)
oversight (p. 607)
privatization (p. 603)
regulatory agencies (p. 580)
revenue agencies (p. 596)
rule making (p. 573)

15 THE FEDERAL COURTS

⋆ **The Legal System**

Within what broad categories of law do cases arise?
How is the U.S. court system structured?

⋆ **Federal Jurisdiction**

What is the importance of the federal court system?
What factors play a role in the appointment of federal judges?

⋆ **The Power of the Supreme Court: Judicial Review**

What is the basis for the Supreme Court's power of judicial review?
How does the power of judicial review make the Supreme Court a lawmaking body?
How does a case reach the Supreme Court? What shapes the flow of cases through the Supreme Court? Once accepted, how does a case proceed?
What factors influence the judicial philosophy of the Supreme Court?

⋆ **Judicial Power and Politics**

How has the power of the federal courts been limited throughout much of American history?
How have the role and power of the federal courts been transformed over the last fifty years?

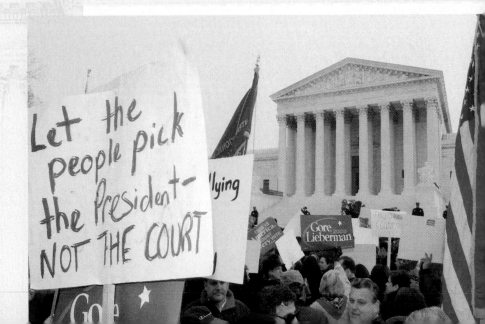

GEORGE W. BUSH WON the 2000 national presidential election. The final battle in the race, however, was not decided in the electoral arena and did not involve the participation of ordinary Americans. Instead, the battle was fought in the courts, in the Florida state legislature, and in the executive institutions of the Florida state government by small groups of attorneys and political activists. During the course of the dispute, some forty lawsuits were filed in the Florida circuit and supreme courts, the U.S. District Court, the U.S. Court of Appeals, and the U.S. Supreme Court.[1] Together, the two campaigns (Bush and Gore) amassed nearly $10 million in legal fees during the month of litigation. In most of the courtroom battles, the Bush campaign prevailed. Despite two setbacks before the all-Democratic Florida supreme court, Bush attorneys won most of the circuit court cases and the ultimate clash before the U.S. Supreme Court in a narrow 5-4 vote. The next day, Al Gore made a speech conceding the election, and on December 18, 2000, 271 presidential electors—the constitutionally prescribed majority—cast their votes for George W. Bush.

The court battle over Florida's twenty-five electoral votes illustrates the political power that the courts now exercise. Over the past fifty years, the prominence of the courts has been heightened by the sharp increase in the number of major policy issues that have been fought and decided in the judicial realm. But since judges are not elected and accountable to the people, what does this shift in power mean for American democracy?

Every year, nearly twenty-five million cases are tried in American courts and one American in every nine is directly involved in litigation. Cases can arise from disputes between citizens, from efforts by government agencies to punish wrongdoing, or from citizens' efforts to prove that a right provided them by law has been infringed upon as a result of government action—or inaction. Many critics of the U.S. legal system assert that Americans have become much too litigious (ready to use the courts for all purposes), and perhaps that is true. But the heavy use that Americans make of the courts is also an indication of the extent of conflict in American society. And given the existence of social conflict, it is far better that Americans seek to settle their differences through the courts rather than by fighting or feuding. ■

T HE framers of the American Constitution called the Supreme Court the "least dangerous branch" of American government. Today, it is not unusual to hear friends *and* foes of the Court refer to it as the "imperial judiciary."[2] Before we can understand this transformation and its consequences, however, we must look in some detail at America's judicial process.

■ **In this chapter, we will first examine the legal system, including the types of cases that the federal courts consider and the types of law with which they deal.**

■ **Second, we will assess the organization and structure of the federal court system as well as the flow of cases through the courts.**

■ **Third, we will consider judicial review and how it makes the Supreme Court a "lawmaking body."** We will also analyze the procedures of and influences on the Supreme Court.

■ **Finally, we will consider the role and power of the federal courts in the American political process, looking in particular at the growth of judicial power in the United States.** We conclude by looking at how this changing role affects liberty and democracy.

■ Previewing Liberty, Equality, and Democracy

The framers saw the role of the judiciary, an unelected institution, as protecting liberty from the potential excesses of democracy, that is, the "tyranny of the majority." In recent years, however, the judiciary has expanded its role in the political process by also playing an active part in helping bring about more political and social equality.

The Legal System

Originally, a "court" was the place where a sovereign ruled—where the king and his entourage governed. Settling disputes between citizens was part of governing. According to the Bible, King Solomon had to settle the dispute between two women over which of them was the mother of the child both claimed. Judging is the settling of disputes, a function that was slowly separated from the king and the king's court and made into a separate institution of government. Courts have taken over from kings the power to settle controversies by hearing the facts on both sides and deciding which side possesses the greater merit. But since judges are not kings, they must have a basis for their authority. That basis in the United States is the Constitution and the law. Courts decide cases by hearing the facts on both sides of a dispute and applying the relevant law or principle to the facts. This is all the more sensitive a matter because courts have been given the authority to settle disputes not only between citizens but between citizens and the government itself, where the courts are obliged to maintain the same neutrality and impartiality as they do in disputes involving two citizens. This is the essence of the "rule of law," that "the state" and its officials must be judged by the same laws as the citizenry. But since judges must apply the law as well as be subject to it, they must conduct themselves as closely as possible by the principle that they are not making personal judgments but are almost mechanistically applying the Constitution and the laws to the facts. There are obviously elements of myth as well as truth in this principle. But the American judicial system, from bottom to top, must have been doing something right because, compared to the other branches, it has been amazingly free of institutional crises during its history.

CASES AND THE LAW

Court cases in the United States proceed under three broad categories of law: criminal law, civil law, and public law.

Cases of **criminal law** are those in which the government charges an individual with violating a statute that has been enacted to protect the public health, safety, morals, or welfare. In criminal cases, the government is always the **plaintiff** (the party that brings charges) and alleges that a criminal violation has been committed by a named **defendant.** Most criminal cases arise in state and municipal courts and involve matters ranging from traffic offenses to robbery and murder. Although the great bulk of criminal law is still a state matter, a large and growing body of federal criminal law deals with matters ranging from tax evasion and mail fraud to the sale of narcotics and acts of terrorism. Defendants found guilty of criminal violations may be fined or sent to prison. Recently, a number of top corporate executives were charged with criminal violations of federal securities and accounting law. Federal criminal law is becoming an increasingly important factor in American life.

Cases of **civil law** involve disputes among individuals or between individuals and the government in which no criminal violation is charged. Unlike criminal cases, the losers in civil cases cannot be fined or sent to prison, although they may be required to pay monetary damages for their actions. In a civil case, the one who brings a complaint is the plaintiff and the one against whom the complaint is brought is the defendant. The two most common types of civil cases involve

criminal law the branch of law that deals with disputes or actions involving criminal penalties (as opposed to civil law); it regulates the conduct of individuals, defines crimes, and provides punishment for criminal acts

plaintiff the individual or organization who brings a complaint in court

defendant the one against whom a complaint is brought in a criminal or civil case

civil law a system of jurisprudence, including private law and governmental actions, to settle disputes that do not involve criminal penalties contracts and torts. In a typical contract case, an individual or corporation charges that it has suffered because of another's violation of a specific agreement between the two. For example, the Smith Manufacturing Corporation may charge that Jones Distributors failed to honor an agreement to deliver raw materials at a specified time, causing Smith to lose business. Smith asks the court to order Jones to compensate it for the damage allegedly suffered. In a typical tort case, one individual charges that he or she has been injured by another's negligence or malfeasance. Medical malpractice suits are one example of tort cases.

In deciding cases, courts apply statutes (laws) and legal **precedent** (prior decisions). State and federal statutes, for example, often govern the conditions under which contracts are and are not legally binding. Jones Distributors might argue that it was not obliged to fulfill its contract with the Smith Corporation because actions by Smith, such as the failure to make promised payments, constituted fraud under state law. Attorneys for a physician being sued for malpractice, on the other hand, may search for prior instances in which courts ruled that actions similar to those of their client did not constitute negligence. Such precedents are applied under the doctrine of *stare decisis,* a Latin phrase meaning "let the decision stand."

A case becomes a matter of the third category, **public law,** when a plaintiff or defendant in a civil or criminal case seeks to show that his or her case involves the powers of government or rights of citizens as defined under the Constitution or by statute. One major form of public law is constitutional law, under which a court will examine the government's actions to see if they conform to the Constitution as it has been interpreted by the judiciary. Thus, what began as an ordinary criminal case may enter the realm of public law if a defendant claims that his or her constitutional rights were violated by the police. Another important arena of public law is administrative law, which involves disputes over the jurisdiction, procedures, or authority of administrative agencies. Under this type of law, civil litigation between an individual and the government may become a matter of public law if the individual asserts that the government is violating a statute or abusing its power under the Constitution. For example, landowners have asserted that federal and state restrictions on land use constitute violations of the Fifth Amendment's restrictions on the government's ability to confiscate private property. Recently, the Supreme Court has been very sympathetic to such claims, which effectively transform an ordinary civil dispute into a major issue of public law.

Most of the important Supreme Court cases we will examine in this chapter involve judgments concerning the constitutional or statutory basis of the actions of government agencies. As we shall see, it is in this arena of public law that the Supreme Court's decisions can have significant consequences for American politics and society.

TYPES OF COURTS

In the United States, systems of courts have been established both by the federal government and by the governments of the individual states. Both systems have several levels, as shown in Figure 15.1. More than 99 percent of all court cases in the United States are heard in state courts. The overwhelming majority of criminal cases, for example, involve violations of state laws prohibiting such actions as murder, robbery, fraud, theft, and assault. If such a case is brought to trial, it will be

precedents prior cases whose principles are used by judges as the bases for their decisions in present cases

stare decisis literally, "let the decision stand." The doctrine that a previous decision by a court applies as a precedent in similar cases until that decision is overruled

public law cases involving the actions of public agencies or officials

The U.S. Court System

Figure 15.1

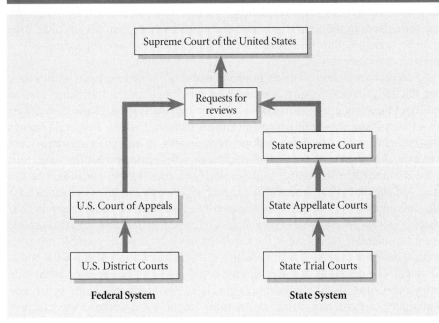

The state and federal court systems parallel each other until they reach the Supreme Court.

Federal System

State System

---

heard in a state **trial court,** in front of a judge and sometimes a jury, who will determine whether the defendant violated state law. If the defendant is convicted, he or she may appeal the conviction to a higher court, such as a state **appellate court,** and from there to a state's **supreme court.** Similarly, in civil cases, most litigation is brought in the courts established by the state in which the activity in question took place. For example, a patient bringing suit against a physician for malpractice would file the suit in the appropriate court in the state where the alleged malpractice occurred. The judge hearing the case would apply state law and state precedent to the matter at hand. (It should be noted that in both criminal and civil matters, most cases are settled before trial through negotiated agreements between the parties. In criminal cases these agreements are called **plea bargains.**)

Although each state has its own set of laws, these laws have much in common from state to state. Murder and robbery, obviously, are illegal in all states, although the range of possible punishments for those crimes varies from state to state. Some states, for example, provide for capital punishment (the death penalty) for murder and other serious offenses; other states do not. However, some acts that are criminal offenses in one state may be legal in another state. Prostitution, for example, is legal in some Nevada counties, although it is outlawed in all other states. Considerable similarity among the states is also found in the realm of civil law. In the case of contract law, most states have adopted the **Uniform Commercial Code** in order to reduce interstate differences. In areas such as family law, however, which covers such matters as divorce and child custody arrangements, state laws vary greatly.

Cases are heard in the federal courts if they involve federal laws, treaties with other nations, or the U.S. Constitution; these areas are the official **jurisdiction** of the federal courts. In addition, any case in which the U.S. government is a party is

trial court the first court to hear a criminal or civil case

appellate court a court that hears the appeals of trial court decisions

supreme court the highest court in a particular state or in the United States. This court primarily serves an appellate function

plea bargains negotiated agreements in criminal cases in which a defendant agrees to plead guilty in return for the state's agreement to reduce the severity of the criminal charge the defendant is facing

Uniform Commercial Code code used in many states in the area of contract law to reduce interstate differences in judicial decisions

jurisdiction the sphere of a court's power and authority heard in the federal courts. If, for example, an individual is charged with violating a federal criminal statute, such as evading the payment of income taxes, charges would be brought before a federal judge by a federal prosecutor. Civil cases involving the citizens of more than one state and in which more than $70,000 is at stake may be heard in either the federal or the state courts, usually depending on the preference of the plaintiff.

Federal courts serve another purpose in addition to trying cases within their jurisdiction: that of hearing appeals from state-level courts. Individuals found guilty of breaking a state criminal law, for example, can appeal their convictions to a federal court by raising a constitutional issue and asking a federal court to determine whether the state's actions were consistent with the requirements of the U.S. Constitution. An appellant might assert, for example, that the state court denied him or her the right to counsel, imposed excessive bail, or otherwise denied the appellant **due process.** Under such circumstances, an appellant can ask the federal court to overturn his or her conviction. Federal courts are not obligated to accept such appeals and will do so only if they feel that the issues raised have considerable merit and if the appellant has exhausted all possible remedies within the state courts. (This procedure is discussed in more detail later in this chapter.) The decisions of state supreme courts may also be appealed to the U.S. Supreme Court if the state court's decision has conflicted with prior U.S. Supreme Court rulings or has raised some important question of federal law. Such appeals are accepted by the U.S. Supreme Court at its discretion.

Although the federal courts hear only a small fraction of all the civil and criminal cases decided each year in the United States, their decisions are extremely important. It is in the federal courts that the Constitution and federal laws that govern all Americans are interpreted and their meaning and significance established. Moreover, it is in the federal courts that the powers and limitations of the increasingly powerful national government are tested. Finally, through their power to review the decisions of the state courts, it is ultimately the federal courts that dominate the American judicial system.

due process of law the right of every citizen against arbitrary action by national or state governments

Federal Jurisdiction

Of all the cases heard in the United States in 2003, federal district courts (the lowest federal level) received 323,604. Although this number is up substantially from the 87,000 cases heard in 1961, it still constitutes about 1 percent of the judiciary's business. The federal courts of appeal listened to 60,847 cases in 2003, and the U.S. Supreme Court reviewed 9,406 in its 2002–2003 term. Most of the cases filed with the Supreme Court are dismissed without a ruling on their merits. The Court has broad latitude to decide what cases it will hear and generally listens to only those cases it deems to raise the most important issues. Only 84 cases were given full-dress Supreme Court review (the nine justices actually sitting *en banc*—in full court—and hearing the lawyers argue the case).[3]

original jurisdiction the authority to initially consider a case. Distinguished from appellate jurisdiction, which is the authority to hear appeals from a lower court's decision

THE LOWER FEDERAL COURTS

Most of the cases of original federal jurisdiction are handled by the federal district courts. Courts of **original jurisdiction** are the courts that are responsible for discovering the facts in a controversy and creating the record on which a judgment is based. Although the Constitution gives the Supreme Court original jurisdiction in several types of cases, such as those affecting ambassadors and those in which a state is one of the parties, most original jurisdiction goes to the lowest courts—the trial courts. (In courts that have appellate jurisdiction, judges receive cases after the factual record is established by the trial court. Ordinarily, new facts cannot be presented before appellate courts.)

There are eighty-nine district courts in the fifty states, plus one in the District of Columbia and one in Puerto Rico, and three territorial courts. These courts are staffed by 665 federal district judges. District judges are assigned to district courts according to the workload; the busiest of these courts may have as many as twenty-eight judges. Only one judge is assigned to each case, except where statutes provide for three-judge courts to deal with special issues. The routines and procedures of the federal district courts are essentially the same as those of the lower state courts, except that federal procedural requirements tend to be stricter. States, for example, do not have to provide a grand jury, a twelve-member trial jury, or a unanimous jury verdict. Federal courts must provide all these things.

THE APPELLATE COURTS

Roughly 10 percent of all lower court and federal agency cases are subsequently reviewed by federal appeals courts. Except for cases filed with the Supreme Court, a properly filed appeal will be heard. The country is divided into twelve judicial circuits, each of which has a U.S. Court of Appeals. Every state, the District of Columbia, and each of the territories is assigned to the circuit in the continental United States that is closest to it. A thirteenth appellate court, the U.S. Court of Appeals for the Federal Circuit, has subject matter rather than a geographical jurisdiction. This court accepts appeals regarding patents, copyrights, and international trade.

Except for cases selected for review by the Supreme Court, decisions made by the appeals courts are final. Because of this finality, certain safeguards have been built into the system. The most important is the provision of more than one judge for every appeals case. Each court of appeals has from six to twenty-eight permanent judgeships, depending on the workload of the circuit. Although normally three judges hear appealed cases, in some instances a larger number of judges sit together *en banc*.

Another safeguard is provided by the assignment of a Supreme Court justice as the circuit justice for each of the twelve circuits. Since the creation of the appeals court in 1891, the circuit justice's primary duty has been to review appeals arising in the circuit in order to expedite Supreme Court action. The most frequent and best-known action of circuit justices is that of reviewing requests for stays of execution when the full Court is unable to do so—primarily during the summer, when the Court is in recess.

THE SUPREME COURT

The Supreme Court is America's highest court. Article III of the Constitution vests "the judicial power of the United States" in the Supreme Court, and this court is supreme in fact as well as form. The Supreme Court is made up of a chief justice and eight associate justices. The **chief justice** presides over the Court's public sessions

chief justice justice on the Supreme Court who presides over the Court's public sessions and conferences. In the Court's actual deliberations and decisions, however, the chief justice has no more authority than his colleagues. Each justice casts one vote. To some extent, the influence of the chief justice is a function of his or her own leadership ability. Some chief justices, such as the late Earl Warren, have been able to lead the court in a new direction. In other instances, forceful associate justices, such as the late Felix Frankfurter, are the dominant figures on the Court.

The Constitution does not specify the number of justices who should sit on the Supreme Court; Congress has the authority to change the Court's size. In the early nineteenth century, there were six Supreme Court justices; later there were seven. Congress set the number of justices at nine in 1869, and the Court has remained that size ever since. In 1937, President Franklin D. Roosevelt, infuriated by several Supreme Court decisions that struck down New Deal programs, asked Congress to enlarge the Court so that he could add a few sympathetic justices to the bench. Although Congress balked at Roosevelt's "court packing" plan, the Court gave in to FDR's pressure and began to take a more favorable view of his policy initiatives. The president, in turn, dropped his efforts to enlarge the Court. The Court's surrender to FDR came to be known as "the switch in time that saved nine."

HOW JUDGES ARE APPOINTED

Federal judges are appointed by the president and are generally selected from among the more prominent or politically active members of the legal profession. Many federal judges previously served as state court judges or state or local prosecutors. Before the president makes a formal nomination, however, the senators from the candidate's own state must indicate that they support the nominee. This is an informal but seldom violated practice called **senatorial courtesy.** Because the Senate will rarely approve a nominee opposed by a senator from his or her own state, the president will usually not bother to present such a nomination to the Senate. Through this arrangement, senators are able to exercise veto power over appointments to the federal bench in their own states. Senators also see nominations to the judiciary as a way to reward important allies and contributors in their states. If the state has no senator from the president's party, the governor or members of the state's House delegation may make suggestions.

senatorial courtesy the practice whereby the president, before formally nominating a person for a federal judgeship, seeks the indication that senators from the candidate's own state support the nomination

Federal appeals court nominations follow much the same pattern. Since appeals court judges preside over jurisdictions that include several states, however, senators do not have as strong a role in proposing potential candidates. Instead, potential appeals court candidates are generally suggested to the president by the Justice Department or by important members of the administration. The senators from the nominee's own state are still consulted before the president will formally act.

In general, presidents endeavor to appoint judges who possess legal experience and good character and whose partisan and ideological views are similar to the president's own. During the presidencies of Ronald Reagan and George H. W. Bush, most federal judicial appointees were conservative Republicans. Bush established an advisory committee to screen judicial nominees to make certain that their legal and political philosophies were sufficiently conservative. Bill Clinton's appointees to the federal bench, on the other hand, tended to be liberal Democrats. Clinton also made a major effort to appoint women and African Americans to the federal courts. Nearly half of his nominees were drawn from these groups.

Once the president has formally nominated an individual, the nominee must be considered by the Senate Judiciary Committee and confirmed by a majority vote in the full Senate. In recent years, the Senate Judiciary Committee has sought to signal the president when it has had qualms about a judicial nomination. After the Republicans won control of the Senate in 1994, for example, Judiciary Committee chair Orrin Hatch of Utah let President Clinton know that he considered two of Clinton's nominees to be too liberal. The president withdrew the nominations.

During President George W. Bush's first two years in office, Democrats controlled the Senate and used their majority on the Judiciary Committee to block eight of the president's first eleven federal court nominations. After the GOP won a narrow Senate majority in the 2002 national elections, Democrats used a filibuster to block action on two Bush federal appeals court nominees, Miguel Estrada and Priscilla Owen. Democratic senators charged that Estrada and Owen were activist conservatives who would use the bench to rewrite federal law. At the same time, though, the Senate voted to confirm several other Bush nominees. On two occasions early in 2004, Bush skirted the Senate confirmation process during a congressional recess and used his power to make appointments when Congress is not in session. Bush named Charles W. Pickering, Sr., and William H. Pryor, Jr., directly to the federal appeals court bench. Both had earlier been blocked by Senate Democrats. Under the Constitution, these appointments last only until the end of the next session of Congress. Throughout the history of the federal judiciary, there have been more than 300 such judicial recess appointments, though few have occurred in recent years. Both Democrats and Republicans saw struggles over lower court slots as practice and preparation for all-out partisan warfare over the next Supreme Court vacancy.

If political factors play an important role in the selection of district and appellate court judges, they are decisive when it comes to Supreme Court appointments. Because the high court has so much influence over American law and politics, virtually all presidents have made an effort to select justices who share their own political philosophies. Presidents Ronald Reagan and George H. W. Bush, for example,

As of 2004, the members of the Supreme Court are (from left to right) Antonin Scalia, Ruth Bader Ginsburg, John Paul Stevens, David Souter, Chief Justice William Rehnquist, Clarence Thomas, Sandra Day O'Connor, Stephen Breyer, and Anthony Kennedy.

appointed five justices whom they believed to have conservative perspectives: Sandra Day O'Connor, Antonin Scalia, Anthony Kennedy, David Souter, and Clarence Thomas. Reagan also elevated William Rehnquist to the position of chief justice. Reagan and Bush sought appointees who believed in reducing government intervention in the economy and who supported the moral positions taken by the Republican Party in recent years, particularly opposition to abortion. However, not all the Reagan and Bush appointees have fulfilled their sponsors' expectations. Bush appointee David Souter, for example, has been attacked by conservatives as a turncoat for his decisions on school prayer and abortion rights. Nevertheless, through their appointments, Reagan and Bush were able to increase the conservatism of the Supreme Court. For his part, President Bill Clinton endeavored to appoint liberal justices. Clinton named Ruth Bader Ginsburg and Stephen Breyer to the Court, hoping to counteract the influence of the Reagan and Bush appointees. (Table 15.1 shows information about the current Supreme Court justices.)

In recent years, Supreme Court nominations have come to involve intense partisan struggle. Typically, after the president has named a nominee, interest groups opposed to the nomination have mobilized opposition in the media, the public, and the Senate. When President Bush proposed conservative judge Clarence Thomas for the Court, for example, liberal groups launched a campaign to discredit Thomas. After extensive research into his background, opponents of the nomination were able to produce evidence suggesting that Thomas had sexually harassed a former subordinate, Anita Hill. Thomas denied the charge. After contentious Senate Judiciary Committee hearings, highlighted by testimony from both Thomas and Hill, Thomas narrowly won confirmation.

Likewise, conservative interest groups carefully scrutinized Bill Clinton's somewhat more liberal nominees, hoping to find information about them that would

Table 15.1	Supreme Court Justices, 2004 (in Order of Seniority)			
NAME	**YEAR OF BIRTH**	**PRIOR EXPERIENCE**	**APPOINTED BY**	**YEAR OF APPOINTMENT**
William H. Rehnquist* *Chief Justice*	1924	Assistant attorney general	Nixon	1972
John Paul Stevens	1920	Federal judge	Ford	1975
Sandra Day O'Connor	1930	State judge	Reagan	1981
Antonin Scalia	1936	Law professor, federal judge	Reagan	1986
Anthony Kennedy	1936	Federal judge	Reagan	1988
David Souter	1939	Federal judge	Bush	1990
Clarence Thomas	1948	Federal judge	Bush	1991
Ruth Bader Ginsburg	1933	Federal judge	Clinton	1993
Stephen Breyer	1938	Federal judge	Clinton	1994

*Appointed chief justice by Reagan in 1986.

While the Supreme Court presents itself to the public as a collegial body, its members are deeply divided along ideological and partisan lines. The current chief justice, William Rehnquist, was appointed to the Court by one Republican president, Richard Nixon, and elevated to chief justice by another Republican president, Ronald Reagan. This photo, from June 1986, shows Reagan announcing Rehnquist's promotion and Antonin Scalia's nomination to take Rehnquist's spot on the Court. At right is retiring chief justice Warren Burger.

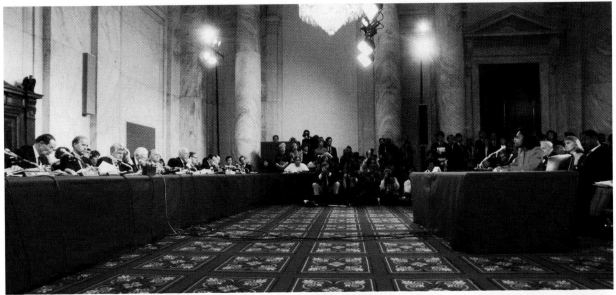

The partisan nature of the Court is also evident during confirmation hearings in the Senate. In testimony before the Senate Judiciary Committee in 1991, Anita Hill alleged that Supreme Court nominee Clarence Thomas had sexually harassed her. Hill's testimony brought nationwide attention to the nomination hearings (above). The Senate subsequently approved Thomas by the narrowest ratification margin in history, 52 to 48.

President George W. Bush saw eight of his first eleven candidates for federal judgeships face partisan opposition from the narrow Democratic majority in the Senate. While Bush has had 201 nominees approved to the federal bench, several prominent judges that he nominated were not approved (right).

sabotage their appointments. During his two opportunities to name Supreme Court justices, Clinton was compelled to drop several potential appointees because of information unearthed by political opponents.

These struggles over judicial appointments indicate the growing intensity of partisan struggle in the United States today. They also indicate how much importance competing political forces attach to Supreme Court appointments. Because these contending forces see the outcome as critical, they are willing to engage in a fierce struggle when Supreme Court appointments are at stake.

The matter of judicial appointments became an important issue in the 2000 and 2004 elections. Democrats charged that, if he was elected, George W. Bush would appoint conservative judges who might, among other things, reverse the *Roe v. Wade* decision and curb abortion rights. Bush would say only that he would seek judges who would uphold the Constitution without reading their own political biases into the document.

From the liberal perspective, the danger of a conservative judiciary was underlined by the Supreme Court's decision in the Florida election case, *Bush v. Gore.* The court's conservative bloc, in recent years, has argued that the states deserve considerable deference from the federal courts. In this instance, however, the Supreme Court overturned a decision of the Florida supreme court regarding Florida election law. The Court ruled that its Florida counterpart had ignored the U.S. Constitution's equal protection doctrine when it mandated recounts in some, but not all, Florida counties. By voting to overrule the Florida court, the Supreme Court's conservative justices appeared to disregard the logic of their own decisions, which had expanded the authority of the states over the past two decades (see Chapter 3). To be sure, the same liberal justices who voted to uphold the Florida court's decision had frequently argued against deferring to the states in previous decisions. Ideological consistency notwithstanding, defenders of the decision argued that it was doctrinally sound and that it averted the chaos that might have ensued if a recount gave Gore the victory and the Florida legislature carried out its threat to appoint Bush electors. Two competing slates of electors might then have sought congressional certification. Critics of the decision, however, asserted that the Court was merely searching for a rubric under which it could ensure Bush's victory. As a result of the Florida contest, there can be little doubt that the next Supreme Court vacancy will generate sharp fighting in Washington.

The Power of the Supreme Court: Judicial Review

judicial review the power of the courts to declare actions of the legislative and executive branches invalid or unconstitutional. The Supreme Court asserted this power in *Marbury v. Madison*

One of the most important powers of the Supreme Court is the power of **judicial review**—the authority and the obligation to review any lower court decision in which a substantial issue of public law is involved. The disputes can be over the constitutionality of federal or state laws, over the propriety or constitutionality of the court procedures followed, or over questions of whether public officers are exceeding their authority. The Supreme Court's power of judicial review has come to mean review not only of lower court decisions but also of state legislation and acts of Congress. For this reason, if for no other, the Supreme Court is more than a judicial agency—it is a major lawmaking body.

The Supreme Court's power of judicial review over lower court decisions has never been at issue. Nor has there been any serious quibble over the power of the federal courts to review administrative agencies in order to determine whether their actions and decisions are within the powers delegated to them by Congress. There has, however, been a great deal of controversy occasioned by the Supreme Court's efforts to review acts of Congress and the decisions of state courts and legislatures.

JUDICIAL REVIEW OF ACTS OF CONGRESS

Since the Constitution does not give the Supreme Court the power of judicial review over congressional enactments, the Court's exercise of it is something of a usurpation. It is not known whether the framers of the Constitution opposed judicial review, but "if they intended to provide for it in the Constitution, they did so in a most obscure fashion."[4] Disputes over the intentions of the framers were settled in 1803 in the case of *Marbury v. Madison.*[5] Although Congress and the president have often been at odds with the Court, its legal power to review acts of Congress has not been seriously questioned since 1803. One reason is that judicial power has been accepted as natural, if not intended. Another reason is that over more than two centuries, the Supreme Court has struck down only some 160 acts of Congress. When such acts do come up for review, the Court makes a self-conscious effort to give them an interpretation that will make them constitutional. In some instances, however, the Court reaches the conclusion that a congressional enactment directly violates the Constitution. For example, in 1998, the Court invalidated a statute through which Congress had given the president the authority to reject specific projects contained in spending bills. The Court ruled that this "line-item veto" power violated the constitutionally mandated separation of powers.[6]

JUDICIAL REVIEW OF STATE ACTIONS

The power of the Supreme Court to review state legislation or other state action and to determine its constitutionality is neither granted by the Constitution nor inherent in the federal system. But the logic of the **supremacy clause** of Article VI of the Constitution, which declares it and laws made under its authority to be the supreme law of the land, is very strong. Furthermore, in the Judiciary Act of 1789, Congress conferred on the Supreme Court the power to reverse state constitutions and laws whenever they are clearly in conflict with the U.S. Constitution, federal laws, or treaties.[7] This power gives the Supreme Court appellate jurisdiction over all of the millions of cases handled by American courts each year.

The supremacy clause of the Constitution not only established the federal Constitution, statutes, and treaties as the "supreme Law of the Land," but also provided that "the Judges in every State shall be bound thereby, any Thing in the Constitution or Laws of the State to the Contrary notwithstanding." Under this authority, the Supreme Court has frequently overturned state constitutional provisions or statutes and state court decisions it deems to contravene rights or privileges guaranteed under the federal Constitution or federal statutes.

The civil rights area abounds with examples of state laws that were overturned because the statutes violated guarantees of due process and equal protection contained in the Fourteenth Amendment to the Constitution. For example, in the

supremacy clause Article VI of the Constitution, which states that laws passed by the national government and all treaties are the supreme law of the land and superior to all laws adopted by any state or any subdivision

1954 case of *Brown v. Board of Education,* the Court overturned statutes from Kansas, South Carolina, Virginia, and Delaware that either required or permitted segregated public schools on the basis that such statutes denied black schoolchildren equal protection of the law. In 1967, in *Loving v. Virginia,* the Court invalidated a Virginia statute prohibiting interracial marriages.[8]

State statutes in other subject matter areas are equally subject to challenge. In *Griswold v. Connecticut,* the Court invalidated a Connecticut statute prohibiting the general distribution of contraceptives to married couples on the basis that the statute violated the couples' rights to marital privacy.[9] In *Brandenburg v. Ohio,* the Court overturned an Ohio statute forbidding any person from urging criminal acts as a means of inducing political reform or from joining any association that advocated such activities on the grounds that the statute punished "mere advocacy" and therefore violated the free speech provisions of the Constitution.[10]

JUDICIAL REVIEW OF FEDERAL AGENCY ACTIONS

Although Congress makes the law, as we saw in Chapters 12 and 14, Congress can hardly administer the thousands of programs it has enacted and must delegate power to the president and to a huge bueaucracy to achieve its purposes. For example, if Congress wishes to improve air quality, it cannot possibly anticipate all the conditions and circumstances that may arise with respect to that general goal. Inevitably, Congress must delegate to the executive substantial discretionary power to make judgments about the best ways to bring about improved air quality in the face of changing circumstances. Thus, over the years, almost any congressional program will result in thousands and thousands of pages of administrative regulations developed by executive agencies nominally seeking to implement the will of the Congress.

Such delegation is inescapable in the modern era. But delegation of power to the executive poses a number of problems for Congress and the federal courts. If Congress delegates broad authority to the president, it risks seeing its goals subordinated to and subverted by those of the executive branch.[11] If Congress attempts to limit executive discretion by enacting precise rules and standards to govern the conduct of the president and the executive branch, it risks writing laws that do not conform to real-world conditions and that are too rigid to be adapted to changing circumstances.[12]

The issue of delegation of power has led to a number of court decisions over the past two centuries, generally revolving around the question of the scope of the delegation. Courts have also been called on to decide whether the rules and regulations adopted by federal agencies are consistent with Congress's express or implied intent.

As presidential power expanded during the New Deal era, one measure of increased congressional subordination to the executive was the enactment of laws that contained few, if any, principles limiting executive discretion. Congress enacted legislation, often at the president's behest, that gave the executive virtually unfettered authority to address a particular concern. For example, the Emergency Price Control Act of 1942 authorized the executive to set "fair an equitable" prices without offering any indication of what those terms might mean.[13] Although the Court initially challenged these delegations of power to the president during the

New Deal, a confrontation with President Franklin D. Roosevelt caused the Court to retreat from its position. Perhaps as a result, no congressional delegation of power to the president has been struck down as impermissibly broad since then. In the last two decades in particular, the Supreme Court has found that so long as federal agencies developed rules and regulations "based upon a permissible construction" or "reasonable interpretation" of Congress's statute, the judiciary would accept the views of the executive branch. Generally, the courts give considerable deference to administrative agencies as long as those agencies have engaged in a formal rule-making process and can show that they have carried out the conditions prescribed by the various statutes governing agency rule making. These include the 1946 *Administrative Procedure Act*, which requires agencies to notify parties affected by proposed rules as well as allow them ample time to comment on such rules before they go into effect.

JUDICIAL REVIEW AND LAWMAKING

Much of the work of the courts involves the application of statutes to the particular case at hand. Over the centuries, however, judges have developed a body of rules and principles of interpretation that are not grounded in specific statutes. This body of judge-made law is called common law.

The appellate courts, however, are in another realm. Their rulings can be considered laws, but they are laws governing the behavior only of the judiciary. They influence citizens' conduct only because, in the words of Justice Oliver Wendell Holmes, who served on the Supreme Court from 1900 to 1932, lawyers make "prophecies of what the courts will do in fact."[14]

The written opinion of an appellate court is about halfway between common law and statutory law. It is judge-made and draws heavily on the precedents of previous cases. But it tries to articulate the rule of law controlling the case in question and future cases like it. In this respect, it is like a statute. But it differs from a statute in that a statute addresses itself to the future conduct of citizens, whereas a written opinion addresses itself mainly to the willingness or ability of courts in the future to take cases and render favorable opinions. Decisions by appellate courts affect citizens by giving them a cause of action or by taking it away from them. That is, they open or close access to the courts.

A specific case may help clarify the distinction. Before the Second World War, one of the most insidious forms of racial discrimination was the "restrictive covenant," a clause in a contract whereby the purchasers of a house agreed that if they later decided to sell it, they would sell only to a Caucasian. When a test case finally reached the Supreme Court in 1948, the Court ruled unanimously that citizens had a right to discriminate with restrictive covenants in their sales contracts but that the courts could not enforce these contracts. Its argument was that enforcement would constitute violation of the Fourteenth Amendment provision that no state shall "deny to any person within its jurisdiction equal protection under the law."[15] The Court was thereby predicting what it would and would not do in future cases of this sort. Most states have now enacted statutes that forbid homeowners to place such covenants in sales contracts.

The 1963 case *Gideon v. Wainwright* extends the point. When the Supreme Court ordered a new trial for Clarence Earl Gideon because he had been denied the right to legal counsel,[16] it said to all trial judges and prosecutors that henceforth they would be wasting their time if they cut corners in trials of indigent defendants. It also invited thousands of prisoners to appeal their convictions. (See Chapter 4 for a further discussion of this case.)

Many areas of civil law have been constructed in the same way—by judicial messages to other judges, some of which are codified eventually into legislative enactments. An example of great concern to employees and employers is that of liability for injuries sustained at work. Courts have sided with employees so often that it has become virtually useless for employers to fight injury cases. It has become "the law" that employers are liable for such injuries, without regard to negligence. But the law in this instance is simply a series of messages to lawyers that they should advise their corporate clients not to appeal injury decisions. In recent years, the Supreme Court has also been developing law in the realm of sexual harassment in the workplace. In one 1998 case, for example, the Court ruled that an employer can be held responsible if one of its employees is sexually harassed by a supervisor, even if the company was unaware of the supervisor's specific behavior.[17]

In Marbury v. Madison *(1803), Chief Justice John Marshall established the Supreme Court's power to rule on the constitutionality of federal and state laws. This power makes the Court a lawmaking body.*

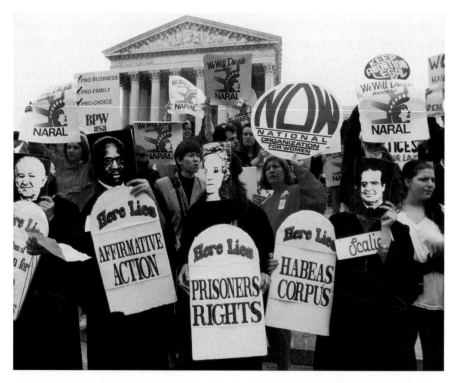

One important policy area in which the Court's decisions have the effect of law is abortion rights. For example, in 1989 the Supreme Court ruled on the constitutionality of a Missouri state law that put limitations on a woman's right to seek an abortion. Given the Court's lawmaking ability, prochoice groups such as the National Organization for Women and the National Abortion and Reproductive Rights Action League filed amicus curiae *briefs and gathered outside the Court in hopes of influencing public opinion.*

The appellate courts cannot decide what types of behavior will henceforth be a crime. They cannot directly prevent the police from forcing confessions from suspects or intimidating witnesses. In other words, they cannot directly change the behavior of citizens or eliminate abuses of government power. What they can do, however, is make it easier for mistreated persons to gain redress.

In redressing wrongs, the appellate courts—and even the Supreme Court itself—often call for a radical change in legal principle. Changes in race relations, for example, would probably have taken a great deal longer if the Supreme Court had not rendered the 1954 decision *Brown v. Board of Education* that redefined the rights of African Americans.

Similarly, the Supreme Court interpreted the doctrine of the separation of church and state so as to alter significantly the practice of religion in public institutions. For example, in a 1962 case, *Engel v. Vitale,* the Court declared that a once widely observed ritual—the recitation of a prayer by students in a public school—was unconstitutional under the establishment clause of the First Amendment. Almost all the dramatic changes in the treatment of criminals and of persons accused of crimes have been made by the appellate courts, especially the Supreme Court. The Supreme Court brought about a veritable revolution in the criminal process with three cases over less than five years: *Gideon v. Wainwright,* in 1963, was just discussed. *Escobedo v. Illinois,* in 1964, gave suspects the right to remain silent and the right to have counsel present during questioning. But the *Escobedo* decision left confusions that allowed differing decisions to be made by lower courts. In *Miranda v. Arizona,* in 1966, the Supreme Court cleared up these

Another policy area in which the federal courts have assumed a dominant role is busing. For example, federal judge W. Arthur Garrity (pictured here) ordered that Boston's schools be desegregated and created an elaborate plan for accomplishing this goal. When opponents of Garrity's plan were denied appeal by the Supreme Court, the plan effectively became law.

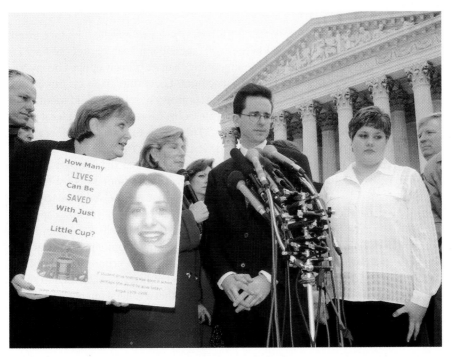

Due process of law is yet another area where federal courts have been critical in "making law" since the 1960s. In 2002, the issue of random drug testing of high school students who participate in extracurricular activities, a policy based on a Supreme Court decision upholding random testing of high school athletes, came before the Court. Lindsey Earls (second from right), a member of the Tecumseh, Oklahoma, high school choir and marching band, challenged the constitutionality of this policy; Sharon Smith, holding the sign, supported it. Earls's challenge was rejected, as the Court ruled that its earlier decision applied to this case as well.

Miranda rule the requirement, articulated by the Supreme Court in *Miranda v. Arizona,* that persons under arrest must be informed prior to police interrogation of their rights to remain silent and to have the benefit of legal counsel

confusions by setting forth what is known as the ***Miranda* rule:** arrested people have the right to remain silent, the right to be informed that anything they say can be held against them, and the right to counsel before and during police interrogation (see Chapter 4).[18] In 2000, the Supreme Court considered overruling *Miranda* in *Dickerson v. United States,* but it decided that the wide acceptance of Miranda rights in the legal culture is "adequate reason not to overrule" it.

One of the most significant changes brought about by the Supreme Court was the revolution in legislative representation unleashed by the 1962 case of *Baker v. Carr*.[19] In this landmark case, the Supreme Court held that it could no longer avoid reviewing complaints about the apportionment of seats in state legislatures. Following that decision, the federal courts went on to force reapportionment of all state, county, and local legislatures in the country.

HOW CASES REACH THE SUPREME COURT

Given the millions of disputes that arise every year, the job of the Supreme Court would be impossible if it were not able to control the flow of cases and its own caseload. The Supreme Court has original jurisdiction in a limited variety of cases defined by the Constitution. The original jurisdiction includes (1) cases between the United States and one of the fifty states, (2) cases between two or more states, (3) cases involving foreign ambassadors or other ministers, and (4) cases brought by one state against citizens of another state or against a foreign country. The most important of these cases are disputes between states over land, water, or old debts. Generally, the Supreme Court deals with these cases by appointing a "special master," usually a retired judge, to actually hear the case and present a report. The Supreme Court then allows the states involved in the dispute to present arguments for or against the master's opinion.[20]

Rules of Access   Over the years, the courts have developed specific rules that govern which cases within their jurisdiction they will and will not hear. In order to have access to the courts, cases must meet certain criteria that are initially applied by the trial court but may be reconsidered by appellate courts. These rules of access can be broken down into three major categories: case or controversy, standing, and mootness.

Article III of the Constitution and Supreme Court decisions define judicial power as extending only to "cases and controversies." This means that the case before a court must be an actual controversy, not a hypothetical one, with two truly adversarial parties. The courts have interpreted this language to mean that they do not have the power to render advisory opinions to legislatures or agencies about the constitutionality of proposed laws or regulations. Furthermore, even after a law is enacted, the courts will generally refuse to consider its constitutionality until it is actually applied.

standing the right of an individual or organization to initiate a court case

Parties to a case must also have **standing**—that is, they must show that they have a substantial stake in the outcome of the case. The traditional requirement for standing has been to show injury to oneself; that injury can be personal, economic, or even aesthetic. In order for a group or class of people to have standing (as in class action suits), each member must show specific injury. This means that a general interest in the environment, for instance, does not provide a group with sufficient basis for standing.

mootness a criterion used by courts to screen cases that no longer require resolution.

The Supreme Court also uses a third criterion in determining whether it will hear a case: that of **mootness.** In theory, this requirement disqualifies cases that are brought too late—after the relevant facts have changed or the problem has been resolved by other means. The criterion of mootness, however, is subject to the discretion of the courts, which have begun to relax the rules of mootness, particularly in cases where a situation that has been resolved is likely to come up again. In the abortion case *Roe v. Wade,* for example, the Supreme Court rejected the lower court's argument that because the pregnancy had already come to term, the case was moot. The Court agreed to hear the case because no pregnancy was likely to outlast the lengthy appeals process.

Putting aside the formal criteria, the Supreme Court is most likely to accept cases that involve conflicting decisions by the federal circuit courts, cases that present important questions of civil rights or civil liberties, and cases in which the federal government is the appellant. Ultimately, however, the question of which cases to accept can come down to the preferences and priorities of the justices. If a group of justices believes that the Court should intervene in a particular area of policy or politics, they are likely to look for a case or cases that will serve as vehicles for judicial intervention. For many years, for example, the Court was not interested in considering challenges to affirmative action or other programs designed to provide particular benefits to minorities. In recent years, however, several of the Court's more conservative justices have been eager to push back the limits of affirmative action and racial preference, and have therefore accepted a number of cases that would allow them to do so. In 1995, the Court's decisions in *Adarand Constructors v. Pena, Missouri v. Jenkins,* and *Miller v. Johnson* placed new restrictions on federal affirmative action programs, school desegregation efforts, and attempts to increase minority representation in Congress through the creation of "minority districts" (see Chapter 10).[21]

Writs Decisions handed down by lower courts can reach the Supreme Court in one of two ways: through a *writ of certiorari,* or, in the case of convicted state prisoners, through a writ of *habeas corpus.* A writ is a court document conveying an order of some sort. In recent years, an effort has been made to give the Court more discretion regarding the cases it chooses to hear. Before 1988, the Supreme Court was obligated to review cases on what was called a writ of appeal. This has since been eliminated, and the Court now has virtually complete discretion over what cases it will hear.

Most cases reach the Supreme Court through the **writ of *certiorari,*** which is granted whenever four of the nine justices agree to review a case. The Supreme Court was once so inundated with appeals that in 1925 Congress enacted laws giving it some control over its caseload with the power to issue writs of *certiorari.* Rule 10 of the Supreme Court's own rules of procedure defines *certiorari* as "not a matter of right, but of sound judicial discretion . . . granted only where there are special and important reasons therefor." The reasons provided for in Rule 10 are these:

writ of *certiorari* a decision of at least four of the nine Supreme Court justices to review a decision of a lower court; from the Latin "to make more certain"

1. Where a state has made a decision that conflicts with previous Supreme Court decisions
2. Where a state court has come up with an entirely new federal question
3. Where one court of appeals has rendered a decision in conflict with another
4. Where there are other inconsistent rulings between two or more courts or states
5. Where a single court of appeals has sanctioned too great a departure by a lower court from normal judicial proceedings (a reason rarely given)

Figure 15.2   How Cases Reach the Supreme Court

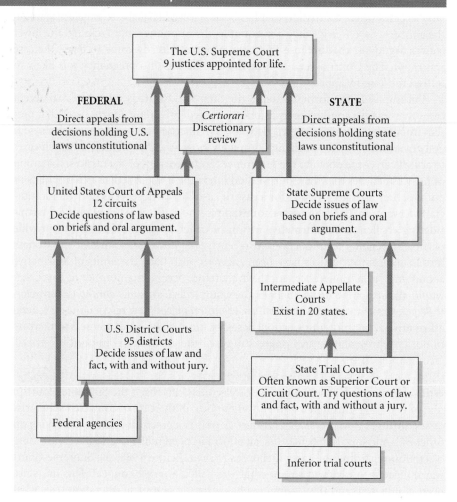

writ of *habeas corpus* a court
order that the individual in custody
be brought into court and shown
the cause for detention. *Habeas
corpus* is guaranteed by the Constitution and can be suspended only
in cases of rebellion or invasion

The **writ of *habeas corpus*** is a fundamental safeguard of individual rights. Its historical purpose is to enable an accused person to challenge arbitrary detention and to force an open trial before a judge. But in 1867, Congress's distrust of southern courts led it to confer on federal courts the authority to issue writs of *habeas corpus* to prisoners already tried or being tried in state courts of proper jurisdiction where the constitutional rights of the prisoner were possibly being violated. This writ gives state prisoners a second channel toward Supreme Court review in case their direct appeal from the highest state court fails (see Figure 15.2). The writ of *habeas corpus* is discretionary; that is, the Court can decide which cases to review.

CONTROLLING THE FLOW OF CASES

In addition to the judges themselves, two other actors play important roles in shaping the flow of cases through the federal courts: the solicitor general and federal law clerks.

The Solicitor General   If any single person has greater influence than individual judges over the federal courts, it is the **solicitor general** of the United States. The solicitor general is the third-ranking official in the Justice Department (below the attorney general and the deputy attorney general) but is the top government lawyer in virtually all cases before the Supreme Court in which the government is a party. The solicitor general has the greatest control over the flow of cases; his or her actions are not reviewed by any higher authority in the executive branch. More than half the Supreme Court's total workload consists of cases under the direct charge of the solicitor general.

The solicitor general exercises especially strong influence by screening cases before any agency of the federal government can appeal them to the Supreme Court; indeed, the justices rely on the solicitor general to "screen out undeserving litigation and furnish them with an agenda to government cases that deserve serious consideration."[22] Typically, more requests for appeals are rejected than are accepted by the solicitor general. Agency heads may lobby the president or otherwise try to circumvent the solicitor general, and a few of the independent agencies have a statutory right to make direct appeals, but these are almost inevitably doomed to ***per curiam*** rejection—rejection through a brief, unsigned opinion by the whole Court—if the solicitor general refuses to participate. Congress has given only a few agencies, including the Federal Communications Commission, the Federal Maritime Commission, and in some cases, the Department of Agriculture (even though it is not an independent agency), the right to appeal directly to the Supreme Court without going through the solicitor general.

The solicitor general can enter a case even when the federal government is not a direct litigant by writing an ***amicus curiae*** ("friend of the court") brief. A friend of the court is not a direct party to a case but has a vital interest in its outcome. Thus, when the government has such an interest, the solicitor general can file as *amicus curiae,* or a federal court can invite such a brief because it wants an opinion in writing. The solicitor general also has the power to invite others to enter cases as *amici curiae.*

In addition to exercising substantial control over the flow of cases, the solicitor general can shape the arguments used before the federal courts. Indeed, the Supreme Court tends to give special attention to the way the solicitor general characterizes the issues. The solicitor general is the person appearing most frequently before the Court and, theoretically at least, is the most disinterested. The credibility of the solicitor general is not hurt when several times each year he or she comes to the Court to withdraw a case with the admission that the government has made an error.

The solicitor general's sway over the flow of cases does not, however, entirely overshadow the influence of the other agencies and divisions in the Department of Justice. The solicitor general is counsel for the major divisions in the department, including the Antitrust, Tax, Civil Rights, and Criminal divisions. Their activities generate a great part of the solicitor general's agenda. This is particularly true of the Criminal Division, whose cases are appealed every day. These cases are generated by initiatives taken by the United States attorneys and the district judges before whom they practice.

Law Clerks   Every federal judge employs law clerks to research legal issues and assist with the preparation of opinions. Each Supreme Court justice is assigned

solicitor general the top government lawyer in all cases before the Supreme Court where the government is a party

per curiam decision by an appellate court, without a written opinion, that refuses to review the decision of a lower court; amounts to a reaffirmation of the lower court's opinion

amicus curiae literally, "friend of the court"; individuals or groups who are not parties to a lawsuit but who seek to assist the Supreme Court in reaching a decision by presenting additional briefs four clerks. The clerks are almost always honors graduates of the nation's most prestigious law schools. A clerkship with a Supreme Court justice is a great honor and generally indicates that the fortunate individual is likely to reach the very top of the legal profession. The work of the Supreme Court clerks is a closely guarded secret, but it is likely that some justices rely heavily upon their clerks for advice in writing opinions and in deciding whether an individual case ought to be heard by the Court. In a recent book, a former law clerk to retired justice Harry Blackmun charged that Supreme Court justices yielded "excessive power to immature, ideologically driven clerks, who in turn use that power to manipulate their bosses."[23]

LOBBYING FOR ACCESS: INTERESTS AND THE COURT

At the same time that the Court exercises discretion over which cases it will review, groups and forces in society often seek to persuade the justices to listen to their problems. Interest groups use several different strategies to get the Court's attention. Lawyers representing these groups try to choose the proper client and the proper case, so that the issues in question are most dramatically and appropriately portrayed. They also have to pick the right district or jurisdiction in which to bring the case. Sometimes they even have to wait for an appropriate political climate.

Group litigants have to plan carefully when to use and when to avoid publicity. They must also attempt to develop a proper record at the trial court level, one that includes some constitutional arguments and even, when possible, errors on the part of the trial court. One of the most effective litigation strategies used in getting cases accepted for review by the appellate courts is bringing the same type of suit in more than one circuit (i.e., developing a "pattern of cases"), in the hope that inconsistent treatment by two different courts will improve the chance of a Supreme Court review.

Congress will sometimes provide interest groups with legislation designed to facilitate their use of litigation. One important recent example is the 1990 Americans with Disabilities Act (ADA), enacted after intense lobbying by public interest and advocacy groups. The ADA, in conjunction with the 1991 Civil Rights Act, opens the way for disabled individuals to make effective use of the courts to press their interests.

The two most notable users of the pattern of cases strategy in recent years have been the National Association for the Advancement of Colored People (NAACP) and the American Civil Liberties Union (ACLU). For many years, the NAACP (and its Defense Fund—now a separate group) has worked through local chapters and with many individuals to encourage litigation on issues of racial discrimination and segregation. Sometimes it distributes petitions to be signed by parents and filed with local school boards and courts, deliberately sowing the seeds of future litigation. The NAACP and the ACLU often encourage private parties to bring suit and then join the suit as *amici curiae.*

One illustration of an interest group employing a carefully crafted litigation strategy to pursue its goals through the judiciary was the Texas-based effort to establish a right to free public school education for children of illegal aliens. The issue arose in 1977 when the Texas state legislature, responding to a sudden public backlash against illegal immigration from Mexico, enacted a law permitting school districts to charge undocumented children hefty tuition for the privilege

Abortion and the Right to Privacy

Although the word "privacy" does not appear in the Bill of Rights, the courts have agreed that such a fundamental right exists. They disagree, however, about exactly from where the protection arises and about how far it should be applied. Nowhere is this disagreement more protracted than on the issue of abortion.

Since its 1973 landmark ruling in *Roe v. Wade*, the Supreme Court has repeatedly found that the right to privacy protects the right of a woman to end a pregnancy via abortion, subject to some court-approved restrictions. Abortion opponents, of course, have rejected the premise of *Roe* that privacy protects an act they consider murder. For example, members of Congress who oppose abortion have succeeded in restricting federal Medicaid funding for abortions. Today's more conservative Supreme Court has allowed states to impose restrictions such as parental notification for minors and twenty-four-hour waiting periods for those seeking abortions.

Supporters of privacy-based protection for abortion argue that, as a matter of law and tradition, a developing fetus cannot be accorded the same legal status as the woman carrying a fetus. If privacy means anything, it must extend to the right of a woman to decide, at least during the early months of pregnancy (when the

vast majority of abortions are performed, and before the point of viability, when the fetus can live outside of the woman), whether or not to have an abortion. For the government to require women to carry most or all pregnancies to term represents extreme government intrusion into the innately personal decision over procreation. The principle of individual liberty must allow women to make such fundamental decisions themselves.

Further, the idea that all abortions are murder means that a fertilized egg does and should possess the same traits as a full-term baby, an idea that is rejected by medical science, most Americans, and many religions. For example, when a spontaneous abortion occurs early in a pregnancy, it is called a "miscarriage," for which funeral services are not held. A late-term spontaneous abortion, called a "stillbirth," evokes a different and more complex response, reflecting the evident difference in development. Abortion laws properly reflect these differences. Finally, the Consti-

tution speaks to the issue by noting that citizenship, and therefore the rights stemming from it, begins at birth.

Opponents of abortion argue that the relative differences observed in fetal development do not obviate the fact that, by genetic makeup, even a fertilized egg is a person. The right to privacy does not and cannot provide an excuse for murder. The absence of birth does not, in and of itself, mean that a fetus is without rights. Even if the Constitution's framers had all agreed that the Bill of Rights protected the liberty associated with privacy, there is no reason to believe that they would have countenanced its extension to abortion. Furthermore, to say that such issues are purely a matter of personal choice is to turn a blind eye to the sort of evil that government has every right to regulate or prohibit. And while pregnancy is a developmental process for the fetus, it is precisely because there is no magic, agreed-upon point at which a fetus becomes a person that the fetus must be protected as a person at all stages.

Women who become pregnant, whether by accident or intent, assume a special obligation to the innocent life they carry. Although some who oppose abortions are willing to allow exceptions for cases of rape or incest, such cases account for only a tiny percentage of all abortions. Legal abortion is harmful in other respects. It demeans respect for life by allowing, even encouraging, abortion as a means of birth control. If later-term abortions are allowed because of, say, fetal defect, it is a short step to euthanasia (so-called mercy killing) of living persons. Above all, the right of a fetus to live must supersede the privacy rights, however defined, of pregnant women.

FOR CRITICAL ANALYSIS

1. If *Roe* were reversed and states made abortion a crime, how would protection of the fetus, beginning with the fertilized egg, be implemented? If a "miscarriage" was induced by abortion, what should be the punishment for the mother? Murder? Criminal negligence? Manslaughter?

2. Thousands of childless couples engage in great effort and endure delays and disappointments in adopting a child. Should government provide incentives to pregnant women to go to term so that more children are available for adoption?

DEBATE

Is the Right to Abortion Constitutional?

Yes Abortion is a sensitive issue. It's one of those topics you try to avoid while you're having dinner with your in-laws. Most people have made up their minds on the issue and have no interest in hearing opposing arguments. However, it is imperative that the issue be discussed, given the impact it has on women across the nation. Abortion is, and must remain, legal.

In 1973, the Supreme Court decided that abortion is constitutional through interpreting the Ninth Amendment as a right to privacy. Contrary to arguments from the antichoice movement, the Supreme Court took a very plausible road to come to this conclusion.

The Constitution does not directly assert that abortion is legal, but the purpose of the Constitution isn't to state whether any particular act is legal or not. The document wasn't written as a list of rules by which to abide. It was written as a blueprint for our government to follow when writing laws. Our founding fathers knew they couldn't foresee the type of legislation America would need 200 years in the future, so they purposely designed the Constitution to be ambiguous. In this way, future congressional representatives would have the power to write laws pertaining to their own society. However, the writers kept certain guidelines in the document to set a standard by which to measure all legislation.

For this reason, the Supreme Court must interpret the Constitution in order to know whether laws written contradict our forefathers' vision of America. The Ninth Amendment states, "The enumeration in the Constitution, of certain rights, shall not be construed to deny or disparage others retained by the people." This directly translates as a right of the people to keep the rights they hold that are not mentioned in the Constitution, one of which being a right to privacy. People have a right to make personal decisions for themselves. The government can't tell you what god to worship, what beliefs to hold, or whether to have children.

That's right—the decision to have children is private. The government has no business telling private citizens they must give birth.

Antichoice activists claim abortion is not a private choice because a fetus is a living human being, and therefore, the decision to stop its growth is equivalent to murder. Whether or not you consider abortion to be murder depends on where you believe life begins. According to the Bible, life begins in the womb.

But we don't base our nation's laws on the Bible. We base them on the Constitution. The religious right must accept that there is a separation between church and state. This is not a Christian society—we don't outlaw adultery, premarital sex, or envy. And there is no reason to believe life starts at conception if you don't consult the Bible. After all, the fetus can't live outside of the womb. It isn't fully formed and it doesn't have a functioning brain. It isn't a life until it's complete. An ear is not a child. A toe is not a child. An organism with two ears, ten toes, and a few working organs isn't a child. It's an organism.

This isn't to say abortion is an easy choice. Before many women have the procedure done, they wrestle with the decision and even second-guess themselves. However, sometimes abortion is the only viable option. Under certain circumstances, which differ depending on the situation of the mother-to-be, it may be the best choice. Unless one has been through similar circumstances, it's unreasonable to judge a woman for choosing to end her pregnancy. Abortion must remain legal because if woman are left without a choice, they could put themselves in danger trying to end their pregnancies themselves.

Women have been having abortions for centuries. Before it became legal, a woman who wished to terminate her pregnancy was forced to have a very dangerous procedure performed on the black market by unqualified doctors who would charge astronomical prices while practically destroying her insides. If she couldn't afford one of these doctors, she might try to perform the procedure herself with a wire coat hanger. This was an unspeakably traumatic experience, and it happened more often then many anti-choice activists want to believe.

But it doesn't have to happen again. If we keep abortion legal, then women can have this procedure completed safely. Abortion is a private decision that should be respected, given the amount of desperation it takes to make.

SOURCE: Rebecca Martin, "The Ninth Amendment Gives Women a Right to Choose," *The Daily Aztec*, (San Diego State University), March 6, 2003.

No

There is an awkward point in many women's lives when they have another human being living inside them. This fact of nature has its advantages and drawbacks. It is an experience completely unique to the gender and seems to be a difficult, yet life-altering experience. However, there is a point of deep responsibility when what a pregnant woman decides to do with her body no longer solely impacts her alone—and this naturally invades her privacy.

The primary divide between people who are prochoice and prolife is most frequently with whether the fetus is a living human being. If you believe a developing fetus is a human life and that human life deserves the protection of the law, then you have to oppose the legality of abortion.

Most of the prochoice arguments deal with issues concerning the mother or social situations alleviated by abortion, which are irrelevant to the issue of whether a fetus is a human being. Obviously, a fetus is alive and uniquely human. The fetus has a gender, a distinctly human genetic make-up, and is capable of reproducing his or her cells. The fetus is a complete human being and needs no genetic additions, just nurturing and time to mature—as are humans existing outside of the womb. You would have to ignore nature and science to argue that he or she is not a living human being.

The second condition, whether the unborn deserve protection from the law, is more subjective. Law is a philosophy created by mankind, and essentially the lines we choose to draw. However, most people recognize a higher moral law—be it through religion or empathy—and believe the worst laws have been in violation of this. Slavery is perhaps the clearest example of a former law that violated this understood morality. Violations of human rights generally occur when people disregard the sanctity of all human life and try to redraw these lines to include only some of human life.

Furthermore, the law already protects the unborn in certain instances. Many healthcare requirements ensure the unborn get proper prenatal care. In addition, if a drunk driver kills a pregnant woman, he or she may be convicted for two counts of manslaughter. There are two definite losses in this situation, and both are justified. However, this shows that when unborn children are wanted, the law will protect them, but when they are unwanted the law permits their deaths—we are allowing people's desires to validate another human's existence. Allowing this strips the inalienable right to life. If the law considers the unborn a human being in a murder case, and punishes a person for violating his or her human right to life, than it should be consistent and protect the unborn in all cases.

Roe v. Wade uses privacy zones, the precedent of which is established in various other Supreme Court cases, to institutionalize something that violates the biggest principle in U.S. law—the right to life. You should not be allowed to have a "privacy zone" where you can legally take the life of another human being. On top of that, the legal precedent is weak, and the Supreme Court majority opinion reads more like the best possible rationalization rather than the most apparent legal conclusion.

U.S. law should protect the unborn, but it doesn't because a lot of pressure was in place to legalize abortion. It conveniently solves several problems such as unwanted pregnancies, deaths in relation to illegal abortions, overpopulation, and the horrible situations where women give birth to babies fathered by rapists. These problems, and more, were dampened when the *Roe v. Wade* decision was made. However, that doesn't justify the solution and make abortion acceptable. It's a visible solution, not a moral one. The Supreme Court responded to these problems and outside pressure instead of doing what was right.

No decent person wants to make a woman have a child she doesn't want. Unfortunately, there is a point where it is necessary to ensure the safety of another human being. Unwanted pregnancy is a horrible thing, but the best solution is to avoid it all together. Improving sex education, increasing accessibility to contraceptives, overwhelmingly condemning rape (which we sadly don't do), and ensuring women are given a choice to have sex can solve many unfortunate situations. However, once the window of prevention is closed, society has a duty to protect the unborn.

SOURCE: Joe Zarro, "Legal Precedent Supporting Sanctity of Unborn Life Is Strong," *The Daily Aztec,* (San Diego State University), March 6, 2003.

of attending public school. A public-interest law organization, the Mexican-American Legal Defense Fund, prepared to challenge the law in court after determining that public opposition precluded any chance of persuading the legislature to change its own law.

Part of the defense fund's litigation strategy was to bring a lawsuit in the northern section of Texas, far from the Mexican border, where illegal immigration would be at a minimum. Thus, in Tyler, Texas, where the complaint was initially filed, the trial court found only sixty undocumented alien students in a school district composed of 16,000. This strategy effectively contradicted the state's argument that the Texas law was necessary to reduce the burdens on educational resources created by masses of incoming aliens. Another useful litigation tactic was to select plaintiffs who, although illegal aliens, were nevertheless clearly planning to remain in Texas even without free public education for their children. Thus, all of the plaintiffs came from families that had already lived in Tyler for several years and included at least one child who was an American citizen by virtue of birth in the United States. By emphasizing the stability of such families, the defense fund argued convincingly that the Texas law would not motivate families to return to the poverty in Mexico from which they had fled, but would more likely result in the creation of a subclass of illiterate people who would add to the state's unemployment and crime rates. Five years after the lawsuit on behalf of the Tyler children began, the U.S. Supreme Court in the case of *Plyler v. Doe* held that the Texas law was unconstitutional under the equal protection clause of the Fourteenth Amendment.[24]

In many states, it is considered unethical and illegal for attorneys to engage in "fomenting and soliciting legal business in which they are not parties and have no pecuniary right or liability." The NAACP was sued by the state of Virginia in the late 1950s in an attempt to restrict or eliminate its efforts to influence the pattern of cases. The Supreme Court reviewed the case in 1963, recognized that the strategy was being utilized, and held that it was protected by the First and Fourteenth Amendments, just as other forms of speech and petition are protected.[25]

Thus, many pathbreaking cases are eventually granted *certiorari* because continued refusal to review one or more of them would amount to a rule of law just as much as if the courts had handed down a written opinion. In this sense, the flow of cases, especially the pattern of significant cases, influences the behavior of the appellate judiciary.

THE SUPREME COURT'S PROCEDURES

The Preparation   The Supreme Court's decision to accept a case is the beginning of what can be a lengthy and complex process (see Figure 15.3). First, the attorneys on both sides must prepare **briefs**—written documents that may be several hundred pages long in which the attorneys explain why the Court should rule in favor of their client. Briefs are filled with referrals to precedents specifically chosen to show that other courts have frequently ruled in the same way that the Supreme Court is being asked to rule. The attorneys for both sides muster the most compelling precedents they can in support of their arguments.

As the attorneys prepare their briefs, they often ask sympathetic interest groups for their help. Groups are asked to file *amicus curiae* briefs that support the claims of one or the other litigant. In a case involving separation of church and

briefs written documents in which attorneys explain, using case precedents, why the court should find in favor of their client

The Supreme Court's Decision-Making Process

Figure 15.3

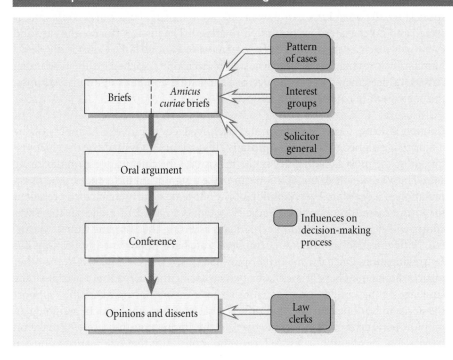

In addition to the individual justices who make up the Supreme Court, various groups and factors also may influence the Court's decision on any given case.

state, for example, liberal groups such as the ACLU and Citizens for the American Way are likely to be asked to file *amicus* briefs in support of strict separation, whereas conservative religious groups are likely to file *amicus* briefs advocating increased public support for religious ideas. Often, dozens of briefs will be filed on each side of a major case. *Amicus* filings are one of the primary methods used by interest groups to lobby the Court. By filing these briefs, groups indicate to the Court where their group stands and signal to the justices that they believe the case to be an important one.

Oral Argument The next stage of a case is **oral argument,** in which attorneys for both sides appear before the Court to present their positions and answer the justices' questions. Each attorney has only a half hour to present his or her case, and this time includes interruptions for questions. Certain members of the Court, such as Justice Antonin Scalia, are known to interrupt attorneys dozens of times. Others, such as Justice Clarence Thomas, seldom ask questions. For an attorney, the opportunity to argue a case before the Supreme Court is a singular honor and a mark of professional distinction. It can also be a harrowing experience, as justices interrupt a carefully prepared presentation. Nevertheless, oral argument can be very important to the outcome of a case. It allows justices to better understand the heart of the case and to raise questions that might not have been addressed in the opposing side's briefs. It is not uncommon for justices to go beyond the strictly legal issues and ask opposing counsel to discuss the implications of the case for the Court and the nation at large.

oral argument stage in Supreme Court procedure in which attorneys for both sides appear before the Court to present their positions and answer questions posed by justices

The Conference   Following oral argument, the Court discusses the case in its Wednesday or Friday conference. The chief justice presides over the conference and speaks first; the other justices follow in order of seniority. The Court's conference is secret, and no outsiders are permitted to attend. The justices discuss the case and eventually reach a decision on the basis of a majority vote. If the Court is divided, a number of votes may be taken before a final decision is reached. As the case is discussed, justices may try to influence or change one another's opinions. At times, this may result in compromise decisions.

Opinion Writing   After a decision has been reached, one of the members of the majority is assigned to write the **opinion**. This assignment is made by the chief justice, or by the most senior justice in the majority if the chief justice is on the losing side. The assignment of the opinion can make a significant difference to the interpretation of a decision. Every opinion of the Supreme Court sets a major precedent for future cases throughout the judicial system. Lawyers and judges in the lower courts will examine the opinion carefully to ascertain the Supreme Court's meaning. Differences in wording and emphasis can have important implications for future litigation. Once the majority opinion is drafted, it is circulated to the other justices. Some members of the majority may decide that they cannot accept all the language of the opinion and therefore write "concurring" opinions that support the decision but offer a somewhat different rationale or emphasis. In assigning an opinion, serious thought must be given to the impression the case will make on lawyers and on the public, as well as to the probability that one justice's opinion will be more widely accepted than another's.

One of the more dramatic instances of this tactical consideration occurred in 1944, when Chief Justice Harlan F. Stone chose Justice Felix Frankfurter to write the opinion in the "white primary" case *Smith v. Allwright*. The chief justice believed that this sensitive case, which overturned the southern practice of prohibiting black participation in nominating primaries, required the efforts of the most brilliant and scholarly jurist on the Court. But the day after Stone made the assignment, Justice Robert H. Jackson wrote a letter to Stone urging a change of assignment. In his letter, Jackson argued that Frankfurter, a foreign-born Jew from New England, would not win the South with his opinion, regardless of its brilliance. Stone accepted the advice and substituted Justice Stanley Reed, an American-born Protestant from Kentucky and a southern Democrat in good standing.[26]

Dissent   Justices who disagree with the majority decision of the Court may choose to publicize the character of their disagreement in the form of a **dissenting opinion.** Dissents can be used to express irritation with an outcome or to signal to defeated political forces in the nation that their position is supported by at least some members of the Court. Ironically, the most dependable way an individual justice can exercise a direct and clear influence on the Court is to write a dissent. Because there is no need to please a majority, dissenting opinions can be more eloquent and less guarded than majority opinions. The current Supreme Court often produces 5–4 decisions with dissenters writing long and detailed opinions that, they hope, will help them to convince a swing justice to join their side on the next round of cases dealing with a similar topic. Thus, for example, Justice Souter wrote a thirty-four page dissent in a 2002 case upholding the use of government-funded

opinion the written explanation of the Supreme Court's decision in a particular case

dissenting opinion a decision written by a justice in the minority in a particular case in which the justice wishes to express his or her reasoning in the case school vouchers to pay parochial school tuition. Souter called the decision "a dramatic departure from basic Establishment Clause principle," which he hoped a "future court will reconsider."[27]

Dissent plays a special role in the work and impact of the Court because it amounts to an appeal to lawyers all over the country to keep bringing cases of the sort at issue. Therefore, an effective dissent influences the flow of cases through the Court as well as the arguments that will be used by lawyers in later cases. Even more important, dissent points out that although the Court speaks with a single opinion, it is the opinion only of the majority—and one day the majority might go the other way.

EXPLAINING SUPREME COURT DECISIONS

The Supreme Court explains its decisions in terms of law and precedent. But although law and precedent do have an effect on the Court's deliberations and eventual decisions, it is the Supreme Court that decides what laws actually mean and what importance precedent will actually have. Throughout its history, the Court has shaped and reshaped the law. In the late nineteenth and early twentieth centuries, for example, the Supreme Court held that the Constitution, law, and precedent permitted racial segregation in the United States. Beginning in the late 1950s, however, the Court found that the Constitution prohibited segregation on the basis of race and indicated that the use of racial categories in legislation was always suspect. By the 1970s and 1980s, the Court once again held that the Constitution permitted the use of racial categories—when such categories were needed to help members of minority groups achieve full participation in American society. In the 1990s, the Court began to retreat from this position, too, indicating that governmental efforts to provide extra help to racial minorities could represent an unconstitutional infringement on the rights of the majority.

Although it is not the only relevant factor, the prime explanation for these movements is shifts in judicial philosophy. These shifts, in turn, result from changes in the Court's composition as justices retire and are replaced by new justices who, as we saw earlier, tend to share the philosophical outlook of the president who appointed them.

Activism and Restraint One element of judicial philosophy is the issue of activism versus restraint. Over the years, some justices have believed that courts should interpret the Constitution according to the stated intentions of its framers and defer to the views of Congress when interpreting federal statutes. The late justice Felix Frankfurter, for example, advocated judicial deference to legislative bodies and avoidance of the "political thicket," in which the Court would entangle itself by deciding questions that were essentially political rather than legal in character. Advocates of **judicial restraint** are sometimes called "strict constructionists," because they look strictly to the words of the Constitution in interpreting its meaning.

The alternative to restraint is **judicial activism.** Activist judges such as the former chief justice Earl Warren believed that the Court should go beyond the words of the Constitution or a statute to consider the broader societal implications of its decisions. Activist judges sometimes strike out in new directions, promulgating new interpretations or inventing new legal and constitutional concepts when they

judicial restraint judicial philosophy whose adherents refuse to go beyond the clear words of the Constitution in interpreting its meaning

judicial activism judicial philosophy that posits that the Court should go beyond the words of the Constitution or a statute to consider the broader societal implications of its decisions believe these to be socially desirable. For example, Justice Harry Blackmun's decision in *Roe v. Wade* was based on a constitutional right to privacy that is not found in the words of the Constitution. Blackmun and the other members of the majority in the *Roe* case argued that the right to privacy was implied by other constitutional provisions. In this instance of judicial activism, the Court knew the result it wanted to achieve and was not afraid to make the law conform to the desired outcome.

Activism and restraint are sometimes confused with liberalism and conservatism. For example, conservative politicians often castigate "liberal activist" judges and call for the appointment of conservative jurists who will refrain from reinterpreting the law. To be sure, some liberal jurists are activists and some conservatives have been advocates of restraint, but the relationship is by no means one to one. Indeed, the Rehnquist court, dominated by conservatives, has been among the most activist courts in American history, striking out in new directions in such areas as federalism and election law.

Political Ideology   The second component of judicial philosophy is political ideology. The liberal or conservative attitudes of justices play an important role in their decisions.[28] Indeed, the philosophy of activism versus restraint is, to a large extent, a smokescreen for political ideology. For the most part, liberal judges have been activists, willing to use the law to achieve social and political change, whereas conservatives have been associated with judicial restraint. Interestingly, however, in recent years some conservative justices who have long called for restraint have actually become activists in seeking to undo some of the work of liberal jurists over the past three decades.

From the 1950s to the 1980s, the Supreme Court took an activist role in such areas as civil rights, civil liberties, abortion, voting rights, and police procedures. For example, the Supreme Court was more responsible than any other governmental institution for breaking down America's system of racial segregation. The Supreme Court virtually prohibited states from interfering with the right of a woman to seek an abortion and sharply curtailed state restrictions on voting rights. And it was the Supreme Court that placed restrictions on the behavior of local police and prosecutors in criminal cases. In a series of decisions between 1989 and 2001, however, the conservative justices appointed by presidents Ronald Reagan and George H. W. Bush were able to swing the Court to a more conservative position on civil rights, affirmative action, abortion rights, property rights, criminal procedure, voting rights, desegregation, and the power of the national government.

The importance of ideology was very clear during the Court's 2000–2001 term. In important decisions, the Court's most conservative justices—Scalia, Thomas, and Rehnquist, usually joined by Kennedy—generally voted as a bloc.[29] Indeed, Scalia and Thomas voted together in 99 percent of all cases. At the same time, the Court's most liberal justices—Breyer, Ginsburg, Souter, and Stevens—also generally formed a bloc with Ginsburg and Breyer and Ginsburg and Souter voting together 94 percent of the time.[30] Justice O'Connor, a moderate conservative, was the swing vote in many important cases. This ideological division led to a number of important 5-4 decisions. As we saw, in the main Florida election law case, *Bush v. Gore,* Justice O'Connor joined with the conservative bloc to give Bush a 5-4 victory.[31] Indeed, more than 33 percent of all the cases heard by the Court in its 2000–2001 term were decided 5 to 4.

The Supreme Court and International Law

For most of its history the American judiciary has been a particularly domestic institution. But in this epoch of globalization, the Court has had to give up what Justice Ruth Bader Ginsburg in 2003 called "our 'island' or 'lone ranger' mentality." Ginsberg went on to note that increasingly the justices were considering the perspectives of comparative and international law.

Along one path of change, numerous cases involving such things as interpreting the terms of an international treaty have arisen over "cross-border transactions" in which international law is not only relevant but could be the governing law. Such cases have given rise to the adoption of the United Nations Convention on Contracts for the International Sale of Goods (CISG), which the United States ratified in 1986. By the mid-1990s, U.S. courts had to deal with an increasing number of such cases, and the lower judges as well as the Supreme Court justices and their law clerks had a difficult time with these because they required research on international law and decisions by foreign courts. In 2003, Justice Stephen Breyer confessed in a speech to the Society of International Law that he and his colleagues had to rely on the lawyers involved in the litigation for applicable foreign precedents to apply. And our various courts continually disagree over the weight to put on the rulings of foreign tribunals: Are these foreign decisions to be taken as precedents in our courts? Or do U.S. courts apply U.S. law to such transnational cases? One U.S. Circuit Court in fact refused to apply a U.S. precedent in a CISG case because it would upset parties relying on the CISG if we substituted "familiar principles of domestic law when the CISG requires a different result." U.S. courts are going to be involved in international regulation of commerce whether they like it or not.

A second path of change, more diffuse and harder to measure, is the extent to which our courts, all the way to the top, can permit themselves to be influenced not only by precedents in cases of international law but also by international opinion and the decisions by foreign legislators and courts in their domestic disputes. The most striking was the 2003 decision that a Texas statute making it a crime for two persons of the same sex to engage in consensual sexual conduct violates the due process clause (*Lawrence v. Texas,* 123 S.Ct. 2472). This opinion overruled a case that had been the leading opinion since 1986 (*Bowers v. Hardwick,* 478 U.S. 186). More controversial

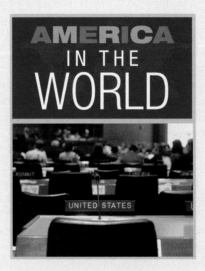

than the ruling itself was part of its argument—that other nations, including Great Britain, had repealed such laws ten years earlier. Another decision of equal import was the Supreme Court holding in 2003 that the University of Michigan's "narrowly tailored use of race" in its admissions decisions did not violate the Equal Protection clause (*Grutter v. Bollinger,* 123 S.Ct. 2325). In her concurring opinion, Justice Ruth Bader Ginsburg noted that the majority opinion was in accord with "international understanding," as found in the United Nations' International Convention on the Elimination of All Forms of Racial Discrimination, ratified by the United States in 1994. Still another was the 2002 decision in which the majority opinion noted that "within the world community the imposition of the death penalty for crimes committed by mentally retarded offenders is overwhelmingly disapproved." Chief Justice Rehnquist and Justice Scalia vigorously dissented on this point: "The viewpoints of other countries simply are not relevant …[and foreign] notions of justice are not always those of our people" (*Atkins v. Virginia,* 536 U.S. 304).

Still another international influence is the UN Treaty to establish an International Criminal Court (ICC), to be given jurisdiction over the conduct of military personnel in any international campaign. Since its creation in 1998, 130 countries have signed the treaty. Although President Clinton signed for the United States, he continued to bargain over terms, and the U.S. Senate has never had to confront a vote on ratification. However, Clinton's signature has committed the United States to avoid acting in any way that would undermine the treaty. Consequently, fears persist that U.S. military personnel could be subject to prosecution if one of the ratifying states comes forward with an allegation that a "war crime" has been committed.

FOR CRITICAL ANALYSIS

1. Who should have jurisdiction if American soldiers at Abu Ghraib Prison in Baghdad are charged by the new Iraqi government with war crimes for mistreating Iraqi prisoners? Iraqi court? American court? ICC?

2. Who should have jurisdiction if an American soldier is arrested by Iraqi police and charged with molesting an Iraqi woman?

Yet the efforts by Reagan and Bush to reshape the federal judiciary were not fully successful. Often in American history, judges have surprised and disappointed the presidents who named them to the bench. Justice Souter, for example, has been far less conservative than President Bush and the Republicans who supported Souter's appointment thought he would be. Likewise, Justices O'Connor and Kennedy have disappointed conservatives by opposing limitations on abortion.

Nevertheless, with a combined total of twelve years in office, Reagan and Bush were also able to exercise a good deal of influence on the composition of the federal district and appellate courts. By the end of Bush's term, he and Reagan together had appointed nearly half of all federal judges. Thus, whatever impact Reagan and Bush ultimately have on the Supreme Court, their appointments will certainly influence the temperament and behavior of the district and circuit courts for years to come.

President Clinton promised to appoint more liberal jurists to the district and appellate courts, as well as to increase the number of women and minorities serving on the federal bench. During his first two years in office, Clinton held to this promise; more than 60 percent of his 128 judicial nominees were women or members of minority groups.[32]

The political struggles of the 1980s and 1990s amply illustrate the importance of judicial ideology. Is abortion a fundamental right or a criminal activity? How much separation must there be between church and state? Does the use of the Voting Rights Act to increase minority representation constitute a violation of the rights of whites? The answers to these and many other questions cannot be found in the words of the Constitution. They must be located, instead, in the hearts of the judges who interpret that text.

Judicial Power and Politics

One of the most important institutional changes to occur in the United States during the past half-century has been the striking transformation of the role and power of the federal courts, and of the Supreme Court in particular. Understanding how this transformation came about is the key to understanding the contemporary role of the courts in America.

TRADITIONAL LIMITATIONS ON THE FEDERAL COURTS

For much of American history, the power of the federal courts was subject to five limitations.[33] First, courts were constrained by judicial rules of standing that limited access to the bench. Claimants who simply disagreed with governmental action or inaction could not obtain access. Access to the courts was limited to individuals who could show that they were particularly affected by the government's behavior in some area. This limitation on access to the courts diminished the judiciary's capacity to forge links with important political and social forces.

Second, courts were traditionally limited in the character of the relief they could provide. In general, courts acted only to offer relief or assistance to individuals and not to broad social classes, again inhibiting the formation of alliances between the courts and important social forces. Third, courts lacked enforcement powers of their own and were compelled to rely on executive or state agencies to ensure compliance with their edicts. If the executive or state agencies were unwilling to assist the courts, judicial enactments could go unheeded, as when President Andrew Jackson declined to enforce Chief Justice John Marshall's 1832 order to the state of Georgia to release two missionaries it had arrested on Cherokee lands. Marshall asserted that the state had no right to enter the Cherokee lands without their assent.[34] Jackson is reputed to have said, "John Marshall has made his decision, now let him enforce it."

Fourth, federal judges are, of course, appointed by the president (with the consent of the Senate). As a result, the president and Congress can shape the composition of the federal courts and ultimately, perhaps, the character of judicial decisions. Finally, Congress has the power to change both the size and jurisdiction of the Supreme Court and other federal courts. In many areas, federal courts obtain their jurisdiction not from the Constitution but from congressional statutes. On a number of occasions, Congress has threatened to take matters out of the Court's hands when it was unhappy with the Court's policies.[35] For example, in 1996 Congress enacted several pieces of legislation designed to curb the jurisdiction of the federal courts. One of these laws was the Prison Litigation Reform Act, which limits the ability of federal judges to issue "consent decrees" under which the judges could take control of state prison systems. Another jurisdictional curb was included in the Immigration Reform Act, which prohibited the federal courts from hearing class action suits against Immigration and Naturalization Service deportation orders. As to the size of the Court, on one memorable occasion, presidential and congressional threats to expand the size of the Supreme Court—Franklin Roosevelt's "court packing" plan—encouraged the justices to drop their opposition to New Deal programs.

As a result of these five limitations on judicial power, through much of their history the chief function of the federal courts was to provide judicial support for executive agencies and to legitimate acts of Congress by declaring them to be consistent with constitutional principles. Only on rare occasions have the federal courts actually dared to challenge Congress or the executive branch.[36]

TWO JUDICIAL REVOLUTIONS

Since the Second World War, however, the role of the federal judiciary has been strengthened and expanded. There have actually been two judicial revolutions in the United States since World War II. The first and most visible of these was the substantive revolution in judicial policy. As we saw earlier in this chapter and in Chapters 4 and 5, in policy areas, including school desegregation, legislative apportionment, and criminal procedure, as well as obscenity, abortion, and voting rights, the Supreme Court was at the forefront of a series of sweeping changes in the role of the U.S. government, and ultimately, in the character of American society.[37]

But at the same time that the courts were introducing important policy innovations, they were also bringing about a second, less visible revolution. During the 1960s and 1970s, the Supreme Court and other federal courts instituted a series of changes in judicial procedures that fundamentally expanded the power of the courts in the United States. First, the federal courts liberalized the concept of standing to permit almost any group that seeks to challenge the actions of an

FOR CRITICAL ANALYSIS

Are the federal courts imperial, or are they merely handmaidens to the elective branches of government? The federal judiciary has a history of approving executive and legislative restrictions on civil liberties during wars and other threats to national security. In the years following *Roe v. Wade,* which voided state laws prohibiting abortion, the Supreme Court has approved almost all efforts by states to restrict abortion to such an extent that it is tantamount to prohibition. The present Supreme Court has approved of almost all efforts by state governments to expand their power over accused persons, despite 1960s cases protecting them. In what respects does the federal judiciary still play any sort of "checks and balances" role?

administrative agency to bring its case before the federal bench. In 1971, for example, the Supreme Court ruled that public interest groups could use the National Environmental Policy Act to challenge the actions of federal agencies by claiming that the agencies' activities might have adverse environmental consequences.[38]

Congress helped to make it even easier for groups dissatisfied with government policies to bring their cases to the courts by adopting Section 1983 of the U.S. Code, which permits the practice of "fee shifting"—that is, allowing citizens who successfully bring a suit against a public official for violating their constitutional rights to collect their attorneys' fees and costs from the government. Thus, Section 1983 encourages individuals and groups to bring their problems to the courts rather than to Congress or the executive branch. These changes have given the courts a far greater role in the administrative process than ever before. Many federal judges are concerned that federal legislation in areas such as health care reform would create new rights and entitlements that would give rise to a deluge of court cases. "Any time you create a new right, you create a host of disputes and claims," warned Barbara Rothstein, chief judge of the federal district court in Seattle, Washington.[39]

class action suit a legal action by which a group or class of individuals with common interests can file a suit on behalf of everyone who shares that interest

Second, the federal courts broadened the scope of relief to permit themselves to act on behalf of broad categories or classes of persons in "class action" cases, rather than just on behalf of individuals.[40] A **class action suit** is a procedural device that permits large numbers of persons with common interests to join together under a representative party to bring or defend a lawsuit. One example of a class action suit is the case of *In re Agent Orange Product Liability Litigation,* in which a federal judge in New York certified Vietnam War veterans as a class with standing to sue a manufacturer of herbicides for damages allegedly incurred from exposure to the defendant's product while in Vietnam.[41] The class potentially numbered in the tens of thousands.

Third, the federal courts began to employ so-called structural remedies, in effect retaining jurisdiction of cases until the court's mandate had actually been implemented to its satisfaction.[42] The best known of these instances was federal judge W. Arthur Garrity's effort to operate the Boston school system from his bench in order to ensure its desegregation. Between 1974 and 1985, Judge Garrity issued fourteen decisions relating to different aspects of the Boston school desegregation plan that had been developed under his authority and put into effect under his supervision.[43] In another recent case, federal judge Leonard B. Sand imposed fines that would have forced the city of Yonkers, New York, into bankruptcy if it had refused to accept his plan to build public housing in white neighborhoods. After several days of fines, the city gave in to the judge's ruling.

Through these three judicial mechanisms, the federal courts paved the way for an unprecedented expansion of national judicial power. In essence, liberalization of the rules of standing and expansion of the scope of judicial relief drew the federal courts into linkages with important social interests and classes, while the introduction of structural remedies enhanced the courts' ability to serve these constituencies. Thus, during the 1960s and 1970s, the power of the federal courts expanded in the same way the power of the executive expanded during the 1930s—through links with constituencies, such as civil rights, consumer, environmental, and feminist groups, that staunchly defended the Supreme Court in its battles with Congress, the executive, and other interest groups.

THINKING CRITICALLY ABOUT THE JUDICIARY, LIBERTY, AND DEMOCRACY

In the original conception of the framers, the judiciary was to be the institution that would protect individual liberty from the government. As we saw in Chapter 2, the framers believed that in a democracy the great danger was what they termed "tyranny of the majority"—the possibility that a popular majority, "united or actuated by some common impulse or passion," would "trample on the rules of justice."[44] The framers hoped that the courts would protect liberty from the potential excesses of democracy. And for most of American history, this was precisely the role played by the federal courts. The courts' most important decisions were those that protected the freedoms—to speak, worship, publish, vote, and attend school—of groups and individuals whose political views, religious beliefs, or racial or ethnic backgrounds made them unpopular.

In recent years, however, the courts have been changing their role in the political process. Rather than serving simply as a bastion of individual liberty against the excessive power of the majority, the judiciary has tried to play an active role in helping groups and forces in American society bring about social and political change in the fight for equality. In a sense, the judiciary has entered the political process and has begun to behave more like the democratic institutions whose sometimes misdirected impulses toward tyranny the courts were supposed to keep in check. This change poses a basic dilemma for students of American government. If the courts have become simply one more part of the democratic political process, then who is left to protect the liberty of individuals?

FOR CRITICAL ANALYSIS

In many ways, courts are expected to be apolitical institutions of government. In what ways are courts, judges, and justices shielded from politics and political pressure? In what ways are they vulnerable to political pressure? Are the courts an appropriate place for politics? What is the danger of having too much or too little political accountability in judicial decision making?

GET INVOLVED

What You Can Do:
File *Amicus Curiae* Briefs

The framers of the Constitution deliberately designed the judiciary to be independent of the ebb and flow of public sentiment. For this reason, federal judges are appointed for life. In many states, judges are appointed or elected for long terms. Citizen participation in the judicial process is, by design, limited.

One way, however, in which citizens can participate in the judicial process is by filing *amicus curiae* briefs. Although *amicus curiae* is translated as "friend of the court," it is better understood to mean an "adjunct adversary" permitted to intervene on behalf of one side or the other in which an important issue, usually constitutional in nature, is involved.

The *amicus curiae* brief has been quite effectively employed by African Americans pursuing civil rights cases. This was of particular importance in the earliest cases, beginning with *Shelley v. Kraemer* in 1948 and culminating with *Brown v. Board of Education* in 1954.[45] The NAACP and related organizations continue to maintain an interest in this method of interest group activity along with their continued efforts to influence Congress. In the past two decades, these "outside" interest groups have been joined by a very important "inside" interest group as an *amicus curiae*, the Congressional Black Caucus (CBC). This is an important caucus in the U.S. Congress, made up of the African American members of Congress (mostly from the Democratic Party). Their primary mission, of course, is to

YOU ARE... an intern
for the clerk of the Federal Court!

Less tends to be known about the American judicial system than either the presidency or Congress. Federal judges are appointed for life, deliberate in secret, and tend to eschew the public spotlight. Other than highly publicized confirmation hearings, or the partisan wrangling over when to vote on nominees, there is little opportunity for the public to get to know about these decision makers. However, it is wrong to think of the courts as nonpolitical. Their decisions often provide political answers to some of the most emotionally charged issues of the day.

In this simulation, you are cast in the role of a college student intern at the clerk of the Federal District Court's office. You will be helping steer court case files to the appropriate court for docket scheduling.

Go to www.wwnorton.com/wtp5

Questions to consider as you conduct the online simulation:

Why do we have federal, state, and local courts instead of a single court system?

How are the courts organized, and which types of courts have which roles?

What criteria do Federal Appellate Courts use to determine which cases to hear?

Are the courts really the least dangerous branch of the U.S. government, or do they verge on becoming an imperial judiciary?

advance the interests of African Americans and other minorities in civil rights legislation. But since there has been little new legislative activity, the CBC has found itself concentrating more on the courts in order to advance its agenda of implementing existing civil rights legislation. Since the passage of the 1982 amendments to the 1964 Civil Rights Act, race has become the most important consideration in drawing voting districts following each decennial census. Drawing the district so as to guarantee that some will elect blacks to send to Congress—a form of "benign gerrymandering" (see Chapter 10)—was at first approved but then came under considerable scrutiny in the federal court system. The Justice Department under presidents Reagan and Bush opposed such districts and took their opposition to the judiciary. Former attorney general Janet Reno defended the so-called majority-minority districts. Both sides went before the Supreme Court accompanied by *amicus curiae* briefs written and promoted by the CBC. Thus, what had been a purely congressional organization became an important interest group directly representing the African American community and other minorities in court.[46]

The *amicus curiae* device is used by groups other than civil rights interests. In fact, a large number of such efforts were made in abortion litigation. Demands for the reversal of *Roe v. Wade* and *Webster v. Reproductive Health Services* included a cast of thousands. Although the Supreme Court receives thousands of letters a day from citizens, the volume increased dramatically during the litigation over *Webster;* on one day in April, the Court's mailroom received 46,000 letters on both sides of the abortion issue. Groups on both sides came forward in greater numbers than ever, and seventy-eight *amicus* briefs were filed, representing the interests of thousands of individuals and over 400 organizations. This was the largest number of *amicus* briefs ever filed on a single case.[47]

No one can say precisely when justice has been done. But we can say that when the voice of the ordinary citizen is heard—and heeded—then we have moved much closer to the ideal of justice.

Summary

Millions of cases come to trial every year in the United States. The great majority—nearly 99 percent—are tried in state and local courts. The types of law are civil law, criminal law, and public law.

Three kinds of cases fall under federal jurisdiction: (1) civil cases involving citizens from different states, (2) civil cases where a federal agency is seeking to enforce federal laws that provide for civil penalties, and (3) cases involving federal criminal statutes or where state criminal cases have been made issues of public law. Judicial power extends only to cases and controversies. Litigants must have standing to sue, and courts neither hand down opinions on hypothetical issues nor take the initiative.

Each district court is in one of the twelve appellate districts, called circuits, presided over by a court of appeals. Appellate courts admit no new evidence; their rulings are based solely on the records of the court proceedings or agency hearings that led to the original decision. Appeals court rulings are final unless the Supreme Court chooses to review them. The Supreme Court has some original jurisdiction, but its major job is to review lower court decisions involving substantial issues of public law.

Federal judges are appointed by the president, subject to confirmation by the Senate. Presidents generally attempt to select judges whose political philosophy is similar to their own. Over time, presidents have been able to exert a great deal of influence over the federal courts through their appointments.

There is no explicit constitutional authority for the Supreme Court to review acts of Congress. Nevertheless, the 1803 case of *Marbury v. Madison* established the Court's right to review congressional acts. The supremacy clause of Article VI and the Judiciary Act of 1789 give the Court the power to review state constitutions and laws.

Both appellate and Supreme Court decisions, including the decision not to review a case, make law. The impact of such law usually favors the status quo. Yet, many revolutionary changes in the law have come about through appellate court and Supreme Court rulings—in the criminal process, in apportionment, and in civil rights. Judge-made law is like a statute in that it articulates the law as it relates to future controversies. It differs from a statute in that it is intended to guide judges rather than the citizenry in general.

Most cases reach the Supreme Court through a writ of *certiorari* or a writ of *habeas corpus.* Once the Court has accepted a case, attorneys for both sides prepare briefs and seek *amicus curiae* briefs from sympathetic groups. Cases are presented to the Court in oral argument, are discussed by the justices during the Court's conference, and are decided by a majority vote of the justices. The Court's opinion is written by a member of the majority. Members of the minority may write dissenting opinions, while other members of the majority may write concurring opinions.

The influence of any individual member of the Supreme Court is limited. Writing the majority opinion for a case is an opportunity for a justice to influence the judiciary. But the need to frame an opinion in such a way as to develop majority support on the Court may limit such opportunities. Dissenting opinions can have more impact than the majority opinion; they stimulate a continued flow of cases around an issue. The solicitor general is the most important single influence outside the Court itself because he or she controls the flow of cases brought by the Justice Department and also shapes the argument in those cases. But the flow of cases is a force in itself, which the Department of Justice cannot entirely control. Social problems give rise to similar cases that ultimately must be adjudicated and appealed. Some interest groups try to develop such case patterns as a means of gaining power through the courts.

In recent years, the importance of the federal judiciary—the Supreme Court in particular—has increased substantially as the courts have developed new tools of judicial power and forged alliances with important forces in American society.

For Further Reading

Abraham, Henry. *The Judicial Process.* 6th ed. New York: Oxford University Press, 1993.

Bryner, Gary, and Dennis L. Thompson. *The Constitution and the Regulation of Society.* Provo, UT: Brigham Young University, 1988.

Davis, Sue. *Justice Rehnquist and the Constitution.* Princeton, NJ: Princeton University Press, 1989.

Graber, Mark A. *Transforming Free Speech: The Ambiguous Legacy of Civil Libertarianism.* Berkeley: University of California Press, 1991.

Kahn, Ronald. *The Supreme Court and Constitutional Theory, 1953–1993.* Lawrence: University Press of Kansas, 1994.

McCann, Michael W. *Rights at Work.* Chicago: University of Chicago Press, 1994.

Mezey, Susan G. *No Longer Disabled: The Federal Courts and the Politics of Social Security Disability.* New York: Greenwood, 1988.

O'Brien, David M. *Storm Center: The Supreme Court in American Politics.* 5th ed. New York: Norton, 2000.

Rosenberg, Gerald. *The Hollow Hope: Can Courts Bring about Social Change?* Chicago: University of Chicago Press, 1991.

Rubin, Eva. *Abortion, Politics and the Courts.* Westport, CT: Greenwood Press, 1982.

Silverstein, Mark. *Judicious Choices: The New Politics of Supreme Court Confirmations.* New York: Norton, 1994.

Study Outline

www.wwnorton.com/wtp5e

Keyword: Review 15

The Legal System

1. Court cases in the United States proceed under three categories of law: criminal, civil, and public.
2. In the area of criminal law, either a state government or the federal government is the plaintiff who alleges that someone has committed a crime.
3. Civil cases are those between individuals or between individuals and the government in which no criminal violation is charged. In deciding these cases, courts apply statutes and legal precedent.
4. Public law involves questions of whether the government has the constitutional or statutory authority to take action.
5. By far, most cases are heard by state courts.
6. Cases are heard in federal courts if the U.S. government is a party in the case or if the case involves federal statutes, treaties with other nations, or the U.S. Constitution.
7. Although the federal courts hear only a fraction of all the cases decided every year in the United States, federal court decisions are extremely important.

Federal Jurisdiction

1. The eighty-nine federal district courts are trial courts of original jurisdiction and their cases are, in form, indistinguishable from cases in the state trial courts.
2. The twelve U.S. courts of appeals review and render decisions in approximately 10 percent of all lower-court and agency cases.
3. Federal judges are appointed by the president and confirmed by a majority vote of the full Senate.
4. The Supreme Court is the highest court in the country and has the power and the obligation to review any lower court decision involving a substantial issue of public law, state legislation, or act of Congress.

5. The Constitution does not specify the number of justices that should sit on the Supreme Court, although since 1869 there have been nine—one chief justice and eight associate justices.
6. The solicitor general can influence the Court by screening cases before they reach the Supreme Court, submitting *amicus* briefs, and shaping the arguments used before the Court.

The Power of the Supreme Court: Judicial Review

1. The Supreme Court's power to review acts of Congress, although accepted as natural and rarely challenged, is not specifically granted by the Constitution.
2. The Supreme Court's power to review state action or legislation derives from the Constitution's supremacy clause, although it is neither granted specifically by the Constitution nor inherent in the federal system.
3. Appeals of lower court decisions can reach the Supreme Court in one of two ways: through a writ of *certiorari*, or, in the case of convicted state prisoners, through a writ of *habeas corpus*.
4. Over the years, courts have developed specific rules that govern which cases within their jurisdiction they hear. These rules of access can be broken down into three categories: case or controversy, standing, and mootness.
5. Groups and forces in society attempt to influence justices' rulings on particular issues.
6. After filing written arguments, or briefs, attorneys present oral argument to the Supreme Court. After oral argument, the justices discuss the case and vote on a final decision.
7. The Supreme Court always explains its decisions in terms of law and precedent.
8. Despite the rule of precedent, the Court often reshapes law. Such changes in the interpretation of law can be explained, in part, by changes in the judicial philosophy of activism versus restraint and by changes in political ideology.

Judicial Power and Politics

1. For much of American history, the power of the federal courts was subject to five limitations: standing, the limited relief courts could provide, the lack of enforcement powers, political appointment, and the power of Congress to change the size and jurisdiction of federal courts.
2. The role of the federal judiciary has been strengthened since World War II by two judicial revolutions. The first revolution was a substantive revolution in several policy areas. The second revolution involved changes in judicial procedures that lessened traditional limitations on the courts.

Practice Quiz

www.wwnorton.com/wtp5e

Keyword: Quiz 15

1. Which of the following is a brief submitted to the Supreme Court by someone other than one of the parties in the case?
   a) *amicus curiae*
   b) *habeas corpus*
   c) solicitor general
   d) *ex post* brief

2. By what term is the practice of the courts to uphold precedent known?
   a) *certiorari*
   b) *stare decisis*
   c) rule of four
   d) senatorial courtesy

3. Which government official is responsible for arguing the federal government's position in cases before the Supreme Court?
   a) the vice president
   b) the attorney general
   c) the U.S. district attorney
   d) the solicitor general

4. Which of the following helps to explain the expanded power of the judiciary since World War II?
   a) changes in judicial procedure
   b) changes in judicial policy areas
   c) Neither a nor b is correct.
   d) Both a and b are correct.

5. What is the name for the body of law that involves disputes between private parties?
   a) civil law
   b) privacy law
   c) household law
   d) common law

6. Under what authority is the number of Supreme Court justices decided?
   a) the president
   b) the chief justice
   c) Congress
   d) the Constitution

7. Which of the following does not influence the flow of cases heard by the Supreme Court?
   a) the Supreme Court itself
   b) the solicitor general
   c) the attorney general
   d) the FBI

8. Which of the following cases involved the "right to privacy"?
   a) *Griswold v. Connecticut*
   b) *Brown v. Board of Education*
   c) *Schneckloth v. Bustamante*
   d) *Marbury v. Madison*

9. Which of the following Supreme Court cases from the 1960s involved the rights of criminal suspects?
   a) *Gideon v. Wainwright*
   b) *Miranda v. Arizona*
   c) *Escobedo v. Illinois*
   d) all of the above

10. Where do most trials in America take place?
    a) state and local courts
    b) appellate courts
    c) federal courts
    d) the Supreme Court

Key Terms

www.wwnorton.com/wtp5e

Keyword: Vocabulary 15

amicus curiae (p. 635)
appellate court (p. 619)
briefs (p. 640)
chief justice (p. 621)
civil law (p. 617)
class action suit (p. 648)
criminal law (p. 617)
defendant (p. 617)

dissenting opinion (p. 642)
due process of law (p. 620)
judicial activism (p. 643)
judicial restraint (p. 643)
judicial review (p. 626)
jurisdiction (p. 619)
Miranda rule (p. 632)
mootness (p. 632)
opinion (p. 642)
oral argument (p. 641)
original jurisdiction (p. 620)
per curiam (p. 635)
plaintiff (p. 617)

plea bargains (p. 619)
precedents (p. 618)
public law (p. 618)
senatorial courtesy (p. 622)
solicitor general (p. 635)
standing (p. 632)
stare decisis (p. 618)
supremacy clause (p. 627)
supreme court (p. 619)
trial court (p. 619)
Uniform Commercial Code (p. 619)
writ of *certiorari* (p. 633)
writ of *habeas corpus* (p. 634)

APPENDIX

THE DECLARATION OF INDEPENDENCE

In Congress, July 4, 1776

The unanimous Declaration of the thirteen united States of America,

When in the Course of human events, it becomes necessary for one people to dissolve the political bands which have connected them with another, and to assume among the powers of the earth, the separate and equal station to which the Laws of Nature and of Nature's God entitle them, a decent respect to the opinions of mankind requires that they should declare the causes which impel them to the separation.

We hold these truths to be self-evident, that all men are created equal, that they are endowed by their Creator with certain unalienable Rights, that among these are Life, Liberty and the pursuit of Happiness.—That to secure these rights, Governments are instituted among Men, deriving their just powers from the consent of the governed. —That whenever any Form of Government becomes destructive of these ends, it is the Right of the People to alter or to abolish it, and to institute new Government, laying its foundation on such principles and organizing its powers in such form, as to them shall seem most likely to effect their Safety and Happiness. Prudence, indeed, will dictate that Governments long established should not be changed for light and transient causes; and accordingly all experience hath shewn, that mankind are more disposed to suffer, while evils are sufferable, than to right themselves by abolishing the forms to which they are accustomed. But when a long train of abuses and usurpations, pursuing invariably the same Object evinces a design to reduce them under absolute Despotism, it is their right, it is their duty, to throw off such Government, and to provide new Guards for their future security.—Such has been the patient sufferance of these Colonies; and such is now the necessity which constrains them to alter their former Systems of Government. The history of the present King of Great Britain is a history of repeated injuries and usurpations, all having in direct object the establishment of an absolute Tyranny over these States. To prove this, let Facts be submitted to a candid world.

He has refused his Assent to Laws, the most wholesome and necessary for the public good.

He has forbidden his Governors to pass Laws of immediate and pressing importance, unless suspended in their operation till his Assent should be obtained; and when so suspended, he has utterly neglected to attend to them.

He has refused to pass other Laws for the accommodation of large districts of people, unless those people would relinquish the right of Representation in the Legislature, a right inestimable to them and formidable to tyrants only.

He has called together legislative bodies at places unusual, uncomfortable, and distant from the depository of their public Records, for the sole purpose of fatiguing them into compliance with his measures.

He has dissolved Representative Houses repeatedly, for opposing with manly firmness his invasions on the rights of the people.

He has refused for a long time, after such dissolutions, to cause others to be elected; whereby the Legislative powers, incapable of Annihilation, have returned to the People at large for their exercise; the State remaining in the mean time exposed to all the dangers of invasion from without, and convulsions within.

He has endeavoured to prevent the population of these States; for that purpose obstructing the Laws for Naturalization of Foreigners; refusing to pass others to encourage their migrations hither, and raising the conditions of new Appropriations of Lands.

He has obstructed the Administration of Justice, by refusing his Assent to Laws for establishing Judiciary powers.

He has made Judges dependent on his Will alone, for the tenure of their offices, and the amount and payment of their salaries.

He has erected a multitude of New Offices, and sent hither swarms of Officers to harrass our people, and eat out their substance.

He has kept among us, in times of peace, Standing Armies without the Consent of our legislatures.

He has affected to render the Military independent of and superior to the Civil power.

He has combined with others to subject us to a jurisdiction foreign to our constitution, and unacknowledged by our laws; giving his Assent to their Acts of pretended Legislation:

For Quartering large bodies of armed troops among us:

For protecting them, by a mock Trial, from punishment for any Murders which they should commit on the Inhabitants of these States:

For cutting off our Trade with all parts of the world:

For imposing Taxes on us without our Consent:

For depriving us in many cases, of the benefits of Trial by Jury:

For transporting us beyond Seas to be tried for pretended offences:

For abolishing the free System of English Laws in a neighboring Province, establishing therein an Arbitrary government, and enlarging its Boundaries so as to render it at once an example and fit instrument for introducing the same absolute rule into these Colonies:

For taking away our Charters, abolishing our most valuable Laws, and altering fundamentally the Forms of our Governments:

For suspending our own Legislatures, and declaring themselves invested with power to legislate for us in all cases whatsoever.

He has abdicated Government here, by declaring us out of his Protection and waging War against us.

He has plundered our seas, ravaged our Coasts, burnt our towns, and destroyed the lives of our people.

He is at this time transporting large Armies of foreign Mercenaries to compleat the works of death, desolation and tyranny, already begun with circumstances of Cruelty & perfidy scarcely paralleled in the most barbarous ages, and totally unworthy the Head of a civilized nation.

He has constrained our fellow Citizens taken Captive on the high Seas to bear Arms against their Country, to become the executioners of their friends and Brethren, or to fall themselves by their Hands.

He has excited domestic insurrections amongst us, and has endeavoured to bring on the inhabitants of our frontiers, the merciless Indian Savages, whose known rule of warfare, is an undistinguished destruction of all ages, sexes and conditions.

In every stage of these Oppressions We have Petitioned for Redress in the most humble terms: Our repeated Petitions have been answered only by repeated injury. A Prince whose character is thus marked by every act which may define a Tyrant, is unfit to be the ruler of a free people.

Nor have We been wanting in attentions to our Brittish brethren. We have warned them from time to time of attempts by their legislature to extend an unwarrantable jurisdiction over us. We have reminded them of the circumstances of our emigration and settlement here. We have appealed to their native justice and magnanimity, and we have conjured them by the ties of our common kindred to disavow these usurpations, which, would inevitably interrupt our connections and correspondence. They too have been deaf to the voice of justice and of consanguinity. We must, therefore, acquiesce in the necessity, which denounces our Separation, and hold them, as we hold the rest of mankind, Enemies in War, in Peace Friends.

We, Therefore, the Representatives of the United States of America, in General Congress, Assembled, appealing to the Supreme Judge of the world for the rectitude of our intentions, do, in the Name, and by Authority of the good People of these Colonies, solemnly publish and declare, That these United Colonies are, and of Right ought to be Free and Independent States; that they are Absolved from all Allegiance to the British Crown, and that all political connection between them and the State of Great Britain, is and ought to be totally dissolved; and that as Free and Independent States, they have full Power to levy War, conclude Peace, contract Alliances, establish Commerce, and to do all other Acts and Things which Independent States may of right do. And for the support of this Declaration, with a firm reliance on the protection of divine Providence, we mutually pledge to each other our Lives, our Fortunes and our sacred Honor.

The foregoing Declaration was, by order of Congress, engrossed, and signed by the following members:

John Hancock

NEW HAMPSHIRE
Josiah Bartlett
William Whipple
Matthew Thornton

MASSACHUSETTS BAY
Samuel Adams
John Adams
Robert Treat Paine
Elbridge Gerry

RHODE ISLAND
Stephen Hopkins
William Ellery

CONNECTICUT
Roger Sherman
Samuel Huntington
William Williams
Oliver Wolcott

NEW YORK
William Floyd
Philip Livingston
Francis Lewis
Lewis Morris

NEW JERSEY
Richard Stockton
John Witherspoon
Francis Hopkinson
John Hart
Abraham Clark

PENNSYLVANIA
Robert Morris
Benjamin Rush
Benjamin Franklin
John Morton
George Clymer
James Smith

George Taylor
James Wilson
George Ross

DELAWARE
Caesar Rodney
George Read
Thomas M'Kean

MARYLAND
Samuel Chase
William Paca
Thomas Stone
Charles Carroll,
  of Carrollton

VIRGINIA
George Wythe
Richard Henry Lee
Thomas Jefferson

Benjamin Harrison
Thomas Nelson, Jr.
Francis Lightfoot Lee
Carter Braxton

NORTH CAROLINA
William Hooper
Joseph Hewes
John Penn

SOUTH CAROLINA
Edward Rutledge
Thomas Heyward, Jr.
Thomas Lynch, Jr.
Arthur Middleton

GEORGIA
Button Gwinnett
Lyman Hall
George Walton

Resolved, That copies of the Declaration be sent to the several assemblies, conventions, and committees, or councils of safety, and to the several commanding officers of the continental troops; that it be proclaimed in each of the United States, at the head of the army.

THE ARTICLES OF CONFEDERATION

Agreed to by Congress November 15, 1777;
ratified and in force March 1, 1781

To all whom these Presents shall come, we the undersigned Delegates of the States affixed to our Names, send greeting. Whereas the Delegates of the United States of America, in Congress assembled, did, on the fifteenth day of November, in the Year of Our Lord One thousand Seven Hundred and Seventy seven, and in the Second Year of the Independence of America, agree to certain articles of Confederation and perpetual Union between the States of New-hampshire, Massachusetts-bay, Rhodeisland and Providence Plantations, Connecticut, New-York, New-Jersey, Pennsylvania, Delaware, Maryland, Virginia, North-Carolina, South-Carolina and Georgia in the words following, viz. "Articles of Confederation and perpetual Union between the states of Newhampshire, Massachusettsbay, Rhodeisland and Providence Plantations, Connecticut, New-York, New-Jersey, Pennsylvania, Delaware, Maryland, Virginia, North-Carolina, South-Carolina and Georgia.

Art. I. The Stile of this confederacy shall be "The United States of America."

Art. II. Each state retains its sovereignty, freedom and independence, and every Power, Jurisdiction and right, which is not by this confederation expressly delegated to the United States, in Congress assembled.

Art. III. The said states hereby severally enter into a firm league of friendship with each other, for their common defence, the security of their Liberties, and their mutual and general welfare, binding themselves to assist each other, against all force offered to, or attacks made upon them, or any of them, on account of religion, sovereignty, trade, or any other pretence whatever.

Art. IV. The better to secure and perpetuate mutual friendship and intercourse among the people of the different states in this union, the free inhabitants of each of these states, paupers, vagabonds and fugitives from Justice excepted, shall be entitled to all privileges and immunities of free citizens in the several states; and the people of each state shall have free ingress and regress to and from any other state, and shall enjoy therein all the privileges of trade and commerce, subject to the same duties, impositions and restrictions as the inhabitants thereof respectively, provided that such restriction shall not extend so far as to prevent the removal of property imported into any state, to any other state, of which the Owner is an inhabitant; provided also that no imposition, duties or restriction shall be laid by any state, on the property of the united states, or either of them.

If any Person guilty of, or charged with treason, felony, or other high misdemeanor in any state, shall flee from Justice, and be found in any of the united states, he shall, upon demand of the Governor or executive power, of the state from which he fled, be delivered up and removed to the state having jurisdiction of his offence.

Full faith and credit shall be given in each of these states to the records, acts and judicial proceedings of the courts and magistrates of every other state.

Art. V. For the more convenient management of the general interests of the united states, delegates shall be annually appointed in such manner as the legislature of each state shall direct, to meet in Congress on the first Monday in November, in every year, with a power reserved to each state, to recall its delegates, or any of them, at any time within the year, and to send others in their stead, for the remainder of the Year.

No state shall be represented in Congress by less than two, nor by more than seven Members; and no person shall be capable of being a delegate for more than three years in any term of six years; nor shall any person, being a delegate, be capable of holding any office under the united states, for which he, or another for his benefit receives any salary, fees or emolument of any kind.

Each state shall maintain its own delegates in a meeting of the states, and while they act as members of the committee of the states.

In determining questions in the united states, in Congress assembled, each state shall have one vote.

Freedom of speech and debate in Congress shall not be impeached or questioned in any Court, or place out of Congress, and the members of congress shall be protected in their persons from arrests and imprisonments, during the time of their going to and from, and attendance on congress, except for treason, felony, or breach of the peace.

Art. VI. No state without the Consent of the united states in congress assembled, shall send any embassy to, or receive any embassy from, or enter into any conference, agreement, or alliance or treaty with any King, prince or state; nor shall any person holding any office or profit or trust under the united states, or any of them, accept of any present, emolument, office or title of any kind whatever from any king, prince or foreign state; nor shall the united states in congress assembled, or any of them, grant any title of nobility.

No two or more states shall enter into any treaty, confederation or alliance whatever between them, without the consent of the united states in congress assembled, specifying accurately the purposes for which the same is to be entered into, and how long it shall continue.

No state shall lay any imposts or duties, which may interfere with any stipulations in treaties, entered into by the united states in congress assembled, with any king, prince or state, in pursuance of any treaties already proposed by congress, to the courts of France and Spain.

No vessels of war shall be kept up in time of peace by any state, except such number only, as shall be deemed necessary by the united states in congress assembled, for the defence of such state, or its trade; nor shall any body of forces be kept up by any state, in time of peace, except such number only, as in the judgment of the united states, in congress assembled, shall be deemed requisite to garrison the forts necessary for the defence of such state; but every state shall always keep up a well regulated and disciplined militia, sufficiently armed and accoutred, and shall provide and constantly have ready for use, in public stores, a due number of field pieces and tents, and a proper quantity of arms, ammunition and camp equipage.

No state shall engage in any war without the consent of the united states in congress assembled, unless such state be actually invaded by enemies, or shall have received certain advice of a resolution being formed by some nation of Indians to invade such state, and the danger is so imminent as not to admit of a delay, till the united states in congress asssembled can be consulted; nor shall any state grant commissions to any ships or vessels of war, nor letters of marque or reprisal, except it be after a declaration of war by the united states in congress assembled, and then only against the kingdom or state and the subjects thereof, against which war has been so declared, and under such regulations as shall be established by the united states in congress assembled, unless such state be infested by pirates; in which case vessels of war may be fitted out for that occasion, and kept so long as the danger shall continue, or until the united states in congress assembled shall determine otherwise.

Art. VII. When land-forces are raised by any state for the common defence, all officers of or under the rank of colonel, shall be appointed by the legislature of each state respectively, by whom such forces shall be raised, or in such manner as such state shall direct, and all vacancies shall be filled up by the state which first made the appointment.

Art. VIII. All charges of war, and all other expences that shall be incurred for the common defence or general welfare, and allowed by the united states in congress assembled, shall be defrayed out of a common treasury, which shall be supplied by the several states in proportion to the value of all land within each state, granted to or surveyed for any Person, as such land and the buildings and improvements thereon shall be estimated according to such mode as the united states in congress assembled, shall from time to time direct and appoint.

The taxes for paying that proportion shall be laid and levied by the authority and direction of the legislatures of the several states within the time agreed upon by the united states in congress assembled.

Art. IX. The united states in congress assembled, shall have the sole and exclusive right and power of determining on peace and war, except in the cases mentioned in the sixth article—of sending and receiving ambassadors—entering into treaties and alliances, provided that no treaty of commerce shall be made whereby the legislative power of the respective states shall be restrained from imposing such imposts and duties on foreigners, as their own people are subjected to, or from prohibiting the exportation of any species of goods or commodities whatsoever—of establishing rules for deciding in all cases, what captures on land or water shall be legal, and in what manner prizes taken by land or naval forces in the service of the united states shall be divided or appropriated—of granting letters of marque and reprisal in times of peace—appointing courts for the trial of piracies and felonies committed on the high seas and establishing courts for receiving and determining finally appeals in all cases of captures, provided that no member of congress shall be appointed a judge of any of the said courts.

The united states in congress assembled shall also be the last resort on appeal in all disputes and differences now subsisting or that hereafter may arise between two or more states concerning boundary, jurisdiction or any other cause whatever; which authority shall always be exercised in the manner following. Whenever the legislative or executive authority or lawful agent of any state in controversy with another shall present a petition to congress stating the matter in question and praying for a hearing, notice thereof shall be given by order of congress to the legislative or executive authority of the other state in controversy, and a day assigned for the appearance of the parties by their lawful agents, who shall then be directed to appoint by joint consent, commissioners or judges to constitute a court for hearing and determining the matter in question: but if they cannot agree, congress shall name three persons out of each of the united states, and from the list of such persons each party shall alternately strike out one, the petitioners beginning, until the number shall be reduced to thirteen; and from that number not less than seven, nor more than nine names as congress shall direct, shall in the presence of congress be drawn out by lot, and the persons whose names shall be so drawn or any five of them, shall be commissioners or judges, to hear and finally determine the controversy, so always as a major part of the judges who shall hear the cause shall agree in the determination: and if either party shall neglect to attend at the day appointed, without shewing reasons, which congress shall judge sufficient, or being present shall refuse to strike, the congress shall proceed to nominate three persons out of each state, and the secretary of congress shall strike in behalf of such party absent or refusing; and the judgment and sentence of the court to be appointed, in the manner before prescribed, shall be final and conclusive; and if any of the parties shall refuse to submit to the authority of such court, or to appear to defend their claim or cause, the court shall nevertheless proceed to pronounce sentence, or judgment, which shall in like manner be final and decisive, the judgment or sentence and other proceedings being in either case transmitted to congress, and lodged among the acts of congress for the security of the parties concerned: provided that every commissioner, before he sits in judgment, shall take an oath to be administered by one of the judges of the supreme or superior court of the state, where the cause shall be tried, "well and truly to hear and determine the matter in question, according to the best of his judgment, without favour, affection or hope of reward:" provided also, that no state shall be deprived of territory for the benefit of the united states.

All controversies concerning the private right of soil claimed under different grants of two or more states, whose jurisdictions as they may respect such lands, and the states which passed such grants are adjusted, the said grants or either of them being at the same time claimed to have originated antecedent to such settlement of jurisdiction, shall on the petition of either party to the congress of the united states, be finally determined as near as may be in the same manner as is before prescribed for deciding disputes respecting territorial jurisdiction between different states.

The united states in congress assembled shall also have the sole and exclusive right and power of regulating the alloy and value of coin struck by their own authority, or by that of the respective states—fixing the standard of weights and measures throughout the united states—regulating the trade and managing all affairs with the Indians, not members of any of the states, provided that the legislative right of any state within its own limits be not infringed or violated—establishing and regulating post-offices from one state to another, throughout all the united states, and exacting such postage on the papers passing thro' the same as may be requisite to defray the expences of the said office—appointing all officers of the land forces, in the service of the united states, excepting regimental officers—appointing all the officers of the naval forces, and commissioning all officers whatever in the service of the united states—making rules for the government and regulation of the said land and naval forces, and directing their operations.

The united states in congress assembled shall have authority to appoint a committee, to sit in the recess of congress, to be denominated "A Committee of the States," and to consist of one delegate from each state; and to appoint such other committees and civil officers as may be necessary for managing the general affairs of the united states under their direction—to appoint one of their number to preside, provided that no person be allowed to serve in the office of president more than one year in any term of three years; to ascertain the necessary sums of Money to be raised for the service of the united states, and to appropriate and apply the same for defraying the public expenses—to borrow money, or emit bills on the credit of the united states, transmitting every half year to the respective states an account of the sums of money so borrowed or emitted,—to build and equip a navy—to agree upon the number of land forces, and to make requisitions from each state for its quota, in proportion to the number of white inhabitants in such state; which requisition shall be binding, and thereupon the legislature of each state shall appoint the regimental officers, raise the men and cloath, arm and equip then in a soldier like manner, at the expense of the united states; and the officers and men so cloathed, armed and equipped shall march to the place appointed, and within the time agreed on by the united states in congress assembled: But if the united states in congress assembled shall, on consideration of circumstances judge proper that any state should not raise men, or should raise a smaller number than its quota, and that any other state should raise a greater number of men than the quota thereof, such extra number shall be raised, officered, cloathed, armed and equipped in the same manner as the quota of such state, unless the legislature of such state shall judge that such extra number cannot be safely spared out of the same, in which case they shall raise officer, cloath, arm and equip as many of such extra number as they judge can be safely spared. And the officers and men so cloathed, armed and equipped, shall march to the place appointed, and within the time agreed on by the united states in congress assembled.

The united states in congress assembled shall never engage in a war, nor grant letters of marque and reprisal in time of peace, nor enter into any treaties or alliances, nor coin money, nor regulate the value thereof, nor ascertain the sums and expenses necessary for the defence and welfare of the united states, or any of them, nor emit bills, nor borrow money on the credit of the united states, nor appropriate money, nor agree upon the number of vessels of war, to be built or purchased, or the number of land or sea forces to be raised, nor appoint a commander in chief of the army or navy, unless nine states assent to the same: nor shall a question on any other point, except for adjourning from day to day be determined, unless by the votes of a majority of the united states in congress assembled.

The congress of the united states shall have power to adjourn to any time within the year, and to any place within the united states, so that no period of adjournment be for a longer duration than the space of six Months, and shall publish the

Journal of their proceedings monthly, except such parts thereof relating to treaties, alliances or military operations, as in their judgment require secrecy; and the yeas and nays of the delegates of each state on any question shall be entered on the Journal, when it is desired by any delegate; and the delegates of a state, or any of them, at his or their request shall be furnished with a transcript of the said Journal, except such parts as are above excepted, to lay before the legislatures of the several states.

Art. X. The committee of the states, or any nine of them, shall be authorised to execute, in the recess of congress, such of the powers of congress as the united states in congress assembled, by the consent of nine states, shall from time to time think expedient to vest them with; provided that no power be delegated to the said committee, for the exercise of which, by the articles of confederation, the voice of nine states in the congress of the united states assembled is requisite.

Art. XI. Canada acceding to this confederation, and joining in the measures of the united states, shall be admitted into, and entitled to all the advantages of this union: but no other colony shall be admitted into the same, unless such admission be agreed to by nine states.

Art. XII. All bills of credit emitted, monies borrowed and debts contracted by, or under the authority of congress, before the assembling of the united states, in pursuance of the present confederation, shall be deemed and considered as a charge against the united states, for payment and satisfaction whereof the said united states and the public faith are hereby solemnly pledged.

Art. XIII. Every state shall abide by the determinations of the united states in congress assembled, on all questions which by this confederation are submitted to them. And the Articles of this confederation shall be inviolably observed by every state, and the union shall be perpetual; nor shall any alteration at any time hereafter be made in any of them; unless such alteration be agreed to in a congress of the united states, and be afterwards confirmed by the legislatures of every state.

And Whereas it hath pleased the Great Governor of the World to incline the hearts of the legislatures we respectively represent in congress, to approve of, and to authorize us to ratify the said articles of confederation and perpetual union. Know Ye that we the undersigned delegates, by virtue of the power and authority to us given for that purpose, do by these presents, in the name and in behalf of our respective constituents, fully and entirely ratify and confirm each and every of the said articles of confederation and perpetual union, and all and singular the matters and things therein contained: And we do further solemnly plight and engage the faith of our respective constituents, that they shall abide by the determinations of the united states in congress assembled, on all questions, which by the said confederation are submitted to them. And that the articles thereof shall be inviolably observed by the states we respectively represent, and that the union shall be perpetual. In Witness whereof we have hereunto set our hands in Congress. Done at Philadelphia in the state of Pennsylvania the ninth day of July, in the Year of our Lord one Thousand seven Hundred and Seventy-eight, and in the third year of the independence of America.

THE CONSTITUTION OF THE UNITED STATES OF AMERICA

[PREAMBLE]

We the People of the United States, in Order to form a more perfect Union, establish Justice, insure domestic Tranquility, provide for the common defence, promote the general Welfare, and secure the Blessings of Liberty to ourselves and our Posterity, do ordain and establish this Constitution for the United States of America.

Article I

Section 1

[LEGISLATIVE POWERS]

All legislative Powers herein granted shall be vested in a Congress of the United States, which shall consist of a Senate and House of Representatives.

Section 2

[HOUSE OF REPRESENTATIVES, HOW CONSTITUTED, POWER OF IMPEACHMENT]

The House of Representatives shall be composed of Members chosen every second Year by the People of the several States, and the Electors in each State shall have the Qualifications requisite for Electors of the most numerous Branch of the State Legislature.

No Person shall be a Representative who shall not have attained to the Age of twenty five Years, and been seven Years a Citizen of the United States, and who shall not, when elected, be an Inhabitant of that State in which he shall be chosen.

Representatives and *direct Taxes*[1] shall be apportioned among the several States which may be included within this Union, according to their respective Numbers, *which shall be determined by adding to the whole Number of free Persons, including those bound to Service for a Term of Years, and excluding Indians not taxed, three fifths of all other Persons.*[2] The actual Enumeration shall be made within three Years after the first Meeting of the Congress of the United States, and within every subsequent Term of ten Years, in such Manner as they shall by Law direct. The Number of Representatives shall not exceed one for every thirty Thousand, but each State shall have at Least one Representative; *and until such enumeration shall be made, the State of New Hampshire shall be entitled to chuse three, Massachusetts eight, Rhode-Island and Providence Plantations one, Connecticut five, New-York six, New Jersey four, Pennsylvania eight, Delaware one, Maryland six, Virginia ten, North Carolina five, South Carolina five, and Georgia three.*[3]

When vacancies happen in the Representation from any State, the Executive Authority thereof shall issue Writs of Election to fill such Vacancies.

The House of Representatives shall chuse their Speaker and other Officers; and shall have the sole Power of Impeachment.

Section 3

[THE SENATE, HOW CONSTITUTED, IMPEACHMENT TRIALS]

The Senate of the United States shall be composed of two Senators from each State, *chosen by the Legislature thereof,*[4] for six Years; and each Senator shall have one Vote.

Immediately after they shall be assembled in Consequence of the first Election, they shall be divided as equally as may be into three Classes. The Seats of the Senators of the first Class shall be vacated at the Expiration of the second Year, of the second Class at the Expiration of the fourth Year, and of the third Class at the Expiration of the sixth Year, so that one third may be chosen every second Year; *and if Vacancies happen by Resignation, or otherwise, during the Recess of the Legislature of any State, the Executive thereof may make temporary Appointments until the next Meeting of the Legislature, which shall then fill such Vacancies.*[5]

No Person shall be a Senator who shall not have attained to the Age of thirty Years, and been nine Years a Citizen of the United States, and who shall not, when elected, be an Inhabitant of that State for which he shall be chosen.

The Vice President of the United States shall be President of the Senate, but shall have no Vote, unless they be equally divided.

---

[1]Modified by Sixteenth Amendment.

[2]Modified by Fourteenth Amendment.

[3]Temporary provision.

[4]Modified by Seventeenth Amendment.

[5]Modified by Seventeenth Amendment.

The Senate shall chuse their other Officers, and also a President pro tempore, in the Absence of the Vice President, or when he shall exercise the Office of President of the United States.

The Senate shall have the sole Power to try all Impeachments. When sitting for that Purpose, they shall be on Oath or Affirmation. When the President of the United States is tried, the Chief Justice shall preside: And no Person shall be convicted without the Concurrence of two thirds of the Members present.

Judgment in Cases of Impeachment shall not extend further than to removal from Office, and disqualification to hold and enjoy any Office of honor, Trust or Profit under the United States: but the Party convicted shall nevertheless be liable and subject to Indictment, Trial, Judgment and Punishment, according to Law.

Section 4
[ELECTION OF SENATORS AND REPRESENTATIVES]

The Times, Places and Manner of holding Elections for Senators and Representatives, shall be prescribed in each State by the Legislature thereof; but the Congress may at any time by Law make or alter such Regulations, except as to the Places of chusing Senators.

The Congress shall assemble at least once in every Year, and such Meeting shall be on the first Monday in December, unless they shall by Law appoint a different Day.[6]

Section 5
[QUORUM, JOURNALS, MEETINGS, ADJOURNMENTS]

Each House shall be the Judge of the Elections, Returns and Qualifications of its own Members, and a Majority of each shall constitute a Quorum to do Business; but a smaller Number may adjourn from day to day, and may be authorized to compel the Attendance of absent Members, in such Manner, and under such Penalties as each House may provide.

Each House may determine the Rules of its Proceedings, punish its Members for disorderly Behaviour, and, with the Concurrence of two thirds, expel a Member.

Each House shall keep a Journal of its Proceedings, and from time to time publish the same, excepting such Parts as may in their Judgment require Secrecy; and the Yeas and Nays of the Members of either House on any questions shall, at the Desire of one fifth of those Present, be entered on the Journal.

Neither House, during the Session of Congress, shall, without the Consent of the other, adjourn for more than three days, nor to any other Place than that in which the two Houses shall be sitting.

[6]Modified by Twentieth Amendment.

Section 6
[COMPENSATION, PRIVILEGES, DISABILITIES]

The Senators and Representatives shall receive a Compensation for their Services, to be ascertained by Law, and paid out of the Treasury of the United States. They shall in all Cases, except Treason, Felony and Breach of the Peace, be privileged from Arrest during their Attendance at the Session of their respective Houses, and in going to and returning from the same; and for any Speech or Debate in either House, they shall not be questioned in any other Place.

No Senator or Representative shall, during the Time for which he was elected, be appointed to any civil Office under the Authority of the United States, which shall have been created, or the Emoluments whereof shall have been encreased during such time; and no Person holding any Office under the United States, shall be a Member of either House during his Continuance in Office.

Section 7
[PROCEDURE IN PASSING BILLS AND RESOLUTIONS]

All Bills for raising Revenue shall originate in the House of Representatives; but the Senate may propose or concur with Amendments as on other Bills.

Every Bill which shall have passed the House of Representatives and the Senate, shall, before it become a Law, be presented to the President of the United States: If he approve he shall sign it, but if not he shall return it, with his Objections to that House in which it shall have originated, who shall enter the Objections at large on their Journal, and proceed to reconsider it. If after such Reconsideration two thirds of that House shall agree to pass the Bill, it shall be sent, together with the Objections, to the other House, by which it shall likewise be reconsidered, and if approved by two thirds of that House, it shall become a Law. But in all such Cases the Votes of both Houses shall be determined by yeas and Nays, and the Names of the Persons voting for and against the Bill shall be entered on the Journal of each House respectively. If any Bill shall not be returned by the President within ten Days (Sundays excepted) after it shall have been presented to him, the Same shall be a Law, in like Manner as if he had signed it, unless the Congress by their Adjournment prevent its Return, in which Case it shall not be a Law.

Every Order, Resolution, or Vote to which the Concurrence of the Senate and House of Representatives may be necessary (except on a question of Adjournment) shall be presented to the President of the United States; and before the Same shall take Effect, shall be approved by him, or being disapproved by him, shall be repassed by two thirds of the Senate and House of Representatives, according to the Rules and Limitations prescribed in the Case of a Bill.

Section 8

[POWERS OF CONGRESS]

The Congress shall have Power

To lay and collect Taxes, Duties, Imposts and Excises, to pay the Debts and provide for the common Defence and general Welfare of the United States; but all Duties, Imposts and Excises shall be uniform throughout the United States;

To borrow Money on the credit of the United States;

To regulate Commerce with foreign Nations, and among the several States, and with the Indian Tribes;

To establish an uniform Rule of Naturalization, and uniform Laws on the subject of Bankruptcies throughout the United States;

To coin Money, regulate the Value thereof, and of foreign Coin, and fix the Standard of Weights and Measures;

To provide for the Punishment of counterfeiting the Securities and current Coin of the United States;

To establish Post Offices and post Roads;

To promote the Progress of Science and useful Arts, by securing for limited Times to Authors and Inventors the exclusive Right to their respective Writings and Discoveries;

To constitute Tribunals inferior to the supreme Court;

To define and punish Piracies and Felonies committed on the high Seas, and Offences against the Law of Nations;

To declare War, grant Letters of Marque and Reprisal, and make Rules concerning Captures on Land and Water;

To raise and support Armies, but no Appropriation of Money to that Use shall be for a longer Term than two Years;

To provide and maintain a Navy;

To make Rules for the Government and Regulation of the land and naval Forces;

To provide for calling forth the Militia to execute the Laws of the Union, suppress Insurrections and repel Invasions;

To provide for organizing, arming, and disciplining, the Militia, and for governing such Part of them as may be employed in the Service of the United States, reserving to the States respectively, the Appointment of the Officers, and the Authority of training the Militia according to the discipline prescribed by Congress;

To exercise exclusive Legislation in all Cases whatsoever, over such District (not exceeding ten Miles square) as may, by Cession of particular States, and the Acceptance of Congress, become the Seat of the Government of the United States, and to exercise like Authority over all Places purchased by the Consent of the Legislature of the State in which the Same shall be, for the Erection of Forts, Magazines, Arsenals, dock-Yards, and other needful Buildings;—And

To make all Laws which shall be necessary and proper for carrying into Execution the foregoing Powers, and all other Powers vested by this Constitution in the Government of the United States, or in any Department or Officer thereof.

Section 9

[SOME RESTRICTIONS ON FEDERAL POWER]

The Migration or Importation of such Persons as any of the States now existing shall think proper to admit, shall not be prohibited by the Congress prior to the Year one thousand eight hundred and eight, but a Tax or duty may be imposed on such Importation, not exceeding ten dollars for each Person.[7]

The Privilege of the Writ of Habeas Corpus shall not be suspended, unless when in Cases of Rebellion or Invasion the public Safety may require it.

No Bill of Attainder or ex post facto Law shall be passed.

No Capitation, or other direct, Tax shall be laid, unless in Proportion to the Census or Enumeration herein before directed to be taken.[8]

No Tax or Duty shall be laid on Articles exported from any State.

No Preference shall be given by any Regulation of Commerce or Revenue to the Ports of one State over those of another; nor shall Vessels bound to, or from, one State, be obliged to enter, clear, or pay Duties in another.

No Money shall be drawn from the Treasury, but in Consequence of Appropriations made by Law; and a regular Statement and Account of the Receipts and Expenditures of all public Money shall be published from time to time.

No Title of Nobility shall be granted by the United States: And no Person holding any Office of Profit or Trust under them, shall, without the Consent of the Congress, accept of any present, Emolument, Office, or Title, of any kind whatever, from any King, Prince, or foreign State.

Section 10

[RESTRICTIONS UPON POWERS OF STATES]

No State shall enter into any Treaty, Alliance, or Confederation; grant Letters of Marque and Reprisal; coin Money; emit Bills of Credit; make any Thing but gold and silver Coin a Tender in Payment of Debts; pass any Bill of Attainder, ex post facto Law, or Law impairing the Obligation of Contracts, or grant any Title of Nobility.

No State shall, without the Consent of the Congress, lay any Imposts or Duties on Imports or Exports, except what may be absolutely necessary for executing it's inspection Laws: and the net Produce of all Duties and Imposts, laid by any State on Imports or Exports, shall be for the Use of the Treasury of the United States; and all such Laws shall be subject to the Revision and Controul of the Congress.

No State shall, without the Consent of Congress, lay any Duty of Tonnage, keep Troops, or Ships of War in time of

---

[7]Temporary provision.

[8]Modified by Sixteenth Amendment.

Peace, enter into any Agreement or Compact with another State, or with a foreign Power, or engage in War, unless actually invaded, or in such imminent Danger as will not admit of delay.

Article II

Section 1

[EXECUTIVE POWER, ELECTION, QUALIFICATIONS OF THE PRESIDENT]

The executive Power shall be vested in a President of the United States of America. *He shall hold his Office during the Term of four Years, and, together with the Vice President, chosen for the same Term, be elected, as follows*[9]

Each State shall appoint, in such Manner as the Legislature thereof may direct, a Number of Electors, equal to the whole Number of Senators and Representatives to which the State may be entitled in the Congress: but no Senator or Representative, or Person holding an Office of Trust or Profit under the United States, shall be appointed an Elector.

The electors shall meet in their respective States, and vote by ballot for two Persons, of whom one at least shall not be an Inhabitant of the same State with themselves. And they shall make a List of all the Persons voted for, and of the Number of Votes for each; which List they shall sign and certify, and transmit sealed to the Seat of the Government of the United States, directed to the President of the Senate. The President of the Senate shall, in the Presence of the Senate and House of Representatives, open all the Certificates, and the Votes shall then be counted. The Person having the greatest Number of Votes shall be the President, if such Number be a Majority of the whole Number of Electors appointed; and if there be more than one who have such Majority, and have an equal Number of Votes, then the House of Representatives shall immediately chuse by Ballot one of them for President; and if no Person have a Majority, then from the five highest on the List the said House shall in like Manner chuse the President. But in chusing the President, the Votes shall be taken by States, the Representation from each State having one Vote; A quorum for this Purpose shall consist of a Member or Members from two thirds of the States, and a Majority of all the States shall be necessary to a Choice. In every Case, after the Choice of the President, the person having the greatest Number of Votes of the Electors shall be the Vice President. But if there should remain two or more who have equal Votes, the Senate shall chuse from them by Ballot the Vice President.[10]

The Congress may determine the Time of chusing the Electors, and the Day on which they shall give their Votes; which Day shall be the same throughout the United States.

No Person except a natural born Citizen, or a Citizen of the United States, at the time of the Adoption of this Constitution, shall be eligible to the Office of President; neither shall any Person be eligible to that Office who shall not have attained to the Age of thirty five Years, and been fourteen Years a Resident within the United States.

In Case of the Removal of the President from Office, or his Death, Resignation, or Inability to discharge the Powers and Duties of the said Office, the Same shall devolve on the Vice President, and the Congress may by Law provide for the Case of Removal, Death, Resignation or Inability, both of the President and Vice President, declaring what Officer shall then act as President, and such Officer shall act accordingly, until the Disability be removed, or a President shall be elected.

The President shall, at stated Times, receive for his Services, a Compensation, which shall neither be increased nor diminished during the Period for which he shall have been elected, and he shall not receive within that Period any other Emolument from the United States, or any of them.

Before he enter on the Execution of his Office, he shall take the following Oath or Affirmation:—"I do solemnly swear (or affirm) that I will faithfully execute the Office of President of the United States, and will to the best of my Ability, preserve, protect and defend the Constitution of the United States."

Section 2

[POWERS OF THE PRESIDENT]

The President shall be Commander in Chief of the Army and Navy of the United States, and of the Militia of the several States, when called into the actual Service of the United States; he may require the Opinion, in writing, of the principal Officer in each of the executive Departments, upon any Subject relating to the Duties of their respective Offices, and he shall have Power to grant Reprieves and Pardons for Offences against the United States, except in Cases of Impeachment.

He shall have Power, by and with the Advice and Consent of the Senate, to make Treaties, provided two thirds of the Senators present concur; and he shall nominate, and by and with the Advice and Consent of the Senate, shall appoint Ambassadors, other public Ministers and Consuls, Judges of the supreme Court, and all other Officers of the United States, whose Appointments are not herein otherwise provided for, and which shall be established by Law: but the Congress may by Law vest the Appointment of such inferior Officers, as they think proper, in the President alone, in the Courts of Law, or in the Heads of Departments.

The President shall have Power to fill up all Vacancies that may happen during the Recess of the Senate, by granting Commissions which shall expire at the End of their next Session.

[9]Number of terms limited to two by Twenty-second Amendment.

[10]Modified by Twelfth and Twentieth Amendments.

Section 3

[POWERS AND DUTIES OF THE PRESIDENT]

He shall from time to time give to the Congress Information of the State of the Union, and recommend to their Consideration such Measures as he shall judge necessary and expedient; he may, on extraordinary Occasions, convene both Houses, or either of them, and in Case of Disagreement between them, with Respect to the Time of Adjournment, he may adjourn them to such Time as he shall think proper; he shall receive Ambassadors and other public Ministers; he shall take Care that the Laws be faithfully executed, and shall Commission all the Officers of the United States.

Section 4

[IMPEACHMENT]

The President, Vice President and all civil Officers of the United States, shall be removed from Office on Impeachment for, and Conviction of, Treason, Bribery, or other high Crimes and Misdemeanors.

Article III

Section 1

[JUDICIAL POWER, TENURE OF OFFICE]

The judicial Power of the United States, shall be vested in one supreme Court, and in such inferior Courts as the Congress may from time to time ordain and establish. The Judges, both of the supreme and inferior Courts, shall hold their Offices during good Behaviour, and shall, at stated Times, receive for their Services, a Compensation, which shall not be diminished during their Continuance in Office.

Section 2

[JURISDICTION]

The judicial Power shall extend to all Cases, in Law and Equity, arising under this Constitution, the Laws of the United States, and Treaties made, or which shall be made, under their Authority;—to all Cases affecting Ambassadors, other public Ministers and Consuls;—to all Cases of admiralty and maritime Jurisdiction;—to Controversies to which the United States shall be a Party;—to Controversies between two or more States;—*between a State and Citizens of another State;*—between Citizens of different States,—between Citizens of the same State claiming Lands under Grants of different States, *and between a State,* or the Citizens thereof, *and foreign States, Citizens or Subjects.*[11]

In all Cases affecting Ambassadors, other public Ministers and Consuls, and those in which a State shall be Party, the supreme Court shall have original Jurisdiction. In all the other Cases before mentioned, the supreme Court shall have appellate Jurisdiction, both as to Law and Fact, with such Exceptions, and under such Regulations as the Congress shall make.

The Trial of all Crimes, except in Cases of Impeachment, shall be by Jury; and such Trial shall be held in the State where the said Crimes shall have been committed; but when not committed within any State, the Trial shall be at such Place or Places as the Congress may by Law have directed.

Section 3

[TREASON, PROOF, AND PUNISHMENT]

Treason against the United States, shall consist only in levying War against them, or in adhering to their Enemies, giving them Aid and Comfort. No Person shall be convicted of Treason unless on the Testimony of two Witnesses to the same overt Act, or on Confession in open Court.

The Congress shall have Power to declare the Punishment of Treason, but no Attainder of Treason shall work Corruption of Blood, or Forfeiture except during the Life of the Person attainted.

Article IV

Section 1

[FAITH AND CREDIT AMONG STATES]

Full Faith and Credit shall be given in each State to the public Acts, Records, and judicial Proceedings of every other State. And the Congress may by general Laws prescribe the Manner in which such Acts, Records and Proceedings shall be proved, and the Effect thereof.

Section 2

[PRIVILEGES AND IMMUNITIES, FUGITIVES]

The Citizens of each State shall be entitled to all Privileges and Immunities of Citizens in the several States.

A Person charged in any State with Treason, Felony or other Crime, who shall flee from Justice, and be found in another State, shall on Demand of the executive Authority of the State from which he fled, be delivered up, to be removed to the State having Jurisdiction of the Crime.

No person held to Service or Labour in one State, under the Laws thereof, escaping into another, shall, in Consequence of any Law or Regulation therein, be discharged from such Service or Labour, but shall be delivered up on Claim of the Party to whom such Service or Labour may be due.[12]

Section 3

[ADMISSION OF NEW STATES]

New States may be admitted by the Congress into this Union; but no new State shall be formed or erected within the Jurisdiction of any other State; nor any State be formed by the Junction of two or more States, or Parts of States, without

---

[11]Modified by Eleventh Amendment.

[12]Repealed by the Thirteenth Amendment.

the Consent of the Legislatures of the States concerned as well as of the Congress.

The Congress shall have Power to dispose of and make all needful Rules and Regulations respecting the Territory or other Property belonging to the United States; and nothing in this Constitution shall be so construed as to Prejudice any Claims of the United States, or of any particular State.

Section 4
[GUARANTEE OF REPUBLICAN GOVERNMENT]

The United States shall guarantee to every State in this Union a Republican Form of Government, and shall protect each of them against Invasion; and on Application of the Legislature, or of the Executive (when the Legislature cannot be convened), against domestic Violence.

Article V
[AMENDMENT OF THE CONSTITUTION]

The Congress, whenever two thirds of both Houses shall deem it necessary, shall propose Amendments to this Constitution, or, on the Application of the Legislatures of two thirds of the several States, shall call a Convention for proposing Amendments, which, in either Case, shall be valid to all Intents and Purposes, as Part of this Constitution, when ratified by the Legislatures of three fourths of the several States, or by Conventions in three fourths thereof, as the one or the other Mode of Ratification may be proposed by the Congress; *Provided that no Amendment which may be made prior to the Year One thousand eight hundred and eight shall in any Manner affect the first and fourth Clauses in the Ninth Section of the first Article;*[13] and that no State, without its Consent, shall be deprived of its equal Suffrage in the Senate.

[13]Temporary provision.

Article VI
[DEBTS, SUPREMACY, OATH]

All Debts contracted and Engagements entered into, before the Adoption of this Constitution, shall be as valid against the United States under this Constitution, as under the Confederation.

This Constitution, and the Laws of the United States which shall be made in Pursuance thereof; and all Treaties made, or which shall be made, under the Authority of the United States, shall be the supreme Law of the Land; and the Judges in every State shall be bound thereby, any Thing in the Constitution or Laws of any State to the Contrary notwithstanding.

The Senators and Representatives before mentioned, and the Members of the several State Legislatures, and all executive and judicial Officers, both of the United States and of the several States, shall be bound by Oath or Affirmation, to support this Constitution; but no religious Test shall be required as a Qualification to any Office or public Trust under the United States.

Article VII
[RATIFICATION AND ESTABLISHMENT]

The Ratification of the Conventions of nine States, shall be sufficient for the Establishment of this Constitution between the States so ratifying the Same.[14]

Done in Convention by the Unanimous Consent of the States present the Seventeenth Day of September in the Year of our Lord one thousand seven hundred and Eighty seven and of the Independence of the United States of America the Twelfth. *In Witness* whereof We have hereunto subscribed our Names,

[14]The Constitution was submitted on September 17, 1787, by the Constitutional Convention, was ratified by the conventions of several states at various dates up to May 29, 1790, and became effective on March 4, 1789.

G:[0] WASHINGTON—
Presidt. and deputy from Virginia

NEW HAMPSHIRE
John Langdon
Nicholas Gilman

MASSACHUSETTS
Nathaniel Gorham
Rufus King

CONNECTICUT
Wm. Saml. Johnson
Roger Sherman

NEW YORK
Alexander Hamilton

NEW JERSEY
Wil: Livingston

David Brearley
Wm. Paterson
Jona: Dayton

PENNSYLVANIA
B Franklin
Thomas Mifflin
Robt. Morris
Geo. Clymer
Thos. FitzSimons
Jared Ingersoll
James Wilson
Gouv Morris

DELAWARE
Geo: Read
Gunning Bedford jun
John Dickinson
Richard Bassett
Jaco: Broom

MARYLAND
James McHenry
Dan of St Thos. Jenifer
Danl. Carroll

VIRGINIA
John Blair—
James Madison Jr.

NORTH CAROLINA
Wm. Blount
Richd. Dobbs Spaight
Hu Williamson

SOUTH CAROLINA
J. Rutledge
Charles Cotesworth
Pinckney
Charles Pinckney
Pierce Butler

GEORGIA
William Few
Abr Baldwin

AMENDMENTS TO THE CONSTITUTION

Proposed by Congress and Ratified by the Legislatures of the Several States, Pursuant to Article V of the Original Constitution.

Amendments I–X, known as the Bill of Rights, were proposed by Congress on September 25, 1789, and ratified on December 15, 1791.

Amendment I

[FREEDOM OF RELIGION, OF SPEECH, AND OF THE PRESS]

Congress shall make no law respecting an establishment of religion, or prohibiting the free exercise thereof; or abridging the freedom of speech, or of the press; or the right of the people peaceably to assemble, and to petition the Government for a redress of grievances.

Amendment II

[RIGHT TO KEEP AND BEAR ARMS]

A well regulated Militia, being necessary to the security of a free State, the right of the people to keep and bear Arms, shall not be infringed.

Amendment III

[QUARTERING OF SOLDIERS]

No Soldier shall, in time of peace be quartered in any house, without the consent of the Owner, nor in time of war, but in a manner to be prescribed by law.

Amendment IV

[SECURITY FROM UNWARRANTABLE SEARCH AND SEIZURE]

The right of the people to be secure in their persons, houses, papers, and effects, against unreasonable searches and seizures, shall not be violated, and no Warrants shall issue, but upon probable cause, supported by Oath or affirmation, and particularly describing the place to be searched, and the persons or things to be seized.

Amendment V

[RIGHTS OF ACCUSED PERSONS IN CRIMINAL PROCEEDINGS]

No person shall be held to answer for a capital, or otherwise infamous crime, unless on a presentment or indictment of a Grand Jury, except in cases arising in the land or naval forces, or in the Militia, when in actual service in time of War or in public danger; nor shall any person be subject for the same offence to be twice put in jeopardy of life or limb; nor shall be compelled in any criminal case to be a witness against himself, nor be deprived of life, liberty, or property, without due process of law; nor shall private property be taken for public use, without just compensation.

Amendment VI

[RIGHT TO SPEEDY TRIAL, WITNESSES, ETC.]

In all criminal prosecutions, the accused shall enjoy the right to a speedy and public trial, by an impartial jury of the State and district wherein the crime shall have been committed, which district shall have been previously ascertained by law, and to be informed of the nature and cause of the accusation; to be confronted with the witnesses against him; to have compulsory process for obtaining witnesses in his favor, and to have the Assistance of Counsel for his defence.

Amendment VII

[TRIAL BY JURY IN CIVIL CASES]

In suits at common law, where the value in controversy shall exceed twenty dollars, the right of trial by jury shall be preserved, and no fact tried by a jury, shall be otherwise reexamined in any Court of the United States, than according to the rules of the common law.

Amendment VIII

[BAILS, FINES, PUNISHMENTS]

Excessive bail shall not be required, nor excessive fines imposed, nor cruel and unusual punishments inflicted.

Amendment IX

[RESERVATION OF RIGHTS OF PEOPLE]

The enumeration in the Constitution, of certain rights, shall not be construed to deny or disparage others retained by the people.

Amendment X

[POWERS RESERVED TO STATES OR PEOPLE]

The powers not delegated to the United States by the Constitution, nor prohibited by it to the States, are reserved to the States respectively, or to the people.

Amendment XI

[Proposed by Congress on March 4, 1794; declared ratified on January 8, 1798.]

[RESTRICTION OF JUDICIAL POWER]

The Judicial power of the United States shall not be construed to extend to any suit in law or equity, commenced or prosecuted against one of the United States by Citizens of another State, or by Citizens or Subjects of any Foreign State.

Amendment XII

[Proposed by Congress on December 9, 1803; declared ratified on September 25, 1804.]

[ELECTION OF PRESIDENT AND VICE PRESIDENT]

The Electors shall meet in their respective states and vote by ballot for President and Vice-President, one of whom, at least, shall not be an inhabitant of the same state with themselves; they shall name in their ballots the person voted for as President, and in distinct ballots the person voted for as Vice-President, and they shall make distinct lists of all persons voted for as President, and of all persons voted for as Vice-President, and of the number of votes for each, which lists they shall sign and certify, and transmit sealed to the seat of the government of the United States, directed to the President of the Senate;—the President of the Senate shall, in presence of the Senate and House of Representatives, open all the certificates and the votes shall then be counted;—The person having the greatest number of votes for President, shall be the President, if such number be a majority of the whole number of Electors appointed; and if no person have such majority, then from the persons having the highest numbers not exceeding three on the list of those voted for as President, the House of Representatives shall choose immediately, by ballot, the President. But in choosing the President, the votes shall be taken by states, the representation from each state having one vote; a quorum for this purpose shall consist of a member or members from two-thirds of the states, and a majority of all the states shall be necessary to a choice. And if the House of Representatives shall not choose a President whenever the right of choice shall devolve upon them, before the fourth day of March next following, then the Vice-President shall act as President, as in the case of the death or other constitutional disability of the President.—The person having the greatest number of votes as Vice-President, shall be the Vice-President, if such number be a majority of the whole number of Electors appointed, and if no person have a majority, then from the two highest numbers on the list, the Senate shall choose the Vice-President; a quorum for the purpose shall consist of two-thirds of the whole number of Senators, and a majority of the whole number shall be necessary to a choice. But no person constitutionally ineligible to the office of President shall be eligible to that of Vice-President of the United States.

Amendment XIII

[Proposed by Congress on January 31, 1865; declared ratified on December 18, 1865.]

Section 1

[ABOLITION OF SLAVERY]

Neither slavery nor involuntary servitude, except as a punishment for crime whereof the party shall have been duly convicted, shall exist within the United States, or any place subject to their jurisdiction.

Section 2

[POWER TO ENFORCE THIS ARTICLE]

Congress shall have power to enforce this article by appropriate legislation.

Amendment XIV

[Proposed by Congress on June 13, 1866; declared ratified on July 28, 1868.]

Section 1

[CITIZENSHIP RIGHTS NOT TO BE ABRIDGED BY STATES]

All persons born or naturalized in the United States, and subject to the jurisdiction thereof, are citizens of the United States and of the State wherein they reside. No State shall make or enforce any law which shall abridge the privileges or immunities of citizens of the United States; nor shall any State deprive any person of life, liberty, or property, without due process of law; nor deny to any person within its jurisdiction the equal protection of the laws.

Section 2

[APPORTIONMENT OF REPRESENTATIVES IN CONGRESS]

Representatives shall be apportioned among the several States according to their respective numbers, counting the whole number of persons in each State, excluding Indians not taxed. But when the right to vote at any election for the choice of electors for President and Vice-President of the United States, Representatives in Congress, the Executive and Judicial officers of a State, or the members of the Legislature thereof, is denied to any of the male inhabitants of such State, being twenty-one years of age, and citizens of the United States, or in any way abridged, except for participation in rebellion, or other crime, the basis of representation therein shall be reduced in the proportion which the number of such male citizens shall bear to the whole number of male citizens twenty-one years of age in such State.

Section 3

[PERSONS DISQUALIFIED FROM HOLDING OFFICE]

No person shall be a Senator or Representative in Congress, or elector of President and Vice-President, or hold any office, civil or military, under the United States, or under any State, who, having previously taken an oath, as a member of Congress, or as an officer of the United States, or as a member of any State legislature, or as an executive or judicial officer of any State, to support the Constitution of the United States, shall have engaged in insurrection or rebellion against the same, or given aid or comfort to the enemies thereof. But Congress may by a vote of two-thirds of each House, remove such disability.

Section 4
[WHAT PUBLIC DEBTS ARE VALID]

The validity of the public debt of the United States, authorized by law, including debts incurred for payment of pensions and bounties for services in suppressing insurrection or rebellion, shall not be questioned. But neither the United States nor any State shall assume or pay any debt or obligation incurred in aid of insurrection or rebellion against the United States, or any claim for the loss or emancipation of any slave; but all such debts, obligations and claims shall be held illegal and void.

Section 5
[POWER TO ENFORCE THIS ARTICLE]

The Congress shall have power to enforce, by appropriate legislation, the provisions of this article.

Amendment XV
[Proposed by Congress on February 26, 1869; declared ratified on March 30, 1870.]

Section 1
[NEGRO SUFFRAGE]

The right of citizens of the United States to vote shall not be denied or abridged by the United States or by any State on account of race, color, or previous condition of servitude.

Section 2
[POWER TO ENFORCE THIS ARTICLE]

The Congress shall have power to enforce this article by appropriate legislation.

Amendment XVI
[Proposed by Congress on July 2, 1909; declared ratified on February 25, 1913.]
[AUTHORIZING INCOME TAXES]

The Congress shall have power to lay and collect taxes on incomes, from whatever source derived, without apportionment among the several States, and without regard to any census or enumeration.

Amendment XVII
[Proposed by Congress on May 13, 1912; declared ratified on May 31, 1913.]
[POPULAR ELECTION OF SENATORS]

The Senate of the United States shall be composed of two Senators from each State, elected by the people thereof, for six years; and each Senator shall have one vote. The electors in each State shall have the qualifications requisite for electors of the most numerous branch of the State legislatures.

When vacancies happen in the representation of any State in the Senate, the executive authority of such State shall issue writs of election to fill such vacancies: *Provided,* That the legislature of any State may empower the executive thereof to make temporary appointments until the people fill the vacancies by election as the legislature may direct.

This amendment shall not be so construed as to affect the election or term of any Senator chosen before it becomes valid as part of the Constitution.

Amendment XVIII
[Proposed by Congress December 18, 1917; declared ratified on January 29, 1919.]

Section 1
[NATIONAL LIQUOR PROHIBITION]

After one year from the ratification of this article the manufacture, sale, or transportation of intoxicating liquors within, the importation thereof into, or the exportation thereof from the United States and all territory subject to the jurisdiction thereof for beverage purposes is hereby prohibited.

Section 2
[POWER TO ENFORCE THIS ARTICLE]

The Congress and the several States shall have concurrent power to enforce this article by appropriate legislation.

Section 3
[RATIFICATION WITHIN SEVEN YEARS]

This article shall be inoperative unless it shall have been ratified as an amendment to the Constitution by the legislatures of the several States, as provided in the Constitution, within seven years from the date of the submission hereof to the States by the Congress.[1]

Amendment XIX
[Proposed by Congress on June 4, 1919; declared ratified on August 26, 1920.]
[WOMAN SUFFRAGE]

The right of citizens of the United States to vote shall not be denied or abridged by the United States or by any State on account of sex.

Congress shall have power to enforce this article by appropriate legislation.

Amendment XX
[Proposed by Congress on March 2, 1932; declared ratified on February 6, 1933.]

Section 1
[TERMS OF OFFICE]

The terms of the President and Vice President shall end at noon on the 20th day of January, and the terms of Senators and Representatives at noon on the 3d day of January, of the years

---

[1]Repealed by the Twenty-first Amendment.

in which such terms would have ended if this article had not been ratified; and the terms of their successors shall then begin.

Section 2
[TIME OF CONVENING CONGRESS]

The Congress shall assemble at least once in every year, and such meeting shall begin at noon on the 3d day of January, unless they shall by law appoint a different day.

Section 3
[DEATH OF PRESIDENT-ELECT]

If, at the time fixed for the beginning of the term of the President, the President elect shall have died, the Vice President elect shall become President. If a President shall not have been chosen before the time fixed for the beginning of his term, or if the President elect shall have failed to qualify, then the Vice President elect shall act as President until a President shall have qualified; and the Congress may by law provide for the case wherein neither a President elect nor a Vice President elect shall have qualified, declaring who shall then act as President, or the manner in which one who is to act shall be selected, and such person shall act accordingly until a President or Vice President shall have qualified.

Section 4
[ELECTION OF THE PRESIDENT]

The Congress may by law provide for the case of the death of any of the persons from whom the House of Representatives may choose a President whenever the right of choice shall have devolved upon them, and for the case of the death of any of the persons from whom the Senate may choose a Vice President whenever the right of choice shall have devolved upon them.

Section 5
[AMENDMENT TAKES EFFECT]

Sections 1 and 2 shall take effect on the 15th day of October following the ratification of this article.

Section 6
[RATIFICATION WITHIN SEVEN YEARS]

This article shall be inoperative unless it shall have been ratified as an amendment to the Constitution by the legislatures of three-fourths of the several States within seven years from the date of its submission.

Amendment XXI

[Proposed by Congress on February 20, 1933; declared ratified on December 5, 1933.]

Section 1
[NATIONAL LIQUOR PROHIBITION REPEALED]

The eighteenth article of amendment to the Constitution of the United States is hereby repealed.

Section 2
[TRANSPORTATION OF LIQUOR INTO "DRY" STATES]

The transportation or importation into any State, Territory, or Possession of the United States for delivery or use therein of intoxicating liquors, in violation of the laws thereof, is hereby prohibited.

Section 3
[RATIFICATION WITHIN SEVEN YEARS]

This article shall be inoperative unless it shall have been ratified as an amendment to the Constitution by conventions in the several States, as provided in the Constitution, within seven years from the date of the submission hereof to the States by the Congress.

Amendment XXII

[Proposed by Congress on March 21, 1947; declared ratified on February 27, 1951.]

Section 1
[TENURE OF PRESIDENT LIMITED]

No person shall be elected to the office of President more than twice, and no person who has held the office of President or acted as President, for more than two years of a term to which some other person was elected President shall be elected to the office of the President more than once. But this Article shall not apply to any person holding the office of President when this Article was proposed by the Congress, and shall not prevent any person who may be holding the office of President, or acting as President, during the term within which this Article becomes operative from holding the office of President or acting as President during the remainder of such term.

Section 2
[RATIFICATION WITHIN SEVEN YEARS]

This article shall be inoperative unless it shall have been ratified as an amendment to the Constitution by the legislatures of three-fourths of the several States within seven years from the date of its submission to the States by the Congress.

Amendment XXIII

[Proposed by Congress on June 16, 1960; declared ratified on March 29, 1961.]

Section 1
[ELECTORAL COLLEGE VOTES FOR THE DISTRICT OF COLUMBIA]

The District constituting the seat of Government of the United States shall appoint in such manner as the Congress may direct:

A number of electors of President and Vice President equal to the whole number of Senators and Representatives in Congress to which the District would be entitled if it were a State, but in no event more than the least populous State; they shall be in addition to those appointed by the States, but they shall be considered, for the purposes of the election of President and Vice President, to be electors appointed by a State; and they shall meet in the District and perform such duties as provided by the twelfth article of amendment.

Section 2
[POWER TO ENFORCE THIS ARTICLE]

The Congress shall have power to enforce this article by appropriate legislation.

Amendment XXIV

[Proposed by Congress on August 27, 1962; declared ratified on January 23, 1964.]

Section 1
[ANTI-POLL TAX]

The right of citizens of the United States to vote in any primary or other election for President or Vice President, for electors for President or Vice President, or for Senator or Representative of Congress, shall not be denied or abridged by the United States or any State by reason of failure to pay any poll tax or other tax.

Section 2
[POWER TO ENFORCE THIS ARTICLE]

The Congress shall have power to enforce this article by appropriate legislation.

Amendment XXV

[Proposed by Congress on July 6, 1965; declared ratified on February 10, 1967.]

Section 1
[VICE PRESIDENT TO BECOME PRESIDENT]

In case of the removal of the President from office or his death or resignation, the Vice President shall become President.

Section 2
[CHOICE OF A NEW VICE PRESIDENT]

Whenever there is a vacancy in the office of the Vice President, the President shall nominate a Vice President who shall take the office upon confirmation by a majority vote of both houses of Congress.

Section 3
[PRESIDENT MAY DECLARE OWN DISABILITY]

Whenever the President transmits to the President pro tempore of the Senate and the Speaker of the House of Representatives his written declaration that he is unable to discharge the powers and duties of his office, and until he transmits to them a written declaration to the contrary, such powers and duties shall be discharged by the Vice President as Acting President.

Section 4
[ALTERNATE PROCEDURES TO DECLARE AND TO END PRESIDENTIAL DISABILITY]

Whenever the Vice President and a majority of either the principal officers of the executive departments, or of such other body as Congress may by law provide, transmit to the President pro tempore of the Senate and the Speaker of the House of Representatives their written declaration that the President is unable to discharge the powers and duties of his office, the Vice President shall immediately assume the powers and duties of the office as Acting President.

Thereafter, when the President transmits to the President pro tempore of the Senate and the Speaker of the House of Representatives his written declaration that no inability exists, he shall resume the powers and duties of his office unless the Vice President and a majority of either the principal officers of the executive department, or of such other body as Congress may by law provide, transmit within four days to the President pro tempore of the Senate and the Speaker of the House of Representatives their written declaration that the President is unable to discharge the powers and duties of his office. Thereupon Congress shall decide the issue, assembling within forty eight hours for that purpose if not in session. If the Congress, within twenty one days after receipt of the latter written declaration, or, if Congress is not in session, within twenty one days after Congress is required to assemble, determines by two-thirds vote of both Houses that the President is unable to discharge the powers and duties of his office, the Vice President shall continue to discharge the same as Acting President; otherwise, the President shall resume the powers and duties of his office.

Amendment XXVI

[Proposed by Congress on March 23, 1971; declared ratified on July 1, 1971.]

Section 1
[EIGHTEEN-YEAR-OLD VOTE]

The right of citizens of the United States, who are eighteen years of age or older, to vote shall not be denied or abridged by the United States or by any State on account of age.

Section 2
[POWER TO ENFORCE THIS ARTICLE]

The Congress shall have power to enforce this article by appropriate legislation.

Amendment XXVII

[Proposed by Congress on September 25, 1789; declared ratified on May 8, 1992.]

[CONGRESS CANNOT RAISE ITS OWN PAY]

No law varying the compensation for the services of the Senators and Representatives, shall take effect, until an election of representatives shall have intervened.

THE FEDERALIST PAPERS

No. 10: MADISON

Among the numerous advantages promised by a well constructed Union, none deserves to be more accurately developed than its tendency to break and control the violence of faction. The friend of popular governments never finds himself so much alarmed for their character and fate, as when he contemplates their propensity to this dangerous vice. He will not fail therefore to set a due value on any plan which, without violating the principles to which he is attached, provides a proper cure for it. The instability, injustice, and confusion introduced into the public councils have, in truth, been the mortal diseases under which popular governments have everywhere perished, as they continue to be the favorite and fruitful topics from which the adversaries to liberty derive their most specious declamations. The valuable improvements made by the American constitutions on the popular models, both ancient and modern, cannot certainly be too much admired; but it would be an unwarrantable partiality to contend that they have as effectually obviated the danger on this side, as was wished and expected. Complaints are everywhere heard from our most considerate and virtuous citizens, equally the friends of public and private faith and of public and personal liberty, that our governments are too unstable, that the public good is disregarded in the conflicts of rival parties, and that measures are too often decided, not according to the rules of justice and the rights of the minor party, but by the superior force of an interested and overbearing majority. However anxiously we may wish that these complaints had no foundation, the evidence of known facts will not permit us to deny that they are in some degree true. It will be found, indeed, on a candid review of our situation, that some of the distresses under which we labor have been erroneously charged on the operation of our governments; but it will be found, at the same time, that other causes will not alone account for many of our heaviest misfortunes; and, particularly, for that prevailing and increasing distrust of public engagements and alarm for private rights which are echoed from one end of the continent to the other. These must be chiefly, if not wholly, effects of the unsteadiness and injustice with which a factious spirit has tainted our public administration.

By a faction I understand a number of citizens, whether amounting to a majority or minority of the whole, who are united and actuated by some common impulse of passion, or of interest, adverse to the rights of other citizens, or to the permanent and aggregate interests of the community.

There are two methods of curing the mischiefs of faction: the one, by removing its causes; the other, by controlling its effects.

There are again two methods of removing the causes of faction: the one, by destroying the liberty which is essential to its existence; the other, by giving to every citizen the same opinions, the same passions, and the same interests.

It could never be more truly said than of the first remedy, that it is worse than the disease. Liberty is to faction what air is to fire, an aliment without which it instantly expires. But it could not be a less folly to abolish liberty, which is essential to political life, because it nourishes faction, than it would be to wish the annihilation of air, which is essential to animal life, because it imparts to fire its destructive agency.

The second expedient is as impracticable, as the first would be unwise. As long as the reason of man continues fallible, and he is at liberty to exercise it, different opinions will be formed. As long as the connection subsists between his reason and his self-love, his opinions and his passions will have a reciprocal influence on each other; and the former will be objects to which the latter will attach themselves. The diversity in the faculties of men, from which the rights of property originate, is not less an insuperable obstacle to a uniformity of interests. The protection of these faculties is the first object of Government. From the protection of different and unequal faculties of acquiring property, the possession of different degrees and kinds of property immediately results; and from the influence of these on the sentiments and views of the respective proprietors, ensues a division of the society into different interests and parties.

The latent causes of faction are thus sown in the nature of man; and we see them everywhere brought into different degrees of activity, according to the different circumstances of civil society. A zeal for different opinions concerning religion, concerning Government, and many other points, as well of speculation as of practice; an attachment to different leaders ambitiously contending for pre-eminence and power; or to persons of other descriptions whose fortunes have been interesting to the human passions, have in turn divided mankind into parties, inflamed them with mutual animosity, and rendered them much more disposed to vex and oppress each other, than to co-operate for their common good. So strong is this propensity of mankind to fall into mutual animosities, that where no substantial occasion presents itself, the most frivolous and fanciful distinctions have been sufficient to kindle their unfriendly passions, and excite their most violent conflicts. But the most common and durable source of factions has been the various and unequal distribution of property. Those who hold and those who are without property have ever formed distinct interests in society. Those who are creditors, and those who are debtors, fall under a like discrimination. A landed interest, a manufacturing interest, a mercantile interest, a moneyed interest, with many lesser interests, grow up of necessity in civilized nations, and divide them into different classes, actuated by different sentiments and views. The regulation of these various and interfering interests forms the principal task of modern Legislation, and involves the spirit of party and faction in the necessary and ordinary operations of Government.

No man is allowed to be judge in his own cause, because his interest would certainly bias his judgment and, not improbably, corrupt his integrity. With equal, nay with greater reason, a body of men are unfit to be both judges and parties at the same time; yet what are many of the most important acts of legislation but so many judicial determinations, not indeed concerning the rights of single persons, but concerning the rights of large bodies of citizens; and what are the different classes of legislators but advocates and parties to the causes which they determine? Is a law proposed concerning private debts? It is a question to which the creditors are parties on one side and the debtors on the other. Justice ought to hold the balance between them. Yet the parties are, and must be, themselves the judges; and the most numerous party, or in other words, the most powerful faction must be expected to prevail. Shall domestic manufacturers be encouraged, and in what degree, by restrictions on foreign manufacturers? are questions which would be differently decided by the landed and the manufacturing classes, and probably by neither with a sole regard to justice and the public good. The apportionment of taxes on the various descriptions of property is an act which seems to require the most exact impartiality; yet there is, perhaps, no legislative act in which greater opportunity and temptation are given to a predominant party to trample on the rules of justice. Every shilling with which they overburden the inferior number is a shilling saved to their own pockets.

It is in vain to say that enlightened statesmen will be able to adjust these clashing interests and render them all subservient to the public good. Enlightened statesmen will not always be at the helm. Nor, in many cases, can such an adjustment be made at all without taking into view indirect and remote considerations, which will rarely prevail over the immediate interest which one party may find in disregarding the rights of another or the good of the whole.

The inference to which we are brought is that the *causes* of faction cannot be removed and that relief is only to be sought in the means of controlling its *effects*.

If a faction consists of less than a majority, relief is supplied by the republican principle, which enables the majority to defeat its sinister views by regular vote. It may clog the administration, it may convulse the society; but it will be unable to execute and mask its violence under the forms of the Constitution. When a majority is included in a faction, the form of popular government, on the other hand, enables it to sacrifice to its ruling passion or interest both the public good and the rights of other citizens. To secure the public good and private rights against the danger of such a faction, and at the same time to preserve the spirit and the form of popular government, is then the great object to which our enquiries are directed. Let me add that it is the great desideratum by which alone this form of government can be rescued from the opprobrium under which it has so long labored and be recommended to the esteem and adoption of mankind.

By what means is this object attainable? Evidently by one of two only. Either the existence of the same passion or interest in a majority at the same time must be prevented, or the majority, having such co-existent passion or interest, must be rendered, by their number and local situation, unable to concert and carry into effect schemes of oppression. If the impulse and the opportunity be suffered to coincide, we well know that neither moral nor religious motives can be relied on as an adequate control. They are not found to be such on the injustice and violence of individuals, and lose their efficacy in proportion to the number combined together, that is, in proportion as their efficacy becomes needful.

From this view of the subject it may be concluded that a pure Democracy, by which I mean a Society consisting of a small number of citizens, who assemble and administer the Government in person, can admit of no cure for the mischiefs of faction. A common passion or interest will, in almost every case, be felt by a majority of the whole; a communication and concert results from the form of Government itself; and there is nothing to check the inducements to sacrifice the weaker party or an obnoxious individual. Hence it is that such Democracies have ever been spectacles of turbulence and contention; have ever been found incompatible with personal security or the rights of property; and have in general been as short in their lives as they have been violent in their deaths. Theoretic politicians, who have patronized this species of Government, have erroneously supposed that by reducing mankind to a perfect equality in their political rights, they would at the same time be perfectly equalized and assimilated in their possessions, their opinions, and their passions.

A Republic, by which I mean a Government in which the scheme of representation takes place, opens a different prospect and promises the cure for which we are seeking. Let us examine the points in which it varies from pure Democracy, and we shall comprehend both the nature of the cure and the efficacy which it must derive from the Union.

The two great points of difference between a Democracy and a Republic are: first, the delegation of the Government, in the latter, to a small number of citizens elected by the rest; secondly, the greater number of citizens and greater sphere of country over which the latter may be extended.

The effect of the first difference is, on the one hand, to refine and enlarge the public views by passing them through the medium of a chosen body of citizens, whose wisdom may best discern the true interest of their country and whose patriotism and love of justice will be least likely to sacrifice it to temporary or partial considerations. Under such a regulation it may well happen that the public voice, pronounced by the representatives of the people, will be more consonant to the public good than if pronounced by the people themselves, convened for the purpose. On the other hand, the effect may be inverted. Men of factious tempers, of local prejudices, or of sinister designs, may, by intrigue, by corruption, or by other means, first obtain the suffrages, and then betray the interests of the people. The question resulting is, whether small or extensive Republics are most favorable to the election of proper guardians of the public weal; and it is clearly decided in favor of the latter by two obvious considerations.

In the first place it is to be remarked that however small the Republic may be, the Representatives must be raised to a certain number in order to guard against the cabals of a few; and that however large it may be they must be limited to a certain number in order to guard against the confusion of a multitude. Hence, the number of Representatives in the two cases not being in proportion to that of the Constituents, and being proportionally greatest in the small Republic, it follows that if the proportion of fit characters be not less in the large than in the small Republic, the former will present a greater option, and consequently a greater probability of a fit choice.

In the next place, as each Representative will be chosen by a greater number of citizens in the large than in the small Republic, it will be more difficult for unworthy candidates to practise with success the vicious arts by which elections are too often carried; and the suffrages of the people being more free, will be more likely to centre on men who possess the most attractive merit and the most diffusive and established characters.

It must be confessed that in this, as in most other cases, there is a mean, on both sides of which inconveniencies will be found to lie. By enlarging too much the number of electors, you render the representative too little acquainted with all their local circumstances and lesser interests; as by reducing it too much, you render him unduly attached to these, and too little fit to comprehend and pursue great and national objects. The Federal Constitution forms a happy combination in this respect; the great and aggregate interests being referred to the national, the local and particular to the State legislatures.

The other point of difference is the greater number of citizens and extent of territory which may be brought within the compass of Republican than of Democratic Government; and it is this circumstance principally which renders factious combinations less to be dreaded in the former than in the latter. The smaller the society, the fewer probably will be the distinct parties and interests composing it; the fewer the distinct parties and interests, the more frequently will a majority be found of the same party; and the smaller the number of individuals composing a majority, and the smaller the compass within which they are placed, the more easily will they concert and execute their plans of oppression. Extend the sphere and you take in a greater variety of parties and interests; you make it less probable that a majority of the whole will have a common motive to invade the rights of other citizens; or if such a common motive exists, it will be more difficult for all who feel it to discover their own strength and to act in unison with each other. Besides other impediments, it may be remarked, that where there is a consciousness of unjust or dishonorable purposes, communication is always checked by distrust in proportion to the number whose concurrence is necessary.

Hence, it clearly appears that the same advantage which a Republic has over a Democracy in controlling the effects of faction is enjoyed by a large over a small republic—is enjoyed by the Union over the States composing it. Does this advantage consist in the substitution of representatives whose enlightened views and virtuous sentiments render them superior to local prejudices and to schemes of injustice? It will not be denied that the representation of the Union will be most likely to possess these requisite endowments. Does it consist in the greater security afforded by a greater variety of parties, against the event of any one party being able to outnumber and oppress the rest? In an equal degree does the increased variety of parties comprised within the Union increase this security? Does it, in fine, consist in the greater obstacles opposed to the concert and accomplishment of the secret wishes of an unjust and interested majority? Here again the extent of the Union gives it the most palpable advantage.

The influence of factious leaders may kindle a flame within their particular States but will be unable to spread a general conflagration through the other States: a religious sect may degenerate into a political faction in a part of the Confederacy; but the variety of sects dispersed over the entire face of it must secure the national Councils against any danger from that source: a rage for paper money, for an abolition of debts, for an equal division of property, or for any other improper or wicked project, will be less apt to pervade the whole body of the Union than a particular member of it; in the same proportion as such a malady is more likely to taint a particular county or district than an entire State.

In the extent and proper structure of the Union, therefore, we behold a republican remedy for the diseases most incident to Republican Government. And according to the degree of pleasure and pride we feel in being republicans ought to be our zeal in cherishing the spirit and supporting the character of federalist.

PUBLIUS

NO. 51: MADISON

To what expedient, then, shall we finally resort, for maintaining in practice the necessary partition of power among the several departments as laid down in the constitution? The only answer that can be given is that as all these exterior provisions are found to be inadequate the defect must be supplied, by so contriving the interior structure of the government as that its several constituent parts may, by their mutual relations, be the means of keeping each other in their proper places. Without presuming to undertake a full development of this important idea I will hazard a few general observations which may perhaps place it in a clearer light, and enable us to form a more correct judgment of the principles and structure of the government planned by the convention.

In order to lay a due foundation for that separate and distinct exercise of the different powers of government, which to a certain extent is admitted on all hands to be essential to the preservation of liberty, it is evident that each department should have a will of its own; and consequently should be so constituted that the members of each should have as little agency as possible in the appointment of the members of the others. Were this principle rigorously adhered to, it would require that all the appointments for the supreme executive, legislative, and judiciary magistracies should be drawn from the same fountain of authority, the people, through channels having no communication whatever with one another. Perhaps such a plan of constructing the several departments would be less difficult in practice than it may in contemplation appear. Some difficulties, however, and some additional expense would attend the execution of it. Some deviations, therefore, from the principle must be admitted. In the constitution of the judiciary department in particular, it might be inexpedient to insist rigorously on the principle: first, because peculiar qualifications being essential in the members, the primary consideration ought to be to select that mode of choice which best secures these qualifications; second, because the permanent tenure by which the appointments are held in that department must soon destroy all sense of dependence on the authority conferring them.

It is equally evident that the members of each department should be as little dependent as possible on those of the others for the emoluments annexed to their offices. Were the executive magistrate, or the judges, not independent of the legislature in this particular, their independence in every other would be merely nominal.

But the great security against a gradual concentration of the several powers in the same department consists in giving to those who administer each department the necessary constitutional means and personal motives to resist encroachments of the others. The provision for defence must in this, as in all other cases, be made commensurate to the danger of attack. Ambition must be made to counteract ambition. The interest of the man must be connected with the constitutional rights of the place. It may be a reflection on human nature that such devices should be necessary to control the abuses of government. But what is government itself but the greatest of all reflections on human nature? If men were angels, no government would be necessary. If angels were to govern men, neither external nor internal controls on government would be necessary. In framing a government which is to be administered by men over men, the great difficulty lies in this: You must first enable the government to control the governed; and in the next place oblige it to control itself. A dependence on the people is, no doubt, the primary control on the government; but experience has taught mankind the necessity of auxiliary precautions.

This policy of supplying, by opposite and rival interests, the defect of better motives, might be traced through the whole system of human affairs, private as well as public. We see it particularly displayed in all the subordinate distributions of power, where the constant aim is to divide and arrange the several offices in such a manner as that each may be a check on the other; that the private interest of every individual may be a sentinel over the public rights. These inventions of prudence cannot be less requisite in the distribution of the supreme powers of the State.

But it is not possible to give to each department an equal power of self-defense. In republican government, the legislative authority necessarily predominates. The remedy for this inconveniency is to divide the legislature into different branches; and to render them, by different modes of election and different principles of action, as little connected with each other as the nature of their common functions and their common dependence on the society will admit. It may even be necessary to guard against dangerous encroachments by still further precautions. As the weight of the legislative authority requires that it should be thus divided, the weakness of the executive may require, on the other hand, that it should be fortified. An absolute negative on the legislature appears, at first view, to be the natural defense with which the executive magistrate should be armed. But perhaps it would be neither altogether safe nor alone sufficient. On ordinary occasions it might not be exerted with the requisite firmness, and on extraordinary occasions it might be perfidiously abused. May not this defect of an absolute negative be supplied by some qualified connection between this weaker branch of the stronger department, by which the latter may be led to support the constitutional rights of the former, without being too much detached from the rights of its own department?

If the principles on which these observations are founded be just, as I persuade myself they are, and they be applied as a criterion to the several State constitutions, and to the federal Constitution, it will be found that if the latter does not perfectly correspond with them, the former are infinitely less able to bear such a test.

There are, moreover, two considerations particularly applicable to the federal system of America, which place that system in a very interesting point of view.

First. In a single republic, all the power surrendered by the people is submitted to the administration of a single government; and usurpations are guarded against by a division of the government into distinct and separate departments. In the compound republic of America, the power surrendered by the people is first divided between two distinct governments, and then the portion allotted to each subdivided among distinct and separate departments. Hence a double security arises to the rights of the people. The different governments will control each other, at the same time that each will be controlled by itself.

Second. It is of great importance in a republic not only to guard the society against the oppression of its rulers, but to guard one part of the society against the injustice of the other part. Different interests necessarily exist in different classes of citizens. If a majority be united by a common interest, the rights of the minority will be insecure. There are but two methods of providing against this evil: The one by creating a will in the community independent of the majority—that is, of the society itself; the other, by comprehending in the society so many separate descriptions of citizens as will render an unjust combination of a majority of the whole very improbable, if not impracticable. The first method prevails in all governments possessing an hereditary or self-appointed authority. This, at best, is but a precarious security; because a power independent of the society may as well espouse the unjust views of the major as the rightful interests of the minor party, and may possibly be turned against both parties. The second method will be exemplified in the federal republic of the United States. Whilst all authority in it will be derived from and dependent on the society, the society itself will be broken into so many parts, interests and classes of citizens, that the rights of individuals, or of the minority, will be in little danger from interested combinations of the majority. In a free gov-

ernment the security for civil rights must be the same as that for religious rights. It consists in the one case in the multiplicity of interests, and in the other in the multiplicity of sects. The degree of security in both cases will depend on the number of interests and sects; and this may be presumed to depend on the extent of country and number of people comprehended under the same government. This view of the subject must particularly recommend a proper federal system to all the sincere and considerate friends of republican government: Since it shows that in exact proportion as the territory of the Union may be formed into more circumscribed Confederacies, or States, oppressive combinations of a majority will be facilitated; the best security, under the republican form, for the rights of every class of citizens, will be diminished; and consequently the stability and independence of some member of the government, the only other security, must be proportionally increased. Justice is the end of government. It is the end of civil society. It ever has been and ever will be pursued until it be obtained, or until liberty be lost in the pursuit. In a society under the forms of which the stronger faction can readily unite and oppress the weaker, anarchy may as truly be said to reign as in a state of nature, where the weaker individual is not secured against the violence of the stronger: And as, in the latter state, even the stronger individuals are prompted, by the uncertainty of their condition, to submit to a government which may protect the weak as well as themselves: So, in the former state, will the more powerful factions or parties be gradually induced, by a like motive, to wish for a government which will protect all parties, the weaker as well as the more powerful. It can be little doubted that if the State of Rhode Island was separated from the Confederacy and left to itself, the insecurity of rights under the popular form of government within such narrow limits would be displayed by such reiterated oppressions of factious majorities that some power altogether independent of the people would soon be called for by the voice of the very factions whose misrule had proved the necessity of it. In the extended republic of the United States, and among the great variety of interests, parties, and sects which it embraces, a coalition of a majority of the whole society could seldom take place on any other principles than those of justice and the general good; and there being thus less danger to a minor from the will of the major party, there must be less pretext, also, to provide for the security of the former, by introducing into the government a will not dependent on the latter, or, in other words, a will independent of the society itself. It is no less certain than it is important, notwithstanding the contrary opinions which have been entertained, that the larger the society, provided it lie within a practicable sphere, the more duly capable it will be of self-government. And happily for the *republican cause,* the practicable sphere may be carried to a very great extent by a judicious modification and mixture of the *federal principle.*

PUBLIUS

PRESIDENTS AND VICE PRESIDENTS

President	Vice President	President	Vice President
1 George Washington (Federalist 1789)	John Adams (Federalist 1789)	16 Abraham Lincoln (Republican 1861)	Hannibal Hamlin (Republican 1861) Andrew Johnson (Unionist 1865)
2 John Adams (Federalist 1797)	Thomas Jefferson (Dem.-Rep. 1797)	17 Andrew Johnson (Unionist 1865)	
3 Thomas Jefferson (Dem.-Rep. 1801)	Aaron Burr (Dem.-Rep. 1801) George Clinton (Dem.-Rep. 1805)	18 Ulysses S. Grant (Republican 1869)	Schuyler Colfax (Republican 1869) Henry Wilson (Republican 1873)
4 James Madison (Dem.-Rep. 1809)	George Clinton (Dem.-Rep. 1809) Elbridge Gerry (Dem.-Rep. 1813)	19 Rutherford B. Hayes (Republican 1877)	William A. Wheeler (Republican 1877)
5 James Monroe (Dem.-Rep. 1817)	Daniel D. Tompkins (Dem.-Rep. 1817)	20 James A. Garfield (Republican 1881)	Chester A. Arthur (Republican 1881)
6 John Quincy Adams (Dem.-Rep. 1825)	John C. Calhoun (Dem.-Rep. 1825)	21 Chester A. Arthur (Republican 1881)	
7 Andrew Jackson (Democratic 1829)	John C. Calhoun (Democratic 1829) Martin Van Buren (Democratic 1833)	22 Grover Cleveland (Democratic 1885)	Thomas A. Hendricks (Democratic 1885)
8 Martin Van Buren (Democratic 1837)	Richard M. Johnson (Democratic 1837)	23 Benjamin Harrison (Republican 1889)	Levi P. Morton (Republican 1889)
9 William H. Harrison (Whig 1841)	John Tyler (Whig 1841)	24 Grover Cleveland (Democratic 1893)	Adlai E. Stevenson (Democratic 1893)
10 John Tyler (Whig and Democratic 1841)		25 William McKinley (Republican 1897)	Garret A. Hobart (Republican 1897) Theodore Roosevelt (Republican 1901)
11 James K. Polk (Democratic 1845)	George M. Dallas (Democratic 1845)	26 Theodore Roosevelt (Republican 1901)	Charles W. Fairbanks (Republican 1905)
12 Zachary Taylor (Whig 1849)	Millard Fillmore (Whig 1849)	27 William H. Taft (Republican 1909)	James S. Sherman (Republican 1909)
13 Millard Fillmore (Whig 1850)		28 Woodrow Wilson (Democratic 1913)	Thomas R. Marshall (Democratic 1913)
14 Franklin Pierce (Democratic 1853)	William R. D. King (Democratic 1853)	29 Warren G. Harding (Republican 1921)	Calvin Coolidge (Republican 1921)
15 James Buchanan (Democratic 1857)	John C. Breckinridge (Democratic 1857)	30 Calvin Coolidge (Republican 1923)	Charles G. Dawes (Republican 1925)

President	Vice President	President	Vice President
31 Herbert Hoover (Republican 1929)	Charles Curtis (Republican 1929)	37 Richard M. Nixon (Republican 1969)	Spiro T. Agnew (Republican 1969) Gerald R. Ford (Republican 1973)
32 Franklin D. Roosevelt (Democratic 1933)	John Nance Garner (Democratic 1933) Henry A. Wallace (Democratic 1941) Harry S. Truman (Democratic 1945)	38 Gerald R. Ford (Republican 1974)	Nelson Rockefeller (Republican 1974)
		39 James E. Carter (Democratic 1977)	Walter Mondale (Democratic 1977)
33 Harry S. Truman (Democratic 1945)	Alben W. Barkley (Democratic 1949)	40 Ronald Reagan (Republican 1981)	George H. W. Bush (Republican 1981)
34 Dwight D. Eisenhower (Republican 1953)	Richard M. Nixon (Republican 1953)	41 George H. W. Bush (Republican 1989)	J. Danforth Quayle (Republican 1989)
35 John F. Kennedy (Democratic 1961)	Lyndon B. Johnson (Democratic 1961)	42 William J. Clinton (Democrat 1993)	Albert Gore, Jr. (Democrat 1993)
36 Lyndon B. Johnson (Democratic 1963)	Hubert H. Humphrey (Democratic 1965)	43 George W. Bush (Republican 2001)	Richard Cheney (Republican 2001)

GLOSSARY

access the actual involvement of interest groups in the decision-making process

administrative adjudication applying rules and precedents to specific cases to settle disputes with regulated parties

administrative regulation rules made by regulatory agencies and commissions

affirmative action government policies or programs that seek to redress past injustices against specified groups by making special efforts to provide members of these groups with access to educational and employment opportunities

agencies of socialization social institutions, including families and schools, that help to shape individuals' basic political beliefs and values

agency representation the type of representation by which representatives are held accountable to their constituency if they fail to represent that constituency properly. This is the incentive for good representation when the personal backgrounds, views, and interests of the representative differ from those of his or her constituency

agenda setting the power of the media to bring public attention to particular issues and problems

Aid to Families with Dependent Children (AFDC) federal funds, administered by the states, for children living with parents or relatives who fall below state standards of need. Replaced in 1996 by TANF

amendment a change added to a bill, law, or constitution

American political community citizens who are eligible to vote and participate in American political life

amicus curiae literally, "friend of the court"; individuals or groups who are not parties to a lawsuit but who seek to assist the Supreme Court in reaching a decision by presenting additional briefs

Antifederalists those who favored strong state governments and a weak national government and who were opponents of the constitution proposed at the American Constitutional Convention of 1787

antitrust policy government regulation of large businesses that have established monopolies

appellate court a court that hears the appeals of trial court decisions

appropriations the amounts of money approved by Congress in statutes (bills) that each unit or agency of government can spend

Articles of Confederation America's first written constitution; served as the basis for America's national government until 1789

attitude (or opinion) a specific preference on a particular issue

authoritarian government a system of rule in which the government recognizes no formal limits but may nevertheless be restrained by the power of other social institutions

autocracy a form of government in which a single individual—a king, queen, or dictator—rules

balance-of-power role the strategy whereby many countries from alliances with one or more other countries in order to counterbalance the behavior of other, usually more powerful, nation-states

bandwagon effect a shift in electoral support to the candidate that public opinion polls report as the front-runner

benign gerrymandering attempts to draw district boundaries so as to create districts made up primarily of disadvantaged or underrepresented minorities

bicameral having a legislative assembly composed of two chambers or houses; opposite of unicameral

bilateral treaties treaties made between two nations

bill a proposed law that has been sponsored by a member of Congress and submitted to the clerk of the House or Senate

Bill of Rights the first ten amendments to the Constitution, which guarantee certain rights and liberties to the people

bills of attainder laws that decree a person guilty of a crime without a trial

block grants federal grants-in-aid that allow states considerable discretion in how the funds are spent

briefs written documents in which attorneys explain, using case precedents, why the court should find in favor of their client

Brown v. Board of Education the 1954 Supreme Court decision that struck down the "separate but equal" doctrine as fundamentally unequal. This case eliminated state power to use race as a criterion of discrimination in law and provided the national government with the power to intervene by exercising strict regulatory policies against discriminatory actions

budget deficit   amount by which government spending exceeds government revenue in a fiscal year

bureaucracy   the complex structure of offices, tasks, rules, and principles of organization that are employed by all large-scale institutions to coordinate effectively the work of their personnel

Bush doctrine   foreign policy based on the idea that the United States should take preemptive action against threats to its national security

Cabinet   the secretaries, or chief administrators, of the major departments of the federal government. Cabinet secretaries are appointed by the president with the consent of the Senate

campaign   an effort by political candidates and their staffs to win the backing of donors, political activists, and voters in the quest for political office

capture   an interest's acquisition of substantial influence over the government agency charged with regulating its activities

categorical grants   congressional grants given to states and localities on the condition that expenditures be limited to a problem or group specified by law

caucus (congressional)   an association of members of Congress based on party, interest, or social group such as gender or race

caucus (political)   a normally closed meeting of a political or legislative group to select candidates, plan strategy, or make decisions regarding legislative matters

checks and balances   mechanisms through which each branch of government is able to participate in and influence the activities of the other branches. Major examples include the presidential veto power over congressional legislation, the power of the Senate to approve presidential appointments, and judicial review of congressional enactments

chief justice   justice on the Supreme Court who presides over the Court's public sessions

citizenship   informed and active membership in a political community

civic engagement   a sense of concern among members of the political community about public, social, and political life, expressed through participation in social and political organizations

civil law   a system of jurisprudence, including private law and governmental actions, to settle disputes that do not involve criminal penalties

civil liberties   areas of personal freedom with which governments are constrained from interfering

civil penalties   regulatory techniques in which fines or another form of material restitution is imposed for violating civil laws or common law principles, for example through negligence

civil rights   obligation imposed on government to take positive action to protect citizens from any illegal action of government agencies as well as from other private citizens

class action suit   a legal action by which a group or class of individuals with common interests can file a suit on behalf of everyone who shares that interest

"clear and present danger" test   test to determine whether speech is protected or unprotected, based on its capacity to present a "clear and present danger" to society

closed caucus   a presidential nominating caucus open only to registered party members

closed primary   a primary election in which voters can participate in the nomination of candidates, but only of the party in which they are enrolled for a period of time prior to primary day

closed rule   a provision by the House Rules Committee limiting or prohibiting the introduction of amendments during debate

cloture   a rule allowing a majority of two-thirds or three-fifths of the members in a legislative body to set a time limit on debate over a given bill

coalition   a group in interests that join together for the purpose of influencing government

coattail effect   the result of voters casting their ballot for president or governor and "automatically" voting for the remainder of the party's ticket

Cold War   the period of struggle between the United States and the former Soviet Union between the late 1940s and about 1990

collective goods   benefits, sought by groups, that are broadly available and cannot be denied to nonmembers

commander in chief   the power of the president as commander of the national military and the state national guard units (when called into service)

commerce clause   Article I, Section 8, of the Constitution, which delegates to Congress the power "to regulate commerce with foreign nations, and among the several States and with the Indian tribes." This clause was interpreted by the Supreme Court in favor of national power over the economy

committee markup   session in which a congressional committee rewrites legislation to incorporate changes discussed during hearings on the bill.

concurrent powers   authority possessed by both state and national governments, such as the power to levy taxes

confederation   a system of government in which states retain sovereign authority except for the powers expressly delegated to the national government

conference a gathering of House Republicans every two years to elect their House leaders. Democrats call their gathering the caucus

conference committee a joint committee created to work out a compromise on House and Senate versions of a piece of legislation

conservative today this term refers to those who generally support the social and economic status quo and are suspicious of efforts to introduce new political formulae and economic arrangements. Conservatives believe that a large and powerful government poses a threat to citizens' freedom

constituency the district comprising the area from which an official is elected

constitutional government a system of rule in which formal and effective limits are placed on the powers of the government

containment the policy used by the United States during the cold war to restrict the expansion of communism and limit the influence of the Soviet Union

contracting power the power of government to set conditions on companies seeking to sell goods or services to government agencies

contributory programs social programs financed in whole or in part by taxation or other mandatory contributions by their present or future recipients. The most important example is Social Security, which is financed by a payroll tax

cooperative federalism a type of federalism existing since the New Deal era in which grants-in-aid have been used strategically to encourage states and localities (without commanding them) to pursue nationally defined goals. Also known as intergovernmental cooperation

cost-of-living adjustments (COLAs) changes made to the level of benefits of a government program based on the rate of inflation

criminal law the branch of law that deals with disputes or actions involving criminal penalties (as opposed to civil law); it regulates the conduct of individuals, defines crimes, and provides punishment for criminal acts

criminal penalties regulatory techniques in which imprisonment or heavy fines and the loss of certain civil rights and liberties are imposed

dealignment large-scale weakening of partisan ties in the electorate

de facto literally, "by fact"; practices that occur even when there is no legal enforcement, such as school segregation in much of the United States today

de jure literally, "by law"; legally enforced practices, such as school segregation in the South before the 1960s

defendant the one against whom a complaint is brought in a criminal or civil case

delegate the role of a representative who votes according to the preferences of his or her constituency

delegated powers constitutional powers that are assigned to one governmental agency but that are exercised by another agency with the express permission of the first

delegates political activists selected to vote at a party's national convention

democracy a system of rule that permits citizens to play a significant part in the governmental process, usually through the election of key public officials

department the largest subunit of the executive branch. The secretaries of the fourteen departments form the Cabinet

deregulation a policy of reducing or eliminating regulatory restraints on the conduct of individuals or private institutions

deterrence the development and maintenance of military strength as a means of discouraging attack

devolution a policy to remove a program from one level of government by delegating it or passing it down to a lower level of government, such as from the national government to the state and local governments

diplomacy the representation of a government to other foreign governments

direct action politics a form of politics, such as civil disobedience or revolutionary action, that takes place outside formal channels

direct democracy a system of rule that permits citizens to vote directly on laws and policies

discount rate the interest rate charged by the Federal Reserve System when commercial banks borrow in order to expand their lending operations; an effective tool of monetary policy

discretionary spending federal spending on programs that are controlled through the regular budget process

discrimination use of any unreasonable and unjust criterion of exclusion

dissenting opinion a decision written by a justice in the minority in a particular case in which the justice wishes to express his or her reasoning in the case

divided government the condition in American government wherein the presidency is controlled by one party while the opposing party controls one or both houses of Congress

double jeopardy the Fifth Amendment right providing that a person cannot be tried twice for the same crime

dual federalism the system of government that prevailed in the United States from 1789 to 1937, in which most fundamental governmental powers were shared between the federal and state governments

due process of law the right of every citizen against arbitrary action by national or state governments

economic expansionist role   the strategy often pursued by capitalist countries to adopt foreign policies that will maximize the success of domestic corporations in their dealings with other countries

elastic clause   Article I, Section 8, of the Constitution (also known as the necessary and proper clause), which enumerates the powers of Congress and provides Congress with the authority to make all laws "necessary and proper" to carry them out

electoral college   the presidential electors from each state who meet after the popular election to cast ballots for president and vice president

electoral realignment   the point in history when a new party supplants the ruling party, becoming in turn the dominant political force. In the United States, this has tended to occur roughly every thirty years

eminent domain   the right of government to take private property for public use

entitlement   eligibility for benefits by virtue of a category of benefits defined by legislation

equal protection clause   provision of the Fourteenth Amendment guaranteeing citizens "the equal protection of the laws." This clause has served as the basis for the civil rights of African Americans, women, and other groups

equal time rule   the requirement that broadcasters provide candidates for the same political office an equal opportunity to communicate their messages to the public

equality of opportunity   a widely shared American ideal that all people should have the freedom to use whatever talents and wealth they have to reach their fullest potential

establishment clause   the First Amendment clause that says that "Congress shall make no law respecting an establishment of religion." This law means that a "wall of separation" exists between church and state

ex post facto laws   laws that declare an action to be illegal after it has been committed

exclusionary rule   the ability of courts to exclude evidence obtained in violation of the Fourth Amendment

executive agreement   an agreement, made between the president and another country, that has the force of a treaty but does not require the Senate's "advice and consent"

Executive Office of the President   the permanent agencies that perform defined management tasks for the president. Created in 1939, the EOP includes the Office of Management and Budget, the Council of Economic Advisers, the National Security Council, and other agencies

executive order   a rule or regulation issued by the president that has the effect and formal status of legislation

executive privilege   power that presidents assert in order to protect the executive branch from Congress and the judiciary. Executive privilege allows presidents to refuse some requests for information from Congress or the judiciary. Justified on the basis of the separation of powers, not the

Constitution, executive privilege is subject to limitation by the courts.

expressed powers   specific powers granted to Congress under Article I, Section 8, of the Constitution

expropriation   confiscation of property with or without compensation

fairness doctrine   a Federal Communications Commission (FCC) requirement for broadcasters who air programs on controversial issues to provide time for opposing views. The FCC ceased enforcing this doctrine in 1985

federal funds rate   the interest rate on loans between banks that the Federal Reserve Board influences by affecting the supply of money available

Federal Reserve Board (Fed) the governing board of the Federal Reserve System, comprising a chair and six other members, all appointed by the president with the consent of the Senate

Federal Reserve System   a system of twelve Federal Reserve Banks that facilitates exchanges of cash, checks, and credit; regulates member banks; and uses monetary policies to fight inflation and deflation

federal system   a system of government in which the national government shares power with lower levels of government, such as states

federalism   a system of government in which power is divided, by a constitution, between a central government and regional governments

Federalist Papers   a series of essays written by James Madison, Alexander Hamilton, and John Jay supporting the ratification of the Constitution

Federalists   those who favored a strong national government and supported the constitution proposed at the American Constitutional Convention of 1787

Fifteenth Amendment   one of three Civil War amendments; guaranteed voting rights for African American men

fighting words   speech that directly incites damaging conduct

filibuster   a tactic used by members of the Senate to prevent action on legislation they oppose by continuously holding the floor and speaking until the majority backs down. Once given the floor, senators have unlimited time to speak, and it requires a vote of three-fifths of the Senate to end a filibuster

fiscal policy   the use of taxing, monetary, and spending powers to manipulate the economy

527 Committees   nonprofit independent groups that receive and disburse funds to influence the nomination, election, or defeat of candidates. Named after Section 527 of the Internal Revenue Code, which defines and provides tax-exempt status for nonprofit advocacy groups

food stamps   coupons that can be exchanged for food at most grocery stores; the largest in-kind benefits program

formula grants   grants-in-aid in which a formula is used to determine the amount of federal funds a state or local government will receive

Fourteenth Amendment one of three Civil War amendments; guaranteed equal protection and due process

framing the power of the media to influence how events and issues are interpreted

free exercise clause the First Amendment clause that protects a citizen's right to believe and practice whatever religion he or she chooses

free riders those who enjoy the benefits of collective goods but did not participate in acquiring them

full faith and credit clause provision from Article IV, Section 1 of the Constitution, requiring that the states normally honor the public acts and judicial decisions that take place in another state

gender gap a distinctive pattern of voting behavior reflecting the differences in views between women and men

General Agreement on Tariffs and Trade (GATT) international trade organization, in existence from 1947 to 1995, that set many of the rules governing international trade

general revenue sharing the process by which one unit of government yields a portion of its tax income to another unit of government, according to an established formula. Revenue sharing typically involves the national government providing money to state governments

gerrymandering apportionment of voters in districts in such a way as to give unfair advantage to one racial or ethnic group or political party

going public a strategy that attempts to mobilize the widest and most favorable climate of public opinion

government institutions and procedures through which a territory and its people are ruled

government corporation a government agency that performs a service normally provided by the private sector

grand jury jury that determines whether sufficient evidence is available to justify a trial; grand juries do not rule on the accused's guilt or innocence

grants-in-aid programs through which Congress provides money to state and local governments on the condition that the funds be employed for purposes defined by the federal government

grassroots mobilization a lobbying campaign in which a group mobilizes its membership to contact government officials in support of the group's position

Great Compromise the agreement reached at the Constitutional Convention of 1787 that gave each state an equal number of senators regardless of its population, but linked representation in the House of Representatives to population

Gross Domestic Product (GDP) index of the total output of goods and services produced in the economy

habeas corpus a court order demanding that an individual in custody be brought into court and shown the cause for detention

Holy Alliance role a strategy pursued by a superpower to prevent any change in the existing distribution of power among nation-states, even if this requires intervention into the international affairs of another country in order to keep a ruler from being overturned

home rule power delegated by the state to a local unit of government to manage its own affairs

"horse race" coverage news coverage emphasizing changes in the candidates' poll standings rather than the issues or positions they espouse

illusion of saliency the impression conveyed by polls that something is important to the public when actually it is not

impeachment the formal charge by the House of Representatives that a government official has committed "Treason, Bribery, or other high Crimes and Misdemeanors"

implementation the efforts of departments and agencies to translate laws into specific bureaucratic routines

implied powers powers derived from the "necessary and proper" clause of Article I, Section 8, of the Constitution. Such powers are not specifically expressed, but are implied through the expansive interpretation of delegated powers

in-kind benefits noncash goods and services provided to needy individuals and families by the federal government

incumbency holding a political office for which one is running

incumbent a candidate running for a position that he or she already holds

independent agency an agency that is not part of a Cabinet department

independent counsel an official appointed to investigate criminal misconduct by members of the executive branch

indexing periodic process of adjusting social benefits or wages to account for increases in the cost of living

inflation a consistent increase in the general level of prices

infomercial a lengthy campaign advertisement on television

informational benefits special newsletters, periodicals, training programs, conferences, and other information provided to members of groups to entice others to join

inherent powers powers claimed by a president that are not expressed in the Constitution, but are inferred from it

institutional advertising advertising designed to create a positive image of an organization

interest group individuals who organize to influence the government's programs and policies

intermediate scrutiny test, used by the Supreme Court in gender discrimination cases, which places the burden of proof partially on the government and partially on the challengers to show that the law in question is constitutional

International Monetary Fund (IMF) an institution established in 1944 that provides loans and facilitates international monetary exchange

investigative journalism   news coverage aimed at ferreting out the facts beneath the claims of public officials and politicians

iron triangle   the stable, cooperative relationships that often develop between a congressional committee, an administrative agency, and one or more supportive interest groups. Not all of these relationships are triangular, but the iron triangle is the most typical

issue network   a loose network of elected leaders, public officials, activists, and interest groups drawn together by a specific policy issue

issue advocacy   independent spending by individuals or interest groups on a campaign issue but not directly tied to a particular candidate

Jim Crow   laws enacted by southern states following reconstruction that discriminated against African Americans

joint committee   a legislative committee formed of members of both the House and the Senate

judicial activism   judicial philosophy that posits that the Court should go beyond the words of the Constitution or a statute to consider the broader societal implications of its decisions

judicial restraint   judicial philosophy whose adherents refuse to go beyond the clear words of the Constitution in interpreting its meaning

judicial review   the power of the courts to declare actions of the legislative and executive branches invalid or unconstitutional. The Supreme Court asserted this power in *Marbury v. Madison*

jurisdiction   the sphere of a court's power and authority

Keynesianism   economic theory, based on the ideas of British economist John Maynard Keynes, that argues that the government can stimulate the economy by increasing public spending or by cutting taxes

Kitchen Cabinet   an informal group of advisers to whom the president turns for counsel and guidance. Members of the official Cabinet may or may not also be members of the Kitchen Cabinet

laissez-faire capitalism   an economic system in which the means of production and distribution are privately owned and operated for profit with minimal or no government interference

legislative initiative   the president's inherent power to bring a legislative agenda before Congress

***Lemon* test**   a rule articulated in *Lemon v. Kurtzman* that government action toward religion is permissible if it is secular in purpose, does not lead to "excessive entanglement" with religion, and neither promotes nor inhibits the practice of religion

libel   a written statement made in "reckless disregard of the truth" that is considered damaging to a victim because it is "malicious, scandalous, and defamatory"

liberal   today this term refers to those who generally support social and political reform; extensive governmental intervention in the economy; the expansion of federal social services; more vigorous efforts on behalf of the poor, minorities, and women; and greater concern for consumers and the environment

libertarian   the political philosophy that is skeptical of any government intervention as a potential threat against individual liberty; one who favors minimal government and maximum individual liberty

liberty   freedom from governmental control

license   permission to engage in some activity that is otherwise illegal, such as hunting or practicing medicine

limited government   a principle of constitutional government; a government whose powers are defined and limited by a constitution

line-item veto   the power of the executive to veto specific provisions (lines) of a bill passed by the legislature

litigation   a lawsuit or legal proceeding; as a form of political participation, an attempt to seek relief in a court of law

lobbying   a strategy by which organized interests seek to influence the passage of legislation by exerting direct pressure on members of the legislature

logrolling   a legislative practice wherein agreements are made between legislators in voting for or against a bill. Unlike bargaining, parties to logrolling have nothing in common but their desire to exchange support

loophole   incentive to individuals and businesses to reduce their tax liabilities by investing their money in areas that the government designates

machines   strong party organizations in late-nineteenth- and early-twentieth-century American cities. These machines were led by "bosses" who controlled party nominations and patronage

majority leader   the elected leader of the majority party in the House of Representatives or in the Senate. In the House, the majority leader is subordinate in the party hierarchy to the Speaker of the House

majority party   the party that holds the majority of legislative seats in either the House or the Senate

majority rule/minority rights   the democratic principle that a government follows the preferences of the majority of voters but protects the interests of the minority

majority system   a type of electoral system in which, to win a seat in the parliament or other representative body, a candidate must receive a majority of all the votes cast in the relevant district

mandate   a claim by a victorious candidate that the electorate has given him or her special authority to carry out promises made during the campaign

mandatory spending   federal spending that is made up of "uncontrollables," budget items that cannot be controlled through the regular budget process

marketplace of ideas   the public forum in which beliefs and ideas are exchanged and compete

Marshall Plan   the U.S. European Recovery Plan, in which over $34 billion was spent for the relief, reconstruction, and economic recovery of Western Europe after World War II

material benefits   special goods, services, or money provided to members of groups to entice others to join

means testing   a procedure by which potential beneficiaries of a public assistance program establish their eligibility by demonstrating a genuine need for the assistance

measurement error   failure to identify the true distribution of opinion within a population because of errors such as ambiguous or poorly worded questions

media momentum   news coverage suggesting that a candidate is rapidly gaining public support

media monopoly   control of multiple sources of news and information by a small number of news agencies

Medicaid   a federally financed, state-operated program providing medical services to low-income people

Medicare   a form of national health insurance for the elderly and the disabled

membership association   an organized group in which members actually play a substantial role, sitting on committees and engaging in group projects

merit system   a product of civil service reform, in which appointees to positions in public bureaucracies must objectively be deemed qualified for the position

midterm elections   congressional elections that do not coincide with a presidential election; also called off-year elections

minority district   a gerrymandered voting district that improves the chances of minority candidates by making selected minority groups the majority within the district

minority leader   the elected leader of the minority party in the House or Senate

minority party   the party that holds a minority of legislative seats in either the House or the Senate

***Miranda* rule**   the requirement, articulated by the Supreme Court in *Miranda v. Arizona*, that persons under arrest must be informed prior to police interrogation of their rights to remain silent and to have the benefit of legal counsel

mobilization   the process by which large numbers of people are organized for a political activity

monetarism   economic theory that contends that the role of the government in the economy should be limited to regulating the supply of money

monetary policies   efforts to regulate the economy through manipulation of the supply of money and credit. America's most powerful institution in the area of monetary policy is the Federal Reserve Board

monopoly   the existence of a single firm in a market that controls all the goods and services of that market; absence of competition

mootness   a criterion used by courts to screen cases that no longer require resolution

most favored nation status   agreement to offer a trading partner the lowest tariff rate offered to other trading partners

multilateralism   a foreign policy that seeks to encourage the involvement of several nation-states in coordinated action, usually in relation to a common adversary, with terms and conditions usually specified in a multicountry treaty

multiple-member district   an electorate that selects all candidates at large from the whole district; each voter is given the number of votes equivalent to the number of seats to be filled

Napoleonic role   a strategy pursued by a powerful nation to prevent aggressive actions against themselves by improving the internal state of affairs of a particular country, even if this means encouraging revolution in that country

nation-state   a political entity consisting of a people with some common cultural experience (nation) who also share a common political authority (state), recognized by other sovereignties (nation-states)

national convention   a national party political institution that serves to nominate the party's presidential and vice presidential candidates, establish party rules, and write and ratify the party's platform

National Security Council (NSC)   a presidential foreign-policy advisory council composed of the president; the vice president; the secretaries of state, defense, and the treasury; the attorney general; and other officials invited by the president

necessary and proper clause   from Article I, Section 8 of the Constitution, it provides Congress with the authority to make all laws "necessary and proper" to carry out its expressed powers

New Federalism   attempts by Presidents Nixon and Reagan to return power to the states through block grants

New Jersey Plan   a framework for the Constitution, introduced by William Paterson, which called for equal state representation in the national legislature regardless of population

New Politics movement   a political movement that began in the 1960s and 1970s, made up of professionals and intellectuals for whom the civil rights and antiwar movements were formative experiences. The New Politics movement strengthened public-interest groups

news enclave   a group seeking specialized information not provided by the mainstream media

nomination   the process through which political parties select their candidates for election to public office

noncontributory programs   social programs that provide assistance to people based on demonstrated need rather than any contribution they have made

North American Free Trade Agreement (NAFTA)   trade treaty between the United States, Canada, and Mexico to lower and eliminate tariffs among the three countries

North Atlantic Treaty Organization (NATO) a treaty organization, comprising the United States, Canada, and most of western Europe, formed in 1948 to counter the perceived threat from the Soviet Union

oligarchy   a form of government in which a small group—landowners, military officers, or wealthy merchants—controls most of the governing decisions

open caucus   a presidential nominating caucus open to anyone who wishes to attend

open market operations   method by which the Open Market Committee of the Federal Reserve System buys and sells government securities, etc., to help finance government operations and to loosen or tighten the total amount of money circulating in the economy

open primary   a primary election in which the voter can wait until the day of the primary to choose which party to enroll in to select candidates for the general election

open rule   a provision by the House Rules Committee that permits floor debate and the addition of new amendments to a bill

opinion   the written explanation of the Supreme Court's decision in a particular case

oral argument   stage in Supreme Court procedure in which attorneys for both sides appear before the Court to present their positions and answer questions posed by justices

original jurisdiction   the authority to initially consider a case. Distinguished from appellate jurisdiction, which is the authority to hear appeals from a lower court's decision

oversight   the effort by Congress, through hearings, investigations, and other techniques, to exercise control over the activities of executive agencies

party activists   partisans who contribute time, energy, and effort to support their party and its candidates

party identification   an individual voter's psychological ties to one party or another

party organization   the formal structure of a political party, including its leadership, election committees, active members, and paid staff

party vote   a roll-call vote in the House or Senate in which at least 50 percent of the members of one party take a particular position and are opposed by at least 50 percent of the members of the other party. Party votes are rare today, although they were fairly common in the nineteenth century

patronage   the resources available to higher officials, usually opportunities to make partisan appointments to offices and to confer grants, licenses, or special favors to supporters

per curiam   decision by an appellate court, without a written opinion, that refuses to review the decision of a lower court; amounts to a reaffirmation of the lower court's opinion

permanent campaign   description of presidential politics in which all presidential actions are taken with reelection in mind

plaintiff   the individual or organization who brings a complaint in court

platform   a party document, written at a national convention, that contains party philosophy, principles, and positions on issues

plea bargains   negotiated agreements in criminal cases in which a defendant agrees to plead guilty in return for the state's agreement to reduce the severity of the criminal charge the defendant is facing

pluralism   the theory that all interests are and should be free to compete for influence in the government. The outcome of this competition is compromise and moderation

plurality system   a type of electoral system in which, to win a seat in the parliament or other representative body, a candidate need only receive the most votes in the election, not necessarily a majority of the votes cast

pocket veto   a presidential veto that is automatically triggered if the president does not act on a given piece of legislation passed during the final ten days of a legislative session

police power   power reserved to the government to regulate the health, safety, and morals of its citizens

policy entrepreneur   an individual who identifies a problem as a political issue and brings a policy proposal into the political agenda

policy of redistribution   a policy whose objective is to tax or spend in such a way as to reduce the disparities of wealth between the lowest and the highest income brackets

political action committee (PAC) a private group that raises and distributes funds for use in election campaigns

political culture   broadly shared values, beliefs, and attitudes about how the government should function. American political culture emphasizes the values of liberty, equality, and democracy

political efficacy   the ability to influence government and politics

political equality   the right to participate in politics equally, based on the principle of "one person, one vote"

political ideology   a cohesive set of beliefs that forms a general philosophy about the role of government

political institution   an organization that connects people to politics, such as a political party, or a governmental organization, such as the Congress or the courts

political machines   local party organizations that controlled local politics in the late nineteenth and early twentieth centuries through patronage and control of nominations

political participation   political activities, such as voting, contacting political officials, volunteering for a campaign, or participating in a protest, whose purpose is to influence government

political parties   organized groups that attempt to influence the government by electing their members to important government offices

political socialization   the induction of individuals into the political culture; learning the underlying beliefs and values that the political system is based on

politics   conflict over the leadership, structure, and policies of governments

poll tax   a state-imposed tax upon voters as a prerequisite for registration. Poll taxes were rendered unconstitutional in national elections by the Twenty-fourth Amendment, and in state elections by the Supreme Court in 1966

popular sovereignty   a principle of democracy in which political authority rests ultimately in the hands of the people

pork barrel   appropriations made by legislative bodies for local projects that are often not needed but that are created so that local representatives can win re-election in their home districts

power   influence over a government's leadership, organization, or policies

precedents   prior cases whose principles are used by judges as the bases for their decisions in present cases

preemption   the principle that allows the national government to override state or local actions in certain policy areas

priming   process of preparing the public to take a particular view of an event or political actor

primary elections   elections used to select a party's candidate for the general election

prior restraint   an effort by a governmental agency to block the publication of material it deems libelous or harmful in some other way; censorship. In the United States, the courts forbid prior restraint except under the most extraordinary circumstances

private bill   a proposal in Congress to provide a specific person with some kind of relief, such as a special exemption from immigration quotas

privatization   removing all or part of a program from the public sector to the private sector

privileges and immunities clause   provision from Article IV, Section 2, of the Constitution, that a state cannot discriminate against someone from another state or give its own residents special privileges

probability sampling   a method used by pollsters to select a representative sample in which every individual in the population has an equal probability of being selected as a respondent

procedural liberties   restraints on how the government is supposed to act; for example, citizens are guaranteed the due process of law

progressive/regressive taxation   taxation that hits the upper income brackets more heavily (progressive) or the lower income brackets more heavily (regressive)

project grants   grant programs in which state and local governments submit proposals to federal agencies and for which funding is provided on a competitive basis

proportional representation   a multiple-member district system that allows each political party representation in proportion to its percentage of the total vote

prospective voting   voting based on the imagined future performance of a candidate

protest   participation that involves assembling crowds to confront a government or other official organization

public goods   goods that are provided by the government because they either are not supplied by the market or are not supplied in sufficient quantities

public interest groups   groups that claim they serve the general good rather than only their own particular interest

public law   cases involving the actions of public agencies or officials.

public opinion   citizens' attitudes about political issues, leaders, institutions, and events

public opinion polls   scientific instruments for measuring public opinion

public policy   a law, rule, statute, or edict that expresses the government's goals and provides for rewards and punishments to promote their attainment

public relations   an attempt, usually through the use of paid consultants, to establish a favorable relationship with the public and influence its political opinions

purposive benefits   selective benefits of group membership that emphasize the purpose and accomplishments of the group

push polling   a polling technique in which the questions are designed to shape the respondent's opinion

rallying effect   the generally favorable reaction of the public to presidential actions taken in foreign policy, or more precisely, to decisions made during international crises

random digit dialing   polls in which respondents are selected at random from a list of ten-digit telephone numbers, with every effort made to avoid bias in the construction of the sample

recall   procedure to allow voters an opportunity to remove state officials from office before their terms expire

redistribution   a policy whose objective is to tax or spend in such a way as to reduce the disparities of wealth between the lowest and the highest income brackets

redistributive programs economic policies designed to control the economy through taxing and spending, with the goal of benefiting the poor

redistricting the process of redrawing election districts and redistributing legislative representatives. This happens every ten years to reflect shifts in population or in response to legal challenges to existing districts

redlining a practice in which banks refuse to make loans to people living in certain geographic locations

referendum the practice of referring a measure proposed or passed by a legislature to the vote of the electorate for approval or rejection

regulated federalism a form of federalism in which Congress imposes legislation on states and localities, requiring them to meet national standards

regulation a technique of control in which the government adopts rules imposing restrictions on the conduct of private citizens

regulatory agencies departments, bureaus, or independent agencies whose primary mission is to impose limits, restrictions, or other obligations on the conduct of individuals or companies in the private sector

regulatory tax a tax whose primary purpose is not to raise revenue but to influence conduct: e.g., a heavy tax on gasoline to discourage recreational driving

representative democracy (or republic) a system of government in which the populace selects representatives, who play a significant role in governmental decision making

reserve requirement the amount of liquid assets and ready cash that banks are required to hold to meet depositors' demands for their money

reserved powers powers, derived from the Tenth Amendment to the Constitution, that are not specifically delegated to the national government or denied to the states

responsible party government a set of principles that idealizes a strong role for parties in defining their stance on issues, mobilizing voters, and fulfilling their campaign promises once in office

retrospective voting voting based on the past performance of a candidate

revenue agencies agencies responsible for collecting taxes. Examples include the Internal Revenue Service for income taxes, the U.S. Customs Service for tariffs and other taxes on imported goods, and the Bureau of Alcohol, Tobacco, and Firearms for collection of taxes on the sales of those particular products

right of rebuttal a Federal Communications Commission regulation giving individuals the right to have the opportunity to respond to personal attacks made on a radio or television broadcast

right to privacy the right to be let alone, which has been interpreted by the Supreme Court to entail free access to birth control and abortions

roll-call vote a vote in which each legislator's yes or no vote is recorded as the clerk calls the names of the members alphabetically

rule making a quasi-legislative administrative process that produces regulations by government agencies

salient interests attitudes and views that are especially important to the individual holding them

sample a small group selected by researchers to represent the most important characteristics of an entire population

sampling error polling error that arises because of the small size of the sample

select committee a (usually) temporary legislative committee set up to highlight or investigate a particular issue or address an issue not within the jurisdiction of existing committees

selection bias polling error that arises when the sample is not representative of the population being studied, which create errors in overrepresenting or underrepresenting some opinions

selective incorporation the process by which different protections in the Bill of Rights were incorporated into the Fourteenth Amendment, thus guaranteeing citizens protection from state as well as national government

senatorial courtesy the practice whereby the president, before formally nominating a person for a federal judgeship, seeks the indication that senators from the candidate's own state support the nomination

seniority priority or status ranking given to an individual on the basis of length of continuous service on a committee in Congress

"separate but equal" rule doctrine that public accommodations could be segregated by race but still be equal

separation of powers the division of governmental power among several institutions that must cooperate in decision making

shadow welfare state social benefits that private employers offer to their workers, such as medical insurance and pensions

single-member district an electorate that is allowed to select only one representative from each district; the normal method of representation in the United States

slander an oral statement, made in "reckless disregard of the truth," which is considered damaging to the victim because it is "malicious, scandalous, and defamatory"

Social Security a contributory welfare program into which working Americans contribute a percentage of their wages, and from which they receive cash benefits after retirement

socioeconomic status status in society based on level of education, income, and occupational prestige

sociological representation a type of representation in which representatives have the same racial, ethnic, religious, or educational backgrounds as their constituents. It is based on the principle that if two individuals are similar in background, character, interests, and perspectives, then one could correctly represent the other's views

soft money money contributed directly to political parties for voter registration and organization

solicitor general the top government lawyer in all cases before the Supreme Court where the government is a party

solidary benefits selective benefits of a group membership that emphasize friendship, networking, and consciousness-raising

sound bites short snippets of information aimed at dramatizing a story rather than explaining its substantive meaning

Speaker of the House the chief presiding officer of the House of Representatives. The Speaker is elected at the beginning of every Congress on a straight party vote. The Speaker is the most important party and House leader, and can influence the legislative agenda, the fate of individual pieces of legislation, and members' positions within the House

speech plus speech accompanied by conduct such as sit-ins, picketing, and demonstrations; protection of this form of speech under the First Amendment is conditional, and restrictions imposed by state or local authorities are acceptable if properly balanced by considerations of public order

split-ticket voting the practice of casting ballots for the candidates of at least two different political parties in the same election

spot advertisement a fifteen-, thirty-, or sixty-second television campaign commercial that permits a candidate's message to be delivered to a target audience

staff agency a legislative support agency responsible for policy analysis

staff organization a type of membership group in which a professional staff conducts most of the group's activities

standing the right of an individual or organization to initiate a court case

standing committee a permanent committee with the power to propose and write legislation that covers a particular subject, such as finance or appropriations

stare decisis literally, "let the decision stand." The doctrine that a previous decision by a court applies as a precedent in similar cases until that decision is overruled

states' rights the principle that the states should oppose the increasing authority of the national government. This principle was most popular in the period before the Civil War

straight-ticket voting the practice of casting ballots for candidates of only one party

strict scrutiny test, used by the Supreme Court in racial discrimination cases and other cases involving civil liberties and civil rights, which places the burden of proof on the government rather than on the challengers to show that the law in question is constitutional

subsidies government grants of cash or other valuable commodities such as land to individuals or organizations; used

to promote activities desired by the government, to reward political support, or to buy off political opposition

substantive liberties restraints on what the government shall and shall not have the power to do

suffrage the right to vote; also called franchise

superdelegate a convention delegate position, in Democratic conventions, reserved for party officials

Supplemental Security Income (SSI) a program providing a minimum monthly income to people who pass a "means test" and who are sixty-five or older, blind, or disabled. Financed from general revenues rather than from Social Security contributions

supremacy clause Article VI of the Constitution, which states that laws passed by the national government and all treaties are the supreme law of the land and superior to all laws adopted by any state or any subdivision

supreme court the highest court in a particular state or in the United States. This court primarily serves an appellate function

tariff a tax on imported goods

tax expenditures government subsidies provided to employers and employees through tax deductions for amounts spent on health insurance and other benefits; these represent one way the government helps to ensure the social welfare of the middle class

Temporary Assistance to Needy Families (TANF) a federal block grant that replaced the AFDC program in 1996

term limits legally prescribed limits on the number of terms an elected official can serve

third parties parties that organize to compete against the two major American political parties

Thirteenth Amendment one of three Civil War amendments; abolished slavery

Three-fifths Compromise the agreement reached at the Constitutional Convention of 1787 that stipulated that for purposes of the apportionment of congressional seats, every slave would be counted as three-fifths of a person

totalitarian government a system of rule in which the government recognizes no formal limits on its power and seeks to absorb or eliminate other social institutions that might challenge it

town meeting a media format in which candidates meet with ordinary citizens. Allows candidates to deliver messages without the presence of journalists or commentators

trial court the first court to hear a criminal or civil case

trustee the role of a representative who votes based on what he or she thinks is best for his or her constituency

turnout the percentage of eligible individuals who actually vote

two-party system a political system in which only two parties have a realistic opportunity to compete effectively for control

tyranny oppressive and unjust government that employs cruel and unjust use of power and authority

uncontrollables budgetary items that are beyond the control of budgetary committees and can be controlled only by substantive legislative action in Congress. Some uncontrollables are beyond the power of Congress, because the terms of payments are set in contracts, such as interest on the debt

unfunded mandates regulations or conditions for receiving grants that impose costs on state and local governments for which they are not reimbursed by the federal government

Uniform Commercial Code code used in many states in the area of contract law to reduce interstate differences in judicial decisions

unilateralism a foreign policy that seeks to avoid international alliances, entanglements, and permanent commitments in favor of independence, neutrality, and freedom of action

unit rule the convention voting system under which a state delegation casts all of its votes for the candidate supported by the majority of the state's delegates

unitary system a centralized government system in which lower levels of government have little power independent of the national government

United Nations (UN) an organization of nations founded in 1945 to serve as a channel for negotiation and a means of settling international disputes peaceably. The UN has had frequent successes in providing a forum for negotiation and on some occasions a means of preventing international conflicts from spreading. On a number of occasions, the UN has been a convenient cover for U.S. foreign policy goals

values (or beliefs) basic principles that shape a person's opinions about political issues and events

veto the president's constitutional power to turn down acts of Congress. A presidential veto may be overridden by a two-thirds vote of each house of Congress

Virginia Plan a framework for the Constitution, introduced by Edmund Randolph, which called for representation in the national legislature based upon the population of each state

War Powers Resolution a resolution of Congress that the president can send troops into action abroad only by authorization of Congress, or if American troops are already under attack or serious threat

whip system a communications network in each house of Congress; whips take polls of the membership in order to learn their intentions on specific legislative issues and to assist the majority and minority leaders in various tasks

white ethnics white immigrants to the United States whose culture differs from that of WASPs

White House staff analysts and advisers to the president, often given the title "special assistant"

white primary primary election in which only white voters are eligible to participate

winner-take-all system a system in which all of a state's presidential nominating delegates are awarded to the candidate who wins the most votes, while runners-up receive no delegates

World Trade Organization (WTO) international trade agency promoting free trade that grew out of the General Agreement on Tariffs and Trade

writ of *certiorari* a decision of at least four of the nine Supreme Court justices to review a decision of a lower court; from the Latin "to make more certain"

writ of *habeas corpus* a court order that the individual in custody be brought into court and shown the cause for detention. *Habeas corpus* is guaranteed by the Constitution and can be suspended only in cases of rebellion or invasion

yellow journalism sensational coverage emphasizing scandals and misdeeds, often with little regard to evidence or analysis

ENDNOTES

Chapter 1

1. Gary Orren, "Fall from Grace: The Public's Loss of Trust in Government," in *Why People Don't Trust Government,* ed. Joseph S. Nye, Jr., Philip D. Zelikow, and David C. King (Cambridge, MA: Harvard University Press, 1997), pp. 80–81.

2. Robert J. Blendon et al., "Changing Attitudes in America," in *Why People Don't Trust Government,* ed. Nye, Zelikow, and King, pp. 207–8.

3. Michael A. Fletcher, "Trust and Interest in Government Soar on College Campuses," *Washington Post,* November 23, 2001, p. A3.

4. Amelia Gruber, "Public Finds Government Inefficient, Study Shows," GovExec.com, August 8, 2003.

5. Joseph S. Nye, Jr., "Introduction: The Decline of Confidence in Government," in *Why People Don't Trust Government,* ed. Nye, Zelikow, and King, p. 4.

6. Orren, "Fall from Grace," p. 81.

7. Owen, "Mixed Signals," p. 98.

8. Michael Walzer, *Spheres of Justice* (New York: Basic Books, 1983), p. 304.

9. This definition is taken from Norman H. Nie, Jane Junn, and Kenneth Stehlik-Barry, *Education and Democratic Citizenship in America* (Chicago: University of Chicago Press, 1996).

10. See Eugen Weber, *Peasants into Frenchmen: The Modernization of Rural France, 1870–1914* (Stanford, CA: Stanford University Press, 1976), chap. 5.

11. See V. O. Key, *Politics, Parties, and Pressure Groups* (New York: Crowell, 1964), p. 201.

12. Harold Lasswell, *Politics: Who Gets What, When, How* (New York: Meridian Books, 1958).

13. Herbert McClosky and John Zaller, *The American Ethos: Public Attitudes toward Capitalism and Democracy* (Cambridge, MA: Harvard University Press, 1984), p. 19.

14. J. R. Pole, *The Pursuit of Equality in American History* (Berkeley: University of California Press, 1978), p. 3.

15. See Judith N. Shklar, *American Citizenship: The Quest for Inclusion* (Cambridge, MA: Harvard University Press, 1991).

16. Cindy Skrzycki, "OSHA Abandons Rules Effort on Repetitive Injury," *Washington Post,* June 13, 1995, p. D1.

17. See Rogers M. Smith, *Liberalism and American Constitutional Law* (Cambridge, MA: Harvard University Press, 1985), chap. 6.

18. The case was *San Antonio Independent School District v. Rodriguez,* 411 U.S. 1 (1973). See the discussion in Smith, *Liberalism and American Constitutional Law,* pp. 163–64.

19. See the discussion in Eileen McDonagh, "Gender Political Change," in *New Perspectives on American Politics,* ed. Lawrence C. Dodd and Calvin Jillson (Washington, DC: Congressional Quarterly Press, 1994), pp. 58–73. The argument for moving women's issues into the public sphere is made by Jean Bethke Elshtain, *Public Man, Private Woman* (Princeton, NJ: Princeton University Press, 1981).

20. On current differences in wealth, see Keith Bradsher, "Gap in Wealth in U.S. Called Widest in West," *New York Times,* April 17, 1995, p. A1; on income inequality, see Gary Burtless and Timothy Smeeding, "America's Tide Lifting the Yachts, Swamping the Rowboats," *Washington Post,* June 25, 1995, p. C3.

21. Kevin Phillips, *The Politics of Rich and Poor: Wealth and the American Electorate in the Reagan Aftermath* (New York: Random House, 1994); and Thomas Byrne Edsall, *The New Politics of Inequality* (New York: Norton, 1984).

22. Kevin Phillips, *Arrogant Capital: Washington, Wall Street, and the Frustration of American Politics* (Boston: Little, Brown, 1994).

23. Joe Stephens, "Hard Money, Strong Arms and 'Matrix,'" *Washington Post,* February 10, 2002, p. 1.

Chapter 2

1. Michael Kammen, *A Machine That Would Go of Itself* (New York: Vintage, 1986), p. 22.

2. The social makeup of colonial America and some of the social conflicts that divided colonial society are discussed in Jackson Turner Main, *The Social Structure of Revolutionary America* (Princeton, NJ: Princeton University Press, 1965).

3. George B. Tindall and David E. Shi, *America: A Narrative History,* 3rd ed. (New York: Norton, 1992), p. 194.

4. For a discussion of events leading up to the Revolution, see Charles M. Andrews, *The Colonial Background of the American Revolution* (New Haven, CT: Yale University Press, 1924).

5. See Carl Becker, *The Declaration of Independence* (New York: Knopf, 1942).

6. See Merrill Jensen, *The Articles of Confederation* (Madison: University of Wisconsin Press, 1970).

7. Reported in Samuel E. Morrison, Henry Steele Commager, and William Leuchtenberg, *The Growth of the American Republic,* vol. 1 (New York: Oxford University Press, 1969), p. 244.

8. Quoted in Morrison et al., *The Growth of the American Republic,* vol. 1, p. 242.

9. Charles A. Beard, *An Economic Interpretation of the Constitution of the United States* (New York: Macmillan, 1913).

10. Madison's notes along with the somewhat less complete records kept by several other participants in the convention are available in a four-volume set. See Max Farrand, ed., *The Records of the Federal Convention of 1787*, 4 vols., rev. ed. (New Haven, CT: Yale University Press, 1966).

11. Farrand, ed., *The Records of the Federal Convention of 1787*, vol. 1, p. 476.

12. Farrand, ed., *The Records of the Federal Convention of 1787*, vol. 2, p. 10.

13. E. M. Earle, ed., *The Federalist* (New York: Modern Library, 1937), No. 71.

14. Earle, ed., *The Federalist*, No. 62.

15. Earle, ed., *The Federalist*, No. 70.

16. Max Farrand, *The Framing of the Constitution of the United States* (New Haven, CT: Yale University Press, 1962), p. 49.

17. Richard E. Neustadt, *Presidential Power* (New York: Wiley, 1960), p. 33.

18. Melancthon Smith, quoted in Storing, *What the Anti-Federalists Were For*, p. 17.

19. "Essays of Brutus," No. 1, in Herbert Storing, ed., *The Complete Anti-Federalist* (Chicago: University of Chicago Press, 1981).

20. Earle, ed., *The Federalist*, No. 57.

21. "Essays of Brutus," No. 15, in Storing, ed., *The Complete Anti-Federalist*.

22. Earle, ed., *The Federalist*, No. 10

23. "Essays of Brutus," No. 7, in Storing, ed., *The Complete Anti-Federalist*.

24. "Essays of Brutus," No. 6, in Storing, ed., *The Complete Anti-Federalist*.

25. Storing, *What the Anti-Federalists Were For*, p. 28.

26. Earle, ed., *The Federalist*, No. 51.

27. Quoted in Storing, *What the Anti-Federalists Were For*, p. 30.

28. Observation by Colonel George Mason, delegate from Virginia, early during the convention period. Quoted in Farrand, ed., *The Records of the Federal Convention of 1787*, vol. 1, pp. 202–3.

29. Clinton Rossiter, ed., *The Federalist Papers* (New York: New American Library, 1961), No. 43, p. 278.

30. See Marcia Lee, "The Equal Rights Amendment: Public Policy by Means of a Constitutional Amendment," in *The Politics of Policy-Making in America*, ed. David Caputo (San Francisco: Freeman, 1977); Jane Mansbridge, *Why We Lost the ERA* (Chicago: University of Chicago Press, 1986); and Donald Mathews and Jane Sherron DeHart, *Sex, Gender, and the Politics of the ERA* (New York: Oxford University Press, 1990).

31. The Fourteenth Amendment is included in this table as well as in Table 2.4 because it seeks not only to define citizenship but *seems* to intend also that this definition of citizenship included, along with the right to vote, all the rights of the Bill of Rights, regardless of the state in which the citizen resided. A great deal more will be said about this in Chapter 4.

32. Earle, ed., *The Federalist*, No. 10.

Chapter 3

1. Andre Henderson, "Cruise Control," *Governing*, February 1995, p. 39. Unemployment benefit figures are from U.S. House of Representatives, Committee on Ways and Means, *1998 Green Book* (Washington, DC: U.S. Government Printing Office, 1998), p. 340.

2. Ken I. Kersch, "Full Faith and Credit for Same-Sex Marriages?" *Political Science Quarterly*, 112 (Spring 1997), pp. 117–36; Joan Biskupic, "Once Unthinkable, Now Under Debate," *Washington Post*, September 3, 1996, p. A1.

3. Linda Greenhouse, "Supreme Court Weaves Legal Principles from a Tangle of Legislation," *New York Times*, June 30, 1988, p. A20.

4. *Hicklin v. Orbeck*, 437 U.S. 518 (1978).

5. *Sweeny v. Woodall*, 344 U.S. 86 (1953).

6. Marlise Simons, "France Won't Extradite American Convicted of Murder," *New York Times*, December 5, 1997, p. A9.

7. Patricia S. Florestano, "Past and Present Utilization of Interstate Compacts in the United States," *Publius* 24 (Fall 1994), pp. 13–26.

8. A good discussion of the constitutional position of local governments is in York Willbern, *The Withering Away of the City* (Bloomington: Indiana University Press, 1971). For more on the structure and theory of federalism, see Thomas R. Dye, *American Federalism: Competition among Governments* (Lexington, MA: Lexington Books, 1990), chap. 1; and Martha Derthick, "Up-to-Date in Kansas City: Reflections on American Federalism" (the 1992 John Gaus Lecture), *PS: Political Science & Politics* 25 (December 1992), pp. 671–75.

9. For a good treatment of the contrast between national political stability and social instability, see Samuel P. Huntington, *Political Order in Changing Societies* (New Haven, CT: Yale University Press, 1968), chap. 2.

10. *McCulloch v. Maryland*, 4 Wheaton 316 (1819).

11. *Gibbons v. Ogden*, 9 Wheaton 1 (1824).

12. The Sherman Antitrust Act, adopted in 1890, for example, was enacted not to restrict commerce, but rather to protect it from monopolies, or trusts, so as to prevent unfair trade practices, and to enable the market again to become self-regulating. Moreover, the Supreme Court sought to uphold liberty of contract to protect businesses. For example, in *Lochner v. New York*, 198 U.S. 45 (1905), the Court invalidated a New York law regulating the sanitary conditions and hours of labor of bakers on the grounds that the law interfered with liberty of contract.

13. The key case in this process of expanding the power of the national government is generally considered to be *NLRB v. Jones & Laughlin Steel Corporation*, 301 U.S. 1 (1937), in which the Supreme Court approved federal regulation of the workplace and thereby virtually eliminated interstate commerce as a limit on the national government's power.

14. *U.S. v. Darby Lumber Co.*, 312 U.S. 100 (1941).

15. W. John Moore, "Pleading the 10th," *National Journal*, July 29, 1995, p. 1940.

16. *United States v. Lopez*, 115 S.Ct. 1624 (1995).

17. *Printz v. United States*, 117 S.Ct. 2365 (1997).

18. *Seminole Indian Tribe v. Florida*, 116 S.Ct. 1114 (1996).

19. See the poll reported in Guy Gugliotta, "Scaling Down the American Dream," *Washington Post*, April 19, 1995, p. A21.

20. Kenneth T. Palmer, "The Evolution of Grant Policies," in *The Changing Politics of Federal Grants,* by Lawrence D. Brown, James W. Fossett, and Kenneth T. Palmer (Washington, DC: Brookings, 1984), p. 15.

21. Palmer, "The Evolution of Grant Policies," p. 6.

22. Morton Grozdins, *The American System,* ed. Daniel J. Elazar (Chicago: Rand McNally, 1966).

23. See Terry Sanford, *Storm over the States* (New York: McGraw-Hill, 1967).

24. James L. Sundquist with David W. Davis, *Making Federalism Work* (Washington, DC: Brookings, 1969), p. 271. George Wallace was mistrusted by the architects of the War on Poverty because he was a strong proponent of racial segregation. He believed in "states' rights," which meant that states, not the federal government, should decide what liberty and equality meant.

25. See Don Kettl, *The Regulation of American Federalism* (Baton Rouge: Louisiana State University Press, 1983).

26. See Advisory Commission on Intergovernmental Relations, *Federal Regulation of State and Local Governments: The Mixed Record of the 1980s* (Washington, DC: Advisory Commission on Intergovernmental Relations, July 1993).

27. Advisory Commission on Intergovernmental Relations, *Federal Regulation of State and Local Governments,* p. iii.

28. Quoted in Timothy Conlon, *New Federalism: Intergovernmental Reform from Nixon to Reagan* (Washington, DC: Brookings, 1988), p. 25.

29. For the emergence of complaints about federal categorical grants, see Palmer, "The Evolution of Grant Policies," pp. 17–18. On the governors' efforts to gain more control over federal grants after the 1994 congressional elections, see Dan Balz, "GOP Governors Eager to Do Things Their Way," *Washington Post,* November 22, 1994, p. A4.

30. Advisory Commission on Intergovernmental Relations, *Federal Regulation of State and Local Governments,* p. 51.

31. For an assessment of the achievements of the 104th and 105th Congresses, see Timothy Conlan, *From New Federalism to Devolution: Twenty-Five Years of Intergovernmental Reform* (Washington, DC: Brookings Institution Press, 1998).

32. Robert Frank, "Proposed Block Grants Seen Unlikely to Cure Management Problems," *Wall Street Journal,* May 1, 1995, p. 1.

33. U.S. Committee on Federalism and National Purpose, *To Form a More Perfect Union* (Washington, DC: National Conference on Social Welfare, 1985). See also the discussion in Paul E. Peterson, *The Price of Federalism* (Washington, DC: Brookings, 1995), esp. chap. 8.

34. Malcolm Gladwell, "In States' Experiments, a Cutting Contest," *New York Times,* March 10, 1995, p. 6.

35. The phrase "laboratories of democracy" was coined by Supreme Court justice Louis Brandeis in his dissenting opinion in *New State Ice Co. v. Liebman,* 285 U.S. 262 (1932).

36. "Motor Vehicle Fatalities in 1996 were 12 Percent Higher on Interstates, Freeways in 12 States that Raised Speed Limits," Press Release of the Insurance Institute for Highway Safety, October 10, 1997.

37. This was a comment from Walter E. Dellinger, President Clinton's acting solicitor general. Linda Greenhouse, "Will the Court Reassert National Authority?" *New York Times,* September 30, 2001, sect. 4, p. 14.

38. Sidney Verba, Kay Lehman Schlozman, and Henry E. Brady, *Voice and Equality: Civic Voluntarism in American Politics* (Cambridge, MA: Harvard University Press, 1995), pp. 66–67.

Chapter 4

1. Clinton Rossiter, ed., *The Federalist Papers* (New York: New American Library, 1961), No. 84, p. 513.

2. Rossiter, ed., *The Federalist Papers,* No. 84, p. 513.

3. Clinton Rossiter, *1787: The Grand Convention* (New York: Norton, 1987), p. 302.

4. Rossiter, *1787,* p. 303. Rossiter also reports that "in 1941 the States of Connecticut, Massachusetts and Georgia celebrated the sesquicentennial of the Bill of Rights by giving their hitherto withheld and unneeded assent."

5. *Barron v. Baltimore,* 7 Peters 243, 246 (1833).

6. The Fourteenth Amendment also seems designed to introduce civil rights. The final clause of the all-important Section 1 provides that no state can "deny to any person within its jurisdiction the equal protection of the laws." It is not unreasonable to conclude that the purpose of this provision was to obligate the state governments as well as the national government to take *positive* actions to protect citizens from arbitrary and discriminatory actions, at least those based on race. This will be explored in Chapter 5.

7. For example, *The Slaughterhouse Cases,* 16 Wallace 36 (1883).

8. *Chicago, Burlington and Quincy Railroad Company v. Chicago,* 166 U.S. 226 (1897).

9. *Gitlow v. New York,* 268 U.S. 652 (1925).

10. *Near v. Minnesota,* 283 U.S. 697 (1931); *Hague v. C.I.O.,* 307 U.S. 496 (1939).

11. *Palko v. Connecticut,* 302 U.S. 319 (1937).

12. All of these were implicitly included in the *Palko* case as "not incorporated" into the Fourteenth Amendment as limitations on the powers of the states.

13. There is one interesting exception, which involves the Sixth Amendment right to public trial. In the 1948 case *In re Oliver,* 33 U.S. 257, the right to the public trial was, in effect, incorporated as part of the Fourteenth Amendment. However, the issue in that case was put more generally as "due process," and public trial itself was not actually mentioned in so many words. Later opinions, such as *Duncan v. Louisiana,* 391 U.S. 145 (1968), cited the *Oliver* case as the precedent for more explicit incorporation of public trials as part of the Fourteenth Amendment.

14. For a lively and readable treatment of the possibilities of restricting provisions of the Bill of Rights, without actually reversing prior decisions, see David G. Savage, *Turning Right: The Making of the Rehnquist Supreme Court* (New York: Wiley, 1992). For an indication that the Supreme Court may in fact be moving toward more restrictions on the Bill of Rights, see Richard Lacayo, "The Soul of a New Majority," *Time,* July 10, 1995, pp. 46–48.

15. *Abington School District v. Schempp,* 374 U.S. 203 (1963).

16. *Engel v. Vitale,* 370 U.S. 421 (1962).

17. *Wallace v. Jaffree,* 472 U.S. 38 (1985).

18. *Lynch v. Donnelly,* 465 U.S. 668 (1984).

19. *Lemon v. Kurtzman,* 403 U.S. 602 (1971). The *Lemon* test is still good law, but as recently as the 1994 Court term, four justices have

urged that the *Lemon* test be abandoned. Here is a settled area of law that may soon become unsettled.

20. *Rosenberger v. Rector and Visitors of the University of Virginia*, 115 S.Ct. 2510 (1995).

21. *Agostini v. Felton*, 117 S.Ct. 1997 (1997). The case being overruled was *Aguilar v. Felton*, 473 U.S. 402 (1985).

22. For good coverage of voucher and charter school experiments, see Peter Schrag, "The Voucher Seduction," *American Prospect*, November 23, 1999, pp. 46–52.

23. *West Virginia State Board of Education v. Barnette*, 319 U.S. 624 (1943). The case it reversed was *Minersville School District v. Gobitus*, 310 U.S. 586 (1940).

24. *Employment Division, Department of Human Resources of Oregon v. Smith*, 494 U.S. 872 (1990).

25. *City of Boerne v. Flores*, 117 S.Ct. 293 (1996).

26. *Wisconsin v. Yoder*, 406 U.S. 205 (1972).

27. *U.S. v. Carolene Products Company*, 304 U.S. 144 (1938), note 4. This footnote is one of the Court's most important doctrines. See Alfred H. Kelly, Winfred A. Harbison, and Herman Belz, *The American Constitution: Its Origins and Development*, 7th ed. (New York: Norton, 1991), Vol. 2, pp. 519–23.

28. *Schenk v. U.S.*, 249 U.S. 47 (1919).

29. *Brandenburg v. Ohio*, 395 U.S. 444 (1969).

30. *McConnell v. FEC*, 124 S.Ct. 34 (2003).

31. *Stromberg v. California*, 283 U.S. 359 (1931).

32. *Texas v. Johnson*, 488 U.S. 884 (1989).

33. *United States v. Eichman*, 496 U.S. 310 (1990).

34. Lizette Alvarez, "Measure to Ban Flag Burning Falls 4 Votes Short in the Senate," *New York Times*, March 30, 2000, p. A24; Adam Clymer, "House, in Ritual Vote, Opposes Flag Burning," *New York Times*, July 18, 2001, p. A20.

35. *Virginia v. Black*, 528 U.S. 343 (2003).

36. For a good general discussion of "speech plus," see Louis Fisher, *American Constitutional Law* (New York: McGraw-Hill, 1990), pp. 544–46. The case upholding the buffer zone against the abortion protesters is *Madsen v. Women's Health Center*, 114 S.Ct. 2516 (1994).

37. *Near v. Minnesota*, 283 U.S. 697 (1931).

38. *New York Times v. U.S.*, 403 U.S. 731 (1971).

39. *New York Times v. Sullivan*, 376 U.S. 254 (1964).

40. *Hustler Magazine v. Falwell*, 108 S.Ct. 876 (1988).

41. *Roth v. U.S.*, 354 U.S. 476 (1957).

42. Concurring opinion in *Jacobellis v. Ohio*, 378 U.S. 184 (1964).

43. *Miller v. California*, 413 U.S. 15 (1973).

44. *Reno v. American Civil Liberties Union*, 117 S.Ct. 2329 (1997).

45. *U.S. v. American Library Association*, 539 U.S. 194 (2003).

46. *Chaplinsky v. State of New Hampshire*, 315 U.S. 568 (1942).

47. *Dennis v. United States*, 341 U.S. 494 (1951), which upheld the infamous Smith Act of 1940, which provided criminal penalties for those who "willfully and knowingly conspire to teach and advocate the forceful and violent overthrow and destruction of the government."

48. *Bethel School District No. 403 v. Fraser*, 478 U.S. 675 (1986).

49. *Hazelwood School District v. Kuhlmeier*, 108 S.Ct. 562 (1988).

50. "The Penn File: An Update," *Wall Street Journal*, April 11, 1994, p. A14.

51. *Meritor Savings Bank, FBD v. Vinson*, 477 U.S. 57 (1986).

52. Charles Fried, "The New First Amendment Jurisprudence: A Threat to Liberty," in *The Bill of Rights and the Modern State*, ed. Stone, Epstein, and Sunstein, p. 249.

53. *Broadcasting Company v. Acting Attorney General*, 405 U.S. 1000 (1972).

54. *Board of Trustees of the State University of New York v. Fox*, 109 S.Ct. 3028 (1989).

55. *City Council v. Taxpayers for Vincent*, 466 U.S. 789 (1984).

56. *Posadas de Puerto Rico Associates v. Tourism Company of Puerto Rico*, 479 U.S. 328 (1986).

57. Fisher, *American Constitutional Law*, p. 546.

58. *Bigelow v. Virginia*, 421 U.S. 809 (1975).

59. *Virginia State Board of Pharmacy v. Virginia Citizens Consumer Council*, 425 U.S. 748 (1976). Later cases restored the rights of lawyers to advertise their services.

60. *44 Liquormart, Inc. and Peoples Super Liquor Stores Inc., Petitioners v. Rhode Island and Rhode Island Liquor Stores Association*, 116 S.Ct. 1495 (1996).

61. *Lorillard Tobacco v. Reilly*, 121 S.Ct. 2404 (2001)

62. *Presser v. Illinois*, 116 U.S. 252 (1886).

63. *Quilici v. Village of Morton Grove*, 695F.2d 261 (7th Cir. 1982); cert denied, 464 U.S. 863 (1983).

64. *In re Winship*, 397 U.S. 361 (1970). An outstanding treatment of due process in issues involving the Fourth through Seventh Amendments will be found in Fisher, *American Constitutional Law*, chap. 13.

65. *Horton v. California*, 496 U.S. 128 (1990).

66. *Mapp v. Ohio*, 367 U.S. 643 (1961). Although Ms. Mapp went free in this case, she was later convicted in New York on narcotics trafficking charges and served nine years of a twenty-year sentence.

67. For a good discussion of the issue, see Fisher, *American Constitutional Law*, pp. 884–89.

68. *National Treasury Employees Union v. Von Raab*, 39 U.S. 656 (1989).

69. *Skinner v. Railroad Labor Executives Association*, 489 U.S. 602 (1989).

70. *Vernonia School District 47J v. Acton*, 115 S.Ct. 2386 (1985).

71. *Chandler et al. v. Miller, Governor of Georgia et al.*, 117 S.Ct. 1295 (1997).

72. *Indianapolis v. Edmund*, 531 U.S. 32 (2000), 121 S.Ct. 447 (2000).

73. *Ferguson v. Charleston*, 121 S.Ct. 1281 (2001).

74. *Kyllo v. U.S.*, 121 S.Ct. 2038 (2001).

75. Corwin and Peltason, *Understanding the Constitution*, p. 286.

76. *Miranda v. Arizona*, 348 U.S. 436 (1966).

77. *Berman v. Parker*, 348 U.S. 26 (1954). For a thorough analysis of the case see Benjamin Ginsberg, "*Berman v. Parker*: Congress, the Court, and the Public Purpose," *Polity* 4 (1971), pp. 48–75. For a later application of the case that suggests that "just compensation"—defined as something approximating market value—is about all a property owner can hope for protection against a public taking of property, see Theodore Lowi et al., *Poliscide; Big Government, Big Science, Lilliputian Politics*, 2nd ed. (Lanham, MD: University Press of America, 1990), pp. 267–70.

78. *Gideon v. Wainright*, 372 U.S. 335 (1963). For a full account of the story of the trial and release of Clarence Earl Gideon, see Anthony Lewis, *Gideon's Trumpet* (New York: Random House, 1964). See also David O'Brien, *Storm Center*, 2nd ed. (New York: Norton, 1990).

79. *Wiggins v. Smith*, 123 S. Ct. 2527 (2003).

80. For further discussion of these issues, see Corwin and Peltason, *Understanding the Constitution*, pp. 319–23.

81. *Furman v. Georgia*, 408 U.S. 238 (1972).

82. *Gregg v. Georgia*, 428 U.S. 153 (1976).

83. *Minerville School District v. Gobitis*, 310 U.S. 586 (1940).

84. *West Virginia State Board of Education v. Barnette*, 319 U.S. 624 (1943)

85. *NAACP v. Alabama ex rel. Patterson,* 357 U.S. 449 (1958).

86. *Griswold v. Connecticut,* 381 U.S. 479 (1965).

87. *Griswold v. Connecticut,* concurring opinion. In 1972, the Court extended the privacy right to unmarried women: *Eisenstadt v. Baird,* 405 U.S. 438 (1972).

88. *Roe v. Wade,* 410 U.S. 113 (1973).

89. *Webster v. Reproductive Health Services,* 109 S.Ct. 3040 (1989), which upheld a Missouri law that restricted the use of public medical facilities for abortion. The decision opened the way for other states to limit the availability of abortion.

90. *Planned Parenthood of Southeastern Pennsylvania v. Casey,* 112 S.Ct. 2791 (1992).

91. *Stenberg v. Carhart,* 120 S.Ct. 2597 (2000).

92. *Bowers v. Hardwick,* 478 U.S. 186 (1986).

93. The dissenters were quoting an earlier case, *Olmstead v. United States,* 27 U.S. 438 (1928), to emphasize the nature of their disagreement with the majority in the *Bowers* case.

94. *Lawrence v. Texas,* 123 S. Ct. 2472 (2003).

95. It is worth recalling here the provision of the Ninth Amendment: "The enumeration in the Constitution, of certain rights, shall not be construed to deny or disparage others retained by the people."

96. *Washington v. Glucksberg,* 117 S.Ct. 2258 (1997).

97. *Washington v. Glucksberg.*

98. *Washington v. Glucksberg.*

99. For an excellent discussion, see David M. O'Brien, *Supreme Court Watch 1997* (New York: Norton, 1998), pp. 117–30.

100. Military Order of November 13, 2001: Detention, Treatment and Trial of Certain Non-Citizens in the War against Terrorism," 66 *Federal Register* 57833, November 14, 2001.

101. Alberto Gonzales, "Martial Justice, Full and Fair," *New York Times,* November 30, 2001, p. A27.

102. *Ex Parte Quirin,* 317 U.S. 1 (1942).

103. Katherine Q. Seelye, "Government Sets Rules for Military on War Tribunals," *New York Times,* March 21, 2002, p. A1; William Safire, "Military Trials Modified," *New York Times,* March 21, 2002, p. A33.

104. George Lardner, Jr., "U.S. Will Monitor Calls to Lawyers," *Washington Post,* November 9, 2001, p. A1.

105. William Safire, "Kangaroo Courts," *New York Times,* September 26, 2001, p. A17.

106. *Rasul v. Bush,* No. 03-334; *Hamdi v. Rumsfeld,* No. 03-6696.

107. *Roe v. Wade.*

108. *Rosenberger v. University of Virginia.*

Chapter 5

1. Paula Baker, "The Domestication of Politics: Women and American Political Society, 1780–1920," *American Historical Review* 89 (June 1984), pp. 620–47.

2. August Meier and Elliot Rudwick, *From Plantation to Ghetto* (New York: Hill and Wang, 1976), pp. 184–88.

3. Jill Dupont, "Susan B. Anthony," New York Notes (Albany, NY: New York State Commission on the Bicentennial of the U.S. Constitution, 1988), p. 3.

4. *Plessy v. Ferguson,* 163 U.S. 537 (1896).

5. Dupont, "Susan B. Anthony," p. 4.

6. The prospect of a Fair Employment Practices law tied to the commerce power produced the Dixiecrat break with the Democratic Party in 1948. The Democratic Party organization of the States of the Old Confederacy seceded from the national party and nominated its own candidate, the then-Democratic governor of South Carolina, Strom Thurmond, who is now a Republican senator. This almost cost President Truman the election.

7. This was based on the provision in Article VI of the Constitution that "all treaties made, . . . under the Authority of the United States," shall be the "supreme Law of the Land." The committee recognized that if the U.S. Senate ratified the Human Rights Covenant of the United Nations—a treaty—then that power could be used as the constitutional umbrella for effective civil rights legislation. The Supreme Court had recognized in *Missouri v. Holland,* 252 U.S. 416 (1920), that a treaty could enlarge federal power at the expense of the states.

8. *Missouri ex rel. Gaines v. Canada,* 305 U.S. 337 (1938).

9. *Sweatt v. Painter,* 339 U.S. 629 (1950).

10. *Smith v. Allwright,* 321 U.S. 649 (1944).

11. *Shelley v. Kraemer,* 334 U.S. 1 (1948).

12. Kermit L. Hall, *The Magic Mirror: Law in American History* (New York: Oxford University Press, 1989), pp. 322–24. See also Richard Kluger, *Simple Justice* (New York: Random House, Vintage Edition, 1977), pp. 530–37.

13. The District of Columbia case came up too, but since the District of Columbia is not a state, this case did not directly involve the Fourteenth Amendment and its "equal protection" clause. It confronted the Court on the same grounds, however—that segregation is inherently unequal. Its victory in effect was "incorporation in reverse," with equal protection moving from the Fourteenth Amendment to become part of the Bill of Rights. See *Bolling v. Sharpe,* 347 U.S. 497 (1954).

14. *Brown v. Board of Education of Topeka, Kansas,* 347 U.S. 483 (1954).

15. The Supreme Court first declared that race was a suspect classification requiring strict scrutiny in the decision *Korematsu v. United States,* 323 U.S. 214 (1944). In this case, the Court upheld President Roosevelt's executive order of 1941 allowing the military to exclude persons of Japanese ancestry from the West Coast and to place them in internment camps. It is one of the few cases in which classification based on race survived strict scrutiny.

16. The two most important cases were *Cooper v. Aaron,* 358 U.S. 1 (1958), which required Little Rock, Arkansas, to desegregate; and *Griffin v. Prince Edward County School Board,* 377 U.S. 218 (1964), which forced all the schools of that Virginia county to reopen after five years of closing to avoid desegregation.

17. In *Cooper v. Aaron,* the Supreme Court ordered immediate compliance with the lower court's desegregation order and went beyond that with a stern warning that it is "emphatically the province and duty of the judicial department to say what the law is."

18. *Shuttlesworth v. Birmingham Board of Education,* 358 U.S. 101 (1958), upheld a "pupil placement" plan purporting to assign pupils on various bases, with no mention of race. This case interpreted *Brown* to mean that school districts must stop explicit racial discrimination but were under no obligation to take positive steps to desegregate. For a while black parents were doomed to case-by-case approaches.

19. For good treatments of this long stretch of the struggle of the federal courts to integrate the schools, see Paul Brest and Sanford

Levinson, *Processes of Constitutional Decision-Making: Cases and Materials*, 2nd ed. (Boston: Little, Brown, 1983), pp. 471–80; and Alfred Kelly et al., *The American Constitution: Its Origins and Development*, 6th ed. (New York: Norton, 1983), pp. 610–16.

20. Pierre Thomas, "Denny's to Settle Bias Cases," *Washington Post*, May 24, 1994, p. A1.

21. See Hamil Harris, "For Blacks, Cabs Can Be Hard to Get," *Washington Post*, July 21, 1994, p. J1.

22. For a thorough analysis of the Office for Civil Rights, see Jeremy Rabkin, "Office for Civil Rights," in *The Politics of Regulation*, ed. James Q. Wilson (New York: Basic Books, 1980).

23. This was an accepted way of using quotas or ratios to determine statistically that blacks or other minorities were being excluded from schools or jobs, and then on the basis of that statistical evidence to authorize the Justice Department to bring suits in individual cases and in "class action" suits as well. In most segregated situations outside the South, it is virtually impossible to identify and document an intent to discriminate.

24. *Swann v. Charlotte-Mecklenberg Board of Education*, 402 U.S. 1 (1971).

25. *Milliken v. Bradley*, 418 U.S. 717 (1974).

26. For a good evaluation of the Boston effort, see Gary Orfield, *Must We Bus? Segregated Schools and National Policy* (Washington: Brookings Institution, 1978), pp. 144–46. See also Bob Woodward and Scott Armstrong, *The Brethren: Inside the Supreme Court* (New York: Simon and Schuster, 1979), pp. 426–27; and J. Anthony Lukas, *Common Ground* (New York: Random House, 1986).

27. *Board of Education v. Dowell*, 498 U.S. 237 (1991).

28. *Missouri v. Jenkins*, 115 S.Ct. 2038 (1995).

29. See especially *Katzenbach v. McClung*, 379 U.S. 294 (1964). Almost immediately after passage of the Civil Rights Act of 1964, a case was brought challenging the validity of Title II, which covered discrimination in public accommodations. Ollie's Barbecue was a neighborhood restaurant in Birmingham, Alabama. It was located eleven blocks away from an interstate highway and even farther from railroad and bus stations. Its table service was for whites only; there was only a take-out service for blacks. The Supreme Court agreed that Ollie's was strictly an intrastate restaurant, but since a substantial proportion of its food and other supplies were bought from companies outside the state of Alabama, there was a sufficient connection to interstate commerce; therefore, racial discrimination at such restaurants would "impose commercial burdens of national magnitude upon interstate commerce." Although this case involved Title II, it had direct bearing on the constitutionality of Title VII.

30. *Griggs v. Duke Power Company*, 401 U.S. 24 (1971). See also Allan Sindler, *Bakke, DeFunis, and Minority Admissions* (New York: Longman, 1978), pp. 180–89.

31. For a good treatment of these issues, see Charles O. Gregory and Harold A. Katz, *Labor and the Law* (New York: Norton, 1979), chap. 17.

32. In 1970, this act was amended to outlaw for five years literacy tests as a condition for voting in all states.

33. Joint Center for Political Studies, *Black Elected Officials: A National Roster—1988* (Washington, DC: Joint Center for Political Studies Press, 1988), pp. 9–10. For a comprehensive analysis and evaluation of the Voting Rights Act, see Bernard Grofman and Chandler Davidson, eds., *Controversies in Minority Voting: The Voting Rights Act in Perspective* (Washington, DC: Brookings, 1992).

34. Ford Fessenden, "Ballots Cast by Blacks and Older Voters Were Tossed in Far Greater Numbers," *New York Times*, November 12, 2001, p. A17.

35. See Douglas S. Massey and Nancy A. Denton, *American Apartheid: Segregation and the Making of the Underclass* (Cambridge, MA: Harvard University Press, 1993), chap. 7.

36. See Jane J. Mansbridge, *Why We Lost the ERA* (Chicago: University of Chicago Press, 1986); and Gilbert Steiner, *Constitutional Inequality* (Washington, DC: Brookings, 1985).

37. *See Frontiero v. Richardson*, 411 U.S. 677 (1973).

38. See *Craig v. Boren*, 423 U.S. 1047 (1976).

39. *Franklin v. Gwinnett County Public Schools*, 503 U.S. 60 (1992).

40. Jennifer Halperin, "Women Step Up to Bat," *Illinois Issues* 21 (September 1995), pp. 11–14.

41. Joan Biskupic and David Nakamura, "Court Won't Review Sports Equity Ruling," *Washington Post*, April 22, 1997, p. A1.

42. *U.S. v. Virginia*, 116 S.Ct. 2264 (1996).

43. Judith Havemann, "Two Women Quit Citadel over Alleged Harassment," *Washington Post*, January 13, 1997, p. A1.

44. *Meritor Savings Bank v. Vinson*, 477 U.S. 57 (1986).

45. *Harris v. Forklift Systems, Inc.*, 510 U.S. 17 (1993).

46. *Burlington Industries v. Ellerth*, 118 S.Ct. 2257 (1998); *Faragher v. City of Boca Raton*, 118 S.Ct. 2275 (1998).

47. New Mexico had a different history because not many Anglos settled there initially. ("Anglo" is the term for a non-Hispanic white generally of European background.) Mexican Americans had considerable power in territorial legislatures between 1865 and 1912. See Lawrence H. Fuchs, *The American Kaleidoscope* (Hanover, NH: University Press of New England, 1990), pp. 239–40.

48. On La Raza Unida Party, see "La Raza Unida Party and the Chicano Student Movement in California," in *Latinos in the American Political System*, ed. F. Chris Garcia (Notre Dame, IN: University of Notre Dame Press, 1988), pp. 213–35.

49. *United States v. Wong Kim Ark*, 169 U.S. 649 (1898).

50. *Lau v. Nichols*, 414 U.S. 563 (1974).

51. Dick Kirschten, "Not Black and White," *National Journal*, March 2, 1991, p. 497.

52. See Robert Pear, "Deciding Who Gets What in America," *New York Times*, November 27, 1994, sec. 4, p. 5.

53. Not all Indian tribes agreed with this, including the Navajos. See Ronald Takaki, *A Different Mirror: A History of Multicultural America* (Boston: Little, Brown: 1993), pp. 238–45.

54. On the resurgence of Indian political activity, see Stephen Cornell, *The Return of the Native: American Indian Political Resurgence* (New York: Oxford University Press, 1990); and Dee Brown, *Bury My Heart at Wounded Knee* (New York: Holt, 1971).

55. See the discussion in Robert A. Katzmann, *Institutional Disability: The Saga of Transportation Policy for the Disabled* (Washington, DC: Brookings, 1986).

56. For example, after pressure from the Justice Department, one of the nation's largest rental-car companies agreed to make special handcontrols available to any customer requesting them. See "Avis Agrees to Equip Cars for Disabled," *Los Angeles Times*, September 2, 1994, p. D1.

57. The case and the interview with Stephen Bokat was reported in Margaret Warner, "Expanding Coverage," *The News-Hour with Jim Lehrer Transcript*, July 1, 1998, on-line News-Hour, http://webcro5.pbs.org.

58. *Bowers v. Hardwick*, 478 U.S. 186 (1986).

59. Quoted in Joan Biskupic, "Gay Rights Activists Seek a Supreme Court Test Case," *Washington Post*, December 19, 1993, p. A1.

60. *Romer v. Evans,* 116 S.Ct. 1620 (1996).

61. *Lawrence v. Texas,* 123 S. Ct. 2472 (2003).

62. From Lyndon B. Johnson, *The Vantage Point* (New York: Holt, Rinehart, and Winston, 1971), p. 166.

63. The Department of Health, Education, and Welfare (HEW) was the cabinet department charged with administering most federal social programs. In 1980, when education programs were transferred to the newly created Department of Education, HEW was renamed the Department of Health and Human Services.

64. *Regents of the University of California v. Bakke,* 438 U.S. 265 (1978).

65. See, for example, *United Steelworkers v. Weber,* 443 U.S. 193 (1979); and *Fullilove v. Klutznick,* 100 S.Ct. 2758 (1980).

66. *Ward's Cove v. Atonio,* 109 S.Ct. 2115 (1989).

67. *Griggs v. Duke Power Company,* 401 U.S. 24 (1971).

68. *Martin v. Wilks,* 109 S.Ct. 2180 (1989). In this case, some white firefighters in Birmingham challenged a consent decree mandating goals for hiring and promoting blacks. This was an affirmative action plan that had been worked out between the employer and aggrieved black employees and had been accepted by a federal court. Such agreements become "consent decrees" and are subject to enforcement. Chief Justice Rehnquist held that the white firefighters could challenge the legality of such programs, even though they had not been parties to the original litigation.

69. *St. Mary's Honor Center v. Hicks,* 113 S.Ct. 2742 (1993).

70. *Adarand Constructors v. Pena,* 115 S.Ct. 2097 (1995).

71. Ann Devroy, "Clinton Study Backs Affirmative Action," *Washington Post,* July 19, 1995, p. A1.

72. *Hopwood v. State of Texas,* 78 F3d 932 (5th Cir., 1996).

73. See Lydia Lum, "Applications by Minorities Down Sharply," *Houston Chronicle,* April 8, 1997, p. A1; R. G. Ratcliffe, "Senate Approves Bill Designed to Boost Minority Enrollments," *Houston Chronicle,* May 8, 1997, p. A1.

74. Linda Greenhouse, "Settlement Ends High Court Case on Preferences," *New York Times,* November 22, 1997, p. A1; Barry Bearak, "Rights Groups Ducked a Fight, Opponents Say," *New York Times,* November 22, 1997, p. A1.

75. *Gratz v. Bollinger,* 123 S. Ct. 2411 (2003).

76. *Grutter v. Bollinger,* 123 S. Ct. 2325 (2003).

77. Michael A. Fletcher, "Opponents of Affirmative Action Heartened by Court Decision," *Washington Post,* April 13, 1997, p. A21.

78. See Sam Howe Verhovek, "Houston Vote Underlined Complexity of Rights Issue," *New York Times,* November 6, 1997, p. A1.

79. There are still many genuine racists in America, but with the exception of a lunatic fringe, made up of neo-Nazis and members of the Ku Klux Klan, most racists are too ashamed or embarrassed to take part in normal political discourse. They are not included in either category here.

80. *Slaughterhouse Cases,* 16 Wallace 36 (1873).

81. See Paul M. Sniderman and Edward G. Carmines, *Reaching beyond Race* (Cambridge, MA: Harvard University Press, 1997).

Chapter 6

1. Alexander Astin et al., "The American Freshman: National Norms for Fall 1994," Cooperative Institutional Research Program of the American Council on Education and the Higher Education Research Institute of the University of California at Los Angeles, 1994.

2. Quoted in the *Tampa Tribune,* January 9, 1995, p. 1.

3. Henry K. Lee, "Tentative Pact between UC, Hunger Strikers," *San Francisco Chronicle,* May 8, 1999, p. A15.

4. Karlene Hanko, "College, University Presidents Pledge to Encourage Participation in Politics," *Daily Pennsylvanian,* July 13, 1999.

5. For a discussion of the political beliefs of Americans, see Harry Holloway and John George, *Public Opinion* (New York: St. Martin's, 1986). See also Paul R. Abramson, *Political Attitudes in America* (San Francisco: Freeman, 1983).

6. See Paul M. Sniderman and Edward G. Carmines, *Reaching beyond Race* (Cambridge, MA: Harvard University Press, 1997).

7. See Angus Campbell et al., *The American Voter* (New York: Wiley, 1960), p. 147.

8. Richard Morin, "Poll Reflects Division over Simpson Case," *Washington Post,* October 8, 1995, p. A31.

9. Paul Farhi, "Black Media Barons Back Sharpton Bid," *Washington Post,* November 9, 2003, p. A4.

10. "Middle-Class Views in Black and White," *Washington Post,* October 9, 1995, p. A22.

11. For data see Rutgers University, Eagleton Institute of Politics, Center for the American Woman in Politics, "Sex Differences in Voter Turnout," August 1994.

12. Donald Green, Bradley Palmquist, and Eric Schickler, *Partisan Hearts and Minds: Political Parties and the Social Identities of Voters* (New Haven, CT: Yale University Press, 2002).

13. David S. Broder, "Partisan Gap Is at a High, Poll Finds," *Washington Post,* November 9, 2003, p. A6.

14. Pamela Johnston Conover, "The Role of Social Groups in Political Thinking," *British Journal of Political Science* 18 (1988), pp. 51–78.

15. See Michael C. Dawson, "Structure and Ideology: The Shaping of Black Opinion," paper presented to the 1995 annual meeting of the Midwest Political Science Association, Chicago, Illinois, April 7–9, 1995. See also Michael C. Dawson, *Behind the Mule: Race, Class, and African American Politics* (Princeton, NJ: Princeton University Press, 1994).

16. Elisabeth Noelle-Neumann, *The Spiral of Silence* (Chicago: University of Chicago Press, 1984).

17. Ole R. Holsti, "A Widening Gap Between the Military and Civilian Society?" John M. Olin Institute for Strategic Studies.

18. Michael X. Delli Carpini and Scott Keeter, *What Americans Know about Politics and Why It Matters* (New Haven, CT: Yale University Press, 1996).

19. Larry M. Bartels, "Homer Gets a Tax Cut: Inequality and Public Policy in the American Mind." Paper prepared for presentation at the annual meeting of the American Political Science Association, Philadelphia, August 2003.

20. Sniderman and Carmines, *Reaching beyond Race,* ch. 4.

21. For an interesting discussion of opinion formation, see John Zaller, *The Nature and Origins of Mass Opinion* (New York: Cambridge University Press, 1992).

22. Gerald F. Seib and Michael K. Frisby, "Selling Sacrifice," *Wall Street Journal,* February 5, 1993, p. 1.

23. Michael K. Frisby, "Clinton Seeks Strategic Edge with Opinion Polls," *Wall Street Journal,* June 24, 1996, p. A16.

24. Joshua Green, "The Other War Room," *Washington Monthly,* April 2002.

25. Peter Marks, "Adept in Politics and Advertising, 4 Women Shape a Campaign," *New York Times,* November 11, 2001, p. B6.

26. See Gillian Peele, *Revival and Reaction* (Oxford, U.K.: Clarendon, 1985). Also see Connie Paige, *The Right-to-Lifers* (New York: Summit, 1983).

27. See David Vogel, "The Power of Business in America: A Reappraisal," *British Journal of Political Science* 13 (January 1983), pp. 19–44.

28. See David Vogel, "The Public Interest Movement and the American Reform Tradition," *Political Science Quarterly* 96 (winter 1980), pp. 607–27.

29. Jason DeParle, "The Clinton Welfare Bill Begins Trek in Congress," *New York Times,* July 15, 1994, p. 1.

30. Joe Queenan, "Birth of a Notion," *Washington Post,* September 20, 1992, p. C1.

31. Zaller, *The Nature and Origins of Mass Opinion.*

32. See Shanto Iyengar, *Is Anyone Responsible? How Television Frames Political Issues* (Chicago: University of Chicago Press, 1991); and Shanto Iyengar, *Do the Media Govern?* (Thousand Oaks, CA: Sage, 1997).

33. Herbert Asher, *Polling and the Public* (Washington, DC: CQ Press, 2001), p. 64.

34. Carl Cannon, "A Pox on Both Our Parties," in David C. Canon et al., eds., *The Enduring Debate* (New York: Norton, 2000), p. 389.

35. John Goyder, Keith Warriner, and Susan Miller, "Evaluating Socio-economic Status Bias in Survey Nonresponse," *Journal of Official Statistics* 18, no. 1 (2002).

36. Michael Kagay and Janet Elder, "Numbers Are No Problem for Pollsters, Words Are," *New York Times,* August 9, 1992, p. E6.

37. Donn Tibbetts, "Draft Bill Requires Notice of Push Polling," *Manchester Union Leader,* October 3, 1996, p. A6.

38. "Dial S for Smear," *Memphis Commercial Appeal,* September 22, 1996, p. 6B.

39. Amy Keller, "Subcommittee Launches Investigation of Push Polls," *Roll Call,* October 3, 1996, p. 1.

40. For a discussion of the growing difficulty of persuading people to respond to surveys, see John Brehm, *Phantom Respondents* (Ann Arbor: University of Michigan Press, 1993).

41. See Richard Morin, "Is Bush's Bounce a Boom or a Bust?" *Washington Post National Weekly Edition,* August 31–September 6, 1992, p. 37.

42. See Thomas E. Mann and Gary Orren, eds., *Media Polls in American Politics* (Washington, DC: Brookings, 1992).

43. For an excellent and reflective discussion by a journalist, see Richard Morin, "Clinton Slide in Survey Shows Perils of Polling," *Washington Post,* August 29, 1992, p. A6.

44. See Michael Traugott, "The Impact of Media Polls on the Public," in *Media Polls in American Politics,* Mann and Orren, eds., pp. 125–49.

45. Benjamin I. Page and Robert Y. Shapiro, "Effects of Public Opinion on Policy," *American Political Science Review* 77 (March 1983), pp. 175–90.

46. Robert A. Erikson, Gerald Wright, and John McIver, *Statehouse Democracy: Public Opinion and Democracy in the American States* (New York: Cambridge University Press, 1994).

47. The results of separate studies by the political scientists Lawrence Jacobs, Robert Shapiro, and Alan Monroe were reported by Richard Morin in "Which Comes First, the Politician or the Poll?" *Washington Post National Weekly Edition,* February 10, 1997, p. 35.

48. David S. Broder, *Democracy Derailed: Initiative Campaigns and the Power of Money* (New York: Harcourt, 2000).

49. Robert Tomsho, "Liberals Take a Cue from Conservatives: This Election, the Left Tries to Make Policy with Ballot Initiatives," *Wall Street Journal,* November 6, 2000, p. A12.

50. Delli Carpini and Keeter. *What Americans Know about Politics and Why It Matters.*

Chapter 7

1. Benjamin Ginsberg and Martin Shefter, *Politics by Other Means* (New York: Basic Books, 1990), p. 24.

2. CNN.com/Inside Politics, February 18, 2003.

3. Samantha M. Shapiro, "The Dean Connection," *New York Times Magazine,* December 7, 2003, p. 58.

4. U.S. Bureau of the Census, *Statistical Abstract of the United States: 1994* (Washington, DC: Department of Commerce, 1994), pp. 567, 576.

5. *Red Lion Broadcasting Company v. FCC,* 395 U.S. 367 (1969).

6. For a criticism of the increasing consolidation of the media, see the essays in Patricia Aufderheide et al., *Conglomerates and the Media* (New York: New Press, 1997).

7. See Leo Bogart, "Newspapers in Transition," *Wilson Quarterly,* special issue, 1982; and Richard Harwood, "The Golden Age of Press Diversity," *Washington Post,* July 22, 1994, p. A23.

8. See Benjamin Ginsberg, *The Captive Public* (New York: Basic Books, 1986).

9. Michael Dawson, "Structure and Ideology: The Shaping of Black Public Opinion," paper presented to the 1995 meeting of the Midwest Political Science Association, Chicago, Illinois, April 7, 1995.

10. See the discussions in Gary Paul Gates, *Air Time* (New York: Harper & Row, 1978); Edward Jay Epstein, *News from Nowhere* (New York: Random House, 1973); Michael Parenti, *Inventing Reality* (New York: St. Martin's, 1986); Herbert Gans, *Deciding What's News* (New York: Vintage, 1980); and W. Lance Bennett, *News: The Politics of Illusion* (New York: Longman, 1986).

11. See Edith Efron, *The News Twisters* (Los Angeles: Nash Publishing, 1971).

12. Rowan Scarborough, "Leftist Press? Reporters Working in Washington Acknowledge Liberal Leanings in Poll," *Washington Times,* April 18, 1996, p. 1.

13. David Firestone, "Steven Brill Strikes a Nerve in News Media," *New York Times,* June 20, 1998, p. 4.

14. Elisabeth Bumiller, "Keepers of Bush Image Lift Stagecraft to New Heights," *New York Times,* May 16, 2003, p. 1.

15. See Tom Burnes, "The Organization of Public Opinion," in *Mass Communication and Society,* ed. James Curran (Beverly Hills, CA: Sage, 1979), pp. 44–230. See also David Altheide, *Creating Reality* (Beverly Hills, CA: Sage, 1976).

16. Garrow, *Protest at Selma.*

17. See Todd Gitlin, *The Whole World Is Watching* (Berkeley, CA: University of California Press, 1980).

18. For a discussion of framing, see Amy Jasperson, et al., "Framing and the Public Agenda," *Political Communication,* vol. 15, no. 2, pp. 205–24.

19. Kathleen Hall Jamieson and Paul Waldman, *The Press Effect* (New York: Oxford University Press, 2003), p. 61.

20. Jamieson and Waldman, *The Press Effect,* p. 56.

21. Eric Lyman, "Hollywood Discusses Role in War Effort," *New York Times,* November 12, 2001, p. B2.

22. See Martin Linsky, *Impact: How the Press Affects Federal Policy-making* (New York: Norton, 1986).

23. Carl Allen, "UB Paper Prints Apology for Story on Student Poll," *Buffalo News,* November 15, 1997, p. 1B.

24. For a good discussion of how to evaluate media biases see Don Hazen and Julie Winokur, eds., *We the Media* (New York: New Press, 1997).

Chapter 8

1. For a discussion of the decline of voting turnout over time, see Ruy A. Teixeira, *The Disappearing American Voter* (Washington, DC: Brookings, 1992). On the 1994 elections, see Paul Taylor, "Behind the Broom of '94: Wealthier, Educated Voters," *Washington Post,* June 8, 1995, p. A12.

2. Sidney Verba, Kay Lehman Schlozman, and Henry E. Brady, *Voice and Equality: Civic Voluntarism in American Politics* (Cambridge, MA: Harvard University Press, 1995), chap. 3, for kinds of participation, and pp. 66–67 for prevalence of local activity.

3. For a discussion of citizen lobbying, see Jeffrey M. Berry, *The New Liberalism: The Rising Power of Citizen Groups* (Washington, DC: Brookings, 1999).

4. Verba, Schlozman, and Brady, *Voice and Equality,* p. 51.

5. Steven J. Rosenstone and John Mark Hansen, *Mobilization, Participation, and Democracy in America* (New York: Macmillan, 1993), chap. 3; and Verba, Schlozman, and Brady, *Voice and Equality,* pp. 71–74.

6. Robert Jackman, "Political Institutions and Voter Turnout in the Democracies," *American Political Science Review* 81 (June 1987), p. 420.

7. See William Julius Wilson, *The Truly Disadvantaged: The Inner City, the Underclass, and Public Policy* (Chicago: University of Chicago Press, 1987); and Douglas Massey and Nancy Denton, *American Apartheid: Segregation and the Making of the American Underclass* (Cambridge, MA: Harvard University Press, 1993).

8. See Michael C. Dawson, *Behind the Mule: Race and Class in African-American Politics* (Princeton, NJ: Princeton University Press, 1994), chaps. 5 and 6.

9. Dawson, *Behind the Mule.*

10. Dana Milbank, "Attacks Shelve GOP Effort to Woo Hispanics," *Washington Post,* December 20, 2001, p. A4.

11. Pei-te Lien, Christian Collet, Janelle Wong, and S. Karthick Ramakrishnan, "Asian Pacific-American Public Opinion and Political Participation," *PS: Political Science* 34(3) (September 2002), p. 628.

12. Anne E. Kornblut, "Bush Plan to Win over Democratic Voters Lags," *Boston Globe* (April 27, 2003), p. A1.

13. Ronald Browstein, "Response to Terror: The Times Poll," *Los Angeles Times,* November 15, 2001, p. A1.

14. Richard Benedetto, "Expectations Have Changed, But Not Support," *USA Today* (March 24, 2003), p. 8A; Bob von Sternberg and Eric Black, "A Political Roundup," *Star Tribune* (November 16, 2003), p. 7A.

15. See Thomas B. Edsall, "Pollsters View Gender Gap as Political Fixture," *Washington Post,* August 15, 1995, p. A11.

16. Richard L. Berke, "Defections among Men to G.O.P. Helped Insure Rout of Democrats," *New York Times,* November 11, 1994, p. A1.

17. "Fact Sheet: Women in Elective Office," Center for the American Woman and Politics, Eagleton Institute of Politics, Rutgers University, January 2002.

18. David S. Broder, "Key to Women's Political Parity: Running," *Washington Post,* September 8, 1994, p. A17.

19. "The Impact of Women in Public Office: Findings at a Glance," Center for the American Woman and Politics (New Brunswick, NJ: Rutgers University, n.d.).

20. *Engel v. Vitale,* 370 U.S. 421 (1962); *Abington School District v. Schempp,* 374 U.S. 203 (1963); *Roe v. Wade,* 410 U.S. 113 (1973).

21. Laurie Goodstein, "Bush's Charity Plan Is Raising Concerns for Religious Right," *New York Times,* March 3, 2001, p. A1.

22. Dana Milbank, "Religious Right Finds Its Center in Oval Office," *Washington Post,* December 24, 2001, p. A2.

23. U.S. Census Bureau, Statistical Abstract of the United States: 2001, Table No. 401, www.census.gov. Accessed February 23, 2002.

24. Michael DeCourcy Hinds, "Youth Vote 2000: They'd Rather Volunteer," Carnegie Reporter 1, No. 2 (Spring 2001), p. 2.

25. Hinds, "Youth Vote 2000," p. 3.

26. See Thomas B. Edsall, "Huge Gains in South Fueled GOP Vote in '94," *Washington Post,* September 27, 1995, p. A8.

27. See Richard A. Brody, "The Puzzle of Political Participation in America," in *The New American Political System,* ed. Anthony King (Washington, DC: American Enterprise Institute, 1978), chap. 8.

28. On the nineteenth century, see Michael E. McGerr, *The Decline of Popular Politics: The American North, 1865–1928* (New York: Oxford University Press, 1986).

29. Verba, Schlozman, and Brady, *Voice and Equality.*

30. See Alexis de Tocqueville, *Democracy in America* (New York: Vintage, 1945).

31. Robert D. Putnam, "Bowling Alone: America's Declining Social Capital," *Journal of Democracy* 6, no. 1 (January 1995), pp. 65–78.

32. On television see Robert D. Putnam, "Tuning In, Tuning Out: The Strange Disappearance of Social Capital in America," *PS: Political Science and Politics* 28, no. 4 (December 1995), pp. 664–83; for a reply see Pippa Norris, "Does Television Erode Social Capital? A Reply to Putnam," *PS: Political Science and Politics* 29, no. 3 (September 1996), pp. 474–80.

33. Michael Schudson, "What If Civic Life Didn't Die?" *American Prospect* 25 (March–April 1996), pp. 17–20.

34. Rosenstone and Hansen, *Mobilization, Participation, and Democracy in America,* p. 59.

35. Robert A. Jackson, Robert D. Brown, and Gerald C. Wright, "Registration, Turnout and the Electoral Representativeness of U.S. State Electorates," *American Politics Quarterly,* vol. 26, no. 3 (July 1998), pp. 259–87. Also, Benjamin Highton, "Easy Registration and Voter Turnout," *Journal of Politics,* vol. 59, no. 2 (April 1997), pp. 565–87.

36. Connie Cass, "'Motor Voter' Impact Slight," *Chattanooga News-Free Press,* June 20, 1997, p. A5. On the need to motivate voters see Marshall Ganz, "Motor Voter or Motivated Voter?" *American Prospect,* no. 28

(September–October 1996), pp. 41–49. On the hopes for Motor Voter see Frances Fox Piven and Richard A. Cloward, "Northern Bourbons: A Preliminary Report on the National Voter Registration Act," *PS: Political Science and Politics* 29, no. 1 (March 1996), pp. 39–42. On turnout in the 1996 election, see Barbara Vobejda, "Just under Half of Possible Voters Went to the Polls," *Washington Post,* November 7, 1996, p. A3.

37. The data in this paragraph is drawn from The Sentencing Project and Human Rights Watch, "Losing the Vote: The Impact of Felony Disfranchisement Laws in the United States," 1998, www.sentencingproject.org/pubs/hrwfvr.html. Accessed February 23, 2002.

38. Chris Uggen and Jeffrey Manza, "Democratic Contraction: Political Consequences of Felon Disenfranchisement in the United States," *American Sociological Review* 67(6), pp. 777–803.

39. Lawrence Bobo and Franklin D. Gilliam, "Race, Sociopolitical Participation, and Black Empowerment," *American Political Science Review* 24, no. 2 (June 1990), pp. 377–93.

40. Rosenstone and Hansen, *Mobilization, Participation, and Democracy in America,* p. 59.

41. Alan Gerber and Donald Green, "The Effects of Canvassing, Phone Calls, and Direct Mail on Voter Turnout: A Field Experiment," Yale University, April 24, 2000, p. 22.

42. Donald P. Green and Alan S. Gerber, "Getting Out the Youth Vote: Results from Randomized Field Experiments," Pew Charitable Trusts, August 6, 2001, p. 27.

43. Erik Austin and Jerome Chubb, *Political Facts of the United States since 1789* (New York: Columbia University Press, 1986), pp. 378–79.

44. Kenneth N. Weine, "Campaigns without a Human Face," *Washington Post,* October 27, 1996, p. C1; see also Margaret Weir and Marshall Ganz, "Reconnecting People and Politics," *The New Majority: Toward Popular Progressive Politics,* ed. Stanley B. Greenberg and Theda Skocpol (New Haven, CT: Yale University Press, 1997), pp. 149–71.

45. Joyce Purnick, "One-Doorbell One-Vote Tactic Re-emerges in Bush-Kerry Race," *New York Times,* April 6, 2004, p. A1.

46. *Buckley v. Valeo,* 424 U.S. 1 (1976).

47. Michael Schudson, "What If Civic Life Didn't Die?" *American Prospect* 25 (March–April 1996), p. 18.

48. See Christopher Lasch, *The Revolt of the Elites and the Betrayal of American Democracy* (New York: Norton, 1995). The idea of the "secession of the rich" comes from Robert Reich, *The Work of Nations* (New York: Knopf, 1991), chaps. 23 and 24.

Chapter 9

1. See Richard Hofstadter, *The Idea of a Party System* (Berkeley: University of California Press, 1969).

2. John Aldrich, *Why Parties: The Origin and Transformation of Political Parties in America* (Chicago: University of Chicago Press, 1995).

3. See Matthew Crenson and Benjamin Ginsberg, *Downsizing Democracy* (Baltimore, MD: Johns Hopkins University Press, 2002).

4. Benjamin Ginsberg, *The Consequences of Consent* (New York: Random House, 1982), chap. 4.

5. For a discussion of third parties in the United States, see Daniel Mazmanian, *Third Parties in Presidential Election* (Washington, DC: Brookings, 1974).

6. See Maurice Duverger, *Political Parties* (New York: Wiley, 1954).

7. Glen Justice, "F.E.C. Declines to Curb Independent Fund Raisers," *New York Times,* May 14, 2004, p. A16.

8. See Harold Gosnell, *Machine Politics Chicago Model,* rev. ed. (Chicago: University of Chicago Press, 1968).

9. For a useful discussion, see John Bibby and Thomas Holbrook, "Parties and Elections," in *Politics in the American States,* ed. Virginia Gray and Herbert Jacob (Washington, DC: Congressional Quarterly Press, 1996), pp. 78–121.

10. For an excellent analysis of the parties' role in recruitment, see Paul Herrnson, *Congressional Elections: Campaigning at Home and in Washington* (Washington, DC: Congressional Quarterly Press, 1995).

11. Duverger, *Political Parties,* p. 426.

12. Duverger, *Political Parties,* chap. 1.

13. Stanley Kelley, Jr., Richard E. Ayres, and William Bowen, "Registration and Voting: Putting First Things First," *American Political Science Review* 61 (June 1967), pp. 359–70.

14. David H. Fischer, *The Revolution of American Conservatism* (New York: Harper & Row, 1965), p. 93.

15. Fischer, *The Revolution of American Conservatism,* p. 109.

16. Henry Jones Ford, *The Rise and Growth of American Politics* (New York: Da Capo Press, 1967 reprint of the 1898 edition), chap. 9.

17. Ford, *The Rise and Growth of American Politics,* p. 125.

18. Ford, *The Rise and Growth of American Politics,* p. 125.

19. Ford, *The Rise and Growth of American Politics,* p. 126.

20. Mark Barabak, "Los Angeles Times Interview: Cruz Bustamente: On Surviving a Bruising First Term as Assembly Speaker," *Los Angeles Times,* August 24, 1997, p. M3.

Chapter 10

1. Clinton Rossiter, ed., *The Federalist Papers* (New York: New American Library, 1961), No. 57, p. 352.

2. *League of United Latin American Citizens v. Wilson,* CV-94-7569 (C.D. Calif.), 1995.

3. *Gray v. Sanders,* 372 U.S. 368 (1963); *Wesberry v. Sanders,* 376 U.S. 1 (1964); *Reynolds v. Sims,* 377 U.S. 533 (1964).

4. *Thornburg v. Gingles,* 478 U.S. 613 (1986).

5. *Shaw v. Reno,* 509 U.S. 113 (1993).

6. State legislatures determine the system by which electors are selected and almost all states use this "winner-take-all" system. Maine and Nebraska, however, provide that one electoral vote goes to the winner in each congressional district and two electoral votes go to the winner statewide.

7. Stephen Ansolabehere and James Snyder, "Campaign War Chests and Congressional Elections," *Business and Politics* 2 (2000): 9–34.

8. Gary W. Cox and Eric Magar, "How Much Is Majority Status in the U.S. Congress Worth?" *American Political Science Review* 93 (1999): 299–309.

9. Jacob Schlesinger and Jeanne Cummings, "To Beat President, Democrats Hone a 5-Point Strategy," *Wall Street Journal,* November 13, 2003, p. 1.

10. Larry J. Sabato, *The Rise of Political Consultants* (New York: Basic Books, 1981).

11. Larry J. Sabato, *The Rise of Political Consultants,* p. 250.

12. Naom Scheiber, "Organization Man: Joe Trippi Reinvents Campaigning," *The New Republic,* November 17, 2003, p. 25.

13. Dana Milbanks, "Virtual Politics," *New Republic,* July 5, 1999, p. 22.

14. M. Ostrogorski, *Democracy and the Organization of Political Parties* (New York: Macmillan, 1902).

15. Timothy Clark, "The RNC Prospers, the DNC Struggles as They Face the 1980 Election," *National Journal,* October 27, 1980, p. 1619.

16. For discussions of the consequences, see Thomas Edsall, *The New Politics of Inequality* (New York: Norton, 1984). Also see Thomas Edsall, "Both Parties Get the Company's Money—But the Boss Backs the GOP," *Washington Post National Weekly Edition,* Sep-tember 16, 1986, p. 14; and Benjamin Ginsberg, "Money and Power: The New Political Economy of American Elections," in *The Political Economy,* ed. Thomas Ferguson and Joel Rogers (Armonk, NY: M. E. Sharpe, 1984).

17. www.fec.gov.

18. www.fec.gov.

19. FEC reports.

20. FEC reports.

21. James Grimaldi and Thomas B. Edsall, "Fundraiser Denies Link between Money, Access," *Washington Post,* May 17, 2004, p. 1.

22. David Broder and Ruth Marcus, "Wielding Third Force in Politics," *Washington Post,* September 20, 1997, p. 1.

Chapter 11

1. Ceci Connolly, "Drugmakers Protect Their Turf," *Washington Post,* November 21, 2003, p. A4.

2. Thomas B. Edsall, "2 Bills Would Benefit Top Bush Fundrais-ers," *Washington Post,* November 22, 2003, p. 1.

3. Clinton Rossiter, ed., *The Federalist Papers* (New York: New American Library, 1961), No. 10, p. 83.

4. Rossiter, ed., *Federalist Papers,* No. 10.

5. The best statement of the pluralist view is in David Truman, *The Governmental Process* (New York: Knopf, 1951), chap. 2.

6. E. E. Schattschneider, *The Semisovereign People* (New York: Holt, Rinehart, and Winston, 1960), p. 35.

7. Betsy Wagner and David Bowermaster, "B.S. Economics," *Washington Monthly,* November 1992, pp. 19–21.

8. David B. Truman, *The Governmental Process* (New York: Knopf, 1951).

9. Mancur Olson, *The Logic of Collective Action* (Cambridge, MA: Harvard University Press, 1965).

10. Timothy Penny and Steven Schier, *Payment Due: A Nation in Debt, a Generation in Trouble* (Boulder, CO: Westview, 1996), pp. 64–65.

11. Kay Lehman Schlozman and John T. Tierney, *Organized Inter-ests and American Democracy* (New York: Harper & Row, 1986), p. 60.

12. John Herbers, "Special Interests Gaining Power as Voter Disil-lusionment Grows," *New York Times,* November 14, 1978.

13. For discussions of lobbying, see Allan J. Cigler and Burdett A. Loomis, eds., *Interest Group Politics* (Washington, DC: Congressional Quarterly Press, 1983). See also Jeffrey M. Berry, *Lobbying for the Peo-ple* (Princeton, NJ: Princeton University Press, 1977).

14. "The Swarming Lobbyists," *Time,* August 7, 1978, p. 15.

15. See Frank Baumgartner and Beth Leech, *Basic Interests* (Princeton, NJ: Princeton University Press, 1998).

16. Steven Brill, *After: How America Confronted the September 12 Era* (New York: Simon & Schuster, 2003).

17. Daniel Franklin, "Tommy Boggs and the Death of Health Care Reform," *Washington Monthly* (April 1995), p. 36.

18. Marie Jojnacki, "Interest Groups' Decisions to Join Alliances or Work Alone," *American Journal of Political Science 41* (1997) pp. 61–87; Kevin W. Hula, *Lobbying Together: Interest Groups Coali-tions in Legislative Politics* (Washington, DC: Georgetown University Press, 1999).

19. Peter H. Stone, "Follow the Leaders," *National Journal,* June 24, 1995, p. 1641.

20. www.commoncause.org, "The Microsoft Playbook: A Report from Common Cause," September 25, 2000.

21. "Edison Electric Institute Lobbying to Weaken Toxic Mercury Standards," http://tristatenews.com, February 28, 2003.

22. John P. Heinz et al., *The Hollow Core: Private Interests in Na-tional Policy Making* (Cambridge, MA: Harvard University Press, 1993).

23. For an excellent discussion of the political origins of the Ad-ministrative Procedure Act, see Martin Shapiro, "APA: Past, Present, Future," 72 *Virginia Law Review 377* (March 1986), pp. 447–92.

24. *Roe v. Wade,* 93 S.Ct. 705 (1973).

25. *Webster v. Reproductive Health Services,* 109 S.Ct. 3040 (1989)

26. *Brown v. Board of Education of Topeka, Kansas,* 74 S.Ct. 686 (1954).

27. See, for example, *Duke Power Co. v. Carolina Environmental Study Group,* 438 U.S. 59 (1978).

28. E. Pendleton Herring, *Group Representation before Congress* (New York: McGraw-Hill, 1936).

29. Ann Devroy, "Gay Rights Leaders Meet President in Oval Office: White House Tries to Play Down Session," *Washington Post,* April 17, 1993, p. 1.

30. Michael Weisskopf, "Energized by Pulpit or Passion, the Public Is Calling," *Washington Post,* February 1, 1993, p. 1.

31. Stephen Engelberg, "A New Breed of Hired Hands Cultivates Grass-Roots Anger," *New York Times,* March 17, 1993, p. A1.

32. Jane Fritsch, "The Grass Roots, Just a Free Phone Call Away," *New York Times,* June 23, 1995, pp. A1 and A22.

33. Richard L. Burke, "Religious-Right Candidates Gain as GOP Turnout Rises," *New York Times,* November 12, 1994, p. 10.

34. Some Americans and even more Europeans would stress only the negative aspect of the softening and adulterating effect of the two-party system on class and other basic subdivisions of soci-ety. For a discussion of how the working class was divided and soft-ened, with native workers joining the Democratic Party and new immigrant workers becoming Republicans, see Gwendolyn Mink, *Old Labor and New Immigrants in American Political Development: Union, Party, and State, 1875–1920* (Ithaca, NY: Cornell University Press, 1986).

35. Elisabeth R. Gerber, *The Populist Paradox* (Princeton, NJ: Princeton University Press, 1999).

36. Rossiter, ed., *The Federalist Papers*, No. 10.

37. Olson, *The Logic of Collective Action*.

38. Steve Ma, telephone interview by author, February 12, 1998.

39. Steve Ma, interview, February 12, 1998.

Chapter 12

1. John F. Harris, "Hillary's Big Adventure," *Washington Post*, January 27, 2002, p. W8.

2. For a discussion of these roles, see Roger Davidson and Walter H. Oleszek, *Congress and Its Members* (Washington, DC: CQ Press, 2002), chap. 5.

3. Herb Asher and Mike Barr, "Popular Support for Congress and Its Members," and Karlyn Borman and Everett Carll Ladd, "Public Opinion toward Congress: A Historical Look," in *Congress, the Press, and the Public*, ed. Thomas E. Mann and Norman J. Ornstein (Washington, DC: American Enterprise Institute and Brookings Institution, 1994), pp. 34, 51, 53.

4. John R. Hibbing and Elizabeth Theiss-Morse, *Congress as Public Enemy: Public Attitudes toward American Political Institutions* (New York: Cambridge University Press, 1995), p. 100.

5. This argument is developed in Hibbing and Theiss-Morse, *Congress as Public Enemy*. For more on the institutionalization of Congress, see Nelson Polsby, "The Institutionalization of the US House of Representatives," *American Political Science Review* 62 (1968): 144–68; on professionalization see Alan Ehrenhalt, *The United States of Ambition: Politicians, Power, and the Pursuit of Office* (New York: Times Books, 1991).

6. For data on religious affiliations of the members of the 105th Congress, see *Congressional Quarterly Weekly Report*, January 4, 1997.

7. For data on occupational backgrounds of the members of the 105th Congress, see *Congressional Quarterly Weekly Report*, January 4, 1997.

8. Marian D. Irish and James Prothro, *The Politics of American Democracy*, 5th ed. (Englewood Cliffs, NJ: Prentice-Hall, 1971), p. 352.

9. For a discussion, see Benjamin Ginsberg, *The Consequences of Consent* (New York: Random House, 1982), chap. 1.

10. For some interesting empirical evidence, see Angus Campbell, Philip Converse, Warren Miller, and Donald Stokes, *Elections and the Political Order* (New York: Wiley, 1966), chap. 11.

11. Congressional Quarterly, *Guide to the Congress of the United States*, 3rd ed. (Washington, DC: Congressional Quarterly Press, 1982), p. 599.

12. John S. Saloma, *Congress and the New Politics* (Boston: Little, Brown, 1969), pp. 184–85. A 1977 official report using less detailed categories came up with almost the same impression of Congress's workload. Commission on Administrative Review, *Administrative Reorganization and Legislative Management*, House Doc. #95-232 (September 28, 1977), vol. 2, especially pp. 17–19.

13. See Linda Fowler and Robert McClure, *Political Ambition: Who Decides to Run for Congress* (New Haven, CT: Yale University Press, 1989); and Alan Ehrenhalt, *The United States of Ambition*.

14. See Barbara C. Burrell, *A Woman's Place Is in the House: Campaigning for Congress in the Feminist Era* (Ann Arbor: University of Michigan Press, 1994), chap. 6; and the essays in Elizabeth Adell Cook, Sue Thomas, and Clyde Wilcox, eds., *The Year of the Woman: Myths and Realities* (Boulder, CO: Westview, 1994).

15. Ruth Marcus and Juliet Eilperin, "Battle for House Fuels Cash Race," *Washington Post*, August 11, 1999, p. A1; Alison Mitchell, "Congress Chasing Campaign Donors Early and Often," *New York Times*, June 14, 1999, p. A1; Gilbert Craig, "Kohn Vows to Win Dairy Price Fight," *Milwaukee Journal Sentinel*, November 21, 1999, p. 1.

16. See Burrell, *A Woman's Place Is in the House;* and David Broder, "Key to Women's Political Parity: Running," *Washington Post*, September 8, 1994, p. A17.

17. "Did Redistricting Sink the Democrats?" *National Journal*, December 17, 1994, p. 2984.

18. *Miller v. Johnson*, 115 S.Ct. 2475 (1995).

19. Joseph J. Schatz, "GOP Hopeful for Quick Resolution on Spending Omnibus in New Year," *Congressional Quarterly Weekly*, December 13, 2003, p. 3080.

20. Timothy Eagan, "Built with Steel, Perhaps, But Greased with Pork," *New York Times*, April 10, 2004, p. A1.

21. www.house.gov/stark/services.html

22. Congressional Quarterly, *Guide to the Congress of the United States*, 2nd ed. (Washington, DC: Congressional Quarterly Press, 1976), pp. 229–310.

23. Richard Fenno, Jr., *Home Style: House Members in Their Districts* (Boston: Little, Brown, 1978).

24. Richard C. Fenno, *Congressmen in Committees* (Boston: Little, Brown, 1973), p. 1; Richard L. Hall, "Participation, Abdication, and Representation in Congressional Committees," in *Congress Reconsidered*, 5th ed., ed. Lawrence C. Dodd and Bruce I. Oppenheimer (Washington DC: Congressional Quarterly Press, 1993), p. 164.

25. Derek Willis, "Republicans Mix It Up When Assigning House Chairmen for the 108th," *Congressional Quarterly Weekly*, January 11, 2003, p. 89.

26. See Thomas E. Mann and Norman J. Ornstein, *Renewing Congress: A First Report of the Renewing Congress Project* (Washington, DC: American Enterprise Institute and Brookings Institution, 1992). See also the essays in Roger H. Davidson, ed., *The Postreform Congress* (New York: St. Martin's, 1992).

27. Richard E. Cohen, "Crackup of the Committees," *National Journal*, July 31, 1999, p. 2210–16.

28. Jeff Plungis, "The Driving Force of Bud Schuster," *Congressional Quarterly Weekly Report*, August 7, 1999, p. 1919.

29. See Robert Pear, "Senator X Kills Measure on Anonymity," *New York Times*, November 11, 1997, p. 12.

30. See John W. Kingdon, *Congressmen's Voting Decisions* (New York: Harper & Row, 1973), chap. 3; and R. Douglas Arnold, *The Logic of Congressional Action* (New Haven, CT: Yale University Press, 1990).

31. Jane Fritsch, "The Grass Roots, Just a Free Phone Call Away," *New York Times*, June 23, 1995, p. A1.

32. Daniel Franklin, "Tommy Boggs and the Death of Health Care Reform," *Washington Monthly,* April 1995, p. 36.

33. Holly Idelson, "Signs Point to Greater Loyalty on Both Sides of the Aisle," *Congressional Quarterly Weekly Report,* December 19, 1992, p. 3849.

34. "GOP Leadership PACs' Fundraising Far Outstrips 1997–98," *Congressional Quarterly Weekly Report,* August 15, 1999, p. 1991.

35. Alison Mitchell, "Underlying Tensions Kept Congress Divided to the End," *New York Times,* November 21, 1999, p. 1.

36. James J. Kilpatrick, "Don't Overlook Corn for Porn Plot," *Chicago Sun-Times,* January 3, 1992, p. 23.

37. Dennis McDougal, "Cattle Are Bargaining Chip of the NEA," *Los Angeles Times,* November 2, 1991, p. F1.

38. Carl Hulse, "Even Some in GOP Call for More Oversight of Bush," *New York Times,* May 31, 2004, p. A13.

39. *U.S. v. Pink,* 315 U.S. 203 (1942). For a good discussion of the problem, see James W. Davis, *The American Presidency* (New York: Harper & Row, 1987), chap. 8.

40. Carroll J. Doherty, "Impeachment: How It Would Work," *Congressional Quarterly Weekly Report,* January 31, 1998, p. 222.

41. See Kenneth A. Shepsle. "Representation and Governance: The Great Legislative Trade-off," *Political Science Quarterly* 103:3 (1988), pp. 461–84.

42. Role of the Public in Government Decisions Survey, January 1999, Roper Center Public Opinion Online, Accession number 0325495; Role of the Public in Government Decisions Survey, January 1999, Roper Center Public Opinion Online, Accession number 0325490.

43. See Hibbing and Theiss-Morse, *Congress as Public Enemy,* p. 105.

44. Larry M. Bartels, "Economic Inequality and Political Representation" (unpublished paper, Department of Politics and Woodrow Wilson School of Public and International Affairs, Princeton University, November 2002).

45. Birnbaum, "Washington's Power 25."

Chapter 13

1. *In re Neagle,* 135 U.S. 1 (1890).

2. James G. Randall, *Constitutional Problems under Lincoln* (New York: Appleton, 1926), ch. 1.

3. Edward S. Corwin, *The President: Office and Powers,* 4th rev. ed. (New York: New York University Press, 1957), p. 229.

4. These statutes are contained mainly in Title 10 of the United States Code, Sections 331, 332, and 333.

5. The best study covering all aspects of the domestic use of the military is that of Adam Yarmolinsky, *The Military Establishment* (New York: Harper & Row, 1971). Probably the most famous instance of a president's unilateral use of the power to protect a state "against domestic violence" was in dealing with the Pullman Strike of 1894. The famous Supreme Court case that ensued was *In re Debs,* 158 U.S. 564 (1895).

6. In *United States v. Pink,* 315 U.S. 203 (1942), the Supreme Court confirmed that an executive agreement is the legal equivalent of a treaty, despite the absence of Senate approval. This case approved the executive agreement that was used to establish diplomatic relations with the Soviet Union in 1933. An executive agreement, not a treaty, was used in 1940 to exchange "fifty over-age destroyers" for ninety-nine-year leases on some important military bases.

7. Raoul Berger, Executive *Privilege: A Constitutional Myth* (Cambridge, MA: Harvard University Press, 1974), pp. 1–14.

8. There is a third source of presidential power implied from the provision for "faithful execution of the laws." This is the president's power to impound funds—that is, to refuse to spend money Congress has appropriated for certain purposes. One author referred to this as a "retroactive veto power" (Robert E. Goosetree, "The Power of the President to Impound Appropriated Funds," *American University Law Review,* January 1962). This impoundment power was used freely and to considerable effect by many modern presidents, and Congress occasionally delegated such power to the president by statute. But in reaction to the Watergate scandal, Congress adopted the Budget and Impoundment Control Act of 1974 and designed this act to circumscribe the president's ability to impound funds by requiring that the president must spend all appropriated funds unless both houses of Congress consent to an impoundment within forty-five days of a presidential request. Therefore, since 1974, the use of impoundment has declined significantly. Presidents have either had to bite their tongues and accept unwanted appropriations or had to revert to the older and more dependable but politically limited method of vetoing the entire bill.

9. For a different perspective, see William F. Grover, *The President as Prisoner: A Structural Critique of the Carter and Reagan Years* (Albany: State University of New York Press, 1988).

10. For more on the veto, see Chapter 13 and Robert J. Spitzer, *The Presidential Veto: Touchstone of the American Presidency* (Albany: State University of New York Press, 1989).

11. Quoted in Richard W. Stevenson, "Focus on Social Security and the Tax Code," *New York Times,* November 5, 2004, p. A1.

12. For a good review of President Clinton's legislative leadership in the first session of his last Congress, see *Congressional Quarterly Weekly,* November 13, 1999, especially the cover story by Andrew Taylor, "Clinton Gives Republicans a Gentler Year-End Beating," pp. 2698–2700.

13. Kenneth F. Warren, *Administrative Law,* 3rd ed. (Upper Saddle River, NJ: Prentice Hall, 1996), p. 250.

14. Theodore J. Lowi, *The End of Liberalism,* 2nd ed. (New York: Norton, 1979), pp. 117–18.

15. *J. W. Hampton & Co. v. U.S.,* 276 U.S. 394 (1928).

16. 48 Stat. 200.

17. David Schoenbrod, *Power without Responsibility: How Congress Abuses the People through Delegation* (New Haven, CT: Yale University Press, 1993), pp. 49–50.

18. Lowi, *The End of Liberalism,* p. 117.

19. *New York Times,* December 23, 1992, p. 1.

20. A substantial portion of this section is taken from Theodore J. Lowi, *The Personal President* (Ithaca, NY: Cornell University Press, 1985), pp. 141–50.

21. All the figures since 1967, and probably 1957, are understated, because additional White House staff members were on "detail" service from the military and other departments (some secretly assigned) and are not counted here because they were not on the White House payroll.

22. The actual number is difficult to estimate because, as with White House staff, some EOP personnel, especially in national security work, are detailed to EOP from outside agencies.

23. Article I, Section 3, provides that "The Vice-President . . . shall be President of the Senate, but shall have no Vote, unless they be equally divided." This is the only vote the vice president is allowed.

24. Samuel Kernell, *Going Public: New Strategies of Presidential Leadership*, 3rd ed. (Washington, DC: Congressional Quarterly Press, 1997); also, Jeffrey K. Tulis, *The Rhetorical Presidency* (Princeton, NJ: Princeton University Press, 1987).

25. Tulis, *The Rhetorical Presidency*, p. 91.

26. Sidney M. Milkis, *The President and the Parties* (New York: Oxford, 1993), p. 97.

27. James MacGregor Burns, *Roosevelt: The Lion and the Fox* (New York: Harcourt, Brace, 1956), p. 317.

28. Burns, *Roosevelt*, p. 317.

29. Kernell, *Going Public*, p. 79.

30. Tulis, *The Rhetorical Presidency*, p. 161.

31. Lowi, *The Personal President: Power Invested, Promise Unfulfilled* (Ithica, NY: Cornell University Press, 1985).

32. Lowi, *The Personal President*, p. 11.

33. Kernell, *Going Public*, p. 114.

34. Harold W. Stanley and Richard G. Niemi, *Vital Statistics on American Politics, 2001-2002* (Washington, DC: Congressional Quarterly Press, 2001), pp. 250–51.

35. Milkis, *The President and the Parties*, p. 128.

36. Milkis, *The President and the Parties*, p. 160.

37. The classic critique of this process is Theodore J. Lowi, *The End of Liberalism* (New York: Norton, 1969).

38. Kenneth Culp Davis, *Administrative Law Treatise* (St. Paul, MN: West Publishing, 1958), p. 9.

39. Elena Kagan, "Presidential Administration," 114 *Harvard Law Review 2245* (2001), p. 2265.

40. For example, Douglas W. Kmiec, "Expanding Power," in Roger Pilon, ed., *The Rule of Law in the Wake of Clinton* (Washington, DC: Cato Institute Press, 2000), pp. 47-68.

41. A complete inventory is provided in Harold C. Relyea, "Presidential Directives: Background and Review," The Library of Congress, *Congressional Research Service Report 98–611*, November 9, 2001.

42. Terry M. Moe and William G. Howell, "The Presidential Power of Unilateral Action," *Journal of Law, Economics and Organization, 15*, no. 1 (January, 1999), pp. 133-34.

43. Moe and Howell, "The Presidential Power of Unilateral Action," p. 164.

44. *Youngstown Sheet & Tube Co. v. Sawyer*, 346 U.S. 579 (1952).

45. Todd Gaziano, "The New 'Massive Resistance'," *Policy Review* (May–June 1998), p. 283.

46. Kagan, "Presidential Administration," p. 2351.

47. Clinton Rossiter, ed., *The Federalist Papers, No. 70* (New York: Signet, 1961), pp. 423–30.

48. Terry Moe, "The Presidency and the Bureaucracy: The Presidential Advantage," in Michael Nelson, ed., *The Presidency and the Political System* (Washington, DC: Congressional Quarterly Press, 2002), pp. 416–20.

Chapter 14

1. U.S. Bureau of the Census, *Statistical Abstract of the United States, 2003* (Washington, DC: U.S. Government Printing Office, 2003), pp. 336, 344.

2. Arnold Brecht and Comstock Glaser, *The Art and Techniques of Administration in German Ministries* (Cambridge, MA: Harvard University Press, 1940), p. 6.

3. This account is drawn from Alan Stone, *How America Got On-Line: Politics, Markets, and the Revolution in Telecommunications* (Armonk, NY: M. E. Sharpe, 1997), pp. 184–87.

4. Gary Bryner, *Bureaucratic Discretion* (New York: Pergamon, 1987).

5. There are historical reasons why American cabinet-level administrators are called "secretaries." During the Second Continental Congress and the subsequent confederal government, standing committees were formed to deal with executive functions related to foreign affairs, military and maritime issues, and public financing. The heads of those committees were called "secretaries" because their primary task was to handle all correspondence and documentation related to their areas of responsibility.

6. 32 Stat. 825; 15 U.S.C. 1501.

7. See William Keller, *The Liberals and J. Edgar Hoover* (Princeton, NJ: Princeton University Press, 1989). See also Victor Navasky, *Kennedy Justice* (New York: Atheneum, 1971), chap. 2 and p. 8.

8. Bryan Bender, "Fighting Terror the Military Campaign/FBI Director; In Afghanistan Visit, Mueller Sees Agents' New Roles," *Boston Globe*, January 24, 2002, p. A13.

9. For more detail, consult John E. Harr, *The Professional Diplomat* (Princeton, NJ: Princeton University Press, 1972), p. 11; and

Nicholas Horrock, "The CIA Has Neighbors in the 'Intelligence Community,'" *New York Times*, June 29, 1975, sec. 4, p. 2. See also Roger Hilsman, *The Politics of Policy Making in Defense and Foreign Affairs*, 3rd ed. (Englewood Cliffs, NJ: Prentice Hall, 1993).

10. *The 9/11 Commission Report: Final Report of the National Commission on Terrorist Attacks upon the United States* (New York: Norton, 2004).

11. Daniel Patrick Moynihan, "The Culture of Secrecy," *Public Interest*, Summer 1997, pp. 55–71.

12. Sean Paige, "A Sunshine Law Still in Shadows," *Insight on the News* 14 (December 28, 1998), p. 14.

13. Dana Milbank, "Under Bush, Expanding Secrecy," *Washington Post*, December 23, 2003, p. A19.

14. See Paul Peterson, *The Price of Federalism* (Washington, DC: Brookings, 1995) for a recent argument that "redistribution" is the distinctive function of the national government in the American federal system.

15. *Budget of the United States Government, FY 2005: Analytical Perspectives* (Washington, DC: U.S. Government Printing Office, 2004), Table 15-1, p. 223.

16. For an excellent political analysis of the Fed, see Donald Kettl, *Leadership at the Fed* (New Haven, CT: Yale University Press, 1986).

17. George E. Berkley, *The Craft of Public Administration* (Boston: Allyn & Bacon, 1975), p. 417. Emphasis added.

18. Correspondent Kelli Arena, "Overhauling the IRS," CNN Financial Network, March 7, 1997.

19. Robert Cohen, "IRS, Ordered to Treat U.S. Taxpayers Better, Collects Billions Less," *Seattle Times*, December 2, 1999, p. A18; David

Cay Johnston, *Perfectly Legal: The Covert Campaign to Rig Our Tax System to Benefit the Super Rich—and Cheat Everybody Else* (New York: Portfolio, 2003).

20. David Cay Johnston, "At IRS, a Systems Update Gone Awry," *New York Times,* December 11, 2003, p. C1.

21. Eric Schmitt, "Washington Talk: No $435 Hammers, but Questions," *New York Times,* October 23, 1990, p. A16.

22. See National Performance Review Savings, www.npr.gov/library/announce/040700.html (accessed on June 13, 2000).

23. Paul C. Light, "Fact Sheet on the New True Size of Government," Center for Public Service (Washington, DC: Brookings Institution, September 5, 2003), www.brookings.org/gs/cps/light20030905.htm).

24. A thorough review of the first session of the 104th Congress will be found in "Republican's Hopes for 1996 Lie in Unfinished Business," *Congressional Quarterly Weekly Report,* January 6, 1996, pp. 6–18.

25. Public Law 101-510, Title XXIX, Sections 2,901 and 2,902 of Part A (Defense Base Closure and Realignment Commission).

26. Ronald Brownstein, "Washington Outlook; Shortsighted States Are Putting Health Care on the Chopping Block," *Los Angeles Times,* December 22, 2003, p. A13.

27. Joshua Chaffin, "Democrats Probe High Cost of Halliburton," *Financial Times,* February 17, 2004, p. 10.

28. The title was inspired by a book by Charles Hyneman, *Bureaucracy in a Democracy* (New York: Harper, 1950). For a more recent effort to describe the federal bureaucracy and to provide some guidelines for improvement, see Patricia W. Ingraham and Donald F. Kettl, eds., *Agenda for Excellence: Public Service in America* (Chatham, NJ: Chatham House, 1992).

29. Clinton Rossiter, ed., *The Federalist Papers* (New York: New American Library, 1961), No. 51, p. 322.

30. The title of this section was inspired by Peri Arnold, *Making the Managerial Presidency* (Princeton, NJ: Princeton University Press, 1986).

31. See Richard Nathan, *The Plot that Failed: Nixon and the Administrative Presidency* (New York: Wiley, 1975), pp. 68–76.

32. For more details and evaluations, see David Rosenbloom, *Public Administration* (New York: Random House, 1986), pp. 186–221; Levine and Kleeman, "The Quiet Crisis"; and Patricia Ingraham and

David Rosenbloom, "The State of Merit in the Federal Government," in *Agenda for Excellence,* ed. Ingraham and Kettl.

33. Lester Salamon and Alan Abramson, "Governance: The Politics of Retrenchment," in *The Reagan Record,* ed. John Palmer and Isabel Sawhill (Cambridge, MA: Ballinger, 1984), p. 40.

34. Colin Campbell, "The White House and the Presidency under the 'Let's Deal' President," in *The Bush Presidency: First Appraisals,* ed. Colin Campbell and Bert A. Rockman (Chatham, NJ: Chatham House, 1991), pp. 185–222.

35. See John Micklethwait, "Managing to Look Attractive," *New Statesman* 125, November 8, 1996, p. 24.

36. Quoted in I. M. Destler, "Reagan and the World: An 'Awesome Stubborness,'" in *The Reagan Legacy: Promise and Performance,* ed. Charles O. Jones (Chatham, NJ: Chatham House, 1988), pp. 244 and 257. The source of the quote is *Report of the President's Special Review Board* (Washington, DC: U.S. Government Printing Office, 1987).

37. Richard E. Cohen, "Crackup of the Committees," *National Journal* (July 31, 1999), p. 2214.

38. *The 9/11 Commission Report,* p. 399–419.

39. *The 9/11 Commission Report,* p. 421.

40. *The 9/11 Commission Report,* p. 422.

41. See Aaron Wildavsky, *The New Politics of the Budgetary Process,* 2d ed. (New York: HarperCollins, 1992), pp. 15–16.

42. The Office of Technology Assessment (OTA) was a fourth research agency serving Congress until 1995. It was one of the first agencies scheduled for elimination by the 104th Congress. Until 1983, Congress had still another tool of legislative oversight: the legislative veto. Each agency operating under such provisions was obliged to submit to Congress every proposed decision or rule, which would then lie before both chambers for thirty to sixty days. If Congress took no action by one-house or two-house resolution explicitly to veto the proposed measure during the prescribed period, it became law. The legislative veto was declared unconstitutional by the Supreme Court in 1983 on the grounds that it violated the separation of powers—the resolutions Congress passed to exercise its veto were not subject to presidential veto, as required by the Constitution. See *Immigration and Naturalization Service v. Chadha,* 462 U.S. 919 (1983).

Chapter 15

1. "In the Courts," *San Diego Union Tribune,* December 7, 2000, p. A14.

2. See Richard Neely, *How Courts Govern America* (New Haven, CT: Yale University Press, 1981).

3. U.S. Bureau of the Census, *Statistical Abstract of the United States* (Washington, DC: Government Printing Office, 1995).

4. C. Herman Pritchett, *The American Constitution* (New York: McGraw-Hill, 1959), p. 138.

5. *Marbury v. Madison,* 1 Cr. 137 (1803).

6. *Clinton v. City of New York,* 55 U.S.L.W. 4543 (1998).

7. This review power was affirmed by the Supreme Court in *Martin v. Hunter's Lessee,* 1 Wheat. 304 (1816).

8. *Brown v. Board of Education,* 347 U.S. 483 (1954); *Loving v. Virginia,* 388 U.S. 1 (1967).

9. *Griswold v. Connecticut,* 381 U.S. 479 (1965).

10. *Brandenburg v. Ohio,* 395 U.S. 444 (1969).

11. See Theodore J. Lowi, *The End of Liberalism,* 2nd ed. (New York: Norton, 1979); also, David Schoenbrod, *Power without Responsibility: How Congress Abuses the People through Delegation* (New Haven, CT: Yale University Press, 1993).

12. Kenneth Culp Davis, *Discretionary Justice* (Baton Rouge: Louisiana State University Press, 1969), pp. 15–21.

13. 56 Stat. 23 (January 30, 1942).

14. Oliver Wendell Holmes, Jr., "The Path of the Law," *Harvard Law Review* 10 (1897), p. 457.

15. *Shelley v. Kraemer,* 334 U.S. 1 (1948).

16. *Gideon v. Wainwright,* 372 U.S. 335 (1963).

17. *Burlington Industries v. Ellerth,* 97-569 (1998).

18. *Engel v. Vitale,* 370 U.S. 421 (1962); *Gideon v. Wainwright,* 372 U.S. 335 (1963); *Escobedo v. Illinois,* 378 U.S. 478 (1964); and *Miranda v. Arizona,* 384 U.S. 436 (1966).

19. *Baker v. Carr,* 369 U.S. 186 (1962).

20. Walter F. Murphy, "The Supreme Court of the United States," in *Encyclopedia of the American Judicial System,* ed. Robert J. Janosik (New York: Scribner's, 1987).

21. *Adarand Constructors v. Pena,* 115 S.Ct. 2097 (1995); *Missouri v. Jenkins,* 115 S.Ct. 2573 (1995); *Miller v. Johnson,* 115 S.Ct. 2475 (1995).

22. Robert Scigliano, *The Supreme Court and the Presidency* (New York: Free Press, 1971), p. 162. For an interesting critique of the solicitor general's role during the Reagan administration, see Lincoln Caplan, "Annals of the Law," *New Yorker,* August 17, 1987, pp. 30–62.

23. Edward Lazarus, *Closed Chambers* (New York: Times Books, 1998), p. 6.

24. *Plyler v. Doe,* 457 U.S. 202 (1982).

25. *NAACP v. Button,* 371 U.S. 415 (1963). The quotation is from the opinion in this case.

26. *Smith v. Allwright,* 321 U.S. 649 (1994).

27. Warren Richey, "Dissenting Opinions as a Window on Future Rulings," *Christian Science Monitor,* July 1, 2002, p. 1.

28. R. W. Apple, Jr., "A Divided Government Remains, and with It the Prospect of Further Combat," *New York Times,* November 7, 1996, p. B6.

29. Linda Greenhouse, "In Year of Florida Vote, Supreme Court Also Did Much Other Work," *New York Times,* July 2, 2001, p. A12.

30. Charles E. Lane, "Laying Down the Law," *Washington Post,* July 1, 2001, p. A6.

31. *Bush v. Gore,* 531 U.S. 98, 121 S.Ct. 525 (2000).

32. *Chicago Daily Law Bulletin,* October 5, 1994.

33. For limits on judicial power, see Alexander Bickel, *The Least Dangerous Branch* (Indianapolis, IN: Bobbs-Merrill, 1962).

34. *Worcester v. Georgia,* 6 Pet. 515 (1832).

35. See Walter Murphy, *Congress and the Court* (Chicago: University of Chicago Press, 1962).

36. Robert Dahl, "The Supreme Court and National Policy Making," *Journal of Public Law* 6 (1958), p. 279.

37. Martin Shapiro, "The Supreme Court: From Warren to Burger," in *The New American Political System,* ed. Anthony King (Washington, DC: American Enterprise Institute, 1978).

38. *Citizens to Preserve Overton Park v. Volpe,* 401 U.S. 402 (1971).

39. Toni Locy, "Bracing for Health Care's Caseload," *Washington Post,* August 22, 1994, p. A15.

40. See "Developments in the Law—Class Actions," *Harvard Law Review* 89 (1976), p. 1318.

41. *In re Agent Orange Product Liability Litigation,* 100 F.R.D. 718 (D.C.N.Y. 1983).

42. See Donald Horowitz, *The Courts and Social Policy* (Washington, DC: Brookings, 1977).

43. *Moran v. McDonough,* 540 F2d 527 (1 Cir., 1976; *cert. denied,* 429 U.S. 1042 [1977]).

44. Clinton Rossiter, ed., *The Federalist Papers* (New York: New American Library, 1961), No. 10, p. 78.

45. Probably the best study of the role of interest groups in the judicial process is that of Clement Vose, "Litigation as a Form of Pressure Group Activity," *Annals of the American Academy of Political and Social Science,* 319 (1958); this was expanded in his book *Caucasians Only: The Supreme Court, the NAACP and the Restrictive Covenant Cases* (Berkeley: University of California Press, 1959).

46. A full account of this role of the CBC and an assessment of its effectiveness will be found in Christina Rivers, unpublished doctoral dissertation, Cornell University, 2000. For an excellent account and assessment of the role of the CBC in Congress, see Paul Frymer, *Uneasy Alliances—Race and Party Competition in America* (Princeton, NJ: Princeton University Press, 1999), chap. 6.

47. Account will be found in David O'Brien, *Storm Center,* pp. 46–48. Other accounts of *amicus* briefs in other cases are also provided there.

ILLUSTRATION CREDITS

p. 1: AP/Wide World Photos; p. 2: AP/Wide World Photos; p. 11: (top left and bottom left) AP/Wide World Photos; p. 11: (top right and bottom right) Bettmann/Corbis; p. 12: AP/Wide World Photos; p. 22: (top left) Bettmann/Corbis; p. 22: (top right) The Library Company of Philadelphia; p. 22: (bottom) Neil Ryder Hoos; p. 23: (top) Dan Habib/Impact Visuals; p. 23: (bottom) Mark Wilson/Getty Images; p. 27: (top) From the Art Collection of the Boatmen's National Bank of St. Louis; p. 27: (bottom) Bettmann/Corbis; p. 28: AP/Wide World Photos; p. 29: (left and right) AP/Wide World Photos; p. 32: Shephard Sherbell/Corbis Saba; p. 36: Reuters/Corbis; p. 40: (top) Bettmann/Corbis; p. 40: (bottom) The Metropolitan Museum of Art, Arthur Hoppock Hearn Fund, 1950 (50.117). Photograph © 1988 The Metropolitan Museum of Art; © Estate of Grant Wood/Licensed by VAGA, New York, NY; p. 41: Library of Congress; p. 42: Courtesy, American Antiquarian Society; p. 45: (right) Bettmann/Corbis; p. 45: (left) The Historical Society of Pennsylvania; p. 47: Library of Congress; p. 48: The Granger Collection, New York; p. 49: The Library of Congress; p. 59: AP/Wide World Photos; p. 66: AP/Wide World Photos; p. 72: (top left) AP/Wide World Photos; p. 72: (top right) Carlos Avila Gonzalez/San Francisco Chronicle/Corbis; p. 72: (bottom left) Rick Friedman/Corbis; p. 72: (bottom right) Jodi Hilton/Corbis; p. 76: Bettmann/Corbis; p. 80: AP/Wide World Photos; p. 91: (left) Collection of the New-York Historical Society; p. 91: (right) Library of Congress; p. 92: (left) PEMCO Webster and Stevens Collection, Museum of History and Industry, Seattle/Corbis; p. 92: (right) Billy E. Barnes/Stock Boston; p. 93: AP/Wide World Photos; p. 94: (top) Reuters/Corbis; p. 94: (bottom) AP/Wide World Photos; p. 95: AP/Wide World Photos; p. 105: Jaon Reed/Reuters/Corbis; p. 108: (top) AP/Wide World Photos; p. 108: (bottom) AP/Wide World Photos; p. 109: (both) AP/Wide World Photos; p. 109: AP/Wide World Photos; p. 114: Chuck Savage/Corbis; p. 127: AP/Wide World Photos; p. 128: (right) Win McNamee/Reuters/Corbis; p. 128: (top left) AP/Wide World Photos; p. 128: (bottom left) AP/Wide World Photos; p. 130: AFP/Getty Images; p. 140: AP/Wide World Photos; p. 141: (left) Bettmann/Corbis; p. 141: (middle) AP/Wide World Photos; p. 141: (right) AP/Wide World Photos; p. 143: (both) AP/Wide World Photos; p. 145: (both) Bettmann/Corbis; p. 151: AP/Wide World Photos; p. 158: AP/Wide World Photos; p. 162: AP/Wide World Photos; p. 172: (top) Bettmann/Corbis; p. 172: (bottom left) Bettmann/Corbis; p. 172: (bottom right) Warder Collection; p. 173: (top) AP/Wide World Photos; p. 173: (bottom) Stanley J. Forman, Pulitzer Prize, 1977; p. 185: Bettmann/Corbis; p. 185: (bottom) Corbis; p. 186: (top) Bettmann/Corbis; p. 186: (bottom) AP/Wide World Photos; p. 187: Wathiq Khuzaie/Getty Images; p. 196: AP/Wide World Photos; p. 197: (top left) AP/Wide World Photos; p. 197: (bottom) AP/Wide World Photos; p. 197: (top right) AP/Wide World Photos; p. 199: Alex Wong/Getty Images; p. 204: Getty Images; p. 209: AP/Wide World Photos; p. 210: Bill Bachman/Right Image; p. 216: (bottom) AP/Wide World Photos; p. 216: (top right) Todd A. Gipstein/Corbis; p. 216: (top left) Wally McNamee/Corbis; p. 217: (left) Jessica Rinaldi/Reuters/Corbis; p. 217: (right) AFP/Getty Images; p. 218: Frederic Larson/San Francisco Chronicle/Corbis; p. 234: (bottom left) AP/Wide World Photos; p. 234: (bottom right) Brooks Kraft/Corbis; p. 234: (top left) Bettmann/Corbis; p. 234: (top right) By permission of Bob Gorrell and Creators Syndicate; p. 239: (top) Bettmann/Corbis; p. 239: (bottom) AP/Wide World Photos; p. 244: (both) AP/Wide World Photos; p. 246: Behrouz Mehri/AFP/Getty Images; p. 248: AP/Wide World Photos; p. 252: Stephen Jaffe/AFP/Getty Images; p. 261: AP/Wide World AP/Wide World Photos; p. 268: (bottom) AP/Wide World Photos; p. 269: (bottom) Anwar Mirza/Reuters/Corbis; p. 269: (top) AFP/Getty Images; p. 272: (top) AP/Wide World Photos; p. 273: (top) © 1963 Charles Moore/Black Star; p. 273: (bottom left) AP/Wide World Photos; p. 273: (bottom right) CNN/Corbis Sygma; p. 277: Namir Noor-Eldeen/Reuters/Corbis; p. 278: (top, bottom left, bottom right) AP/Wide World Photos; p. 279: AP/Wide World Photos; p. 284: AP/Wide World Photos; p. 288: Reuters/Corbis; p. 299: Faleh Kheiber/Reuters/Corbis; p. 301: Chicago Historical Society; p. 303: Library of Congress; p. 307: (top left) AP/Wide World Photos; p. 307: (top right) © B. Daemmrich/The Image Works; p. 309: Rebecca Cook/Reuters/Corbis; p. 316: Brown Brothers; p. 317: (top left and bottom) AP/Wide World Photos; p. 317: (top right) Courtesy Danny Clinch; p. 322: AP/Wide World Photos; p. 326: AFP/Getty Images; p. 332: (top) Library of Congress; p. 332: (bottom) Bettmann/Corbis; p. 333: (top and bottom) AP/Wide World Photos; p. 335: (top)

ANSWER KEY

CHAPTER 1
1. d
2. b
3. c
4. d
5. c
6. d
7. d
8. a
9. a
10. a

CHAPTER 2
1. b
2. b
3. b
4. d
5. c
6. c
7. d
8. d
9. d
10. a

CHAPTER 3
1. b
2. c
3. d
4. c
5. c
6. b
7. a
8. d
9. c
10. d

CHAPTER 4
1. a
2. c
3. b
4. a
5. d
6. d
7. b
8. a
9. a
10.

CHAPTER 5
1. b
2. a
3. b
4. b
5. c
6. b
7. d
8. d
9. d
10. a

CHAPTER 6
1. c
2. a
3. d
4. c
5. d
6. b
7. d
8. b
9. a
10. b

CHAPTER 7
1. c
2. b
3. d
4. c
5. d
6. a
7. b
8. a
9. d
10. a

CHAPTER 8
1. d
2. d
3. a
4. c
5. d
6. d
7. a
8. c
9. c
10. d

CHAPTER 9
1. a
2. d
3. c
4. d
5. b
6. c
7. c
8. a
9. c
10. d

CHAPTER 10
1. a
2. b
3. c
4. d
5. a
6. a
7. b
8. a
9. d
10. c

CHAPTER 11
1. a
2. d
3. c
4. a
5. a
6. c
7. d
8. d
9. b
10. a

CHAPTER 12
1. a
2. d
3. c
4. c
5. a
6. c
7. b
8. a
9. a
10. c

CHAPTER 13
1. b
2. a
3. a
4. b
5. a
6. c
7. a
8. b
9. c

CHAPTER 14
1. b
2. a
3. c
4. d
5. a
6. a
7. d
8. d

CHAPTER 15
1. a
2. b
3. d
4. d
5. a
6. c
7. c
8. a
9. d
10. a

INDEX